SCIENTIFIC FOUNDATIONS OF DEVELOPMENTAL PSYCHIATRY

Scientific Foundations of Developmental Psychiatry

Edited by
MICHAEL RUTTER

UNIVERSITY PARK PRESS
Baltimore

DEDICATION
To Jerry Shields and Jack Tizard—social scientists of outstanding quality

© Michael Rutter 1981

First published in North America by
UNIVERSITY PARK PRESS
300 North Charles Street
Baltimore, Maryland 21201

First published by
William Heinemann Medical Books Ltd
23 Bedford Square
London, England

ISBN 0-8391-1690-X
LCCN 81-51259

Printed in Great Britain

CONTENTS

SECTION I

INFLUENCES ON DEVELOPMENT

SECTION II

BODY FUNCTIONING

v

SECTION V

THEORIES AND APPROACHES

LIST OF CONTRIBUTORS

MARTIN C. O. BAX, B.M., B.Ch.
Thomas Coram Research Unit, 41, Brunswick Square, London WC1N 1AZ.

K. J. CONNOLLY, B.Sc., Ph.D., F.B.Ps.S.
Professor of Psychology, University of Sheffield.

J. F. DUNN, M.A.(Cantab), (Fellow of King's College, Cambridge).
Scientific Officer, Assistant Director, Medical Research Council Unit on the Development and Integration of Behaviour, University of Cambridge.

E. J. EBELS
Reader in Neuropathology, University of Groningen, The Netherlands.

U. FRITH, Dip.Psych., Ph.D.
M.R.C. Scientific Staff, M.R.C. Developmental Psychology Unit, Drayton House, Gordon Street, London WC1H 0AN.

P. J. GRAHAM, F.R.C.P., F.R.C.Psych.
Walker Professor of Child Psychiatry, Institute of Child Health, London WC1.

W. W. HARTUP, B.S., M.A., Ed.D.
Professor of Child Psychology, and Director, Institute of Child Development, University of Minnesota, USA.

R. A. HINDE, F.R.S., Sc.D.(Cantab).
Royal Society Research Professor, Hon. Director, M.R.C. Unit on Development and Integration of Behaviour, University of Cambridge.

P. HOWLIN, B.A., M.Sc., Ph.D.
Lecturer, Department of Psychology/Department of Child and Adolescent Psychiatry, Institute of Psychiatry, De Crespigny Park, London SE5 8AF.

C. N. JACKLIN, Ph.D.
Senior Research Associate, Department of Psychology, Stanford University, California, USA.

E. E. MACCOBY, Ph.D.
Barbara Kimball Browning Professor of Psychology, Stanford University, California, USA.

N. J. H. MADGE, B.A., M.Sc.
Now at London School of Economics, Houghton Street, London WC2A 2AE.

B. MAUGHAN, B.A.
Research Worker, Department of Child and Adolescent Psychiatry, Institute of Psychiatry, De Crespigny Park, London SE5 8AF.

H. F. L. MEYER-BAHLBURG
College of Physicians and Surgeons of Columbia University, New York, USA.

P. MORTIMORE, B.Sc., M.Sc., Ph.D.
Now Director, Research and Statistics Group, Inner London Education Authority, The County Hall, London SE1 7PB.

J. E. OUSTON, B.Sc., Ph.D.
Research Worker, Department of Child and Adolescent Psychiatry, Institute of Psychiatry, De Crespigny Park, London SE5 8AF.

DAVID QUINTON, M.A.
Department of Child and Adolescent Psychiatry, Institute of Psychiatry, De Crespigny Park, London SE5 8AF.

J. L. RAPOPORT, M.D.
Chief, Unit on Childhood Mental Illness, N.I.M.H., Bethesda, Maryland, USA and Associate Professor of Psychiatry and Pediatrics, Georgetown University, School of Medicine, Washington, DC, USA.

D. B. ROSENBLATT, B.A., M.Sc.
Research Officer, Bedford College, Honorary Lecturer, Paediatric Dept., St Mary's Hospital Medical School, London.

MICHAEL RUTTER
Professor of Child Psychiatry, Department of Child and Adolescent Psychiatry, Institute of Psychiatry, De Crespigny Park, London, and Fellow of the Center for Advanced Study in the Behavioral Sciences, Stanford, California, USA.

D. SHAFFER, M.B., B.S., M.R.C.P., M.R.C.Psych., D.P.M.
Clinical Professor of Psychiatry, College of Physicians and Surgeons of Columbia University, New York. Director, Dept. of Child Psychiatry in the Presbyterian Hospital of New York, USA.

J. SHIELDS,* B.A., Hon.M.D.(Zurich).
Reader in Psychiatric Genetics, Institute of Psychiatry, University of London.

H. W. STEVENSON
Professor of Psychology, University of Michigan, Ann Arbor, Michigan, USA.

C. J. L. STOKMAN
College of Physicians and Surgeons of Columbia University, New York, USA.

E. A. TAYLOR, M.A., M.B., M.R.C.P., M.R.C.Psych.
Senior Lecturer in Child and Adolescent Psychiatry, Institute of Psychiatry, Hon. Consultant Psychiatrist, Bethlem Royal and Maudsley Hospitals, and King's College Hospital, London.

J. TIZARD,* Ph.D.
Research Professor of Child Development, University of London Institute of Education, and Director of the Thomas Coram Research Unit, 41, Brunswick Square, London WC1N 1AZ.

B. C. L. TOUWEN, M.D.
Senior Scientific Co-worker, Dept. of Developmental Neurology, State University of Groningen, The Netherlands.

P. H. VENABLES, B.A., Ph.D., Hon. D.Sc.
Professor of Psychology, University of York.

R. D. WALK, Ph.D.
Professor of Psychiatry, George Washington University, Washington, DC, USA.

D. J. WOOD, B.A., Ph.D.
Lecturer, Dept. of Psychology, University of Nottingham, Nottingham NE7 2RD.

* Deceased

ACKNOWLEDGEMENTS

I am most grateful to Martin Bax who first suggested the need for this book and who provided extremely helpful advice during the whole period from the book's conception to its completion. Brian Foss played a major role in formulating ideas on the book's content and in suggesting possible authors for chapters; I am most indebted to him for invaluable assistance, without which the book might not have been started. Also I wish to thank Richard Emery who not only made many helpful suggestions during the planning stage, but who provided publishing support and guidance throughout. The book was completed while a Fellow at the Center for Advanced Study in the Behavioral Sciences, Stanford, California, and thanks are due to the Grant Foundation, the Foundation for Child Development, the Spencer Foundation and the National Science Foundation (BNS78–24671).

Joy Maxwell deserves special thanks for helping in innumerable ways; in typing manuscripts, in subediting chapters, in checking references, and in reading proofs. I would also like to thank Mrs. Doreen Blake for careful preparation of the index.

The untimely death of both Jerry Shields and Jack Tizard during the course of the book's production has resulted in not only great personal sadness but also a deep sense of loss to the field of developmental psychiatry, to which, in their very different ways, each contributed an enormous amount. As a mark of this contribution, and more particularly of my own debt to them both, this book is dedicated to Jerry and Jack.

SECTION I

INFLUENCES ON DEVELOPMENT

1. INTRODUCTION

MICHAEL RUTTER

DEVELOPMENT AS A UNIFYING CONCEPT IN PSYCHIATRY

Psychiatry encompasses a wide range of disorders extending from exaggerations of normal emotions to disease states which represent a more or less complete break with normality. But perhaps most conditions fall somewhere between the two with phenomena such as thought disorder, hallucinations or delusions which are clearly pathological, but yet with elements, such as responsiveness to environmental change, which mark continuities with normality. As a consequence no one type of aetiological explanation is adequate to account for the causes and course of all psychiatric conditions. Different clinical problems need to be tackled in different ways, and even with a single condition a combination of approaches may be needed both to achieve understanding of the pathological processes involved and to bring about an effective therapeutic intervention.

Nevertheless, as Eisenberg (1977) has eloquently argued, a developmental perspective constitutes one essential underlying concept in the psychiatry of both adults and children. It is not just that some disorders involve a distortion of personality development, or that some have their roots in physical or experiential traumata in childhood, or that some involve a genetically determined interference with the normal developmental process, or that some last for so many years that considerations of developmental causes and consequences are unavoidable. Rather it is that the process of development constitutes the crucial link between genetic determinants and environmental variables, between sociology and individual psychology, and between physiogenic and psychogenic causes. Development thus encompasses not only the roots of behaviour in prior maturation, in physical influences (both internal and external) and in the residues of earlier experiences, but also the modulations of that behaviour by the circumstances of the present. It is in that sense that the adjective 'developmental' is applied to psychiatry in the title of this book.

It should not be taken as a synonym for child psychiatry, not only because the scientific foundations of child psychiatry extend beyond the study of development (*see* Rutter and Hersov, 1977), but also because adult psychiatry necessarily involves a major developmental component. The chapters of this volume aim to provide a critical appraisal of those aspects of development which are particularly relevant to an understanding of psychiatric disorders. This means that the book has to cover many of the topics relevant to the study of child development as a whole (*see e.g.* Mussen *et al.*, 1979) and to social and personality development (*see e.g.* Mischel, 1976; Lamb, 1978). However, it differs both in its balance and emphasis (so that aspects of development of most interest to clinicians receive greater attention) and in its orientation (so that normal development is viewed with a particular eye to its implications for clinical pathology).

CONTINUITIES AND DISCONTINUITIES IN DEVELOPMENT

In arguing that a developmental perspective is necessary in adult as well as in child psychiatry, it is not, of course, suggested that all adult disorders have their origins in childhood, or that psychiatric conditions arising during the years of adulthood can only be understood by reference to the process of development as it took place in childhood. Far from it. It is evident that many mental illnesses arise for reasons which have little to do with happenings during the early years. Nevertheless, this is of interest in its own right. A developmental perspective must take account of continuities *and* discontinuities between childhood and adult life. The empirical data make clear that both occur. This book is not concerned with an analysis of the course and development of psychiatric disorders as such; rather it seeks to provide a scientific backcloth made up of the findings and issues in the study of normal development against which the developmental aspects of psychopathology may be considered. But, in this introductory chapter it may be useful to make brief mention of some of the clinical concerns which raise developmental questions.

Behavioural antecedents in childhood of adult disorders

The adult disorder which shows the strongest continuities with childhood problems is that of antisocial behaviour. As evident from Robins' (1978) four longitudinal studies of very different populations, antisocial behaviour in adult life has usually been preceded by similar behaviour in childhood; only quite rarely does it arise for the first time in adult life. West and Farrington's (1977) study of London males produced similar findings, but also demonstrated that persistent delinquency tended to be associated with a whole constellation of characteristics including aggressiveness, irregular work habits, immoderation in the pursuit of immediate pleasure and lack of conventional social restraints. It seems that persistent antisocial behaviour is associated with certain distinctive features of personality functioning and that this pattern begins in childhood but persists into adult life. On the other hand, continuities in antisocial behaviour are not the same as continuities in criminal record (see Farrington, 1979). About two-fifths of adult offenders have not been convicted as juveniles. Moreover, however measured, the continuities looking *forwards* are much less than those looking *backwards*. Most delinquent children do *not* become antisocial adults. Important questions remain on what is different about those children in whom the delinquencies constitute a 'passing phase' rather than an enduring pattern of behaviour.

The findings with respect to adult neurosis and depression are rather different, although it must be said that the evidence is less satisfactory (see Cox, 1976; Rutter and Madge, 1976). Many adults develop emotional disorders for the first time in adult life, without ever having shown disturbance during childhood. This seems to occur most frequently in the case of depressive disorders and especially with manic-depressive psychosis. Only quite uncommonly do bipolar cyclical psychoses begin before puberty and there do not seem to be any identifiable behavioural childhood antecedents of manic-depressive disorder. It is also the case that most children with emotional disorders become normal adults, although their risk of adult psychiatric disorder is substantially raised above that for individuals without disturbance in childhood. If disorder persists into adult life it usually takes the form of neurosis or depression, but there is little continuity with respect to the particular types of emotional symptomatology. Perhaps most striking of all, there is a shift in the pattern of emotional disturbance during adolescence (see Rutter, 1979a). Depressive feelings become much more common and there is a change from the roughly equal sex ratio for emotional disorders seen during childhood to the marked female preponderance evident in adult life. These issues are considered in more detail in Chapter 25.

Schizophrenia usually does not become manifest until later adolescence or early adult life. However, as a variety of research strategies have shown (see e.g. Offord and Cross, 1969; Watt and Lubensky, 1976; Watt, 1976) about half of schizophrenic adults have shown behavioural abnormalities in childhood. Few of these abnormalities are evident in early childhood but most are apparent by early adolescence. No clear-cut syndrome identifies pre-schizophrenic states but on the whole it has been found that pre-schizophrenic boys appear irritable, aggressive, negativistic and defiant while the girls are more likely to seem shy, introverted and excessively compliant. The meaning of these sex differences in the childhood antecedents of adult schizophrenia remains obscure. Furthermore, little is known on the significance of whether or not schizophrenia shows non-psychotic behavioural precursors in childhood. The matter warrants further study (Rutter, 1972a).

On the whole, the majority of developmental disorders of childhood (language delay, specific reading retardation, primary enuresis, etc.) have cleared up or at least greatly diminished by the time adulthood is reached. Moreover, whereas psychiatric disorders arising in early or middle childhood show quite strong associations with developmental delays and with both specific and general cognitive deficits, this does not seem to be the case with disorders in which the onset is during or after adolescence (Rutter et al., 1976). On the other hand, adult sequelae of developmental problems are common. Many children with specific developmental delays of speech or language continue to have serious reading difficulties long after their spoken language has become fluent and extensive (see Rutter and Yule, 1973 and Benton and Pearl, 1978). These 'dyslexic' difficulties often persist well into adult life, although by then, spelling problems may be more severe than reading deficits as such.

Several longitudinal studies have looked at the inter-correlations between behavioural or personality ratings over the years (see Chapter 9 in which Dunn discusses the matter in more detail). Generally, it has been found that measures during the pre-school years have little predictive value for an individual's behaviour during and after adolescence; but that there is a moderate degree of consistency between the early school years and adolescence. There are also moderate, but only moderate, levels of continuity in personality functioning between adolescence and adult life (see Rutter, 1979a). Some data (Bronson, 1967; Gersten et al., 1976) suggest that behaviour may not always show increasing stability with increasing age; instead there may be a temporary period of transient fluctuations during adolescence which is not necessarily of great prognostic importance. However, the evidence is too sparse for firm conclusions on this point. Certainly, the inter-correlations over time from middle childhood to adult life across the adolescent years are not very high and changes in overt behaviour are common. Whether or not these changes are interpretable within an overall consistency in personality pattern (as Block, 1971, suggests) remains uncertain. The issues with respect to adolescent functioning are more fully discussed in Rutter (1979a).

Childhood experiences and adult disorder

There are many data which indicate statistical associations between childhood experiences and adult problems but the developmental *meaning* of these associations remains surprisingly ill-understood. There is, of course, the basic question of whether they represent *causal* connections in which the adverse experiences play a part in the aetiology of psychiatric disorders. However, the pattern of findings indicates that in many instances they almost certainly do (see Rutter, 1972b and Rutter and Madge, 1976). So far as adult disorders are concerned, even when this is accepted, three other issues remain only partially resolved. First, there is the question of so-called 'sleeper' effects; that is whether events or happenings can have a *delayed* effect in leading to disorder in later years even when there are no immediate observable behavioral consequences. Such delayed effects of early experiences can only be studied with respect to experiences which are restricted to early childhood and which do not continue throughout the whole of development. Unfortunately, childhood adversities tend to be very persistent and some of the continuities in people's behaviour may just mean that they are continuing to respond to the same contemporaneous (*not* earlier) stresses, but that the stresses have not altered. Few data are available to test for the possibility of sleeper effects and the findings so far are contradictory (*see* Rutter, 1979a for a fuller discussion).

Secondly, there is the related issue of vulnerabilities—namely whether early experiences can predispose to or protect from disorder, not by any direct effect but rather through an influence on a person's susceptibility to later stresses or psychosocial traumata. Brown and Harris (1978) have argued for the operation of this mechanism in relation to possible links between childhood bereavement and adult depressive disorder, and Rutter (1979b) has considered some of the very limited available evidence on protective or ameliorating factors. It seems likely that the concept may have some validity but few empirical data are available to test the notions involved at all adequately.

Thirdly, there is the vexed issue of 'sensitive' or 'critical' periods in development; the idea that happenings at a particular developmental phase have an effect far greater than at any other stage and that certain events *have* to occur during the 'critical' period if normal development is to proceed thereafter. On the whole, the empirical data suggest that this does *not* apply to any marked degree with most aspects of human development (*see* Clarke and Clarke, 1976; Rutter, 1979c). However, as discussed in Chapter 22, the development of social bonds or attachments in early childhood may constitute a *partial* exception to these generally negative findings.

The major point is that it is not enough to know that there is, or is not, an association between childhood experiences and adult psychiatric conditions. If this knowledge is to increase our understanding of the nature of the psychopathological disorders or if it is to lead to more effective therapeutic interventions, it is essential to appreciate the various biological and psychosocial processes involved in development and the several ways in which they may be affected by both positive and stressful experiences.

Biological influences on development

As Shields brings out very clearly in Chapter 2, genetic factors influence the whole of development and at no time in life can it be said that they have ceased to exert their effects. Twin studies indicate that hereditary influences shape not only the outcome of personality development but also its timing and the various fluctuations in maturation involved. Moreover, as illustrated by the responses to blood transfusion or tissue transplantation, stresses in later life can evoke latent genetic potentialities. However, the delayed effects of genetic factors are not confined to stress responses. Many genetic diseases, such as Huntington's Chorea, have a late age of onset which cannot be explained by life stresses. Carriers of the gene cannot be identified in early life, though there is an indication that the gene may have an effect on IQ before psychiatric or neurological symptoms are shown. Precisely what is involved developmentally in these delayed genetic effects remains uncertain.

Various physical factors, including body build at age of puberty, have been found to be associated with psychosocial functioning, as discussed by Rapoport in Chapter 4. Some of these associations persist into adult life. The mechanisms involved remain ill-understood (*see also* Rutter, 1979a) and it appears that the effects are rather different in boys and girls. This constitutes another developmental topic, with implications for both child and adult psychiatry, worth further study.

It has been well demonstrated by both epidemiological and longitudinal studies (*see* Rutter, 1977; Rutter and Chadwick, 1979) that brain damage is associated with a marked increase in both cognitive deficits and psychiatric problems during childhood, and also during adult life (*see* Lishman, 1978). It is important to appreciate that it is not just a matter of an immediate effect consequent upon loss of brain substance. In the first place, the effects of *abnormal* brain functioning are at least as important as those of lost function. Secondly, processes of both adaptation and of altered brain function go on for many years after the injury. The changing pattern of EEG abnormalities and of type of epileptic fit associated with 'hypsarrhythmia' and drop attacks in early childhood provides one example of continuing developmental change; the development of fits during adolescence in autistic children provides another; and the later development of schizophrenia in individuals with temporal lobe epilepsy provides a third.

Another different type of biological influence is illustrated by the effects of prenatal sex hormone exposure on later psychosexual and behavioural development (discussed in Chapters 26 and 28). Precisely *how* this exerts its effect is not yet known but it is clear that this is a mode of developmental influence of considerable potential importance and possibly wide implications.

At several points in this chapter so far, reference has been made to 'personality development' and to the various factors which may influence it. Before proceeding further, it may be as well to pause to consider just what is meant by this term.

CONCEPTS OF PERSONALITY

The concept of personality is a rather imprecise one, with almost as many definitions as theorists who have attempted to define it (Mischel, 1976). Nevertheless, in general it is taken to mean a person's distinctive style or pattern of thought, emotions, adaptation and behaviour. In that sense, this book could be said to be about the development of personality as it takes place during the childhood years. None of the chapters is explicitly concerned with the notion of personality as such and there is very little reference to any concept of the 'whole' personality. Nevertheless, in considering the empirical findings in the chapters to follow, on the development of, say, language, aggression or emotions, it is useful to have some idea of how personality development as a whole has been viewed by different theorists. In other words what is this 'thing'—personality—the development of which is being considered?

Personality types

For many years people tended to discuss personality in terms of specific categories or types. Thus, Hippocrates described temperaments as 'choleric', 'melancholic', 'sanguine' or 'phlegmatic'. More recently, Jung proposed the psychological categories of 'introverts' and 'extraverts'. These typologies are attractive in terms of their simplicity and their consonance with popular stereotypes. However, it has long been obvious that although people may approximate to one or other of these types, personalities do not constitute discontinuous varieties which fit readily into discrete pigeon holes. Rather, human characteristics differ in degree as well as form to constitute an almost infinite variety of personalities with no one person quite like any other.

As a result, the concept of personality types as a means of describing normal variations in personality has been virtually abandoned. But the approach still persists, and may have some validity, in the field of *abnormalities* of personality. Psychiatric classifications almost always include codings for various different types of personality disorders. Most of these categories have little, if any, empirical support, but it has been argued that the concept of 'sociopathy' or 'antisocial personality disorder' may have utility (Robins, 1966). Thus, as already mentioned, West and Farrington (1977) have provided evidence on the extent to which persistent delinquency is associated with a predictable life pattern of social relationships and leisure pursuits; and Robins (1978) has pointed to the high consistency of findings with respect to the childhood predictors of adult antisocial behaviour. Both sets of data seem to point to the existence of some kind of antisocial or sociopathic personality type; Schulsinger's (1972) data suggest that it may involve a genetic component. However, it remains uncertain how far the consistency in behaviour reflects an enduring biological predisposition and how far it simply reflects the persistence of environmental pressures and constraints (*see* below). Moreover, it has yet to be determined how far this form of personality type is qualitatively distinct, rather than quantitatively different, from normal personality variations.

Personality traits

Psychologists have tended to respond to the evidence that, on the whole, discrete types do not exist, by using *trait* rather than type variables. Like personality types, traits are generally assumed to constitute basic underlying dispositions that account for consistencies in behaviour (Guilford, 1959). The difference lies in the fact that traits are considered to be continuous dimensions, so that individual differences may be assessed in terms of the degree or extent to which a person exhibits a particular trait. Psychometric approaches, usually using questionnaires of some form, have been developed to provide quantitative scores for a person's position on each trait distribution. Thus, measures are available to assess dimensions such as 'neuroticism' or 'introversion-extraversion' (Eysenck and Eysenck, 1975). The trait approach to personality has proved successful to the extent that such traits can indeed be measured in a reliable fashion and that they provide a modest level of prediction for the ways in which people will behave. However, there is continuing disagreement on which trait dimensions are basic and on how many should be used to describe personality variations. There is also controversy on the extent to which traits have a fundamental biological basis so that the observed behaviours reflect some underlying physiological substrate.

Situation-Specificity

But the major attack on trait theory has come from psychologists who pointed to the very considerable extent to which an individual's behaviour alters from situation to situation (Mischel, 1968). Thus, in apparent opposition to the findings on the persistence and pervasiveness of antisocial behaviour, it has been observed that such behaviour is much more likely to be elicited in some environmental settings than in others (*see* Mayhew *et al.*, 1976). Attention shifted from a focus on individual personality characteristics to a focus on the environment as a source of behavioural variation.

Behaviourists argued that what people do is a function of patterns of reward or reinforcement. Thus, Patterson (1977), in a study of family interactions in the home showed that coercion tended to increase the likelihood that a child's hostile behaviour or social aggression would persist. Similarly, experimental studies of teacher–child interaction in the classroom have shown that a focus on disruptive behaviour tends to perpetuate its occurrence (Becker *et al.*, 1967). Some behaviourists have suggested that this constitutes a complete explanation. As Skinner (1957) put it, 'the artist paints what reinforces him visually'. According to this view there is no need to invoke any concept of personality predisposition or internal motivation.

However, the emphasis on environment was by no means confined to behaviourists. Social ecologists, too, noted the extent to which particular environments facilitated or inhibited particular behaviours through their impact on the people in them. Thus, Bronfenbrenner (1979) has summarized many of the empirical findings showing that this applies to family functioning; and Rutter *et al.* (1979) have provided evidence on the importance of school influences.

The attack on trait theories came also from sociologists who pointed to the extent to which behaviours were a function of the labels applied to them (Scheff, 1966; Lemert, 1967; Cicourel, 1968). According to this view, delinquency persists not because of any inherent characteristic of the person but rather because the very labelling of people as delinquents tends to perpetuate their involvement in antisocial behaviour. The finding that delinquent behaviour is more likely to persist if it results in a court appearance than if it does not (Farrington, 1977) provides some empirical support for a labelling effect.

As a result of these several (rather different) arguments it came to be widely accepted that situation-variability was so great that it made the study of personality traits almost redundant.

Interactionist views

It is now clear that this view went well beyond the evidence (*see* Bowers, 1973). Although it is undoubtedly true that behaviour is more situation-specific than trait theory acknowledged, it is also the case that situations are more person-specific than situationism theory had allowed. The importance of personality traits was shown by the great individual variation in people's responses to any one situation; but the need to invoke environmental determinants was equally evident in the extent to which any person's mode of functioning altered from situation to situation. A pooling of studies suggested that, overall, the variation accounted for by persons was about as much as that accounted for by situations (Bowers, 1973), but even the sum of the two left most of the variation still unexplained.

However, the evidence also suggested that the effects do not simply summate. Rather there is an *interaction* between persons and situations (Bowers, 1973; Bem and Allen, 1974; Bem and Funder, 1978; Mischel, 1973; Lamb, 1978). This interaction takes many different forms, only some of which are understood as yet. For example, the genotype may determine an individual's responsiveness to particular environmental influences. This may involve damage from elements which are harmless to others (as with phenylketonuria and a normal diet); an increased vulnerability to common stresses; or a *different* response to specific environments. Examples of both ordinal and disordinal genetic-environment interactions are provided by Shields in Chapter 2. Non-genetic physical factors, too, may alter how a person responds to environmental circumstances—as illustrated by the finding that deaf children may show a more normal development when reared by deaf parents than when brought up by hearing parents, presumably because the former are more aware of the importance of gestural and other non-verbal cues for the hearing-impaired child (Meadow, 1975). Temperamental variables may not only determine how an individual responds to a particular environment but also may change the *effective* environment itself, through their effect on other people's behaviour. Examples of this form of interaction are given by Dunn in Chapter 9 and also, with respect to sex differences, by Maccoby and Jacklin in Chapter 8. Past experiences, too, may shape an individual's response to new situations. This is evident for example in terms of both the protective effect of previous happy separation experiences and the enhanced vulnerability stemming from earlier stressful separations in relation to children's responses to later separations (*see* Chapter 5). Similarly, the prior experience of success or failure will influence how a person responds to the challenge of a new task (Mischel, 1973). A person's cognitive structuring of the environment will also affect his reaction to it (Mischel, 1973, 1976). This is shown by the effects of the expectancies people bring to a situation, by the ways in which a stimulus is defined (something which is perceived as dangerous by one person may be seen as challenging by another), and by the effects of group norms or values. It is because of factors of this kind that the effects of alcohol on a person's behaviour at a party tended to be very different from the effects on the same person's behaviour when he has a drink on his own in his hotel room just before going to bed.

The importance of interaction effects of different kinds are well brought out by Hinde in Chapter 5 when discussing family dynamics. Not only do relationships always involve mutual influences, but also the behaviour of one individual to another is affected by the relationships of each with others, and furthermore, family interactions are affected by influences from outside in terms of the broader sociocultural environment (*see also* Chapter 7).

Ideographic versus nomothetic approaches

It is evident that, as a consequence, it is difficult to make valid, broad, sweeping generalizations about human behaviour. Attention must be paid to the specificities of person-situation interactions. That does not mean that no generalizations are possible, but it does mean that valid 'laws' of personality development and of human behaviour must provide ways of accounting for these interactions. So far only limited progress has been made in this direction. However, not everyone would agree that this is the right avenue to explore in any case. Rather than pursue nomothetic principles of general applicability, it may be suggested that it is preferable to take an ideographic approach which explicitly focuses on the *individuality* of human beings—not just in the degree to which they show particular traits or even in terms of the traits which are relevant to them, but more generally in terms of the idiosyncrasies which make each person uniquely different from all others. In essence that has been the approach of the novelist who seeks to bring out the features which make a person *different* from everyone else. It is supposed to contrast with that of the scientist who tries to establish the *communalities* in behaviour between individuals which enables him to generalize from one person to the next and in so doing to derive principles or laws of universal applicability. However, in many respects the dichotomy is a false one. Both the novelist and the scientist are interested in predicting from one situation to the next; variability is not synonymous with either capriciousness or unpredictability.

Perhaps, as suggested by Bem (Bem and Allen, 1974; Bem and Funder, 1978), Mischel (1973, 1976) and others, the answer lies in attempting to derive nomothetic principles which apply to the idiographic circumstances of person-situation interactions. Personality development must mean *psychosocial* development in which attention is paid to the biology of the individual in the ecological context of his psychosocial environment.

Overlap between systems

For the most part, the chapters of this book are organized according to different facets of development—psychosexual development, moral development, language, intelligence, etc. This is convenient for a discussion of the processes involved and for a consideration of the theoretical issues. However, it is obvious that this separation between systems is rather artificial. In practice the development of one aspect of personality functioning is often dependent on changes in another. Thus, as discussed in the relevant chapters, there are effective links between cognition and language, between attachment and peer relationships, and between moral concepts and intelligence. On the other hand, as shown by the results of unusual experiences or of biological anomalies, personality development does not necessarily proceed evenly as a whole across all fronts. Thus, social development and intellectual development tend to be affected by rather different kinds of influences and even the different aspects of psychosexual development are not necessarily consonant with one another. These questions of overlap or lack of overlap are discussed in individual chapters when the issues seem to have particular theoretical or practical relevance.

Rational and irrational explanations

In the discussion so far, there has been an implicit assumption that personality development can be described and accounted for in purely rational terms. However, psychodynamic theories deny this assumption in their emphasis on unconscious motivations. Psychoanalytic theories are concerned more with conflicts *within* an individual's psychic structure than with conflicts or stresses *between* an individual and his external environment. There is an emphasis on hypothetical constructs such as the superego, libido or depressive position, rather than on overt behaviour (Dare, 1977). Moreover, there is a concentration on the understanding of current experiences in terms of earlier mental and life processes. Much attention is paid to the operation of psychic defence mechanisms (repression, projection, sublimation, etc.), by which the organism deals with anxiety or threat. Meaning is attributed to apparently meaningless behaviour through the invoking of these universal defence mechanisms. The approach is ideographic in its focus on the meaning of individual behaviours in terms of unique events, but is nomothetic in its use of general psychodynamic principles held to apply to everyone.

The whole style and type of explanation utilized by psychoanalytic theories make them very different from all other theories of personality development. However, to a considerable extent the differences are more evident in the language and terminology used than in the broad concepts which are employed. Thus, social-learning theory (*see* Bandura, 1971 and Mischel, 1976), like psychoanalysis, is concerned with the effects on behaviour of the mental representation and manipulation of events, with symbolic activities, and with the personal meaning of situations. It is accepted that human beings are not passive bundles of responses; rather they actively interpret and evaluate their environment, internalizing their experiences in ways which will influence their later behaviour. Moreover, learning can take place without awareness, so introducing the possibility of unconscious thought processes. In short, the differences between psychoanalytic theories and social-learning theories do not concern the invoking of cognition or of personal meaning. On the other hand, there are very major differences in the types of thought processes and of mental mechanisms which are considered to be operating. These differences lead to contrasting predictions of behaviour and to quite different modes of therapeutic intervention.

THEORIES OF DEVELOPMENT

These considerations raise the question of the place of theories in any discussion of development. It will be noted that this volume contains no chapters which have as their main intent an account or critical appraisal of any of the major developmental theories, although evaluations of theoretical contributions to specific issues are to be found in most of the individual chapters. The omission was deliberate. Nor does the book follow any unifying theoretical approach or construct. This, too, was deliberate. It is not that theories are unimportant in either research or clinical practice. To the contrary, they are essential as a means of ordering ideas and of making sense out of factual findings. The mindless collection of factual information is not the way that science proceeds. Almost always, the strategies and tactics of research are guided by some theoretical concept and frequently the studies are explicitly designed to test or contrast various hypotheses. Also, it is not that the theories are necessarily wrong in what they propose (*see* Baldwin, 1967 for a balanced critique of developmental theories). To the contrary, most of the theories provide convincing partial explanations of some aspects or features of the course of personality development.

The limitations are of a rather different kind. Firstly, it is immediately obvious that no one theory constitutes anything like a complete explanation of the developmental process. For example, almost all theorists acknowledge the role of genetic factors in development, the importance of biological maturation, and the relevance of brain pathology. But these variables are generally passed over rapidly as in some way playing an unspecified part in whatever variance is left unexplained. Only very rarely is there any attempt to provide even the most elementary form of integration. Secondly, none of the theories provides any explanation for many of the crucial developmental phenomena of greatest concern to clinicians. For example, few of the theories focus on either the nature or the determination of individual differences. Similarly, few pay any attention to the major sex differences apparent in many aspects of development. Furthermore, most ignore many of the major changes which are so striking during childhood—for example, the development of peer relationships (discussed in Chapter 23), or the functions of play (discussed in Chapter 24), or the emotional changes evident during adolescence (discussed in Chapter 25). It is as a consequence of these considerations that theoretical issues are relegated to a rather minor role in some chapters whereas they form a more major critical focus in others. The result is a rather inelegant patchwork quilt of ideas, but that is the state of the art. A tidy, conceptually complete model could only have been achieved at the cost of writing a work of fiction. However, the crucial motivating importance of theoretical concerns as a stimulus to thought and to empirical investigation, as well as an essential means of bringing conceptual order into factual chaos is implicit (and often explicit) in all that follows. These essays on different facets of the scientific basis of developmental psychiatry aim to capture the excitement of the development of ideas as they now engage the attention of researchers, as well as providing an account of those aspects of developmental knowledge which are of immediate practical relevance to the clinical psychiatrist or pediatrician.

REFERENCES

Baldwin, A. L. (1967). *Theories of Child Development.* New York: Wiley.

Bandura, A. (1971). *Social Learning Theory.* Morristown, N.J.: General Learning Press.

Becker, W. C., Madsen, C. H., Arnold, C. R. and Thomas, D. R. (1967). The contingent use of teacher attention and praise in reducing classroom behavior problems. *J. Spec. Educ., 1,* 287–307.

Bem, D. J. and Allen, A. (1974). On predicting some of the people some of the time: the search for cross-situational consistencies in behavior. *Psychol. Rev., 81,* 506–520.

Bem, D. J. and Funder, D. C. (1978). Predicting more of the people more of the time: assessing the personality of situations. *Psychol. Rev., 85,* 485–501.

Benton, A. L. and Pearl, D. (Eds.) (1978). *Dyslexia: An appraisal of current knowledge.* New York: Oxford University Press.

Block, J. (1971). *Lives Through Time.* Berkeley: Bancroft Books.

Bowers, K. S. (1973). Situationism in psychology: an analysis and a critique. *Psychol. Rev., 80,* 307–336.

Bronfenbrenner, U. (1979). *The Ecology of Human Development: experiments by nature and design.* Cambridge, Mass.: Harvard University Press.

Bronson, W. C. (1967). Adult derivatives of emotional expressiveness and reactivity-control: developmental continuities from childhood to adulthood. *Child Develop., 38,* 801–817.

Brown, G. W. and Harris, T. (1978). *Social Origins of Depression.* London: Tavistock Publications.

Cicourel, A. V. (1968). *The Social Organization of Juvenile Justice.* London: Wiley (Re-issued with a new introduction, Heinemann Educational Books, 1976).

Clarke, A. and Clarke, A. (Eds.) (1976). *Early Experience: Myth and Evidence.* London: Open Books.

Cox, A. (1976). The association between emotional disorders in childhood and neuroses in adult life. *In:* H. M. Van Praag (Ed.) *Research in Neuroses.* Utrecht: Bohn, Scheltema & Holkema.

Dare, C. (1977). Psychoanalytic theories. *In:* M. Rutter and L. Hersov (Eds.) *Child Psychiatry: Modern Approaches.* Oxford: Blackwell Scientific.

Eisenberg, L. (1977). Development as a unifying concept in psychiatry. *Brit. J. Psychiat. 131,* 225–237.

Eysenck, H. J. and Eysenck, S. B. G. (1975). *Manual of the Eysenck Personality Questionnaire (Junior and Adult).* London: Hodder & Stoughton.

Farrington, D. P. (1977). The effects of public labelling. *Brit. J. Criminol., 17,* 112–125.

Farrington, D. P. (1979). Longitudinal research on crime and delinquency. *In:* N. Morris and N. Tonry (Eds.) *Crime and Justice—1978: An Annual Review of Criminal Justice Research.* Chicago: University of Chicago Press. (In press.)

Gersten, J. C., Langner, T. S., Eisenberg, J. G., Simcha-Fagan, O. and McCarthy, E. D. (1976). Stability and change in types of behavioral disturbance of children and adolescents. *J. abn. Child Psychol., 4,* 111–128.

Guilford, J. P. (1959). *Personality.* New York: McGraw Hill.

Lamb, M. E. (Ed.) (1978). *Social and Personality Development.* New York: Holt, Rinehart and Winston.

Lemert, E. M. (1967). *Human Deviance, Social Problems, and Social Control.* Englewood Cliffs: N.J.: Prentice-Hall.

Lishman, W. A. (1978). *Organic Psychiatry.* Oxford: Blackwell.

Mayhew, P., Clarke, R. V. G., Sturman, A. and Hough, J. M. (1976). *Crime as Opportunity.* Home Office Research Study No. 34. London: HMSO.

Meadow, K. P. (1975). The development of deaf children. *In:* E. M. Hetherington (Ed.) *Review of Child Development Research, Vol. 5.* Chicago: University of Chicago Press.

Mischel, W. (1968) *Personality and Assessment.* New York: Wiley.

Mischel, W. (1973). Toward a cognitive social learning reconceptualization of personality. *Psychol. Rev., 80,* 252–283.

Mischel, W. (1976). *Introduction to Personality, 2nd edition.* New York: Holt, Rinehart and Winston.

Mussen, P. H., Conger, J. J. and Kagan, J. (1979). *Child Development and Personality, 5th edition.* New York: Harper & Row.

Offord, D. R. and Cross, L. A. (1969). Behavioural antecedents of adult schizophrenia. *Arch. gen. Psychiat., 21,* 267–283.

Patterson, G. R. (1977). Accelerating stimuli for two classes of coercive behaviors. *J. abn. Child Psychol., 5,* 335–350.

Robins, L. (1966). *Deviant Children Grown Up.* Baltimore: Williams & Wilkins.

Robins, L. (1978). Sturdy childhood predictors of adult antisocial behavior: replications from longitudinal studies. *Psychol. Med., 8,* 611–622.

Rutter, M. (1972a). Childhood schizophrenia reconsidered. *J. Autism Child. Schiz., 2,* 315–337.

Rutter, M. (1972b). *Maternal Deprivation Reassessed.* Harmondsworth: Penguin.

Rutter, M. (1977). Brain damage syndromes in childhood: concepts and findings. *J. Child Psychol. Psychiat., 18,* 1–21.

Rutter, M. (1979a). *Changing Youth in a Changing Society: patterns of adolescent development and disorder.* London: Nuffield Provincial Hospitals Trust.

Rutter, M. (1979b). Protective factors in children's responses to stress and disadvantage. *In:* M. W. Kent and J. E. Rolf (Eds.) *Primary Prevention of Psychopathology: Vol. 3: Promoting Social Competence and Coping in Children.* Hanover, N.H.: University Press of New England.

Rutter, M. (1979c). Maternal deprivation 1972–1978: New findings, new concepts, new approaches. *Child Develop, 50,* 283–305.

Rutter, M. and Chadwick, O. (1979). Neuro-behavioural associations and syndromes of 'Minimal Brain Dysfunction'. *In:* F. C. Rose (Ed.) *Clinical Neuro-Epidemiology.* Tunbridge Wells, Pitman Medical. (In press.)

Rutter, M., Graham, P., Chadwick, O. and Yule, W. (1976). Adolescent turmoil: fact or fiction? *J. Child Psychol. Psychiat. 17,* 35–56.

Rutter, M. and Hersov, L. (Eds.) (1977). *Child Psychiatry: Modern Approaches.* London: Blackwell Scientific.

Rutter, M. and Madge, N. (1976). *Cycles of Disadvantage.* London: Heinemann Educational.

Rutter, M., Maughan, B., Mortimore, P., Ouston, J. with Smith, A. (1979). *Fifteen Thousand Hours: Secondary Schools and their effects on Children.* London: Open Books.

Rutter, M. and Yule, W. (1973). Specific reading retardation. *In:* L. Mann and D.A. Sabatino (Eds.) *The First Review of Special Education.* Philadelphia: Buttonwood Farms.

Scheff, T. (1966). *Being Mentally Ill: a sociological theory*. Chicago: Aldine.

Schulsinger, F. (1972). Psychopathy: heredity and environment. *Internat. J. Ment. Health*, **1**, 190–206.

Skinner, B. F. (1957). *Verbal Behaviour*. London: Methuen.

Watt, N. F. (1976). Longitudinal changes in the social behavior of children hospitalized for schizophrenia as adults. *J. nerv. ment. Dis.*, **155**, 42–54.

Watt, N. F. and Lubensky, A. W. (1976). Childhood roots of schizophrenia. *J. consult. clin. Psychol.*, **44**, 353–375.

West, D. J. and Farrington, D. P. (1977). *The Delinquent Way of Life*. London: Heinemann Educational.

2. GENETICS AND MENTAL DEVELOPMENT

JAMES SHIELDS

Longitudinal studies
    Cognitive development
    Age of menarche
    Temperament

Personality tests
    Age-dependent anomalies

Schizophrenia, developmental aspects

Interaction

Nature of genetic factors
    Chromosomes
    Single genes with major effects
    Polygenic inheritance

Attempts to partition the causes of variation
    Heritability and other components
    Path analysis of influences on wealth
    Plurality of approaches

Concluding Remarks

A book about development cannot afford to neglect genetics. The genes provide the code for specific enzymes, and the information they contain regulates the operation of these enzymes, switching their production on and off in response to internal and external stimuli. In this way they exert a major control on development, speeding up one process, slowing down another, or waiting until the environment is ripe to trigger it off. They determine the capacity of the organism to respond to a particular environment in a certain way. It is often implied that genes merely influence intrauterine development and perhaps early physical maturation too; everything that happens later on is, according to this view, the result of subsequent interaction between the environment and the infant's congenital characteristics, these themselves being the product of both genetic and prenatal environmental factors. A child's behaviour is thus largely determined by such things as his physical condition at birth, his size, features, skin colour and so on and how these are perceived and reacted to by his parents and peers. This is a mistaken view. At no time in life can it be said that the genes have ceased to exert their effects. They influence not only the colour of our hair but when it turns grey or grows thin on top. Throughout childhood, adolescence, adult life and senescence, there is a dynamic interplay between environment and genetic constitution. New stresses can evoke latent genetic potentialities, in addition to responses that have been previously learned. The simplest example is the response to blood transfusion or tissue transplantation. Many genetic diseases, such as Huntington's chorea, have a late age of onset, and cannot be explained by the interaction of life stresses in a person of a particular appearance or temperament, brought up in a particular childhood environment. Only rarely, however, will the response be reducible to the molecular level, as in the above examples.

Genetic influences in child and adolescent psychiatry have already been reviewed comprehensively (Shields, 1977), and this chapter will not cover the same ground again. Instead, examples will be given of some of the few genetic studies that have investigated the same subjects at different ages or in some other way have tried to clarify the ways in which the development of a disorder may be under genetic control. There will be some discussion of the concept of genetic-environmental interaction, the complex pathway from genotype to phenotype, the nature of the genetic influences, and of attempts to say how much rather than just whether individual differences in a characteristic depend on genetic differences. Firm conclusions will be few. It is often a case of the less the knowledge, the greater the disagreement. But from what emerges I hope it will be clear that the inborn potentialities of the child and the adult cannot just be ignored, even if little definite can be said about them.

Before describing the developmental studies, a brief word on methods of genetic investigation in clinical psychiatry. In the case of the commoner disorders of behaviour and mood, these rely mainly on twin studies and adoption studies. This is because of the difficulty of disentangling biological from social heredity in most other types of family investigation. In the past the twin method was severely criticized and very few adoption studies existed. In recent years, however, it has been shown that many of the pitfalls of twin studies can be successfully avoided, and the extent of many of the supposed biases has been evaluated and found to be less extreme than was claimed by the critics. Adoption studies have been found more feasible than previously thought. Both types of investigations agree in finding most conditions to be subject to both genetic and environmental influences, whether these are cognitive traits or personality disorders. This has been so even with some features defined by social or legal criteria.

Crude environmental theories that attribute variation almost entirely to social variation between families, emotional differences within families and exogenous brain damage have been found inadequate. Adopted-away children still show some resemblance to their biological parents; MZ twins do not have to be brought up together in an extremely similar environment for them to be alike; and minor or major brain dysfunction due to injury before or after birth accounts for little of the total variation in behaviour. But the far from perfect concordance in MZ twins reared together is the strongest evidence we have of the importance of environmental factors peculiar to the individual, and is a warning against genetic over-interpretation. Support for the above statements will be found in Cohen *et al.* (1977), Gottesman and Shields (1976a, b), Loehlin and Nichols (1976), Matheny *et al.* (1976), Mednick *et al.* (1974), Schepank (1974) and Shields (1976, 1978) and in some of what follows.

The hypothesis of genetic influences on behaviour has survived successive attempts at refutation. However, it is the genes that are inherited. All characteristics are acquired as a result of heredity and environment acting together on their development. Sometimes the processes by which the information coded in the genes is translated into behaviour in response to varying nurture may be the same for all members of our species, and sometimes they may depend on individual genetic differences. It is conceivable that variation in a characteristic might be mainly environmental at one age and mainly genetic at another.

LONGITUDINAL STUDIES

I shall first describe briefly three longitudinal studies of development, relating to the growth of intelligence, sexual maturation, temperament and personality test scores. Based mainly on twins, they provide some evidence for genetic differences in rates of development.

Cognitive development

Over the years since 1957 the Louisville Twin Study has recruited twins from Board of Health birth records. R. S. Wilson (1977) has recently summarized its findings on mental development. Over 400 pairs of twins, representing a wide range of socioeconomic environments, have participated. Most of the twins were tested for consecutive periods of at least four years between the ages of 3 months and 6 years. Tests were carried out at the ages of 3, 6, 9, 12, 18 and 24 months and at $2\frac{1}{2}$, 3, 4, 5 and 6 years. The Bayley mental tests, mostly concerned with sensorimotor coordination, were used at the earlier ages and

Wechsler intelligence tests at the later ages. MZ twins showed some remarkable similarities in spurts and lags in development as well as in their abilities at each age, while DZ pairs, particularly at later ages, were less alike in these respects. Three of Wilson's profiles illustrate the point. In Fig. 1A both MZ twins show an upward trend after a low

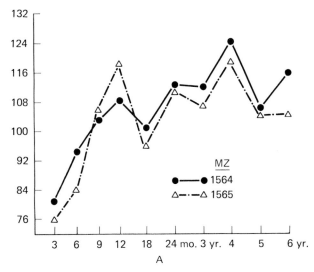

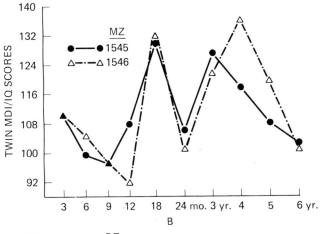

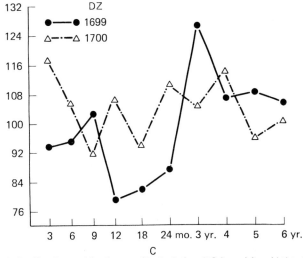

Fig. 1. Profiles of mental development (Bayley Index of IQ Scores) from birth to 6 years in 3 pairs of twins. (From Wilson, 1977)

beginning. In another MZ pair (Fig. 1B) both twins show similar spurts and lags. This is in contrast to the DZ pair shown in Fig. 1C. The conclusion was supported by analysis of all pairs. Table I shows the within-pair correlation in respect of changes from age to age and in overall level at five interlocking periods.

TABLE I

TWIN RESEMBLANCE FOR TRENDS IN PRE-SCHOOL MENTAL DEVELOPMENT
(AFTER WILSON, 1977)

Ages	Age-to-age change		Overall level	
	rMZ	rDZ	rMZ	rDZ
3–12 months	·49	·20	·88	·79
6–24 months	·64	·53	·84	·73
18–36 months	·47	·35	·90	·72
3–5 years	·47	·17	·93	·74
4–6 years	·41	·11	·90	·66

The number of MZ pairs in each period varied from 35 to 58 and the number of DZ pairs from 44 to 60. All but one of the MZ:DZ comparisons were statistically significant.

Wilson concluded that 'the most powerful determinant of mental development was the genetic blueprint supplied for each twin by the parents'. The DZ twins became less concordant during the pre-school years, while being continuously exposed to the same family environment. Such differential treatment by the parents as occurred was frequently evoked by the demands of the child. No relationship could be demonstrated between presumed differential treatment and measures of intelligence in DZ twins. 'The alleged potency of these variables,' says Wilson, 'is based on conjecture, not on empirical data, and as an explanation it is without substance.... Indeed, the parental treatment is typically in the opposite direction—to minimize differences and attempt to bring both twins to a common level.'

Accordingly the genotype is the major though not the only determinant of the child's capacities. As Nancy Bayley herself concluded, each child—or each zygote, in Wilson's opinion—is a law unto itself as regards development. The contribution of the parents, according to Wilson, is to provide a family environment that is suitably supportive and stimulating—or perhaps discouraging, as he might have added if he had been considering temperamental or intellectual development.

The Louisville study also sheds light on the effect of prenatal and perinatal hazards on the intellectual development of twins. By the age of 6 the twins had made up most of their earlier retardation compared to singletons: at all percentiles from the 5th to the 95th the means of twins and singletons were within three points of each other. Being the second-born twin had no effect on intellectual development, despite any greater hazard at birth compared with the first-born. After the first six months the correlation between birth weight and developmental status declined to a modest ·10 or ·15. However, there was a preponderance of low scores when both twins weighed under 1750 g at birth, i.e. in those where gestational age was short. On the other hand, in MZ pairs with a big difference in birth weight the im-

balance of prenatal nutrition had only a very minor influence on IQ, accounting for no more than 1% of the total score variance.

Age of menarche

Fischbein's (1977) investigation of pubertal development in a representative sample of normal Swedish twins has the advantage that it was based, not on recall, but on information mostly obtained at six-monthly intervals between the ages of 10 and 16. The girl twins' resemblance in menarcheal age (Table II) confirms three previous reports and indicates that physical maturity is strongly regulated by hereditary factors. There has also been a marked secular trend towards earlier menarche of about four months per decade over more than a century, and towards accelerated growth generally (Tanner, 1962). This does not affect the above conclusion any more than increased stature over the years affects conclusions about genetic causes of differences in height within a population at a given time.

TABLE II

RESEMBLANCE IN AGE AT MENARCHE IN TWINS (LONGITUDINALLY COLLECTED
DATA OF FISCHBEIN, 1977)

Zygosity	Number of pairs	Intrapair Difference (years)	Intrapair Correlation r
MZ	28	0·29	0·93
DZ	48	0·71	0·62

If precocious or retarded maturity can lead to disturbed behaviour, this may represent one of many indirect genetic influences on psychiatric development. Postmenarcheal girls tend to be more intelligent than premenarcheal girls of the same age, and the same appears to be true within MZ twin pairs aged between 12 and 15 (Shields, 1954a). However, Shields's (1962) findings, both in MZ twins brought up apart and in those brought up together, that the twin whose periods were said to have started first did better than her co-twin on intelligence tests as an adult have yet to be confirmed.

Temperament

The New York Longitudinal Study of temperament and development (Thomas and Chess, 1977) is not specifically a genetic investigation, though its predominantly middle class Jewish sample included a few pairs of twins. Earlier study of these twins (Rutter, et al., 1963) produced evidence of genetic influences on activity level and reaction patterns such as withdrawal and adaptability.

One MZ pair was brought up apart without contact between the twins and has now been followed up for 16 years. When they were aged 2, both twins had highly irregular sleep patterns and were markedly intense in their expression of negative moods. Parental handling was very different in the two families. In one, the parents were consistent and affectionate, and were able to ignore the crying when it was apparent it did not reflect discomfort. The night awakening diminished and disappeared without any behaviour problems developing. The other parents could not bear to hear the infant scream, picked her up, soothed her and fed her. This reinforced the night crying pattern. At 28 months they were advised to ignore this and the tantrum behaviour in the daytime. The sleep problem then gradually disappeared, and subsequent development was without incident.

At the age of 16 these twins showed remarkable similarities in their behaviour. Both were adaptable and persistent, and they continued to show intense emotional expressiveness. They were doing well in school, had an active social life, and both displayed interest in music and acrobatics. Their striking temperamental similarity in adolescence was thought to be the result of the same genetic factors appropriately reinforced in a similar sociocultural environment.

Thomas and Chess stress that factors other than genetic ones may be equally or more influential in shaping temperament. Obstetrical and birth difficulties, or perinatal brain damage, however, did not appear to them to be as important for temperament, as is claimed by proponents of the minimal brain dysfunction syndrome (Wender, 1971). Of greatest importance was the goodness of fit, or lack of fit, between the child's inherent characteristics and the parents' response to them. The child himself can play an active role in his development from birth on. They were impressed by the breadth and scope of individual differences: natural populations are genetically heterogeneous, and polymorphism is desirable.

In support of the role they give to genetic factors in the development of temperament, Thomas and Chess quote a study from Norway by Torgersen (see Torgersen and Kringlen, 1978) in which 53 pairs of infant twins were investigated using their NYLS protocol for obtaining temperamental data. At 2 months of age there were significant differences between MZ and DZ twins in some categories, and by 9 months in all 9 categories—activity level, rhythmicity, approach-withdrawal, adaptability, threshold of responsiveness, intensity of reaction, quality of mood, distractability, and persistence. There was a tendency for MZ twins to grow more alike and DZ twins to grow less alike. There was no evidence that the mothers treated MZ twins more similarly than DZ twins, or reported them to be more alike than they really were. Most of the mothers had no definite opinion regarding the zygosity. At 2 months, only one mother thought her twins were MZ, though most of them were.

There is support from other studies that some psychiatric behaviour problems are transient reactions to environmental circumstances, and may have little bearing on later mental health. In the separated twins studied by Shields (1962) changes of environment in childhood could be seen to have had an upsetting effect on several twins, without any lasting influence. Similarly, in Heston's (1966) study of children reared in a variety of institutional and foster home settings there are several examples of behaviour disorders occurring as a reaction to unsuitable placement. Later mental health, however, was more

closely related to the biological parentage. Schizophrenia occurred only among those with schizophrenic mothers.

Such findings, if extended and generalized, might seem to support the idea of there being a large homeostatic element in the genetic control of development. Environmental influences might throw development off course for a time, but unless these influences were extreme or multiple, or continually reinforced or, perhaps, occurred at critical periods, these fluctuations would sooner or later tend to right themselves. Within limits, the individual's final state would be that channelled by his genetic programme.

In view of the evolved plasticity of human behaviour—variable from individual to individual—the above view may be less true for behavioural than for physical development. It will then be a question of how extreme and how reinforced environmental influences have to be for them to have a lasting effect on development? They might not have to be very great for the development of some characteristics. Even MZ twins reared together show that environmental factors are often of critical importance. With regard to diagnosable psychiatric disorder MZ concordance rates of well over 50% are the exception rather than the rule. This points to the importance of influences peculiar to the individual rather than simply to the shared family environment. These can be early or later influences, or both. Among the early influences is the tendency for twins to cast themselves or to be cast by the parents in different roles, such as the leader and follower. Later influences include acquired physical illness and relationships in marriage and at work. However, the occurrence of childhood behaviour disorder was seen by Shields (1954a) to be related also to harmful family environments such as disturbed parental relations. Genetic factors appeared to influence temperament and the kind of symptom shown more than the occurrence of the disorder. It could further be shown (Shields, 1954b) that when there was quarrelling between the parents, the twins tended to get on badly with one another too. The 6 out of 36 MZ pairs where the twins were antagonistic or indifferent to one another all came from the 16 homes where the psychological family environment was rated as poor or bad—a highly significant difference. A close mutual twin relationship seemed to characterize stable families, rather than being a morbid reaction to parental neglect, as has sometimes been maintained. Disturbed inter-personal relationships are not an environmental influence which necessarily rules out genetics. They are the result of a two-way process and may depend on a child's inherent characteristics.

PERSONALITY TESTS

There is a dearth of reports of personality measures on the same group of twins, or other relatives, at different ages to discover whether those aspects of behaviour which show evidence of genetic determination at one age are the same as those that do so at a later stage of development. However, the same tests administered to different groups of twins at about the same age are liable to produce inconsistent findings. This is true whether the tests are those constructed in Minnesota (the MMPI) or at the Maudsley (the MPI and its successors). In view of present test unreliability and the frequent drop in sample size in longitudinal studies, one should not expect firm conclusions to be obtained.

Eaves and Eysenck (1976) analysed the 11 neuroticism items common to two personality tests given two years apart to a large sample of normal twins.* Since these were adults, changes cannot be attributed to development in the usual sense. The analysis of variability of response produced the intriguing suggestion of a genetic component in inconsistency of response: the heritability of inconsistency, as estimated by the authors, was ·47.

Much of the psychometric evidence for a genetic contribution to personality comes from high school twins. Loehlin and Nichols's (1976) study of 850 such pairs is a recent example. The pioneer follow-up by Dworkin et al. (1976) of adolescent twins into young adulthood is therefore of considerable interest. Only 42 of Gottesman's (1965, 1966) Boston sample of 147 pairs of twins, aged around 16 when originally tested on the Minnesota Multiphasic Personality Inventory and the California Psychological Inventory, could be retested around the age of 28. Dworkin et al. found a substantial change in those personality scales that showed significant genetic variance at the two ages. Rather more scales showed genetic influence in adolescence only than in adulthood only. The MMPI scales labelled Anxiety and Dependency were two that showed significant genetic variance in both adolescence and adulthood, and in adolescence-to-adulthood personality change. Various possible explanations of these age differences were put forward. Among them were the effects of gene regulation, the accelerated rate of development in adolescence, changes in the environmental variance, and the possibility that a scale might measure different traits at different ages. It was not possible to say which explanation best accounted for the results.

Age-dependent anomalies

The comparison of patients' sibs at different ages may sometimes point to anomalies genetically related to the disorder in question that are detectable only at certain stages of development. When Metrakos and Metrakos (1961) examined the sibs of centrencephalic epileptics, they found similar EEG 3/sec spikes and waves in 45% of those aged between $4\frac{1}{2}$ and $16\frac{1}{2}$, but a considerably lower prevalence in younger and older age groups. Such a high rate in sibs suggested the contribution of a major gene. Doose et al. (1967) investigated the EEGs of the sibs of children whose convulsive disorders were associated with an abnormal theta rhythm. Once again the prevalence of a theta rhythm in sibs was high and remarkably age dependent. Between the ages of 2 and 4 as many as 54% of 46 sibs showed this abnormality, compared with 12% of 60 controls. The records were judged blind.

* See Shields (1976, Table 1) for a comparison of the results.

Information about developmental disorders in parents is difficult to obtain and evaluate, especially if they have found ways round their difficulty. There is evidence from studies by Hallgren (1950), Bakwin (1973), Rutter et al. (1970), De Fries et al. (1978) and others of a genetic component, perhaps a major one, in many cases of specific reading retardation. In this, unlike other childhood behaviour and educational difficulties, nearly 100% of MZ twins are concordant, and approaching 50% in DZ twins (Shields, 1975). Marked regional variation in prevalence (Berger et al., 1975) indicates that genetic factors are not the only ones of importance, however. In Baltimore, Finucci et al. (1976) have tested the families of 20 children with specific reading problems in a way that ingeniously detects adults who may have compensated for a similar disability in themselves. Their tests included the reading of words written upside down or backwards, nonsense passages, and unrelated sentences at increased speed. 45% of first degree relatives were classified as disabled readers, considerably more than in a comparison group. Males were more often affected than females. The pedigrees resembled those of Hallgren's (1950) larger Swedish study and are more consistent with his theory of a major dominant gene with reduced manifestation, particularly in females, than with polygenic inheritance. Finucci et al. suggest that their material is genetically heterogeneous and that examination of visual evoked EEG responses might identify subgroups. To summarize the findings in reading retardation, people seem to differ genetically in how easily they acquire reading skills. Environmental factors and other skills influence whether a difficulty becomes a disability and how successfully it is overcome.

In Japan Abe and co-workers (see Shields, 1973) report resemblance in respect of sleep disturbances such as insomnia, sleepwalking and teeth-grinding and other behaviours between children seen in infant welfare clinics and their parents when they were the same age. Information about the parents was obtained from grandparents. Abe (1972) has also reported a significant association between certain phobias and other symptoms in childhood and adulthood. This was in the mothers of the children referred to above.

The relationship between childhood and adult psychiatric disorder has been extensively discussed by Rutter (1972) and Cox (1976). Though a few individuals suffer from phobic or obsessional disorders as children and adults, there are many discontinuities. Despite surface similarities between child and adult neurosis, most of the so-called neurotic traits of childhood are seen to be nothing of the kind. Adult psychiatric disorder need not have its roots in childhood.

SCHIZOPHRENIA, DEVELOPMENTAL ASPECTS

The high risk studies (Garmezy, 1974a, b) are the nearest we have to a prospective investigation of the development of schizophrenia. Despite many interesting observations and hypotheses concerning perinatal factors, psychophysiological measures, attention and other variables, not always confirmed, no firm conclusions can yet be drawn from these studies about what is inherited or how psychotic development might be prevented (Erlenmeyer-Kimling, 1975; Hanson, Gottesman and Heston, 1976; Hanson, Gottesman and Meehl, 1977; Mednick et al., 1974; Shields and Gottesman, 1977; van Dyke et al., 1974). The subjects are usually the children of schizophrenic parents. Without knowing which of them eventually become schizophrenic, it is difficult to tell how far their behavioural characteristics are genetic or environmental in origin, or are typical for the majority of schizophrenics who do not have psychotic parents. Only the Danish study by Mednick and Schulsinger has followed up its subjects into early adult life (H. Schulsinger, 1976). Not all schizophrenics are premorbidly schizoid, and children who are pathologically shy and withdrawn seldom become schizophrenic adults. No trait in these high risk children has yet been found to be more simply inherited and less mixed in aetiology than schizophrenia itself for it to be a satisfactory indicator of a schizophrenia-prone genotype and hence a more promising subject for genetic investigation in the population (Shields et al., 1975).

In a twin study of infantile autism in 20 pairs of twins Folstein and Rutter (1977) found that in all but one of the discordant MZ pairs the unaffected twin had a definite, although not always the same, cognitive or language abnormality. This, they considered, is what might be inherited in autism. Other factors such as early brain injury would determine whether the characteristic symptoms developed or not. It was not suggested, however, that all forms of language impairment were genetically related to autism, in the way it is sometimes suggested that all 'schizoid' features are on the same genetic dimension as schizophrenia. Infantile autism itself is not genetically related to schizophrenia.

The most detailed retrospective reconstruction of the development of schizophrenia in more than one family member must be that of the Genain quadruplets by Rosenthal (1963) and his collaborators. The quadruplets were monozygotic and all eventually became schizophrenic. What was inherited, according to Rosenthal, was the 'general pattern of unfolding subtype syndromes', but the sequence could be truncated at any stage. The illnesses of the quadruplets, which were mainly catatonic in form, differed in severity and outcome, the process having progressed further in some of them than in others. From an early age the quads were temperamentally alike in that they all had 'low energy levels, were rather placid, "sweet", introverted ... and would take little initiative either with respect to general activities or interpersonal relationships'. Furthermore, they were reared in an unreasonably constrictive environment. The psychiatric differences between them could be related to their different life experiences and relationships within this family. The genes thus seem to have had an influence on the form of the eventual illness as well as on early temperament.

Gottesman and Shields (1972) also speak of the 'unfolding of schizophrenia' over time, depending both on 'diathesis' and 'stress'. In a schematic diagram (Fig. 2), suggested by the case histories of their Maudsley twin series, they illustrate the development of four hysterical persons with an above-average genetic predisposition to schizophrenia. Two of them are a pair of discordant MZ twins. G3 has the highest genetic liability. He develops a schizoid personality and becomes a chronic schizophrenic without remission. Twins A and B start with the same, lesser genetic loading (G2), though one more typical of the average schizophrenic. Twin A encounters stresses

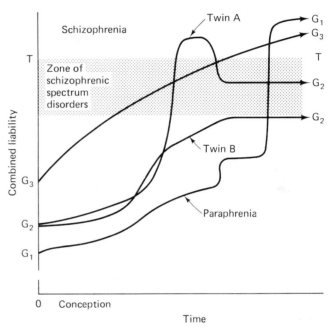

Fig. 2. Schematic proposal for how diathesis interacts with stress in the development of schizophrenia. (From Gottesman & Shields, 1973)

which over time result in an overt schizophrenic illness. This improves with treatment, but he remains an impoverished, eccentric personality within the zone of 'spectrum disorders'. Twin B has got by without detectable abnormality, though his total genetic and environmental liability may have brought him close to the zone of spectrum disorder. G1 has less genetic predisposition than most schizophrenics, but stresses such as the death of a spouse and the onset of deafness lead to a late onset paraphrenia.

The introductory remarks to the chapter and the examples given so far from longitudinal studies, age-related anomalies and schizophrenia, indicate that genetic and environmental influence can each make a contribution to development at any age. Genetically determined characteristics present at birth and early experience may colour subsequent development, but in the past the importance of early experience appears to have been exaggerated (Clarke and Clarke, 1976). Equally clear is the conclusion that the effect of a particular environment on a child or adult may depend on his or her genetic constitution; and conversely, the way an individual's unique genetic constitution manifests itself in behaviour may depend on the nature of the environment he encounters. In other words, genes and environment interact.

INTERACTION

Assessing the parts played by heredity and environment in psychological development is made no easier by the different meanings given to the term interaction. Sometimes genetic-environmental interaction may mean no more than the obvious fact that both genes and environment are necessary if development is to occur at all. It could be that either genetic variation or environmental variation, provided it was compatible with life, made no difference as to how a particular characteristic developed. More usually, interaction is taken to imply that both have an influence: vary the genotype or vary the environment in certain relevant ways and the outcome will be different. The nature and extent of genetic and environmental influences, and how extreme they have to be for them to have a marked effect, will be a matter for investigation. It could well be that a number of genetic factors and a number of environmental factors each independently influenced a characteristic, such as stature or anxiety, and did so in an additive manner. Some individuals might possess a genetic-biochemical constitution such that, in any given environment, they would manifest more anxiety than others who were genetically less predisposed; but increase the anxiety-provoking stresses, and the manifest anxiety of both groups of individuals would increase to a similar extent.

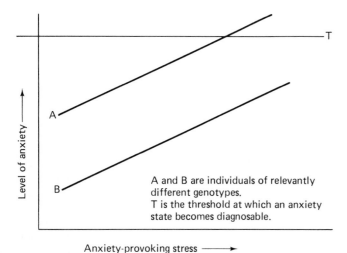

Fig. 3. Additive model of genetic-environmental co-action.

In the more technical, statistical use of the term, these additive effects do not constitute interaction, even though a given stressor or set of stressors would be sufficient to lead some individuals but not others to develop a diagnosable anxiety state requiring treatment (Fig. 3). A more neutral term to cover this use of the word would be co-action of genetic and environmental factors. For interaction in the strict sense to occur, changes in the

environmental variables would have to affect individuals of different constitution to a different extent (ordinal interaction) or in opposite ways (disordinal interaction). The subject is discussed by Erlenmeyer-Kimling (1972).

Ordinal interaction may occur in the case of some sex differences, boys being more sensitive to certain kinds of stress than girls (Rutter, 1970). Genotype x environment interaction seems to be indicated in criminal behaviour. In Hutchings and Mednick's (1974) study of all male Copenhagen adoptees born 1927–41 the highest rate of criminality, 36%, occurred in those where both the adoptive and the biological father had a criminal record. The relevant findings are shown in Fig. 4. Being reared by a criminal adoptive father (hatched bars) increased the incidence of registered criminality in adoptees significantly more when the biological father had a criminal background (shown on the right of the figure) than when the biological father was not known to the police—an example of ordinal interaction.

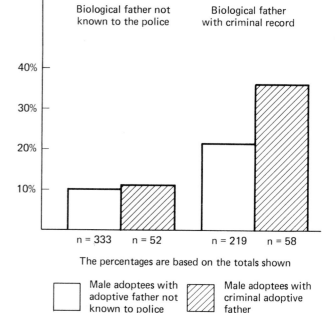

Fig. 4. Percentage of registered criminality in Danish male adoptees. (Data of Hutchings & Mednick, 1974)

An instructive example of disordinal gene-environment interaction on growth is provided by the plant golden rod *Solidago virgaurea* (Thoday, 1969). Populations of the plant found in southern Sweden are taller than those in northern Norway. The natural habitat of the Swedish variety is shady, while the Norwegian variety is exposed to the light. One might be tempted to conclude that a simple relationship between light and growth explained the difference—the shadier the environment, the taller the eventual height. However, experimental transplantation of the two varieties, each grown under high and low intensity of light, shows the situation to be more complex. The two varieties differ genetically, having adapted to different habitats. Both react profoundly to the environmental variable of light intensity, but they do so in opposite directions (Table III). A low intensity, instead of making the Norwegian variety taller, has a dwarfing effect; it requires a high intensity of light to grow to medium height. The Swedish variety on the other hand thrives in shade; a strong exposure to the sun reduces its stature to the medium size of the Norwegian variety in its natural habitat.

TABLE III

GOLDEN ROD: HEIGHT OF PLANT
(AFTER THODAY, 1969)

	Experimental environment	
Natural habitat of plants	High intensity of light	Low intensity of light
Exposed, northern Norway	Medium	Dwarf
Shaded, southern Sweden	Medium	Tall

In mental handicap, the inborn errors of metabolism may provide examples of disordinal interaction. The low phenylalanine diet, which is beneficial to the intellectual development of the PKU homozygote, could hardly be anything but detrimental to anyone else! Identical forms of treatment may also have the opposite effects in people of different personality. According to Eysenck's theory (Eysenck and Wilson, 1976), introverts are more responsive to conditioning than extraverts and so should be more easily socialized. Extraverts are more liable to hysterical (dissociative) and psychopathic (antisocial) disorders, while introverts are more liable to anxiety, depressions and obsessions. Stimulation is a more effective treatment for extraverts, sedation for introverts. Opposite (disordinal) reactions to sedative drugs have been observed. Following their administration, the performance of introverts with high anxiety improved, while that of extraverts with low anxiety worsened. The theory also predicts that introverts, being chronically more aroused, should show better long-term memory and extraverts better short-term memory. On a memory test, introverts' recall score, low at first, increased with the length of recall interval (1 min to 24 h.), while that of extraverts, high at first, fell. There is evidence from several twin studies that extraversion-introversion and Eysenck's independent dimension of neuroticism are both under some degree of genetic control, though each dimension may not be as unitary as the theory originally proposed (Eaves and Eysenck, 1975). Whereas there is disordinal interaction between extraversion-introversion and the effects of treatment, this is apparently not so as regards the causes of extraversion-introversion itself. The genetic and environmental factors that contribute to scores on Eysenck's personality questionnaires fit a simple additive model (Jinks and Fulker, 1970; Eaves and Eysenck, 1975, 1976)—co-action, not interaction.

The existence of interaction, ordinal or disordinal, underlines the importance of fitting the treatment to the individual: what is best for one may not be best for another. If interaction were disordinal and, for instance, giving up smoking raised morbidity in some people but reduced it in others, general policy recommendations could not be made unless one could accurately predict how an individual would react. Clinically it may be important to identify interaction effects and take account of them when one can. To do this with scientific accuracy is seldom possible in the present state of our knowledge, though we may all do it intuitively in everyday life. For other purposes it may be more desirable to iron out trivial interaction in order to obtain a clear general picture. For example, in designing personality questionnaires, items can be omitted to which the sexes respond differently.

NATURE OF THE GENETIC FACTORS

Mankind shares many developmental processes with other animal life, and our uniquely developed capacities for speech, learning and the transmission of culture have been acquired through natural selection. We are not concerned here with the evolutionary aspects of mental development but rather with individual differences.

Chromosomes

The most far-reaching single genetic influence on social and emotional development, and on the predisposition to disorders of many different kinds, is the inheritance of an XX or an XY sex chromosomal constitution. By a simple switch mechanism the presence or absence of the Y chromosome determines the formation and maturation of the primary sex character, either testes or ovaries. The secondary sex characters in turn depend on the hormones produced by the primary sex characters. In normal development the boy and the girl will indulge in, and be encouraged to indulge in, different kinds of behaviour. The ensuing biosocial interactions result in existing sex differences in behaviour. Other influences can disrupt normal development. For example, in rare instances an abnormal autosomal gene may prevent an XY individual from responding to testosterone, resulting in the development of female genitalia and feminine gender orientation—in other words an XY female. Flooding the organism with sex hormones belonging to the other sex can transform sexual behaviour.

Extra or missing sex chromosomes resulting from errors in cell division can influence cognitive and emotional development. Males with Klinefelter's syndrome (47, XXY) and triple-X females (47, XXX) are found to excess in subnormality hospitals, and the larger the number of extra X chromosomes (48, XXXY, 49, XXXXY, etc.) the lower the IQ. The increased liability of XXY individuals to develop behaviour disorders is unlikely to be simply a psychogenic reaction to their hypogonadism, since it was not shown by hypogonadal patients who were not XXY (Theilgaard et al., 1971; Wakeling, 1972.) Both XXY and XYY males have a somewhat increased risk for admission to mental hospitals and to prisons compared with the normal XY, and XYYs have a twenty-fold risk for admission to a high security hospital or penal-mental institution such as Carstairs (Hook, 1973; Hamerton, 1976). This cannot be accounted for by their tall stature, since tall XY males do not have a similarly increased risk of incarceration on account of menacing behaviour. Nor can it be accounted for by poverty, since chromosome anomalies are no respecters of social class (Walzer and Gerald, 1975). Furthermore, the rare XXYY individual has a 100-fold risk of admission to a penal-mental institution. But it is a myth that XYY males are destined to become violent psychopaths. They are if anything less violent than other people in the institutions to which they are admitted, and the great majority are not in trouble with the law at all. From such studies as have been done of XYYs not ascertained through surveys of psychiatric and penal populations there is the suggestion that some are prone to impulsive behaviour, which is not the same thing as violent crime (Noel *et al.*, 1974; Nielsen and Christensen, 1974; Dorus *et al.*, 1976; Witkin *et al.*, 1976; Zeuthen *et al.*, 1975). There may be an excess of XYYs seen at fertility clinics, and sex chromosome abnormalities have been found in children with severe speech retardation (Garvey and Mutton, 1973). Only by prospective surveys from birth shall we know the extent and nature of the risks. Some of the problems of work of this kind have been sensitively discussed by those engaged in it (Hamerton, 1976; Walzer *et al.*, 1976). Nevertheless, protests about such investigations were so strong that Walzer and Gerald's Boston study had to be abandoned.

In Edinburgh, 14 XYY boys, all under 8 years of age and some of them still very young, have been followed up from birth. A preliminary report (Ratcliffe, 1976) gives a hint that early behaviour problems in such boys may be concentrated in a group that shows an early spurt in growth at about the age of $2\frac{1}{2}$ years. The four boys who showed behaviour disorder were all above the 90th percentile for height. The four were basically timid children with occasional outbursts of aggression and exaggerated responses to stimuli. The mothers found them difficult to control. Four of the 14 boys had delayed speech, but the range of IQ was normal.

According to some reports (Kahn *et al.*, 1969, 1976; Nielsen, 1971; Say *et al.*, 1977) minor variants in the shape or length of chromosomes, such as a long Y chromosome, are also found more often than one might expect in certain child psychiatric and delinquent populations.

It has been suggested (Polani, 1977; Soudek and Laraya, 1974) that the effect of sex-chromosome anomalies on brain function and behaviour could in some way be attributed to an imbalance of normally inactive 'heterochromatin'.

Down's syndrome (trisomy-21) is the only common disorder caused by an extra autosome. It accounts for about a quarter of admissions to hospitals for the severely subnormal. Unlike sex chromosome abnormalities, there is no disagreement here about the causal relationship: for once, the extra chromosomal material is both necessary and (except in the case of some mosaics) sufficient for the syndrome to occur. But, as with the sex chromosome abnormalities, we know little about the causes of the non-disjunction in the first instance, or the mechanisms by which it produces the cognitive or other abnormalities. Patients with Down's syndrome live longer than they used

to, and the brains of those dying in their thirties or forties have been found to show changes like those in Alzheimer's presenile dementia (Ellis *et al.*, 1974).

In conclusion, there is evidence of a genuine association between chromosome anomalies and behavioural or cognitive disorders which is worth exploring further. We know little about the mechanisms. Except in the case of Down's syndrome, chromosomal anomalies account for only a very small proportion of the persons seen by the psychiatrist or the magistrate, and even so may not be the only cause of the trouble. Furthermore, most individuals with sex chromosome anomalies are not found in hospitals or prisons.

Single genes with major effects

Occasionally a rare gene in single dose (dominant inheritance) or in double dose (recessive inheritance) can be the major cause of a disorder. The many rare recessive inborn errors of metabolism, of which phenylketonuria (PKU) is the commonest, are a good example. From the point of view of the present discussion, PKU illustrates a number of points. First, even in this relatively clear-cut disease it is still not fully understood exactly how a mutant liver enzyme produces its effects on the developing brain. Caspari (1977) suggests that toxic products, resulting from the elevated level of phenylalanine in the blood, interfere with the action of other enzymes necessary for the synthesis of neurotransmitter substances. Second, the influence of the genes on intelligence is indirect, their primary effect being the inability to metabolize phenylalanine. Third, discovery of the single cause has led to the one appropriate treatment for avoiding the secondary effects on intelligence—a low phenylalanine diet which prevents the building up of the toxic substances. Once a single causal element such as a particular gene has been identified and studied, holding other factors constant, genetic-environmental co-action will be seen to be interactional rather than additive. A particular diet, infective agent, type of rearing or whatever, will produce an unwanted reaction in an individual of one particular genotype but not in another. Most of the instructive examples which Eisenberg (1977) gives in his stimulating paper on developmental psychiatry come from single-gene disorders such as galactosaemia and G6PD. Fourth, though in PKU a particular gene and a particular diet are necessary for mental deficiency to occur, it still makes sense to talk here of a genetic disease, since the genotype is rare and the noxious environmental element is the normal diet.

In Huntington's chorea, a late-onset neurological disorder, usually with psychiatric complications, inheritance is dominant. Carriers of the gene cannot yet be identified in early life, though there is an indication that the gene has an effect on IQ before psychiatric or neurological symptoms are shown (Lyle and Gottesman, 1977). At postmortem there is a loss of GABA (gamma-aminobutyric acid) in the basal ganglia of the brain (Bird and Iversen, 1974).

In PKU and Huntington's chorea, family pedigrees are

consistent with simple Mendelian inheritance, where all those with the necessary genes are affected. In other psychiatric disorders family data can sometimes be shown to be consistent with the hypothesis that all those cases that occur on a genetic basis are accounted for by the same gene, but that only some gene carriers—perhaps a small minority—exhibit the condition. But this hypothesis of monogenic inheritance with reduced manifestation is not the only one consistent with the data. In the case of schizophrenia, for example, all the experts go out of their way to say that one cannot at present decide between monogenic and polygenic inheritance. The latter usually fits the data just as well. To resolve problems about mode of transmission, progress in other fields will probably be necessary. In the case of the commoner childhood behaviour disorders, however, it would smack of 'geneticism' to think in terms of one gene, one problem. Yet even here monogenic or 'Single Major Locus' hypotheses are sometimes put forward, as for instance by Kidd et al. (1976) in the case of stammering. The single gene hypothesis seems more credible for specific reading retardation, as noted previously. Its advocates can point to the possibility of a perceptual anomaly underlying many cases, and to the existence of normal variants in perception, such as colour blindness and the inability to taste phenylthiocarbamide (PTC), which are both dependent on single pairs of genes.

Polygenic inheritance

The most natural assumption, in the case of common disorders and traits that vary quantitatively, is that causation will be multifactorial. Insofar as hereditary influences are concerned, it will likely be a question of the combined effects of anything from a few to a very large number of genes at different loci, i.e. of polygenic inheritance. No one gene will be necessary for the disorder or trait to occur. The combination of genes present will vary from case to case. Some people will be more genetically predisposed than others to develop a particular condition under the same environment. Individuals will differ, partly for genetic reasons, in the kinds of stress to which they are most sensitive and in the kinds of reaction they are most prone to develop.

In polygenic inheritance we are mainly dealing with the remote, indirect effects of genes that also carry out other functions more closely related to their primary biochemical effects. These genes will usually be normal, polymorphic variants and not gross biochemical errors as in PKU. On account of the wide range of human genetic diversity, every individual with the exception of genetically identical twins will be found to have a unique biochemical constitution (Harris, 1975), and this is likely to be reflected—here more directly, there more indirectly—in many of his neurochemical, physiological and psychological characteristics. Since we are concerned with the remote effects of genes, often on intervening variables, environmental influences of many kinds will be interwoven with the genetic ones. On account of the multiple causes in an individual case and the different combination

of causes from one case to the next, there will be no single cure to match a single cause as in PKU. The most appropriate treatment will vary with the individual. However, provided a given set of environmental influences tends to act on a skill or disability in the same direction in all cases, public health programmes directed at raising the level of the skill in the population can still be expected to have some effect.

It would be unwise to expect any clear answer to the question of what is inherited. Temperamental categories, such as those of Thomas and Chess (1977) and Graham et al. (1973), and the constellations into which they fall, such as Easy Child, Difficult Child, and Slow to Warm Up, may be important for understanding childhood behaviour disorders, but they are no easier to analyse genetically than behaviour disorders themselves. It might be thought that biological traits would give a better indication of 'what is inherited' in polygenic disorders. But the more interesting psychophysiological measures and evoked EEG responses present equally great problems with regard to the most stable and meaningful trait for genetic analysis. Though various hypotheses have been put forward, there is no agreement about their relationship to the neuroses and developmental behaviour disorders. It remains to be seen whether the prospective investigation by Schulsinger et al. (1975) of the psychophysiology and behaviour of children in different educational settings in Mauritius will shed light on the development of psychiatric disorder including schizophrenia. Buchsbaum et al. (1976) have been investigating and following up students with the lowest and highest levels of MAO (monoamine oxidase) activity. It was originally thought that low MAO activity might be a genetic marker for schizophrenia. The students with low MAO activity and their families had an increased prevalence of psychiatric and legal problems but not schizophrenia.

The genetical model put forward by Slater (Slater and Cowie, 1971) as appropriate for the deviations of personality and the behaviour disorders connected with them (neuroses and others) is both polygenic and pluridimensional. The inverse relationship found in soldiers of the Second World War between the degree of stress undergone and the number of markers indicating abnormality of personality suggested that variation in neurotic predisposition was quantitative in nature and hence polygenic. However, the relationship between type of personality and type of symptom suggested qualitative as well as quantitative variation. The relationship was stronger between some traits and symptoms than others, being closest in the case of obsessions. By the laws of chance an individual breaking down would be more likely to show moderate deviations along a number of dimensions rather than an extreme deviation on one and none on any of the others. Hence the mixture of stresses and symptoms found in practice. The genetic make-up of the individual, according to Slater, determines a constitution which is subject to influences from the environment from conception onwards. Some of these early influences affect the development and maturation of the individual. These genetic and environmental factors combine to produce relatively stable personality traits. Not only will polygenes contribute to personality traits that can be inferred from ordinary behaviour, but it is also supposed that the genes provide predispositions that are not manifest in everyday life but which will show up when the individual is subjected to special stress. Among these reactions would be the symptomatology of the neuroses. The complex series of relationships between genes, environment, personality and neurotic reaction are shown in a simplified diagram (Fig. 5). One would, says Slater, draw the arrows thick or thin according to how one quantified the contribution from the various factors in any individual case. Later on we shall refer to attempts by means of 'path analysis' to quantify the routes by which genetic and environmental factors, via schooling or otherwise, influence something very different—wealth.

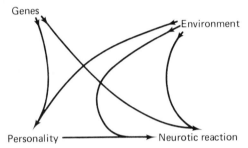

Fig. 5. Simplified picture of Slater's model of the interrelationships between genes, environment, personality and neurotic reaction. (From Slater & Cowie, 1971)

Once a neurotic reaction of behaviour disorder has reached a certain stage, still other influences, social and psychological, can come into play which perpetuate the disorder and may lead to its escalation in a vicious circle. Alternatively, appropriate social or medical intervention may lead to improvement and to a more hopeful set of learning experiences for the individual. Studies of neurotic and personality disorders in twins indicate that severity of the disturbance is not under much genetic control. Severe chronic anxiety neurosis and obsessional symptoms led, in one twin, to a prefrontal leucotomy as a treatment of last resort and to her death after the operation. Her MZ co-twin had definite but much less incapacitating traits and symptoms of a similar nature, but these were never severe enough to lead her to seek psychiatric treatment.

If Slater's theory is over-general, this is because of the relative scarcity of reliable data about the incidence of the various neurotic and personality disorders in the families of patients and in the general population. Polygenic theories, usually unidimensional, have been more widely applied to traits that can be measured and found to be normally distributed, using statistical methods first developed by R. A. Fisher. Height and IQ are the classical examples. Similar biometrical methods have been used to analyse personality questionnaire data.

Polygenic theory can be extended to threshold characters, such as congenital malformations and diseases like stroke, diabetes and duodenal ulcer. What are assumed to be normally distributed here are the many factors, genetic and environmental, that contribute to the liability to developing the disease—including blood pressure, for instance, in the case of stroke. The disease develops once a threshold of liability is passed. The model works reasonably well for schizophrenia (Gottesman and Shields, 1967, 1972; Matthysse and Kidd, 1976) where the data are rather more suitable than in the non-psychotic disorders.

Whatever method of analysis is applied, the evidence for the existence of genetic factors comes from the logic and findings of careful family, twin and adoption studies which try to rule out alternative hypotheses that exclude genetic factors.

ATTEMPTS TO PARTITION THE CAUSES OF VARIATION

Heritability and other components

If it is agreed that heredity makes a contribution to development, it seems reasonable to ask, in respect of any particular characteristic, how great that contribution is. That is a more sensible question than asking whether it is due to heredity *or* environment. It would certainly be convenient if the comparison of MZ and DZ twin concordance rates for schizophrenia, or the correlations for IQ between pairs of relatives from the same and different environments, could be neatly summarized in a single statistic. Such attempts generally make use of the concept of heritability. Agricultural geneticists have found this to be a useful tool in analysing quantitative characters such as fertility and milk yield in order to predict the possibility of improving a strain by selective breeding. Heritability is an estimate of the proportion of the variability of the trait that can be accounted for by genetic variation, of any kind (broad heritability) or that which is due only to the additive effects of genes (narrow heritability).

It should be clear that heritability does not say anything about the relative importance of heredity and environment in determining the characteristics of an individual considered in isolation: obviously they are both equally necessary, whether we are thinking of traits that everyone possesses like having two eyes, a nose and a mouth, or traits that differ, normal or abnormal. Nor is heritability an intrinsic property of a trait. It applies to the distribution of individual differences in a population, and its value depends on the degree of effective genetic and environmental variation in that population. Ignoring the tints and dyes applied by the hairdresser, differences in hair colour in northern Europe can be shown to be almost entirely attributable to genetic variation. In China this cannot be shown, since everyone has black hair. A heritability of zero would not mean that genes had no influence on the colour of the hair. There are justifiable doubts about some of Sir Cyril Burt's data, but he was very clear about the limitations of heritability. 'To an omnibus inquiry', what is the relative influence on a trait of heredity as opposed to environment, 'there can be no single answer. We can only try to determine, for this or that type of environment, for this or that population, and for this or that type of assessment, how far the observable results appear to be influenced by each of the two main groups of factors' (Burt, 1958). Since many different methods have been proposed for calculating heritability, he might have added that the estimate also depends on which method is used. Holzinger's widely used index, derived from MZ and DZ correlation coefficients or variances, is no longer thought to be a satisfactory estimate of either broad or narrow heritability (Smith, 1974). It is also widely recognized that heritabilities obtained from within populations cannot be assumed to apply to differences between populations, such as racial groups that might differ in relevant environments.

One problem about a heritability estimate, according to an eminent expert, is what you do with it when you have got it. Of course, it can be of interest to compare estimates made at different ages, or after different lengths of exposure to an environment, and based on tests of more than one kind; and it is of great importance to compare estimates derived from relatives varying in degree of environmental similarity. In the case of IQ, heritabilities obtained from twin studies and from adoption studies are in good agreement (Loehlin, 1978). But what does heritability tell us about how manipulation of existing environmental factors will effect the trait in the population? In a general way, the higher the heritability the less effect can be expected. Only if it is virtually 100% will environmental manipulation have no effect at all. Even if heritability is quite high, as are most estimates for IQ, changes in environment, if they are marked, can have a significant influence, as was shown in Scarr and Weinberg's (1976) study of Black children adopted into White families well above average in education and occupation. However, a high heritability in a population need not mean that less extreme environmental modification will always be in vain—there will be some individuals for whom effective modifications can be found; and it tells us nothing about what the effects on a population of a *new* environment might be. If heritability of a disorder is high, we shall probably have to look outside the range of environments experienced by the population from which the estimate was obtained in order to find the most effective prevention or treatment.

A single figure such as heritability estimate obviously cannot do justice to all the subtleties. The theory on which the Fisherian analysis of variance approach is based assumes that the multiple causes of a variable trait are approximately additive in their effects and that the trait itself is uniform in its aetiology. These assumptions are likely to turn out to be over-simplifications. The more that is known about single contributory factors, the greater the importance we would probably have to lay on interaction; and the more thoroughly a cognitive or temperamental dimension like intelligence or neuroticism is studied, the more likely is it that it will turn out to consist of elements of rather different kinds. Nevertheless, the simple additive homogeneous model is parsimonious and it has consequences that can be tested. It has proved useful as a working hypothesis in animal and plant genetics. So it seems unfair to dismiss biometric analysis of human attri-

butes on the grounds that the situation *may* be more complicated than the simple model allows, and, as the Medawars (1977) do, to reject any formulation of heritability for a behaviour trait as 'utterly unacceptable' and 'the enthusiastic misapplication of not fully understood genetic principles in situations where they do not apply'. (A more thoughtful and less sweeping criticism is that by Caspari, 1977.)

For most biometrical and behaviour geneticists heritability is only part of the picture. They are equally if not more concerned with the more interesting though more difficult tasks of partitioning the variance into further components such as the proportion due to assortative mating (or like marrying like) and dominance or other interaction effects between genes. Many analyses suggest that some of the genes that enhance IQ are dominant over those that do not. In this way clues may be provided about the genetic architecture and evolutionary history of the trait. Interaction between genes and environment is thought to play little part in determining the distribution of IQ scores (Jinks and Fulker, 1970), but the influence of a correlation between genotype and environment is more difficult to evaluate. This can occur either through persons of different genotypes selecting environments appropriate for them, or it may occur through their partly genetically determined behaviour resulting in their being exposed to different kinds of environment. These environments may aim either to augment or reduce the genetic effects. For example, the intellectually bright child might receive greater educational attention than the less bright, whereas attempts are likely to be made to bring the sluggish and the over-active child closer to the social norm. Furthermore, the different environments may be appropriate or inappropriate for the child's normal healthy development, and they may be effective or ineffective. A constraint here would be an unbiased estimate of the heritability of the trait.

In principle, non-additive effects and genotype-environmental correlation can be detected (Eaves *et al.*, 1977). It is increasingly appreciated, however, that very large samples of strategic groups such as twins are required to test the various models of variation. Martin *et al.* (1978) have calculated that at least 600 pairs of twins would be needed to reject the simpler hypotheses with 95% certainty if they are wrong.

Path analysis of influences on wealth

Heritability and such analyses may seem rather static, bound to the here and now. The multifactorial approach can be extended to explore the mechanisms. A few years ago, when the controversy about heredity and intelligence had flared up once again, a minor stir was created by a press report of genetic influences on wealth. Taubman (1977) analysed questionnaire items about income and occupation completed by over 4000 pairs of American adult male twins. Heritabilities were calculated which were modest compared with those usually reported for IQ, but it nevertheless surprised or enraged many people to hear it said that income and occupational status might be even remotely influenced by genetic differences.

With complex variables such as these, where genetic influence, if any, will be partial and indirect, a multifactorial structured analysis of some of the components would be of greater interest than a single estimate of heritability. Fulker (1978) reanalysed Taubman's data using the technique of 'path analysis' in order to deduce how far the genetic, family environmental and other influences on income and occupational status were the same as those that determined length of schooling. The details of the method need not concern us. The latent variables are derived from the variances and correlations of the data. No doubt other approaches applied to the same data might come up with somewhat different sets of figures; and there is no reason to suppose that the same relationships would hold in cultures with an educational system and a distribution of wealth different from that in present-day USA. Fig. 6 nevertheless is of interest in

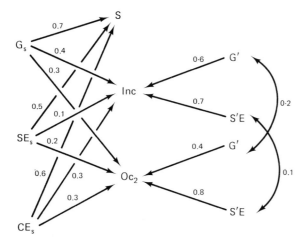

Latent variables:

G_s = genetic influences on schooling
SE_s = specific environmental influences on schooling
CE_s = common family influences on schooling

G¹ = residual genetic influences
SE¹ = residual specific environmental influences

Observed variables:

S = schooling (years)
Inc = adult income (log $)
Oc₂ = adult occupational status

Fig. 6. Path analysis Taubman's (1977) twin study of wealth. (From Fulker, in press)

showing a recent, thoughtful application of the path analysis approach which is increasingly favoured today. The straight arrows bear the 'path' coefficients that indicate their relative influence, other factors being held constant. The arrows coming to Income and Occupation from the left are those genetic and environmental variables that influence schooling. It will be seen that genes such as those that affect IQ (Gs), and shared family influences on years of schooling (CEs), have a moderate and approxi-

mately similar influence; the correlations are ·3 and ·4. Other specific environmental influences on schooling (SEs), such as chance illnesses, have only a trivial influence on the later observed variables (correlations of ·1 and ·2). The arrows coming from the right are the residual genetic and environmental influences that are not specifically related to schooling. These apparently have a greater influence on income and occupation, with correlations up to ·7 and ·8. The genetic influences might be thought to be those related to temperament and special skills rather than to IQ, and the most important environmental factors, according to Fulker, probably relate to market imperfections—and simply to luck.

The coefficients on the arrows of Fig. 6 are somewhat analogous to the thickness or thinness of the arrows of Fig. 5 which Slater suggested might be introduced to indicate their relative importance. However, sufficient information is not available to quantify the genetic, family environmental and other factors in the neuroses and psychoses and to show how far these operate via their effects on previous personality or otherwise.

Plurality of approaches

We know little enough about the causes of behavioural variation and how they operate, so we should hesitate before rejecting any approach that might be promising. Until we know more about some of the particular genetic and environmental elements concerned in a disease or disorder, the statistical multifactorial model, despite its recognized limitations, may, as Curnow and Smith (1975) put it, have a role as 'a temporary tool useful during a period of ignorance for estimating risks and for providing indicators about the relations between different diseases and the relation of diseases with measurable continuous characters. Major breakthroughs must come from more fundamental research'.

It is, however, only one approach. Those whose interest is the development and treatment of psychiatric disorder may prefer clinical studies to those, however large, of wealth, police records, personality questionnaire scores or standardized IQ tests. Several genetic studies have been made without the investigators seeing a single one of their subjects. This is not only true, understandably enough, for the huge Taubman study of wealth. It is also true for Loehlin and Nichols' (1976) study of cognitive and personality measures in 850 American high school twins, whose parents also completed a detailed questionnaire; for the Eaves and Eysenck (1975, 1976) analyses of the responses of some 500 volunteer adult twins to a postal personality inventory; and for the Hutchings and Mednick (1974) study of registered criminality in Danish adoptees and their fathers, on which Fig. 4 was based. It also applies to some smaller studies, including the highly influential first report of mental illness in the families of 33 schizophrenic adoptees (Kety et al., 1968). (Though this was based on information from records only, its findings have subsequently been confirmed by interviews with the relatives (Kety et al., 1975).) Direct observation and interviews with patients and their family members are often essential for the genetic study of development or of psychiatric disorder. Appropriate accessible samples will usually be small and standards of investigation, even in the best studies, far from ideal.

The matching of nationwide registers of twins and psychiatric cases in Denmark (Fischer, 1973) produced no more than 21 MZ pairs in which one or both of the twins were schizophrenic, and many of these could not be personally investigated because they had died. Nevertheless, this and other small but well-designed studies have established the existence of genetic factors in schizophrenia and suggested hypotheses about related disorders and reasons for discordance.

Identical twins brought up apart are rare and one would hardly expect them to be placed into different homes at random. Yet the comparison of the case histories of twins with the supposedly most and the least similar environments is instructive and can produce unexpected findings (Shields, 1978). The case history approach has its uses, as well as biometrical analysis. As regards developmental data, information here is usually limited to retrospective self-reports by adults. With this reservation, Shields (1962) found so-called childhood neurotic traits were a little less concordant in MZ twins brought up apart (45%) than in those brought up together (57%). In both groups concordance was more frequent than discordance in respect of enuresis (three 'separated' pairs were concordant, none discordant), aggressive behaviour disorders, sleep disturbances other than sleep-walking, and emotional difficulties during adolescence. Sleep-walking, tics and over-dependency were among traits that were more often discordant than concordant.

In his Mapother lecture, Eisenberg (1977) spoke of development as a unifying concept in psychiatry. Human geneticists have shown an increasing concern with development. Gedda and Brenci (1973, 1975) introduced the term chronogenetics to refer to the timing of genetically determined processes as seen, for example, in the development of twins; Gottesman (1974) proposed the cross-fertilization of ontogenetic psychology and developmental genetics; and the proceedings of a specially organized conference on developmental human behaviour genetics was published (Schaie *et al.*, 1975), in which leading American behaviour geneticists took part and discussed each other's views. We have already referred to the growing interest in prospective studies of children at high risk for developing psychiatric disorder. For many, ethology (*e.g.* Bowlby, 1971) also provides a unifying concept; and from the long perspective of the evolution of behaviour in animals, E. O. Wilson (1975) presented his stimulating though controversial views of sociology as an extension of sociobiology. Mankind has evolved the means of non-organic transmission of information, and attempts have been made to incorporate cultural inheritance into genetic models, taking account, for instance, of the parents' skills as teachers as well as their genotypes (Cavalli-Sforza and Feldman, 1973).

Some of these attempts to establish links between gene action and social behaviour in the development of the species or the individual have been immensely stimulat-

ing. They encourage interdisciplinary contacts. The focus on development and mechanisms helps to counteract the false view that psychological geneticists are only interested in measuring heritability. But, while the developmental concept makes us more aware of complexities and interactions, this approach does not lead to any easy practical applications. It is more difficult to collect and analyse data at several points of time than at one point only. Except in bacteria, little is known about the biological mechanisms that switch genes on and off, though Davidson and Britten (1973) have put forward a theoretical scheme about the complexities of gene regulation in animals, for which there is thought to be some evidence. Despite advances in disciplines such as neurochemistry, for some time to come we shall probably have to rely on such deductions about the roles and interaction of genetic and environmental influences on behaviour disturbances as can be obtained from some of the approaches suggested in this chapter. Well-designed family and epidemiological studies, with improved clinical and other assessments, and with or without the parallel study of biological variables and the use of multivariate analysis, will still be needed. The variety of approaches is desirable.

CONCLUDING REMARKS

This chapter has been concerned with the contribution of genetic diversity to individual differences. The attention given to developmental aspects of psychiatric disorder and to some of the mechanisms believed to be implicated has led to an emphasis, in many of the accounts, on maturation and epigenetic development—on the unfolding of genetic potentialities and the carrying out of instructions provided by the individual's genetic blueprint. But I have stressed that these instructions depend on environmental input. Nature and Nurture are both essential for development. Differences in Nature may have little effect on some processes or reactions (*e.g.* gross physical trauma): in other words, everyone's instructions will be much the same. For other processes or reactions differences in Nature will be paramount (*e.g.* Down's syndrome, inborn errors of metabolism, Huntington's chorea). More often both sets of factors will have an influence: the response of Nature will depend on Nurture, and the effects of Nurture depend on Nature. The points at issue will be their relative influence in different conditions, and to what extent the contributing causes combine additively, or to what extent there is interaction in the statistician's sense of the word.

It is of interest and importance to try to identify major genetic influences on behaviour such as chromosome abnormalities and the effects of single genes, and to explore their complex interactions. Most individual differences, however, are likely to be due to the combined effect of many genes (polygenic influences), together with many environmental factors. Multivariate analysis will have an appropriate role to play here. The genetic influence on behaviour and psychiatric disorder is always indirect, even in PKU where it is via the diet. In polygenic inheritance it will usually be very indirect and remote, though not necessarily of little effect. The genes, it has been stressed, can exert their influence at any stage of life from conception onwards. Often it may be through the contribution they make during childhood development to cognitive skills and features of temperament or personality. But the genes also show their effects at later stages, for example in the form of an illness such as manic-depressive psychosis. Disorders of adult life are not merely an outcome of childhood maladjustment.

If the influence of genes on traits, symptoms and disorders is usually remote, dependent on the environment, and variable as to when it shows its effect, it is hardly surprising that there are many uncertainties and differences of opinion, even as to its existence. For instance, a psychiatrist who is completing a prospective study of twins from birth to 5 years says he is 'increasingly suspicious that by the time one has worked out all the interrelationships between parent behaviour and child behaviour, the genetic component (in early personality differences) may well disappear altogether' (Costello, 1976). Perhaps they may come into play later.

Despite these uncertainties and lack of firm knowledge, the writer believes that the evidence from the best epidemiological, family, twin and adoption studies, clinical and psychometric, points to the pervasive influence of genetic variation, sometimes major and specific, sometimes minor and nonspecific. Genetic principles predict differences as well as similarities within families, in a way that purely environmental theories do not. The segregation of many genes, as in polygenic inheritance, results in a wide range of differences within a sibship. It is likely that cognitive and temperamental differences, partly genetically determined, explain why some children show superior talent despite an extremely unfavourable upbringing, and why many succeed in breaking out of cycles of disadvantage (Rutter and Madge, 1976). The recognition of genetic differences adds to one's respect for human individuality.

Not surprisingly, there are differences among geneticists, psychiatrists and social scientists about the interpretation of the findings. These individual differences must be respected too, though I would venture to suggest that they, at least, do not rest on a genetic basis.

REFERENCES

Abe, K. (1972). Phobias and nervous symptoms in childhood and maturity: persistence and associations. *British Journal of Psychiatry*, **120**, 275–283.

Bakwin, H. (1973). Reading disability in twins. *Developmental Medicine and Child Neurology*, **15**, 184–187.

Berger, M., Yule, W. and Rutter, M. (1975). Attainment and adjustment in two geographical areas. II. The prevalence of specific reading retardation. *British Journal of Psychiatry*, **126**, 510–519.

Bird, E. D. and Iversen, L. L. (1974). Huntington's chorea. Post-mortem measurement of glutamic acid decarboxylase, choline acetyltransferase and dopamine in basal ganglia. *Brain*, **97**, 457–472.

Bowlby, J. (1971). *Attachment and Loss. Vol. 1: Attachment*. Penguin, Harmondsworth, Middx.

Buchsbaum, M. S., Coursey, R. D. and Murphy, D. L. (1976). The biochemical high-risk paradigm: behavioral and familial correlates of low platelet monoamine oxidase activity. *Science*, **194**, 339–341.

Burt, C. (1958). The inheritance of mental ability. *American Psychologist*, **13**, 1–15.

Caspari, E. W. (1977). Genetic mechanisms and behavior. In: *Genetics, Environment and Intelligence*, ed. A. Oliverio, North-Holland Publishing Co., Amsterdam, 3–22.

Cavalli-Sforza, L. L. and Feldman, M. W. (1973). Cultural versus biological inheritance: phenotypic transmission from parents to children (a theory of the effect of parental phenotypes on children's phenotypes). *American Journal of Human Genetics*, **25**, 618–637.

Clarke, A. M. and Clarke, A. D. B. (1976). *Early Experience: Myth and Evidence*. The Free Press, New York.

Cohen, D. J., Dibble, E. and Grawe, J. M. (1977). Fathers' and mothers' perceptions of children's personality. *Archives of General Psychiatry*, **34**, 480–487.

Costello, A. (1976). Are mothers necessary? *The Listener*, 21 October.

Cox, A. (1976). The association between emotional disorders in childhood and neuroses in adult life. In: *Research in Neurosis*, ed. H. M. van Praag, Bohn, Scheltema and Holkema, Utrecht, 40–58.

Curnow, R. N. and Smith, C. (1975). Multifactorial models for familial diseases in man. *Journal of the Royal Statistical Society*, A, **138**, 131–169.

Davidson, E. H. and Britten, R. J. (1973). Organization, transcription, and regulation in the animal genome. *Quarterly Review of Biology*, **48**, 565–613.

DeFries, J. C., Singer, S. M., Foch, T. T. and Lewitter, F. I. (1978). Familial nature of reading disability. *British Journal of Psychiatry*, **132**, 361–367.

Doose, H., Gerken, H. and Völzke, E. (1967). Elektrencephalographische Untersuchungen über die Genetik zentrencephaler Epilepsien. *Zeitschrift für Kinderheilkunde*, **101**, 242–257.

Dorus, E., Dorus, W., Telfer, M. A., Litwin, S. and Richardson, C. E. (1976). Height and personality characteristics of 47,XYY males in a sample of tall non-institutionalized males. *British Journal of Psychiatry*, **129**, 564–573.

Dworkin, R. H., Burke, B. W., Maher, B. A. and Gottesman, I. I. (1976). A longitudinal study of the genetics of personality. *Journal of Personality and Social Psychology*, **34**, 510–518.

van Dyke, J. L., Rosenthal, D. and Rasmussen, P. V. (1974). Electrodermal functioning in adopted-away offspring of schizophrenics. *Journal of Psychiatric Research*, **10**, 199–215.

Eaves, L. and Eysenck, H. (1975). The nature of extroversion: a genetical analysis. *Journal of Personality and Social Psychology*, **32**, 102–112.

Eaves, L. and Eysenck, H. (1976). Genotype x age interaction for neuroticism. *Behavior Genetics*, **6**, 359–362.

Eaves, L. J., Last, K., Martin, N. G. and Jinks, J. L. (1977). A progressive approach to non-additivity and genotype-environmental covariance in the analysis of human differences. *British Journal of Mathematical and Statistical Psychology*, **30**, 1–42.

Eisenberg, L. (1977). Development as a unifying concept in psychiatry. *British Journal of Psychiatry*, **131**, 225–237.

Ellis, W. G., McCulloch, J. R. and Corley, C. L. (1974). Presenile dementia in Down's syndrome. *Neurology*, **24**, 101–106.

Erlenmeyer-Kimling, L. (1972). Gene-environment interactions and the variability of behavior. In: *Genetics, Environment, and Behavior: Implications for Educational Policy*, ed. L. Ehrman, G. Omenn and E. Caspari, Academic Press, New York, 181–208.

Erlenmeyer-Kimling, L. (1975). A prospective study of children at risk for schizophrenia: methodological considerations and some preliminary findings. In: *Life History Research in Psychopathology*, Vol. 4, ed. R. D. Wirt, G. Winokur and M. Roff, University of Minnesota Press, Minneapolis, 23–46.

Eysenck, H. J. and Wilson, G. D., ed. (1976). *A Textbook of Human Psychology*. MTP Press, Lancaster.

Finucci, J. M., Guthrie, J. T., Childs, A. L., Abbey, H. and Childs, B. (1976). The genetics of specific reading disability. *Annals of Human Genetics*, 40, pt. 1, 1–23.

Fischbein, S. (1977). Onset of puberty in MZ and DZ twins. *Acta Geneticae Medicae et Gemellologiae*, **26**, 151–157.

Fischer, M. (1973). Genetic and environmental factors in schizophrenia. *Acta Psychiatrica Scandinavica*, Supplement 238.

Folstein, S. and Rutter, M. (1977). Infantile autism: a genetic study of 21 twin pairs. *Journal of Child Psychology and Psychiatry*, 18, 297–321.

Fulker, D. W. (1978). Multivariate extensions of a biometrical model of twin data. In *Twin Research: Psychology and Methodology,* ed. W. E. Nance, Alan R. Liss Inc., New York, 217–236.

Garmezy, N. (with Streitman, S.) (1974a). Children at risk: The search for the antecedents of schizophrenia. Part 1. Conceptual models and research methods. *Schizophrenia Bulletin*, 1 (Experimental issue No. 8), 14–90.

Garmezy, N. (1974b). Children at risk: The search for the antecedents of schizophrenia. Part 2. Ongoing research programs, issues, and intervention. *Schizophrenia Bulletin*, 1 (Experimental issue No. 9), 55–125.

Garvey, M. and Mutton, D. E. (1973). Sex chromosome aberrations and speech development. *Archives of Disease in Childhood*, 48, 937–941.

Gedda, L. and Brenci, G. (1973). Chronogenetics. *Acta Geneticae Medicae et Gemellologiae*, 22, 3–17.

Gedda, L. and Brenci, G. (1975). Twins as a natural test of chronogenetics. *Acta Geneticae Medicae et Gemellologiae*, 24, 15–30.

Gottesman, I. I. (1965). Personality and natural selection. In: *Methods and Goals in Human Behavior Genetics*, ed. S. G. Vandenberg, Academic Press, New York, 63–80.

Gottesman, I. I. (1966). Genetic variance in adaptive personality traits. *Journal of Child Psychology and Psychiatry*, 7, 199–208.

Gottesman, I. I. (1974). Developmental genetics and ontogenetic psychology: overdue detente and propositions from a matchmaker. In: *Minnesota Symposia on Child Psychology*, Vol. 8, ed. A. D. Pick, University of Minnesota Press, Minneapolis.

Gottesman, I. I. and Shields, J. (1967). A polygenic theory of schizophrenia. *Proceedings of the National Academy of Sciences*, 58, 199–205.

Gottesman, I. I. and Shields, J. (1972). *Schizophrenia and Genetics: a Twin Study Vantage Point*. Academic Press, New York, London.

Gottesman, I. I. and Shields, J. (1976a). A critical review of recent adoption, twin, and family studies of schizophrenia: behavioral genetics perspectives. *Schizophrenia Bulletin*, 2, 360–401.

Gottesman, I. I. and Shields, J. (1976b). Rejoinder: toward optimal arousal and away from original din. *Schizophrenia Bulletin*, 2, 447–453.

Graham, P., Rutter, M. and George, S. (1973). Temperamental characteristics as predictors of behavior disorders in children. *American Journal of Orthopsychiatry*, 43, 328–339.

Hallgren, B. (1950). Specific dyslexia ('congenital word-blindness'): a clinical and genetic study. *Acta Psychiatrica et Neurologica Scandinavica*, Supplement 65.

Hamerton, J. L. (1976). Human population cytogenetics: dilemmas and problems. *American Journal of Human Genetics*, 28, 107–122.

Hanson, D. R., Gottesman, I. I. and Heston, L. L. (1976). Some possible childhood indicators of adult schizophrenia inferred from children of schizophrenics. *British Journal of Psychiatry*, 129, 142–154.

Hanson, D. R., Gottesman, I. I. and Meehl, P. E. (1977). Genetic theories and the validation of psychiatric diagnoses: implications for the study of children of schizophrenics. *Journal of Abnormal Psychology*, 86, 575–588.

Harris, H. (1975). *The Principles of Human Biochemical Genetics*, 2nd ed. North-Holland Publishing Co., Amsterdam, Oxford.

Heston, L. L. (1966). Psychiatric disorders in foster home reared children of schizophrenic mothers. *British Journal of Psychiatry*, 112, 819–825.

Hook, E. B. (1973). Behavioral implications of the human XYY genotype. *Science*, 179, 139–150.

Hutchings, B. and Mednick, S. A. (1974). Registered criminality in the adoptive and biological parents of registered male adoptees. In: *Genetics, Environment and Psychopathology*, ed. S. A. Mednick, F. Schulsinger, J. Higgins and B. Bell, North-Holland Publishing Co., Amsterdam, Oxford, 215–227.

Jinks, J. L. and Fulker, D. W. (1970). A comparison of the biometrical genetical, MAVA and classical approaches to the analysis of human behavior. *Psychological Bulletin*, 73, 311–349.

Kahn, J., Carter, W. I., Dernley, N. and Slater, E. T. O. (1969). Chromosome studies in remand home and prison populations. In: *Criminological Implications of Chromosome Abnormalities*, ed. D. J. West, Institute of Criminology, Cambridge, 44–48.

Kahn, J., Reed, F. S., Bates, M., Coates, T. and Everitt, B. (1976). A survey of Y chromosome variants and personality in 436 Borstal lads and 254 controls. *British Journal of Criminology*, 16, 233–244.

Kety, S. S., Rosenthal, D., Wender, P. H. and Schulsinger, F. (1968). The types and prevalence of mental illness in the biological and adoptive families of adopted schizophrenics. In: *The Transmission of Schizophrenia*, ed. D. Rosenthal and S. S. Kety, Pergamon, Oxford, 345–362.

Kety, S. S., Rosenthal, D., Wender, P. H., Schulsinger, F. and Jacobsen, B. (1975). Mental illness in the biological and adoptive families of adopted individuals who have become schizophrenic: a preliminary report based on psychiatric interviews. In: *Genetic Research in Psychiatry*, ed. R. R. Fieve, D. Rosenthal and H. Brill, Johns Hopkins University Press, Baltimore and London, 147–165.

Kidd, K. K., Records, M. A. and Kidd, J. R. (1976). Genetic analysis of stuttering. Fifth International Congress of Human Genetics, Mexico. *Excerpta Medica, International Congress Series 397*, 83 (abstract).

Loehlin, J. (1978). MZ's apart and other ways to the same destination. In: *Twin Research: Psychology and Methodology*, ed. W. E. Nance, Alan R. Liss, Inc., New York.

Loehlin, J. C. and Nichols, R. C. (1976). *Heredity, Environment, & Personality: A Study of 850 Sets of Twins*, University of Texas Press, Austin and London.

Lyle, O. E. and Gottesman, I. I. (1977). Premorbid psychometric indicators of the gene for Huntington's disease. *Journal of Consulting & Clinical Psychology*, 45, 1011–1022.

Martin, N. G., Eaves, L. J., Kearsey, M. J. and Davies, P. (1978). The power of the classical twin study. *Heredity*, 40, 97–116.

Matheny, A. P. Jr., Wilson, R. S. and Dolan, A. B. (1976). Relations between twins' similarity of appearance and behavioral similarity: testing an assumption. *Behavior Genetics*, 6, 343–351.

Matthysse, S. W. and Kidd, K. K. (1976). Estimating the genetic contribution to schizophrenia. *American Journal of Psychiatry*, 133, 185–191.

Medawar, P. B. and Medawar, J. S. (1977). *The Life Science: Current Ideas of Biology*. Wildwood House, London.

Mednick, S. A., Schulsinger, F., Higgins, J. and Bell, B., ed. (1974). *Genetics, Environment and Psychopathology*. North-Holland Publishing Co., Amsterdam, Oxford.

Metrakos, K. and Metrakos, J. D. (1961). Genetics of convulsive disorders. II. Genetic and electroencephalographic studies in centrencephalic epilepsy. *Neurology*, 11, 474–483.

Nielsen, J. (1971). Prevalence and a 2½ years incidence of chromosome abnormalities among all males in a forensic psychiatric clinic. *British Journal of Psychiatry*, 119, 503–512.

Nielsen, J. and Christensen, A.-L. (1974). Thirty-five males with double Y chromosome. *Psychological Medicine*, 4, 28–37.

Noël, B., Duport, J. P., Revil, D., Dussuyer, I. and Quack, B. (1974). The XYY syndrome: reality or myth? *Clinical Genetics*, 5, 387–394.

Polani, P. E. (1977). Abnormal sex chromosomes, behaviour and mental disorder. In: *Developments in Psychiatric Research*, ed. J. M. Tanner, Hodder and Stoughton, London, 89–128.

Ratcliffe, S. G. (1976). The development of children with sex chromosome abnormalities. *Proceedings of the Royal Society of Medicine*, 69, 189–192.

Rosenthal, D. and colleagues. (1963). *The Genain Quadruplets*. Basic Books, New York.

Rutter, M. (1970). Sex differences in children's responses to family stress. In *The Child in his Family*, ed. E. James Anthony and C. Koupernik, Wiley-Interscience, New York, 165–196.

Rutter, M. L. (1972). Relationships between child and adult psychiatric disorders. *Acta Psychiatrica Scandinavica*, 48, 3–21.

Rutter, M., Korn, S. and Birch, H. G. (1963). Genetic and environmental factors in the development of 'primary reaction patterns'. *British Journal of Social and Clinical Psychology*, 2, 161–173.

Rutter, M. and Madge, N. (1976). *Cycles of Disadvantage*. Heinemann, London.

Rutter, M., Tizard, J. and Whitmore, K. (1970). *Education, Health and Behaviour*, Longman, London.

Say, B., Carpenter, N. J., Lanier, P. R., Banez, C., Jones, K. and Coldwell, J. G. (1977). Chromosome variants in children with psychiatric disorders. *American Journal of Psychiatry*, **134**, 424–426.

Scarr, S. and Weinberg, R. A. (1976). IQ test performance of black children adopted by white families. *American Psychologist*, **31**, 726–739.

Schaie, K. Warner, Anderson, V. E., McClearn, G. E. and Money, J. (1975). *Developmental Human Behavior Genetics*, Lexington Books, D. C. Heath Ltd., Farnborough, Hants.

Schepank, H. (1974). *Erb- und Umweltfaktoren bei Neurosen*. Tiefenpsychologische Untersuchungen an 50 Zwillingspaaren. Monographien aus dem Gesamtgebiete der Psychiatrie, Psychiatry Series, Band 11, Springer-Verlag, Berlin, Heidelberg, New York.

Schulsinger, F., Mednick, S. A., Venables, P. H., Raman, A. C. and Bell, B. (1975). Early detection and prevention of mental illness: the Mauritius project. *Neuropsychobiology*, **1**, 166–179.

Schulsinger, H. (1976). A ten-year follow-up of children of schizophrenic mothers: clinical assessment. *Acta Psychiatrica Scandinavica*, **53**, 371–386.

Shields, J. (1954a). Personality differences and neurotic traits in normal twin schoolchildren. *Eugenics Review*, **45**, 213–246.

Shields, J. (1954b). The social development of twins. *Case Conference*, August, 5–14.

Shields, J. (1962). *Monozygotic Twins Brought up Apart and Brought up Together*. Oxford University Press, London.

Shields, J. (1973). Heredity and psychological abnormality. In: *Handbook of Abnormal Psychology*, 2nd ed., ed. H. J. Eysenck. Pitman Medical, London, 540–603.

Shields, J. (1975). Some recent developments in psychiatric genetics. *Archiv für Psychiatrie und Nervenkrankheiten*, 220, 347–360.

Shields, J. (1976). Heredity and environment. In: *A Textbook of Human Psychology*, ed. H. J. Eysenck and G. D. Wilson, MTP Press, Lancaster, 145–160.

Shields, J. (1977). Polygenic influences. In: *Child Psychiatry: Modern Approaches*, ed. M. Rutter and L. Hersov. Blackwell Scientific Publications, Oxford, 22–46.

Shields, J. (1978). Genetics. In: *Schizophrenia: Towards a New Synthesis*, ed. J. K. Wing, Academic Press, New York, 53–87.

Shields, J. (1978). MZA twins: their use and abuse. In: *Twin Research: Psychology and Methodology*, ed. W. E. Nance, Alan R. Liss, Inc., New York.

Shields, J. and Gottesman, I. I. (1977). Obstetric complications and twin studies of schizophrenia: clarifications and affirmations. *Schizophrenia Bulletin*, **3**, 351–354.

Shields, J., Heston, L. L. and Gottesman, I. I. (1975). Schizophrenia and the schizoid: the problem for genetic analysis. In: *Genetic Research in Psychiatry*, ed. R. R. Fieve, D. Rosenthal and H. Brill, Johns Hopkins University Press, Baltimore and London, 167–197.

Slater, E. and Cowie, V. (1971). *The Genetics of Mental Disorders*, Oxford University Press, London.

Smith, C. (1974). Concordance in twins: methods and interpretation. *American Journal of Human Genetics*, **26**, 454–466.

Soudek, D. and Laraya, P. (1974). Longer Y chromosome in criminals. *Clinical Genetics*, **6**, 225–229.

Tanner, J. M. (1962). *Growth at Adolescence*, 2nd ed. Blackwell Scientific Publications, Oxford.

Taubman, P., ed. (1977). *Kinometrics: The Determinants of Socioeconomic Success Within and Between Families*, North Holland Publishing Co., Amsterdam.

Theilgaard, A., Nielsen, J., Sørensen, A., Frøland, A. and Johnsen, S. G. (1971). *A psychological-psychiatric study of patients with Klinefelter's syndrome, 47,XXY*. Publication of the University of Aarhus, Copenhagen, Munksgaard.

Thoday, J. M. (1969). Limitations to genetic comparison of populations. *Journal of Biosocial Science*, Supplement No. 1, *Biosocial Aspects of Race*, ed. G. A. Harrison and J. Peel, Blackwell Scientific Publications, Oxford, 3–14.

Thomas, A. and Chess, S. (1977). *Temperament and Development*. Brunner/Mazel, New York.

Torgersen, A. M. and Kringlen, E. (1978). Genetic aspects of temperamental differences in infants. *Journal of the American Academy of Child Psychiatry*, **17**, 433–444.

Wakeling, A. (1972). Comparative study of psychiatric patients with Klinefelter's syndrome and hypogonadism. *Psychological Medicine*, **2**, 139–154.

Walzer, S. and Gerald, P. S. (1975). Social class and frequency of XYY and XXY. *Science*, **190**, 1228–1229.

Walzer, S., Richmond, J. B. and Gerald, P. S. (1976). The implications of sharing genetic information. In: *Psychiatry and Genetics: Psychosocial, Ethical, and Legal Considerations*, ed. M. A. Sperber and L. F. Jarvik, Basic Books, Inc., New York, 147–162.

Wender, P. (1971). *Minimal Brain Dysfunction in Children*. Wiley-Interscience, New York.

Wilson, E. O. (1975). *Sociobiology, the New Synthesis*. The Belknap Press of Harvard University Press, Cambridge, Mass. and London.

Wilson, R. S. (1977). Mental development in twins. In: *Genetics, Environment and Intelligence*, ed. A. Oliverio, North-Holland Publishing Co., Amsterdam, 305–334.

Witkin, H. A., Mednick, S. A., Schulsinger, F., *et al.* (1976). Criminality in XYY and XXY men. *Science*, **193**, 547–555.

Zeuthen, E., Hansen, M., Christensen, A.-L. and Nielsen, J. (1975). A psychiatric-psychological study of XYY males found in a general male population. *Acta Psychiatrica Scandinavica*, **51**, 3–18.

3. MATURATION OF THE CENTRAL NERVOUS SYSTEM

INTRODUCTION

An understanding of the *mechanisms* involved in the maturation of the central nervous system is obviously important for anyone interested in the processes of normal and abnormal psychological development. However, the very many detailed changes in each and every part of the brain are likely to be of less interest to clinicians than to basic scientists. Accordingly, in this chapter, most attention is paid to the principles and issues involved in the chief morphological processes in brain maturation. Examples are largely taken from the cerebellum as this provides a convenient model for the analysis of developmental processes of presumably wider significance. Other aspects of brain maturation (such as neurochemical or neurophysiological changes) are outside the scope of the chapter, but brief mention is made of a few features which relate to morphology. There is also a short discussion of presumed regulatory mechanisms, followed by comments on plasticity in the developing CNS and the possibilities of repair. Finally, attention is drawn to some principles concerning vulnerability of the maturating brain and to some aspects of human developmental neuropathology. A selective list of references (chosen with regard to their availability) is given to provide readers with access to a more detailed consideration of the points raised.

AN ANALYSIS OF SOME MORPHOGENETIC EVENTS

In order to analyse processes of development it is useful to consider various morphogenetic events in isolation even though in reality they are so closely related that sharp boundaries cannot be drawn. These categories include: cell proliferation, cell migration, cell differentiation and, as a special case of the latter, the formation of synapses. Under normal developmental conditions cell death too can be an important morphogenetic factor.

Cell proliferation

Cell proliferation in the developing CNS is neither ubiquitous nor continuous. To the contrary, it occurs in a narrow time- and place-bound pattern (Berquist and Källén, 1954; O'Rahilly and Gardner, 1971). In the very early stages of CNS development proliferation takes place in the germinal cells of the neural tube. When later, larger congregates of proliferating elements occur these are referred to as matrices. The most conspicuous of these are the subependymal layer, bordering the ventricular surface, and the external granular layer (EGL) covering the immature cerebellum.

Cell proliferation can be studied to some extent with conventional light microscopic techniques. But a major impetus for this study has been the introduction of a method that directly visualizes DNA-synthesis. Radioactive thymidine, injected intravenously or intraperitoneally, is incorporated into the DNA of cells that are engaged in its synthesis at the time when the injected thymidine is available (for about 2 hours after injection). This incorporation can be demonstrated by means of autoradiography, revealing the radioactive label, now present within the DNA. Thus in animals killed shortly after injection there is a demonstration of those cells in the process of DNA-synthesis. Continuing mitotic activity of such labelled cells leads to a dilution of the label until it is below the level of detectability. The intensity of the label after longer intervals, therefore, is an indication of the number of divisions a cell underwent after the incorporation of the label. Examination of the tissues at various intervals after injection, together with quantitative or semi-quantitative assessments of the degree of labelling, thus gives an impression of the dynamics of the process of proliferation. Also within the matrices a distinction can be made between those cells which are still synthesizing DNA and those that no longer do so and embark upon their future career as neuroblasts and neurons. In this way the relation between the phases of proliferation and differentiation can be directly visualized.

The technique has another important application with respect to those cells which do not continue dividing but become 'post-mitotic' (such as neurons). After these cells stop dividing they preserve for the rest of their lifespan whatever label they have acquired during the final episode(s) of DNA-synthesis. So by the injection of thymidine at various stages of development, and by performing autoradiography on adult brains, the approximate 'date of birth' of the labelled neurons can be assessed. The technique is not helpful for the glial cells as they preserve mitotic capacity and some degree of activity in later life.

The EGL of small rodents (rats, mice) lends itself very well to analysis with this method, because the cerebellum is relatively easy to study and the bulk of proliferative activity takes place after birth (circumventing the need of intrauterine injections of the labelled thymidine). The findings obtained with this technique confirm and substantially refine earlier findings and assumptions. In the early stages of the EGL the whole population of its cells is engaged in proliferative activity. Later on two zones emerge, an outer (subpial) zone consisting of dividing cells and an inner one in which the great majority of cells no longer take up the thymidine (Fujita, 1967). Fujita suggested three stages in matrix development: a first with exclusively proliferative activity, and two others in which, in addition to mitotic activity, cells start to differentiate into neuroblasts and glial cell-precursors, respectively. Here, as in other situations (but not everywhere), there seems to be mutual exclusion between mitotic activity and differentiation. The first steps of neurogenesis occur in the matrix-regions. Glial cells however maintain their potential to divide even far away from their source of origin; in fact, during myelinogenesis a burst of proliferation occurs at the site of myelin deposition in the cells concerned (*i.e.* the prospective oligodendrocytes).

Two major questions can be raised with regard to cell proliferation in the developing CNS. The first one concerns the lay-out of the time-schedule for proliferation in the various regions, the second the regulatory mechanisms operating within the proliferating systems themselves. No real answer can be given to the first question at present. We do not know what causes the normal sequence to occur; we only know that development takes place in an ordered pattern and that a specific, limited, period of time is available for each proliferating system. For the understanding of some aspects of abnormal development it is essential to realize that if this period is not 'used', lasting damage occurs. The regulation of mitotic activity within a group of cells with proliferative potential is the subject of very extensive and intensive research today. Studies range from the observations of the behaviour of groups of cells (*in vivo* or *in vitro*) to very detailed molecular analysis of, for instance, surface and other characteristics of the cells involved. The observation of cell proliferation under normal *in vivo* conditions clearly points to species-specific tissue- and region-bound regulatory mechanisms. So the EGL (being used here as an example) follows a very narrow time-schedule for its growth, presence and decline, which is characteristic for a certain species. This schedule is held to even under markedly pathological conditions: for instance, after partial damage the EGL may show marked regenerative proliferation—but it still disappears at the normal time. Under other abnormal conditions, however, such as thyroid hormone deficiency, the time-table of the EGL can be disturbed. Experiments with *in vitro*-conditions led to the concepts of 'cell density-dependent growth inhibition' (Dulbecco and Elkington, 1973; Mierzejewski and Rozengurt, 1977; Stokes and Rubin, 1967): once the surface available for the growth has been covered by proliferating cells, normal cells (in contrast with malignant cells) stop further mitotic activity, and of 'contact-inhibition' of cell division (Martz and Steinberg, 1972). The exact mechanisms of these phenomena remain to be elucidated. But the results from experiments on the EGL suggest that *in vivo* comparable phenomena may exist. The width of the EGL and the proportion of dividing and non-dividing cells vary in the course of time, but both are specific for a certain age of the animal. The EGL can be easily destroyed, such as by suitable doses of X-rays (to which the dividing cells are highly sensitive). After incomplete destruction the EGL regenerates; but for an occasional slight and temporary 'overshoot' this regeneration results in an increase in thickness until the age-appropriate thickness is reached again. Thereafter the EGL follows the normal age-dependent pattern of decline (Ebels, Peters and Thijs, 1975). Mechanisms similar to those responsible for the cell-density dependence of growth *in vitro* may well be operative here. Regulatory factors discussed so far operate over a restricted area. They seem to comprise direct cell interaction between similar or different types of cells. An example of the latter is the proliferative activity of glial cells preceding myelination. Shortly before the deposition of myelin starts, a very marked mitotic activity occurs in the precursors of the oligodendrocytes. The well-established fact that the axon diameter is a determinant for myelin-formation (Friede, 1972) and the very close relation between the dividing glial cells and the structures (axons) to be myelinated warrant the assumption that the interaction between the axons, increasing in diameter, and the neighbouring as yet uncommitted glial cells induces the proliferation of the latter. Other factors also known to influence proliferative activity will be discussed later in the chapter.

Cell differentiation

At a certain stage of its evolution a division occurs in the EGL between a compartment of cells that continue to divide and an inner one in which proliferation no longer takes place. Although all matrix cells in the CNS look rather similar, the various types of cells originating from them can easily be identified on the basis of their morphological characteristics: not only can glial cells be distinguished from neurons, but also a Purkinje cell from an anterior horn-cell or one from Clarke's column; the small granule cells in the cerebellum, hippocampus or olfactory region show less marked developmental changes.

The acquiring of adult characteristics (morphological, chemical and physiological) is the result of a process of differentiation. This process requires an extensive elaboration and re-organization of the nuclear and perinuclear structures, which can be studied with various tools. Even within the field of morphology alone different techniques can be used: light microscopy (including impregnation methods, histochemistry and enzymehistochemistry, labelling and injection procedures) scanning and transmission electron microscopy. Alterations also occur at the periphery of the cell; these include the growth of processes and the establishment of structures for various types of contact with other cells. From the marked differences between the various types of adult cells it is evident that qualitative and quantitative aspects of differentiation vary over a considerable range. The changes within the nucleus and perikaryon reflect both the metabolic alterations the cells undergo, and also the activities at the periphery of the cells. The latter may be exemplified by changes in the cytoplasm of the Purkinje cells. During the phase of massive growth of the larger dendritic branches the nucleus is located at the opposite site from the dendritic pole; the cytoplasm is jammed with organelles and shows high activity of various enzymes. When the emphasis of peripheral growth shifts towards the axon, the nucleus migrates towards the centre of the cell and a marked area of cytoplasm emerges between the nucleus and the site of origin of the axon. The differences in morphologic appearance between various types of neurons are directly and intimately related to the functional and metabolic peculiarities of each type (although the details of this are ill-understood). Neurons can be subdivided into macroneurons and microneurons. In general the macroneurons in a particular region originate and differentiate earlier than the microneurons. This can conveniently be observed in the cerebellum, where in rats and mice the Purkinje cells are formed before birth, the Golgi cells around birth, but the very numerous granule cells only in the second and third weeks after birth (Altman, 1966; 1969). It appears as if gross networks are established first. In many situations the efferent cells in such a chain of neurons are seen to mature before the afferent ones (Barron, 1946). Another feature of this seemingly 'retrograde' development is the observation that dendrites develop only after the axon reaches its peripheral destination. This sequence of events may contribute to the time-schedule of developmental processes. Later on, these networks are enriched by the intercalated microneurons.

It is important to realize that the neuronal elements, once they emerged from the population of dividing cells, have lost the capacity ever to divide again (under all but perhaps some very exceptional and artificial conditions [Cone and Cone, 1978]). This implies that loss of neurons is irrevocable apart from recruitment of new elements from a pool of undifferentiated dividing cells—which is possible only to a limited extent in time and in number.

Changes due to differentiation, although less spectacular, are observed in neuroglial cells. Morphological changes in astrocytes and in perineuronal oligodendrocytes are inconspicuous. The cells concerned with the deposition of myelin however show a stage of temporary high cytoplasmic activity, as inferred from the high content of ribonucleic acid, protein and oxydative enzymes, which appears to be the expression of the myelination-associated metabolism. The changing properties and characteristics of cells during differentiation have important implications for their vulnerability to noxious agents and factors. The concept of 'indirect signs of differentiation', based on the very changes in vulnerability during maturation, is relevant in this connection.

Factors involved in the local regulation of mitotic activity have already been considered. With a view to the seemingly mutual exclusion of proliferation and differentiation (at any rate for neurons) these same factors must also be important determinants for differentiation. In vitro-studies have shown that changes in the culture medium (for instance in protein content or ionic concentrations) directly influence the balance between proliferation and non-proliferation (here to be equated with differentiation). Comparable factors may operate in vivo. The balance between proliferation and differentiation in the EGL can be disturbed experimentally. The fact that under normal and experimental conditions the division of the EGL into a proliferative and differentiating compartment depends on the attainment of a certain thickness suggests that gradients of nutritional or metabolic factors may be important. The distance from the arachnoid space (and perhaps also from developing bloodvessels) may determine these presumed gradients.

Cell migration

During CNS development many cells change their position with regard to other cells or structures (Sidman and Rakic, 1973). A relatively clear example can be observed (and was already beautifully illustrated by Ramón y Cajal!) in the cerebellum. Whereas the EGL lies at the outside of the Purkinje cells (covering the subpial surface of the cerebellum) the mature granule cells derived from it lie underneath the Purkinje cell-layer. This change of position is often referred to as resulting from an inward migration of the granule cells. What is meant is a change in the relative position of the *nuclei* of Purkinje and granule cells. This need not necessarily imply, however, a real migration of one cell as a whole with regard to another—it can also result from an alteration of the site of the nucleus within the cytoplasm. The picture presented by conventional staining techniques with their emphasis on the nucleus may be misleading. Another cause of possible mis-interpretation may be an inclination to conceive of developmental changes as a discontinuous series of states instead of a flowing series of continuous alterations. This pitfall is especially relevant to the morphologist studying slides from which the dynamics of the processes going on are of course completely absent. Real migration only occurs when cells as a whole change their position with regard to fixed spatial landmarks; the latter are difficult (or even impossible) to find in a system that changes as a whole all the time. Parts of cells do, of course, change position with regards to neighbouring elements by the growth or resorption of processes or by movement of structures within the cell, especially the nuclei (Meller and Tetzleff, 1975).

At first glance it may seem superfluous to stress what might seem mere points of semantics. But for an understanding of development it is necessary to conceive of it as occurring within a living system composed of cells that display some sort of amoeboid activity all the time. A static picture of migration misleadingly turns it into some sort of magic where cells seem to be endowed with foreknowledge of their future destiny. Migratory phenomena are more appropriately seen as the result of continuous changes in configuration of cells establishing permanent or temporary contacts with other cells in a growing and continuously changing environment. So the downward migration of the cerebellar granule cells can be interpreted as the result of differential growth of the cells with a shift, within the changing cells, of nucleus and perinuclear structures. It is tempting to raise the possibility that already during this re-shaping contacts are being made between dendritic branches of the Purkinje cells and the downward growing granule cells (Uzman, 1960). It is also conceivable that cells that originate from the same source but later become separated (such as the Purkinje cells and the neurons of the central cerebellar nuclei) remain in contact with each other rather than first completely separate and subsequently grow processes towards each other.

Even when we try to reduce so-called migration to the result of differential growth, the mechanisms for this apparent migration remain to be elucidated. But in a sense the problem is then reduced to a more familiar field: that of ordered growth of processes ultimately leading to the formation of specific connections with such structures as bundles and tracts (Sidman and Wessells, 1975). Here a tendency for self-increasing order may become manifest: pre-existing structure may act as a guidance for further elaboration (Weiss, 1934; 1961). These pre-existing orderly relations may exist from very early stages onwards (as suggested for those between Purkinje cells and neurons of the central nuclei). Conversely, absence or disturbance of this 'primary' order may cause abnormal development, such as is often interpreted as resulting from abnormal migration.

The following experiments, taken from our own work, may serve to illustrate other important determinants for normal migratory patterns (Ebels, 1972; Ebels and Peters, 1974). These experiments were set up to analyse the pathogenesis of so-called ectopic cells—generally interpreted as signs of disturbed migration. In the cerebellar cortex granule cells may occasionally be located within the molecular layer instead of the granular layer. Often this arrest of migration is explained by a decreased capacity to fully migrate. We tried to explain their position along the lines indicated above: as a result of a disturbed balance of cell growth. We showed that such ectopic granule cells can be produced very consistently by well-defined experimental means; the effects of experimental disturbance are time- and dose-related (we mainly used X-irradiation). It is important to know that the ectopic granule cells form normal connections with ingrowing mossy fibres (their major afferent partners). It appears that as a result of the experimental disturbance the development of the granule cells is retarded (secondary to regeneration of the partially destroyed EGL) whereas the ingrowth of the mossy fibres follows the normal time-schedule. Mossy fibres that do not contact granule cells in

the normal area (the granular layer) continue their growth and invade the molecular layer where they may meet belatedly 'migrating' granule cells. According to this hypothesis, seemingly abnormal migration can be interpreted as the result of a disturbance of the balances in time and in number preserved under normal developmental conditions.

The formation of synapses

Teleologically the formation of synapses is the ultimate goal of the developmental processes in the maturing CNS. It also gives a special flavour to the development of the CNS in comparison with that of other organs. Synapses occur between all parts of neurons (Peters, Palay and Webster, 1976); but the majority occurs between axons and dendrites or cell bodies. Morphologically synapses are characterized by special features of the membranes involved and by the presence of synaptic vesicles. Special excrescenses (spines) may be present at the postsynaptic site. Many aspects of synapse formation lie outside the scope of this presentation. The molecular events involved in synapse formation (comprising the manufacture of synaptic structures as well as the establishment of specific cell preferences) are the subject of much investigation today (Appel, 1975; Barondes, 1975, 1976).

Even though many aspects of synapse formation are still only partly or poorly understood, we may postulate some necessary conditions for a normal wiring pattern to develop. The number of cells concerned and their position have to be within a certain range. Also the patterns of the growth of the cell processes and their terminal branches must be structured in time, place and number. Under normal conditions there is an obvious balance between the synaptic partners. Many data point to at least some (often a high) degree of special preference of one type of cell for another—but the partners must be there at the right moment to express this affinity. Spatial relationships are sometimes easy to understand, as when cells are formed in close connection. In other cases (such as the axons of the Betz cells reaching the anterior horn cells from the motor cortex) processes grow over large distances until they meet their partner of choice; are they so fastidious, or do they not encounter possible partners earlier on? It appears as if the establishment of permanent synaptic contact means the end of further growth (perhaps resembling the *in vitro* phenomenon of 'contact inhibition'); without such contact growth may continue beyond the normal boundaries as was observed for the mossy fibres invading the molecular layer when they did not encounter a granule cell within the normal area.

In order to marshal the many and manifold data and ideas on synapse formation we should like to raise three questions:

(i) Is the formation of synaptic structures the result of an interaction between the synapting cells, or is it an autonomous process on one or both sides?

(ii) What is the degree of specificity of synaptic connections?

and (iii) Are synapses under normal developmental conditions permanent or can they be temporary?

(i) It seems an attractive presumption that such a specialized contact between two cells as the synapse results from an interaction between the two cells concerned. That such interaction is not necessarily a functional one was shown by *in vitro* experiments in which all electrical activity was suppressed but synaptic contact nevertheless did develop (Crain, Peterson and Bornstein, 1968); of course quite different types of interaction may operate.

It is not possible to decide whether the local apposition of two cell surfaces engaged in synapse-formation during normal development also implies direct 'inductive' interaction. This can only be studied under suitable abnormal conditions. Occasionally, it is possible to eliminate one synaptic partner to see what happens. This can be done by destroying one partner (and not affecting the other) by such means as X-irradiation, viruses, or drugs; comparable conditions also occur spontaneously *in vivo* in animals with genetically determined disturbances of CNS development.

Recent evidence from such investigations demonstrates that development of synaptic structures (especially the post-synaptic ones) can occur in the absence of the other (afferent) partner. But other observations suggest the contrary: especially in the more peripheral parts of the dendritic tree postsynaptic development seems to depend on the presence of the afferent elements (Hartkop and Jones, 1976; Hirano, 1978; Sotelo and Privat, 1978). Thus, different mechanisms may operate in different systems or in various parts of the same system. Even the opposite of synapse-induction may occur. Sometimes a superabundant anlage of postsynaptic structures is reduced to the final pattern under the influence of afferent fibres (Larramendi, 1969; Sotelo and Arsenio-Nunes, 1976; Sotelo, Hillman, Zamora and Llinas, 1975; Sidman and Wessells, 1975). Accordingly, all three possible mechanisms (induction, reduction and autonomy) operate.

(ii) Many factors suggest a high degree of specificity in synapse-formation. The strongest is the fundamentally similar wiring pattern of the CNS in all members of a certain species. Experiments into the establishment or re-establishment of synaptic connections, and also *in vitro* investigations of the formation of aggregates of cells derived from various regions of the CNS, both point to specific synapse–favouring properties (undoubtedly determined by the surface characteristics of the cells involved). But this specificity is not absolute; cells which do not form synapses under normal conditions have been shown to be able to do so in abnormal situations (Chung, 1975; Gaze, 1974; Jacobson and Hunt, 1973; Moscona, 1976; Roth and Marchese, 1976; Sotelo and Privat, 1978).

(iii) The synapse is such an elaborate result of local differentiation that the *a priori* assumption that under normal conditions they are permanent structures, seems reasonable. But it has been suggested, from Cajal onward, that this is not necessarily so. Cajal himself suggested that the synapses established in early cerebellar development between the afferent climbing fibres and the soma of the Purkinje cells were resorbed later and replaced by those between climbing fibres and the major dendritic branches (Cajal, 1911). If this were true then it would be a strong counter-argument against our assumption. It is, however, very well possible here that the original synapses are not resorbed, but (during the growth of the Purkinje cells and their dendritic system) move upward from the soma to the larger dendritic branches. There are other, stronger, arguments in favour of changing inter-neuronal relationships during normal development (though the more spectacular ones have been described in lower animals) (Gaze, 1974). This would fit in with the conclusion that synaptic specificity is not absolute; cells have their preference but may change allegiance!

In conclusion it seems that two sets of factors are of paramount importance in synapse-formation: cellular characteristics on one hand, determining the degrees of preference, and on the other the availability of cells and cell processes for contact.

Cell death

Three kinds of regulatory mechanism can be suggested for the determination of the ultimate number of cells: an *a priori*-balance, a positive and a negative adjustment to need. As discussed below, the rate of the production of neuron-precursors in the matrices does not seem to be influenced by the presence or absence of possible afferent partners. An example of possible positive adjustment to need might be the proliferation of glial cells in relation with myelination. But negative adjustment in the form of cell death is an important feature in some situations. Two types of spontaneous cell death are in fact observed. One, occurring within proliferative compartments (Lewis, 1975), seems of very minor morphogenetic significance. The other type involves already post-mitotic cells (neuroblasts) that have migrated away from their site of origin, and has been described in various regions of the developing CNS (Cowan, 1973; I-Wu Chu-Wang and Oppenheim, 1978; Oppenheim, I-Wu Chu-Chang and Maderdrut, 1978; Prestige, 1970, 1974). It is most striking in the spinal cord where a massive anlage of potential motor neurons is considerably reduced to the periphery-determined requirement. It is assumed that those cells die that fail to make sufficient functional peripheral contact. This assumption is supported by experiments in which the 'peripheral load' is altered—which results in a corresponding change in the rate of death of the spinal neuroblasts. The same mechanism is assumed to operate in other regions, where it may be more difficult to demonstrate it directly because of the more complex connective conditions.

Speculations have been raised on the 'reason why' of this remarkable phenomenon. It has been suggested that dying cells pass information on to the surviving ones, that the developing nervous system 'needs' more cells than later on, or that there may be a sort of 'selection pressure' to make enough cells (Prestige, 1974; Sidman, 1970). A possibility is that the balance between proliferation and non-proliferation in matrices (needed for the production of sufficient post-mitotic elements) can only be obtained at the cost of over-production. But none of these suggestions provides a really satisfactory explanation. The death of the spinal neuroblasts that failed to establish sufficient peripheral connections is an example of what one might call 'retrograde' death. Situations have also been described in which cells that do not receive normal afferent connections die ('anterograde' cell death) (Prestige, 1974). But in both instances cells die only when certain responsible mechanisms operate in very specific phases of their development. The effect is most severe at the time when connections are normally being established.

SOME OTHER ASPECTS OF THE MATURATION OF THE CNS

No attempt is being made in this chapter to cover, even cursorily, all aspects of the maturation of the CNS. Even within the domain of morphology some features of major functional significance (such as the development of blood vessels, ependyma and choroid plexus) have been left out completely. However, brief mention must be made of the impressive developmental changes during chemical, electrophysiological and behavioural maturation.

Chemical analysis reveals marked and numerous changes in the maturing CNS (Ford, 1973; Himwich, 1974; Richter, 1975; Sokoloff, 1974). Some of these can easily be correlated with morphological alterations: an increase in DNA reflects an increase in the number of cells, an increase in the specific components of the myelin sheaths can be correlated with the morphologically demonstrable development of myelin. Differentiation of cells implies an increase in such cell constituents as RNA, proteins (enzymes), and lipids. During CNS development there is a decrease in water content and the amount of extracellular space (Bondareff, 1973; Selzer, Myers and Holstein, 1972). The ratio between the volumes occupied by cell nuclei, perinuclear cytoplasm and cell processes ('neuropil') changes, resulting in a decrease in cellularity as measured by the number of cells (= cell nuclei) per unit of volume or surface-area. There are drastic metabolic changes of all kinds. An increase in aerobic metabolism is accompanied by an increase in vascularization. The development of capillaries and their changing relation with the surrounding elements (plus changing metabolic requirements) account for the changes in exchange and transport phenomena between blood and brain, resulting in the establishment of the so-called blood brain-barrier. The changes mentioned so far are of a more general type, occurring (with regional variation) all over the CNS. More specific alterations are observed when, for instance, (putative) transmittor substances (Coyle, 1974) or such surface-associated elements as are supposed to be involved in cell recognition are analysed.

A major advantage of chemical over morphological investigation is that quantification of results is inherent to chemical procedures of analysis, whereas morphological results are most often the result of subjective assessment. This gain however is offset by loss of information about cellular detail and localization. A recurrent problem in the interpretation of many chemical data, obtained during CNS maturation, is the fact that all parameters continuously change: there is no constant value of reference (Himwich, 1973). Are results best expressed pro unit of fresh or of dry weight, with reference to DNA or to protein? In order to discover more specific changes it may be necessary to analyse small, circumscribed areas of the CNS, homogeneous groups of cells or specific cell fractions. This is now possible by means of appropriate technical procedures. Such refinements on the chemical side to some degree annihilate the disadvantages of chemical analysis when compared with morphological approaches. Progress on the morphological side (comprising such techniques as histo- and enzymehistochemistry, labelling and injection procedures, transmission and scanning electron microscopy, immunological methods) builds further bridges between the two lines of approach and gives rise to promising results. But the gap still exists, factually and conceptually, and will require much patient effort and mutual understanding and cooperation between morphologist and chemist in order to be closed as far as possible.

Wider still seems the gap between morphology and electro-physiology. Neurons are cells specialized in receiving, integrating and transmitting certain stimuli. They are able to do so because of their configuration and contact with other cells, their specialized membrane properties and the production of substances involved in transmitting the impulse from one cell to another. Thus in order for a neuron to act effectively, the sites of functional contact with other cells must have been established, the membrane must have acquired the potential to generate and propagate impulses, and the machinery for the production and the transport of the neurotransmittor substances must function. The development of these varying properties is a major part of neuronal differentiation and growth. Cone has shown that for somatic cells there is an inverse correlation between the size of the membrane potential and mitotic activity (Cone, 1971). So the facts that neurons have a high membrane potential and have lost the capacity to divide seem to be closely connected. Neurons have been shown to be able to resume mitosis under some very abnormal conditions, in which—significantly—their membrane potential is considerably reduced! (Cone and Cone, 1978). One can conceive of the emerging physiological properties of the CNS (including the electro-encephalogram as a sort of epiphenomenon) as the result of interactions between neurons of various types (macro- and microneurons, excitatory and inhibitory ones) integrated in a network of increasing complexity and stability—with the conduction-velocity being speeded up by the development of myelination.

Behavioural aspects of development are outside the

scope of this chapter. It is tempting for the morphologist and the student of behaviour alike to try and draw links between the structure of the nervous system and the expression of its potential as revealed by the various aspects of behaviour (Bernhard, Kolmodin and Meyerson, 1967; Bodian, 1970; Humphrey, 1964; Lindsley, 1974; Purpura, Shofer, Housepian and Nobacjm, 1964; Scheibel and Scheibel, 1964, 1971). The capacities of small networks of neuron-like elements can be predicted from a knowledge of the properties of the constituting elements and their interaction. But for higher levels of complexity this is no longer possible. Here the statement of one of the greatest of investigators of the nervous system, Ramón y Cajal, seems still valid: 'La psychologie peut mieux aider à la connaissance du cerveau que celle-ci a la connaissance des phénomènes psychologiques' (Cajal, 1911). We can say that for a given member of a certain species to behave 'normally' its brain has to be within the normal range. Most people with abnormally large brains are not super-intelligent, but mentally subnormal! A normal brain is a necessary (and, to a large extent perhaps also sufficient) condition for normal behaviour.

REGULATORY MECHANISMS

'The brain and all its sundry cells observe degree, priority and place, office and custom—in this line of order.'

As with all development, the maturation of the CNS is an ordered process. This is evident from the time- and region-bound bursts of proliferative activity, the transition from proliferation to differentiation, the steps leading towards the various types and sub-types of cells, the growth and branching of the processes arriving at the right moment at the proper place to establish appropriate connections. It is clear that precise regulatory mechanisms must be involved. Some such possible mechanisms have already been noted.

It is important to realize that, in a morphological (or biochemical) study of normal development, only temporal and spatial relationships can be observed. It is impossible from such studies to differentiate between coincidence and causative relation. Sometimes it is possible to do so in suitable experimental conditions, including 'experiments of nature' in the form of mutant animals with more or less well-defined derangement of CNS development. 'Take degree away—and see, what discord follows': studies of selected and selective states of disorder may help us grasp the essence of order.

It is also essential to be aware of the various levels of complexity and hierarchy on which regulatory mechanisms can be sought. So we have seen that the proliferative characteristics of groups of cells can be analysed to some extent in terms of 'group-behaviour', for which various possible regulatory mechanisms can be postulated. An obvious next step is to try and specify such mechanisms in molecular terms. The same holds for differentiation and growth of processes. But even if much fuller knowledge of

molecular parameters of development were obtained, this would not by itself provide us with real understanding of what goes on at higher levels of complexity (as so succinctly expressed by Paul Weiss: 'One plus one does not equal two' [Weiss, 1967]). As in all biology, so in our field of interest the extrapolation of findings from one level to another constitutes a major problem in itself.

It may be helpful to distinguish between two sets of regulatory mechanisms. The first operates over a narrow range, by direct cell-interaction or through spatially restricted microenvironmental conditions. Phenomena such as cell-density dependence of growth and contact inhibition suggest the operation of very local factors. The phenomena occurring just prior to and during myelination also point to direct cell interaction. This may play a role, too, in the formation of synaptic structures. The fact that spontaneous cell death seems to be regulated by a process of 'supply and demand' indicates some form of direct cell interaction (or rather, cell communication). The question has been raised as to whether 'afferent' fibres influence proliferative activity within matrices; the evidence available seems to negate such influence, at any rate as far as the proliferation of neuron-precursors is involved.

The second set of mechanisms comprises those which are not locally restricted but operate over a much wider field. These include nutritional states and hormone levels (Balàsz, 1974; Prescott, Read and Coursin, 1975; Winnick, 1975). Severe undernutrition during the stages of cell proliferation results in a reduced number of neurons in the adult animal. The same factor during differentiation leads to under-sized cells. Among hormones, the influence of the level of thyroid hormone has been extensively studied. Hyperthyroidism accelerates cell proliferation but also brings it to a premature close—with the result of a permanent deficiency of neurons. Hypothyroidism, on the other hand, retards cell proliferation, which however is continued beyond the normal span, so that ultimately a normal number of neurons is reached. Hypothyroidism has also been shown to retard myelination (which may be due to a direct effect on the myelinating cells or secondary to reduced or retarded axonal growth). Other hormones (sex hormones, cortico-steroids), too, have been demonstrated to influence CNS development. The influence of the so-called Nerve Growth Factor (Mobley, Server, Ishii, Riopelle and Shooter, 1977), although restricted in its scope to sympathetic and dorsal ganglia, is very impressive.

There remains, within this second category, a group of factors, often rather loosely referred to as 'enriched' or 'poor environments'. Among the better defined and extensively studied is the influence of the presence or absence of visual stimuli on the development of the visual system (Blakemore, 1974, 1977; Hubel, Wiesel and LeVay, 1977; Lund and Lund, 1977; Rakic, 1977; Rose, 1977). It has been shown that visual experience in the early postnatal period to some extent influences the morphological and functional maturation of this system. Much more difficult is the exact interpretation of those studies where the variable factor consists of more loosely defined environmental factors (the frequency of handling, the space and companionship allotted to animals) summarized as 'experience'. Several workers have demonstrated measurable effects of variations in experience on various parameters of brain development (Kolata, 1975; Rose, 1977; Rosenzweig, Bennett and Diamond, 1972). There is an obvious and understandable temptation to extrapolate such findings into the human situation and apply them to the educational situation in man. Whether the experiments and their results provide a strong enough base for such a rather risky enterprise remains questionable!

The development of the CNS is a process in which continuous interactions of all kinds operate all the time. But on the other hand many changes occurring, though well coordinated, seem to be rather autonomous. An impressive example of a large degree of autonomy is the occasional finding of very highly organized CNS-tissue in completely foreign and presumably non-functional surroundings, as shown by cerebellar cortex in teratomas of the ovary! Which of both lines, interaction or autonomy, is emphasized depends on the particular situation studied but also on the viewpoint of the investigator.

The orderliness of the developmental processes has been stressed up to now. But this does not necessarily imply that everything is completely pre-determined (Bekoff and Fox, 1972). There are many examples of self-increasing ordered complexity, such as the outgrowth of bundles of processes (Sidman and Wessells, 1975; Willshaw and Von der Marburg, 1976). Results of cell interaction may lead to further interaction; microenvironmental changes may give rise to events that in turn result in critical environmental alterations determining further developmental changes. Randomness may well be involved. From a certain matrix different types of cells emerge. Do we have to assume that individual matrix cells are already predestined to their future role? Some people think so but it is doubtful. It does not really matter which particular cell turns into a basket or a granule cell, provided the normal number of each type is ultimately reached. Such randomness may operate, for example, through the type of partner available for synaptic contact. Here quantitative and temporal aspects become critical: the availability of partners has to be within the normal range of time, number, place and variety. When this range is disturbed normal connections are no longer made or made at abnormal sites (as was shown for the ectopic granule cells), or abnormal connections may become established.

So, in the development of the CNS 'macrodeterminacy may not be reducible to microdeterminacy' (Paul Weiss, 1970) and we seem to encounter Jacques Monod's two categories, 'Hasard' and 'Nécessité' (Monod, 1970). In the words of Jacobson 'the genetic control of morphogenesis may be relatively simple, and may consist of a programmed sequence of changes in cellular adhesiveness and in cellular motility . . . it is simpler and more economical to specify a developmental programme than to specify the final structure in detail' (Jacobson, 1970).

PLASTICITY AND REGENERATION IN THE DEVELOPING CNS

It is well established that, with very limited exceptions (Kaplan and Hinds, 1977; Raisman, 1978), loss of neurons from the mature mammalian brain is irreplaceable and its effect therefore permanent. It has often been assumed that regenerative activity after damage to neuronal processes too is absent from such brains (Guth, 1975). That recovery of function may occur after cerebrovascular accidents or trauma is not in contradiction with this. Such recovery can largely be accounted for by the disappearance of secondary changes including oedema or disturbed circulation. There is growing evidence, however, that structural recovery too can occur (Barlow and Gaze, 1977; Guth and Clemente, 1975; Raisman, 1978; Young, 1977). Axons, in the mature mammalian brain, do show the phenomena of regeneration and of sprouting—but they do not replace the severed parts over more than a tiny distance. It has also been demonstrated that loss of synaptic contacts, due to degeneration of presynaptic elements, is replaced by new contacts, which may be of a different kind from the original ones (Raisman, 1978). But both the limited regrowth of axons and the reoccupation of vacant synaptic sites by other elements prevent a reconstitution of the *status quo ante*. So, although there is some degree of regenerative activity and structural integrity may be restored to some extent, this need not result in functional recovery. Attempts to improve the situation have mainly concentrated on enhancing axonal growth (Guth, 1975). But it may also be important to prevent vacated synaptic sites from being occupied by 'unwanted' partners. We wish, of course, to improve the final outcome after damage to the brain. The most important way of doing so is by counteracting the secondary changes (oedema, circulatory insufficiency etc.) and their effects. Whether it is also possible to directly improve functional recovery by medication or physiotherapy is uncertain.

It is pertinent to ask whether the absence of repletion of dead neurons and the limited extent of regeneration also hold for the developing CNS. There is no good reason to assume that neurons and neuroblasts in the maturing CNS differ from neurons in the adult brain with regard to reacquisition of proliferative capacity. Any compensation for loss of neurons has to result from additional manufacture by proliferating systems (as has been shown to occur) or from reduced spontaneous death of neuroblasts. But both phenomena, cell proliferation and spontaneous cell death, are time- and region-bound. It is therefore only 'then' and 'there' that neuronal loss can be compensated. For neuroglial cells, especially the astrocytes, the situation is different as they preserve mitotic potential; in fact, an increase in the number of astrocytes is a well-known reaction under many pathological conditions.

It is very difficult, if at all possible, to compare plasticity, growth and regeneration of nerve cell processes in the mature and the developing CNS. Kerr (1975) has stated that 'Plasticity is the ability of the CNS neurons to grow *beyond the normal developmental period* or to re-establish old or *develop new connections* or regenerate after injury'—(added emphasis). However, this is only partly applicable to a growing system, in which processes grow and new connections are being established all the time. The statement by the same author that 'there appears to be general agreement that a greater degree of neuroplasticity is present in immature than in mature animals' therefore has to be scrutinized for its actual meaning and content. We stated earlier that cell connections seem to be based on relative, rather than on absolute, affinity between the partners involved. If one of them is not present or available at the right moment and the right place, other connections can be made, provided other suitable and not-yet committed cells are present. It is a matter of semantics whether one wishes to call these 'new' or 'aberrant' connections. But the far greater degree of freedom in the developing CNS in this respect may well impress as greater plasticity.

The end of the growth of neuronal processes seems to be related to the establishment of mature synaptic connections. As long as this has not occurred, processes in the developing CNS can *continue* to grow (which is different from *resumed* growth in Kerr's definition) even beyond the normal boundaries. Thus, the molecular layer of the cerebellum may be invaded by mossy fibres under pathological conditions, whereas normally they do not grow beyond the granular layer. This, again, *suggests* greater plasticity of the developing system in comparison with the mature one. So it is not surprising that the immature CNS seems to possess greater regenerative and reparative potential than the adult CNS. But the term plasticity is not strictly applicable to both in the same sense.

There is yet another pitfall in comparisons between the effects of damage to the mature and the developing CNS; the immature system may react to the same kind of injury in a different way. As these reactions (such as circulatory disturbance, oedema, glial—especially astrocytic—reaction) are important determinants for recovery, such differences have to be taken into account when comparing recovery of mature and immature brains. In the case of glial reaction, for example, the cause of the difference may be the immature state of the astrocyte, or the absence of the particular stimulus operating in the mature tissue (Osterberg and Wattenberg, 1965).

Many reactions to injury (for example, compensation of cell loss) can be considered beneficial for the individual concerned. But in principle disruptive effects can also occur (as after regeneration in the mature CNS). The formation of aberrant connections ('re-wiring') may have negative functional effects, even though this may not be demonstrable at the clinical level.

In summary, where plasticity and the potential for repair are concerned, neither the mature and the immature CNS, nor even the various developmental stages, can be strictly compared with each other. As long as the system is not yet structurally determined, developmental byways are open and compensatory mechanisms may exist that are no longer available in the mature system. And, no doubt, the same holds from the functional point of view.

These wider options become manifest when normal development is disturbed—which is one of the reasons why the immature CNS appears to have a larger degree of plasticity and greater possibilities for repair after damage.

THE VULNERABILITY OF THE DEVELOPING CNS—SOME PRINCIPLES INVOLVED

Inevitably the maturing CNS, in which so many complex and intricate changes go on all the time, must be vulnerable to a wide range of noxious influences. Happily in mammals this vulnerability is counteracted by the protection the intrauterine environment provides against external factors (physical, chemical and microbiological). But another type of protection may also be present: foetal metabolic deficiencies can be compensated by the maternal organism; this may explain why some inborn errors of metabolism do not exert their influence until after birth. Nevertheless, many cases of intra-uterine brain damage do occur in man and in animals and can also be induced experimentally. The resulting effects can profitably be studied in terms of more or less circumscribed disturbances of normal development. Later in this chapter we comment briefly on some aspects of human developmental neuropathology; here we consider some concepts relevant for an understanding of phenomena to be observed.

A basic concept underlying 'pathological' thinking implies that vulnerability of cells to noxious agents is directly related with the physical and chemical peculiarities of those cells. Therefore, one may expect that for a given agent the reactions of a Purkinje cell, a motor neuron, a granule cell or a glial element will vary considerably. During the course of development even larger variations must be expected: the same cell may react differently to the same damaging factor according to its very stage of maturation. Changes in degree of vulnerability of a certain type of cell may occur gradually or more abruptly; the latter is observed when marked maturational changes take place within a relatively short period of time. For such periods the term *critical periods* has been coined (Davison and Dobbing, 1968; LaVelle, 1964). Another term used as a common denominator is that of *vulnerable periods* (Dobbing, 1968); this is used to describe periods of high susceptibility of the maturing CNS to damaging factors. One has to be aware of the limitations of these and similar concepts. Like the so-called blood brain-barrier they have no intrinsic explanatory power but only serve as a sort of short-hand description of sets of phenomena, and are only useful as such. Their real content has to be specified for each particular instance. A third concept of potential usefulness in the context of our discussion is that of *selective vulnerability*. For the mature CNS this implies that certain regions are much more vulnerable to the same noxious agent than others. This can be observed in the developing CNS too; but here we see a *changing pattern of selective vulnerability*—each maturational stage displaying its own characteristics in this respect (Richardson, 1973). In the following we shall be more specific and give some examples.

The high vulnerability of proliferating cells to various agents such as X-rays, drugs and toxins, certain viruses, is well known. The ultimate effect of the action of such an agent on the developing CNS depends (*inter alia*) on the maturational stage at which it operates (Ebels, 1970), and can be predicted from knowledge of the time-schedule and location of proliferative activity in the CNS. For instance, early postnatal irradiation of the brains of rats and mice will cause severe damage to the cerebellum as this passes through a phase of high proliferative activity—other areas, such as the brain stem and also the cerebral cortex, being much less vulnerable at that period. High vulnerability is also seen in the proliferating glial cells in the white matter prior to myelination. The same holds for infection with certain drugs, toxins and viruses (Jones, Mickelsen and Yang, 1973; Margolis, Kilham and Johnson, 1971; Shimada and Langman, 1970a, b). Other viruses however (such as the virus of poliomyelitis) have a distinct preference for mature cells. Sensitivity to anoxia (in itself a spectacular illustration of selective vulnerability) increases with increasing maturation of the cells affected (Jílek, Fischer, Krulich and Trojan, 1964). Undernutrition (in severe degrees, as employed experimentally) results in a decreased number of cells—when operative during stages of cell proliferation. But it has a different effect on differentiating systems, where it reduces the growth of the maturing cells (Winnick, 1975).

The concept of *indirect signs of differentiation* has been mentioned already. This was based on observations that cells may change considerably with regard to their vulnerability to certain agents, without showing concurrent morphological alterations. A striking example is provided by the cerebellar granule cells in connection with irradiation (and other agents). Whereas morphologically these cells show only minor maturational changes (in the cell bodies), their susceptibility changes very much over the period of their development from matrix cells into mature elements. Also, in chickens the reaction of motor neuroblasts to axotomy markedly changes over a period when these cells show little alteration and look like being in a type of resting phase (Houthoff and Drukker, 1977).

AN EXCURSION INTO HUMAN PATHOLOGY

So far in this chapter no particular attention has been paid to man. To the contrary, data and formulations have been presented in a way which is applicable to CNS development in all mammals. Some specific aspects of the human situation must now be considered. Two facets of CNS development in man are of immediate importance: its time-schedule and time-scale on one hand, and the relative lengths of the intra- and extrauterine periods of CNS maturation on the other (Dobbing and Sands, 1970, 1973; Lemire, Loeser, Leech and Alvord, 1975; O'Rahilly and Gardner, 1971). The first, among other things, determines the effect of the action of potentially noxious agents operative at a certain developmental period, the second the exposure to or shielding from environmental influences. From the second month in utero onwards, brain weight increases exponentially until some time during the year after birth. Hereafter the growth slows down, but continues for at least another five years. The largest increase takes place after birth: brain weight of the newborn is about 350 grams, of an adult male 1350 grams and of an adult woman about 1300 grams. In young children brain weight accounts for a larger percentage of total body weight than in adults. Under poor nutritional conditions the brain is relatively privileged over other organs (such as the liver): in dystrophic children brain weight is higher in relation to total body or liver weight than in normal children of the same age.

The first phase of neural tube formation is accomplished at the end of the first intrauterine month. Over the next four months regional differentiation occurs. In the cerebral cortex a laminar pattern can be distinguished already at two months. The eye also develops within about the first two months. A division of the colliculi into a superior group, related with vision, and a posterior one, connected with hearing, begins within the second month. The olfactory nerves enter the brain at about seven weeks; after three months the adult pattern has been established (Lemire *et al.*, 1975).

As in other mammals, so in man the development of the cerebellum is a late phenomenon (Friede, 1973; Roesman, 1974). In the newborn the weight of the infratentorial region is only 5–7% of the total brain weight, whereas in the adult it is 11–14%. The molecular layer of the cerebellar cortex acquires its adult thickness at about eight months after birth; the involution of the EGL accelerates between the second and fourth months after birth, with remnants persisting up to well into the second year of life. The total number of cells in the brain (estimated on the basis of its DNA content) increases after birth in all regions of the brain but most markedly in the cerebellum (Dobbing and Sands, 1970). Increase in the later stages of development (of the various parts of the CNS) is due to an increase in the number of glial cells. Cellularity, as measured as the amount of DNA pro unit of fresh weight, however decreases already before birth with the exception of the cerebellum. The increase in weight is then accounted for by the growth of cell processes and myelin sheaths (Dobbing and Sands, 1973).

These and comparable data, in combination with the ideas on the vulnerability of the developing CNS (see above), can be used to interpret neuropathological observations related with the developmental period in man (Friede, 1976; Ostertag, 1956; Smith, 1974). The much larger time-scale in man as compared with the rat and mouse implies that the vulnerable periods for various agents are much longer and less well-defined. Vulnerability lasts longer—but the deleterious effect of a single exposure will be smaller. To understand the pathogenesis of abnormal developmental patterns it is essential to distinguish between damage to systems in very early stages (such as proliferating matrices) and that to structures already more or less established (such as the cerebral or cerebellar cortex). In the following we shall refer to these two categories as 'primary' and 'secondary' developmental damage. It is important to realize that primary damage affects not only the structure directly involved but also others with which it is in some way connected. A distinction between the two types of damage is hampered by the fact that histological reactions such as occur after damage to mature structures (*e.g.* gliosis) may be scanty or even absent after damage to more immature counterparts (Osterberg and Wattenberg, 1965). The absence of reactive changes therefore cannot be used as an conclusive argument in favour of primary damage. But even then some clues may remain. We studied several cases of cerebellar atrophy or hypoplasia, with profound loss of neurons (Purkinje and granule cells). Experiments on rats, in which the EGL was destroyed at various stages of its development, showed that early and complete destruction results in a severely hypoplastic cerebellum without granule cells, in which the Purkinje cells are scattered irregularly over the cortex without the formation of a real Purkinje cell-layer (Ebels, 1970). The same picture was observed in some human cases too, and interpreted as the result of primary damage to the EGL. Other severely atrophic cerebella, however, revealed some preservation of a Purkinje cell-layer even when most of these cells were gone. This was interpreted as resulting from destruction of a cerebellum in which normal development had progressed to a well-layered cortex (an example of secondary damage). For other situations other parameters may be invoked to try and distinguish between the two categories. The practical importance of such a distinction lies in the clues it may possibly provide as to the aetiology of the laesion.

It is obvious that the primary developmental abnormalities constitute a very wide range—due to the different cytotoxic effects of the various agents operative at different developmental stages. We already referred to the high vulnerability of proliferating systems to various agents. The fact that cerebellar proliferation occurs late makes it especially vulnerable to exogenous factors. But in lissencephaly the cerebellum is largely normal, whereas the cerebral cortex is markedly malformed; here some factor must have operated in utero and have disappeared at the time of cerebellar growth. In so-called true microencephaly too, the cerebral hemispheres are usually more affected than the cerebellum. To explain cases of microencephaly in which the various parts of the CNS preserve normal mutual proportions, one is tempted to adduce factors operative over a long developmental period (undernutrition, chronic viral infection, or possibly abnormal hormone levels). In all these instances it is likely that more or less widespread damage to matrices has occurred. Olfactory hypoplasia is an example of a condition that can occur as a 'primary' lesion, but also secondary to hydranencephaly or anencephaly (Friede, 1976). It is much more difficult to explain the occasionally encountered hypertrophy (hyperplasia) affecting restricted areas of the CNS, *a fortiori* when it is asymmetrical as in most cases of cerebellar hypertrophy (Ambler, Pogacar and Sidman, 1969; Oppenheim, 1955; Pritchett

and King, 1978). But it has been shown that hyperplastic growth in the embryonic brain can be induced experimentally, by disturbances of the interaction between the substratum and the neural tube (Källén, 1965).

The proliferation of glial cells just prior to myelination (itself a 'vulnerable' period) was assumed to be causally related to contact with growing axons. Hypomyelination may be due to glial insufficiency, but also to insufficient growth of axons (itself part of disturbed growth of the neuron as a whole, such as may occur *e.g.* in undernutrition). To elucidate the pathogenesis of hypomyelination it is therefore imperative to see whether the axons reached their 'critical' diameter. In some instances myelination seems to have proceeded during the intrauterine period but to have come to a standstill after birth. In many of these cases the cause of this is unknown, but in a few patients metabolic errors have been described. It is attractive to suppose that in utero the child was protected against the effects of the metabolic derangement by the maternal influence.

An impressive and important example of changing patterns of vulnerability to one and the same factor during maturation is the reaction to hypoxia. Not only does this pattern change, but also the histological type of reaction of the sensitive cells, which in immature stages do not show the classical type of ischaemic change seen in adult neurons (Friede, 1976). The changing pattern of vulnerability is certainly caused by the differential maturation of various groups of neurons although other factors (such as changing circulatory conditions) may play a role too. It has been suggested that the neurons suffering most in kernicterus (in which hypoxia is an important factor) are those with the most advanced degree of differentiation at the time.

We have been (perhaps somewhat unfairly) sceptical about cell migration as a morphogenetic event. Still, it remains a useful descriptive term and has often been invoked to explain the pathogenesis of various developmental abnormalities, such as malformations of the cerebral cortex (agyria, microgyria, pachygyria) and dysplasias and heterotopias. We already mentioned that such abnormalities may be limited to part of the brain (*e.g.* the cerebellum being normal in cases of agyria of the cerebral hemispheres). Such observations point to noxious factors operative over a limited period of time only. Ectopism of cerebellar granule cells according to the interpretation of our own experiments suggests a noxious agent of moderate destructive potential against the EGL operative at a fairly specific stage.

We postulated that upsetting the normal numerical and temporal balances during development might directly influence the establishment of functional contacts, especially synapses—resulting in the absence or decrease of normal connections or the establishment of abnormal ones. It needs no further explanation that sufficient detailed and quantitative data cannot be obtained from human material. There have been reports in the literature on synaptic abnormalities observed in human material, but they have to be interpreted with caution. Even when present, such changes need not constitute the primary pathological derangement: in fact they may very well represent secondary alterations. The very limited amount of fresh (biopsy) material available for detailed study (in the case of a brain biopsy derived from one single region only) makes it hazardous to generalize from any findings obtained.

The possible protection against metabolic errors afforded by the intrauterine situation has been noted. It also shields the foetus from many other noxious agents, notably infectious ones. Only a few infectious agents are known to be important causes of intrauterine infection involving the CNS (Intrauterine Infections, 1973). The damage caused by such an infection depends on the time of infection and on the agent involved. During parturition and afterwards many more agents may find their way towards the CNS. It is to be expected that early infection persisting over a long period of time may result in micro-encephaly—as has indeed been described for rubella and cytomegaly infections (Friede, 1976; Smith, 1974). With later occurrence of the infection the effect may be assumed to shift gradually towards decreasing developmental abnormalities (with the possible exception of cerebellar damage) and ultimately come to resemble that seen in adults. As direct signs of inflammation may be completely lacking afterwards when the infection affects very immature tissue, it may be difficult to establish the infectious nature of a malformation. This is the case, for example, with stenosis of the aqueduct due to viral infection affecting the ependymal cells (Johnson, 1975), and with cerebellar hypoplasia due to viral infection of the EGL (Margolis, Kilham and Johnson, 1971). The latter in its endstage is indistinguishable from hypoplasia due to physical or chemical agents. Therefore, on the one hand, it may be very difficult or even impossible to prove a viral aetiology for such (and other) malformations, but on the other it leaves the possibility open in cases where other causes are absent (the assumption of a viral aetiology being impossible to disprove).

CONCLUSIONS

Some aspects of the maturation of the CNS have been discussed. Analysis of this development shows very conspicuous changes for all parameters studied. Seen as a whole, the process of maturation seems fairly smooth and gradual; detailed examination however shows more sudden alterations, giving rise to such phenomena as vulnerable and critical periods. The orderliness of the maturational processes, the underlying temporal and numerical balances, and also the difficulties in distinguishing between coincidence and causative relation have all been emphasized. Damage by noxious influences can be explained partly by their direct deleterious effects, partly by these effects upsetting the balances just mentioned (and so influencing further development). For an understanding of normal and abnormal human development, extrapolation from findings in animals (especially those obtained from well designed experiments) may be useful, if only the dangers of the extrapolation are realized.

Some issues of more or less direct social or clinical importance have emerged. It was stated that in nearly all respects the immature brain, in its various stages, is a quite different system from the mature one. This implies that these various developmental stages all have their own more or less specific pattern of reaction to damaging factors. For some (e.g. anoxia) the vulnerability increases with increasing maturation; for others, very likely the majority, the opposite is true (as for certain viruses, many drugs, X-rays). The immature brain, morphologically and functionally, impresses as having greater effective plasticity than the adult one. As long as the development is not yet finished, developmental strategies can be changed as a reaction to damage, especially with regards to compensation for loss of neurons (by such mechanisms as increased proliferation of matrix cells or reduced spontaneous cell death), continued growth of neuronal processes and the formation of (normal or aberrant) synapses. These compensatory mechanisms will finally result in permanent changes in the structure.

The grosso modo similar structure of the brains of all (normal) members of a certain species implies that genetic factors, acting directly or indirectly on the developing CNS, are the major determinants of brain development. This normal pattern can however be upset by sufficiently grave changes in the 'milieu interne' (such as severe hormonal dysbalance or undernutrition) and by many exogenous factors, provided they get access to the developing brain, which in utero is largely protected from them. The question was raised whether, besides viruses, drugs, X-rays and severe functional depletion (as operative in the visual system under experimental conditions), less well defined influences such as 'enriched' or 'poor' environment may be considered to have a direct and measurable effect on brain development. Some workers have claimed that this is indeed the case, and the results of their experiments are suggestive evidence. But there should not be too easy an extrapolation to the human situation. Such influences must be strong enough to upset the regulatory mechanisms operative during brain development! This does not, of course, imply that the development of the brain of individuals of a certain species is not under some sort of environmental control. But this may result more from some degree of freedom (at least temporarily present) than from direct determination of developmental processes.

Even when assuming that genetic factors are indeed the main determinants of brain development, this does not mean that every single step is under direct genetic control; to the contrary, that would seem an unlikely strategy. If only the developmental programme is specified but not every single step, that implies that there must be some freedom within the genetically determined boundaries of normal development. What exactly these boundaries are is impossible to ascertain. For the time being we have to satisfy ourselves with rather vague notions, and as human beings can only assume that optimal environmental conditions (whatever these may be) favour an optimal development of the brain.

It may disappoint those primarily interested in disturbed behaviour that there has been so little discussion on relationships between the structure of the CNS and the behavioural possibilities, under normal and abnormal conditions (Dobbing and Smart, 1974; Rodier, 1977; Rodier and Reynolds, 1977; Tizard, 1974; Towbin, 1969a, b). The statement that a normal brain is a necessary condition for normal behaviour is perhaps a little more than just a platitude. The concept of normality, whether applied to structural or to behavioural features of the CNS, is a statistical one. No one doubts that certain structural conditions are abnormal: a brain weight of less than 1000 or more than 2000 grams in an adult man is definitely abnormal; certain kinds of behaviour too are judged by everyone to fall outside the normal range. But even in clearly pathological cases the correlation between structure and behaviour is by no means always clear. Even such gross anomalies as an absence of the corpus callosum or severe hypoplasia of the cerebellum do not always lead to gross behavioural disturbance. On the other hand investigation of the brains of even severely mentally retarded people does not always reveal distinct structural abnormalities. Moreover, people with very large brains are mentally subnormal rather than super-intelligent. Even much more difficult, of course, is an evaluation of the possible significance of much smaller deviations from the normal than those just mentioned, such as a somewhat low brain weight or minor structural irregularities. Do we have to assume that even for minor behavioural aberrations a physical (or chemical) substrate must be present? Does 'minimal brain damage' exist? Of course it does in the morphological sense. But does it really matter whether there are a few ectopic granule cells in the cerebellar cortex or whether the gyral pattern of the brain seems somewhat irregular—matter in terms of behaviour? We do not know, and perhaps we may never come to know. The correlation between 'brain and behaviour' may be more a Kantian idea than a reality within conceivable range. Little hope to substantiate this correlation may be better than false hope—and to realize the limitations of our possibilities is preferable to unwarranted expectations!

REFERENCES

Altman, J. (1966). Autoradiographic and histological studies of post-natal neurogenesis. II. *J. comp. Neur.* **128**, 431.

Altman, J. (1969). Postnatal development of the cerebellar cortex in the rat. III. Maturation of the components of the granular layer. *J. comp. Neur.* **145**, 465.

Ambler, M., Pogacar, S., Sidman, R. (1969). Lhermitte-Duclos disease (granule cell hypertrophy of the cerebellum). *J. Neuropath. exp. Neur.* **28**, 622.

Appel, S. H. (1975). Neuronal recognition and synaptogenesis. *Exp. Neur.* **48**, 52.

Balàsz, R. (1974). Influence of metabolic factors in brain development. *Brit. med. Bull.* **30**, 126.

Barlow, H. B., Gaze, R. M., eds. (1977). A discussion on structural and functional aspects of plasticity in the nervous system. *Phil. Trans. roy. Soc. Lond.* B 278 no 961.

Barondes, S. H. (1975). Towards a molecular basis of neuronal recognition. In: *The nervous system. Vol. I 'The basic neurosciences'*, D. B. Tower, (ed.) New York: Raven Press.

Barondes, S. H., (ed.) (1976). *Neuronal Recognition*. New York: Plenum Press; London: Chapman and Hill.

Barron, D. H. (1946). Observations on the early differentiation of the motor neuroblasts in the spinal cord of the chick. *J. comp. Neur.* **85**, 149.

Bekoff, M., Fox, M. W. (1972). Postnatal neural ontogeny: environment-dependent or environment-expectant? *Developm. Psychobiol.* **5**, 323.

Bergquist, H., Källén, B. (1954). Notes on the early histogenesis and morphogenesis of the central nervous system in vertebrates. *J. comp. Neur.* **100**, 627.

Bernhard, C. G., Kolmodin, G. M., Meyerson, B. A. (1967). On the prenatal development of function and structure in the somesthetic cortex of the sheep. In: *Progress in Brain Research, vol. 26: Developmental Neurology*. C. G. Bernhard and J. P. Schadé (eds). Amsterdam/London/New York: Elsevier.

Blakemore, C. (1974). Development of functional connexions in the mammalian visual system. *Brit. med. Bull.* **30**, 152.

Blakemore, C. (1977). Genetic instructions and developmental plasticity in the kitten's visual cortex. *Phil. Trans. roy. Soc. Lond.* B 278, 425.

Bodian, D. (1970). A model of synaptic and behavioral ontogeny. In: *The Neurosciences, Second Study Program*. F. O. Schmitt, (ed). New York: Rockefeller University Press.

Bondareff, W. (1973). Age changes in the neuronal microenvironment. In: *Development and Aging in the Nervous System*. M. Rockstein, ed. New York/London: Academic Press.

Cajal, Ramón y (1911). *Histologie du système nerveux*. Tome II (traduite par L. Azoulay) Paris: Maloine (re-edited by the CSIC, Madrid, 1955).

Chung, Shin-Ho (1975). Synaptic remodelling in the mutant cerebellum. *Nature* **257**, 86.

Cone, C. D. Jr. (1971). Unified theory on the basic mechanisms of normal mitotic control and oncogenesis. *J. theor. Biol.* **30**, 151.

Cone, C. D., Cone, C. M. (1978). Evidence of normal mitosis with complete cytokinesis in central nervous system neurons during sustained depolarization with ouabain. *Exp. Neur.* **60**, 41.

Cowan, W. M. (1973). Neuronal death as a regulative mechanism in the control of cell number in the nervous system. In: *Development and aging in the nervous system*. M. Rockstein, (ed). New York/London: Academic Press.

Coyle, J. T. Jr. (1974). Development of Central Catecholaminergic Neurons. In: *The Neurosciences, Third Study Program*. F. O. Schmitt and F. G. Worden, (eds). Cambridge, Mass./London: M.I.T. Press.

Crain, S. M., Peterson, E. R., Bornstein, M. B. (1968). Formation of functional connections between explants of various mammalian. In: *Growth of the Nervous System*—Ciba Foundation symposium. G. E. W. Wolstenholme and M. O'Connor, (eds). London: Churchill.

Davison, A. N., Dobbing, J. (1968). Critical periods. In: *Applied Neurochemistry* (Ch. II). A. N. Davison and J. Dobbing, (eds). Oxford/Edinburgh, Blackwell.

Dobbing, J. (1968). Vulnerable periods. In: *Applied Neurochemistry*. A. N. Davison and J. Dobbing, (eds). Oxford/Edinburgh, Blackwell.

Dobbing, J., Sands, J. (1970). Timing of neuroblast multiplication in developing human brain. *Nature* **226**, 639.

Dobbing, J., Sands, J. (1973). Quantitative growth and development of human brain. *Arch. Dis. Childh.* **48**, 757.

Dobbing, J., Smart, J. L. (1974). Vulnerability of developing brain and behaviour. *Brit. med. Bull.* **30**, 164.

Dulbecco, R., Elkington, J. (1973). Conditions limiting multiplication of fibroblastic and epithelial cells in dense cultures. *Nature* **246**, 197.

Ebels, E. J. (1970). The influence of age upon the effect of early postnatal X-irradiation on the development of the cerebellar cortex in rats. *Acta neuropath.* **15**, 298.

Ebels, E. J. (1972). Studies on ectopic granule cells in the cerebellar cortex—with a hypothesis as to their aetiology and pathogenesis. *Acta neuropath.* **21**, 117.

Ebels, E. J., Peters, I. (1974). Studies on ectopic granule cells in the cerebellar cortex. II. The 'date of birth' of the ectopic and normal granule cells after low-level X-irradiation. *Acta neuropath.* **27**, 271.

Ebels, E. J., Peters, I., Thijs, A. (1975). Studies on ectopic granule cells in the cerebellar cortex. III. An investigation into the restoration of the external granular layer after partial destruction. *Acta neuropath.* **31**, 103.

Ford, D. H. (1973). Selected changes in the developing postnatal rat brain. In: *Development and Aging in the Nervous System*. M. Rockstein, (ed). New York/London: Academic Press.

Friede, R. L. (1972). Control of myelin formation by axon caliber. *J. comp. Neur.* **144**, 233.

Friede, R. L. (1973). Dating the development of the human cerebellum. *Acta neuropath.* **23**, 48.

Friede, R. L. (1976). *Developmental Neuropathology*. Wien/New York, Springer.

Fujita, S. (1967). Quantitative analysis of cell proliferation and differentiation in the cortex of the postnatal mouse cerebellum. *J. Cell Biol.* **32**, 277.

Gaze, R. M. (1974). Neuronal specificity. *Brit. med. Bull.* **30**, 122.

Guth, L. (1975). History of central nervous system regeneration research. *Exp. Neur.* **48**, 3.

Guth, L., Clemente, C. D., eds. (1975). Growth and regeneration in the central nervous system. *Exp. Neur.* **48**, no. 3, part 2.

Hartkop, T. H., Jones, M. Z. (1976). Methylazoxymethanol-induced aberrant Purkinje cell dendritic development. *J. Neuropath. exp. Neur.* **36**, 519.

Himwich, W. A. (1973). Problems in interpreting neurochemical changes occurring in developing and aging animals. In: *Progress in Brain Research*, vol. 40, 'Neurobiological aspects of maturation and aging'. D. H. Ford, (ed). Amsterdam/London/New York: Elsevier.

Himwich, W. A. (ed.) (1974). *Biochemistry of the Developing Brain* (2 vols.). New York: Dekker.

Hirano, A. (1978). Neuronal and glial processes in neuropathology. *J. Neuropath. exp. Neur.* **37**, 365.

Houthoff, H. J., Drukker, J. (1977). Changing patterns of axonal reaction during neuronal development. *Neuropath. appl. Neurobiol.* **3**, 441.

Hubel, D. H., Wiesel, T. N., LeVay, S. (1977). Plasticity of ocular dominance columns in monkey striate cortex. *Phil. Trans. roy. Soc. Lond.* B **278**, 411.

Humphrey, T. (1964). Some correlations between the appearance of human fetal reflexes and the development of the nervous system. In: *Progress in Brain Research*, vol. 4, 'Growth and Maturation of the Brain'. D. P. Purpura and J. P. Schadé, (eds). Amsterdam/London/New York: Elsevier.

Intrauterine infections (1973). *Ciba Foundation Symposium* no. 10 (*New Series*). Amsterdam/London/New York: Elsevier.

I-Wu Chu-Wang, Oppenheim, R. W. (1978). Cell death of motoneurons in the chick embryo spinal cord (I and II). *J. comp. Neur.* **177**, 33 and 59.

Jacobson, M. (1970). Development, specification and diversification of neuronal connections. In: *The Neurosciences, Second Study Program*. F. O. Schmitt, (ed). New York: Rockefeller University Press.

Jacobson, M., Hunt, R. K. (1973). The origin of nerve-cell specificity. *Sci. Amer.* **228**, 26.

Jílek, L., Fischer, J., Krulich, L., Trojan, S. (1964). The reaction of the brain to stagnant hypoxia and anoxia during ontogeny. In: *Progress in Brain Research*, vol. 9, 'The Developing Brain'. W. A. and H. E. Himwich, (eds). Amsterdam/London/New York: Elsevier.

Johnson, R. T. (1975). Hydrocephalus and viral infections. *Developm. Med. Child Neur.* **17**, 807.

Jones, M., Mickelsen, O., Yang, M. (1973). Methylazoxymethanol neurotoxicity. In: *Progress in Neuropathology*, vol. II. H. M. Zimmerman, (ed). London/New York: Grune and Stratton.

Källén, B. (1965). Proliferation in the embryonic brain with special reference to the overgrowth phenomenon and its possible relationship with neoplasia. In: *Progress in Brain Research*, vol. 14, 'Degeneration patterns in the nervous system'. M. Singer and J. P. Schadé, (eds). Amsterdam/London/New York: Elsevier.

Kaplan, M. S., Hinds, J. W. (1977). Neurogenesis in the adult rat. *Science* **197**, 1092.

Kerr, F. W. L. (1975). Structural and functional evidence of plasticity in the central nervous system. *Exp. Neur.* **48**, 16.

Kolata, G. B. (1975). Behavioral development: effects of environment. *Science* **189**, 207.

Larramendi, L. H. M. (1969). An analysis of synaptogenesis in the cerebellum of the mouse. In: *Neurobiology of Cerebellar Evolution and Development*. R. R. Llinàs, (ed). Chicago: American Medical Association.

LaVelle, A. (1964). Critical periods of neuronal maturation. In: *Progress in Brain Research*, vol. 9, 'The Developing Brain'. W. A. and H. E. Himwich, (eds). Amsterdam/London/New York: Elsevier.

Lemire, R. J., Loeser, J. D., Leech, R. W., Alvord Jr, E. C. (1975). *Normal and Abnormal Development of the Human Nervous System*. Hagerstown: Harper and Row.

Lewis, P. D. (1975). Cell death in the germinal layers of the postnatal rat brain. *Neuropath. appl. Neurobion.* **1**, 21.

Lindsley, D. B. (1974). Ontogenetic development of brain and behaviour. In: *Brain Mechanisms and the Control of Behaviour*. W. Ross Adey *et al.*, (eds). London: Heinemann.

Lund, R. D., Lund, J. (1977). Plasticity in the developing visual system: the effect of retinal lesions made in young rats. *J. comp. Neur.* **169**, 133.

Margolis, G., Kilham, L., Johnson, R. H. (1971). The parvoviruses and replicating cells: insights into the pathogenesis of cerebellar hypoplasia. In: *Progress in Neuropathology* vol. I. H. M. Zimmerman, (ed). New York/London: Grune and Stratton.

Martz, E., Steinberg, M. S. (1972). The role of cell-cell contact in 'contact' inhibition of cell division. *J. cell. Physiol.* **79**, 189.

Meller, K., Tetzlaff, W. (1975). Neuronal migration during the early development of the cerebral cortex. *Cell Tissue Res.* **163**, 313.

Mierzejwski, K., Rozengurt, E. (1977). Density-dependent inhibition of fibroblast growth is overcome by pure mitogenic factors. *Nature* **269**, 155.

Mobley, W. C., Server, A. C., Ishii, D. N., Riopelle, R. J., Shooter, E. M. (1977). Nerve Growth Factor. *New Engl. J. Med.* **297**, 1096, 1149 and 1211.

Monod, J. (1970). *Le Hasard et La Nécessité*. Paris: Editions du Seuil.

Moscona, A. A. (1976). Cell recognition in embryonic morphogenesis and the problem of neuronal specificities. In: *Neuronal Recognition*. S. H. Barondes, (ed). New York: Plenum Press; London: Chapman and Hall.

Oppenheim, D. R. (1955). A benign 'tumour' of the cerebellum. Report on two cases of diffuse hypertrophy of the cerebellar cortex with a review of nine previously published cases. *J. Neur. Neurosurg. Psychiat.* **18**, 199.

Oppenheim, R. W., I-Wu Chu-Wang, Maderdrut, J. L. (1978). Cell death of motoneurons in the chick embryo spinal cord. III. *J. comp. Neur.* **177**, 87.

O'Rahilly, R., Gardner, E. (1971). The timing and sequence of events in the development of the human nervous system during the embryonic period. *Z. Anat. Entwickl.-Gesch.* **134**, 1.

Osterberg, K. A., Wattenberg, L. W. (1965). Enzyme induction in immature glia. *Proc. Soc. exp. Biol. Med.* **118**, 477.

Ostertag, B. (1956). Grundzüge der Entwicklung und Fehlentwicklung, die formbestimmenden Faktoren, and Die Einzelformen der Verbildungen. In: *Handbuch der speziellen pathologischen Anatomie und Histologie*, XIII. Band, 4. Teil. W. Scholz, (ed). Berlin/Göttingen/Heidelberg: Springer.

Peters, A., Palay, S. L., Webster, H. de F. (1976). *The Fine Structure of the Nervous System*. Philadelphia/London/Toronto: Saunders.

Prescott, J. W., Read, M. S., Coursin, D. B. (1975). *Brain Function and Malnutrition*. New York: John Wiley.

Prestige, M. C. (1970). Differentiation, degeneration and the role of the periphery: quantitative considerations. In: *The Neurosciences, Second Study Program*. F. O. Schmitt, (ed). New York: Rockefeller University Press.

Prestige, M. C. (1974). Axon and cell numbers. *Brit. med. Bull.* **30**, 107.

Pritchett, P. S., King, T. I. (1978). Dysplastic gangliocytoma of the cerebellum. *Acta neuropath.* **42**, 1.

Purpura, D. P., Shofer, R. J., Housepian, E. M., Nobacjm, C. R. (1964). Comparative ontogenesis of structure-function relations in cerebral and cerebellar cortex. In: *Progress in Brain Research* vol. 4, 'Growth and maturation of the brain'. D. P. Purpura and J. P. Schadé, (eds). Amsterdam/London/New York: Elsevier.

Raisman, G. (1978). What hope for repair of the brain? *Ann. Neur.* **3**, 101.

Rakic, P. (1977). Prenatal development of the visual system. *Phil Trans. roy. Soc. Lond.* B **278**, 245.

Richardson, F. (1973). Insults to the brain: differential effects of aging. In: *Development and aging in the nervous system*. M. Rockstein, (ed). New York/London: Academic Press.

Richter, D. (1975). Neurochemical aspects of the growth and development of the brain. In: *Growth and development of the brain: nutritional, genetic and environmental factors* (International Brain Research Organization Monograph Series, vol. 1). M. A. B. Brazier, (ed). New York: Raven Press.

Rodier, P. M. (1977). Correlations between prenatally-induced alterations in CNS cell populations and postnatal function. *Teratology* **16**, 235.

Rodier, P. M., Reynolds, S. S. (1977). Morphological correlates of behavioral abnormalities in experimental congenital brain damage. *Exp. Neur.* **57**, 81.

Roesman, U. (1974). Weight ratio between the infratentorial and supratentorial portions of the central nervous system. *J. Neuropath. exp. Neur.* **33**, 164.

Rose, S. P. R. (1977). Early visual experience, learning and neurochemical plasticity in the rat and the chick. *Phil. Trans. roy. Soc. Lond.* B **278**, 307.

Rosenzweig, M. R., Bennett, E. L., Diamond, M. C. (1972). Brain changes in response to environment. *Sci. Amer.* **226**, 22.

Roth, S., Marchese, R. B. (1976). An *in vitro* assay for retinotectal specificity. In: *Neuronal Recognition*. S. H. Barondes, (ed). New York: Plenum Press; London: Chapman and Hall.

Scheibel, M. E., Scheibel, A. (1964). Some structural and functional substrated of development in young rats. In: *Progress in Brain Research*, vol. 9, 'The developing brain'. W. A. and H. E. Himwich, (eds). Amsterdam/London/New York: Elsevier.

Scheibel, M. E., Scheibel, A. (1971). Selected structural-functional correlations in postnatal brain. In: *Brain development and behavior*. M. B. Sterman, D. J. McGinty and A. M. Adolfini, (eds). New York: Academic Press.

Selzer, M. E., Myers, R. E., Holstein, S. B. (1972). Maturational changes in brain water and electrolytes in rhesus monkey with some implications for electrogenesis. *Brain Res.* **45**, 193.

Shimada, M., Langman, J. (1970a). Repair of the external granular layer of the hamster cerebellum after prenatal and postnatal administration of methylazoxymethanol. *Teratology* **3**, 119.

Shimada, M., Langman, J. (1970b). Repair of the external granular layer after postnatal treatment with 5–fluorodeoxyuridine. *Am. J. Anat.* **129**, 247.

Sidman, R. L. (1970). Cell proliferation, migration and interaction in the developing central nervous system. In: *The Neurosciences, Second Study Program*. F. O. Schmitt, (ed). New York: Rockefeller University Press.

Sidman, R. L., Rakic, P. (1973). Neuronal migration, with special reference to developing human brain. *Brain Res.* **62**, 1.

Sidman, R. L., Wessells, N. K. (1975). Control of direction of growth during the elongation of neurites. *Exp. Neur.* **48**, 237.

Smith, J. F. (1974). *Pediatric Neuropathology*. New York: McGraw-Hill.

Sokoloff, L. (1974). Changes in enzyme activities in neural tissues with maturation and development of the nervous system. In: *The Neurosciences, Third Study Program*. F. O. Schmitt and F. G. Worden, (eds). Cambridge, Mass./London: M.I.T. Press.

Sotelo, C., Arsenio-Nunes, M. L. (1976). Development of Purkinje cells in absence of climbing fibers. *Brain Res.* **111**, 389.

Sotelo, C., Hillman, D. E., Zamora, A. J., Llinás, R. (1975). Climbing fiber deafferentiation: its action on Purkinje cell dendritic spines. *Brain Res.* **98**, 574.

Sotelo, C., Privat, A. (1978). Synaptic remodelling of the cerebellar circuitry in mutant mice and experimental cerebellar malformations. *Acta neuropath.* **43**, 19.

Stoker, M. G. P., Rubin, H. (1967). Density dependent inhibition of cell growth in culture. *Nature* **215**, 171.

Tizard, J. (1974). Early malnutrition, growth and mental development in man. *Brit. med. Bull.* **30**, 169.

Towbin, A. (1969a). Mental retardation due to germinal matrix infarction. *Science* **164**, 156.

Towbin, A. (1969b). Organic causes of minimal brain dysfunction. *J. am. med. Assoc.* **217**, 1207.

Uzman, L. L. (1960). The histogenesis of the mouse cerebellum as studied by tritiated thymidine uptake. *J. comp. Neur.* **114**, 137.

Weiss, P. (1934). *In vitro* experiments on the factors determining the course of the outgrowing nerve fiber. *J. exp. Zool.* **68**, 393.

Weiss, P. (1961). Guiding principles in cell locomotion and cell aggregation. *Exp. Cell Res.* **18**, 260.

Weiss, P. (1967). One plus one does not equal two. In: *The Neurosciences, a Study Program*. G. C. Quarton, T. Melchenuk and F. O. Schmitt, (eds). New York: Rockefeller University Press.

Weiss, P. A. (1970). Neural development in biological perspective. In: *The Neurosciences, Second Study Program*. F. O. Schmitt, (ed). New York: Rockefeller University Press.

Willshaw, D. J., Von der Marburg, C. (1976). How patterned neural connections can be set up by self-organization. *Proc. roy. Soc. Lond.* B **194**, 431.

Winnick, M. (1975). Effects of malnutrition on the maturing central nervous system. In: *Advances in Neurology,* vol. 12, 'Current Reviews'. M. J. Friedlander, (ed). New York: Raven Press; Amsterdam: North-Holland Publishing Co.

Young, J. Z. (1977). Concluding remarks (to a symposium on plasticity in the nervous system). *Phil. Trans. roy. Soc. Lond.* B **278**, 435.

4. CONGENITAL ANOMALIES, APPEARANCE AND BODY BUILD

JUDITH L. RAPOPORT

INTRODUCTION

A variety of circumstances are known in which an individual's physical characteristics may be associated with alterations in psychological development. The improvement in medical care for handicapping conditions, for example, has greatly increased the number of children with permanent anatomical deformities who would not have survived in previous times and these children are forced to face the issues inherent in physical limitation, altered self-image, and altered environmental interaction.

A second type of association between physical appearance and behavioural developmental deviation is through congenital contributors to behaviour which are also evidenced by relatively minor physical variations in size or body build, and/or the appearance of minor anatomical deviation (such as epicanthal folds or low set ears). Some of these anomalies may not be particularly socially evident (such as minor dental irregularities). The congenital insult or genetic defect responsible for these features might also affect behavioural factors such as energy level, aggression, or attention span which, in turn, interact with environmental factors to contribute to behavioural outcome.

Body build, the tendency towards angularity of form or plumpness, for example, is somewhat intermediate between these two poles in that while genetic contributions to somatotype have been demonstrated, there are also stereotypes directed towards 'lean' vs. 'plump' individuals, and the relative contributions of congenital and social influences remain a matter of debate. Similarly, the age of physiological maturation is partially under control of genetic and CNS influences and also brings marked change in social interactions.

Clinicians concerned with childhood psychopathology need to be aware of all of these areas. Handicapped individuals will continue to require a disproportionate share of mental health services (Rutter, *et al.*, 1970) and the relative importance of congenital and environmental factors remains a relatively unexplored area in child psychiatric research.

PHYSICAL HANDICAP AND PSYCHOLOGICAL DEVELOPMENT

The vast literature on emotional impact of physical handicap has been summarized by Wright (1960) and McDaniel (1976). It consists primarily of case studies and clinical surveys which stress the high emotional morbidity of the parents and children due to the difficulties inherent in accepting a handicapped child into family and community and the severity of stress which a handicapped child imposes upon his family.

Physical handicap is likely to influence development in a number of ways. One frequent and immediately obvious effect of physical handicap is that of decreased attractiveness of the afflicted individual. There is some evidence that physical attractiveness *per se*, even in the absence of physical handicap, will show a relationship to personal-social development in children and adolescents. Bersheid and Walster (1972) found that unattractive preschool children were less popular than attractive preschoolers and undesirable behaviours (aggression, dependency) were more likely to be attributed to them. Salvia, Sheare and Algozzine (1975) examined the relationship between physical attractiveness and social acceptance and self-concept for 440 grade school children; their findings indicate that attractive children were more socially accepted and had higher self-concept than did their unattractive peers. Similarly, Lerner and Lerner (1977) showed significant (but modest) correlation between physical attractiveness and peer relationships among fourth- and sixth-grade children. Finally, facial pictures of black and white delinquents were rated as significantly less attractive than pictures of control groups, as judged by some race raters (Cavior and Howard, 1973). The authors speculate that peers and caretakers may react differently to transgressions of unattractive children than to attractive ones, thereby contributing to a negative cycle of interaction.

Certainly concepts of attractiveness or unattractiveness are not limited by physical attributes, as voice quality, or in one study even the sound of a child's name (Bagley and Evan-Wong, 1970) may show a relationship to social acceptance. However, such attributes are beyond the scope of this review.

Considerable work has been carried out on the socially averse consequences of physical handicap (Barker, Wright, Meyerson and Gonick, 1953; Goffman, 1963; Wright, 1960). Richardson has shown considerable uniformity for children's preference order for drawings of five different physical handicaps and the absence of handicap. The drawings, in decreasing order of preference were: no handicap, a child with crutches and a leg brace, a child in a wheelchair, a child with left forearm amputation, a child with slight facial disfigurement, and an obese child (Richardson *et al.*, 1961; Goodman *et al.*, 1963). This preference order was obtained both from Negro and white children, with and without handicaps.

Several studies have demonstrated the striking effects that a handicapped infant or child may have on the family (Cummings, Bayley and Rie, 1966) and on the relation between parents' attitude towards the child, the distortion in their perception of the child's condition, and the emotional status of the child (Hewett and Newson, 1970; Hare *et al.*, 1966; Gath, 1977; Walker *et al.*, 1971). Most research has focused on family correlates of functional incapacity in patients with physical or mental handicaps. Families of such children tend to overestimate the handicapped child's IQ (Jensen and Kogen, 1962; Boles, 1959), which may reflect a human need to maintain hope where any ambiguity is possible, although this distortion often leads to conflict between the family and clinics or agencies.

Studies of the effect of disability from congenital heart disease on the child's family have shown the clinically striking feature of protectiveness by the mother, and in one study, a clear relationship between maternal overestimation of the severity of the cardiac condition and overprotection of the child, and with the disruption of family life by the handicapped child (Offord and Aponte, 1967). An area that is often neglected is the adverse effect of the handicapped child on the physically normal siblings (Poznanski, 1969).

A variety of mechanisms may contribute to the increased degree of psychopathology which is present in handicapped children. Central nervous system damage, for example, may be part of the primary illness, as even in 'peripheral' conditions such as congenital heart disease there is evidence that those children who were cyanotic had lower IQ's than those who were acyanotic (Silbert *et al.*, 1969). Thus CNS damage may even contribute to behavioural responses seen with cardiac illness in childhood.

The specific handicap will, of course, have a direct effect upon the life of the child and this varies greatly with the nature of the disability. For example, there remains considerable disagreement over the severity and even existence of chronic psychological disability in children with cleft palate. The evidence from most studies utilizing structured personality tests and objectively scored projective techniques supports the contention that children with cleft lip and/or palate do not display significant emotional maladjustment. However, some studies have reported some adjustment difficulties, reduced creativity and extrapunitive needs (Richman, 1976).

Behavioural evaluation of children with physical handicap from peripheral causes, however, has often supported the notion that deformity in the absence of CNS impairment may have a surprisingly low incidence of overt psychiatric disturbance (Seidel *et al.*, 1975; McFie and Robertson, 1973) in some cases, in spite of seriously handicapping conditions necessitating profound restriction of mobility and independence.

An unusually perceptive clinical report of young children with a variety of severe handicapping conditions, with and without central nervous system involvement (Minde *et al.*, 1972), has stressed the age-specific responses of handicapped children during their period of entry into special school. These authors described the complexity of stresses during this critical period (school entry) in which the children typically must face a long period of travel to special school facilities, the marked dependency in the school setting of these children who had often been overprotected at home, the realization, with special school placement, that there were children much older who were still afflicted with similar problems, and the increasing isolation from normal peers. The authors noted a depressive response (severe in about one-third of the children) with marked hopelessness, refusal to continue with school work, and gradual emergence into emotional readiness to incorporate the handicap as part of the life of the child.

The Minde study points up the importance of the question of special school placement for physically handicapped children. Anderson (1973) has studied moderately or severely disabled children who were being educated in ordinary primary schools. In her excellent report, *The Disabled Schoolchild*, she demonstrated the difficulty that parents of handicapped children of normal intelligence have in obtaining satisfactory school placement for their children. In the group of 99 children whose parents had chosen ordinary (rather than special) school placement, school satisfaction was high, and social contacts with non-handicapped peers and academic achievement were quite comparable to that for non-handicapped controls. Anderson's study was not ideally controlled (this was not a 'randomly assigned' group), however, the impressive level of adjustment for the non-neurologically handicapped children provides strong argument for continuation of such 'experimental' placement of the physically handicapped child in ordinary school settings, and for the need for some appropriate preparation for the schools so that this integration can function well.

Dorner (1976) has reported a standardized psychiatric evaluation of adolescents with spina bifida in which 46 adolescents were interviewed to find out how they felt about their situation. This study understandably focused on the adolescents' concern with sexual and child rearing ability. Periods of marked unhappiness were common (85%), including periods of severe misery and even suicidal thoughts, particularly for girls. What was striking was the lack of realistic information which these teenagers had about their condition and their potential for future sexual and childbearing activity. Another important finding of this study was the good adjustment found in some of the adolescents with severe impairment. As the mortality rate for patients born with spina bifida was greatly decreased in the 1950s, when a shunt operation for the treatment of hydrocephalus was first employed, many survivors are now approaching childbearing age. Thus this is a growing problem for society and a most poignant one for the families of the more handicapped adolescents.

The point is that any study of psychological vulnerability needs to be age-appropriate. It is also most sensible to address those concerns that are directly and appropriately related to the specific physical disability that is present, *i.e.*, concerns over sexual functioning will appear in adolescence while concerns over physical mobility will be prominent at an earlier age.

Recent epidemiological studies have added useful distinctions about the particular type of illness and associated stress of the child and family. For example, while any chronic illness will have some effect upon the afflicted child, asthmatic children show an increase of two to three times more psychiatric difficulty than do the non-handicapped population, and these children have predominantly emotional difficulties (Rutter *et al.*, 1970). When physical handicap is also associated with central nervous system dysfunction (as with cerebral palsy or epilepsy), then the risk is about four times that of the general population (Rutter *et al.*, 1970; Seidel *et al.*, 1975), although there is no specificity as to the type of behavioural disturbance.

MINOR PHYSICAL ANOMALIES AND EARLY DEVELOPMENTAL DEVIATION

Minor anatomical deviations of head, eyes, ears, mouth and extremities are often part of a diagnosable chromosomal disorder. Syndromes involving a great variety of such features form a sizeable part of the modern pediatric literature. There is a growing body of literature which has linked some of these minor anatomical abnormalities, often associated with Downs Syndrome, with behavioural deviance in studies of both clinic and normal school populations with normal intelligence and no known chromosomal abnormality. Previous work had shown that variations in hair patterns, size and shape of eyes, ears, fingers and toes are associated selectively with alterations of the central nervous system. Smith and Bostian (1964), for example, demonstrated that these anomalies are four times as common within a group of retarded patients as in a group of normal controls or in patients with known congenital anomalies such as cardiac defects or cleft palate. As these physical stigmata are known to be found early in fetal development (Smith, 1970), they provide a 'calendar marker' for early fetal maldevelopment.

Such findings were of rather incidental interest to child psychiatrists until more recent studies have indicated that with populations of children with behavioural deviance and normal intelligence, such minor anomalies may be more frequent than for control groups.

Goldfarb (1967) had reported a higher frequency of minor anomalies in schizophrenic populations compared with controls. Following this study, Waldrop and associates took Goldfarb's measures that discriminated among groups, provided scoring weights, and standardized the assessment. Waldrop's scale is shown in Table I. Using

TABLE I

LIST OF MINOR PHYSICAL ANOMALIES AND SCORING WEIGHTS

Anomaly	Scoring Weights
Head	
Head circumference	
>1·5 S.D.	2
1><1·5 S.D.	1
'Electric' hair	
Very fine hair that won't comb down	2
Fine hair that is soon awry after combing	1
Eyes	
Epicanthus	
Where upper and lower lids join at the nose, point of union is: deeply covered	2
partly covered	1
Hypertelorism	
Approximate distance between tear ducts:	
1·5 S.D.	2
1·25 to 1·5 S.D.	1
Ears	
Low set	
Bottom of ears in line with:	
Mouth (or lower)	2
Area between mouth and nose	1
Adherent lobes	
Lower edges of ears extend:	
Upward and back towards crown of head	2
Straight back towards rear of neck	1
Malformed	1
Asymmetrical	1
	Scoring Weights
Anomaly	
Mouth	
High palate	
Roof of mouth steepled	2
Roof of mouth moderately high	1
Furrowed tongue	1
Hands	
Fifth finger	
Markedly curved inward towards other fingers	2
Slightly curved inward towards other fingers	1
Single transverse palmar crease	1
Feet	
Third toe	
Definitely longer than second toe	2
Appears equal in length to second toe	1
Partial syndactyly of two middle toes	1
Gap between first and second toe (approx. ¼ inch)	1

this scale, Waldrop and co-workers showed that pre-schoolers having a weighted score of five or more of these anomalies are more likely to have fast moving, frenetic play and to require more frequent intervention by the teacher (Waldrop, Pedersen and Bell, 1968). Waldrop has extended these findings to older populations and, most interestingly, has recently reported that grade school girls with higher anomalies are more likely to be negativistic and *withdrawn* compared with controls all within a normal school system.

Rapoport and her group have used this measure in clinical studies. Among a group of 81 boys attending a

Hyperactivity Clinic, approximately one-quarter had a weighted anomaly score of five or more and those with a high score were more likely to have a father with a history of hyperactivity or a mother who had had obstetrical difficulties during this and previous pregnancies. In addition, the high anomaly children were more likely to have been difficult infants (more headbanging, tantrums, fussiness about eating) as well as to have had an earlier onset of the hyperactivity (before age 3) compared with the rest of the sample who were, of course, all hyperactive boys being evaluated for stimulant drug treatment in a pediatric setting (Quinn and Rapoport, 1974; Rapoport, Quinn and Lamprecht, 1974).

One interpretation of these findings is that a high number of those minor anomalies indicate a genetically determined disorder. This idea was explored by an examination of the fathers of this sample (for whom a special scoring system had to be assembled). When a blind rater evaluated the fathers, it was found that those with a history of childhood hyperactivity had a higher mean score than did the fathers who had not had behaviour and learning problems during their grade school years.

In separate studies, Firestone has replicated the finding that hyperactive children seen in a clinical setting have higher scores of anomalies than age matched behaviourally normal controls (Firestone et al., 1976). The higher anomaly score is, of course, not specific to hyperkinetic syndrome; as noted previously, the first non-retarded population with reported high scores concerned 'schizophrenic' children, and autistic and learning disordered populations have been found to have higher scores than did neurotic or normal age matched controls (Steg and Rapoport, 1975). Similarly, Campbell et al. (1978), found young autistic children to have higher anomaly scores than did their siblings. This latter finding is particularly intriguing as Chess and co-workers have reported a marked increase in autistic symptomatology in children with the rubella syndrome (Chess et al., 1971). As rubella has its effect primarily in the first third of pregnancy, these findings point to the first months of fetal development as a critical period during which central nervous system insult may lead to subsequent behavioural deviance.

One possibility which must be considered is that children with multiple minor anomalies of this sort may be perceived as unattractive by their parents and teachers and so treated in a less favourable manner. This, however, does not appear to be the case. As part of their initial study, full-face photographs of a sample of 80 hyperactive boys were rated for attractiveness by a pediatric nurse and a grade school teacher. While there was surprisingly good agreement between the two raters on attractiveness (interrater person $r=\cdot72$), there was no significant correlation between the rating of attractiveness and the weighted anomaly score ($r=\cdot01$).

The presence of minor anomalies provides a 'red flag' for possible congenital toxic insult or genetic predisposition to developmental deviation in a child; it is clear that this list of anatomical anomalies is an arbitrary one; there are many other possible minor anatomical variations of genetic interest and, furthermore, high anomaly does not describe a homogeneous subgroup of children by any means. As most of these anomalies are detectable at birth and anomalies are stable between birth and 12 years of age (Waldrop and Halverson, 1971) the use of minor anomalies as part of a screening programme might, together with other measures, provide some measure of risk which would be of research and, possibly, clinical usefulness.

To pursue the possibility, 933 normal white newborns were screened during a 14 month period for the presence of these anomalies and high and low anomaly groups were followed prospectively, for evidence of intellectual or temperamental deviance between the high and low anomaly groups.

Infants were rated at 6 months for temperamental characteristics and at 1 and 2 years of age. Psychological testing and clinical interview and examination were carried out as well.

At age 1 (Quinn et al., 1977) there was a significant though low association between parental rating of 'irritability', hyperactivity, and the newborn anomaly score. More interestingly, among high anomaly infants, there was a significant association between either obstetrical difficulties or family history of learning and behaviour problems with the presence of activity and 'difficulty' in the 1 year old, while this association was not present for low anomaly infants.

While the statistical relationships were interesting, it was clear that, taken by itself, a score of minor anomalies would be of no clinical use as there were many false positives; that is, many children with high anomaly scores did not seem to present any problems whatsoever and this was also the case at age 2 (Burg et al., 1978). While infants with higher anomaly scores (identified at birth) were more likely to be rated as irritable at age 2, this measure was not a major contributor to prediction of behaviour disorder for males or females. However, the small subgroup of infants (6 of 126) who were *consistently* irritable on evaluation at both ages one and two were all from the high anomaly group ($p<\cdot01$), indicating perhaps more diagnostic usefulness of transituational irritability.

BODY BUILD AND BEHAVIOUR IN CHILDHOOD AND ADOLESCENCE

An extensive network of associations between body build and characteristics of behaviour in adults and adolescents has been described by Sheldon (1942) and also in children and adolescents (Walker, 1974a, 1974b). Other investigators have confirmed some of Sheldon's observations, although the associations have often been lower than those Sheldon reported (Lindzey, 1973).

To oversimplify somewhat, Sheldon's initial ratings of physique were carried out from nude photographs of the individual, using front, side and back views. Three somatotypes were described: endomorphy, which is, roughly speaking, roundness and plumpness of physique; mesomorphy (heaviness of bone and muscle development) and ectomorphy (linearity and attenuation of build). More recently, Sheldon and co-workers (1969) have described a new somatotyping technique called the Trunk Index and a number of findings have subsequently been published using this rating. This latter method, using actual relatively objective indices of age, height, ponderal index (height/cube root of weight) and trunk index is less open to observer bias although relatively little has been published using this method.

It is of interest to child psychiatrists that many of Sheldon's studies were carried out in adolescent populations. For example, over an eight year period, Sheldon and his collaborators (1949) conducted a study of physique and behaviour with residents of a rehabilitation home for boys in Boston. In comparison with college students, the delinquent subjects showed a cluster of mesomorphs, particularly endomorphic mesomorphs. This study has been criticized for possible contamination of measures as Sheldon himself executed both sets of measures (morphologic and temperamental). However, some subsequent studies, which have involved better controls and more objective analysis of the data, have yielded similar results.

The best known study was that conducted by Glueck and Glueck (1950, 1956) of 500 delinquents and 500 non-delinquents matched for age, ethnic background, intelligence and place of residence. Independent ratings of physique, without knowledge of the classification of the subjects, provided strong support for Sheldon's finding. That is, approximately 60% of the delinquents were mesomorphic while only 30% of the non-delinquents were in this category. Normal subjects were more likely to be ectomorphic (over 40%) while less than 15% of the delinquents were ectomorphs. Similarly, Epps and Parnell (1952) showed that female delinquents were likely to be shorter, heavier, and more muscular than female (non-delinquent) college students (Epps and Parnell, 1952).

There is, naturally, considerable debate over the locus of the association between body build and behaviour, as it is possible that genetic factors responsible for physique might have pleiotrophic behavioural effects and highly likely as well that there are social stereotypes associated with physical appearance.

The studies on somatotype and behaviour in young children are of particular interest in this regard as it can be argued that there may be less social learning in a nursery school population than in adolescent groups.

Walker has carried out extensive work on somatotyping young children from their growth data (Walker, 1974a, 1974b). In an earlier study, however, using Sheldon's original techniques of rating from nude photographs, Walker studied 73 boys and 52 girls attending the Gesell Institute Nursery School during a two year period. The children ranged in age from $2\frac{1}{2}$ years to almost 5. The sample was generally from a middle- and upper-middle-socioeconomic group. As judged from parent attitude scores, the children's mothers were relatively homogeneous in their permissive, supportive attitudes towards childbearing.

An extensive set of rating scales was assembled for judging nursery school behaviour. Of the 15 teachers who contributed to the ratings, only three knew that they were to be used for physique-behaviour comparisons. A total of 292 predictions had been made prior to the study on the basis of Sheldon's work with adults and adolescents. The results strongly supported most of the predictions. Specifically, 73% of the ratings were confirmed in the expected direction and 21% were confirmed at the ·05 level of confidence, while only 3% were disconfirmed at the 5% level. Predictions were more successful for boys than for girls. The best predictions were those with mesomorphy; for boys, close to half the predictions made were confirmed. Ectomorphy had intermediate success as a predictor, while relations with endomorphy predicted close to chance for both girls and boys.

Characteristics of boys and girls high in mesomorphy are a dominating assertiveness (leader in play, competitive, easily angered, etc.), high energy output, and fearlessness. The girls combine this with warmth and cheerful sociability. Both boys and girls showed an association of aloofness with ectomorphy (not social, inplay, day dreams) and emotional restraint. However, for the males, the items defined a somewhat more vulnerable appearing child (slow to recover from upsets, dislikes gross motor play, looks to adults rather than to peers for approval).

It is striking that these associations were similar to those described by Sheldon for college aged men, though the strength of associations is not as strong as he reported.

A study with normal English 7-year-olds (Davidson et al., 1957) found a low but significant association between intelligence and endomorphy. In this study, ectomorphs tended to have higher standards, be more meticulous and have somewhat more disturbed behaviour. The methodology is not described in detail but the results are of interest and, as with other somatotype studies, seem more clear-cut for males than for females.

Verdonck and Walker (1976) carried out a similar study with a Dutch group of 75 boys and 51 girls, ages 6–14, in a residential treatment centre in Holland. Their findings were similar, in spite of differences in culture, and the fact that these subjects were mildly to moderately disturbed. Among the boys, mesomorphy was related to energy level while ectomorphy was related to unsociability. For girls, the results were less clear as both energy level and unsociability were related positively with mesomorphy but negatively with endomorphy and ectomorphy.

These authors do not have a simplistic explanation for these associations and consider the possible influence of social stereotypes on these results. That is, the descriptions might be of stereotypes and not of children, and body build-behavioural expectancies have been demonstrated in young children (Staffieri, 1972). In addition, they hypothesize that there may be basic organismic associations (children with different physiques may differ in toughness and possibly drive strengths). Secondarily, children with different physiques may have different life experiences.

Other measures of body build have been related to childhood behavioural deviance. Eggins et al. (1975) have reported a 19% greater mean percentile height (but not weight) for neurotic boys compared with conduct-disordered boys (all age 11 and under) attending a child guidance clinic. There are several possible mechanisms for such an association which that study could not unravel, but should this prove a reliable finding, it would fit, in a general way, with other somatotype behavioural associations reported above.

MATURATION AND PSYCHOLOGICAL DEVELOPMENT

Statistically, pubertal development begins around age 11 in girls and age 13 in boys (Marshall and Tanner, 1969); however, individual variation within medically normal groups will cover as much as eight years.

A variety of factors are associated with accelerated pubertal development. There is a clear association between body build and maturation rate in women. Pubertal changes in women are, morphologically speaking, a matter of decreasing linearity in body build during adolescence; women who mature earlier are less slender at maturity than are their later maturing peers and this difference is present prior to puberty (McNeill and Livson, 1963). For males the relationship between body build and maturation seems less clear (Livson and McNeill, 1962). As pubertal development is controlled in part by brain maturation, it is plausible to assume that mental growth might be associated with pubertal development. Early studies indicated that early maturing boys were more socially accepted, and less aggressive than a comparison group of late maturing boys (Mussen and Jones, 1958; McCandless, 1960), while interestingly, this difference was slight for girls (Jones and Mussen, 1958). This early research is methodologically weak, but it raises interesting and important questions that have not been fully explored in later work. Douglas, Ross and Simpson (1968) found that early maturing boys and girls make higher academic scores at 8 years and later, and stay on longer in school than do late maturers. As proportionately more early maturing children in their sample came from small families, however, the authors do not attribute their finding to biological influence. Even if this association between early maturation and family size is not replicated in future studies, the marked social effects of early puberty may well account for differential achievements of early maturers rendering biological hypotheses superfluous. During the preadolescent and adolescent periods, there has been substantial evidence for a general relationship between physical and mental precocity (Nisbet and Illsley, 1963; Douglas and Ross, 1964). On the other hand, there is controversy as to the continuity of early maturing subjects' precocity in the post-adolescent period.

Studies of children with clearly abnormal pubertal development have been impressive in their failure to demonstrate any social or psychological disturbances that one might anticipate from such physical deviance from peers. Money and Merideth (1967) and Money and Alexander (1969) have reported on a series of cases with idiopathic precocious puberty (pubertal onset before age 6) and that associated with the adrenogenital syndrome. The most striking finding is that of an elevated verbal IQ. The authors do not believe this intellectual superiority to be an artifact of their sampling, but feel it reflects either a direct hormonal influence on nervous system development or is secondary to the precocious social contacts. The authors do not favour the second explanation, that of social stimulation, as they point out that the accelerated verbal IQ was associated with the entire age range of their sample of 35 children with idiopathic sexual precocity and, furthermore, note that the accelerated verbal IQ had also been found in their cases of adrenogenital syndrome which had been successfully treated with cortisone.

The association is, of course, not absolute since both high and low intelligence have been reported in association with pubertal precocity. What is of considerable interest is the lack of any major psychiatric illnesses or sexual perversions in these cases (Money and Alexander, 1969) and the apparent adaptability (school acceleration seeking older playmates) which these children can show.

There is perhaps more general interest in the interaction between age of puberty and psychiatric disorders of children and adolescents. The few studies which have been carried out however, do not permit any clear conclusions to be drawn. In one study, for example (Littlemore et al., 1974), psychiatrically disturbed adolescents over age 14 had a slightly delayed wrist bone age in comparison with controls, however this was not true for younger children. There is considerable lore that the onset of puberty per se produces beneficial changes in hyperactive boys, but no one has provided hard data so far to support this notion. Such studies are waiting to be done.

DISCUSSION AND SUMMARY

Explanations for the associations between physical characteristics and behaviour vary; it can be argued that the child's habits may influence physical development so that athletic children will tend towards mesomorphy, etc., and there are certainly instances where a child's habits are known to influence appearance, as with finger sucking and anterior tooth alignment (Infante, 1976). The point is that the demonstration of a relation between anatomical features and behaviour in school age children will be interpreted in different ways, and it is likely that there *are* several possible mechanisms which can form these associations. Moreover, our knowledge of the multiple factors involved in the development of behaviour problems in childhood precludes any simple association between anatomical features and a resultant 'personality' or syndrome.

What research has shown so far is a low though significant association between anomalies, or body build, and some behaviours. It is unlikely that screening for these features early in life would be of any value; such efforts to detect 'high risk' populations run the danger of doing more harm than good through identification of many 'false positives'. On the other hand, the theoretical implications of these associations remain enormously interesting and careful study of physical and physiological differences in relation to psychiatric disorder may illuminate underlying mechanisms of importance for Child Psychiatry.

REFERENCES

Anderson, E. M. (1973). *The Disabled Schoolchild*. London: Methuen & Co.

Bagley, C. and Evan-Wong, L. (1970). Psychiatric disorder and adult and peer group rejection of the child's name. *J. Child Psychol. Psychiat.*, **11**, 19–27.

Barker, R., Wright, B., Meyerson, L. and Gonick, M. R. (1953). Adjustment to Physical Handicap and Illness: *A Survey of the Social Psychology of Physique and Disability*. New York: Social Science Research Council.

Bersheid, E. and Walster, E. (1972). Beauty and the best. *Psychology Today*, **5**, 42–45.

Boles, G. (1959). Personality factors in mothers of cerebral palsied children. *Genet Psychol. Monogr.*, **59**, 159–218.

Burg, C., Hart, D., Quinn, P. and Rapoport, J. (1978). *Minor physical anomalies*: A newborn screening and two year follow-up. *J. Autism Child. Schizo.*, **8**, 427–439.

Campbell, M., Geller, B., Small, A. M., Petti, T. A. and Ferris, S. H. (1978). Minor physical anomalies in young psychotic children. *Am. J. Psychiat.* **135**, 573–575.

Cavior, N. and Howard, L. (1973). Facial attractiveness and juvenile delinquency among black and white offenders. *J. Abnorm Child Psychol.*, **1**, 202–213.

Chess, S., Korn, S. J. and Fernandez, P. B. (1971). *Psychiatric disorders of children with rubella*. New York: Brunner/Mazel.

Cummings, S. T., Bayley, H. and Rie, H. (1966). Effects of the child's deficiency on the mother: A study of mothers of mentally retarded, chronically ill and neurotic children. *Am. J. Orthopsychiat.*, **36**, 595–608.

Davidson, M., McInnes, R. and Parrell, R. (1957). The distribution of personality traits in seven-year-old children: A combined psychological, psychiatric and somatotype study. *Br. J. Educ. Psychol.*, **27**, 48–61.

Dorner, S. (1976). Adolescents with spina bifida. How they see their situation. *Arch. dis. Child.*, **51**, 439–444.

Douglas, J. and Ross, J. (1964). Age of puberty related to educational ability, attainment and school leaving age. *J. Child Psychol. Psychiat.*, **5**, 185–196.

Douglas, J. B., Ross, J. M. and Simpson, H. R. (1968). *All Our Future*. London: Peter Davies.

Eggins, L., Barker, P. and Walker, R. J. (1975). A study of the heights and weights of different groups of disturbed children. *Child Psychiatry Hum. Dev.*, **5**, 203–208.

Epps, P. and Parnell, R. (1952). Physique and temperament of women delinquents compared with women undergraduates. *Br. J. Med. Psychol.*, **25**, 249–255.

Firestone, P., Lewey, F. and Douglas, V. (1976). Hyperactivity and physical anomalies. *Can. Psychiatr. Assoc. J.*, **21**, 23–26.

Gath, A. (1977). The impact of an abnormal child upon the parents. *Br. J. Psychiat.*, **130**, 405–410.

Glueck, S. and Glueck, E. (1956). *Physique and Delinquency*. New York: Harper.

Glueck, S. and Glueck, E. (1950). *Unraveling Juvenile Delinquency*. New York: Harper.

Goffman, E. (1963). *Stigma*. Englewood Cliffs, New Jersey: Prentice Hall.

Goldfarb, W. (1967). Factors in the development of schizophrenic children: An approach to subclassification. In Romano, J. (ed.): *The Origins of Schizophrenia*. New York: Excerpta Medica Foundation, pp. 70–91.

Goodman, N., Richardson, S., Dornbusch, S. and Hastorf, A. (1963). Variant reactions to physical disabilities. *Am. Sociol. Rev.*, **28**, 429–435.

Hare, E., Laurence, K., Payne, H. and Rawnsley, K. (1966). Spina bifida cystica and family stress. *Br. Med. J.*, **2**, 757–760.

Hewett, S. and Newson, J. (1970). *The Family and the Handicapped Child*. London: Allen & Unwin.

Infante, P. (1976). An epidemiological study of finger habits in pre-school children as related to malocclusion, socioeconomic status, race, sex and size of community. *J. Dent. Child.*, **43**, 33–38.

Jensen, G. and Kogan, K. (1962). Parental estimates of future achievement of children with cerebral palsy. *J. Ment. Defic. Res.*, **6**, 56–64.

Jones, M. C. and Mussen, P. H. (1958). Self conceptions, motivations and interpersonal attitudes of early and late maturing girls. *Child Dev.*, **29**, 491–501.

Lerner, R. M. and Lerner, J. V. (1977). Effects of age, sex and physical attractiveness on child–peer relations, academic performance, and elementary school adjustment. *Dev. Psychol.*, **13**, 585–589.

Lindzey, G. (1973). Morphology and behavior, in Lindzey, G., Hall, C., Manosevitz, M. (eds): *Theories of Personality: Primary Sources and Research*. New York: Wiley.

Littlemore, D., Metcalfe, E. and Johnson, A. L. (1974). Skeletal immaturity in psychiatrically disturbed adolescents. *J. Child. Psychol. Psychiat.*, **15**, 133–138.

Livson, N. and McNeill, D. (1962). Physique and maturation rate in male adolescents. *Child Dev.*, **33**, 145–152.

McCandless, B. (1960). Rate of development, body build and personality. *Psychiatric Research Reports*, **13**, 42–57.

McDaniel, J. W. (1976). *Physical Disability and Human Behavior*, 2nd Edition. New York: Pergamon Press.

McFie, J. and Robertson, J. (1973). Psychological test results of children with thalidomide deformities. *Dev. Med. Child Neurol.*, **15**, 719–727.

McNeill, D. and Livson, N. (1963). Maturation rate and body build in women. *Child Develop.*, **34**, 25–32.

Marshall, W. A. and Tanner, J. M. (1969). Variations in pattern of pubertal changes in girls. *Arch. dis. Child.*, **44**, 291–303.

Minde, K., Hackett, J., Killou, D. and Silver, S. (1972). How they grow up: 41 physically handicapped children and their families. *Am. J. Psychiat.*, **128**, 1554–1560.

Money, J. and Alexander, D. (1969). Psychosexual development and absence of homosexuality in males with precocious puberty. Review of 18 cases. *J. Nerv. Ment. Dis.*, **148**, 111–123.

Money, J. and Clopper, R. (1974). Psychosocial and psychosexual aspects of errors of pubertal onset and development. *Human Biology*, **46**, 173–181.

Money, J. and Meredith, T. (1967). Elevated verbal IQ and idiopathic precocious sexual maturation. *Pediatr. Res.*, **1**, 59–65.

Mussen, P. H. and Jones, M. C. (1958). The behavior inferred motivations of late and early maturing boys. *Child Dev.*, **29**, 61–67.

Nisbet, J. and Illsley, R. (1963). The influence of early puberty on test performance at the age of eleven. *Br. J. Educ. Psychol.*, **33**, 176–196.

Offord, D. and Aponte, J. F. (1967). Distortion of disability and effect on family life. *J. Am. Acad. Child Psychiat.*, **6**, 499–511.

Poznanski, E. (1969). Psychiatric difficulties of siblings of handicapped children. *Clin. Pediatr.*, **8**, 232–234.

Quinn, P., Burg, C. and Rapoport, J. (1977). Minor physical anomalies: A newborn screening and one year follow-up. *J. Am. Acad. Child Psychiat.*, **16**, 662–669.

Quinn, P. and Rapoport, J. (1974). Minor physical anomalies and neurological studies in hyperactive boys. *Pediatrics*, **53**, 742–747.

Rapoport, J., Prandoni, C., Renfield, M., Lake, C. R. and Ziegler, M. (1977). Newborn dopamine-B-hydroxylase, minor physical anomalies and infant temperament. *Am. J. Psychiat.*, **134**, 676–679.

Rapoport, J., Quinn, P. and Lamprecht, F. (1974). Minor physical anomalies and plasma dopamine-B-hydroxylase activity in hyperactive boys. *Am. J. Psychiat.*, **131**, 386–390.

Richardson, S., Goodman, N., Hastorf, A. and Dornbusch, S. (1961). Cultural uniformity in reaction to physical disabilities. *Am. Sociol. Rev.*, **26**, 241–247.

Richman, L. (1976). Behavior and achievement of cleft palate children. *Cleft Palate J.*, **13**, 4–10.

Rutter, M., Tizard, J. and Whitmore, K. (Eds). (1970). *Education, Health and Behaviour*. London: Longmans.

Salvia, J., Sheare, J. and Algozzine, B. (1975). Facial attractiveness and personal-social development. *J. Abnorm. Child Psychol.*, **3**, 171–178.

Seidel, U., Chadwick, O. and Rutter, M. (1975). Psychological disorders in crippled children. A comparative study of children with and without brain damange. *Dev. Med. Child. Neurol.*, **17**, 563–573.

Sheldon, W. H. (1949). *Varieties of delinquent youth: An introduction to constitutional psychiatry*. New York: Harper.

Sheldon, W. H. (1942). *The Varieties of Temperament*. New York: Harper.

Sheldon, W. H., Lewis, N. and Tenney, A. (1969). Psychotic patterns and physical constitution: A thirty year follow-up of 3800 psychiatric patients in New York State, in Siva Sankar, D. V. (ed). *Schizophrenia: Current Concepts and Research*. New York: P.J.D. Publications, pp. 838–912.

Silbert, A., Wolff, P. H., Mayer, B., Rosenthal, A. and Nadas, A. S. (1969). Cyanotic heart disease and psychological development. *Pediatrics*, **43**, 192–200.

Smith, D. W. (1970). *Recognizable patterns of human malformation*. Philadelphia: W. B. Saunders.

Smith, D. and Bostian, K. (1964). Congenital anomalies associated with idiopathic mental retardation. *J. Pediatr.*, **65**, 189–196.

Staffieri, J. R. (1972). Body build and behavioral expectancies in young females. *Dev. Psychol.*, **6**, 125–127.

Steg, J. and Rapoport, J. (1975). Minor physical anomalies in normal, neurotic, learning disabled and severely disturbed children. *J. Autism Child Schizo.*, **5**, 299–307.

Verdonck, P. F. and Walker, R. N. (1976). Body build and behavior in emotionally disturbed children. *Genet. Psychol. Monogr.*, **94**, 149–173.

Waldrop, M. and Halverson, C. (1971). Minor physical anomalies and hyperactive behavior in young children, in Hellmuth, J. (ed). *The Exceptional Infant, Vol. 2*. New York: Brunner/Mazel, pp. 343–381.

Waldrop, M., Pedersen, F. and Bell, R. (1968). Minor physical anomalies and behavior in preschool children. *Child Dev.*, **39**, 391–400.

Walker, R. N. (1962). Body build and behavior in young children. I. Body build and nursery school teachers' ratings. *Monogr. Soc. Res. Child Dev.* 27 No 3 (serial no. 84).

Walker, R. N. (1963). Body build and behavior in young children. II. Body build and parents' ratings. *Child Dev.*, **34**, 1–23.

Walker, R. N. (1974a). Standards for somatotyping children. I. Predicting young adult height from children's growth data. *Ann. Hum. Biol.*, **1**, 149–158.

Walker, R. N. (1974b). Standards for somatotyping children. II. Predicting somatotyping ponderal index from children's growth data. *Ann. Hum. Biol.*, **1**, 289–299.

Walker, J., Thomas, M. and Russell, I. (1971). Spina bifida and the parents. *Dev. Med. Child Neurol.*, **13**, 462–476.

Wright, B. A. (1960). *Physical Disability: A Psychological Approach*. New York: Harper & Row.

5. FAMILY INFLUENCES

R. A. HINDE

Introduction

Family dynamics
    The family
    The network of relationships within the family

Family disruption
    Death and illness in the family
    Rearing in social isolation or in institutions
    Temporary separation

Family disharmony
    Family disharmony and antisocial behaviour
    Family interaction patterns in disturbed families

Intellectual development

Sex role development and related issues

Socialization, discipline and moral development

INTRODUCTION

Family influences on child development comprise the interacting consequences of multiple interacting factors: there is no easy route to an understanding of the resultant complexity. The techniques employed range from epidemiological surveys to frame-by-frame analyses of video-taped sequences, and include studies of 'normal' families as well as comparisons between normals and those containing a wide variety of clinical and sub-clinical disorders. This chapter can therefore do no more than survey some representative areas. In general I have tended to emphasize studies concerned with the family as a unit rather than with particular relationships within it, to select areas that illustrate the problems of studying the long-term effects of factors, to focus on data rather than theory, and to cite only recent work but to include references to reviews of earlier literature. Genetic studies are reviewed in Chapter 2.

The first main section, on family dynamics, is intended to build up a background picture of the family as a complex system. A necessary consequence of the family's complexity is that each characteristic of the family and each type of experience that a child may have within the family (*i.e.* each independent variable) may be related to many outcome measures (*i.e.* dependent variables), and each dependent variable to many independent ones. For those reasons, no scheme for classifying material on family influences can be satisfactory. I have chosen to devote two sections to groups of independent variables—various types of parental deprivation and separation, and various aspects of 'family disharmony'—and the final three to groups of dependent variables. In selecting the latter, I have omitted some that have been extensively reviewed recently (*e.g.* aggression, Berkowitz, 1973; de Wit and Hartup, 1974; Crabtree and Moyer, 1977), and others that for which even the important independent variables cannot yet be specified with precision. Studies of infancy form the subject matter of other chapters and few are cited here.

FAMILY DYNAMICS

The Family

'The Family' usually means a unit of father, mother and children. That such units are found in only a few of man's non-human primate relatives (Hinde, 1974), and are by no means common to all human societies (Fox, 1970), are important issues if the future course of society is under consideration. Studies of immigrant populations (*e.g.* Raveau, 1970) and the impact of westernizing influences on simpler societies (*e.g.* Huffer, 1973) reveal how flexible human familial arrangements can be. But the fact remains that in Western society the two-parent family is the norm: children lacking such a family sooner or later demand an explanation of their circumstances. This chapter, therefore, is concerned with influences operating on a child developing within a presumptively two-parent nuclear family; the extent to which such family influences are determined by cultural norms is not explored. It is important to remember that the generality of many of the findings discussed may be limited in that most are based on studies in Western Europe or North America.

The network of relationships within the family

The child has a relationship with each family member

The newborn's social world lies largely within his mother's arms, and it is not surprising that most studies have been concerned with maternal influences on development. That these influences are not all that matter is now apparent, and there is a growing literature on the role of other family members. Much of this centres on the father. The father's emotional response to a newborn is at least comparable with that of the mother (Greenberg and Morris, 1974); and infants respond individually to their fathers by at least 7 months of age (Lamb, 1976), and probably much younger. However, at least in two-parent families, the father–child relationship comes to differ in kind from the mother–child one: even whilst playing, the two parents play in different ways (Bau and Lewis, 1974; Lamb, 1976, 1977). Some of the evidence about the ways in which the father affects the child's development will be considered later (see also reviews by Lamb, 1976; Lewis and Weinraub, 1976).

In non-human primates the role of the father varies greatly between species (Mitchell and Brandt, 1972; Rowell, 1974): in some it is minimal, whilst in others the father carries the infant almost as much as the mother (Ingram, 1975). Of almost universal importance, however, are (half-) siblings and peers. In species with a matrilineal social structure, interactions with elder siblings and peers of other families within the same group or lineage are conspicuous (*e.g.* Fady, 1969; Ruppenthal

et al., 1974; Berman, 1978). Drawing on evidence that there were few signs of deficiencies in the social behaviour of rhesus monkeys brought up with peers but without mothers, that infants reared on inanimate surrogate mothers with access to peers were only slightly and temporarily retarded in comparison with mother-raised infants with access to peers, and that rhesus infants reared in isolation from other animals can subsequently be rehabilitated by experience with peers, Harlow and Harlow (1965, 1969) have claimed that peer contact alone is paramount and even sufficient for normal development. With a reservation mentioned below, these studies establish experimentally that peer interactions can play an important part in social development (see also Sackett and Ruppenthal, 1973). Evidence for the importance of peer–peer relationships in the human case is now considerable (Hartup, 1976; Banks and Kahn, 1975; Apolloni and Cooke, 1975) and some of it will be mentioned later (see Lewis and Rosenblum, 1975). (Here, and in one or two other cases, I have felt that specific issues were well illustrated from studies of non-human primates. It will be apparent that these studies involved exploitation of the differences between monkey and man (*e.g.* diversity, simplicity, susceptibility to experimentation) rather than assumptions of close similarity.)

Relationships always involve mutual influence

All relationships, including those of the growing child with other family members, involve mutual influences: to consider the child as passive clay moulded by its parents or by forces generated within the family is thus quite false. Correlational evidence suggests that the individual characteristics of the baby soon after birth may affect the mother–infant relationship both then (Osofsky and Danzger, 1974; Dunn and Richards, 1977) and later (Dunn, 1977); and there is now considerable evidence that the behaviour of older children affects their parents' behaviour to them (Bell, 1968; McPherson, 1970; Osofsky and O'Connell, 1972; Harper, 1975. Indeed it is almost impossible for adults to treat children in predetermined ways; the children's differing natures elicit different behaviours from them (Yarrow, Waxler and Scott, 1971). Reciprocal influences are similarly present in every other dyad within the family (*e.g.* Crago, 1972).

One corollary of this is that, when a relationship is under study, great caution is necessary in ascribing measures of behaviour to one partner or the other, as every measure is liable to be influenced by both (Dunn, 1975; Hinde and Herrmann, 1977); how quickly a mother responds when her baby cries, often used as a measure of maternal behaviour, is surely influenced by how often it has cried recently.

Relationships affect each other

Furthermore, the family consists of a network of relationships: the behaviour of one individual to another is affected by the relationships of each with others. The arrival of a baby monkey affects the mother's relationships with her group companions (*e.g.* Seyfarth, 1976; Hinde and Proctor, 1977), and the mother–infant relationship is affected by the mother's relationship with her peers (Hinde, 1974). For this reason the Harlows' conclusion that peer–peer interaction is *more* important for normal development than mother–infant is suspect: it was based on a comparison of peer–infant dyads without mothers and mother–infant dyads without peers, and neglected triadic complexities.

In man, children may have a deep effect on the nature of a marriage—though opinions differ as to the nature of that effect (Slater and Woodside, 1951; Fletcher, 1966; Glenn, 1975; Humphrey, 1975). (The proceedings of a conference on 'Contributions of the child to marital quality and family interactions through the life-span' to be edited by Lerner, R. M. and Spanier, G. D. (1979, Acad. Press) were not available at the time of writing.) Once children are born the parents' behaviour to the children is correlated with the nature of their marriage. For example Kemper and Reichler (1976) found that parents satisfied with their marriages rewarded their children more and punished their children less than less-satisfied parents. They also found that in marriages with an egalitarian power structure mothers tended to reward daughters and punish sons more, and fathers to punish sons and daughters less, than in marriages with husband or wife markedly dominant. Such differences may underlie the relationship, found by Matteson (1974), between the self-esteem of adolescents and the marital satisfaction expressed by their parents. Of course such influences are probably reciprocal, handling of the children affecting marital quality as well as vice versa. Temporary absences of the father may affect the mother's attitude to the children (Marsella, Dubanoski and Mohs, 1974); the arrival of the second born affects the parents' relationship with the first (Dunn and Kendrick, in prep.); and the sex of the first child may affect parental attitudes to the second (*e.g.* Cicirelli, 1975). Whilst studies cited later show that paternal absence may have considerable influence on personality development, its effects can be ameliorated by the presence of an older male sibling (Wohlford *et al.*, 1971). Such examples could be multiplied almost indefinitely: the ramifications of the effects of change in one focus on the rest of the family is perhaps best shown by Burton's (1975) study of the consequences for the family of a chronically sick child (*see also* Gath, 1978) and Rutter's (1966) analysis of the effects on the family of a sick parent. Evidence that parents of children with some sort of mental disorder are more likely to be psychiatrically disturbed themselves has recently been reviewed by Rutter (1977b).

Quite apart from the importance for any one relationship of influence from others, the degree to which the relationships within a family influence each other may be an important dimension. Hoffman (1975) found that the families of delinquent boys might be either 'disengaged', with the members often operating in a manner uninfluenced by others, or 'enmeshed', with any move towards independence by one member countered by others.

The family structure changes with time

The relationships of a child with each family member inevitably change as both grow older. To ascribe changes in a relationship to changes in one or other partner is not always easy. Whilst at first sight it might seem that the changing nature of the parent–offspring relationship is a consequence of the child's development, there is evidence from monkeys that the rate of change is determined more by changes in the mother than by changes in the infant (Hinde, 1974; Hinde and Herrmann, 1977): such considerations probably apply also to man (Hinde, 1978). However even in monkeys the relative roles of mother and infant in the growth of independence by the latter may be affected by third parties (Suomi, in press; Berman, 1978), and in the human case the father may play an important role (Lamb, 1976).

Family structure is influenced from outside

The nuclear family is often embedded within an extended family, whose members may affect the child's development: where an extended family is not present, comparable contributions may come from non-relatives. This is true not only in the obvious case of nurturance during childhood, but also, for instance, during adolescence. In other cultures, the mother's brother in patrilineal systems, and the father's brother in matrilineal ones, may provide a tolerant extra-nuclear-family adult who assists the adolescent towards independence (J. Goody, 1969; M. Fortes, personal communication). In our own, clinical evidence suggests that psychological maturation during adolescence may require a balance between the individual, the nuclear family, extra-parental adults and the peer group (Miller, 1970).

In any case each family and each family member is involved to a greater or lesser extent in the extra-familial world (*e.g.* Bott, 1957). Satisfactions and disappointments, success and failure, occupations and preoccupations outside the family will have repercussions inside, and vice versa. I will mention here only one category of such external influences—the family's life circumstances and social class. These are consistently found to be associated with the incidence of psychiatric disorders (*e.g.* Kolvin *et al.*, 1971). They may have an immediate effect on the parents: in a US sample depressive symptoms were more common in low income groups (Schwab *et al.*, 1976), and in London, Richman (1974, 1977) found more complaints of depression and loneliness amongst women living in flats than amongst women living in houses (*see also* Sainsbury and Collins, 1966). In a recent more detailed study Brown *et al.* (1975) not only identified some primary aetiological events for the occurrence of depressive symptoms, but also showed that working-class mothers were more vulnerable to their effects. This was primarily because working-class mothers were more likely to lack the ameliorating influence of an intimate adult relationship. Of particular interest was the finding in this study that vulnerability of the mother was increased by the presence of young children at home. It is pertinent here that mothers with psychiatric problems are likely to have children with behaviour problems: whilst one must be careful about inferring causation from correlation, this could be another way in which the child can affect the parents, with probable consequences for the child.

Although studies of parent–child interaction and family dynamics repeatedly show class differences to be important, the basic ways in which class affects the variables being measured are often hard to specify. Newson and Newson (1970), on the basis of a Nottingham (England) sample, proposed four generalizations about the differences between the children of middle-class (white-collar workers and above) and working-class (manual workers other than foremen) parents: middle-class children (a) are more future orientated; (b) lead more sheltered lives; (c) are expected to learn communication skills of many kinds as early as possible and (d) are subject to different types of parental control. In a more detailed study of a particular issue, Dunn and Kendrick (1977) found that, whilst interacting with their children, middle-class mothers made more and better use of representational material than working-class mothers.

E. Goody (1974), in a discussion of parental roles from an anthropological perspective, links some aspects of class differences to the constraints on fathers in their extrafamilial functions. She argues that in most societies the parental roles involve nurturance, training in role skills, status placement in the social system, and sponsorship into full adult status. In our society nurturance is the province of the mother, training in role skills is delegated to teachers and others and, in a working-class family, the father has neither status to pass on nor resources to assist his son. In such circumstances, Goody suggests, the father can therefore do little for his son, and may not even be able to provide him with a model of how to be an effective adult.

Another, though related, category consists of the social conventions in the society. These become conspicuous when societies are compared or when conventions change. A current example is the increase in the number of mothers in employment: this is discussed later.

The case of child abuse

Many of the points just mentioned are illustrated by recent findings on child abuse. Lystal (1975) emphasizes that this is related to variables at a number of different levels. At one extreme lie the cultural norms that allow or condone violent behaviour. Second, the social variables operating on the family: child-abuse is often associated with unemployment or demeaning social status. Third, there are psychological variables, such as enforced long-term intimate social contact. Parent–child interaction in the families concerned seems to have particular characteristics—the parents use physical punishment and love withdrawal as sanctions, material rewards, and demand instant obedience: at the same time the parent may be relatively careless about the child's whereabouts (Smith and Hanson, 1975). These characteristics seem to be

under parental control, but they are often associated with marital problems and, in the more remote past, a history of deprivation and/or family history that includes an aggressive parental model (Spinetta and Rigler, 1972; Rutter and Madge, 1976). Furthermore the parental behaviour is elicited by the particular child, whose special characteristics (or at least the characteristics that the parent perceives him to have) contribute to the abuse (Friedrich and Boriskin, 1976; George and Main, 1979).

Thus present knowledge shows that child-abuse varies with multiple factors, general and specific in nature, in the remote and immediate past, and on interactions between those factors. It is not easy to evaluate their relative importance especially as this will depend on the precise questions being asked. Thus cultural norms may be important only when cross-cultural comparisons are made; and the association between child abuse and unemployment may be due to aetiological factors they share in the parents' earlier experience, and not a matter of immediate causation. Again, whilst battered children may differ in certain characteristics from other children, they may have acquired those characteristics as a result of their home environment (George and Main, *l.c.*): certainly the existence of such differences does not imply that parental characteristics are unimportant, or that their siblings should not be considered at risk. This sort of complexity is ubiquitous in the study of family influences.

Relationships and structures as self-regulating

As a network of inter-related relationships between individuals, each of whom changes with time and is subjected to multiple influences from outside, how can the family have any stability? There must surely be multiple forces tending to cause each family to fragment, and to induce marked change over successive generations.

First, a general point that comes from recent developments in learning theory. Individuals are not susceptible to all the influences that impinge on them: even within the range of things an individual could learn, there are constraints on what he will actually learn, and he is predisposed to learn some things more than others (Seligman and Hager, 1972; Hinde and Stevenson-Hinde, 1973). The importance of such predispositions is illustrated by some sex differences—for instance young girls are more amenable to many of the demands of socialization than young boys (*e.g.* Martin, 1975). By virtue of early training, and perhaps even by virtue of their genetic constitution, most people are predisposed to maintain a degree of stability in the social structures of which they are part. Disruptive forces therefore meet opposition.

Second, the course of development is in some degree self-regulatory. That this may be true of behaviour in general has been suggested by Bateson (1976a). It seems certainly to be true of behaviour whose development depends on an inter-individual relationship, like that between mother and child (Bell, 1974; Dunn, 1976). Relationships themselves, though changing with time, may have self-regulatory properties. The partners may for instance seek a particular goal (*e.g.* an ideal marriage) whatever the current state ('global stability'), or provided the current state is within certain limits ('asymptotic stability'). Or they may avoid certain states ('stability boundaries'), or be constrained directly by social pressures (Hinde and Stevenson-Hinde, 1976). Even the rhesus monkey mother–infant relationship is profitably regarded as self-regulatory, tending to regain its previous state after temporary disruption by separation (Hinde, 1977). While childhood psychopathy, including conduct disorders, is related to adult psychopathology (Robins, 1966), there is little relation between other forms of childhood (Rutter, 1972b) or adolescent (Allport, 1961) psychopathology and adult disorders: this may reflect the potency of such self-regulatory mechanisms. Furthermore, as a number of writers have argued, the family has self-regulatory properties, and its structure may remain stable despite considerable buffeting from outside (*e.g.* Fleck, 1976; Wertheim, 1975). The development of the regulatory mechanisms is of course itself a further problem (Bateson, 1976a).

Summary of cause-effect relations and family influence on child development

Implicit in the previous sections, and in current views of behavioural development (*e.g.* Martin, 1975), is the conclusion that simple relations between particular influences in infancy or childhood and subsequent behaviour will be the exception rather than the rule. The particular case of perinatal trauma, whose effects seem to be dissipated by high socioeconomic status but amplified by a poor social environment, has been discussed by Sameroff and Chandler (1975); and Dunn (1976), in a critical review, has emphasized some of the difficulties in predicting the longer-term consequences of early individual differences. Some of the reasons for this complexity in the relations between early and late individual differences are summarized here:

(i) Children differ at birth as a result of genetic and prenatal influences (*e.g.* Bell *et al.*, 1971). Such differences involve susceptibility to environmental influences on development (Dunn, Chapter 9, this volume). Thus any attempt to relate child characteristics to environmental factors encounters noise from the start.

(ii) Each character of behaviour depends on multiple influences, some widespread in their effects and some specific to one or a few types of behaviour (Bateson, 1976b, 1978).

(iii) The multiple factors influencing any one aspect of behaviour may interact in complex ways. This is true even of the mother–infant relationship of the relatively simple rhesus monkey living in a simplified group-cage environment: of six independent variables assessed, all except one were found to affect the relationship, but none produced effects that were consistent when the others were varied (White and Hinde, 1975). In development, such interactions could result in a measured variable depending not on a particular experience (such as loss of a parent in early life) but on a pattern of experiences (such as loss of a parent followed by low social status) (*see* discussion by Denenberg, 1978).

(iv) Many of the more important influences on behavioural development involve intra-familial relationships. But interactions within each relationship depend on both individuals (*above*), and are affected by each individual's other relationships within the family (*above*).

(v) All individuals and relationships change with time, both in their properties and in their susceptibility to influences (*above*). Furthermore, even if individuals or relationships maintain certain core characteristics, the overt behaviour through which those characteristics are expressed may change with time. One possible consequence of this is that an influence at one time may produce an effect immediately afterwards, no apparent effect a little later, but an effect considerably later on ('sleeper effects,' *see e.g.* Dunn 1976; *see also* Bateson, 1978).

(vi) All individuals and relationships are subject to influences from outside the family (*above*).

(vii) Influences potentially important for development may have little, moderate or marked effects because:

　i. Their effect depends on association with other factors at particular times (*see above*).

　ii. Individuals are not passively responsive to all potential influences in their environment, but select actively from those they encounter (*above*).

　iii. Most influences do not have a continuous effect, but operate only when above a threshold value (Hinde, 1977). For example, role-taking skills appear to require a certain amount of early social experience, but further experience of the same kind does not produce differential effects (West, 1974).

　iv. Relationships have self-regulatory properties (*above*). For this reason, an influence that appears to be important in the short term may be unimportant in the long term. If these regulatory properties are effective only when deviance exceeds a threshold, they may protect against 'abnormality' but not against differences within the 'normal range'. In the range of potential deviance within which they have some influence only the joint action of several independent variables may be enough to distort development (*e.g.* Hinde, 1977).

All this means that techniques for assessing the importance of a given independent variable that depend on comparing groups in which that variable is present or absent, while other factors are held constant, are likely to be effective only for robust variables not subject to marked interactional effects (*e.g.* Birtchnell, 1973). As we shall see later many variables are in fact of this type, and the more sophisticated surveys have considerable power even in unmasking interactions. But it follows from the above that negative findings, even from large samples, are difficult to interpret, and it is for instance difficult to know how much weight to give to the fact that many studies have found no relationship between child-rearing practices and subsequent child characteristics (*e.g.* Caldwell, 1964). One cannot conclude that, because a given variable produces no measurable effect in the context of one constellation of associated variables, it will not do so in another; nor that, if it produces no effect during one subsequent period, it will not do so in another; nor, contrariwise, that because it produces an effect at one age, it will matter in the long run.

But no one who has been associated with developmental problems needs to be told that they are complex: the point being made here is that a combination of large scale surveys with small scale and even case history studies is essential. To assess the importance of one variable which interacts with many others, and to establish a cause-effect relationship that operates over a long time span, with subjects having many intervening experiences, large scale surveys are essential. But their success may depend on prior identification of the interacting variables, and this may depend on data, formal or informal, on single cases. And when large scale studies do help in identification of the relevant variables, they are likely to be less useful in studies of developmental processes. Prevention and/or therapy may be possible simply by controlling the relevant variables, but often this is not possible, and understanding of the mechanisms of development is essential.

FAMILY DISRUPTION

Death and illness in the family

If development is affected by the family social environment, we might expect the most adverse effects to be produced by the total loss of a family member in death. Curiously, although adults are more prone to psychiatric breakdown in the years following the death of a parent (Birtchnell, 1975), there is remarkably little evidence that the death of a parent in childhood produces adverse effects in later childhood or adolescence. Rutter (1971) cites a number of studies in which parental death was followed by at most a very slight increase in psychiatric disturbance, and others that found no relation with childhood neurosis. The effects of parental death on childhood disturbance are thus not nearly so great as might be expected.

Four points must be made here. First, some effects of parental death would certainly be found if more fine-grained measures were used. Second, we may be dealing with a sleeper effect (*see above*): the effects may be inconspicuous in the immediately ensuing years, but become apparent later. Childhood bereavement seems to be accompanied by increased susceptibility to depressive disorders in adulthood (*e.g.* Bowlby, 1973; Brown *et al.*, 1975), though this has not been demonstrated in all studies (Rutter, 1971). There is also some indication that early parental death may affect later marriage patterns, though the influence may be indirect. For example Birtchnell (1974) suggests that a correlation between a high incidence of maternal bereavement and early divorce in men may have been a consequence of desperate attempts to escape from the parental home leading to early marriage; and Hilgard, Newman and Fisk (1960) suggest that the marriage of men whose fathers died

before they were 19 may be delayed by their over-dependent mothers.

A third issue is that the consequences of parental death in childhood may vary with age—a matter often neglected in epidemiological studies, though Rutter (1972a) has suggested that the long-term effects may be greatest if the parent died when the child was 2–3 years old. In so far as the child's response to bereavement depends on its cognitive development, it is certain to change with age (*cf* Koocher, 1973).

Finally, loss of a parent by divorce or separation may be associated with sequelae different from those of early bereavement (*e.g.* Gay and Tonge, 1967; Rutter, 1972a, Jacobson *et al.*, 1975). Such effects may result not from the loss itself, but from the accompanying disharmony, and will be considered later.

Rearing in social isolation or in institutions

If the effects of death of a parent are less severe than might be expected, what about those of long or short term parental deprivation? Bowlby (1944) suggested that separation from the mother during the first five years of life was one of the major factors in delinquency, and a number of studies have shown that maternal deprivation in childhood can be associated with some subsequent susceptibility to psychological disturbance (Ainsworth, 1962; Brown *et al.*, 1975). It will be convenient to consider successively extreme social deprivation and institution rearing, and then the questions of temporary separations and day care.

Rearing in near-total social isolation is of course extremely rare in man. Available evidence indicates that, if isolation is terminated within a few years and special remedial measures are used, considerable recovery of cognitive functioning is possible (Clarke and Clarke, 1976): data on social behaviour are lacking. Monkeys reared in various degrees of social isolation usually show markedly aberrant social behaviour, the effects being strongest in males (Harlow and Harlow, 1965, 1969; Anderson and Mason, 1974): though 'therapy' is possible (Harlow and Suomi, 1971), it is not yet clear whether recovery is complete.

Not surprisingly institution-rearing can produce long-term deleterious consequences. Children reared in institutions may show language retardation and impaired cognitive functioning (*e.g.* Ainsworth, 1962), and anti-social/neurotic disorders in girls are often associated with earlier experience of residential care (Wolkind, 1974). Children with Down's Syndrome do less well in institutions than at home (Francis, 1971; Stedman and Eickorn, 1964; Centerwall and Centerwall, 1960). Even infants less than 1 year old may be affected by an institutional environment—for instance they explore less than home-reared infants (Collard, 1971).

However institutions differ markedly in quality, and some studies have revealed no difference or even improvement in intellectual functioning (*e.g.* Skeels, 1966). The important question therefore is whether children reared in any type of institution *necessarily* differ from those reared at home. The most interesting data have come from a long-term comparison of children in 'high quality' residential nurseries in UK with home-reared controls (Tizard and Rees, 1974, 1975; Tizard, 1977). At 2 the children did not differ in non-verbal IQ from working-class home-reared controls, though they were behind on language development and differed in a number of ways in their social behaviour. Children who remained in the nurseries to 4 showed no differences in IQ from the home-reared controls, and showed no higher incidence of behaviour pathology (including bed-wetting), but did differ in their social behaviour with adults. They tended to be more demanding, but were less likely to form deep relationships, than family-reared children. Those adopted before 4 by middle-class parents formed good attachments with their adoptive parents and showed improved language development and IQ by 4. However both the adopted children and those still in institutions at 4 showed some atypical aspects in their affectional behaviour, including abnormal overt friendliness to strangers. At 8 years most children who had been adopted before the age of 4 had an above average IQ, while children restored to their natural mothers had increased less and were of average IQ and below average in school attainment. Most of the children left in the institution after $4\frac{1}{2}$ decreased in IQ between 2 and 8. However, the social problems remained, the previously institutionalized children showing a great desire for attention and difficulties in forming good relationships with their peer group. Whilst overall conclusions must thus be made with caution, it seems that early institutional rearing does not necessarily have an adverse effect on intellectual development and may even enhance it. If adopted by about 4, IQ may yet be markedly influenced by the child's new environment. There are, however, likely to be long-term consequences of early institutionalization on social behaviour which are less easily reversible.

Temporary separation

It is claimed that, after birth, separations between mother and infant measurable in hours may have long-term sequelae: there is some evidence that interaction between them then may affect infant development and the mother–infant relationship until the infant is at least 2 years old, and possibly longer (e.g. Klaus and Kennell, 1976). Whether the differences between babies more or less continuously with their mothers and those separated briefly from them are due to the separation per se, or to some other factor such as the altered expectations of the mothers consequent upon paediatric intervention, is an open issue (Richards, 1978).

Our main concern here is with later separations lasting a few days to a few weeks. That such separations produce immediate effects on the child is beyond dispute: Bowlby (e.g. 1969) and Robertson (1953) have described the child's response in terms of three phases—protest, involving much crying and distress; despair, in which the child seems apathetic and withdrawn; and detachment, in which he appears to be uninterested in his parents. The symptoms are most marked in children between 6 months and 4 years, but are not invariant even then. They are much less marked if, during the period of separation, the child receives personal attention in a family setting than if he or she is in an institution (Robertson and Robertson, 1971).

Early data on the consequences of separation experiences, such as those accompanying hospitalization, have been reviewed by Ainsworth (1962) and Bowlby (1969). In general, this earlier evidence seemed to show that a few weeks separation between mother and child was liable to produce long-term consequences. However Rutter (1971, 1972a) argued that, whilst emotional distress might persist for some months after reunion, long-term consequences of a single hospital admission were very uncommon except in cases where the separation experience took place against a background of family discord or pathology. More recent findings come from Douglas's (1975) analysis of data on children born in 1946 in UK. Whilst some preschool children appeared to profit from a stay in hospital, prolonged or repeated hospital admissions in early childhood were associated with an increased risk of behaviour disturbance or delinquency in adolescence. Most vulnerable were children highly dependent on their mothers or under stress at home (e.g. from the birth of a sibling or family disharmony) at the time of the break. Quinton and Rutter (1976) confirmed these findings on the basis of a different sample, though they point out that a necessary effect of early hospital admissions on later psychiatric or behavioural/emotional disturbance is not proven. In particular, the effect was greater in disadvantaged homes, the evidence suggesting that children from such homes are more susceptible to the stresses of repeated hospital admissions. As discussed elsewhere, separation experiences in childhood may be related to aspects of later behaviour other than those studied by these workers: for instance in a group of primiparous British women an early separation experience tended to be associated with an unmarried status, teenage pregnancy, psychiatric treatment, a high score on a 'malaise' inventory, etc. (Wolkind et al., 1976; See also Frommer and O'Shea, 1973).

The general conclusions to be drawn here are that repeated or prolonged separation experiences are most likely to be associated with long-term sequelae if accompanied by a disturbed family background, and that the precise nature of the consequences depend on the sex of the child and a considerable number of other variables. Even the effects of a disturbed family background are small if the child has a good relationship with one or other parent (Rutter, 1972a). However it will be necessary to survey a wider range of dependent variables before full conclusions can be drawn.

Comparative evidence is of some interest here. Monkey infants separated from their mothers show similar phases of protest, despair and (rarely) detachment (Hinde and Spencer-Booth, 1971; Suomi, 1976), and in certain circumstances a separation experience can produce long-term effects (Hinde and Spencer-Booth, 1971; Hinde et al., 1978). But the severity of the symptoms varies with the species; the pre- and post-separation mother–infant relationship and thus also with the pre- and post-separation relationships of mother and infant with other social companions; the nature and duration of the separation experience; the availability of alternative sources of mothering during separation; the sex, age and other characteristics of the infant; and the mother's and infant's previous experience of separation. Furthermore the effects of separation seem to involve a threshold: only if this is exceeded is the resilience of the mother–infant relationship unable to restore development to its normal course (Hinde and McGinnis, 1977; *see also* Suomi, 1976).

Finally we come to very short separations, such as those experienced by the children of working mothers in day-care. Here it must be remembered that not only are there good and bad day-care centres, but that day-care must be considered as an alternative to homes of widely differing quality (J. Tizard, 1976). Where disadvantaged homes are concerned, the child may well profit from any form of day-care, since the alternative would be less satisfactory. For example, Robinson and Robinson (1971) found that day-care can enhance intellectual development, especially in children from underprivileged backgrounds (*see also* Caldwell, 1972). Douglas (1975) found that hospitalization had less effect on the children of working mothers and that children with experience of day-care show less disturbance on transfer to a new facility. Indeed even longer separations, provided they are of a happy kind, may reduce susceptibility to subsequent unhappy ones (Stacey *et al.*, 1970). As to possible ill effects of day-care, a number of studies show no tendency for the children of working mothers to become delinquent or to be susceptible to psychiatric disorder (*e.g.* Douglas, 1968; Rutter, Tizard and Whitmore, 1970). However, where more subtle dependent variables are used, the situation is by no means so clear. Taking a stand on the principle that the mother–child relationship matters, Murray (1975) reviews evidence that the full-time employment of mothers of disadvantaged infants hinder the development of an optimal mother–infant relationship, and argues that even care by a grandmother may create conflicts in the mother, who may feel that her relationship with her child is not so close as she would wish (or, perhaps, as she believes her culture decrees). Whether such conflicts in the mother affect the child in the long run is a further issue on which evidence is lacking. In this context it is significant that, whilst Caldwell *et al.* (1970) found no significant difference in attachment to the mother between home-reared and day-care children at 30 months, the same children tended to be less cooperative with adults and more aggressive than a control group when they later entered nursery school (Schwarz *et al.*, 1974). Whilst such effects may not occur in all cases (Macrae and Herbert-Jackson, 1976), these are not isolated findings. Moore (1964) found that children who had had substitute care before 5 years of age tended to conform less, to be more self assertive, less susceptible to being punished, less effectively toilet trained and less averse to dirt than a home-reared group. Similarly Blehar (1974), using the Ainsworth strange-situation technique to compare 20 day-care children with 20 home-reared children, found qualitative disturbances in the mother–child relationship in day-care children, their nature depending on the age at which day-care started. Cornelius and Denney (1975) found no difference in dependency amongst 4 and 5 year olds, though there was a suggestion that the day-care children were less sex-typed. The effect on sex role stereotypes varies with the children's age (Marantz and Mansfield, 1977).

In a critical review L. W. Hoffman (1974) found no support for the hypothesis that a working mother's absence *need* result in emotional or cognitive deprivation for the child. However there was evidence that the working mother provides a different role model for the child, that employment affects the mother's emotional state (in the direction of greater satisfaction and/or guilt), that child care practices are affected, and that the child receives less adequate supervision.

In summary, it would seem that there is no evidence that good day-care produces any *marked* intellectual deficit or behavioural pathology: indeed children from underprivileged homes may profit from it. There are, however, reasons for thinking that children may be affected by day-care in lesser ways, some possibly desirable but some not: the balance between these two depends in part on the home background to which day-care is an alternative. But in evaluating the consequences of a mother working the possible effects on the mother of *not* working must also be considered: full or part-time work appears to protect women from developing depression (Brown *et al.*, 1975), which might in turn affect the child.

FAMILY DISHARMONY

Family disharmony and antisocial behaviour

We have seen that the consequences of separation experiences *per se*, unless prolonged or repeated, were less than might be expected: the human mother–child relationship has regulatory properties which, in an harmonious family, enable it to recover from the acute effects of a separation experience. However this was true only where the parents had a reasonably 'good' marriage. Boys from families where there was marital discord were more likely later to show antisocial behaviour if they had had a separation experience. Indeed family discord is in itself associated with behaviour problems in adolescence. Rutter *et al.* (1975) found that four sets of variables (family discord, parental deviance, social disadvantage and certain school characteristics) were associated with child deviance and disorder both within an Inner London Borough and in the Isle of Wight, and also differed between the two areas. In so far as they could be considered causal, those variables accounted for the greater discord and deviance in London. The importance of emotional disharmony is indicated also by evidence that children from broken homes tend to function better than children from unhappy unbroken ones (review, Biller, 1976; Rutter, 1977a).

Similar conclusions emerge from studies of the current status of families containing a delinquent. For instance Peterson and Becker (1965) found more marital instability and a more negative interpersonal atmosphere in the homes of delinquents. A study by Megargee *et al.* (1971) is of special interest in showing a similar trend amongst adolescents not labelled as delinquents: those found to be less 'socialized' on the California Personality Inventory Socialization Scale tended to come from homes showing more marital instability and a more negative atmosphere.

Whilst it is at least possible that a child's antisocial behaviour can cause marital discord, rather than vice versa, the epidemiological evidence indicates that the parental discord precedes the child's antisocial behaviour. It is however likely that the child's behaviour may exacerbate the discord (Rutter, 1971). Of course none of this evidence implies that lack of harmony in the home is *the* cause of delinquency: mental illness and criminality in the parents and poor housing conditions are also associated with aggressiveness and delinquency (*e.g.* Robins and Lewis, 1966; Frommer, Mendelson and Reid, 1972).

The next question is why some children are more affected than others. One important issue here is the child's sex. Parental discord, whilst sometimes associated with delinquency in girls (Koller, 1971) seems to produce deviant behaviour in boys more than in girls. Rutter (1971) ascribes this to a greater susceptibility to psychological stresses amongst males than amongst females, but it remains possible that choice of other dependent variables (*e.g.* marital history) would show that girls were susceptible in other ways.

A second important issue is age. Although the earlier work suggested a greater susceptibility to separation experiences in younger children, there is little evidence concerning susceptibility to family disharmony. However Wallerstein and Kelly (1975) have shown that the response at the time of parental separation and one year later varied with the age of the child. The youngest children showed regression, fretfulness, and bewilderment; the middle group underwent 'early super ego development'; and the oldest were relatively unaffected.

Third, children vary in susceptibility by virtue of their own personality characteristics. Rutter (1971) found deviant behaviour to be more likely in children who lacked fastidiousness, malleability, and regularity in their eating and sleeping patterns. This may be related to the finding that such children are more likely than other family members to be the target of parental criticism during periods of family stress (Rutter, 1978).

Family interaction patterns in disturbed families

If delinquency is associated with disharmony, we may ask what aspects of disharmony produce this effect, and whether there are patterns of family interaction associated with other types of disturbance.

Stimulated in large measure by the still unsubstantiated double-bind theory of schizophrenia (Bateson *et al.*, 1956; *see below*), many investigators have compared the communication patterns to be found in normal families with those in families containing a disturbed member. They have attempted to assess differences between normal families and families containing a disturbed member in such measures as the dominance or coalition patterns between family members, how easily differences of opinion are resolved, how much the individuals speak and to whom, where control resides, and the extent to which the utterances of one family member 'disqualify' or invalidate the messages, and even the claims for self recognition, of other members (Danziger, 1976; Watzlawick *et al.*, 1967). In view of the difficulties of recording and analysing family interaction patterns, especially when it is far from clear which are the most appropriate dependent variables, it is hardly surprising that the results of this work are contradictory and confusing (Schuham, 1967; Olson, 1972; Riskin and Faunce, 1972). Nevertheless the work has established that families do have patterns of interaction that are stable over time (*e.g.* Murrell, 1971), and the clinical significance of such differences is now established in a few areas.

In a recent critical review of this work, Jacob (1975) pointed out the methodological weaknesses in the earlier studies and confined himself to the 57 studies available up to June 1973 in which direct observation procedures had been used. The studies were divided according to whether schizophrenic (*i.e.* containing a schizophrenic member) or disturbed but non-schizophrenic families were being compared with controls, and according to the nature of the dependent variables. When studies were compared, conclusions could be 'tentative at best and mixed or almost entirely nonsignificant at worst'. Amongst the more substantial findings were:

(a) Schizophrenic families communicate with less clarity and accuracy than normal families.

(b) Non-schizophrenic disturbed families tend to have egalitarian power structures as compared with the more hierarchical structures found in normal families.

(c) Fathers are more influential in normal than in non-schizophrenic disturbed family groups.

(d) Normal families show more positive affect and less negative affect than non-schizophrenic disturbed families.

Even these conclusions (except perhaps the last) must be hedged with reservations, and the extent of their validity is far from clear. Amongst the reasons for the generally contradictory nature of the findings Jacob discusses first the lack of clarity in the diagnostic status of the families used. It is well known that the category of schizophrenia is itself often broadly defined, and 'schizophrenic' families with good or bad premorbid histories may give quite different results. And difficulties of definition are not limited to schizophrenia: Hetherington, Stouwie and Ridberg (1971) found differences in family interaction patterns between each of three groups of delinquents as differentiated by Quay (1965). Other methodological problems mentioned by Jacob include the variety of measurement techniques used and the often tenuous relations between the measures and explanatory constructs;

confusion between differences at the family, dyadic and individual level; and inadequate attention to demographic factors. To these may be added the usual question of direction of effect: family interaction patterns could be affected by, for instance, the disgrace or self doubts consequent upon the institutionalization of one of its members (Duncan, 1971). Most careful researchers attempt to control for this, but some do not. It must also be emphasized that studies of two groups differing along one dimension may be too simple minded. Gassner and Murray (1969) found that with high marital conflict boys show more disturbance in mother dominated families and girls in father dominated ones. But with low marital distress, disturbance was not related to parent dominance. Finally the artificiality of the situations used in many of the studies must be mentioned: it has for instance been shown that the distribution of emotional expressiveness amongst family members varies with the situation (Waxler and Mishler, 1970; Lytton, 1971), so that the validity of laboratory studies must be questioned.

In this review relatively little attention has so far been paid to studies using other observational or experimental techniques. This is in part due to relative unreliability of the interview and questionnaire techniques formerly used in this area (*see* discussion by Rutter and Brown, 1966; Jacob, 1975). However interviewing techniques have recently become more sophisticated, with emphasis on distinguishing between concrete happenings in the family and feelings or attitudes about these events or about the individuals involved (*e.g.* Rutter and Brown, *l.c.*), on focusing on specific relationships rather than using global measures of the family, and on distinguishing a number of dimensions of feelings and temperaments. Reference to some of the findings using such instruments has already been made. As another example, an interview method has recently produced important information about relapse from schizophrenic illness after discharge from hospital. Using an 'index of expressed emotion' based on the number of critical comments made by a relative about the patient, hostility and marked emotional over-involvement, Brown, Birley and Wing (1972) were able to predict relapse within nine months after discharge: 58% of patients from homes with a high index, but only 16% of those from homes with a low index, relapsed. Their findings have been replicated by Vaughn and Leff (1976), who also found the index useful in predicting relapse in depressed patients. Seligman's (1975) hypothesis that patients can learn 'helplessness' seems likely to be relevant here. Whether the characteristics of family interaction revealed as important in these studies are involved also in the initial aetiology of the disorders is so far unproven, but seems likely.

Some further aspects of family interaction patterns are mentioned later.

INTELLECTUAL DEVELOPMENT

As discussed in the introductory sections, family characteristics and family experiences may have diverse effects on the growing child, and the extent of these effects may vary with the impact of other independent variables. In the preceding sections we have focused on the effects of some of the major independent variables. Here and in the next two sections we shall turn to some of the outcome measures, trying to trace their aetiology.

Like every other aspect of behavioural development, intellectual functioning is affected by many factors. We have already seen that it may, but need not, be affected by institutional rearing (p. 53): here we are concerned with intra-familial influence. It is convenient to consider first the relatively gross variables of family size and birth order.

In many societies, first children contribute more to parental status, and themselves receive more respect and have more power, than their siblings (Fortes, 1974; Rosenblatt and Skoogberg, 1974). In our own society first borns are more likely to show high achievement (Altus, 1966). And beyond that, although there are contradictory findings (*e.g.* McCall and Johnson, 1972), relations between birth order and intelligence or achievement are to be found also for later born family members. The most comprehensive survey (Breland, 1974), based on about 800 000 participants in the US National Merit Scholarship Qualification Test, showed that children's scores tended to decrease with family size and with birth order, except that only children scored lower and twins much lower than would otherwise have been expected. Zajonc (1976) has recently proposed a 'confluence' model to explain these and other similar data. This suggests that the intellectual growth of each family member depends on that of all the others, and thus on the family configuration. The relevant variable is considered to be some function of the average absolute intellectual levels of the family members, intellectual level being a quantity comparable to mental age. The intellectual level of a newborn is regarded as zero, and the intellectual environment to which a first born is exposed to be the average of the intellectual levels of his father, his mother and himself. Since intellectual level increases with age, birth spacing is crucial for determining the intellectual environment of subsequent children. Because the first born is likely still to have an intellectual level considerably less than either of the parents, the addition of a fourth family member will bring the average intellectual level of the family below that encountered by the first born. However the older the first born (*i.e.* the longer the birth gap), the higher his intellectual level and thus the higher the average for the family when the next child arrives.

This model brings together a wide range of factors:

(a) The evidence for differences in intellectual test performance with family size in four large national surveys (Scotland, France, Netherlands and US).

(b) The decrease in performance with birth order in two of these surveys. The absence of such an effect in the other two is explicable by the longer birth intervals.

(c) Lower intellectual performance by children who have lost one parent.

(d) Associations of temporal changes in family patterns with changes in intellectual performance.

(e) Association of differences in family patterns between different countries and/or ethnic groups with differences in intellectual performance.

(f) Associations of differences in average birth order of males and females with differences in their intellectual performance.

The unexpectedly low performance scores of only children are ascribed to an additional factor—the effect of acting as a teacher or interlocutor to younger sibs (*see also* Breland, *l.c.*). Last children often show unexpectedly high or low scores, and this may be due to an interplay between their lack of a teacher role and the longer birth interval that usually separates last and penultimate sibling (*see also* McGurk and Lewis, 1972). Last children also never have to adjust to the arrival of a younger sib (Dunn and Wooding, personal communication).

These birth order effects are in practice quite small. In considering the mechanisms underlying them, Zajonc emphasized both that the confluence model provided only a partial interpretation of some of the phenomena with which he was concerned, and that the 'average intellectual level' was at best a crude concept, whose effects must be distorted by differences in the quantity and nature of interactions within families of a given configuration. It must be remembered here that even newborns tend to differ according to the spacing of their mother's previous pregnancies, those born to mothers who had had a large number of closely spaced pregnancies being more lethargic than those to mothers who had had fewer pregnancies more widely-spaced (Waldrop and Bell, 1966). For this and a host of other reasons it is not surprising that the nature of mother–infant interaction varies with the birth order (Jacobs and Moss, 1976; Cicirelli, 1975) in ways that may well affect the development of intellectual functioning. Furthermore the later born children may encounter not only a different degree of parental supervision, but also more crowded physical surroundings. It must also be remembered that the presence of many young children may make mothers more vulnerable to stress-induced depression (Brown *et al.*, 1975), and this may in turn affect the intellectual development of the children. Finally large families are often associated with social disadvantage.

Whilst achievement and/or IQ has often been found to be related to social class indices such as parental occupation, education or income, detailed assessments of parent/child interaction do in fact provide better predictions of IQ scores than social class (*e.g.* Bloom, 1964). In considering some representative studies, it is important to remember that some activities are more influenced by environmental variables than others, and that different activities are related to different independent variables (Cattell, 1963). With that in mind, we may ask which members of the family are important, and in what ways.

First, two representative studies concerned primarily with the role of the mother may be mentioned. Jones (1972) compared high-verbal with low-verbal fifth grade boys matched for general intelligence, basing her assessment of the home situation on an interview with and assessments of the mother. The higher verbal boys had parents with a higher interaction index, higher academic and vocational aspirations, who had provided more opportunity for the use and development of language, and who had had higher occupational status (*see also* Bing, 1963).

In a study comparing the home environments of language-delayed with normal preschool children, Wulbert *et al.* (1975) used the Caldwell Inventory of Home Stimulation—an instrument with which the mother's behaviour is observed in an interview about the child. With the language-delayed children the scores were lower on five of the six subcategories. Summarizing their results, the authors write '... On the whole the mothers of the normal children enjoyed them, actively encouraged their development, and took pride in their accomplishments. However the language-delayed children were a source of great frustration to their mothers...' The poor interaction was of course reciprocal in nature: as usual, the correlations permitted no certain deductions about causation (*see also* Jeffree and Cashdan, 1971).

Development occurs over time, so that interaction with the parent may affect cognitive development over a long period. Bradley and Caldwell (1976) assessed children with the Bayley Scales at 6 months and Stanford-Binet scales at 3 years. Increases in test performance were associated with maternal involvement with the child and the provision of play materials. Decreases in test scores were related to inadequate organization of the physical and temporal environment. Other studies relating aspects of the mother–child relationship to the child's IQ are reviewed by Honzik (1976; *see also* Yarrow *et al.*, 1973): in general the evidence that maternal involvement or warmth affects IQ is stronger for boys than for girls, and indicates that the early years are more important than later. The father also plays an important role (review by Radin, 1976). In the first place, a number of studies show that children with a father present at home perform better than children without (*e.g.* Blanchard and Biller, 1971; Santrock, 1972). The difference seems to lie in the realization of potential rather than in IQ, and has been ascribed to poor motivation in the father-absent child.

As might be expected, the consequences of father-loss vary both with its cause and with the age of the child: Santrock (1972) found that, when assessed in terms of IQ and achievement, father-absence due to divorce, desertion or separation was most deleterious in the first two years of life, but father-absence due to death was most detrimental if it occurred between 6 and 9.

Second, when the father is present, relationships between paternal nurturance and intellectual functioning in boys have been demonstrated (Radin, 1972; Jordan, Radin and Epstein, 1975). The effect on girls is much smaller or absent.

The studies cited so far have endeavoured to assess the influence of certain characteristics of either the father or the mother. In real life families usually have both, and their influences interact. Thus in a study of the development of descriptive categorizing styles, Davis and Lange's

(1973) correlational analyses suggested that the mother–father unit, rather than either parent simply, was the essential agent. Most investigators, however, have examined separately the behaviour of each parent to the child. Walberg and Marjaribanks (1973) used an instrument based on the assumptions that each cognitive ability depends on certain environmental forces. They identified eight 'environmental press areas'—press for achievement, activeness, intellectuality, independence, English, language, and Father dominance and Mother dominance. Each of these was assessed by interviews with fathers and mothers of 185 11-year-old Canadian boys. These home-environment process measures, their socio-economic indicators and their family structure measures were canonically correlated with four mental abilities (verbal, number, spatial and reasoning). Higher scores on all four abilities were associated with higher levels of all press measures. Higher verbal but lower number ability was associated with higher socioeconomic level and parent–son mutual involvement in activities.

Three further studies showing a relation between parental child-rearing practices or attitudes and school performance may be mentioned here. Heilbrun and Waters (1968) found that children who were sensitive to reinforcement and expected only 'negative reinforcement' from their parents tended to underachieve in school, whilst those who were sensitive to reinforcement and anticipated positive reinforcement did well. In a later study Heilbrun (1971) found that children experiencing mothers as more controlling and hostile were especially susceptible to evaluative cues by others and less creative. Barton, Dielman and Cattell (1974) related the fifteen mothers' factors and eleven fathers' factors in a Child Rearing Practices Questionnaire, to school achievement. Some of these factors were significantly correlated with achievement: high punishment and low use of reason by the mother, and early authoritative discipline by the father, were negatively correlated with achievement, whilst items showing that the mother showed much warmth and was tolerant were positively correlated. Frequent use of praise and reward by the father were negatively correlated with achievement. Other factors correlated with grade scores in particular areas. The authors stress that direction of causation must not be assumed from the correlations.

At this point we may ask if studies of family interaction patterns throw any further light on the mechanisms underlying the effect of birth order. There is general agreement that first borns not only perform better but also have higher educational aspirations than their later born siblings (e.g. Glass, Neulinger and Brim, 1974). Such differences are likely to be related to the more intense but less relaxed interaction with the parents experienced by first borns (Hilton, 1967). They have also been related to 'dependency', a concept that has suffered greatly from imprecise usage (Martin, 1975). Unfortunately the hypotheses put forward are somewhat contradictory. Some authors (e.g. Rosen, 1961; Adams and Phillips, 1972) theorize that first borns receive more training in independence from their parents, and that this leads to

greater need for achievement later. According to Glass, Neulinger and Brim's (1974) data, this is especially true for the better educated parents. Others stress that the first born receives more and/or more inconsistent mothering, leading to greater dependency (Schachter, 1959). This greater dependency of first borns is especially marked if the age gap is small (Cornoldi and Fattori, 1976), and may lead in turn to greater (Staples and Walters, 1961; Harwood, 1973) or less (Gilmore and Zigler, 1964) susceptibility to social reinforcers. While greater dependency in first borns has been invoked as an explanation for their intellectual success, greater dependency *conflict* has been advanced as a reason for the greater proneness to alcoholism of male, but not female, last borns (Blane, Barry and Barry, 1971). Such speculations seem endless, and their generality is called into question by the findings of McGurk and Lewis (1972), and Deutsch (1975), who, admittedly using fairly small samples and different techniques, found that second borns showed more dependency behaviour than either first borns or later borns. Furthermore, many speculations about the bases of birth order differences run into difficulties over the anomalous position of the only child (*e.g.* Unruh, Grosse and Zigler, 1971). Douglas (1968), discussing data derived from over 5000 children born in Great Britain during one week in 1946, stresses the diversity of factors that may operate to produce differences related to family size and birth order: so far little clear progress has been made in disentangling their relative importance.

It must be also emphasized that progressive changes in intelligence with birth order may depend on influences from the siblings, as well as from the parents. Although the decrease in IQ with birth order, and the tendency to lower performance in institution-reared children, might suggest that sibling or peer-interaction tends to dilute parent- or adult-interaction, this is certainly not all there is to it. This is especially clear in studies of the influence of the sex of a sibling. In general, children with a male elder sibling tend to be superior in ability and achievement to children with a female sibling (*e.g.* Schoonover, 1959), but older sisters are better than older brothers at teaching their siblings, even though they show no difference in ability to teach unrelated children. The younger siblings are more willing to accept help from an older sister than from an older brother (Cicirelli, 1973, 1974, 1975; Bates, 1975).

A variety of mechanisms has been suggested to account for sibling effects on abilities and achievement, including differential parental treatment and sibling rivalry, and modelling (Sutton-Smith and Rosenberg, 1970).

Discussion of the processes by which family interactions affect intellectual development are beyond the scope of this chapter, though data are accumulating rapidly. Mention may be made of recent studies of language acquisition, and especially of how the mother adjusts the complexity of her utterances to the developing child (*e.g.* Snow, 1972), and uses representational material as a forum for increasingly rich verbal exchange (Dunn and Kendrick, 1977). The reader is referred to later chapters in this volume for further discussion.

SEX ROLE DEVELOPMENT AND RELATED ISSUES

The problem of sex role development is concerned with such questions as the extent to which the individual identifies himself as male or female, the extent to which he behaves in ways that are culturally accepted as masculine or feminine, and the nature of his sexual object choice. While these issues are not always fully correlated, there is clear evidence that the sex assigned to a child by its parents can affect its sex role development (Money, Hampson and Hampson, 1957). From the start, therefore, development of sex-typical behaviour may be influenced by the family. What the family considers as sex-typical is, of course, in fact culturally determined, and most of the studies considered here refer to US families unaffected by recent changes in views of the relative roles of the sexes.

That mothers treat male and female children differently has been established in a number of studies (*e.g.* Lewis and Weinraub, 1974): for example, mothers tend to talk more to daughters, and to encourage physical contact more with girls and independence with boys. How far such differences in maternal treatment result from sex differences in child behaviour is not here relevant: at the least mothers' differential behaviour seems likely to enhance sex differences.

More interest has centred on the father's part in sex role development. The evidence has recently been reviewed by Biller (1976) and Lamb (1976), and only a few points will be mentioned here. A number of studies have demonstrated an effect of father absence on sex-role behaviour or preference, especially in boys (*e.g.* Lynn and Sawrey, 1959; Badaines, 1976); but not girls (Birtchnell, 1974). The nature of the effect is variable: most studies show a tendency towards feminine sex role behaviour and cognitive style, but some show 'compensatory' (and sometimes fragile) masculinity. The variability of findings in this area no doubt reflects the diversity of other factors operating. The age at separation, the reason for it (death, separation or work-enforced temporary absences), and the maternal response to it are amongst the more important. For example Hetherington (1972) found that the daughters of divorcees showed more attention-seeking from males, and early heterosexual behaviour, while daughters of widows showed inhibition and rigidity (*see also* Uddenberg, 1976).

When an alternative adult male is present the effects of father loss may be smaller (*e.g.* Oshman and Manosevitz, 1976): this may be a direct result of the relationship between the new male and the child, an effect of the male presence on the child's mother or, in some studies, an artifact arising because mothers who re-marry are more adaptable psychologically than those who do not. Peers, especially elder peers, also influence sex role behaviour, and can partially compensate for absence of a parent (*e.g.* Koch, 1956; Bigner, 1972).

Not surprisingly, findings on the influence of parents on sex role behaviour in intact families are not wholly consistent. That masculine fathers tend to have feminine daughters seems clear, though paternal influences may be both direct and indirect (Biller and Weiss, 1970). The prediction of simple modelling theory that masculine fathers will tend to have masculine sons is less well supported, though a boy's perception of his father's masculinity and influence in the family appears to be a better predictor than the father's masculinity or dominance as assessed directly (Biller, 1976). Furthermore the evidence (reviewed Lamb, *l.c.*, Biller, *l.c.*) indicates the quality of the father–child relationship to be important, warm and nurturant fathers tending to have masculine sons and feminine daughters, especially when the father is himself masculine. Siblings also play a role in the development of sex-typical traits (*e.g.* Leventhal, 1970; Langlois *et al.*, 1973). Sutton-Smith and Rosenberg (1970) suggest that close birth spacing facilitates appropriate dependency in girls, and wide spacing fosters culturally acceptable independence in boys: they also present evidence that the relative importance of ordinal position and sex of sibling change with age.

Research in this area has reached a point where the natures of most of the important variables are clear, but hard-headed investigations of their full subtlety and of the manner in which they interact are only just beginning. In this context, the study by Block, Lippe and Block (1973) merits special mention. These authors emphasize that sex-role typing interacts with socialization, and summarize their data in terms of four categories of individuals.

(i) Sex appropriate, socialized individuals tend to come from families where the parents have clearly differentiated roles, are healthy and fully available throughout adolescence, and where the like-sex parent provides the more salient model for identification.

(ii) Sex inappropriate, socialized individuals had parents who presented more complex role models for their children, and were less stereotyped in their own definitions of masculinity and femininity. Sex role acquisition involves identification with positive aspects of both parents, who are not themselves prototypical sex role examples, and by emulation of the opposite sex parent.

(iii) Sex appropriate unsocialized individuals tended to have a neurotic and rejecting same sex parent, but a seductive opposite sex parent. Here the sex role seems to be acquired by complementary reactions to the opposite sex parent rather than by modelling.

(iv) Sex inappropriate unsocialized individuals tended to come from families with conflict and psychopathology.

Block *et al.* pointed out that high socialization involves selection from amongst the various aspects of the appropriate sex role those of a more positive nature (*e.g.* conservation and nurturance for females, initiative and instrumentality for males) and suppression of those of a more negative nature (*e.g.* anxiety for females, aggressiveness for males). Socialization thus encourages males to acquire some female features (*e.g.* conscientiousness) but does not make females more masculine.

Consideration of the aetiology of homosexuality is beyond the scope of this chapter, but it is worth noting that the earlier emphasis on maternal dominance (*e.g.*

Stephen, 1973) has not received universal support (*e.g.* Bené, 1965), and that once again the qualities of the relationships with both parents, and the differences between those relationships, may turn out to be important (Robertson, 1972).

SOCIALIZATION, DISCIPLINE AND MORAL DEVELOPMENT

We have already seen that, whilst marked family disharmony is associated with delinquency and deviant behaviour, relations between psychopathology and communication patterns within the family have proved far more tenuous than at first seemed likely. However, interesting data are emerging from studies of the consequences of different types and degrees of parental control: while the issues are complex, research findings are pointing towards a balance between the extremes of discipline and permissiveness that have been advocated in the past, with weight on the importance of the timing and appropriateness of each, and an overall emphasis on the quality of the parent–child relationship.

Experimental studies have been concerned primarily with the effectiveness of different types of parental control in the immediately ensuing period, or at a later time in a similar context. It is generally agreed that both reward for good behaviour (*e.g.* Aronfreed, 1968) and punishment for deviant behaviour can be effective. Punishment is more effective if given immediately rather than later, at fairly high intensity, consistently, and especially if accompanied by cognitive explanations. Relationship with the punisher, and the context, are also important issues (*e.g.* Parke, 1969; Hoffmann, 1970; Martin, 1975). Punishment for aggressive behaviour must be made with great care, for whilst reducing aggression towards or in the presence of the punisher, it may result in increased aggression elsewhere (Ilfield, 1970; Feshbach, 1970).

The important implication of such studies is that family members should respond appropriately to different types of antisocial behaviour, distinguishing between those that are most effectively met by attention, ignoring or punishment. It is, however, equally important that positive social behaviour should be encouraged, and this also requires fine discrimination permitting appropriate rewards. Furthermore the verbal content of the parents' remarks should be consistent with the associated affect and non-verbal signals (Bugental *et al.*, 1971; Bugental and Love, 1975). And both punishment and reward are more likely to be effective in the context of warm and intimate parent–child relationships.

Important as experimental studies are, it is also essential to know what happens in real life situations. In recent years sophisticated studies of family interaction patterns have begun to appear, and two may be mentioned here. Patterson (*e.g.* 1975) has used both observational and experimental techniques to study antisocial behaviour. First a group of 'coercive' types of behaviour, found with high frequency in aggressive children and used by them to control family members, were identified—*e.g.* Disapproval, Negativism, Non-compliance, Physical Negative, Tease and Humiliate. Patterson then attempted to account for variations in the frequency of these coercive skills. By studying sequences in dyadic interchanges between family members, he identified two kinds of stimuli—those associated with the initiation of coercive behaviour, and those associated with its immediate recurrence or maintenance. Other variables, such as hunger and fatigue, may influence the effectiveness of such stimuli. Laboratory experiments showed at least some of these stimuli to be effective, and an elaborate analysis of one case proved their predictive power.

The utility of this approach for understanding the genesis of behaviour disorders remains to be proven. The extent to which the behaviour studied proved to be under stimulus control might indicate that the analysis was of interest only for understanding the immediate determinants of aggression, and not those of long-term propensity. However Patterson has also shown that when a child shows an 'hostile' response, family members in problem families are five times more likely to respond in a manner which will increase the probability of another hostile response than are family members of non-problem families. Furthermore, for the clinical sample parental attempts to punish coercive behaviour were followed by bursts of such behaviours, whilst in the normal sample it was suppressed. This suggests further avenues for inquiry concerning the bases of this difference.

In another study involving the analysis of sequences of behaviour in family settings, Lytton and Zwirner (1975) emphasize that the tactics which bring immediate compliance are not necessarily those that will bring overall obedience in the long run. The probability of compliance by $2\frac{1}{2}$ year olds was highest after parental suggestions and progressively lower after parental commands and reasoning. Physical control and negative actions by the parent before verbal controls were likely to weight the balance towards non-compliance rather than compliance, whilst positive or neutral actions had the opposite effects. By contrast, in the long term the best predictors of overall compliance were the mother's consistency in rule enforcement, the amount she played with the child, and her use of psychological rewards and reasoning. Use of psychological punishment, material rewards and (the father's) physical punishment were negatively associated with compliance.

Ultimately the parental aim must be the development of a mode of conduct that depends not on actual punishments and rewards but on an internal 'conscience' and set of moral values. Research findings on this issue are of variable value, in part because of the difficulty of obtaining reliable measures of a childs' 'moral stage' (Kohlberg, 1971; Kurtlines and Greif, 1974; Hoffmann, 1970). The literature has recently been reviewed by Hogan (1974) and Lickona (1976), and only a few points will be mentioned.

Here as elsewhere parental influences apparently start early: Stayton, Hogan and Ainsworth (1971) found that maternal sensitivity was strongly related to obedience in

11 month olds. In preschool children, an authoritative parental pattern (*i.e.* one in which attempts are made to direct the child's behaviour not in a rigid but in a rational, issue-oriented manner) seems most likely to produce socially responsible attitudes (Baumrind, 1967). With children of elementary school age, frequent use of inductive discipline (that is, techniques which demonstrate the consequences of the child's behaviour for others) by the mother is associated with a moral orientation marked by independence of external sanctions and high feelings of guilt. Fear of detection and punishment, by contrast, is associated with use by the mother of physical punishment, maternal deprivation, or the threat of such punishments. Withdrawal of love does not appear to augment internalization. Although these generalizations are based on correlational evidence (and much of it derived from middle-class families) there are strong reasons for believing that the parental influence is causal (M. L. Hoffman, 1975; *see also* West and Farrington, 1973; Gutkin, 1975). This does not imply that the parental influence is wholly autonomous, for it inevitably results from interaction between parent and child. Indeed Denny and Duffy (1974) showed that the nature of the moral reasoning used by the mother is related to the moral stage reached by the child.

It is far from clear how the parental influence acts. Identification with the parent, fostered by a warm and respectful child–parent relationship, appears to be important in the modelling of aggressive behaviour (*e.g.* Bandura, 1971), and is likely also to be important in the acquisition of moral principles. Hoffmann (1971) believes that identification is not sufficient: while it may contribute to the recognition of moral principles, in the absence of authority it will not lead to their application in practice.

Whilst most research has been concerned with the mother, absence of the father can affect conscience development in boys, but not apparently in girls. As with sex-typical behaviour, the father's role seems to be most effective if he has a warm relationship with the child. However the effects of father absence may be mediated at least in part through effects on the mother, women without husbands expressing less affection to sons than women with husbands (Hoffman, 1971). In addition, siblings can have an influence: for example Dielman, Barton and Cattell (1974), studying a sample of 298 junior high-school children, found that those with sisters scored more highly on 'guilt proneness' than those with brothers. Finally, in adolescence the peer group comes to be increasingly important as a determinant both of moral attitudes and of moral conduct (*e.g.* Reich, 1970). Interestingly, the influence of the peer group on moral behaviour varies with the wider context of culture in which family and peer-group are placed. Thus American children could be induced to misbehave more readily if they believed their behaviour to be monitored by peers, and less readily if they believed it to be monitored by parents. Soviet children were less ready to misbehave under both conditions (Bronfenbrenner, 1970; Bixenstine, DeCarte and Bixenstine, 1976).

CONCLUSION

It has been possible only to indicate the nature of current work on a few selected aspects of family influences on development. In conclusion, it is appropriate to emphasize a few of the caveats implicit in the preceding sections.

In considering family influences, we are concerned with the interacting consequences of multiple interacting factors, with no clear boundaries to our realm of discourse. A certain scepticism about the generality of simple answers even to simple questions is certainly healthy. In dealing with this complexity, some guide lines may be available from General Systems Theory: Wertheim's (1975) classification of family systems is an example of its value. But as yet our knowledge even of which are the relevant independent variables is too crude for any general attempt at formalization to be profitable, and the veneer of sophistication that lip service to a systems approach brings can be misleading.

The need for a range from epidemiological to case history studies has been emphasized: we need to know both what the important variables are, and how they act and interact. In each case we must beware of the seductive appeal of variables that are easy to measure, and pursue rather those likely to be meaningful in the context.

Family influences are exerted through interpersonal relationships. Within a relationship, what individuals do together may be less important than the quality with which they interact, and the actual quality of their interactions may be less important than the quality those interactions are perceived to have. Relationships are mutual, so we must beware of conclusions about effects from purely correlational evidence. Relationships exist in time, so there is a limit to what either short-term experiments, or retrospective questionnaires which evoke answers relating primarily to the present, can tell us (Hinde, in press).

The experiences of a child are likely to be important only in relation to the way in which the child conceptualizes his experience. Meaning is crucial, but this is not an excuse for woolly research. Some experiences have similar meanings to all or virtually all individuals: where they do not, it is the meaning of experience, rather than (or as well as) experience that we must seek to quantify.

Relationships affect relationships, and within a relationship the meaning of experience varies with previous and other concurrent experience—that is, with the context. The plea for a multivariate approach is hackneyed, but the inherent difficulties are so great that it is perhaps not inappropriate to repeat it.

But given an awareness of those difficulties, the possibilities of considerable advance in the next decade or two seem considerable. Clearly if knowledge gained is to continue to be useful as social conditions change, it must be concerned ultimately not with which independent variable in the presence of which other independent variables affects which dependent variable in a particular culture, but rather with the mechanisms of process—mechanisms here implying principles common to diverse social conditions.

ACKNOWLEDGEMENTS

I am grateful to Judy Dunn, Mary Main, Michael Rutter and Joan Stevenson-Hinde for their comments on earlier drafts. During the preparation of this chapter my work was supported by the Medical Research Council, the Royal Society and the Grant Foundation.

REFERENCES

Adams, R. L. and Phillips, B. N. (1972). Motivational and achievement differences among children of various ordinal birth positions. *Child Dev.*, **43**, 155–164.

Ainsworth, M. D. (1962). The effects of maternal deprivation: a review of findings and controversy in the context of research strategy. In *Deprivation of Maternal Care*. Geneva: W.H.O.

Allport, G. W. (1961). *Pattern and growth in personality*. New York: Holt, Rinehart & Winston.

Altus, W. D. (1966). Birth order and its sequelae. *Science*, **151**, 44–48.

Anderson, C. O. and Mason, W. A. (1974). Early experience and complexity of social organization in groups of young rhesus monkeys (*Macaca mulatta*). *J. of comp. physiol. Psychol.*, **87**, 681–690.

Apolloni, T. and Cooke, T. P. (1975). Peer behavior conceptualized as a variable influencing infant and toddler development. *Am. J. Orthopsychiat.*, **45**, 4–17.

Aronfreed, J. (1968). *Conduct and Conscience*. New York: Academic Press.

Badaines, J. (1976). Identification, imitation, and sex-roles preference in father-present and father-absent black and Chicago boys. *J. Psychol.*, **92**, 15–24.

Bau, P. L. and Lewis, M. (1974). Mothers and fathers, girls and boys attachment behavior in the one-year-old. *Merrill-Palmer Quart.*, **20**, 195–204.

Bandura, A. (1971). Vicarious and self-reinforcement processes. In *The Nature of Reinforcement*. Ed. R. Glaser, New York and London: Academic Press.

Banks, S. and Kahn, M. D. (1975). Sister-brotherhood is powerful: sibling subsystems and family therapy. *Family Process*, **14**, 311–337.

Barton, K., Dielman, T. E. and Cattell, R. B. (1974). Child rearing practices and achievement in school. *J. gen. Psychol.*, **124**, 155–165.

Bates, E. (1975). Peer relations and the acquisition of language. In *Friendship and Peer Relations*. Eds. M. Lewis and L. A. Rosenblum. New York: Wiley.

Bateson, G., Jackson, D. D., Haley, J. and Weakland, J. (1956). Toward a theory of schizophrenia. *Behavioral Science*, **1**, 251–264.

Bateson, P. P. G. (1976a). Rules and reciprocity in behavioural development. In *Growing Points in Ethology*. Eds. P. P. G. Bateson and R. A. Hinde, pp. 401–421. Cambridge: Cambridge University Press.

Bateson, P. P. G. (1976b). Specificity and the origins of behaviour. *Adv. Study Behav.*, **6**, 1–20.

Bateson, P. P. G. (1978). How does behaviour develop? In *Perspectives in Ethology*, **3**, *Social Behavior*. Eds. P. P. G. Bateson and P. H. Klopfer 55–66. New York: Plenum.

Baumrind, D. M. (1967). Child care practices anteceding three patterns of preschool behavior. *Genetic Psychol. Monographs*, **75**, 43–88.

Bell, R. Q. (1968). A reinterpretation of the direction of effects in studies of socialization. *Psychol. Rev.*, **75**, 81–95.

Bell, R. Q. (1974). Contributions of human infants to caregiving and social interaction. In *The Effects of the Infant on its Caregiver*. Eds. M. Lewis and L. Rosenblum. New York: Wiley.

Bell, R. Q., Weller, G. M. and Waldrop, M. F. (1971). Newborn and preschooler. *Monogr. Soc. Child Res. Child Dev*. No. 142.

Bené, E. (1965). On the genesis of male homosexuality. *Brit. J. Psychiat.*, **111**, 815–821.

Berkowitz, L. (1973). Control of aggression. In *Review of child development*, vol. 3. Eds. B. M. Caldwell and H. N. Ricciuti. University of Chicago Press.

Berman, C. M. (in press). The analysis of mother–infant interaction in groups: possible influence of yearling siblings. In *Proceedings of the Sixth International Primatological Congress*, 1976. Behaviour volume. London: Academic Press.

Berman, C. M. (1978). The development of social relationships among free-ranging rhesus monkeys. Ph.D. thesis, University of Cambridge.

Bigner, J. J. (1972). Sibling influence on sex-role preference of young children. *J. genet. Psychol.*, **121**, 271–282.

Biller, H. B. (1976). The father and personality development: paternal deprivation and sex role development. In *The role of the father in child development*. Ed. M. Lamb. New York: Wiley.

Biller, H. B. and Weiss, S. D. (1970). The father–daughter relationship and the personality development of the female. *J. genet. Psychol.*, **116**, 79–93.

Bing, E. (1963). Effect of child-rearing practices on the development of differential cognitive abilities. *Child Dev.*, **34**, 631–648.

Birtchnell, J. (1973). How appropriate is the epidemiological approach to the investigation of the familial causation of mental illness? *Brit. J. med. Psychol.*, **46**, 365–371.

Birtchnell, J. (1974a). Some possible early family determinants of marriage and divorce. *Brit. J. med. Psychol.*, **47**, 121–127.

Birtchnell, J. (1974b). The effect of early parent loss upon the direction and degree of sexual identity. *Brit. J. med. Psychol.*, **47**, 129–137.

Birtchnell, J. (1975). Psychiatric breakdown following recent parent death. *Brit. J. med. Psychol.*, **48**, 379–390.

Bixenstine, V. E., de Corte, M. S. and Bixenstine, B. A. (1976). Conformity to peer-sponsored misconduct at four grade levels. *Dev. Psychol.*, **12**, 226–236.

Blanchard, R. W. and Biller, H. B. (1971). Father availability and academic performance among third-grade boys. *Dev. Psychol.*, **4**, 301–305.

Blane, H. T., Barry, H. and Barry, H. (1971). Sex differences in birth order of alcoholics. *Brit. J. Psychiat.*, **119**, 657–661.

Blehar, M. C. (1974). Anxious attachment and defensive reactions associated with day care. *Child Dev.*, **45**, 683–692.

Block, J., Lippe, A. von der and Block, J. H. (1973). Sex role and socialization patterns. *J. consult. clin. Psychol.*, **41**, 321–341.

Bloom, B. S. (1964). *Stability and change in human characteristics*. New York: Wiley.

Bott, E. (1957). *Family and social networks*. London: Tavistock Publications.

Bowlby, J. (1944). Forty-four juvenile thieves: their characters and home life. *Int. J. Psycho-anal.*, **25**, 19–52 and 107–127.

Bowlby, J. (1969). *Attachment and Loss*, vol. I, *Attachment*. London: Hogarth.

Bowlby, J. (1973). *Attachment and Loss*, vol. II. London: Hogarth Press.

Bradley, R. H. and Caldwell, B. M. (1976). Early home environment and changes in mental test performance in children from 6 to 36 months. *Dev. Psychol.*, **12**, 93–97.

Breland, H. M. (1974). Birth order, family configuration and verbal achievement. *Child Dev.*, **45**, 1011–1019.

Bronfenbrenner, U. (1970). Reaction to social pressure from adults versus peers among soviet day school and boarding school pupils in the perspective of an American sample. *J. pers. soc. Psychol.*, **15**, 179–189.

Brown, G. W., Birley, J. L. T. and Wing, J. K. (1972). Influence of family life on the course of schizophrenic disorders: a replication. *Br. J. Psychiat.*, **121**, 241–258.

Brown, G. W., Bhrolchain, M. N. and Harris, T. (1975). Social class and psychiatric disturbance among women in an urban population. *Sociology*, **9**, 225–254.

Bugental, D. B. and Love, L. (1975). Nonassertive expression of parental approval and disapproval and its relationship to child disturbance. *Child Dev.*, **46**, 747–752.

Bugental, D. E., Love, L. E., Kaswan, J. W. and April, C. (1971). Verbal-nonverbal conflict in parental messages to normal and disturbed children. *J. abn. Psychol.*, **77**, 6–10.

Burton, L. (1975). *The Family Life of Sick Children*. London: Routledge & Kegan Paul.

Caldwell, B. M. (1964). The effects of infant care. In *Review of Child Development Research*, vol. 1. Eds. M. L. and L. W. Hoffman. New York: Russell Sage Foundation.

Caldwell, B. M. (1972). What does research teach us about day care: for children under three. *Children Today*, **1**, reprinted Am. Prog. Child Psychiat. and Child Dev., 1973. New York: Brunner/Mazel.

Caldwell, B. M., Wright, C. M., Honig, A. S. and Tannenbaum, J. (1970). Infant day care and attachment. *Am. J. Orthopsychiat.*, **40**, 397–412.

Cattell, R. B. (1963). Theory of fluid and crystallized intelligence: a critical experiment. *J. educ. Psychol.*, **54**, 1–22.

Centerwall, S. A. and Centerwall, W. R. (1960). A study of children with mongolism reared in the home compared to those reared away from the home. *Pediatrics*, **25**, 678–685.

Cicirelli, V. G. (1973). Effects of sibling structure and interaction on children's categorization style. *Devl. Psychol.*, **9**, 132–139.

Cicirelli, V. G. (1974). Relationship of sibling structure and interaction to younger sib's conceptual style. *J. genet. Psychol.*, **125**, 37–49.

Cicirelli, V. G. (1975). Effects of mother and older sibling on the problem solving behaviour of the younger child. *Dev. Psychol.*, **11**, 749–756.

Clarke, A. M. and Clarke, A. D. B. (1976). *Early experience: myth and evidence*. London: Open Books.

Collard, R. B. (1971). Exploratory and play behaviors of infants reared in an institution and in lower- and middle-class homes. *Child Dev.*, **42**, 1003–1015.

Cornelius, S. W. and Denney, N. W. (1975). Dependency in day-care and home-care children. *Dev. Psychol.*, **11**, 575–582.

Cornoldi, C. and Fattori, L. C. (1976). Age spacing in firstborns and symbiotic dependence. *J. pers. soc. Psychol.*, **33**, 431–434.

Crabtree, J. M. and Moyer, K. E. (1977). *Bibliography of Aggressive Behavior*. New York: Alan Rhiss.

Crago, M. A. (1972). Psychopathology in married couples. *Psychol. Bull.*, **77**, 114–128.

Danziger, K. (1976). *Interpersonal communication*. New York, Oxford: Pergamon.

Davis, A. J. and Lange, G. (1973). Parent-child communication and the development of categorization styles in pre-school children. *Child Dev.*, **44**, 624–629.

Denenberg, V. H. (1978). Paradigms and paradoxes in the study of behavioural development. In *The origins of the infant's social responsiveness*. Ed. E. B. Thoman. Hillsdale, N.J.: L. Erlbaum Assoc.

Denny, N. W. and Duffy, D. M. (1974). Possible environmental causes of stages in moral reasoning. *J. genet. Psychol.*, **125**, 277–283.

Deutsch, F. (1975). Birth order effects on measures of social activities for lower-class preschoolers. *J. genet. Psychol.*, **127**, 325–326.

Dielman, T. E., Barton, K. and Cattell, R. B. (1974). Adolescent personality and intelligence scores as related to family demography. *J. genet. Psychol.*, **124**, 151–154.

Douglas, J. W. B. (1968). *The School and the Home*. London: MacGibbon & Kee.

Douglas, J. W. B. (1975). Early hospital admissions and later disturbances of behaviour and learning. *Develop. med. Child Neurol.*, **17**, 456–480.

Duncan, P. (1971). Parental attitudes and interactions in delinquency. *Child Dev.*, **42**, 1751–1765.

Dunn, J. (1975). Consistency and change in styles of mothering. In *Parent-Child Interaction*. Ciba Foundation Symposium. Amsterdam: ASP.

Dunn, J. B. (1976). How far do early differences in mother-child relations affect later development? In *Growing Points in Ethology*, pp. 481–496. Eds. P. P. G. Bateson and R. A. Hinde. Cambridge: Cambridge University Press.

Dunn, J. B. (1977). Patterns of early interaction: continuities and consequences. In *Studies in mother–infant interaction*. Ed. H. R. Schaffer. London: Academic Press.

Dunn, J. B. (in press). Changes in family relationships with the birth of a sibling. In *Atti del IV Congresso Internazionale della ISSBD*. Franco Angeli, Minlano, 1977, vol. 1.

Dunn, J. (1980). Individual differences in temperament. (This volume.)

Dunn, J. B. and Richards, M. P. M. (1977). Observations on the developing relationship between mother and baby in the neonatal period. In *Studies in mother–infant interaction*. Ed. H. R. Schaffer. London: Academic Press.

Dunn, J. B. and Kendrick, C. (1977). Play in the home and its implications for learning. In *Biology of Play*. Eds. B. Tizard and D. Harvey. Spastics International Medical Publications.

Fady, J.-C. (1969). Les jeux sociaux: le compagnon de jeux chez les jeunes. Observations chez *Macaca irus*. *Folia Primat.*, **11**, 134–143.

Feshbach, S. (1970). Aggression. In *Carmichael's Manual of Child Psychology*, vol. 2. Ed. P. H. Mussen. New York: Wiley.

Fleck, S. (1976). A general systems approach to severe family pathology. *Am. J. Psychiat.*, **133**, 669–673.

Fletcher, R. (1966). *The family and marriage in Britain*. London: Penguin.

Fortes, M. (1974). The first born. *J. Child Psychol. Psychiat.*, **15**, 81–104.

Fox, R. (1970). Comparative family patterns. In *The family and its future*, Ed. K. Elliott. London: Churchill.

Francis, S. H. (1971). The effects of own-home and institution-rearing on the behavioural development of normal and mongol children. *J. Child Psychol. Psychiat.*, **12**, 173–190.

Friedrich, W. N. and Boriskin, J. A. (1976). The role of the child in abuse: a review of the literature. *Am. J. Orthopsychiat.*, **46**, 580–590.

Frommer, E. A., Mendelson, W. B. and Reid, M. A. (1972). Differential diagnosis of psychiatric disturbance in pre-school children. *Br. J. Psychiat.*, **121**, 71–74.

Frommer, E. A. and O'Shea, G. (1973). The importance of childhood experience in relation to problems of marriage and family building. *Br. J. Psychiat.*, **123**, 157–160.

Gassner, S. and Murray, E. (1969). Dominance and conflict in the interactions between parents of normal and neurotic children. *J. abn. Psychol.*, **74**, 33–41.

Gath, A. (1978), *Down's Syndrome and the Family—Early Years*. London: Academic Press.

Gay, M. J. and Tonge, W. L. (1967). The late effects of loss of parents in childhood. *Br. J. Psychiat.*, **113**, 753–759.

George, C. and Main, M. (1979). Social interactions of young abused children. *Child Dev.*, **50**, 306–318.

Gilmore, J. and Zigler, E. (1964). Birth order and social reinforcer effectiveness in children. *Child Dev.*, **35**, 193–200.

Glass, D. C., Neulinger, J. and Brim, O. G. (1974). Birth order, verbal intelligence and educational aspiration. *Child Dev.*, **45**, 807–811.

Glenn, N. D. (1975). Psychological well-being in the post-parental stage: some evidence from national surveys. *J. Marriage and the Family*, **37**, 105–112.

Goody, E. (1974). Parental roles in anthropological perspective. In *The Family in Society*. London: H.M.S.O.

Goody, J. (1969). *Comparative Studies in Kinship*. Stanford: Stanford Univ. Press.

Greenberg, M. and Morris, N. (1974). Engrossment: the newborn's impact upon the father. *Am. J. Orthopsychiat.*, **44**, 520–531.

Gutkin, D. C. (1975). Maternal discipline and children's judgement of moral intentionality. *J. genet. Psychol.*, **127**, 55–62.

Harlow, H. F. and Harlow, M. K. (1965). The affectional systems. In *Behavior of Nonhuman Primates*, vol. 2. Ed. A. M. Schrier, H. F. Harlow and F. Stollnitz. New York: Academic Press.

Harlow, H. F. and Harlow, M. K. (1969). Effects of various mother–infant relationships on rhesus monkey behaviors. In *Determinants of Infant Behaviour*, vol. 4. Ed. B. M. Foss. London: Methuen.

Harlow, H. F. and Suomi, S. J. (1971). Social recovery by isolation-reared monkeys. *Proc. Natl. Acad. Sci.*, **68**, 1534–1538.

Harper, L. V. (1975). The scope of offspring effects: from caregiver to culture. *Psychol. Bull.*, **82**, 784–801.

Hartup, W. W. (1976). Peer interaction and the behavioural development of the individual child. In *Psychopathology and Child Development*. Eds. E. Schopler and R. J. Reichler, pp. 203–218. New York: Plenum Press.

Harwood, B. T. (1973). Expressed preferences for information seeking behaviors and their relationship to birth order. *J. genet. Psychol.*, **123**, 123–131.

Heilbrun, A. B. (1971). Maternal child rearing and creativity in sons. *J. genet. Psychol.*, **119**, 175–179.

Heilbrun, A. B. and Waters, D. (1968). Underachievement as related to perceived maternal child rearing and academic conditions of reinforcement. *Child Dev.*, **39**, 913–921.

Hetherington, E. M. (1972). Effects of father absence on personality development in adolescent daughters. *Dev. Psychol., 7,* 313–326.

Hetherington, E. M., Stouwie, R. J. and Ridberg, E. H. (1971). Patterns of family interaction and child-rearing attitudes related to three dimensions of juvenile delinquency. *J. abn. Psychol., 78,* 160–176.

Hilgard, J., Newman, M. and Fisk, F. (1960). Strength of adult ego following childhood bereavement. *Am. J. Orthopsychiat., 30,* 788–798.

Hilton, I. (1967). Differences in the behaviour of mothers towards first and later-born children. *J. pers. soc. Psychol., 7,* 282–290.

Hinde, R. A. (1974). *Biological Bases of Human Social Behaviour.* New York: McGraw-Hill.

Hinde, R. A. (1977). Mother–infant separation and the nature of interindividual relationships: experiments with rhesus monkeys. *Proc. Roy. Soc. Lond. B., 196,* 29–50.

Hinde, R. A. (1978). Social development: a biological approach. In *Human Growth and Development* (Wolfson College Lecture, 1976). Eds. J. Bruner and A. Garton. London: Oxford University Press.

Hinde, R. A. (in press). *Towards Understanding Relationships.* London: Academic Press.

Hinde, R. A. and Herrmann, J. (1977). Frequencies, durations and derived measures and their correlations in studying dyadic and triadic relationships. In *Studies in mother–infant interaction.* Ed. H. R. Schaffer. London: Academic Press.

Hinde, R. A., Leighton-Shapiro, M. and McGinnis, L. (1978). Effects of various types of separation experience on rhesus monkeys 5 months later. *J. Child Psychol. Psychiat., 9,* 199–211.

Hinde, R. A. and McGinnis, L. (1977). Some factors influencing the effects of temporary mother–infant separation—some experiments with rhesus monkeys. *Psychol. Med., 7,* 197–212.

Hinde, R. A. and Proctor, L. P. (1977). Changes in the relationships of captive rhesus monkeys on giving birth. *.Behaviour, 61,* 304–321.

Hinde, R. A. and Spencer-Booth, Y. (1971). Effects of brief separation from mother on rhesus monkeys. *Science, 173,* 111–118.

Hinde, R. A. and Stevenson-Hinde, J. (1973). *Constraints on Learning: Limitations and Predispositions* (Eds.) London: Academic Press.

Hinde, R. A. and Stevenson-Hinde, J. (1976). Towards understanding relationships: dynamic stability. In *Growing Points in Ethology.* Eds. P. P. G. Bateson and R. A. Hinde, pp. 451–479. Cambridge: Cambridge University Press.

Hoffman, L. W. (1974). Effects of maternal employment on the child—a review of the research. *Dev. Psychol., 10,* 204–228.

Hoffman, L. (1975). 'Enmeshment' and the too richly cross-joined system. *Family Process, 14,* 457–468.

Hoffman, M. L. (1970). Moral development. In *Carmichael's Handbook of Child Psychology,* Ed. P. H. Mussen. Vol. 2. New York: Wiley.

Hoffman, M. L. (1971a). Identification and conscience development. *Child Dev., 42,* 1071–1082.

Hoffman, M. L. (1971b). Father absence and conscience development. *Dev. Psychol., 4,* 400–406.

Hoffman, M. L. (1975). Moral internalization, parental power, and the nature of parent–child interaction. *Dev. Psychol., 11,* 228–239.

Hogan, R. (1974). Moral conduct and moral character. *Psychol. Bull., 79,* 217.

Honzik, M. P. (1976). Value and limitations of infant tests: an overview. In *Origins of intelligence.* Ed. M. Lewis. New York: Plenum Press.

Huffer, V. (1973). Australian aborigine: transition in family grouping. *Family Process, 12,* 303–315.

Humphrey, M. (1975). The effect of children upon the marriage relationship. *Br. J. med. Psychol., 48,* 273–279.

Ilfield, F. W. (1970). Environmental theories of violence. In *Violence and the Struggle for Existence.* Eds. D. N. Daniels, M. F. Gilula and F. M. Ochberg, Boston: Little, Brown.

Ingram, J. (1975). Husbandry and observation methods of a breeding colony of marmosets (*Callithrax jaechus*) for behavioural research. *Lab. Anim. 9,* 249–259.

Jacob, T. (1975). Family interaction in disturbed and normal families: a methodological and substantive review. *Psychol. Bull., 82,* 33–65.

Jacobs, B. S. and Moss, H. A. (1976). Birth order and sex of siblings as determinants of mother–infant interaction. *Child Dev., 47,* 315–322.

Jacobson, S., Fasman, J. and Di Masco, A. (1975). Deprivation in the childhood of depressed women. *J. nerv. ment. Dis., 160,* 5–14.

Jeffree, D. M. and Cashdan, A. (1971). The home background of the severely abnormal child: a second study. *Br. J. med. Psychol., 44,* 27–34.

Jones, P. A. (1972). Home environment and the development of verbal ability. *Child Dev., 43,* 1081–1086.

Jordan, B. E., Radin, N. and Epstein, A. (1975). Paternal behaviour and intellectual functioning in pre-school boys and girls. *Dev. Psychol., 11,* 407–408.

Kemper, T. D. and Reichler, M. L. (1976). Marital satisfaction and conjugal power as determinants of intensity and frequency of rewards and punishments administered by parents. *J. genet. Psychol., 129,* 221–234.

Klaus, M. and Kennell, J. H. (1976). *Maternal–infant bonding.* St. Louis: C. V. Mosby.

Koch, H. (1956). Attitudes of young children toward their peers as related to certain characteristics of their siblings. *Psychol. Monogr., 70,* 426.

Kohlberg, H. (1971). From is to ought: how to commit the naturalistic fallacy and get away with it in the study of development. In *Cognitive development and epistemology.* Ed. T. Mischel, New York: Academic Press.

Koller, K. M. (1971). Parental deprivation, family background and female delinquency. *Br. J. Psychiat., 118,* 319–327.

Kolvin, I., Ounsted, C., Richardson, L. M. and Garside, R. F. (1971). The family and social background in childhood psychoses. *Br. J. Psychiat., 118,* 396–402.

Koocher, G. P. (1973). Childhood, death and cognitive development. *Dev. Psychol., 9,* 369–375.

Kurtlines, W. and Greif, E. B. (1974). The development of moral thought: review and evaluation of Kohlberg's approach, *Psychol. Bull., 81,* 453–470.

Lamb, M. E. (1976). (Ed.) *The role of the father in child development.* New York: Wiley.

Lamb, M. E. (1977). Father–infant and mother–infant interaction in the first year of life. *Child Dev., 48,* 167–181.

Langlois, J. H., Gottfried, N. W. and Seay, B. (1973). The influence of sex of peer on the social behavior of preschool children. *Dev. Psychol., 8,* 93–98.

Leventhal, G. S. (1970). Influence of brothers and sisters on sex-role behavior. *J. pers. soc. Psychol., 16,* 452–465.

Lewis, M. and Rosenblum, L. R. (1975). *Friendship and Peer Relations.* New York: Wiley.

Lewis, M. and Weinraub, M. (1974). Sex of parent and sex of child: socioemotional development. In *Sex Differences in Behavior,* Eds. P. Richart et al.. New York: Wiley.

Lewis, M. and Weinraub, M. (1976). The father's role in the child's social network. In *The role of the father in child development.* Ed. M. Lamb, New York: Wiley.

Lickona, T. (1976). (Ed.) *Moral development and behavior.* New York: Holt, Rinehart and Winston.

Lynn, D. and Sawrey, W. (1959). The effects of father absence on Norwegian boys and girls. *J. abn. soc. Psychol., 59,* 258–262.

Lystal, M. H. (1975). Violence at home: a review of the literature. *Am. J. Orthopsychiat., 45,* 328–345.

Lytton, H. (1971). Observation studies of parent–child interaction: a methodological review. *Child Dev., 42,* 651–684.

Lytton, H. and Zwirner, W. (1975). Compliance and its controlling stimuli observed in a natural setting. *Dev. Psychol., 11,* 769–779.

McCall, J. N. and Johnson, O. G. (1972). The independence of intelligence from family size and birth order. *J. genet. Psychol., 121,* 207–213.

Macrae, J. W. and Herbert-Jackson, E. (1976). Are behavioural effects of infant day-care program-specific? *Dev. Psychol., 12,* 269–270.

McGurk, H. and Lewis, M. (1972). Birth order: a phenomenon in search of an explanation. *Dev. Psychol., 7,* 366.

McPherson, S. (1970). Communication of intents among parents and their disturbed adolescent children. *J. abn. Psychol., 76,* 98–105.

Marantz, S. A. and Mansfield, A. F. (1977). Maternal employment and the development of sex-role stereotyping in the five- to eleven-year-old girls. *Child Dev., 48,* 668–673.

Marsella, A. J., Dubanoski, R. A. and Mohs, K. (1974). The effects of father presence and absence upon maternal attitudes. *J. genet. Psychol.*, **125**, 257–263.

Martin, B. (1975). Parent–child relations. In *Child Development and Research*, vol. 4. Eds. F. D. Horowitz, M. Hetherington, S. Scarr-Salapatek and G. Sregal. Chicago: University of Chicago Press. pp. 463–540.

Matteson, R. (1974). Adolescent self-esteem, family communication, and marital satisfaction. *J. Psychol.*, **86**, 35–47.

Megargee, E. I., Parker, G. V. C. and Levine, R. V. (1971). Relationship of familial and social factors to socialization in middle-class college students. *J. abn. Psychol.*, **77**, 76–89.

Miller, D. (1970). Parental responsibility for adolescent maturity. In *The Family and its Future*. Ed. K. Elliott. London: Churchill.

Mitchell, G. D. and Brandt, E. M. (1972). Paternal behavior in primates. In *Primate Socialization*. Ed. F. Poirier, New York: Random House.

Money, J., Hampson, J. G. and Hampson, J. L. (1957). Imprinting and the establishment of gender role. *Arch. neurol. Psychiat.*, **77**, 333–336.

Moore, T. (1964). Children of full-time and part-time mothers. *Int. J. soc. Psychiat.*, Congress Issue, 1–10.

Murray, A. D. (1975). Maternal employment reconsidered: effects on infants. *Am. J. Orthopsychiat.*, **45**, 773–790.

Murrell, S. A. (1971). Family interaction variables and adjustment of non-clinic boys. *Child Dev.*, **42**, 1485–1494.

Newson, J. and Newson, E. (1970). Changes in concepts of parenthood. In *The Family and its Future*. Ed. K. Elliott. Ciba Foundation Symposium. London: Churchill.

Olson, D. H. (1972). Empirically unbinding the double bind: review of research and conceptual reformulations. *Family Process*, **11**, 69–94.

Oshman, H. P. and Manosevitz, M. (1976). Father absence: effects of stepfathers upon psychological development in males. *Dev. Psychol.*, **12**, 479–480.

Osofsky, J. D. and Danzger, B. (1974). Relationships between neonatal characteristics and mother–infant interaction. *Dev. Psychol.*, **10**, 123–130.

Osofsky, J. D. and O'Connell, E. J. (1972). Parent–child interaction. *Dev. Psychol.*, **7**, 157–168.

Parke, R. D. (1969). Effectiveness of punishment as an interaction of intensity, timing, agent nurturance, and cognitive structuring. *Child Dev.*, **40**, 211–235.

Patterson, G. R. (1975). A three-stage functional analysis for children's coercive behaviors: A tactic for developing a performance theory. In *New developments in behavioral research: Theory, methods, and applications*. Eds. B. C. Etzel, J. M. LeBlanc and D. M. Baer. New Jersey: Lawrence Erlbaum Associates Inc.

Peterson, D. R. and Becker, W. C. (1965). Family interaction and delinquency. In *Juvenile Delinquency*. Ed. H. C. Quay. Princeton: Van Nostrand.

Quay, H. C. (1965). Personality and delinquency. In *Juvenile Delinquency*. Ed. H. C. Quay. Princeton: Van Nostrand.

Quinton, D. and Rutter, M. (1976). Early hospital admissions and later disturbances of behaviour: an attempted replication of Douglas's findings. *Dev. Med. Child Neurol.*, **18**, 447–459.

Radin, N. (1972). Father–child interaction and the intellectual functioning of four-year-old boys. *Dev. Psychol.*, **6**, 353–361.

Radin, N. (1976). The role of the father in cognitive, academic and intellectual development. In *The role of the father in child development*. Ed. M. Lewis, New York: Wiley.

Raveau, F. H. M. (1970). Future family patterns and society. In *The Family and its Future*. Ed. K. Elliott, Ciba Foundation Symposium. London: Churchill.

Reich, C. A. (1970). *Greening of America*. New York: Random House.

Richards, M. P. M. (1978). Possible effects of early separation on later development of children—a review. In *Early Separation and Special Care Nurseries*, Eds. F. S. W. Brimblecombe and M. P. M. Richards. London: Heinemann Med. Books.

Richman, N. (1974). The effects of housing on pre-school children and their mothers. *Dev. Med. Child Neurol.*, **16**, 53–58.

Richman, N. (1977). Behaviour problems in pre-school children: family and social factors. *Brit. J. Psychiatry*, **131**, 523–527.

Riskin, J. and Faunce, E. E. (1972). An evaluative review of family interaction research. *Family Process*, **11**, 365–455.

Robertson, G. (1972). Parent–child relationships and homosexuality. *Br. J. Psychiat.*, **121**, 525–528.

Robertson, J. (1953). Some responses of young children to loss of maternal care. *Nursing Times*, **49**, 382–386.

Robertson, J. and Robertson, J. (1971). Young children in brief separation: a fresh look. *Psychoanal. Study of the Child*, **26**, 264–315.

Robins, L. N. (1966). *Deviant Children Grown Up*. Baltimore: Williams & Wilkins.

Robins, L. N. and Lewis, R. G. (1966). The role of the antisocial family in school completion and delinquency: a three generation study. *Sociology Quart.*, **7**, 500–514.

Robinson, H. B. and Robinson, N. M. (1971). Longitudinal development of very young children in a comprehensive day care programme: the first two years. *Child Dev.*, **42**, 1673–1683.

Rosen, B. C. (1961). Family structure and achievement motivation. *American Sociological Review*, **26**, 575–585.

Rosenblatt, P. C. and Skoogberg, E. L. (1974). Birth order in cross-cultural perspective. *Dev. Psychol.*, **10**, 48–54.

Rowell, T. E. (1974). Contrasting adult male roles in different species of nonhuman primates. *Arch. Sex. Behav.*, **3**, 143–149.

Ruppenthal, G. C., Harlow, M. K., Eisele, C. D., Harlow, H. F. and Suomi, S. J. (1974). Development of peer interactions of monkeys reared in a nuclear-family environment. *Child Dev.*, **45**, 670–682.

Rutter, M. (1966). Children of sick parents: an environmental and psychiatric study. *Maudsley Monograph* No. 16. London: Oxford University Press.

Rutter, M. (1971). Parent–child separation: psychological effects on the children. *J. Child Psychol. Psychiat.*, **12**, 233–250.

Rutter, M. (1972a). *Maternal deprivation reassessed*. Harmondsworth: Penguin.

Rutter, M. (1972b). Relationships between child and adult psychiatric disorders. *Acta Psychiatrica Scandinavica*, **48**, 3–21.

Rutter, M. (1977a). Separation, loss and family relationships. In *Child Psychiatry*. Ed. M. Rutter and L. Hersov. Oxford: Blackwell.

Rutter, M. (1977b). Other family influences. In *Child Psychiatry. Ibid.*

Rutter, M. (1978). Family, area and school influences in the genesis of conduct disorders. In *Aggression and Antisocial Behaviour in Childhood and Adolescence*. Eds. L. Hersov, M. Berger and D. Shaffer. Oxford: Pergamon.

Rutter, M. and Brown, G. W. (1966). The reliability and validity of measures of family life and relationships in families containing a psychiatric patient. *Social Psychiatry*, **1**, 38–53.

Rutter, M. and Madge, N. (1976). *Cycles of Disadvantage: a review of research*. London: Heinemann.

Rutter, M., Tizard, J. and Whitmore, K. (eds.) (1970). *Education, Health and Behaviour*. London: Longman.

Rutter, M., Yule, B., Quinton, D., Rowlands, O., Yule, W. and Berger, M. (1975). Attainment and adjustment in two geographical areas. III, Some factors accounting for area differences. *Br. J. Psychiat.*, **125**, 520–533.

Sackett, G. P. and Ruppenthal, G. C. (1973). Development of monkeys after varied experiences during infancy. In 'Ethology and Development', Ed. S. A. Barnett. *Clinics in Developmental Medicine*, **49**. London: Heinemann.

Sainsbury, P. and Collins, J. (1966). Some factors relating to mental illness in a new town. *J. Psychosom. Res.*, **10**, 45.

Sameroff, A. J. and Chandler, M. J. (1975). Reproductive risk and the continuum of caretaking causality. In *Review of Child Development Research, 4*. Ed. F. D. Horowitz, M. Hetherington, S. Scarr-Salapatek and G. Sregal. Chicago: Univ. of Chicago Press.

Santrock, J. W. (1972). Relation of type and onset of father absence to cognitive development. *Child Dev.*, **43**, 455–469.

Schachter, S. (1959). *The psychology of affiliation*. Stanford: Stanford Univ. Press.

Schoonover, S. M. (1959). The relationship of intelligence and achievement to birth order, sex of sibling and age interval. *J. educ. Psychol.*, **50**, 143–146.

Schuham, A. I. (1967). The double bind hypothesis a decade later. *Psychol. Bull.*, **68**, 409–416.

Schwab, J. J., Holzer, C. E., Warkeit, G. J. and Schwab, R. J. (1976). Human ecology and depressive symptomatology. In *The range of normal in human behaviour*. Ed. J. H. Masserman, New York: Grune & Stratton.

Schwarz, J. C., Strickland, R. G. and Krolick, G. (1974). Infant day care: behavioral effects at preschool age. *Dev. Psychol.*, **10**, 502–605.

Seligman, M. E. P. (1975). *Helplessness*. San Francisco: Freeman.

Seligman, M. E. P. and Hager, J. L. (1972). *Biological boundaries of learning.* New York: Appleton-Century-Crofts.

Seyfarth, R. (1976). Social relationships among adult female baboons. *Anim. Behav.*, **24**, 917–938.

Skeels, M. (1966). Adult status of children with contrasting early life experiences. *Monogr. Soc. Res. Child Dev.*, **31**.

Slater, E. and Woodside, M. (1951). *Patterns of marriage*. London: Cassell.

Smith, S. M. and Hanson, R. (1975). Interpersonal relationships and child-rearing practices in 214 parents of battered children. *Br. J. Psychiat.* **127**, 513–525.

Snow, C. E. (1972). Mother's speech to children learning language. *Child Dev.*, **43**, 549–565.

Spinetta, J. J. and Rigler, D. (1972). The child-abusing parent. *Psychol. Bull.*, **77**, 296–304.

Stacey, M., Dearden, R., Pill, R. and Robinson, D. (1970). *Hospitals, Children and their Families.* London: Routledge & Kegan Paul.

Staples, F. R. and Walters, R. H. (1961). Anxiety, birth order and susceptibility to social influence. *J. abn. soc. Psychol.*, **62**, 716–719.

Stayton, D. J., Hogan, R. and Ainsworth, M. D. S. (1971). Infant obedience and maternal behavior: the origins of socialization considered. *Child Dev.*, **42**, 1057–1069.

Stedman, D. J. and Eickorn, D. H. (1964). A comparison of the growth and development of institutionalized and home reared mongolids during infancy and childhood. *Am. J. ment. Defic.* **69**, 391–401.

Stephen, W. G. (1973). Parental relationships and early social experiences of activist male homosexuals and male heterosexuals. *J. abn. Psychol.*, **82**, 506–513.

Sutton-Smith, B. and Rosenberg, B. G. (1970). *The Sibling*. New York: Holt, Rinehart & Winston.

Suomi, S. J. (1976). Factors affecting responses to social separation in rhesus monkeys. In *Animal Models in Human Psychopathology*. Ed. G. Serban and A. Kling. New York: Plenum.

Suomi, S. J. (in press). Mechanisms underlying social development: a re-examination of mother–infant interactions in monkeys. Minnesota Sym. *Child Psychol.*, **10**.

Tizard, B. (1977). *Adoption: a second chance*. London: Open Books.

Tizard, B. and Rees, J. (1974). A comparison of the effects of adoption, restoration to the natural mother, and continued institutionalization on the cognitive development of 4-year-old children. *Child Dev.*, **45**, 92–99.

Tizard, B. and Rees, J. (1975). The effect of early institutional rearing on the behaviour problems and affectional relationships of 4-year-old children. *J. Child Psychol. Psychiat.*, **16**, 61–74.

Tizard, J. (1976). Working mothers: effects of day care on young children. In *Mothers in Employment: Trends and Issues*. Ed. N. Fonda and P. Moss, Papers from a Conference held at Brunel University, May, 1976.

Uddenberg, N. (1976). Mother–father and daughter–male relationships: a comparison. *Arch. sex. Behav.*, **5**, 69–79.

Unruh, S. G., Grosse, M. E. and Zigler, E. (1971). Birth order, number of siblings and social reinforcer effectiveness in children. *Child Dev.*, **42**, 1153–1163.

Vaughn, C. E. and Leff, J. P. (1976). The influence of family and social factors on the course of psychiatric illness. A comparison of schizophrenic and depressed neurotic patients. *Br. J. Psychiat.*, **129**, 125–137.

Walberg, A. J. and Marjoribanks, K. (1973). Differential mental abilities and home environment. *Dev. Psychol.*, **9**, 363–368.

Waldrop, M. F. and Bell, R. W. (1966). Effects of family size and density on newborn characteristics. *Am. J. Orthopsychiat.*, **36**, 544–550.

Wallerstein, J. S. and Kelly, J. B. (1975). The effects of parental divorce: experiences of the preschool child. *J. Am. Acad. Child Psychiat.*, **14**, 600–616.

Watzlawick, P., Beavin, J. H. and Jackson, D. D. (1967). *Pragmatics of Human Communication*. New York: Norton.

Waxler, N. E. and Mishler, E. G. (1970). Experimental studies of families. In *Advances in Experimental Social Psychology*, Ed. L. Berkowitz, New York: Academic Press.

Wertheim, E. S. (1975). The science and typology of family systems. 2. Further theoretical and practical considerations. *Family Process*, **14**, 285–300.

West, D. J. and Farrington, D. P. (1973). *Who becomes delinquent?* London: Heinemann.

West, H. (1974). Early peer-group interaction and role-taking skills: an investigation of Israeli children. *Child Dev.*, **45**, 1118–1121.

White, L. and Hinde, R. A. (1975). Some factors affecting mother–infant relations in rhesus monkeys. *Anim. Behav.*, **23**, 527–542.

Wit J. de and Hartup, W. W. (1974). *Determinants and origins of aggressive behavior*. Paris: Mouton.

Wohlford, P., Santrock, J. W., Berger, S. E. and Liberman, D. (1971). Older brother's influence on sex-typed, aggressive and dependent behavior in father-absent children. *Dev. Psychol.*, **4**, 124–134.

Wolkind, S. N. (1974). Sex differences in the aetiology of antisocial disorders in children in long term residential care. *Br. J. Psychiat.*, **125**, 125–130.

Wolkind, S. N., Druk, S. and Chares, L. P. (1976). Childhood separation experiences and psychosocial status in primiparous women: preliminary findings. *Br. J. Psychiat.*, **128**, 391–396.

Wulbert, M., Inglis, S., Kriegsmann, E. and Mills, B. (1975). Language delay and associated mother–child interactions. *Dev. Psychol.*, **11**, 61–70.

Yarrow, L. J., Goodwin, M. S., Manheimer, H. and Milowe, I. D. (1973). Infancy experiences and cognitive and personality development at ten years. In *The Competent infant: research and commentary*. Eds. L. J. Stone, H. T. Smith, and L. B. Murphy. New York: Basic Books.

Yarrow, M. R., Waxler, C. Z. and Scott, P. M. (1971). Child effects on adult behavior. *Dev. Psychol.*, **5**, 300–311.

Zajonc, R. B. (1976). Family configuration and intelligence. *Science*, **192**, 227–236.

6. SCHOOL INFLUENCES

JANET OUSTON, BARBARA MAUGHAN AND PETER MORTIMORE

School is an important part of most children's lives; for eleven years they are expected to spend much of their time in the classroom. But until recently there has been little academic interest in whether some schools are more successful than others in helping children to develop their full potential. Most parents have been concerned with the quality of education their children receive, assuming that the school, its formal curriculum and its general ethos, will have important effects on both personality development and academic attainment. In contrast, educationalists have argued that intellectual ability and family background are the main factors which determine success at school. The recent emphasis on the importance of the preschool years in determining subsequent development has also led to an under-valuing of the possible contribution which schooling might make. Generally, it has been considered that the able child from a middle-class family would be successful anywhere, whereas the less able, working-class child would be very likely to fail. Although there have always been individuals who do not conform to this pattern, it seemed that, for the majority, these were the overwhelmingly powerful influences. This view has been supported by many research studies (*e.g.* Douglas *et al.*, 1968; Ainsworth and Batten, 1974) which show that family background and measured ability were the most important factors in explaining differences in attainment during adolescence. However, both these studies suggested that some schools might foster better attainment than others, but neither were able to follow up this possibility. Subsequent research, which will be reviewed in this chapter, has confirmed that schools do differ in how successful they are with very similar groups of pupils. In examining differences of this kind it is usual to compare schools in terms of their mean scores on a variety of measures. Even if these mean scores are found to be significantly different from one another this does not imply that, within each school, the range of scores between individual children has altered. A successful school may raise the level of attainments of all its pupils even though the performance of the most able remains superior.

LARGE SCALE SURVEYS OF SCHOOLING AND ATTAINMENT

In the United States anxiety about the low academic performance of children from minority groups led to the setting up of the Equality of Educational Opportunity Survey (Coleman, 1966). Its aim was to examine the schooling provided for children from ethnic minority groups and to identify ways in which it might be improved. However, the results were very different from those which had been expected, since no relationship was found between the amount of resources available to schools and the attainments of their pupils. Differences in attainments could be explained by the personal and family characteristics of the pupils regardless of the level of school resources. There was little evidence that schools attended by minority group children were, on the indices used, much less favoured than those of other children.

Jencks and his colleagues (1972) re-examined the data collected for both Project Talent and the Coleman Report, attempting to relate educational attainment to both family background and schooling. They concluded that, if all high schools were equally effective, differences in attainment would be reduced by less than one per cent. Jencks concluded that schools merely reflect the inequalities which exist between families, and have very little independent influence on children's development.

COMPENSATORY EDUCATION PROGRAMMES

The widely-held view that compensatory education programmes have little long-term effect has also contributed to the popular belief that schools in general are unlikely to have much impact on the course of children's development.

During the last fifteen years compensatory education programmes for young children have been introduced throughout the USA; 'Head Start' for children between the ages of 3 and 5 years and 'Follow Through' for those up to 7. These programmes have been directed towards children from poor families, with the intention of reducing the inequality in educational attainment which existed between these children and those from more favoured circumstances. It was assumed that boosting the attainments of disadvantaged children before the start of compulsory schooling would enable these children to keep up with the performance of other children.

The effectiveness of these programmes has been evaluated both nationally and project by project; early reports (*e.g.* that of the Westinghouse Learning Corporation, 1969) generally concluded that they had not fulfilled the high hopes which had been held for them. Although many of the programmes did promote measurable gains in attainment these dissipated during the first two years of regular schooling so that by the age of 7 or 8 the gap between the disadvantaged children and their more advantaged peers again started to widen. Several reasons have been suggested to explain this finding: that the programmes themselves were not very effective, that the curriculum of the early years of regular schooling was not designed to follow on from the preschool programmes, or that the more advantaged children merely caught up with the progress made by the 'Head Start' children. Miller and Dyer (1975) examined the effectiveness of different types of 'Head Start' programme, demonstrating that the most structured approaches had the greatest immediate impact on attainment test scores, whereas the much less structured Montessori programmes showed greater longer term gains.

The findings were not clear cut, showing variations according to the sex, age and subsequent educational experience of the children involved: they also reported that children who were not 'Head Start' participants tended to catch up those who were during the first two years of school. The 'Follow Through' series of programmes were devised for children in the first two or three years of regular schooling, but using similar approaches to teaching as had been used in 'Head Start'. Stallings (1975) reported similar findings to those of Miller and Dyer; that structured 'Follow Through' programmes led to greater gains in tests of arithmetic and reading, while less structured programmes boosted scores on non-verbal reasoning and on several behavioural measures.

The possible long-term advantages of special programmes for young children is still being examined, many recent reports suggesting that earlier conclusions might have been unduly pessimistic. Cookson (1978) and Lewin (1977) both give details of follow up studies of adolescents who had taken part in 'Head Start' programmes. They report that, although the initial gains seemed to be lost rather quickly after the start of regular schooling, by the age of 14 the 'Head Start' children were, in one study, a year ahead of others in tests of writing, language and arithmetic skills. They were also far less likely to be receiving special education and to be more realistic in their career expectations. The importance of parental involvement in preschool programmes is also stressed and it may be this factor which is of crucial importance in determining their long-term success. Evaluators are also being urged to consider a wider range of outcomes; House, Glass, McLean and Walker (1978), in their review of the evaluation of 'Follow Through', point out that there may be many advantages to be gained from intervention programmes other than improved scores on attainment tests, and that these should also be included in any subsequent evaluation.

STUDIES OF SCHOOL DIFFERENCES

Recent work, both in the USA and in England and Wales has reopened the question of differences between schools in their impact on children's development. This has happened for several different reasons. First, it is possible that the measures of both individuals and schools used in the American surveys might actually conceal real differences between schools. Recent studies which have used examination results rather than IQ tests as their outcome measures support this suggestion. Secondly, it might be important to examine the effects of schools on children even if families exert a more powerful influence on their development. Schools may be more open to modification than homes and families and even small improvements in schooling might be of value to the individual child. Finally, if the recent findings on the long-term effects of 'Head Start' are confirmed by other research teams, it seems very likely that some schools for older children may also have positive effects on their development.

This chapter will review many different studies, all of which have been concerned with differences in outcomes between schools. None of the studies look at the differences between children who go to school and those who do not; all assume that children receive approximately the same amount of schooling. Rutter and Madge (1976) and Jencks *et al.* (1972) both review comparisons between children who attend school and those who do not; nearly all research on this topic shows that children who do not go to school have a depressed level of attainment compared with those who attend regularly. The impact of political and economic factors on schools will also not be examined here (*see* Eggleston, 1977, for a review of these).

OUTCOMES OF SCHOOLING

Schools are expected to influence many different aspects of the development of children in their care. These range from the very practical, such as teaching the basic skills, to the greater intellectual demands of learning history, mathematics or a foreign language. Schools are also expected to influence their pupils in many broader ways, to direct their moral and social development and to help them become well-functioning adults (see Dreeben, 1968). It has not been possible for studies of school influences to look at such a wide variety of objectives, and existing studies of schools have generally been concerned with such things as examination pass rates, delinquency and attendance rates. This limited range of measures reflects the requirements of a comparative methodology (see Tizard et al., 1975, for a discussion of this point) and also the difficulty in collecting more complex data. The assumption is generally made that, firstly these are widely accepted objectives of schooling, and secondly, that schools which are successful in these will also be successful in their less tangible objectives.

The 'outcomes' of schooling which have been considered by researchers fall into three categories: first of all there are those which are concurrent with being a pupil, for example, attendance and behaviour in school. These can be seen as indicators of the child's immediate response to school, but may well bear no relationship either to behaviour outside school or to subsequent adult life. Indeed, a study of high school drop-outs in the USA has shown that they tend to fare rather better in the short term than other students who completed high school but did not go to college. Their higher rates of pay were accounted for by the longer time which they had had at work; in this study it did not seem that dropping out of school had a positively harmful effect as might have been predicted (Bachman, 1971). Reynolds et al. (1976) and our own study of 12 London schools (Rutter et al., 1979) have shown that ordinary secondary schools do differ considerably in their attendance rates, and the London research also demonstrated clear differences between schools in their pupil's behaviour. Our measures of behaviour covered many aspects of school life such as behaviour in lessons, graffiti and damage to school property and so on. Heal (1978) has also shown differences between primary schools in their pupils' behaviour. Concurrent behaviour has also been used as an indicator of outcome in studies of other kinds of institutions such as children's homes, hospitals, and special schools for delinquents (the 'approved school' studies). As all these institutions have a therapeutic purpose one of their aims is the modification of children's current behaviour, and this can be considered as an outcome which may be quite independent of longer term consequences such as rates of reconviction. Several of these studies are reported in Tizard et al. (1975).

The second type of outcome occurs concurrently with schooling, but is likely to have more far reaching consequenses. What is learnt at school comes into this category, both in terms of formal knowledge of the school curriculum and also all the more informal knowledge which children acquire at school. We have used exam pass rates and delinquency rates as indicators of this type of outcome. Being a delinquent during the school years does not, of course, usually lead to a criminal adult life any more than obtaining five examination passes at 'Ordinary' level leads directly to successful employment, but both are factors which may be influenced by the school and also have an effect on the young person's life long after leaving school.

Several research teams have reported differences between schools in academic attainment. Our own study (Rutter et al., 1979) has shown consistent differences between schools in their academic attainment. Reynolds et al. (1976) have reported similar findings for their study of secondary modern schools in South Wales, as has Davis (1977) in Leicestershire. Brimer et al. (1978) also showed that schools differ in the success of the pupils in the 'Ordinary' level exam. Several studies have also demonstrated differences between schools in their delinquency rates: Power et al. (1972) showed that a very small number of schools accounted for the majority of delinquent boys in an inner London borough, similar findings have been reported by Gath et al. (1977) in his study of an outer London suburb, and also by Reynolds et al. (1976), Rutter et al. (1979) and Cannan (1970). Farrington (1972) suggested that schools may have some part to play in the development of delinquency but in subsequent reports of this study (Farrington and West, 1973) the importance of school factors has received little emphasis, all differences between schools being explained by the characteristics of the children admitted.

The third type of outcome includes all those possible effects of schooling which only become apparent during adult life. These might include, for example, success in employment or in family life. Gray et al (1980) have recently interviewed a sample of school leavers from the London Secondary Schools Study to investigate this issue. Follow-up studies of this kind will enable this long-term outcome of schooling to be examined in more detail than is possible in retrospective studies.

The variations between schools in their exam pass rates or their delinquency rates are striking but in themselves they do not indicate a school influence on children. This is because schools also vary greatly in their intakes. Schools with a large proportion of highly intelligent pupils are likely to have a much higher exam pass rate than schools with a majority of less able children. The key question is whether schools differ from one another *after* allowances have been made for the differences between the children entering each school.

CONTROLLING FOR DIFFERENCES IN INTAKE

One of the simplest methods of controlling for preexisting differences between the children admitted to a school is to limit the sample so that differences on any particular variable are reduced to a minimum. Reynolds et al. (1976) argue that their schools are homogenous in intake and that it is not necessary to control for differences between the schools, whereas Brimer *et al.* (1978) limit their study to a sample of children taking GCE 'O' level examinations in London. Most research workers have, however, accepted that their schools do differ in intake and have attempted to allow for these differences before making comparisons between schools. The 'controlling' variable is generally chosen on the basis of its correlation with the outcome measure, and, in the case of examination performance the obvious control variable is a measure of ability taken on entry to the secondary school. The London study (Rutter *et al.*, 1979) found a strong relationship between examination performance and measures of verbal reasoning at the age of 10 years so this verbal reasoning score was used as a control variable. In other cases statistical controls are much more difficult to apply as there are few good predictors available and they may not have such direct intuitive validity. The second problem associated with the control of pre-existing differences between schools is the choice of statistical technique. There has been considerable debate about the most appropriate method (*see* Nunnally, 1975) and also whether analysis should be based on the school, the classroom or the pupil as the unit of analysis. This question is considered in detail by Gray and Satterly (1976) in their review of Bennett's (1976) study of teacher styles and pupil progress.

TWO CONTROLLED STUDIES OF SCHOOL OUTCOMES

Reynolds *et al.* (1976) have reported data on the attendance, delinquency, academic attainment and employment rates of 9 secondary modern schools in South Wales which admit very similar pupils. Attendance rates varied from 77% to 89%, the number of first offenders per annum from 4% to 10%, from 8% to 53% obtained entry to the local technical college, and unemployment rates 4 months after leaving school varied from nil to 7%. He demonstrated that the schools were comparable in intake on the Raven's Progressive Matrices Test. Also, their catchment areas had very similar proportions of the population employed in either semi-skilled or unskilled work.

The first report on the London schools study (Rutter *et al.*, 1975) showed similar results to that of Douglas (1964); that primary schools varied both in their levels of attainment and in the number of children reported as showing difficult behaviour at school. As these data were collected at the end of primary schooling, when the children were 10 years old, it was not possible to tell whether the differences between schools reflected differences in intake, differences in the education provided, or a combination of both factors. It was, however, possible to follow up these children at the age of 14 years using the 10-year-old data as a baseline against which to assess the progress made in the secondary school. Differences between schools were found in both attainment and in behaviour. A second follow-up of the same children at the

age of 16 years again demonstrated significant differences between schools in examination pass rates, attendance rates and the rates of delinquency, even after controlling for differences in intake (Rutter *et al.*, 1979). The measure of in-school behaviour referred to earlier also showed marked differences between schools, but, because it was not based on the performance of individuals it could not be directly controlled on a pupil-by-pupil basis. It is interesting to note that there was no significant relationship between the relative position of schools on this measure and the proportion of pupils in the cohort who had been reported as showing difficult behaviour in school at the age of 10 years. This supports the suggestion that the behaviour observed in the secondary school was a response to the secondary school, not merely a continuation of patterns of behaviour established at primary school.

BALANCE OF INTAKE

The statistical controls which have been discussed above all relate to *individual* children. There is a second characteristic of school intakes which has not so far been considered; that is the effect of variations in the balance of intake (*e.g.* with respect to the proportion of less able children) on the *total group* of children. The London study (Rutter *et al.*, 1979) showed that the balance of the intake related to the measures of school outcome. This was particularly evident in the area of academic attainment where a very adverse balance appeared to depress the performance of all the children. As none of the schools in this study received a very favourable intake it was not possible to look at the effects of balance at both ends of the range. But even after taking differences in balance into account, some schools still appeared to be more successful than others.

Two other interesting points resulted from our study of intake balance. First of all, we found that it was the intellectual balance of the intake, rather than the social mix, which was the important factor. Schools which admitted a high proportion of children with low academic attainments were much less successful than other schools even after allowing for individual differences between the children. This finding was not repeated when social mix was considered, in that schools with a relatively high proportion of children from middle-class families were not particularly successful once individual differences had been taken into account.

Secondly, there was no relationship between our measure of school practice (to be discussed in detail later) and our measures of balance. It did not appear that the type of children admitted influenced the schools' day-to-day practice. Rather, it seemed that the intake balance affected the peer group and that it was this aspect of the school which was related to outcome. This relationship was particularly strong with respect to delinquency, and it seems very likely that the differences in outcome observed resulted from the nature of the peer group rather than directly from differences in school practice.

Many other writers have stressed the importance of the peer groups in the development of delinquent behaviour (Sugarman, 1967) and our findings add support to their views.

RELATIONSHIPS BETWEEN OUTCOMES

The studies reviewed above show that schools do differ in their outcomes and that significant differences remain even after taking into account the characteristics of the intake to the schools. Our own study of 12 London schools (Rutter *et al.*, 1979) and the South Wales study (Reynolds *et al.*, 1976) both examined several outcomes, and both showed that schools which had good academic attainment also had high attendance rates and low levels of delinquency, the rank correlations of schools' relative positions ranging from 0·50 to 0·85 indicating that schools had similar, but not identical, positions on each measure of outcome. In-school behaviour and subsequent employment also showed similar patterns. These findings suggest that schools have rather consistent patterns of performance across a variety of indicators of outcome.

STABILITY OF SCHOOL DIFFERENCES

So far this chapter has focused on the outcome of schooling of a single age group of children. The proposal that the differences found relate to school functioning would be considerably strengthened if it could be shown that a similar pattern existed for other age groups of children passing through the same schools. Three of the studies already mentioned have considered this question and in all three stable patterns of outcome were found. Power *et al.* (1972) looked at the stability of delinquency rates in a London borough over an eleven year period from 1958 to 1969 and found a marked similarity in rates from year to year. Reynolds *et al.* (1976) collected data on his schools over a nine-year period whereas Rutter and his colleagues (1979) were only able to examine outcomes over a three-year period but in both studies stable patterns emerged. These three sets of findings certainly support the hypothesis that schools do influence their pupils' performance in very consistent ways from year to year. They also suggest that the outcome measures collected are good indicators of a school's impact on the progress of its pupils as a whole rather than just reflections of the performance of one particular age-group of pupils.

THE RELATIONSHIP BETWEEN SCHOOL PROCESSES AND OUTCOME

The research reviewed so far suggests that schools differ in their outcomes even after allowances have been made for differences in intake and that the level of these outcomes remains fairly stable from year to year. What is it about some schools which enables them to be consistently more successful than others? It has already been suggested that this cannot be accounted for by differences in the intake of schools, nor by the differences in the balance of intake. One possible factor which has been considered is that of a neighbourhood effect; might the apparent differences between schools actually reflect differences in the schools' catchment areas? Cannan (1970), Power *et al.* (1972) and Rutter *et al.*, (1979) have all looked at this possibility and all report the same negative findings. Delinquency rates did vary from ward to ward but these variations did not account for the differences between schools. Power reported that some schools with low delinquency rates actually drew many of their pupils from high delinquency areas and vice versa, suggesting that schools were having an effect which was independent of any possible area effects. Other outcomes of schooling have not been examined for a similar neighbourhood effect, but it does seem to be unlikely in view of the negative findings on delinquency. The source of the differences in outcomes between schools appears to lie within the school itself, and the remainder of this chapter will be concerned with studies which suggest the particular aspects of schooling which might be most powerful in promoting good progress.

In general, school studies fall into three broad categories. First of all there are those which are based on large scale surveys such as the Coleman study (Coleman, 1966) and the follow-up survey to the Plowden Report (Ainsworth and Batten, 1974). The second group of studies are those which are concerned with the functioning of single schools such as the work of Hargreaves (1967) and Lacey (1970). This approach permits very detailed descriptions to be made of the functioning of particular groups within the school but does not provide any guide as to how applicable these findings might be to other similar schools. The third type of studies are those which are essentially a compromise between the survey and the case study in that a small number of schools examined allowing comparisons to be made between schools using data which is more detailed than that which can be obtained from surveys. Ideally, all three approaches need to be used as each has advantages which cannot be matched by the others.

School resources

Coleman (1966), Shaycoft (1967) and Jencks *et al.* (1972) report that differences between the schools in the Equality of Educational Opportunity Survey and in Project Talent in their financial resources did not appear to be related to outcome. This has sometimes been interpreted as meaning that schools made no difference to outcome but, as Shaycoft (1967) points out, it merely suggests that these are not the important variables for those who are concerned with school differences to consider. Both Reynolds *et al.* (1976) and Rutter *et al.* (1979) support this conclusion since both research projects were undertaken within the same Local Education Authorities; the school differences found could not be explained in either study by differences in financial support. Summers and

Wolfe (1977) in their analysis of the effects of schooling in Philadelphia have shown that some resource variables do relate to differences in outcome when they are linked in the statistical analysis to sub-groups of children rather than to the school as a whole. They demonstrated that changes in attainment were related to differences in resources and in teacher characteristics but that these relationships became weaker when data about individual children were aggregated to produce group scores. The more aggregated the data the more powerful the background factors of family income, race and IQ appeared. This study suggests that schools do not have a similar impact on all their pupils and that there are powerful interactions between pupil characteristics and school characteristics. This has already been noted by researchers involved in case studies of single schools (*e.g.* Hargreaves, 1967) but has not yet been followed up by those concerned with comparative studies of a larger number of schools. The London research, for example, assumed that all school process variables affect all children in the school in very similar ways; the design made it impossible to examine the impact of particular processes on particular groups of pupils. As studies of school process become more sophisticated it will be important to consider this question in more detail.

School size

Many different aspects of schooling have been examined during the last 20 years, an early concern being that of school size. Barker and Gump (1964) showed that pupils in large schools were less likely to be involved in after-school activities than were those attending small schools. Ross *et al.* (1972), in her study of 12 comprehensive schools also reported similar findings, but noted that most of their large schools were in urban areas and it may be the location, rather than the size of the school which accounts for the difference. Also, English schools seem to have far fewer after-school activities than schools in the USA so it may be unwise to make direct comparisons between them. Our study (Rutter *et al.*, 1979) of London schoolchildren showed very little participation in activities of this kind and there were no relationships with school size. Galloway (1976) in his study of persistent absenteeism in 30 secondary schools found no relationship between non-attendance and size of school.

Class size and pupil–teacher ratio

There is very little evidence that either class size or pupil–teacher ratio are related to successful school outcomes. Within the very limited range of class size found in most schools there is some evidence to suggest that larger class size is associated with better attainments (Rutter and Madge, 1976). This finding may well reflect the fact that schools with particular difficulties are often given extra teachers, which are not available in more successful schools. It also seems likely that only very small classes would permit radical changes in teaching style.

GROUPING PRACTICES

Another topic which has been examined in several studies is the impact of different grouping practices on children's learning. Lunn (1970) showed no differences in outcome of junior school classes taught in streamed and mixed ability groups. A recently reported study of Banbury School (Postlethwaite and Denton, 1978) shows that the types of grouping used during the first two years of the secondary school influenced the subject's choices made by children at the end of the third year, and also, to a lesser extent, the examination pass rates at the end of the fifth year. There was a trend for children at both ends of the ability range to do better if taught in mixed ability classes, but there were no differences in the performance of the children from the middle of the ability range. These findings certainly suggest the value of further work on this topic as they refer to the effects of grouping during the first two years only, since all the pupils were taught in streamed groups or sets from the third year onwards.

Hargreaves (1967) and Lacey (1970) have also been concerned with grouping practices and their impact on children's progress. Both studies showed that sub-groups evolved in accord with the streaming system used by the schools, the bottom streams becoming delinquent and developing anti-school norms. Neither of these studies were concerned with the longer term outcomes of schooling but Lacey's follow-up study of the same school after it had changed to mixed ability grouping showed that the less able boys improved their examination performance, whereas the more able boys' pass rate was unaffected (Lacey, 1974). This study, in contrast to the Banbury study, was undertaken in a selective school so that the definition of 'less able' is rather different in the two studies. The less able children at Banbury were defined as those with verbal reasoning quotients of less than 85, whereas the 'less able' at Lacey's school were actually above average in measured IQ. Ross *et al.* (1972) also suggests that mixed ability grouping may help to prevent the formation of particularly difficult classes.

TEACHER EXPECTATIONS

The research evidence on the effects of teacher expectations on pupils' attainment shows no clear pattern. Rosenthal and Jacobson (1968) reported that experimentally induced expectations had positive effects on children's attainment test scores. Subsequent attempts to replicate these results have generally been unsuccessful and their validity has been questioned (Brophy and Good, 1974). In contrast, expectations already held by teachers do seem to have small effects on progress (Pilling and Pringle, 1978). Our own study of London schools (Rutter *et al.*, 1979) showed a close relationship between the number of children expected to pass their school leaving examinations and the schools' success rate. This might, of course, be explained by the teachers' knowledge of their pupils' ability: but it was striking that two of the schools with relatively few able children in their intake had both high teacher expectations and successful outcomes.

TEACHER–CHILD INTERACTION

Much of educational research is concerned with the effects of particular types of classroom interaction, focusing on differences between teachers rather than on school differences. This research can be considered under three broad headings: the style of the lesson, the amount and type of feedback provided and the methods of group management and discipline which the teacher uses. Bennett (1976) looked at the relationship between teaching style and change in performance on tests of reading, mathematics and English during the final year at junior school. In general, Bennett found that children taught by teachers using a 'formal' style showed greater gains than those taught in 'informal' classrooms. There are, however, some difficulties in interpreting this study; first of all the schools varied in whether secondary school placement was on a selective or a comprehensive system. Even though the largest gain scores overall were made by children in the 'formal' group, the highest scoring sub-group were the children taught by informal methods in a selective district. There were also difficulties in interpreting exactly what the formal/informal dichotomy meant in practical terms; some teachers are very informal in their use of the classroom but highly structured in their planning and recording of pupils' work. Other research studies have looked at the patterns of verbal interaction between teachers and pupils using structured observation schedules such as that devised by Flanders (1970). Many of these studies have demonstrated the positive outcomes which result from indirect teaching and from the use of praise in the classroom.

Feedback to pupils about their performance and behaviour has also been extensively studied, either using the experimental paradigm developed from behaviour modification theory, or by focusing on naturally occurring praise and criticism. Both kinds of positive feedback have been shown to be valuable, but the findings are less clear with respect to negative feedback. Much of the interest in group management has resulted from the work of Kounin (1970). From observations of a large number of classrooms he developed a series of hypotheses relating to successful management in the classroom, showing how skill in maintaining a smooth flow of activities with little overt discipline led to greater pupil involvement. Brophy and Evertson (1976) reported very similar findings.

Classroom studies ignore the possibility that individual pupils may react in different ways to very similar educational environments, although Brophy and Evertson (1976) compare the classroom behaviour and attainments of children from different socio-economic groups, and many observers have reported sex differences in children's performance at school. Dunkin and Biddle (1974), in their excellent review of several hundred observational studies, suggest that future work on classroom teaching should give greater emphasis to the individual differences of this kind.

SCHOOL PRACTICE

Several research studies have been concerned with the relationship between school practice and academic outcome. McDill and Rigsby (1973) found a small relationship between performance on a standardized test and the schools' score on an 'academic emphasis' scale constructed from the replies of both pupils and teachers to a questionnaire. As this was not a longitudinal study it was not possible to control satisfactorily for what the pupils were like before entering high school, so that differences between schools might well have been underestimated. Our own study has also shown that schools with high scores on a variety of measures of academic emphasis have better outcomes than schools with lower scores.

Douglas et al. (1968) and Ainsworth and Batten (1974) report that examination results relate closely to three types of background variables, to the measured ability of the child, to family background and to type of school attended (both studies being undertaken in selective areas). Both studies identified some schools which appeared to be more successful than the majority of schools in the study. Ainsworth and Batten (1974) report that their small group of 'successful' schools were large, well-equipped and with well-trained teachers. They had a low teacher–pupil ratio, an emphasis on examinations and homework and a flexible streaming system. There were also more out-of-school activities, few positions of responsibility for pupils, an authoritarian head teacher and little formal provision for welfare. It seems likely that this last finding might reflect the absence of the need for such provision in a school which was generally rather successful rather than that formal provision for welfare was unproductive.

The London research team studied the ways in which differences in outcomes are related to differences in school practice. We found that the size of schools and the major differences in organization (such as dividing the school into house or year groups for administrative purposes and for pastoral care) did not relate to differences in outcome. Most of the schools in the study were streamed so it was not possible to look at the impact of ability groupings in this study, but it was clear that the few mixed ability schools were neither very successful nor very unsuccessful when compared with the streamed or banded schools. Schools which were successful varied in many ways from their less successful neighbours. We have grouped these into six broad categories. The first is concerned with academic emphasis within the school, with items such as the setting of homework, the use of the library and the amount of children's work displayed on the walls—these all showed positive relationships to successful outcomes. Our own work, along with that of the Young Leavers' Project (Schools' Council, 1968), shows that school pupils think that their schools should primarily be concerned with academic and work oriented goals and the successful schools in our study were trying to meet this. These schools offered more children the opportunity of being successful at school; this seems likely to make older pupils more enthusiastic about attending school and prevent them from becoming alienated from its objectives.

Our second category, lesson management style, also suggests that our more successful schools were more work oriented. In these, more of the teachers' lesson time was spent on the topic of the lesson, as opposed to preparing equipment or handing out pens and pencils; also the lessons were set up to involve the whole class most of the time. Little of the lesson was spent on disciplinary interventions so there were few interruptions to the children's learning. Bennett (1978) reviews several studies which report similar findings: good organization allowed teachers in successful schools to spend more of their lessons teaching and good classroom management gave their pupils more time to learn.

All the schools in our study used both sanctions and rewards for their pupils; it was very noticeable, however, that punishments of various kinds were much more common than rewards or praise. But when we examined the relationship between levels of punishment and outcome we found no links between them. Schools with high levels of punishment were neither particularly successful nor unsuccessful nor were they those which admitted particularly difficult pupils. Informal punishments, in the form of slaps and the like, related to poor outcome and may reflect the stress which teachers experience in the less well-functioning schools. It also seems probable that behaviour of this kind sets a poor model for pupils to follow. In contrast, praise did relate to successful outcome; the successful schools being much more likely to praise their pupils both in lessons and in school assembly. A related finding was that these schools provided better working conditions for their pupils; classrooms were clean and attractive with little damage or graffiti, children reported having been on more out-of-school outings and that they would consult a member of staff about a personal problem if they needed to.

Our next group of findings relate to the extent to which pupils are expected to take responsibility at school. In the more successful schools it was the usual practice for the children, rather than the teachers, to keep their own textbooks, folders, pens and pencils, and to bring them to lessons. Similarly, children were expected to take responsibility for other pupils by holding positions such as form captain or homework monitor; they also reported the number of times they had taken part in a school assembly and this, too, related to outcome. Encouraging children to be more involved in their schooling in these ways may lead to a closer identification with the school and its aims. Our final set of findings come from interviews with teachers, and here the pattern which emerges is one of staff working together, having common standards of discipline, rather than each teacher planning his own work in isolation from other members of staff. Teachers reported that, in the successful schools, decisions were made at senior level but that their own views could be represented. The overall pattern which emerges is one of order without excessive punishment; of well managed, work orientated lessons; of concern for children's needs, appreciation of good work and behaviour, and an assump-

tion that they will take a responsible part in their own schooling. Teachers in the successful school cooperated more with their colleagues than did those in other schools, and this may well have provided both support for individuals and consistency in dealing with the problems which inevitably arise in the daily life of an inner-city school.

Reynolds and his colleagues have not yet published details of their school process measures but preliminary results (Reynolds and Murgatroyd, 1977) indicate that they also have identified aspects of school practice which discriminate between more and less successful schools.

King (1973) was not concerned with long term outcomes of schooling but with factors which related to pupil participation. He was particularly interested in relating a school's score on a measure of participation to differences in school organization. No overall relationships were found although there were some between particular age groups and types of schools. Our own work, together with that of Reynolds *et al.*, has shown that considerable differences exist between schools in the same administrative category so that grouping schools to these categories may have concealed any interesting relationships between school practice and pupil participation.

SCHOOL CLIMATE AND ATMOSPHERE

Some research teams have been concerned with much broader concepts than those already discussed, such as school climate (or atmosphere) and pupils' perceptions of their schools. Clegg and Megson (1968) described their impressions of the differences in atmosphere between more and less successful schools, and supported these observations by showing that the positive relationship between corporal punishment and delinquency could not be explained by the quality of the housing in the schools' catchment area. Halpin and Croft (1962) developed a series of questionnaires for teachers which were used to give a school a profile on six organizational climates. Teachers were asked to either agree or disagree with a series of statements describing the behaviour of other teachers and the school principal. The six climates ranged from the 'open' climate with high teacher morale to the 'closed' where morale was very low. Schools were not expected to fall into only one category but to have a distinctive profile across all six. This work has been extended by Finlayson (1973) to include the perceptions of pupils as well as those of teachers, and also to include a section on teachers' perceptions of heads of departments as well as of head teachers. Finlayson and Loughran (1975) used the pupil perception scales to examine the differences in boys' perceptions of their teachers and their fellow pupils in four schools matched on various social indicators but differing in the delinquency rates. Pupils in high delinquency schools perceived their teachers as being more authoritarian and their schools as being less committed to learning than did the pupils in low delinquency schools. There were, however, no differences between the perceptions of delinquents and non-delinquents in the high delinquency schools. In the low delinquency schools the delinquents were nearly all in the bottom streams of the schools, adding support to Hargreaves' view of streaming, so it was not possible to look at the perceptions of these boys independently of their position in the streaming system. Finlayson suggested that the pupils' responses to the rating scales indicate that teachers in high delinquency schools are perceived as 'defensive and authoritarian' in their interactions with groups of pupils rather than with particular individuals, a point which we have also considered in our examinations of different styles of classroom management.

STUDIES OF OTHER INSTITUTIONS

Many other studies undertaken in settings other than ordinary schools suggest possible ways of considering the relationship between school process and outcome. The well-known small group studies of Sherif (1961) and of White and Lippitt (1960) demonstrate the ways in which the structure and leadership of small groups of children determines the patterns of interaction between them. These studies were, however, based on small groups of volunteers in contrast to a school class which usually consists of far more children in compulsory attendance. Several studies of children living in residential care (reported in Tizard, 1975) demonstrate the powerful effects of different programmes on children's concurrent behaviour and also show how the quality of relationships between staff may have unintended consequences for the inmates. Many of these comparative studies of institutions have come to similar conclusions, that different 'treatments' lead to differences in concurrent behaviour but are less likely to influence long term outcomes. The institutional studies may provide useful hypotheses which would repay exploration in ordinary schools. but their findings are not directly applicable as they are nearly all based on small residential establishments for 'deviant' children in contrast to the ordinary day school serving a wide range of 'normal' children.

CONCLUSIONS

Studies of school differences and of their effects on the development of children are only just beginning. Recent research, reviewed in this chapter, has shown that schools do differ in how effective they are with comparable groups of children. It has also been shown that the features which relate to success are not external to the school and hence impossible to change; the key features are nearly all aspects of school practice, which although difficult to change, are open to modification by teachers. We do not yet know how great the long-term effect of school differences are; it seems very likely that, as in studies of other institutions, concurrent outcomes may be the most responsive to schooling. A child with behavioural or emotional problems may well find that a good school is a powerful positive influence in his life, whereas a less well functioning school becomes an additional source of stress.

It is not yet possible to match a particular child to the type of school which might be most appropriate for him, but it seems that successful schools exert a positive influence on children from across the ability range and from a variety of home backgrounds. It is also impossible to make direct comparisons between the relative importance of home and school on a child's development, but even if it could be clearly demonstrated that home influences were the most important, the contribution which a good school might make to a child should not be underestimated. Most of the research reviewed here has been based on inner-city schools serving many disadvantaged inner-city families. The schools themselves are often in old buildings with very restricted sports facilities and playgrounds. Yet some of them function extremely well, providing good teaching in a pleasant and supportive environment. The pupils are well behaved, the lessons orderly and enjoyable, and even the older pupils attend regularly. Not all inner-city schools are 'blackboard jungles'!

Measures of school outcomes show consistent patterns from year to year, suggesting that school functioning is very resistant to change. Of course, schools do alter, but exactly how this happens in not yet completely understood. It would, however, appear to be important for those concerned with children in difficulties to be aware of the positive support which a good school can provide; also to consider ways of working with teachers, helping them to improve their own schools so that, in the long term, fewer children will need help from child guidance clinics or other specialized agencies.

REFERENCES

Ainsworth, M. E. and Batten, E. O. (1974). *The Effects of Environmental Factors on Secondary Educational Attainment in Manchester: A Plowden Follow Up*. London: Macmillan Education.

Bachman, E. (1971). *Youth in Transition: dropping-out, problem or symptom*. Michigan: Ann Arbor.

Barker, R. G. and Gump, P. V. (1964). *Big School, Small School*. Stanford Calif., Stanford U.P.

Bennett, S. N. (1976). *Teaching Styles and Pupil Progress*. London: Open Books.

Bennett, S. N. (1978). Recent Research on Teaching: a dream, a belief, and a model. *British Journal of Educational Psychology*, **48**, 127–147.

Brimer, M. A., Madaus, G. F., Chapman, B., Kellaghan, T. and Wood, R. (1978). *Sources of Difference in School Achievement*. Slough: National Foundations for Educational Research.

Brophy, J. E. and Evertson, C. M. (1976). *Learning from Teaching: a developmental perspective*. Boston: Allyn and Bacon.

Brophy, J. E. and Good, T. L. (1974). *Teacher–Student Relationships—Causes and Consequences*. New York: Holt, Rinehart and Winston.

Cannan, C. (1970) Schools for delinquency. *New Society*, **16**, 1004.

Clegg, A. and Megson, B. (1968) *Children in Distress*. Harmondsworth: Penguin Books.

Coleman, J. S. (1966). *Equality of Educational Opportunity*. Washington: U.S. Government Printing Office.

Cookson, C. (1978). Teenagers begin to reap the benefits of Head Start. *Times Educational Supplement*, 9.6.78.

Davis, D. (1977). Where comprehensives score. *Times Educational Supplement*, 25.3.77.

Douglas, J. W. B. (1964). *The Home and the School*. London: Macgibbon and Kee.

Douglas, J. W. B., Ross, J. M. and Simpson, H. R. (1968). *All Our Future.* London: Peter Davies.

Dreeben, R. (1968). *On What is Learned in School.* Reading, Mass.: Addison-Wesley.

Dunkin, M. J. and Biddle, B. J. (1974). *The Study of Teaching.* New York: Holt, Rinehart and Winston.

Eggleston, J. (1977). *The Ecology of the School.* London: Methuen.

Farrington, D. (1972). Delinquency begins at home. *New Society,* **21,** 495–497.

Farrington, D. and West, D. (1973). *Who Becomes Delinquent?* London: Heinemann.

Finlayson, D. J. (1973). Measuring school climate. *Trends in Education.* April 1973.

Finlayson, D. J. and Loughran, J. L. (1975). Pupils' perceptions in low and high delinquency schools. *Educational Research,* **18,** 138–145.

Flanders, N. (1970). *Analysing Teacher Behaviour.* Reading, Mass: Addison-Wesley.

Galloway, D. (1976). Size of school, socio-economic hardship, suspension rates and persistent unjustified absence from school. *British Journal of Educational Psychology,* **46,** 40–47.

Gath, D., Cooper, B., Gattoni, F. and Rockett, D. (1977) *Child Guidance and Delinquency in a London Borough.* Maudsley Monographs, No. 24. Oxford: University Press.

Gray, G., Smith, A. and Rutter, M. (1980). School attendance and the first year of employment. In: Hersov, L. and Berg. I. (Eds). *Out of School: Modern perspectives in truancy and school refusal.* London: Wiley (in press).

Gray, J. and Satterly, D. (1976). A chapter of errors: 'Teaching Styles and Pupil Progress' in retrospect. *Educational Research,* **19,** 45–56.

Halpin, A. W. and Croft, D. B. (1962). *Organisational Climate of Schools.* Midwest Administrative Center, University of Chicago.

Hargreaves, D. (1967). *Social Relations in a Secondary Modern School.* London: Routledge and Kegan Paul.

Heal, K. H. (1978). Misbehaviour among schoolchildren: the role of the school in strategies for prevention. *Policy and Politics,* **6,** 321–332.

House, E. R., Glass, G. V., McLean, L. D. and Walker, D. F. (1978). No simple answer: a critique of the Follow Through evaluation. *Harvard Educational Review,* **48,** 128–160.

Jencks, C. *et al.* (1972). *Inequality: a reassessment of the effect of family and schooling in America.* Harmondsworth: Penguin Books.

King, R. (1973). *School Organisation and Pupil Involvement: a study of secondary schools.* London: Routledge and Kegan Paul.

Kounin, J. S. (1970). *Discipline and Group Management in Classrooms.* New York: Holt, Rinehart and Winston.

Lacey, C. (1970). *Hightown Grammar: the school as a social system.* Manchester: University Press.

Lacey, C. (1974). 'Destreaming in a "pressured" academic environment.' In: Eggleston, J. (Ed.) *Contemporary Research in the Sociology of Education.* London: Methuen.

Lewin, R. (1977). 'Head Start' pays off. *New Scientist,* **73,** 508–509.

Lunn, J. (1970). *Streaming in the Primary School.* Slough: National Foundation for Educational Research.

McDill, E. L. and Rigsby, L. C. (1973). *Structure and Process in Secondary Schools.* Baltimore: Johns Hopkins U.P.

Miller, L. B. and Dyer, J. L. (1975). Four preschool programs: their dimensions and effects. *Monographs of the Society for Research in Child Development,* **40,** Serial No. 162.

Nunnally, J. C. (1975). 'The study of change in evaluation research: principles concerning measurement, experimental design, and analysis.' In: Struening, E. L. and Guttentag, M. (Eds.) *Handbook of Evaluation Research.* New York: Sage Publications.

Pilling, D. and Pringle, M. (1978). *Controversial Issues in Child Development.* London: Paul Elek.

Postlethwaite, K. and Denton, C. (1978). *Streams for the Future?* Banbury: Pubansco Publications.

Power, M. J., Benn, R. T. and Morris, J. N. (1972). Neighbourhood, school and juveniles before the courts. *British Journal of Criminology,* **12,** 111–132.

Reynolds, D., Jones, D. and St Leger, S. (1976). Schools do make a difference. *New Society,* **37,** 321–323.

Reynolds, D. and Murgatroyd, S. (1977). 'The sociology of schooling and the absent pupil.' In: Carroll, H. M. C. (Ed.) *Absenteeism in South Wales: studies of pupils, their homes and their secondary schools.* The Faculty of Education, University College of Swansea.

Rosenthal, R. and Jacobson, L. (1968). *Pygmalion in the Classroom.* New York: Holt, Rinehart and Winston.

Ross, J., Bunton, W. J., Evison, P. and Robertson, T. S. (1972). *A Critical Appraisal of Comprehensive Schooling: a research report.* Slough: National Foundation for Educational Research.

Rutter, M. and Madge, N. (1976). *Cycles of Disadvantage.* London: Heinemann.

Rutter. M., Maughan, B., Mortimore, P. and Ouston, J. (1979). *Fifteen Thousand Hours.* London: Open Books.

Rutter, M., Yule, B., Quinton, D., Rowlands, O., Yule, W. and Berger, M. (1975). Attainment and adjustment in two geographical areas: III. Some factors accounting for area differences. *British Journal of Psychiatry,* **126,** 520–533.

Schools' Council (1968). *Enquiry I: Young School Leavers, Part 2.* London: H.M.S.O.

Shaycoft, M. (1967). *The High School Years: growth in cognitive skills.* Pittsburgh: American Institutes for Research and School of Education, University of Pittsburgh.

Sherif, M., Harvey, O. J., White, B. J., Hood, W. R. and Sherif, C. W. (1961). *Intergroup Conflict and Co-operation: the Robbers' Cave experiment.* Norman, Oklahoma: University of Oklahoma Book Exchange.

Stallings, J. (1975). Implementation and child effects of teaching practices in Follow Through classrooms. *Monographs of the Society for Research in Child Development,* **40,** Serial No. 163.

Sugarman, B. (1967). Involvement in youth culture, academic achievement and conformity in school: an empirical study of London schoolboys. *British Journal of Sociology,* **18,** 151–164.

Summers, A. A. and Wolfe, B. L. (1977). Do schools make a difference? *American Economic Review,* **67,** 639–652.

Tizard, J., Sinclair, I. and Clarke, R. (1975). *Varieties of Residential Experience: research issues in the care and treatment of children.* London: Routledge and Kegan Paul.

Westinghouse Learning Corporation, Ohio University (1969). *The Impact of Head Start: an evaluation of the effects of Head Start on children's cognitive and affective development.* Washington D.C.: Clearinghouse for Federal Scientific and Technical Information.

White, R. and Lippitt, R. (1960). 'Leader behaviour and member reaction in three "social climates".' In: Cartwright, D. and Zander, A. (Eds.) *Group Dynamics in Research and Theory.* New York: Harper and Row.

7. CULTURAL AND COMMUNITY INFLUENCES

DAVID QUINTON

The wide variations in childhood experiences which exist within Western societies, together with differences in development associated with them, have been a fruitful source for the elaboration and testing of particular theories. In particular, social class differences have been used as 'natural experiments' through which to explore the variables associated with normal and abnormal development. In the majority of psychological investigations social variations have been examined in terms of differences in the patterns of primary care taking experiences and the relationships between mothers and children. More recently the scope of enquiry has been widened to include comparative studies of development within widely differing cultural settings (*e.g.* Leiderman *et al.*, 1977). The purpose of much of this research has been to see whether certain invariant patterns of child rearing exist and also to use the differences in child rearing circumstances to examine whether the relationships between particular social patterns and particular developmental outcomes observed within Western industrialized cultures apply more generally. The major focus of research has primarily involved what may be broadly termed 'family influences'. These are examined in Chapter 4 and will not be reviewed here. The purpose of this chapter is to explore some of the broader social and environmental variations and to consider their relevance for development.

STUDIES IN DIFFERENT CULTURES

Accounts from different cultures have shown the wide variations which exist both in the physical circumstances which surround the developing child and the patterns of child rearing experienced (*e.g.* Narrol, 1970; Barry and Paxson, 1971). Thus infants' physical movements may be virtually unrestricted or highly limited by being bound much of the time to a cradle board; the child may be carried nearly all the time by an adult or only picked up in emergencies; parental reactions to crying may vary from indifference or punitiveness to a highly nurturant response; weaning may begin below the age of 6 months and be severely applied or be delayed until after the age of 2; the early development of motor skills may be punished or strongly encouraged; the biological mother may be the exclusive care taker or the majority of care may be provided by others. In later childhood socialization may continue in nuclear family households or the child may be fostered by relatives; control may be exercised predominantly by parents or the child may be transferred with his peers to separate accommodation and trained by other adults, or major aspects of socialization may be taken by older peers (Mayer, 1970). Wide variations between cultures have also been reported in adult behaviour or 'personality' (Child, 1968) and in perceptual and cognitive skills (Lloyd, 1972).

Cultural differences of this magnitude provide tempting natural experiments for the investigation of the links between cultural variables and development. Studies of these links have taken two principal forms (*see* Leiderman *et al.*, 1977). Firstly, there have been a series of cross-cultural comparisons based on anthropological accounts which have examined whether particular child-rearing practices are associated with adult personality characteristics or with particular forms of social organization. Secondly, there have been a number of more recent studies of child-rearing patterns and child development in different cultures in which the general applicability of developmental processes observed in Western societies has been tested in other settings (*e.g.* Ainsworth, 1967; Leiderman *et al.*, 1977).

Cross-cultural studies

Cross-cultural studies have largely been concerned with correlations between broadly defined variables at the cultural level, usually on the basis of data from the world ethnographic sample (Murdock, 1967). Comparisons have been made firstly to see whether there are any relationships between environmental circumstances, social structure and child-rearing patterns, and secondly to see whether these patterns are associated with adult behaviour. Most of these studies report comparisons between pairs of variables only: thus they may examine child-rearing and the economy or child-rearing and political complexity, but seldom consider the one relationship whilst controlling for the other. With respect to environment and social structure a number of correlations have been reported. Thus Barry and his colleagues have compared child-rearing practices in agricultural or herding economies (which have accumulation of food resources) and hunting and gathering societies (which do not). The former group of societies emphasize responsibility and obedience in child-rearing whilst the latter emphasized achievement, self-reliance and independence (Barry et al., 1959). In like manner, the encouragement of competitiveness and responsibility in children has been shown to be positively related to the extent to which animal husbandry is an important part of subsistence economies. The stress on self-reliance decreases and on obedience increases with an increasing number of levels in the political structure (Barry et al., 1976).

Interpretations of such differences have made the non-controversial assumption that in part they reflect cultural adaptions to particular environmental circumstances and constraints (Le Vine, 1977) and that they have developed in order to produce adults fitted for the maintenance of particular social systems (Whiting, 1977). Thus, Le Vine suggests the extent to which infants are carried depends on environmental hazards. However, it is unlikely that it will be possible to determine the extent to which *particular* circumstances produce *particular* child-rearing patterns, since a wide variety of systems are likely to be effective in adaptation to particular circumstances. Moreover the cultural variety which exists within broadly similar ecologies suggest that cultural patterns are not strongly determined by environmental factors. This is supported by the generally modest associations found in these correlation studies.

From a developmental perspective however the *reasons* for variations in cultural patterns are less important than a consideration of their effects. Unfortunately the evidence which can be drawn from a majority of cross-cultural studies on this question is limited. This is firstly because the data on different cultures are of a widely varying character and quality and depend mostly on reports of modal patterns, and secondly because the data are largely deficient in any detailed information on child development. It is thus possible neither to investigate within culture variations nor satisfactorily to examine particular developmental issues.

The approach to developmental questions in the majority of cross-cultural research has been to examine the association between child-rearing patterns and certain adult characteristics. For example Bacon and her colleagues report a relationship between suspicion and distrust in adulthood and socialization methods which involve strongly dependent child–mother relationships in infancy and an abrupt and punitive transition to independence (Bacon et al., 1963). However, it is not possible

with these cross-cultural data to distinguish between those adult behaviours which reflect stable internal characteristics of individuals ('personality') and those which depend primarily on custom or external constraints.

A related area of investigation has been that between child-rearing patterns and the expressive system of society such as magico-religious beliefs. Whiting, using a psychoanalytic framework, has argued that the adaptation of child-rearing practices to ecological circumstances is frequently at variance with the optimal developmental environment for individuals. This results in conflicts which are expressed in adult personality and in the expressive aspects of the culture. Correlations which support this view have been reported by Spiro and D'Andrade (1958) who showed significant associations in a sample of 11 societies between the severity of child-rearing practices, especially in feeding and toilet training, and the belief that the good or ill-will of the gods is contingent upon individual behaviour.

The dangers of circularity in any approach which examines associations at the cultural level were anticipated in the writings of Mead (1928, 1930, 1953, 1954) and Benedict (1934, 1938, 1949) who argued that differences between cultures in adult behaviour and personality could not be explained by differences in child-rearing practices. Rather they saw both personality and child-rearing as expressions of general cultural preferences or themes. These themes are communicated to the child through all its interactions with the culture, not only with its parents but also with the expressive features such as art or drama. The effects of child-rearing practices on development are seen as depending primarily on the nature of the messages transmitted through them. In this the affective tone and social relationships associated with a particular technique are of more importance than the method itself (Benedict, 1949).

Whilst Mead and Benedict are correct in questioning the possibility of making causal inferences from comparisons at the cultural level, they have been justifiably criticized for the circularity of their own position. This stretches cultural relativity to a degree which denies any possibility of using cross-cultural comparisons to investigate the effects of child-rearing patterns (*e.g.* Le Vine, 1973). However, it should be remembered that they were concerned to counteract the naïve determinism and ethnocentricity of many developmental theories of their time. It is clear that they accepted that particular child-rearing practices had implications for individual development (Benedict, 1949) but that they wanted to emphasize the degree to which particular methods—*e.g.* swaddling—had different consequences depending on wider aspects of social organization and values.

Despite the limitations of the broad cross-cultural approach a number of interesting associations have been reported. Bacon *et al.* (1963) examined the correlates of theft and of crimes against the person in 48 societies. The extent of both types of crime was positively related to prolonged mother–infant sleeping arrangements and to limited father–child involvement. Theft was significantly more common in societies which were low in indulgence towards their children and placed a punitive emphasis on responsibility, self-reliance, achievement and obedience. Personal crime was more common in societies with an abrupt and punitive socialization to independence. Higher rates of both types of crime are argued to be associated with a lack of opportunity for children to identify with male figures. Theft is seen as associated with techniques which encourage feelings of deprivation of love and personal crime with techniques which abruptly break previously close relationships and engender feelings of hostility and suspicion. On the other hand Lester (1967) suggests that there may be no relationship cross-culturally between societies where children are physically punished and the level of aggression amongst adults. Such contradictory findings are not unexpected, given the generally modest correlations provided in most cross-cultural comparisons and given the variable nature of the data.

Two cross-cultural studies have examined the relationship between stressful child-rearing practices such as head moulding or body piercing (Landauer and Whiting, 1964) or mother–infant separation (Gunders and Whiting, 1968) and adult stature. They found that stature was significantly increased in societies with such practices and drew parallels between this finding and the results of earlier animal studies into the relationship between stress and later physical development. Although rigorous controls could not be applied the relationships appeared to remain when genetic, nutritional and climatic factors were taken into account.

Comparative child development studies

The problems inherent in the cross-cultural studies described in the previous section have led to alternative approaches. Whiting recognized the weakness in the comparability of existing data and the necessity of examining intracultural variations. The Six Culture Study (Whiting and Whiting, 1975) attempted a more systematic examination of the relationship between social organization, child-rearing patterns and child behaviour. Although the work was limited by very small sample sizes, and problems of maintaining comparability between research teams in different parts of the world, it supported other findings (*e.g.* Barry *et al.*, 1976) of broad links between social organization and child-rearing patterns. The degree of cultural complexity was measured, following Murdock (1973), on the basis of features including occupational specialization, a cash economy, the degree of political and legal centralization, and the extent of hierarchical organization. Whiting and his colleagues argued that simpler societies require a high degree of cooperation within family units, kin networks and communities. More complex societies need to place more emphasis on competition and achievement. The data support this hypothesis. Observations of children showed that those in simpler societies were more nurturant and responsible whilst those in more complex societies were more attention-seeking and competitive. However, the relationship was also affected by the type of residence,

independent of cultural complexity. Children raised in nuclear households were more sociable and less aggressive than those brought up under other arrangements. There was evidence, however, that within culture variation was considerable.

Other research workers have begun to use cultural variations as an opportunity for examining particular developmental issues. The majority of detailed studies of child development in different societies have so far concentrated on variations of patterns of primary care taking and mother–child relationships. Ainsworth (1967), for example, investigated mother–infant attachment in Baltimore and amongst the Ganda. She found that maternal behaviours encouraging secure attachment were similar in the two cultures but that separation protest was greater amongst Ganda children, even when security of attachment was taken into account. This seemed to be explained by cultural differences in the pattern of mother–infant contact. Konner (1977) has studied infancy amongst the !Kung, a group of hunter-gatherers in the Kalahari Desert. In this society, infancy is characterized by much higher mother–child physical contact than is the case amongst American and English samples. The infants are carried on their mothers' backs for long periods in an upright and non-restrictive sling. The evidence suggests that, at the age of 1 year, the !Kung infants are advanced in motor development compared with children in Western societies. However, these variations may be largely explained by genetic differences. Konner also reports certain advances in cognitive development and the genetic explanation is less plausible in this case. In addition, cross-cultural studies mentioned above suggest that cultural factors can affect physical development even when biological differences are taken into account.

Comparative studies of this kind represent a promising new departure in the study of development but the problems of interpreting differences remain formidable. Variations which seem clearly cultural in nature may be strongly influenced by other factors, such as nutrition (Chavez *et al.*, 1974), whilst physiological factors such as maternal blood pressure may be strongly influenced by social factors (Blurton-Jones *et al.*, 1979). If major problems exist in explaining inter-cultural differences in the behaviour of infants, even greater difficulties remain concerning the long-term importance of many variations found in child-rearing patterns and associated developmental differences. Dunn (1976) has pertinently pointed out that since human infants are very adaptable a wide range of cultural patterns may be equally adequate for achieving the same developmental ends. This implies that differences or lack of differences observed at any one point in time may have little long-term relevance. We do not yet know the necessary conditions for specific developmental outcomes. Equally, we as yet know little about possible 'sleeper' effects of particular early experiences. For example, children reared during their early years in adequate residential nurseries, have at the age of 4 levels of intellectual development and rates of behaviour disturbance similar to working-class children (Tizard and Rees, 1974, 1975). At the age of 8, however, differences in the children's behaviour and attainments were related both to their institutional experience and to the quality of later parenting. The attachment to adults of children either adopted or restored to their natural parents seemed to depend mostly on parental attitudes and behaviour, and although none of the children were intellectually retarded, the adopted group had the highest mean IQ and reading attainments. However, both groups of children were reported by parents as being more attention seeking than the controls. This was also true at school where, in addition, the children had more problems with peer relationships (Tizard and Hodges, 1978).

There are thus difficulties in deciding at what age comparisons should be made and how they should be assessed. Interpreting differences becomes more difficult the longer the child experiences the impress of widely varying cultures and the more the context in which the behaviour occurs varies. At present we do not know whether any particular child-rearing patterns have long-term consequences. It is clear that later cultural factors, as described in the next section, have marked modifying effects on early experiences but the mechanisms involved are not yet understood.

The cultural mediation of early experiences

The diversity of child-rearing practices suggests that a wide variety of infant experiences is compatible with satisfactory development, providing that they are associated with appropriate cultural expectations and support. It is not known however whether such cultural patterns operate by containing the adverse effects of early experiences or whether the psychological effects of particular circumstances are markedly affected by the cultural expectations which surround them. A number of examples can be given.

Goody (1970) has examined the relationship between the fostering of children and later social performance amongst the Gonja of northern Ghana. In Western societies fostering usually occurs in conditions of family crisis and is considered potentially damaging to the child. Norms amongst the Gonja allow patralineal kin to claim children from their natural parents at the age of 7 or 8 and to bring them up for the rest of their childhoods. The evidence suggests that approximately 50% of adults undergo this kind of kin-fostering experience. Comparisons between fostered and non-fostered children as adults showed that there were no differences in their later success within the political system or the stability of their marriages.

The impact of marital breakdown provides a second example. In Western society the association between marital discord and disruption and behavioural deviance or delinquency, is well established (Rutter, 1972). However, in societies where frequent marital breakdown is part of the customary pattern there is generally little association with later developmental problems in the children. This appears to be because compensating social structures exist which support the mother materially and in child rearing. Thus, amongst the Nez Perces indians of Idaho a

high rate of marital breakdown was traditionally balanced by a system of discipline which was largely located in the community, rather than in the family. Only when this external system of control began to decline did marital breakdown become associated with delinquent behaviour (Ackerman, 1971).

Thirdly, variations in values within the same broad cultural area have been shown to alter the effects of particular variables. Christensen (1960) compared pre-marital pregnancy, sex norms and marital stability in three western areas: Utah, an area with traditional proscriptions against pre-marital intercourse; Indiana, an 'average' American county; and Denmark, a society in which pre-marital pregnancy is common and subject to little censure. Cultural norms affected the rate of pre-marital pregnancy in the three areas in the expected direction. Permissiveness in Denmark was related to the longest delay between pre-marital conception and marriage itself and the smallest divorce-rate differential between pre- and post-marital pregnancy cases. In Utah, pre-marital pregnancy led rapidly to marriage but was associated with a high divorce rate. In Indiana, the rates were midway between the two other cultures. Thus, within broadly similar cultural circumstances, variations in cultural values may affect the outcome of the 'same' event.

Summary

The evidence of wide variation in child-rearing patterns itself demonstrates some of the range of experience which infants and children can undergo and still emerge as satisfactorily functioning adults in the context for which they are socialized. Since some of those experiences when manifest as atypical patterns in other cultures lead to adverse outcomes, it follows that there must be regulating processes within the culture for which they are typical, which modify their effects in a satisfactory fashion. Dovetailing of particular patterns of socialization in non-Western societies has so far not been studied from the perspective of its effects on child development. Some investigation by which very different routes lead to similar adult outcomes would be fruitful, especially if it were possible to identify those points at which particular processes of socialization broke down.

COMMUNITY AND DEVELOPMENT IN WESTERN SOCIETIES

Wide variations in both emotional and cognitive development within Western industrialized societies have been observed for many years. The majority of the evidence on community or cultural influences is concerned with differences between social class or status groupings, or between geographical areas.

SOCIAL CLASS DIFFERENCES

Social class is classically defined in terms of a person's relationship to the ownership of the means of production or to his bargaining power within the labour market. The most usual indicator of social class is the status accorded to particular occupations (*e.g.* OPCS, 1970; Goldthorpe and Hope, 1974). Many studies have shown that there is considerable agreement within the general populations of a number of industrialized countries on the general status to be accorded to particular occupations (Reiss, 1961; Hodge *et al.*, 1964).

It is important to understand however that the general agreement on the status of occupations and the different family patterns associated with them, do not imply that occupational groupings necessarily represent social groups sharing localities, common values or a sense of class identity. Although people generally agree on their ranking of occupations their perception of their own position within the class structure is only in moderate agreement with such occupational classifications (Runciman, 1972).

Because status can be conferred by other factors apart from occupation, status categorizations in research are sometimes made using a wider series of indicators than occupational status alone (*e.g.* West, 1969; Hollingshead and Redlich, 1958). Such classifications generally strengthen the association between status and particular dependent variables. However, these indices should be viewed with caution for a number of reasons. Firstly, they may confound position in the economic structure with personal characteristics. Secondly, they may obscure the relatively wide variation in patterns of life which can occur in similar occupational groupings and thus may reinforce stereotypes of class related lifestyles. Finally, they may make it impossible to analyse the separate contributions of the individual elements in the index to the particular associations being studied.

Social class and intellectual development

There is a substantial amount of evidence that consistent relationships exist between social class and various aspects of development. These have been documented most clearly with respect to IQ and scholastic attainment (*e.g.* Plowden, 1967; Douglas *et al.*, 1968). In the National Child Development Study, for example, parental social class was the variable which related most strongly to reading attainment at age 7 (Davie *et al.*, 1972).

Developmental variations have often been linked with differences in child-rearing practices and parent–child relationships within different social groups. Such differences have been shown both for general life styles (Lockwood, 1958; Kohn, 1969; Runciman, 1972; Young and Willmott, 1973) and for specific aspects of child rearing (Bronfenbrenner, 1959; Newson and Newson, 1963 and 1968). The most consistent evidence comes from the Newsons' work in Nottingham. They have shown for example that working-class parents of 4-year-old children play with their children and talk to them less often than parents with non-manual occupations. Working-class parents intervene less in children's quarrels and encourage them to hit back more. Their disciplinary methods are more likely to involve smacking and less likely to involve reasoning.

With respect to differences in intellectual development, particular interest has been focused on the relationships between these social class differences and language style. It is known that variations in the quality of a linguistic environment relate to language development. This has been shown both in studies of children in residential nurseries (Tizard *et al.*, 1972; Tizard and Rees, 1974) and in experimental studies (Rutter and Mittler, 1972). There is evidence that social class differences exist which reflect this environmental difference (Hess and Shipman, 1965, 1967). For example, middle-class mothers engage in more dialogue with their children and are involved in more discussion over play and ideas (Wootton, 1974). They express thoughts and concepts in a more precise way and take less for granted (Brandis and Henderson, 1970). These differences are reflected in the children's language: middle-class children are more explicit in their language use and more able to elaborate without presuming on the listener's knowledge of the context; working-class children on the other hand tend to be less explicit and to make assumptions which are only intelligible with knowledge of the context (Hawkins, 1969).

The relationship between class position and language style has been particularly stimulated by the work of Bernstein. He described the differences in language use in terms of 'elaborated' or 'restricted' codes or styles of speaking. An elaborated code is one in which the speaker selects from a relatively extensive range of syntactic alternatives to express ideas or concepts in such a way that the message could be understood in its own right, without the knowledge of the speaker or the context. In contrast, the restricted code is one where the range of syntactic alternatives is severely limited and where the understanding of the message is largely dependent upon the knowledge of the speaker, the circumstances in which he spoke and the setting of the conversation. Practice in the use of elaborated codes confers particular advantages for the performance of intellectual tasks. It is hypothesized that working class children are at a disadvantage in such tasks because of their use of predominantly restricted codes. Bernstein's work has been the subject of recent criticism (Lawton, 1968; Coulthard, 1969) and at present the nature of the relationship between social class differences in language use and development are unclear. Similarly the extent to which working class children are limited to restricted code styles is debatable. Robinson (1965) has convincingly shown, for example, that children using predominantly working-class language styles are able to use more elaborated middle-class forms when the occasion demands.

Although a number of explanations have been proposed, the reasons for these persisting social class differences in language use and scholastic attainment are unclear. Genetic factors probably play some part in general linguistic ability but it is implausible to suggest that they explain social class differences in language styles.

Most sociological theories link these differences in

language use to variations in the life experiences and expectations of different social classes. Kohn (1969) has argued strongly that position within the class structure is related to the development of values and attitudes which stress conformity and obedience to external standards on the one hand, or on the other the ability to act on the basis of individual judgment, in the belief that decisions and actions can be consequential. Working-class parents tend to emphasize values of conformity, whilst middle-class parents stress self-direction. An emphasis on conformity is the inevitable result of conditions of life that allow little freedom of action or little reason to feel in control of the future: a belief in self-direction develops through a contrasting set of experiences in which the child learns that his actions will affect the future course of events. These variations in attitudes are seen to be related to language styles, to variations in child-rearing practices and to the values stressed in bringing up children. Kohn showed these differences occur both in America and in Italy and that they are not a function of race or religion. However, within class groupings the level of education has an effect on the extent of self-directed values although it does not obliterate the effects of class. Kohn links the variations in parental values to the extent to which work experience allows the individual to make decisions or control his activities.

The statistical correlations on which this view is based are generally low. Nevertheless they are in agreement with evidence that shows that those in less socially advantaged positions face a restricted range of life options. Such circumstances are associated with orientation towards present gratification rather than planning for the future and emphasize the importance of personal relationships and group solidarity over individual achievement (Blum and Rossi, 1968). Although these data undoubtedly reflect broad differences in orientation between the classes, theories based upon them tend to underestimate the degree of variation in values and child-rearing practices which exist within social strata as well as the relatively high level of social mobility that now exists in most Western societies. Nevertheless differences (between non-manual and manual families) in family style and especially language use, clearly exist and relate to intellectual development. At present the importance of these differences and the mechanisms through which they operate remain to be established. The fact that more consistent relationships are found between class and attainment than class and behaviour may suggest that certain features of language use and the home environment are more pervasive characteristics of the class structure than are the factors which are of consequence for emotional and behavioural development. However, the findings may also be affected by the fact that intellectual performance is easier to measure.

Social class and behavioural problems

Evidence for differences between social groups in emotional and behavioural development is based almost entirely on cross-sectional data concerning deviance,

delinquency or psychiatric problems. Against popular assumptions, epidemiological studies have shown that, in contrast with adult disorders, the prevalence of psychological problems in childhood and adolescence is not generally related to social class as measured by the father's occupation (Rutter, Tizard and Whitmore, 1970). There is a tendency for delinquency and conduct disorders to be more common in families of semi or unskilled occupational status. However, this association is only found at the extreme lower end of the class scale and is only found in some populations. In general the association is more consistently apparent when low social status is associated with other aspects of disadvantage (e.g. West, 1969) and this may account for the more consistent finding of differences between geographical areas in the rates of particular problems. This is considered in the next section.

AREA DIFFERENCES IN DELINQUENCY AND PSYCHIATRIC DISORDER

Ecological correlations

Earlier studies both in Britain and America examined the relationship between the social characteristics of particular areas of cities and varying rates of crime and delinquency (Burt, 1925; Shaw and McKay, 1942). Since then numerous investigations confirmed these patterns. These area variations in rates of delinquency tend to be associated with indices of social disadvantage such as poverty, overcrowding and low social status. However, the areas vary quite considerably both in size and in the nature of the physical environment. Thus they may be older city slums (Lander, 1954; Mays, 1954), or new housing estates (Mannheim, 1948; Morris, 1957; Jones, 1934). They may vary between boroughs (Wallis and Maliphant, 1967); wards (Power et al., 1972; Edwards, 1973); enumeration districts (Gath et al., 1975); or even streets (Jephcott and Carter, 1954). There is evidence that such areas may show considerable stability over time, both in rates of crime and delinquency and in social characteristics. Wallis and Maliphant (1967) showed that the distribution of offenders in London was the same as it had been in Burt's original study. Hunter (1971) showed that there was considerable persistence in the distribution of social characteristics within Chicago. Castle and Gittus (1957) found a similar distribution of social problems in Liverpool as those noted 20 years earlier (Jones, 1934).

There are a number of problems in explaining area differences in rates of deviance on the basis of ecological correlations. Firstly reliance on official crime and delinquency statistics involves the danger of biases resulting from variations in police practice. Secondly, only limited conclusions can be drawn about the causes of criminality, because the nature of the association between the deviant behaviour and other area characteristics is not known. Fallacious causal inferences may be drawn as Robinson (1950) has shown, since the aggregated figures for the indices of adversity which characterized the areas may not refer to the deviant individuals (the 'ecological fallacy').

Epidemiological studies

These problems are avoided by epidemiological approaches in which social variables and psychological characteristics are assessed on samples of individuals representative of particular populations for geographical areas. Epidemiological studies have been carried out in metropolitan and small town areas in Britain (Rutter, Tizard and Whitmore, 1970).

The most revealing in terms of explaining area differences are those which apply the same measurement procedures to contrasting populations. Such investigations have been undertaken in Denmark (Kastrup, 1977); in Norway (Lavik, 1977) and England (Quinton and Rutter, 1980). Kastrup found few differences between a large municipal area and a small rural one in rates of children's problems. Lavik conducted a similar investigation of adolescents representative of contrasting areas of Oslo and compared them with a similar group from a rural valley 300 kilometres to the north. In Oslo there was a marked increase in behaviour disorders and school problems, especially in boys. The increase in urban problems was related to family disruption, social class and school attainment. These factors seem to have more influence in the urban than in the rural setting. Variations in rates of disorder between the different areas of Oslo were very small.

The most detailed study of the relationship between child disorder and family, social and educational factors in different areas is that by Rutter and his colleagues (Rutter et al., 1975 (a), 1975 (c), Berger et al., 1975; Quinton and Rutter, 1980). In a comparative study of the Isle of Wight, an area of small towns, and one inner London borough, the total population of 10-year-old children was screened for behavioural disorder, using teachers' questionnaires. Representative samples of families in both areas were then interviewed. The findings on disorder were similar to those in the Oslo study: rates of psychiatric problems in children were found to be twice as high in the London borough as they were on the island. These differences were related to parental criminality and psychiatric disorder and to family disruption and to social disadvantage in both geographical areas.

Summary

The evidence overwhelmingly suggests that large and often stable differences between areas in rates of delinquency and psychiatric disorder in children do exist. In general these rates are highest in cities, with a downward gradient through industrial towns, country towns and rural communities. In so far as these differences reflect the effects of family variables on development, they are the concern of a previous chapter. The key question here, therefore, is the extent to which area differences in children's problems can be explained with reference to such family factors alone. This has been examined in the inner London and Isle of Wight study (Rutter and Quinton, 1977). Rates of disorder were found to be twice as high in the London borough as on the island. Child disorder within each geographical area was found to be related to certain family factors. These were family discord and disruption, parental psychiatric disorder and criminality, and family disadvantage as indicated by low social status and overcrowding. All these factors were found to be much more common in the London borough but when the two populations were standardized for the amount of family adversity, the differences in rates of psychiatric disorder almost disappeared. It was thus concluded that the high rate of problems in London could almost entirely be explained by family factors. Influences outside the family may become increasingly important through the teenage years—for example clear effects of differences in secondary schooling have been shown (Rutter et al., 1979). It is apparent, however, that factors within the family continue to be strongly related to deviance over the early teens (West and Farrington, 1973; Power et al., 1972; Rutter et al., 1976).

The remainder of this chapter will consider some of the major social variables frequently thought to be related to variations in family patterns and development in different areas and some of the theories advanced to explain these differences.

Community decay

Higher rates of problems in urban areas are often interpreted as reflecting inevitable differences in the quality of life in different environments and in variations in the stability and integration of communities. Some investigations have dealt primarily with the greater number of adverse factors in towns and cities, without relating these to more general features of urban life: others have drawn on these facts to suggest that there is something in urban living itself which is more stressful and by implication less conducive to normal development (Wirth, 1938; Milgram, 1970). These inferences are generally drawn without the essential characteristics of 'community' having been defined or the relevance of these characteristics to child development having been determined. This imprecise usage is regrettable. In addition it is essential to grasp that all the evidence on community differences in development is based on comparisons of geographical areas which are either administratively defined, such as wards or boroughs, or defined with reference to particular social indicators or both. The alternative strategy of selecting areas for comparison on the basis of other indicators of the community, such as the connectedness of social networks, for example, has not been attempted. Very few studies provide evidence even on the kind and extent of social contacts and support within area samples and none have related the connectedness of networks or the effectiveness of informal social controls to patterns of child development and delinquency. Whether community organization and integration are of importance in this has yet to be discovered.

The word community is now commonly used to refer simply to particular localities which are homogeneous in certain respects. As a minimum the word community ought to imply that the inhabitants generally share a similar style of life, common values, a high level of social interaction and support, and a feeling of distinctness from other areas (Dennis *et al.*, 1957; Young and Wilmott, 1957; Frankenberg, 1966; Luloff and Wilkinson, 1977). Such communities have been more easily identified in rural areas, where the clear territorial demarcation is apparent. There they may still retain some features of social organization in addition to these more general characteristics, thus they may have an active political structure and a well-defined and articulated local culture, maintained by a system of informal social controls.

In the past, some urban as well as rural areas were characterized by considerable occupational homogeneity and stability of population. This pattern is becoming increasingly less common, although it still occurs in areas which rely heavily on single industries or employers. Where such areas exist, it has been proper to speak of them as communities. However, it is unlikely that communities of this sort were as common a feature of urban areas as is supposed. Victorian administrators shared our contemporary concerns with the lack of or breakdown in urban communities (Glass, 1968). There are reasons for supposing that the existence of distinct and settled communities in major cities has been overemphasized. This is likely to be the case since there is less overlap in urban areas between the various factors which encourage community feeling. Distinct districts are not obviously demarcated; the shopping, leisure and service facilities used by the inhabitants of any particular area often do not lie within it. The consequence is that local social organization generally does not develop beyond a series of overlapping personal networks. The degree of connectedness of these appears to be mainly a function of length of residence (Kasarda and Janowitz, 1974), and the need to maximize potential supports in marginal economic circumstances (Lomnitz, 1977). Where areas have a stable population this connectedness and stability may be considerable and may generate a sense of local identity. This seems to have been the case in Bethnal Green (Young and Wilmott, 1957). However, identification is primarily with a personal network linked through kinship ties. Concern with the area as such is restricted to a small local territory, often one or two streets or turnings. This is exemplified in Gans's (1962) study of Italian Americans living in the west end of Boston prior to redevelopment. Even within such a culturally distinct group, attachment to the locality was low. Most people were simply concerned with its convenience for work and downtown shopping. They took little interest in the area as a physical and social unit. They were primarily concerned with their own families and peer groups and with their own streets, not with the population as a whole. Only when redevelopment threatened did any sense of common interest or identity emerge.

It is often suggested that both child and adult disorders are associated with the breakdown of community patterns of help and support. Although redevelopment disturbs social networks and settled neighbourhoods and can have adverse psychological effects (Fried, 1963) there is little evidence to support the idea that urban areas are characterized by a major breakdown of individual social networks. For example, the inner London area studied by Rutter and Quinton is one which has been subject to major redevelopment. Nevertheless, families there have contacts with kin and friends just as frequently as families on the Isle of Wight and they have equally supportive relationships with them (Quinton and Rutter, 1980). In neither area is adult or child disorder or the quality of marital relationships related to the pattern of social contact. Multiple problem families have often been found to lack support or contact or to have poor relationships with kin (Schaffer and Schaffer, 1968; Wilson and Herbert, 1978; Quinton, 1980). However, this seems to be linked to psychological problems associated with adverse personal histories, rather than to lack of potential support as such.

Migration

The definition of the cultural boundaries within or across which migration occurs is problematic. Thus individuals or families may move into an area which is clearly linguistically and culturally similar or they may move to a different language area but remain within a substantially similar cultural environment in other respects. Alternatively their language may be apparently similar but the cultural context different. Or, finally, they may move into an area which is different both in language and culture. Each kind of migration imposes particular stresses, even when the language and culture are broadly the same. This is the case for example when peasant families move into urban areas. At present however the implications of these various kinds of migration from a developmental point of view have been little studied.

Migration to different cultures

Much of the existing evidence concerning developmental differences in groups migrating to different cultures concerns families of West Indian, African or Asian origin now living in Great Britain. It should be noted that the majority of in-migrants to the United Kingdom are white, English-speaking persons, moving within a broadly similar cultural context. However, developmental implications of this kind of movement have been little studied. Recent research on migration into mainland Europe has been concerned with the children and families of migrant workers from Turkey, Yugoslavia or other areas into France, Germany and the Iberian peninsula but as yet there is little information on these groups (Poustka *et al.*, 1977).

Studies of new commonwealth migrants to Great Britain have generally shown that the children have both deficits in academic attainment and more behavioural problems in school than their white peers. The reasons for these differences are not yet well understood. The increase in behavioural problems has largely been examined with respect to the children of West Indian parentage. The limited evidence which exists both from epidemiological studies (Rutter *et al.*, 1975b) and studies of child guidance clinics (Nicol, 1971) suggests that migration itself is not an important factor for the age groups studied. Moreover, problem behaviour is largely confined to school (Rutter *et al.*, 1974) and this suggests that difficulties in adapting to the school environment may be more important. These difficulties may include both conflicts between the expectations of home and school, the effects of racial discrimination and the effects of educational retardation. There is as yet no clear evidence whether the excess of school disturbance in comparison with white peers is diminishing or not.

The gap in academic attainment between the children of these migrant groups and those of indigenous parents has been shown to be less the longer the child's experience in the English school system is (*e.g.* ILEA, 1969; Little *et al.*, 1968; Yule *et al.*, 1975). It seems likely that the kind and quality of educational experience is again a more important variable than migration itself. Asian children who have been in the country several years have levels of performance similar to white children (Ashby, Morrison and Butcher, 1971). Despite this improvement, however, studies on children of West Indian parentage show a continuing deficit in performance (Little, 1978). The reasons for this continuing difference is not well understood. Until recently genetic explanations have been strongly advanced but these have seldom been supported by evidence which compares children with clearly similar childhood experience (*see* Rutter and Madge, 1976). When this has been done, in the case of children reared in institutions for example, few differences have been found (Tizard and Rees, 1974). Since the gap between white children and the children of West Indian parentage is apparent at the time of school entry and remains much the same throughout the years of schooling, it is possible that the differences are due to family patterns which have a strong and continuing impact from the early years. There is evidence of differences in family patterns between different racial groups which may reflect variations in the quality of early intellectual stimulation, although there are no adequate studies of family life in the early years which compare developmental differences both within and between groups. The evidence which exists shows that Asian families regardless of social class have child-rearing patterns which contain many of the features of middle-class indigenous groups, whereas this is not true of migrants from the West Indies. James (1974) for example described the strong ties within Sikh families in Britain and the child-rearing practices related to their religious and cultural values. Although the upbringing of girls tends to emphasize preparation for marriage and motherhood, all children are encouraged to question and explore. Similarly, research in Nottingham and Derby on 200 Punjabi speaking families by Dosanjh (1972) found a much greater emphasis upon rewards rather than punishments in child-rearing in comparison with both West Indian and English families. Withdrawal of love was rarely used as a method of control. Studies of West Indian parents on the other hand have revealed rather different child-rearing techniques, despite a similar level of warmth towards and concern for the children. Thus, at 1 year of age West Indian children are more frequently discouraged from touching and playing with objects in the home (Hood *et al.*, 1970) and at 3 years make fewer outings with their parents, play fewer games with them and have fewer toys (Pollack, 1972). At the age of 10 they have been shown to be more disciplined by their parents than are their white peers (Rutter *et al.*, 1975b). These differences are associated with other patterns which affect the amount of parent–child interaction and the quality of early child care. Asian families appear to have more successfully maintained extended family ties and this means that children can be cared for within the family if the mother has to go out to work. The migration patterns of West Indian families have meant that extended family support is less available. Since mothers of necessity frequently work long hours in order to help with family finance and house purchase, they are more likely to have to rely on child minding, often of a poor quality.

Families from different cultural backgrounds consequently import cultural practices which in conjunction with their new social circumstances facilitate or hinder their accommodation to the developmental norms of their host communities.

Migration within countries

Population movements within countries are now a major feature of community change but although internal migration has been shown to explain the greater concentration of various adult psychiatric problems such as schizophrenia (Goldberg and Morrison, 1963) and criminality (Morris, 1957) in poorer city areas, no clear cut evidence for the adverse effects of internal migration on family life has yet been found. Nor is there any clear relationship with those family variables known to relate to the majority of developmental problems. Thus, internal migration is not associated with the depressive and neurotic conditions which are the most common adult disorders amongst inner city parents (Birchnell, 1971). In the inner London–Isle of Wight comparative study rates of disorder in parents and children born and bred in inner London were similar to those moving in from elsewhere. The same pattern was true for the Isle of Wight. In addition, it is known that children of out-migrants from the London area have rates of disorders similar to those remaining there (Rutter, Quinton and Yule, 1980). Moreover, within a European-born sample, parents of children received into care in London are only marginally more likely to be migrants than the parents in the general population (Quinton, 1980). Internal migration patterns may affect families in more indirect ways through their impact on individual feelings of environmental stability and their sense of control over individual circumstances, but this has not yet been investigated.

Within area migration has been little studied. It seems plausible that the large differences in rates of delinquency between contiguous wards of similar physical characteristics in many cities may be related to small scale adjustments over a number of years. It is known that certain disadvantaged groups are much more geographically mobile within a small area than are more stable families (Quinton, 1980). It is not known to what extent lower rates of disorder in more rural areas are due to selective out-migration of problem families.

Sub-cultural influences

A number of sociological theories explain these differing rates of deviant behaviour as a consequence of inequalities within the social structure. In these theories social disadvantage is seen as causally related to deviance, not primarily through its effect on development but rather by promoting the emergence of adaptive patterns which enable those whose access to various resources through legitimate channels is blocked to acquire them by other means (Cloward and Ohlin, 1961). These patterns may or may not have an abnormal psychological component. Some writers have stressed the importance of status frustration as a motivating force in individual deviant acts (Cohen, 1956). Others see crime and delinquency as behaviours accepted within the normal value systems of certain disadvantaged groups without this status frustration element (Downes, 1966; Wilmott, 1969; Mays, 1954, 1972). In both cases the definition of deviance itself is seen as part of separate values through which those in control of resources try to restrict the access of others. This is evident in social control procedures to which those committing particular acts are more likely to be labelled as deviant if they come from lower social class groups (Cicourel, 1968).

The argument that delinquency is a normal part of this local sub-culture has been most strongly advanced by Mays (1954, 1972). In a study of patterns of delinquency among 80 boys from a Youth Club in an under-privileged part of Liverpool he found that over three-quarters admitted undetected offences of an indictable nature. He argued that delinquency in this area was part of an identifiable lower working-class pattern of behaviour to which the majority of normal and healthy boys had to conform. He did not see such delinquency either as a reflection of individual maladjustment or as resulting from status frustration. This view received some support from Wilmott's (1969) study which showed that amongst adolescent boys in east London petty thieving was a normal pattern of behaviour for the social group and was regarded lightly by most local people. Such delinquency was generally a passing phase unconnected with feelings of frustration. However, there is ample evidence from self-report studies both in Great Britain (Belson, 1968) and in the United States (Nye et al., 1958; Akers, 1964; Clark and Wenninger, 1962; Dentler and Monroe, 1961) that transitory delinquencies are very common and are largely unrelated to social class.

Some studies have shown delinquency and disorder to be related to social status when official delinquency is considered (Morris, 1957; Douglas et al., 1966) but others have found no such association (Palmai et al., 1967; West and Farrington, 1973). On balance the evidence suggests that the occupational status of a family is not generally related to deviance or disorder on its own, although the relationship is more consistently found when persistent offending is considered and when class is associated with other indicators of disadvantage. For these reasons it is still possible that areas with particular 'deviant' sub-cultures of the kind suggested by Mays may exist. For this to be the case certain known associations between maladjustment and family disruption and delinquency should be less strong in areas when normal cultural components play a large part in deviant behaviour. In general the evidence does not support this expectation and thus both in Britain (Stott, 1960, 1966) and in the United States (Conger and Miller, 1966) studies have shown that general maladjustment is as common in delinquents from lower-class backgrounds as it is from those in middle-class homes. Similarly, family disorganization and disruption is equally related to delinquency in all social classes. This is also found in epidemiological studies in child psychiatric disorders (Rutter et al., 1975c). It is important to note that many of the additional factors used in composite indices of low status involve aspects of family functioning. In addition, if delinquency were generally part of the normal peer group culture, delinquents in disadvantaged areas should not show increased disturbance in their peer relationships. This is not the case (Conger and Miller, 1966). Roff et al. (1972) have shown that boys rejected by their peers are the more likely to become delinquent. Similarly, West and Farrington (1973) demonstrated that delinquents tend to be less popular with their peers.

Finally, if sub-cultural arguments could be strongly considered, rates of deviance should be relatively constant within sub-divisions of the socially homogeneous geographical areas. This is generally not so. Several studies have indicated that within area variation is as great if not greater than that between larger and more socially distinct districts (Power et al., 1972; Edwards, 1973; Jephcott and Carter, 1954).

The evidence suggests that transitory delinquencies are a common feature of adolescent life in all social classes and are thus not related to cultural patterns or to values within particular social groups. Persistent offending is commoner in those from homes of low social status but predominantly when these are characterized by greater degrees of family disorganization. This seems unlikely to be part of a common pattern of life sanctioned by the community. Delinquent families are in the minority, even in severely deprived areas. They are less well integrated into them and have poorer relationships with kin and friends (Wilson and Herbert, 1978). In addition, parents themselves are equally likely to complain about their children's behaviour in these groups as they are in any other (Glueck and Glueck, 1950). This does not entirely discount the possibility that certain pockets of delinquency may exist in particular areas and may develop self-justifying and self-perpetuating sets of values. In areas where gang delinquency is common, groups may develop norms of behaviour centred round delinquent acts. In general, such value systems are better viewed in the context of small group processes rather than as reflections of the more enduring transmitted cultural patterns within the population as a whole or within major divisions of it.

Differential association

Sutherland (1939) argued that criminal behaviour was learned by association with those who commit crime so that the chances of becoming deviant are more determined by the frequency and consistency of a person's contact with those who are already deviant. This view, therefore, does not rest on the argument that deviant behaviour is part of the normal culture of certain areas. It is true that becoming delinquent is more likely in areas already high in delinquency and where there is frequent association with other offenders (Power et al., 1972; Rutter et al., 1979). It is also known that the probability of becoming delinquent is raised in high delinquency schools even when individual background factors are taken into account (Rutter et al., 1979). This suggests that differential association may be important in some cases. Nevertheless, the problem with Sutherland's approach lies both in explaining initial differences in area rates of deviance and the differential recruitment amongst those equally in touch with criminal activities. It is possible that this process is more related to transitory delinquencies than to persistent offending but the extent to which this is the case is not known.

Labelling and variations in police practice

Although it has been argued that variations in rates of delinquency cannot be explained primarily in terms of cultural variations related to social class or disadvantage, evidence suggests that differential probabilities of identification related to social class do exist together with differences in processing of those identified (Cicourel, 1968; Lemert, 1967). Labelling is the process through which identification as a delinquent leads to a subsequent career of delinquency through more intrusive police surveillance, the effects on life chances and increased probability of differential association. Such labelling has been shown to affect future careers and attitudes (West and Farrington, 1977; Robins, 1966; Gold and Williams, 1969; Gold, 1970). West and Farrington (1977) have shown that after controlling for initial level of delinquent activity self-reported delinquent acts increase in frequency if a boy is convicted but decrease over the same time if he is not.

Labelling may partly account for social class differences in official delinquency figures when these occur. However, since the association of deviance with social class on its own is not strong, even when official statistics are considered, it is unlikely that labelling as a class-rated control procedure plays a major part in determining differences in rates of delinquency between areas or social groups.

Physical environment

The fact that inner city environments are often seen as less pleasant than small town ones is sometimes taken as evidence that they have a directly adverse effect on development. It is true that certain environmental features are commonly associated with family problems. Thus overcrowding is consistently shown to relate to delinquency (West and Farrington, 1973; Ferguson, 1952) and to poor academic attainment (Douglas, 1964; Birch and Gussow, 1970; Rutter et al., 1970; Davie et al., 1972). However, overcrowding is generally associated with lower social status and larger family size. The relative importance of these individual factors has yet to be firmly established. On the one hand it has been shown that single adverse factors, of which overcrowding is one, do not relate to an increased risk of disorder in 10-year-old children (Rutter, 1979). On the other hand, data from the National Child Development Study has suggested that adverse circumstances may affect school attainments, even when other circumstances are taken into account (Davie et al., 1972).

Psychiatric problems and marital difficulties in adults have not generally been shown to relate to current environmental circumstances (Quinton and Rutter, 1980) or to improvements in environments (Hare and Shaw, 1965; Taylor and Chave, 1964). Housing styles do not generally appear to affect psychological functioning in the absence of other stresses. Thus living in flats is not consistently related to adult psychological problems (Moore, 1974). However, little is yet known about the ways in which living conditions determine family patterns or, conversely, the ways in which cultural patterns mediate the effects of environments. The importance of the latter may be quite large. Mitchell (1971) has shown that families in Hong Kong tolerate degrees of overcrowding which would seem to be unacceptable in the West. This is related principally to the acceptance of extended family obligations. Overcrowding causes more difficulties when non-kin are involved. Another major problem in investigating the influence of the built-in environment on development is the difficulty of taking previous housing history, cultural factors, and the effects of disruption of social networks into account. The Newsons (1968) for example showed variations in patterns of supervision and control in middle-class and working-class families. They linked these differences to the presence of privately supervisable play space. In general, working-class parents exercise less control over their children's behaviour outside the home, possibly because of greater social problems inherent in intervening in disputes in communal play areas. However, working-class mothers on new estates continue to show similar patterns. This suggests that one consequence of poor housing circumstances may be their effects on parental control of the children. Parents in overcrowded conditions are more likely to allow or encourage their children to play outside the home (Mitchell, 1971; Newson and Newson, 1968; Jephcott and Carter, 1954). This tendency may be reinforced by the effects of overcrowding on family relationships.

Another consequence of urban environments is likely

to be an increase in the risk of certain types of deviance because of inevitably great problems for formal and informal social controls, and because of the greater concentration of certain objects of delinquency such as motor vehicles. Thus types of offence are known to differ by type of environment (Clark and Wenninger, 1962). However, these wide variations in rates of deviance and disorder are often found in similar contiguous physical environments (Jephcott and Carter, 1954; Edwards, 1973; Power *et al.*, 1972). It is extremely unlikely that any straightforward relationship between environment and developmental problems exists.

Nevertheless, some environments do seem to become inimical to habitation. Thus the Pruitt-Igoe development in St. Louis or the 'Piggeries' in Liverpool were abandoned by tenants because of violence and vandalism. This has been linked to features of design. Yancey (1971) suggested that the lack of development of neighbourly relationships in Pruitt-Igoe was related to the lack of any semi-public spaces which might be necessary for safe informal connections to be established. Newman (1973) has argued that the lack of defensible space—personal territory which allows individuals to know their neighbours and spot strangers—is conducive to high rates of vandalism and delinquency. His initial evidence comparing two housing estates has been criticized on the grounds that the differences were explained by the intake (Hiller, 1973). Later studies by Newman have suggested that although the characteristics of the residents were a better predictor of crime and vandalism than was the design, the best predictions involved both personal characteristics and design features (Newman, 1974).

Urban stress and vulnerability

The study of area and class differences in developmental problems has yet to produce convincing explanations of the mechanisms which link wider social and environmental variables with that overlap of family adversity which has been shown to have detrimental effects on development. The evidence suggests that there are features of life in some areas which promote family difficulties (Rutter and Quinton, 1977), but the nature of those features remain notoriously elusive. One by one major variables, such as class, housing or social relationships fail to provide clear answers. Psychological explanations have fallen back on more general notions. Milgram (1970) has suggested that a number of patterns of city life are adaptations to the problem in 'information overload'. Thus an excess of stimuli from the environment causes people to restrict social interactions and limit helping behaviour. By implication, increased psychiatric problems may also stem from this source. Direct evidence in support of this view is lacking, but the fact that city life has more adverse effects only on the psychological well-being and marital relationships of those in more adverse circumstances suggests that a relative absence of ameliorating factors may be more important. This receives some support from Brown *et al.* (1975) who showed that working-class women in a similar inner city area were somewhat

more subject to severe life events or major long-term difficulties involving threatened or actual major loss or chronic problems with housing, money, children, family, health or marriage. However, only under certain conditions were they more likely than middle-class women to develop psychiatric problems in the face of such stresses. These conditions included the presence of small children and the lack of a confiding relationship with a husband or boyfriend. Similarly, McCarthy and Saegart (1978) showed that people were more likely to feel crowded and dissatisfied in high-rise than in low-rise dwellings but that this only applied to those of lower social status. The reasons for the greater vulnerability of working-class families in these circumstances are still largely a matter of speculation. They are likely to involve less personal control over various aspects of life such as housing, fewer economic resources to help in coping with stress, and perhaps with more restricted personal coping skills. The speed of environmental change and population turnover may also effect psychological well-being, especially when this change is very apparent and beyond the control of the inhabitants. Thus rates of delinquency increased in areas with a high influx of West Indian families even though they themselves do not contribute to that increase (Lambert, 1970). For the rehoused Boston Americans described by Gans, feelings of depression or loss were common two or three years after being moved (Fried, 1963). It may be that the lack of positive experiences rather than the presence of negative ones is a key feature. Phillips (1968) found that stress was related to psychological disturbance but that this was more common in lower social groups and that it was related more to the lack of positive experiences than to the presence of negative ones. Positive experiences were less common for those in the lower social classes.

CONCLUSIONS

The relationship between cultural and community factors and differences in development is extremely complex and, as yet, very little understood. The evidence strongly suggests that in all societies the major direct influences come through the primary caretakers or what may be generally called 'family influences'. However, the family patterns which relate to satisfactory development in one cultural context may be those which are indicators of later developmental problems in others. This provides much scope for research into the necessary conditions for adequate development, however that may be defined, and for the study of compensating cultural mechanisms. At present, however, the evidence presents challenges rather than solutions and indicates the complexity of the problems which are yet to be tackled.

REFERENCES

Ackerman, L. A. (1971). Marital Instability and Juvenile Delinquency amongst the Nez Perces. *American Anthropologist*, **73**, 595–603.
Ainsworth, M. D. S. (1967). *Infancy in Uganda: Infant Care and the Growth of Love*. Baltimore: Johns Hopkins University Press.

Akers, R. L. (1964). Socio-Economic Status and Delinquent Behaviour: a retest. *J. Res. Crime Delinq.*, **1**, 38–46.

Ashby, E., Morrison, A. and Butcher, H. J. (1971). The abilities and attainments of immigrant children. *Research in Education*, **4**, 73–80.

Bacon, M. K., Child, I. L. and Barry, H. III (1963). A Cross Cultural Study of Correlates of Crime. *J. Abnorm. Soc. Psychol.*, **66**, 291–300.

Barry, H. III, Child, I. L. and Bacon, M. K. (1959). The Relation of Child Training to Subsistence Economy. *American Anthropologist*, **61**, 51–63.

Barry, H. III. Josephson, L., Lauer, E. and Marshall, C. (1976). Traits Inculcated in Childhood: Cross-Cultural Codes 5. *Ethnology*, **15**, 83–114.

Barry, H. III and Paxson, L. M. (1971). Infancy and Early Childhood: Cross Cultural Codes. *Ethnology*, **10**, 466–508.

Belson, W. A. (1968). The Extent of Stealing by London Boys. *Advancement of Science*, **25**, 171–184.

Benedict, R. F. (1934). *Patterns of Culture*. Boston: Houghton Mifflin.

Benedict, R. F. (1938). Continuities and Discontinuities in Cultural Conditioning. *Psychiatry*, **1**, 161–167.

Benedict, R. F. (1949). Child Rearing in Certain European Countries. *Amer. J. Orthopsychiat.*, **19**, 342–350.

Berger, M., Yule, W. and Rutter, M. L. (1975). Attainment and Adjustment in two Geographic Areas. II The Prevalence of Specific Reading Retardation. *Brit. J. Psychiat.*, **126**, 510–519.

Birch, H. G. and Gussow, J. D. (1970). *Disadvantaged Children: Health, Nutrition and School Failure*. New York: Grune and Stratton.

Birchnell, J. (1971). Social Class, parental social class, and social mobility in psychiatric patients and general population controls. *Psychol. Med.*, **1**, 209–221.

Blum, Z. D. and Rossi, P. M. (1968). Social Class Research and Images of the Poor: A Bibliographic Review. In: Moynihan, D. P. (Ed.) *On Understanding Poverty*. New York: Basic Books.

Blurton-Jones, N., Woodson, R. W. and Chisholm, J. S. (1979). Cross-cultural perspectives on the significance of social relationships in infancy. In Shaffer, D. and Dunn, J. F. (Eds.) *The First Year of Life*. London: Wiley.

Brandis, B. and Henderson, D. (1970). *Social Class, Language and Communication*. London: Routledge and Kegan Paul.

Bronfenbrenner, U. (1959). Socialization and Social Class through time and space. In: Maccoby, E., Newcomb, J. M. and Hartley, E. L. (Eds.) *Readings in Social Psychology (3rd Edition)*. London: Methuen.

Brown, G. W., Bhrolchain, M. N. and Harris, T. (1975). Social Class and Psychiatric Disturbance among women in an Urban Population. *Sociology*, **9**, 225–254.

Burt, C. (1925). *The Young Delinquent*. London: Univ. of London Press.

Castle, I. M. and Gittus, E. (1957). The distribution of social defects in Liverpool. *Sociological Review*, **5**, 43–64.

Chavez, A., Martinez, C. and Yaschine, T. (1974). The Importance of Nutrition and Stimuli on Child Mental Development. In: Cravioto, J., Hambraeus, L. and Vahlquist, B. (Eds.) *Early Malnutrition and Mental Development*. Uppsala: Almquist and Wiksell.

Child, I. L. (1968). Personality in Culture. In: Borgatta, E. F. and Lambert, W. W. (Eds.) *Handbook of Personality Theory and Research*. Chicago: Rand McNally.

Christensen, H. T. (1960). Cultural relativism and pre-marital sex norms. *Amer. Sociol. Rev.*, **25**, 31–39.

Cicourel, A. V. (1968). *The Social Organization of Juvenile Justice*. New York: John Wiley.

Clark, J. P. and Wenninger, E. P. (1962). Socio-Economic Class and area as correlates of illegal behaviour among juveniles. *Amer. Sociol. Rev.*, **27**, 826–834.

Cloward, R. A. and Ohlin, L. E. (1961). *Delinquency and Opportunity: a theory of Delinquent Boys*. Glencoe, Ill.: Free Press.

Cohen, A. K. (1956). *Delinquent Boys: the Culture of the Gang*. London: Routledge and Kegan Paul.

Conger, J. J. and Miller, W. C. (1966). *Personality, Social Class and Delinquency*. New York: John Wiley.

Coulthard, M. (1969). A discussion of restricted and elaborated codes. *Educational Review*, **22**, 38–50.

Davie, R., Butler, N. and Goldstein, H. (1972). *From Birth to Seven: a report on the National Child Development Study*. London: Longman.

Dennis, N., Henriques, F. M. and Slaughter, C. (1957). *Coal is our Life*. London: Eyre and Spottiswoode.

Dentler, R. A. and Monroe, L. J. (1961). Early Adolescent Theft. *Amer. Sociol. Rev.*, **26**, 733–743.

Dosanjh, J. S. (1972). A comparative study of the child rearing of English and Punjabi immigrants in Nottingham and Derby. Unpublished Ph.D. thesis: University of Nottingham.

Douglas, J. W. B. (1964). *The Home and the School*. London: MacGibbon and Kee.

Douglas, J. W. B., Ross, J. M., Hammond, W. A. and Mulligan, D. G. (1966). Delinquency and Social Class. *Brit. J. Crim.*, **6**, 294–302.

Douglas, J. W. B., Ross, J. M. and Simpson, H. R. (1968). *All our Future: A longitudinal study of secondary education*. London: Peter Davis.

Downes, D. M. (1966). *The Delinquent Solution: a study in sub-cultural theory*. London: Routledge and Kegan Paul.

Dunn, J. (1976). How far do early differences in mother–child relations affect later development? In: Bateson, P. P. G. and Hinde, R. A. (Eds.) *Growing Points in Ethology*. London: Cambridge University Press.

Edwards, A. (1973). Sex and area variations in delinquency rates in an English city. *Brit. J. Criminol.*, **13**, 121–137.

Ferguson, T. (1952). *The Young Delinquent in his Social Setting*. Oxford: Oxford University Press.

Frankenberg, R. (1966). *Communities in Britain*. London: Penguin Books.

Fried, M. (1963). Grieving for a lost home. In: Duhl, L. J. (Ed.) *The Urban Condition*. New York: Basic Books.

Gans, H. J. (1962). *The Urban Villagers: Group and Class in the Life of Italian-Americans*. New York: Free Press.

Gath, D., Cooper, B., Gattoni, F. and Rockett, D. (1975). *Child Guidance and Delinquency in a London Borough*. Institute of Psychiatry, Maudsley Monograph No. 24. Oxford: Oxford Univ. Press.

Glass, R. (1968). Urban Sociology in Great Britain. In: Pahl, R. E. *Readings in Urban Sociology*. Oxford: Pergamon Press.

Glueck, S. and Glueck, E. T. (1950). *Unravelling Juvenile Delinquency*. New York: The Commonwealth Fund.

Gold, M. (1970). *Delinquent Behaviour in an American City*. Belmont, California: Brooks/Cole.

Gold, M. and Williams, J. R. (1969). National Study of the Aftermath of Apprehension. *Prospectus*, **3**, 3–12.

Goldberg, E. M. and Morrison, S. L. (1963). Schizophrenia and Social Class. *Brit. J. Psychiat.*, **109**, 785–802.

Goldthorpe, J. H. and Hope, K. (1974). *The Social Grading of Occupations: a new approach and scale*. Oxford: Clarendon Press.

Goody, E. (1970). Kinship fostering in the Gonja: Deprivation or advantage. In: Mayer, P. (Ed.) *Socialization: the Approach from Social Anthropology*. London: Tavistock.

Gunders, S. M. and Whiting, J. W. M. (1968). Mother–Infant separation and physical growth. *Ethnology*, **7**, 196–206.

Hare, E. H. and Shaw, G. K. (1965). *Mental Health on a New Housing Estate*, Maudsley Monograph No. 12. London: Oxford University Press.

Hawkins, P. R. (1969). Social Class, the Nominal Group and references. *Language and Speech*, **12**, 125–135.

Hess, R. D. and Shipman, V. C. (1965). Early experience and the Socialization of Cognitive Modes in Children. *Child Develop.*, **36**, 869–886.

Hess, R. D. and Shipman, V. C. (1967). Cognitive Elements in Maternal Behaviour. In: Hill, J. P. (Ed.) *Minnesota Symposia on Child Psychology* Vol. 1. Minneapolis: Univ. of Minnesota Press.

Hiller, W. (1973). In defence of Space. *J. Roy. Inst. Brit. Architects.*, **80**, 539–544.

Hodge, R. W., Seigel, P. M. and Rossi, P. H. (1964). Occupational Prestige in the United States 1925–63. *Amer. J. Sociol.*, **70**, 286–302.

Hollingshead, A. B. and Redlich, F. C. (1958). *Social Class and Mental Illness*. New York: Wiley.

Hood, C., Oppe, T. E., Pless, I. B. and Apte, E. (1970). *Children of West Indian Immigrants: a study of one-year-olds in Paddington*. London: Institute of Race Relations.

Hunter, A. (1971). The Ecology of Chicago: Persistence and Change, 1930–1960. *Amer. J. Sociol.*, **77**, 425–444.

Inner London Education Authority (1969). Literacy survey—a summary of interim results of the study of pupils' reading standards. ILEA Document.

James, R. G. (1974). *Sikh Children in Britain*. London: Institute of Race Relations: Oxford University Press.

Jephcott, A. P. and Carter, M. P. (1954). *The Social Background and Delinquency*. Nottingham: Univ. of Nottingham.

Jones, D. C. (Ed.) (1934). *The Social Survey of Merseyside*. London: Hodder and Stoughton.

Kasarda, J. D. and Janowitz, M. (1974). Community Attachment in Mass Society. *Amer. Sociol. Rev., 39*, 328–339.

Kastrup, M. (1977). Urban–Rural differences in 6-year-olds. In: Graham, P. J. (Ed.) *Epidemiological Approaches in Child Psychiatry*. London: Academic Press.

Kohn, M. L. (1969). *Class and Conformity: a study in values*. Homewood, Ill.: The Dorsey Press.

Konner, M. (1977). Infancy among the Kalahari Desert San. In: Leiderman, P. H., Tulkin, S. R. and Rosenfeld, A. (Eds.) *Culture and Infancy*. New York: Academic Press.

Lambert, J. (1970). *Crime, Police and Race Relations*. London: Oxford University Press.

Landauer, T. K. and Whiting, J. W. M. (1964). Infantile Stimulation and adult stature of human males. *American Anthropologist, 66*, 1007–1028.

Lander, B. (1954). *Towards an Understanding of Juvenile Delinquency*. New York: Columbia Univ. Press.

Lavik, N. (1977). Urban–Rural differences in rates of disorder. In: Graham, P. J. (Ed.) *Epidemiological Approaches in Child Psychiatry*. London: Academic Press.

Lawton, D. (1968). *Social Class, Language and Education*. London: Routledge and Kegan Paul.

Leiderman, P. H., Tulkin, S. R. and Rosenfeld, A. (Eds.) (1977). *Culture and Infancy*. New York: Academic Press.

Leighton, D. C., Harding, J. G., Macklin, D. B., Macmillan, A. M. and Leighton, A. H. (1963). *The Character of Danger*. New York: Basic Books.

Lemert, E. M. (1967). *Human Deviance, Social Problems and Social Control*. Englewood Cliffs, New Jersey: Prentice-Hall.

Lester, D. (1967). The relationship between discipline experiences and the expression of aggression. *American Anthropologist, 69*, 734–737.

Le Vine, R. A. (1973). *Culture, Behaviour and Personality*. Chicago: Aldine Publishing Co.

Le Vine, R. A. (1977). Child Rearing as Cultural Adaptation. In: Leiderman, P. H., Tulkin, S. R. and Rosenfeld, A. (Eds.) *Culture and Infancy*. New York: Academic Press.

Little, A. N. (1978). *Educational Policies for Multi-Racial Areas*. Goldsmith's College Inaugural Lecture. London: University of London, Goldsmith's College.

Little, A., Mabey, C. and Whitaker, G. (1968). The Education of Immigrant Children in Inner London Primary Schools. *Race, 9*, 439–452.

Lloyd, B. B. (1972). *Perception and Cognition: a cross-cultural perspective*. Harmondsworth: Penguin Books.

Lockwood, D. (1958). *The Black Coated Worker*. London: Allen and Unwin.

Lomnitz, L. A. (1977). *Networks and Marginality*. New York: Academic Press.

Luloff, R. E. and Wilkinson, K. P. (1977). Is the community alive and well in the city? *Amer. Sociol. Rev., 42*, 827–828.

McCarthy, D. and Saegert, S. (1978). Residential density, social overload and social withdrawal. *Human Ecology, 6*, 253–272.

Mannheim, H. (1948). *Juvenile Delinquency in an English Middle Town*. London: Kegan Paul, Trench, Trubner.

Mayer, P. (Ed.) (1970). *Socialization: the Approach from Social Anthropology*. London: Tavistock.

Mays, J. B. (1954). *Growing Up in the City*. Liverpool: University Press.

Mays, J. B. (Ed.) (1972). *Juvenile Delinquency, the Family and the Social Group: a reader*. London: Longmans.

Mead, M. (1928). *Coming of Age in Samoa*. New York: William Morrow.

Mead, M. (1930). *Growing up in New Guinea*. New York: William Morrow.

Mead, M. (1953). National Character. In: Kroeber, A. L. (Ed.) *Anthropology Today*. Chicago: University of Chicago Press.

Mead, M. (1954). The Swaddling Hypothesis: its reception. *American Anthropologist, 56*, 395–409.

Milgram, S. (1970). The Experience of Living in Cities. *Science, 167*, 1461–1468.

Mitchell, R. E. (1971). Some Social Implications of High Density Housing. *Amer. Sociol. Rev., 36*, 18–29.

Moore, N. C. (1974). Psychiatric Illness and Living in Flats. *Brit. J. Psychiat., 125*, 500–507.

Morris, T. P. (1957). *The Criminal Area*. London: Routledge and Kegan Paul.

Murdock, G. P. (1967). *Ethnographic Atlas*. Pittsburg: University of Pittsburg Press.

Murdock, G. P. (1973). Measurement of Cultural Complexity. *Ethnology, 12*, 379–392.

Narrol, R. (1970). What have we learned from cross-cultural surveys? *American Anthropologist, 72*, 1227–1288.

Newman, O. (1973). *Defensible Space*. London: Architectural Press.

Newman, O. (1974). Unpublished paper presented at NACRO Conference on 'Architecture Planning and Urban Crime'.

Newson, J. and Newson, E. (1963). *Infant Care in an Urban Community*. London: Allen and Unwin.

Newson, J. and Newson, E. (1968). *Four Years Old in an Urban Community*. London: Allen and Unwin.

Nicol, A. R. (1971). Psychiatric disorder in the children of Caribbean Immigrants. *J. Child Psychol. Psychiat., 12*, 233–281.

Nye, F. E., Short, J. F. and Olson, V. J. (1958). Socioeconomic Status and Delinquent Behaviour. *Amer. J. Sociol., 63*, 381–389.

Office of Population Censuses and Surveys (1970). *Classification of Occupations*. London: HMSO.

Palmai, G., Storey, P. B. and Briscoe, O. (1967). Social Class and the Young Offender. *Brit. J. Psychiat., 113*, 1073–1082.

Phillips, D. L. (1968). Social Class and Psychological Disturbance: the influence of positive and negative experiences. *Social Psychiatry, 3*, 41–46.

Plowden, Lady (1967). *Children and their Primary Schools* Vol. 2. Central Advisory Council for Education (England): HMSO.

Pollack, M. (1972). *Today's Three Year Olds in London*. London: Heinemann/SIMP.

Poustka, F., Schwarzbach, M. B., Schmidt, M. H. and Eisert, H. G. (1977). Planning an Epidemiological Study in Mannheim. In: Graham, P. J. (Ed.) *Epidemiological Approaches in Child Psychiatry*. London: Academic Press.

Power, M. J., Benn, R. T. and Morris, J. N. (1972). Neighbourhood, School and Juveniles before the Courts. *Brit. J. Criminol., 12*, 111–132.

Quinton, D. L. (1980). Parents with Children in Care. 1. Childhood Experiences and Current Circumstances. (In preparation.)

Quinton, D. L. and Rutter, M. L. (Eds.) (1980). *The Child, His Family and the Community*. London: John Wiley. (In preparation.)

Reiss, A. J. (1961). *Occupations and Social Status*. Glencoe, Ill.: Free Press.

Robins, L. N. (1966). *Deviant Children Grown Up*. Baltimore: Williams and Wilkins.

Robinson, W. P. (1965). The Elaborated Code in Working Class Language. *Language and Speech, 8*, 243–252.

Robinson, W. S. (1950). Ecological correlations and the behaviour of individuals. *Amer. Sociol. Rev., 15*, 351–357.

Roff, M., Sells, S. B. and Golden, M. M. (1972). *Social Adjustment and Personality Development in Children*. Minneapolis: Univ. of Minnesota Press.

Runciman, W. G. (1972). *Relative Deprivation and Social Justice*. Harmondsworth: Penguin Books.

Rutter, M. (1972). *Maternal Deprivation Reassessed*. Harmondsworth: Penguin.

Rutter, M. (1979). Protective Factors in Children's Responses to Stress and Disadvantage. In: Kent, M. W. and Rolf, J. E. (Eds.) *Primary Prevention of Psychopathology: Vol. 3: Social Competence in Children*. Hanover N.H.: University Press of New England.

Rutter, M., Cox, A., Tupling, C., Berger, M. and Yule, W. (1975a). Attainment and Adjustment in Two Geographical Areas: 1. The prevalence of psychiatric disorder. *Brit. J. Psychiat., 126*, 493–509.

Rutter, M., Graham, P., Chadwick, O. and Yule, W. (1976). Adolescent Turmoil: fact or fiction? *J. Child Psychol. Psychiat.,* **17,** 35–56.

Rutter, M. and Madge, N. (1976). *Cycles of Disadvantage.* London: Heinemann SIMP.

Rutter, M., Maughan, B., Mortimore, P. and Ouston, J. with Smith, A. (1979). *Fifteen Thousand Hours.* London: Open Books.

Rutter, M. and Mittler, P. (1972). Environmental Influences on Language Development. In: Rutter, M. and Martin, J. A. M. (Eds.) *The Child with Delayed Speech.* Clinics in Developmental Medicine, No. 43. London: Heinemann/SIMP.

Rutter, M. and Quinton, D. L. (1977). 'Psychiatric Disorder': ecological factors and concepts of causation. In: McGurk, H. (Ed.) *Ecological Factors in Human Development.* Amsterdam: North Holland.

Rutter, M., Quinton, D. L. and Yule, B. (1980). *Family Pathology and Disorder in the Children.* London: John Wiley. (In preparation.)

Rutter, M., Tizard, J. and Whitmore, K. (Eds.) (1970). *Education, Health and Behaviour.* London: Longmans.

Rutter, M., Yule, B., Morton, J. and Bagley, C. (1975b). Children of West Indian Immigrants. III Home Circumstances and Family Patterns. *J. Child Psychol. Psychiat.* **16,** 105–124.

Rutter, M., Yule, W., Berger, M., Yule, B., Morton, J. and Bagley, C. (1974). Children of West Indian Immigrants: I Rates of Behavioural Deviance and of Psychiatric Disorder. *J. Child Psychol. Psychiat.,* **15,** 241–262.

Rutter, M., Yule, B., Quinton, D., Rowlands, O., Yule, W. and Berger, M. (1975c). Attainment and Adjustment in Two Geographical Areas: III Some factors accounting for area differences. *Brit. J. Psychiat.,* **126,** 520–533.

Schaffer, H. R. and Schaffer, E. B. (1968). *Child Care and the Family.* London: Bell.

Shaw, C. R. and McKay, H. D. (1942). *Juvenile Delinquency and Urban Areas.* Chicago: Univ. of Chicago Press.

Spiro, M. E. and D'Andrade, R. G. (1958). A Cross-cultural Study of Some Supernatural Beliefs. *American Anthropologist,* **60,** 456–466.

Stott, D. H. (1960). The Prediction of Delinquency from non-delinquent Behaviour. *Brit. J. Delinq.,* **10,** 195–210.

Stott, D. H. (1966) *Studies of troublesome Children.* London: Tavistock Publ.

Sutherland, E. H. (1939). *Principles of Criminology.* Philadelphia: Lippincott.

Taylor, G. and Chave, G. (1964). *Mental Health and Environment.* London: Longmans.

Tizard, B., Cooperman, O., Joseph, A. and Tizard, J. (1972). Environmental effects on language development: a study of young children in long stay residential nurseries. *Child Develop.,* **43,** 337–358.

Tizard, B. and Hodges, J. (1978). The effects of early institutional rearing on the development of 8-year-old children. *J. Child Psychol. Psychiat.,* **19,** 99–118.

Tizard, B. and Rees, J. (1974). A comparison of the effects of adoption, restoration of the natural mother, and continued institutionalization on the cognitive development of 4-year-old children. *Child Develop.,* **45,** 92–99.

Tizard, B. and Rees, J. (1975). The effects of early institutional rearing on the behaviour problems and affectional relationships of 4-year-old children. *J. Child Psychol. Psychiat.,* **16,** 61–73.

Wallis, C. P. and Maliphant, R. (1967). Delinquent areas in the County of London: Ecological Factors. *Brit. J. Criminol.,* **7,** 250–284.

West, D. J. (1969). *Present Conduct and Future Delinquency.* London: Heinemann Educational Books.

West, D. J. and Farrington, D. P. (1973). *Who Becomes Delinquent?* Second report of the Cambridge Study in delinquent development. London: Heinemann Educational Books.

West, D. J. and Farrington, D. P. (1977). *The Delinquent Way of Life.* London: Heinemann Educational Books.

Whiting, J. W. M. (1977). A model for Psychocultural Research. In: Leiderman, P. H., Tulkin, S. R. and Rosenfeld, A. (Eds.) *Culture and Infancy.* New York: Academic Press.

Whiting, J. B. B. and Whiting, J. W. M. (1975). *Children of Six Cultures: a psycho-cultural analysis.* Cambridge, Mass.: Harvard University Press.

Wilmott, P. (1969). *Adolescent Boys of East London.* Harmondsworth: Penguin Books.

Wilson, H. and Herbert, G. W. (1978). *Parents and Children in the Inner City.* London: Routledge and Kegan Paul.

Wirth, L. (1938). Urbanism as a way of life. *American Journal of Sociology,* **44,** 1–24.

Wootton, A. J. (1974). Talk in the Homes of Young Children. *Sociology,* **8,** 277–295.

Yancey, W. L. (1971). Architecture, interaction and social control. *Environment and Behaviour,* **3,** 3–21.

Young, M. and Wilmott, P. (1957). *Family and Kinship in East London.* London: Routledge and Kegan Paul.

Young, M. and Wilmott, P. (1973). *The Symmetrical Family: a study of work and leisure in the London region.* London: Routledge and Kegan Paul.

Yule, W., Berger, M., Rutter, M. L. and Yule, B. (1975). Children of West Indian immigrants. II Intellectual performance and reading attainment. *J. Child Psychol. Psychiat.,* **16,** 1–18.

8. PSYCHOLOGICAL SEX DIFFERENCES

ELEANOR E. MACCOBY and CAROL NAGY JACKLIN

PSYCHOLOGICAL SEX DIFFERENCES

This chapter deals with contrasts in the way males and females think, feel, and behave, in the aspects of their lives that are not specifically sexual. The development of the sexual aspects of psychological differentiation—the formation of a sexual identity, the growth of sexual object choice, and the emergence of sexual attitudes and behaviour—are also, of course, of considerable interest to developmental psychiatry. But the presence or absence of sex differences in intellectual abilities and in the aspects of interpersonal feelings and relationships that are not specifically sexual is a topic that has come to have increasing importance in its own right. It bears upon the definitions of sex roles, and upon the extent to which societies can change or shape these definitions to meet the rapidly changing conditions of modern life.

In the present chapter we will be concerned first of all with identifying some of the realities of sex differences, whatever the cause. That is, we will summarize some of the evidence concerning sex differences in cognitive functioning and in social behaviour, as they occur in childhood, adolescence and adulthood. Since this paper is necessarily a very brief presentation of complex issues, we must remind the reader of the following points:

(1) Comparisons of groups of males and groups of females yield *average* differences: in all known aspects of psychological functioning, even when there is a consistent average difference, there is considerable overlap between the distributions of males and females. In other words, there are many women and girls with characteristics more like those of the average male, and many men and boys who feel and behave in ways that closely resemble the usual female pattern.

(2) Most studies have been done with white, middle-class American children. We will include cross-cultural evidence wherever it is available, but we will not always know how far existing evidence can be generalized to different populations than the ones primarily studied.

(3) There is a bias in indexing and publishing towards positive findings. When a study finds differences, this fact is likely to be noted in publication; an absence of differences is likely to be ignored. Thus reviews of published literature may exaggerate the extent or frequency of sex differences.

(4) When a difference is found, it is often assumed to be a 'natural' (i.e., unlearned) dimension of difference between the sexes. In fact, the cause of a difference is a separate and more difficult issue than the mere existence of a difference, and causal factors must be the focus of research specifically designed to uncover them.

We will discuss the nature and adequacy of the documentation of those sex differences that have some foundation in fact, and will point out areas in which promising research is being done. And finally, we will be concerned with the genetic and social forces which join to produce the differences. On the matter of causality, the evidence will be somewhat fragmentary.

SEX DIFFERENCES IN COGNITIVE FUNCTIONING

Verbal ability

On the average, girls achieve higher scores on tests of verbal ability beginning at about age 11–13. During the early school years, the sexes perform quite similarly on a variety of tests of verbal abilities, although there are more boys who have difficulty learning to read. It may be that language has an earlier onset in girls: recent work by Schachter *et al.* (1978) and Nelson (1973) would suggest that this is the case. The tests which yield sex differences from age 11 on measure a variety of verbal skills, depending on the ages for which the tests are designed; female superiority is found in vocabulary, reading comprehension, verbal fluency, verbal analogies and opposites, and verbal reasoning problems. The verbal abilities of both boys and girls improve through adolescence but the rate of improvement is often found to be greater in girls than boys. The average differences are quite small, and there is a possibility that, at least in the United States, the sex differences in verbal ability in late adolescence are diminishing. In the most recent nationwide American College Entrance examinations administered by the Educational Testing Service, average female scores no longer exceed average male scores. So far an explanation for the disappearance of the traditional sex difference in college-bound young adults is not at hand. In earlier work, it has been found that there are similar proportions of boys and girls earning high scores on verbal tests, but that there tends to be a higher concentration of males among low scorers (*see* Maccoby and Jacklin (1974) for a detailed review).

Mathematical ability

Boys and girls learn to count, and achieve number conservation, at approximately the same age. Through the early school years, their performance in traditional arithmetic and on 'new maths' (*e.g.* sets and intersection of sets) is closely comparable. From 11 years to 18 years, boys make more rapid progress than girls. By the end of high school their average scores are consistently higher.

Visual-spatial ability

After approximately the age of 11–13 boys obtain higher average scores on tests of spatial visualization. (There are some reports of differentiation at an earlier age.) These tests measure the ability to perform rotations of the mental representations of two-dimensional or three-dimensional figures. This ability increases in both sexes during adolescence, but the rate of increase is greater for boys. It is not at present clearly understood what kinds of real-life skills make use of this visual-spatial rotational skill, nor whether there are alternative methods—verbal methods, for example—for approaching the tasks in which visual-spatial skills are useful.

A good deal of recent research has focused on causal factors which might underly the above sex differences. It was thought earlier that spatial ability involved a recessive genetic factor which was carried on the x chromosome and hence sex-linked. Vandenberg and Kuse (in press) have shown that a statistical error led to a slight overestimation of the significance of these early findings. But more important, two more recent studies (DeFries *et al.*, 1976, and Spuhler 1976), using a wide battery of spatial tests and—at least in the DeFries study—a large sample of families, have found no evidence of a pattern of within-family correlations that would point to the influence of an x-linked gene.

Another major effort to locate a physiological component in cognitive sex differences had involved studies of brain localization. When one side of the brain solves problems more quickly (or more accurately) than the other side, the brain is said to be 'lateralized' for that type of problem. There are sex differences in brain laterality (Bryden, in press). Witelson (1977) has reported that boys are lateralized earlier than girls for certain functions involving haptic perception of forms. This is a kind of performance in which there is usually no average sex difference. But even in the absence of mean differences, there may be a sex difference in the function served by lateralization. Witelson finds that those boys who are *not* lateralized early show deficits in the verbal sphere. Girls,

by contrast, do not appear to need haptic-perceptual lateralization for high-level verbal functioning.

Waber has taken a different approach to lateralization, arguing that the rate of sexual maturation at adolescence affects the level of lateralization that is reached, with early maturers of either sex having the rate of lateralization slowed down at an earlier age. Greater lateralization, she argues, fosters high levels of visual-spatial ability, and the fact that girls undergo sexual maturation at an earlier age than boys, on the average, would help to explain the fact that boys continue to show rapid growth in this ability to a later age than girls do. Waber (1977) has some data consistent with her hypothesis. Further work needs to be done to confirm the initial Waber findings, and to give greater attention to the problem of which functions, if any, have their lateralization affected by the rate of sexual maturation. It is now clear that 'lateralization' is not a unitary phenomenon. Individuals can be lateralized for certain functions and not others, and the developmental timetable for lateralization varies from one kind of function to another. The work on lateralization is currently a very active field of research (*see* Chapter 14), but linkages to sex differences in cognitive functioning have not yet been clearly demonstrated.

At puberty, differences between males and females in the circulating levels of sex hormones are greatly increased. Research is in progress, investigating additional possible links between these hormones and cognitive performance, beyond whatever effects may be produced by the action of hormones upon brain lateralization (*see* Petersen, in press, for a review). So far, this work is only in the initial stages and clear findings have not emerged.

Work on the effects of socialization pressures, and sex-role related attitudes and experiences, has also been very active. It has been shown that experience with sex-typed toys during the preschool years is associated with performance on cognitive tests (Connor and Serbin, 1977).

Some current research is investigating the hypothesis that girls' accumulating deficit in maths during the late teens stems primarily from the fact that they take fewer courses in maths when they get into the grade levels where they have a choice of academic programme. Some earlier work (Project Talent, Flanagan *et al.*, 1961) compared male and female high school seniors where the sexes were matched with respect to the number of maths courses taken. In that study, male students still scored higher on maths achievement tests. A more recent study by Fennema and Sherman (1977) of 9–12th grade students all of whom were in maths course appropriate for their grade found no sex differences in two out of four schools tested. In a similar vein, deWolf (1977) studied 16 to 18-year-olds taking a pre-college test battery, and found no sex differences in mathematical or spatial ability when type of mathematics coursework was equated. (Sex differences were still found in mechanical ability.) Thus evidence is accumulating that the number of maths courses taken is indeed related to the previously found sex differences in mathematical ability in the upper school years. Of course the possibility exists that girls drop out of mathematics courses because they lack mathematical ability and find these courses especially difficult. But the belief held by many girls (and no doubt by their counsellors as well) that girls are unlikely to need maths and science courses for their future lives, also undoubtedly leads to the avoidance of maths courses in school. At present, the evidence is insufficient to permit assigning weights to these several factors.

Peer pressures have also been identified as a probable factor affecting sex differences in intellectual performance. Just at the age when the intellectual differences emerge most clearly—during the teenage years—peer pressures for sex-appropriate behaviours intensify. (*See* Fox, 1976, for a full discussion of peer pressure, especially as it impacts upon mathematically precocious girls.) Furthermore, it is at this same age that children of the two sexes begin to differ in their views about what sort of intellectual skills will be needed in their future lives (*See* Fennema and Sherman, 1977; Hilton and Berglünd, 1974) and their expectations match their differential performance fairly directly.

Perhaps the clearest evidence for differential socialization of boys and girls, and the possible effects of these socialization practices upon intellectual performance, comes from studies of the way children of the two sexes are dealt with in school. In preschool classes, girls are more likely to get positive reinforcement from a teacher if they stand close to her rather than at a distance. With boys, reinforcement tends to be unaffected by how far away from the teacher the child is located (Serbin *et al.*, 1973). Perhaps as a consequence of these differential patterns, girls tend to remain closer to their teachers. Teachers, for their part, tend to stay in the area of the school room where the materials for fine motor activities (*e.g.* clay, puzzles, drawing materials, beads for bead-stringing) are displayed. If teachers do move to other areas—outdoor activity areas, or indoor areas where blocks and wheeled toys are kept—girls tend to move to these areas along with the teachers (Serbin, 1977). We see here a mechanism whereby girls' preferences for certain kinds of toys and activities could be formed. And as noted above, there are correlations between the types of toys a child plays with and its later cognitive abilities.

During the school years, children encounter both textbooks and tests which embody sex stereotypes (Saario, Jacklin and Title, 1973). Illustrations in textbooks show female characters less frequently than male ones, and when female characters appear, they are frequently shown as passive on-lookers while boys are shown as 'doers'.

Interactions with teachers also show differentiation. Dweck and her colleagues (1978; Dweck and Gilliard, 1975) have done a series of studies pointing to a source of motivational deficit in girls. Boys receive most of their classroom criticism for 'misbehaving' (*e.g.* for being noisy, moving about the classroom too freely, roughhousing with other boys, being messy) rather than for making mistakes in carrying out their academic work. For girls, a different pattern has been found. When they are praised, it is likely to be for neatness, compliance—for being 'nice', 'pretty', 'good', or 'quiet' while any criticism given to girls tends to be for academic shortcomings, such as for mis-spelled words or mistakes on maths problems. This is true even though girls do not make more such mistakes, on the average, than boys. Perhaps as a consequence of these feedback patterns, boys come to believe that when they do poor academic work it is because they have not tried hard enough; girls, on the contrary, come to attribute their own failures to lack of ability. These attributions then contribute to differential reactions to academic failure. How strongly a child persists in attempting to solve a difficult problem is a function of positive and negative feedback patterns. Individuals who have received largely negative feedback for previous efforts tend to give up more easily. (The reader may recognize this pattern under the label 'learned helplessness'.) Girls give up more easily after academic failure than boys, but if the feedback contingencies are experimentally changed, 'learned helplessness' can be moderated or eliminated. Dweck has shown, with a group of girls who were extreme in their tendency to stop trying even after small failures, that if the girls are encouraged to believe that their failures are due to lack of effort rather than lack of ability, their willingness to persist in difficult tasks is considerably improved.

SOCIAL BEHAVIOUR

Aggression

In a review of a large number of studies most of which were done with children, Maccoby and Jacklin (1974) concluded that aggression is the social behaviour in which the sexes most clearly differ. More recent reviews, including experimental studies with adults (*see* review by Frodi, Macaulay and Thome, 1977) and further cross-cultural work (*see* review by Edwards and Whiting, 1978) generally support the conclusion that the male is the more aggressive member of the human species and that this is true at all ages and in all cultures where relevant studies have been made. Among adults, Frodi *et al.* find some indication that sex differences are weaker (or may disappear altogether) if subjects have been experimentally angered, suggesting that women can be as aggressive as men if and when an aggressive response is clearly justified in self-defence.

A rather surprising fact emerging from the review by Frodi *et al.* is that the greater aggressiveness of the male appears most clearly in the experimental situation (introduced by Buss) where the subject ostensibly functions as a research assistant in a learning experiment, and is asked to administer shock to a learner whenever the learner makes a mistake. This is a situation in which hurting another person is done in compliance with the demands of an experiment. It can be viewed as a situation in which the subject's aggression has a pro-social purpose. In view of the fact that in a number of studies females have been found to be somewhat more compliant to the demands of an authority figure than males, it might be expected that the Buss situation would be one where the usual sex difference in aggression would disappear or even be reversed. On the contrary, however, in the Buss experiments, women subjects more often refuse to administer shock, and characteristically give lower levels of shock to the 'learner' than do male subjects. Frodi *et al.* consider the possibility that women moderate the severity of their aggressive behaviour out of fear of retaliation from the victim, and they cite experiments showing that this is *not* the factor that underlies the sex difference found in this experimental situation. Rather, the greater female tendency to empathize with the victim, and to feel guilt over hurting others, seems to be implicated. They also find that women and girls, more often than men and boys, report experiencing anxiety over their own aggression and over any aggression displayed by others in their presence.

The more recent reviews continue to find, as did Maccoby and Jacklin (1974), that males are more aggressive both physically and verbally. There is some indication that a higher proportion of female aggressive acts, when they do occur, take verbal rather than physical forms. Thus the female bias towards verbal aggression is a proportional matter. It does not mean that females show more verbal aggression than males.

What do we know about the causes of the sex differences in aggression? We know that aggression can be learned, and we know that there are strong differences among different cultures and sub-cultures in how much aggression is allowed. Still, when research is done in other cultures if sex differences are found, males show more aggression than females. In animal studies aggression has been linked to hormones. Greater amounts of the male hormone, testosterone, produces more aggression in male and female rodents, and primates. However we also know from animal studies, that the resting level of testosterone (and probably other hormones as well) are themselves changed when primates have 'success' or 'failure' experiences. The relation of hormones to behaviour and behaviour to hormones is an active area of research. Much further work needs to be done before we can evaluate the contributions of socialization and biological predisposition to aggressive behaviour. There is reason to suspect that the effects of the two kinds of factors are not merely additive, but interactive. That is, the presence of certain biological determiners may cause an individual (or a sex) to react differently to environmental events, and hence learn differently, than would otherwise be the case.

Lest sex differences be overemphasized, it might be wise to underline the fact that aggression is a relatively rare thing in real-life interaction, except in warfare or other institutionalized and socially required forms of injury. An observer must watch a group of preschool children over a considerable period of time to see enough instances of fighting to permit reliable assessment of individual or group aggressive tendencies. And the frequency of fighting diminishes markedly as the children grow older. While there are certain deviant families and other social groups in which members frequently become involved in cycles of mutual hostility with one another, the more usual pattern of interaction in families or friendship groups is dispassionate or has a positive affective tone. Indeed, one of the reasons that psychologists interested in studying aggression in adults have turned to experimental laboratory procedures is that they find they must arrange situations so as to increase the frequency of the behaviour artificially; otherwise, the normally-occurring base rates are too low for study. Thus, to say that men are more aggressive than women does not imply that men are highly aggressive. Aggression is under good control, or virtually absent, within most small face-to-face human groups. Aggression *between* groups, of course, is another matter.

Social group formation and functioning

Some of the reasonably well-supported generalizations are these:

1. Boys are likely to play in larger groups than girls. Among children of nursery school age, boys tend to play in groups of four or five while girls tend to play in pairs or threesomes (Waldrop and Halverson, 1975).

2. Play groups are largely sex-segregated, and this segregation begins as early as age 3. Edwards and Whiting report that in the several cultures they studied, there is more hostility in cross-sex interactions, and more positive social interactions in same-sex pairs. When children just under 3 years of age are brought together in previously unacquainted pairs, play is more active in same-sex pairs than in mixed-sex pairs (Jacklin and Maccoby, 1978), indicating that even at this early age, children are reacting, in their play, to something about a partner's sex, and that young children find a same-sex partner somehow more compatible.

3. Dominance hierarchies are a more prominent feature of male play groups than female ones. Boys direct more dominance attempts towards one another, and the hierarchy tends to become more clearly established than among girls. That is, children in a classroom show considerable agreement as to which boys are 'tougher' than which other boys. There is less agreement about girls' position in a 'toughness' hierarchy (Omark and Edelman, 1973). In boys' play groups, the interaction is likely to involve a considerable amount of active running and body-contact (rough and tumble) play; girls' play is quieter, and involves more mutual nurturance (Edwards and Whiting, 1978).

The relation between aggression and dominance hierarchies is not well understood. A popular hypothesis is that the formation of hierarchies reduces the need for fighting among groups of individuals who continue to be involved in interaction with one another over a period of time. It has been shown (Strayer, 1977) that normal children respect the dominance hierarchy, in that their aggressive encounters tend to be confined to children closest to them in the hierarchy. Deviant, hyper-aggressive children, by contrast, become involved in fights with children much higher or much lower on the dominance scale than themselves. It may be, then, that the greater tendency of males to display dominance behaviours towards one another is related to their higher levels of aggression, which make hierarchies more functionally necessary in male groups. Or both dominance and aggression may be related to the male tendency to congregate in larger groups. So far, the developmental literature has yielded only slim clues as to the nature of these linkages.

It would be useful to know more too, about athletic skills and interest, and their relation to heirarchies, group size, aggression, and competitive versus cooperative behaviour. Is it the case that boys' greater interest in active, out-door sports grows out of the early group play characterized by dominance attempts and rough-and-tumble play? Or does the sports interest come first, and generate the larger group size and formation of dominance hierarchies that characterizes boys' play groups? And does boys' experience in organized, active sports equip them with a set of interactive skills which are useful for certain adult roles, just as girls' greater experience in care-giving functions during childhood may equip them for efficient functioning in a different set of adult roles? We know very little about the role that childhood play groups have in preparing children for adult functioning.

Sociability and pro-social behaviour

Girls are traditionally believed to have deeper, more significant ties to other persons than boys. This is thought to take both positive and negative forms—that is, to imply that girls are more dependent on others and more anxious about whether they have others' approval and affection, and that they have a greater sympathy for others' distress and hence a greater willingness to help others. What is the current state of our knowledge concerning these matters?

1. As far as the dependency side of the picture goes, these stereotypes are not supported by the evidence. In laboratory studies of very young children, the two sexes are very similar with respect to the standard measures of attachment to parents (*e.g.* separation protest, proximity seeking, smiling and vocalizing to parents, etc.). Maccoby and Jacklin (1974) did not find any tendency for girls to be more responsive to social approval than boys. Edwards and Whiting report that in a number of cultures boys make more dependency demands than girls do.

2. Both sexes show an active interest in peers. If there is a difference in the 'need' for peer interaction, it may favour boys; at least, at certain ages they are likely to spend a larger proportion of their time involved in such interaction.

3. There does not appear to be a clear sex difference in young children's sociability towards adults outside the family. As noted above, Serbin *et al.*, (1973) did find a tendency for girls of nursery-school age to remain closer to the teacher—a tendency which may be in part a reflection of the boys' greater involvement in active outdoor play with a number of peers, as well as of the teachers' differential reinforcement patterns. We do not know how general the Serbin findings will prove to be. Attachment studies with younger children frequently involve a 'stranger' episode, and the children's readiness to approach an unfamiliar adult is scored. Such studies usually do not find a sex difference in the children's sociability towards strange adults.

4. With respect to the willingness to help others, the literature on altruism suggests that such willingness is greatly influenced by circumstances. Whether one individual helps another depends on the role relationships between the potential helper and the person needing help, on the sexes and ages of the various persons involved, and on the nature of the help required. No tendency for one sex to be more helpful than the other across all, or most, situations can be discerned.

There is an exception to the general picture of sex-equality in altruism. Women and girls more frequently give help, nurturance and care to young children. (*See* for example, O'Bryant and Brophy, 1976) and show more interest in infants (Feldman and Nash, 1978; Frodi and Lamb, 1978). This is a generalization which holds across human cultures and across various species of primates lower than humans. Even in societies where women's work is needed for the general economic welfare, and where equalitarian ideologies or economic pressures or both have led to the organization of group child care to free women for work (*e.g.* the kibbutzim of Israel, and the child-care centres of China, Sweden, and the Soviet Union) the people working as caretakers of young children are almost exclusively female. Given the universal female dominance in child care, there is nevertheless enormous variation among human cultures (and among sub-human primate species as well) in the amount of participation by males in this vital social function.

Edwards and Whiting (1978) report that, in the several cultures for which they have observational data, girls are more nurturant towards infants in almost all instances, and that this sex difference may be discerned even in the reactions towards infants of children as young as 2–4 years. Boys direct more dominant aggressive actions towards children younger than themselves.

The reasons for the sex difference in nurturance is simply not known at present. Considering the cross-cultural universality and the fact that the same tendencies are found in sub-human primates, it is not unlikely that hormonal or other biological factors are involved or at least *were* involved at earlier points when deep cultural patterns were being established. Breast-feeding obviously plays a role in producing high levels of nurturant interactions between mothers and their infants, establishing a pattern which may carry over into the post-weaning period. However, there is as yet no direct evidence that breast-feeding by itself leads to an elevated level of mother–child interaction once the infant is weaned. There may be other biological factors making females, especially those that have recently given birth, more responsive to infants and young children.

Recent work with animals finds that post-partum females, even though they are less sensitive to most environmental stressors than other animals, show heightened sensitivity to distress cues emanating from the young. Also they are in a state of readiness to have their own stress reactions reduced by contact with the young (*see* review by Mendoza, Coe, Smotherman, Kaplan and

Levine, 1978). However, the parallel experiments have not been done with males, and therefore it is only an inference that this form of mutual soothing is more effective with post-partum females than it would be for adult males who formed attachments.

Clearly, socially-defined roles must also be involved. Girls are more likely to be *assigned* child-care functions from an early age. Furthermore, as soon as they are aware of their own sex identity and that of the people around them, they can easily observe that it is primarily females who are responsible for child care in the culture as a whole; therefore it would come to seem 'natural' to girls that they should be the ones to assume a care-taking role when the opportunity arises. It is hardly possible to find a human situation in which such cultural shaping factors have not been at work. Hence they can never be ruled out, and so far it is not possible, therefore, to examine biological factors in 'pure' form uncomplicated by interactions with social roles.

There is another respect in which females probably show greater positive social response than males. This is in empathic responding to others' distress. A recent review by Hoffman (1977) summarized the findings of studies where the sexes were compared with respect to whether they shared the affective state of others. In 16 independent samples covering a wide age range, females showed higher levels of empathic response, on the average, in all 16. The difference between male and female subjects was not usually large, and the within-sex variation was substantial, so that the sex differences were not significant in a number of the studies cited; nevertheless the direction of the differences between sex groups was entirely consistent. Hoffman shows that the tendency for females to be more empathic is *not* a result of greater attention to, nor understanding of, other people's emotional states. Males are as accurate as females in their assessment of the emotions others are experiencing. The sex difference lies in whether the observer *shares* (experiences vicariously) the emotional state of the other. It should be noted that in most of the work cited by Hoffman, sex of subject is confounded with sex of the target person whose emotional state is being responded to. We cannot be sure, then, whether females are more empathic regardless of the sex of the target, whether observers (regardless of their sex) tend to be more empathic towards female targets, or whether both things are true.

Is there any sense in which girls can be described as more 'sociable' than boys? In terms of the amount of time spent in social interaction, the answer must be no, as we have seen. There do seem to be some qualitative characteristics of the social interactions in female pairs or groups, however, that could be taken to mean that they interact in a more 'sociable' (that is, positive) way than is the case with male-male or cross-sex interactions. The cross-cultural evidence cited by Edwards and Whiting shows that girls more often approach their mothers simply for social play, games, or offering to share in the mother's on-going activity; boys tend to approach 'egoistically'—that is, making a demand for some form of service, or attempting to dominate or control the other. The

mother, on her side, focuses her interaction with her son on control and discipline, while with a daughter she is more involved in teaching and joint activity. Block (in press) has given questionnaires to a number of different groups of parents from different cultural backgrounds and having children of a range of ages, and finds that mothers are quite consistently more likely to say 'the child and I shared warm times together' if the child is a daughter. Furthermore, college-aged young women in six different countries are more likely to say that they 'shared warm times' with their mothers than are young men of the same age. There seems to be a greater mutuality between mother–daughter pairs. The same may be said of the interactions within girl-girl pairs, as contrasted with boy-boy pairs in the Edwards and Whiting data. Current observational studies of parent–child interactional sequences, and of peer play, are investigating whether mutual responsiveness (reciprocity) is indeed a more common feature of female dyads. At present the most that can be said is that some evidence is accumulating in favour of this hypothesis, and that more will be known shortly. In the Block work, there is also evidence for greater 'sharing of warm times' between fathers and daughters than between fathers and sons. It is possible, then, that there is also greater 'mutuality' between father–daughter pairs, and that what we are seeing, in the case of adult–child interactions, is not the characteristics of an all-female dyad, but of any dyad involving a female child. There is insufficient data on father–child interactions across a range of ages to establish the point.

In our efforts to understand the social behaviour of males as compared with females, we have shifted our focus from individuals to larger social groups. Same-sex groupings function differently from mixed-sex groupings; and all-male groupings function differently, in some respects, from all-female groupings. When we are studying the social behaviour of the children of a given sex, we cannot separate the effects of a child's own behaviour from that of the partners with whom the child is interacting. Children's behaviour is, to a large extent, a function of the company they keep. Since children do tend to assort themselves into same-sex groups, statements about the social behaviour of boys versus girls automatically become statements about boys as they interact with boys, versus girls as they interact as members of female groups. We do not know whether the crucial factor is the behavioural dispositions of the actor or the eliciting characteristics of the partner. In a sense it may not matter, but it is well to be aware that descriptions of social behaviour must, by their very nature, be descriptions of a dyad or a larger social system.

DIFFERENTIAL SOCIALIZATION

At several points so far, we have touched upon parental socialization pressures, and how this may differ for the sexes. Several generalizations appear warranted at this time:

a. Social science evidence was hardly needed to show

that parents select sex-typed clothing and toys for their children. It is of some importance to note however, that research confirms the popular intuition that the emphasis on sex-appropriate items is greater for boys. There is more pressure on boys *not* to play with girls' toys or engage in girlish activities, than there is on girls to avoid masculine interests. Decoration of a child's room also follows sex-stereotypes: stripes, bold colours and rugged materials for boys' rooms, pastel colours, floral themes and ruffles for girls' rooms (Rheingold and Cook, 1975).

b. Parents, particularly fathers, play more roughly with boys, and this differential treatment begins in the first year of life.

c. Parents use harsher punishment with boys, and find it more difficult to punish girls.

d. Fathers and sons seem especially likely to have an authoritarian relationship: fathers are likely to say that they have firm rules for their sons, do not let their sons question their decisions, and do not allow their sons to show anger towards them—more likely than they are to say these things about daughters, and more likely than mothers are to say them about children of either sex. For the most part, grown sons agree, in retrospect, that their fathers did indeed take an authoritarian stance. This contrasts with a greater degree of mutual trust and openly expressed affection between mothers and daughters, and in some respects, between fathers and daughters as well.

One can hardly fail to see an analogy between the relationships of fathers and sons and the relationships of male peers. Fathers and sons engage in rough-and-tumble play; dominance issues are salient between them, and coercive physical force is used to enforce dominance relationships. It is as though fathers' reactions to sons have something in common with their reactions to other males; the size difference of course establishes the direction of the dominance relationship—at least through most of childhood—and paternal reactions are influenced by the compassion and protective commitment that looms so large in parenthood. Nevertheless, the male-male element appears to be present.

As noted earlier, evidence is beginning to accumulate that girls develop a somewhat more harmonious relationship with their parents, on the average, than boys. Perhaps for this reason, the relationship is less vulnerable to stress. Hetherington's (*see* for example Hetherington, Cox and Cox, 1978) studies of divorce have shown that there is a more rapid deterioration of the mother-child relationship with sons than with daughters in the post-divorce period. Hetherington finds that in normal, intact families girls are more compliant than boys to parental directives, and that children of both sexes are more compliant to the demands of their fathers than of their mothers. After divorce, it is with boys that the father's back-up authority is especially missed by mothers attempting to guide and manage the children alone. When the mother-son relationship deteriorates into more frequent cycles of mutual coercion, the boy shows the effects outside the home—in his school work, and in his relationship with peers. The work of Wallerstein and Kelly (1975, 1976) on divorcing families confirms in every detail the greater vulnerability of boys to post-divorce familial stress.

In our earlier review (Maccoby and Jacklin, 1974) we summarized a mixed bag of studies on socialization of boys and girls *vis-à-vis* aggressive behaviour. Some studies involve observations and others interviews or questionnaires administered to parents. There was no consistent evidence that parents were more permissive, or less punitive, towards aggression in boys than in girls. Almost all the studies dealt with parental treatment of quite young children. The more recent work of Jeanne Block (in press) brings out some interesting issues concerning the perceptions of children and parents from a wider range of ages. Block has used a questionnaire, the Child Rearing Practices Report (CRPR), with five samples of American parents: in one sample, the parents had children of age 3–4 years; in another, aged 3–11 years (these children were all chronically ill); in another, the children were 12 years of age; one sample was made up of the parents of children in high school, and the fifth of parents of college students. In another phase of the study, college-aged young people were asked to fill out the CRPR, describing the way in which they had been reared when still at home. Young people from several countries (in England and Western Europe, as well as in the United States) were asked about their mothers' child-rearing practices; only US students were asked about their fathers.

While the comparisons of parents of sons with parents of daughters did not usually yield significant differences within the individual samples, there were some consistent trends across samples, and the same was true for the reports of young men and women concerning how they had been raised. Fathers and daughters were in fairly good agreement: both said that the fathers had tried to keep their daughters from fighting or playing rough games. (The exception was found when fathers of preschool children were questioned: here the fathers were more concerned to keep their *sons* from fighting.) But there are some interesting discrepancies in perception between the two generations when it comes to mothers' treatment of sons and daughters. Young men are more likely than young women to recollect that their mothers didn't allow rough games, and tried to get them to keep clean. Mothers report, on the other hand, that they hold up stricter standards to daughters than sons when it comes to avoiding rough games and keeping clean. It would seem that mothers, in responding to questionnaires (particularly retrospectively) are expressing a *value* for cleanliness and gentle behaviour that applies especially to girls. Children, again retrospectively, report on the pressure that they experienced. Which is a more accurate representation of the socialization pressure that was actually brought to bear upon the children? We can only suspect that the children are reporting on the number of times mothers actually scold about rough play or soiled clothing—issues which probably more often arise with boys. Mothers' reports, on the other hand, may reflect how they felt on the rarer occasions when their daughters did engage in rough play or get their clothes dirty. Both reports no doubt reflect something important about socialization pressures, but the difficulties in interpreting the findings point to the value of observational data to help clarify findings based upon questionnaires.

In studies of socialization, it is extraordinarily difficult to identify cause and effect. Do boys engage in more rough-and-tumble play with one another because their fathers have initiated such play in the child's infancy, or is it the case that fathers engage in this kind of play more often with sons because boys respond more positively to it? Do boys receive more physical punishment because parents believe they should be treated without pampering, so as to make them 'tough', or have parents discovered that milder pressures are not as effective with sons as they are with daughters? Are parents gentler with girls because girls are more compliant, or are girls more compliant because their parents have been gentler? Again, we do not know. The most we can say at present is that influence probably goes in both directions, so that any on-going relationship between a parent and child reflects a history of previous events where the actions and reactions of each participant have been important in 'shaping' the other.

IMPLICATIONS FOR PSYCHOSOCIAL ISSUES

We have been discussing the psychological characteristics of the two sexes. Since our topic has been 'sex differences', we have emphasized the differences and not the similarities, although we have tried periodically to note the fact that in many ways, males and females are psychologically very much alike. Considering the differences, there appear to be some that are not due entirely to social shaping, as well as some that are. It is well to bear in mind that even for those differences where biological predispositions are implicated, the within-sex variation is extremely large, so that there are many individuals who share the characteristics more commonly associated with the opposite sex; and, also, behaviour that an individual is biologically 'primed' to acquire must be learned, and is therefore subject to social shaping. Furthermore, any disposition is likely to manifest itself under a rather narrow set of eliciting conditions, and not take the form of a generalized 'trait'.

Does the existence of some dispositions that have biological foundations commit us to the view that the two sexes are destined to have different status, roles and occupations in life? It would be very difficult indeed to make the case that most men's occupations call especially for spatial or mathematical ability, and most women's for verbal ability. With rare exceptions, the work assignments to the two sexes seem to be made on an entirely different basis. In some instances (e.g. professional prizefighter) it is clear that the male's greater strength and aggressiveness are required and make it inevitable that men will continue to predominate in this occupation. However, it is surprising how often the division of labour between the sexes is such that women are called upon for greater feats of physical strength during their daily lives than men: witness the cultures where only the women bear heavy burdens upon their heads or do the heavy agricultural labour. Perhaps women, with their lower levels of strength and aggression, have been less willing or less able to protest onorous assignments.

It has been argued (see Goldberg, 1973) that wherever a biological difference exists, societies will—and should—socialize individuals so as to emphasize the difference. Girls should be trained to be submissive, Goldberg holds, because otherwise in adulthood they would be destined to be frustrated in encounters with men, who would inevitably dominate them because of their biological advantage in strength and aggressiveness. Perhaps in a culture where authority is maintained by brute force, such a course would be wise. But in modern cultures, it is more and more the case that leadership in groups of mature human beings is exercised through persuasion, inspiration, and task competence, and neither sex has an intrinsic advantage in these domains. Human social groups can make choices concerning the kind of society they want to have. In the interests of adaptation between the sexes, a society could either train its girls to accept male coercion, or it could train its boys to moderate their aggression and teach both sexes the skills of positive social interaction. There seems to be no reason why one approach should be regarded as more 'natural' than the other. It is our view that social institutions and social practices are not merely reflections of the biologically inevitable. A variety of social practices are viable within the framework set by biology, and human beings, being less driven by predetermined behaviour patterns than lower animals, are in a position to select those socialization processes that foster the life styles they most value.

REFERENCES

Block, J. H. Another look at sex difference in the socialization behaviors of mother and fathers. In J. Sherman and F. Denmark (Eds.), *Psychology of Women: Future direction of research*, New York: Psychological Dimensions, Inc., in press.

Bryden, M. P. Evidence for sex differences in cerebral organization. In M. A. Wittig and A. C. Petersen (Eds.), *The Development of Sex-related Differences in Cognitive Functioning*, New York: Academic Press, in press.

Connor, J. M. and Serbin, L. A. (1977). Behaviorially based masculine—and feminine—activity preference scales for preschoolers: Correlates with other classroom behaviors and cognitive tests. *Child Develop.*, **48**, 1411–1416.

DeFries, J. C., Ashton, G. C., Johnson, R. C., Kuse, A. R., McClearn, G. E., Mi, M. P., Rashad, M. N., Vandenberg, S. G. and Wilson, J. R. (1976). Parent-offspring resemblance for specific cognitive abilities in two ethnic groups. *Nature*, **261**, 131–133.

DeWolf, V. A. (1977). High school mathematics preparation and sex differences in quantitative abilities, *EAC Reports 77–17* (Report of the Educational Assessment Center, University of Washington, Seattle).

Dweck, C. S., Davidson, W., Nelson, S. and Enna, B. (1978). Sex differences in learned helplessness: The contingencies of evaluation feedback in the classroom and (III) An experimental analysis. *Developmental Psychology*, **14**, 268–276.

Dweck, C. S. and Gilliard, D. (1975). Expectancy statements as determinants of reactions to failure: Sex differences in persistent and expectancy change. *Journal of Personality and Social Psychology*, **32**, 1077–1084.

Edwards, C. P. and Whiting, B. (1978). Sex differences in children's social interaction. In sex differences and the effects of modernization on family life cross-culturally. Report to Ford Foundation.

Feldman, S. S. and Nash, S. C. (1978). Interest in babies during young adulthood. *Child Develop.*, **49**, 617–622.

Fennema, E. and Sherman, J. (1977). Sex-related differences in mathematics achievement, spatial visualization and affective factors. *American Education Research Journal*, **14**, 51–71.

Flanagan, J. C., Dailey, J. T., Shaycroft, M. F., Gorham, W. A., Orr, D. B., Goldberg, I. and Neyman, C. A., Jr. (1961). *Counselor's technical manual for interpreting test scores* (Project Talent), Palo Alto, California.

Fox, L. H. (1976). Sex differences in mathematical precocity: Bridging the gap. In D. P. Keating (Ed.), *Intellectual talent: Research and development.* Johns Hopkins University Press, Baltimore and London.

Frodi, A. and Lamb, M. (1978). Sex differences in responsiveness to infants: a developmental study of psychophysical and behavioral responses. *Child Develop.*, **49**, 1182–1188.

Frodi, A., Macaulay, J. and Thome, P. R. (1977). Are women always less aggressive than men? A review of the experimental literature. *Psychological Bulletin*, **84**, 634–660.

Goldberg, S. (1973). *The Inevitability of Patriarchy.* New York, William Morrow & Co., Inc.

Hetherington, E. M., Cox, M. and Cox, R. (1978). Aftermath of divorce. In J. H. Stevens, Jr. and M. Mathews (Eds.) *Mother–child, Father–child Relationships.* Washington, D.C.: National Association for the Education of Young Children.

Hilton, T. L. and Berglund, G. W. (1974). Sex differences in mathematics achievement: A longitudinal study. *Journal of Educational Research*, **67**, 231–237.

Hoffman, M. L. (1977). Sex differences in empathy and related behaviors. *Psychological Bulletin*, **84**, 712–722.

Jacklin, C. N. and Maccoby, E. E. (1978). Social behavior at 33 months in same-sex and mixed-sex dyads. *Child Development*, in press.

Maccoby, E. E. and Jacklin, C. N. (1974). *Psychology of Sex Differences.* Stanford, Calif.: Stanford University Press.

Mendoza, S. P., Coe, C. L., Smotherman, W. P., Kaplan, J. and Levine, S. (1978). Functional consequences of attachment: A comparison of two species. In *Early experience and behavior*, Smotherman, W. P. and Bell, R. W. (Eds.), in press.

Nelson, K. (1973). Structure and strategy in learning to talk. *Monograph of the Society for Research in Child Development*, (1–2, Serial No. 149).

Omark, D. R. and Edelman, R. (1973). Peer group social interactions from an evolutionary perspective. Paper presented at the Society for Research in Child Development Conference, Philadelphia.

O'Bryant, S. L. and Brophy, J. E. (1976). Sex differences in altruistic behavior. *Developmental Psychology*, **12**, 554.

Petersen, A. C. Hormones and cognitive functioning in normal development. In M. A. Wittig and A. C. Petersen (Eds.), *The Development of Sex-related Differences in Cognitive Functioning.* New York: Academic Press, in press.

Rheingold, H. L. and Cook, K. V. (1975). The contents of boys' and girls' rooms as an index of parents' behavior. *Child Development*, **46**, 459–463.

Saario, T. N., Jacklin, C. N. and Title, C. K. (1973). Sex role stereotyping in the public schools. *Harvard Educational Review*, **43**, 386–416.

Schachter, F. F., Shore, E., Hodapp, R., Chalfin, S. and Bundy, C. (1978). Do girls talk earlier?: Mean length of utterance in toddlers. *Developmental Psychology*, **14**, 388–392.

Serbin, L. A. (1977). Sex stereotyped play behavior in the preschool classroom: Effects of teacher presence and modeling. Paper presented at the biennial meetings of the Society for Research in Child Development, New Orleans, Louisiana.

Serbin, L. A., O'Leary, K. D., Kent, R. N. and Tonick, I. J. (1973). A comparison of teacher response to the pre-academic and problem behavior of boys and girls. *Child Development*, **44**, 796–804.

Spuhler, K. P. (1976). Family resemblance for cognitive performance: An assessment of genetic and environmental contributions to variation. Unpublished doctoral dissertation, University of Colorado.

Strayer, J. (1977). Social conflict and peer-group status. In F. F. Strayer (Ed.). Ethological perspectives on preschool social organization. Report of Research, no. 5, Department of Psychology, University of Quebec at Montreal, April.

Vandenberg, S. G. and Kuse, A. R. Spatial ability: A critical review of the sex-linked major gene hypothesis. In M. A. Wittig and A. C. Petersen (Eds.), *The Development of Sex-related Differences in Cognitive Functioning*, New York: Academic Press, in press.

Waber, D. P. (1977). Sex differences in mental abilities, hemispheric lateralization, and rate of physical growth at adolescence. *Developmental Psychology*, **13**, (1), 29–38.

Waldrop, M. F. and Halverson, C. F., Jr. (1975). Intensive and extensive peer behavior: Longitudinal and cross-sectional analyses. *Child Development*, **46**, 19–26.

Wallerstein, J. S. and Kelly, J. B. (1975). The effects of parental divorce: Experiences of the preschool child. *Journal of the American Academy of Child Psychiatry*, **14**, 600–616.

Wallerstein, J. S. and Kelly, J. B. (1976). The effects of parental divorce: Experiences of the child in later latency. *American Journal of Orthopsychiatry*, **46**, 256–269.

Witelson, S. F. (1977). Early hemisphere specialization and interhemispheric plasticity: an empirical and theoretical review. In S. H. Segalowitz and P. A. Gruber (Eds.) *Language development and neurological theory*, New York: Academic Press.

9. INDIVIDUAL DIFFERENCES IN TEMPERAMENT

JUDITH DUNN

INTRODUCTION

Even in the early weeks of life there are marked individual differences between babies. How do these differences between babies relate to later differences between children? Is there good evidence for continuity in temperamental traits from infancy? How do such differences affect the other family members, particularly those who care for the baby? Are they related to the child's vulnerability to stress? What part do they play in shaping the course of the child's development? These questions involve issues of central importance to our understanding of how human beings develop; they also reflect an urgent practical issue—how far can we predict which children are likely to suffer from disorders later? This chapter will discuss these questions in the light of findings from recent research.

INDIVIDUAL DIFFERENCES IN INFANCY

There are individual differences in many aspects of the behaviour of newborn babies: in sucking and mouthing (Korner *et al.*, 1968; Bell *et al.*, 1971), in spontaneous startles (Korner, 1969), in motor activity (Campbell, 1968), in autonomic reactivity (Steinschneider, 1967), in irritability (Korner, 1971; Bernal, 1972), in visual alertness (Korner, 1974; Barten *et al.*, 1971), and in response to a variety of laboratory and experimental interventions (*e.g.* Brazelton, 1973). It is difficult to trace how far these individual differences persist from the very early days. Babies develop so quickly that their behaviour becomes transformed within a few months. Even when a physical response looks similar at two different ages its meaning and the circumstances which elicit it and influence it may be very different: the crying of a hungry 3-week-old means something very different from the crying of a 3-year-old whose toy has just been taken. One approach to the study of the persistence of individual differences, which attempts to avoid the difficulties imposed by the baby's rapid development and the changing meaning of particular items of behaviour, is to examine the *style* of children's behaviour—the broad pattern of how they behave, rather than the particular details of what they do. Differences in such broad temperamental attributes were examined in a longitudinal study in New York by Thomas, Chess and Birch and colleagues (1963; Thomas and Chess, 1977). They showed that early in infancy the babies in their sample differed consistently in a number of respects. Nine temperamental traits were differentiated from the mother's description of the child: activity level; regularity of sleeping, hunger and elimination patterns; adaptability to altered circumstances; tendency to approach or withdraw from new situations or people; threshold of sensory responsiveness; quality of mood; intensity of emotional expression; distractibility and attention span. Further studies based on this approach have shown that these particular broad descriptive categories can be used with a good measure of agreement between those rating the interview descriptions. Assigning a child's behaviour to such global descriptive categories does, however, present a number of difficulties during the first year of life. For instance, should differences in the vigour and rate of sucking be considered as differences in intensity, in threshold of responsiveness, or in activity? With small babies such broad categories are inevitably interpretative. And when attempts are made to assess individual differences in the broad traits by measures of detailed behaviour, the results suggest that the uni-dimensional temperamental traits may well be over-simple constructs. The breadth of such traits apparently masks differing patterns of consistency in individual differences which more fine-grain direct assessments of behaviour do reveal. (Dunn, 1979.) Such methodological problems certainly raise doubts about the reliability of our present procedures for identifying accurately and consistently the characteristics of particular infants. But while more systematic work using both direct observation and assessment of behaviour and rating of temperament is certainly needed, it is already clear from a number of studies using either technique that individual differences in infancy have important implications for the course of development, and for the child's vulnerability to later stress.

ORIGINS OF INDIVIDUAL DIFFERENCES

Studies of twins using both ratings of temperament and direct observation of behaviour have shown that hereditary factors are important in contributing to individual differences between children. Torgersen and Kringlen (1978) studied 53 same-sex twin pairs, looking at the temperamental traits identified in the New York Longitudinal Study. They found that the differences between dizygotic twins at 2 months were significantly greater than the differences between monozygotic twins for only two traits, but that by 9 months the differences were significant for all nine traits. (It is important to note that in this study the 'majority' of mothers were apparently unaware of the zygosity of their children.) Rutter et al. (1963) found evidence, in a small sample of twins from the New York Longitudinal Study, for the importance of genetic factors in these temperamental traits during the first year of life. After the first year the evidence for genetic components was much less strong. Early smiling behaviour (Freedman and Keller, 1963; Repucci, 1968) and a variety of other aspects of social behaviour (Vandenberg, 1969; Scarr, 1969) have been found to show heritability.

Apart from the evidence provided by these few twin studies of the importance of hereditary factors, there is little clear information on the origins of temperamental differences. This is in part a consequence of the close association between individual differences in children and individual differences in their parents or caregivers. It is often difficult, or impossible, to separate these, or to understand the direction of causal link between them. Where, for instance, an association between individual differences in infants and perinatal difficulties is reported, the link between environmental event and baby behaviour could be formed in a number of different ways. Two studies have found, for instance, that babies born after a long labour and much maternal medication were more likely to cry frequently and to wake frequently in the newborn period, (Bernal, 1973; Blurton Jones et al., 1978). The perinatal events themselves may have affected the babies directly (see e.g. Prechtl, 1965). But it is also possible that differences between the fetuses had contributed to the difficulties in labour, and had produced, quite independently, differences in sleeping and crying in the newborn period. Yet another possibility is that the more anxious mothers tended to have longer labours, and also tended to interact with their babies in a way that led to shorter sleeps and more frequent crying. A further possibility might well be that the irritable crying and short sleeping are a result of feeding problems, the behaviour of the baby then being not a result of the direct effect of the stressful labour on the baby, but rather reflecting the problems both mother and baby experience in feeds after a difficult delivery (Dunn and Richards, 1977). While the association between perinatal events and behavioural differences in the newborn period is not as yet well understood, the existence of such links has been described in a number of studies. (Moore and Ucko, 1957; Rosenblatt and Packer, 1979; Prechtl, 1965.)

It is sometimes suggested that children with organic brain damage differ in their temperamental characteristics from those without such damage. But there is little systematic information on the issue. Behaviour problems are more common in mentally retarded children (Rutter, 1971), but we do not know how far these effects reflect temperamental differences; temperamental features are reported to be often normal in mentally retarded children (Chess and Korn, 1970; Baron, 1972). Some studies have reported an association between congenital physical anomalies, and hyperactivity and impulsiveness (e.g. Waldrop et al., 1968). Ucko (1965) found that children whose birth records suggested that they had suffered neonatal asphyxia differed on neonatal characteristics: they were more irregular over sleeping, unadaptable, sensitive to noise, anxious over starting school, and particularly difficult to manage, in comparison with a control group matched for socioeconomic background. There was, however, no evidence for a direct relationship between these behavioural difficulties and organic brain damage.

Wide cross-cultural differences have been shown in studies of newborn babies; differences in response to soothing and in self-quieting ability are particularly marked. Brazelton and Collier (1969), for instance, compared a group of Zinanteco babies from Mexico with a sample of babies from the US: all the babies had had drug-free deliveries. The American babies cried more intensely, and slept more deeply. The Indian babies stayed in a quiet alert state for longer than the American babies. It is not clear whether these differences are attributable to genetic or environmental factors, differences in caregiving style, for example, being very marked between cultures. Whatever their origin, such differences in the behaviour of babies are likely to have important consequences for the patterns of interaction between baby and caregiver.

SEX DIFFERENCES

There are conflicting reports on the extent and nature of sex differences in infancy (see review by Maccoby and Jacklin, 1975 and Chapter 7 in this volume). Differences in taste discrimination and in tactile sensitivity have been confirmed (Bell and Costello, 1964; Nisbet and Gurwitz, 1970; Lipsitt and Levy, 1959). And in later childhood differences in style of play, and in aggressive behaviour, have been repeatedly reported in a variety of cultures (Maccoby and Jacklin, 1975). It is clear that social pressures are of great importance in influencing some of the differences between boys and girls (such as e.g. the greater dependence and conformity often described for girls); however there is also evidence that hormonal factors are important in accounting for the differences in aggressive behaviour (Money and Ehrhardt, 1968).

Since boys are more physically vulnerable than girls from conception onwards, in any sample of children that is not carefully screened for perinatal problems the behaviour of more boys than girls is likely to be affected by a difficult delivery. But some sex differences in the behaviour of very young children are apparent even in samples carefully selected to exclude those who had experienced difficult deliveries (Pedersen and Bell, 1970). The more rapid rate of maturation in girls means that at any one age there are likely to be differences between the sexes which can be attributed to developmental rate. Sex differences have also been noted in the response of children to family discord and separation experiences (Rutter, 1970). It is not known whether this association is linked to differences in temperament.

CONTINUITIES AND DISCONTINUITIES IN INDIVIDUAL DIFFERENCES

The persistence of individual differences in behaviour has been examined in a number of longitudinal studies (reviewed by Berger, 1973). The methods used in these studies range from the interview-based ratings of global temperamental traits in the New York Study (Thomas *et al.*, 1963), ratings of observed behaviour in the Fels study (Kagan and Moss, 1962), observation of children's behaviour during cognitive testing in the Berkeley Growth Study (Schaefer and Bayley, 1963), to the use of detailed and careful measures of observed behaviour, as in Kagan's study of attentional processes (Kagan, 1971), or in Bell and colleagues (1971) study of children at the newborn and preschool stages.

Individual differences between children in these studies are considered from very divergent theoretical viewpoints. The term 'temperament' for instance is used only in discussion of infants and young children; in the study of older children individual differences are described in terms of a number of different theories of personality development, in which the 'traits' or aspects of behaviour studied inevitably differ widely. These different approaches to the study of personality do of course emphasize very different aspects of continuity and change in development, with the plasticity of developmental processes emphasized by theories derived from social learning theory, and the stability of personality emphasized by psychoanalytic theories, which stress the long-term effects of early experience.

In spite of the very wide range of approaches to the description of individual differences in childhood, there is considerable agreement among the studies that from about 3 years on there is some consistency of individual differences from year to year, though there may be marked changes over longer periods. However, it is necessary to qualify this generalization in a number of important respects which will be considered next.

FACTORS INFLUENCING THE CONTINUITY OF INDIVIDUAL DIFFERENCES

Developmental changes from infancy

Babies develop quickly during the first 18 months. Within the first year there are two periods of particularly rapid development, during which there appear to be major changes in organization, reflected for example in changes in patterns of sleep, wakefulness, the EEG, autonomic responses, and responses to people and environmental changes (Emde *et al.*, 1976). This rapid development presents problems for those attempting to assess the extent of continuity in individual differences. It means first that individual differences at any one age may reflect differences in rate of maturation rather than differences in temperament, and second, that the meaning of a particular response may change markedly in the course of the first year. Individual differences in infancy may reflect differences in adaptation to a particular stage of development. In different phases of development the baby shows very different responses to the outside world and to people: if these responses reflect adaptations peculiar to that phase of development, individual differences may not necessarily persist beyond the phase in question or relate in any consistent way to individual differences at later stages. There may in fact be a real discontinuity in the patterns of association between measures, with the developmental changes in organization.

Apparent discontinuities in the consistency of individual differences between children as they grow up may also reflect the difficulty the investigator has in deciding which behaviour measures might be related at different ages.

Finally, discontinuities in individual differences reflect the effects of environment on patterns of temperament. Although the term 'temperament' is sometimes used as if it reflects constitutional characteristics of the child, it should certainly not be supposed that temperamental characteristics are not modifiable, or that they are not affected by the environment in which the child grows up (Thomas and Chess, 1977).

How far do the developmental changes of later childhood and adolescence alter the continuity of individual differences? Studies of adolescence have reported that marked swings of mood, feelings of misery, depression anxiety and self-depreciation are particularly common among 14-year-olds (Rutter *et al.*, 1976; Masterson, 1967). It is, however, quite unclear how individual differences in early childhood relate to the appearance of such feelings during adolescence. It is also unclear how such feelings are related to psychiatric disorder (the patterns of psychiatric disorder among adolescents do show an increase in the prevalence of depression (Graham and Rutter, 1977; Graham and Rutter, 1973; Rutter *et al.*, 1976). Much of the information which is at present available on the consistency of individual differences in later childhood and adolescence derives from follow-up studies of behaviour disorders (*see below* 'Follow up Studies of Behaviour Disorders').

Continuity and discontinuity of individual differences in patterns of parental behaviour

It is probable that continuity in patterns of interaction with parents contribute in an important way to the persistence of individual differences in children (*see* Chapter on family influences). The results of one of the very few studies which has followed children from birth to adulthood, the Fels study, demonstrates very clearly the significance of environmental influences on patterns of continuity (Kagan and Moss, 1962). Many of the measures of individual differences between the children at ages 6–10 years were moderately good predictors of later behaviour. The degree of continuity was also closely related, however, to the extent to which the behaviour fitted sex-role standards prevailing in the culture of the population studied. For instance, 'passivity' in girls in early childhood was closely related both to direct measures of passivity later, and to measures of conformity to parents, timidity in social situations, and absence of physical aggression. This 'passivity' dimension was much more stable for girls than for boys. In contrast, measures of aggression showed much greater stability for boys. Individual differences in these measures in the 6–10 year age period were good predictors of later aggressive behaviour. Individual differences in behaviour indicating 'intellectual mastery' showed good continuity for both sexes from the 6–10 year age period to adulthood. These results emphasize the impact of cultural expectations and standards in determining both behavioural change and stability.

Discontinuities in the individual differences in parental response to the developing child may also contribute importantly to discontinuities in individual differences. In one longitudinal study it was found that at the stage when children began to understand speech, and to become more effective communicators, patterns of individual differences in maternal responsiveness, which had been very stable over the course of the first year, disappeared. New patterns of individual differences in maternal behaviour appeared, as the mothers responded in different ways to the development of language and communication skills in their children (Dunn, 1977).

Nature of sample

The stability of individual differences from early infancy varies very markedly with the nature of the sample studied. Just as exceptionally low scores on DQ tests in the first year show some predictive significance, while scores within the more normal range do not (McCall *et al.*, 1972; McCall, 1976), it has been shown that children whose behaviour is extreme on some dimensions will continue to differ markedly from the rest of the sample in later years. In Kagan's longitudinal study there were several examples of remarkable continuity in individual differences for children who scored at the extreme of the behavioural measure being examined (Kagan, 1971). Studies of the effects of perinatal trauma on later development show very different results according to the character of the sample of families which is studied:

differences in the early months attributable to the perinatal events disappear unless they are combined with continuing conditions of social deprivation. These effects of extreme perinatal hazard have been reviewed by Sameroff and Chandler (1975). Parallel results for a medically low-risk sample show continuity between neonatal differences and behaviour at 4 or 5 years for the children from low SES background; however, for the middle-class children in the sample, the neonatal differences disappeared. Amongst other factors the effects of differences in parental response and attentiveness during the second and third years may well have served to swamp the variation between children which could be traced from the neonatal stage (Dunn, 1979).

Processes of self-regulation in development

For many different reasons, then, individual differences in the early months may not persist to later childhood. Studies such as those reviewed by Sameroff and Chandler on the effects of perinatal trauma suggest that the developing child may be 'buffered' in some way against traumatic experiences. The importance of some sort of 'self-righting' process in development has been stressed by many biologists (Waddington, 1957; Bateson, 1976). They point out that in many developmental processes there may be several possible routes to a particular developmental outcome. This is an important idea for psychologists to consider, since there are several aspects of development where a wide range of environmental variables may be influential on a relatively narrow range of outcomes. Studies of language development, for instance, have shown that with different mother–child pairs there may be considerable differences in the routes along which language competence develops (Nelson, 1973), and children with physical handicaps may make conceptual discoveries in quite different ways from those of children with no such handicap (Gouin-Decarie, 1969). Recent follow-up studies of children who spent their first years in residential nurseries or in deprived circumstances illustrate well the point that if placed in moderately favourable environments children do show considerable powers of recovery from early trauma, restricted or difficult circumstances. (Clarke and Clarke, 1976.) Such studies underline the importance of taking real account of the flexibility of developmental processes.

Linking studies of early and late childhood

The very different theoretical approaches to the study of temperament and personality in early and late childhood present particular problems to those attempting to link the findings of studies of these phases of development, since such very different 'traits' or 'dimensions' of individual differences in behaviour are discussed in them. The disparities in approach reflect the major conceptual difficulties posed by any attempt to relate the behaviour of a young child to that of a relatively sophisticated adolescent. What measures should be used to compare 'malleability' in a 3-year-old with the behaviour of an adolescent?

Since social norms necessarily influence the expression of a 'trait' to very different degrees and in very different ways at different ages, how is it possible to distinguish the evidence for the impact of cultural learning from the evidence for the stability or change of the 'trait' under investigation? The difficulties we encounter in trying to link the findings of studies of very young children with those of adolescents are thus far from being simply the results of trivial problems of method. They derive from major theoretical problems in the understanding of human development. Some theoretical models highlight aspects of individual differences in which considerable instability can be found. Others highlight aspects in which much consistency has been demonstrated. This disparity in itself does not give one grounds for doubting the validity of either set of findings. But it does suggest the need for more careful comparison, between the various theoretical models, of the meaning of the concepts of personality and of personal identity which they use.

INDIVIDUAL DIFFERENCES AND LATER DISORDER

Much of the interest shown in early differences between children arises from the hope that prediction of vulnerability to later disorder will become possible. A number of studies involving very different samples of children, and using very different methods of assessing individual differences, have now demonstrated that there are associations between particular constellations of individual differences and later behaviour problems. Two studies, for instance, have now found associations between sleeping problems in the second year, and individual differences that can be traced to the neonatal period (Bernal, 1973; Blurton-Jones *et al.*, 1978). In the study in Cambridge by Bernal and Richards the group of children who had sleep problems in the second year had also been slower to establish regular breathing and crying at birth, had reacted more quickly by crying in a test situation, and were more irritable and slept for shorter periods during the first 10 days of life. These differences in sleeping patterns continued until after the children were 3. At 5 years the sleeping-problem children were significantly more likely to score above the median on a rating of behaviour problems (Dunn, 1979).

In the New York Longitudinal study comparisons were made between the temperamental traits of the children referred for psychiatric help (usually for mild behavioural disturbance), and those of the rest of the sample (Rutter *et al.*, 1964). In the second year, before behavioural disturbance was evident, the pattern of temperamental characteristics did differentiate the children who were to develop problems later. A pattern of irregularity in sleep and feeding, predominantly miserable or irritable mood, lack of adaptability to new circumstances, and an intensity of emotional response was more common among those children who were referred for psychiatric help in later years.

Studying a very different sample, a group of working-class families with one parent receiving care for psychiatric problems, Graham and colleagues (1973) assessed temperamental differences between the children in a similar way, and reported a very similar association between temperament and later disorder. Irregularity of eating, sleeping and elimination habits, lack of malleability and a lack of fastidiousness were more common among the children who one year later showed behavioural disorder. They also tended to be negative in mood, and intense in their emotional reactions. When these temperamental characteristics were combined to form a temperamental adversity index, it was found that the children with high scores were one year later three times as likely as the low scoring children to show psychiatric disorder at home, and eight times as likely to show behavioural deviance at school. This striking result underlines the importance of taking account of children's temperament in understanding the development of behavioural problems. It is possible that the assessment of temperament was in fact picking up the early signs of disorder at home: certainly some items of temperament as measured in this way are difficult to distinguish from what would be considered disorders of behaviour. However a measure of disorder in behaviour at home in fact predicted less well the deviance at school one year later.

It should also be noted that in the New York Longitudinal Study two-thirds of the children later referred for psychiatric help did not fit the pattern of temperament outlined. Similarly in the sleep problem study several of the 5-year-olds who scored high on behavioural problems had *not* been children with sleep problems, and vice versa. While the association between pattern of temperament and later disorder is clear, individual differences in the first two years (at least as we are now able to identify them) should not be used as though they were predictors of great power.

Individual differences in temperament have also been linked with variations in other important developmental processes, which are not intrinsically indices of emotional state. Difficulties in learning to read, for example, have been linked with temperamental differences. A number of studies have found associations between restlessness, impulsiveness, poor concentration and reading difficulties. Epidemiological studies, for instance, have found that children with reading difficulties show poor concentration on tasks which do not involve reading (Rutter *et al.*, 1970; Malmquist, 1958), and studies by De Hirsch and colleagues (1966) and by Kagan (1965) have found characteristics of hyperactivity and impulsiveness to be more common among children who had reading difficulties.

Follow-up studies of behaviour disorder

A number of studies show that from age 6–7 years individual differences in the incidence of some behaviour problems display some consistency over several years (Robins, 1966, 1972). The Berkeley Guidance Study, for instance, showed that if destructiveness, demandingness, sombreness, jealousy or shyness were present at 6–7 years such features were likely to be present at adolescence (Macfarlane et al., 1954). Children with many symptoms at the earlier age also tended to have many symptoms in later childhood and adolescence. Several studies have shown that difficulty in relationships with peers is associated with persistent behaviour disorders (Roff et al., 1972; Cowen et al., 1973). Disorders in middle or late childhood and adolescence do often persist for several years (Zax et al., 1968; Graham and Rutter, 1973; Cowen et al., 1973). Conduct disorders in particular show strong continuity, and a poor prognosis for adulthood (Robins, 1972). While better prognosis had been reported for emotional disorders (Robins, 1972), two recent studies have shown that emotional problems do persist to adolescence in many cases. In a follow-up study of the total population of children in the Isle of Wight, it was shown that 46% of the children who suffered from emotional disorder at 10 years had important problems at 14 years (Graham and Rutter, 1973). Similar rates of persistence were found in a study of London children (Cox and Rutter, 1977). Studies of children with hyperkinetic disorders indicate that while the hyperactivity itself may diminish with age, the children continue to be more distractible, restless and impulsive than their peers (Cantwell, 1977). There is frequently a continuing pattern of antisocial behaviour, depression, educational retardation and psychosis.

INDIVIDUAL DIFFERENCES AND THE COURSE OF DEVELOPMENT

In what ways do individual differences between children affect the course of their development?

Influence on others

There is an intimate association between some individual differences in children, and differences in the way their parents behave towards them. What do such associations mean? On the one hand, studies of parent–child interaction in infancy have shown that differences between children must be taken into account when assessing parent behaviour. Yet the complexity of the causal relations within parent–child interactions make it very difficult to interpret unequivocally even highly specific behavioural data. In one longitudinal study, for example, marked differences in the maternal responsiveness to the children were observed when the children were 14 months old (Dunn, 1977). These differences were correlated with differences in the child's behaviour at 14 months (the frequency of vocal demands), and also with measures of maternal affectionate behaviour, and differences in reactivity among the children during the neonatal period. These close associations between differences in mother behaviour, and differences in child behaviour, found at each age point in the study, mean that the links between age points must be expressed in terms of continuity in differences between mother–child dyads,

differences in interactive style, and cannot be taken simply as indices of continuity in the behaviour of either the mother or the child.

Other studies have demonstrated more direct effects of differences between children on their caregivers. Yarrow (1963) showed that individual differences between the children cared for by a foster mother influenced the maternal behaviour shown by the mother. Studies of interaction in families with a congenitally handicapped child have shown distinctively associated differences in parental behaviour (Cummings et al., 1966). More generally, sequential analyses of behavioural interactions between child and mother, which have been developed in a number of studies (Bell, 1971; Lewis, 1972; Yarrow et al., 1971; Clarke-Stewart, 1973), demonstrate the complex dynamics of the mutual influence of child and mother. In studying the patterns of interaction highlighted in this way we have moved beyond the simple recognition that children can influence their parents and can begin to look much more precisely at the particular ways in which a child influences his environment.

Much less is known about the precise ways in which temperamental differences between children affect their interaction with their families, as there have been very few studies which combine direct observation with assessment of temperament. Information is particularly sparse on the effects of temperamental differences in school-age children on parents and on peers. It seems very probable that parents will vary in their reaction to children of difficult temperament. In the study of sleep-problem children it was found that similar patterns of regular waking which were regarded as a major problem by some parents were regarded as 'normal' by others. Just as similar patterns of lively and demanding behaviour may be found to be intolerably wearing by some parents and enjoyable by others, so too similar parental styles will be experienced very differently by children with different temperamental make-up. This seems a reasonable supposition, on the basis of everyday observation and clinical experience. However, it is notable that there has been very little systematic study beyond early childhood of the mutual influence of child temperament and parental behaviour.

Range of experience, and variation in responses to the environment

It is clear that individual differences may shape the course of children's development not only by influencing the way people behave towards the children, but more generally by affecting the range of the child's life experience. In the Cambridge longitudinal study for instance it was found that the children who had been sleep problems in the first year were at 3 years of age particularly difficult to manage. They were more likely to be described by their mothers as stubborn and difficult, as unfriendly towards strangers, more likely to have difficulty in toilet or in feeding behaviour in strange situations, and as especially reluctant to be left with other adults by their mothers. This group of children were in fact taken out less frequently, and their mothers left them with other people less often.

We cannot of course assume that the difficulties of managing the children *led* to their comparative isolation—the direction of the causal link might have been in the other direction. But whatever the origin of the isolation, children with this particular temperamental make-up were less used to meeting new people, and to enjoying this contact, and had less experience of coping with separation experiences.

Children who are active, curious and investigative may enjoy the experience of new situations, and gain from a range of experiences far wider than that experienced by more withdrawn and passive children. A recent longitudinal study of a group of middle-class children found that girls who at 15 months were easy and sociable were more likely than their less easy-going peers to be sent to nursery school early (Blurton-Jones *et al.*, 1978). Boys in this sample, on the other hand, were more likely to be sent to nursery school early if they were particularly difficult to manage at 15 months. Again individual differences between children may be important in explaining the differences between children's responses to mildly stressful experiences. Schaffer (1965) found in a study of babies in an institution that the most active babies were the least likely to show developmental retardation. It is quite probable that part of the explanation for this 'protective' effect of differences in activity level lies in the way nurses respond to individual differences in children. A study of infants in a newborn nursery (Campbell, 1974, quoted in Rutter, 1977) indicated that the active babies got more attention from the nurses than the less active babies.

Individual differences between children then influence the range of experience to which children are exposed. They also affect the way in which particular environmental circumstances are experienced by the child. By definition, differences in malleability or adaptability will affect the degree of stress or unhappiness experienced by the child when he is faced by changes in his circumstances or by a new environment. Such changes are recurrent features of young children's lives. By the ages of 5 or 6, many children have had to cope with changes in home circumstances, family size or structure, regular separations from their mothers, being with groups of other children for longer periods, facing the demands of school situations, as well as the more obvious demands of socialization pressures from their family—going to bed alone, coping with toileting on their own, dressing and feeding themselves, conforming to family routines and expectations. The costs and benefits of such experiences will obviously vary greatly according to the particular temperament and sensitivity of the child.

Vulnerability to stress

It has been frequently noted that children vary greatly in their response to stressful situations. Differences in children's response to separation from the mother have already been mentioned. The study of first-born children's response to the arrival of a sibling showed that temperamental differences are associated with particular aspects of disturbed behaviour after the birth of the sibling. The birth of the sibling is associated with a constellation of changes for the first child, including a marked decrease in maternal attention, and an increase in prohibitive behaviour by the mother. Breakdown in sleeping patterns and toilet training, and increases in clinging behaviour were more common in those children who were rated as extreme in intensity of emotional expression, unmalleable, and predominantly negative in mood. The children who had sleeping problems before the birth of the sibling also responded to the new situation with a distinctive pattern of changes in behaviour. (It is interesting to note that the mothers attributed much of the disturbed behaviour of the children to the changes in routine experienced by the children, while being cared for by father or grandmother. The mothers were clearly very conscious of the difficulties such children have in coping with changes.) This study also illustrates the escalation of difficulties for children of such temperamental traits: when the children are upset they become much more difficult for their mothers to handle, and however well-meaning the mother may be, the interaction between mother and child almost always becomes tenser, and the exchange between the two becomes dominated to a greater extent by confrontation (Dunn and Kendrick, 1980).

It has been noted that some children seem to be more 'accident-prone' than others. Carey (1970) reports that babies with a pattern of temperament characterized by irregularity, low adaptability, emotional intensity, negative mood and withdrawal, were significantly more likely to sustain lacerations requiring sutures during the first 2 years of life than children who had different temperamental characteristics. Similarly in the Cambridge longitudinal study the sleep problem group had had more accidents by 3 years of age than the rest of the sample. It is not clear whether such associations reflect more reckless exploring behaviour by the children, or less close maternal supervision.

Children with organic brain damage are known to be more likely to develop psychiatric problems, even where there is no evidence of family discord or psychosocial stress (Shaffer, 1977). It is not at present known, however, how this association arises.

CONCLUSION

It is clear that individual differences between children must be taken into account in attempts to understand patterns of family interaction. Such differences are of great importance in their influence on the way people behave towards children, on the way children cope with changing circumstances and stressful experiences, on the children's range of experiences and on their perception of, and thus their reactions towards, those experiences. These individual differences do show some consistency over time, and they are implicated in the later development of psychiatric disorder. But it would be deeply misleading to imply that by identifying a child's temperamental characteristics we could predict developmental outcome with any certainty. Understanding the course of development means taking into account the complexity of mutual influences within the family, the dynamics of these interactions over time, the social and cultural environment of the family, the stresses to which it is exposed, and so on. In particular the adaptability and flexibility of the developmental process has to be remembered. While temperamental differences are certainly important in influencing the way children react to such situations, these temperamental differences can themselves be modified by the experience of the child. For different analytical or practical purposes it may be more appropriate to stress the consistency of individual differences, or to emphasize the comparative flexibility of the processes of development and the continuing possibilities for change in developing children. There is, of course, evidence for both. To understand the part which temperamental differences play in shaping development, and in determining an individual's vulnerability to psychiatric disorder, we need to be sensitive to the full complexity of the interactions between an individual child and his environment throughout childhood.

REFERENCES

Baron, J. (1972). Temperament profile of children with Down's syndrome. *Devel. Med. and Child Neurol.*, **14**, 640–643.

Barten, S., Birns, B. and Rouch, J. (1971). Individual differences in the visual pursuits behaviour of neonates. *Child Dev.*, **42**, 313–319.

Bateson, P. P. G. (1976). Rules and reciprocity in behavioural development. In P. P. G. Bateson and R. A. Hinde (Eds.) *Growing Points in Ethology*. Cambridge: Cambridge University Press.

Bell, R. Q. (1971). Stimulus control of parent or caregiver behaviour by offspring. *Devel. Psychol.*, **4**, 61–72.

Bell, R. Q. and Costello, N. (1964). Three tests for sex differences in tactile sensitivity in the newborn. *Biologica. Neonatorum*, **7**, 335–347.

Bell, R. Q., Weller, G. M. and Waldrop, M. F. (1971). Newborn and preschooler: organization of behaviour and relations between periods. *Monog. Soc. Res. Child Devel.*, **36** (1–2, Serial; no. 142).

Berger, M. (1973). Early experience and other environmental factors: Studies with humans. In H. J. Eysenck (Ed.) *Handbook of Abnormal Psychology*. London: Pitman Medical.

Bernal, J. F. (1972). Crying during the first 10 days and maternal responses. *Develop. Med. and Child Neurol.*, **14**, 362–372.

Bernal, J. F. (1973). Night-waking in the first 14 months. *Develop. Med. and Child Neurol.*, **15**, 760–769.

Blurton-Jones, N., Fereira, M. C. R., Farquhar-Brown, M. and MacDonald, L. (1978). The association between perinatal factors and later night waking. *Dev. Med. Child Neurol.*, **20**, 427–434.

Brazelton, T. B. and Collier, C. A. (1969). Infant development in the Zinacanteco Indians of Southern Mexico. *Pediatrics*, **44**, 274–290.

Brazelton, T. B. (1973). *Neonatal Assessment Scale*. London: Heinemann Medical Books.

Cambell, D. (1968). Motor activity in a group of newborn babies. *Biologica Neonatorum*, **13**, 257–270.

Cantwell, D. (1977). Hyperkinetic syndrome. In M. Rutter and L. Hersov (Eds.). *Child Psychiatry: Modern Approaches*. Oxford: Blackwell.

Carey, W. B. (1970). A simplified method for measuring infant temperament. *J. Pediat.*, **77**, 188–194.

Chess, S. and Korn, S. (1970). Temperament and behaviour disorders in mentally retarded children. *Arch. Gen. Psychiat.*, **23**, 122–130.

Clarke, A. M. and Clarke, A. D. B. (Eds.) (1976). *Early Experience: Myth and Evidence*. London: Open Books.

Clarke-Stewart, A. K. (1973). Interactions between mothers and their young children: characteristics and consequences. *Monog. Soc. Res. Child Dev.*, **38**, Serial No. 153.

Cowen, E. L., Pederson, A., Babigian, H., Izzo, L. D. and Trost, M. A. (1973). Long-term follow-up of early detected vulnerable children. *J. cons. clin. Psychol.*, **41**, 438–446.

Cox, A. and Rutter, M. (1977). Diagnostic appraisal and interviewing. In M. Rutter and L. Hersov (Eds.) *Child Psychiatry: Modern Approaches*. Oxford: Blackwell.

Cummings, S. T., Bayley, M. C. and Rie, H. E. (1966). Effects of the child's deficiency on the mother: a study of mothers of mentally retarded, chronically ill and neurotic children. *Amer. J. Orthopsychiat.*, **36**, 595–608.

De Hirsch, K., Jansky, J. J. and Langford, W. S. (1966). *Predicting Reading Failure*. New York: Harper.

Dunn, J. F. (1977). Patterns of early interactions: continuities and consequences. In H. R. Schaffer (Ed.) *Studies in Mother–Infant Interaction*. London: Academic Press.

Dunn, J. F. (1979). The first year of life: continuity in individual differences. In D. Shaffer and J. Dunn (Eds.) *The First Year of Life*. London: Wiley.

Dunn, J. F. and Kendrick, C. (1980). The arrival of a sibling: changes in patterns of interaction between mother and first born child. *J. Child Psychol. Psychiat.* (in press).

Dunn, J. F. and Richards, M. P. M. (1977). Observations on the developing relationship between mother and baby in the neonatal period. In H. R. Schaffer (Ed.) *Studies in Mother–Infant Interaction*. London: Academic Press.

Emde, R. N., Gaensbauer, T. J. and Harmon, R. J. (1976). Emotional expression in infancy. *Psychological Issues 10 no. 1*. Monograph 37.

Freedman, D. G. and Keller, B. (1963). Inheritance of behaviour in infants. *Science*, **40**, 196.

Gouin-Decarie, T. (1969). A study of the mental and emotional development of the thalidomide child. In B. H. Foss (Ed.) *Determinants of Infant Behaviour vol. 4*. Methuen: London.

Graham, P. and Rutter, M. (1973). Psychiatric disorders in the young adolescent: a follow-up study. *Proc. Roy. Soc. Med.*, **66**, 1226–1229.

Graham, P. and Rutter, M. (1977). Adolescent disorders. In M. Rutter and L. Hersov (Eds.) *Child Psychiatry: Modern Approaches*. Oxford: Blackwell, 407–427.

Graham, P., Rutter, M. and George, S. (1973). Temperamental characteristics as predictors of behavior disorders in children. *Amer. Journal Orthopsych.*, **43**, 328–339.

Kagan, J. (1965). Reflection-impulsivity and reading ability in primary grade children. *Child Dev.*, **36**, 609–628.

Kagan, J. (1971). *Change and Continuity in Infancy*. New York: Wiley.

Kagan, J. and Moss, H. A. (1962). *Birth to Maturity: a Study in Psychological Development*. New York: Wiley.

Korner, A. F. (1969). Neonatal startles, smiles, erections and reflex sucks as related to state, sex and individuality. *Child Dev.*, **40**, 1039–1053.

Korner, A. F. (1971). Individual differences at birth: implications for early experience and later development. *Amer. Journal Orthopsychiat.*, **41**, 608–619.

Korner, A. F. (1973). Sex differences in newborns with special reference to differences in the organization of oral behaviour. *J. Child Psychol. Psychiat.*, **14**, 19–29.

Korner, A. F. (1974). The effect of the infant's state, level of arousal, sex and ontogenetic stage on the caregiver. In M. Lewis and L. Rosenblurm (Eds.) *The Effects of the Infant on its Caregiver*. New York: Wiley.

Korner, A. F., Chuck, B. and Dontchos, S. (1968). Organismic determinants of spontaneous oral behaviour in neonates. *Child Dev.*, **39**, 1145–1157.

Lewis, M. (1972). State as an infant-environment interaction: an analysis of mother–infant interactions as a function of sex. *Merrill-Palmer Quarterly*, **18**, 95–121.

Lipsitt, L. P. and Levy, N. (1959). Electrotactual threshold in the human neonate. *Child Dev.*, **30**, 547–554.

Maccoby, E. and Jacklin, E. N. (1975). *The Psychology of Sex Differences*. London: Oxford University Press.

Malmquist, E. (1958). *Factors Leading to Reading Disabilities in the First Grade of Elementary School*. Stockholm: Almquist.

Masterson, J. F. (1967). *The Psychiatric Dilemma of Adolescence*. London: Churchill.

McCall, R. B. (1976). Toward an epigenetic conception of mental development. In M. Lewis (Ed.) *Origins of Intelligence*. New York: Plenum Press.

McCall, R. B., Hogarty, P. S. and Hurlburt, N. (1972). Transitions in infant sensorimotor development and the prediction of childhood I.Q. *Amer. Psychologist*, **27**, 728.

Money, J. and Ehthardt, A. A. (1968). Prenatal hormonal exposure: possible effects on behaviour in man. In R. P. Michael (Ed.) *Endocrinology and Human Behaviour*. Oxford: Oxford University Press.

Moore, T. and Ucko, L. E. (1957). Night waking in early infancy. *Arch. Dis. Childh.*, **32**, 333–342.

Nelson, K. (1973). Structure and strategy in learning to talk. *Monogr. Soc. Res. Child Devel.*, no. 149.

Nisbett, R. E. and Gurwitz, S. B. (1970). Weight, sex, and the eating behaviour of human newborns. *J. Comp. Physiol. Psychol.*, **73**, 245–253.

Pedersen, F. and Bell, R. Q. (1970). Sex differences in preschool children without histories of complications of pregnancy and delivery. *Devl. Psychol.*, **3**, 10–15.

Prechtl, H. F. (1965). Prognostic value of neurological signs in the newborn infant. *Proc. Roy. Soc. Med.*, **38**, 3–4.

Quinn, P. O. and Rapoport, J. L. (1974). Minor physical anomalies and neurological status in hyperactive boys. *Pediatrics.*, **53**, 742–747.

Repucci, E. M. (1968). Hereditary influences upon distribution of attention in infancy. Unpublished doctoral dissertation. Harvard University Press.

Robins, L. N. (1966). *Deviant Children Grown Up*. Baltimore: Williams & Wilkins.

Robins, L. N. (1972). Follow-up studies of behaviour disorders in children. In H. L. Quay and J. S. Werry. *Psychopathological Disorders in Childhood*. New York: Wiley.

Rosenblatt, D. and Packer, M. (1979). Issues in the study of social behaviour in the first weeks of life. In D. Shaffer and J. Dunn (Eds.) *The First Year of Life*. London: Wiley.

Rutter, M. (1970). Sex differences in children's response to family stress. In E. J. Anthony and C. Koupernik (Eds.) *The Child in His Family*. London: Wiley.

Rutter, M. (1971). Psychiatry. In J. Wortis (Ed.) *Mental Retardation: an Annual Review vol. 3*. New York: Grune and Stratton.

Rutter, M. (1977). Individual differences. In M. Rutter and L. A. Hersov (Eds.) *Child Psychiatry: Modern Approaches*. Oxford: Blackwell, 3–21.

Rutter, M., Korn, S. and Birch, H. (1963). Genetic and environmental factors in the development of 'primary reaction patterns'. *Brit. J. Soc. Clin. Psychol.*, **2**, 161–173.

Rutter, M., Birch, H., Thomas, A. and Chess, S. (1964). Temperamental characteristics in infancy and the later development of behaviour disorders. *Brit. J. Psychiat.*, **110**, 651–661.

Rutter, M., Graham, P., Chadwick, O. F. D. and Yule, W. (1976). Adolescent turmoil: fact or fiction? *J. Child Psychol. Psychiat.*, **17**, 35–56.

Rutter, M., Tizard, J. and Whitmore, K. (Eds.) (1970). *Education, Health and Behaviour*. London: Longman.

Sameroff, A. J. and Chandler, M. J. (1975). Reproductive risk and the continuum of caretaking casualty. In F. D. Horowitz, M. Hethernyton, S. Scarrsalapatek and G. Sregel (Eds.) *Review of Child Development Research vol. 4*. Chicago: University of Chicago Press.

Scarr, S. (1969). Social introversion-extraversion as a heritable response. *Child Develop.*, **40**, 823–832.

Schaefer, E. and Bayley, N. (1963). Maternal behaviour, child behaviour, and their intercorrelations from infancy through adolescence. *Monogr. Soc. Res. Child Devl.*, **28**, 1–27.

Schaffer, H. R. (1965). Changes in developmental quotient under two conditions of maternal separation. *Brit. J. Soc. Clin. Psychol.*, **4**, 39–46.

Shaffer, D. (1977). Brain Injury. In M. Rutter and L. A. Hersov (Eds.) *Child Psychiatry: Modern Approaches*. Oxford: Blackwell.

Stacey, M., Dearden, R., Pill, R. and Robinson, D. (1970). *Hospitals, Children and their Families: the report of a Pilot Study*. London: Kegan Paul.

Steinschneider, A. (1967). Developmental psychophysiology. In Y. Brackbill (Ed.) *Infancy and Early Childhood*. Glencoe: Free Press.

Thomas, A. and Chess, S. (1977). *Temperament and Development*. New York: Brunner/Mazel.

Thomas, A., Chess, S., Birch, H. G., Hertzig, M. E. and Korn, S. (1963). *Behavioural Individuality in Early Childhood*. New York: New York University Press.

Tizard, B. and Rees, J. (1975). The effect of early institutional rearing on the behaviour problems and affectional relationships of 4-year-old children. *J. Child Psychol. Psychiat.*, **16**, 61–73.

Torgersen, A. M. and Kringlen, E. (1978). Genetic aspects of temperamental differences in infants. *H. Amer. Acad. Child Psych.*, **17**, 433–444.

Ucko, L. E. (1965). A comparative study of asphyxiated and non-asphyxiated boys from birth to 5 years. *Develop. Med. Child Neurol.*, **7**, 643–657.

Vandenberg, S. G. (1969). Contributions of twin research to psychology. In M. Manosevitz, G. Lindzey and D. D. Thiessen (Eds.) *Behavioural Genetics*. New York: Appleton-Century-Crofts.

Waddington, C. H. (1957). *The Strategy of the Genes*. London: Allen and Unwin.

Waldrop, M., Pedersen, F. A. and Bell, R. Q. (1968). Minor physical anomalies and behaviour in pre-school children. *Child Dev.*, **39**, 391–400.

Yarrow, L. J. (1963). Research in dimensions of early maternal care. *Merrill-Palmer Quarterly*, **9**, 101–114.

Yarrow, M. R., Waxlev, C. Z. and Scott, P. M. (1971). Child effects on adult behaviour. *Develop. Psychol.*, **5**, 300–311.

Zax, M., Cowen, E. L., Rapoport, J., Beach, D. R. and Laird, J. D. (1968). Follow-up study of children identified early as emotionally disturbed. *J. Cons. Clin. Psychol.*, **32**, 369–374.

10. LEARNING

HAROLD W. STEVENSON

Learning involves a change in an individual's performance as a function of experience. Several implications of this statement should be emphasized before we begin our discussion of the learning process. Learning itself can never be observed directly, for changes in the organization and activity of the central nervous system involved in learning are unobservable by us. We are forced, therefore, to make inferences about learning by observing how these changes are manifested in an individual's performance. When changes in performance are evident, we assume learning has occurred; when performance remains unchanged, we assume that no learning has taken place. Unfortunately, our deductions may be incorrect. We may make errors, not only in inferring whether or not learning has occurred, but also in attempting to describe what has been learned.

These errors occur because the conditions we impose on performance may prevent the child from showing what has been learned. This can be illustrated by an example. Children learn aggressive responses by observing aggression displayed on television or in real life. After observing such aggressive incidents, boys have been found to demonstrate aggression more frequently than do girls. Should we conclude, therefore, that girls learn less about aggression through observation than do boys? A slight change in the conditions under which aggression is tested produces different results (Bandura, 1965). Rather than place children in a free-play situation, as is typically the case in studies of aggression, children are offered a small prize for the recall of each aggressive response they have seen displayed. Sex differences disappear; girls recall the aggressive responses as well as boys. The difference, then, is not in what had been learned, but in the conditions under which the learning was performed. Girls display

less aggression in their everyday behaviour, but we would be wrong if we interpreted this as being an indication that girls are less able to learn the content of aggressive acts.

Physical state also plays an important role in determining whether or not learning will be displayed. The child who is fatigued or the child who is in an unusually high state of arousal may perform in a manner different from that found under more typical conditions. We must recognize from the beginning, therefore, an elementary, but critically important point: there is an imperfect correspondence between learning and performance. Before concluding that learning has not occurred or—even more importantly—that a child may lack the ability to learn, careful consideration must be given to the possibility that performance might be quite different with a change in conditions. Repeatedly, conclusions about individual children or about children from various social and cultural groups have had to be changed when more appropriate conditions for evaluating their learning have been introduced.

INFANT LEARNING

No greater change in contemporary psychology has occurred than in our conception of the learning and memory capacities of the human infant. Until recently, it was doubted whether the very young infant was capable of learning, and older infants were viewed as reactive organisms, ones whose responses were controlled by the stimulus conditions imposed by the environment. We now have firm evidence that babies are able to learn from their earliest days of life and that rather than being passive recipients of stimulation, infants are active organisms, seeking and organizing their own stimulus input (*see* Stone, Smith and Murphy, 1973).

Operant conditioning

An example of very early learning can be found in studies of operant conditioning, a type of conditioning in which responses are strengthened through the systematic application of reward. When the cheek of a newborn infant is stroked, the infant tends to rotate its head towards the source of stimulation. This reflexive response occurs about one-third of the time. Can the frequency with which this reflexive response occurs be increased by rewarding the infant following each rotation of the head? That is, can we modify the infant's behaviour by increasing the likelihood that the behaviour will lead to some consequence of importance to the infant?

This question was studied with 2- to 5-day-old infants by Siqueland and Lipsitt (1966). They sought to determine whether operant conditioning would occur, and whether the neonate is capable of differentiating between conditions that do and do not lead to reinforcement. Their experimental procedure was somewhat complicated. When a tone preceded the stroke to the cheek, a head-turn was reinforced by allowing the infant to suck on a nipple which yielded a small amount of dextrose solution. When the stroke was preceded by a buzz, the dextrose solution was withheld. Clear evidence of the ability to learn and to discriminate between reinforced and non-reinforced stimuli was found. Responses to the tone soon doubled in frequency while the proportion of responses made to the buzz remained unchanged. Neonates had learned the appropriate cue for turning their heads.

The experiment was pursued into a second phase in which the relation between stimulus and reinforcement was reversed. The buzzer, which had been the negative stimulus, led to reinforcement. The infant now received no dextrose solution following head-turns to the tone, the previously positive stimulus. The infants were able to reverse their pattern of response. The frequency of response to the buzzer (the previously negative stimulus) now exceeded that to the tone (the previously positive and now negative stimulus). Conditioning, conditioned discrimination, and reversal of conditioning had been demonstrated with babies less than 5 days old. The babies displayed a competence in learning that even skilled observers would have thought to be impossible a few decades ago.

Classical conditioning

Further evidence of early learning comes from studies utilizing classical conditioning procedures. In classical conditioning a previously neutral stimulus becomes capable, through its repeated association with an effective stimulus, of functioning as an effective stimulus. Clifton (1974), for example, asked whether heart rate could be conditioned. Heart rate typically increases in young infants upon the presentation of a positive stimulus and decreases when a negative stimulus appears. A sound was presented repeatedly to 1- to 5-day-olds prior to the presentation of the glucose. The infants were strongly influenced by their experience. There was a dramatic decrease in heart rate when, on test trials, the nipple was not placed in the infants' mouths after the appearance of the tone. The infants acted as if they were anticipating the appearance of the nipple, and when it failed to appear they responded as they would to a negative stimulus by showing a decrease in heart rate. Studies such as this offer further evidence of the modifiability of the behaviour of the young infant through the creation of a systematic, predictable environment.

Practical applications

A word should be said about the usefulness of conditioning procedures in practical settings. A mother vocalizes, but her infant fails to seek out the source of the sound. One's first guess is that the infant is deaf. But it also is possible that the infant is severely retarded or autistic. How might one confirm or reject the possibility of deafness? Both operant and classical conditioning procedures may be used clinically to answer such a question. In a typical case involving the use of classical conditioning, a tone of a given frequency is sounded just before a slight shock is delivered to the infant's foot. The child makes a reflexive motor response to the unpleasant shock. This procedure is repeated a number of times and then the shock is omitted. Does the child make the response to the tone that previously had been made only following the shock? If the initial phase of the testing is successful, the limits or hearing can be established by testing the child with other sounds than that initially used as the conditioned stimulus.

Habituation

A third, commonly used method for assessing the influence of experience on infant behaviour is found in studies of habituation. Habituation describes the phenomenon whereby stimuli initially effective in producing a particular form of behaviour become ineffective with repeated presentation. A coloured slide of a yellow square appears before a young infant. The infant looks intently at the square. The slide is removed and after several seconds is presented again. This procedure is repeated many times. Each appearance of the square engages the infant's attention for shorter and shorter periods of time until eventually the infant regards it with only a hasty glance. Habituation has occurred. A slide of a red circle is substituted for the yellow square. The infant shows dishabituation; once again the infant looks intently at the screen (see Tighe and Leaton, 1976).

The selective nature of infant perception is evident in a study by Miller (1972). Four-month-olds were shown a complex figure, such as a circle surrounding two crossed lines and a pair of dots. Miller used complex figures because they can be broken down into their components, making it possible to ascertain which aspects of the stimulus were being attended to by the infant. The components were presented separately both before and after the habituation trials with the total figure. The components were differentially salient; a hierarchy appeared among them and the hierarchy differed for different children. Some infants looked longest at the circle, others at the cross, and still others at the dots. After the habituation trials had been conducted with the composite figure, infants spent less time observing the component that had been most salient for each infant at the beginning of the study. Little change was found in the amount of time spent in observing the other two components. In other words, the infants appear to have responded selectively to the complex figure and habituation was evident for the component to which the infant had directed its attention longest during the pre-training trials.

The habituation paradigm has proved to be a powerful tool for studying the psychological characteristics of young infants. Human infants have been shown to be sensitive, selective organisms, responding to certain aspects of their environments and ignoring others. Their worlds are not the buzzing confusions described by William James, but appear to be much more highly organized, and to take on meaning as events become predictable and lead to useful consequences. Events that have no utility gradually are ignored, while those that prove to yield important consequences lead the infant to modify its behaviour. Environments appear not to be equipotential in their ability to elicit an infant's response; what is responded to differs for different infants. Moreover, some infants are slow to change their responses; others adapt readily to new events. From the time of birth there are large differences among infants in their readiness for learning. How these individual differences influence later development remain unclear. We know, however, that the view of the human infant as clay to be moulded by the environment is incorrect; resistances and pliabilities lie within the infant that lead to outcomes which cannot be predicted by knowledge of stimulus events alone.

REINFORCEMENT AND PUNISHMENT

To the degree that controls can be imposed upon environmental events, the opportunity exists for perpetuating or changing human behaviour. Behaviour can be strengthened by reinforcement, and weakened by the withdrawal of reinforcement. The nucleus of the idea is simple, but there are many complicated ramifications. What shall be used as a reinforcer? When should reinforcement be given? What if the responses to be reinforced are not manifested by the child? When should punishment be used? These will be considered in turn.

Reinforcers

What is reinforcing to a child may be something that is shared by other children or may be idiosyncratic. If a child is hungry, it is likely that food will be an effective reinforcer. Most children like to see novel events, to be told they are doing well, or to receive supportive responses from their peers and adults. Other objects and events may be highly desirable to some children and of little interest or value to others. It cannot be assumed, therefore, that what is an effective reinforcer for one child will be equally effective as a reinforcer for another child, nor even that what is effective at one time will be a successful reinforcer at a later time.

Isolating effective reinforcers may be difficult. For example, we observe the behaviour of a self-mutilating child, who keeps an open wound by banging against sharp edges. What type of reinforcement could be maintaining this behaviour? We observe that head-banging is more frequent when adults are present. Could it be that the reinforcement is the solicitous response of adults to the child's self-destructive acts? Could the child be using this response as a means of obtaining positive social responses? The effectiveness of adult social response as a reinforcer can be confirmed by systematically varying the relation between the child's behaviour and adults' responses (Lovaas and Bucher, 1974). As long as adults respond sympathetically, the child continues the self-destructive behaviour. When adults are instructed to ignore the behaviour and to respond positively at other times, the frequency of self-mutilating behaviour is found to decrease. Careful analysis revealed an unusual means of obtaining reward.

Applying reinforcement

Without control over the child's access to reinforcement, it is difficult to impose requirements upon the child. For example, efforts to use television viewing as a reinforcer may prove unsuccessful if television is accessible at a friend's house. Controlling resources in the everyday environment is very difficult, a fact that may account for why many of the most successful demonstrations of the application of reinforcement principles occur in institutions, where it is easier to control the availability of resources.

It also is necessary to apply reinforcement contingently (see Bandura, 1969, Chapter 4). By this we mean that access to reinforcement must be dependent upon the performance of a particular type of behaviour. Desirable stimuli applied in a non-contingent, random fashion may produce a warm and pleasant environment, but their potentiality for changing behaviour is unfulfilled unless a contingent relation exists between the child's behaviour and their presence.

Finally, the relation between response and reinforcement must be consistent (Hilgard and Bower, 1975, Chapter 7). Children find it difficult to understand how the two are related if reinforcers appear in an erratic manner. During the early phases of learning, consistent reinforcement leads to more rapid changes in performance. Later, behaviour can be maintained and strengthened by a schedule of partial reinforcement, whereby reinforcement occurs only a portion of the times the behaviour appears. Reinstituting reinforcement on a single trial maintains the behaviour in full force. This, of course, is a problem for the parent who is trying to withdraw reinforcement in an effort to eliminate undesirable behaviour. The child, denied a desired object, discovers in the manipulable parent that by persisting, the object reappears. One of the most difficult problems encountered in living and working with children is that of attempting to be consistent in the application and withdrawal of reinforcement. It is hard to reward desired behaviour systematically, and even more difficult to be consistent in withholding reinforcement.

Behavioural shaping

Attempting to develop new forms of behaviour in children may be a tedious task. To solve this problem, behavioural shaping often is employed (e.g. Lovaas, Berberich, Perloff and Schaeffer, 1966). Initially, any response is reinforced that lies within the domain of the behaviour the adult wishes to generate; reinforcement is withheld following other responses. Step by step, closer and closer approximations to the desired response are required for reinforcement. Through selective application of reinforcement and non-reinforcement the child is guided into making the desired responses in the appropriate situations.

Among the most compelling studies of the application of reinforcement principles are those in which efforts have been made to teach psychotic children to speak (Lovaas, 1966). A variety of reinforcing agents were used, including food, close physical contact, and warm social response. Since psychotic children frequently are inattentive, the child initially was reinforced merely for looking at the adult. After the child had learned to attend, reinforcement was given for any type of vocalization. When the output of vocalizations increased, the child was reinforced only if the vocalization occurred after the adult's vocalization. After this contingency was learned, the child was required to imitate what the adult said. Simple sounds were selected, but training in imitative vocalization continued with the introduction of a large variety of sounds, words, phrases and, eventually, sentences. The children learned to speak. It should be pointed out, however, that after extraordinarily long and arduous involvement with the experimental procedures, the children's language had a ritualistic quality and they rarely conducted truly interesting conversations. Even with prolonged and systematically regulated reinforcement, there are limitations in the degree to which new behaviours can be learned.

Punishment

Some persons, faced with the question of when punishment should be used, deny its effectiveness. Others are less negative. Walters and Grusec (1977), for example, end their discussion of the research on punishment with the conclusion that punishment 'will always be a necessary tool of behavioural change'. Evidence can be produced to support both negative and positive views. Since there are reasons, both humane and ethical, why psychological research on punishment with children is relatively sparce, it may be some time before evidence will be available to resolve this argument.

Three reasons are often cited as to why punishment is ineffective. First, strong punishment can produce high emotional arousal. We know that such a state is not optimal for learning. Punishing a child for making errors may, therefore, produce an emotional state that precludes efficient learning of the correct response. A second criticism is that punishment fails to teach the child what should be done. The child should understand not only what should not be done, but also what kind of response should be made. Punishment, at best, is effective in reducing the tendency to perform the inappropriate response. Third, mild forms of punishment may acquire reinforcing qualities. Harsh words or even physical abuse may constitute the only form of response which a child is capable of eliciting from parents or siblings and may, in this atypical manner, take on reinforcing value. These are not kinds of stimuli that constitute healthy sources of reinforcement.

Among positive values of punishment, the most frequently discussed is its ability to suppress behaviour.

Presentation of a single electric shock after the performance of a self-mutilating response, for example, will result in immediate suppression of this form of behaviour. Whether suppression occurs only in the presence of the punitive agent, a point often made by critics of the use of punishment, the tendency to suppress certain responses may be a valuable and sufficient goal in itself. Preventing a child from running into the street or from hitting other children are important accomplishments for persons entrusted with the care of children. Second, children may be more strongly motivated to isolate relevant cues when both reinforcement and punishment are employed. Reinforcement for correct response and withdrawal of reinforcers or mild punishment for incorrect response may be more informative than the provision of reinforcement alone. Finally, cessation of punishment or escape from punishment may be used as forms of reinforcement. Children readily learn that following the performance of a response, punishment will cease or be withheld. For example, presenting a noxious stimulus when the child fails to make a social response has been used as a means of developing social responsiveness in autistic children. Children quickly learn that a noxious stimulus can be avoided if an appropriate response is made.

Through vivid and sometimes dramatic examples, psychologists have demonstrated that behaviours can be created or suppressed, strengthened or weakened by carefully arranging the situation so that responses lead to systematic consequences. Some consider the application of these principles to be among psychology's major accomplishments. The principles are derived from a large line of laboratory research and continually are being subjected to experimental analysis. Their successful application does not necessarily lead us to a mechanistic view of children's learning. By saying that a world is systematic is equivalent to saying that it is predictable. When we speak of making predictions, we are describing an organism whose behaviour is controlled by cognitive processes rather than through the mechanistic association of stimulus and response.

DEVELOPMENTAL CHANGES

Generally, older children learn more rapidly than younger children. Maturation and experience are the sources of these developmental changes. Maturation of the central nervous system expands the growing child's capacities for learning. Older children also have broader and more varied experiences than younger children. The greater the number of situations in which the child must learn, the more skills the child can bring to new learning situations. The child learns how to sit still, listen to directions, maintain attention, isolate relevant cues, associate responses with their outcomes, rehearse and employ other useful learning and memory strategies. In other words, the child learns how to learn.

While rate of maturation is resistant to change, it may be quite easy to provide children with skills that are of assistance in learning. Two illustrations will be helpful.

Steady improvement in performance as children grow older can be easily demonstrated in many types of learning tasks. Show pairs of pictures of common objects to children between the ages of 5 and 18 years; ask them to name each object, and then instruct them that the members of each pair are to be remembered. After all the pairs have been displayed, one member of each pair is presented and the child is asked to recall the second member of the pair. Five-year-olds require many more presentations of the pairs than do 7-year-olds. Successive age groups require even fewer trials before they are able to recall all of the pairs perfectly.

A reasonable deduction is that the differences in performance reflect developmental changes in the capacity to learn. This deduction can quickly be shown to be false. Jensen and Rohwer (1965), for example, tested children in the manner described and also in a second condition in which the children were asked to construct a sentence relating the objects in each pair of pictures. After the single trial in constructing sentences, the experiment proceeded as it did for the first group of subjects. A dramatic effect was obtained from this single change in procedure. After the age of 5, developmental changes in performance for the most part disappeared. Seven-year-olds differed little from 14-year-olds, or even from 18-year-olds. Only the 5-year-olds failed to benefit from constructing the sentences.

The purpose of the study was to demonstrate that differences in performance may be due not to a difference in learning ability, but to differences in children's tendencies to generate strategies. Older children may quickly realize that the stimuli can be related meaningfully by linking them in a sentence. Younger children have difficulty in generating such strategies spontaneously and rely on rote learning unless strategies are suggested to them. Strategies appear spontaneously as children grow older, both because older children are more capable of generating them, and also because they have found such efforts to be useful in previous learning situations.

A second example comes from a study we have recently completed in Peru (Stevenson, Parker, Wilkinson, Bonnevaux, and Gonzales, 1978). We chose Peru because it is a country where only a portion of children attend school. Five- and 6-year-olds were given a variety of learning, memory, and problem-solving tasks. When 6-year-olds attended school, there were developmental changes in performance. The 6-year-olds, as expected, were better than the 5-year-olds on nearly every task. Entirely different results appeared with 6-year-olds who did not attend school. Their performance differed on very few tasks from that of the 5-year-olds. The rapid changes in performance we often attribute to the advances in developmental status accompanying increases in age may, then, be a result of the influences of schooling as well as of age. When all children in a society attend school, we cannot separate the contribution of these two variables. The aspects of attending school that contribute most strongly to developmental changes are not clear, but the demands for verbalization, solving complex problems, and abstract thinking must be important. From studies such as the two that have just been discussed, we are led to conclude that we should not be too ready to dismiss the possibility of complex forms of learning by children. Certain kinds of experiences may have remarkable effects in improving their performance.

LANGUAGE

The acquisition of language releases the child from the world of here-and-now by making it possible for objects and events—present, past, and anticipated—to be represented through language. Other modes of representation, such as images and movements, occur, but none allows as ready and fluent manipulation of concepts and operations as does language. The power gained from being able to store large amounts of information in the form of words, to formulate verbal hypotheses, to use words as mnemonic aids, and to construct sets of verbal propositions permits the older child to reach remarkably advanced levels of behaviour.

In the young child, the relation between language and behaviour is not so obvious. Early in life, the two are related in an overt manner: 'Get my ball', the 2-year-old says in instructing himself to pick up the ball. It does not take long, however, before performance is divorced from the manifest aid of language. The directive and representational functions of language become interiorized and unavailable to observation. Because the functions must be deduced rather than observed, and because young children cannot tell us how they go about learning, controversy has existed about the early origins of complex mental activity. Some views, such as the Soviet position, posit that complex learning and higher forms of thinking develop only to the degree that the child acquires language. Others, such as the famous Swiss psychologist, Piaget, have argued that the emergence of higher mental processes and of language are parallel rather than interdependent processes. Words, according to this view, may be helpful but are not necessary for abstract thinking and complex forms of learning.

Current research tends to support the second position. With proper training, young children perform far more complex tasks than had been thought possible. Deducing relationships, for example, had been assumed to be rare before the relation could be represented verbally. It is easy to see the basis of this assumption. Show a 3-year-old three circles of different size; hide a piece of candy under the middle-sized circle. Now substitute cards bearing a second set of circles, all much larger than the first set. The child does not transfer the relation from the first to the second situation and chooses randomly. This is very different from the behaviour of 6- or 7-year-olds, who consistently choose the middle-sized member of the second set. These children can represent the relation among the stimuli verbally and are able to tell us that they use this as a means of directing their response.

What would happen if we were to teach younger children to verbalize the relation? Before every choice on the initial task, children are told to tell themselves, 'Choose the middle-sized one', or 'Don't choose the big or little one'. The training is ineffective. The children again respond randomly to the second task. Could it be, then, that young children fail to demonstrate transfer, not because they did not learn the rule well, but because they failed to understand that a rule learned in one situation is applicable to other situations? If this is true, children could be shown that the response is not restricted to situations with certain absolute properties. Beatty and Weir (1966) have done this with 3- and 4-year-olds, who typically have difficulty in transferring concepts such as largest, smallest and middle-sized. Two sets of three squares were presented during the original training, one small set and one large set. Choices of the middle-sized member of each set led to reward. The correct response to the two sets used during original training was learned rapidly, and when the children were given a third set of squares, their choices indicated strong evidence of their ability to transfer the rule. Having learned that choices of the middle-sized square were correct for two sets, they easily transferred the rule to the third set of squares—despite the fact that neither before nor after the games did they give any evidence of understanding what the term middle-sized meant.

Three-year-olds do not know words to describe the concepts of roundness or angularity. Furthermore, without prior training it is extremely difficult for them to use these concepts. Caron (1968) sought to develop pre-training experiences that might lead these young children to employ the concepts correctly. Many sets of figures were constructed in which the differentiating attribute was the roundedness or pointedness of a portion of the figure. The figures were paired in a problem where the correct choice was dependent on the selection of the figures that contained one of these characteristics. Some children consistently had to pick the stimulus with a rounded portion; others had to pick the stimulus with a pointed portion. For some children the figures were initially presented only in part. Rather than use the fully represented figure, only the portion of each figure that contained the distinctive attribute was visible. Very gradually, over a long series of trials, the full figure was faded in. By seeing only the critical feature at first, 3-year-olds gave clear evidence of having used the concepts. But there was no indication that the concepts had been represented in words. The children could not tell the experimenter at the end of the study how they had solved the problem, nor could they pick out the 'round' and 'pointed' figures when they were directed to do so.

Similar results were obtained with other groups of children who were asked to fit the stimulus figures into a hollow V shape. Figures with an angular portion fitted into the V, but the others did not. The child was to go through the stimuli, placing figures that fitted the shape into one pile and those that did not into another. When the children later were required to apply the concept of roundness or angularity, they were highly successful. Again, they could not give a verbal explanation of how they solved the problem, nor were they able to identify the figures that possessed the attribute described by the adult.

These studies offer an interesting insight into how we can improve young children's ability to acquire and transfer information. Demonstration of concepts through multiple examples conveys what cannot be readily assimilated through verbal instructions. Words may be the natural means of transmitting knowledge among older children and adults, but they are not the most effective medium for instructing young children.

OBSERVATIONAL LEARNING

If we regard learning as the process of extracting and accumulating information from the environment, it is apparent that one of the most efficient means of gaining such information is through observation. Observing the efforts of another person makes it unnecessary to go through one's own trial and error processes in order to find out what is relevant for producing certain effects. Useful information is obtained immediately, without practice and without tangible forms of reinforcement. A great deal of children's everyday learning occurs in this way.

Television has heightened our awareness of how much children learn through observation, and it is from research on television viewing that some of the most striking illustrations of observational learning are found. Many studies have dealt with aggressive behaviour, for one of the public's great concerns is the possibility that children learn aggressive responses through observing violence displayed on television. The studies do little to relieve this concern. Children do imitate aggression that they have observed. This is demonstrated convincingly in many studies, among which is an especially interesting one by Friedrichs and Stein (1973).

The study was conducted with three groups of young children who were attending nursery school. Each group was shown one of three types of television programmes several times a week for a month. The programmes consisted of aggressive cartoons, prosocial segments depicting cooperation, sympathy, and other positive forms of social behaviour, or neutral films with minimal aggressive and prosocial content. No effort was made to modify the children's out-of-school television viewing.

The frequency of prosocial and aggressive behaviours displayed by the children in their daily social interactions at nursery school were determined before and after the month of television viewing. Both types of behaviour were influenced by the programmes, but not all children were equally affected. Aggressive films increased the aggressive behaviour of aggressive children. That is, aggressive behaviour increased among the half of the children who had been above the group median in aggression before the programmes were viewed. Children below the median in aggression displayed no significant increase in their daily aggressive behaviour. This is a disturbing finding, for it indicates that the influence of aggressive materials may be strongest among individuals who already tend to display such behaviour. Comparable results were not found for prosocial behaviour. Only children below the median in socio-economic status showed positive influences of viewing the prosocial programmes. Why the effects were not found among the more economically advantaged children is not clear.

Among the techniques available for changing children's behaviour, one of the most effective is to provide them with models who are successful and appealing. Children imitate the behaviour of individuals who are successful to a greater degree than if the model's behaviour is ineffective, and they are more likely to imitate a model whose behaviour is approved by other persons (Bandura, 1977). Preferences, attitudes, sex roles, styles of speech and dress—all are presumably influenced by observation. Children often learn through imitation what they cannot otherwise be taught or told. If they attend carefully and remember what has been observed, children will imitate the model's behaviour when appropriate motivational conditions arise. As in all forms of learning, observational learning does not occur with equal ease for all persons or all types of behaviour. For example, motor responses, such as swimming, may be less influenced by the observation of skilled swimmers than is practice and feedback about correct and incorrect movements. Observation may be insufficient for learning sequences of acts, although the components may be learned if they are performed in a readily discriminable manner. However, even affective states such a fear can be reduced by observing the behaviour of other, unfearful individuals.

INDIVIDUAL DIFFERENCES

There is great variability both among and within individuals in the rate at which learning occurs. The variability that exists among individuals is readily evident. From the time of birth there are large differences within any group in the rate at which the members learn. It is less obvious that within the same individual there typically is a large amount of variability in the rate at which learning occurs in different types of situations. A child may be slow in learning one type of material, but may astound us in the speed with which a second task is mastered.

Part of the variability must be related to biological factors, but about this we have only conjecture and no facts. Instead, psychologists interested in studying individual differences in learning have spent most of their time in assessing the types of individual differences that exist, the relation of individual differences in learning among various types of tasks, and in investigating other characteristics of children that contribute to differences in performance on learning tasks.

One of the questions that has been asked is whether there is a general learning ability. The answer is essentially negative (*see* Stevenson, 1972). Only a small portion of the variability in performance on one task is related to variability in another task. Rather than being dependent upon a single ability, adequate performance appears to be a product of a great many factors, including those related to attention, perception, memory and motivation. Consequently, large differences within the same child may arise

when the child is faced with tasks that are differentially dependent upon these different factors. We cannot place children in such broad categories as good learners and bad learners, and it is a great disservice to children when attempts to do this are made.

Some clues to the problems of predicting rate of learning lie in the relation of learning to personality (*e.g.* Naylor, 1972). It is unfortunate that we have so little information about this matter. There are hints, such as the findings that anxious children learn less readily than do less anxious children and that learning is more rapid if children have a high need for achievement and high self-esteem. At present, however, we have only a vague understanding of how such personality characteristics exert their influence on children's learning.

Human learning is an exceedingly complex phenomenon, and the difficulties in understanding its operation are compounded by developmental changes and large individual differences among children. Nevertheless, research of the past several decades has shown that children's learning is susceptible to scientific analysis, and a large amount of information has been obtained. It is impossible in a brief chapter to present more than a cursory sample of this information. The pace of the research continues to accelerate, and within the coming years we should be able to offer clearer and clearer delineations of what the favourable conditions are for rearing and educating children.

REFERENCES

Bandura, A. (1965). Influence of model's reinforcement contingencies on the acquisition of imitative responses. *Journal of Personality and Social Psychology*, **1**, 589–595.

Bandura, A. (1969). *Principles of Behavior Modification*. New York: Holt, Rinehart & Winston.

Bandura, A. (1977). *Social learning theory*. Englewood Cliffs: Prentice-Hall.

Beatty, W. E. and Weir, M. W. (1966). Children's performance on the intermediate-size problem as a function of two training procedures. *Journal of Experimental Child Psychology*, **4**, 332–340.

Caron, A. J. (1968). Conceptual transfer in preverbal children as a consequence of dimensional training. *Journal of Experimental Child Psychology*, **6**, 522–542.

Clifton, R. K. (1974). Heartrate conditioning in the newborn infant. *Journal of Experimental Child Psychology*, **18**, 9–21.

Friedrichs, L. C. and Stein, A. H. (1973). Aggressive and prosocial television programs and the natural behavior of preverbal children. *Monographs of the Society for Research in Child Development*, **38**, Whole No. 131.

Hilgard, E. R. and Bower, G. H. (1975). *Theories of Learning*. Englewood Cliffs, N.J.: Prentice-Hall.

Jensen, A. R. and Rohwer, W. D., Jr. (1965). Syntactical mediation of serial and paired-associate learning as a function of age. *Child Development*, **36**, 601–608.

Lovaas, O. I. (1966). A program for the establishment of speech in psychotic children. In J. K. Wing (Ed.), *Early childhood autism*. New York: Pergamon.

Lovaas, O. I., Berberich, J. P., Perloff, B. F. and Schaeffer, B. (1966). Acquisition of imitative speech by schizophrenic children. *Science*, **151**, 705–707.

Lovaas, O. I. and Bucher, B. D. (Eds.) (1974). *Perspectives in behavior modification with deviant children*. Englewood Cliffs: Prentice-Hall.

Miller, D. J. (1972). Visual habituation in the human infant. *Child Development*, **43**, 483–493.

Naylor, F. D. (1972). *Personality and Educational Achievement.* Sydney: Wiley.

Siqueland, E. R. and Lipsitt, L. P. (1966). Conditional head turning in human newborns. *Journal of Experimental Child Psychology*, **3,** 356–376.

Stevenson, H. W. (1972). The taxonomy of tasks. *In* F. J. Monks, W. W. Hartup and J. de Wit (Eds.) *Determinants of Behavioral Development.* New York: Academic Press.

Stevenson, H. W., Parker, T., Wilkinson, A., Bonnevaux, B. and Gonzales, M. (1978). Schooling, environment, and cognitive development: A cross-cultural study. *Monographs of the Society for Research in Child Development*, Whole No. 175.

Stone, L. J., Smith, H. T. and Murphy, L. B. (Eds.) (1973). *The Competent Infant: Research and Commentary.* New York: Basic Books.

Tighe, T. J. and Leaton, R. N. (Eds.) (1976). *Habituation: Perspectives from child development, animal behavior, and neurophysiology.* Hillsdale, N.J.: Erlbaum.

Walters, G. C. and Grusec, J. E. (1977). *Punishment.* San Francisco: Freeman.

11. FEEDING AND SLEEPING

JUDITH DUNN

Feeding and sleeping
    Developmental changes in feeding

Factors influencing feeding patterns
    Scheduling of feeds and weaning
    Breast and bottle feeding
    Nutritional effects

Feeding problems in infancy and early childhood
    Family factors in feeding disorder
    Failure to thrive
    Anorexia nervosa

Sleeping
    Developmental changes in physiology and
       organization of sleep
    Transition from wakefulness to sleep
    Night-waking and difficulties in settling

Sleepwalking, sleeptalking and night terrors

Conclusion

FEEDING AND SLEEPING

A baby's patterns of feeding and sleeping are of central concern to his mother from the moment that he is born. Difficulties, or deviations from the expected pattern, can cause great anxiety in the early weeks, and throughout the preschool period they remain a source of distress with real potential for damaging the relationship between mother and child. Feeding also has a place of special significance in theories of psychological development. Oral experiences in infancy have been particularly stressed in psychoanalytic theories, with the child's experience of gratification or frustration in the feeding relationship with the mother seen as having long-term implications for personality development (Abraham, 1927). Three particular aspects of the feeding situation—the source of food (breast or bottle), the flexibility of schedule, and the technique of weaning—have been claimed to affect the gratification experienced by the child. The translation of psychoanalytic theory into the language of social learning then extended interest in feeding. More recently psychoanalysts have become increasingly interested in other aspects of interaction between mother and baby, and have laid less emphasis on oral influences on development (Dare, 1977). It is clear that the development of attachment between mother and child does not depend primarily on the feeding experience (Bowlby, 1969), but since so much of the early communication between mother and baby centres on feeding, this remains a focus of much interest for those concerned with the early relationship between mother and child.

Developmental changes in feeding

The newborn baby is born with considerable skill at finding and sucking from the nipple or bottle: if his face close to the mouth is stroked he will turn towards the stimulus with open mouth, and this 'rooting' reflex is followed by a 'placing' reflex. He fastens onto the stimulus and begins to suck. Sucking techniques adapt very quickly to differences in the way his milk is provided, and once a baby has experienced a bottle teat, which is designed to provide a 'supernormal' sucking stimulus, he may be less willing to suck from the breast. If he is fed 'on demand' (whenever he cries and seems inconsolable by holding) he may take as many as 12 feeds a day during the first fortnight (Illingworth *et al.*, 1952). Over the next few weeks he settles to a regular routine of four-hourly feeds, and eventually moves onto three meals a day. By 3 to 4 months, if solid food is placed on the back of his tongue, he can successfully pass it backwards and swallow it. By 3 months, most babies have ceased to wake for a night feed, although some continue for several more weeks.

FACTORS INFLUENCING FEEDING PATTERNS

Individual differences

From the earliest days there are marked individual differences in how regularly the baby demands feeds. One study which followed babies from 3 months for several years found some evidence for continuity from the first to the fourth year of life in these individual differences in regularity of bodily function, both feeding and sleeping (Thomas *et al.*, 1963). While parental patterns of caretaking are obviously of great importance in establishing a rhythm for feeds, it is also clear that babies differ very much in the ease with which they can be encouraged to fit into a routine. Individual differences between babies in sucking behaviour are also marked from birth. Some babies suck very excitedly and vigorously. Others are much more placid. Some react rapidly and intensely to any interruption or frustration. Others are much calmer. The causes of these differences are not well understood, although the course of delivery, and the medication which the mother has received during labour, have been shown to affect the course of feeds and the baby's non-nutritive sucking behaviour (Richards and Bernal, 1973; Brazelton, 1961). It is very likely that such differences in sucking do contribute to the relative ease or difficulty of the early feeds, and thus to the confidence of the mother.

The importance of early experience

These early feeds seem of particular importance for the developing child's patterns of feeding: clinical observations by Middlemore (1942), Gunther (1955), and Isbister (1954) have shown that if a baby has difficulty during the first few feeds in taking the nipple well in, or if he has difficulty breathing while feeding because his nose is occluded by the breast, he may react adversely, even by actively refusing the breast. Clinical experience has also suggested that if the first feed is given very soon after delivery, when the baby is in a particularly alert state, breast-feeding goes especially well (MacKeith and Wood, 1977).

Support for this clinical view is provided in the findings of an interview study of 2000 women, which showed that mothers who put their babies to the breast within four hours of birth were much more successful in breast-feeding than those who waited eight hours or more (Martin, 1978).

The idea that this postnatal period may be of special importance for feeding, and for the developing relationship between mother and child more generally, has received support from a study of Guatemalan mothers and babies. Kennell et al. (1975) showed that if mother and baby were allowed 'extended contact' with each other for some hours after birth, rather than experiencing the usual hospital routine separation, the duration of breast-feeding was significantly increased, and other aspects of mother–child interaction were affected. But it should be noted that the consequences of particular early experiences may be very different in different groups. When parallel studies were carried out in groups of mothers in Stanford (Leiderman and Seashore, 1975) and Oxford (Whiten, 1977) these early effects disappeared after a few weeks. It seems likely that the fading of the effects was a function of the very different social background of the families in Oxford and Stanford; unlike the Guatemalan mothers, these were well educated, in good economic circumstances, in nuclear family units. In discussing the effects of varying postnatal contact between mother and baby, Kennell et al. employ the metaphor of imprinting, taken from animal studies, describing the postnatal period as a 'sensitive period'. But it is not clear that the results require this interpretation. Richards (1978) has suggested instead that the intervention by paediatricians gives the mother much needed support, and affects their entire conception of mothering. For mothers living in very difficult circumstances, this intervention may be extremely important.

It has also been suggested that there is a 'sensitive period' for the introduction of solid foods. Illingworth and Lister (1964), on the basis of clinical experience, maintain that if a baby is not allowed the experience of tasting and swallowing solids in the fourth month, his interest in eating solids may be drastically affected. More systematic work is needed on the question of early appetite generally.

Scheduling of feeds and weaning

The success of breast-feeding can be importantly affected by the flexibility of feeds in the early weeks. In a study of 80 families in Cambridge it was found that the breast-fed babies (who were fed on a roughly four-hourly schedule), cried more frequently, and slept for shorter periods than the bottle-fed babies, and that this frequent crying led many mothers to feel that they were failing to supply enough breast milk, and to abandon the attempt (Bernal, 1972). When they gave their babies bottle milk, the babies slept for much longer periods, and the mothers concluded that they had been right to assume that their milk supply had been inadequate. But there is quite a different explanation for the different patterns of sleeping in breast- and bottle-fed babies. If the composition of milk of various mammals and the periodicity of their nursing sessions is compared, a correlation is found between the protein content of the milk and the interval between feeds. This association cuts across taxonomic groupings. The protein content of breast milk places humans among the continuous contact, frequent feeding species. Bottle milk with its higher protein is comparable to the milk of species with longer feed intervals (Ben Shaul, 1962). It is thus possible that the breast-fed babies would have experienced no difficulties if they had been fed more often.

Flexibility of schedule, and the timing and manner of weaning, have been thought to be of central importance in the child's experience of oral gratification or frustration, and thus of long-term significance in personality development. However, no clear and consistent relationship has been demonstrated between flexibility of infant feeding, or weaning, and later personality. Caldwell (1964) in a detailed early review, pointed out how methodological problems had contributed to this confusing and inconclusive picture. Particularly notable is the failure to study individual differences between children in their reaction to different aspects of the feeding situation, which is surely of particular importance in attempting to examine the consequences of the gratification or frustration experienced by the child.

The findings of research into the relationship between feeding and oral symptoms such as thumb-sucking are also conflicting. The studies suggest that both short individual feed times in early infancy and late weaning are associated with prolonged thumb-sucking. There is a tendency for longer opportunity for nutritive sucking to be associated with greater emotional response to weaning. The reaction to limitation of nutritive sucking then varies with the developmental phase: if a baby's sucking experience is frustrated, this is likely to have different consequences according to his stage of development (Yarrow,

1954). The relationship between the development of thumb-sucking and sleeping habits is discussed below.

Breast and bottle feeding

It is now well established that for a baby's physical health, breast milk has considerable advantages over its substitutes (MacKeith and Wood, 1977). It is much more difficult to assess the possible advantages of breast-feeding for the child's psychological development, although much research effort has been devoted to looking for associations between feeding method and behavioural differences later (Caldwell, 1964).

It is hard to separate the effects of feeding method *per se* from the wide range of factors, social or nutritional, which are likely to be associated with the different feeding methods. The incidence and duration of breast-feeding differs markedly with variations in class, region, culture and community. For instance the social class and educational level of the mother are closely related to differences in attitude to breast-feeding in the UK and USA, and attitude to breast-feeding is closely related to success in feeding once breast-feeding is attempted (Newton and Newton, 1967; Bernal, 1972). This relationship between measures of class and education and the decision to breast-feed means that a whole range of attitudes to other aspects of child rearing will co-vary, and thus complicate the attempt to assess the effects of feeding method on the development of the child. It should preclude the use of 'duration of breast-feeding' as a measure which reflects some basic aspect of maternal acceptance or rejection. However, the question of how far mothers who decide to breast-feed, and who succeed in doing so, *differ* in their interaction with their children from bottle-feeding mothers remains important. Very little is known about the direct effects on the mother of lactation and nursing. Parallel studies with animals which separate the effects of the hormonal state, suckling experience and presence of the young, and which demonstrate that lactating individuals are more ready to show maternal behaviour than non-lactating individuals are often cited in writing about humans (Newton and Newton, 1967). But their implications for humans should be interpreted with great caution. Such studies can only be very distant analogies, as the more we learn of the differences in attitude, personality and social context of those choosing to breast-feed rather than bottle-feed, the more aware we are of how important these variables are in relation to physiological variables in determining maternal behaviour in humans.

Direct observation of interaction between mother and baby during feeds has shown considerable differences in patterns of interaction between breast- and bottle-feeds (Dunn and Richards, 1977). Breast-fed babies were touched and kissed more, and breast-feeding mothers patterned their talking and touching more closely to the babies' activities. Breast-feeding mothers responded more quickly to their baby's crying. Several investigators have reported greater responsiveness and higher levels of activity in breast-fed babies. But both the interpretation and the evaluation of these differences present problems.

Many of the differences in behaviour and interaction may simply be due to the breast-fed babies being hungrier in the first two weeks. Given the correlations with social class we cannot attribute this effect simply to feeding techniques. The observational data do suggest that there may be a closer and more intimate interaction during breast-feeding, but they do not enable us to conclude that bottle-fed babies are deprived of similar intimacy in other contexts, since feeding interaction may play a rather different role in the two groups. Furthermore follow-up studies of the two groups throughout the next four years found no differences attributable to feeding method.

Nutritional effects

In developing countries the importance of breast-feeding in the health of children cannot be over-emphasized (MacKeith and Wood, 1977). In Western countries, breast-fed babies are also more resistant to infection, and are less likely to suffer from hypernatraemia. The study of the physiological consequences of different dietary intakes during the early months—for example the effects on the myelinization process of differences in lipid intake—is an area of very active research. It has been shown that breast-feeding enables the baby to regulate the quantity of milk required for his own individual needs (Ounsted and Simons, 1976). The demonstration by Dobbing that the human brain growth spurt continues after birth underlines the importance of these advantages for the developing baby, during early infancy (Dobbing, 1974). Differences in neurological status have indeed been reported between breast-fed and bottle-fed babies aged 2 months, with significantly fewer breast-fed babies rated as being of questionable neurological status (Ounsted and Simons, 1976).

Breast milk changes in composition during the course of a feed: at the end of the feed it contains much more lipid and protein. Hall (1975) has suggested that this change in composition and consequently in tastes, may be linked to the way breast-fed babies stop feeding even though there is milk still available in the breast. She proposes that this provides an appetite-satiety control mechanism, which bottle milk with its constant composition cannot provide. In effect, the composition of the breast-feed can thus be varied according to the baby's needs at the time.

FEEDING PROBLEMS IN INFANCY AND EARLY CHILDHOOD

Feeding problems are reported particularly frequently by parents during the first six months, and during the preschool years (Bentovim, 1973). Richman *et al.* (1975) found food fads reported by parents of 13% of the children in a random sample of 3-year-olds in London. Roberts and Schoelkopf (1951) found 10% of a sample of 283 2½-year-olds in Rochester, USA, were finicky over food. In their study of Nottingham families, the Newsons' (1968) found that 30% of 4-year-olds were described as variable or finicky, and that 42% of the mothers were mildly or very concerned about the amount their child ate. Sears *et al.* (1957) report similar findings. Crisp and colleagues found that among the children of the National Survey 16% were overweight in relation to their height, and 16% were underweight (Crisp *et al.*, 1970).

Are these feeding difficulties in young children related to problems in infancy? A number of studies suggest that preschool feeding problems begin in early infancy (*e.g.* Brandon, 1970; Bentovim, 1970). But these reports are obtained retrospectively, and the connection cannot be taken as firmly established. Even if patterns of feeding behaviour are shown to be consistent from early infancy, it cannot be assumed that the cause of a continuing difficulty in feeding is a consistent pattern of maternal mismanagement, as the presentation of some psychiatric case histories suggests. It has already been noted that studies of infancy have provided ample evidence for the striking individual differences between young babies, and these are particularly evident in sucking and feeding behaviour. To understand the association between patterns of feeding in infancy and later difficulties there can be no substitute for detailed longitudinal study which takes account of individual differences in babies early on, as well as differences in parental caregiving. We do not at present have such information.

Just how hard it is to separate out the various influences on the feeding patterns and the weight gain of a developing child can be illustrated by the data on obesity in childhood. Both genetic and environmental factors have been found to influence childhood obesity. Twin studies by Shields (1962) and Bjorsen (1976) have demonstrated that genetic factors are important. Familial patterns of obesity, however, often reflect culturally transmitted attitudes to eating. On the issue of continuity, some studies find evidence for significant individual stability in body weight and shape over time. Crisp *et al.* (1970) found individual differences consistent between 4 years and 20 years for the National Survey sample. Charney *et al.* (1976), in a longitudinal study of 366 individuals now 20–30 years old found a significant association with adult obesity for those infants who exceeded the 75th percentile, independent of their height: while birth weight was important in this link, the weight gain over the first 6 months appeared particularly influential. Fisch *et al.* (1975) in a prospective study of 3000 children found that neonates who were extremely lean or obese tended to be extreme in body shape at 4 years, and at 7 years, though the associations decreased in strength. Eid (1970) also found excessive weight gain in infancy related to being overweight at 6, 7, or 8 years. That infantile or juvenile obesity leads inevitably to fatness in adult life has, however, been disputed by others. Garn (1976) maintains that the measures used in these studies are poor. Lack of stability in fatness is also indicated, for some socio-economic groups, in the epidemiological evidence from a number of national surveys that there is an inversion of relative fatness in socio-economic groups with development. Poor girls in the US are leaner than middle-class girls, but poor women are fatter. (Garn and Clark, 1976.) The apparent contradictions in some of these studies may in part reflect changes in dietary habits over the last 15 years.

Fat infants and children have higher lipid levels than those who are lean, and it has been argued that high levels of fat cells can be induced during the first year by overfeeding, and that maternal feeding patterns can thus lead inevitably to continuing fatness. (Brook, 1972.) However, this remains a speculative hypothesis, as the methodology of assessing numbers of fat cells requires refinement (Widdowson and Shaw, 1973).

It is hard to identify with confidence precisely what causes continuity in the excessive gaining of weight from infancy. The National Survey data showed a relationship between high birth weight and later fatness. But the origins of high birth weight are very complex, with genetic, socio-cultural, metabolic, and parity factors all potentially important, as well as maternal nutrition before and during pregnancy. As Crisp *et al.* (1970) point out, the maternal feeding pattern may be related to constitutional and cultural aspects of the mother's life style and to her personality and attitude to pregnancy. Any of these may be *independently* related to her patterns of interaction with the baby, including the feeding interaction.

Meanwhile it should be noted that even comparatively simple and apparently well-established relationships, such as the association of bottle-feeding and early introduction of solids with obesity in infancy and later childhood (Taitz, 1971) require re-examination, in light of recent evidence. De Sweit and Fayers (1977) in a study of 758 babies found no such association. And several studies now report no difference between breast-fed and bottle-fed babies in the incidence of fatness later (Charney *et al.*, 1976; Eid, 1970). It is possible that recent changes in attitude to feeding practices on the part of both medical authorities and parents—specifically an increase in the discouragement of overfeeding and in attention to the details of bottle-feeding practices—may explain the apparent conflict between these results.

Family factors in feeding disorder

Feeding problems are, it has been noted, common among preschool children, along with other 'neurotic' symptoms such as ritualistic behaviour, fears, and sleep problems. How far these symptoms form definite groups which could be considered clinical entities we do not know, although it is clear that the degree of concern aroused by a particular behaviour problem will depend on the way the child functions in other respects, and on the attitude and tolerance of the family and community in which he is living (Richman, 1977a). Among children referred to clinics, and in epidemiological studies in the community, associations are reported between disorders in the child, and parental psychiatric illness (Rutter, 1966; Rutter *et al.*, 1970). Feeding problems often form part of such 'significant' disorder, and are particularly associated with maternal illness. Brandon (1970) studying a 'malady' group of 11-year-olds with a very high rate of feeding disorder, and a group of children with feeding disorder drawn from a control population, reported an association between psychiatric stress in the mothers, poor marital relations, and poor parent–child relations. He emphasized the importance of poor mother–child relationships in contributing to eating disorders, stressing that in the groups he studied eating disorders were associated with early feeding difficulties in infancy, toilet training problems, and stuttering. Again, caution should be exercised in making assumptions about the direction of causality here.

Failure to thrive

Just as there are many possible contributing causes of obesity, so too there are many reasons why children fail to grow adequately. Familial patterns of growth may reflect a genetic pattern, or may indicate family attitudes to eating and exercise. But difficulties in the early relationships which a child forms which are of particular importance in affecting children's growth patterns. The term 'deprivation dwarfism' has been used to describe children brought up in conditions of extreme deprivation, who are very small for their age. Such children also often show marked delay in sexual maturation; they usually come from very disturbed families (Patton and Gardner, 1963; Koluchova, 1976) or from very poor quality residential institutions (Widdowson, 1951; Fried and Mayer, 1948). When admitted to hospital these children usually gain weight very rapidly.

How do the stressful or depriving conditions in which the children have been reared affect their somatic growth? It has been argued that emotional deprivation has led to the failure to grow properly *in spite* of adequate food intake (Silver and Finkelstein, 1967). It is certainly clear that emotional disturbance may be associated with slowed somatic growth. But the link between emotional disturbance and failure to grow is not clearly understood. Endocrine disturbance, and changes in intestinal absorption have been thought to contribute to the disturbance in growth (Talbot *et al.*, 1947). However, there are a number of important points to take into account in interpreting the results of the studies of children who fail to thrive.

1) First, many of the studies of children who fail to grow indicate that the children are suffering from inadequate food intake (Whitten *et al.*, 1969; Apley *et al.*, 1971; McCarthy, 1974). For instance, Whitten and colleagues studied 13 emotionally deprived infants, and showed that the children ate well when fed by people other than their mothers, even in hospital conditions which were designed to simulate the 'deprived' home circumstances. Eleven of the children accelerated in weight gain in hospital, and extra 'mothering' did not affect the rate of weight gain. From other evidence the investigators deduced that the mothers did neglect to feed the children when they were not being observed, and that their statements about the child's intake were not reliable.

Some studies report that children receiving an adequate diet (or with voracious appetites) still fail to grow if they remain in particularly unhappy or depriving circumstances (Fried and Mayer, 1948; Widdowson, 1951). The study by Widdowson of children in an institution with a harsh supervisor certainly suggests that dietary supplements may not improve growth unless the emotional circumstances also improve. However, in both these studies it is not clear what food the children actually *consumed*. It certainly seems plausible that the stressful circumstances may have affected the children's appetites.

2) Growth failure is sometimes associated with hormonal dysfunction. Powell and colleagues (1967) reported deficiencies in growth hormone and ACTH in 13 children of very short stature, from disturbed homes. However, it is not clear that endocrine abnormalities are the primary cause of growth failure; they could well result from the malnutrition. Other studies of children who fail to thrive have reported normal levels of growth hormone and steroid output (Silver and Finkelstein, 1967; Apley *et al.*, 1971). McCarthy (1974), in a review of the 'failure to thrive' syndrome, discusses in detail the problems involved in interpeting the results of the endocrine studies; he concludes that insufficiency of growth hormone cannot be the complete explanation of failure to thrive, which is more likely to be in terms of nutrition.

3) McCarthy (1974) points out some important developmental consequences of periods of reduced food intake in early childhood. The body's mechanisms of adaptation, which are of great complexity, can ensure that once the body is undersized it tends to remain small by adjustment of the normal enzyme and hormone action, so that health may be preserved with reduced food intake, but at the cost of slowing of growth. This slowing of growth seems to be most conspicuous if this bodily adaptation takes place in the first three years.

4) It is possible that changes in intestinal function may contribute to the failure to grow. However, there is not clear evidence that malabsorption of food or changes in metabolism play a major part in contributing to most cases of failure to thrive.

The research on failure to thrive then illustrates a number of points of general importance in the development of children. The failure of growth which results from emotional disturbance in young children provides a dramatic illustration of the powerful and long-term effects that can result from distortion in the early parent–child relationship. Attempts to understand the 'failure to thrive' syndrome must include a careful focus on the emotional environment in which the child is growing up. It is notable that McCarthy and Booth (1970) attributed the emotional deprivation which they found to be associated with failure to thrive to difficulties in the mothers' own childhood—a theme which recurs in discussion of difficulties in the mother–child relationship. It is important that research into the variables affecting children's appetite and feeding patterns should examine both the developing child's relationship and his behaviour in some detail. It is possible, for instance, that some of the symptoms which accompany the failure to thrive, such as inertia and solitariness, will themselves contribute to the slow growth (McCarthy, 1974).

While there is good evidence for nutritional deprivation as a major cause for slowing of growth in these children it is not clear whether the link between this insufficient food intake and the emotionally upsetting home circumstances is disturbance of appetite and feeding patterns, or lack of food provided. There is encouraging clinical evidence for the body's ability to 'catch up' with accelerated growth when circumstances improve, but the limits on the possibilities for such improvement are not well understood.

The important effects of malnutrition on brain growth in infancy, and the related effects on personality and intelligence are beyond the scope of this chapter (*see* Dobbing, 1974).

Anorexia nervosa

Since this chapter is primarily concerned with developmental issues, rather than with the description of disease states, anorexia nervosa is not discussed here. The subject is reviewed by Tolstrup (1975).

SLEEPING

Developmental changes in the physiology and organization of sleep

The sleep of the full term newborn baby is broken up into short periods, alternating with even shorter periods of wakefulness. Over the early months the temporal patterning of sleep and waking periods changes, with longer periods of sleep and wakefulness being sustained, and a diurnal pattern becoming established. Parmelee *et al.* (1964), in a study of 46 infants followed from birth to 16 weeks, demonstrated that there was a relatively small decrease in the total amount of sleep over 24 hours, but that the number of hours in the longest sustained sleep doubled and the longest awake period increased by one half. The ability to sustain prolonged sleep is enormously increased with maturation. There are wide individual differences between infants in how much they sleep, and these differences show some consistency over the next two years (Bernal, 1973).

Electrophysiological studies of very young infants have shown marked changes in the nature and organization of sleep in these early weeks. In adult sleep, two states of different physiological activity have been described: phases of quiet sleep (Non-REM sleep), which are divided into four stages according to the EEG characteristics, and phases of Rapid Eye Movement sleep (REM sleep) characterized by irregular heart and respiration rate, and synchronous eye movements. The phase of REM sleep is associated with dreaming, but some mental activity is reported to occur in particular states of Non-REM sleep (Foulkes, 1967). With the newborn baby, it is not possible to classify the physiological phases simply: besides phases of sleep which resemble active REM sleep and quiet sleep there are phases which Anders classifies as 'indeterminate'. (In premature babies this indeterminate state predominates—Anders and Weinstein (1972) suggest that it represents an immature stage of poorly organized sleep.) The proportion of this 'indeterminate'

sleep phase decreases over time and by 3 months it has usually disappeared. The quiet sleep phase shows marked EEG changes with age; by 3 months the electrophysiological characteristics can be classified in the same way as those of adult Non-REM sleep. While the newborn baby at term spends 45–50% of sleep time in active REM sleep, and 35–45% in quiet sleep, with increasing age these proportions change, with quiet sleep increasing and REM sleep decreasing, so that by 8 months there is twice as much quiet sleep as REM sleep, and by 10 years the normal adult proportions of 20% REM and 80% quiet sleep are reached.

What is the significance of this predominant state of 'active' REM sleep in the very young infant? Roffwarg *et al.* (1966) have suggested that the REM system constitutes a source of stimulation necessary for the maturation of the higher centres of the brain. They argue that during the period of uterine and early postnatal life the infant is cut off from stimulation and that, since growth and maintenance of neural tissues are enhanced by stimulation, the excitation from the REM system is important in providing the stimulation necessary for the maturing brain. This hypothesis does not, of course, explain the cyclic nature of activity in the brain.

Over the early weeks there are changes too in the temporal organization of the phases of REM and Non-REM sleep. While adults start sleep with a long period of Non-REM, and have most of their REM sleep in the last $\frac{1}{3}$ of the night, infants start with a period of active REM. The establishment of a diurnal rhythm takes some time: some studies report indications of patterning in the first 10 days (Sander *et al.*, 1970), but others refer to diurnal rhythms established by 3–4 months. It is at this age that most babies begin to 'sleep through' the night. Moore and Ucko (1957) report 70% of babies sleeping through by 3 months, and a further 16% sleeping through by 6 months: 10% of babies in their study never settled in this way during the first year.

How far do environmental influences affect these developmental changes in the organization of sleep? The establishment of diurnal rhythm probably is affected by environmental clues (Sander *et al.*, 1970), but the decrease in REM sleep is generally attributed to CNS maturation (Roffwarg *et al.*, 1966). Since quiet sleep is a state which requires complex feedback mechanisms to maintain regularity in respiration and heart-rate, Stern *et al.* (1969) suggests that the changes in proportion are an important reflection of CNS maturation. Quiet sleep is usually the first state to show alterations under pathological conditions (Prechtl, 1968; Lenard, 1970) and the sleep polygram has been used to demonstrate abnormalities in babies suffering neurological damage. It has been shown that, with various kinds of prenatal and perinatal pathology, the neonatal brain loses its ability to maintain the state of quiet sleep (Schulte *et al.*, 1972). Infants with mild birth trauma, infants of diabetic or toxaemic mothers, and infants of heroin-addicted mothers all show abnormalities in the organization of quiet sleep (Dreyfus-Brisac and Monod, 1970; Schulte *et al.*, 1969).

Transition from wakefulness to sleep: swaddling and thumb-sucking

The use of techniques such as swaddling or binding young children has been extremely widespread in many different societies (Lipton *et al.*, 1965), and some research has been carried out to investigate the influence of such practices on the behaviour and physiological state of infants. Lipton, Steinschneider and Richmond carried out experiments on swaddling in babies, and showed that infants who were swaddled slept more, had lower heart-rate variability, fewer startles and reduced levels of activity in response to stimulation than infants who were not swaddled. They concluded that the motor restraint imposed by the swaddling was reducing the overall arousal level of the infant by decreasing the proporioceptive stimuli reaching the reticular formation of the brain. But studies by Brackbill (1973) showed that the effect of swaddling was not simply one of motor restraint. She demonstrated that continuous stimulation from a variety of sources (swaddling, noise, light, or temperature) had a profound effect on the infant's state. Motor activity, heart-rate variability, and irregularity of respiration were all reduced, and the baby spent more time in quiet sleep. Swaddling was the most effective kind of continuous stimulation. It is not known what long term effects regular swaddling may have on a child's development (*but see* Chisholm and Richards, 1978).

The calming and soothing effects of continuous stimulation, which Brackbill showed can dramatically affect a young infant's state, are also to be seen in older children who are using comfort objects of a strokable or suckable kind. In these cases the comforting effects obviously depend too on the significance which the child attributes to the objects.

The way in which a child is put to sleep has been shown to affect the development of thumb-sucking habits. Ozturk and Ozturk (1977) studying a sample of Turkish children left to fall asleep alone, without the opportunity of sucking breast or bottle, or of being rocked, were much more likely to develop thumb-sucking habits.

Individual differences: night-waking and difficulties in settling

Disturbances of sleep such as regular waking in the night, and difficulty over settling to sleep are reported in several studies to be common in the preschool years. Two separate studies of 14–15-month-olds have reported regular night-waking in about 23% of their samples (Bernal, 1973; Blurton-Jones *et al.*, 1978). Roberts and Schoelkopf (1951), in their study of 783 2½-year-olds in the USA, report that 21% had bedtime or sleep problems; a study of a random sample of 3-year-olds in a London borough reported 13% as having difficulty settling at night, and 14% as waking during the night (Richman *et al.*, 1975), and another study of a London borough found night-waking in 17% of children under 2, and 11% of children over 2 (Bax and Hart, 1977).

In much of the earlier discussion of sleep problems, night-waking and settling difficulties were attributed to problems represented by the particular stage of ego development through which children were passing in their second and third years. Fraiberg reports that sleep problems which persist appear first at this time (Fraiberg, 1950). Settling difficulties, for example, have been seen as related to anxiety over separation from the mother. This emphasis on the anxiety over bedtime separation seems quite plausible: young children do quite often develop elaborate rituals over the bedtime separation. In the study by Roberts and Schoelkopf (1951) 90% of the 2½-year-old children had bedtime routines, and 33% had very elaborate rituals. A study by Luce and Segal (1969), which investigated children's experiences during the night when alone, showed that children reported many more frightening and upsetting experiences than their parents reported for them. The authors stress that parents underestimate children's fears about being alone at night and going to sleep, and they attribute sleep problems to parents' unwillingness to recognize and discuss this anxiety. It is worth noting that other cultures often lay very much stress than American or British people do on the importance of children becoming independent and on learning to cope with separation experiences: their attitudes to children's sleeping habits may thus differ greatly. In Japan, for instance, children sleep with adults until they are 10 years old, and it is rare for a child to sleep alone at any stage until 15 years old (Caudill and Platt, 1966). The high frequency with which children sleep with their parents expresses the great value placed on mutual dependence within the family in Japan.

That particular stresses can contribute to sleeping difficulties is also suggested by the finding that after the birth of a sibling night-waking can develop, or become worse as a problem (Dunn and Kendrick, 1979). However, two longitudinal studies indicate that night-waking does not necessarily begin during a particular phase of development and that there is marked continuity in differences (and difficulties) over sleeping from birth onwards. Children who were regular night-wakers in their second year were in the newborn period irritable babies who slept little, cried frequently and throughout their first year slept less than the rest of the sample. The night-waking children tended to have had more difficult deliveries than those who slept soundly (Bernal, 1973; Blurton Jones *et al.*, 1978). In the first of these studies the night-waking children continued to have difficulty over sleep either in waking or refusing to settle, for the next two years; at 5 years they were more likely to score above average on behaviour difficulties. Moore and Ucko (1957) also report an association between anoxia and night-waking. Some continuity in individual differences was reported for children with irregular sleeping and feeding habits in the New York Longitudinal Study (Thomas, Chess and Birch, 1963), while a study in London using a similar assessment of temperament found this irregularity in bodily functions to be associated with later development of disturbance (Graham *et al.*, 1973).

Do patterns of parental care contribute to the problems

of night-waking and difficulty over settling? An association between maternal anxiety and sleep problems is reported by Gottfarb *et al.* (1961) and by Ragins and Schachter (1971); but it is unclear that maternal anxiety is a cause rather than a consequence of the problem. Parental mishandling is frequently cited as an important cause of sleep problems (Moore and Ucko, 1957; Illingworth, 1966). But the results of the two longitudinal studies do not support this attribution. Continuity in individual differences in sleep patterns from the earliest days could arise either through consistency in a particular pattern of child-rearing (for instance the consistent response of an over-anxious or over-protective parent), through the consistent individual differences in the children's behaviour, or through an interaction between a particular style of child-rearing with a particular pattern of reactivity on the child's part. The findings of the Blurton Jones study show that obstetric factors, and the behaviour of the child in early infancy were the best indicators of night-waking in the second year, and accounted for the associated maternal behaviour—results very similar to those found in the Bernal study.

SLEEPWALKING, SLEEPTALKING, AND NIGHT TERRORS

Before the development of electrophysiological techniques, these disorders were thought to be associated with dreaming. Sleepwalking, for instance, was seen as the 'acting out' of dreams (Pierce *et al.*, 1961; Sours *et al.*, 1963). However, recent physiological research studies suggests that these episodes must be dissociated from dreams. The great majority of such episodes occur in the first three hours of sleep, when the individual is in Non-REM quiet sleep; in only 10% of recordings do they occur in REM sleep (Anders and Weinstein, 1972). The individual has no recall of the episode, or of dreaming; during the episode he is extremely difficult to arouse or waken. Children suffering from these disorders do in fact have normal REM sleep patterns (Kales *et al.*, 1968).

Sleepwalking

It is reported that 15% of children between 5–12 years sleepwalk at least once (Kales *et al.*, 1968); sleepwalking is more common among boys than girls, and may be associated with nocturnal enuresis. The EEG during an episode shows characteristic paroxysmal bursts: since these patterns occur in 85% of 6–11-month-olds, and decrease to 3% in 7–9-year-olds, Kales and colleagues have suggested that somnambulists suffer from CNS immaturity (1968). A twin study suggests that genetic factors may be involved in the disorder. Identical twins show greater concordance in sleepwalking than fraternal twins (Bakwin, 1970). It is thought that episodes of sleepwalking and talking and of night terrors are associated with stress: individuals who have had long periods without such episodes revert under stress (Anders and Weinstein, 1972). As the children grow up, the episodes of sleepwalking and talking usually decrease, and eventually disappear.

Night terror (pavor nocturnus)

Episodes of night terror occur during arousal from Stage 4 Non-REM sleep to a waking EEG pattern. The child's heart-rate rapidly increases, there is rapid and irregular breathing, and crying and screaming. Kales *et al.* (1968) reports on incidence of 1–3% among children aged 5 to 12 years. Gastaut and Broughton (1965) found that children with night terrors rarely had daytime anxiety, and were considered psychiatrically normal. As with sleepwalking, episodes of night terror subside as the child grows up; if they continue into adolescence and adulthood more serious problems are indicated.

Research with the sleep polygraph has given us a much more precise description of these episodes of arousal during sleep; it has made clear that they differ in important respects from nightmares (REM anxiety dreams). But there are many unanswered questions about their occurrence. Why are particular individuals susceptible to them? There are some suggestions that there are physiological differences associated with their occurrence (Broughton, 1968), and the link with stressful events is often cited in discussion of case material. The age link is seen by Keith (1975) as indicating that the episodes 'occur in consequence of sexual and aggressive conflicts of anal/oedipal periods of psychosexual development'. But while it is clear that during the early childhood years children are having to cope with particular developmental problems, there is not at present evidence to justify the link between specifically psychosexual conflicts, and episodes of sleepwalking or *pavor nocturnus*.

Studies of sleep fall into three very separate groups—the neuro-physiology of sleep in infancy, the polygraphic study of sleep disorders in older children, and at a grosser level of description the epidemiological study of sleep disorder. Very little is known about the links between these three: how far individual differences in early infancy are related to the sleep disorders of middle childhood is just one of the many important developmental questions to which answers are not yet available.

CONCLUSION

Feeding and sleeping problems are very common in early childhood. It is still very unclear what relationship there may be between these difficulties in infancy and the preschool period, and later disturbance of feeding and sleeping. For many young children these disturbances are probably essentially developmental problems. This does *not* mean that these difficulties should be dismissed lightly. It is clear from community studies of families with young children that there is a high rate of depression in mothers with young children, particularly those living in difficult circumstances (Brown *et al.*, 1975; Richman, 1974). Studies of clinic populations and community surveys have shown that there is a relationship between psychiatric illness and the incidence of behaviour problems, such as disorders of feeding and sleeping, in young children. Richman (1977b) found that mothers of preschool children with behaviour problems were significantly more likely to suffer from depressive illness than mothers of a matched group of control children. This association could reflect the mothers' perception of the children, alternatively the children's behaviour problems could be contributing to the mothers' depression, or there could be an interaction between the two, with each exacerbating the other. While we are not at present in a position to assess with confidence the causal links between maternal illness and the disturbed behaviour of the child, the prevalence of both should alert us to the importance of providing support and help for families where young children present such problems of management such as difficulties over feeding and sleeping.

REFERENCES

Abraham, K. (1927). The influence of Oral Eroticism on Character Formation. *In Selected Papers on Psycho-Analysis*. London: Hogarth.

Anders, T. F. and Weinstein, P. (1972). Sleep and its disorders in infants and children. *Pediatrics*, **50**, 312–324.

Apley, J., Davies, J., Davis, D. R. and Silk, B. (1971). Non-physical causes of dwarfism. *Proc. Roy. Soc. Med.*, **64**, 135–138.

Bakwin, H. (1970). Sleep-walking in twins. *Lancet*, **2**, 446–447.

Bax, M. and Hart, H. (1977). Health needs of preschool children. *Archiv. Dis. Childhood*, **51**, no. 11, 848–52.

Ben Shaul, D. M. (1962). Int. Zoo. Year Book, **4**, 333. Quoted in N. Blurton Jones (Ed.) *Ethological Studies of Child Behaviour*. Cambridge: Cambridge University Press.

Bentovim, A. (1970). The clinical approach to feeding disorders of childhood. *J. Psychosom. Med.*, **14**, 267–276.

Bentovim, A. (1973). Disturbed and under five. *Spec. Educ.*, **62**, 31–35.

Bernal, J. F. (1972). Crying during the first 10 days of life, and maternal responses. *Devel. Med. Child Neurol.*, **14**, no. 3, 362–372.

Bernal, J. F. (1973). Night-waking in infants during the first year. *Develop. Med. Child Neurol.*, **15**, 760–769.

Bjorsen, M. (1976). The aetiology of obesity in children. *Acta Ped. Scand.*, **65**, 279–287.

Blurton Jones, N., Fereira, M. C. R., Farquhar-Brown, M. and MacDonald, L. (1978). The association between perinatal factors and later night waking. *Dev. Med. Child Neurol.*, **20**, 427–434.

Bowlby, J. (1969). *Attachment and Loss, Vol. 1, Attachment*. London: Hogarth Press.

Brackbill, Y. (1973). Continuous stimulation reduces arousal level: stability of the effects over time. *Child Devel.*, **44**, 43–46.

Brandon, S. (1970). An epidemiological study of eating disturbances. *J. Psychosom. Med.*, **14**, 253–257.

Brazelton, T. B. (1961). Effects of maternal medication on the neonate and his behavior. *J. Pediat.*, **58**, 513–518.

Brook, C. G. D. (1972). Evidence for a sensitive period in adipose cell replication in man. *Lancet*, **2**, 624–627.

Broughton, K. J. (1968). Sleep disorders—disorders of arousal? *Science*, **159**, 1070–1078.

Brown, G. W., Bhrolchain, M. N. and Harris, T. (1975). Social class and psychiatric disturbance among women in an urban population. *Sociol.*, **9**, 225–254.

Caldwell, B. M. (1964). The effects of infant care. In M. L. Hoffman and L. W. Hoffman (Eds.) *Review of Child Development Research Vol. I*. New York: Russell Sage Foundation.

Caudill, W. and Plath, D. W. (1966). Who sleeps by whom? Parent–child involvement in urban Japanese families. *Psychiat.*, **29** (4), 344–366.

Charney, E., Goodman, H. C., McBride, M., Lyon, B. and Pratt, R. (1976). Childhood antecedents of obesity. *New Engl. Journ. Med.*, **295**, 6–9.

Chisholm, J. S. and Richards, M. P. M. (1978). Swaddling, cradleboards and the development of children. *Early Human Develop.*, **2**, 255–275.

Crisp, A. H., Douglas, J. W. B., Ross, J. M. and Stonehill, E. (1970). Some developmental aspects of disorders of weight. *J. Psychosom. Med.*, **14**, 327–345.

Dare, C. (1977). Psychoanalytic theories. In M. Rutter and L. Hersov (Eds.) *Child Psychiatry: Modern Approaches*. Oxford: Blackwell.

De Sweit, M. and Fayers, P. (1977). Effects of feeding habit on weight in infancy. *Lancet*, **i**, 892–894.

Dobbing, J. (1974). Later development of the brain and its vulnerability. In J. A. Davis and J. Dobbing (Eds.) *Scientific Foundations of Pediatrics*. London: Heinemann Medical Books.

Dunn, J. and Kendrick, C. (1979). The arrival of a sibling: approaching the study of a developmental context. *Alti del IV congresso Internazionale della I.S.S.B.D.* Milano: Franco Angeli.

Dunn, J. and Richards, M. P. M. (1977). Observations on the developing relationship between mother and baby in the neonatal period. In H. R. Schaffer (Ed.) *Studies in Mother–Infant Interaction*. London: Academic Press.

Eid, E. E. (1970). Follow-up study of physical growth in children who had excessive weight gain in the first 6 months of life. *Brit. Med. J.*, **2**, 74–76.

Fisch, R. O., Bilek, M. K. and Ulstrom, R. (1975). Obesity and leanness at birth and their relationship to body habitus in later childhood. *Pediat.*, **56**, no. 4, 521–528.

Foulkes, D. (1967). Non-Rapid eye movement orientation. *Exp. Neurol. (suppl.)*, **4**, 28–38.

Fraiberg, S. (1950). On the sleep disturbance of childhood. *Psycho-analytic Study of the Child*, **5**, 285–309.

Fried, R. and Mayer, M. F. (1948). Socio-economic factors accounting for growth failure in children living in an institution. *J. Pediat.*, **33**, 444–56.

Fries, H. (1974). Secondary amenorrhea, self-induced weight reduction and anorexia nervosa. *Acta Psych. Scand. Suppl.*, 248.

Garn, S. M. (1976). The origins of obesity. *Amer. J. Dis. Childh.*, **130**, 465–467.

Garn, S. M. and Clark, D. C. (1976). Trends in fatness and the origins of obesity. *Amer. Acad. Ped.*, **57**, 443–456.

Gastaut, H. and Broughton, R. J. (1965). A clinical and polygraphic study of episodic phenomena during sleep. In J. Wortis (Ed.) *Recent Advances in Biological Psychiatry*. New York: Plenum Press.

Gottfarb, L., Lagercrantz, R. and Lagerdahl, A. (1961). Sleep disturbances in infancy and early childhood. *Acta Pediat. Scand.*, **50**, 212–213.

Graham, P. (1977). Psychosomatic relationships. In M. Rutter and L. Hersov (Eds.) *Child Psychiatry: Modern Approaches*. Oxford: Blackwell.

Graham, P., Rutter, M. and George, S. (1973). Temperamental Characteristics as predictors of behaviour disorder in children. *Amer. J. Orthopsych.*, **43**, 328–339.

Gunther, M. (1955). Instinct and the nursing couple. *Lancet*, **1**, 575–578.

Hall, B. (1975). Changing composition of human milk and early development of an appetite control. *Lancet*, **1**, 779–781.

Illingworth, R. S. (1966). Sleep problems of children. *Clin. Pediat.*, **5**, 45–48.

Illingworth, R. S. and Lister, J. (1964). The critical or sensitive period, with special reference to certain feeding problems in infants and young children. *J. Pediat.*, **65**, 839–848.

Illingworth, R. S., Stone, D. G. H., Jowett, G. H. and Scott, J. F. (1952). Self-demand feeding in a maternity unit. *Lancet* **i**, 683–687.

Isbister, C. (1954). A clinical study of the draught reflex in human lactation. *Arch. Dis. Childh.*, **29**, 66–71.

Kales, J., Jacobson, A. and Kales, A. (1968). Sleep disorders in children. *Prog. Clin. Pathol.*, **8**, 63.

Keith, P. R. (1975). Night terrors. *J. Amer. Acad. Child Psychiat.*, **14**, 477–489.

Kennell, J. H., Trause, M. A. and Klaus, M. H. (1975). Evidence for a sensitive period in the human mother. *In Parent—Infant Interaction*. Ciba Foundation Symposium no. 53. Amsterdam: Elsevier.

Koluchova, J. (1976). A report on the further development of twins after severe and prolonged deprivation. In A. M. and A. D. B. Clarke (Eds.) *Early Experience: Myth and Evidence*. London: Open Books.

Leiderman, P. H. and Seashore, M. J. (1975). Mother–infant neonatal separation: some delayed consequences. *In Parent–Infant Interaction*. Ciba Foundation Symposium No. 53. Amsterdam: Elsevier.

Lenard, H. G. (1970). Sleep studies in infancy. *Acta Pediat. Scand.*, **59**, 572–581.

Lipton, E., Steinschneider, A. and Richmond, J. (1965). Swaddling; a child care practice. Historical, cultural, and experimental observations. *Pediatrics, 35*, 519–567.

Luce, G. G. and Segal, J. (1969). *Insomnia: The Guide for Troubled Sleepers*. New York: Doubleday.

MacKeith, R. and Wood, C. (1977). *Infant Feeding and Feeding Difficulties*. Edinburgh: Churchill Livingstone.

Martin, J. (1978). *Instant feeding 1975. Practice and attitudes in England and Wales*. London H.M.S.O.

McCarthy, D. (1974). Effects of emotional disturbance and deprivation (maternal rejection) on somatic growth. In J. A. Davis and J. Dobbing (Eds.) *Scientific Foundations of Paediatrics*. London: Heinemann Medical Books.

McCarthy, D. and Booth, E. M. (1970). Parental rejecting and stunting of growth. *J. Psychosom. Res., vol. 14*, 259–265.

Middlemore, M. P. (1942). *The Nursing Couple*. London: Hamish Hamilton.

Moore, T. and Ucko, L. E. (1957). Night-waking in early infancy Part I. *Archiv. Dis. Childh., 32*, 333–342.

Newton, N. and Newton, M. (1967). Psychologic aspects of lactation. *New Engl. J. Med.*, **277**, 1179–1188.

Newson, J. and Newson, E. (1968). *Four Years Old in an Urban Community*. London: Allen and Unwin.

Ounsted, M. K. and Simons, C. D. (1976). Infant feeding, growth and development. *Curr. Med. Res. Opin., 4*, 60–72.

Ozturk, M. and Ozturk, O. M. (1977). Thumb-sucking and falling asleep. *Brit. J. Med. Psychol., 50*, 95–103.

Parmelee, A. H., Wenner, N. H. and Schulz, H. R. (1964). Infant sleep patterns: from birth to 16 weeks of age. *J. Pediat., 65*, no. 4, 576–582.

Patton, R. G. and Gardner, L. I. (1963). *Growth Failure in Maternal Deprivation*. Springfield: C. C. Thomas.

Pierce, C. M., Whitman, R. M., Maas, J. W. and Gay, M. L. (1961). Enuresis and dreaming. *Archiv. Gen. Psychiat., 4*, 166–170.

Prechtl, H. F. R. (1968). Polygraphic studies of the full-term newborn. In R. MacKeith and M. Bax. (Eds.) *Studies in Infancy*. Clinics in Developmental Medicine, No. 27. London: Heinemann Medical Books.

Ragins, N. and Schachter, J. (1971). A study of sleep behaviour in two-year-old children. *J. Amer. Acad. Child Psychiat., 10*, 464–480.

Richards, M. P. M. (1978). Possible effects of early separation on later development of children—A review. In F. S. W. Brimblecombe, M. P. M. Richards and N. R. C. Roberton (Eds.) *Separation and Special-care Baby Units*. Clinics in Developmental Medicine, No. 68. London: Heinemann Medical Books.

Richards, M. P. M. and Bernal, J. F. (1973). Effects of obstetric medicine on mother–infant interaction and infant development. *Proc. 3rd Int. Cong. Psychosom. Med. Obstet. Gynaec.* Basel: Karger.

Richman, N. (1974). The effects of housing on preschool children and their mothers. *Devel. Med. Child Neurol., 16*, 53–58.

Richman, N. (1977a). Behaviour problems in preschool children: family and social factors. *Brit. J. Psychiat., 131*, 523–527.

Richman, N. (1977b). Disorders in preschool children. In M. Rutter and L. Hersov (Eds.) *Child Psychiatry: Modern Approaches*. Oxford: Blackwell.

Richman, N., Stevenson, J. and Graham, P. (1975). Prevalence of behaviour problems in 3-year-old children: an epidemiological study in a London borough. *J. Child Psychol. Psychiat., 16*, 272–287.

Roberts, K. E. and Schoelkopf, J. A. (1951). Eating, sleeping and elimination practices in a group of 2½-year-old children. *Amer. J. Dis. Childh., 82*, 121.

Roffwarg, H. P., Dement, W. and Fisher, C. (1966). Ontogenetic development of the human sleep-dream cycle. *Science, 152*, 604–619.

Rutter, M. (1966). *Children of Sick Parents: an Environmental and Psychiatric Study*. Institute of Psychiatry. Maudesley Monographs No. 16. London: Oxford University Press.

Rutter, M. (1972). *Maternal Deprivation Reassessed*. Harmondsworth, Middx.: Penguin.

Rutter, M., Graham, P. and Yule, W. (1970). *A Neuropsychiatric Study in Childhood*. Clinics in Developmental Medicine, No. 35/36. London: Heinemann Medical Books.

Sallade, J. (1973). A comparison of the psychological adjustment of obese vs. non-obese children. *J. Psychosom. Research, 17*, 89–96.

Sander, L. W., Stechler, G., Barns, P. and Julia, H. (1970). Early mother–infant interaction and 24-hour patterns of activity and sleep. *J. Amer. Acad. Child Psychiat., 9*, 103–123.

Schulte, F. J., Lasson, U., Paul, U., Nolte, R. and Jurgens, U. (1969). Brain and behavioral maturation in newborn infants of diabetic mothers. *Neuropaed., 1*, 36–43.

Schulte, F. J., Hinze, G. and Schrempf, G. (1972). Maternal toxaemia, fetal malnutrition and bioelectric brain activity of the newborn. In C. D. Clemente, D. P. Purpura and F. E. Mayer. *Sleep and the Maturing Nervous System*. New York: Academic Press.

Sears, R. R., Maccoby, E. F. and Levin, H. (1957). *Patterns of Child-rearing*. New York: Row Peterson.

Shields, J. (1962). *Monozygotic Twins Brought Up Apart and Brought Up Together*. London: Oxford University Press.

Silver, H. K. and Finkelstein, M. (1967). Deprivation dwarfism. *J. Pediat., 70*, 317–324.

Sosa, R., Kennell, J. H., Klaus, M. and Urrulia, J. J. (1976). The effect of early mother–infant contact on breastfeeding and growth. In *Breast-feeding and the Mother*. Ciba Foundation Symposium 45 (New Series). Amsterdam: Elsevier.

Sours, J., Franklin, P. and Indermill, R. (1963). Somnambulism. *Archiv. Gen. Psychiat., 9*, 400–413.

Stern, E., Parmelee, A. H., Akiyama, Y., Schulz, H. R. and Wenner, N. H. (1969). Sleep cycle characteristics in infants. *Pediat., 43*, 65–70.

Taitz, L. S. (1971). Infantile overnutrition among artificially fed infants in the Sheffield region. *Brit. med. J., 1*, 315–316.

Talbot, N. B., Sobel, E. H., Burke, B. S., Lundermann, E. and Kaufman, S. B. (1947). Dwarfism in healthy children: its possible relation to emotional, nutritional and endocrine disturbances. *New Engl. J. Med.* **236**, 783–793.

Thomas, A., Chess, S., Birch, H. G., Hertzig, M. E. and Korn, S. (1963). *Behavioral Individuality in Early Childhood*. New York: New York University Press.

Tolstrup, K. (1975). Treatment of anorexia neurosa in childhood and adolescence. *J. Child. Psychol. Psychiat., 16*, 75–78.

Widdowson, E. M. (1951). Mental contentment and physical growth. *Lancet, 1*, 1316–1318.

Widdowson, E. M. and Shaw, W. T. (1973). Full and empty fat cells. *Lancet, 2*, 905.

Whiten, A. (1977). Assessing the effects of perinatal events on the success of the mother–infant relationship. In H. R. Schaffer (Ed.) *Interactions in Infancy*. London: Academic Press.

Whitten, C. F., Pettitt, M. G. and Fischoff, J. (1969). Evidence that growth failure from maternal deprivation is secondary to undereating. *J. Amer. Med. Assn., 209*, 1675–1682.

Yarrow, L. J. (1954). The relationship between nutritive experiences in infancy and non-nutritive sucking in childhood. *J. Genet. Psychol., 84*, 149–162.

12. THE DEVELOPMENT OF BLADDER CONTROL

DAVID SHAFFER

INTRODUCTION

The development of bladder control in the young child is a complex process. There is evidence that it requires not only the, presumably innately determined, maturation of complex neurological pathways and of anatomical structures surrounding the bladder, but also environmental conditions which favour the child learning to void at appropriate times and places during the day and to contain or accommodate to nocturnal urine flow without wetting the bed.

Most children will have completed this process by the age of 3. However many do not, so that by the age of 5, frequent wetting, especially at night, is a common and distressing problem and one that is often, although by no means always, associated with behaviour or emotional difficulties.

This chapter summarizes observations which detail the stages of normal development and examines both biological and environmental factors which appear to contribute to normal development of bladder control and to its failure.

WHEN DO CHILDREN BECOME DRY?

Night time dryness

Although most children will have become dry by the time they start school a significant proportion will still be wet at night (*see* de Jonge 1973 for a review). Although most of these children will gradually—and predictably—become dry during middle childhood, a small proportion—about 1%—will still not be dry at night when they have reached the age of 18 (Thorne 1944).

A judgement about when persistent incontinence becomes 'abnormal' can be made using both statistical and clinical criteria: according to the age by which most children have become dry; by variations with age in the probability of becoming dry and by the age at which persistent wetters include significant numbers of children who have those difficulties which are known to co-exist with enuresis in older children.

The statistical perspective is best judged from clinically unselected samples, studied longitudinally, in which information is collected reliably and at frequent intervals during that part of early childhood when change is most likely to take place.

A number of studies provide this information, and despite having been carried out in very different populations they yield remarkably similar information. Oppell *et al.* (1968a) studied a clinically unselected cohort of mature black and white children in the city of Baltimore as a control for a study on prematurity. Kaffmann and Elizur (1977) studied a smaller, but similarly unselected population of children reared in a Kibbutz. Miller *et al.* (1960) studied an unselected sample of families in Newcastle upon Tyne. All used similar criteria of incontinence (one to three nights wet per month) and obtained information at regular intervals starting at infancy. Other studies on larger populations (*see* de Jonge, 1973 for a summary) have either examined groups of children attending special clinics, have relied upon parents' retrospective accounts or else have failed to define the frequency of night wetting.

In the Baltimore study, black boys were slower to become dry than either white boys or black or white girls up until the age of 6. Thereafter, bedwetting was significantly more common in black children of either sex. All of the studies have shown a tendency for girls to achieve continence before boys. By age 3 years over a half of all children and by the age of 4 over two-thirds of all children are dry by night.

These studies also show that the probability of becoming dry during the following year changes markedly during this period. To take the Baltimore male sample as an example: over 40% of wet 2-year-olds were to become dry before the age of 3, 20% of wet 3-year-olds before age 4 but only 6% of wet 4-year-olds would become dry before age 5. Thereafter the probability of becoming dry remains low (*see also* Douglas and Blomfield, 1958 and Miller *et al.* 1960). Rutter *et al.* (1973) examined continence patterns in a total population of 5-year-olds who were re-examined at age 7 years. Only four of the 158 wet

5-year-olds (*i.e.* 1.5%) were to become dry during the following two years. In the Israeli study Kaffman and Elizur (1977) 21 children were wet at age 6 years and 19 were wet between the ages of 7 and 9 years. However it is not clear whether only two of the 21 had become dry during this period or whether the children wet at age 7 to 9 included any late onset enuretics. On the basis of these findings, it seems that persistent wetting at age 4 is a more unusual and potentially persistent condition than wetting at age 3.

In their total population study Rutter *et al.* (1973) demonstrated that psychiatric disorder was significantly more common in bed wetters than in non bed wetters, at least between the ages of 5 and 14. As suggested above, a further method for deciding when persistent night time incontinence should be regarded as clinically abnormal, is to look at the association between wetting and behaviour problems at various ages. This was done by Kaffman and Elizur (1977) who obtained behaviour problem ratings from the house mothers of the 161 children in their study. Results have been presented for ages 3 and 4 years. Three-year-old wetters had no more problems than 3-year-olds who were dry. However, children who were still wet at night by age 4 were significantly more likely to have behaviour problems than those who were dry at that age.

Taken together these approaches would suggest that wetting up until age 3 is 'normal' but that children who are wet after that age differ qualitatively in that more, although by no means all, will have other difficulties and that the likelihood of their becoming dry during the following year is significantly reduced.

Day time continence

Gesell and Amatruda (1941) summarized the process of becoming dry as follows:

15 months: Will pass urine frequently when put on the pot. Does not ask to go on the pot. Does not defer micturition until put on the pot. Frequent 'accidents'.
18 months: As above but defers micturition for a reasonable time and has infrequent accidents.
24 months: Makes needs known in a regular and consistent fashion.
36 months: Goes to the lavatory alone both in the day and the night.

However, there are many deviations from this orderly process, which is clearly dependent on both motor and language skills as well as on the maturity of 'bladder control' mechanisms.

Roberts and Schoellkopf (1951) interviewed the parents of 783 2½ year-olds. They found that although continence during the day usually came before dryness at night, the order was by no means uniform. Fifty per cent of children were consistently dry during the day by age 2½ but 16% of the children who were still wetting during the daytime were dry at night. By age 3 years as many as one in five of all children are still wet during the day at least once a month (Oppell *et al.*, 1968a; de Jonge, 1969.)

Roberts and Schoellkopf also found significant sex differences in how often children made their toileting needs known to a parent. Boys needed reminding to go to the toilet four times as often as girls.

By age 5 years, day wetting occurs more often among girls than boys (Rutter *et al.*, 1973). Day wetting at this age is very frequently associated with night wetting and day time wetters are significantly more likely to have an associated behaviour problem than children who only wet at night.

Secondary incontinence

A number of children who acquire continence at an early age will start to wet, usually at night and usually after an incident involving some form or psycho-social stress (*see* Shaffer, 1977 for a review). Such children are known as 'secondary', 'onset' or 'regressive' enuretics. Longitudinal studies (*e.g.* Oppell *et al.*, 1968a; Miller *et al.*, 1960) suggests that as many as a third of children who are found to be persistently enuretic after age 7 have previously been continent for at least six months, most often between the ages of 2 and 3 years. This comes as a surprise to many clinicians for it seems that relatively few parents recall the history of early continence when their children are referred for treatment in middle childhood.

CONSTITUTIONAL FACTORS AND THE DEVELOPMENT OF CONTINENCE

Genetic factors

Approximately 70% of all enuretic children have a parent or a sibling who is or was enuretic after age 5 (Bakwin, 1961). Twin studies (Hallgren, 1960; Bakwin, 1973) show a higher concordance for persistent bed wetting in monozygotic than in dizygotic twins. It is not known which mechanisms are inherited and the area is open for further research. It would however be reasonable to suppose that any inherited delay in acquiring continence is mediated by a structural or functional difference in the genito-urinary apparatus and/or its neurological control.

The physiology of continence

Under normal circumstances bladder continence is maintained through progressive accommodation to bladder filling by the smooth muscle of the bladder. This can probably be accounted for by the viscous and elastic properties of the bladder wall, for in animals the portion of the cystometrogram prior to the voiding contraction is not affected by anaesthesia, nerve transection or even death (Stephenson, 1978). Other mechanisms which contribute to the maintenance of continence include the physical properties of the internal urethral orifice and compression exerted both by the musculature of the urethra and bladder neck itself and by the action of the pelvic floor muscles (Zinner *et al.*, 1976).

The bladder fills at an average rate of about one millilitre per minute, by a train of small squirts from the ureter. The rate of urine production is increased by exercise and fluid intake and is subject to circadian rhythms. The rhythm of water excretion is such that output is usually at its nadir between midnight and 5 a.m. Mature cyclical rhythms are not usually acquired until after the first year of life (Hellbrugge, 1960).

During filling, the bladder conforms its shape to external limiting or compressing structures. Pressure within the filling bladder remains at about 10 cm of water when the person is prone and increases to about 20 cm of water in the sitting or upright position (Zinner and Paquin, 1963).

As the bladder continues to fill to capacity, afferent impulses inhibit the pontine and sacral micturition reflex centres preventing the pelvic nerves from producing a coordinated bladder contraction (Stephenson, 1978). Normally, a person is unaware of bladder filling, unless the bladder is excessively distended.

When urination is desired and the time and place are appropriate the bladder neck descends (Lapides, 1958) and the pelvic floor muscles, which support the base of the bladder, relax. Isometric contractions occur in the bladder wall and the intravesical pressure rises. There is some question about whether the urethra dilates as an active process but the net result is that it shortens, the bladder neck assumes a funnel shape and micturition commences.

An important coordinating centre concerned with sensations indicating the urge to micturate and with motor behaviour facilitating the emptying of the bladder, is located in the septal and preoptic areas lateral to the third ventricle, above the hypothalamus and below the amygdalum and the hippocampus (Hess, 1957). It is from this centre that sphincter and detrusor activity is controlled, being mediated through: (a) parasympathetic nerve fibres which travel through the caudal part of the spinal cord between the second and fourth sacral segments (these are by and large concerned with active contraction and bladder emptying); and (b) sympathetic fibres (these affect relaxation of the bladder wall but also innervate the bladder neck) which leaves the cord from all of the thoracic and the first two lumbar roots and which travel to the bladder in the hypogastric nerves (Nathan, 1976).

Voluntary control over the micturition reflex develops during infancy and originates from a region of the medial wall of the anterior frontal cortex and that part of the cingulate gyrus which envelopes the genu of the corpus callosum. Lesions in this part of the brain result in micturition with little prior sensation and in incontinence at night (Andrew and Nathan, 1965).

Physiological abnormalities and enuresis

There is some evidence that a proportion of children who are slow to acquire continence have abnormalities of the anatomical structures which reinforce continence and that some also show a disturbance of bladder function.

The evidence for abnormality of structure was reported by Hutch (1972) who, with his colleagues at Stanford University, performed lateral cystograms on 93 children below the age of 3, on 200 non-enuretics and on 89 enuretics aged between 4 and 14 years. All of the children aged under 3 years had 'rounded' 'base plates', i.e. a radiological representation which is thought to indicate a sub-optimal arrangement of the bladder muscles surrounding the vesico-urethral orifice. Non-enuretic children aged 4 and over showed a 'flat', i.e. optimal, 'base plate', significantly more often than enuretic children of the same age. Hutch has suggested that the optimum muscular structure results from local tissue growth around the vesico-urethral junction, rather than from any change in neurological function. However, it is clear that the maintenance of continence is not solely dependent upon the base plate, which is thought rather to reinforce other continence maintaining mechanisms under conditions of increased intra-vesical pressure. In keeping with this hypothesis Hutch found that the presence or absence of a mature base plate was imperfectly related to continence. Some continent children had immature, rounded plates and vice-versa.

Bladder function is disturbed in many enuretics. This was noted by Starfield (1967) who compared the maximum volume passed at the time of a single micturition by a large group of enuretics and by their non-enuretic siblings after they had received a standard fluid load. She found that, on average, the maximum volume passed by the enuretics was substantially less than that passed by controls of the same age, although there was a good deal of overlap between enuretics and non-enuretics. Starfield suggested that frequency and urgency were the clinical correlates of these findings. Certainly these symptoms are reported more often in enuretics than non-enuretics. Thus, Hallgren (1956) found that 24% of a representative sample of 7-year-old enuretics had frequency compared with only 1·5% of a control group.

More light has been shed on this phenomenon by cystometric studies in which intra-vesical pressure changes have been recorded during artificial filling of the bladder. Pompeius (1971) studied a group of enuretics and found that even among those with no known associated infection or other structural abnormalities, bladder filling was associated with both a more rapid rise in pressure for a given volume and with larger amplitude micturition contractions than expected. Bates (1971) has introduced the term 'unstable bladder' to describe this phenomenon and defines it as the occurrence of detrusor contractions which the patient is unable to inhibit. Whiteside and Turner-Warwick (1976) confirm that unstable bladders occur in children with enuresis and on the basis of clinical studies in previously enuretic adults suggest that the functional abnormality may be present from birth and continue on into adult life, even after enuresis has ceased, with the persistence of such symptoms as frequency and urgency.

The causes of bladder 'instability' are unknown although it seems as if it may be affected by habitual volume. Thus, when a bladder is artificially kept empty, contractile responses to filling are exaggerated (Yeates, 1973). Conversely, there are clinical reports that forced dilation reduced bladder instability (Dunn et al., 1976) although other workers (Pengelly *et al.*, 1978) have failed to replicate these findings. These observations raise the question of whether bladder instability in enuretics is a consequence rather than a cause of night time incontinence or frequency, *i.e.* that the bladder of the child who is incontinent at night never experiences a degree of filling sufficient to reduce inherent instability. However the findings by Whiteside and Arnold (1975) that cystometric patterns and the symptoms of urgency and frequency persist after continence has been achieved and by Shaffer *et al.* (1978) that functional bladder volume is little changed when continence is acquired through conditioning treatment, would suggest that instability is an independent phenomenon. Finally, differences in bladder capacity in wet and dry children are functional rather than anatomical in origin. This has been demonstrated by Troup and Hodgson (1971) who found that bladder volumes under anaesthesia were similar in enuretics and non-enuretics even though cystometric findings with the same subjects when conscious, showed that the enuretics had smaller functional volumes than non-enuretics.

Depth of sleep

Sleep studies have shown that the stage of sleep when enuresis occurs is in part a function of when the enuretic event takes place. Taking this factor into account the sleep stage at which an enuretic event occurs is proportionate to the time spent in that stage (Kales *et al.*, 1977; Mikkelsen *et al.*, 1978). Sophisticated sleep studies such as those quoted above have compared the overall composition of sleep staging between enuretics with standards established for non-enuretics and have found no overall differences in proportions of sleep stages other than those which can be explained by the child walking or being woken after being wet. The report by some researchers that enuresis rarely takes place during REM sleep (Ritvo *et al.*, 1969) seems to be a consequence of the fact that enuretic events are relatively uncommon during the early hours of sleep when REM sleep is most prominent. The implications of these findings are that the failure of the child to respond to sensations of bladder tension or distension are not secondary to deep sleep.

Association with other delays

A delay in becoming continent bears some similarities to other developmental disorders such as developmental reading and language delays. Thus persistent wetting is more prevalent in boys (although the sex differences are not so marked as they are with either of these conditions) and a positive family history is commonly found. An important difference is that an appreciable number of children who are enuretic in middle childhood have been through an earlier period of continence. This is clearly different from reading, language or motor competency delays in which skills once acquired, are, for the most part, retained.

Developmental delays tend to be associated with each other. Does this hold for enuresis? Certainly developmental delays are not infrequently found in samples of enuretics attending clinics. Kaffman and Elizur (1977) in a survey of children attending special clinics found higher rates of motor and speech abnormalities in enuretic patients than in non-enuretic patients, as did Lickorish (1964). However these findings may be representative only of enuretics who also have psychiatric problems. Does it hold for other enuretics? The evidence on this point is sparse. Kaffman and Elizur (1977) found no delay in continence milestones in those few children in their *non-clinic*, representative sample who were retarded on motor and speech milestones. Oppell *et al.* (1968a) similarly found no relationship between delay in continence and other milestones but did note that children with demonstrable neurological abnormalities were significantly more likely to be slow in becoming dry. Douglas and Blomfield (1958) reporting on the British National Study found that children who were still wet at the age of 6 were more likely to have associated speech defects noted at a school medical examination. However the nature of the speech abnormalities was not specified. Nor does enuresis appear to be related to intelligence. Both Oppell *et al.* (1968a) and Rutter *et al.* (1973) have confirmed this in their studies among clinically unselected groups.

Delays in acquiring continence have been noted in low birth weight children. Neligan *et al.* (1976) found that low weight for dates infants were more likely to be wet than either normal controls or low birth weight, short gestation (premature) children at age 6 years. However, differences between prematures and low weight for dates children were no longer apparent at age 7 years. Kaffman and Elizur (1977) found that all of the premature born children in their sample were still wetting at the age of 4, and Oppell *et al.* (1968a) noted that low birth weight infants were significantly slower in acquiring both day and night time continence than infants whose birth weight was over $2\frac{1}{2}$ kilograms. These findings cannot easily be accepted as evidence of a developmental delay as the later developmental correlates of low birth weight are in general ill understood and in many cases can be accounted for by associated adverse environmental factors (Werner *et al.*, 1971).

Enuresis is commonly found to be associated with encopresis. Hallgren (1956) in a survey of a large school population found that 13% of children who were still wetting at age 7 had had episodes of faecal incontinence since the age of 3 compared with only 3% of a control group. However the neuromuscular mechanisms involved in faecal continence overlap to some extent with those involved in urinary control. A finding of associated difficulties therefore is not necessarily indicative of a more generalized developmental delay.

In summary, studies of clinically unselected groups, do not indicate any clear relationship between delays in acquiring continence and other forms of developmental delay other than encopresis. In addition the intermittent nature of delayed sphincter control is different in quality to the patterns of acquiring competence that are found in other developmental disorders.

PSYCHOSOCIAL FACTORS AND BECOMING DRY

The foregoing section on constitutional abnormalities in enuretics can be summarized as showing that some disturbances of anatomy and physiology are common but that they are not in themselves 'sufficient' to explain persistent wetting and that there is a real possibility that the physiological differences are secondary to repeated nocturnal incontinence rather than causal. It is therefore necessary to examine psychosocial and environmental factors as well.

The broad social correlates of persistent wetting have been examined in a number of studies. Rutter *et al.* (1973) found only weak and inconsistent relationships between persistent bed wetting and parental occupation at ages 9 and 10 years and Stein and Sussar (1967) Oppell *et al.* (1968b) and Blomfield and Douglas (1956) found that social class differences pertained mainly to girls and mainly to children who had first been dry and then relapsed. Miller *et al.* (1960) found that enuresis was unrelated to parental occupation, but was more common in severely disadvantaged families who were dependent on welfare and who offered a depriving environment for their children.

Rutter *et al.* (1973) have suggested that the failure to demonstrate a consistent relationship between delayed continence and social class can be interpreted as showing that there is no consistent, *culturally linked*, parental behaviour or style of child rearing that leads to enuresis. This certainly seems likely. However, there are a number of psychosocial influences which still require examination.

These include the possibilities that: (a) certain styles of toilet training—perhaps more characteristic of individual families than of any social class or cultural group—delay or facilitate continence; and (b) certain disruptions and stresses during that period of childhood when continence is normally acquired, lead to a delay in becoming dry; and (c) concomitant emotional or behavioural disturbance leads to a delay in becoming dry.

Toilet training

Quite opposing predictions about the effect of toilet training practices have been made in the past. On the one hand, it has been suggested that early training might lead to rebellion and to the subsequent and conscious use by the child of wetting as a mechanism to punish the parent (Huschka, 1942). Conversely, learning theorists have suggested that early training will increase the probability of early acquired and sustained continence.

A number of problems hinder the examination of this issue. Most studies rely upon retrospective parental report and parents are seldom asked—even assuming they were able—to report on the various behavioural components that constitute toilet training. Indeed a great many cannot recall any discrete process of training at all (Lovibond, 1964; Klackenburg, 1955).

At least three aspects of toilet training need to be considered: (a) the age at which a child is provided with a structured opportunity for appropriate voiding, *i.e.* potting; (b) the quality and amount of reinforcement and encouragement that is given both for urination in an appropriate place, for the child indicating to the parent that it wishes to go to the toilet, and for withholding elimination, especially at night; and (c) the quality and amount of punishment that is given for inappropriate elimination.

Timing of training

Parents are commonly advised to delay the onset of training until the child is 'ready' and this is often said to be after the age of 2 years (Brazelton, 1962, 1973; Ben Yaakov, 1972). However it seems that few parents are tempted to accept this advice. Douglas and Blomfield (1958) found that over half a large National British sample of Mothers had first held their infants on a pot within two weeks of birth. Sears *et al.* (1957) found that over a half of a group of Californian mothers were regularly potting their child before the age of 9 months, and that most parents started to pot their child between the age of 5 and 9 months (*i.e.* a time when most infants can sit unsupported). Klackenburg (1955) in Sweden and Lovibond (1964) in Australia found that between 35% and 40% of mothers start to pot their infants before the age of 3 months and that between 80% and 90% have done so by the time the child reaches the age of 9 months. A different situation pertains in Israel when children on kibbutzim are trained by a metapalet, often on the basis of published guidelines. In a sample of children reared in a number of kibbutzim Kaffman and Elizur (1977) found that only 4% had started to be trained by the age of 14 months and that the modal time for the start of training was 20 months.

Most natural mothers seem to disregard child development manuals and start training well before the end of the first year. Fortunately this does not seem to influence later continence to any significant extent. Lovibond (1964) found no differences between the mothers of enuretics and non-enuretics in the time of starting training. Sears *et al.* (1957) and Blomfield and Douglas (1956) reported similar findings. Sears found that among the relatively small proportions of mothers who started to train their child after the age of 18 months, the time taken to become dry was slightly shorter than if training was started at an earlier age, but the differences were so slight that the overall effect was that the earlier training started the earlier the child became dry.

However the study by Kaffman and Elizur described above suggests that if training is delayed beyond 20 months the likelihood of persisting incontinence is significantly *increased*. Thus, whereas only 5% of the children whose training had started before 20 months were still wet between the ages of 6 and 8, nearly four times as many of the children whose training had started after 20 months were wetting at that age. These results are important not only because the differences were so large but also because the timing of the training was determined by convention rather than any individual characteristics of the child or metapalet.

To summarize, it seems that most mothers start to train their children when they are able to sit on a pot independently, that this is a sensible practice and is more likely to lead to later continence than delaying potting until a notional stage of 'readiness'.

Reinforcement

Encouragement for appropriate elimination is written into most management manuals and is probably common, although perhaps not universal, amongst normal parents. However, a good parent's spontaneous pleasure at noting appropriate elimination falls short of the more elaborate meticulous and efficient approach to reinforcement that has been used by some psychologists.

In an earlier report, Madsen (1965) described a single case in which a 19-month-old child, who had previously been potted regularly without any systematic reinforcement, rapidly became dry when given an edible reward for passing urine in a pot. Pumroy and Pumroy (1965) described how offering an after-dinner mint to their 26-month-old children resulted in an increase in both requests to be allowed to urinate and also appropriate urination in a pot. Foxx and Azrin (1973) have adapted a number of the principals of social learning to develop a programme which, in their study, produced day time continence within 48 hours in 34 2- to 3-year-old children.

The children were trained in their own homes by a specially trained 'instructor'. A distraction free environment was created by removing all toys and by arranging for the childs' parents to be away from home during the training period. A large number of 'learning trials' (i.e. urinations) were brought about by encouraging the liberal intake of fluids and both social (i.e. hugging, kissing, and praising) and edible reinforcements were given not only for passing urine in a chamber pot but also for certain essential preliminary behaviours such as indicating an urge to pass urine, for getting out the pot and for removing pants. Other aids to the learning process were the use of a pot which provide a signal to the instructor as soon as micturition had started (enabling the instructor to provide reinforcement for appropriate behaviour with a minimum of delay) and the use of a wetting doll as a model for imitative learning. The negative elements, or punishers, which were used in the programme included reprimand, withdrawing attention for several minutes after an accident and making the child change their pants themselves. Foxx and Azrin found that in all cases day time continence was brought about within 48 hours and that 30% of children who became dry during the day also became dry at night. The children seemed to enjoy the training episode and no adverse sequelae were noted.

Harsh training

Another element of the training procedure is the degree of harshness or punitiveness that the parents apply to the child for a failure to appropriately pass urine or faeces. As mentioned above, an element of disapproval would be likely to aid efficient training but undue harshness would be likely to create unwanted effects. Sears et al. (1957) found that the expression of some disapproval by parents was usual when their young children were incontinent. However, about one in five parents recalled having used more severe punishment. The parents who reported being punitive or harsh in this way were more likely to have recalled that the children showed emotional problems during training (recalled retrospectively). There are several possible explanations for this reported association. On the one hand it may have been that the punitive approach by the mother caused the emotional distress at the time of training. It could also have been that difficult children elicit a more punishing approach from their parents (see Thomas and Chess, 1977). A further possibility is that parents who are harsh during toilet training also exhibit punitive methods in other areas of parenting and that this leads to emotional upsets. Sears provided some evidence that this is so. Mothers who had been harsh during toilet training also used more physical punishment generally and used less reasoning in their parenting practices. They had higher anxiety levels about their ability to rear their children, and they showed less warmth toward their children. Although harsh toilet training was associated with more emotional disturbance during the process it did not necessarily delay becoming dry, and rather more of the children who had received harsh training were dry before the age of 2 than was expected. The study did not establish whether harshness during the initial training was more or less likely to be followed by secondary incontinence.

Night time training

Night time training or 'lifting' bears some similarities to day time training. However, the procedure appears to be adopted less often than day time training. Lovibond (1964) found that fewer than 40% of his sample had ever wakened their child at night, and that there were no differences between the parents of enuretics and nonenuretics in this respect. Roberts and Schoellkopf (1951) interviewed a large sample of the parents of 2½-year-old American children (predominantly middle class) and found that fewer than one in five of the children were ever lifted at night. Boys who were still wetting at night were more likely to be lifted, which is perhaps not surprising, but which is also a poor testament to the effectiveness of the process.

Summary

It seems clear that intensive and well timed toilet training, emphasizing praise and reinforcement, facilitates the acquisition of continence in most children. This raises the interesting possibility that enuresis, whether it be diurnal or nocturnal, is a consequence of inadequate or inept early training experiences, and that the consistently reported relationships between enuresis and either sub-optimal home experiences or hospitalization at a crucial age (*see* below) may be accounted for by improper training. However, whether training interacts with any anatomical or physiological differences to cause enuresis remains to be studied.

Early stressful events

Miller (1960) in his study of a thousand Newcastle families noted that children who were admitted to hospitals between the ages of 2 and 5 years were significantly more likely to continue to wet during middle childhood than children who had not been admitted to hospital. Douglas (1973) examined this finding in a more detailed fashion using data derived from the British National Survey of 4500 children born in Great Britain in the first week of March 1946. Douglas found that a number of early life events were associated with an increased prevalence of enuresis at age 4½ years. These included a break up of a family through death, divorce, or separation; temporary separation from the mother; and admission to hospital. Many of the increases were small and not statistically significant. However by summating events, 16% of children who had experienced four or more during the first 4 years of life, were still wetting at age 6 compared with 8·7% of children who had experienced none. At age 15 years, 3% of the children who had experienced four or more early events were wet compared with 1·5% of the children with no events. In a more detailed analysis of the correlates it was noted that the effect of earlier events was more marked for girls than for boys; that there were no effects from a single hospitalization, but that if a child was admitted to a hospital three or more times during early childhood the likelihood of later enuresis increased three-fold. The effect of separation from a parent was especially marked if it was a consequence of a death or separation from a mother, and the effect of a break up of a family were most marked if it involved the child going into care or being separated from its siblings.

Kaffman and Elizur (1977) also examined early separation from parents. This affected 14 out of a total of 161 children in the Kibbutz study. All three of the children who were separated from their mothers during this time wet at age 7; children who had experienced a separation from fathers were also significantly less likely to achieve bladder control by age 4 than those who had not. Separations from fathers were mainly for military service. None of the other stress events that Douglas had reported were found to be significantly related to delay in becoming dry.

These studies therefore suggest that the experience of stress during a time when continence is normally acquired may lead to persisting incontinence. The mechanisms through which they do so are not known. The most commonly advanced hypothesis is that the emotional distress associated with a separation from a parent or an admission to hospital interferes with the process of learning but it may be that such events act not only through stress but by interfering with other aspects of optimal learning conditions. Expectations for continence among children in

hospitals may be low so that the contingences for incontinence may be different both during and after admission. Parents who are otherwise under stress or distracted may pay less attention to praise or punishment for continence or incontinence. Stein and Susser (1965) noted that incontinence was generally more prevalent in institutionalized children, and this, too, may reflect a reduction in training efficacy or a lowering of expectations.

Yet another explanation of the link between early stress events and incontinence is that a delay in becoming dry is a sign of an underlying emotional disorder. This will be dealt with in the following section.

Emotional disturbance

Rutter *et al.* (1973) have shown that enuretics in middle childhood and early adolescence have higher rates of psychiatric disturbance than non-enuretics although by no means all incontinent children are disturbed. Although the association is clear there is no definitive evidence that the association, when it exists, is a causal one. Evidence concerning the relationship has to be gleaned from a number of sources, many of them contradictory and none of them directly responsive to the issue. These have been more extensively reviewed elsewhere (*see* Shaffer, 1973).

One way in which the issue can be studied is through an examination of the events which precede the onset of secondary enuresis. Werry and Cohrssen (1967) studied a group of cases referred to a clinic for secondary enuresis and noted that the commonest antecedent reported by the parent was some environmental change or event which would be expected to provoke a high level of anxiety. Hallgren (1957) noted that 55% of cases of secondary enuresis in an unselected population had been precipitated by an event that might be expected to have adverse emotional consequences on the child. However, Hallgren also noted that most of the children who started to wet after the stress event had been described as 'nervous' before the onset of their enuresis, a finding supported by Rutter *et al.* (1973) in their longitudinal study of children between the ages of 5 and 7. These findings could be interpreted as showing that in a psychologically vulnerable child additional stress may lead to the onset of enuresis but equally it seems that for many of the children disturbance is probably present during the process of normal acquisition of continence and does not delay the process.

If emotional or behaviour disturbance was the cause of delayed continence one might expect to find that the disturbances would usually be similar in type. One might also expect to find that treatment directed towards the causal disturbance would lead to a reduction in wetting (*see* Shaffer, 1973 for a review). However disturbed enuretic children do not appear to have any characteristic form of psychiatric problem (Achenbach and Lewis, 1971; Lickorish, 1964 and Rutter *et al.*, 1973) and enuretic children with associated psychiatric disturbance seemed to respond well to systematic treatment whether it be behavioural (Jehu *et al.*, 1976) or psychopharmacological (Shaffer *et al.*, 1968). They do not respond well to psychotherapy (De Leon and Mandell, 1966).

Of course there are other explanations for an association between wetting and emotional disturbance. Thus it is possible that the associated disturbance is a consequence of wetting rather than its cause. If this were so we might expect to find that older enuretics, for whom the symptom was more discrepant, or that very frequent wetters would be especially likely to be disturbed. However the relationship is as strong in very young wetters as it is for enuretics in their teens and is as strong for children who wet every night as for those who are only wet occasionally (Rutter *et al.*, 1973).

A more plausible explanation might be that those same adverse circumstances which interfere with the learning of continence also interfere with the learning of other social behaviours or else are associated with a good deal of stress and thus quite independently lead to psychiatric disorder. If a constitutional hypothesis is to be examined along similar lines one would expect that constitutional factors which make learning more difficult for the persistently incontinent child also predispose to the development of emotional disturbance. At the present time there is little evidence to support these hypotheses which must remain unproven.

SUMMARY

Most children become dry before the end of their fourth year. Children who are still incontinent after that time are relatively less likely to become dry within a given short term period and are more likely to have other associated problems and in particular emotional and behavioural difficulties. Delay in becoming dry runs in families. Children who are enuretic may show anatomical immaturities of the structure surrounding the bladder neck and may also have 'irritable' bladders which can be demonstrated on X-ray and are manifest as symptoms of urgency and frequency. The precise link between these constitutional deviation, and delay in becoming dry is not clear at this time.

Becoming dry involves learning and parenting behaviours which opitimize the learning process are associated with early dryness. Conversely if the teaching of continence is delayed later incontinence is more likely. Factors which interfere with the optimal conditions for learning, such as stress events and family disturbance are found to be associated with delayed learning although at this stage a causal link can only be surmised.

ACKNOWLEDGEMENTS

This work was supported in part by NIMH Psychiatric Education Branch, Grant No. MH07715/17.

I would like to thank Dr. John Stephenson of the Institute of Psychiatry, London, for his helpful comments and advice.

REFERENCES

Achenbach, R. and Lewis, M. (1971). A proposed model for clinical research and its application to encopresis and enuresis. *J. Amer. Acad. Child Psychiat.*, **10**, 535–554.

Andrew, J. and Nathan, P. W. (1965). The cerebral control of Micturition. *Proc. Roy. Soc. Med.*, **58**, 553–555.

Bakwin, H. G. (1961). Enuresis in Children. *J. Pediat.*, **58**, 806–819.

Bakwin, H. G. (1973). The genetics of bed-wetting. Chapter 9. In: *Bladder Control and Enuresis*. Kolvin, I., MacKeith, R. C. and Meadow, S. R. (Eds.) Clinics in Develop. Med. Nos. 48/49. London: Heinemann/S.I.M.P.

Bates, C. P. (1971). Continence and Incontinence. *Ann. Roy. Coll. Sugr. Engl.*, **49**, 18–34.

Ben Yaakov, Y. (1972). Methods of kibbutz collective education during early childhood. In: *Growing up in Groups*. J. Marcus (Ed.). New York: Garden and Breach.

Blomfield, J. M. and Douglas, J. W. B. (1956). Bed-wetting—prevalence among children age 4–7. *Lancet* **1**, 850–852.

Brazelton, T. B. (1962). A child oriented approach to toilet training. *Pediatrics*, **29**, 121–128.

Brazelton, T. B. (1973). 'Is enuresis preventable'? In: *Bladder Control and Enuresis*. Kolvin, I., MacKeith, R. C. and Meadow, S. R. (Eds.) Clinics in Develop. Med. Nos. 48/49. London: Heinemann/S.I.M.P.

De Jonge, G. A. (1969). *Kinderen met Enuresis Een Epidemiologisch en Klinisch Onderzoek*. Assen: Van Gorcum.

De Jonge, G. A. (1973). Epidemiology of enuresis: A survey of the literature. In *Bladder Control and Enuresis*, Kolvin, I., MacKeith, R. C. and Meadow, S. R. (Eds.) Clinics in Develop. Med. Nos. 48/49. London: Heinemann/S.I.M.P.

De Leon, J. and Mandell, W. (1966). A comparison of conditioning and psychotherapy in the treatment of functional enuresis. *J. Clin. Psychol.*, **22**, 326–330.

Douglas, J. W. B. (1973). Early disturbing events and later enuresis. In *Bladder Control and Enuresis*, Kolvin, I., MacKeith, R. C. and Meadow, S. R. (Eds.) Clinics in Develop. Med. Nos. 48/49. London: Heinemann/S.I.M.P.

Douglas, J. W. B. and Blomfield, J. M. (1958). *Children under five*. London: Allen & Unwin.

Dunn, M., Smith, J. C. and Ardran, G. M. (1974). Prolonged bladder distension as a treatment of urgency and urge incontinence of urine. *Brit. J. Urol.*, **46**, 645–652.

Foxx, R. M. and Azrin, N. H. (1973). Dry Pants: a rapid method of toilet training children. *Behav. Res. and Therapy*, **11**, 435–442.

Gesell, A. and Amatruda, C. S. (1941). *Developmental Diagnosis— Normal and Abnormal Child Development*. New York: Harper.

Hallgren, B. (1956). Enuresis: 1. A study with reference to the morbidity and symptomatology, *Acta Psych. Neuro. Scandinavia*. **31**, 379–403.

Hallgren, B. (1957). Enuresis: A clinical and genetic study. *Acta Psych. Neurol. Scand.* Suppl. 114 (32) 1–159.

Hallgren, B. (1960). Nocturnal enuresis in twins. *Acta Psych. Neurol. Scand.*, **35**, 73–90.

Hellbrugge, T. (1960). The development of circadian rhythms in infants. Cold Spring Harbour. *Symp. Quant. Biol.* 25, 311–323.

Hess, W. R. (1957). *The Functional Organisation of the Diencephalon*. New York: Grune and Stratton.

Huschka, M. (1942). The child's response to coercive bowel training. *Psychosom. Med.*, **4**, 301–308.

Hutch, J. A. (1972). *Anatomy and Physiology of the Bladder, Trigone and Urethra*. New York: Appleton Century Crofts.

Jehu, D., Morgan, R. T. T., Turner, R. K. and Jones, A. (1976). A controlled trial of the treatment of nocturnal enuresis in residential homes for children. *Behav. Res. and Therapy*, **15**, 1–11.

Kaffman, M. and Elizur, E. (1977). Infants who become enuretics. A longitudinal study of 161 kibbutz children. *Monogr. Soc. Res. in Child Dev.*, Vol. 42, No. 2, Serial No. 170.

Kales, A., Kales, J., Jacobson, A. *et al.* (1977). Effects of imipramine on enuretic frequency and sleep stages. *Pediatrics*, **60**, 431–436.

Klackenburg, A. (1955). Primary enuresis: When is a child dry at night? *Acta Paed. Scand.*, **44**, 513–518.

Lapides, J. (1958). Structure and function of the internal vesical sphincter. *J. Urol.*, **80**, 341–353.

Lickorish, J. R. (1964). One hundred enuretics. *J. Psychosom. Res.*, **7**, 263–267.

Lovibond, S. H. (1964). *Conditioning and Enuresis*. Oxford: Pergamon.

Madsen, C. H. (1965). Positive reinforcement in the toilet training of a normal child. In: *Case Studies in Behaviour Modification*. Ullman, L. P. and Krasner, L. (Eds.). New York: Holt Rinehart and Winston.

Mikkelsen, E. J., Rapoport, J. L., Nee, L., Grunev, C., Mendelsohn, W. and Gillin, J. C. (1979). Childhood enuresis. I. Sleep patterns and Psychopathology. *Arch. gen. Psychiat.* (In press.)

Miller, F. J. W., Court, S. D. M., Walton, W. S. and Knox, E. G. (1960). *Growing up in Newcastle*. pp. 159–153. London: Oxford University Press.

Nathan, P. W. (1976). The central nervous connections of the bladder. In: *Scientific Foundations of Urology*. D. I. Williams and G. D. Chisholm (Eds.) **2**, 51–58. London: Heinemann.

Neligan, G. A., Kolvin, I., Scott, D. Mc. and Garside, R. F. (1976). *Born too soon or born too small*. Clinics in Developmental Medicine No. 61. London: Heinemann/S.I.M.P.

Oppell, W. C., Harper, P. A. and Rider, R. V. (1968a). The age of attaining bladder control. *Pediatrics*, **42**, 614–626.

Oppell, W. C., Harper, P. A. and Rider, R. V. (1968b). Social, psychological and neurological factors associated with nocturnal enuresis. *Pediatrics*, **42**, 627–641.

Pengelly, A. W., Stephenson, T. P., Milroy, E. J. G., Whiteside, C. G. and Turner-Warwick, R. (1978). Results of prolonged bladder distension as treatment for detrusor instability. *Brit. J. Urol.*, **50**, 243–245.

Pompeius, R. (1971). Cystometry in paediatric enuresis. *Scan. J. Urol. Nephrol.*, **5**, 222–228.

Pumroy, D. K. and Pumroy, S. S. (1965). Systematic observation and reinforcement in toilet training. *Psychological Reports*, **16**, 467–471.

Ritvo, E. R., Ornitz, E. M., Gottlieb, F., Poussaint, H. F., Maron, B. J., Ditmon, K. S. and Blinn, K. A. (1969). Arousal and non-arousal enuretic events. *Am. J. Psychiat.*, **126**, 77–84.

Roberts, K. E. and Schoellkopf, J. A. (1951). Eating, sleeping and elimination practices of a group of 2½ yr. olds. *Am. J. Dis. Child.* **82**, 144–152.

Rutter, M., Yule, W. and Graham, P. (1973). Enuresis and behavioural deviance: Some epidemiological considerations. Chapter 17. In: *Bladder Control and Enuresis*. Kolvin, I., MacKeith, R. C. and Meadow, S. R. (Eds.) Clinics in Develop. Med. Nos. 48/49. London: Heinemann/S.I.M.P.

Sears, R., Maccoby, E. M. and Levin, H. (1957). *Patterns of Child Rearing*. Evanston: Row Patterson.

Shaffer, D. (1973). 'The association between enuresis and emotional disorder: a review of the literature'. In: *Bladder Control and Enuresia*. Kolvin, I., MacKeith, R. C. and Meadow, S. R. (Eds.) Clinics in Develop. Med. Nos. 48/49. London: Heinemann/S.I.M.P.

Shaffer, D. (1977). 'Enuresis'. In: *Child Psychiatry: Modern Approaches*. (Eds.) Rutter, M. and Hersov, L. Oxford: Blackwell Scientific.

Shaffer, D., Costello, A. J. and Hill, I. D. (1968). Control of enuresis with Imipramine. *Arch. Dis. Childh.*, **43**, 665–671.

Shaffer, D., Turgeon, L. and Hedge, B. (1978). 'Psychiatric disturbance and enuresis'. Paper presented at 25th Annual Meeting of the American Academy of Child Psychiatry. San Diego, California.

Starfield, S. B. (1967). Functional bladder capacity in enuretic and non-enuretic children. *J. Paediat.*, **70**, 777–781.

Stein, Z. A. and Susser, M. W. (1965). Socio-medical study of enuresis among delinquent boys. *Brit. J. Prev. Soc. Med.*, **19**, 174–181.

Stein, Z. and Susser, M. (1967). Social factors in the development of sphincter control. *Dev. Med. Child Neurol.*, **9**, 692–706.

Stephenson, J. (1978). Personal communication.

Thomas, A. and Chess, S. (1977). *Temperament and Development*. New York. Brunner/Mazel.

Thorne, F. C. (1944). The incidence of Nocturnal enuresis after age of 15 years. *Amer. J. Psychiat.*, **100**, 686–689.

Troup, C. W. and Hodgson, N. B. (1971). Nocturnal functional bladder capacity in enuretic children. *J. Urol.*, **105**, 129–132.

Werner, E., Bierman, J. M. and French, F. (1971). *The Children of Kauai. A longitudinal study from the prenatal period to age ten*. Honolulu: University of Hawaii Press.

Werry, J. S. and Cohrssen, J. (1967). Enuresis: An aetiologic and therapeutic study. *J. Paediat.*, **67**, 423–431.

Whiteside, C. G. and Arnold, E. P. (1975). Persistent primary enuresis a urodynamic assessment. *Brit. Med. J.*, **1**, 364–369.

Whiteside, C. G. and Turner-Warwick, R. (1976). Urodynamic studies the unstable bladder. In: *Scientific Foundations of Urology*. (Eds.) D. I. Williams and G. D. Chisholm. London: Heinemann.

Yeates, W. K. (1973). Bladder function in normal micturition. In: *Bladder Control and Enuresis*. Kolvin, I., MacKeith, R. C. and Meadow, S. R. (Eds.) Clinics in Develop. Med. Nos. 48/49. London: Heinemann/S.I.M.P.

Zinner, N. R. and Paquin, A. J. (1963). Clinical urodynamics: I. Studies of intravesical pressure in normal human female subject. *J. Urol.*, **90**, 719–730.

Zinner, N., Ritter, R. C. and Sterling, A. M. (1976). The mechanism of micturition. In: *Scientific Foundations of Urology*. (Eds.) D. I. Williams and G. D. Chisholm. **2**, 39. London: Heinemann.

13. MOTOR DEVELOPMENT AND MOTOR DISABILITY

KEVIN CONNOLLY

INTRODUCTION

The striking feature about human skills is not their uniqueness but their ubiquity. Every healthy baby, without any formal training, acquires the ability to walk, run, reach, grasp and manipulate objects. A major task of childhood is to develop means of exerting control over the environment. From birth through childhood and into adult life we acquire various means of accomplishing this. We achieve ways of controlling our environment in varying degrees and we gradually, though quickly, acquire the power to influence circumstances and events by developing skills; social skills, intellectual skills and motor skills. This chapter is about motor skills, but they have many features in common with intellectual skills.

Because of the ubiquity of skill there is a tendency to reserve the term skilled to particular kinds of performance—a skilled trade, or to particular levels of performance, test cricket or virtuoso performance on a musical instrument. The ostensibly simple acts of walking, or picking up an object, or speaking are all skills in that they require the coordination of sensory information and muscular responses to attain some specifiable goal. Skills are examples of purposive behaviour. When we speak of an individual as skilled we mean that he has mastered some task with a degree of efficiency, he can organize and orchestrate his behaviour into a programme of action directed at achieving a goal. To describe a person as skilled is not to make an absolute judgement. Driving a car, writing, playing a recorder, or catching a ball are all skilled activities but different people exhibit varying degrees of competence or mastery at different times and at different ages. In the course of everyday life we see so many examples of skilled behaviour that we tend to ignore the commonplace and treat only as remarkable examples of outstanding performance or serious failure to perform adequately as in the case of the handicapped. However, in general the elements and essential features seen in the behaviour of world-class performers are also exhibited by the young infant.

The motor behaviour of babies and young infants typically appears staccato and halting when compared with the smoothly orchestrated performance of older children and adults. The stumbling of the 12-month-old as he begins to walk independently, clutching at one support after another in his attempts to remain upright for a few moments, is very different a year later when the same child can run for a ball. An interesting and informative example of differences in motor performance in children is provided by Kay (1970) who analysed films of three children aged 2, 5 and 15 catching a ball. The results

TABLE 1

	2 year old	5 year old	15 year old
General strategy	Almost nil	Some features; say approximately 50 per cent	Complete
Hand movements	Static	Intentional, appropriate but excessive	Directed and effective
Timing and coordination	Almost nil	Effective but slow	Coordinated and unhurried
Eye gaze	On thrower	On thrower, ball and hands	On ball
Stance	Rigid	Jerky	Adaptive

Summary of performance of three children catching a ball (after Kay, 1970).

TABLE 2

Order of Skill	Characteristics	Median Age Achieved
First	Passive postural control of upper trunk region, includes lifting chin and chest when prone, making stepping movements, tensing muscles for lifting, straightening knees. Sitting when held.	Less than 20 weeks
Second	Postural control of entire trunk, represented by sitting alone momentarily, by swimming movements and by child standing with help.	25–30 weeks
Third	Entails active attempts at locomotion, characterized by poorly coordinated motor activity when infant prone. Great deal of overlap with second and fourth periods.	30–40 weeks
Fourth	Locomotion by creeping or walking when supported, reflecting greatly improved postural control.	40–50 weeks
Fifth	Complete postural control during locomotion.	62–64 weeks

Five orders of skill distinguished by Shirley (1931)

summarizing the performance of these three children are shown in Table 1. Our problem is to understand how changes of the kind described here come about. In general terms it would appear that a number of factors are involved. As they develop children are able to perform movements more rapidly and with greater accuracy, the trade-off between speed and accuracy also changes. Asking a child to respond accurately but rapidly does not impose the same stress on the 15-year-old that it does on the 5-year-old. The general observation that older children are able to take on tasks of increasing complexity, which demand higher levels of skill that younger children cannot match, suggests that the capacity to isolate the important features of a task and selectively programme activity by way of strategies is one means by which these developments are effected. The differences in eye gaze patterns by the children Kay (*op. cit.*) studied provide an example of this.

Two major and fundamental skills which gradually appear in infancy in a broadly developed sequence are independent locomotion and the capacity to reach and grasp objects. These two complex activities form the substrate for other skilled activities and they are both fundamental to exerting control over the environment.

THE DEVELOPMENT OF LOCOMOTION

One of the most complete and important longitudinal studies of postural control and locomotion was carried out by Shirley (1931). On the basis of her investigations Shirley divided motor reactions into five orders of skill which are broadly summarized in Table 2. On the basis of this work motor development was thought to follow an orderly sequence of stages, each stage in the sequence being a prerequisite for succeeding stages. Thus the sequence would be; head control, sitting, swimming,

creeping and finally independent walking. The development of upright locomotion has been studied by detailed investigations of these five stages.

Head control

Four groups of head control response have been distinguished. The first group, which are presumably reflexive responses, involve head turning or head raising. Shirley (1931), found that head turning and head raising responses were present in 88% of her sample by the third week after birth. Gesell (1938) considered head lifting when prone to be fully established by the time the infant was about 4 months old. The second group of responses

Fig. 1. Tonic-neck reflex in a young infant.

involving the head is the ocular-neck reflex. This reflex is a bending backwards of the head to a flash of light (Peiper, 1963). The third type of head movement is the asymmetric tonic-neck reflex. When the infant's head is turned to the right or left there is (i) an extension of the ipsilateral arm and (ii) a flexion of the contralateral arm (Fig. 1). The importance of the tonic-neck reflex has been discussed by Gesell (1938) and White (1970) and is considered in more detail below. The fourth class of head movements involve head control. The tensing of the neck muscles for controlling the head is a relatively late development. Most of the published developmental inventories list this as the first phase in the sequence which will culminate in the assumption of an erect posture and walking.

Sitting

The age at which infants sit with support and sit independently has been logged in various normative inventories but the achievement of sitting itself has been the subject of less research. McGraw (1941) analysed independent sitting in an attempt to identify structures regulating these anti-gravity muscles. Complete control over sitting involves getting from an erect to a sitting position as well as from a supine to a sitting position. McGraw concluded on the basis of her studies that there was no definite reflex sitting posture comparable to the subcortical stepping or swimming movements.

Swimming

Our information on swimming movements in the human infant is sparse. Mumford (1897) described swimming-like movements of the newborn and Watson (1919) made some experimental observations, but the most systematic information available comes from McGraw (1939) who described coordinated swimming

movements in 42 infants who ranged in age from 11 days to 2 years. From the neonatal period up until about 4 months the infant exhibits rhythmical associated flexor-extensor movements of the arms and legs (Fig. 2A). After about 4 months the rhythmicity and pattern of the early behaviour becomes disorganized (Fig. 2B). Towards the beginning of the second year children again begin to show organized flexor-extensor movements of the limbs particularly the legs (Fig. 2C). McGraw describes the quality of these movements as being distinctly different from

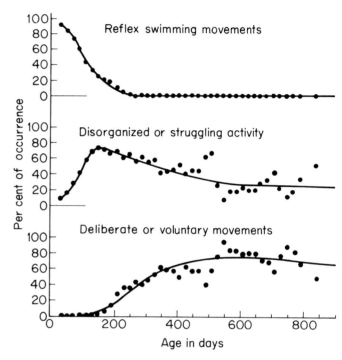

Fig. 3. The appearance of the three phases of aquatic behaviour in infants described by McGraw as a function of chronological age. (From McGraw, 1939)

Fig. 2. Three phases in the development of aquatic behaviour in the human infant. (A) Reflex swimming movements. (B) Disorganised behaviour. (C) Voluntary or deliberate movements. The drawings were made by tracing successive frames of 16 mm ciné film illustrating the quality of consecutive movements at different chronological ages and developmental stages. (From McGraw, 1939)

those of the newborn and suggests that they are more deliberate and apparently voluntary. The changes in the three phases of swimming are shown in Fig. 3.

Creeping

The first detailed study of the infant's attempts at prone progression was made by Burnside (1927) who distinguished 'hitching' from crawling and creeping in a small sample of nine babies. Hitching was defined as progression in a sitting position whilst in the case of crawling the abdomen was in contact with the floor and the baby pulled himself along only by the arms with the legs dragging behind. In creeping the posture adopted by the infant is with hands and knees in contact with the surface. Shirley (1931) listed seven stages as making up the creeping sequence; chin up—chest up—knee push—rolling—rock or pivot—'scooting' backwards—creeping. Ames (1937) who carried out a longitudinal analysis of 20 infants described 14 stages in prone progression which are similar to, though more detailed than, those of Shirley (1931).

Erect posture and locomotion

The most detailed study dealing with the assumption of an erect posture and the development of locomotion is Shirley's (1931). The steps she described in the assumption of an erect posture were as follows:

1. Tensing the muscles when lifted.
2. Sitting with support.
3. Lifting the head when lying supine.
4. Sitting alone momentarily.
5. Standing when supported under the armpits.
6. Sitting alone.
7. Standing with support gained by holding.
8. Sitting down from a standing position.
9. Standing alone and unsupported.

Once an erect posture can be maintained walking usually follows. This next stage is heavily dependent upon the child being able to distribute his weight carefully and to coordinate the activity of sets of muscles. As soon as an upright posture is adopted there are only two points of contact with the surface—the feet. Since these are very

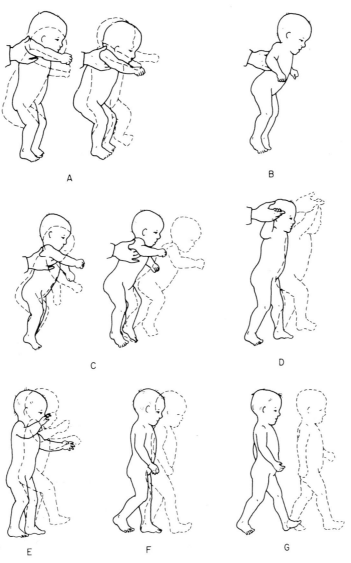

Fig. 4. Phases in the development of erect locomotion described by McGraw (1945).

small and the child's centre of gravity high an unstable equilibrium results (Burnside, 1927).

Shirley (1931) described progress towards walking in four stages:

(i) the early period of stepping
(ii) period of standing with help
(iii) period of walking when led
(iv) period of walking alone.

From records of 20 babies (from 17–78 weeks) Shirley observed that initially the babies supported under the armpits danced or pranced with only their toes touching the floor. This was replaced by stepping acts when support was provided. When standing with support babies bore most of their weight and maintained their balance by outstretched arms. On the basis of her data Shirley found that the sooner this point was reached the earlier the walking (rank correlation between age of standing with support and independent walking was ·80). The third stage was marked by a change in speed of walking and an increase in the width of step. In the fourth stage of walking alone the increase in speed of walking continues and there is a decrease in width of step. The correlation between age of walking with support and walking independently was ·88.

The points made by Shirley are illustrated in Fig. 4 which shows the phases in the development of erect independent locomotion described by McGraw (1943). Normative data on locomotor development, which has aroused such interest because it marks an important stage in the child's transition from dependence to independence, have been summarized by Aldrich and Norval (1946).

THE DEVELOPMENT OF PREHENSION

The human hand is a most remarkable device irrespective of whether one looks at it through the eyes of an anatomist, a physiologist or a psychologist and it is prob-

At birth
Traction Response
Stimulus: Stretch shoulder adductors and flexors
Response: All joints flex

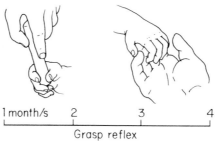

1 month/s   2   3   4
Grasp reflex

(Initial component)   (Fully formed)
S. Contact between thumb and index   S. Distally moving contact medial palm
R. Thumb and index adduct alone   R. All fingers flex

3 months 4   5   6   7   8   9   10   11
Instinctive grasp reaction

S. Contact radial or ulnar side   S. Contact hand (any part)   S. Contact hand (any part)
R. Hand orients   R. Hand gropes   R. Hand grasps

Fig. 5. Evolution of the automatic grasping responses of infants. (From Twitchell, 1965)

ably the most elegant and skilful organ ever developed through natural selection.

The earliest responses of the human hand to stimulation have been described by Hooker (1938). In response to stroking the palm lightly with a hair at 10½ weeks gestational age the four fingers flex synergistically. By about the twelfth week of gestation the thumb also responds by flexing across the palm. This crude prehensive pattern slowly wanes but it is usually present in a weakened form between 18 and 19 weeks of gestational age. As with walking voluntary prehensile activity is based on reflex substrates which develop and change during the first few months of postnatal life. Twitchell (1965) has investigated in considerable detail the grasp reflex and distinguished three kinds of automatic grasping responses in infants during the first four months of postnatal life. The first of these, the traction response, is a flexor synergy of the upper limb which is elicited by stretching the flexor and adductor muscles of the shoulder. The second, the grasp reflex, consists of flexion-adduction of the fingers and is elicited by a contact stimulus to the palm. It emerges between 1 and 3 months of age. The third, the instinctive grasp reaction, is a complex exploratory and prehensile response, also elicited by a contact stimulus to the hand and developing gradually between the fourth and tenth months (*see* Fig. 5).

During the period when the traction response is dominant no voluntary prehension occurs though an object placed in the infant's hand may be held momentarily. More effective prehension involving visually directed reaching occurs after about the age of 4 months and is preceded by the maturation of the grasp reflex. At this stage the whole hand is involved in grasping even when the infant is attempting to pick up small objects for which this is a very inefficient tactic. When the more precise grasp involving finger–thumb opposition appears is disputed. Bower (1977) claims that it is present in very young babies but it is not functionally efficient until after 6 months.

For the hand to be used efficiently as an instrument of skilled activity it has to be projected into the visual field. This is discussed by Twitchell (1970) but well coordinated projections of the limb into space occur only following the appearance of the instinctive grasp reaction. Most of the studies on the development of prehension emphasize the importance of visually directed reaching but Twitchell's elegant analysis shows that the appearance of and integration of grasping, and also the avoiding automatisms, are necessary for the development of normal voluntary prehension. During development the avoiding and grasping reactions to a contact stimulus appear in an overlapping fashion and in an orderly sequence. In the initial stages of visually directed reaching an object is approached from above and grasped only after contact with the palm. With the appearance of the orientation phase of the instinctive grasp reaction and the acquisition of individual reflex responses to contact on individual digits the hand adapts to the object. The radial aspect of the hand is then directed towards the object and dexterity is improved (Fig. 6).

Visually directed reaching has been the subject of several studies (Halverson, 1931; Piaget, 1952; White, Castle and Held, 1964). Halverson's investigations began when the infants were 4½ months old and went on to the end of the first year. In contrast Piaget and White *et al.* concentrated their attention largely on the period between the first and the fifth month and provide a stepwise analysis which culminates in visually directed reaching at around 5 months.

The human adult exhibits a number of characteristic properties in reaching, grasping and manipulating. The first of these is lateralization of function—handedness (*see* Chapter 14). Functional asymmetry in the adult is remarkably stable, especially when the hands are acting in collaboration as in many, perhaps most, kinds of tool use. The problem is to understand how collaboration between the hands, functional asymmetry and lateralization of functions are related during development. In a series of elegant and insightful observations de Schonen (1977) has outlined this process.

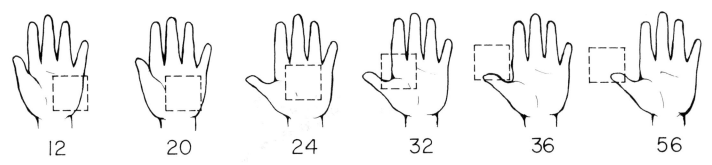

Fig. 6. Changes in the position in which an object is grasped, note shift from ulnar to radial side of hand. (After Halverson, 1932)

Many investigations have reported a sensory-motor bias to the right side in infancy. Tonic-neck reflexes (TNR) are directed to the right about 80% of the time (Turkewitz, Gordon and Birch, 1968). Also hand position during sleep and wakefulness has been found to be asymmetric in that the majority of babies have only one hand fisted, usually the right (Cobb, Goodwin and Saelens, 1966). Caplan and Kinsbourne (1976) report that the mean duration of grasp in 2-month-old babies is longer in the right than the left hand.

The newborn if placed in a supine position with the head directed to one side will exhibit a tonic-neck reflex with the ipsilateral arm extended and the contralateral arm in a flexed posture (Fig. 1). For the majority of babies the TNR is to the right and it has been used by Gesell and Ames (1947) to predict handedness at age 10. If an object is placed in the visual field the ipsilateral arm will be extended towards it in the TNR as a consequence of head orientation. This is seen by de Schonen (*op. cit.*) as providing a means of controlling the direction and extension of each arm separately. The relationship between a seen object and an extension of the ipsilateral arm provides an opportunity to develop control over arm orientation relative to a visual target. At this stage reaching is rarely observed to an object presented in the midline, perhaps due to competition between the two arms. This coordination between the arms exists initially via the tonic-neck reflex, one arm is moved towards an object in reaching whilst the other maintains a stable position in flexion. Without this asymmetry in movement initiation it is difficult to see how the differentiation in spatial control relative to a target could come about. Asymmetry and coordination are thus necessary conditions for the development of differentiation and complementary arm control.

During the third month the TNR disappears and the infant lifts one arm in the midsaggital plane of the trunk and with his head in the midline position visually inspects his hand (sustained hand regard, White, 1970). A functional asymmetry is evident since the orientated activities of the arms are differentially practised, usually the right hand is extended first and more frequently.

The next major phase described by de Schonen involves the infant in lifting both arms in the midline, the two hands clasp and are virtually fixated. Each arm is now performing two functions, one postural the other concerned with orientated movements, at the same time and in a coordinated manner. This clasping of the two hands in the midline position permits the beginning of mutual manipulation, it also represents the first visually orientated activity which is symmetrical and coordinated. Symmetry in coordinated arm movements appears only after functional asymmetry has been practised in unilateral orientated movements. During the first few months the infant has learned to control the position and movement of each arm relative to three kinds of spatial reference; (a) external objects, (b) the head and the trunk in the frontal plane, (c) to the other arm when it is still or moving symmetrically.

At around 16 weeks reaching is visually elicited but not visually guided; there is no evidence of local correction when the hand comes close to an object and no adjustment in the speed of the movement. By about 22 weeks the infant begins to visually control the whole trajectory of his reaching. From around 24–26 weeks bimanual coordination is evident in reaching. Complementary hand functions are now programmed from the beginning of an action; in reaching for a block one hand is extended to the surface but before contact for the supporting function is made the other hand begins its reach to the object (Fig. 7). The hands are now coordinated in an orchestrated pattern of action designed to achieve a specific goal.

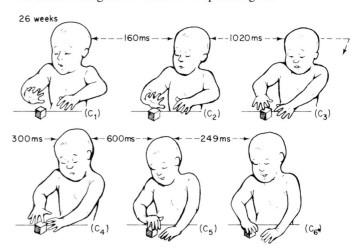

Fig. 7. Examples of successive stages in reaching for an object drawn from a video tape recording. (From de Schonen, 1977)

From these initial patterns of visually elicited and visually monitored actions the child is now launched on a career of fine and dextrous manual activities which culminate in a range of tool-using skills. Many further changes take place over quite a long period of time as hand function and manual skills are further differentiated and mastered (Connolly and Elliott, 1972; Connolly, 1973; Elliott and Connolly, 1974).

THE QUESTION OF ORIGINS

From the preceding sections on the development of locomotion and prehensile functions it is evident that the origin of skilled motor behaviour is tied into a reflex substrate. How 'reflex' and 'voluntary' motor activity are related is an important and as yet unresolved question. The traditional explanation for motor development is in terms of 'maturation'. The principal proponent of this viewpoint was Gesell (1954) who explained the ontogeny of behaviour in terms of a number of basic principles (Connolly, 1970b). In essence the maturationist viewpoint is that development proceeds satisfactorily in the absence of any *specific* environmental events, though this is not to say that the environment is unimportant. Bruner and Bruner (1968) have argued that before voluntary programmed actions can become effective there must be a recession of reflex activity. The components of voluntary skilful activity are not in their view the reflex actions which have been described, and it is assumed that these reflex actions are suppressed by the maturation of cortical inhibitory processes. An alternative hypothesis has recently been advanced by Zelazzo (1976) who argues that the reflexes do not disappear but are incorporated into, and retain their identity within a hierarchy of controlled behaviour. The evidence for Zelazzo's view is sparse and we still lack a suitable theoretical model but it is more likely that some functional interrelationship exists between 'reflexive' and 'voluntary' behaviour than the alternative sharp dichotomy, which is not in itself an explanation.

If the human neonate is held in an upright position he will assume a generally flexed posture, and if supported in this posture with the feet just touching a firm horizontal surface the infant will engage in rhythmical stepping movements known as 'primary walking' (Peiper, 1963). Primary walking is a reflex and an interesting question concerns the relation which this may have to true or secondary walking. An early investigation by Andre-Thomas and Dargassies (1952) reported that if babies were practised in primary walking then this advanced the onset of secondary walking. More recently in a better designed study Zelazzo, Zelazzo and Kolb (1972) have also shown that brief daily exercise of the walking and placing reflexes in the newborn leads to a high rate of responding by 8 weeks and to a significantly earlier onset of independent walking. The authors suggest that there may be a critical period during which the walking reflex can be transformed intact from a reflexive to an instrumental action. They argue further that reflexive actions are responsive to operant or instrumental control so that reflexive components can be incorporated into a smoother and less stereotyped system.

So far we have few data which bear on this possibility and the theoretical position is only sketchily stated but the idea provides an initial, albeit crude, approach to the relationship of reflex to voluntary action and hopefully will help us to grapple with the mystery surrounding the origins of voluntary action in infancy.

TOWARDS A THEORY OF SKILL DEVELOPMENT

A number of theories concerning the acquisition of skill by adults have been advanced. These have been for the most part based in learning theory (for example *see* Bilodeau, 1966; Adams, 1971; Schmidt, 1975; Russell, 1976). Attempts have also been made to link these models of motor skill acquisition with ideas on motor development in children (Connolly, 1977). Much of the now vast literature on adult skilled behaviour has analysed performance and changes in performance characteristics as skills are acquired. Of course, changes in performance characteristics occur in childhood as a consequence of development and these are considered below. However, the problem faced by the young child in first learning a skill, say learning to use a tool such as a

spoon, is not identical to that facing an adult learning to use a new tool, for example, in the course of an apprenticeship. The carpenter's apprentice has already a long history of achievement in manual skills; he is used to translating a sensory analysis of a problem and its requirements for solution into an appropriate action programme designed to achieve a specified goal. Consider, for example, the grip which a young child first employs in grasping a pencil and contrast it with the grip that an adult would use with any new precision tool presented to him (Fig. 8). The adult's past history and experience of solving motor problems will affect the way in which he addresses a new problem; his knowledge of his own body and its properties, of objects and of previous attempts to use objects will influence his strategy.

Fig. 8. 'Precision' or 'adult' grip on a pencil.

Skilled motor behaviour involves the organization of movements in space and time into a programme of action specifying an objective to be achieved. The relationship between the end and the means used to attain the end is a central feature of skilled performance and the ability to adapt means to achieve ends is an important characteristic of skill. Once a child has mastered walking he can do it (with varying degrees of difficulty and success) in sand, uphill, downhill, etc. In each case the activity is walking but the environmental conditions and constraints vary greatly. Another feature of the flexibility of skilled behaviour is its creative attributes, we use our hands in similar but not *identical* ways for a great range of actions and from time to time we perform novel actions in attaining a particular goal.

Movement as such should not be confused with skill, movements are best seen as accompaniments of skill but not defining features. Let us consider writing which is certainly a highly developed human skill. If I want to write the initial letter of my name I would do it usually with a pencil held in my right hand in a characteristic posture but if pressed I could hold the pencil in my teeth and make a passable shot at writing C that way. It would not be as skilful but no doubt I could improve my performance greatly with practice. In both these examples the end product would be essentially the same but the means used to produce it are quite different, different muscles and different movements are involved. The relationship between movements, actions and skills is an important consideration (Connolly, 1975). If we think of a child learning to write we see that this involves not only learning a sequence of appropriate postures and movements but also some higher level activity in which the child must learn about writing in terms of a temporal and spatial sequence of strokes.

From the nature of skill outlined above it is evident that in developing a skill a child is involved in constructing a programme of action directed towards a particular goal, the activity is purposeful and presumes intention on the part of the child. The notion of a programme itself implies that it is made up of components or units; the skill itself is the correct construction and development of the whole sequence. What then are these components which go to make up an action programme; can they be identified and what is their nature? Fitts and Posner (1967) in thinking about skills as hierarchically organized sequences of action drew a parallel with computing and likened skills to sub-routines under the control of an executive programme. Bruner (1970) and Connolly (1970b, 1973) have also used this metaphor and pressed it further. A sub-routine is an act necessary but not sufficient for the execution of a more complex hierarchically organized sequence, the whole sequence itself in the correct context constituting what is generally thought of as the skill. At this level skill is very much a cognitive activity and an individual needs to have at his disposal a set of sub-routines which may be combined together into an action programme on the basis of certain combinatorial rules. The great variety of human motor skills probably stems not from a wide range of sub-routines but from the combinatorial rules used to deploy them and from variations on parameters such as force, speed, and time, etc. If we consider manual skills this becomes more evident. The hand itself is first and foremost a prehensile organ, a device for holding things. The range of prehensile patterns exhibited by the adult is remarkably small (Napier, 1966) as are the distinct forms of movement made by the hand. However, the way in which this limited set of components can be sequentially organized into skilled actions is large.

A specific and familiar example may serve to make clear the general analysis given above. Let us imagine a task which most young children in a culture like ours will encounter and master. Such a situation is provided by a tool-using activity such as eating with cutlery. Consider the following circumstances, a child aged about 3 (and hence already quite skilled and experienced) is given a boiled egg to eat. The egg sits in an eggcup on a table in front of the child who is provided with a small spoon. The detail of the description of the ensuing encounter of the child and the egg could vary over a wide range, from simply, 'eats with a spoon', to a minute analysis of the postures and movements employed. My purpose, however, is simply to indicate the great complexity of such commonplace actions which we take for granted. In order to solve the problem of eating the egg with the spoon the child must already have a richly developed cognitive system. He must have some idea of what he is aiming at—intention is implied on his part. Further, he must know something of the use and properties of a spoon, in itself a formidable achievement when one is called upon to explain it, which we shall assume. The child must pick up the spoon and hold it both appropriately (correct

configuration of the hand on the spoon) and securely. Once this is done the child must take the spoon, correctly orientated, to a specific target location—the egg. The spoon must then be inserted into the egg, which requires postural adjustment of the spoon in the hand and the hand itself by the whole upper limb. Inside the egg controlled force must be applied through the spoon, here quite fine tolerance limits apply, too little force and the spoon is not loaded, too much and the egg is destroyed. Once this is done further postural adjustments must be made to extract the loaded spoon from the egg. The final part of the action consists in transporting the loaded spoon (which on the return journey must be managed under a different set of constraints if the egg is to remain on the spoon) to another target, the mouth, and there unloading it. Eating a boiled egg is such a commonplace activity that it causes little amazement and holds no puzzlement for most of us but try and build a machine to do this, or gain some insight into the difficulty by watching the young child gain a mastery of the task. To master a skill such as this it is necessary first to master certain essential components such as holding a spoon in an adequate stable configuration. Once this is done the spoon can be grasped and used effectively for purposes other than eating boiled eggs. From the example described sub-routines are likely to be grip patterns on a tool (which are affected by the purpose to which the tool will be put, Napier, 1966) postural adjustments of the tool in the hand, maintaining an orientation within defined tolerance limits by some combination of supination and pronation, and so forth.

To summarize then, skills are seen as developing from the deployment of a limited number of highly practised sub-routines by a set of combinatorial rules (a grammar) to create a wide range of action programmes which are goal directed.

PLANS AND CONTROL

The description given above of the child eating with a spoon was of a staccato process of the kind associated with a simple robot; take spoon to egg, then insert, then load, then extract, etc. In the early stages of acquiring skill the child's performance is a little like that but the ultimate smooth performance shown by children executing such actions is very different. To some extent the improvements which are so evident will follow the modularization of sub-routines and the refinement of the motor syntax but these alone will not provide an adequate explanation of the changes.

Once a general plan emerges, even though only coarsely, performance can be shaped, refined and modified by practice. An approximately successful outcome is in itself rewarding—watch the child learning to feed himself. Practice is not a rote repetition of action (Bernstein, 1967; Connolly, 1975) and is best seen as the search for optimal motor solutions to appropriate problems, the central programme may therefore change and not merely the means of execution. The sub-routines become increasingly reliable and predictable (I can readily grasp a whole range of different spoons or drinking vessels) and thus require less of the child's attention and information processing capacity which can then be devoted to other features of the task. The sub-routine is freed from a dependence upon a specific context and so assumes an integrity of its own. For example, the adult precision grip (Connolly and Elliott, 1972) on a pencil, in which the pencil is held between the volar surface of the partially flexed thumb and first finger with the lateral radial surface of the second finger providing stabilizing support, once mastered can be used on other tools such as chalk, a paintbrush or a probe. The pattern of the grip itself has other important consequences because it permits the small finger movements which I need to write cursive script. Another grip pattern, the palmar grip (Fig. 9), does

Fig. 9. 'Power' grip on a pencil.

not permit these small intrinsic movements with which I can move the pen relative to the hand. With such a grip I can only form letters by moving the whole hand and arm relative to the body. Writing is possible this way but we are likely to judge it less skilful because it takes longer and requires more energy expenditure.

Skills are learned and involve the coordination of movements in time and space. Although the tolerance limits on any given movement may be well within the capability of the average person quite a high degree of temporal precision is required to orchestrate the agonist and antagonist muscle groups. How this is accomplished is obviously an important question. Simple, or even complex, stimulus-response models are quite inadequate to account for the complexity of human performance. As Lashley (1951) pointed out some skilled activities, such as piano playing, take place too rapidly for the behavioural units to be related to each other as chained kinaesthetic feedback from the periphery. Responses are created not elicited. Matching intentions (in this context motor acts) with outcomes involves questions of control and monitoring. An important feature in the establishment and regulation of intentional voluntary action relates to the opportunity to compare what is planned with the outcome so that any necessary corrections can be made. Feedback and knowledge of results are important to adults, and perhaps more so to children. Broadly speaking two alternative types of model have been suggested, closed-loop and open-loop. A good deal of controversy surrounds these alternatives, which are seen by some as mutually exclusive, and the literature is peppered with experimental reports supporting one or the other (see Glencross, 1977).

In the case of closed-loop theories feedback from the peripheral nervous system is seen as necessary and sufficient for motor control whereas open-loop theorists argue that motor acts can be carried out in the absence of feedback, movement being regulated centrally. The evidence concerning these alternatives is equivocal and the position emphasised here is that both central *and* peripheral processes are involved in the control of skilled movement. This position is strengthened by the evidence from developmental studies.

Several models providing the basic logic of a control system using sensory feedback from peripheral receptors have been devised. One of the most fully developed models for movement control is that described by Bernstein (1967) who argues that any self-regulating system must contain a number of elements as minimum requirements. These are:

1. an *effector*, the source of motor activity which is regulated along the given parameter,
2. a *control element*, which conveys to the system in one way or another the required value of the parameter to be regulated,
3. a *receptor*, which perceives the factual course of the value of the parameter and signals it to,
4. a *comparator device*, which perceives the discrepancy between the factual and required values with its magnitude and direction,
5. a *recoder*, an apparatus which encodes the data provided by the comparator device into correlation information which is transmitted by feedback linkages to,
6. a *regulator*, which controls the function of the effector along a given parameter.

The relationship between these elements is shown in Figure 10. The required value of the parameter to be regulated is known as the sollwert (Sw), the factual course of the parameter as the istwert (Iw) and any discrepancy detected by the comparator as the deltawert (Δw). The system requires the constant comparison of the intended outcome, the Sw, with what actually happens, the Iw, to generate the crucial Δw which is then translated into any necessary correction signal. There is thus a plan, a check upon the outcome in relation to the plan, and a means whereby error correction can be accomplished.

Closed-loop models of this kind have a number of obvious strengths and advantages in trying to understand how a child acquires skilled motor behaviour but they do not cope adequately with what we observe in relation to motor skill as the child develops. In any feedback system there are time lags whilst feedback information is processed. Such time lags would lead to a jerky performance which whilst perhaps common in the motor behaviour of young infants is less in evidence in the older child and exactly what the skilled adolescent does not exhibit. In contrast to the jerky output from a closed-loop system an open-loop model which is not dependent upon peripheral feedback will be smooth. The open-loop view proposes that higher centres in the central nervous system provide all the information necessary for specifying a movement

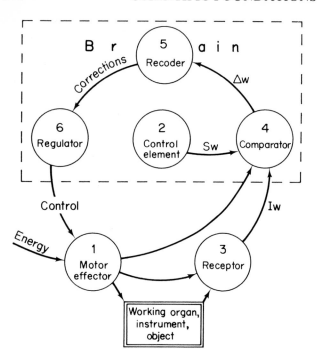

Fig. 10. Bernstein's model for a closed-loop system of voluntary activity directed towards objects or states of the environment. (After Bruner, 1970)

pattern and that sufficient control is obtained from the corollary discharge. In the course of skill development there is presumably a shift from jerky closed-loop control to smooth open-loop programmes which free the child to some degree from feedback involvement. Something of this sort happens when a child masters sub-routines, they are overlearned and the need for peripheral feedback is inversely proportional to the capacity of the central nervous system to predict the outcome of motor commands. Once the appropriate tolerance limits on a movement are appreciated all that is required for a satisfactory outcome is that the movement should be within the limits.

A vital aspect of understanding skill development lies in appreciating the properties of the control element in Bernstein's diagram and with it the notion of feedforward. Feedforward involves using a model to predict what is about to happen so that the outcome of a series of movements can be computed before the outcome materializes. A model, plan, programme or whatever one chooses to call it allows for anticipation and thus for smooth, efficient and elegantly orchestrated actions. In the case of the boiled egg problem described above the changes in postural orientation of the spoon can be begun before the spoon reaches the egg, and the build up to applying the required force to load the spoon can be begun or prepared for before contact is made between the spoon and the inside of the egg, and so forth (for further discussion of feedforward *see* Connolly, 1977). Although as yet we know little about the nature of the transition from a closed-loop form of control to an open-loop form in the course of skill acquisition it gives us a means of appreciating the nature of some important developmental changes which take place during childhood.

CHANGES IN PERFORMANCE CHARACTERISTICS

All children, with the possible exception of some who are severely handicapped, will be skilled operators on their environment. However, the quality or degree of skill which they show will vary greatly and some will be far enough outside the appropriate norms to merit the description 'unskilled' in everyday language. Motor skill and its expression is of course a function of many factors. Irrespective of speed, accuracy, delicacy of movement and cognitive capacity not every small boy can become a Don Bradman or every little girl a Margot Fonteyn. Temperament, motivation and opportunity all play their part. Leaving such considerations aside and focussing on 'motor features' in isolation there will be, as in all biological systems, individual differences in performance. In addition to and overlaying individual differences there are also age trends in performance capabilities which account for some of the greater differences in skill through childhood.

Although speed, in an absolute sense, is rarely crucial over a vast range of adult skilled behaviour it may be a limiting factor in the performance of children, and of old people. However, since motor skills involve organized sequences of goal directed movements the temporal aspects are fundamental. In relation to a skilled operation three kinds of time constraint can be distinguished. These are; reaction time (the time elapsing between the onset of a signal and the beginning of a response), the intervals between successive components in a motor programme (the timing of the component parts) and movement time itself (the speed with which a movement can be made).

In comparison with adults and older children the very young appear generally slow and seem incapable of reacting rapidly enough to changing circumstances. In 1892 Bryan used speed of tapping to measure what he called the speed of muscular movement and found that the gain in speed was almost linear to the age of 16. Goodenough and Brian (1929) and Goodenough and Tinker (1930) subsequently confirmed these findings. Using quite different, but practiced tasks, Connolly (1968) and Connolly *et al.* (1968) found steady and substantial changes in the speed of motor performance as a function of age.

Gilbert (1894) in an extensive study on a large number of children found that reaction time (RT) decreased as a function of increasing age over the age range 6–17 years. Several other studies have confirmed this trend (Bellis, 1932/33; Philip, 1934) and suggested a sex difference in favour of boys, though the evidence for this is equivocal (Jones, 1937). More recently Surwillo (1971) has reported experiments on simple and two-choice reaction time experiments with children whose age ranged from 4–17 years. In the case of simple RT he found a correlation of $-\cdot87$ with age and for two-choice RT a correlation with age of $-\cdot86$.

In a card sorting task carried out by children aged 6, 8, 10, 12 and 14 and by a group of young adults Connolly (1970a) found systematic changes with age in decision time (Fig. 11) and movement time. Information process-

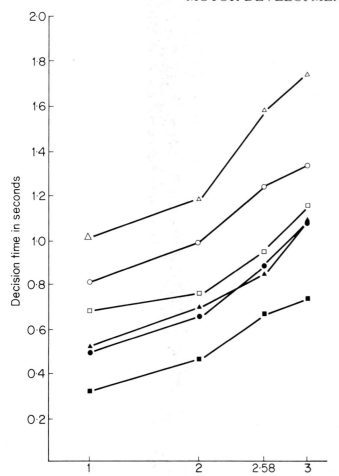

Fig. 11. Decision time as a function of entropy per card (binary digits) for a range of age groups; △ 6 years, ○ 8 years, □ 10 years, ▲ 12 years, ● 14 years, ■ adults. (From Connolly, 1970)

process information more rapidly and efficiently, to make faster and more consistent movement decisions and to execute movements more rapidly. The data on their ability to time intervals between movements accurately and consistently are still sparse but it does not seem improbable or unreasonable to speculate that this will show progressive developmental change. It is unlikely that all these changes will occur at a constant rate and such evidence as is presently available suggests that the greater changes occur during the period from 6–12. However, much more systematic research is needed to establish this and to uncover the mechanisms involved.

The efficiency of computing is a function of two classes of variables, 'hardware' and 'software'. Hardware involves the computing machinery itself (the components from which the computer is constructed and its size) whilst 'software' relates to the quality of the programming used to drive it. This has been used by Connolly (1970b) as an analogy to understand changes in the speed of motor behaviour and in timing which occur with development. Hardware changes in the nervous system may be related to changes in connectivity, myelination or the balance between facilitatory and inhibitory transmitters. Other types of relevant hardware change relate to mechanical factors such as increases in muscle bulk. Software changes are cognitive developments reflecting the programming or the way in which the machine is used. Parsimony in the number of steps or operations necessary to solve a motor problem will result in increased efficiency. A third class of variables which could affect temporal aspects of motor performance comes from an interaction of hard and software factors. With the progressive establishment of organized neural networks, enriched continually by experience, the effective functioning size of the brain may be increased and consequently the capacity of the central processing machinery enlarged. Such changes may then permit the parallel processing of information.

Most of our everyday skilled activities do not require great strength though limitations in strength will impose certain constraints on the motor skill capabilities of children. Carron and Bailey (1974) have shown in a longitudinal study of boys aged 10 through 16, significant increments in strength over this period even when height and weight are factored out. They report also a high stability of individual differences in strength. As with speed, absolute levels of strength, within broad limits, are not likely to be of very great significance in relation to most skilled activities. However, the ability to exert controlled forces with some degree of precision and certainty is clearly very important for skilled activity. Consider the young child when first scribbling with a pencil; invariably he exerts far more force than is necessary, often to the extent of scarring the surface of a table or tearing the paper. With older children this is not a problem, force can be harnessed and controlled quite readily though we know almost nothing of the typical pattern of secular changes.

In the case of accuracy of movement such evidence as we have indicates that children acquire the capability of making accurate movements early in life. Connolly *et al.*

ing, measured in terms of decision time, was three times faster in adults than in 6-year-olds. Young children thus not only face a relatively more difficult problem with tasks which require that greater amounts of information be processed but they are also constrained by the speed at which movements, once programmed, can be executed.

There is little experimental data available which bear on the question of timing (the temporal linking of components in an action programme). Gardner (1971) investigated the ability of children aged 6, 8 and 11 to duplicate rhythmic patterns of different lengths. The children were required to listen to a sequence of rhythms, 4, 5, 6, 7 or 8 taps in length and then reproduce these, the interval between any two taps being 1 sec or ⅓ sec. The results indicate that the accuracy with which children can perform the task increases with increasing age. Rothstein (1972) in an experiment designed to examine the ability of children to solve a timing problem found improvements in performance over the range 5–11 years. Developmental changes such as these are likely to affect the individual's capacity to orchestrate the component movements of a skill.

In summary these experiments indicate that as children mature from around 4 to early adulthood they are able to

(1968) found no differences in the accuracy with which children between 6 and 10 performed on a target task though significant differences in speed and differences in the strategy employed were found. It is likely that the trade off between speed and accuracy will vary with age so that the accuracy of motor performance will be more adversely affected by speed demands in younger children, this, however, probably relates primarily to the timing variables discussed above and to the rate at which information can be processed.

MOTOR DISABILITY AND HANDICAP

Gross pathology and motor handicap is not difficult to identify though it is often difficult to predict the extent of handicap in the young baby. As the child matures and fails to acquire the usual skills the extent of any deficit gradually becomes apparent to parents and doctors alike. The problem of predicting the degree of deficit during the infantile period is made more difficult by the considerable variance shown in a normal population (Gesell and Amatruda, 1965). As the child develops the perseverance of abnormal signs coupled with the failure to show the usual developmental progress enables a diagnosis of handicap to be made with greater confidence. In all but the very severe cases it remains difficult however to predict the degree of motor handicap which the child will present later.

Leaving aside severe forms of cerebral palsy and other congenital anomalies of the central nervous system less severe motor disability is difficult to identify in infancy for a number of reasons. The concept itself when applied to children is a relative one. Expected levels of performance vary with age and so too do the criteria on which disability can be diagnosed. In this respect disability in children is more difficult to assess than disability in adults, if an adult is unable to perform adequately when an attempt has been made to teach a particular behaviour then he has a disability. Because of variation in the rate and timing of development this is more difficult to ascertain in children. If we consider an adult who has sustained some injury to the brain his performance following this can be compared with his previous level of competence, or failing that with the minimal levels of normal adult functioning. In contrast with children we are dealing with a function which has not developed rather than one which has been impaired. Children who suffer some form of disability also learn to compensate for it in different ways and to different degrees. This may make disabilities easier to identify in younger children before compensating tactics have been acquired, on the other hand with younger children it is more difficult to be specific about appropriate expectations of normal achievements. Consequently a discrepancy in performance has to be more clearly marked before it can be recognized and diagnosed as such. It is not therefore surprising that many specific difficulties are identified only when a child enters school and can be readily compared with others on a range of activities.

Discounting the cases of severe handicap it is rare to find total disability in any one area of performance, no doubt because of the characteristic interaction of abilities. Broadly speaking there are two approaches to identifying disability; if a child is distinctly different from the norm for his age on some aspect of performance or if some aspect of his performance does not accord with what would be expected on the basis of other aspects of his behaviour then there is a *prima facie* case for presuming a disability. The confidence with which such a judgement can be made depends on the age of the child, it is easier if the child is older, and the degree of deviation from the norm, it is easier the further the child is outside the norm. These procedures are similar to those employed in diagnosing intellectual disability; a mismatch between chronological age and mental age or an aberrant score on some subtests in an instrument such as the WISC.

Motor deficit or disability can be classed in a number of ways. For example, by the limb or body parts which are affected, by the type of neuromuscular dysfunction presented, *e.g.* poliomyelitis, muscular dystrophy, spasticity, athetosis, etc., or by the skills affected, *e.g.* walking, writing, catching, etc. The most useful classification, especially for less severe forms of disability, is the functional one which attempts to evaluate the extent and nature of the specific functional deficit. The identification, diagnosis, assessment and treatment of motor disability is a complex task the difficulty of which is attested by the fact that although many individuals suffer from a wide range of disabilities of varying degrees of severity relatively little progress has been made in remediation.

Motor disabilities can result from input problems (perceptual), central processing problems (cognitive strategies, timing, etc.) or output problems (effector dysfunction) or all of these. The less severe the deficit the more inadequate are the concepts which we have available for analysing the difficulties. For example, the concept of minimal brain damage or dysfunction appears to be untestable. Clumsiness is a source of many problems in school for children with disorders of praxis and gnosis. Because such children do not show overt neurological signs the disorder is less easily recognized and consequently the children may receive less sympathetic understanding and special help. The outcome is often frustration which reflects badly on the child's academic achievement and social interactions with peers, parents and teachers. Gubbay *et al.* (1965) studied a group of 21 children presenting with severe clumsiness and poor school performance. All these children manifested cognitive and performance defects which could be classified as various forms of apraxia and agnosia. They suggested a variety of causes for the syndrome including; inadequate establishment of cerebral dominance, delayed maturation and structural lesions in one or both parietal lobes. They concluded that the condition was more common than usually thought and that the children required individual care by specially trained teachers. Support for this was provided by Brenner *et al.* (1967) who conducted a survey of visuo-motor ability in a sample of 810 healthy school children in Cambridge from which they identified 54 cases

(6·7 per cent) where the performance was sufficiently deficient to suggest specific developmental failure. Fourteen of these children were matched with an equal number from the sample who showed no evidence of impairment on age, sex, handedness, verbal IQ and home and school background. These two groups were then followed up for three years. The children with visuomotor defects were found to be inferior to the controls on tests of spatial judgement and manual skill. In addition they presented a variety of educational problems, particularly in spelling and arithmetic, and showed evidence of a high incidence of maladjustment.

There has been a great deal of interest in 'minimal brain dysfunction' and its remediation over the past decade including some exaggerated claims for 'cure'. There have also been several sustained attempts to develop training programmes to ameliorate the difficulties (*see* Wedell, 1973). These programmes can be grouped into those attempting an improvement on specific skills and those aimed at achieving a more general behavioural or educational adequacy. Ayres (1968) devised a training programme based on physiotherapy which traced poor motor organization to inadequate inhibition of infantile motor reflexes. Ayres compared a group of 8-year-old children given her training programme with a control group who did not receive it, measuring their progress on the Illinois Test of Psycholinguistic Abilities, the Frostig Developmental Test of Visual Perception and on the Southern California Battery of tests. The results from this study showed no significant improvement on the part of those children given the training programme. Kephart (1960) identified four basic aspects of motor organization as being of particular significance; posture and maintenance of balance, locomotion, manipulation, and receipt and propulsion (catching and relation to moving objects). An extensive battery of activities to foster these was devised but investigations have not supported the postulated benefit for reading attainment. These and other studies (reviewed by Wedell, 1973) provide little support for any improvement in skilled motor behaviour but it should be born in mind that their efficacy has usually been evaluated by educational attainment. Training programmes based on a more detailed analysis of motor skill, grounded in an appropriate theoretical framework and evaluated by appropriate and sensitive tests may well show that impairments in skilled motor behaviour can be ameliorated.

Motor disability is spread along a continuum and cannot very sensibly be divided into mild and severe but until adequate tests and profiles of motor function are devised its classification remains crude. Tests of motor development such as the Lincoln-Oseretsky Motor Development Scale (Sloan, 1955) are of very limited value because their theoretical basis is questionable. On the other hand tests of motor impairment (Stott, Moyes and Henderson, 1972; Henderson and Stott, 1977) may well prove to be useful screening instruments with which to identify children in the school-age population who show some degree of motor disability. Once these children are identified, teachers and parents should be encouraged to recognize the special difficulties which they have and guard against a host of possible secondary problems stemming from underachievement, lack of educational attainment and adverse effects on self image. It follows too from screening the population to identify children with 'minor' motor disability that they should receive a more detailed evaluation of their deficit and that carefully designed remediation programmes should be prepared and evaluated.

In the case of gross motor handicap such as that resulting from severe cerebral palsy there have been few attempts at specific motor training other than by physiotherapy (Bobath, 1966) and occupational therapy. Connolly (1968) devised a means of applying operant techniques to training the accuracy and speed of a target response and similar techniques are now used in several remediation programmes for the severely handicapped. A further and more sophisticated development of this approach has been used by Harrison and Connolly (1971) and Harrison (1975). This involves augmenting the feedback normally available to a subject through an alternative input channel. Using surface electrodes to monitor EMG activity in forearm flexor muscles spastic subjects were taught to reliably repeat a range of tension levels in a single muscle group. The use of augmented feedback (display of the EMG signal or verbal information) provided the individual with an unambiguous measure of ongoing activity and a clear definition of error and improvement in performance, Using these techniques young adults with severe spasticity were enabled to execute with quite remarkable precision a range of responses of varying complexity (Fig. 12).

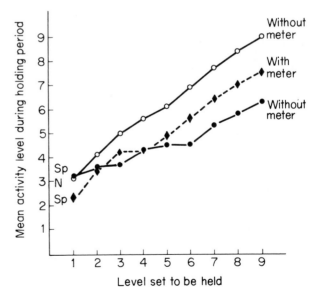

Fig. 12. Mean activity level held by spastic (Sp) subjects with and without augmented feedback and normal (N) subjects without augmented feedback when instructed to hold constant a range of nine tension levels in the forearm flexor. (From Connolly and Harrison, 1976)

A major problem in devising and evaluating methods of motor training for handicapped individuals reflects the lack of any very adequate model of good motor control (Connolly and Harrison, 1976). The importance of a theoretical framework on which methods of training and rehabilitation can be based has been stressed by Connolly (1975). In the case of a spastic child, for example, the retention of 'primitive' reflexes and the presence of abnormal reflex patterns are difficulties which must be dealt with in some fashion before motor control and skill can be improved. Hyperactivity of the motoneurones gives rise to a situation in which muscle contraction can be triggered by sensory stimuli or by activity in related muscle groups. The spastic child thus faces an enormously complex task in mapping the various pathways available in his neuromuscular system and defining interactions going on between the forces present. The child must plan movements not only to initiate specific action programmes but also to avoid concomitant activity which may hamper the achievement of a particular goal.

REFERENCES

Adams, J. A. (1971). A closed-loop theory of motor learning. *J. Mot. Behav.,* **3,** 111–150.

Aldrich, C. A. and Norval, M. A. (1946). A developmental graph for the first year of life. *J. Pediat.,* **29,** 204–308.

Ames, L. B. (1937). Sequential patterning of prone progression in the human infant. *Genet. Psychol. Monog.,* **19,** 409–460.

Andre-Thomas, C. and Dargassies, A. (1952). *Etudes neurologiques sur le nouveau-ne et le jeune nourrison.* Paris: Masson.

Ayres, A. J. (1968). Effect of sensorimotor activity on perception and learning in neurologically handicapped children. Unpublished report, University of Southern California.

Bellis, C. J. (1932/33). Reaction time and chronological age. *Soc. exp. Biol. Med. Proc.,* **30,** 801–803.

Bernstein, N. (1967). *The co-ordination and regulation of movements.* Oxford: Pergamon Press.

Bilodeau, E. A. (1966). *Acquisition of skill.* London: Academic Press.

Bobath, K. (1966). *The motor deficit in patients with cerebral palsy.* London: Spastics International Medical Publications/Heinemann.

Bower, T. G. R. (1977). *A primer of infant development.* San Francisco: Freeman.

Brenner, W. M., Gillman, S., Zangwill, O. L. and Farrell, M. (1967). Visuo-motor disability in school children. *Brit. Med. J.,* **4,** 259–262.

Bruner, J. S. (1970). The growth and structure of skill. In Connolly, K. J. (Ed.), *Mechanisms of motor skill development.* London: Academic Press.

Bruner, J. S. and Bruner, B. M. (1968). On voluntary action and its hierarchical structure. *Internat. J. Psychol.,* **3,** 239–255.

Bryan, W. L. (1892). On the development of voluntary motor ability. *Amer. J. Psychol.,* **5,** 125–204.

Burnside, H. L. (1927). Coordination in the locomotion of infants. *Genet. Psychol. Monog.,* **2,** 279–372.

Caplan, P. J. and Kinsbourne, M. (1976). Baby drops the rattle: asymmetry of duration of grasp by infants. *Child Develop.,* **47,** 532–534.

Carron, A. V. and Bailey, D. A. (1974). Strength development in boys from 10 through 16 years. *Monog. Soc. Res. Child Develop.,* **39,** Ser. No. 157.

Cobb, K., Goodwin, R. and Saelens, E. (1966). Spontaneous hand positions of newborn infants. *J. Genet. Psychol.,* **108,** 225–237.

Connolly, K. (1968). Some mechanisms involved in the development of motor skills. *Aspects of Educ.,* **7,** 82–100.

Connolly, K. (1970a). Response speed, temporal sequencing and information processing in children. In Connolly, K. (Ed.), *Mechanisms of motor skill development.* London: Academic Press.

Connolly, K. (1970b). Skill development: problems and plans. In Connolly, K. (Ed.), *Mechanisms of motor skill development.* London: Academic Press.

Connolly, K. (1973). Factors influencing the learning of manual skills by young children. In Hinde, R. A. and Hinde, J. S. (Eds.), *Constraints on learning.* London: Academic Press.

Connolly, K. (1975). Behaviour modification and motor control. In Kiernan, C. C. and Woodford, F. P. (Eds.), *Behaviour modification with the severely retarded.* Amsterdam: Elsevier, North-Holland.

Connolly, K. (1975). Movement, action and skill. In Holt, K. S. (Ed.), *Movement and child development.* London: Spastics International Medical Publications/Heinemann.

Connolly, K. (1977). The nature of motor skill development. *J. Hum. Movement Stud.,* **3,** 128–143.

Connolly, K., Brown, K. and Bassett, E. (1968). Developmental changes in some components of a motor skill. *Brit. J. Psychol.,* **59,** 305–314.

Connolly, K. and Elliott, J. (1972). The evolution and ontogeny of hand function. In Blurton Jones, N. (Ed.), *Ethological studies of child behaviour.* Cambridge: Cambridge University Press.

Connolly, K. and Harrison, A. (1976). The analysis of skill and its implications for training the handicapped. In Siva Sankar, D. V. (Ed.), *Mental Health in Children,* Vol. III. Westbury, New York: PJD Publications.

de Schonen, S. (1977). Functional asymmetries in the development of bimanual co-ordination in human infants. *J. Hum. Movement Stud.,* **3,** 144–156.

Elliott, J. and Connolly, K. (1974). Hierarchical structure in skill development. In Connolly, K. and Bruner, J. (Eds.), *The growth of competence.* London: Academic Press.

Fitts, P. M. and Posner, M. I. (1967). *Human performance.* Belmont, California: Brooks/Cole.

Gardner, H. (1971). Children's duplication of rhythmic patterns. *J. Res. Music Educ.,* **19,** 355–360.

Gesell, A. (1938). The tonic neck reflex in the human infant: Its morphogenic and clinical significance. *J. Pediat.,* **13,** 455–464.

Gesell, A. (1954). The ontogeny of infant behaviour. In Carmichael, L. (Ed.), *Manual of child psychology.* London: Wiley.

Gesell, A. and Amatruda, C. (1965). *Developmental diagnosis.* 2nd Ed. New York: Hoeber Medical Division, Harper and Row.

Gesell, A. and Ames, L. B. (1947). The development of handedness. *J. Genet. Psychol.,* **70,** 155–175.

Gilbert, J. A. (1894). Researches on the mental and physical development of school children. *Stud. Yale Psychol. Lab.,* **2,** 40–100.

Glencross, D. (1977). Control of skilled movements. *Psychol. Bull.,* **84,** 14–29.

Goodenough, F. L. and Brian, E. R. (1929). Certain factors underlying the acquisition of motor skills by preschool children. *J. exp. Psychol.,* **12,** 127–155.

Goodenough, F. L. and Tinker, M. A. (1930). A comparative study of several methods of measuring finger tapping in adults. *J. Genet. Psychol.,* **38,** 146–160.

Gubbay, S. S., Ellis, E., Walton, J. N. and Court, S. D. M. (1965). Clumsy children, a study of apraxis and agnostic defects in 21 children. *Brain,* **88,** 295–312.

Halverson, H. M. (1931). An experimental study of prehension in infants by means of systematic cinema records. *Genet. Psychol. Monog.,* **10,** 107–286.

Harrison, A. (1975). Studies of neuromuscular control in normal and spastic individuals. In Holt, K. S. (Ed.), *Movement and child development.* London: Spastic International Medical Publications/Heinemann.

Harrison, A. (1975). Training spastic individuals to achieve better neuromuscular control using EMG feedback. In Holt, K. S. (Ed.), *Movement and child development.* London: Spastic International Medical Publication/Heinemann.

Harrison, A. and Connolly, K. (1971). The conscious control of fine levels of neuromuscular firing in spastic and normal subjects. *Develop. Med. Child Neurol.,* **13,** 762–771.

Henderson, S. E. and Stott, D. H. (1977). Finding the clumsy child: Genesis of a test of motor impairment. *J. Hum. Movement Stud.,* **3,** 38–48.

Hooker, D. L. (1938). Origin of grasping movement in man. *Proc. Amer. Phil. Soc.,* **79,** 597–606.

Jones, H. E. (1937). Reaction-time and motor development. *Amer. J. Psychol.,* **50,** 181–194.

Kay, H. (1970). Analysing motor skill performance. In Connolly, K. (Ed.), *Mechanisms of motor skill development.* London: Academic Press.

Kephart, N. C. (1960). *The slow learner in the classroom.* Columbus: Merrill.

Lashley, K. S. (1951). The problem of serial order in behavior. In Jeffress, L. P. (Ed.), *Cerebral mechanisms in behavior: the Hixon symposium.* London: Wiley.

McGraw, M. (1939). Swimming behavior of the human infant. *J. Pediat.,* **15,** 485–490.

McGraw, M. (1941). Development of neuro-muscular mechanisms as reflected in the crawling and creeping behavior of the human infant. *J. Genet. Psychol.,* **59,** 83–111.

McGraw, M. (1943). *The neuromuscular maturation of the human infant.* New York: Columbia University Press.

Mumford, A. A. (1897). Survival movements of human infancy. *Brain,* **20,** 290–307.

Napier, J. R. (1966). Functional aspects of the anatomy of the hand. In Pulvertaft, R. G. (Ed.), *The hand: Clinical surgery.* 7th Ed. London: Butterworths.

Peiper, A. (1963). *Cerebral function in infancy and childhood.* New York: Consultants Bureau.

Philip, B. R. (1934). Reaction-times of children. *Amer. J. Psychol.,* **46,** 379–396.

Piaget, J. (1952). *The origins of intelligence in the child.* London: Routledge and Kegan Paul.

Rothstein, A. L. (1972). Effect of age, feedback, and practice on ability to respond within a fixed time interval. *J. Mot. Behav.,* **4,** 113–119.

Russell, D. G. (1976). Spatial location cues and movement production. In Stelmach, G. E. (Ed.), *Motor control: issues and trends.* London: Academic Press.

Schmidt, R. A. (1975). A schema theory of discrete motor skill learning. *Psychol. Bull.,* **76,** 383–393.

Shirley, M. M. (1931). *The first two years, a study of twenty-five babies.*

Vol. 1. Postural and locomotor development. Minneapolis: University of Minnesota Press.

Sloan, W. (1955). The Lincoln-Oseretsky motor development scale. *Genet. Psychol. Monog.,* **51,** 183–252.

Stott, D. H., Moyes, F. A. and Henderson, S. E. (1972). *A test of motor impairment.* Slough: NFER Pub. Co.

Surwillo, W. W. (1971). Human reaction time and the period of the EEG in relation to development. *Psychophysiol.,* **8,** 468–482.

Turkewitz, C., Gordon, B. W. and Birch, H. G. (1968). Head turning in the human neonate: effects of prandial condition and lateral preference. *J. comp. physiol. Psychol.,* **59,** 198–192.

Twitchell, T. (1965). The automatic grasping responses of infants. *Neuropsychologia,* **3,** 247–259.

Twitchell, T. E. (1970). Reflex mechanisms and the development of prehension. In Connolly, K. (Ed.), *Mechanisms of motor skill development.* London: Academic Press.

Watson, J. B. (1919). *Psychology from the standpoint of a behaviorist.* Philadelphia: Lippincott.

Wedell, K. (1973). *Learning and perceptuo-motor disabilities in children.* London: Wiley.

White, B. L. (1970). Experience and the development of motor mechanisms in infancy. In Connolly, K. (Ed.), *Mechanisms of motor skill development.* London: Academic Press.

White, B. L., Castle, P. and Held, R. (1964). Observations on the development of visually directed reaching. *Child Develop.,* **35,** 349–364.

Zelazzo, P. R. (1976). From reflexive to instrumental behavior. In Lipsitt, L. P. (Ed.), *Developmental psychobiology.* New Jersey: Erlbaum.

Zelazzo, P. R., Zelazzo, N. A. and Kolb, S. (1972). 'Walking' in the newborn. *Science,* **176,** 314–315.

14. LATERALITY

B. C. L. TOUWEN

INTRODUCTION

The term laterality indicates the asymmetric functioning of a paired faculty. This definition must be further specified. In the first place there are at least four paired faculties: hands, feet, eyes, ears. Thus laterality must be specified for the faculty under consideration. In the second place one must distinguish between simple and complex motor tasks. These include those which can be carried out with either faculty, such as opening a door or picking up an object, and tasks which are done by one faculty-member better (more easily, faster, more adequately) than by the other, such as writing. Laterality denotes the member of a paired faculty which is used preferentially for the complex motor skills. It presupposes a certain specialization of the faculty in question, which is most evident in the case of the hands. It does not imply that the opposite faculty-member is universally inferior, *i.e.* for all functional activities. Therefore laterality must not only be specified with regard to a particular faculty, but also with regard to the task under consideration.

Laterality is an objectively measurable phenomenon: it can be observed and tested. Its subjective counterpart is *preference*, *i.e.* hand-preference, preferred ear, preferred eye as reported by the questioned subject. Self-reported preferences, however, need not always be the same as measured laterality (Benton *et al.*, 1962).

Dominance

Laterality and preference must not be confused with *dominance*; a concept of lateralized specialization of the cerebral hemispheres of the brain. The dominant hemisphere is the hemisphere that makes its presence felt because it can speak (Blakemore, 1977), that is the hemisphere in which speech and language are localized. This view of dominance was put forward by Vygotsky (1962) but Gazzaniga (1974) suggested an alternative view. This stressed the decision-making and integrative functions which control the various information-processing activities of the brain; and lead to a 'final cognitive path'. This dominance includes but is not limited to language.

Originally, cerebral dominance was derived from lateralized hand-function, by anatomical knowledge of the central pathways controlling manual skills. Thus a right-handed person was thought to have a left hemispheral dominance. Clinical experience also suggested that in the majority of persons language mechanisms were localized unilaterally in the brain on the side concerned with the more skilled hand. As a consequence, handedness became the indicator for speech and language localization, and by derivation for the surmised hemispheric dominance. This is an example of circular reasoning, however, and further clinical experience showed that such a simple relationship could not be maintained. It appeared, for example, that many left-handed persons had a left hemisphere localization of language, just like right-handers. Apparently it is possible for one and the same individual to have a right hemisphere which is dominant for handedness and a left hemisphere which is dominant for language and speech.

In other left-handers a bilateral representation of speech and language functions had to be assumed. Thus, language lateralization is a relative phenomenon, at least in some individuals. Accordingly, Buffery (1978) proposed that the term 'dominance' should be discarded. Rather, 'cerebral predominance' should be used only for specified skills (*e.g.* verbal skills or spatial skills). A term like 'predominance' moreover has the advantage that it takes into account the repeatedly found variability of the degree of cerebral functional asymmetry by task and by person (Buffery, 1978). The introduction of intracorotid injection of sodium amytal for the cerebral localization of speech by Wada (1949), Wada and Rasmussen (1960) and Branch *et al.* (1964) confirmed that the relationship between handedness and language-localization in the brain may vary, especially in left-handers, but to a certain degree in right-handed persons as well.

A further argument for the view that there is not one 'dominant' or 'major' hemisphere, but rather a brain with specialized 'predominances' for specified skills is furnished by the studies on patients who had undergone a cerebral commissurotomy ('split-brain' studies, Sperry, 1968; 1973, Sperry *et al.*, 1969; Kreuter *et al.*, 1972; Preilowski, 1972; Gazzaniga *et al.*, 1977; LeDoux *et al.*, 1977). Admittedly these studies are hampered by the fact that they concern patients with usually unilateral lesions, often of long standing; yet the neuropsychological test-results suggest that there is a functional specialization of both hemispheres. In right-handed patients the left hemispheres turned out to be specialized for verbal- and language-related functions, whereas the right hemisphere appeared specialized for visuo-spatial functions.

If one uses the term dominance for the hemisphere which generates language and speech, one should keep in mind that this does not necessarily imply a universal superiority of that hemisphere over the other, the 'sub ordinate' or 'minor' hemisphere. In certain respects that 'minor' hemisphere may excel over the 'dominant' one, *e.g.* in spatial analysis and complex visual recognition.

Consequently, it would be wise to specify 'dominance' for the function under consideration. Perhaps it would be better still to replace it by terms like 'lateralized function' or 'lateralized specialization' of the brain, with a specification of the particular function which is meant (*see also* Buffery, 1978).

Non-human species

Laterality is not unique for humans. It has been described in, for example, monkeys (Warren, 1977), mice (Annett, 1976; Collins, 1977), rats (Annett, 1976) and cats (Webster, 1972, 1977), mainly with regard to the forepaws. Lateralized specialization of the brain seems to be poorly developed in the subhuman species but the data are equivocal. Hamilton (1977) did not find indications of hemispheral specialization for visual discrimination in monkeys; but Dewson (1977) found a hemispheric specialization for auditory dependent activities. Warren (1977) concluded that handedness in monkeys does not reflect a functional asymmetry of their brains, but Stamm *et al.* (1977) claimed the opposite. Lehman (1978) suggested that 'intrinsic and/or experimental developmental biases' constitute the basis of lateral preferences in rhesus monkeys. Yeni-Komshian and Benson (1976) reported anatomical temporal lobe asymmetry in chimpanzees, similar to but less than that found in man. It is tempting to speculate that there is a relation between the anatomical asymmetry and the chimpanzee's demonstrated ability to learn sign language (Gardner and Gardner, 1969). Nelson *et al.* (1977), Webster (1977) and Glick *et al.* (1977) found some indications for lateral hemispheric specialization in rabbits, cats and rats respectively but they stated that these were but rough analogues to what is found in man. Nottebohm (1977), on the other hand, reported left hemispheric specialization for vocalization in canaries.

ASSESSMENT AND INCIDENCE OF LATERALITY

Why assess laterality?

The answer to this question has two aspects. The first aspect is historical, and goes back to the time when handedness was thought to determine hemispheric dominance. Hemispheric dominance implied the localization of language organization in the brain, and was therefore important for neurosurgeons. But with the introduction of the Wada test and unilateral ECT (electro convulsive therapy) by Cohen *et al.* (1968) and Pratt *et al.* (1971) more accurate means for the localization of language become available.

The second aspect of the answer relates to the fact that right-handedness occurs more frequently than left-handedness. As a result the question was raised whether left-handedness should be regarded as a variation in otherwise normal individuals, or as a sign of an abnormal functioning of the brain (*see* Hardyck and Petrinovich, 1977). Research focused on the relationship between laterality and hemispheral specialization in order to find out whether the assessment of laterality could be used as a diagnostic means for the detection of disturbed brain functioning. At the same time, however, research on the relationship between laterality and hemispheric specialization increased knowledge on the differential activities of the brain and their determinants in normal individuals. This last aspect came to be increasingly emphasized.

Brain specialization

Both motor and sensory faculties (hands, eyes, and ears) are 'portes d'entree' for the (neuropsychological) study of asymmetrically organized brain functions. It is noteworthy that the connotation of laterality of ears and eyes in this context is different from the common meaning of eye and ear preference (*i.e.* the preferred eye or ear for peeping through a hole, viewing with a gun, or listening to a distant sound, respectively). With asymmetrical brain functions, laterality of eyes and ears (or rather of visual fields and ears), denotes a differential use of the left and right perceptors for verbal and non-verbal stimuli, which is a central rather than a peripheral phenomenon. Eye and ear preference can be influenced by the quality of the peripheral organ. Refraction-anomalies or other differences in visual acuity, as well as peripheral deafness as a result of recurrent otitis media, may determine the choice of the preferred eye or ear.

Types of assessment

The incidence of any measurable phenomenon depends to a large extent on the mode of assessment. This is particularly evident in the case of handedness. In general two basically different types of approach can be distinguished: the subjective and the objective, *i.e.* verbal report or performance. The subject can simply be asked whether he is right-handed, left-handed or ambidextrous, or he can be requested to fill in a questionnaire about the hand used in various familiar daily activities (*e.g.* Oldfield, 1971; Raczkowski *et al.*, 1974; Bryden, 1977). The objective approach varies from the simple observation of which hand is used for writing (the least reliable method, considering the number of left-handers who have learned to write with their right hand), to complex batteries of tests consisting of familiar and unfamiliar motor tasks (*e.g.* Passian *et al.*,1969; Suchenwirth, 1969; Steingrüber, 1971; Provins and Cunliffe, 1972a). The two modes of approach do not necessarily agree, especially in left-handers (Provins and Cunliffe, 1972b; Hardyck and Petrinovich, 1977). Self-report is particularly unreliable; subjects who classified themselves as left-handers turned out to be right-hand performers in 10–17%, self-classified right-handers were wrong in about 3% (Benton *et al.*, 1962; Satz *et al.*, 1967). Zurif and Carson (1970) found no reliable association between handedness assessed by questionnaire and manual dexterity measures. Naturally this depends on the type and number of questions and the type and number of dexterity measures. Variations in hand-use may be particularly common in unfamiliar motor tasks and the literature suggests that the percentage of left- and mixed-handers increases in parallel with the size and unfamiliarity of the test battery.

Incidence of handedness

Moderate to strong left-handedness is said to occur in about 10% of humans (Hardyck and Petrinovich, 1977). According to Subirana (1969) one quarter of the population is preponderantly right-handed; one third shows right predominance; one quarter shows mixed or double-handedness, and one sixth a left predominance. Pure left-handedness would amount to about 1% or less of the population, and would nearly always have a pathological aetiology. Perhaps the same can be said of exclusive right-handedness. It is clear, that handedness cannot be regarded as a uniform property, but rather as a degree of differentiation between preferred and non-preferred hand performance (Barnsley and Rabinovitch, 1973). In other words, estimation of handedness does not imply that the preferred hand has universal superior manual skills (Bresson *et al.*, 1977). For example, in young children who showed strong preference for the right hand Ingram (1975) found that the left hand performed better at hand posture and finger spacing tasks.

Foot preference

Footedness is measured by asking the subject to kick a medially presented ball, to stand on one leg or to hop. It is noteworthy that balance mechanisms as well as voluntary motor activity are involved in these. In children below the age of about 8 years the preferred leg for football and for standing on one leg often differs. Presumably this is an effect of the differential development of the mechanisms for balance and for complex motor activities. It has been argued that foot preference should be less influenced by cultural pressures and by education than handedness (Benson and Geschwind, 1968). In the case of kicking and hopping—which belong to popular games—this view may be questioned.

Foot preference is generally considered to follow hand preference, except in originally left-handed persons who have been converted into right-handedness at a very early age. However, Warren (1977) claims that there is no relationship between the laterality of the various faculties and it is a common experience to find a cross hand- and foot-laterality (*e.g.* right-handedness with left-footedness) without any history of an enforced change of hand preference.

Eye preference

The common meaning of the term eye preference implies the eye preferred for monocular tasks. But the optical pathways of each eye project to both hemispheres; the visual (half-)fields project one-sidedly (contralaterally). Nevertheless most people have a clear preference for one eye which, according to Coren (1974), is the right eye in about 60%. Such monocular eye preference is a motor activity rather than a sensory experience. Subirana (1969) suggested that eye preference follows hand preference. Coren (1974) and Warren (1977) query this. Eye preference for monocular tasks is measured by asking the subject to peep through a hole or tube or by means of the cover test. In this test the subject is asked to point at a distant object, then each eye is covered in turn. The subject has to say with which eye open the alignment of finger and object is the least disturbed. A variation of this test is the pointing-test (*i.e.* which eye is aligned with the finger and arm with which the subject is asked to point at the examiner's nose). A set of tests has been discussed by Gronwall and Sampson (1971) but they emphasize the weakness of the interrelationships between these tests. Gur and Gur (1977) have stressed the distinction which must be made between 'sighting-dominance' and 'acuity-dominance', meaning eye-preference for sighting (*e.g.* the pointing test) and the preferred eye in tests of visual acuity (measured with the Snellen chart) respectively. They found complex relationships in a group of right-handed subjects; sighting and acuity preference were associated in females only, but an association with handedness was found only for sighting preference, and that only in males.

Visual fields

The assessment of differences between the visual half-fields refers to the processing of the sensory information in the hemispheres. Nobody has a conscious preference for one of his two visual half-fields; however, it is possible to analyse functional differences between the hemispheres by measuring differences in the processing of stimuli which are presented separately or subsequently to the two visual half-fields, *i.e.* to the individual hemispheres. This is done by means of tachistoscopy (*see* below).

Ear preference

Ear preference for monaural tasks (*e.g.* which ear would you put against the door if you would not be able to resist the temptation to eavesdrop?) is rarely assessed. Again, as in monocular eye preference, it is a motor pattern (*i.e.* directing one side of the head to a sound-source) rather than a sensory one. It is thought to follow handedness, but naturally the condition of the ear will have a large influence.

The central pathways of the ears project to both hemispheres but under conditions of competition the contralateral projection is said to preponderate (Quinn, 1972; Berlin, 1977; Springer, 1977). Therefore monaural stimulation given simultaneously to both ears (dichotic listening) can be used in order to collect information about the hemispheric specialization for auditory stimulation. Colbourn queries the value of these neuropsychological instruments mainly on methodological grounds. He pleads for a further elaboration of the concept of laterality before such sophisticated techniques are applied (Colbourn, 1978).

THE RELATIONSHIP BETWEEN LATERALITY AND HEMISPHERIC SPECIALIZATION

Speech and language localization

The assessment of hemispheric specialization for speech and language by the Wada test and ECT techniques has been mentioned above. The development of tachistoscopy and dichotic listening tasks has considerably increased the possibilities for a sophisticated analysis of hemispheric functional asymmetry. Clinical experience had shown that some left-handed patients with a left-sided hemispheric lesion lose speech, whereas others only do so after a right-sided lesion. Branch *et al.* (1964) noted the importance of the child's age at the time of the left hemisphere injury. In patients with injuries in infancy or at least before five years speech was localized in the right hemisphere in two thirds, and in the left hemisphere in one third of the cases. When there was no evidence of an early left hemisphere damage, one third of the patients appeared to have a right hemispheric, and two thirds a left hemispheric localization. Ten per cent of right-handed patients were found to have a right hemispheric speech localization. Of course these results refer to neurosurgical patients, subjected to the Wada test as part of the preparation for neurosurgical treatment. Still, the left-handed group seems to be less homogeneous than the right-handed group. Following Weinstein and Sersen (1961) and Bryden (1965), Hecaen and Sauget (1971) showed that the familial history has also to be taken into account. Among familial left-handed persons with unilateral hemispheric lesions verbal deficits were equally likely

for left-sided and right-sided lesions. For the non-familial left-handed group the frequency of language disturbances was greater with left-sided lesions. There was also a strong relationship with the *intensity* of left-handedness; the weakly left-handed (on motor performance tests) mainly belonged to the group of the familial left-handed, whereas the non-familial left-handers were usually strongly left-handed. Ramier and Hecaen (1977) applied a 'verbal fluency' test, and did not find significant differences in scores between left-handers with right or left lesions, or with anterior and posterior lesions. In right-handers the scores differed significantly. They could not replicate the original finding of a difference between familial and non-familial left-handers, but they concluded that there was a lesser localization of language functions in left-handed persons.

Tachistoscopy

Tachistoscopic studies point in the same direction. In right-handed subjects verbal stimuli appeared to be identified more readily when presented in the right visual field (projecting to the left hemisphere) and non-verbal stimuli in the left visual field. However, familial left-handers show a tendency to be more accurate in the identification of verbal material in the left visual field, whereas non-familial left-handers behave like right-handed subjects (Zurif and Bryden, 1969; Bryden, 1973). Kershner and Gwan-Rong Jeng (1972) found that among bilingual (Chinese and English) subjects, right-eyed persons processed verbal materials faster and more accurately than left-eyed persons, who were better at processing non-verbal material. However, in both groups there appeared to be a right visual field (*i.e.* left hemisphere) superiority for verbal stimuli, and a left visual field superiority for non-verbal stimuli. Jeeves (1972) found that when unstructured visual stimuli were supplied, the responses occurred more quickly if the input went to the right hemisphere first, than if they were first presented to the left hemisphere, but the difference was significant only in right-handed subjects. Geffen *et. al.* (1972) concluded that the spatial comparison of letters is carried out in the right hemisphere, but that comparison on a verbal level occurs in the left hemisphere in close connection with the language mechanisms. The relationship between handedness and efficiency of visual-field localization, however, remains unclear, with results from different studies contradictory (Hardyck and Petrinovich, 1977).

Dichotic listening

Kimura (1961) has been one of the first to use dichotic listening tests in order to establish the lateralization of language and speech in the brain. The argument is that the auditory perception on the same side as the speech centres should be recalled most quickly and most adequately. Naturally the dichotic listening test can be modified by using melodies or other non-verbal stimuli, vocal music which combines verbal and non-verbal stimuli, etc. It was found that the right ear is the preferred ear for verbal material (in right-handers and non-familial left-handers) and that the left ear is more effective in identifying non-verbal stimuli (Bradshaw *et al*. 1972a and b; Gates and Bradshaw, 1977). However, there is no exclusive specialization, but rather a continuum: with an increasing verbal load the left hemisphere becomes preponderant, whereas an increasing non-verbal load calls in the right hemisphere. There should be a relationship with handedness in right-handers and non-familial left-handers: in these categories right ear (as well as right eye) preference (measured with dichotic listening tests and tachistoscopy) would prevail (Zurif and Bryden, 1969). The close cooperation of both hemispheres in auditory tasks has been demonstrated by Gates and Bradshaw (1977), who found that rhythmic properties of music are identified more readily by the hemisphere opposite to the ear preferred for verbal material, whereas the melodic properties are best perceived via the other ear. To complicate matters further, Gregory *et al*. (1972) argue that pure rhythmic stimuli (*i.e.* not offered as a part of music) are perceived fastest by the right hemisphere in right-handers, probably by the ipsilateral pathway. Berlin (1977) concluded that dichotic listening may be a correlate of laterality for speech and language functions, but that it is not an index for the strength of that laterality.

Specialization of the hemispheres and variability

Springer (1977) and Wada and Davis (1977) state that both the nature of the stimulus and the kind of processing needed in the brain—analytic versus holistic—appear to determine all the functional asymmetries to be observed. In right-handers, and probably in non-familial left-handers as well, the left hemisphere subserves analytic, rhythmic, temporally regulated, sequential motor, language and language-related functions. In contrast, the right hemisphere is specialized for visuo-spatial and holistic tasks, which are more diffusely represented. In familial left-handers a more bilateral representation is thought to be the rule. But in both right-handers and left-handers there is interlinking between the two hemispheres (*e.g.* Semmes, 1968; Sperry, 1968, 1973; Eccles, 1973; Kimura and Archibald, 1974; Wolff and Hurwitz, 1976; Wolff *et al*. 1977). Notwithstanding the differences between the functional activities of both hemispheres, it is evident that there is a large individual variability both in the left-handed and in the right-handed population (Bradshaw *et al*., 1972a and b; Dimond and Beaumont, 1972; Kreuter *et al*., 1972; Luria, 1973; Hicks *et al*., 1975; Ingram, 1975; Doms-Lissens, 1976; Hecaen, 1976; Burklund and Smith, 1977).

Naturally, part of this variability results from the variability of methods used in assessing laterality, and hemispheral specialization: the complexity of the tasks and the subject's amount of training and experience with the particular tasks affect the results. Moreover, the findings concerning laterality as well as hemispheral functional asymmetry concern giving statistics which are not directly applicable to individuals. However, both genetic and experiential factors will inevitably lead to large inter-

individual variability. Such variability becomes particularly evident when detailed questions are asked about the specific functional organization of the brain. Careful assessment of lateralized functions is needed in each case, and caution is required in drawing conclusions about clinical dysfunction from test findings.

The assessment of the various kinds of laterality and their relationships with hemispheric specialization plays a valuable role in the research into the mechanics of the brain. However, the variability of the relationships which are found throw doubt upon their value as a reliable indicator of the presence or absence of neurological dysfunction.

PROCESSES INVOLVED IN THE DEVELOPMENT OF LATERALITY

Genetics

The causation of laterality is still a matter of dispute. Collins (1977) for instance, states flatly that there is no evidence supporting the existence of right and left genes in animal or human populations; however, he admits the possibility of a genetic maintenance of laterality in a (right)-biased world. Annett (1972, 1976) on the other hand, maintains that right-handedness at least is inherited and she assumes accidental variation to be one of the causes of left-handedness. Others take an intermediate position (Morgan, 1977; Levy, 1977; Dawson, 1977), claiming that inherited as well as environmental factors cause left-handedness. Bakan *et al*. (1973) suggested an inherited familial tendency to birth stress, based on the finding that the frequency of birth stress appeared to be about twice as great among left-handers as among right-handers. However, the argument is doubtful because the chance of a potential right-hander becoming left-handed due to perinatal difficulties (damaging the left hemisphere) is much larger than the other way round, given the much larger number of right-handers and potential right-handers in any population. Coren and Porac (1977) find that in 50 centuries of handedness there does not seem to be a trend of increasing right-handedness, based on a close inspection of pictorial art showing manual activities. This perhaps can be considered as an argument for a physiologic rather than an environmental theory of the causation of handedness—though this does not necessarily imply a genetic causation.

Ontogenesis

Zangwill (1967) regarded both hemispheres as equipotential at birth, a view which is supported by Hecaen (1976), on the grounds that the preserved side can take over from the damaged one in young patients with unilateral lesions. Cernacek (1977) suggested that left-handed children who are trained to become right-handed, develop a left hemispheric localization of speech and language as a result of this training. Clinical data on right-handed patients who underwent a left-sided hemispherectomy or extensive left hemisphere damage suggest that there are at least traces of a language specialization in the right hemisphere (Smith, 1969; Smith and Burklund, 1966; Doms, 1976; Burklund and Smith, 1977). Others such as Jeeves (1972), Seth (1973), Suchenwirth (1969), Bresson *et al.* (1977) and Kinsbourne and Hiscock (1977) contend that there is an asymmetric functional specialization of the brain already at very early ages—the newborn period or earlier. Of course does this not refute the possibility of a shift in the case of unilateral brain damage (Hecaen, 1976; Cernacek, 1977), or a growth of the lateralization of a particular function, *e.g.* handedness, with increasing age (Passian *et al.*, 1969). Taylor (1976) concluded, on the basis of a study of patients with temporal lobe impairment, that hemispheric specialization may change during development, if necessary. This is in accordance with Semmes' (1968) observation that hemispheric specialization cannot be too rigid in early life, since compensations may occur when there are lesions. Moreover, this change occurs differently for males and females. Based on the finding that 'male cerebral maturation proceeded slower than in the female, and right hemisphere maturation proceeded faster than in the left', Taylor (1976) suggests a differential effect of early brain lesions in men and women. Witelson (1977a) is of the opinion that there remains a certain degree of what she calls 'interhemispheral plasticity' after hemispheric specialization (which in her view is actualized by environmental factors though based on a preprogrammed potential) has been established. This plasticity decreases in stages, and the right hemisphere may lose it earlier than the left. Also Witelson pointed to the existence of sex differences, specially in the degree of specialization of the right hemisphere, which would be stronger in (young and adult) males than in females, whereas the specialization of the left hemisphere for language functions showed some sex difference in adults only.

Sex differences in specialization and in maturation of the specialization are reported by others as well (Buffery, 1976, 1978; Bakker *et al.*, 1976; Davis and Wada, 1978), and are considered to play a role in the well-known differences between boys and girls with regard to specific learning difficulties.

There is evidence from both anatomical and electrophysiological studies of asymmetries in brain from a very early age. Heschl (1878) noted that the left transverse temporal gyrus—which was named after him—was usually larger than the comparable area on the other hemisphere. This has been confirmed as far as adults are concerned for the whole so-called planum temporale (Benson and Geschwind, 1968; Geschwind and Levitsky, 1968; Teszner *et al.*, 1972; Witelson and Pallie, 1973; Rubens, 1977); in general about 65% favour the left side and about 11% favour the right. Some work has been done on newborn and fetal brains with comparable results (Witelson and Pallie, 1973; Chi *et al.*, 1977; Teszner *et al.*, 1972). Witelson and Pallie (1973) reported a possible sex difference in left–right asymmetry of the planum in neonates: the asymmetry was less clear in males than in females. Wada *et al.* (1975) found indications of sex

differences in the degree of the asymmetry of the planum temporale, but also in the frontal operculum where Broca's area is found. The planum temporale appeared somewhat larger on both sides in males than in females, in infants, but only on the left side in adults. However, this sex difference was statistically not significant. In adults they found significantly more reversal asymmetries in females (*i.e.* right planum larger than left) than in males. The frontal operculum tended to be somewhat larger in adult males than in females, and females had a somewhat larger left frontal operculum, but the differences were not significant. Considerable individual differences were noted, especially in the early gestational stage. McRae *et al.* (1968) found asymmetries in the length of the occipital horn of the lateral ventricles of the brain; these asymmetries were remarkably less obvious in left-handed persons.

Also the decussation of the pyramidical tracts and their size appears to show some asymmetry. Benson and Geschwind (1968) mention their own and Yakovlev and Rakic's (1966) findings that the pyramidal tract from the left hemisphere usually starts to cross before that of the right hemisphere, and that in most cases the pyramidal tract is greater on the right side of the cord than on the left. They suggest that hand preference depends on an increased innervation available on one side of the cord, which results in a finer manipulative control on that side. This asymmetry may be acquired during development, however. Galaburda *et al.* (1978) reviewed the literature on the anatomical asymmetries, and concluded that there is good evidence for morphological left–right differences in humans from the prenatal period onwards, especially in right-handed individuals. Although there are great individual differences in the extent of asymmetries, they claim that the finding of asymmetry is so consistent that a functional meaning cannot be dismissed. On the contrary the finding of a morphological asymmetry (with *e.g.* the CTG scan) may be of help in the understanding of particular clinical conditions, such as individual differences in recovery from aphasia-producing lesions. LeMay (1977) reported on asymmetries of the skull, measured with the help of CTT (computerized transaxial tomography). She found that the right frontal lobe had the greater width of the two in about 60% of her group of 120 right-handed subjects, whereas in about 19% the left frontal lobe had a larger width; the left occipital pole was wider in 66% and the right occipital pole in 10%. For left-handers these percentages were 40, 26, 31 and 26 respectively. LeMay found that the non-familial left-handers as a group resembled the right-handers.

A good review of the evidence of anatomical asymmetry has been published by Witelson (1977b), who concluded that an anatomical asymmetry is already present in infants, to an extent comparable to that in adults. In her view this signifies that 'hemispheral specialization is operational from the start for whatever behaviour the infant is capable of'. The origin of this specialization remains unknown. Kimura (1977) suggested that a major function of the left hemisphere (in the majority of right-handed people) is the control of changes in limb or articulatory posture: the analysis of 'internal' spatial location information; while the right hemisphere is involved rather in spatial analysis of 'external' stimuli. In her opinion this control makes complex verbal and motor skills (language and praxia functions) possible: speech and language are not primary but derivative functions of the left (dominant) hemisphere.

Preferences in newborns

The majority of newborns show a predilected head position to the right, associated with an asymmetry to auditory, visual and tactile stimuli, favouring the right side (Turkewitz, 1977). There is a remarkable age influence. Immediately after birth the right-preference of the head position can be abolished by keeping the head in a centred position for about 15 minutes. At an age of 75–100 hours the majority of babies keep their right preference, even after this procedure. It is attractive to surmise that the right preference immediately after birth is innate, but still malleable, while after 75–100 hours of life the 'right-biased world' has reinforced the right-preference. LeMay's findings may be considered as one of the environmental influences which promote the right-sided preference.

Cohen (1972) found that the majority of his 4-month-old subjects tended to turn to a stimulus on the right more rapidly than to a stimulus on the left; they also looked longer at the stimulus when it was presented on the right. Furthermore, measurements of scanning movements showed that at birth already many infants favoured the right side of a homogeneous stimulus (Salapatek, 1975).

EEG and ERP

Studies relating EEG measures to laterality have produced ambiguous results. Crowell *et al.* (1973) found that bilateral photic stimulation of newborns caused a photic driving of the EEG which usually started in the right hemisphere. They considered this as an early sign of asymmetric hemispheral specialization. Others, such as Provins and Cunliffe (1972b) and Donchin *et al.* (1977), have contended that there is no conclusive evidence of a relation between EEG measures and handedness, eye or ear preference and cerebral dominance. Studies on ERP (evoked potentials) show a similar picture. Thatcher (1977) found asymmetric auditory evoked potentials on linguistic stimuli, but not on non-linguistic ones; Gates and Bradshaw (1977) found that melody gave rise to ERP more often on the right, whereas rhythm more often brought about ERP on the left half of the brain. Kutas and Donchin (1974) inferred from the evidence of ERP on squeezing that left-handers showed less asymmetry than right-handers. Wada and Davis (1977) concluded, on the basis of click and flash evoked potentials in infants, that asymmetries can shift from the left to the right depending on the subject's state, or his experience. The asymmetries which can be found already in very young babies, are in their view related to more fundamental processes than

language. However, Donchin *et al.* (1977), Eason *et al.* (1967), and Gott and Boyarsky (1972) conclude that so far ERP studies do not justify any unequivocal pronouncement on the relation between laterality and hemispheric specialization.

Development with age

The common view is that handedness will be consolidated at about age 5 although its first appearance may occur much earlier, even in infancy. In the majority of cases this is in favour of the right hand, although many infants seem to start favouring their left hand (*see* Young, 1977). De Schonen (1977) suggests that right hemisphere specialization, subserving spatial localization, takes the lead. This enables the infant to localize an object spatially by reaching for it with the left hand, and subsequently reaching for and grasping the object with the right hand, steered by the left hemisphere which is specialized for motor skill (*see also* Bresson *et al.*, 1977).

Footedness would be stable at about 7 years of age, eye preference at about the same time and ear preference at age 8 or 9. All kinds of environmental factors have a steering influence, ranging from intelligence (mentally retarded children do not develop strong hemispheric specialization (Kershner and Gwan-Rong Jeng, 1972)) to motor agility and favourite games.

CLINICAL SIGNIFICANCE

Historically left-handedness has a bad reputation (Hardyck and Petrinovich, 1977). This has led to the popular conception that left-handedness stands for clumsiness (yet some outstanding painters such as Leonardo da Vinci, Michelangelo and Pablo Picasso are reported to have been left-handed).

In the literature there is only dubious evidence that left-handedness and mixed laterality are signs of brain dysfunction. Hardyck and Petrinovich (1977) concluded: 'There is usually just enough of a relationship to suggest a possible link and never enough of one to establish firmly a solid correlation.' The number of studies in which a relationship is refuted is increasing. Calnan and Richardson (1976) reported on 11-year-old schoolchildren, and found no difference between right and left-handers for mathematics, speech problems or writing problems; there was also only a low correlation between left-handedness and reading problems, explaining but a small part of the variance. The main relationship was found between the left-handedness of the children and the teachers' report about their 'poor control of hands'. This poor control could not be objectified. Reading problems have been a main focus of attention of many researchers. They have been said to be more prevalent among left-handed and mixed- (or ambi)-handed children, and this is interpreted as a result of a maturational delay or dysfunction of the left hemisphere (Zangwill, 1960; Satz and Van Nostrand, 1972; Zurif and Carson, 1970). However, Leong (1976) argues that 'the hemispheric specialization proceeds from the lateralization of gross and fine motor skills followed by the lateralization of sensori-motor functions to the lateralization of speech and language', so that any disturbance in this process may lead to developmental lags. Pizzamiglio (1976) emphasizes that learning to read and write depends on spatial and visual abilities as well as linguistic ones. Thus the disturbance of many more lateralized functions may result in specific learning difficulties. Witelson (1976) argues that developmental dyslexia may be associated with either lack of right hemisphere specialization for spatial processing, or a dysfunction in left hemispheric processing of linguistic functions. Satz (1976) concludes that the relation between hemispheric dominance and reading disability remains a problem with many contradictory findings and suggested relationships. This conclusion indirectly confirms the argument put forward in the beginning of the chapter, that the notion of 'hemispheric dominance' as such should be discarded (cf. Buffery's 1978 'predominance' for specific functions).

Benson and Geschwind (1968), Rutter et al. (1970), and Kinsbourne and Hiscock (1977), argue that in the case of a relationship there will be rather a common origin than a causal relationship. They offer the rational explanation that in a world with predominantly right-handed persons, the mere chance to shift to left-handedness after incurring an unilateral hemisphere damage, e.g. at birth, is much larger than the other way round, and this may explain the higher amount of left- or mixed-handed children among the mentally retarded, in groups of special school pupils, etc. It is remarkable in this respect that most studies on the relation between dysfunction (behavioural, cognitive, neurological) and laterality make no distinction between familial and non-familial left-handers. As mentioned above, the latter often have a hemispheric specialization which, handedness excepted, is directly comparable to that of right-handers, whereas the familial left-handers more often turn out to have a bilateral localization in many respects.

It is important to make this distinction if one holds the view that either a shift to the opposite hemisphere, or a bilateral localization of a function induces the occupation of available 'brain-space' at the expense of other functions (e.g. speech and language in the left hemisphere, or visuospatial functions in the right hemisphere), as for example Levy (1969), Miller (1971), or Zurif and Carson (1970), and Satz and Van Nostrand (1972) do. Left-handers on the basis of a damage to the left hemisphere will often belong to the category of non-familial left-handers, unless the production of children at risk of a cerebral damage at birth would be a familial characteristic. On the other hand non-familial left-handedness may also occur as a 'variation' (Annett, 1976), so that even if 'pathological' left-handers will mainly be found among the non-familial left-handed population, still it is not permitted to invert the relation and to claim that left-handedness—(especially non-familial)—is a sign of pathology. This is also valid for 'developmental diagnosis': Cernacek (1977) could not find a relationship between the degree of handedness, considered as a measure of the degree of lateralization of the brain, and

mental development in infants between 12 and 40 months of age. Furthermore, Crinella et al. (1971), did not find any predictive relationship between a variety of neuropsychological measurements and the intensity of lateral preference, at various ages between 7 and 21 years. It is particularly interesting that they did not find any relationship with lateral disagreement, i.e. crossed-handedness, and/or footedness and/or eye preference.

Still, McBurney and Dunn (1976) found a relationship between the congruity of (right) handedness, footedness and eyedness and the degree of language development in young children. Buffery (1976), however, found a wide variety of lateral congruity and non-congruity for handedness and eyedness and the specialized verbal and spatial hemispheric abilities in intelligent young university students. The notion of crossed laterality as such does not seem to be a sufficient condition for learning disorders. Finally, as far as specialized cerebral mechanisms are concerned, Witelson (1977c) has suggested that some types of reading disability in normally intelligent children may be based on a (developmental) deficiency of left hemisphere specialization, favouring a bilateral spatial holistic processing instead of a well differentiated left and right hemisphere specialization (linguistic, sequential, analistic and spatial, parallel, holistic processing respectively). However, it may as well be, as Badian and Wolff (1977) suggested, that there exists a deficit in the interhemispheric cooperation. Witelson based her view on a study of right-handed reading impaired boys; Badian and Wolff based theirs on a group of reading disabled children consisting of right-handers (19) and left-handers (9). Admittedly the number of left-handers outnumbers somewhat the expected frequency of left-handers in a random population. Yet this fact alone does not relate left-handedness to the quality of reading, neither does it permit a generalization to left-handedness as a sign of brain dysfunction. The least that one can say, therefore, is, to quote Buffery (1976): 'The relationship of various patterns of lateral congruity to learning disorders in general remains enigmatic.'

CONCLUSION

It can be concluded that the simple fact that a patient is found to be left-handed or left-footed, or shows a crossed laterality for hands, feet and eyes, does not furnish proof of an impaired brain function. From a neurologist's point of view, laterality in itself cannot be considered as a neurological sign, as laterality is not a uniform characteristic with a uniform significance, either in left-handed, or in right-handed individuals. Rather it is the other way round. It may be worthwhile, in patients with signs of brain impairment, to study lateralized brain functions because they may lead to insights into the origin and the background of the brain dysfunction. Observed laterality is a very complex expression of brain mechanisms which requires a complex neuropsychological assessment. The concept of 'laterality' as a simple sign of brain function is gravely mistaken.

The term 'laterality' is meaningless if it is not specified. But, as we have seen, the attempt to specify 'laterality' in relation to left or right specialized 'brainedness' shows the enormous complexity of brain organization; an organization which changes during development, which may 'compensate' along various lines for disrupting early lesions, which seems to be different in men and women, and which can be influenced by environmental conditions to a till now unknown degree. It appears worthwhile, therefore, to focus for a while on the environmental variability as an important parameter, for the establishment of specialized brain mechanisms, keeping in mind at the same time whatever preprogrammed or innate global designs there may be. The assessment of laterality or dominance in whatever specified way can never be used as a neurological (screening) test. In patients with proven brain dysfunction, it may sometimes be of great help in the analysis of the dysfunction and in the considerations about eventual treatment.

REFERENCES

Annett, M. (1972). The Distribution of Handedness. *Brit. J.P. Psychol.* **63**, 343–358.

Annett, M. (1976). Handedness and the cerebral representation of speech. *Ann. Hum. Biol.* **3**, 317–328.

Badian, N. A. and Wolff, P. H. (1977). Manual asymmetries of motor sequencing in boys with reading disability. *Cortex*, **13**, 343–349.

Bakan, P., Dibb, G. and Reed, P. (1973). Handedness and birthstress. *Neuropsychol.* **11**, 363–366.

Bakker, D. J., Teunissen, J. and Bosch, J. (1976). Development of laterality-reading patterns. In: Knights, R. M. and Bakker, D. J. (Eds.) *The Neuropsychology of Learning Disorders*. Baltimore: University Park Press, 207–220.

Barnsley, R. H. and Rabinovitch, M. S. (1973). Handedness and 'Automatization' cognitive style. *Canad. J. Psychol. Rev. Canad. Psych.* **27**, 7–15.

Benson, F. D. and Geschwind, N. (1968). Cerebral Dominance and its Disturbances. *Ped. Clin. North America*, **15**, 759–769.

Benton, A. L., Meyers, R. and Polder, G. J. (1962). Some aspects of handedness. *Psych. Neurol. Basel.* **144**, 321–337.

Berlin, C. I. (1977). Hemispheric Asymmetry in Auditory Tasks. In: Harnad, S.; Doty, R. W.; Goldstein, L.; Jaynes, J.; Krauthamer, G. (Eds.): *Lateralization in the Nervous System*. New York: Academic Press, pp. 303–324.

Blakemore, C. (1977). *Mechanisms of the Mind*. Cambridge: Cambridge University Press.

Bradshaw, J., Geffen, G. and Nettleton, N. (1972a). Our two brains. *New Scientist*, 15–6–72, p. 628–631.

Bradshaw, J., Nettleton, N. C. and Geffen, G. (1972b). Ear asymmetry and delayed auditory feedback: effects of task requirements and competitive stimulation. *J. Exp. Psychol.* **94**, 269–275.

Branch, C., Milner, B. and Rasmussen, T. (1964). Intracarotid Sodium Amytal for the Lateralization of Cerebral Speech Dominance. *J. Neurosurgery*, **21**, 399–405.

Bresson, F., Maury, L., Pierraot-Le Bonniec, G. and De Schonen, S. (1977). Organization and Lateralization of reaching in infants: an instance of asymmetric functions in hands collaboration. *Neuropsychol.* **15**, 311–320.

Bryden, M. P. (1965). Tachistoscopic recognition, handedness and cerebral dominance. *Neuropsychologia*, **3**, 1–8.

Bryden, M. P. (1973). Perceptual asymmetry in vision: Relation to handedness, eyedness, and speech lateralization. *Cortex*, **9**, 419–435.

Bryden, M. P. (1977). Measuring Handedness with Questionnaires. *Neuropsychol.* **15**, 617–624.

Buffery, A. W. H. (1976). Sex differences in the neuropsychological development of verbal and spatial skills. In: Knights, R. M. and Bakker, D. J. (Eds.) *The Neuropsychology of Learning Disorders*. Baltimore: University Park Press, 187–205.

Buffery, A. W. H. (1978). Neuropsychological aspects of language development: an essay on cerebral dominance. In: Waterson, N. and Snow, C. (Eds.) *The Development of Communication*. New York: Wiley and Sons, Inc., 25–46.

Burklund, C. W. and Smith, A. (1977). Language and the cerebral hemispheres. *Neurology*, **27**, 627–633.

Calnan, M. and Richardson, K. (1976). Developmental correlates of handedness in a national sample of 11-year-olds. *Ann. Hum. Biol.* **3**, 329–342.

Cernacek, J. (1977). Physiologische und klinische Manifestationen der Hirndominanz. *Fortschritte der Neurol. und Psychiatr.* **45**, 306–320.

Chi, J. G., Dooling, E. C. and Gilles, F. H. (1977). Left–right Asymmetries of the temporal speech areas of the Human Fetus. *Arch. Neurol.* **34**, 346–348.

Cohen, B. D., Noblin, C. D., Silverman, A. J. and Penick, S. B. (1968). Functional Asymmetry of the Human Brain. *Science*, **162**, 475–477.

Cohen, L. B. (1972). Attention-getting and attention-holding processes of the infant visual preferences. *Child Dev.* **43**, 869–879.

Colbourn, C. J. (1978). Can laterality be measured? *Neuropsychologia*, **16**, 283–289.

Collins, R. L. (1977). Towards an admissible genetic model for the inheritance of the degree and the direction of asymmetry. In: Harnad, S., Doty, R. W., Goldstein, L., Jaynes, J., Krauthamer, G. (Eds.): *Lateralization in the Nervous System*. New York: Academic Press, 137–151.

Coren, S. (1974). The development of ocular dominance. *Develop. Psychol.* **10**, 304.

Coren, S. and Porac, C. (1977). Fifty centuries of righthandedness: the Historical Record. *Science*, **198**, 631–632.

Crinella, F. M., Beck, F. W. and Robinson, J. W. (1971). Unilateral dominance is not related to neuropsychological integrity. *Child Dev.* **42**, 2033–2054.

Crowell, D. H., Jones, R. H., Kapuniai, L. E. and Nakagawa, J. K. (1973). Unilateral Cortical Activity in Newborn Humans: an early index of Cerebral Dominance? *Science*, **180**, 205–208.

Davis, A. E. and Wada, J. A. (1978). Speed dominance and handedness in the normal human. *Brain and Language*, **5**, 42–55.

Dawson, J. L. M. B. (1977). Theory and method in biosocial psychology: a new approach to cross-cultural psychology. In: Loeb Adler, L. (Ed.): *Issues in crosscultural research. Ann. New York Acad. Sciences*, **285**, 46–66.

De Schonen, S. (1977). Functional asymmetries in the development of bimanual coordinations in infants. *J. Human Movement Studies*, **3**, 144–156.

Dewson, J. H. (1977). Preliminary Evidence of Hemispheric Asymmetry of Auditory Function in Monkeys. In: Harnad, S., Doty, R. W., Goldstein, L., Jaynes, L., Krauthamer, G. (Eds.): *Lateralization in the Nervous System*. New York: Academic Press, 63–71.

Dimond, S. J. and Beaumont, J. G. (1972). Hemispheric control of hand function in the human brain. *Acta Psychol.* **36**, 32–36.

Doms-Lissens, M. C. (1976). The role of the non-dominant hemisphere in recovery from aphasia. *Paper Vth Int. Symp. on Rehabilitation in Neurology*. Prague, 15–17 Sept. 1977.

Donchin, E., Kutas, M. and McCarthy, G. (1977). Electrocortical Indices of Hemispheric Utilization. In: Harnad, S., Doty, R. W., Goldstein, L., Jaynes, J. and Krauthamer, G. (Eds.): *Lateralization in the Nervous System*. New York: Academic Press, 339–385.

Eason, R. G., Groves, P., White, C. T. and Oden, D. (1967). Evoked Cortical Potentials: relation to visual field and handedness. *Science*, **156**, 1643–1646.

Eccles, J. C. (1973). *The Understanding of the Brain*. New York: McGraw Hill.

Galaburda, A. M., LeMay, M., Kemper, T. L. and Geschwind, N. (1978). Right–left asymmetries in the brain. *Science*, **199**, 852–856.

Gardner, R. A. and Gardner, B. T. (1969). Teaching sign language to a chimpanzee. *Science*, **165**, 664–672.

Gates, A. and Bradshaw, J. L. (1977). The role of the cerebral hemispheres in music. *Brain and Language*, **4**, 1–29.

Gazzaniga, M. S. (1974). Cerebral dominance viewed as a decision system. In: Dimond, S. and Beaumont, J. (Eds.) *Hemispheric Functions in the Human Brain*. London: Halstead Press, 367–382.

Gazzaniga, M. S., LeDoux, J. E. and Wilson, D. H. (1977). Language, praxis, and the right hemisphere: clues to some mechanisms of consciousness. *Neurology*, **27**, 1144–1147.

Geffen, G., Bradshaw, J. L. and Nettleton, N. C. (1972). Hemispheric asymmetry: verbal and spatial encoding of visual stimuli. *J. Exp. Psychol.* **95**, 25–31.

Geschwind, N. and Levitsky, W. (1968). Human Brain: Left–right asymmetries in temporal speech region. *Science*, **161**, 186–187.

Glick, S. D., Jerussi, T. P. and Zimmerberg, B. (1977). Behavioural and Neuropharmacological Correlates of Nigrostriatal Asymmetry in Rats. In: Harnad, S., Doty, R. W., Goldstein, L., Jaynes, J. and Krauthamer, G. (Eds.): *Lateralization in the Nervous System*. New York: Academic Press, 213–251.

Gott, P. S. and Boyarsky, L. L. (1972). The relation of cerebral dominance and handedness to visual evoked potentials. *J. Neurobiol.* **3**, 65–77.

Gregory, A. H., Harriman, J. C. and Roberts, L. D. (1972). Cerebral dominance for the perception of rhythm. *Psychon. Sci.* **28**, 75–76.

Gronwall, D. M. A. and Sampson, H. (1971). Ocular dominance: a test of two hypotheses. *Brit. J. Psychol.* **62**, 175–185.

Gur, R. and Gur, R. (1977). Correlates of Conjugate Lateral Eye Movement in Man. In: Harnad, S., Doty, R. W., Goldstein, L., Jaynes, J. and Krauthamer, G. (Eds.): *Lateralization in the Nervous System*. New York: Academic Press, 261–281.

Hamilton, C. R. (1977). Investigations of perceptual and mnemonic lateralization in monkeys. In: Harnad, S., Doty, R. W., Goldstein, L., Jaynes, J. and Krauthamer, G. (Eds.): *Lateralization in the Nervous System*. New York: Academic Press, 45–62.

Hardyck, C. and Petrinovich, L. F. (1977). Left handedness. *Psychol. Bull.* **84**, 385–404.

Hécaen, H. (1976). Acquired aphasia in children and the ontogenesis of hemispheric functional specialization. *Brain and Language*, **3**, 114–134.

Hécaen, H. and Sauget, J. (1971). Cerebral dominance in left-handed subjects. *Cortex*, **7**, 19–48.

Heschl, R. (1878). *Über die vordere quere Schlafenwindung des menschlichen Grosshirns*. Braumüller: Vienna, Austria.

Hicks, R. E., Provenzano, F. J. and Rybstein, E. D. (1975). Generalized and lateralized effects of concurrent verbal rehearsal upon performance of sequential movements of the fingers by the left and right hands. *Acta Psychologica*, **39**, 119–130.

Ingram, D. (1975). Motor asymmetries in young children. *Neuropsychologica*, **13**, 95–102.

Jeeves, M. A. (1972). Hemisphere differences in response rates to visual stimuli in children. *Psychon. Sci.* **27**, 201–203.

Kershner, J. R. and Gwan-Rong Jeng, A. (1972). Dual functional hemispheric asymmetry in visual perception: effects of ocular dominance and post exposural processes. *Neuropsychologie*, **10**, 437–445.

Kimura, D. (1961). Cerebral dominance and the perception of verbal stimuli. *Canadian J. Psychol.* **15**, 166–171.

Kimura, D. (1977). Acquisition of a motor skill after left-hemisphere damage. *Brain*, **100**, 527–542.

Kimura, D. and Archibald, Y. (1974). Motor functions of the left hemisphere. *Brain*, **97**, 337–350.

Kinsbourne, M. and Hiscock, M. (1977). Does cerebral dominance develop? In: Segalowitz, S. J. and Gruber, F. A. (Eds.): *Language Development and Neurological Theory*. New York: Academic Press, 171–191.

Kreuter, Ch., Kinsbourne, M. and Trevarthen, C. (1972). Are disconnected cerebral hemispheres independent channels? A preliminary study of the effect of unilateral loading on bilateral finger tapping. *Neuropsychologia*, **10**, 453–461.

Kutas, M. and Donchin, E. (1974). Studies of squeezing: handedness, responding hand, response force, and asymmetry of readiness potential. *Science*, **186**, 545–548.

LeDoux, J. E., Wilson, D. H. and Gazzaniga, M. S. (1977). A divided mind: observations on the conscious properties of the separated hemisphere. *Ann. Neurol.* **2**, 417–421.

Lehman, R. A. W. (1978). The handedness of rhesus monkeys–1. *Neuropsychologia*, **16**, 33–42.

LeMay, M. (1977). Asymmetrics of the skull and handedness. *J. Neurol. Sci.* **32**, 243–253.

Leong, Che. K. (1976). Lateralization in severely disabled readers in relation to functional cerebral development and synthesis of information. In: Knights, R. M. and Bakker, D. J. (Eds.) *The Neuropsychology of Learning Disorders*. Baltimore: University Park Press, 221–231.

Levy, J. (1969). Possible basis for the evolution of lateral specialization of the human brain. *Nature*, **224**, 614–615.

Levy, J. (1977). The origins of lateral asymmetry. In: Harnad, S., Doty, R. W., Goldstein, L., Jaynes, J. and Krauthamer, G. (Eds.): *Lateralization in the Nervous System*. New York: Academic Press, 195–209.

Luria, A. R. (1973). *The Working Brain* (repr. ed. 1976). Harmondsworth: Penguin Education.

McBurney, A. K. and Dunn, H. G. (1976). Handedness, footedness, eyedness: A prospective study with special reference to the development of speech and language skills. In: Knights, R. M. and Bakker, D. J. (Eds.) *The Neuropsychology of Learning Disorders*. Baltimore: University Park Press, 139–147.

McRae, D. L., Brandt, C. L. and Milner, B. (1968). The occipital horns and cerebral dominance. *Neurology*, **18**, 95–98.

Miller, E. (1971). Handedness and the pattern of human ability. *Br. J. Psychol.* **62**, 111–112.

Morgan, M. (1977). Embryology and Inheritance of Asymmetry. In: Harnad, S., Doty, R. W., Golstein, L., Jaynes, J. and Krauthamer, G. (Eds.): *Lateralization in the Nervous System*. New York: Academic Press, 173–195.

Nelson, J. M., Phillips, R. and Goldstein, L. (1977). Interhemispheric EEG Laterality Relationships following Psychoactive Agents and during Operant Performance in Rabbits. In: Harnad, S., Doty, R. W., Goldstein, L., Jaynes, J. and Krauthamer, G. (Eds.): *Lateralization in the Nervous System*. New York: Academic Press, 451–471.

Nottebohm, F. (1977). Asymmetries in Neural Control of Vocalization in the Canary. In: Harnad, S., Doty, R. W., Goldstein, L., Jaynes, J. and Krauthamer, G. (Eds.): *Lateralization in the Nervous System*. New York: Academic Press, 23–45.

Oldfield, R. C. (1971). The assessment and analysis of handedness. The Edinburgh Inventory. *Neuropsychologie*, **9**, 97–113.

Passian, J., Suchenwirth, R. and Ferner, U. (1969). Die Lateralization der manuellen Leistung in Abhängingkeit vom Lebensalter. *Fortschritte der Neurologie-Psychiatrie*, **37**, 319–331.

Pizzamiglio, L. (1976). Cognitive approach to hemispheric dominance. In: Knights, R. M. and Bakker, D. J. (Eds.) *The Neuropsychology of Learning Disorders*. Baltimore: University Park Press, 265–272.

Pratt, R. T. C., Warrington, E. K. and Halliday, A. M. (1971). Unilateral ECT as a test for cerebral dominance, with a strategy for treating left-handers. *Br. J. Psychiat.* **119**, 79.

Preilowski, B. F. B. (1972). Possible contribution of the anterior forebrain commissures to bilateral motor coordination. *Neuropsychologia*, **10**, 267–277.

Provins, K. A. and Cunliffe, P. (1972a). The reliability of some motor performance tests of handedness. *Neuropsychologia*, **10**, 199–206.

Provins, K. A. and Cunliffe, P. (1972b). The relationship between EEG activity and handedness. *Cortex*, **8**, 136–146.

Quinn, P. T. (1972). Stuttering, cerebral dominance and the dichotic word test. *Med. J. Australia*, **2**, 639–643.

Raczkowski, D., Kalat, J. W. and Nebes, R. (1974). Reliability and validity of some handedness questionnaire items. *Neuropsychologia*, **12**, 43–47.

Ramier, A. M. and Hécaen, H. (1977). Les déficits au test de 'Fluence Verbale' chez les sujets gauchers avec lésions hémisphériques unilatérales. *Rev. Neurol.* **133**, 571–574.

Rubens, A. B. (1977). Anatomical asymmetries of human cerebral cortex. In: Harnad, S., Doty, R. W., Goldstein, L., Jaynes, J. and Krauthamer, G. (Eds.): *Lateralization in the Nervous System*. New York: Academic Press, 503–516.

Rutter, M., Graham, P. and Yule, W. (1970). A neuropsychiatric study in childhood. *Clin. Dev. Med.* **35/36**. London: SIMP/Heinemann.

Salapatek, P. (1975). Pattern Perception in Early Infancy. In: Cohen, L. B. and Salapatek, Ph. (Eds.): *Infant Perception: From Sensation to Cognition*. Vol. I: Basic visual processes. New York: Academic Press.

Satz, P. (1976). Cerebral dominance and reading disability: An old problem revisited. In: Knights, R. M. and Bakker, D. J. (Eds.): *The Neuropsychology of Learning Disorders*. Baltimore: University Park Press, 273–294.

Satz, P., Achenbach, K. and Fennell, E. (1967). Correlations between assessed manual laterality and predicted speech laterality in a normal population. *Neuropsychologia*, **5**, 295–310.

Satz, P. and Van Nostrand, G. K. (1972). Developmental Dyslexia: an evaluation of a theory. In: Satz, P. and Ross, J. (Eds.): *The Disabled Learner: Early Detection and Intervention*. Rotterdam: Univ. of Rotterdam Press.

Semmes, J. (1968). Hemispheric specialization: a possible clue to mechanism. *Neuropsychologia*, **6**, 11–26.

Seth, G. (1973). Eye-hand coordination and 'handedness': a developmental study of visuomotor behavior in infancy. *Br. J. Educ. Psychol.* **43**, 35–49.

Smith, A. (1969). Nondominant Hemispherectomy. *Neurology (Minn.)*, **19**, 442–445.

Smith, A. and Burklund, C. W. (1966). Dominant hemispherectomy: preliminary report on neuropsychological sequelae. *Science*, **153**, 1280–1282.

Sperry, R. W. (1968). Plasticity of neural maturation. *Dev. Biol.* (suppl.), **2**, 306–327.

Sperry, R. W. (1973). Lateral specialization of cerebral function in surgically separated hemispheres. In: McGuigan, F. J. and Schoonover, R. A. (Eds.): *The Psychophysiology of Thinking*. New York: Academic Press.

Sperry, R. W., Gazzaniga, M. S. and Bogen, J. E. (1969). Interhemispheric relationships: The neocortical commissures; syndromes of hemisphere disconnection. In: Vinken, P. J. and Bruyn, G. W. (Eds.): *Handbook of clinical neurology* (vol. 4). Amsterdam: North Holland Publishing Company.

Springer, S. P. (1977). Tachistoscopic and Dichotic Listening Investigations of Laterality in Normal Human Subjects. In: Harnad, S., Doty, R. W., Goldstein, L., Jaynes, J. and Krauthamer, G. (Eds.): *Lateralization in the Nervous System*. New York: Academic Press, 325–336.

Stamm, J. S., Rosen, S. C. and Gadotti, A. (1977). Lateralization of Functions in the Monkey's Frontal Cortex. In: Harnad, S., Doty, R. W., Goldstein, L., Jaynes, J. and Krauthamer, G. (Eds.): *Lateralization in the Nervous System*. New York: Academic Press, 385–402.

Steingrüber, H. J. (1971). Zur Messung der Händgett. *Zschr. exp. angew. Psychol.* **18**, 337–357.

Subirana, A. (1969). Handedness and cerebral dominance. In: Vinken, P. J. and Bruyn, G. W. (Eds.): *Handbook of Clinical Neurology*. Vol. 4. Amsterdam: North Holland Publishing Company, 248.

Suchenwirth, R. (1969). Bedingungen der Händigkeit und ihre Bedeuting für die Klinik der Hemisphërenprozesse. *Der Nervenarzt*, **40**, 509–517.

Taylor, D. C. (1976). Developmental stratagems organizing intellectual skills: Evidence from studies of temporal lobectomy for epilepsy. In: Knights, R. M. and Bakker, D. J. (Eds.) *The Neuropsychology of Learning Disorders*. Baltimore: University Park Press, 149–171.

Teszner, D., Tzavaras, A., Gruner, J. and Hecaen, H. (1972). L'asymétrie droite-gauche du planum temporale; à propos de l'étude anatomique de 100 cerveaux. *Revue Neurologique*, **126**, 444–449.

Thatcher, R. W. (1977). Evoked-Potentials correlates of Hemispheric Lateralization during semantic Information-processing. In: Harnad, S., Doty, R. W., Goldstein, L., Jaynes, J. and Krauthamer, G. (Eds.) *Lateralization in the Nervous System*. New York: Academic Press, 429–448.

Turkewitz, G. (1977). The development of Lateral Differences in the Human Infant. In: Harnad, S., Doty, R. W., Goldstein, L., Jaynes, J. and Krauthamer, G. (Eds.): *Lateralization in the Nervous System*. New York: Academic Press, 251–260.

Vygotsky, L. (1962). *Thought and Language*. New York: Wiley and Sons, Inc.

Wada, J. A. (1949). A new method for the determination of the side of cerebral speech dominance. A preliminary report on the intracarotid injection of sodium-amytal in man. *Igaku to Seibutsugaku*, **14**, 221.

Wada, J. A., Clarke, R. and Hamm, A. (1975). Cerebral hemispheric asymmetry in humans. *Arch. Neurol.* **32**, 237–246.

Wada, J. A. and Davis, A. E. (1977). Fundamental nature of human infant's brain asymmetry. *Le Journal Canadien des Sciences Neurologiques*, **4**, 203–207.

Wada, J. A. and Rasmussen, T. (1960). Intracarotid injection of sodium amytal for the lateralization of cerebral speech dominance. Experimental and clinical observations. *J. Neurosurgery*, **17**, 266–282.

Warren, J. M. (1977). Handedness and cerebral dominance in monkeys. In: Harnad, S., Doty, R. W., Goldstein, L., Jaynes, J. and Krauthamer, G. (Eds.): *Lateralization in the Nervous System*. New York: Academic Press, 151–172.

Webster, W. G. (1972). Functional asymmetry between the cerebral hemispheres of the cat. *Neuropsychologia*, **10**, 75–87.

Webster, W. G. (1977). Hemispheric Asymmetry in Cats. In: Harnad, S., Doty, R. W., Goldstein, L., Jaynes, J. and Krauthamer, G. (Eds.) *Lateralization in the Nervous System*. New York: Academic Press, 471–480.

Weinstein, S. and Sersen, E. A. (1961). Tactual sensitivity as a function of handedness and laterality. *J. Comp. Physiol. Psychol.* **54**, 665–669.

Witelson, S. F. (1976). Abnormal right hemisphere specialization in developmental dyslexia. In: Knights, R. M. and Bakker, D. J. (Eds.) *The Neuropsychology of Learning Disorders*. Baltimore: University Park Press, 233–255.

Witelson, S. F. (1977a). Early hemisphere specialization and interhemispheric plasticity: an empirical and theoretical review. In: Segalowitz, S. J. and Gruber, F. A. (Eds.) *Language Development and Neurological Theory*. New York: Academic Press, 213–287.

Witelson, S. F. (1977b). Anatomic asymmetry in the temporal lobes: its documentation, phylogenesis and relationships to functional asymmetry. In: Dimond, S. J. and Blizard, D. A. (Eds.) *Evolution and lateralization of the brain*. *Ann. New York Acad. Sciences*, **299**, 328–354.

Witelson, S. F. (1977c). Developmental dyslexia: Two right hemispheres and none left. *Science*, **195**, 309–311.

Witelson, S. F. and Pallie, W. (1973). Left hemisphere specialization for language in the newborn: neuroanatomical evidence of asymmetry. *Brain*, **96**, 641–646.

Wolff, P. H. and Hurwitz, I. (1976). Sex differences in finger tapping: a developmental study. *Neuropsychol.* **14**, 35–41.

Wolff, P. H., Hurwitz, I. and Moss, H. (1977). Serial organization of motor skills in left- and right-handed adults. *Neuropsychol.* **15**, 539–546.

Yakovlev, P. I. and Rakic, P. (1966). Patterns of decussation of bulbar pyramids and distribution of pyramidal tracts on two sides of the spinal cord. *Trans. Amer. Neurol. Assoc.* **91**, 366–367.

Yeni-Komshian, G. H. and Benson, D. A. (1976). Anatomical study of cerebral asymmetry in the temporal lobe of humans, chimpanzees, and rhesus monkeys. *Science*, **192**, 387–389.

Young, G. (1977). Manual Specialization in Infancy: Implications for Lateralization of Brain Function. In: Segalowitz, S. J. and Gruber, F. A. (Eds.) *Language Development and Neurological Theory*. New York: Academic Press, 289–311.

Zangwill, O. L. (1960). *Cerebral dominance and its relation to psychological function*. Edinburgh: Oliver and Boyd.

Zangwill, O. L. (1967). Speech and the minor hemisphere. *Acta Neurol. Psychiatr. Belg.* **67**, 1013–1020.

Zurif, E. B. and Bryden, M. P. (1969). Familial handedness and left–right differences in auditory and visual perception. *Neuropsychol.* **6**, 179–189.

Zurif, E. B. and Carson, G. (1970). Dyslexia in relation to cerebral dominance and temporal analysis. *Neuropsychol.* **8**, 351–361.

15. AUTONOMIC REACTIVITY

PETER H. VENABLES

INTRODUCTION

The discussion of autonomic reactivity in the context of developmental psychiatry is needed not so much because of a major interest in the physiological aspects of this section of the nervous system itself, but rather because of the extent to which indices of autonomic activity can lead to a broader understanding of aspects of the developing organism which may not otherwise be accessible to observation.

In some instances autonomic reactivity may be used as an indicant of general reactivity to the environment and as such may be particularly important in reflecting the child's reaction to his surroundings before the development of speech. On the other hand autonomic reactivity may be viewed as a major component of emotional responsivity and may be useful as such in the interpretation of patterns of overt behaviour. However, the point of view which will receive major attention here is that autonomic reactivity may be most fruitfully seen as a part of the response of a total system. Then, provided the recording methods are adequate, the total experimental situation is fully understood and the response measures are interpreted in the context of data not only from children but also from adults and from animals, measurement of autonomic reactivity may be very fruitful.

The main difficulty of a review of this area arises from the patchiness of the data. For instance, the large amount of data that is collected on heart rate measures with neonates and infants before the age of one year is not reflected in an equally prolific spread into later years. Similarly, whereas there is a lot of data on cardiovascular activity in the infant the amount of data on the electrodermal system is sparse. Most of the work which is available is cross-sectional and longitudinal studies are rarities.

In a companion volume (Davis and Dobbing, 1974), Shinebourne (Chapter 13b) presents age normative data on tonic cardiovascular indices. Virtually no comparable baseline data are available on phasic cardiovascular activity or indeed on any of the other measures discussed in this chapter. This, therefore, inevitably results in the presention of islets of data gathered in points in developmental time without continuous reference one to the other. Because of this lack of age-related norms interpretation of data is not straightforward and care always has to be taken to examine how far an aspect of autonomic responsivity may be limited by the stage of the child's physiological development before any interpretation can be made that, for instance, lack of a particular response is due to some limitation imposed by a higher function.

A review of some of the available literature from a general point of view is to be found in Steinschneider (1967). Reviews from the standpoint of the cardiac literature are available in Graham and Jackson (1970), Clifton (1974) and Lewis (1974).

To a very large extent the systems which have been used as indicators of autonomic activity in children have been the same as those used in adults. The major research investment is in electrodermal and cardiac activity, where the measurement variables are skin conductance, skin potential and heart rate. Other cardiovascular aspects such as blood pressure and vasomotor activity have been used much less frequently. Other available measures are respiration and pupillary activity but the data from these sources are sparse. Because, as indicated above, three major reviews of the available literature on cardiac reactivity have been presented, this present chapter will give somewhat more attention to the data on electrodermal activity.

Electrodermal activity is of two kinds, 'exosomatic' where the conductivity of the skin to an imposed potential is measured and 'endosomatic' where no external source is imposed by the potential difference between two electrodes on the skin surface is measured. In the first instance the variable measured is labelled skin conductance (SC) and in the second, skin potential (SP).

Very full descriptions of the physiological mechanisms underlying these measurements are given by Edelberg (1971, 1972), Venables and Christie (1973) and Fowles (1974). It is, however, possible to say in summary, without too much distortion of the facts, that electrodermal indices reflect activity mediated by the sympathetic division of the autonomic nervous system, albeit by a cholinergic final pathway. The higher levels of control of this system are best viewed as layers of a hierarchical system (*e.g.* Wang, 1964) with major influence on activity from the bulbar and brain stem reticular formations, the hypothalamus, the amygdala and hippocampus in the limbic system and finally the cortex. The interest of electrodermal activity is thus not confined to the extent to which it reflects autonomic activity in any simple fashion but rather how far it may provide, under particular circumstances, indices of subcortical activity. Electrodermal activity is only normally recordable from palmar and plantar surfaces (*see* Rickles and Day, 1968) and is a function, particularly in the case of skin potential, of the local electrode–electrolyte conditions. It is thus unlike other electrophysiological measures where types of electrodes and electrolytes are chosen only to provide the best conduction pathway for transmission of the signal which appears at the skin surface from some underlying source.

Unlike singly innervated electrodermal activity, cardiac activity reflects the balance between sympathetic and parasympathetic influences on the heart. At any one time it is not possible to say, without further investigation, whether heart rate deceleration is a result of increased parasympathetic or decreased sympathetic activity. Gunn, Wolf, Block and Person (1972), Cohen and McDonald (1974) and Forsyth (1974) provide very full descriptions of the physiological basis of cardiac control. The important point to bear in mind is that when examining the effect of a stimulus situation on cardiac activity the

cerned with the control of electrolyte retention or excretion via ductal sodium pump pathways.

In a manner parallel to that of the control of electrodermal activity, the control of the heart may be seen as resulting from the functioning of a hierarchical system. The main difference between cardiac and electrodermal activity, however, probably lies in the degree of systematic feedback control exercised in the former. For instance, an increase in sympathetic activation causes an increase in heart rate and blood pressure, the increase in blood pressure stimulates baroreceptors in the carotid sinus and the aortic arch and these provide signals to the vasomotor centre in the medulla. This in turn results in an increase in vagal activity causing a slowing of the heart. While there is thus control of the heart at this medullary level further control is exercised in the hypothalmus, the limbic system and the cortex.

MEASUREMENT

Electrodermal activity

Techniques for the measurement of electrodermal activity are dealt with fully by, for example, Edelberg (1967), Venables and Martin (1967), Lykken and Venables (1971), Venables and Christie (1973) and Grings (1974).

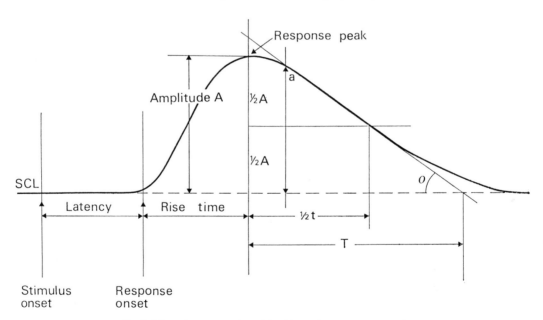

Fig. 1. Schematic representation of the skin conductance response (SCR).

activity is that of a constrained system with two influences in balance and maintaining a life support function. On the other hand in the case of electrodermal activity the system appears more 'open' and without the limiting effects of dual innervation. It should not, however, be thought, as perhaps has been the case in the past, that the activity of the skin is in a sense passive and not concerned in vital functions. At least part of electrodermal activity is con-

In summary it can be said that over the last 15 years there has been a fairly strong move to standardization of procedures. Most workers now use a constant voltage system for measuring skin conductance and are thus able to record skin conductance directly rather than as skin resistance as had been the case with constant current systems with the subsequent necessity of reciprocal conversion. There has, too, been an adoption of silver/silver chloride electrodes, in part at least because they are readily available commercially. Most workers also use physiological levels of sodium or potassium chloride as the electrolyte although the base medium in which the saline is used is still the subject of investigation and the use of different media may result in the non-comparability of data from different laboratories. Probably the largest amount of data has been collected using a hydrating medium such as agar-agar or starch paste and the continued use of these may be worthwhile to enable comparable data to be collected. It is well established that skin conductance varies with the size of electrode employed. Consequently the use of small electrodes with children automatically results in lower values of conductance than those obtained with adults which may have used larger electrodes.

Fig. 1 shows the form of the skin conductance response (SCR). The components of the phasic response which may be measured are amplitude, latency, rise time and half-recovery time. Other variables measuring tonic activity are skin conductance level (SCL) and numbers of spontaneous fluctuations (NSF) which have the same waveform as elicited responses but which do not appear to be initiated by any overt stimulus. Skin potential is usually measured using similar electrode and electrolyte techniques to those used in skin conductance measurement. The electrodes are used in conjunction with a DC preamplifier capable of measuring levels of potential (SPL) between 0 and -70 mV, negativity being at the palmar or plantar surface with reference to a limb electrode. This potential is usually backed off or bucked by an equal and opposite potential to enable responses to be recorded at a higher level of amplification and presented around an artificial but known, zero point. Skin potential responses (SPR) may have a maximum amplitude of around 5 mV and have a waveform which is uniphasic negative or biphasic (negative/positive) or more rarely uniphasic positive. The latency of the negative component is comparable with that of the SCR.

Cardiac activity

Methods for the recording of cardiac activity are fairly straightforward and are dealt with by Brener (1967) and Schneiderman, Dauth and Van Dercar (1974). Normally, it is only heart rate, rather than the particular form of the cardiac waveform, which is of interest in the present context. A direct readout in terms of rate is provided by the use of a cardiotachometer; however, because of the large amount of data which results from recording cardiac material, increasing use is made of computers in analysis. Successive R waves of the electrocardiogram are used to measure interbeat intervals (which are of course reciprocally related to heart rate—HR). The data may then be retained as successive interbeat intervals or converted to heart rate. Use of the computer enables the data to be referred to a real time base and expressed as heart rate or interbeat intervals (IBIs) at seconds or half seconds. This is in contrast to the more traditional cardiotachometer output which is in terms of HR at successive beats.

Whereas the recording of cardiac activity for rate measurement is relatively simple, the analysis of the data presents considerable difficulty. Three major factors underlie this difficulty. Firstly, any analysis of phasic heart rate changes has to recognize that the ongoing (resting) heart rate is undergoing cyclic changes and phasic responses have to be viewed as deviations from this changing baseline. Secondly, the extent of phasic changes is related to the tonic level of activity at the beginning of the change and the law of initial value, LIV (Wilder, 1957, 1958) needs to be taken into account. Thirdly, as successive heart rates or IBIs are not independent, it is not strictly legitimate to use straightforward analysis of variance techniques in the analysis of heart rate trends. Thus the method of preference is some form of time series analysis. The arguments for and against different analytic methods are presented in Graham and Jackson (1970), Gatchel and Lang (1973), Wilson (1974), Jones, Crowell and Kapuniai (1969) and Crowell, Blurton, Kobayashi, McFarland and Yang (1976). The methods involved in dealing with the law of initial value (LIV) are discussed by Lacey (1956), Block and Bridger (1962), Benjamin (1963, 1967) and Steinschneider and Lipton (1965).

A further factor which is of major importance in work with infants, but which has been neglected in work with older children, although it may be of importance here too, is that of 'state' measured on the sleep–wakefulness–alertness–agitation continuum.

Very full discussion of the importance of taking into account the state of infants at the time of testing is given by Prechtl (1965), Prechtl and Beintema (1964), Hutt, Lenard and Prechtl (1969). Berg, Berg and Graham (1971), for instance, showed that different patterns of cardiac responsivity was obtained in infants rated as 'Sleepy', 'Drowsy', 'Alert', 'Fussy' or 'Crying'.

In part, differences in state may be dealt with statistically by application of procedures which 'undo' (Benjamin, 1967) the effects of the 'Law of Initial Values'. But it is better for the experimenter to be aware of the necessity for controlling for the state of the subject (if possible) rather than to have to compensate for it at a later stage.

DEVELOPMENTAL ASPECTS OF ELECTRODERMAL ACTIVITY

Tonic activity

Kaye (1964) conducted a study in which he measured the skin conductance levels of 112 newborn children between birth and 96 hours. Measures were taken from palmar, plantar and calf sites. One group was tested serially over each of the four days, another group was tested only once during the four-day period. Equal numbers of male and female children were included in each group. The data show a fall in conductance from birth to those testing sessions between 8–15 hours and following this a consistent rise in conductance on each day of the remainder of the four-day period. Kaye suggests that the initial fall in conductance may be due to local skin changes during the first few hours after birth. Weller and Bell (1965) studied the plantar skin conductance level of 40 newborns between the ages of 60 and 110 hours, in relation to six levels of state at time of testing. This state measure was correlated significantly with skin conductance. Higher levels of behavioural activity were positively related to higher levels of conductance.

The data from Kaye and Weller and Bell are very comparable in absolute terms. The mean value of conductance for Weller and Bell data is 11·01 micromhos, and that for children of the same age from Kaye's sample have a mean value (judged from graphical presentation) of 12·0–13·0 micromhos. Both workers used ⅝″ diameter electrodes although of different metals.

Consistently collected data from birth to adulthood which might make possible statements about age trends in skin conductance do not appear to be available. A cross-sectional study now being analysed (Venables, Fletcher, Mednick, Schulsinger and Cheeneebash, 1980) on 640 subjects in 5 age groups from 5 to 25 years on the island of Mauritius suggests that a peak value of conductance level is reached at about age 5 which then declines to about age 15 in males after which it rises again to age 25. In females, however, there is no rise in conductance level after age 15. As there are racial differences in skin conductance level (*e.g.*, Juniper and Dykman, 1967) with, for instance, negroes showing lower conductance levels than whites, the generalizability of these data must be questioned. They are in some accord with very old material of Jones (1930) which reports that only 5% of his adult subjects showed as high levels of conductance as those of his infant subjects. Between the ages of 7 and 10 years Wenger and Ellington (1943) report no differences in skin conductance level due to either age or sex, findings which the Mauritius data support for this age range.

Phasic activity

Crowell, Davis, Chun and Spellacy (1965) examined the electrodermal responsivity of infants seen first between 20 and 43 hours after birth and then 24 hours later. A plantar electrode placement was used. The stimuli were lights of two intensities, tones of two intensities, a puff of nitrogen on the abdomen, clicks, flashes and an odour. Of the total number of stimuli presented, only 18% evoked responses. Of these the smallest number was to light stimuli and the largest, 26%, to the most intense (80dB) tone. The latencies of the SCR are short (0·7–1·4 secs) in comparison to adult values. Data from Venables, Fletcher, Mednick, Schulsinger and Cheeneebash (1979), however, suggest that latency is a significant function of age, and increases from about 1·7 secs at age 3 to 2·2 secs at age 20 for identical stimuli. The recovery times for the SCR from Crowell *et al.*'s data range from 2·4–3·8 secs, values which do not differ from those found in adult data under similar stimulating conditions. The most outstandingly different figure from that usually encountered is that for rise time where the value of 8·9 secs for auditory stimuli is well outside adult range.

Crowell *et al.*, report that females produce more responses, a finding which would be in line with the report of higher SCLs in females in the Weller and Bell (1965) data cited above. The finding of these authors that neonates are capable of producing SCRs is in accord with the position of Jones (1930) although he used slightly older children and in contradiction to the earlier work of Peiper (1924). Again there appears to be no basis for normative developmental data over later years from a white population. Data from Venables, Fletcher, Mednick, Schulsinger and Cheeneebash (1979) suggest no marked developmental changes in response amplitude or recovery time in their Mauritian study. However, one of the major effects of age appears to be the extent to which electrodermal responses may be readily elicited. Table 1

TABLE I

MEAN PERCENTAGES OF SUBJECTS RESPONDING TO MEDIUM INTENSITY AUDITORY STIMULI, BY AGE.

			Age (years)				
	0*	3†	5	10	15	20	25
% responding	18	44	74	87	95	90	88

* Data from Crowell *et al.*, 1965
† Data from 3–25 from Venables, 1978

presents data from two sources which illustrate this point. Crowell, Davis, Chun and Spellacy (1965) report data which indicates that neonates respond to 18% of stimuli presented. Venables (1978) reports data from subjects aged 3, 5, 10, 15, 20 and 25 years of age. These data are in the form of percentage of subjects responding to 75 dB 1000 Hz stimuli. Although these two sources of data are not strictly comparable they serve to illustrate the point of a low level of electrodermal responsivity at birth rising to a maximal value at age 15. These data should only be viewed as illustrative, as clearly responsivity depends on the nature of the stimuli used and the gain of the amplifying system employed for recording. Stechler, Bradford and Levy (1966) provide data to show that a stimulus in the form of a puff of air directed at the abdomen in neonates produced SPRs of 2 mV or more on 63% of trials. This is in contrast to the data from Crowell *et al.* (1965) cited above showing that similar stimulation only produced 18% of SCRs. In support of this difference in skin conductance and skin potential reactivity in infants, Campos, Tursky and Conway (1970) and Appel, Campos, Silverman and Conway (1971) have shown that white noise or thermal stimuli presented to 1-month old infants produced skin potential responses but did not elicit skin conductance responses.

These data on electrodermal activity are in accordance with work on eccrine sweating reported by Verbov and Baxter (1974) who showed that it was possible to detect sweating on the palm at the age of 24 hours. This report is in contrast to that of earlier material which suggest that palmar sweating does not occur until 2–3 months after birth.

In summary both skin conductance and skin potential appear to be recordable from birth onwards, although the degree of skin conductance responsivity appears to be somewhat low at birth. This low responsivity may, of course, be in part due to low levels of sensitivity to stimuli used. However, the apparent orderliness of increase in responsivity from birth to age 15 evident in the SCR as shown in Table 1 suggests that deficiency in responding is to be allocated to the response mechanisms rather than to the sensivity of receptor organs which do not show, on the basis of other data, evidence of graded development with age.

The data from Venables *et al.* (1979) show that the rate of habituation over the first six orienting stimuli presented to the subjects shows an increase to age 15 with hardly any habituation being shown at age 3. Douglas (1972), p. 543, suggests that the hippocampus may not become functional in man until age 4. This suggestion set alongside the data of Pribram and McGuiness (1975) showing the role of the hippocampus in SCR habituation may provide some explanation for the minimal habituation at age 3.

Stern (1968) provides further data which suggest state development in orienting. His subjects were groups of 6-year-olds and 12-year-olds and the SCR to a 6 sec tone was measured. There was no difference between the two groups in the response to the onset of the tone. However, there was a marked deficit in the 6-year-old group in habituation of the response to tone offset. Stern suggests that the extent to which the subject can develop a concept of the length of a stimulus the quicker should be the habituation of the terminal orienting response. The data thus suggest a deficiency in 6-year-olds in what Stern denotes as 'time-binding'.

DEVELOPMENTAL TRENDS IN CARDIAC ACTIVITY

Tonic activity

Data on developmental changes in tonic activity are presented in Table 2. The changes in level of heart rate with age are marked and need to be borne in mind when investigating the effect of other variables. Perhaps more importantly they present changes in a baseline from which deviations in the form of phasic responses are made. While there is by no means universal agreement that the Law of Initial Values is always operative, the recognition that it sometimes is necessitates that phasic data are examined in respect to the age-related tonic level before strong statements can be made that phasic changes are themselves independently age related.

Phasic activity

Extensive reviews of this area are available in Steinschneider (1967), Graham and Jackson (1970), Lewis (1974) and Clifton (1974) and it would be redundant to reiterate at length the material which they fully present. The nature-direction of the heart rate response depends upon the type of stimulus used to elicit it. Graham and Clifton (1966) in a major review of this field suggest that low intensity stimuli eliciting an *orienting response* are usually accompanied by heart rate *deceleration* and stimuli of a high enough intensity to elicit a *defensive* response produce a heart rate *acceleration*. The limits of 'high' and 'low' intensity auditory stimuli cannot be stated without further reservations as Hatton, Berg and Graham (1970) show that there is a marked effect of onset rise time; at 90 dB fast onsets produce heart rate acceleration and slow onsets heart rate deceleration. Furthermore, the nature of the auditory stimulus is important. Graham and Slaby (1973) showed that an 85 dB white noise elicited a diphasic (HR) response of marked acceleration followed by deceleration while an equally intense 1000 Hz pure tone elicited a triphasic response of deceleration–acceleration–deceleration.

With visual stimuli, interesting material normally elicits a deceleratory response interpreted by Lacey (*e.g.* 1967) as indicating the organism's 'openness' to the environment or the 'bradycardia of attention'. In contrast, visual stimuli containing material which has to be 'processed', *e.g.* requiring problem solving or mental arithmetic are usually accompanied by heart rate acceleration.

Up to the time of Graham and Jackson's (1970) review the general finding was that all stimuli produce heart rate acceleration in the newborn and it was not until the age of 3 or 4 months that deceleratory responses became evident. Later work has suggested that the universal finding of acceleration in newborns has to be modified. It now appears that a deceleratory response is likely to be observed in the fully awake neonate and at least part of the reason for acceleration being the commonest form of response is because neonates spend so much time asleep. Other studies, *e.g.* Sameroff, Cashmore and Dykes (1973), Kearsley (1973) and Pomerleau-Malcuit and Clifton (1973) have shown that deceleratory responses may be given by neonates to visual stimuli, to auditory stimuli with slow rise times and to vestibular stimulation. Schacter, Williams, Khachaturian, Tobin, Kruger and Kerr (1971) report mixed acceleration and deceleration to click stimuli.

In summary, in the light of the later data it is not possible to state unequivocally that neonates are

TABLE II

DEVELOPMENTAL CHANGES IN HEART RATE.

	Heart Rate (beats/min.)				
Age	Min.	5%	Mean	95%	Max.
0–24 hours	85	94	119	145	145
1–7 days	100	100	133	175	175
8–30 days	115	115	163	190	190
1–3 months	115	124	154	190	205
3–6 months	115	111	140	179	205
6–12 months	115	112	140	177	175
1–3 years	100	98	126	163	190
3–5 years	55	65	98	132	145
5–8 years	70	70	96	115	145
8–12 years	55	55	79	107	115
12–16 years	55	55	75	102	115

Reproduced from Shinebourne, 1974 (with permission).

incapable of deceleratory responses as had earlier seemed to be the case.

The heart rate response may be elicited at earlier ages than birth. Sontag, Steele and Lewis (1969), and Tanaka and Arayama (1969), for instance, showed that the heart rate response of the foetus in the third trimester of pregnancy was primarily accelerative. Berkson, Wasserman and Behrman (1974) in a study of premature infants showed that cardiac response was typically accelerative.

In 4-month-old infants, Berg, Berg and Graham (1971) showed that a decelerative response was generally given in the alert state and to slow rise time auditory stimuli, and that rapid rise time and states other than alert wakefulness interacted to produce increasing evidence of response acceleration.

This pattern of response is in general that which is reported in adults. Data from older children (9-year-olds) also show an adult pattern (Klorman and Lang, 1972), thus suggesting that an essentially adult pattern of response is established quite early in the child's life.

NON AGE RELATED ASPECTS OF AUTONOMIC ACTIVITY DURING DEVELOPMENT

Weller and Bell (1965) in their study of skin conductance level in neonates, in addition to the effects of 'state' already mentioned, reported the influence of two other variables. Female children had significantly higher conductance levels than males, and children of primiparous mothers had significantly lower conductance levels than children of multiparous mothers. Possible factors confounded with the parity variable are maternal age, length of labour and method of delivery. Weller and Bell suggest that the higher conductance levels of children born to multiparae may indicate a more rapid rate of overcoming lethargy and other residues of birth in these children. They suggest the need to seek confirmation of these results and to establish continuity of these characteristics beyond the first few days of life. This challenge does not appear to have been taken up despite its obvious interest.

Data from a high-risk study in Mauritius (Schulsinger, Mednick, Venables, Raman and Bell, 1975; Venables, 1978) in which 1800 3-year-olds were tested psychophysiologically enabled the effect of mothers' parity to be tested at age 3. Skin conductance level was marginally greater (rather than lower) in those subjects who were only children at the time of testing (p = ·08) in comparison to those who had older brothers or sisters. The two groups of children were, however, significantly different in the numbers of spontaneous fluctuations (NSF) in skin conductance which they produced (p<·001). The NSF were higher in only children than in those with sibs. The extent of equivalence of SCL and NSF as measures of tonic activity is supported by data from Kimmel and Hill (1961). The finding of a lower level of skin conductance in the newborn infants of primiparous as compared with multiparous mothers thus appears to

have been reversed when age 3 is reached. Clearly further studies on this variable are required.

Other more lasting effects on electrodermal activity have been reported by Schulsinger and Mednick (1975) as part of their study on children at familial risk for schizophrenia (Mednick and Schulsinger, 1968). Analysis of their data on both high risk (having a schizophrenic mother) and low risk (having a normal mother) samples showed that amplitude of the SCR and the speed of its recovery were greater in children who had suffered birth complications even when measured 15 years later. This analysis was confirmed with more substantial statistical procedures and reported by Mednick, Schulsinger, Teasdale, Schulsinger, Venables and Rock (1978). Thus, again, the hypothesis that the low conductance shown by the children of primiparous mothers might be due to the more difficult labour in the case appears to be contradicted by these data. Although skin conductance level was measured in one instance and amplitude in the other, these two measures are normally positively correlated.

Schulsinger and Mednick (1975) also report data on the effect of separation on skin conductance activity. The basis for the material was a separation scale 'which expresses the degree to which a child has been free of, or deprived of, the direct or individual care of a parent or parent substitute in the first five years of life'. High degree of separation, in contrast to a low degree, was associated with SCRs of short latency and high amplitude. This finding applies to children who are both at high and low risk for schizophrenia. In contrast, short recovery of the SCR which is related to high genetic risk for schizophrenia does not appear to be related to separation.

The important feature of these data (which have not yet been replicated) is that they indicate that an environmental stressor before age 5 has a lasting effect to age 15. Other data are available which give some indication of the mechanisms which may be involved in the initial production of separation effects.

Hofer and his colleagues (e.g. Hofer, 1975) have shown, using rats as subjects, that there is an interaction between control of heart rate and the role of the mother in supplying nutrition. Heart rate of 2-week-old rats decreased by 40% during 12 to 16 hours after separation from the mother even though fed four hourly.

Meares and Horvath (1974) extended these findings on rats to human infants. They showed that although apparently receiving the same amount of milk, the children of mothers who showed impairment of attention to their children had heart rates during feeding which did not rise in comparison to a control period. This was in contrast to the children of mothers whose attention was not diverted to external stimuli but who paid full attention to their children during feeding who showed increases of heart rate on receiving milk. These data have some parallels to that reported on adult subjects by Christie, Cort and Venables (1976) where it was shown that those subjects who showed heart rate increases on ingestion of food showed lower electrodermal activity (SPL) than those who showed no heart rate increase after food.

The manner in which heart rate interacts with situational determinants of behaviour is exemplified by the work of Sroufe and his colleagues (*e.g.* Sroufe and Waters, 1977). These workers showed, for instance, that wariness in children was associated with heart rate acceleration (a defensive response as described earlier); if, however, there was behavioural avoidance (*e.g.* turning the body away from a stranger) then no heart rate acceleration was seen. They showed gaze aversion in infants followed heart rate acceleration and then subsequent to gaze aversion, heart rate returned to basal level. At this point the infant looked at the stranger again and this could lead to further HR acceleration and then gaze aversion. Learning to modulate arousal in relation to the behavioural reaction to new circumstances appears to happen at a very early age and may readily become a regular reaction pattern.

Another set of data showing an interaction between physiological and behavioural variables is described by Buck (1976). There is a fairly well established concept of a reciprocal relationship between overt and physiological responses. For instance, subjects classed as repressors, showing and reporting little disturbance to unpleasant events, show larger physiological responses than those who show and report large behavioural signs of activation (Byrne, 1964). Similarly, Buck (1977) provides data to show that children aged 4–6 whose spontaneous facial expressions and gestures in relation to emotionally loaded slide pictures could be interpreted by their mothers (via television) showed less electrodermal reactivity than those children who were 'non-communicators'. The importance of these data appears to lie in the extent to which they illustrate the symmetrical interaction between behavioural and physiological events and indicate the necessity to view autonomic activity not merely as having a passive response role but taking part in the modulation of behaviour.

SOME APPLICATIONS; MEASUREMENT OF AUTONOMIC REACTIVITY IN CLINICAL STATES

'Hyperactivity'; 'minimal brain dysfunction'

The data on autonomic activity in children with these labels is not entirely consistent. Dykman, Ackerman and Clements (1971) and Cohen and Douglas (1972) report no differences in electrodermal and cardiac data between hyperactive and control children. However, at the same time, Satterfield and Dawson (1971) reported a lower SCL and fewer spontaneous fluctuations in electrodermal activity in hyperactive as compared to normal children. In a later study, Satterfield, Cantwell, Lesser and Podosin (1972) reported that there was a difference in autonomic activity in those hyperactive children who were good, as against poor methylphenidate responders. Those who had indices indicating a low arousal level (*e.g.* a mean SCL of 16·7 micromhos) showed better clinical improvement under medication than those showing a high arousal level (*e.g.* a mean SCL of 24·4 micromhos—controls having a mean level of 20·0 micromhos). Zahn, Abate, Little and

Wender (1975) carried out a study in which they made a much more extensive investigation of electrodermal activity than had been undertaken by earlier workers in addition to recording heart rate. These workers report no difference in SCL, numbers of spontaneous fluctuations in SC or in basal heart rate between normal and hyperactive children off drugs. They do, however, report differences in responses measured. The hyperactive children in comparison to the normal children show more 'sluggish' SCRs with slower latencies, longer rise times, smaller amplitudes and longer recoveries. The phasic heart rate response of these children also showed smaller deceleration than normal to orienting tone stimuli. In contrast to the Satterfield data the children who showed little clinical improvement with methylphenidate showed lower SCLs than those who improved clinically under medication.

Zahn *et al.* suggest that on the basis of the data available there are two possible models to account for hyperactivity; the one which he favours is that although hyperactive children do not differ from normals in resting, non-medicated levels of arousal, their optimal arousal level, that is, the level producing optimal performance, is higher than normal. This is a modified version of the under-arousal hypothesis of Satterfield which suggests that hyperkinetic behaviour provides the sensory inflow which is necessary to achieve higher and optimal levels of arousal. Porges (1976) presents data on hyperactive children in the context of the concept of autonomic balance, that is, the balance between the activity of the sympathetic and parasympathetic nervous system. The method which Porges uses to measure balance is a complex one and involves the estimation of a coherence function which 'identifies the percentage of heart rate activity shared with respiration'. Porges then uses this measure to examine the autonomic balance of hyperactive children on and off methylphenidate in comparison to that of normal children. His data suggest that hyperactive children off drugs exhibited sympathetic dominance whereas the normal child shows more parasympathetic dominance. The effect of low doses of methylphenidate is to move the balance of the hyperactive child in the direction of parasympathetic dominance; high doses of medication did not have this effect. The clinical improvement with the low dose paralleled the change in autonomic balance.

Porges reviews data which in contrast to that of Satterfield and Zahn suggest a high arousal view of hyperactivity, that is, that the high behavioural activity goes with high physiological arousal. The difference in stance arises particularly perhaps because of the emphasis on heart rate rather than electrodermal indices. Porges, Walter, Korb and Sprague (1975), for instance, show that hyperactive children tend to show heart rate accelerative rather than decelerative responses to stimuli requiring attention—as do, in fact, Zahn *et al.*—and they appropriately suggest that this indicates sympathetic dominance in the hyperactive children.

The difficulty lies in explaining how methylphenidate produces a picture of heart rate deceleration, when it is much simpler to explain how this activating drug produces increases in arousal which are in line with the low arousal model of Satterfield. Porges suggests that the model of Anisman (1975) is appropriate to his data and in relation to the success of sympathomimetic drugs in treating behavioural reactivity. He suggests that 'these catecholaminergic agonists elicit a cholinergic rebound which may facilitate mediated inhibitory behaviors'.

The data which appear to suggest that low physiological reactivity is the accompaniment of high behavioural activity and vice versa are in line with data which have already been reviewed (p. 165). More directly relevant data are presented by Helper, Garfield and Wilcott (1963) in a study of 'emotionally disturbed children'. They showed that high autonomic reactors are rated as less appropriate in affective expression than low reactors. High reactors on SCL were rated as less active motorically than low reactors.

The data available to date suggest that stimulant medication often produces a reduction in behavioural activity and thus supports the notion of reciprocity between overt and covert levels of arousal. However, at this time results of measurement of autonomic activity do not enable strong indications about which functional model may be appropriate to be made.

Refractoriness and delinquency

Follow-up studies of hyperkinetic children suggest that some develop anti-social behaviour in adolescence and later (e.g. Menkes, Rowe and Menkes, 1967; Weiss, Minde and Werry, 1971). Satterfield et al. (1972) suggest that it is 'the hyperkinetic children who come from families with alcoholism and mental illness who do not respond to stimulant treatment and who become anti-social adolescents and adults'. There is thus a possible link from the work on hyperactivity to later difficulty, which may be shown in school. Data also exist which suggest that there are parallels between the behaviour of psychopaths and refractoriness in normal adolescents. Davies and Maliphant (1971a), for instance, show that refractory adolescent boys have high scores on the Pd scale of the M.M.P.I. The general finding (e.g. Hare, 1970) is that psychopaths exhibit small sluggish skin conductance responses with a low mean SCL. Most workers have not shown a consistent relationship between tonic heart rate and psychopathic behaviour and there are few data to show that psychopaths differ from normals in reactivity to simple stimuli; where they do differ is in anticipatory cardiac activity prior to a noxious stimulus.

A study on refractory adolescents by Davies and Maliphant (1971b) suggests that the parallel between psychopathy and refractoriness while provocative is not exact. This study shows that the refractory children had lower mean base heart rates than controls. (Refractory group 75·6 bpm, controls 84·2 bpm.) Change of heart rate under threat or stress was also lower in refractory than in non-refractory boys.

Support for this finding comes from a large scale investigation reported by Wadsworth (1976) based on a sample drawn from the study of Douglas and Blomfield

(1958). At school medical examinations which took place when the children in the study were 11 years of age, pulse rate was noted. A sub-population of 1813 males was examined and delinquents defined as those who according to records either made a court appearance or were cautioned by the police between the ages of 8 and 21 years. Two hundred and sixty-nine subjects were thus classified. The heart rates of the delinquent boys tended to be lower than those who were not delinquent and this was especially the case in those who were sexual offenders or who committed violent crimes.

Additional data in accord with these results is provided by Little (personal communication) who found that 9- and 11-year-old children rated as anti-social by their teachers had lower heart rates than those not so rated. No difference in heart rate between anti-social children and others was found in a group of 7-year-olds.

Zahn et al. (1975) reported that hyperactive children showed 'sluggish' skin conductance responses with lower amplitudes, slower rise times and longer recovery times. Siddle, Nicol and Foggitt (1973) reported lower SCR magnitude as a function of anti-social behaviour in a group of Borstal boys rated as exhibiting high, medium and low anti-social behaviour. A further analysis of the data by Siddle, Mednick, Nicol and Foggitt (1976) showed that the groups were also distinguished on SCR recovery time, the most anti-social children showing the longest recovery time.

Not enough data are available to enable other than tentative statements to be made about the autonomic concomitants of anti-social behaviour in children. There are suggestions, however, of some parallels between this and hyperactivity on the one hand and adult psychopathic behaviour on the other (Hare, 1970), the most evident characteristic being low levels of activity and the sluggish nature of the response.

Children at risk for later psychiatric breakdown

Garmezy (1974) has extensively reviewed the data available on children at risk for schizophrenia. Most of this work uses the 'familial' risk model where one or both of the children's parents are diagnosed as schizophrenic. The pioneering study using measures of autonomic system functioning as major indices is that started in 1962 by Mednick and Schulsinger. These workers have reported their work on several occasions, e.g. Mednick and Schulsinger (1968), Schulsinger and Mednick (1975), Mednick, Schulsinger, Teasdale, Schulsinger, Venables and Rock (1978). In summary it can be said that the strongest predictor of later breakdown with schizophrenic symptoms approximating to Schneider's (1959) first rank list is the recovery limb of the SCR. The SCR measured in 1962 of those who ten years later exhibited schizophrenic symptoms is characterized by short recovery and high amplitude. A single measure which combines these two variables is recovery rate which empirically is correlated with both variables. Mednick et al. (1978) show that an index derived by the product of recovery rate and percentage of responses exhibited to a standard stimulus procedure is a strong predictor of later breakdown in males but not in females.

A derivation of this type of study was mounted in Mauritius in 1972 by Mednick, Schulsinger and Venables. Preliminary reports are to be found in Bell, Mednick, Raman, Schulsinger, Sutton-Smith and Venables (1975), Schulsinger, Mednick, Venables, Raman and Bell (1975), Venables, Mednick, Schulsinger, Raman, Bell, Dalais and Fletcher (1978) and Venables (1978). A population of 1800 3-year-olds was psychophysiologically screened and, from these, 200 were selected for further study. Of these approximately three quarters had electrodermal characteristics which placed them in three sub-classes, having characteristics of (a) fast recovery rate, comparable to those children in Copenhagen who later exhibited breakdown, (b) long recovery time, comparable to those children who show hyperactivity and anti-social behaviour, (c) no electrodermal activity, analogous to a large proportion of the adult schizophrenic population (Gruzelier and Venables, 1972). The other quarter of the sample had 'normal' electrodermal activity.

Venables *et al*. (1978) report a follow-up, in a play situation, of these children at age 6½ years. In summary, the data show that there was an interaction between risk group status and the exposure (or not) experienced by half the group to being placed in a nursery school. The fast recovery rate group, whether or not they had been in a nursery school, showed more constructive play than those control children who had not been in a nursery school; these latter children in turn showed much less constructive play than those control children who had been in a nursery school. The children exhibiting no electrodermal responsivity at age 3 showed less constructive play than the remainder and were more often to be found on the outside of the group, watching and not participating. The group with long electrodermal recovery times, particularly if they had been in the nursery school, show more social interaction with their peers and adults than the remainder of the group.

In summary, these studies indicate that it is possible to predict both later adult behaviour and also intermediate stages of childhood behaviour from autonomic measures taken some years earlier.

CONCLUSIONS

It will be evident from the material which has been reviewed that there are probably more lacunae in the data than fully satisfactory coverage. Nevertheless, sufficient results are available to indicate the value of work in the area, both in its own right and as an essential underpinning for more behavioural studies. A valuable procedural advance would be the adoption of more standardized techniques which would provide age-related norms against which deviations could be viewed. However, in the meantime robust findings transcend the variation in techniques used and provide a useful basis from which to undertake further studies.

ACKNOWLEDGEMENTS

This review was prepared while in receipt of grant no. MH 27777 from the U.S. Public Health Service and grant no. 6883/I.5 from the Wellcome Trust.

REFERENCES

Anisman, H. (1975). Time dependent variations in aversively motivated behaviors: Nonassociative effects of cholinergic and catecholaminergic activity. *Psychological Review*, **82**, 359–385.

Appel, M. A., Campos, J. J., Silverman, S. Z. and Conway, E. (1971). Electrodermal responding of the human infant. Paper presented at the meeting of the Society for Research in Child Development, Minneapolis.

Bell, B., Mednick, S. A., Raman, A. C., Schulsinger, F., Sutton-Smith, B. and Venables, P. H. (1975). A longitudinal psychophysiological study of three year old Mauritian children: Preliminary report. *Developmental Medicine and Child Neurology*, **17**, 320–324.

Benjamin, L. S. (1963). Statistical treatment of the law of initial values (LIV) in autonomic research: A review and a recommendation. *Psychosomatic Medicine*, **25**, 556–566.

Benjamin, L. S. (1967). Facts and artifacts in using analysis of covariance to 'undo' the law of initial values. *Psychophysiology*, **4**, 187–206.

Berg, K. M., Berg, W. K. and Graham, F. K. (1971). Infant heart rate response as a function of stimulus and state. *Psychophysiology*, **8**, 30–44.

Berkson, G., Wasserman, G. A. and Behrman, R. E. (1974). Heart rate response to an auditory stimulus in premature infants. *Psychophysiology*, **11**, 244–246.

Block, J. D. and Bridger, W. H. (1962). The law of initial values in psychophysiology: A reformulation in terms of experimental and theoretical considerations. *Annals of the New York Academy of Science*, **98**, 1229–1241.

Brener, J. (1967). Heart rate. In P. H. Venables and I. Martin (Eds.) *A Manual of Psychophysiological Methods*. Amsterdam: North-Holland. Chapter 3.

Buck, R. (1976). *Human Motivation and Emotion*. New York: Wiley.

Buck, R. (1977). Non-verbal communication of affect in pre-school children: Relationships with personality and skin conductance. *Journal of Personality and Social Psychology*, **35**, 225–236.

Byrne, D. (1964). Repression-sensitization as a dimension of personality. In B. A. Maher (Ed.) *Progress in Experimental Personality Research*. New York: Academic Press.

Campos, J. J., Tursky, B. and Conway, E. (1970). Skin potential and skin resistance responses of the very young infant. Paper presented at the meeting of the Society for Psychophysiological Research, New Orleans, November.

Christie, M. J., Cort, J. and Venables, P. H. (1976). Individual differences in post prandial state: laboratory explorations with palmar skin potentials. *Journal of Psychosomatic Research*, **20**, 501–508.

Clifton, R. K. (1974). Cardiac conditioning and orienting in the infant. Chapter 24 in P. A. Obrist, A. H. Black, J. Brener and L. V. di Cara (Eds.) *Cardiovascular Psychophysiology*. Chicago: Aldine.

Cohen, D. H. and MacDonald, R. L. (1974). A selective review of central neural pathways involved in cardiovascular control. Chapter 2 in P. A. Obrist, A. H. Black, J. Brener and L. V. di Cara (Eds.) *Cardiovascular Psychophysiology*. Chicago: Aldine.

Cohen, N. J. and Douglas, V. I. (1972). Characteristics of the orienting response in hyperactive and normal children. *Psychophysiology*, **9**, 238–245.

Crowell, D. H., Blurton, L. B., Kobayashi, L. R., McFarland, J. L. and Yang, R. K. (1976). Studies in early infant learning: Classical conditioning of the neonatal heart rate. *Developmental Psychology*, **12**, 373–397.

Crowell, D. H., Davis, C. M., Chun, B. J. and Spellacy, F. J. (1965). Galvanic skin reflex in newborn humans. *Science*, **148**, 1108–1111.

Davis, J. A. and Dobbing, J. (Eds.) (1974) *Scientific Foundations of Paediatrics*. London: Heinemann.

Davies, J. G. V. and Maliphant, R. (1971a). Refractory behaviour at school in normal adolescent males in relation to psychopathy and early experience. *Journal of Child Psychology and Psychiatry*, **12**, 35–41.

Davies, J. G. V. and Maliphant, R. (1971b). Autonomic responses of male adolescents exhibiting refractory behaviour in school. *Journal of Child Psychology and Psychiatry*, **12**, 115–127.

Douglas, J. W. B. and Blomfield, J. M. (1958). *Children Under Five.* London: Allen and Unwin.

Douglas, R. J. (1972). Pavlovian conditioning and the brain. In R. A. Boakes and M. S. Halliday (Eds.) *Inhibition and Learning.* London: Academic Press. Chapter 20.

Dykman, R. A., Ackerman, P. T. and Clements, S. D. (1971). Specific learning difficulties: An attentional deficit syndrome. In H. R. Myklebust (Ed.) *Progress in Learning Difficulties.* New York: Grune and Stratton.

Edelberg, R. (1967). Electrical properties of the skin. Chapter 1 in C. C. Brown (Ed.) *Methods in Psychophysiology.* Baltimore: Williams and Wilkins.

Edelberg, R. (1971). Electrical properties of the skin. Chapter 15 in H. R. Elden (Ed.) *Biophysical Properties of the Skin.* New York: Wiley.

Edelberg, R. (1972). Electrical activity of the skin: Its measurement and uses in psychophysiology. In N. S. Greenfield and R. A. Sternbach (Eds.) *Handbook of Psychophysiology.* New York: Holt, Rinehart and Winston. Chapter 9.

Fowles, D. C. (1974). Mechanisms of electrodermal activity. In R. F. Thompson and M. M. Patterson (Eds.) *Bioelectric recording techniques.* Part C. New York: Academic Press. Chapter 9.

Forsyth, R. P. (1974). Mechanisms of the cardiovascular response to environmental stressors. In P. A. Obrist, A. H. Black, J. Brener and L. V. di Cara (Eds.) *Cardiovascular Psychophysiology.* Chicago: Aldine. Chapter 1.

Garmezy, N. (with Streitman, S.) (1974). Children at risk: The search for the antecedents of schizophrenia. Part II Ongoing research programs, issues and intervention. *Schizophrenic Bulletin*, **8**, 14–90 and **9**, 55–125.

Gatchel, R. J. and Lang, P. J. (1973). Accuracy of psychophysical judgements and physiological response amplitude. *Journal of Experimental Psychology*, **98**, 175–183.

Graham, F. K. and Clifton, R. K. (1966). Heart rate change as a component of the orienting response. *Psychological Bulletin*, **65**, 305–320.

Graham, F. K. and Jackson, J. C. (1970). Arousal systems and infant heart rate responses. In H. Reese and L. Lipsitt (Eds.) *Advances in Child Development and Behavior, Vol. 5.* New York: Academic Press.

Graham, F. K. and Slaby, D. A. (1973). Differential heart rate changes to equally intense white noise and tone. *Psychophysiology*, **10**, 347–362.

Grings, W. W. (1974). Recording of electrodermal phenomena. In R. F. Thompson and M. M. Patterson (Eds.) *Bioelectric recording techniques Part C.* New York: Academic Press. Chapter 10.

Gruzelier, J. H. and Venables, P. H. (1972). Skin conductance orienting activity in a heterogeneous sample of schizophrenics. *Journal of Nervous and Mental Disease*, **155**, 277–287.

Gunn, C. G., Wolf, S., Block, R. T. and Person, R. J. (1972). Psychophysiology of the cardiovascular system. In N. S. Greenfield and R. A. Sternbach (Eds.) *Handbook of Psychophysiology.* New York: Holt, Rinehart and Winston.

Hare, R. D. (1970). *Psychopathy.* New York: Wiley.

Hatton, H. M., Berg, W. K. and Graham, F. K. (1970). Effects of acoustic rise time on heart rate response. *Psychonomic Science*, **19**, 101–103.

Helper, M. M., Garfield, S. L. and Wilcott, R. C. (1963). Electrodermal activity and rated behavior in emotionally disturbed children. *Journal of Abnormal and Social Psychology*, **66**, 600–603.

Hofer, M. A. (1975). Infant separation responses and the maternal role. *Biological Psychiatry*, **10**, 149–153.

Hutt, S. J., Lenard, H. G. and Prechtl, H. F. R. (1969). Psychophysiological studies in newborn infants. In L. P. Lipsitt and H. W. Reese (Eds.) *Advances in Child Development and Behaviour Vol. 4.* New York: Academic Press.

Jones, H. E. (1930). The galvanic skin reflex in infancy. *Child Development*, **1**, 106–110.

Jones, R. H., Crowell, D. H. and Kapuniai, L. E. (1969). Change detection model for serially correlated data. *Psychological Bulletin*, **71**, 352–358.

Juniper, K. and Dykman, R. H. (1967). Skin resistance, sweat-gland counts, salivary flow, and gastric secretion: Age, race, and sex differences and intercorrelations. *Psychophysiology*, **4**, 216–222.

Kaye, H. (1964). Skin conductance in the human neonate. *Child Development*, **35**, 1297–1305.

Kearsley, R. (1973). Neonatal response to auditory stimulation: A demonstration of orienting behavior. *Child Development*, **44**, 582–590.

Kimmel, H. D. and Hill, F. A. (1961). A comparison of two electrodermal measures of response to stress. *Journal of Comparative and Physiological Psychology*, **54**, 395–397.

Klorman, R. and Lang, P. J. (1972). Cardiac responses to signal and non-signal tasks in 9 year olds. *Psychonomic Science*, **28**, 299–300.

Lacey, J. I. (1956). The evaluation of autonomic responses: Toward a general solution. *Annals of the New York Academy of Science*, **67**, 123–143.

Lacey, J. I. (1967). Somatic response patterning and stress: Some revisions of activation theory. In M. H. Appley and R. Trumbull (Eds.) *Psychological Stress.* New York: Appleton-Century-Crofts. Chapter 2.

Lewis, M. (1974). The cardiac response during infancy. In R. F. Thompson and M. M. Patterson (Eds.) *Bioelectric recording techniques Part C.* New York: Academic Press. Chapter 8.

Lykken, D. T. and Venables, P. H. (1971). Direct measurement of skin conductance: A proposal for standardization. *Psychophysiology*, **8**, 656–672.

Meares, R. and Horvath, T. (1974). A physiological approach to the study of attachment: The mother's attention and her infant's heart rate. *Australian and New Zealand Journal of Psychiatry*, **8**, 72–76.

Mednick, S. A. and Schulsinger, F. (1968). Some pre-morbid characteristics related to breakdown in children with schizophrenic mothers. In D. Rosenthal and S. S. Kety (Eds.) *The Transmission of Schizophrenia.* New York: Pergamon Press, 267–291.

Mednick, S. A., Schulsinger, F., Teasdale, T. W., Schulsinger, H., Venables, P. H. and Rock, D. R. (1978). Schizophrenia in high-risk children: Sex differences in pre-disposing factors. Chapter in G. Serban (Ed.) *Cognitive Defects in the Development of Mental Illness.* New York: Brunner/Mazel.

Menkes, M. M., Rowe, J. S. and Menkes, J. H. (1967). A twenty-five year follow up study on the hyperkinetic child with minimal brain dysfunction. *Pediatrics*, **39**, 393–399.

Peiper, A. (1924). Untersuchungen uber der galvanischer Hautreflex (Psychogalvanischer Reflex) im Kindesalter. *Jahrbuch fur Kinderheilk*, **107**, 139–150.

Pomerleau-Malcuit, A. and Clifton, R. K. (1973). Neonatal heart rate responses to tactile, auditory and vestibular stimulation in different states. *Child Development*, **44**, 485–496.

Porges, S. W. (1976). Peripheral and neurochemical parallels of psychopathology: A psychophysiological model relating autonomic imbalance to hyperactivity, psychopathy and autism. In H. W. Reese (Ed.) *Advances in Child Development and Behavior Vol. 11.* New York: Academic Press.

Porges, S. W., Walter, G. F., Korb, R. J. and Sprague, R. L. (1975). The influences of methylphenidate on heart rate and behavioral measures of attention in hyperactive children. *Child Development*, **46**, 727–733.

Prechtl, H. F. R. (1965). Problems of behavioral studies in the newborn infant. In D. S. Lehrman and R. Hinde (Eds.) *Advances in the Study of Behavior Vol. 1.* New York: Academic Press.

Prechtl, H. F. R. and Beintema, D. J. (1964). The neurological examination of the full-term newborn infant. *Clinics in Developmental Medicine No. 12.* London: Heinemann.

Pribram, K. H. and McGuiness, D. (1975). Arousal, activation and effort in the control of attention. *Psychological Review*, **82**, 116–149.

Rickles, W. H. and Day, J. L. (1968). Electrodermal activity in non palmar sites. *Psychophysiology*, **4**, 421–435.

Sameroff, A., Cashmore, T. F. and Dykes, A. (1973). Heart rate deceleration during visual fixation in human newborns. *Developmental Psychology*, **8**, 117–119.

Satterfield, J. H., Cantwell, D. P., Lesser, L. I. and Podosin, R. L.

(1972). Physiological studies of the hyperkinetic child I. *American Journal of Psychiatry*, **128**, 1418–1424.

Satterfield, J. H. and Dawson, M. E. (1971). Electrodermal correlates of hyperactivity in children. *Psychophysiology*, **8**, 191–197.

Schacter, J., Williams, T. A., Khachaturian, Z., Tobin, M., Kruger, R. and Kerr, J. (1971). Heart rate response to auditory clicks in neonates. *Psychophysiology*, **8**, 163–179.

Schneider, K. (1959). *Clinical Psychopathology*. M. W. Hamilton (trans.). New York: Grune and Stratton.

Schneiderman, N., Dauth, G. W. and Van Dercar, D. H. (1974). Electrocardiogram: Techniques and analysis. In R. F. Thompson and M. M. Patterson (Eds.) *Bioelectric Recording Techniques Part C*. New York: Academic Press. Chapter 7.

Schulsinger, F. and Mednick, S. A. (1975). Nature-nurture aspects of schizophrenia: Early detection and prevention. In M. H. Lader (Ed.) *Studies of Schizophrenia*. Ashford: Headley. Chapter 6.

Schulsinger, F., Mednick, S. A., Venables, P. H., Raman, A. C. and Bell, B. (1975). Early detection and prevention of mental illness: The Mauritian project. *Neuropsychobiology*, **1**, 166–179.

Shinebourne, E. A. (1974). Growth and development of the cardiovascular system. In J. A. Davis and J. Dobbing (Eds.) *Scientific Foundations of Paediatrics*. London: Heinemann. Chapter 13B.

Siddle, D. A. T., Mednick, S. A., Nicol, A. R. and Foggitt, R. H. (1976). Skin conductance recovery in anti-social adolescents. *British Journal of Social and Clinical Psychology*, **15**, 425–428.

Siddle, D. A. T., Nicol, A. R. and Foggitt, R. H. (1973). Habituation and overextinction of the GSR component of the orienting response in anti-social adolescents. *British Journal of Social and Clinical Psychology*, **12**, 303–308.

Sontag, L. W., Steele, W. G. and Lewis, M. (1969). The fetal and maternal cardiac response to environmental stress. *Human development*, **12**, 1–9.

Sroufe, L. A. and Waters, E. (1977). Heart rate as a convergent measure in clinical and developmental research. *Merrill-Palmer Quarterly*, **23**, 3–27.

Stechler, G., Bradford, S. and Levy, H. (1966). Attention in the newborn: Effect on motility and skin potential. *Science*, **151**, 1246–1248.

Steinschneider, A. (1967). Developmental psychophysiology. In Y. Brackbill (Ed.) *Infancy and Early Childhood*. New York: Free Press. Chapter 1.

Steinschneider, A. and Lipton, E. L. (1965). Individual differences in autonomic responsivity, problems of measurement. *Psychosomatic Medicine*, **27**, 446–456.

Stern, J. A. (1968). Toward a developmental psychophysiology: My look into the crystal ball. *Psychophysiology*, **4**, 403–420.

Tanaka, Y. and Arayama, T. (1969). Fetal responses to acoustic stimuli. *Practice in otorhinolaryngology*, **31**, 269–273.

Venables, P. H. (1978). Psychophysiology and psychometrics. *Psychophysiology*. **15**, 302–315.

Venables, P. H. and Christie, M. J. (1973). Mechanisms, instrumentation, recording techniques and quantification of responses. In W. F. Prokasy and D. C. Raskin (Eds.) *Electrodermal activity in psychological research*. New York: Academic Press. Chapter 1.

Venables, P. H., Fletcher, R. P., Mednick, S. A., Schulsinger, F. and Cheeneebash, R. (1980). Aspects of development of electrodermal and cardiac activity between 5 and 25 years. In preparation.

Venables, P. H. and Martin, I. (1967). Skin resistance and skin potential. In P. H. Venables and I. Martin (Eds.) *A Manual of Psychophysiological Methods*. Amsterdam: North-Holland. Chapter 2.

Venables, P. H., Mednick, S. A., Schulsinger, F., Raman, A. C., Bell, B., Dalais, J. C. and Fletcher, R. P. (1978). Screening for risk of mental illness. In G. Serban (Ed.) *Cognitive Defects in the Development of Mental Illness*. New York: Brunner/Mazel.

Verbov, J. and Baxter, J. (1974). Onset of palmar sweating in newborn infants. *British Journal of Dermatology*, **90**, 269–276.

Wadsworth, M. E. J. (1976). Delinquency, pulse rates and early emotional deprivation. *British Journal of Criminology*, **16**, 245–256.

Wang, G. H. (1964). *Neural Control of Sweating*. Madison: University of Wisconsin Press.

Weiss, G., Minde, K. and Werry, J. S. (1971). The hyperactive child VIII: Five year follow up. *Archives of General Psychiatry*, **24**, 409–414.

Weller, G. M. and Bell, R. Q. (1965). Basal skin conductance and neonatal state. *Child Development*, **36**, 647–657.

Wenger, M. A. and Ellington, M. (1943). The measurement of autonomic balance in children. *Psychosomatic Medicine*, **5**, 241–253.

Wilder, J. (1957). The law of initial values in neurology and psychiatry: Facts and problems. *Journal of Nervous and Mental Diseases*, **125**, 73–86.

Wilder, J. (1958). Modern psychophysiology and the law of initial values. *American Journal of Psychotherapy*, **12**, 199–221.

Wilson, R. S. (1974). CARDIVAR The statistical analysis of heart rate data. *Psychophysiology*, **11**, 76–85.

Zahn, T. P., Abate, F., Little, B. C. and Wender, P. H. (1975). Minimal brain dysfunction, stimulant drugs and autonomic nervous system activity. *Archives of General Psychiatry*, **32**, 381–387.

SECTION III

COGNITION

16. PERCEPTION

RICHARD D. WALK

Perception refers to the process by which we sense the world. We sense its objects and its patterns of varying complexity, we sense its heights and its depths, its bright colours and neutral colours, its roughness and smoothness. We interpret its sounds, in direction and in meaning and some sounds, whether musical or speech sounds, are only understood by a few. We also respond to a variety of tastes and odours. Given the complex physical world, how do we come to respond as we do? Do we come equipped to respond to all of its qualities in all of their complexity? Do we mature to respond to it? Must we learn through experience with the world? Nativism, maturation and empiricism have been mentioned above, and stressed in different ways by theorists and researchers, as foundations for perception ever since the study of perception began.

A general answer, founded in recent research, would seem to be that the perceptual world is organized from birth. This seems to stress nativism, but both maturation and experience also play important roles in perception.

The perceptual world is organized from birth in the sense that elementary discrimination of pattern, colour, taste, space, sound and touch can be demonstrated at a very early age. After the first few weeks the senses develop towards finer discrimination, though the precise course of this development and the role of experience in it is not yet one on which all agree. For hearing, for example, some sounds discriminated soon after birth may be lost through normal experience in the speech environment of one's native language.

This chapter will consider perception with particular reference to the perception of the child and then will shift to focus on disorders of perception. The chapter will be divided into three main portions: the basic analysers, perception and development, and perceptual abnormalities. The basic analysers will consider, in brief, the perceptual equipment of the infant at birth and thereafter as regards basic discrimination by the sense organs. The section on perceptual development will focus on form perception, space perception and auditory perception. Disorders of perception will treat, in brief, stereopsis, synchrony of movement (perception and aging, and perception and the brain). The chapter is brief. Excellent treatments of perceptual development can be found in Gibson (1969) and in Pick and Pick (1970) and of general perception in Kaufman (1974) and in Hochberg (1978).

THE BASIC ANALYSERS

All of the sensory systems of the infant are developed at birth and all function. For further information on normal development *see* Peiper (1963) and Kessen, Haith and Salapatek (1970). While all of the sensory systems are developed enough to function at birth, not all are equally developed, some are more immature at birth than others. The sequence of sensory development in the embryo is tactual, then vestibular, auditory and, finally, visual (Gottlieb, 1971).

The visual system develops late. The infant can see at birth with visual acuity of 20/150 to 20/400, but the eyes are not well coordinated, convergence of both eyes develops during the first 4–6 months, accommodation develops over the first 2 months, the fovea of the eye is immature at birth and develops during the next 4 months. Behaviourally, the neonate fixates on contours in the environment, but it does not search the visual stimulus; initial search is quite passive. Researchers who work with the visual perception of very young infants generally observe where one eye is looking because of the faulty eye coordination.

An example of research that reveals information on basic visual capacities is research which shows that the young infant can discriminate colours. Bornstein, Kessen and Weiskopf (1976) used an habituation paradigm to investigate the colour perception of 4-month-old infants. They hypothesized that wavelengths across a colour boundary would be discriminated while wavelengths of equal distance on the colour continuum within a colour-naming boundary would not be discriminated. The wavelengths were equated for luminance. The infants were habituated to one wavelength (exposed to it until it no longer elicited so much attention) and then presented, in random order, with (1) the old wavelength, (2) a new wavelength that crossed a colour boundary, (3) a new wavelength equally distant from the old one that crossed no colour boundary. The infants looked more at the new colour than at the old habituated one or at the new wavelength within the same colour category. By this method, the infants divided the spectrum into colours of blue, green, yellow and red, showing excellent perception of colours.

Auditory structures are much more advanced at birth than are visual structures. The cochlea has adult dimensions at birth, for example, and myelination of the auditory nerve is complete, while myelination of the visual nerve is completed during the first year. But the auditory cortex, as with other cortical structures, is very immature at birth so that the cortical evoked response is the last of the auditory potential components to attain maturity. The auditory threshold of the infant, however, is only about 10 db less than that of the adult, not a large amount.

The newborn has more tastebuds than the adult and discriminates tastes, particularly sugars, from birth. Salt, sour and bitter are more difficult to distinguish. The newborn also discriminates different concentrations of glucose and sucrose (Nowlis and Kessen, 1976). In their experiment the amount of pressure exerted by the tongue was a function of the concentration level of the substance, and more pressure was exerted for sucrose than for glucose. This technique shows both discrimination between substances and of concentrations within a substance.

Newborn infants discriminate among odours. Infants reacted to acetic acid, anise, asafoetida and phenylethyl alcohol more than to a control neutral odour (Engen, Lipsitt and Kaye, 1963). The sensitivity of the infants also increased over the first four days after birth. The threshold for a reaction to an asafoetida solution declined from a strength of 60% needed on the first day to about a 15% solution required for a reaction on the fourth day.

While the basic sensory systems are developed at birth or soon after, the brain develops much more slowly, reaching adult size around age 6. The attentional systems also mature slowly. When the young infant searches a stimulus with its eyes the search is awkward, often confined to a part of the field, a search that continues to improve throughout infancy and afterwards. Studies of eye movements during visual search after infancy continue to show, as the child matures, more and more attention to the most informative portions of the stimulus, with the adult pattern of visual searching not reached until after the age of 6 years. The same is true of tactual scanning. The 3-year-old child is relatively passive in palpating a bar to estimate its length, and active searching with the fingers continues to develop over the early school years. While a study of the basic analysers shows us that the sensory systems are functional at an early age, the study of attention shows that it takes many years before the child can utilize the sensory systems to extract complex information as efficiently from the environment as can the adult.

PERCEPTION AND DEVELOPMENT

This section is divided into three parts: visual form perception, visual space perception, and auditory perception. This is just a partial sampling of the field; both Gibson (1969) and Pick and Pick (1970) give more extended treatments, in depth as well as in breadth.

Form perception

When does the infant develop the perception of form? What is the course of this development? Is there improvement, and, if so, when is the improvement completed?

The infant appears to have rudimentary form perception at birth. Fantz (1961) has shown that the newborn will fixate (look at) patterns rather than at plain surfaces. This is defined as a 'preference' (more attention to) vertically striped black and white stripes than to plain grey. This preference can be used as a measure of visual acuity and over the first 5 months the infant improves from acuity of about 20/400 in the first month to about 20/100 at 5 months, a preference for $\frac{1}{8}$ in stripes over grey at birth to $\frac{1}{32}$ in stripes over grey at 5 months.

The infant also appears to have a preference for sheer amount of contour or changes in transition from one edge to another. Black and white checkered patterns illustrate such patterns and the infant prefers to look at finer and finer checkered patterns as it matures, even when the other stimulus pattern is also checkered. In other patterns where the elements are not checked the preference simply seems to be that of the most contoured, a preference that changes with age. The fascination with such patterns by the young infant is such as to suspect that the infant is using contour to help develop the visual system.

With advanced development the infant changes from a preference for contour to a preference for more organized properties of the visual stimulus. The 1-month-old looks more at vertical stripes than at a bullseye pattern of equivalent contour. By 3-4 months of age the bullseye pattern is preferred, an apparent preference for curved elements over straight lines (Ruff and Birch, 1974).

The maturing infant also prefers face-like stimulus patterns (Gibson, 1969). The emergence of the preference for face-like patterns is difficult to trace because some features of interest for the youngest infants, birth to 1 month, may simply be for interesting contours or attraction to the eyes. After 2 months of age the infant looks more at a regular face than at one made of the same elements but 'scrambled' so the arrangement is no longer a face but a rather weird one. At around 2-3 months the eyes become especially important to the infant and by age 5 months the mouth is noticed. Around 6 months of age female faces begin to be differentiated from male faces and around 6-7 months of age the infant can tell familiar faces from unfamiliar ones.

The study of facial recognition permits a slight digression. The 1-2-month-old infant smiles to real faces but also to a piece of white cardboard with black ovals on it. The smile is one facial expression that is universally recognized. Even in primitive cultures that have apparently never before seen photographs the smiling face is recognized as such. Consider, too, the rhesus monkey. If reared in isolation, with no contact with other monkeys, and then shown photographs, the infant rhesus recognizes the pictures that show the threat gesture, the gesture that maintains dominance relations within the colony (Sackett, 1966). Is it not hopeful for the future of man that an affiliative expression, the smile, is recognized so early and so universally?

When does form perception begin? When is it fully developed? The infant appears to have rudimentary form perception at birth and then to discriminate more and more fine distinctions, and also to focus on more organized aspects of the visual stimulus patterns. But one cannot say that the perception of form is completed by 6–7 months of age. The perception of form continues to improve until the early school years and perhaps thereafter. Two examples will suffice. Children starting to read have difficulty discriminating b's from d's and p's from q's, a mirror image reversal. Davidson (1935) reported that 87% of kindergarten children confused b with d and 96% confused q with p. It was not until the age of 7½ that 75% of her subjects made no errors. Children are also much worse than adults in discriminating hidden figures, figures hidden within other figures. Ghent (1956) had young children discriminate figures that overlapped each other and figures where the figure to be found was embedded within another one. By age 7–8 the children were perfect in searching for overlapping figures, but they were still making errors in searching for embedded ones. If one may extrapolate from this: a child who is less than 10 years of age might not be of much help on a hunt where eggs or prey were to be found that blended in with the background. The deficit is not an acuity one but, rather, a perceptual-cognitive one in separating out organized patterns that share contours. We will return to this topic when brain damage is discussed under perceptual abnormalities.

Form perception develops, thus, from perception of simple aspects of visual form.to more complex aspects of form perception. Forms themselves are complex and we have no consensus on how they should be classified. The development seems to be one of identification of simple figures in infancy through differentiation of complex figures sometime before puberty, but sophisticated form perception probably requires extensive training: artists and architects would be examples of those whose form perception skills are of a higher order.

Space perception

Space perception is like form perception in that it appears to be present at birth and then to develop towards increased precision. The exact course of this development has so far been sketched in only its vaguest outlines.

What measure of space perception do we use? There are many, and they may depend on the maturity of other systems. For example, bring an object towards the eye of an infant and it will blink its eyes, an indicator, with proper controls, that the child discriminates distance in some rudimentary form. An earlier recognition of the approaching object might appear through another muscular response or through an autonomic response like heart-rate.

The reaction to an approaching object is a good example of both the disagreements and the complexities in the assessment of early space perception. Bower, Broughton and Moore (1970b) and Ball and Tronick (1971) found that infants less than 1 month old responded to the approach of a real object or to an expanding shadow by pulling their heads back and raising their arms as if to avoid a blow. Yonas et al. (1977) failed to replicate these results in young infants. Instead, they found no such reactions in 1–2-month-olds, the beginnings of discrimination in 4–5-month-olds, and avoidance reactions in 8–9-month-olds. However, White (1971) found that the eye blink response to an approaching object developed between 2 and 4 months of age. Not unrelated to the topic are studies of the individual cells in the visual cortex. Such cells, termed 'zoom' cells because they react to approaching objects, have been found in the human adult (Marg and Adams, 1970) and the rhesus monkey (Zeki, 1974). We have no way of knowing whether visual cortical cells in the human infant react to approaching objects. Suppose they did, and no other reaction could be discovered in the nervous system. When, by this measure, would 'space perception' be present in the human? With the reaction of the cortical cell? At a later time when the heart-rate changed in response to the approach of the object? When the eyes blinked? When the child put up its hand to avoid a collision?

Infants also reach out towards objects. Bower, Broughton and Moore (1970a) found that infants 6 to 11 days old reached towards a bright orange sphere, and were accurate, on the average, within 5° (1·5 cm). Bower (1972) also found that 7–15-day-old infants would reach towards a solid object, but they would not reach to its photograph, indicating the discrimination of solid from flat as well.

Another indicator of space perception is stereoscopic vision, the combination of two flat images to produce visual depth. Bower et al. (1970a) had young (8–31-day-old) infants wear goggles with polaroid filters. Light projected from a real object through the filters produced a three-dimensional virtual object 8 inches in front of the child when the goggles were worn. Precise reaching to the virtual object was the index of the presence of stereoscopic vision.

Visual placing is reaching out towards a visual surface. The infant must be supported by its trunk to leave the hands free. The response, also called the 'parachute response' (Paine and Oppé, 1966), develops about the age of 6 months. This figure derives from recent research by C. P. Walters (unpub.) and is about two months ahead of the norms in Paine and Oppé (1966). The Walters' research was better controlled than previous research and used visual surfaces presented beneath glass. The infants showed a placing response when the surface was directly under the glass but usually they did not respond if the surface was some distance below the glass. The reaction is illustrated in Fig. 1.

Crawling infants (7–12 months old) will avoid a visual

Fig. 1. An infant making a visual placing response. The pattern is under transparent plastic. Photo by L. A. Rothblatt.

cliff, approaching a visual surface that is close to them and avoiding a visual surface some distance from them. A heavy plate of glass makes the physical surface the same for both sides (Walk and Gibson, 1961). Schwartz, Campos and Baisel (1973) placed 5-month and 9-month-old infants on the glass of the deep side, the visual surface some distance below the child. The heart rate of the 5-month-olds decelerated over the apparent depth, which they interpreted as 'attention,' and the heart rate of the 9-month-olds accelerated, interpreted by them as 'fear'. Walk (1969) found that more 7–9-month-olds were coaxed over the deep side of the visual cliff than were 10–13-month-olds, when the visual surface was 10 inches below the glass, though no age differences appeared for visual depths of 20 inches and 40 inches. The interpretation was that the difference was not in space perception *per se*, but in the discrimination by motion parallax. Much older children were taught by Carpenter and Carpenter (1958) to push a panel when vertical $\frac{1}{8}$ inch stripes moved. The threshold for the detection of motion was much better for the 8-year 5-month-old than it was for the 6-year 9-month-old child. This means that even as late

as 8–9 years of age children may be improving in their detection of movement.

What does this all mean? A first guess is that space perception is present very early, probably innately, and that it continues to improve for many years thereafter. Improve in what way? Does stereoscopic vision improve as well as motion discrimination?

The strategy so far has been to investigate the earliest appearance of spatial responses. At the present time there is some disagreement as to the earliest indicators of space perception, but general agreement that they are present by 2–4 months of age. The precise course after that, the influences on it, a general understanding of spatial relations in all their complexity as related to perceptual development—this is for the future.

Auditory perception

The auditory system, it will be remembered, is better developed than the visual system at birth. One would expect auditory behaviour to be better developed as well.

The infant recognizes the voice of the mother when it is less than 1 week old (André-Thomas and Autgaerden, 1966). In this experiment the voice of the mother and the voice of a stranger called to the infant, and the infant looked to the mother, not to the stranger. For one mother, with twins, one twin looked at her when she called its own name, not when she called for its twin. The André-Thomas and Autgaerden research is supported by other research on the recognition of the mother's voice in early infancy (Hammond, 1970; Mills and Melhuish, 1974).

The infant also can discriminate the source of sound at birth. The most frequently cited experiment is that of Wertheimer (1961) who noticed that the newborn oriented towards clicking noises with head and eyes towards the source of the sound. Subsequent work (Leventhal and Lipsitt, 1964) has confirmed that sounds are locatable at birth but it is questionable whether neonates also turn their eyes to *visually* locate the sound.

Auditory stimulation and the motor responses of the human infant are apparently synchronized soon after birth, as if the sound of human speech had a special meaning from the very beginning. The infants, 1 to 4 days of age, were played human voices and other sounds on a tape recorder. The infants were filmed as the tape was played. The infants moved synchronously to the human voices, American English and Chinese, and their movement was not synchronized nearly as precisely to tapping sounds and to disconnected vowel sounds (Condon, 1977). This experiment shows that the infant at birth is 'programmed' to respond to human speech, responding to the special nature of human communication months before it utters its first word.

Interesting developmental research on audition concerns the development of the perception of language (*see* Strange and Jenkins, 1978, for a fuller treatment of this topic). This research is particularly relevant to the nature-nurture issue and to the role of experience in perception. While the picture is by no means clear as yet, the findings are exciting.

We perceive certain sounds categorically (Eimas *et al.*, 1971). A speech synthesizer can vary voice onset time to produce a continuous consonant series from b to p or d to t (the first consonant of these pairs is voiced, the second voiceless). We both hear and discriminate categorically: at a certain point on the continuum we shift from hearing 'd' to hearing 't'. This is very different from pitch or colour. We may only verbally identify or label a few colours or a few pitches, but we can discriminate thousands of them.

The discrimination of the young infant can be measured by habituation procedures (previously discussed for infants for the discrimination of colours). If the experimenter keeps presenting a sound like a 'b', the infant will habituate to it, meaning that the heart rate might decline slightly or the number of sucks per minute on a pacifier might decrease as the infant gets used to hearing the 'b' sound. If the experimenter makes a sound on the synchronizer that sounds like a 'p' to us, the infant detects the change and shows it by a change in heart rate or by sucking more. This experiment was performed by Eimas, Siqueland, Jusczyk and Vigorito (1971) using a sucking response with 1- and 4-month-old infants to show that soon after birth infants perceive consonant sounds categorically.

Research with adults, however, reveals that the language one speaks may change the points where the categorical distinctions are made or even eliminate them altogether. The r–l distinction is made in English, not in Japanese. A synthetic r–l continuum was perceived correctly by Americans, but not discriminated by Japanese adults (Miyawaki *et al.*, 1975). American infants, 2–3 months old, on the other hand, did discriminate the r–l distinctions (Eimas, 1975). This could mean that infants can discriminate the r–l sound even though some adults cannot, though, obviously, the next step is to carry out the Eimas (1975) research with Japanese infants. Another example of a change in categorical perception is from the b–p continuum. Americans only make two discriminations as voice onset time changes, from an initial 'b' to a final 'p'. But the Thai make three distinctions on the same continuum, a 'b', a 'p', and a 'pʰ'. While one cannot be too dogmatic because experiments have not examined all of the possibilities with infants, the additional 'pʰ' may be an example of a sound that is not perceived in infancy but can be perceived through experience with a language that makes such distinctions.

The above examples serve only as an introduction to an extensive field; Strange and Jenkins (1978) treat the topic in greater depth. We can conclude, however, that the young infant perceives speech sounds categorically and that adults cannot perceive distinctions that other languages make. The course that experience in a linguistic environment after birth takes is not yet clear, but one may tentatively hypothesize that, (1) the child learns from the linguistic environment distinctions that are new, ones the child could not perceive as an infant, and (2) some discriminations atrophy, the child loses the ability to make distinctions that could be perceived when it was an infant. The details of the process that takes place, now being investigated vigorously, are important for theoretical reasons to understand the role of experience in language perception, and also for such practical uses as the time to start learning a second language, or the possibility that, through training, we can learn to hear the distinctions we no longer can perceive.

PERCEPTUAL ABNORMALITIES

The discussion on perceptual abnormalities will be divided into four sections: the development of stereopsis, synchronization of movement, perception and ageing and perception and the brain. The section treats just a sample of possible perceptual disfunctions and is only meant to be illustrative and not, even by topic, meant to be a representative brief treatment of this area. Dyslexia, for example, is a topic that has perceptual components, but the area is too confusing even to try to discuss with a few representative illustrations.

Development of stereopsis

While all infants occasionally exhibit deviations of gaze, leading the parent to worry whether the child will be cross-eyed (esotropic), only a few infants actually are potential esotropes. This can be corrected by surgery. Does the child then have stereopic vision?

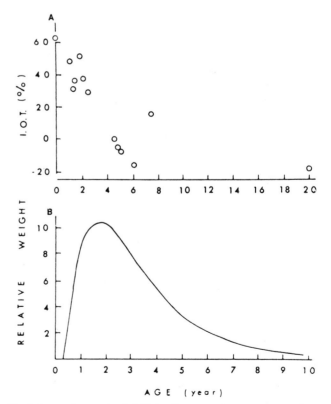

Fig. 2. Interocular transfer (I.O.T.) for 12 congenital esotropes operated on at various ages. The normal subject is plotted at zero years. After Banks, Aslin and Letson (1975).

One method of investigating this topic is through the tilt after-effect. If we stare at lines that are tilted from the vertical, then look at true vertical lines, the vertical lines will now seem to be tilted in the opposite direction. The normal binocular person can look at the tilted lines with one eye, keeping the other eye closed, and then look at the vertical lines with the formerly closed eye only and still get a tilt after-effect. The interocular transfer effect is about 60–65% of the effect with just one eye used for both exposure and test. Individuals who are esotropic get no tilt after-effect through interocular transfer. Banks, Aslin and Letson (1975) related congenital esotropia to age of surgery. All esotropes had been diagnosed as esotropic before 4 months of age. The surgery was performed from 1 year to as long as 19 years after the initial diagnosis.

Fig. 2 shows the interocular transfer as a function of age at the time of the operation. The earlier the operation, the better the transfer, and, from this, Banks *et al.* (1975) deduced the sensitive period for the development of binocular vision. As long as the child was operated on before the age of 2 years, the interocular transfer was fairly normal, the sensitive period being, they felt, from the age of 1–3 years. If the child was not operated on until after the third year, the possibility of stereopsis was drastically reduced. This experiment shows that perceptual tests can both assess binocularity and help to pinpoint the optimal period for surgery.

Synchronization of movement

The synchrony of body movement with speech sounds in the neonate was described earlier. As Condon (1977) points out, synchronization of movement and sound is present in normal behaviour, present, for example, in two individuals conducting a conversation. But the synchronization of movement may take strange forms in disabled individuals. The autistic child may exhibit no response to a sound at all, then one second later respond to the sound as if it were now present. The delayed reaction is often very precise (*e.g.* ⅔ sec later), and it may occur several times, a multiple response to sound. Children with reading problems may also give multiple responses to sound, though they are more in synchrony with the actual sound than are autistic children.

Perception and ageing

The perceptual system changes with age. It is well known that the capacity to accommodate the eye changes with age, the lens becomes less elastic and accommodation declines from about 6 diopters at age 30 to a little better than 3 diopters at age 50. Dark-adaptation changes similarly. The older individual adapts more slowly to the dark, requires more illumination to read comfortably, and very old individuals are particularly susceptible to the effects of glare. Szafran (1968) studied pilots aged 28–61. He found that even in a signal detection task where the ageing eye is at a disadvantage the individual differences in performance overshadowed the age differences. In an auditory detection task the older subjects actually did

somewhat better than the younger ones with white noise as a distractor, though one would expect some hearing loss in the older pilots. From this Szafran inferred that the improved strategy was the result of experience, and this would minimize any loss from impaired peripheral receptors. Szafran concluded that one's discrimination and choice need not decline with advancing years, at least within the years that he studied.

Perception and the brain

Many perceptual tasks are sensitive to brain injury. The tasks are used not only as an aid in the diagnosis of brain injury itself, but also to help localize the portion of the brain that has been injured. It may be very difficult to determine, for example, the exact location of the injury for a patient with cerebral stroke. A patient may be schizophrenic and he may be brain damaged (or he may be both). A patient with a history of alcoholism may or may not have brain damage. The use of these tests, along with other measures, helps to separate out those with organic brain damage from those without it.

The perceptual tasks to be discussed have been given for research purposes to a population with known brain injury. A significant difference between such individuals and controls indicates that a certain portion of the brain is related to performance on the perceptual task. But a significant difference does not mean that every individual with brain injury is worse than the controls: some brain injured may even be better than some of the controls. Identical sites of brain injury may lead to very different behavioural consequences. This means that diagnosing a patient as one with organic brain damage is fraught with pitfalls, requiring considerable patience and clinical skill. With these cautions in mind, a few perceptual tasks are discussed. Most of the material that follows is from Lezak (1976).

A digit span test is a test of attention and memory. In this test the subject is simply presented with a number of digits and asked to repeat them back to find the ceiling of performance. The subject is also asked to repeat the sequence of digits backward. The digit span test is sensitive to any kind of brain injury, particularly to left hemisphere damage. Many intellectual functions reflect overlearned behaviour, such as vocabulary tests, and they are not as sensitive to brain injury. The measure of interest in the use of this test is very poor performance or a large discrepancy between digits repeated forward and backward.

The block design test is a test that presents the subject with a series of designs and the task is to copy them exactly, looking back and forth from the model design to the subject's copy of it, and using a series of blocks that have a different colour or design on each of the six sides. The designs to be copied range from the very simple to the very complex. The block design test is particularly sensitive to damage to the right hemisphere and to the left parietal lobe.

Finding simple designs embedded in more complex designs involves the ability to look at a simple form and find it in the complex form despite common overlapping contours (*see* Fig. 3). The task involves both perception and memory. This task was originally designed by Gottschaldt in the 1920s to show that extensive experience with the simple figure gave no particular advantage in finding the simple figure in the complex one, that the perceptual organization of the whole figure was strong enough to override experience with the parts. The task is no longer viewed as a test of nativism versus empiricism, of experience against immediate perceptual organization, but varieties of the task itself have been important for the study of perceptual development and of brain injury.

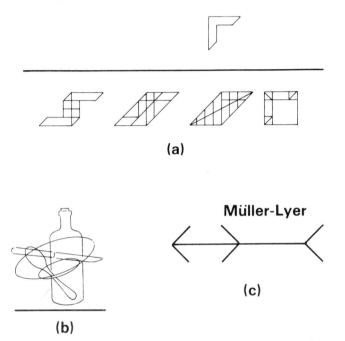

(a)

Müller-Lyer

(c)

(b)

Fig. 3. Illustrative perceptual tasks. (a) The embedded figure test. The subject must find the top figure in the lower ones. (b) The overlapping figures test. The subject names all objects. After Ghent (1956). (c) The Müller-Lyer illusion. The horizontal line is variable and the subject sets the figure so that the two horizontal lines appear equal in length.

The hidden figure task differentiated brain injured from normals in a study of veterans with head wounds compared to controls. Any injury to the brain impaired performance and only the aphasics were significantly worse then other brain injured (Teuber and Weinstein, 1956). The Korsakoff syndrome is a chronic amnesic state associated with alcoholism and the inadequate diet, primarily thiamine deficiency, of alcoholics. Talland (1965) gave the embedded figure test to Korsakoff patients and found the task too difficult for them. Whereas Teuber and Weinstein's (1956) worst group, the aphasics, scored at about 50% of the performance of the controls, Talland's patients averaged less than 10% of the control performance.

While in some instances simple figures may be hidden within larger complex figures, the figures themselves may simply overlap each other. Overlapping figures (*see* Fig. 3) are simpler than embedded figures for children (Ghent, 1956), but the overlapping figures are still somewhat

difficult for younger children. Bisiach *et al.* (1976) found that only adult patients with visual field defects were significantly worse than the controls; other brain injured patients were no different from controls and it did not matter whether the lesion was in the right or the left hemisphere.

Cerebral palsied patients are particularly liable to make spatial errors on the Bender-Gestalt test. This means that they leave a gap between the elements of the patterns in copying (a spatial gap), and they also have a tendency when copying the figures to rotate them, a spatial rotation as compared to normal subjects.

Front lobe lesions appear to affect visual searching. Teuber (1964) found that his subjects with gunshot wounds in the frontal lobes did very poorly in trying to find the match for a figure flashed on the screen. The match for the central figure was found in the visual field around the central portion. The deficit for those with unilateral frontal lesions was for objects in the field opposite to the lesion.

The right hemisphere of the brain is the non-language hemisphere for most people (*see* Chapter 14). Individuals with damage to the right temporal lobe cannot recognize music easily or a common sound like that of a barking dog. Damage to the right hemisphere also affects recognition of faces.

The Müller-Lyer illusion, illustrated in Fig. 3, has a long history in psychology. Susceptibility to the illusion, seeing the middle line as longer in the figure with the non-arrowlike obliques, has been related to the influence of cultural experience, the construction of the eye, and other factors. Basso, Bisiach and Faglioni (1974) used the Müller-Lyer illusion with brain injured patients and found that those with visual field defects in the left hemisphere were less suceptible to the illusion than were controls or other brain injured, including those with right hemisphere visual field defects. On the other hand, those with right visual field defects were much less accurate in discriminating the length of lines. The reason for these different results is not clear.

A few examples of research on perception and brain injury have been presented. The warning presented at the beginning of this section should be remembered: these are group differences, and individual cases may or may not agree with the group differences. It is only in the context of a full understanding of normal development that deviations from the normal can be isolated and understood. The illustrative material presented, combined with references on normal development, help to gain some understanding, but to get beneath the surface one needs the combination of practical experience and academic background found in the clinical neuropsychologist.

REFERENCES

André-Thomas and Autgaerden, S. (1966). *Locomotion from Pre- to Post-natal Life*. Clinics in Developmental Medicine No. 24. London: Heinemann.

Ball, W. and Tronick, E. (1971). Infant responses to impending collision: Optical and real. *Science,* **171**, 818–820.

Banks, M. S., Aslin, R. N. and Letson, R. D. (1975). Sensitive period for the development of human binocular vision. *Science*, **190**, 675–677.

Basso, A., Bisiach, E. and Faglioni, P. (1974). The Müller-Lyer illusion in patients with unilateral brain damage. *Cortex*, **10**, 26–35.

Bisiach, E., Capitani, E., Nichelli, P. and Spinnler, H. (1976). Recognition of overlapping patterns and focal hemisphere damage. *Neuropsychologia*, **14**, 375–379.

Bornstein, M. H., Kessen, W. and Weiskopf, S. (1976). The categories of hue in infancy. *Science*, **191**, 201–202.

Bower, T. G. R. (1972). Object perception in infants. *Perception*, **1**, 15–30.

Bower, T. G. R., Broughton, J. M. and Moore, M. K. (1970a). Demonstration of intention in the reaching behavior of neonate humans. *Nature*, **228**, 679–681.

Bower, T. G. R., Broughton, J. M. and Moore, M. K. (1970b). Infant responses to approaching objects: An indicator of response to distal variables. *Perception and Psychophysics*, **9**, 193–196.

Carpenter, B. and Carpenter, J. T. (1958). Perception of movement by young chimpanzees and human children. *Journal of Comparative and Physiological Psychology*, **51**, 782–784.

Condon, W. S. (1977). A primary phase in the organization of infant responding behavior. In: H. R. Schaffer (Ed.) *Studies in Mother–infant Interaction*. London: Academic Press, 153–176.

Davidson, H. P. (1935). A study of the confusing letters, B, D, P, Q. *Journal of Genetic Psychology*, **47**, 458–468.

Eimas, P. D. (1975). Auditory and phonetic coding of the cues for speech: Discrimination of the [r–l] distinction by young infants. *Perception and Psychophysics*, **18**, 341–347.

Eimas, P. D., Siqueland, E. R., Jusczyk, P. and Vigorito, J. (1971). Speech perception in infants. *Science*, **171**, 303–306.

Engen, T., Lipsitt, L. P. and Kaye, H. (1963). Olfactory responses and adaptation in the human neonate. *Journal of Comparative and Physiological Psychology*, **56**, 73–77.

Fantz, R. L. (1961). The origin of form perception. *Scientific American*, **204** (5), 66–72.

Ghent, L. (1956). Perception of overlapping and embedded figures by children of different ages. *American Journal of Psychology*, **69**, 575–587.

Gibson, E. J. (1969). *Principles of perceptual learning and development*. New York: Appleton-Century-Crofts.

Gottlieb, G. (1971). Ontogenesis of sensory function in birds and mammals. In: E. Tobach, L. R. Aronson and E. Shaw (Eds.) *The Biopsychology of Development*. New York: Academic, 67–128.

Hammond, J. (1970). Hearing and response in the newborn. *Developmental Medicine and Child Neurology*, **12**, 3–5.

Hochberg, J. E. (1978). *Perception*. Englewood Cliffs, N. J.: Prentice-Hall. 2nd ed.

Kaufman, L. (1974). *Sight and Mind: An introduction to visual perception*. New York: Oxford University Press.

Kessen, W., Haith, M. M. and Salapatek, P. H. (1970). Human infancy: A bibliography and guide. In: P. H. Mussen (Ed.) *Carmichael's Manual of Child Psychology*. 3rd ed., Vol. 1. New York: Wiley, 287–445.

Leventhal, A. S. and Lipsitt, L. P. (1964). Adaptation, pitch discrimination and sound localization in the neonate. *Child Dev.*, **35**, 759–767.

Lezak, M. D. (1976). *Neuropsychological Assessment*. New York: Oxford University Press.

Marg, E. and Adams, J. E. (1970). Evidence for a neurological zoom system in vision from angular changes in some receptive fields of single neurons with changes in fixation distance in the human visual cortex. *Experientia*, **26**, 270–271.

Mills, M. and Melhuish, E. (1974). Recognition of mother's voice in early infancy. *Nature*, **252**, 123–124.

Miyawaki, K., Strange, W., Verbrugge, R. R., Liberman, A. M., Jenkins, J. J. and Fujimura, O. (1975). An effect of linguistic experience: The discrimination of [r] and [l] by native speakers of Japanese and English. *Perception and Psychophysics*, **18**, 331–340.

Nowlis, G. H. and Kessen, W. (1976). Human newborns differentiate differing concentrations of sucrose and glucose. *Science*, **191**, 865–866.

Paine, R. S. and Oppé, T. E. (1966). *Neurological Examination of Children*. Clinics in Developmental Medicine Nos. 20 and 21. London: Heinemann.

Peiper, A. (1963). *Cerebral Function in Infancy and Childhood*. New York: Consultants Bureau.

Pick, H. L., Jr. and Pick, A. D. (1970). Sensory and perceptual development. In: P. H. Mussen (Ed.) *Carmichael's Manual of Child Psychology*. 3rd ed. Vol. 1. New York: Wiley, 773–847.

Ruff, H. A. and Birch, H. G. (1974). Infant visual fixation: The effect of concentricity, curvilinearity, and number of directions. *Journal of Experimental Child Psychology*, **17**, 460–473.

Sackett, G. P. (1966). Monkeys reared in isolation with pictures as visual input: Evidence for innate releasing mechanism. *Science*, **154**, 1468–1473.

Schwartz, A. N., Campos, J. J. and Baisel, E. J., Jr. (1973). The visual cliff: Cardiac and behavioral responses on the deep and shallow sides at five and nine months of age. *Journal of Experimental Child Psychology*, **15**, 86–89.

Strange, W. and Jenkins, J. J. (1978). Role of linguistic experience in the perception of speech. In: R. D. Walk and H. L. Pick, Jr. (Eds.) *Perception and Experience*. New York: Plenum, 125–169.

Szafran, J. (1968). Psychophysiological studies of aging in pilots. In: G. A. Talland (Ed.) *Human Aging and Behavior*. New York: Academic, 37–74.

Talland, G. A. (1965). *Deranged memory*. New York: Academic Press.

Teuber, H.-L. (1964). The riddle of frontal lobe function in man. In: J. M. Warren and K. Akert (Eds.) *The Frontal Granular Cortex and Behavior*. New York: McGraw-Hill, 410–477.

Teuber, H.-L. and Weinstein, S. (1956). Ability to discover hidden figures after cerebral lesions. *Archives of Neurology and Psychiatry*, **76**, 369–379.

Walk, R. D. (1969). Two types of depth discrimination by the human infant with five inches of visual depth. *Psychonomic Science*, **14**, 253–254.

Walk, R. D. and Gibson, E. J. (1961). A comparative and analytical study of visual depth perception. *Psychological Monographs*, **75** (15, Whole No. 519).

Walters, C. P. Unpublished studies of visual placing. Fairfax, Va.: Dept of Psychology, George Mason University.

Wertheimer, M. (1961). Psychomotor coordination of auditory and visual space at birth. *Science*, **134**, 1692.

White, B. L. (1971). *Human Infants: Experience and psychological development*. Englewood Cliffs, N.J.: Prentice-Hall.

Yonas, A., Bechtold, A. G., Frankel, D., Gordon, F. R., McRoberts, G., Norcia, A. and Sternfels, S. (1977). Development of sensitivity for impending collision. *Perception and Psychophysics*, **21**, 97–104.

Zeki, S. M. (1974). Cells responding to changing image size and disparity in the cortex of the rhesus monkey. *Journal of Physiology*, **242**, 827–841.

17. DEVELOPMENT OF ATTENTION

ERIC TAYLOR

A child is surrounded by signals from his world. Some are important, need to be analysed and may need a response; others are irrelevant and if they direct the child's behaviour he will be chaotic and inefficient. It is essential for survival that signals be dealt with in an orderly way. The study of attention aims to specify how children adopt strategies for sampling the information of the environment.

It is clear that many processes will be involved. Attention can be directed, switched, captured, distributed, divided, narrowed, sustained or withheld. In a voluminous literature it has been defined in too many ways even to list. It sometimes seems that the only thing held in common by the definitions is the word itself, which deludes investigators into believing that they are all talking about one thing. Yet, it continues to be used: introspectionist, behaviourist and cognitive schools of psychology have all found it an essential concept. Indeed, its vagueness may be part of its attraction, for it represents a bridge between disciplines as different as psychopathology, experimental psychology and neurophysiology.

Attention has proved an important dimension in adults' descriptions of children's behaviour. Ratings by parents and teachers suggest that children are very often regarded as inattentive. In an epidemiological study of 9–12-year-olds (Rutter *et al.*, 1970) 30% of the general population were described as showing poor concentration. Several studies have examined the dimensions used by parents and teachers in describing children's problems. A typical method is to carry out a factor analysis on the intercorrelations of items from a questionnaire about behaviour. It is a repeated finding that one such factor can be regarded as 'inattentiveness', and is made up from descriptions such as 'day dreaming', 'clumsy', 'short attention span', 'inattentive' and 'passive', (Peterson *et al.*, 1961; Conners, 1969; Quay, 1964 and Werry *et al.*, 1975). Concentration is more often rated as poor in younger children (Macfarlane *et al.*, 1954), and so can be seen as an ability which changes as the individual develops.

Such a description, however, may mean many things. 'Distractibility' may imply that the child is not motivated to do the tasks he is given, or that they are too difficult for him to persist at; it may mean that he explores all stimuli, or all prominent stimuli, or simply that the values he gives to stimuli are not those of the rater; it may mean that he becomes fatigued very rapidly and changes task frequently as a result. The methods of the experimental psychologist are needed to unravel the different possibilities.

One general view of attention has guided a lot of thinking on education. This proposes that: a) we slowly develop the ability to attend closely to specific details and ignore other things; b) this development and its pathology are based on the maturing of the brain; c) poor attention causes widespread failure in learning; d) this requires help, *e.g.* by excluding distracting events and teaching the child to ignore them. We shall not find it possible to agree with all these points; but they do emphasise the importance of study in this area.

In this chapter we will consider first the evidence we have on how selective abilities in perception develop, then some of the ways in which individuals may differ, and finally the implications of these differences for psychological development and clinical conditions.

NORMAL DEVELOPMENT

The direction of attention

Even in the first days of life there is evidence that information about the environment is sampled systematically. Mendelson and Haith (1976) have demonstrated ordered differences in the way that neonates scan with their eyes, depending on whether they are in the light or the dark and on whether or not a sound is also present. It appears that it is not entirely necessary to learn what one must examine; some strategies of examination are innate. Nevertheless, it is only gradually that certain qualities of a stimulus come to be preferentially regarded.

The direction of attention is a behaviour which can be studied in different ways. Firstly, an observer can record which way the sense organs (particularly the eyes) are pointed. This has the merit of directness, and the weakness of saying nothing about attention at a central level: it is not necessarily the child who stares most fixedly at the blackboard who is concentrating hardest on the lesson.

Secondly, performance on a test can be measured, and changed performance taken as an index of changed attention to the test material. This will only be completely valid if it is possible to exclude other factors (such as intelligence, learning and motivation) affecting performance. They can seldom be excluded altogether, even when the test is as simple as reaction time.

Thirdly, physiological measures can be taken of variables known to change when an individual concentrates on an important stimulus—such as heart rate, skin resistance and EEG. These are passive indicators, and need not reflect psychologically meaningful changes. They often measure only the responsiveness to the whole environment which Berlyne (1970) classified as the 'intensive' aspect of attention, rather than the selective attention to one part of the environment which is our major theme.

Lessons from all these methods have to be combined. On the whole they teach a coherent story of the changes with age in the determiners of attention.

Initially, features of the stimulus itself determine whether it will be processed (Pick et al., 1975). The neonate looks at a moving stimulus with a lot of light–dark contrast, in preference to one which is still and homogenous (Salapatek and Kessen, 1966; Fantz, 1966). His eyes fixate on the edges of contours; if there are no edges in the visual field his eyes continue to search around (Mendelson and Haith, 1976). It may be that figures with a moderate amount of edge evoke more steadfast gaze than figures with none or a great deal (Karmel, 1969).

Similarly, in the sense of hearing, an intermittent tone produces more behavioural effect (in this case, motor quieting) than does a continuous tone (Brackbill et al., 1966); and an intense tone produces more cardiac deceleration than does a quiet tone (Moffitt, 1973).

By the age of 2 to 4 months the physical properties of the stimulus are no longer the major determinants. The previous experience of the infant begins to play a role, and the novelty of the stimulus starts to evoke his attention (Fantz, 1964). Wetherford and Cohen (1973) demonstrate that visual attention wanes when stimuli are repeated and so lose their novelty; this habituation of attention is much more common at 10–12 weeks of life than at 6–8 weeks. The older infants look longer at the novel stimuli; the younger infants are less discriminating and, if anything, prefer familiar stimuli.

This change coincides with a number of neurological changes. Between 2 and 3 months the average evoked response of the EEG to stimuli becomes more complicated and more like the adult response; the alpha-rhythm appears in the EEG, and the growth of occipital neurones levels off (Ellingson, 1967). It is also the time when some of the physiological components of the orienting reflex, such as deceleration of the heart rate, start to appear to novel stimuli (Graham and Jackson, 1970). These parallel changes make it possible that the preference for novelty is based on maturation of the brain. Evidence for this is hard to find, but it is supported by Fagan et al.'s (1971) study of premature and full-term babies. Both groups preferred novelty at 50 weeks' conceptual age, regardless of their experience.

The effects of novelty may be considered as one example of a general effect of discrepancy from what the infant expects. Kagan (1970) argues that the relationship between attending and discrepancy is curvilinear and that a moderate degree of discrepancy best attracts the gaze. He supports the argument with data on clay masks which resemble a face more or less closely. At the age of 2 months, neither an accurate model nor a distorted mask attract attention differentially: both are unfamiliar. By 4 months the distorted mask is gazed at for longer; it is now optimally discrepant. By 12 months the two masks are again equivalent; the concept of 'face' is now very firmly established. Such an explanation has evident weaknesses, notably the difficulty of specifying what concepts the child has. (The most persuasive evidence quoted by Kagan found the predicted, curvilinear relationship between the attention paid to a test stimulus and its discrepancy from a stimulus which had frequently been presented to the child in the past. This, in effect, controlled the child's concept experimentally.) The above experiment with the masks also showed that when children reached the age of 18 months, they began once more to gaze for longer periods at the distorted mask. The distorted mask is starting to become more 'interesting': it can evoke more hypotheses than a normal face. Discrepancy is no longer so important.

By the age of 4 years, novelty is no longer the major determinant of attention, although it retains some power. Grabbe and Campione (1969) show that in a discrimination learning task children look not at the novel stimuli but at what has previously been rewarded. Also by this age, a familiar environment is scanned systematically and with less tendency to fixate on the most salient points; with increasing age this becomes more securely established as the strategy of sampling stimuli. Wright and Vlietstra (1975) present the evidence for this view, and show how perceptual exploration (on the basis of passive reaction to what is salient and novel) gradually gives way to active, logically organized search. Such a procedure is *independent* of the salience of the environment, *systematic* and *flexible*.

Independence. The concept that one's exploration becomes increasingly independent of the accidental features of the environment is very close to Piaget's account of decentration (Piaget, 1961). Distractibility can be seen as a failure of this independence, and is considered below. It follows that many of the findings on distractibility in clinical conditions can be interpreted in terms of a developmental delay. The degree of independence shown, however, may depend upon the kind of test used. White (1966) shows that, up to the age of 5 years, extraneous stimulus variation does interfere with learning; beyond that age it is actually beneficial. Odom and Guzman (1972) also showed that a salient dimension, when it was relevant to the task, increased the accuracy and speed of responding. It seems that some dependence on salient features of the environment persists if it is helpful for problem-solving. A teacher may use this by presenting the material to be learned in novel and interesting ways.

System in scanning becomes more logical. Braine (1965), for example, finds that younger children start by fixing their eyes on a focal point in a pattern and working away from it, while older children work systematically from top to bottom. In touch also (Zaporozhets, 1965), one becomes increasingly active, exhaustive and organized in the way one explores.

Delay in this ability has not been related to clinical conditions. However, an unsystematic sampling strategy is a part of the concept of impulsiveness considered below, and is therefore relevant to the literature which argues that learning-disordered and hyperactive children are characterized by a severe degree of impulsiveness.

Flexibility also increases with age. In manual exploration of a shape for example, young children may explore only one feature (*e.g.* shape) while older children explore more dimensions (*e.g.* texture) as well (Lehman, 1972). Does this represent a failure of system? Not so; the older children also explore one feature only if they have previously been told which one was relevant, and exceed the younger children in consistency. They have more successfully adapted their strategy to the changing demands of the task. This is a key ability for successful functioning. It is essential that plans are tailored to the needs of the situation and changed easily. We do not know directly how this ability relates to clinical conditions. However, the ability to shift attention rapidly from one sense to another is one kind of flexibility, and has been related to difficulties in learning to read (*e.g.* by Katz and Deutsch, 1973). One consequence of a delay in the development of flexibility could be a tendency to perseverate on one kind of activity, as is sometimes seen in individuals with impaired concentration.

The dividing of attention

In many situations we need to pay attention to two things at the same time. A child may be expected to listen to his teacher's voice and also concentrate on the notebook in which he writes what is being said. Modern industry and military machines place heavy demands on their operators to observe several things at once, and accordingly a large body of experiment and theory has grown up to give an account of this ability in adults. Broadbent (1958, 1971) has given a persuasive and widely accepted account; in this view the ability to process two kinds of stimuli simultaneously depends upon the amount of information which they contain. When two sources of information compete for processing, the individual copes by switching his attention from one to the other, and processing them in series.

In spite of the importance of this ability, and in spite of the theoretical interest of the adult work, it has scarcely been studied in children, and little can be said about its development. Hale and Morgan (1973) presented compound stimuli to children; they found that 8-year-olds were better able than 4-year-olds to attend to more than one feature. Inglis and Sykes (1967) found that with increasing age children were increasingly able to report items which had been presented, simultaneously, one to each ear. They considered that this was due to improvement in memory. Maccoby (1969) used a similar task. She caused children to hear words spoken simultaneously by two different voices. Recalling what had been said by both voices was much harder than recalling one voice only, and was relatively harder for the younger children. This, too, showed a developmental trend towards successful division of attention; furthermore, unlike that of Inglis and Sykes, her analysis suggested that it was indeed a perceptual ability—and not attributable to memory changes.

Increasing ability to process more than one source of information is also suggested by the incidental learning experiments considered under 'selective attention' below. It may well be a more important way than ignoring distractors of accounting for resistance to distraction.

If so, it would be important to know how to train it. For the present one can only regard it as a topic in need of study.

Selective attention

By contrast with the above situation, many tasks will require that only one stimulus is responded to but many other stimuli are present. The child in a classroom may be expected thoroughly to understand his teacher's voice and to ignore all the sounds of a noisy class which also reach his ears. If he fails to do this he will be regarded as distractible. One way of achieving this selection would be to process all the stimuli received, and then to choose the most relevant from amongst them. A much more efficient strategy would be to exclude irrelevant information from being processed at all.

Is this latter strategy necessary, and can it be achieved? Broadbent (1958) showed that the adult human subject had a limited capacity for processing information. Stimuli, if they are easily discriminable on the basis of their physical properties, can be ignored by filtering through only those which belong to a physical class previously chosen as relevant. Later work (Treisman, 1969; Deutsch and Deutsch, 1963) showed that this ignoring was not total. The theory has therefore been amended (Broadbent, 1971) to allow both for 'filtering', in which some stimuli are attenuated on the basis of physical properties, and for 'pigeon-holing', in which the surviving stimuli are assigned to different categories on the basis of decisions about the probabilities and relative importance of the categories.

It is not clear how far this approach can be applied to development through childhood, but it generates interesting questions about how the ability to be selective develops. The first of these questions is: *are older children less distracted by irrelevant information?* The answer depends upon the details of the setting, but usually it is 'yes'. Distractibility is not found in every experiment which seeks it (Doleys, 1976), and even within a single experiment the effect of irrelevant stimuli can be to improve performance at one time and to worsen it at another (Belmont and Ellis, 1968). Yet, we have already seen that the pattern of scanning becomes more systematic and therefore less influenced by irrelevant stimuli. Indeed, several studies show a clear effect of age. Maccoby (1969) has described how Maccoby and Leifer (unpublished) asked children to repeat words read out to them and found, as expected, that kindergarten children were less competent than second and fourth graders. When an extra word in a different voice was also read out, the distraction made more difference to the younger children. Doyle (1973) obtained similar results. White (1966) found that irrelevant variation in visual stimuli interfered with learning in children up to 5 years, while over that age it was often actually helpful. Hagen and Hale (1973), on the other hand, found that an auditory task interfered with visual learning, but that there was no effect of age in their children (who were all over 7). However, since this auditory task required a response, it would not have been an efficient strategy to exclude the auditory task by the operation of selective attention.

The second question is: *what accounts for this developmental trend?* Maccoby (1967, 1969) showed that peripheral factors, such as auditory acuity and sensitivity, are not sufficient. Some central, attentional process is involved.

Pick *et al*. (1972) found an increase with age in schoolchildren's ability to select relevant visual cues when other visual cues were present. Instructions beforehand were more effective than instructions given after the visual presentation. In other words, while looking, children could adopt some strategy which let them exclude unwanted information. Older children were better at using previous instructions; perhaps they could understand them better. On the other hand, Maccoby (1969) found no such trend on her selective listening task. Instructions beforehand certainly led to better performance than instructions afterwards, but children of different ages were equally able to use this information. Yet, as we have seen, younger children made many more errors in this test. In other words, the younger children were less good at excluding irrelevant stimuli, even though they had understood the basis for discriminating what was relevant. This points to the notion that 'filtering' may develop slowly and limit the capacity for selective listening.

It is also possible that older children do better in such tasks by virtue of an increased ability to process 'distracting' as well as relevant stimuli. The next question to arise is therefore: *do older children retain more information about a distractor?* We have supposed so far that the answer is 'no'. If selective attention functions as above, it follows that some of the increasing ability to respond accurately to a relevant stimulus is obtained at the price of a decreasing accuracy of response to stimuli that are not relevant to a task in progress.

Incidental learning offers a powerful way of examining this. Hagen and Hale (1973) tested the ability of children of different ages to recall the positions in which they had seen picture cards of animals. They were instructed beforehand in the task, and were presumed to be concentrating on it. In addition, at the end of the experiment, they were asked to recall features of the cards on which they had not been asked to concentrate. On the main task there was a clear trend for accuracy of recall to increase with age, as expected. The incidental learning task, however, showed no such improvement with age. There had been increased selectiveness in the older children. Yet it was not until the age of about 12 years that performance on the incidental task actually declined, and so this cannot explain the trend to better performance on the main task up to this age. Siegel and Stevenson (1966) found a curvilinear relation between age and incidental learning, which at first improved and then declined, again at about 10–12 years.

The preschool child is rather exclusive in his pattern of attending and focuses intensely (although, as we have seen, he is relatively unsystematic in the choice of what to focus on). Perhaps his selective attention and his ability to divide attention are both developing thereafter, and the interplay of these leads to the curved graph of incidental learning. The implication for the teacher is that he needs to consider an individual child's ability to take in information, not to suppose that it is constant for a given age.

Fourthly, we may ask: *are there qualities of a distracting stimulus that make it harder to ignore?* The question is of practical importance in education. The theory of filtering argues that physical similarity to the relevant stimuli should be the major distractor, and, of course, any 'distractor' which requires a response will be admitted to processing and so be capable of disrupting (or enhancing) other activity. While these are important (Pick *et al*., 1975), other qualities are effective, too. Salience and novelty are sometimes, although not always, distracting. A social stimulus is more distracting to somebody who has previously been socially isolated. A full theory will need to take account of decisions (and therefore of motivation) as well as the mechanical ability to exclude stimuli.

In all these studies the instructions are crucial. The experimenter may be quite clear that one set of stimuli is irrelevant, but the child's perceptions may be different. It is seldom a wise strategy to ignore the rest of the world completely, no matter how definite one's instructions. To be 'distractible' is therefore sometimes to be efficient. Garner (1962) has suggested how an individual could increase his rate of transmission of information by increasing the number of dimensions to which he attends. Perhaps this leads to attending to many dimensions; in the experimenter's view this is taking account of redundant features of the stimulus, but from the perspective of the child it makes the information easier to grasp. The incentives to a child to respond selectively are seldom systematically manipulated; to do so would illuminate the element of decision involved.

Sustained attention

Many tasks with which a child is confronted require that he persists with accuracy at a lengthy task in spite of frustration and boredom. Correspondingly, a 'short attention span' is a frequent comment about children not progressing well in the classroom.

This is clearly a highly complex function, depending on many abilities. Motivation must affect it but even under conditions of good motivation there is a considerable range in maintaining accuracy and speed. The Coding subtest of the WISC (Cohen, 1959) illustrates changes with age and IQ. Some studies, such as that of Doyle (1973), have examined the effect of fatigue on repetitive tasks and found it to be more disruptive in younger children.

Voluminous adult work has shown that many factors affect sustained vigilance (Stroh, 1971). Responsiveness is not maintained continuously; rather one functions like a single information-processing channel that is occasionally switched to something else. Brief lapses of attention account for many of the errors made. Tests such as the WISC coding subtest are not a good measure of this, since lapses of attention can be made up for by rapid work between them. Rather one needs a test in which brief stimuli, requiring a response, are presented unpredictably.

This condition is met by the various forms of the Continuous Performance Test (CPT) (Rosvold et al., 1956), and by some kinds of reaction time test. Different stimuli are presented in rapid succession. The child's task is to respond to one kind of stimulus only: perhaps to a tone that is lower than the others, or to one particular letter as different letters are flashed onto a screen. This kind of test is in some ways rather simple: very little learning is required, and the perceptual discrimination involved can also be made quite easy. Nevertheless, mistakes are made, both in omitting responses to target stimuli and in making incorrect responses. The test has a high face validity of measuring sustained attention, but like any performance measure is vulnerable to other influences. We know surprisingly little about its reliability, its stability or normative data, but it has proved popular with clinical researchers. The reason for its popularity is its robust relationship with psychiatric symptomatology. Poor performance has been found by several researchers in groups of hyperactive children (Sykes et al., 1971), children with learning disorders (Noland and Schuldt, 1971), people with epilepsy (Mirsky and van Buren, 1965), those on anticonvulsant medication (Hutt et al., 1968), adult schizophrenics (Wohlberg and Kornetsky, 1973), and the children of schizophrenics (Rutschman et al., 1977). Performance in 'hyperactive' children is improved by amphetamine-type drugs which can also improve behaviour (Barkley, 1977).

It is therefore worth asking further questions about the test, including: how does normal ability develop? Strikingly little work has been done on this by comparison with the clinical studies and with other topics in attention. Levy (1978) found a marked improvement between 48 and 66 months, and presents some norms. In this study, omitting a response was seen as a failure of attention (and these errors correlated significantly with reaction time), while incorrect responses were seen as impulsiveness, a failure of inhibition (and correlated with a rapid style on a test of

drawing a line slowly). The distinction is perhaps oversimple, and indeed the two kinds of error were correlated. But further consideration of the patterns of error would seem in order.

What factors account for poor performance? Poor persistence is only one of the possible answers: if it is important, then mistakes will cluster towards the end. There is some support for this; for instance, the harmful effect of anticonvulsants is not seen in a short test, but only in a longer one (Hutt et al., 1968). However, the usual analyses combine information from all stages of the test, and so say rather little about persistence. Diminished responsiveness, reckless impulsiveness, slow reactions, and low IQ could all lead to the final common path of a poor performance. The patterns of error may distinguish among these, and the methods of signal detection theory (Swets et al., 1961), seem appropriate but are seldom applied. The effects of manipulating motivation can also be examined.

Is the test relevant to everyday life? Intuitively, persistence seems very important. The young child's concentration is often intense but short-lived; the ability to sustain it is acquired much more slowly. Kupietz and Richardson (1978) have related vigilance in the laboratory to attentiveness in the classroom, and found that omission and commission errors on their test were both correlated with 'off-task' behaviour (such as playing or singing) in the classroom.

One process, or many?

This account has emphasized the variety of processes that are involved in 'attending', without considering how far they are separate in practice. If there are strong associations between the different tests which measure these abilities, then one can reasonably regard them as reflecting a major underlying process, the ability to attend. If there are no such associations, then it would be wiser to think of attention only as a word denoting a broad area of study. Unfortunately, the evidence on these associations is scanty. In the work on adults, no single operational definition of attention has emerged. Factor analysis of a battery of tests (Wittenborn, 1943) did suggest one factor of selective attention; but attempts to replicate this have failed (Moray, 1969). In a few studies on children, there are correlations (admittedly weak) between different tests. Keogh and Margolis (1976) report a 'component analysis' of attentional problems. Tests thought to measure selective attention, sustained attention and impulsiveness turned out to show rather low correlations with IQ; their correlations with each other were higher, but still small. Douglas (1972) mentions a factor analysis of a battery of tests administered to normal children, as well as to some who were diagnosed as hyperactive. The largest factor has loadings from many tests, notably those requiring the control of impulsive responding and some of those requiring recognition of a figure in a confusing background. Impulsiveness (*see below*) is positively but weakly associated with sustained and with selective attention in normals, the learning-disordered, and the hyperactive.

Until further evidence appears, one is encouraged to suppose that these tests are measuring something in common which is different from IQ. Yet the small size of the associations between tests argues against the idea that they measure a single process. Further, we have not been able clearly to define the relationship of these tests to intelligence. This should qualify the discussion which follows of the causes and consequences of individual differences.

INDIVIDUAL VARIATION

Most of the investigations so far considered have studied the normal course of development, and not the extent of variation. Indeed, one purpose of laboratory investigation is to reduce the range of variation. Even so, it is clear that substantial variation exists. Even in infancy, some children consistently orient towards a single feature, while others alternate their gaze (Salapatek and Kessen, 1973).

It is much less clear whether there is stability in this variation, whether the ability to attend is a lasting property of a child. It is usually assumed that this is true. The interest of the work reviewed below on the aetiology of inattentiveness is dependent on attentiveness being a stable quality. But evidence for or against the proposition is very seldom sought. Maccoby (1967) examined correlations between the scores on the two split halves of a single experiment. The correlations were around 0·65 indicating a moderate stability. There was less agreement between the scores of individuals in different experimental conditions. It may be that the different ways of measuring attentional abilities differ in their reliability, and that some of them give more enduring and stable ways of describing individuals. The clinician would be helped by more systematic research on this point.

Poor attention has been said to be a result of brain damage (Strauss and Lehtinen, 1947), of minimal brain dysfunction (Clements, 1966) and of adverse social circumstances (Goldfarb, 1945). We have seen that some selective abilities advance with age, and may therefore be impaired by developmental delay. What are the other sources of variation in attention?

Brain dysfunction

Selectiveness seems to be a property of nervous system functioning at all levels. Hubel and Wiesel (1962) have shown how individual neurones in the sensory regions of the brain respond selectively to particular sensory configurations. Although this ability is present at birth, it regresses if adequate stimulation is not forthcoming. An anatomical basis has also been suggested for the ways in which the brain can regulate its own input. Electrical stimulation of the association areas of the cortex in monkeys and cats causes a change in the evoked potentials measured in various parts of the sensory tracts (Spinelli and Pribram, 1966). This corticofugal influence extends as far peripherally as the cochlear nucleus and

optic tract (Dewson et al., 1966). We do not yet know about developmental changes in such systems.

It is therefore possible that neurological differences could be responsible for differences between individuals in sampling information from the environment. Dykman et al. (1971) assert that this is the case. There are at present two possible sources for evidence in humans bearing on this proposition. The first is the study of those known to be brain-damaged, to determine the effects of brain lesions on attention. The second is the study of individuals differing in their attention by the methods of neurophysiology and clinical neurology.

The ability of the brain-damaged to attend is a problem which has attracted experiments for over 30 years; so far with little consensus. Werner and Strauss (1939) found that brain-damaged children were chaotic in copying a pattern of coloured marbles: this was in large part attributable to interference by the pattern of the background on which the marbles were arranged. Since then, several studies have showed brain-damaged children to be more distractible than controls (Deutsch and Zawel, 1966; Schulman et al., 1965; Kaspar et al., 1971), while a few have not demonstrated this (Crosby, 1972; Browning, 1967). Unfortunately, the criteria for both brain damage and distractibility tend to be idiosyncratic. Furthermore, the effect of brain damage can be confounded with that of lowered IQ. There may indeed be an association of poor attention with low IQ, but it is not easy to decide on the direction of causality.

The brain-damaged are also more likely to be rated as poor in attention by those who know them (Rutter et al., 1970); and are less good at sustaining vigilance (Grassi, 1970; Rosvold et al., 1956).

However, other factors might account for inattentiveness in such populations: behaviour disorder, for instance, is more common in the brain-damaged, and might mediate the change in concentration. Shaffer et al. (1974) studied groups of children, with and without brain damage, with and without conduct disorder. Impairment of attention was not a characteristic of brain damage per se; rather it was present in the children whose behaviour was disturbed, whatever their neurological status. Rutter et al. (1970) found rather little effect of brain damage on rated attention when psychiatric disorder was allowed for. These studies are by no means final, and we can conclude little about any cerebral basis for attention. Nor do we know much about the effect of subcortical lesions, which in adults seem to be especially harmful to the ability to be vigilant (McDonald and Burns, 1964).

Neurophysiological studies have also failed to give any definite answer, in part because the work linking physiological and psychological measures has not yet been done. There is some evidence from the study of clinically derived groups, which is relevant but far from decisive. We shall see in a later section of this chapter that children with learning disorders have abnormalities both on psychological tests of attention and on some physiological variables. These physiological measures are known to be affected by characteristics of a stimulus that are related to attention: for instance, the autonomic changes of the orienting reflex are evoked by novelty and task-relevance of a stimulus (Sokolov, 1960). The alpha rhythm of the EEG tends to be replaced by more rapid frequencies when one concentrates. The later parts of the averaged evoked potential response of the EEG vary with the instructions given about the stimulus (Shagass, 1972). The contingent negative variation (Walter, 1967) is a change of potential in the EEG which appears under conditions of expectancy. While these measures do seem to be altered in children with difficulties in learning, it is hard to know whether this difference is accounted for by differences in attention or by other variables. What evidence there is (*e.g.* Sroufe, 1971) argues that children deficient in a test of attention (*e.g.* speed of reaction) are also impaired in their orienting reflexes (indexed by cardiac deceleration). If there is truly an association between these classes of variables, it would help to validate the construct of attention. But it would not prove that the psychological differences were caused by neurological changes. All these physiological measures are no more than forms of behaviour. It might seem that, because they involve physical quantities, they are more fundamental than psychological tests, but this is not necessarily true. They could as well be the result as the cause of changes in attention. It will be for future research to spell out any contribution from biological causes. Recent work with adults has suggested that biochemical changes (in dopamine-beta-hydroxylase, in platelet monoamine oxidase and in dopaminergic mechanisms) may be associated with individual differences in attention in the normal population (Spring *et al.*, 1977); this should have major implications for developmental studies.

Psychosocial factors

Some evidence indicates that abilities related to attention are also related to the psychological environment. Kagan (1970) found that visual fixation times on stimuli increased with increasing parental education in the age range 13 to 27 months. Hansley and Busse (1969) studied the scanning abilities of young children from families in poverty; they were given triangular figures, which led to triangular scanning, a response of more immature children (Elkind and Weiss, 1967). The mature strategy of left-to-right scanning was infrequent in the young children from poor backgrounds.

Hagen and Hale (1973) describe work by Wagner on cross-cultural differences in a central-incidental learning task. Children from Mexican towns showed a similar pattern to those of American children: central task performance increased with age, while incidental task performance increased from approximately 7 years to approximately 13 years, and then declined. Children from rural Mexico, however, showed a very different pattern: there was no overall increase with age in central task performance, and the decline in incidental learning did not take place until somewhere between 20 and 27 years of age.

In the case of sustained attention, Levy (1978) has found that upper-class children in an Australian suburb showed an earlier capacity for correct performance on a CPT than did their lower-class fellows. There are many differences between different cultural groups and we do not know which are responsible. Evidence from institutionalized children suggests that there is something in the environment of an institution which does not encourage development of these abilities (Goldfarb, 1945). Even in a more modern children's home, which has overcome some of the disadvantages of older settings, Tizard and Rees (1975) have found the residents to be poor in attention as described by their caretakers.

One may reasonably suppose that the psychological environment is responsible, but the precise factors are not clear. It is possible that the more explicit verbal habits of higher-class families (Hess and Shipman, 1965) provide clearer strategies for identifying and isolating what is relevant. Wynne and Singer (1963) suggested that more confusing communications were characteristic of some families, that these were reflected in more confused strategies of focal attention in the children and that this was of importance in the aetiology of schizophrenia. Their study, however, was not replicated by Hirsch and Leff (1975). Bee (1967) also studied a normal population, and examined the family interaction patterns associated with high or low distractibility in the children. She found that the parents of distractible children made more specific suggestions about how problems should be solved. It does not follow that this interaction caused this 'distractibility'.

Campbell (1973) found, also in a normal population, that impulsive children differed from reflective in a dissimilar way: their mothers were less directive. Surprisingly, hyperactive children came from families more like those of the reflective. If indeed psychological experience can modify attention so much, it should be possible to demonstrate the effects of training experimentally. In several studies (Douglas, 1972) it has appeared that such training is possible.

Genetic inheritance

Very little can yet be said on the inheritance of attention. The need to control for IQ becomes particularly strong. Interest so far has focused on the families, and particularly the children of schizophrenic patients. Genetic factors may play a role in the development of cognitive impairment in the relatives (Mednick *et al.*, 1974) and the inability to resist distraction is one of the cognitive problems (Anthony, 1972). On the other hand, Cohler *et al.* (1977) found that depression in mothers was even more harmful than schizophrenia for the cognitive development of their children, and that there was no significant relationship between the performances of mother and child on tests of attention. It is possible that an attention defect is a rather non-specific associate of psychopathology.

Sex differences

On the whole, boys and girls do not differ greatly in their ability to resist distraction, or to sustain concentration. One reliable and interesting difference between the sexes is in the greater tendency of boys to pay attention to novelty. This has been shown in their exploration of a new toy (Hutt, 1972). Habituation experiments are relevant to this: they show that male infants habituate visual attention more rapidly (Cornell and Strauss, 1973) and also dishabituate more completely with a novel stimulus. In both cases one can infer that boys are responding more to novelty. The early onset and the constancy of this finding in other species (Hutt, 1972) have been taken to imply that a biological difference is involved.

Even if this is true, cultural differences will interact. Sustained attention, indexed by visual fixation time, is more closely related to parental education (Kagan, 1970) and to home interactions (Moss and Robson, 1968) for girls than it is for boys.

Other psychological differences

It will not have escaped the reader that 'attention' has been used as a hypothetical construct to explain different kinds of behaviour. Other constructs—especially intelligence and motivation—can also explain some of the same changes, and they may indeed interact with attention. A child may, for instance, sustain attention poorly in class yet be engrossed by the television. Poor attention has been associated with low intelligence, whether assessed by clinical ratings (Rutter et al., 1970) or by tests of vigilance, of figure-ground perception and of distractibility (McGhie, 1969). Zeaman and House's (1963) analysis of discrimination learning in the retarded has been much quoted as evidence that the step which was impaired in retardates was that of identifying the relevant dimension; this is rather different from the ability to attend selectively to what is relevant; but it emphasizes how attention might affect intelligence, how IQ might lead directly to low scores on performance tests which purport to measure attention; or poor attention and low intelligence may be common results of a single aetiology.

Cognitive styles

Several times it has been proposed that individuals are characterized by an enduring tendency to adopt one kind of approach in a wide range of problem-solving tasks. These approaches are rather different from the developmental differences we have been considering: they are thought of as being consistent for one individual through different developmental stages.

Witkin et al. (1962) suggested the value of a dimension of field dependence v. independence. This reflects individual differences in the ability to analyse an item separately from the field, or background, in which it is embedded. It is also supposed to reflect individual differences in whether a stimulus array is perceived as a whole or analysed into details. It is associated with emotional dependence and with poor impulse control. It can be seen as a special case of selectively attending to one source of information among many.

Klein (1954) suggested flexible v. constricted control as a useful dimension. This is associated with the ability to

ignore some of the ways in which stimuli may vary. It is clear that both these dimensions are conceptually linked to the ability to ignore distraction. It is possible that both developmental delay and persistent cognitive style are explanations for individual differences on these dimensions.

The most widely invoked cognitive style is that of impulsivity v. reflectiveness (Kagan et al., 1964). This dimension is intended to explain some of the individual differences in children's problem-solving which is not accounted for by IQ or verbal ability. It refers to an enduring disposition to respond quickly and inaccurately—against slowly and accurately—in tasks where there is considerable uncertainty about which response to give. The reliability and stability of measures of this, such as the Matching Familiar Figures Test, are not as high as one would wish (Egeland and Weinberg, 1976). Its interest lies in its pattern of relationships with other abilities. Messer (1976) concludes that impulsive children are less concerned about making errors and get worse grades in school. From our point of view, impulsive children use less systematic strategies of scanning test material (Ault et al., 1972), they score worse on a Continuous Performance Test of sustained attention (Zelniker et al., 1972), and they are rated by their teachers as having a shorter attention span (Ault et al., 1972). Zelniker and Jeffrey (1976) have argued that the underlying tendency is the strategy of processing test material globally rather than analysing it in a detailed way: in some tests this is an advantage, in others a handicap. There are other interpretations of the underlying dimension: the controversy reflects the problem, of disentangling the ability to attend from the choice of where to direct one's attention.

CONSEQUENCES OF VARIATIONS IN ATTENTION

Important implications have been suggested for the ability to learn, and for the development of psychiatric symptoms.

Learning

We have seen that children differ in their ability to sample information efficiently, and that this ability is a function of age. Is it possible that these differences are the cause of the differences between children in their ability to learn in the classroom?

Failure to learn classroom subjects, even in spite of a normal IQ, is a common and important source of problems in childhood. It is often associated with abnormalities of behaviour. Several authors (e.g. Dykman et al., 1971; Ross, 1976) have argued that the common feature in most cases of learning disorder is a deficiency in attending selectively to task-relevant features of the environment. It is easy to imagine how this might happen. Frequently, a child is expected to discriminate on the basis of stimulus features which are not salient. In understanding speech, for instance, much of the necessary information is not accentuated by intensity, contrast or novelty of the sounds. Failure to focus attention on the relevant dimensions of the stimulus could well lead to impaired comprehension. Gross distractibility could lead to learning nothing; even lesser degrees of distractibility might, in theory, disrupt performance. Some kinds of learning would be badly affected by a failure of persistence, while others could more readily be achieved within the limits of a short attention span. This emphasizes how strong an interaction there is likely to be between the demands of a particular test and the ability of a child to attend to it. In treatment this could be very important, since tasks might be presented by a teacher in ways which avoid a specific difficulty in taking in the information. However, it might also be that children can spontaneously adopt strategies of learning that make up for any weakness of attention; it is therefore necessary to examine the evidence relating to whether attention deficits are capable of causing learning deficits and whether they do in practice cause them.

In the first place, a number of studies have used a learning test as their measure of changes in attention. The well-known studies described by Hagen and Hale (1973), by Odom and Guzman (1972) and by Zeaman and House (1963) have already been quoted. There are potential problems of interpretation, for adequate attention is only one of the necessary conditions for learning (which include aptitude, memory, recall and motivation) and they are confounded if a single measure of learning is used. Nevertheless, it has been possible for some researchers to conclude from experimental operations that attending to relevant dimensions is a limiting factor. For instance, the analysis by Ross and Ross (1976) of the way children learn to reverse a discrimination led to the conclusion that the choice of dimension to be attended to was of first importance. This process is similar to the formation of learning set; it would necessarily be affected by a failure to maintain concentration, but also by decisions about what is relevant.

These studies, taken together, argue that changes in selecting information are capable of affecting the learning of experimental tasks. It remains an inference that this would also apply to learning in the classroom, but the inference is very plausible.

A second source of evidence is the large number of studies in which children who have a learning problem (typically a delay in learning to read) have been compared with normal children on the basis of their performance on psychological tests which are believed to measure abilities related to attention. These yield a mixture of results, some positive and some negative, which serve again to emphasize the need to distinguish between different kinds of attention.

The ability to ignore distraction is a case in point. One way of measuring this is to require a child to work at a task even though the experimenter is also producing loud sounds, or flashing lights, or recordings of speech, or other stimuli quite different from the task. A number of such studies have been reviewed by Doleys (1976) with the conclusion that there is only 'a myriad of inconsistent and contradictory results'. For every study which seems to show that children with learning disorders are more distractible than their peers, others can be quoted to show that they are not inferior. It may be that the exact natures of the task and the distractor are critical; but, if so, we do not know what the critical features are.

There is, however, another way in which distraction has been produced: by embedding a figure in an irrelevant or misleading background. This test of 'field-independence' gives more consistent results. Tarver and Hallahan (1974) have reviewed several such studies, which lead to a clear conclusion that the learning-disordered are inferior to normals in recognizing embedded figures. It remains open whether this finding reflects a problem of selecting information, of spatial analysis, or of interest and familiarity in the test material. From the practical point of view one must note that children who read badly still have difficulties even when external distraction is kept to a minimum, even in a sound-proof room; but that clear presentation of material to be learned is helpful.

If resistance to distraction is indeed important, then one would expect to find differences on tests of central—as opposed to incidental—learning. Hallahan et al. (1973) showed that those with learning disorders were indeed less selective, being impaired on central learning but not on incidental. Pelham and Ross (1977) found that children with reading problems were not only worse at central learning but were actually better than normal controls at incidental learning. Such a finding is powerful, because it cannot be explained by the simple expectation that people with impaired learning will do badly in a wide range of psychological tests. It also suggests an unexpected strength that educators could capitalize on and a weakness that might be overcome by specific training or by extra attention to the organization of teaching material to enhance its relevance.

So far we have considered only the problem of deficiency in selective attention. Over-selective attention might also bring problems. For instance, Lovaas et al. (1971) claimed a marked absence of incidental learning in mentally retarded autistic children. They suggested that this could lead directly to impairment of social learning, but there is no proof that incidental learning is particularly important (and later research showed that the results were a consequence of low mental age—Schover and Newsom, 1976).

Other problems have been identified. Children with learning difficulties are poor at shifting attention between stimuli in different senses (Katz and Deutsch, 1963). They show a delay in the development of the ability to organize and store material from two different senses presented together (Senf, 1969). They do badly on tests of vigilance (Anderson et al. 1973; Noland and Schuldt, 1971). Their reaction time is prolonged (Rourke and Czudner, 1972). It is not clear how far it helps to improve vigilance (e.g. by feedback and reward), but it is worth trying.

The tendency to make impulsive, unconsidered responses to stimuli is likely to disrupt the learning of difficult tasks, and to produce many errors in performance. It is therefore important that several studies (Keogh and Donlon, 1972; Messer, 1970; Hallahan *et al.*, 1973; Douglas, 1972; Conners *et al.*, 1969), have shown that children with problems in academic learning but normal IQs are in general more impulsive than other children of the same age.

Physiological studies can be construed as giving support to the notion that children with learning problems pay less attention to events in their environment. They show smaller autonomic orienting responses than normal controls (Dykman *et al.*, 1971; Sroufe *et al.*, 1973) (as do the slower learners among normal children, according to Cousins, 1976); they also have smaller amplitudes of the averaged evoked responses of the EEG (Sobotka and May, 1977; Conners, 1970; Preston *et al.*, 1974), more asymmetrical evoked responses (John *et al.*, 1977), smaller amplitude of the contingent negative variation (Fenelon, 1968; Dykman *et al.*, 1971), and less attenuation of the alpha-rhythm while listening to instructions or performing mental arithmetic (Fuller, 1977).

In summary, there are good grounds for considering that an altered pattern of responsiveness to stimuli is associated with learning disorder; but we have rather little information on the mechanism of this association. It is easy to see that deficiencies of attention *could* cause poor performance in tests of learning. If this is the reason for the association, several predictions follow:

a) Within the affected group, those with the worst attention should have the most severe difficulties. There is little evidence on this point one way or the other.

b) Defects of attention should be detectable in children before learning problems develop, and should predict difficulties in learning. This point also needs to be examined. Suggestive evidence comes from Rourke and Orr (1977) who found that at age 7 the best predictor of reading level 4 years later was a test of underlining which was thought to be chiefly a test of attention. It may well be that hyperactive behaviour predicts difficulty in learning (Weiss *et al.*, 1975), but hyperactivity and inattentiveness are not necessarily the same.

c) Effective treatment of poor attention should lead to improvements in learning. This too is unclear. Stimulant drugs often improve the ability to attend (Barkley, 1977) and to inhibit impulsive responding (Sykes *et al.*, 1971). Yet even when they do so, academic performance is not necessarily improved (Gittelman-Klein and Klein, 1976). Psychological treatment can diminish impulsiveness but does not necessarily improve reading achievement.

It is, accordingly, not proven that poor attention is a major cause of poor learning. It still makes sense to take particular pains over clarity of presentation of material when teaching slow learners. The research findings that exist are enough to justify encouraging systematic scanning of a whole task before responding; and demonstrat-ing what parts of a task convey the relevant information. Nevertheless, research needs to continue.

Behaviour

Some children with disordered behaviour, and particularly those with the American diagnosis of 'hyperactivity' or 'minimal brain dysfunction', seem to have a pattern of unselectiveness and impulsiveness in their responses to stimuli which is similar to that encountered in disorders of learning (Douglas, 1972; Cantwell, 1977; Ross and Ross, 1976). One can speculate about the cause: an inability to attend and a failure of inhibition might lead to behaviour being directed by stimuli irrelevant to the demands of the task of the moment. The consequent chaotic behaviour would lead to the description of 'overactivity'. Cognitive explanations of behaviour in these terms have a considerable pedigree: ever since Kraepelin's (1896) concept of 'hyperprosexia' in the brain-damaged, the idea has persisted that some individuals show an excessive response to stimuli by reason of organic brain dysfunction, and that this causes chaotic and disruptive behaviour (Strauss and Lehtinen, 1947; Luria, 1961). Physiological studies do not bear this out. The typical neurophysiological pattern of those with disordered behaviour is one of diminished and unselective responsiveness (Taylor, 1979). This lack of selectiveness, however, reinforces the suggestion that poor attention is an important associate of conduct problems. We do not know why this is, nor which comes first. Even if poor attention is the cause of other difficulties, we do not know that its effects are specific to any one kind of behaviour. Perhaps conduct problems develop in reaction to school failure caused by poor attention; perhaps poor attention acts by impairing relationships with other people.

Poor attention is not associated only with hyperactivity, nor only with conduct disorder. Several kinds of attention are impaired in a wide range of psychiatric diagnoses (McGhie, 1969; Meldman, 1970; Garmezy, 1977). This may be a rather non-specific consequence of psychopathology. However, it seems that impaired attention is present in some patients during remission from psychiatric illness and in their relatives (Mednick *et al.*, 1974; Wohlberg and Kornetsky, 1973) and is accordingly a candidate for an aetiological factor. At the level of speculation, deficits in selective attention might be able to cause psychiatric problems rather directly. One example is the possibility that intrusion of irrelevant material might underlie thought disorder—particularly 'overinclusive thinking', and so participate in the genesis of schizophrenia. Kopfstein and Neale (1972) found a small relationship between tests of overinclusive thinking and of vigilance. Another example is the notion that selecting different parts of the environment for processing is a powerful way of coping with anxiety, can be an alternative to action, and underlies a dimension of personality described by Pribram (1967) as 'affect *v.* effect', or emotionality *v.* acting out. A breakdown of the ability to select would therefore be a cause of enhanced anxiety. A third speculation (Grim, Kohlberg and White, 1968) is that the ability to regulate one's input from the external world is reflected in the ability to resist external temptation and achieve internal standards of morality. Evidence on all these possibilities is tenuous, to say the least. They are mentioned to emphasize the explanatory power of the concepts of attention.

CONCLUSIONS

Any short account of so large a field is necessarily partial. There are, however, important gaps in our understanding of the development of attention. Some of its components are well studied, others scarcely at all. The interest of clinicians in individual differences and the reasons for them has usually remained separate from the interests of developmental psychologists, and the two groups have favoured different experimental paradigms. How do these studies relate to the 'story' outlined at the beginning of this chapter?

First of all, attention is not unitary and it is not simply the exclusiveness of concentration which increases with age. Indeed, preschool children sometimes focus on objects at least as intensely as adults. Rather, age brings an increase in the use of systematic, logical strategies of exploring the world; in the ability to be flexible and selective in one's approach to information; and in maintaining one's responsiveness for longer periods.

Children do indeed differ in these functions. Brain damage is probably capable of causing poor attention in a small number of children, but there is little evidence that individual differences in the general population are caused by neurological disability. The psychological environment plays a substantial role.

Poor attention is in all probability a factor in learning problems. Techniques are becoming available for improving the abilities to select and to persist, but it is not yet clear whether they will help more than a minority of children with disorders of learning. Poor attention is also associated with several kinds of psychiatric symptoms; whether symptoms are caused by poor attention and whether treatment of the attention problem is helpful remain unanswered questions. Indeed, the whole field is characterized by unanswered questions; they augur well for its fertility.

REFERENCES

Anderson, R. P., Halcomb, C. G. and Doyle, R. B. (1973). The measurement of attentional deficits. *Exceptional Children*, **39**, 534–539.

Anthony, E. J. (1972). A clinical and experimental study of high-risk children and their schizophrenic parents. In Kaplan, A. R. (Ed.) *Genetic Factors In Schizophrenia*. Springfield, Ill.: Charles C. Thomas.

Ault, R. L., Crawford, D. E. and Jeffrey, W. E. (1972). Visual scanning strategies of reflective, impulsive, fast-accurate and slow-inaccurate children in the Matching Familiar Figures test. *Child Dev.*, **43**, 1412–1417.

Barkley, R. A. (1977). A review of stimulant drug research with hyperactive children. *J. Child Psychol. Psychiat.*, **18**, 137–166.

Bee, H. (1967). Parent–child interaction and distractibility in nine-year-old children. *Merrill-Palmer Quarterly*, **13**, 175–190.

Belmont, J. M. and Ellis, N. R. (1968). Effects of extraneous stimulation upon discrimination learning in normals and retardates. *Amer. J. Ment. Def.*, **72**, 525–532.

Berlyne, D. E. (1970). Attention as a problem in behaviour theory. In Mostofsky, D. I. (Ed.) *Attention: Contemporary Theory and Analysis*. New York: Appleton-Century-Crofts.

Brackbill, Y., Adams, G., Crowell, D. H. and Gray, M. C. (1966). Arousal levels in newborns and preschool children under continuous auditory stimulation. *Exper. Child Psychol.*, **3**, 176–188.

Braine, L. G. (1965). Age changes in the mode of perceiving geometric forms. *Psychonomic Science*, **2**, 155–156.

Broadbent, D. E. (1958). *Perception and Communication*. Oxford: Pergamon Press.

Broadbent, D. E. (1971). *Decision and Stress*. London: Academic Press.

Browning, R. M. (1967). Effect of irrelevant peripheral visual stimuli on discrimination learning in minimally brain-damaged children. *J. Consult. Psychol.*, **31**, 371–376.

Campbell, S. (1973). Mother–child interaction in reflective, impulsive and hyperactive children. *Devel. Psychol.*, **8**, 341–349.

Cantwell, D. (1977). Hyperkinetic syndrome. In Rutter, M. and Hersov, L. (Eds.) *Child Psychiatry: Modern Approaches*. Oxford: Blackwell Scientific.

Clements, S. D. (1966). *Minimal Brain Dysfunction in Children*. (NINDB Monograph No. 3, USPHS Publication No. 1415). Washington, D.C.: U.S. Dept. of Health, Education and Welfare.

Cohen, J. (1959). The factorial structure of the WISC at ages 7·6, 10·6 and 13·6. *J. Consult. Psychol.*, **23**, 285–299.

Cohler, B. J., Grunebaum, H. U., Weiss, J. L., Garner, E. and Gallant, D. H. (1977). Disturbance of attention among schizophrenic, depressed and well mothers and their young children. *J. Child Psychol. Psychiat.*, **18**, 115–136.

Conners, C. K. (1969). A teacher rating scale for use in drug studies with children. *Amer. J. Psychiatry*, **126**, 884–888.

Conners, C. K. (1970). Cortical visual evoked response in children with learning disorders. *Psychophysiology*, **7**, 418–428.

Conners, C. K., Kramer, K. and Guerra, F. (1969). Auditory synthesis and dichotic listening in children with learning disabilities. *J. Special Education*, **3**, 163–170.

Cornell, E. H. and Strauss, M. S. (1973). Infants' responsiveness to compounds of habituated visual stimuli. *Devel. Psychol.*, **9**, 73–78.

Cousins, L. (1976). Individual differences in the orienting reflex and children's discrimination learning. *Psychophysiology*, **13**, 479–487.

Crosby, K. G. (1972). Attention and distractibility in mentally retarded and intellectually average children. *Amer. J. Ment. Def.*, **77**, 46–53.

Deutsch, J. A. and Deutsch, D. (1963). Attention: some theoretical considerations. *Psychological Review*, **70**, 80–90.

Deutsch, C. P. and Zawel, D. (1966). Comparison of visual and auditory perceptual functions of brain-injured and normal children. *Perceptual and Motor Skills*, **22**, 303–309.

Dewson, J. H., Nobel, K. W. and Pribram, K. H. (1966). Corticofugal influence at cochlear nucleus of the cat: some effects of ablation of insular-temporal cortex. *Brain Research*, **2**, 151–159.

Doleys, D. M. (1976). Distractibility and Distracting Stimuli: Inconsistent and Contradictory Results. *The Psychological Record*, **26**, 279–287.

Douglas, V. I. (1972). Stop, look and listen: The problem of sustained attention and impulse control in hyperactive and normal children. *Canadian J. Behavioral Science*, **4**, 259–281.

Doyle, A.-B. (1973). Listening to Distraction: A developmental study of selective attention. *J. Exper. Child Psychol.*, **15**, 100–115.

Dykman, R. A., Ackerman, P. T., Clements, S. D. and Peters, J. E. (1971). Specific learning disabilities: An attentional deficit syndrome. In Myklebust, H. R. (Ed.) *Progress In Learning Disabilities.*, vol. 2, New York: Grune & Stratton.

Egeland, B. and Weinberg, R. A. (1976). The Matching Familiar Figures test: a look at its psychometric credibility. *Child Dev.*, **47**, 483–491.

Elkind, D. and Weiss, J. (1967). Studies in perceptual development, III: Perceptual exploration. *Child Dev.*, **38**, 553–561.

Ellingson, R. J. (1967). Study of brain electrical activity in infants. In Lipsitt, L. P. and Spiker, G. C. (Eds.) *Advances in Child Development and Behaviour*. New York: Academic Press.

Fagan, J. F., Fantz, R. L. and Miranda, S. B. (1971). Infants' attention to novel stimuli as a function of postnatal and conceptual age. Paper presented at the meeting of the Society for Research in Child Devel., Minneapolis.

Fantz, R. L. (1964). Visual experience in infants: decreased attention to familiar patterns relative to novel ones. *Science,* **146,** 668–670.

Fantz, R. L. (1966). Pattern discrimination and selective attention as determinants of perceptual development from birth. In Kidd, A. H. and Rivoire, J. J. (Eds.) *Perceptual Development in Children.* New York: International Universities Press.

Fenelon, B. (1968). Expectancy waves and other complex cerebral events in dyslexic and normal subjects. *Psychonomic Science,* **13,** 253–254.

Fuller, P. W. (1977). Computer-estimated alpha attenuation during problem solving in children with learning disabilities. *Electroencephalography and Clinical Neurophysiology,* **42,** 149–156.

Garmezy, N. (1977). The Psychology and Psychopathology of Attention. *Schizophrenia Bulletin,* **3,** 360–369.

Garner, W. (1962). *Uncertainty and Structure as Psychological Concepts.* London: Wiley.

Gittelman-Klein, R. and Klein, D. (1976). Methylphenidate Effects in Learning Disabilities: Psychometric changes. *Arch. Gen. Psychiat.,* **33,** 655–664.

Goldfarb, W. (1945). Effects of psychological deprivation in infancy and subsequent stimulation. *Amer. J. Psychiat.,* **102,** 18–33.

Grabbe, W. and Campione, J. C. (1969). A novelty interpretation of the Moss-Harlow effect in preschool children. *Child Dev.,* **40,** 1077–1084.

Graham, F. K. and Jackson, J. C. (1970). Arousal systems and infant heart rate responses. In Reese, H. W. and Lipsitt, L. P. (Eds.) *Advances In Child Development and Behaviour, Vol. 5.* New York: Academic Press.

Grassi, J. R. (1970). Auditory vigilance performance in brain-damaged, behaviour disordered and normal children. *J. Learning Disabilities,* **3,** 302–305.

Grim, P. F., Kohlberg, L. and White, S. H. (1968). Some relationships between conscience and attentional processes. *J. Person. Soc. Psychol.,* **8,** 239–252.

Hagen, J. W. and Hale, G. A. (1973). The development of attention in children. In Pick, A. D. (Ed.) *Minnesota Symposia on Child Psychology,* vol. 7. Minneapolis: University of Minnesota Press.

Hale, G. A. and Morgan, J. S. (1973). Developmental trends in children's component selection. *J. Exper. Child Psychol.,* **15,** 302–314.

Hallahan, D. P., Kauffman, J. M. and Ball, D. W. (1973). Selective attention and cognitive tempo of low achieving and high achieving sixth grade males. *Perceptual and Motor Skills,* **36,** 579–583.

Hansley, C. and Busse, T. V. (1969). Perceptual exploration in Negro children. *Devel. Psychol.,* **1,** 446.

Hess, R. D. and Shipman, V. C. (1965). Early experience and the socialisation of cognitive modes in children. *Child Dev.,* **36,** 869–886.

Hirsch, S. R. and Leff, J. P. (1975). *Abnormalities in Parents of Schizophrenics.* London: Oxford University Press.

Hubel, D. and Weisel, T. (1962). Receptive fields, binocular interaction, and functional architecture in the cat's visual cortex. *Jnl. of Physiology,* **160,** 106–154.

Hutt, C. (1972). Neuroendocrinological, Behavioural and Intellectual Aspects of Sexual Differentiation in Human Development. In Ounsted, C. and Taylor, D. C. (Eds.) *Gender Differences: Their Ontogeny and Significance.* Edinburgh: Churchill Livingstone.

Hutt, S. J., Jackson, P. M., Belsham, A. B. and Higgins, G. (1968). Perceptual-motor behaviour in relation to blood phenobarbitone level. *Develop. Med. Child Neurol.,* **10,** 626–632.

Inglis, J. and Sykes, D. H. (1967). Some sources of variation in dichotic listening performance in children. *J. Exper. Child Psychol.,* **5,** 480–488.

John, E. R., Karmel, B. Z., Corning, W. C., Easton, P., Brown, D., Ahn, H., John, M., Harmony, T., Prichep, L., Toro, A., Gerson, I., Bartlett, F., Thatcher, R., Kaye, H., Valdes, P. and Schwartz, E. (1977). Neurometrics. *Science,* **196,** 1393–1410.

Kagan, J. (1970). The determinants of attention in the infant. *Amer. Scientist.* **58,** 298–306.

Kagan, J., Rasman, B. L., Day, D., Albert, J. and Phillips, W. (1964). Information processing in the child: significance of analytic and reflective attitudes. *Psychological Monographs,* **78,** (1, whole No. 578).

Karmel, B. Z. (1969). The effect of age, complexity and amount of contour on pattern preferences in human infants. *J. Exper. Child Psychol.,* **7,** 338–354.

Kaspar, J. C., Millichap, J. G., Backus, R., Child, D. and Schulman, J. L. (1971). Study of the relationship between neurological evidence of brain damage in children and activity and distractibility. *J. Consult. Clin. Psychol.,* **36,** 329–337.

Katz, P. and Deutsch, M. (1963). Relation of auditory-visual shifting to reading achievement. *Perceptual Motor Skills,* **17,** 327–332.

Keogh, B. K. and Donlon, G. McG. (1972). Field independence, impulsivity and learning disabilities. *J. Learning Disabilities,* **5,** 331–336.

Keogh, B. and Margolis, J. (1976). A Component Analysis of Attentional Problems of Educationally Handicapped Boys. *J. Abnorm. Child Psychol.,* **4,** 349–359.

Klein, G. S. (1954). Need and regulation. In Jones, M. R. (Ed.) *Nebraska symposium on Motivation.* Lincoln: University of Nebraska Press.

Kopfstein, J. H. and Neale, J. M. (1972). A multivariate study of attention dysfunction in schizophrenia. *J. Abnorm. Psychol.,* **80,** 294–298.

Kraepelin, E. (1896). *Psychiatrie. Ein Lehrbuch für Studirende und Aerzte,* 5th edition. Leipzig: Barth.

Kupietz, S. and Richardson, E. (1978). Children's vigilance performance and inattentiveness in the classroom. *J. Child Psychol. Psychiat.,* **19,** 145–154.

Lehman, E. B. (1972). Selective strategies in children's attention to task-relevant information. *Child Dev.,* **43,** 197–210.

Levy, F. (1978). The Development of sustained attention and inhibition in children. Unpublished manuscript.

Lovaas, O. I., Schreibman, L., Koegel, R. and Rehm, R. (1971). Selective responding by autistic children to multiple sensory input. *J. Abnorm. Psychol.,* **77,** 211–222.

Luria, A. R. (1961). *The role of speech in the regulation of normal and abnormal behaviour.* (Ed.) Tizard, J. Oxford: Pergamon Press.

Maccoby, E. E. (1967). Selective auditory attention in children. In Lipsitt, L. and Spiker, C. (Eds.) *Advances in Child Development and Behaviour,* Vol. 3. New York: Academic Press.

Maccoby, E. E. (1969). The development of stimulus selection. In Hill, J. P. (Ed.) *Minnesota Symposium on Child Psychology,* vol. 3. Minneapolis: University of Minnesota Press.

Macfarlane, J. W., Allen, L. and Honzik, M. P. (1954). *A Developmental Study of the Behaviour Problems of Normal Children between 21 months and 14 years.* Berkeley: University of California Press.

McDonald, R. D. and Burns, S. B. (1964). Visual vigilance and brain damage: an empirical study. *J. Neurol. Neurosurg. and Psychiat.,* **27,** 206–209.

McGhie, A. (1969). *Pathology of Attention.* Harmondsworth: Penguin.

Mednick, S. A., Schulsinger, F., Higgins, B. and Bell, B. (Eds.) (1974). *Genetics, Environment and Psychopathology.* Amsterdam: North-Holland Research Series.

Meldman, M. J. (1970). *Diseases of Attention and Perception.* Oxford: Pergamon Press.

Mendelson, M. J. and Haith, M. M. (1976). The Relation Between Audition and Vision in the Human Newborn. *Monographs of the Society for Research In Child Develop.,* Serial No. 167, **41** (4), 1–72.

Messer, S. (1970). The effect of anxiety over intellectual performance in reflection-impulsivity in children. *Child Dev.,* **41,** 723–735.

Messer, S. B. (1976). Reflection-impulsivity: a review. *Psychol. Bull.,* **83,** 1026–1052.

Mirsky, A. and van Buren, J. (1965). On the nature of the 'absence' in centrencephalic epilepsy: a study of some behavioural, electroencephalographic and autonomic factors. *Electroencephalography and Clinical Neurophysiology,* **18,** 334–348.

Moffitt, A. R. (1973). Intensity discrimination and cardiac reaction in young infants. *Devel. Psychol.,* **8,** 357–359.

Moray, N. (1969). *Attention: Selective Processes in Vision and Hearing.* London: Hutchinson Educational.

Moss, H. A. and Robson, K. S. (1968). Maternal influences on early social-visual behaviour. *Child Dev.* **39,** 401–408.

Noland, E. C. and Schuldt, W. J. (1971). Sustained attention and reading retardation. *J. Exper. Education,* **40,** 73–75.

Odom, R. and Guzman, R. D. (1972). Development of hierarchies of dimensional salience. *Devel. Psychol.,* **6,** 271–287.

Pelham, W. and Ross, A. (1977). Selective Attention in children with reading problems: a developmental study of incidental learning. *J. Abnorm. Child Psychol.*, **5**, 1–8.

Peterson, D. R., Quay, H. C. and Tiffany, T. L. (1961). Personality factors related to juvenile delinquency. *Child Dev.*, **32**, 355–372.

Piaget, J. (1961). *Les Mécanismes Perceptifs*. Paris: Presses Universitaires de France.

Pick, A. D., Christy, M. D. and Frankel, G. W. (1972). A developmental study of visual selective attention. *J. Exper. Child Psychol.*, **14**, 165–175.

Pick, A. D., Frankel, D. G. and Hess, V. L. (1975). Children's Attention: The Development of Selectivity. In Hetherington, E. M. (Ed.) *Review of Child Development Research*, Vol. 5. Chicago and London: The University of Chicago Press.

Preston, M. A., Guthries, J. T. and Childs, B. (1974). Visual evoked responses in normal and disabled readers. *Psychophysiology*, **11**, 452–457.

Pribram, K. H. (1967). The New Neurology and the biology of emotion: a structural approach. *Amer. Psychol.*, **22**, 830–838.

Quay, H. C. (1964). Personality dimensions in delinquent males as inferred from the factor analysis of behaviour ratings. *J. Research in Crime and Delinquency*, **1**, 33–37.

Ross, A. O. (1976). *Psychological Aspects of Learning Disabilities and Reading Disorders*. New York: McGraw-Hill.

Ross, D. M. and Ross, S. A. (1976). *Hyperactivity: Research, Theory and Action*. New York: Wiley.

Rosvold, H. E., Mirsky, A. F., Sarason, I., Bransome, E. D. and Beck, L. H. (1956). A continuous performance test of brain damage. *J. Consult. Psychol.*, **20**, 343–352.

Rourke, B. P. and Czudner, G. (1972). Age differences in auditory reaction time of 'brain-damaged' and normal children under regular and irregular preparatory internal conditions. *J. Exper. Child Psychol.*, **14**, 372–378.

Rourke, B. P. and Orr, R. R. (1977). Prediction of the Reading and Spelling Performances of Normal and Retarded Readers: A Four Year Follow-Up. *J. of Abnorm. Child Psychol.*, **5**, 9–20.

Rutschman, J., Cornblatt, B., and Erlenmeyer-Kimling, L. (1977). Sustained attention in children at risk for schizophrenia. *Arch. of Gen. Psychiat.*, **34**, 571–575.

Rutter, M., Graham, P. and Yule, W. (1970). *A Neuropsychiatric Study in Childhood*. London: Heinemann.

Salapatek, P. and Kessen, W. (1966). Visual scanning of triangles by the human newborn. *J. Exper. Child Psychol.* **3**, 155–157.

Salapatek, P. and Kessen, W. (1973). Prolonged investigation of a plane geometric triangle by the human newborn. *J. Exper. Child Psychol.*, **15**, 22–29.

Schover, L. R. and Newsom, C. D. (1976). Overselectivity, developmental level, and overtraining in autistic and normal children. *J. Abnorm. Child Psychol.* **4**, 289–298.

Schulman, J. L., Kasper, J. C. and Throne, F. M. (1965). *Brain Damage and Behaviour: A Clinical-Experimental Study*. Illinois: Charles C. Thomas.

Senf, G. M. (1969). Development of immediate memory for bisensory stimuli in normal children and children with learning disorders. *Devel. Psychol. Monographs*, **1**, (6, Pt. 2).

Shaffer, D., McNamara, N. and Pincus, J. H. (1974). Controlled observations on patterns of activity, attention and impulsivity in brain-damaged and psychiatrically disturbed boys. *Psychol. Med.*, **4**, 4–18.

Shagass, C. C. (1972). *Evoked Brain Potentials in Psychiatry*. New York: Plenum Press.

Siegel, A. W. and Stevenson, H. W. (1966). Incidental learning: a developmental study. *Child Dev.*, **37**, 811–818.

Sobotka, K. and May, J. (1977). Visual evoked potentials and reaction time in normal and dyslexic children. *Psychophysiology*, **14**, 18–24.

Sokolov, Ye. N. (1960). Neuronal models and the orienting reflex. In Brazier, M. A. (Ed.) *The Central Nervous System and Behaviour*. New York: Josiah Macey Jr. Foundation.

Spinelli, D. N. and Pribram, K. H. (1966). Changes in visual recovery functions produced by temporal lobe stimulation in monkeys. *Electroencephalography and Clinical Neurophysiology*, **20**, 44–49.

Spring, B., Nuechterlein, K. H., Sugarman, J. and Matthysse, S. (1977). The 'New look' in Studies of Schizophrenic Attention and Information Processing. *Schizophrenia Bulletin*, **3**, 470–482.

Sroufe, L. A. (1971). Age changes in cardiac deceleration within a fixed foreperiod reaction time task: An index of attention. *Devel. Psychol.*, **5**, 338–343.

Sroufe, L. A., Sonies, B., West, W. and Wright, F. (1973). Anticipatory heart rate deceleration and reaction time in children with and without referral for learning disability. *Child Dev.*, **44**, 267–273.

Strauss, A. A. and Lehtinen, L. E. (1947). *Psychopathology and Education of The Brain-Injured Child*. New York: Grune & Stratton.

Stroh, C. M. (1971). *Vigilance: the problem of sustained attention*. Oxford: Pergamon Press.

Swets, J. A., Tanner, W. P. and Birdsall, T. G. (1961). Decision processes in perception. *Psychological Review*, **68**, 301–340.

Sykes, D. H., Douglas, V. I., Weiss, G. and Minde, K. (1971). Attention in hyperactive children and the effect of methylphenidate (Ritalin). *J. Child Psychol. Psychiat.*, **12**, 129–139.

Tarver, S. A. and Hallahan, D. P. (1974). Attention Deficits in Children with Learning Disabilities: A Review. *J. Learning Disabilities*, **7**, 560–569.

Taylor, E. (1979). Psychophysiology: Childhood Disorders. In Van Praag, H. M., Lader, M. H., Rafaelsen, O. J. and Sachar, E. J. (Eds.) *Handbook of Biological Psychiatry*, Vol. 2. New York: Marcel Dekker.

Tizard, B. and Rees, J. (1975). The effect of early institutional rearing on the behaviour problems and affectional relations of four-year-old children. *J. Child Psychol. Psychiat.*, **16**, 61–73.

Treisman, A. M. (1969). Strategies and models of selective attention. *Psychological Review*, **76**, 282–299.

Walter, W. G. (1967). Slow potential changes in the human brain associated with expectancy, decision and intention. *Electroencephalography and Clinical Neurophysiology Supplement*, **26**, 123–130.

Weiss, G., Kruger, E., Danielson, U. and Elman, M. (1975). Effect of long-term treatment of hyperactive children with methylphenidate. *Canadian Med. Assoc. J.*, **112**, 159–165.

Werner, H. and Strauss, A. (1939). Types of visuomotor activity in the relation to low and high performance ages. *Proceedings of the American Association of Mental Deficiency*, **44**, 163–168.

Werry, J. S., Sprague, R. L. and Cohen, M. N. (1975). Conners' Teacher Rating Scale for use in drug studies with children—an empirical study. *J. Abnorm. Child Psychol.*, **3**, 217–229.

Wetherford, M. J. and Cohen, L. B. (1973). Developmental changes in infant visual preferences for novelty and familiarity. *Child Dev.*, **44**, 416–424.

White, S. H. (1966). Age differences in reaction to stimulus variation. In Harvey, O. J. (Ed.) *Experience, structure and adaptability*. New York: Springer.

Witkin, H. A., Dyk, R. B., Paterson, H. F., Goodenough, D. R. and Karp, S. A. (1962). *Psychological Differentiation: Studies of Development*. New York: Wiley.

Wittenborn, J. (1943). Factorial equations for tests of attention. *Psychometrika*, **8**, 19–35.

Wohlberg, G. W. and Kornetsky, C. (1973). Sustained Attention in Remitted Schizophrenics. *Arch. of Gen. Psychiat.*, **28**, 533–537.

Wright, J. C. and Vlietstra, A. G. (1975). The Development of Selective Attention: From Perceptual Exploration to Logical Search. In Reese, H. W. (Ed.) *Advances In Child Development and Behaviour*, vol. 10. New York: Academic Press.

Wynne, L. C. and Singer, M. T. (1963). Thought disorder and family relations of schizophrenics. *Arch. Gen. Psychiat.*, **9**, 191–206.

Zaporozhets, A. V. (1965). The development of perception in the preschool child. *Monographs of the Society for Research in Child Development*, **30**, (2, whole No. 100), 82–101.

Zeaman, D. and House, B. J. (1963). The role of attention in retardate discrimination learning. In Ellis, N. R. (Ed.) *Handbook of Mental Deficiency*. New York: McGraw-Hill.

Zelniker, T. and Jeffrey, W. E. (1976). Reflective and Impulsive Children: Strategies of Information Processing Underlying Differences in Problem Solving. *Monographs of the Society for Research in Child Development*. **41** (5, whole No. 168), 1–59.

Zelniker, T., Jeffrey, W. E., Ault, R. and Parsons, J. (1972). Analysis and modification of search strategies of impulsive and reflective children on the Matching Familiar Figures test. *Child Dev.*, **43**, 321–335.

18. LANGUAGE

PATRICIA HOWLIN

Jesperson, (1922) regarded the essence of language as 'human activity—activity on the part of one individual to make himself understood, and activity on the part of the other to understand what was in the mind of the first. These two individuals ... the speaker and the hearer should never be lost sight of if we want to understand the nature of language'. Language is never the rather static skill which many definitions make it appear; rather it is a dynamic, active, social process affecting almost all man's behaviour.

The meaning of language

Before discussing language development in the young child it is important to clarify the various meanings attributed to this term. Sometimes it is used to refer simply to the actual ability to speak—that is, to produce words or sounds; at other times it may refer to all the skills, including symbolic thought, comprehension and the use and understanding of verbal and non-verbal cues which are essential for communication. As early as 1916, de-Saussure recognized this confusion in terminology and stressed the need to distinguish between the executive skills used in speaking and the more fundamental ability to comprehend and use the basic rules of a language for the purpose of communication. Chomsky (1965) also emphasized the difference between 'Performance', or the actual use of speech, and 'Competence' or the speaker's knowledge (not necessarily expressed in verbal terms) of the rules of his language. Such distinctions are important since the inability to speak does not necessarily mean that language is absent. Thus, the ability to communicate with, and respond to others, as well as the facility for symbolic thought, or 'internal language' may exist even though speech is entirely lacking. For example, William James (1890) recorded the many thoughts of a deaf-mute; Smith *et al.* (1947) found that even after curare resulted in total paralysis and inability to speak, thinking processes were not impaired; Lenneberg (1964) showed that congenital anarthria did not prevent the understanding of language propositions and concepts; and Furth (1966) has demonstrated that deaf children lacking anything resembling normal speech can perform at a relatively high level on tests involving symbolic reasoning.

In sharp contrast it may be possible to possess speech but yet be totally lacking in comprehension or the capacity for abstract thought or inner language. A well-trained Mynah bird, for example, may have excellent *speech* but absolutely no language.

In the following chapter therefore, 'language' refers to the basic ability to communicate and to the capacity for symbolic thought. 'Speech' refers to the ability to produce words and sounds. Similarly 'Speech Disorders' refer to defects in the production of sound, and the ability to speak. 'Language disorder' involves a central deficit in the processing and use of language and language related skills.

Language—its relationship with social and emotional development

The growth of language in the young child does not take place in isolation but is closely related to growth in both cognitive and social skills. The association between speech and language difficulties and subsequent problems in other areas has been demonstrated in a number of studies. Solomon (1961) found that children with speech defects were much more likely to be reported as having social and emotional problems than controls. Rutter *et al*. (1970) in the Isle of Wight Study also showed that speech difficulties were twice as common in boys with psychiatric disorders as in the general population. Children with more severe *language* problems are likely to show high rates of behaviour disturbance. For example, deaf children frequently have additional emotional and behavioural problems (Lewis, 1968). Children with developmental dysphasia tend to show more disturbance in behaviour and social skills than normal children, particularly when they are younger (Wing, 1969; Rutter, 1977). Autistic children invariably show severe social, emotional and behavioural problems in addition to profound language impairment.

Language handicaps are common in children referred to psychiatric clinics (Ingram, 1959; Chess and Rosenberg, 1974; Friedlander *et al*., 1974). This association between language retardation and psychiatric disturbance is also found in the general population. Stevenson and Richman (1978) found behaviour disturbances in 59% of children with language delay; a rate four times that in the total population. Impaired social relationships, mood, activity and over-activity were the commonest problems. The Isle of Wight Study findings (Rutter *et al*., 1970) on a much smaller group were very similar.

It is not possible on the basis of the associations reported in the above studies to determine whether communication problems are the cause or the consequence of behavioural difficulties; or whether both result independently from some further aetiological factors. However, since language delays are frequently reported by parents as occurring *before* other difficulties it seems probable that in many children behavioural disturbances may result from the problems in communication rather than vice versa.

It is important, however, 'to get the perspective right' (Rutter, 1972). Many children with language handicaps do *not* show psychological problems, and thus language retardation cannot *directly* lead to social/emotional problems. Rutter suggests five different ways in which a language handicap may *indirectly* lead to emotional or behavioural disturbance: through educational failure, through impaired social relationships caused by communication difficulties, through lack of social integration, through the effects of teasing and rejection by other children, and through associated brain damage. In addition, Richman (1977), and Stevenson and Richman (1978) stress the importance of social and family factors in the development of behaviour problems, since they found a strong association between adverse social conditions and language delay and behaviour problems.

Whatever the mechanisms, any child with a speech or language handicap should be regarded as being 'at risk' for social/emotional difficulties. The implications for diagnosis and appropriate treatment are obvious. This requires a knowledge of how language develops in the normal child.

STAGES IN LANGUAGE DEVELOPMENT

Early responses to language and the growth of understanding

Language development does not begin simply when the child uses his first word or his first approximation to 'Mama'. The ability to communicate, and to respond to communication by others appears at a much earlier age, long before the acquisition of verbal skills. As early as twelve *hours* post-delivery there is some evidence (Condon and Sandler, 1974) that new-born infants synchronize their actions with the sound of an adult voice.

At 1 month the child is able to make fine discriminations between speech sounds (Eimas *et al*., 1971; Morse, 1972). By 3 months the infant can respond differentially to normal and exaggerated (or 'baby-talk') intonations and is able to differentiate between friendly and hostile voices. At this age, too, prelinguistic 'conversations' between the child and his mother are well established. Thus, whenever the mother speaks, the child is likely to respond with vocalizations of his own, which in turn are followed by more speech by his mother. (Freedle and Lewis, 1977; Olson, 1972).

This early responsiveness to the mother's voice frequently gives the impression that the child is able to understand a great deal of what is said to him, although Lewis (1951) showed that infants respond more to intonation patterns than to the actual words used. Gradually, however, as the same combinations of sounds are daily associated with the same familiar objects the child learns to recognize particular words. Understanding of simple commands, such as 'clap hands' or 'wave bye bye' and of words, such as 'No', 'Mummy' or 'Daddy' or the child's own name, tends to occur at about 8 to 9 months and before the end of the first year children are able to make associations between *familiar* objects and specific words. However, at this age these same words may not be applied to similar but unfamiliar objects. The word 'music', for example, may be associated with a record player in the child's own room, but not recognized in other situations for many months (Bloom, 1973).

The relationship between the use and understanding of language

While normal children seem able to understand at least a limited number of words well before they are a year old, the actual *use* of such words generally appears sometime later. Lewis (1951), for example, suggests that there is a gap of about 1 month between the child's understanding of words, and the clear use of words or word approximations to name objects.

The relationship between the child's early understanding and use of words, however, is a complicated one. For instance, the first words children use are not necessarily the first words they understood. Moreover, from 9 or 10 months onwards, some children produce echolalic words often without understanding them. Experimental investigations of whether comprehension necessarily precedes production are contradictory. Some studies show that production actually *precedes* comprehension (Keeney and Smith, 1971; Chapman and Miller, 1975); others that comprehension is ahead of production (Fraser, Bellugi and Brown, 1963; Lovell and Dixon, 1967; Nelson, 1973); others that both develop together. In fact, it seems probable that whether or not the child comprehends a particular word before he uses it depends both on situational context and on the specific word or structure investigated. However, on the whole comprehension and production probably develop more or less in parallel, perhaps with comprehension being slightly in advance of production.

If language is to develop normally the child must possess the ability to associate the spoken word with the actual object or person it refers to. Blind children, for example, because they are denied the visual cues so important in language learning are generally delayed in language development. Intellectual retardation or other cognitive impairment, such as that found in autism, may also severely affect the child's ability to make the association between spoken words and the objects to which they refer. Deaf children, too, because of their inability to hear the words spoken around them are invariably severely delayed in their acquisition of language.

Early vocalizations

Expressive and receptive language skills do not develop in isolation, and as the infant's responsiveness to sound and his understanding develop so too does the range of his vocalizations. For the first 2 months or so of life the main sounds produced (apart from coughs, hiccoughs, yawns, etc.) are those used to express distress, excitement and contentment. Gradually the infant's cries become more differentiated and can be reliably interpreted by parents as expressing requests, greetings, hunger or surprise (Ricks, 1975). At about the age of 3–4 months the infant also begins to produce combinations of vowel and consonant sounds known as 'babbling'. Over the next few months these sounds increase rapidly in range and complexity, with many new sounds appearing as the child's teeth develop. Such sounds are used both in social interaction with the parents and for the child's own entertainment, and by the age of 7 to 8 months the child may spend a great deal of his time in 'self soliloquy'.

It is at this stage that as well as learning to amuse himself, the child becomes more aware of the value of his vocalizations in influencing others around him. Often by 9 months or so the child is able to use rising or falling intonations differentially to signify 'requests' or 'statements'. Vocalizations also become more clearly differentiated according to whether the child is alone, or with an adult, and whether the adult, or the situation he is in is familiar or strange.

Shortly afterwards speech cadences begin to be heard and there is consistent imitation of heard sounds, occasionally leading to approximations to words such as 'Mama', 'Dada' and 'Baba'. By the age of 1 year, longer and more inflected 'sentence' patterns are produced; appropriate use of words such as 'Ta', 'Mama', 'Dada', 'Bye-bye' begins, as well as onomatopaeic sounds such as 'Choo Choo', (for train) or 'Brrm Brrm' (for car).

The relationship of babble to later language development

There is considerable disagreement about the role of babbling in later language acquisition. Jakobsen (1968) and Lenneberg (1967) suggest that there is a little connection between babbling sounds and later speech sounds but Oller *et al.* (1976) view babble as a direct precursor of later phonological development and cite evidence to show that babbling sequences can predict the phonetic sequences later used in first words. In addition, some children, just before they begin to speak, produce complex strings of babbled sounds which, at a distance, may be indistinguishable from real speech. Many children also continue to babble for some months after the onset of speech and may use babbling intonations to express certain notions (such as requests or rejection) even after they have acquired some words (Menn, 1971).

It has been argued by behaviourists (Mowrer, 1958) that, by selective reinforcement of the child's babble, parents narrow down the baby's repertoire to just those sounds which occur in the language spoken around them. However, this view has not been supported by subsequent research. Firstly, many of the sounds which appear in children's first words have never occurred in earlier babble. Conversely, certain sounds used in babble cannot be produced in the child's first words. The sounds [l] and [r], for example, are very frequent in babbling, but are amongst the latest sounds children master when they begin to talk.

Secondly and perhaps more importantly, most parents do not seem to be in the least selective about the sounds they want their infants to produce, and generally they encourage all vocalizations indiscriminately. Dodd (1972) has shown that even if parents do try to reinforce babble, they succeed simply in increasing the *amount* of babble used by the child, the *range* of sounds does not increase.

It now seems most likely that while some elements of the linguistic system emerge gradually out of the babbling period other aspects do not. Clark and Clark (1977) postulate that while experience with babbling may be a necessary preliminary to gaining articulatory control of the speech organs, there is no particular reason to expect a *direct* connection between the specific sounds produced in babbling and those produced later on.

That at least an indirect relationship exists between babble and later language development is suggested by studies of children who fail to acquire normal language. Autistic children, for example, rarely seem to produce normal patterns of babble; the sounds they make are infrequent, limited in range and lacking in conversational intonations. Retarded children tend to exhibit immature patterns of babble and to be delayed in their acquisition of speech inflections. Deaf children, too, show abnormal development of babbling. Lenneberg (1967) suggests that they go through a short period of apparently normal babbling which then stops, although some infants with central deafness may show impaired sound production from birth (Murphy, 1964). Unless a child is very profoundly deaf babble usually continues, but without the development of speech inflections, up to about 9 months. Thereafter many sounds begin to disappear and by 12 months only very primitive sounds may remain. For the early diagnosis of deafness, therefore, and possibly of many other language disorders as well, the recognition that a child is failing to develop 'mature' patterns of babble is extremely important. It is also suggested (Murphy, 1964) that if early vocalizations can be maintained in the deaf child, later retardation in speech development may be reduced.

The importance of non-verbal communication

Language, as already stated, does not involve simply the acquisition of verbal skills, but includes, too, many non-verbal skills necessary in communication.

The young infant responds to his mother's voice not only with vocalizations of his own but with physical signs of response—such as seeking eye contact, smiling, and lifting his arms in anticipation of being picked up. Gradually gestures become more differentiated, and by the age of about 10 or 11 months of age the child begins to show, give and to point to objects. These early 'speech acts' are used predominantly to obtain adult attention or invoke aid, as well as to signal protest, pleasure or interest in events. To begin with they are accompanied with word-like sounds, which are relatively invariant—the same sound, such as 'Da' being used to accompany all requests. Later, gestures are associated with clearer words which at

first tend to be rather stereotyped and restricted in range; for example, 'Give' used when asking for any object, or 'Dada' or 'Mama' used to gain attention. Gradually the range of words expands, so that the child is able to express his needs more precisely and in many different contexts.

The failure to develop normal, non-verbal patterns of communication may well herald later and more profound language difficulties as well as affecting the quality of the relationship between the child and his mother. Blind children, for example, although they may react to physical contact and to the sound of their mother's voice cannot make direct eye contact. The importance of eye-to-eye gaze in early mother–child interaction has been noted in a number of studies (Greenman, 1963; Robson, 1967; Vine, 1973; Jaffe *et al.*, 1973). If this is reduced, as it is with blind babies, social and verbal interaction between mother and child may be seriously affected.

Deaf children, on the other hand, do not respond to speech sounds but usually show normal responsiveness to facial expression and to gestures. Often, indeed, it is because of this very responsiveness, and their use of non-verbal forms of communication that a firm diagnosis of deafness may be considerably delayed.

Their behaviour contrasts markedly with that of autistic children who are frequently reported as being unresponsive not only to their mother's voice but to her facial expression and to her physical gestures. Such children also fail to use gesture to initiate social interaction themselves and this lack of both non-verbal and verbal communication skills is often apparent very early in the child's development.

The emergence of first words

The emergence of a child's first words has long been a topic of interest for workers in the field of child development. Early studies tended to consist of researchers' diaries, of the speech used by their own children. Probably the best known are those of Leopold (1939–49) and Piaget (1951). More recently, sophisticated analyses have replaced the diary technique although the subjects are still, almost invariably, the investigator's own children (Halliday, 1976; Greenfield and Smith, 1976).

Analyses of early utterances have, typically, centred on two main areas: the *types* of words used by child developing language and the *meanings* they express.

Types of words used

After their early 'echolalic' use of words, the first functional words which children use refer to familiar people and objects which they encounter daily (Nelson, 1973). Thus, 'Mama' and 'Dada' are commonly reported by gratified parents as being the first meaningful utterances to appear. By the time children acquire a vocabulary of 50 words (between 1 year 3 months–2 years) most use some words for people, food, body parts, clothing, animals, household items and vehicles.

At first, children tend to be very precise in their use of certain words—the word 'Daddy', for example, refers only to their father and no one else; 'cat' refers only to their own cat. At about 14 or 15 months when language begins to expand more rapidly these words may suddenly acquire many different meanings. Thus 'Daddy' may be used to refer to any male the child sees (to the possible embarrassment of his mother on the bus!); 'Cat' may be used to indicate all animals, and even any object which possess the 'catty' quality of having four legs. By about 3 years of age, as the child's vocabulary increases this 'over-generalization' begins to decrease, and the child once again becomes more specific in his labelling.

To begin with, too, the child's first words are used mainly to identify objects and people which he sees around him. By the latter half of the second year, however, language becomes more flexible, and the child is able to progress from simple labelling to asking for, and talking about, objects which are not present. This progression from associative labelling to symbolic naming is often considered the first stage in the development of true language. Nouns are generally the first to appear, with verbs appearing shortly after. Prepositions, adjectives and adverbs are next to appear at about 2 years of age, while correct use of pronouns does not usually emerge until sometime later. Conjunctions rarely appear until about 30 months (McCarthy, 1954).

The meanings expressed in first utterances

As soon as the child's use of language progresses beyond simple labelling it is clear that a single word can express many different meanings. The word 'Daddy' may be used in a variety of contexts to identify Daddy's hat, to inquire where Daddy has gone, or to convey pleasure on Daddy's return from work.

The fact that the words used by a young child are capable of expressing much more than their face value would suggest has, of course, been recognized by mothers down the ages, but linguists have been slower in accepting this. Stevenson wrote in 1893: 'In the infants speech these words are not nouns but equivalent to whole sentences. When a very young child says "water", he is not using the word merely as the name of the object so designated, but with the value of an assertion, something like, "I want water", or "There is water".' However, it is only recently that the 'holophrastic' nature of first utterances has been more widely accepted. Young children mean more than they say, but it is difficult to correctly interpret their meaning. Nevertheless, Greenfield and Smith (1976) have recently shown that reliable interpretations *are* possible. They found that by using information from context and intonation, independent raters, one of whom was the mother, could reach a high level of agreement in their interpretation of single words. The different speech functions they identified for two children are summarized in Table I, and similar relationships have also been reported by Bloom (1973). To date, however, detailed, reliable investigations of children's first words, are still rather limited in number, and more studies are needed to validate the generality of the findings of Greenfield and Bloom.

TABLE I

PREDOMINANT FUNCTIONS EXPRESSED IN EARLY ONE-WORD UTTERANCES
(from Greenfield and Smith, 1976)

Semantic Function	Example of Word Used	Instance
Performative	'Bye'	Saying goodbye
Volition	'Up'	Asking to be picked up
Indicative object	Door	Pointing at door
Volitional object	Bread	Reaching for bread
Agent	Mummy	Naming mother
Action or state of agent	Down	When about to get down
Action or state of object	Gone	When mother looking for lost needle
Object	Juice	When drinking juice
Dative	Dada	Offering bottle to father
Object and location/other object	Milk	Referring to milk in fridge
Animate being and location/other object	Daddy	Pointing to Father's books
Location	Chair	Putting toy on chair
Modification of Event	Again	Holding out hand to be washed

Two word utterances

By the age of 2 years the average child is able to understand several hundred words and has a spoken vocabulary of about 200. Within a few months of using their first words children begin to combine single words together to form phrases. At first these word combinations may be invariate and used by the child as single words—as, for example, in 'Wanna' or 'Get-up' where the child shows no recognition that he is actually using more than one word. Following this intermediate stage more general use of two-word utterances usually develops fairly rapidly. There is some evidence (Slobin, 1970) of cross-cultural similarities in the structure of these early utterances, a finding which has led to the search for some 'universal' characteristics in early language development. Braine's notion (1963) of 'Pivot' and 'Open'* classes of words which went together in certain predictable and invariant combinations was for a time heralded as one of these much sought after 'linguistic universals'. Unfortunately, it was soon found that the rules postulated by Braine did not hold true for children speaking different languages, nor indeed for most English-speaking children, and the notion of Pivot Grammar has now been largely jettisoned (Bloom, 1970; Braine, 1976). Chomskian theories of transformational grammar (*see* Greene, 1972 for a useful introduction) have also been employed in the analysis of early utterances. However, since there is little agreement amongst linguists as to how such analyses should be carried out, and since analyses of this kind apply predominantly to the sentences used by competent, adult speakers, rather than to the relatively a-grammatical structures used by young children, this approach has not proved very

---

* 'Pivot' words comprised a small group of words, such as 'Allgone', 'My', 'It', etc. which appeared in a fixed position in the utterance—*e.g.* 'Allgone teddy', 'Push it', 'My Daddy'. Open words were a much larger class of words, which could appear alone, or in combination and had no fixed position.

fruitful. Much more useful information on the development of language at this stage has been gained by studying the *meanings* rather than the structure of children's first phrases.

Semantic relations in two-word utterances

At the two-word level children continue to use language much as in the same way as they used single words, *i.e.* to gain attention or to request help from an adult. Their new-found skill in combining words, however, makes it possible for them to express many new and different relationships. A number of cross-cultural studies (Slobin, 1970; Bowerman, 1973; Bloom, 1970 and Brown, 1973) indicate that certain prevalent relationships are expressed in early two-word utterances (*see* Table II).

TABLE II

PREDOMINANT RELATIONSHIPS IN EARLY TWO-WORD UTTERANCES
(from Clark and Clark, 1971)

Semantic Relationship	Example of Utterance
Assertions	
Presence of object	That car. See sock
Denial of Presence	Allgone shoe. No set
Location of Object	There doggie. Pennyinnere
Possession of Object	Mama dress. Kendall chair
Quality of Object	Pretty boat. Big bus
Ongoing event	Mummy sleep. Hit ball
Requests:	
For Action	More taxi. Want ball
For information	Where doggie? Sit water?
Refusal	No more

Children's grasp of language at this stage enables them to identify the presence of objects, and to assert that objects are in particular places, belonging to particular people, or have particular attributes. They can describe ongoing events, as well as deny the existence of objects or events. In addition the child at this stage is able to make requests for actions and objects, he can ask for information, and make so called 'negative requests' or refusals.

The use of early language

In the discussion so far the emphasis has been on the development of communicative language. Nevertheless, by no means all of the child's speech is used to communicate, and in the early stages there is a lot of 'echolalia' or repetitions of other's speech. When children are first learning to talk they frequently go through a stage of echoing the last few words of what is said to them. Some writers consider that echolalia is merely a function of the child's poor understanding of language, although others (Stewart and Hamilton, 1976) suggest that it may also play an important role in building up the child's vocabulary. In normal children echolalia usually ceases about the age of 2½ years. Prolonged echolalia when it does occur is almost always associated with mental retardation or with specific language disorders, particularly autism. It also occurs in a number of blind children.

The egocentric nature of children's speech is apparent, too, in children's early spontaneous utterances. Although the 1-year-old child can use words to label or ask for objects, he also speaks at times without apparently caring who, if anyone, is listening to him. As time goes on this egocentric use of speech often increases. The child will talk happily to himself, using speech to describe or control his own actions. There is frequent repetition of certain words and phrases, particularly when the child is alone in bed, and by the age of 2½ to 3 years these solitary monologues may become quite lengthy (Weir, 1962).

Early language and the development of play

These verbal 'rituals' which the child goes through when alone are often used later when the child is involved in parallel play with other children (Garvey, 1977). Playing with language in this way is considered important not only in the child's acquisition of vocabulary, but also in the development of symbolic thought and in social and imaginative play. If early 'play with language' does not develop, play in other areas may also be deficient.

Certainly, children who show language delay are also impaired in their use of toys and in their symbolic play, and these abnormalities become more marked as the children grow older (Lovell *et al.*, 1968; Weiner, 1969; Hulme and Lunzer, 1966; Weiner *et al.*, 1969).

Autistic children, even those who eventually develop perfectly good grammatical speech, are particularly handicapped in their play. Unlike children with other language handicaps (*e.g.* developmental dysphasia) they rarely show imaginative play, and remain grossly impaired in their capacity for symbolic language.

Speech delayed and mentally handicapped children also tend to show more limited play than children with normal language, although all except the most severely handicapped generally show some evidence of 'inner language'.

Young deaf children on the other hand usually show good imaginative play, often having an imaginary playmate like normal children (Newson and Newson, 1970). Even in deaf children with very poor speech and comprehension, imaginative play sequences may appear quite normal (Gregory, 1976). Blind children are often delayed in imaginative play, just as they are in verbal language. They tend to catch up later, however, and Fraiberg and Adelson (1973) link the development of imaginary play with dolls, with the emergence of self-referencing pronouns such as 'me' and 'i'.

The capacity for imaginative play is closely related to the later development of symbolic thought and unless children do develop such skills language ability is likely to remain profoundly impaired. Fortunately there is some evidence that play, and hence subsequent language development, may be fostered by special training. Hulme and Lunzer (1966) showed that if free play were encouraged retarded children could quickly learn to play spontaneously. Rosenblatt (1977) trained mute aphasic children in specific play activities and found both an increase in play and improvements, albeit limited, in their use of language.

Later stages in language development

During the second year of life the child's understanding of language grows rapidly. He is able to follow most simple instructions, to understand more and more of adult conversation and to appreciate nursery rhymes and familiar stories. Articulation improves; pretend play with toys begins to develop and imitative gestural games such as pat-a-cake and peek-a-boo are greatly enjoyed. Probably the most rapid period of development, however, takes place between the years of 2 and 5. During this time vocabulary increases to several thousand words, utterance length increases by approximately one word per year, and the child is able to use his language for many different purposes.

By the time he is 2 years old and has reached the level of two-word utterances the child's dialogue with parents is well established. He can initiate conversation, answer questions, and make his needs and wishes perfectly clear. Admittedly his speech lacks the niceties of English Grammar, but it is perfectly adequate as long as he only has to communicate with familiar adults, who understand the idiosyncracies of his speech and are usually only too willing to indulge his requests. With increased cognitive development, however, the child begins to require more sophisticated language skills to describe events around him, and to make his wishes known. Gradually, too, his environment begins to expand and he moves from the realms of the cot and playpen to a richer, more exciting world. As his range of experiences increases so too does his need to express more ideas, and to communicate with people outside the immediate family circle. Simple, two-word utterances, lacking in grammatical inflections, become inadequate to convey everything he needs to express, and hence more sophisticated language skills become necessary.

THE DEVELOPMENT OF SYNTACTICAL RULES

The use of morphemes

Having reached the two-word stage of language development, the child's next step is to elaborate and clarify his utterances. To begin with this is done by using additional 'functor' words—such as prepositions, adjectives, articles, and pronouns, which help to modulate the meaning of his utterances, and by adding inflections or 'morphemes' to nouns and verbs.

Amongst English-speaking children of between 2 and 4 years of age there appears to be a fairly regular pattern in the acquisition of such rules. (Brown, 1973; De Villiers and De Villiers, 1973). The first inflection to appear, and the easiest to use correctly is the 'ing' ending on the present progressive verbs (running, jumping, eating, etc.). The prepositions 'in' and 'on' tend to be next to appear; then comes the plural 's' ending (cats, books, etc.) the irregular past tense (saw, was, etc.) the 's' possessive ending (Daddy's, Mummy's); the articles 'a' and 'the' and the regular forms of the past tense (jumped, played, etc.)

and the third person present endings on verbs (jumps, runs, plays, etc.). The use of the verb 'to be', and the use of auxiliary verbs, is acquired rather later, sometime towards the end of the fourth year.

Correct use of morpheme rules does not develop overnight but tends to go through four main stages (Cazden, 1968; Brown, 1973). These stages of learning are typically:

1) Little or no use of the inflections or morpheme

   [*e.g.* 'I dance' for 'I danced',
   'I eat'—for 'I ate'.]

2) Occasional use of the correct morpheme, but with many omissions

   [*e.g.* I ate dinner
   I dance yesterday]

3) Correct use of the morpheme in regular forms, but overgeneralization to irregular forms

   [*e.g.* I danced,
   I eated.]

4) Correct use of both regular and irregular forms

   [*e.g.* I danced,
   I ate.]

Acquisition of these rules, however, does not necessarily follow a steady pattern and learning may often appear somewhat erratic. Many children will go through a short period of using a rule correctly, but then, as the number of inflected words they use begins to increase, so too does the number of errors they make. Totally correct usage, even of the relatively simple rules described above may not be acquired until as late as 5 or 6 years of age.

The use of transformational rules

Elementary transformations consist of a sequence of operations, such as addition, deletion or re-ordering, which effect changes on the underlying structure of a sentence. In this way various sentence types are derived from basic simple, active declarative sentences. Thus if the rules for forming a negative transformation are applied to the sentence 'I can go', the sentence: 'I cannot go' will result; if an interrogative transformation is used the sentence: 'Can I go?' will result.

In the preschool years the normal child acquires many transformational rules leading to a highly complex level of language usage. Again, emergence of these rules is not a sudden phenomenon, but they develop gradually and, at times, rather erratically. Because of the variation in children's development it is not possible to predict, with any degree of accuracy, the ages at which different structures occur. Brown (1973), for example, reports enormous differences in rule acquisition between just three children of similar middle-class, well-educated backgrounds. The problems involved in analysis of thousands upon thousands of utterances has also meant that the number of transformational rules studied in any detail remains rather limited. The development of imperatives, negatives and interrogative transformations has been studied in some detail, and a certain common pattern of acquisition can be seen to emerge. At first the child uses different intonations to express the differences between questions and commands, as in 'See chair?' or 'Want book!' Later specific words, such as 'Look' or 'Give' are used to express imperatives, often accompanied by a concomitant action such as pointing or holding out the hand; 'No' plus the relevant noun and often shaking of the head is used to express negation, as in 'No biscuit' (indicating that an object is not in its usual place), 'No bed' (indicating refusal to go to bed) or 'No naughty' (indicating denial of his mother's assertion). Questions are expressed by 'wh' words, initially 'where?' and 'what?' and later 'who?' and 'why?', but in an uninverted form as in 'Why you can't sit down?'

Only much later do deletions and inversions of word order occur as in 'Can't' or 'Won't', or 'What is that?', but even at this stage many errors may persist as in 'What did I doed?', 'I not naughty', etc.

The development of other language rules

Up to a few years ago it had been generally accepted that the normal child's acquisition of the basic rules of his language was complete by the age of about 5 years. Many language tests, for example, reflect this in that the upper limit for the test is about 6 years (Reynell, 1969). However it is now clear that language development is by no means complete at this age.

Use and comprehension of the passive transformation, for example, occurs at a relatively late age and until about 5½ to 6 years passives tend to be interpreted as if they were simple active sentences having a subject-verb-object order. Thus the phrase, 'The boy was kissed by his Mummy' would normally be interpreted as if the *boy* were doing the kissing. At about 6 years of age correct use and understanding of passives begins to emerge, although performance is still very variable and depends very much on context and on the meaningfulness of the utterance to the child. Similar stages are also found in the development of complex sentences, involving pronominal and adverbial clauses.

Other rules may not be acquired until much later. Carol Chomsky (1969) showed that the acquisition of rules such as those underlying indirect questions may not be complete until the age of 10 years or even later. Myerson (1975) found that certain morpheme rules governing noun-endings may not be established until the age of 17 or later.

Furthermore, other structures which were generally considered to be easily acquired by young children now appear to be not quite so simple as was first thought. The use of relational terms, such as big and small, more and less, fat and thin, even I and you, often causes difficulties for young children. In an experimental context, at least, it has been demonstrated that children of about 2½ to 3 years tend to confuse the meanings of such word pairs. They begin by using *neither* word correctly; later they use words such as big, tall, more and fat correctly but not their opposites of small, short, less and thin. Not until sometime between 3 and 4 years is consistently correct use of both forms attained. Prepositions also cause similar difficulties for young children and for a long time use and understanding of words such as 'in', 'on' or 'under' seems to be governed more by context than by the words themselves (*e.g.* 'on' is always used in association with a flat surface, 'in' with objects which can be identified as containers, Clark, 1973). Menyuk (1977) provides an extremely readable account of language acquisition at different ages.

Our knowledge of normal language development is based on studies of very few children, many of whom are the 'outrageously precocious' (Bates *et al.*, 1977) offspring of linguists and psychologists. Research with less advantaged groups is needed but some conclusions are possible now. Language development is more complex than once thought but there are certain patterns to this development. Also, however, the way in which language develops appears to be very much governed by the child's general cognitive development and by the environment in which he is raised.

COGNITIVE DEVELOPMENT AND THE ACQUISITION OF LANGUAGE

In the normal child cognitive, social and linguistic abilities are closely related. Progress in each one of these areas will be affected by, and in turn affect, development in the others; thus it is somewhat artificial to discuss language acquisition in isolation from other skills.

Studies of child language development have shown that stages in both verbal and preverbal communication are closely linked to stages in sensori-motor development. For instance, the child's first gestures and his use of objects to attain adult attention does not develop until he reaches Piaget's sensori-motor stage 5 (*i.e.* the stage at which he begins to explore new uses for objects rather than simply repeating old actions).

Words do not appear until a later period corresponding to Piaget's sensori-motor stage 6 (*i.e.* the capacity for mental representation and the use of symbols).

As more complex utterances develop they are generally preceded by a brief period during which the child expresses more complex ideas but does not mark these linguistically. For example, it is only *after* semantic relationships have been expressed in a simple, unmarked form, that children begin to use syntactical rules to express these explicitly. Thus, phrases such as 'Mummy hat' or 'More biscuit' will precede 'Mummy's hat', and 'More biscuits'. In other words, the child's concepts of plurality or possession develop shortly before his ability to express these grammatically.

Often too, more complex ideas are conveyed initially by using combinations of simple terms already in the child's repertoire. For instance, the emergence of three-word phrases may be preceded by the use of a number of two-word utterances in conjunction. Bloom (1973) records the use of phrases such as 'Lois read . . . read book . . . Lois book' occurring shortly before the use of utterances such as 'Lois read book'. Also, before children use plural phrases, such as 'They are green', they tend to use two singular phrases, such as 'That one is green and that one is green'. Again the child's concept of plurality is clearly developed but there is some time lapse before he acquires the linguistic forms to express this concept.

Later on, cognitive development is also important in the expression of more complex terms. Hypothetical statements ('If Daddy comes early', 'If we go to Grannie's') do not appear until the child has some capacity for pretend play or the ability to refer to possibilities rather than actual facts (Cromer, 1968). The use of verb tenses is highly dependent on children's understanding of time (Antinucci and Miller, 1975). The use of prepositions can be related to the development of spatial notions (Parisi and Antinucci, 1970), and the use of locatives (such as behind, in front of, *etc.*) can be predicted from performance on spatial tasks (Johnston, 1973).

A number of related experiments by Inhelder (1969), Sinclair (1969) and Ferreiro and Sinclair (1971) have shown that children's ability to perform Piaget-type tasks of conservation and temporal order is closely linked to their use of related linguistic structures. It has also been observed by Goodson and Greenfield (1975) that the strategies used by children in tasks involving seriation, embedding, and manipulation of objects closely parallel the early strategies used in language development. Moreover, evidence that the development of cognitive structures occurs *before* the development of linguistic structures is suggested by the finding that training in the linguistic terms used in such tasks does not improve performance; instead correct performance tends to precede the correct use of terms such as big and small, more and less.

Additional evidence on the nature of relationship between cognition and language is found in studies reported by Brown (1973) and Slobin (1973). Work by Roger Brown *et al.* (1973) has shown that the order of acquisition of a particular structure is highly correlated with measures of the syntactic and semantic complexity of such structures. Slobin also stresses the influence of cognition on language development, and postulates some rules which help to predict the order of acquisition of linguistic structures. Amongst these 'rules', which seem to apply to children of different nationalities, are:

(1) The tendency to acquire semantically consistent or regular rules early and without significant error. Hence the very regular 'ing' ending on present progressive verbs, such as jumping, running, etc., is learned more easily than the past tense which has both regular and irregular forms.

(2) The tendency to preserve the structure of a sentence as a closed entity and to avoid rearrangement of linguistic units. Thus, sentences involving inversions of word order (*e.g.* questions) or additional clauses are more difficult to process than simple, active, sentences.

(3) The tendency for word order in child language to follow a fixed subject-verb-object word order. For this reason sentences such as passives which deviate from this order tend to be misinterpreted.

Although language and cognitive development are clearly related, the precise nature of this relationship is still unclear. For example, if, within a particular language, a concept is linguistically very complex to express, the linguistic complexity may override the conceptual complexity in determining the order of its emergence. Bilingual children, for instance, may use certain structures earlier in one language rather than another if the means of expressing such terms are particularly difficult in this language. Slobin (1973), Richards (1977) and Bates *et al.* (1977) suggest that it may be extremely misleading to adhere rigidly to the notion that cognitive development is a prerequisite to language development. Social development too, may play an important role and Bates *et al.* (1977), somewhat facetiously propose over 30 000 different models for the possible interrelations of cognitive, social, linguistic development. It seems most likely, in fact, that no one particular model is correct, and that the relationship between language and cognition is never static, but shifts and varies according to the experience of the individual child, and his developing linguistic, social and cognitive skills.

Because of the intrinsic relationship between cognitive and linguistic skills it is hardly surprising that if cognitive development is impaired, so, too, is language development. Over half of children with an IQ below 70 show severe language delay and language handicap is particularly marked in children with an IQ below 50. In children with an IQ below 20, comprehension and spoken language are almost always absent (Gould, 1977). However, different subgroups of retarded children tend to show different patterns of language disability, and this is possibly related to the nature of their cognitive impairment. Autistic children, for example, show a much profounder deficit in both their use and understanding of language than retarded children of a similar non-verbal mental age. Their failure to develop normally can often be traced back to a very early age. They may fail to show normal exploratory use of objects which is typical of infants at about 3 or 4 months old. Their manipulation of objects also tends to remain somewhat rigid and stereotyped, they do not develop novel ways of dealing with objects, nor can they cope well with new situations (*i.e.* Piaget's sensori-motor stage 4—which usually begins about 6–8 months). It has been shown that in normal children communicative gestures and the use of objects to gain adult attention do not develop until the child learns to use objects in a meaningful way. Thus if the child fails to develop, from a very early age, those skills which are closely linked to subsequent language and development, it is likely that a profound communication handicap will result.

In contrast to autistic children, other handicapped children, such as those with Down's Syndrome may show no specific language deficits. They are slow to develop in both verbal *and* non-verbal areas but there is no great disparity between their overall mental age and their language age (although the high rate of speech defects in these children often result in communication problems). However, some children with arrested hydrocephalus may show relatively good expressive skills, at least at a superficial level, in spite of their limited comprehension. Some children with mild intellectual retardation show much severer delay in language development and profoundly retarded children are frequently more delayed in language than in other areas (Morley, 1965). Why language delay is greater in some retarded children than others is not known, and probably many other factors such as brain damage, hearing loss, or psychosocial deprivation play an important role.

LANGUAGE AND ENVIRONMENT

Although the development of language is dependant on the child's development in other areas of cognitive functioning, the child's environment is also important. Unless a child hears language spoken around him he will not learn to talk and, of course, whether he spoke Chinese or English is entirely dependant on his language environment.

Behaviourist views of language acquisition (Skinner 1957; Staats, 1968; Lovaas, 1977) are based on the premise that children learn language by imitating what they hear and by being selectively reinforced for their imitations. Cognitive aspects of the child's development are almost entirely ignored; so much so that Skinner (1957), for example, considered thought to be simply a form of 'covert speech'. In 1959 Chomsky made his now famous attack on Skinnerian theories stressing the absurdity of strictly behaviourist notions of language development. He pointed out that it would be almost impossible, through selective reinforcement alone, to shape the infants imitations, first of the sounds, then of the words and phrases it hears, until eventually it learns *all* the rules of the language, so that novel and previously unheard utterances can be generated. George Miller, too (1964), estimated that if an English-speaking child were to learn to use only 1000 sentences of 20 words long in this way it would take something in the order of 100,000,000,000 centuries simply to listen to them. Clearly not a particularly economical means of learning language! Moreover it is now becoming clear from recent research that children are often extremely bad imitators; also parents are not very good at selective reinforcement.

Parental influences on language development

The association between adult's speech to children, and the ways in which children themselves develop language has in recent years been a topic of much investigation. Research has focused primarily in two main areas:

a) Are there specific ways in which the linguistic form of parent's utterances influences the language development of their children?

b) Is there more general evidence to show that the amount and quality of the verbal interaction between mother and child affects language development?

Mother's language to infants:
Studies of language content

The distinctive nature of mother's speech to their infants has recently been the subject of many different studies of mother–child interaction (*see* Farwell, 1973; Snow, 1977; Snow and Ferguson, 1977). The use of a special language when talking to infants, sometimes called 'baby-talk' or 'motherese', seems to be universal (Ferguson, 1964); it is not only restricted to mothers, even 3- and 4-year-old children adopt a different style when talking to babies (Shatz and Gelman, 1973; Sachs and Devin, 1976). The involuntary nature of this form of communication seems to be demonstrated by the finding that even very education-oriented parents who intend never to use 'baby-talk' succeed in avoiding only a few common features, such as the diminutive, and 'unwittingly use about 100 others' (Brown, 1977).

What then are the features which distinguish so clearly between adult speech to adults, and adult speech to children?

When talking to babies and young children adults use a higher pitch, special intonation patterns (Garnica, 1977) and their utterances are shorter, slower, and more distinct (Broen, 1972; Phillips, 1973). Syntactically, utterances are not necessary over-simplified (Newport *et al.*, 1977) but the semantic content tends to be limited to the semantic constructions the child himself uses (Snow, 1977). There is also a predominance of deictic utterances (*i.e.* pointing out objects and situations to the child—'Here's Teddy', 'That's your nose', etc. (Newport *et al.*, 1977).

In addition mothers frequently 'expand' or provide adult versions of their children's utterances, the child's single word 'cat' typically being met with a response such as 'Yes, that's the cat, isn't she pretty.' There is frequent use of stock phrases, such as 'Good boy', 'That's fine', 'Never mind' (Cross, 1977); and a very high level of self-repetitions which seem to be used predominantly to ensure that the child is responding, and responding correctly, to what is said. Thus the mother may repeat, 'Go get the duck . . . the duck . . . yes get it . . . that's right . . . get the duck' until the child eventually does so (Cross, 1977). Virtually all the conversation tends to centre around the here-and-now environment; there is an almost exclusive use of the present tense (Snow, 1977); and mothers tend to speak about any object primarily when their child is looking at it to ensure that conversation focuses on items of interest to the child (Collis, 1975).

Cross (1977) summarizes the many ways in which mother's speech is finely tuned to the child's own psycholinguistic development, particularly to his level of understanding. It seems probable that factors such as high pitch, different intonation patterns, frequent repetitions and shorter, more distinct utterances, are effective in helping mothers to attract their children's attention and in making it easier for children to understand what is said. Shorter utterances are also more suited to the young child's memory span, whilst limitations of semantic content may aid the child's comprehension.

Cross suggests that many aspects of maternal speech may have a direct effect on children's language acquisition; a suggestion which receives some support from a number of other studies. For example, investigations by Newport et al., 1977; Snow, 1977 and Nelson, 1973 indicate that there are positive correlations between children's language development, and mothers' use of deictic utterances, imitations, expansions and reinforcement. Directions on the other hand tend to be negatively correlated with progress in language development.

However, correlational studies should not be used to infer causal relationships, and in fact experimental studies have failed to find any *direct* relationship between speech used by mothers and the language development of their children.

Work by Brown and his colleagues (1969), for example, has found that although corrections and reinforcements do occur, they are used *not* in response to the grammatical content of the child's utterance—but to the truth value of what the child says. Grammatically correct but untrue statements will be corrected, while true, but grammatically incorrect statements will usually be reinforced. Thus if child says 'We went to Grannies yesterday', when he had not done so, he is likely to be rebuked; if on the other hand he says truthfully 'We wented to the shops' this is more likely to meet with his mother's approbation. According to reinforcement theory, this should, of course, result in children growing up always speaking the truth but doing so in very bad grammar! Instead most children learn to speak perfectly well; it is the veracity of their utterances which is frequently in doubt.

Moreover, even if parents do attempt to correct their children's utterances, this apparently has little effect on the child.

McNeil (1968), for example, quotes the following dialogue:

Child : Nobody don't like me.
Mother : No, say 'nobody likes me'
Child : Nobody don't like me.

9 repetitions of this dialogue

Mother : No, now listen carefully; say '*nobody likes me*'
Child : Oh! Nobody don't likes me

Experimental studies by Cazden (1968), Feldman (1971) and Brown and Hanlon (1970), Nelson *et al.*

(1973) failed to show any direct relationship between changes in the numbers of expansions, imitations and reinforcements used by parents or teachers and subsequent language development in the child. Nor is there any evidence that frequency of a particular rule or construction in mother's speech influences acquisition of that rule by the child. Cromer (1974), for example, points out that the use of the perfect tense emerges fairly consistently at around 4 years of age in most children, but this is not preceded by any sudden increase in usage by parents. And, Brown (1973) concludes, following his extensive investigations of parental speech: 'there is no clear evidence at all that parental frequencies influence the forms we have studied'.

In summary, therefore, although adults' speech to children seems to be ideally suited to the limited expression and comprehension of the listener, there is little hard evidence to show that any particular aspect of mother's speech directly influence language acquisition in their children. Shatz and Gelman (1977) point out that it would be quite unreasonable to assume that children's language development is influenced predominantly by the speech modifications used by their parents. Many other aspects of the child's cognitive and social development will also influence the growth of language.

Studies of language quality

Although no direct links have been established between specific types of utterance used by parents, and improved, or impoverished, language development in their children, there can be no doubt that the general language environment in which children are reared does affect language skills.

Tizard et al., for example (1972) carried out an investigation of language development in residential nurseries and found a close relationship between the amount and quality of staff talk to children and the language level of the children themselves. Thus, the children who were most advanced in their language development, particularly in their comprehension, tended to come from nurseries where adults talked a lot to the children, used a high level of informative speech, and responded to the children's questions. Their findings are also supported by studies of language development in children reared by their natural parents. A longitudinal study of Elardo et al. (1977) of children at 6 months, 24 months, and 3 years of age found that the verbal responsiveness of the mother, and the amount of verbal interaction with the child were among the most important variables related to language competence in the children. Clarke-Stewart (1973) also found that children's early language development (as well as their cognitive and social development) was correlated with the amount of verbal stimulation given by mothers, although there was little relationship between the specific content of mothers' speech and children's language competence.

Evidence of more general parental influences on language acquisition can also be found in studies of the relationship between language and social class.

Social class

Low social class has frequently been associated with impoverished language development (McCarthy, 1954, Douglas *et al.*, 1968).

Bernstein (1962) found that even when intelligence level was controlled, working-class boys used shorter words, made fewer pauses and used a longer phrase length than middle-class boys. He suggested that the two groups used rather distinct forms of language, or linguistic 'codes'. Differences were attributed to the different language environments in which the children were reared. However, the relationships between speech codes and social class are both broad and complex (Bernstein, 1970), with theoretical explanations sometimes ambiguous (Lawton, 1968). Social class groups are by no means homogeneous, and differences between family types will also have a marked effect on communication patterns.

In general, however, Bernstein suggests that the emphasis placed on the encouragement of verbal skills and the expression of abstract concepts which is more typical of middle-class homes results in children developing more 'elaborated' language codes; children from working-class homes, on the other hand, tend to use more 'restricted' language codes which although useful in contacts with families and peer groups, are less effective in the current educational system. Bernstein emphasizes that it is not that working-class children lack access to more elaborated codes and wider ranges of syntactic structures, it is simply that they *use* them less. He also points out that there are constraints imposed on middle-class children's use of language, and in certain situations working-class modes of communication are *more* functional than middle-class styles.

Other studies have also shown social class differences in language. Hess and Shipman (1968) and Nelson (1973) found that working-class mothers tend to be less reinforcing and more 'rejecting' than middle-class mothers. They use a higher rate of directions but fewer questions, and fewer instances of naming objects than middle-class mothers; factors which are significantly correlated with poorer language skills in their children. Admittedly not all investigations have shown such large differences between working-class and middle-class language styles (Tizard, 1980), and studies by Snow *et al.* (1976) and Dunn *et al.* (1977) suggest that the context in which verbal interaction is examined may influence results. However, in general, studies of class differences all tend to support the existence of a relationship between children's language development and the style and frequency of mothers attempts to encourage discourse.

Children of deaf parents

Since children reared in an environment where verbal expression is not encouraged are known to be at risk, one might assume that children born to deaf parents, who obviously cannot respond to their verbalizations, would be grossly retarded in language development. However, most hearing children of deaf parents who are reared in an otherwise 'normal' environment, show no obvious language problems. Rates of speech and language problems in hearing children of deaf parents tend to be somewhat higher than in the general population but this seems to be related to the severity of speech impairments in the parents. Children of deaf mothers with virtually no intelligible speech are more likely to show problems than children whose mothers have some understandable speech (Schiff and Ventry, 1976).

Rather surprisingly, deaf children of deaf parents often show a higher level of attainment in language and many other skills, than do deaf children of hearing parents (Lenneberg, 1967; Critchley, 1967; Schlesinger and Meadow, 1972). Probably gestural communication with parents and verbal contact with other adults helps to avoid severe language problems. Lenneberg suggests that many children of deaf parents may, in effect, become 'bilingual' developing one system of communication for use with their parents and another for use outside the home.

Children of bilingual parents

Although children of bilingual parents face even more problems than monolingual children when learning to talk, in that they have to learn words in two languages rather than one, there is little evidence that this results in any permanent language deficit. Children who learn two, or even more languages from the outset are somewhat slower in acquiring language than other children but the language retardation is usually short-lived.

Longer-lasting problems, however, do seem to occur in children who have to learn a second language or cultural dialect *later* in life. Such children are usually limited in vocabulary and on verbal intelligence tests in this language (Darcy, 1953; Soflieti, 1955) although this is not invariably true (Tenezakis, 1975). Despite the problems of having to learn a second language in later life the advantages of learning two languages generally seem to outweigh the disadvantages.

Work by Peal and Lambert (1962), Slobin (1973) and Ervin-Tripp (1973), suggest that learning two languages may result in both linguistic and cognitive advantages to the child. This view is supported by a recent study by Ben-Zeev (1977) on monolingual and bilingual Hebrew- and English-speaking children. Bilingual children did less well on tests of vocabulary but they performed better on tests of processing verbal material and were more advanced in perceptual skills than monolingual children.

However, if a child does have difficulties in learning to talk, having to cope with two languages may well compound the problem. In such cases, therefore, it usually seems advisable for parents to restrict themselves to one language, at least to begin with.

Family structure

Language acquisition is also affected by family size and to the child's position in the family. Large family size has been consistently related to delays in language development, and the same association applies to language-related skills such as reading (Douglas, 1964; Douglas *et* al., 1968; Rutter et al., 1970). The correlation between large family size and language delay holds true across all social classes although the relationship is less strong in professional families than in a working-class population (Rutter and Mittler, 1972). It is suggested (Rutter and Mittler, 1972) that a child's growth in vocabulary is affected by the extent to which he converses with adults, whose language is more complex and varied, or with children whose linguistic skills are much more immature. Children from small families and first-born children have the opportunity for more intense verbal interaction with adults and therefore would be expected to reach a higher level of language ability than children from large families whose main verbal contact is with other children. This view is supported by the finding that children's vocabulary scores fall as the number of preschool children in the family increases (Douglas et al., 1968).

Multiple births

Another 'family structure' which seems to affect language development is the occurrence of twins or other multiple births. Children of multiple births begin to talk several months later than single children and verbal intelligence is often well below the level of their non-verbal skills. These differences are even more marked in twins from higher social-class groups (Mittler, 1972). As well as showing overall immaturity in language development twins and triplets frequently use more mime and gesture in communication than other children. They may even develop their own private language which is incomprehensible to everyone except the other twin (Zazzo, 1960). Since there is some evidence (Record et al., 1970) that language delays are less marked in twins whose co-twin is stillborn or dies early in infancy, it seems possible that they are caused less by genetic factors or perinatal damage than by the children's environment. That is, twins, triplets and others have less individual verbal contact with their parents than single babies, and a much higher proportion of verbal interaction with children of exactly their own age.

LANGUAGE DEVELOPMENT IN CHILDREN WITHOUT FAMILIES

The discussion so far has focused predominantly on the influences of different family structures on the development of language—but what of children who are deprived entirely of a normal family life?

Children reared in extreme isolation

Instances of severe social deprivation are fortunately rare but almost all the reported cases have shown gross language retardation, if not complete absence of speech. Perhaps one of the best known of such cases is the 'Wild Boy of Aveyron' described by Itard (1962) but Clarke and Clarke (1976) and Langmeier and Matejcek (1975) also describe a number of other children suffering from severe deprivation. The extent of the language impairment and the prognosis in such children varies according to the severity of the deprivation, the presence of previously existing impairment, and the age at which intervention begins. Many feral children, for example, are probably abandoned *because* of their abnormal development, and their retardation cannot be attributed solely to the deprivation which they suffer. If such children do have severe congenital defects, the effects of later intervention will probably be limited. Thus Victor, the 'Wild Boy', described by Itard failed, despite intensive and prolonged training, to develop anything other than a few word approximations.

On the other hand young children with no apparent congenital defects appear to make remarkably good progress despite appalling conditions. Brown (1958), for example, describes a non-speaking child of a deaf-mute, retarded mother found in Ohio at the age of 6. After two years of therapy, by the time she was 8, she had developed almost normal language. Older children seem to make less progress. Curtiss et al. (1974) discuss the case of Genie, a girl found at the age of 14 having lived a life of horrific abuse and almost total confinement. She rarely heard any spoken language—her father and brother who were her main caretakers only barked or growled at her like dogs—and any sounds which she made were punished by severe beatings. The subsequent progress of Genie after her rescue makes fascinating reading (Curtiss, 1977). From being mute she rapidly developed a large and extensive vocabulary and used many two- to three-word utterances. The complexity of her phrase speech over the last 5½ years, however, has remained limited. She has good comprehension of speech, but her own utterances are lacking in many morphemes and functor words such as pronouns or prepositions. She uses only primitive transformations to express negation, interrogatives, etc., and her speech lacks normal intonations. In addition she uses little spontaneous speech; she *never* uses interjections or 'automatic' utterances such as 'Please', 'Hi', 'Well!'; and she shows little in the way of non-verbal gesturing—such as shaking her head or raising her eyebrows in surprise.

Although firm evidence is lacking it seems that Genie was not severely retarded or abnormal at birth and subsequent retardation in her language and social behaviour is attributed solely to her 'inhuman' childhood.

Differences in ultimate language level according to the age at which the child was 'rescued' raises the question of the existence of critical periods in human language development. That is, in the absence of any complicating factors, such as neurological impairment, is there an age after which it is 'too late' to develop mature language? The concept of critical periods has given rise to considerable debate in recent years, particulary in the field of animal learning. There appeared to be, for example, good evidence for the existence of critical periods in the development of vocal and social behaviour in many animals (e.g. in birds, Thorpe, 1961, Lorenz, 1965; in dogs, Scott, 1963 and in primates, Harlow, 1965). However, follow-up studies have since shown that the effects of early deprivation can to a great extent be overcome by subsequent experience (Novak and Harlow, 1975; Hinde, 1970; Klinghammer, 1967). For most aspects of development the notion of fixed, critical periods, after which particular functions will not develop, must be rejected. Connolly (1972) has suggested that there may be nevertheless 'sensitive periods' during development when the growth of specific skills is more likely to be facilitated because of the biological or emotional readiness of the individual. If, for any reason learning does not occur at this stage, it may be more difficult for optimal development to occur later. Nevertheless, even sensitive periods, if they do exist, should not be considered as fixed, in that the environmental circumstances before, during and after them will all play a major role in determining the degree and quality of later acquisition.

Certainly if sensitive periods do exist in language learning these are very extended. Lenneberg, for example, notes that ... 'Between the ages of 3 and the early teens the possibility for primary language acquisition continues to be good ... After puberty the ability for self organization and adjustment to the physiological demands of verbal behaviour quickly declines.'

More extensive follow-up studies of children deprived of normal language development will be needed before it can be established whether complete language development is impossible after a certain age. After all, Genie was 14 years old before she had the opportunity to learn to talk. It would not seem unreasonable to expect her to need many more years experience before she is able to catch up with her peers.

Children reared in impoverished environments

Although few children have the misfortune to grow up in conditions of severe isolation many do suffer varying degrees of social and emotional deprivation with subsequent retardation in their language skills. Thus, impoverished language development is frequently associated with a deprived home background (Stevenson and Richman, 1978), or with inadequate child minding (Prince, 1960). In the past, language retardation has been common in children who spend prolonged periods of their life in institutional care (Lenneberg, 1967). However, although institutions (especially those for mentally handicapped children—(Lyle, 1960), *may* impede language development, this need not be so. Tizard *et al.* (1972) found that children reared in residential nurseries with a high rate of verbal interaction were not delayed in their acquisition of language, in spite of a lack of close personal relationships between staff and children. The concept of 'institutional retardation' is misleading. It is the *type* of institution in which children grow up, not institutionalization *per se*, which affects their development. The fact that separation from parents does not necessarily affect language development is also supported by studies of children brought up in Kibbutzim who generally show good linguistic and cognitive skills (Kohen-Raz, 1968).

Environmental factors certainly influence language

development, but exactly how they do so remains rather obscure. Mothers alter their speech styles according to the linguistic and cognitive immaturity of their offspring, but apparently there are no *direct* associations between the specific types of utterance they use and the language development of their children. Nevertheless, children require active experience of communication in order to develop communication skills themselves. Environments which lack this are systematically associated with language delay. Simply hearing language spoken is not enough to facilitate language development; conversely an environment in which speech is rarely heard but in which other communication skills are encouraged (as in the homes of deaf parents) is not associated with language retardation.

LANGUAGE DEVELOPMENT AND NEUROLOGICAL AND SENSORY IMPAIRMENT

The child's capacity for learning from his environment may be impaired by neurological damage or other sensory impairment. If the child's ability to receive or process incoming stimuli from his environment is defective, language development will almost certainly be affected.

Blindness severely limits the young child's ability to associate the words he hears with the objects which they name and the onset of language in blind children is usually delayed. In addition, echolalia is more common and more persistent in blind than normal children (Fay, 1973; Fraiberg, 1971); they also tend to go through a longer period of constant questioning than do normal children (McCarthy, 1954).

Deafness, too, is almost always associated with multiple language handicaps. An inability to hear speech sounds leads to problems in learning to speak intelligibly. In addition deaf children often have severe difficulties in language-related skills such as reading and writing. However, they show less evidence of impairment in other areas of language—such as imaginative play or symbolic reasoning, which might be expected to result from their limited verbal abilities (Furth and Youniss, 1976). They tend to be inferior on tasks of symbolic logic when compared with hearing controls, but this deficit may be overcome with appropriate training. Furth (1966) suggests that early delays in symbolic development could be avoided if the children received appropriate communication training.

Neurological impairment

Neurological damage frequently affects control of the muscular apparatus needed for speech. Occasionally such deficits result in total loss of intelligible speech although leaving comprehension and verbal reasoning unimpaired (Lenneberg, 1967). Frequently, however, severe problems in processing language accompany the speech abnormalities. Cerebral palsy (which occurs in about 2–3 children per thousand) is particularly associated with language retardation and executive speech defects. About half of such children suffer speech or language defects which severely limit their ability to communicate.

Recovery from neurological impairment depends a great deal on when the damage was incurred and the extent of the lesion. In young children, as long as the damage is restricted to one hemisphere, the 'plasticity' of the brain (*see* Chapter 3) makes it possible for the undamaged hemisphere to take over even if it was the dominant hemisphere which was originally affected. Many children, for example, with severe congenital unilateral cerebral palsy of the dominant hemisphere eventually achieve perfectly normal language. Similarly traumatic aphasia caused by damage to the dominant hemisphere after birth is often remarkably short-lived and reversible. After a delay following the injury language development may proceed quite normally (Lenneberg, 1967). If the damage is sustained after puberty, when the various functions of the brain are better defined and fixed, recovery is less likely. Also if there is damage to *both* hemispheres there is little opportunity for language functions to be 'taken over' by undamaged areas and language impairment is likely to be severe.

Developmental language delays

Although language delay is usually associated with other handicaps—such as neurological malfunction, sensory impairment, or intellectual retardation, the failure to develop language can occur in the apparent absence of additional impairments. Many children with congenital aphasia and autistic children, may show severe language delay although their non-verbal abilities remain intact.

Specific developmental dysphasia

Stevenson and Richman (1976) report that between five and six children per 1,000 show severe expressive language delay not associated with general retardation. These tend to be much more common in boys than in girls, and there is often a family history of delayed language development or reading difficulties. Most of the children with a specific expressive language disorder have a normal understanding of language, although some problems in comprehension may occur (Morley, 1965). Specific *receptive* dysphasia is much less frequent, probably 'much less' than 1 per 10,000 (Rutter, 1972), and unlike expressive dysphasia is often accompanied by a partial high tone hearing loss.

Early Childhood Autism is a less common condition than specific developmental dysphasia, occurring in about 2–4 children per 10,000 (Lotter, 1966). Like dysphasia it is more frequent in boys than girls [with a ratio of about 4 to 1] and is associated with a family history of language delay. Unlike dysphasic children, autistic children generally have a severe impairment in both expressive and receptive language skills. Use and comprehension of language is invariably delayed and many children fail to develop language at all. In those who do learn to speak their use of language is often very bizarre, repetitive,

echolalic and stereotyped, with little spontaneous social usage. Gesture and other non-verbal aspects of communication are impaired, as is also imaginative play and abstract thought. There is associated mental retardation in some three-quarters of the children. [For a much more detailed discussion of autism *see* Rutter, 1977; Kanner, 1973.]

Non-verbal aspects of communication

In addition to the spoken word, messages may be conveyed non-verbally by signs, facial gesture or body movements, and in writing. Although the importance of non-verbal aspects of communication was first stressed by Darwin in 1872, the detailed study of this aspect of language did not really begin until the mid-1960s. Argyle (1972) suggests that the two main functions of non-verbal communication are to manage the immediate social situation and to sustain verbal communication. It may also be used as a replacement for spoken language—as in the sign language of the deaf, or the gestural language of certain Australian Aborigines (Brun, 1969).

If facial expression, eye contact, or body gestures are inappropriate or lacking, social interaction is markedly affected. This is particularly noticeable in autistic children, some of whom may eventually develop perfectly good grammatical speech, but because of their failure to make eye contact and their lack of facial expression and other gestures they continue to appear very bizarre in a social situation. Poor eye contact and lack of facial expressiveness is also associated with other psychotic conditions such as schizophrenia and depression. Deaf and blind children, on the other hand, generally show quite normal patterns of facial expression (Eibl-Eibesfeldt, 1972).

If non-verbal communication is affected by impairment of muscular control—as in the case of Moebius syndrome described by Woolf (1977) where the patient was incapable of smiling—social interaction may be greatly affected, even though other communication skills are unimpaired.

Writing

Traditional Grammarians have, in the past, tended to assume that written language is 'purer' and in some ways superior to spoken language. Contemporary linguists, in contrast, maintain that spoken language is primary and that writing is principally a means of representing speech in another medium (Lyons, 1969). Speech is, after all, much older and more widespread than writing. The relationship between spoken and written language varies from culture to culture. In English the association is very close; in French the two are more independent; and in languages such as Chinese written and spoken forms are very different.

The ability to read and write greatly extends man's scope for communication, and may be a vital adjunct to spoken language if for some reason the ability to speak is impaired. Aphasic patients, for example, can sometimes communicate well in writing although unable to speak.

Braille allows the blind to read and write with ease in any language, although there is evidence that the processes involved are rather different to those involved in ordinary reading and writing. Thus Hermelin and O'Connor (1971) found that processing of the tactile stimuli first takes place in the non-dominant hemisphere, whereas in the non-blind the processing of written material involves the dominant hemisphere. For the deaf, too, reading and writing skills are very important for communication although evidence suggests that they may well have many difficulties in these areas (Myklebust, 1964; Moores, 1970; Furth and Youniss, 1976).

Non-verbal methods of communication may be important in treating children with language handicaps. If a child does not respond to verbal training programmes, training in other systems of communication may be more effective. Sign Language (Paget *et al.*, 1972; Walker, 1977) or written or symbolic languages (Marshall and Hegrenes, 1972; Hughes, 1974; McDonald and Schulz, 1973; De Villiers and Naughton, 1974; Bonvillian and Nelson, 1976; La Vigna, 1977) may constitute alternatives to spoken language.

In the past many therapists, particularly those involved with deaf children, have claimed that alternative communication systems, such as sign language, would be harmful to children in that they would inhibit any motivation to speak. Recently several studies (Moores, 1970; Brasel and Quigley, 1977) have shown that deaf children who are taught sign-language are superior in language ability to children who are trained solely in oral communication. In addition several studies have shown that the acquisition of a non-verbal communication system actually facilitates language development in children who had not previously learned to talk (De Villiers and Naughton, 1974; Fulwiler and Fouts, 1976; Schaeffer *et al.*, 1977; Deich and Hodges, 1977).

THE TREATMENT OF LANGUAGE DISORDERS

When to begin treatment

The age at which children begin to speak varies considerably from child to child. As an approximate guide, however, two thirds of children say their first single word between 9 and 12 months, and the same proportion begin to use phrases between 17 and 24 months (Morley, 1965). Nevertheless many children do not reach these milestones at the prescribed ages and yet still develop normally. Others who learn to speak late may then go on to develop quite normal speech but may show difficulties in related subjects such as reading and writing. Still others show a persisting handicap in language development.

This variability in onset of language and the differing progress of children who show early delay raises many problems for the clinician. Since many children show no permanent deficits following an initial delay, the advice 'Don't worry, he'll grow out of it' may be quite appropriate. Other children, if not given early help, will not 'grow

out of it' and for them such advice may be extremely harmful. The difficulty lies in deciding *which* children are seriously at risk (*see* Rutter, 1972).

On the whole, if the child seems to be developing normally in other areas, if, for example, his babble has developed quite normally, if he understands simple commands and if he uses and responds to non-verbal cues, there is probably little reason to worry if he is late in using his first word. After all, if non-verbal communication is well developed there is no great urgency for the child to begin to speak.

If a child who is late in speaking is showing delays in other areas, too, then there is more serious cause for concern. Inadequate babble, limited social responsiveness, poor manipulative play with objects, all indicate the presence of a much more serious problem needing early remediation. In addition, even in the absence of additional deficits, any prolonged delay in speaking should be taken seriously. In practice, therefore, it is probably safest to assume that children who are not using words by 18 months or phrases by $2\frac{1}{2}$ to 3 years should also be regarded as being at risk.

It is generally accepted that the earlier treatment for language disorders begins the more chance there is of avoiding serious problems later. There is, it is true, little experimental evidence to support this assumption, but in the absence of evidence to the contrary it would seem wisest to begin intervention as soon as possible. In particular, early intervention may help to avoid the many behavioural problems which occur in a child who can neither understand or make himself understood.

If for some reason treatment is not given at an early age this does not mean that later intervention is unlikely to be successful. Many retarded children are very late in learning to talk, and some autistic children do not begin to speak until the age of 8 or 9 or even older. Even if there seems little chance of teaching a delayed child to use words, there are many other ways of improving his communication and comprehension. Perhaps the best general advice to someone about to undertake the treatment of a language-delayed child is 'the earlier the better . . . but it's never *too* late!'

Language delay or deviant language

Early work by Menyuk (1964, 1969), Menyuk and Looney (1972) and Lee (1966) had suggested qualitative differences in the language of normal and retarded children. In contrast, the findings of later studies (Lenneberg *et al.*, 1964; Newfield and Schlanger, 1968; Freedman and Carpenter, 1976; Leonard *et al.*, 1976), indicate that the syntactic and semantic relationships expressed by language handicapped children are generally similar to those used by normal children of similar mental age (see Morehead and Morehead, 1976, for a fuller discussion of this topic). Even with autistic children there is little evidence to support the view that their syntactical development is abnormal (Pierce and Bartolucci, 1977). Most children with language difficulties are quantitatively but not qualitatively different to normal children in their use of language.

This needs to be taken into account when planning programmes for the language-handicapped child. Instead of arbitrarily selecting different aspects of speech and language to work on, account should be taken of the child's overall developmental level and the training programme designed according to the child's mental age. There is little point in trying to teach a delayed child to use structures which even perfectly normal 3-, 4- or 5-year-olds have difficulty with.

In designing a programme, therefore, it is important to bear in mind Cromer's comment (1974) that different subgroups of language-handicapped subjects may possess different language abilities and that to refer to, or treat them, as a homogeneous group is likely to produce conflicting results.

Methods of treatment

Language difficulties, as we have seen, may be caused by many different factors, and the methods to treat speech and language disorders will depend on the needs of each individual child.

Certain speech defects, such as those caused by abnormalities of the tongue, palate or vocal organs, can sometimes be alieviated by surgery. Similarly, children with hearing problems may be helped by the provision of an hearing aid.

Unfortunately the number of children whose speech can be dramatically improved by surgical or mechanical interventions is rather small, and many children will require prolonged therapeutic intervention if they are to overcome their handicap. Speech therapy, and more recently behaviour modification techniques, are the most usual forms of treatment for children with speech and language problems as well as for children with hearing problems.

Speech therapy

If a child has problems in production of sounds this may be helped by a variety of speech therapy techniques. It is impossible in a chapter of this length to do justice to the numerous methods employed by speech therapists in the remediation of voice and articulation problems. Breathing and voicing exercises, together with specific training in mouth and tongue movements, are used to develop the child's correct use of speech sounds. In addition to direct teaching methods, more indirect methods involving games and play situations may be used to draw the child's attention to the sounds he is making and to help him recognize and correct his own errors (Van Riper, 1972). Some children's difficulties in articulation and comprehension may result predominantly from poor auditory discrimination. Systematic training to teach the child to recognize differences between words and sounds is important, but many children with poor auditory discrimination also benefit from training in the use of visual cues (e.g. lip movements, Nelson et al., 1976). Training in

accurate reading and writing, too, is important to develop the child's awareness of differences between words and syllables (Renfrew, 1972). Many children have no obvious difficulties in discriminating speech sounds but are unable to produce certain specific sounds or particular combinations of words and consonants (thus they may be able to produce a particular sound in isolation but not if it is adjacent to another sound). Thus treatment will vary according to each child's individual patterns of speech production, and careful assessment of the child prior to treatment is required. Renfrew (1972) recommends the use of 'oral gymnastics' in the remediation of such problems, but direct motor-kinaesthetic training (Nelson and Evans, 1968) may also be needed for certain children. Most speech therapists stress the importance of feedback either from the child's teachers and parents or through electronic means, to enable the child to monitor both his errors and his progress (Shearer, 1972; Deal et al., 1976).

Speech therapy is not restricted solely to children with disorders of speech but is also used with children who show developmental delays in language. With such children the emphasis is on building up the child's confidence to communicate and express himself. Therapy in such cases often covers many different areas, and may involve increasing the child's ability to converse and to respond to questions about his activities, as well as developing his descriptive language skills. The development of comprehension and 'language awareness' and of play activities is also important.

The obvious necessity of developing language-related skills as well as working directly on speech has led a number of therapists to focus more specifically on the creation of a 'talking environment' for the child. Ewing and Ewing (1954) insisted that before any formal lessons in speech training could begin, the child's 'language readiness' must be demonstrated. They claimed that the child must desire to communicate before teaching begins but unfortunately ways of preparing the child for reaching this stage are generally rather ill-defined. Another major problem with this approach is that these indirect methods may be quite inappropriate for children who lack motivation to speak. Frostig (1976) advises a combined approach to speech training—emphasizing the development of the child's comprehension and his visual, kinaesthetic and auditory awareness in the early stages of training and then moving on to more direct teaching methods later.

However, a study by Fenn (1976) indicated that general enrichment programmes had almost no effect on language development, only children given direct training made significant progress over a year of treatment. It seems, therefore, that from the onset of training, direct methods to improve a child's particular deficits are likely to prove most effective.

Recent studies of therapeutic techniques (Crystal, et al., 1976; Ingram, 1976; Lee, 1974; Lee et al., 1975) stress the need for a detailed analysis of language problems in all areas—comprehension, expression, syntax, phonation and intonation before treatment begins. Remediation programmes are then based on individual analyses of children's problems. Training closely follows patterns of development in normal children, and techniques are carefully adapted to the child's general level of development.

Such techniques, incorporating as they do detailed individual analyses, and direct training methods based on knowledge from normal psycholinguistic research, would seem to be much more promising than the rather vague programmes described by many earlier writers. Unfortunately the effectiveness of these methods has still to be evaluated and, in fact, assessment of speech therapy techniques generally is sadly lacking. A search of the speech therapy literature reveals only a handful of evaluative studies, and the results of these are rather contradictory. For example, Wilson (1966) found that mildly mentally retarded children receiving speech therapy showed *no* significant reduction in articulation errors as compared with an untreated control group. Alvord (1977) on the other hand found that speech training methods were more effective in reducing articulation defects than no treatment at all. In neither of these studies are the therapeutic techniques involved described. The study by Fenn (1976) suggests that direct speech training methods are more effective than general enrichment programmes. And Nelson et al. (1976) found that direct training in the motor skills necessary for producing sounds was more effective than imitation training alone.

Few other controlled, evaluative studies of speech therapy seem to be available, perhaps because of the very many different methods which are subsumed under this name. Nevertheless, on the basis of very limited evidence it seems probable that direct training methods, at least, are likely to be effective with children who possess normal social skills and who make spontaneous attempts to communicate.

However, problems arise if the child is able to talk albeit in a limited fashion, but lacks the motivation to do so. O'Connor and Hermelin (1963), for example, found that many severely subnormal children *could* answer questions but would not do so unless provided with tangible rewards.

For children who lack the normal child's spontaneous desire to communicate, alternative methods may be needed.

Operant language training

Although the language of normal children does not seem to be particularly influenced by the use of prompting, correction or reinforcement techniques, there is considerable evidence that such methods are valuable in training children who have failed to develop language (Yule and Berger, 1972).

Very briefly, operant training methods involve the direct prompting of the sounds or words which the therapist wishes to increase and the reinforcement of the child's attempts to imitate those sounds. Gradually reinforcement is given for closer and closer approximations to the therapist's prompts, until the child is imitating readily. Later the same methods are used to increase the child's use of words and phrases; later still the use of appropriate spontaneous speech can be trained (*see* Sloane and Macaulay, 1968 for a fuller description). The successful use of behaviour modification techniques to increase language skills has been demonstrated with many different children: autistic, language-delayed, deaf, electively mute and mentally retarded. There are also a number of control studies which indicate that operant methods are more effective than general programmes designed to increase the child's 'language readiness' (Ney et al., 1971). Nevertheless, the results of operant training programmes are variable: some claim to produce almost normal spontaneous speech after a relatively short period; others, after literally thousands of training trials have little or no success (Lovaas, 1977). To some extent the language level of the child before treatment is important for outcome. Thus, mute children with little or no comprehension tend to do less well than children who are echolalic or using a few words when training begins. Of course, initial language level is not the only factor influencing outcome and many other variables, such as the child's IQ, the age at which treatment began, and levels of social and play development are probably also important.

Critics of a behaviour modification approach to teaching language have suggested that all such programmes achieve is to teach children to 'parrot' what they hear more effectively. Even amongst behaviour therapists themselves doubt has been expressed as to whether operant training can produce more than simple associative learning (Weiss and Born, 1967). Despite such doubts many studies now show that generalized rule acquisition *can* be taught and that spontaneous, generative language usage does develop, albeit rather slowly. Guess et al. (1974), for example, report a number of studies in which retarded children were successfully taught to use a variety of simple morpheme rules. An increasing number of well controlled studies of operant language training in recent years have shown that, without doubt, operant programmes are of value in increasing language skills. However, exactly which aspects of language acquisition are influenced by these methods remains uncertain (Rutter, 1980). Do such methods simply increase the child's motivation to speak and therefore speed up language learnings, or do they actually influence the ultimate level of language acquisition?

The results of the study by Hemsley et al. (1978) suggest that it may be the rate of learning, not the final level of language which is mostly affected. Autistic children, treated by operant methods, showed significant gains in their spontaneous use of language as compared with a short-term control group, and their use of simple grammatical rules also improved. A longer-term follow-up, indicated that untreated autistic children had also made progress in their language development, although at a slower rate. The same study also found that whereas the experimental children made impressive improvements in their use of functional language to communicate, increases in the syntactical complexity of their utterances were much less marked (Howlin, 1980). It is postulated that the children who respond to operant programmes already possess at least some of the cognitive pre-requisites for language learning, and that behavioural methods are responsible for motivating the children to use their inherent linguistic abilities. If the basic, cognitive skills needed for language acquisition are lacking—as in the case of children who are profoundly handicapped in comprehension and expressive skills—operant tech-niques to train verbal communication are unlikely to be successful. In other words, operant techniques seem to be of value in increasing the child's 'Performance', they are less likely to influence basic language 'Capacity' (Chomsky, 1965).

Early intervention programmes

In addition to methods which focus directly on the child's speech or language handicap, improvements in the child's overall environment may result in improvements in language skills. These are discussed in Chapter 20. Briefly, it appears that compensatory programmes can be successful in improving the child's functioning in many areas, including language, but the results tend to be short-lived unless the programmes are maintained when children begin school. (Abelson *et al.*, 1974; Blank and Solomon, 1969).

CONCLUSIONS

In recent years psycholinguistic studies of normal chil-dren together with investigations of abnormal language development have added greatly to knowledge. Neverthe-less, much remains to be learned about both language acquisition and language handicap. The mechanisms underlying the development of communication skills, and the nature of the relationship between cognitive, social and language development are still largely unexplored areas. We have progressed a little (*see* Cromer, 1980) from over-simplified behaviourist views of language acquisition and from the rather mystical and Cartesian notion of Chomsky's (1971) 'Language Acquisition Device'. However, as Miller in 1965 pointed out in his 'Preliminaries to Psycholinguistics' language remains 'complex, arbitrary, improbable, mentalistic—and no amount of wishful theorizing will make it anything else. In a word . . . language is exceedingly complicated'. Perhaps in the future careful research will help more than 'wishful theorizing' in unraveling some of the complications.

REFERENCES

Abelson, W. D., Zigler, E. and de Blasi, C. L. (1974). Effects of a four year follow-through program on economically disadvantaged chil-dren. *J. Ed. Psychol.* 66, 756–771.

Alvord, D. J. (1977). Innovation In Speech Therapy: A Cost Effective Program. *Exceptional Child,* 43, 518–523.

Antinucci, F. and Miller, R. (1975). How Children talk about what happened. *J. Child. Lang.* 3, 167–189.

Argyle, M. (1972). Human Social Interaction. In R. Hinde (Ed.) *Non-Verbal Communication.* Cambridge: Cambridge University Press.

Bates, E., Benigni, L., Bretherton, I., Camaioni, L. and Volterra, V. (1977). From Gesture to the First Word: On Cognitive and Social Pre-requisites. In: M. Lewis and L. Rosenblum (Eds.) *Interaction, Conversation and the Development of Language.* New York: John Wiley.

Ben-Zeev, S. (1977). The Influences of Bilingualism on Cognitive Strategy and Cognitive Development. *Child Develop.*, 48, 1009–1018.

Bernstein, B. (1962). *Social Class, Linguistic Codes and Grammatical Elements. Language and Speech,* 5, 221–240.

Bernstein, B. (1970). Social Class Language and Socialisation. In: B. Bernstein (Ed.) *Class, Codes and Control. Vol. I: Theoretical Studies Towards a Sociology of Language.* London: Routledge and Kegan Paul.

Blank, M. and Solomon, F. A. (1969). How Shall the Disadvantaged Child Be Taught. *Child Develop.,* 40, 47–61.

Bloom, L. (1970). *Language Development: Form and Function in Emerging Grammars.* Cambridge, Mass.: M.I.T. Press.

Bloom, L. (1973). *One Word at a Time: The Use of Single Word Utter-ances Before Syntax.* The Hague: Mouton.

Bonvillian, J. D. and Nelson, K. E. (1976). Sign Language Acquisition in a Mute Autistic Boy. *J. Speech and Hear. Disorders,* 41, 339–347.

Bowerman, M. (1973). Structural Relationships in Children's Utter-ances Syntactic or Semantic? In: T. E. Moore (Ed.) *Cognitive Development and the Acquisition of Language.* New York: Academic Press.

Braine, M. D. (1963). The Ontogeny of English Phrase Structure: the first phrase. *Language,* 39, 1–14.

Braine, M. D. (1976). Children's First Word Combinations. *Monog. of Soc. for Research in Child Devel. Vol. 41.*

Brasel, K. and Quigley, S. (1977). Influences of Certain Language and Communication Environments in Early Childhood on the Develop-ment of Language in Deaf Individuals. *J. Speech Hear. Res.* 20, 95–107.

Broen, P. A. (1972). The Verbal Environment of the Language-Learning Child. *Monographs of American Speech and Hearing Association No. 17. December 1972.*

Brown, R. (1958). *Words and Things.* New York: The Free Press.

Brown, R. (1973). *A First Language: The Early Stages.* London: Allen and Unwin.

Brown, R. (1977). Introduction to: C. Snow and C. A. Ferguson (Eds.) *Talking to Children.* Cambridge: Cambridge University Press.

Brown, R. and Bellugi, U. (1964). Three Processes in the Child's Acquisition of Syntax. *Harvard Educational Review,* 34, 133–151.

Brown, R., Cazden, C. and Bellugi, U. (1969). The Child's Grammar from I to III in J. P. Hill (Ed.) *Minnesota Symposia on Child Psychol-ogy. Vol. 2.* Minneapolis: University of Minnesota Press.

Brown, R. and Hanlon, C. (1970). Derivational Complexity and Order of Acquisition In Child Speech. In J. R. Hayes (Ed.) *Cognition and the Development of Language.* New York: Wiley.

Brun, T. (1969). *The International Dictionary of Sign Language.* London: Wolfe.

Cazden, C. (1968). The Acquisition of Noun and Verb Inflections. *Child Develop.,* 39, 433–448.

Chapman, R. and Miller, J. F. (1975). Word Order in Early 2 and 3 word utterances: Does Production Precede Comprehension. *J. Speech Hear. Res.,* 18, 355–371.

Chess, S. and Rosenberg, M. (1974). Clinical Differentiation Between Children with Initial Language Complaints. *J. Autism and Child. Schiz.,* 4, 99–109.

Chomsky, C. (1969). The Acquisition of Syntax in Children from 5 to 10. *Research Monograph No. 57.* Cambridge, Mass: M.I.T. Press.

Chomsky, N. (1959). Review of B. F. Skinner, Verbal Behavior. *Language,* 35, 26–58.

Chomsky, N. (1965). *Aspects of the Theory of Syntax.* Cambridge, Mass.: M.I.T. Press.

Chomsky, N. (1971). Recent Contributions to the Theory of Innate Ideas. In: J. R. Searle (Ed.). *The Philosophy of Language.* Oxford: Oxford University Press.

Clark, E. V. (1973). What's in A Word? On the Child's Acquisition of Semantics in his First Language. In T. E. Moore (Ed.) *Cognitive Development and the Acquisition of Language.* New York: Academic Press.

Clark, H. and Clark, E. V. (1977). *Psychology and Language: An Introduction to Linguistics*. New York: Harcourt Brace.

Clarke, A. M. and Clarke, A. D. B. (1976). *Early Experience: Myth and Evidence*. London: Open Books.

Clarke-Stewart, K. A. (1973). Interactions between Mothers and their Young Children: Characteristics and Consequences. *Monographs of the Society for Research in Child Development*, **38**, Nos 6–7. Serial No. 153.

Collis, G. (1975). The Integration of Gaze and vocal behaviour in the mother–infant dyad. Paper presented at Third International Child Language Symposium. London: September 1975.

Condon, W. S. and Sandler, L. W. (1974). Syncrhony demonstrated between Movement of the Neonate and Adult Speech. *Child Develop.* **43**, 456–462.

Connolly, K. (1972). Learning and the Concept of Critical Periods in Infancy. *Develop. Med. Child Neurol.*, **14**, 705–714.

Critchley, E. (1967). Language Development of Hearing Children in a deaf Environment. *Devel. Med. Child Neurol.*, **9**, 274–280.

Cromer, R. F. (1968). *The Development of Temporal Reference during the Acquisition of Language*. Unpublished Doctoral Dissertation. University of Harvard.

Cromer, R. F. (1974). The Development of Language and Cognition: The Cognition Hypothesis. In B. Foss (Ed.) *New Perspectives in Child Development*. Harmondsworth: Penguin Education.

Cromer, R. F. (1980). Normal language development: recent progress. In Hersov, L. A., Berger, M. and Nicol, A. R. (Eds.), *Language and Language Disorders in Childhood*. Oxford: Pergamon (in press).

Cross, T. G. (1977). Mothers' Speech Adjustments: the contribution of selected child listener variables. In C. Snow and C. Ferguson (Eds.) *Talking to Children: Language Input and Acquisition*. Cambridge: Cambridge University Press.

Crystal, D., Fletcher, P. and Garman, M. (1976). The Grammatical Analysis of Language Disability: A Procedure for Assessment and Remediation. In D. Crystal and J. Cooper (Eds.) *Studies in Language Disability and Remediation 1*. London: Edward Arnold.

Curtiss, S. (1977). *Genie: A Psycholinguistic Study of a Modern-Day 'Wild Child'*. New York: Academic Press.

Curtiss, S., Fromkin, V., Krashen, S. and Rigler, M. (1974). The Linguistic Development of Genie. *Language*, **30**, 328–354.

Darcy, N. T. (1953). A review of the literature on the effects of bilingualism upon the Measurement of Intelligence. *J. Genet. Psychol.*, **82**, 21–57.

Darwin, C. (1872). *The Expression of the Emotions in Man and Animals*. London: John Murray.

Deal, R. E., McClain, B. and Sudderth, J. F. (1976). Identification, Evaluation, Therapy and Follow-up for Children with Vocal Nodules in a Public School Setting. *J. Speech Hear. Disorders*, **41**, 390–397.

Deich, R. and Hodges, P. (1977). *Language Without Speech*. London: Souvenior Press.

de Saussure, F. (1974). *Course in General Linguistics*. Translated by Wade Baskin. London: Fontana.

De Villiers, J. and De Villiers, P. (1973). A Cross-sectional Study of the Acquisition of Grammatical Morphemes in Child Speech. *J. Psychol. Res.* **2**, 267–278.

De Villiers, J. and Naughton, J. M. (1974). Teaching a symbol language to autistic children. *J. Consult. Clin. Psychol.* **42**, 111–117.

Dodd, B. (1972). Effects of Social and Vocal Stimulation in Infant Babbling. *Develop. Psychol.* **7**, 80–83.

Douglas, J. W. B. (1964). *The Home and The School*. London: MacGibbon and Kee.

Douglas, J. W. B., Ross, J. M. and Simpson, H. R. (1968). *All Our Future*. London: Peter Davies.

Dunn, J., Wooding, C. and Hermann, J. (1977). Mother's speech to young children: Variation in Context. *Develop. Med. Child Neurol.* **19**, 629–639.

Eibl-Eibesfeldt, L. (1972). Similarities and Differences between cultures and expressive movements. In R. Hinde (Ed.) *'Non-Verbal Communication'* London: Cambridge University Press.

Eimas, P. D., Siqueland, E. R., Jusczyk, P. and Vigorito, J. (1971). Speech perception in Infants. *Science*, **171**, 303–306.

Elardo, R., Bradley, R. and Caldwell, B. M. (1977). A Longitudinal Study of the Relation of Infants' Home Environments to Language Development of Age Three. *Child Develop.* **48**, 595–603.

Ervin-Tripp, S. (1973). *Language Acquisition and Communicative Choice*. Stanford: Stanford University Press.

Ewing, E. R. and Ewing, A. W. G. (1954). *Speech and the Deaf Child*. Manchester: Manchester University Press.

Farwell, C. (1973). The Language Spoken to Children. Papers and Reports on Child Language Development No. 5, 31–62. Stanford University, Stanford, California.

Fay, W. H. (1973). On the echolalia of the blind and of the autistic child. *J. Speech Hear. Res.*, **38**, 478–489.

Feldman, C. (1971). *The Effects of Various Types of Adult Responses in the Syntactic Acquisition of Two to Three year olds*. Unpublished paper. University of Chicago. Mimeo.

Fenn, G. (1976). Against Verbal Enrichment. In P. Berry (Ed.) *Language and Communication in the Mentally Handicapped*. London: Edward Arnold.

Ferguson, C. (1964). Baby Talk in Six Languages. *American Anthropologist*, **66**, 103–114.

Ferreiro, E. and Sinclair, H. (1971). Temporal Relations in Language. *Internat. J. Psychol.* **6**, 39–47.

Fraiberg, S. (1971). Intervention in Infancy: A Program for blind infants. *J. Child Psychiat. Psychol.* **10**, 381–405.

Fraiberg, S. and Adelson, E. (1973). Self Representation in Language and Play. Observations of Blind Children. *Psychoanalytical Quarterly*, **42**, 539–544.

Fraser, C., Bellugi, U. and Brown, R. (1963). Control of Grammar in Imitation, Comprehension and Production. *J. Verbal Learning and Verbal Behaviour*, **2**, 121–135.

Freedle, R. and Lewis, M. (1977). Prelinguistic Conversations. In: M. Lewis and L. Rosenblum (Eds.) *Interaction, Conversation and the Development of Language*. New York: John Wiley.

Freedman, P. and Carpenter, L. (1976). Semantic Relations used by Normal and Language Impaired Children at Stage I. *J. Speech Hear. Res.* **19**, 748–795.

Friedlander, B. Z., Wetstone, H. S. and McPeek, D. L. (1974). Systematic Assessment of Selective Language Listening Deficit in Emotionally Disturbed Children. *J. Child Psychol. Psychiat.* **15**, 1–12.

Frostig, M. (1976). *Education for Dignity*. New York: Grune and Stratton.

Fulwiler, R. L. and Fouts, R. S. (1976). Acquisition of American Sign Language by a non-communicating autistic child. *J. Autism. Child Schiz.* **6**, 43–51.

Furth, H. G. (1966). *Thinking Without Language: Psychological Implications of Deafness*. New York: Free Press.

Furth, H. G. and Youniss, J. (1976). Formal Operations: A Comparison of Deaf and Hearing Adolescents. In: D. Morehead and A. Morehead (Eds.) *Normal and Deficient Child Language*. Baltimore: University Park Press.

Garnica, O. (1977). Some Prosodic and Paralinguistic features of speech to young children. In: C. Snow and C. Ferguson (Eds.) *Talking to Children: Language Input and Acquisition*. Cambridge: Cambridge University Press.

Garvey, C. (1977). Play with Language. In B. Tizard and D. Harvey (Eds.) *Biology of Play*. Clinics in Developmental Medicine No. 62. London: Heinemann/S.I.M.P.

Goodson, B. D. and Greenfield, P. M. (1975). The Search for Structural Principles in Children's Manipulative Play: A parallel with Linguistic Development. *Child Develop.* **46**, 734–736.

Gould, J. (1977). Language Development and Non Verbal Skills in Severely Mentally Retarded Children. *J. Ment. Defic. Res.* **20**, 129–145.

Greene, J. (1972). *Psycholinguistics: Chomsky and Psychology*. Harmondsworth: Penguin.

Greenfield, P. and Smith, J. H. (1976). *The Structure of Communication in Early Language Development*. New York: Academic Press.

Greenman, G. (1963). Visual behaviour of newborn infants. In: A. Solnit and S. Provence (Eds.) *Modern Perspectives in Child Development*. New York: International Universities Press.

Gregory, H. (1976). *The Deaf Child and His Family*. London: Allen and Unwin.

Guess, D., Sailor, W. and Baer, D. M. (1974). To Teach Language to Retarded Children. In: R. L. Schiefelbush and L. L. Lloyd (Eds.) *Language Perspectives—Acquisition, Retardation and Intervention*. London: MacMillan.

Halliday, M. A. K. (1976). *Learning How to Mean: Some Explorations in the Development of Language.* London: Edward Arnold.

Harlow, H. E. (1965). The Affectional Systems. In: A. M. Schrier, H. E. Harlow and F. Stollnitz (Eds.) *Behavior of Non-Human Primates.* Vol. 2. New York: Academic Press.

Hemsley, R., Howlin, O., Berger, M., Hersov, L., Holbrook, D., Rutter, M. and Yule, W. (1978). Treating autistic children in a family context. In: M. Rutter and E. Schopler (Eds.) *Autism: A Reappraisal of Concepts and Treatment.* New York: Plenum.

Hermelin, B. and O'Connor, N. (1971). Right and Left handed Reading of Braille. *Nature 231, No. 5303,* 470.

Hess, R. D. and Shipman, V. C. (1968). Early Experience and the socialisation of Cognitive Modes in Children. *Child Develop.* **36,** 869–888.

Hinde, R. A. (1970). *Animal Behaviour* (2nd Edition) London: McGraw Hill.

Howlin, P. (1980). The home treatment of autistic children. In: Hersov, L. A., Berger, M. and Nichol, A. R. (Eds.). *Language and Language Disorders in Childhood.* Oxford: Pergamon. (In press.)

Hughes, J. (1974). Acquisition of a non-verbal 'language' by aphasic children. *Cognition* 1974/5, **3,** 41–55.

Hulme, I. and Lunzer, E. A. (1966). Play, Language and Reasoning in Subnormal Children. *J. Child Psychol. Psychiat.* **7,** 107–124.

Ingram, D. (1976). Phonological Disability in Children. *Studies in Language Disability and Remediation,* **2.** D. Crystal and J. Cooper (Eds.) London: Edward Arnold.

Ingram, T. T. S. (1959). Specific Developmental Disorders of Speech in Childhood. *Brain,* **82,** 450–467.

Inhelder, B. (1969). Memory and Intelligence in the Child. In: D. Elkind and J. Flavell (Eds.) *Studies in Cognitive Development.* New York: Oxford University Press.

Itard, J. M. G. (1962). *The Wild Boy of Aveyron.* Translation by G. Humphrey and M. Humphrey. New York: Appleton Century Crofts.

Jaffe, J., Stern, D. and Peery, J. (1973). 'Conversational' Coupling of Gaze Behaviour in Prelinguistic Human Development. *J. Psycholinguistic Research,* **2,** 321–329.

Jakobsen, R. (1968). *Child Language, Aphasia and Phonological Universals.* The Hague: Mouton.

James, W. (1890). *The Principles of Psychology.* London: Macmillan.

Jesperson, O. (1922). *Language, Its Nature, Development and Origin.* London: Allen and Unwin.

Johnston, J. R. (1973). *Spatial Notions and the Child's Use of Locatives in an Elicitation Task.* Paper presented at the Stanford Child Language Research Forum. Stanford. April 1973.

Kanner, L. (1973). *Childhood Psychosis: Initial Studies and New Insights.* New York: Wiley.

Keeney, T. J. and Smith, N. D. (1971). Young Children's Imitation and Comprehension of Sentential Singularity and Plurality. *Language and Speech,* **14,** 373–382.

Klinghammer, E. (1967). Factors Influencing Choice of Mate in Altricial Birds. In: H. W. Stevenson, E. H. Hess and H. L. Rheingold (Eds.) *Early Behaviour: Comparative and Developmental Approaches.* New York: Wiley.

Kohen-Raz, R. (1968). Mental and Mohr Development of Kibbutz Institutionalised and home reared infants in Israel. *Child Develop.* **39,** 489–504.

Langemeier, J. and Matejcek, Z. (1975). *Psychological Deprivation in Childhood.* Queensland: University of Queensland Press.

La Vigna, G. W. (1977). Communication Training in Mute Autistic Adolescents Using the Written Word. *J. Autism Child. Schiz.* **7,** 135–149.

Lawton, D. (1968). *Social Class, Language and Education.* London: Routledge and Kegan Paul.

Lee, L. (1966). Developmental Sentence Types: a method for comparing normal and deviant syntactic development. *J. Speech Hear. Disorders,* **31,** 311–330.

Lee, L. (1974). *Developmental Sentence Analysis: A Grammatical Assessment Procedure for Speech and Language Disorders.* Evanston 111: Northwestern University Press.

Lee, L., Koenigsknecht, R. A. and Mulhern, S. T. (1975). *Interactive Language Development teaching: the clinical presentation of grammatical structure.* Ill.: Northwestern University Press.

Lenneberg, E. H. (1964). A Biological Perspective of Language. In:

E. H. Lenneberg (Ed.) *New Directions in the Study of Language.* Cambridge, Mass.: M.I.T. Press.

Lenneberg, E. H. (1967). *Biological Foundations in the Study of Language.* New York: Wiley.

Lenneberg, E. H., Nichols, I. A. and Rosenberger, E. F. (1964). *Primitive Stages of Language Development in Mongolism Disorders of Communication Vol: XLII*: Research publications A.R.N.M.D. 119–139.

Leonard, L. B., Bolders, J. and Miller, J. (1976). An examination of the semantic relations reflected in the language of normal and language disordered children. *J. Speech Hear. Res.* **19,** 357–370.

Leopold, W. F. (1939–49). *Speech development of a bilingual child. 4 volumes.* Ill.: Northwestern University Press.

Lewis, M. (1951). *Infant Speech: A Study of the beginnings of language.* (2nd Ed.). London: Routledge and Kegan Paul.

Lewis, M. (1968). *Language and Personality in Deaf Children.* Slough: N.F.E.R.

Lorenz, K. (1965). *Evolution and the Modification of Behaviour.* Chicago: University of Chicago Press.

Lotter, V. (1966). Epidemiology of Autistic Conditions in Young Children. I. Prevalence. *Soc. Psychiatry,* **1,** 124–137.

Lovaas, O. I. (1977). *The Autistic Child: Language Development Through Behavior Modification.* New York: Wiley.

Lovell, K. and Dixon, E. M. (1967). The Control of Grammar in Imitation, Comprehension and Production. *J. Child Psychol. Psychiat.* **8,** 31–39.

Lovell, K., Hoyle, H. W. and Siddak, N. Q. (1968). A Study of Some Aspects of the Play and Language of Young Children with Delayed Speech. *J. Child Psychol. Psychiat.* **9,** 41–50.

Lyle, J. G. (1960). The Effects of an Institution Environment upon the verbal development of institutionalised children II. Speech and Language. *J. Ment. Def. Res.* **4,** 1–13.

Lyons, J. (1969). *Introduction to Theoretical Linguistics.* London: Cambridge University Press.

McCarthy, D. S. (1954). Language Development in Children. In: L. Carmichael (Ed.) *Manual of Child Psychology.* 2nd Edition. New York: Wiley.

McDonald, E. T. and Schultz, A. R. (1973). Communication Boards for Cerebral Palsied Children. *J. Speech Hear. Disorders,* **38,** 73–88.

McNeil, D. (1968). Developmental Psycholinguistics. In: F. Smith and G. A. Miller (Eds.) *The Genesis of Language.* Cambridge, Mass.: M.I.T. Press.

Marshall, N. R. and Hegrenes, J. (1972). The Use of Written Language as a Communication System for an Autistic Child. *J. Speech Hear. Disorder,* **2,** 258–261.

Menn, L. (1971). Phonotactic rules in beginning speech. *Lingua,* **26,** 225–251.

Menyuk, P. (1964). Comparison of Grammar of Children with Functionally Deviant and Normal speech. *J. Speech Hear. Research,* **7,** 109–121.

Menyuk, P. (1969). *Sentences Children Use.* Cambridge, Mass.: M.I.T. Press.

Menyuk, P. (1977). *Language and Maturation.* Cambridge, Mass.: M.I.T. Press.

Menyuk, P. and Looney, P. L. (1972). A Problem of Language Disorder: Length Versus Structure. *J. Speech Hear. Research,* **15,** 264–279.

Miller, G. A. (1964). The Psycholinguists. *Encounter,* 5, **23,** (July) 29–37.

Miller, S. R. (1965). Some Preliminaries to Psycholinguistics. *American Psychologist,* **20,** 15–20.

Mittler, P. (1972). Language Development and Mental Handicaps. In: M. Rutter and J. A. M. Martin (Eds.) *The Child with Delayed Speech.* Clinics in Developmental Medicine No. 43. London: Heinemann/S.I.M.P.

Moores, D. (1970). Psycholinguistics and Deafness. *Amer. Ann. Deaf.* **115,** 37–48.

Morehead, D. and Morehead A. (Eds.) (1976). *Normal and Deficient Child Language.* Baltimore: University Park Press.

Morley, M. E. (1965). *The Development and Disorders of Speech in Childhood.* Second Edition. Edinburgh: Livingstone.

Morse, P. A. (1972). The Discrimination of Speech and Non-speech Stimuli in Early Infancy. *J. Experimental Child Psychology,* **14,** 477–492.

Mowrer, O. H. (1958). Hearing and Speaking: an analysis of language learning. *J. Speech Hear. Dis.,* **23**, 143–152.

Murphy, K. (1964). Development of Normal Vocalization and Speech. In: C. Renfrew and K. Murphy (Eds.) *The Child Who Does Not Talk.* Clinics in Developmental Medicine No. 13. London: Heinemann/S.I.M.P.

Myerson, R. (1975). A Developmental Study of Children's Knowledge of Complex Derived Words of English. Paper presented at International Reading Association: New York City.

Myklebust, H. R. (1964). *The Psychology of Deafness, Sensory Deprivation, Learning and Adjustment.* (2nd edition) New York: Grune and Stratton.

Nelson, K. (1973). Structure and Strategy in Learning to Talk. *Monographs of the Society for Research in Child Development,* **38**, Nos. 1 and 2.

Nelson, K., Carskaddon, G. and Bonvillian, J. (1973). Syntax Acquisition: Impact of Experimental Variation in Adult Verbal Interaction with the Child. *Child Develop.,* **44**, 497–504.

Nelson, R. O. and Evans, I. M. (1968). The Combination of Learning Principles and Speech Therapy Techniques in the Treatment of Non-communicating Children. *J. Child Psychol., Psychiat.* **9**, 111–124.

Nelson, R. O., Peoples, A., Hay, Johnson, R. and Hay, W. (1976). The Effectiveness of Speech Training Techniques Based on Operant Conditioning: A Comparison of Two Methods. *Mental Retardation,* **14**, 34–38.

Newfield, M. U. and Schlanger, B. B. (1968). The Acquisition of English Morphology by Normal and Educable Mentally Retarded Children. *J. Speech Hear. Research,* **11**, 693–706.

Newport, E. L., Gleitman, H. and Gleitman, L. R. (1977). Mother, I'd rather do it myself: Some effects and non-effects of maternal speech style. In: C. Snow and C. Ferguson (Eds.) *Talking to Children: Language Input and Acquisition.* Cambridge: Cambridge University Press.

Newson, E. and Newson, J. (1970). *Four Years Old in an Urban Community.* Harmondsworth: Penguin.

Ney, P. G., Palvesky, A. E. and Markely, J. (1971). Relative Effectiveness of Operant Conditioning and Play Therapy in Childhood Schizophrenia. *J. Autism Child. Schiz.* **1**, 337–349.

Novak, M. A. and Harlow, H. F. (1975). Social Recovery of Monkeys Isolated in the First Year of Life. *Develop. Psychol.* **11**, 453–455.

O'Connor, N. and Hermelin, B. (1963). *Speech and Thought in Severe Subnormality.* Oxford: Pergamon.

Oller, K., Wieman, L., Doyle, N. and Ross, C. (1976). Infant Babbling and Speech. *J. Child Lang.* **3**, 1–11.

Olson, D. R. (1972). Language Use for Communicating, Instructing and Thinking. In: R. Freedle and J. B. Carroll (Eds.) *Language Comprehension and the Acquisition of Knowledge.* Washington D.C.: Winston/Wiley.

Paget, R., Gorman, P. and Paget, G. (1972). *A Systematic Sign Language.* Mimeographed Manual, London.

Parisi, D. and Antinucci, F. (1970). Lexical Competence. In: G. Flores d'Arcais and W. Levelt (Eds.) *Advances in Psycholinguistics.* Amsterdam: North-Holland Press.

Peal, E. and Lambert, W. E. (1962). The Relationship of Bilingualism to Intelligence. *Psychol. Monographs,* **76**, No. 27, whole No. 546.

Phillips, J. (1973). Syntax and Vocabulary of Mother's Speech to Young Children: Age and Sex Comparisons. *Child Develop.* **44**, 182–185.

Piaget, J. (1951). *Play, Dreams, and Imitation in Childhood.* New York: Norton.

Pierce, S. and Bartolucci, G. (1977). A Syntactic Investigation of Verbal Autistic Mentally Retarded and Normal Children. *J. Autism Child. Schiz.* **7**, 121–134.

Prince, C. S. (1960). Mental Health Problems in Pre-school West Indian Children. *Matern. Child Care,* **3**, 483–486.

Rebelsky, F., Starr, R. and Lukia, Z. (1967). Language Development: The First Four Years. In Y. Brackbill (Ed.) *Infancy and Early childhood.* London: Collier-Macmillan.

Record, R. G., McKeown, T. and Edwards, G. H. (1970). An Investigation of the difference in measured intelligence between twins and single births. *Ann. Human Genetics,* **34**, 11–17.

Renfrew, C. E. (1972). Speech Therapy. In M. Rutter and J. A. M. Martin (Eds.) *The Child with Delayed Speech.* Clinics in Developmental Medicine No. 43. London: Heinemann. S.I.M.P.

Reynell, J. (1969). *Reynell Developmental Language Scales.* Windsor: N.F.E.R.

Richards, M. P. M. (1977). Interaction and the Concept of Development: The Biological and the Social Revisited. In M. Lewis and L. Rosenblum (Eds.) *Interaction, Conversation and the Development of Language.* New York: Wiley.

Richman, N. (1977). Behaviour Problems in Pre-school Children: family and social factors. *Brit. J. Psychiat.* **131**, 523–527.

Ricks, D. (1975). Verbal Communication in Pre-Verbal Normal and Autistic Children. In O'Connor, N. (Ed.) *Language, Cognitive Deficits and Retardation.* London: Butterworths.

Robson, K. (1967). The role of eye-to-eye contact in maternal–infant attachment. *J. Child Psychol. Psychiat.,* **8**, 13–25.

Rosenblatt, D. (1977). Developmental Trends in Infant Play. In B. Tizard and D. Harvey (Eds.) *Biology of Play.* Clinics in Developmental Medicine No. 62. London: Heinemann/S.I.M.P.

Rutter, M. (1972). Clinical Assessment of Language Disorders in the Young Child. In: M. Rutter and J. A. M. Martin (Eds.) *The Child with Delayed Speech.* Clinics in Developmental Medicine No. 43. London: Heinemann/S.I.M.P.

Rutter, M. (1977). Infantile Autism and other Child Psychoses. In: M. Rutter and L. Hersov (Eds.) *Child Psychiatry: Modern Approaches.* Oxford: Blackwell.

Rutter, M. (1980). Language training with autistic children: How does it work and what does it achieve. In: Hersov, L. A., Berger, M. and Nicol, A. R. (Eds.). *Language and Language Disorders in Childhood.* Oxford: Pergamon. (In press.)

Rutter, M., Graham, P. and Yule, W. (1970). *A Neuropsychiatric Study in Childhood.* Clinics in Developmental Medicine No. 35/36. London: Heinemann/S.I.M.P.

Rutter, M. and Mittler, P. (1972). Environmental Influences on Language Development. In Rutter, M. and Martin, J. A. M. (Eds.) *The Child with Delayed Speech.* Clinics in Developmental Medicine No. 43. London: Heinemann/S.I.M.P.

Sachs, J. and Devin, J. (1976). Young Children's Knowledge of Age-Appropriate Speech Styles. *J. Child Lang.,* **3**, 81–98.

Schaeffer, B., Vollinzas, G., Musil, A. and McDowell, P. (1978). Spontaneous verbal language for autistic children, through signed speech. *J. Child Psychol. Psychiat.* (In press.)

Schiff, N. B. and Ventry, I. M. (1976). Communication Problems in Hearing Children of Deaf Parents. *J. Speech Hear. Res.,* **41**, 348–358.

Schlesinger, H. S. and Meadow, K. P. (1972). *Sound and Sign: Childhood Deafness and Mental Health.* Berkeley: University of California.

Scott, J. P. (1963). The Process of Primary Socialisation in Canine and Human Infants. *Monographs of the Society for Research in Child Development.* Vol. 31.

Shatz, M. and Gelman, R. (1973). The Development of Communication Skills: Modifications in the Speech of Young Children as a function of Listener. *Monographs of the Society for Research in Child Development,* **38**, No. 5, Serial No. 152.

Shatz, M. and Gelman, R. (1977). Beyond Syntax: The Influences of Conversational Constraints on Speech Modifications. In C. Snow and C. Ferguson (Eds.) *Talking to Children: Language Input and Acquisition.* Cambridge: Cambridge University Press.

Shearer, W. A. (1972). Diagnosis and Treatment of Voice Disorders in School Children. *J. Speech Hear. Disord.* **37**, 215–221.

Sinclair, H. (1969). Developmental Psycholinguistics. In D. Elkin and J. Flavell (Eds.) *Studies in Cognitive Development.* New York: Oxford University Press.

Skinner, B. F. (1957). *Verbal Behaviour.* New York: Appleton Century Crofts.

Sloane, H. N. and MacAulay, B. D. (1968). *Operant Procedures in Remedial Speech and Language Training.* Boston: Houghton Miflim.

Slobin, D. I. (1970). Universals of grammatical development in children. In G. B. Flores d'Arcais and J. W. Levett (Eds.) *Advances in Psycholinguistics.* Amsterdam: North-Holland.

Slobin, D. I. (1973). Cognitive Pre-requisites for the Development of Grammar. In C. A. Ferguson and D. I. Slobin (Eds.) *Studies of Child Language Development.* New York: Holt Rinehart and Winston.

Smith, E. M., Brown, H. O., Toman, J. E. and Goodman, L. S. (1947). The Lack of Cerebral Effects of D-tubocuraine. *Anesthesiology,* **8**, 1–14.

Snow C. (1977). The Development of Conversation between Mothers and Babies. *J. Child Lang.*, **4**, 1–22.

Snow, C., Arlman-Rupp, A., Hassing, Y., Jobse, J., Joosten, J. and Vorster, J. (1976). Mother's Speech in Three Social Classes. *J. Psycholinguistic Research*, **5**, 1–20.

Snow, C. and Ferguson, C. (1977). (Eds.) *Talking to Children: Language Input and Acquisition*. Cambridge: Cambridge University Press.

Soflieti, J. P. (1955). Bilingualism and Biculturalism. *J. Educ. Psychol.*, **46**, 222–227.

Solomon, A. L. (1961). Personality and Behaviour Patterns of Children with functional defects of articulation. *Child Develop.* **32**, 731–737.

Staats, A. W. (1968). *Learning, Language and Cognition*. New York: Holt Rinehart and Winston.

Stevenson, A. (1893). The Speech of Children. *Science*, **21**, 118–120.

Stevenson, J. and Richman, N. (1976). The Prevalence of Language Delay in a Population of Three Year Old Children and its Association with General Retardation. *Develop. Med. Child Neurol.* **18**, 431–441.

Stevenson, J. and Richman, N. (1978). Behaviour, language and development in three-year-old children. *J. Autism Child. Schiz.* **8**, 299–313.

Stewart, D. M. and Hamilton, M. L. (1976). Imitation as a Learning Strategy in the Acquisition of Vocabulary. *J. Experimental Child Psychology*, **21**, 380–392.

Tenezakis, M. D. (1975). Linguistic Subsystems and Concrete Operations. *Child Develop.* **46**, 430–436.

Thorpe, W. H. (1961). *Bird Song*. Cambridge: Cambridge University Press.

Tizard, B. (1980). Nursery School Children's Conversation with Teachers and Parents. In: Hersov, L. A., Berger, M. and Nichol, A. R. (Eds.). *Language and Language Disorders in Childhood*. Oxford: Pergamon. (In press.)

Tizard, B., Cooperman, O., Joseph, A. and Tizard, J. (1972). Environmental Effects on Language Development: A Study of Young Children in Long Stay Residential Nurseries. *Child Develop.* **43**, 337–358.

Van Riper, C. (1972). *Speech Correction. 5th Edn.* New York: Prentice-Hall.

Vine, I. (1973). The role of facial-visual signalling in early social development. In M. von Cranach and I. Vine (Eds.) *Social Communication and Movement*. New York: Academic Press

Walker, M. (1977). *The Revised Makaton Vocabulary*. London: Royal Association for the Deaf and Dumb.

Weiner, A. E. (1969). Speech Therapy and Behavior Modification: A Conspectus. J. Special Education, **3**, 285–290.

Weiner, B. J., Ottinger, D. R. and Tilton, J. R. (1969). Comparisons of the Toy Play Behaviour of Autistic, Retarded and Normal Children: A reanalysis. *Psychological Reports*, **25**, 223–226.

Weir, R. H. (1962). *Language in the Crib*. The Hague: Mouton.

Weiss, H. H. and Born, B. (1967). Speech Training or Language Acquisition? A distinction when speech training is taught by operant conditioning procedures. *Am. J. Orthopsychiat.*, **37**, 49–55.

Whorf, B. L. (1956). *Language Thought and Reality*. In J. B. Carroll (Ed.) Cambridge Mass. and New York: M.I.T. Press and Wiley.

Wilson, F. B. (1966). Efficacy of Speech Therapy with Educable Mentally Retarded Children. *J. Speech Hear. Res.*, **9**, 423–433.

Wing, L. (1969). The Handicaps of Autistic Children: A Comparative Study. *J. Child Psychol. Psychiat.*, **10**, 1–40.

Woolf, P. G. (1977). Arson and Moebius' Syndrome: A case Study of Stigmatisation. *Medicine Science and the Law*, **17**, 68–70.

Yule, W. and Berger, M. (1972). Behaviour Modification Principles and Speech Delay. In M. Rutter and J. A. Martin (Eds.) *The Child with Delayed Speech*. Clinics in Developmental Medicine No. 43. London: Heinemann/S.I.M.P.

Zazzo, R. (1960). *Les Jumeaux: Le Couple et la Personne*. Paris: Presses Universitaires de France.

19. READING AND SPELLING SKILLS

UTA FRITH

What is reading skill?
What is spelling skill?
The development of reading and spelling skills

Prerequisites for Reading and Spelling
Speech sound
Graphic symbols
Sound-symbol and symbol-symbol relationships
Linguistic awareness

Early Stages in Reading and Spelling
Decoding skills and instant word recognition
Multi-level processing

Later Stages in Reading and Spelling
Comprehension
Automaticity
Flexibility
Speed
Sources of failure in reading and spelling

Reading and spelling are complex and astonishing accomplishments. They are not biological functions for which the brain may be uniquely equipped, but highly artificial processes which depend on specific learning and instruction. Reading and writing create and use visible language, and hence these skills are primarily language skills. However, they are also prime examples of cognitive skills, that is, they crucially involve perception, attention, memory and thinking. The invention of the alphabet has made language visible in a particular and interesting way which is not without problems. Thus, when considering the nature of reading and spelling skills the specific requirements of an alphabetic writing system have to be taken into account.

What is reading skill?

It is tempting to simplify this question by defining reading and writing as the translation of graphic symbols into speech sounds. If this was all there was to it, learning to read would just mean learning to decode from visual into auditory modality. Once this translation into the auditory mode had taken place the already established system that is responsible for understanding speech would come into operation. Comprehension of meaning would therefore not strictly be part of reading. As we shall see, this definition of reading is much too narrow. After all, what we call reading includes such different activities as scanning a phone book, enjoying a novel, appreciating poetry, perusing scribbled notes, recognizing street signs, skimming a magazine, or studying scientific text. These different examples of reading activity have at first glance little in common, and it would certainly seem inadequate to characterize them essentially as visual-auditory translations. There is little doubt that the aim of reading in all these examples is to get meaning from graphic symbols. There appear to be two distinctly different ways of achieving this aim. One is a direct way which goes from written word to meaning without prior translation into sound. Evidence for this direct way comes, for example, from such reading errors as 'spaceman' for 'astronaut', or from the difficulty of understanding a sentence like 'two bee or knot too be'. In the first example, the reader must have understood the correct meaning but nevertheless could not produce the correct sound of the word. In the second example, the correct sound is present, but nevertheless the reader is misled by the odd graphic representation of the words and may not get the meaning. The other way of getting meaning is indirect and depends on the translation of graphic symbols into speech sounds first. The translation is necessary whenever novel or unfamiliar words or names have to be read aloud, *e.g.* 'Epaminondas'. The skilled reader may use either route, the direct or the indirect one, by eye, or by ear, in order to go from script to meaning, as the task demands (Bradshaw, 1975). When reading poetry, where sound appreciation is essential, he would translate the words into sounds; on the other hand, reading the list of ingredients on a packaged food label he might not attempt even covertly to pronounce any chemical compounds mentioned. These two ways of getting meaning from script are also useful when considering the widely different skills of beginning and advanced readers, and moreover they may well be keys to describing individual differences in reading strategies (Baron and McKillop, 1975; Baron and Strawson, 1976). Thus, some readers may predominantly read by ear, others by eye.

The two ways in which meaning is comprehended from print can be distinguished also from another point of view. One way starts from an analysis of perceptual features through various higher order stages of analysis and finally arrives at meaning. This is known as the 'bottom up' model. In contrast, the 'top down' model starts from hypotheses as to what the meaning of a word or text might be and then seeks confirmatory evidence from the perceptual data. Discussions of these models are provided, for example, by Rumelhart (1976) and by Allport (1979). The 'bottom up' model may appear at first more plausible and straightforward, but it cannot easily account for certain phenomena in reading. One such phenomenon is that more letters can be perceived in a given time when these letters form a word than when they form a random string (Huey, 1908). Also, words are perceived more accurately than non-words under very brief exposure to the point that individual letters within words are identified more accurately than within non-words (Wheeler, 1970). If the reader proceeded from single letters through various stages of analysis to a final stage of constructing the word

as a whole this would be difficult to explain. These 'word superiority' effects do not depend on an extremely high level of reading skill; surprisingly, quite a modest amount of reading proficiency is sufficient for such effects to appear.

A tight demonstration that a guess of the meaning of a word can indeed precede proper perceptual analysis has been provided by Marcel (1979). Words were presented briefly and masked subsequently so that people could not be sure whether or not they had seen anything at all. They could nevertheless guess the meaning of the words presented better than chance. But they could not guess their perceptual (graphic or phonological) features. For example, if people had to choose a word as similar to what was flashed on the screen, they would choose a word that was similar in meaning rather than one that looked alike or sounded alike. Thus, if the actually presented word was flower, people might guess 'tulip' rather than 'flour' or 'lower'. From these and related findings it must be concluded that crucial aspects of word recognition proceed without conscious awareness. Furthermore, these high speed processes function in such a way that deep meaning may well be apprehended as fast or faster than surface aspects of words.

The 'top down' model puts particular emphasis on the role of internal knowledge in reading, that is, the hypotheses and guesses that guide reading. The 'bottom up' model stresses the importance of the perceptual aspects, that is, the data present on the printed page. Both sources of information are clearly necessary for successful reading. Using internal knowledge enables the reader to read under very poor conditions, such as 'illegible' handwriting, fragmented script or fancifully ornamented lettering. Knowledge of syntax can be used to guess whether a word that cannot be deciphered is a noun; knowledge of the writer's intention can be used to guess its meaning. On the other hand, we can pronounce written words, which we have never seen before and whose meaning is totally unknown to us. Although it may be questioned to what extent we can call either of these examples reading, they show that if both processes are powerful on their own, they must be formidable in combination. Normal skilled reading presumably works so well because of such a combination. Perfect comprehension is achieved when the reader has analysed and understood the text at surface (perceptual) as well as deep (semantic) levels. Hence it can be argued that these multi-level processes are not well described by either 'top down' or 'bottom up' models, but they require interaction of these levels.

For research as well as teaching purposes a task analysis of reading is essential. Traditionally reading ability has been seen as the outcome of a number of underlying subskills (*e.g.* Vernon, 1977). Thus, it has been assumed that normal ability in such subskills as visual and auditory discrimination, cross-modal integration, and sequencing, would guarantee normal reading. Abnormal functioning of these processes would mean reading retardation. Naturally, in the assessment of reading problems one has to allow for different subskills to be relevant at different ages (Satz *et al.* 1971). Thus, for example, reading retardation at a very early stage might be linked with perceptual problems, whereas reading retardation at a later stage might be linked with specific cognitive problems. However, there are children without any deficit in any of the subskills usually considered but yet who cannot read and there are children who *can* read despite some deficit in these same skills. Examples of serious deficits that do not necessarily prevent reading are poor vision, poor hearing, poor speech, and low intelligence. Therefore differentiation between good and poor readers in terms of relevant subskills is often disappointingly weak. A detailed analysis of the reading process itself, taking account of its basis in language, and the specific problems inherent in an alphabetic writing system, may lead to new subskills being considered.

What is spelling skill?

The essence of alphabetic writing is that speech sounds (phonemes) are represented by letters (graphemes). To do this there are sound-letter correspondence rules specially adapted for a particular language. The significant advantage of writing systems based on the alphabetic principle is that with a limited set of symbols and rules, in theory, one can write down any word even if one has not seen it before. Moreover, applying these same sound-letter rules in reverse, *i.e.* going from letter to sound, in theory, one can pronounce any written word. Reading 'by ear' and spelling therefore have much in common. However, sound-letter correspondence rules do not govern the entire orthography of most languages, much as spelling reformers have been campaigning for this. In English, for example, it is estimated that only about half the words could be spelled correctly following strict sound-letter correspondence rules. Therefore, in practice, one can *not* write any new word and also one can *not* just use the rules in reverse for reading. There are various reasons why additional rules and word-specific information are necessary to govern the 'other half' of spelling. Some of these reasons are discussed by Haas (1970) and Scragg (1974). Spelling reformers hold that it would be best to adopt purely phonetic spelling with a 1:1 correspondence of phonemes and graphemes. If this was adopted we could not distinguish between the written forms of words that have identical sound (sail-sale). But this would only be one of many other disadvantages of such a system (Haas, 1970).

In English orthography many words are spelled in such a way as to represent a direct meaning-letter correspondence, rather than merely a sound-letter correspondence. Reading 'by eye' and spelling in these terms also have much in common. Our memory has information about what words look like, that is, not as pictures, but as specific sequences of letters. Thus we can spell without the use of sound based rules. Simon (1976) has provided a model of spelling that is based on phonological as well as visual information. In skilled writers the vast majority of spelling errors as well as unintentional slips of the pen are phonetically accurate. This suggests that spelling could be viewed as a two stage process: first, from the sound of the word

one or more graphic representations are generated, according to the appropriate grapheme-phoneme rules. Second, the correct graphic representation is chosen according to specific information about the sequence of letters in the word. For example, the sound /thɛər/ could be represented as their or there. Indeed, it is here assumed that in the first instance both representations are generated. This sometimes results in a typical phonetic misspelling. However, for correct spelling, a second step is necessary that enables a decision about which of the two forms is correct. This step may either draw on deep linguistic rules, or failing this, rely on rote memory for specific words.

Whether we think of phonological or visual strategies, reading and spelling abilities are closely related. However, there are sufficient differences to result in marked dissociations between these skills. Thus, Boder (1973) showed that not all words that are in a child's sight vocabulary, *i.e.* can be read instantly, can also be spelled correctly, though she found greater congruence in normal than in retarded readers. Read (1971) showed that very young children can write words with invented spellings based on the sounds of individual letters following a strictly phonetic strategy, but cannot afterwards read these words. Bryant and Bradley (1979) demonstrated that 6-year-olds use predominantly a 'phonics' strategy for spelling and a 'look-and-say' strategy for reading. They found that particular words were more likely to be spelled than read correctly (*e.g.* upset) and other words were more likely to be read than spelled correctly (*e.g.* pretend). Interestingly the children could be made to read the words, that they could spell but not read, by inducing them to adopt a phonics strategy. This was done simply by presenting these words in a set of non-words that could *only* be read by sounding. With increasing age these preferences for different strategies for spelling and reading probably diminish. However, in some cases, a discrepancy between reading and spelling remains, such that there are highly skilled adult readers who are nevertheless atrocious spellers. Frith (1978) showed that this group may well use different and non-overlapping strategies for reading and writing.

The development of reading and spelling skills

A very thorough account of reading acquisition is provided by Gibson and Levin (1975). Following their framework, we shall first consider pre-reading skills which include learning of speech sounds, of graphic symbols and of the equivalence of heard sound and seen symbol. Second, we shall look at the early stages, concerned mainly with the learning of decoding and spelling skills. Third, we shall look at the later stages which are mainly concerned with building up automatic strategies for perfect multilevel comprehension.

It would be foolhardy to mention actual age levels in a developmental account of literacy skills. Given that there are eight hundred million illiterate adults in the world, these skills must be regarded as overwhelmingly determined by external factors (Bataille, 1976). These range from political conditions and cultural desirability of academic achievement, to school entrance age and teaching methods. There are simply too many factors which significantly advance or retard the age at which a certain degree of skill may be expected, to provide a meaningful time scale. However, even if we confine ourselves only to internal factors, as is the case in the following brief account, we can only talk of stages, not ages. For most developmental processes only a stage by stage but not a year by year time course makes sense. An adult without any prior experience in reading has to go through the same stages, in the same order, when acquiring literacy, as a child: Charlemagne when he learned to read in his old age shared some of the problems of a modern precocious baby when coming to grips with letters.

It would be more accurate to talk about the *acquisition* of reading and writing skills rather than their *development* which may be thought to carry biological undertones. However, the use of this term can be justified since we know too little about learning and instructional processes. Therefore it seems wise to take an unspecific 'growth-in-time' view that does not exclude either internal maturational or external factors, or their interaction.

As with other functions, development is not a smooth and gradual process. At each stage, the accumulation of learning has to be used for a break-through into a qualitatively different level of skill. That is, apparently from one day to the next a child can 'read', can 'spell', can 'learn from print'. These break-throughs, however, are not achieved with equal ease by all children, and sometimes are not achieved at all. Even so-called illiteracy does not necessarily imply a total lack of reading skill, as in the pre-reader, but can often be precisely defined as retardation of skill at a particular level.

PREREQUISITES FOR READING AND SPELLING

Speech sound

The alphabet is a device for representing speech sounds. It is very different in nature from other writing systems using pictographs and logographs. In these systems one can for instance draw pictures of objects or actions, one can use arbitrary graphic symbols to denote whole words without in the least depending on speech sound. Obviously these systems must develop thousands of symbols and are therefore very unwieldy. In contrast, syllabaries and alphabets do depend on speech sound and can make do with relatively few symbols. The alphabet graphically represents 'phonemes', which drastically limits the number of possible symbols. The phoneme is a smaller unit than the syllable. It is an abstraction that disregards variations due to sound context, but instead refers to classes of sounds. This abstraction and reduction makes the alphabet the most economical and versatile system for writing down language. However this is achieved at a cost. The unit of the phoneme is a very artificial one which has to be learned by the child as a difficult new concept. Speech sound is not experienced in

ready-made phoneme segments. This is suggested by the work of Liberman and her colleagues (1977). For a young child it is easiest (though by no means self evident) to segment speech into words. Next, the child can learn to segment words into syllables. This can be taught, for example, by tapping out words rhythmically (*e.g.* 'e-le-phant'). Last of all, and often only after considerable practice with rhyming and other segmentation tasks, the child achieves insight into the concept of phonemes. In order to understand the concept of letters it is necessary to understand phonemes, yet in order to understand phonemes it is very useful to understand what letters mean. It seems therefore that understanding of the sound units and the letters representing them must be acquired almost simultaneously. A young child who has just learned 'a is for apple', 'b is for ball' cannot be expected to have the slightest idea why there is a relationship between a and apple. He would learn 'a is for ball' equally well. Nobody knows what suddenly will make this child realize the nature of the relationship. It seems easiest to separate the first letter sound from the rest of the word and only after this can be done, can the child be expected to separate out letter sounds in middle positions.

While the notion of segmentation of words into phonemes is one aspect of preparing to read, the converse notion of blending of letters into a word sound is another. Blending is often held to be a basic prerequisite of reading which may be lacking in reading disabled children (*e.g.* Naidoo, 1972). To the reader who is already familiar with the use of the alphabet it seems a reasonable way to teach somebody to read by sounding out 'kuh-ah-tuh' for 'cat'. However, the young child not only has difficulty in recognizing that 'kuh-ah-tuh' can be blended into the sound 'cat' but he also has not learned the abitrary convention that this word contains three sound elements. The same problem would arise for readers of syllabaries, *e.g.* Japanese, in which consonants do not exist. Thus, Japanese children starting to learn English have great difficulty with the concept of consonants. One method teachers use is to ask them to imagine, *e.g.* the sound /ka/ minus the /a/. An interesting account of how Japanese children learn to read with a syllabary, with apparently great ease at the age of 4, is given by Sakamoto (1980).

Having achieved phoneme segmentation the child experiences the first and possibly most important of break-throughs in the development of reading skill. Some children will take much longer than others, a few may never properly understand it at all. Thorough and illuminating discussions of this crucial process of phoneme acquisition and its relevance to reading have been provided by Gleitman and Rozin (1977) and Liberman *et al.* (1977).

Graphic symbols

Graphic symbols inhabit the artificial world of two-dimensional space. The laws of this space are quite different from ordinary space. Thus upside-down and mirror reversed configurations have to be distinguished because each change in orientation may denote a different symbol. Some letters are very difficult to write for a young child (*e.g.* N) because they contravene his natural action tendency to go in a threading motion starting from top left (*e.g.* n), (Goodnow and Levine, 1973). This perceptual learning, both for recognition and production of graphic symbols, goes on for quite a long time in the pre-reading and early reading stages. The authoritative account of perceptual learning is provided by Gibson (1969). Reese and Lipsitt (1970) give useful discussions of orientation discrimination.

With learning to handle graphic symbols, as with other functions, there are marked individual differences in the pace of learning. Poor readers often seem to be plagued by persistent problems in this area in that they confuse graphic symbols. However, it has been frequently pointed out that reversal errors (*e.g.* b-d-p-q) in both reading and writing occur only as frequently in poor readers as one would expect from their reading level, *i.e.* no more than in equally unskilled but younger normal readers. This seems to suggest that these errors should be considered a secondary consequence of being an unskilled reader and not a primary cause. It is important to point out that confusions of letters are not due to an inability to discriminate small visual differences. Even infants, if tested with appropriate techniques can be shown to differentiate between lines of different orientation. The confusion probably arises due to a difficulty with a differential labelling or coding in memory. That is, the problem with say, b-d, is to know and to remember which is which (*e.g.* Frith, 1971). Initial stages of sensory perception, *i.e.* the discrimination of visual or of auditory features, are unlikely to be major sources of reading problems. One reason for this statement is that the partially sighted or partially hearing do on the whole show normal literacy levels. Even the deaf (Markides, 1976; Conrad, 1977), if inner language is intact, can be normal readers. Nevertheless, there are many who hold that peripheral optical or acoustical defects should not be ignored and may sometimes be easy to remedy.

Sound-symbol and symbol-symbol relationships

The ability to segment speech sound and the ability to recognize and produce correct graphic symbols if added together do not constitute reading. The translation of written into spoken language is another process that is required in addition. Seeing and hearing and writing and speaking have to be related in terms of letter and phoneme units. In a much quoted study, Birch and Belmont (1964) presented dot patterns visually and asked them to be matched to taps presented auditorily. They showed that poor readers failed at this task and concluded that a failure in cross-modal coding, *i.e.* from one sensory modality to the other, was a cause of reading problems. Vande Voort *et al.* (1972) however, demonstrated that intra-modal coding, *i.e.* from one type to another type of material presented to the same sense was also deficient in poor readers. Other authors, reviewed by Vellutino (1977), have also argued against any special role of cross-modality integration in reading and reading failure.

Instead, it could be suggested that the sound-symbol relationships in reading are as easy or as difficult to acquire as any symbol-symbol relationships. This is a basic cognitive skill about which we know very little. However, it is clear that if a disability in this general skill existed, reading would certainly be adversely affected. The labelling or coding problems that probably underlie letter confusions, as mentioned in the previous section, would have to be considered in relation to this skill.

Symbol-symbol relationships are also involved in memory for sequences. This skill has attracted much attention in reading research (*e.g.* Bakker, 1972) because it seems obvious that reading and writing depend on knowing the right order of letters. Apparent support for this view comes from the occurrence of letter order errors, such as was for saw in beginners and in poor readers. However, it has been shown, as with letter reversals, that amount of order errors, which incidentally rarely exceeds 10% of all errors, is entirely predicted by reading level (Nelson, 1979). Therefore, it is possible to argue that sequencing ability, far from being a prerequisite, actually depends on reading experience. In any case, the importance of memory for the specific order of elements is seriously questioned by recent linguistic theories. These theories suggest that language productions and hence words in a sentence and letters in a word, are governed by hierarchical rules rather than merely sequential ones (Cromer, 1978).

Linguistic awareness

It would be possible to quote a large number of skills in which one has to have achieved a certain level as prerequisites for learning to read (*e.g.* memory for sequences, habitual left to right scanning, syntactic competence, vocabulary size). However, all of these are really basic milestones in mental development that happen regardless of whether or not reading will be acquired later. It seems trivial to mention that a child must possess for example a reasonable memory span and must have learned how to learn in order for any literacy teaching to be successful. Clearly, these factors are part of normal growing up, and it is not surprising that if a child is taught reading before he has reached a certain level of maturity his learning will be slow and problematic.

Of all the prerequisites that one could mention linguistic awareness is especially important. Linguistic awareness is not the same as linguistic competence. It refers to the possibility of looking at language, as it were, from the outside. This ability develops quite slowly and shows itself for example in the appreciation of purely verbal games or jokes, or in the realization that sound, meaning and syntax are not identical. For example, a child has to learn that a grammatically correct sentence can nevertheless be nonsense. A child has to learn to recognize what reading really means, he has to learn what defines a sentence, a word as opposed to a pseudo-word, or a letter string (Reid, 1966).

Written language often deviates from spoken language and has its own special rules that literary tradition has elaborated. Instead of being aided by melody, emphasis, pauses and accompanying gestures in speech, the reader is aided by punctuation, capitalization, paragraph structuring, headings, *etc*. Most of this the reader is never taught explicitly. It seems, however, that the ability to stand back and think about language, its sound, its visual representation, is essential for the higher levels of reading skill.

EARLY STAGES IN READING AND SPELLING

Decoding skills and instant word recognition

Two very distinct approaches that most beginning readers adopt, whether or not they are taught explicitly, are 'phonics' and 'look and say'. The 'phonics' approach is properly defined as decoding of graphemes to phonemes and learning spelling rules. This is the essence of alphabet use as we have seen earlier, and no reader can avoid decoding when it comes to unknown words. Nevertheless, many beginning readers do avoid decoding if they can recognize a word by other means, say, a distinctive shape. They thus treat words almost as if they were Chinese logographs. Even the more advanced reader often uses only partial decoding, *e.g.* the beginning sounds of a word. The 'look-and-say' approach is a useful short-cut at all stages of reading, and in the early stages often the only way to build up motivation in the arduous and slow task of learning the correct letter and sound correspondences, the numerous rules governing them and their almost innumerable exceptions. A true break-through is achieved when a child can tackle any new word by decoding without the overwhelming effort this at first implies. Both segmenting and blending of phonemes suddenly becomes easy and obvious.

Spelling probably has to be learned by a mixture of rule learning, rote drill and a more obscure process that is based on producing analogies with known words. Very little is as yet known about this learning, but some discussion is provided by Peters (1970). It is important to remember that sound-letter correspondence rules are not a sufficient basis for becoming a competent speller. Many words have to be learned by rote, by the aid of mnemonics, or by word-specific cues. Nevertheless in spite of the demanding nature of this task, children on their way to becoming good spellers need not spend inordinate time and effort in order to master this skill.

The acquisition of decoding skills is a relatively slow process, and it is therefore not surprising that the short-cut of instant word recognition is used very much in the meantime. Many words are distinctive enough in terms of length or spelling pattern so that they can be recognized as graphic patterns. This instant recognition is considerably improved if as a basis for guessing not only distinctive graphic detail is used but also other clues that are normally provided in the context. Goodman (1970) and Smith (1973) have emphasized the legitimate use of this strategy. They argue that guessing should not be constantly discouraged for the supposed benefit of pure 'phonics'. Indeed, at highly skilled stages of silent reading, particularly at high speed, where accuracy is secondary, such guessing strategies are probably used extensively.

Multi-level processing

Right from the beginning reading and spelling involve attention and performance on several interrelated tasks at once. Perception, memory and linguistic analysis are all required to function at a demanding pace. Timing and coordination is required which has to be achieved through practice. Often at first, when one kind of analysis, say sound segmentation, is carried out, this is so slow that the segments analysed have not been retained in memory and the child has to start again. Similarly, while he recognizes individual words he loses track of the sentence or wider context. The specific aids of story context, paragraphs, sentences, words, spelling patterns, letters, have to become an overlearned framework in order to code, store and retrieve the data that the eye picks up and internal knowledge supplies. Once coordination and integration is achieved it is possible to talk about reading for pleasure or reading to learn. La Berge and Samuels (1974) have provided a theoretical framework that distinguishes accuracy and automaticity of reading performance. They suggest that voluntary *attention* for processing is necessary at first, but that it is becoming less necessary as automaticity is achieved.

LATER STAGES IN READING AND SPELLING

Once the state is reached where reading and writing become something to be used for other purposes, *e.g.* enjoyment, learning, communication, the process seems to be no longer comparable with the beginner's attempts at reading. The break is such that it also defines a boundary which a large proportion of readers never transgress. They read only with effort and concentration and may well therefore avoid it. However, it may be that basic requirements in a literate society are adequately met by a relatively low level of decoding and word recognition skills. It would be important to find out whether any noticeable disadvantage may result other than in academic pursuits, given that communication is increasingly served by audio-visual means.

Comprehension

Comprehension of written language and comprehension of spoken language are not necessarily parallel in their development. Guthrie and Tyler (1976) found that poor readers were worse than good readers only on reading comprehension but not on listening comprehension. They attributed this failure to poor decoding skills and showed that it could not have been due to poor psycholinguistic processing strategies. Thus, for efficient reading comprehension specific learning must occur which is not parasitic on speech comprehension. This learning may well be dependent on practice in decoding and word recognition skills.

Although the comprehension of meaning is always a prominent aim at all levels of reading skill, it can become more refined and deeper when other aspects of reading have become overlearned. It seems likely that the reader can parcel the information in bigger units and can know how to get a global overview of context and structure of a text. Thus the unit for meaning may be a paragraph while earlier it was a sentence, earlier still a word. Rothkopf and Kaplan (1972) have investigated study skills and described various techniques of using questions during reading to increase efficiency of learning.

Deeper level comprehension of linguistic units also benefits spelling. The more one knows about derivations of words and relationships between word families, the clearer their spelling and the precise reason for the spelling become. For example, in order to spell the word 'consignment' one does not have to rely on rote memory in order to decide between consignment, concinement or consynement. One can instead use the knowledge that the root is -sign.

Automaticity

In terms of the model proposed by La Berge and Samuels (1974) automaticity of the various processing levels is what truly distinguishes the skilled from the unskilled reader.

Skilled readers report the experience that they can read out aloud with correct diction and yet at the same time be pre-occupied with their thoughts elsewhere so that they themselves have no comprehension of the text. This shows that the decoding and word recognition work can be carried out with very little conscious attention. It has already been mentioned earlier that the meaning of a word can also be understood without conscious processing (Marcel, 1979).

An interesting phenomenon due to automatic processing skills is the compulsive nature of reading: one cannot easily avoid reading print, even when one tries to ignore it. One famous instance of this is the Stroop phenomenon where colour words are printed in either appropriate or inappropriate inks. The task is to name the colour of the ink regardless of the word. Typically, it takes longer to name the ink colour when it is incongruent with the word, (e.g. the word 'green' written in red letters), which proves that the meaning of the word is understood very quickly indeed. This effect can be obtained already at very early stages of reading skill.

In spelling, the automatic production of letter sequences is very impressive. This has little to do with practised motor movements, as it applies to oral, written or typed spelling. As in reading, one would assume that automaticity frees attention which can then be devoted to other aspects of the complex task of writing.

Flexibility

The skilled reader can adapt his strategies to the demands of the task. With very difficult text it is likely that he uses decoding into speech in order to slow down his pace of reading; with very trivial text his reading may be extremely fast and 'direct', i.e. without sound entering into the comprehension process. Thus, a newspaper article may be summarized without the ability to give a verbatim repetition. On the other hand the typical strategy of the highly skilled reader seems to be processing surface detail as well as deeper meaning. Good readers are able to report more about graphic details of a text than poor readers, and at the same time are better able to report its meaning.

Speed

One possible further achievement that the advanced reader may aim for is to read at a very high speed. Speed reading courses are offered and these use a variety of methods. Their claims and results have been critically examined by Gibson and Levin (1975) who conclude that depending on the nature of the text, speed reading inevitably occurs at a cost. Most advanced readers have flexible enough strategies to adjust their reading speed to the requirements of a situation.

It has been argued that efficient eye movement strategies can be learned in order to speed up reading. One way would be to fixate on as large as possible an area of print, another to move the eye economically and with accurate aim without backtracking. Improvement of peripheral vision has been suggested to be crucial at this stage. However, research by McConkie and Rayner using computer technology (e.g. Rayner and McConkie, 1977) has shown that though peripheral vision is important it is not used very markedly by skilled readers. From Buswell's (1937) careful frame by frame analysis of films of eye movements during reading one can also conclude that where the eye happens to fixate and for how long is difficult to predict. These studies also showed that backtracking occurs quite often at high levels of skill. It is therefore likely that it is pointless to search for optimal eye movement strategies.

Sources of failure in reading and spelling

From what has been said before it is clear that causes of poor reading may often not be mysterious at all. Any child who has normal intellectual abilities should by sheer practice and experience become as good a reader and writer as he is a speaker and listener. However, social disadvantages of all kinds often result in poor motivation to learn, and in poor opportunities for practice.

This means that there are many different causes of reading and spelling failure. The most obvious ones, and those to be ruled out first when trying to account for a child's reading failure, are environmental. Rutter (1977) has reviewed the most important of these causes, such as poor family circumstances, poor schooling, and disadvantaged geographical areas. In addition to these more general factors that adversely affect academic achievements one must also consider specific factors inherent in a teaching-learning situation. These factors have strong effects, positive as well as negative, on reading performance. Thus, reading level may vary from school to school, even in the same area with similar sociological background, and even from class to class, within the same school. It is commonplace that the personality of the teacher, the ability to motivate children and to encourage them over failure crucially determine success or failure of a particular method. A concise discussion of teaching methods and their relationships to varying trends in reading standards has been provided by Morris (1972). Feitelson (1980) has described the remarkable case of a sudden large-scale reading failure, its tracing back to misguided teaching strategies, and its reversal into reading success.

There are also less obvious causes of reading and spelling failure. There are children who apparently bring all the requirements of adequate intelligence and adequate environmental conditions, who even with intensive remedial teaching fail to develop into good readers. This condition is well known under the diagnostic label 'dyslexia'. This term is borrowed from adult neurology, where it is known that certain brain lesions can lead to severe loss of previously good reading and/or writing skills. It has sometimes been questioned whether such a condition really exists in children who never acquire normal reading and spelling skills. Rutter and Yule (1975) have clarified this doubt on purely statistical grounds. They point out that if reading ability is normally distributed, obviously there must be 50% above average and 50% below average readers. Moreover, reading achievement can normally be quite well predicted on the basis of (WISC) intelligence test scores. The fact that it cannot be predicted perfectly means that some children achieve more and others less than expected on the basis of their intellectual abilities. It was further found that there are more under-achievers than would balance the over-achievers. Rutter and Yule could thus demonstrate a 'hump' at the lower end of the distribution of scores. This suggests, therefore, that there are some bad readers that do not really belong to the low end of the presumably normal distribution of reading scores, but are in excess of the proportion of children normally expected at this level. Their reading failure must be due to specific but as yet unknown causes. Thus, there are two kinds of reading failure: one being a case of poor achievement in keeping with poor achievement in other subjects and in IQ tests, the other being a case of unexpectedly poor achievement. In both kinds not only internal factors but also environmental factors are determinants of the extent and incidence of the handicap.

A common research strategy is to compare poor readers with good readers of the same age and intelligence on tasks that are thought to be relevant to reading. When poor readers fail on such a task (e.g. letter naming), it is tempting to conclude that this task failure also accounts for their reading failure. However, one can equally conclude that their reading failure accounts for their task failure. For instance, letter naming may become fast and efficient as a consequence of reading experience, and if so, naming slowness cannot be considered a *cause* of reading failure. A comparison of poor readers with younger, normally reading children of the same level of reading skill may solve this cause and effect problem: if the poor readers show a deficit in relation to such a younger comparison group, then an explanation of reading failure may be at hand. If poor readers perform just as one would expect on the basis of their reading age, but not their chronological age, they are often said to show a 'developmental or maturational lag'. This notion is of course not explanatory. It is just another word for retardation—unless it could be demonstrated that sheer passage of time (*i.e.* maturation) will improve matters and that the retarded children will catch up at some point.

A child may not progress in his reading skill and also fail on a variety of tasks that are related to reading skill, because one of the hurdles in the acquisition of reading has not been surmounted. If we consider the problematic steps in the acquisition process we can get some indication of why a child may be held back at a certain level. Such an approach has been excellently presented by Vernon (1977).

The first and probably the most difficult hurdle is the understanding of the concept of phonemes. A deficit here may well be the most important internal source of reading failure (Savin, 1972; Bradley and Bryant, 1978). Since phoneme segmentation is *the* most important prerequisite of alphabetic writing systems a failure at this stage precludes normal reading. However, the reader could make some progress with a non-alphabetic strategy. He can attempt to recognize words as if they were logographs. In an interesting experiment Rozin *et al.* (1971) showed that severely retarded readers were able to read stories using a small set of Chinese symbols with only very few lessons. However, this method is not a practicable solution to reading retardation.

Failure at later points in the development can occur in the acquisition of rules that govern phoneme-grapheme correspondence, and rules that govern grapheme-phoneme correspondence. Nevertheless, even when these processes are seriously deficient, reading can still be practised as instant word recognition. This strategy makes use of distinctive visual features of words and semantic and syntactic context cues. Usually, even the very poor reader can fall back on this strategy and achieve some degree of competence. If this skill was impaired, there would be widespread congnitive handicap, not just reading disability. Normally, reading and writing by eye and by ear would complement each other to give optimal flexibility. The reader is not consciously aware of most of the complex processing that is involved, which is sketched out in 'top-down' and 'bottom-up' models of word recognition. It is likely that a breakdown occurs if only one of the functions fails to become overlearned or automatic. Such highly interdependent systems will not be workable unless each function is adequately working. Reading solely by ear or solely by eye, would remain a laborious process needing maximum attention so that little could be gained for overall comprehension or study.

A point of breakdown at an advanced stage of reading development can arise from the demands of comprehension skills that are specific to written language. For this, a high level of linguistic awareness is essential that enables the reader to internalize the specific grammar of written as opposed to spoken language. Thus, even at very high levels of skill there can be failure in terms of how text is analysed and comprehended.

Causes for failure in spelling must be considered separately, especially in cases where reading ability greatly exceeds spelling ability. Here a specific cause for the spelling problem must be postulated, while in cases where disability extends to both functions a single cause may possibly account for both. Nelson and Warrington (1974) have indeed suggested that a language deficit would account for a failure in both reading and spelling. They supported this claim by showing that verbal intelligence test scores are lower in a group of reading-and-spelling retarded children than in a group of spelling-only retarded children, which had also been found by Naidoo (1972). What causes specific spelling problems is, however, entirely obscure at present. Spelling is still an unexplored and by no means a trivial skill. It must involve such different kinds of learning as rote associations, rules and analogies, but only speculation exists at present whether here is a source of the deficits. An accomplished speller is implicitly also accomplished at the linguistic analysis of words. A poor speller misses out on this accomplishment. This could be a secondary consequence of his handicap, but it could also be a contributing cause.

The question arises whether the psychological factors that may become sources of reading failure can be reduced to neurological or physiological ones. There is much speculation but minimal evidence exists as to what brain lesions would account for developmental dyslexia. The most promising hypothesis is damage to the left hemisphere which is predominantly concerned with verbal and analytical processing. Research supporting this hypothesis is almost exclusively based on studies with adults. For children, Rourke and Finlayson (1978) have shown indirectly that academic performance can be related to brain processes. They found evidence to support the hypothesis that children with with specific reading and spelling impairment have a relatively dysfunctional left hemisphere and a relatively intact right hemisphere. The opposite conclusion was drawn for children with specific mathematical impairment. Other work on neurological indices in relation to reading disability is reviewed by Rutter (1978) and Vernon (1977). Current research in neurolinguistics is reported in the volumes edited by Whitaker and Whitaker (1976). O'Connor and Hermelin (1978) have pointed out that brain damage in infancy or childhood in contrast to lesions in later life, usually has the effect of lowering ability throughout the range of cognitive functions, reading included. The hypothesis that some brain damage may occur that specifically retards reading acquisition and little else is therefore particularly challenging. Hopefully, such new research tools as computerized axial tomography will throw more light on the relationships between psychological dysfunction and brain processes. Techniques for studying regional cerebral blood flow during reading (Lassen et al., 1978) and related activities would seem particularly useful in future research.

We have looked at some basic processes of reading and spelling which showed that we are dealing with immensely complex skills. They are primarily language skills but also show the characteristics of high level visual-perceptual processing. In addition these skills depend on internal knowledge which is used in precise pre-conscious analysis. Therefore, normal reading and spelling must be seen as part of cognitive and linguistic development. Any abnormalities in these skills may well point to some basic retardation or failure in cognition and language functions. However, one must also consider abnormalities that seem to have specific causes intrinsic to the processes involved in reading and writing in an alphabetical system. The normal development of reading and writing skills shows that there are special hurdles that have to be overcome at each stage. Each hurdle may be a source of a specific reading or writing problem and may block progress over and above a particular achievement level. It is plausible that the earlier in the developmental sequence a breakdown occurs the more severe the effect will be. Nevertheless, each stage has its special problems. Even at a high level of literacy refinements in strategy still continue with continuing practice. Thus, good readers too have problems with some material and nobody is a really perfect speller. It would be impossible to say when the development of reading and writing comes to a stop. It is perhaps not surprising with these amazingly complex skills that we have not penetrated much into the mystery of how they are acquired and finally mastered.

REFERENCES

Allport, D. A. (1979). Word recognition in reading: a tutorial review: In P. A. Kolers, M. Wrolstad, H. Bouma (Eds). *Processing of visible language*. New York: Plenum Publ. Corp.

Bakker, D. J. (1972). *Temporal order in disturbed reading*. Rotterdam: University Press.

Baron, J. and McMillop, B. J. (1975). Individual differences in speed of phonetic analysis, visual analysis, and reading. *Acta Psychologica*, 39, 91–96.

Baron, J. and Strawson, C. (1976). Use of orthographic and word-specific knowledge in reading words aloud, *J. Exp. Psychol. Human Perception and Performance*, 2, 386–393.

Bataille, L. (Ed.) (1976). *A turning point for literacy*. Oxford: Pergamon Press.

Birch, H. G. and Belmont, L. (1964). Auditory-visual integration in normal and retarded readers. *Amer. J. Orthopsychiat.*, 34, 852–861.

Boder, E. (1973). Developmental dyslexia: a diagnostic approach based on three atypical reading-spelling patterns. *Develop. Med. Child. Neurol*, 15, 664–683.

Bradley, L. and Bryant, P. E. (1978). Difficulties in auditory organisation as a possible cause of reading backwardness. *Nature*, 271, 746–747.

Bradshaw, J. L. (1975). Three interrelated problems in reading: a review. *Memory and Cognition*, 3, 123–134.

Bryant, P. E. and Bradley, L. (1979). Why children sometimes write words which they do not read. In: Frith, U. (Ed.) *Cognitive Processes in Spelling*. London: Academic Press.

Buswell, G. T. (1937). *How adults read*. Supplementary educational monographs, No. 45. Chicago: University of Chicago Press.

Conrad, R. (1977). The reading ability of deaf school-leavers. *Brit. J. Educ. Psychol.* 47, 138–148.

Cromer, R. F. (1978). The basis of childhood dysphasia: a linguistic approach. In: Maria Wyke (Ed.). *Developmental Dysphasia*. New York: Academic Press. 85–134.

Feitelson, D. (1980). Relating instructional strategies to language idiosyncrasies in Hebrew. In: R. L. Venezky and J. F. Kavanagh (Eds.) *Orthography, Reading, and Dyslexia*. Baltimore: University Park Press (in press).

Frith, U. (1971). Why do children reverse letters? *Brit. J. Psychol.*, **62**, 459–468.

Frith, U. (1978). From print to meaning and from print to sound. *Visible Language.* **12**, 43–54.

Gibson, E. J. (1969). *Principles of Perceptual Learning and Development.* New York: Prentice Hall.

Gibson, E. J. and Levin, H. (1975). *The Psychology of Reading.* Cambridge, Mass.: MIT Press.

Gleitman, L. R. and Rozin, P. (1977). The structure and acquisition of reading. I: relations between orthographies and the structure of language. In: A. S. Reber and D. L. Scarborough (Eds.). *Toward a Psychology of Reading*. Hillsdale: Erlbaum. 1–53.

Goodman, K. S. (1970). Reading; a psycholinguistic guessing game. In: H. Singer, and R. B. Ruddell (Eds.). *Theoretical Models and Processes in Reading.* Intern. Read. Assoc., Newark, Del.

Goodnow, J. J. and Levine, R. A. (1973). The grammar of action: sequence and syntax in children's copying. *Cognitive Psychol.* **4**, 82–98.

Guthrie, J. T. and Tyler, S. J. (1976). Psycholinguistic processing in reading and listening among good and poor readers. *J. Reading Behaviour.*

Haas, W. (1970). Phonographic translation. Manchester: University Press.

Huey, E. B. (1908). *The Psychology and Pedagogy of Reading.* First published 1908, reprinted 1968. Cambridge, Mass.: MIT Press.

La Berge, D. and Samuels, S. J. (1974). Toward a theory of automatic information processing in reading. *Cognitive Psychol.*, **6**, 293–323.

Lassen, N. A., Ingvar, D. H. and Skinhøj, E. (1978). Brain function and blood flow. *Scientific American*, **239**, 50–59.

Liberman, I. Y., Shankweiler, D., Liberman, A. M., Fowler, C. and Fischer, F. W. (1977). Phonetic segmentation and recoding in the beginning reader. In: A. S. Reber and D. L. Scarborough (Eds.). *Toward a psychology of reading.* Hillsdale: Erlbaum. 207–225.

Marcel, A. J. (1979). Conscious and unconscious perception: the effects of visual masking on word processing. *Cognitive Psychol.* (In press.)

Markides, A. (1976). Comparative linguistic proficiencies of deaf children taught by two different methods of instruction—manual versus oral. *The Teacher of the Deaf*, **74**, 307–347.

Morris, J. (1972). The first 'R': yesterday, today and tomorrow. In: A. Melnik and J. Merritt (Eds.). *Reading Today and Tomorrow.* London: University of London Press.

Naidoo, S. (1972). *Specific dyslexia.* London, Pitman.

Nelson, H. (1979). Analysis of spelling errors in normal and dyslexic children. In: U. Frith (Ed.). *Cognitive Processes in Spelling.* London: Academic Press.

Nelson, H. E. and Warrington, E. K. (1974). Developmental spelling retardation and its relation to other cognitive abilities. *Brit. J. Psychol.*, **65**, 265–274.

O'Connor, N. and Hermelin (1978). *Seeing and Hearing and Space and Time.* New York, London: Academic Press. 4–7.

Peters, M. (1970). *Success in Spelling. A study of the factors affecting improvement in spelling in the junior school.* Cambridge: Cambridge Institute of Education.

Rayner, K. and McConkie, G. W. (1977). Perceptual processes in reading; the perceptual spans. In: A. S. Reber and D. L. Scarborough (Eds.). *Toward a Psychology of Reading*. Hillsdale: Erlbaum. 183–205.

Read, C. (1971). Lessons to be learned from the preschool orthographer. In: E. H. Lenneberg and E. Lenneberg (Eds.). *Foundations of Language Development*, **2.** New York: Academic Press. pp. 328–346.

Reese, H. W. and Lipsitt, L. P. (1970). *Experimental child psychology: perceptual development.* New York: Academic Press. pp. 363–410.

Reid, J. F. (1966). Learning to think about reading. *Educational Research*, **9**, 56–62.

Rothkopf, E. and Kaplan, R. (1972). Exploration of the effect of density and specificity of instructional objectives on learning from text. *J. Educat. Psychol.*, **63**, 295–302.

Rourke, B. P. and Finlayson, M. A. J. (1978). Neuropsychological significance of variations in patterns of academic performance: verbal and visual-spatial abilities. *J. Abn. Child Psychol.* **6**, 129–133.

Rozin, P., Poritsky, S. and Sotsky, R. (1971). American children with reading problems can easily learn to read English represented by Chinese characters. *Science*, **171**, 1264–1267.

Rumelhart, D. G. (1977). Towards an interactive model of reading. In: S. Dornic (Ed.). *Attention and Performance*, **6**. Hillsdale: Erlbaum.

Rutter, M. (1978). Prevalence and types of dyslexia. In: A.L. Benton and D. Pearl (Eds.). *Dyslexia: An appraisal of current knowledge.* New York: Oxford University Press.

Rutter, M. and Yule, W. (1975). The concept of specific reading retardation. *J. Child Psychol. Psychiat.* **16**, 181–197.

Sakamoto, T. (1980). Reading of Hiragana. In: R. L. Venezky and J. F. Kavanagh (Eds.). *Orthography, Reading, and Dyslexia*. Baltimore: University Park Press (in press).

Satz, P., Rardin, D. and Ross, J. (1971). An evaluation of a theory of specific developmental dyslexia. *Child Dev.*, **42**, 2009–2021.

Savin, H. B. (1972). What the child knows about speech when he starts to learn to read. In: J. F. Kavanagh and I. G. Mattingly (Eds.). *Language by Ear and Eye.* Cambridge, Mass.: MIT Press.

Scragg, D. G. (1974). *A history of English spelling.* Manchester: University Press.

Simon, D. P. (1976). Spelling, a task analysis. *Instructional Science*, **5**, 277–302.

Smith, F. (1973). *Psycholinguistics and reading.* New York: Holt, Rinehart and Winston.

Vande Voort, L., Senf, G. M. and Benton, A. L. (1972). Development of audio-visual integration in normal and retarded readers. *Child Dev.* **44**, 1260–1272.

Vellutino, F. R. (1977). Alternative conceptualizations of dyslexia: evidence in support of a verbal deficit hypothesis. *Harvard Educat. Rev.*, **47**, 334–354.

Vernon, M. D. (1977). Varieties of deficiency in the reading process. *Harvard Educat. Rev.*, **47**, 396–410.

Wheeler, D. D. (1970). Processes in word recognition. *Cognition*, **1**, 59–85.

Whitaker, H. and Whitaker, H. A. (Eds.), (1976). *Studies in Neurolinguistics.* Vols. **1, 2, 3**. New York, London: Academic Press.

20. COGNITIVE DEVELOPMENT

D. J. WOOD

INTRODUCTION

In this chapter we explore three different images of the child. One sees the child as an actor in the world, discovering reality largely on his own and always through *action*. Contingent on this image is the argument that the child's construction of reality and the essential structure of his thinking is different—in different ways at different times—from that of mature adults. It also holds that adults can do nothing to affect the essential structure of the child's thinking. If they attempt to shake his view of the world by imposing their own interpretations and logic on his experiences they can only serve to demoralize and frustrate him. His ideas, even his 'errors' in thinking are the natural and inevitable consequence of the stages of mental evolution. So, the proper unit of analysis in thinking about human mental or cognitive development is the organism-in-nature. This approach obviously stresses universals in human thought and has little or nothing to say about individual differences in thinking.

The second image construes the child as essentially and primarily a social being. Its advocates hold that the transmission of thoughts is a cultural affair. They ask how the child could possibly evolve alone all those ideas and technologies of thought and action which are the culmination of the experiences of countless past generations. They see the proper unit of analysis as the child-in-culture and see interpersonal relationships—and language particu-

larly—as the fundamental avenues through which the transmission of knowledge takes place.

The third perspective—less fairly represented than the other two in the following pages—sees the child more as an observer, in the sense that he gains understanding through perceptual experiences—through listening, watching and feeling, not simply through action. In recent years, we have seen the re-emergence of this emphasis both in the study of the sensory abilities of young babies and in the challenging proposition that the child learns language 'naturally' by listening and speaking and not by being taught.

Rather than treating each perspective in chain, though they are introduced in this way, we return to them several times considering their implications for various aspects of the child's mental development. But before we consider these, a word of warning. There is very little in the following pages by way of clear recommendations about the solution to clearly defined, practical problems. Rather, the aim is to explore the three perspectives just outlined and to see what follows from them in terms of how we should construe children—their thinking, their errors, their understanding and their social needs.

CHILD AS ACTOR: THOUGHT AND ACTION

Philosophers and psychologists have often given re-birth to the notion that movement and action educate the senses. When we look at an object, for example, what is there to inform us that what lies within its contour is solid and that what lies outside it may not be? How can we know whether the image that falls on the eyes is that of a small object close to or a large object far away; that a coin, say, which is seen other than straight on remains circular and is not, as it appears, elliptical? How can these and the many other judgements which must be made to preserve the identity and characteristics of real objects possibly be based on the intangibility of visual information alone? Touch is a different matter. The world resists movements of the body, a contour can be felt and its extent left in no doubt, its distance may be measured by attempts to take hold of it, and so on. And while the appearance of objects changes under the control of movement they remain in touch all the time, aspects of their feel remain invariant and help supply the initial basis for judgements of 'constancy' and identity. The circular object becomes elliptical as the hands are turned—but, if it is kept in the same grasp its feeling in the hand remains unchanged. And the elliptical can be made circular again simply by *reversing* the movements made. Objects, like one's hand, become smaller as they are moved away from the face; and more distant objects become larger as one moves towards them.

So movement and touch can be talked of as the foundation stones for perceptual judgements and our understanding of the world and its contents. What we see, given such an approach, is ambiguous in a variety of ways, and it is only through the tangibility of movements and touch that we can discover what lies behind this inevitable tissue of ambiguity.

In many respects, Piaget's theory of the development and structure of intelligence embodies the contemporary form of this constructive approach to perception (*see* Piaget and Inhelder, 1958, for an overview). Thought, argues Piaget, is internalized (or, as some would have it 'interiorized') action. The neonate, for Piaget, is not equipped to perceive the world in any integrated fashion. He experiences a succession of discrete sensory 'tableaux' which simply drift in and out of awareness; first they are and then they are not. Even where these separate events in awareness relate to his own body—say the feel of a limb about to move, the eventual sight of it intruding into his visual field, even here, the necessary and intimate relationships between different momentary events are not appreciated. In other words, as the child feels what he will eventually come to know as his own arm about to move there is no *anticipation* of the fact that very soon a particular impression will be gained visually. The great task and a major achievement of infancy and very early childhood, is the realization of these intimate and necessary relationships between different aspects of experience. The child gradually *constructs* a model of his own bodily experience. He discovers the relationships between the various sensory and motor aspects of events. So, in time, the feeling he gets as he begins to move his arm becomes coordinated with the visual scheme to which it will give rise—the child anticipates what his experience will be like in the very near future. Thus, thought begins to substitute for action—but it has taken its nature from that action. What is imagined are the effects that action will have on future feelings. The total experience of transition between different states of an event has been cut down and short-circuited in a mental internalization of the physical act.

As the infant constructs his model of the relationships between action and sensation he also begins to find out about the world. Initially, he knows it in terms of what he can immediately do to it—objects and events are *assimilated* in terms of the actions which he can perform on them. The sensory schemes which an object presents to him may or may not be capable of assimilation—*e.g.* perhaps they can be sucked perhaps they cannot, or later, reached and grasped. If a state of the world can be assimilated in this way, then it becomes known and remembered in terms of the schemes of action to which it is subjugated. If it cannot be assimilated, if reality *resists* fulfilment of the attempted acts, then his mental structures must be further differentiated to *accommodate* the new ambiguity in his experience. Eventually new actions may be discovered which serve to re-unite this untouchable or 'unactable-upon' experience with the rest of his knowledge of the world. He will discover what he has to do in order to act in some way on an event, to bring together the many sensory-motor facets which it presents. So, for example,

as he starts to crawl or walk he will discover that movements towards an untouchable object may render it tangible. Now the visual scheme to which it gives rise can at last be coordinated with other sensory-motor impressions of smell, taste, touch, weight and so on. His knowledge of the event can be 'filled out' through action on it.

Where there is a great discrepancy between assimilation and accommodation—a division in his knowledge of the world which leaves events unknown in many of their action properties—then the child is in a natural and intolerable state of disequilibrium. This guarantees the motivation and 'direction' of behaviour and provides the 'place' in his mental structures which relevant experiences and discoveries will eventually serve to fill. As knowledge of an event is filled out and, hence brought under control, so equilibrium will be restored—as it must be given the nature of reality as it is experienced by organism in nature. Thus, Piaget blends a basic rationalism—the assertion that reality exists and is discovered by all of us in essentially the same form—with an environmentalism, which holds that each of us must discover and construct the nature of that reality ourselves.

When a child is in the early stages of this '*sensory-motor*' period his behaviour and his failure to solve certain problems betray the uncoordinated nature of his sensory-motor impressions.

One of Piaget's best known and intensively investigated family of demonstrations concerns the stages which the child goes through during this first period in the development of object permanence, the 'first invariant'. Initially the infant can hold no concept of an object which endures in time. Out of immediate sensation means out of mind. Since the different sensory-motor aspects of the object are uncoordinated the child has available no actions to bring about 'retrieval' of the object. Even if it disappears merely to re-appear at a different location the infant cannot initially comprehend its identity because there are no self-produced actions coordinating the two distinct sensory impressions. Only when the child has achieved such sensory-motor coordination can he know that an object can be re-claimed through certain activities and only then can the concept of the object (distinct from any particular event of which it forms a part), begin to emerge. Thus, the child must construct the notion of the object.

So, when a reaching child in these early stages is shown an attractive object which is then placed in his full view beneath a cloth or other covering he will not search for it—even though he may be physically capable of reaching out to the point in space occupied by the covered object. Out of sight is out of mind.

These and other phenomena demonstrate for Piaget that our concepts do not come about primarily through perceptual experience. The 'image' is not suddenly or even gradually imprinted by observation; it is constructed. It is not simply a memory trace outliving activity on the retinae and their servant neurones but a sensory-motor structure built up through activity involving the whole body. What happens when we see or hear and *know*, is a complex assimilation to an integrated system of connections between actions and sensations.

INTUITIVE THINKING

As the infant strives towards the achievement of this 'first invariant' in his experiences he starts to free himself from the dictates of his immediate situation. He develops an ability mentally to represent actions and to re-live past experiences without the trigger of a perceptual scheme. He starts to *anticipate* what his experience will be in the immediate future, to the extent that the quality and nature of that experience is dictated by his own actions. In short, he begins to internalize acts—to anticipate the effects of full-blown physical execution mentally, prior to the act. With anticipation comes the beginning of choice and decision—voluntary suppression of acts whose anticipated consequences are undesirable. And the mirror image of anticipation, recollection, also becomes possible. The achievement of object permanence endows the infant with a currency for representing absent actions and the events with which they are coordinated. Now the deliberate importation of past experiences to try and meet the demands of the present can begin—deliberate problem solving through trial and effect starts to emerge.

However, according to Piagetian theory, the child has still a long way to go before his thinking mirrors reality—his *construction* of that reality has only just begun. From the end of the sensory-motor period at around 18 months or so, through to the development of logical, operational thinking at around 7 years, his mental activity, though often intuitively sound, will *not* reflect the constraints imposed by logic. This essential illogicality is betrayed by the young child's failure to solve a whole range of practical, moral and inter-personal problems. The widely known 'conservation' demonstrations invented by Piaget exemplify this lack of logic in the child and give some insights into the nature of his pre-logical view of things. Shown two identically shaped beakers, each filled to the same level, a pre-operational child of around 5 or so will judge that they contain the same amount to drink. Then, as he watches on, the liquid from one beaker is poured into another of a different shape—such as one which is taller and thinner. When the child is again asked to judge whether the two quantities are the same, he will usually say that the one which stands highest, in the narrower beaker, holds more to drink. Pour the liquid back into its original container and he will again pronounce them equal.

The reason why the child cannot reach a logically compelling conclusion, why he cannot see that the quantity of liquid *must*, inescapably be equivalent to that in the original vessel—rests in his incapacity to coordinate mental actions. He can look at the new container and see that the liquid inside is higher; he can be induced to look at the width to see that it is also narrower (when he may well change his judgement announcing that the other container holds more). What he cannot do, according to Piaget, is to coordinate these judgements in a system of operations. He cannot *simultaneously* represent changes in different dimensions so as to coordinate his different acts of attention to spatially displaced aspects of the situation. He looks first at one location, then, perhaps at another. And with each change in centration comes a new judgement. And his thinking, limited as it is to one mental act at a time, only moves in one direction. He cannot internally reverse a mentally represented act—cannot 'see' that a change in a given dimension can be reversed by a logically annulling action such as pouring the liquid back into the original beaker.

It is this 'one act deep' restriction on the child's thinking which leads him to be dominated by what he currently senses. So, although action leads perception in the sense that what the child sees, hears or feels is only understood in terms of the actions with which they are coordinated in his experience, his judgement (or sense of act-consequence) cannot be logically connected with any judgements prior to it or made subsequently. The child has freed his mentality from the demands of immediate stimulation but only to execute isolated, uncoordinated mental actions. His thinking is not yet governed by a system of operations rooted in the logical structure of reality; these have yet to be constructed.

Throughout this pre-operational period the child is constructing a reservoir of intuitive knowledge—discovering connections between action in the world and its natural consequences. He re-discovers all the banal stuff of daily experience—that as he pulls harder on a piece of elastic it gets longer; as he tips the milk bottle further and holds it tipped for longer his glass gets fuller; the more he walks the further he goes; the faster someone runs into him the more they hurt; and so on. The natural dynamics governing the working of his mind will eventually enable him to coordinate first systems of internalized actions—or operations as they then become—later he will create systems of systems as he discovers how changes brought about by different species of actions with perceptually quite different materials may be related on some common dimension or in terms of a common effect on the world. Ultimately, his logic may be wrested entirely out of practical contexts, articulated as a body of tacit rules which can be applied to symbols and to hypothetical statements to produce logically ordered arguments which refer to no known, experienced or concrete states of the world. Scientific and formal logical thinking can then emerge.

So, the rules and conventions of mathematical-logical thinking, Piaget's focus, are man-made in the sense that they must be constructed actively through experience. But they are also natural, universal and inevitable—the ultimate realization of organism-in-nature. When we ask 'where does logic come from' or, with Lewis Carroll, why it 'grasps us by the throat', the reply is that it arises out of the structure of behaviour and that it is inevitable and its conclusions necessary because no sensory-motor, or intuitive experiences of reality fall outside its mandate.

PERCEPTUAL KNOWLEDGE

Piaget's theory, as we have seen, effectively subjugates perception to action. A strong interpretation of his 'motor' hypothesis would lead us to suppose that distinctions between different sensory impressions only arise when they are coordinated with a self-produced action. Two sounds; two visual displays; two tastes and so forth; all should be distinguished in terms of a differential movement or action which gives rise to them and *not* distinguished where no such actions exist. Put this way the hypothesis already looks extremely doubtful. And experimental studies on a wide variety of fronts ranging from taste preferences in babies through to their differential responses to various visual stimuli, show that it is virtually untenable.

Fantz's (1961) early work on visual preferences in infants, for example, revealed systematic though complex responses by neonates to different visual displays. In particular, face-like cartoons elicited a good deal of attention; three-dimensional models of faces even more so. And whilst it is still not clear what features or combinations of features serve to elicit these preferences, it remains true that extremely young infants will respond selectively—they see, and what they see constrains what they do. It is doubtful whether they have lived long enough to differentiate such visual displays (or features which they possess) through self-produced activities, so it looks very likely that what they are perceiving dictates in part what they do; and not the other way round as the motor theory holds. Similar results have been found for auditory perception of both non-speech and speech sounds (*e.g.* Eisenberg, 1964).

More recent work by Bower (1974) and other researchers goes beyond the conclusion that perception may initially direct movement to suggest that the child's earliest experiences are highly organized. Sensory-motor structures are not constructed but given.

For example, according to a motor hypothesis, the child should only discover that objects get systematically smaller as they move away when he himself has manipulated objects and moved closer and farther away relative to them. However, experiments suggest that such movements are *not* necessary to discover such fundamental properties of space, size and shape. Somehow, this 'knowledge' is largely built in, or pre-wired.

However, even if we take this generation of studies as evidence that the infant's sensory-motor experience is organized and structured, there are results from other lines of work which at first sight seem to produce totally contradictory results. First, let us consider briefly examples of the lines of research being referred to.

Working with different species of animals—kittens and macaques—Held and his colleagues at MIT have produced strong evidence to suggest that self-produced movements are necessary precursors to the adaptive and skilled use of visual information (*e.g.* Held, 1965). In one study, macaques were reared from birth in a special environment. One infant monkey was placed inside a container which supported his body but left his arms free to move. He wore a large collar of an opaque material so that he could not see the movements of his arm. So although he learned, for example, to pull on strings underneath the contraption in order to pull food or objects towards him over the collar, he never ever caught sight of his own movements. Another macaque was placed in a set-up which was identical except that his collar was transparent and he could see his own movements.

After a period in these environments both animals were freed from their yokes and their movements in trying to reach objects observed on film. The 'transparent' collared macaque was perfectly adept; the one who had never seen his limbs did not reach initially; rather he displayed rather bizarre, uncoordinated movements of his arms. This study, in company with many others, some involving human beings, suggests that experience and *action* are necessary for the integration of movement and vision. If the nervous system is to respond differentially to a self-produced change in sensory events on the one hand, and an externally produced sensory change on the other (*e.g.* to 'know' that the hand moving into the visual field is 'caused' by the sensation of the bodies' movements and not due to external events) then it is necessary to first *discover* the relationships between action and perception—as the motor copy theories would predict.

How then are we to reconcile these apparently contradictory results—results which suggest on the one hand, that the human infant's experiences are organized, and on the other that many other, lower species must *discover* such relationships. To paraphrase Bower, it would seem that perception is innate in the human infant but learned in the kitten or the monkey! The key to the paradox lies perhaps in a distinction between structured *movements* on the one hand, and premeditated, more or less skilled *actions* on the other. When the baby experiences a visual impression in his upper-right-hand visual field, let us suppose, as some evidence suggests, that his right arm and hand tend to get activated and move into that region of visual space. Such structured movements would greatly simplify the task facing the infant of *discovering* those relationships so that he can exploit them—initially, perhaps, by inhibiting them; by deciding that the *natural* movement of his arm towards that particular location of space should *not* take place and so on. Even with very simple mechanical systems the discovery task facing a totally unstructured mechanism which is simply activated to move anything anywhere on being stimulated is quite formidable (Lee and Wood, 1973). Once the infant has discovered the time course and consequences of an experience—the growing feeling of tension in his arm, what he will come to know as its movements, the visual changes to which it gives rise and, finally, perhaps tactile contact with an object—once this *natural* sequence of events has been experienced and discovered, then it can be exploited in the realm of *action*. We would expect, then, some processes within the infant's nervous system which effectively *model* and extract patterns from the organized sequences of actions which experience creates. With the construction of such models then the *exploitation* of movements can occur—intelligence, intention and problem solving can commence.

What we are suggesting, then, is that the sensori-motor structures which Piaget describes in fact are the product of a second-order process. The infant does have to discover the relationships between facets of his experience as this perspective suggests, but underlying those movements is a natural structure. Put this way, the infant is modelling, controlling, inhibiting and exploiting an integrity already present in his experience.

In a recent book Vurpillot (1976) has brought together an impressive collection of studies with older children to reach a somewhat similar position. She offers an interpretation and development of Piagetian theory which puts his particular brand of motor copy theory in an interestingly new light. She argues that Piagetian theory does *not* deny the existence of structured, 'gestalt'-like processes underlying perceptual experience. At first sight, this would seem to run counter to certain statements Piaget has made about the nature of perception. He talks of the visual image in the following terms, for example:

> 'the image is an internalised act of imitation; a copy or transfer not of the object as such, but of the motor response required to bring action to bear upon the object. Thus ... the perception is a *scheme* of action (Piaget and Inhelder, 1956, p. 294).

However, the position is more subtle than this statement might lead us to suspect. The key lies in the notion of 'centration'. Vurpillot gives evidence to show that when a young child—up to age of 7 or so—is looking at a visual display, then the impression he gains from each act of attention or centration *is* organized into a pattern or 'gestalt', as our own intuitions would suggest. However, the field of centration is limited. If the child is looking at a large display, or trying to compare two displays which are spatially displaced then the processes involved are qualitatively different. To compare two points removed in space takes *time*, it demands *memory* and a *decision process*. For accurate judgement, the observer must *integrate* each act of centration in some central plan or programme and that plan must take account of all the likely relevant features of the display. Now, argues Vurpillot, it is this secondary level of planning and rational decision-making which differentiates the performance of the non-logical, pre-operational child from that of his concrete operational elders. As we have already seen, the pre-operational child, according to Piagetian theory, cannot logically integrate successive judgements—he cannot rationally coordinate experiences and hence is dominated by his (albeit structured) momentary perceptions.

Here again, then, the key would seem to lie in the suggestion of two levels of organization—one probably innate and based in the dynamics of perceptual organization and the other learned, developed to overcome, coordinate and control the dictates of momentary stimulation.

But the really important distinction within the Piagetian framework is the central claim that the pre-operational child is pre-logical and thus when trying to handle problems of control and coordination he effectively fails to reflect the nature of reality. This sets the stage for an examination of another important line of work which challenges this central notion. Is the young child really pre-logical?

IS THE YOUNG CHILD ILLOGICAL?

One of the large legacy of phenomena bequeathed to psychology by Piaget involves a seriation task. A child is shown a series of sticks varying systematically in size. These can be lined up to create a series ascending stepwise from large to small. A pre-operational child confronted with the sticks in a jumble and asked to copy a series will usually fail. He may put small by large, one pair at a time, but since he cannot see that a given stick may, at the same moment in time, be the 'larger' of one pair and the 'smaller' of another—his thinking is one-act deep—he cannot proceed to make larger series. He cannot logically coordinate individual acts of comparison and arrangement. Similarly, if he is first shown two of the sticks and they are of different colour such that, for example, a blue one is larger than a yellow one and then shown that a red one is larger than the blue one, he cannot reliably make the logical inference that the red one is necessarily larger than the yellow one. The Piagetian explanation, of course, is that he cannot mentally coordinate successive judgements.

Peter Bryant (1974) offers a different explanation. He argues that the young child's failure to make logical inferences—a 'weakness' he shares, on occasion, with all adults—does not betoken the lack of logical capacities but essentially a failure of memory. Using the seriation task he first ensured that his child subjects remembered the result of each comparison—knew that the blue was longer than the red, and so on. Only then, when he had determined this, did he ask them to make the inference. Many of them managed to do so. One possible objection to this experiment is that the children had learned through drill, the absolute size of the various sticks and were actually able to picture in some way the length of each one. So just as they might know that Mummy was 'so high' and their young friend only 'so high', they could work out that one must be taller without seeing them together and without making any logical inferences. However, other studies by Bryant indicate that this is not likely to be the case for the seriation tasks. These show that children have tremendous difficulty in making such *absolute* judgements of size—their 'natural' aptitude seems to be for *relative* coding—appreciating that one thing is bigger than another rather than the observation that one has absolute size 'x' and another some other absolute size—this children find extremely difficult to do. He therefore concludes that the child does not operate on the basis of isolated, absolute perceptual judgements, but to perceptual *relationships* and that his failure to chain together different judgements in a logically compelling manner is due not to prelogicality but to a failure of performance factors like limited memory capacity.

Several years ago in a book about children's failures to handle intelligence test problems, Margaret Donaldson (1963) made a similar point about the nature of errors in thinking. She found that many children failed to solve problems not because they lacked the actual mental operations possessed by children who did solve them but because of factors like 'losing hold' of information they were trying to work with. In other words, those who would come out as less intelligent or less advanced in their thinking did not differ structurally in their mental abilities but in the speed, accuracy and retentiveness of their problem solving.

In a recent book she has identified other factors which underlie children's mistakes in reasoning (Donaldson, 1978). In this new book she says quite explicitly that it is these and not logical incapacity which underlie young children's failures to solve Piagetian problems. One factor, which we examine more fully later, is to do with the child's general orientation towards abstract, logical problems themselves. She argues that children who have had little or no school experience have a quite different attitude towards problems. To solve a formal problem the child must adopt a hypothetical attitude towards it, *accept* that such a state of affairs *might* exist, set it up mentally and then work on it. If he fails to solve a problem, any one of these aspects might be responsible—he may not accept or possess the necessary hypothetical attitude, may not be able to break through the wordy demands of the experimenter to *see* what the problem is, or he may not possess the necessary logical operations to solve the problem. In her book, Donaldson reports experiments which show that if the content and wording of Piagetian problems are changed so that they become more familiar and clear to the child, then his capacity to solve them increases considerably. Once he sees, accepts and comprehends the problem he *can* reason logically about it. These results and her interpretations, as she points out, are consistent with Bruner's (1971) view that factors like schooling and learning to read engender a 'hypothetical' attitude in the child which expands the range of problems he can solve. We return to this hypothesis and the reasoning behind it later in the chapter.

Another important factor identified by Donaldson, one with far-reaching educational implications, concerns the *social context* within which tests of children's mental abilities take place. Many Piagetian test situations confront the child with a characteristic state of affairs. He is shown something—two beakers with the same amount to drink in, say—then the adult does something to these and the child is again asked to give a judgement. If the child *changes* his judgement this may mean that he cannot 'see' the logic of the situation, as Piaget holds. But it might also be the case that, left to his own judgement, he *would* reach a logical conclusion but because an all-powerful adult has *done* something and then asked him to reconsider, then there really *must* have been some change which he, ignorant little soul that he is, cannot yet comprehend. He abdicates the reasoning process because of the characteristic power and knowledge relationship which he holds with adults. In an ingenious experiment, one of Donaldson's students put this idea to the test in the following way. First, he set up a Piagetian situation and asked the child to make a judgement (this was a test of the child's conservation of number). But instead of transforming the situation himself, he so arranged the situation that a 'naughty teddy bear' who was hanging around the laboratory came along and 'naughtily' produced the change. When the problem

was presented *this* way the child was much more likely to give a 'logical' reply than if the same transformation of the task was done by an adult. Donaldson goes on to show that where the power relationship is varied, where a child feels in charge of a situation rather than the victim of it, then his apparent level of ability rises significantly.

This important line of thought is consistent with arguments put forward by people like Labov (1970) to account for the apparently lower intellectual skills of black children, and by cross-cultural researchers (Cole and Scribner, 1974) to account for the apparent 'illogicality' of non-schooled African tribesmen. The implications of this argument for the testing and evaluation of young children are self-evident. Below, we look at the positive side of this social dimension in the development of the child's intelligence.

CHILD AND ADULT

Bryant's work suggests that if an adult constructs the experimental test situation carefully enough he can reveal logical abilities in the child. Donaldson has argued that the social context of the test situation is a major determinant of the child's performance. We now examine more fully different views about the general part played by adults and their wider culture in the child's cognitive development. First, we should make it clear that Piaget does *not* say that social factors are unimportant in development. Indeed, he identifies them as one of the four cornerstones of intelligence (Piaget 1967, 1958). However they are still offered a rather lowly status and play no part in determining the actual structure of the child's thinking. If an adult talks to a child, for example, or attempts to teach him things in a way which is well beyond his current stage of thinking, the child will naturally distort what he sees and hears to fit his own, pre-logical theory about things. Attempts to push him into logical comprehension can only demoralize him and leave him feeling uncertain. His 'errors' must be left alone, they are natural, productive and inevitable. Adults can help to 'tighten' his thinking and lubricate the transition between stages by presenting him with situations that will heighten his awareness of contradictions between his dying, old view of things and his newly emerging view. But the child can only appreciate these contradictions when he is ready, they alone cannot push him into new realms of thought. It follows then, that language too must play a secondary role in the development of logical thinking, since the child's comprehension of what others say to him is determined by his mental structures. If the talk is too advanced it goes 'over his head' and will stay there until he has evolved through his own action and experience to the necessary stage of development. But is language so unimportant in intellectual development?

When theorists like Bryant (1974) and Bruner (1971) claim to show that the young child *can* reason logically and grasp abstract concepts, the Piagetian response is that they are simply drilling the child into (for him) arbitrary responses and mere parroting. But for Bruner such educated masteries are the very basis of intellectual development. They are not misguided attempts to artificially accelerate growth but the very stuff and process of development itself. Underlying this different perspective on adults, their language and culture lies a quite different conception of knowledge.

Intelligent, creative thinking is characterized by Bruner as a highly *heuristic* business. He emphasizes the strategic, often problem—or discipline—specific mental activities which characterize clever thinking. In teaching the child how to think powerfully and adaptively about any given body of knowledge it is necessary to introduce him to the 'forms of connection, the attitudes, hopes, jokes and frustrations that go with it'. Not a case of waiting for logic, then, but of teaching *skills*.

At a more general level, Bruner regards mental activity as part of the fabric of society. The operations of thought must interlock with the tools of culture; with the media, institutions, language, procedures and physical mechanisms which comprise society's intellectual and behavioural technology. So, where Piaget stresses an intimate continuity and reciprocal relationships between physical reality and mental structures, Bruner emphasizes the reciprocity of thought and culture. And that culture embodies many *different* tools, methods and disciplines. Consequently, individuals within a given society may have differential access to cultural knowledge and, hence, embody different skills and different mental structures. Development for Piaget comprises inevitable changes across a broad front, performance across tasks and disciplines being bounded by the same basic theory of the world. But, for Bruner, the image is more that of streams penetrating to different degrees into the territories of cultural knowledge. At any one time an individual may be advanced to highly abstract, symbolic levels of reasoning in one domain of experience, yet locked at an intuitive or sensory-motor level in many others. Mental growth for Piaget is a series of widely spaced, great triumphs; for Bruner it is a relatively fast succession of minor victories. For Piaget, all knowledge must eventually take on one ultimate underlying form, for although the potential content of formal systems is indeterminate the underlying properties of the operation which comprise them are fixed. For Bruner, knowledge may expand and change *structurally* as a culture acquires new tools and technologies.

So, then, where Piaget characterizes the infants early experiences in basically asocial terms—leaving the infant watching his hands, listening to his own noises, feeling his body in motion and, eventually, observing the results of actions in the world, Bruner adds a fundamental cultural dimension. The infant, for Bruner, is primarily adapted not only to a physical world but to a social one (Bruner, 1972). This image of the child is of an inherently social being surrounded by natural teachers who eventually pass on their own culturally evolved mental abilities to the child.

In the following pages we will first explore this social image of the infant. Later, we will look briefly at the relationships between language, culture and thought.

THE SOCIAL INFANT

A number of studies suggest that the infant's perceptual world is somewhat different to that of adults (Tronick, 1972; Harris and McFarlane, 1974).

In vision, for example, under certain conditions of stimulation the infant appears to exhibit a form of functional 'tunnel' vision. If he is shown two stimuli, one a static object and the other a rotating one, he will usually show a preference for the moving one. However, suppose the infant is 2 months old and we first get him looking at the static object. Next we introduce the moving one. Now if the new target falls within 20° of his current point of fixation he will turn to look at it. However, he will *not* if it lies outside that 'tunnel'. Considerably older children will turn their eyes through 90°. This, together with some evidence that the infant has a short, fixed focal length suggests that he is somewhat screened from visual stimulation. He is operating within a narrow visual field which gradually expands as he gets older and more knowledgeable. Juxtapose this evidence with the infant's known attraction to face-like objects and the structure of the feeding situation which puts him into close visual proximity with his feeder's face, and we have a high probability of sustained attention by infant to mother. Such characteristics of early infant experience Bruner labels 'shield adaptations'; biological mechanisms which ensure a high probability of early attachment between the infant and the adults around him. He is pre-adapted to the social world. The story goes further. Other studies, those of the learning capacities of infants (*e.g.* Papousek, 1967) show that very young babies can learn the short-term contingencies between their own actions and sensory events. For example, if mum appears in view each time they turn their heads in a particular direction, they will soon pick up the contingency and start to turn their heads 'deliberately' in order to 'make' her appear. The character of their movements change as they are conditioned to suggest that they are moving away from chance movements to deliberate actions. But the time between action and sensory 'consequence' must be quite short or the infant will not pick up the relationship. So, any situation in which a movement by the infant becomes the signal for, or cause of a (nonnoxious) change in conditions of stimulation, are capable of being picked up by the infant and repeated. Now the best advice available for reacting quickly and predictably to the child, one able to spot a potentially controllable movement by him and able to act as though they are controlled by it, is, of course, another human being. Other people are therefore qualified to become just about the most attractive feature of the infant's world. And it seems that other people get satisfaction and even reassurance from establishing such reciprocal exchanges with babies. For a mother, it may be one of the first signs that all is well, that her child can see her, hear her, that he finds her interesting and that he really is a clever boy or girl. (Perhaps for these reasons mothers detect handicap in their child before the medical profession does so.) These early activities by the child are one barometer that adults can use to show that all is well.

The suggestion is, then, that the behaviour of infant and adult are destined to become intertwined and integrated. Such must be the case, reasons Bruner, for a species such as ours. There must be some biological foundations for adult–child bonding since in a species where the young show a long and protracted incompetence, they must have some general *guarantee* that they will be shielded from trouble and nurtured.

These early, reciprocal patterns of exchange between adult and child are, for Bruner, the first avenues through which the adult begins to transmit language, thought and culture to the child. They are the basis of language acquisition and the start of the long apprenticeship whereby the child will be schooled in the ways of his society—as manifest in the actions of those around him. Where Piaget charts the growth of knowledge through the child's interactions with the physical world, Bruner sees the process as one of transferring thoughts, concepts and attitudes to the child from his elders who, in turn, have received them from earlier generations and developed them further in their own lifetime.

Another important difference between these two perspectives on the nature of early childhood experiences lies in the conception they yield of language and its acquisition, and to major differences in related ideas about the role played by language in the development of thinking.

LANGUAGE AND COMMUNICATION

One problem which is exciting a good deal of interest currently concerns the basis of the child's acquisition of language (*see* Chapter 18). Thanks to the impetus and direction established by Chomsky's (1957, 1965) theory of language (Chapter 18), linguists and psychologists have achieved in recent years a greatly modified and elaborated view of the young child's speech (*e.g.* McNeil, 1970). It now seems to be generally accepted that children do not start their linguistic careers by putting words together at random. Their early attempts to express themselves seem to be systematic and rule governed. The Chomskian school of thought holds that this systematic quality in the child's speech is a direct manifestation of an innate linguistic ability. The child possesses an inborn knowledge of the fundamental structure of language and this, quite naturally and inevitably, leads him to discover the precise nature and underlying rules of his host language from the often corrupt, non-grammatical speech which he hears.

So, when we ask the Chomskian where the child gets his hypotheses from about the relationships between speech and meaning, the answer is that they arise out of some form of neurological hardware which is the result of evolution. However, there are serious doubts about the ability of Chomsky's characterization of the growth of language to properly describe the speech of young children (Brown, 1973) and other candidates have arisen in more recent years which, in part at least, free us from the somewhat terminal conclusion that language has a special status and that its acquisition rests in an innate, indepen-

dent system. In short, others now argue that language acquisition and language structure are expressions of more general cognitive functions (*see* Cromer, 1974). Two such alternatives which are relevant here arise out of the general perspectives considered above—Piaget's and Bruner's.

Hermina Sinclair-de-Zwart (1969), a principal advocate of the Piagetian approach to language, points out that the child does not generally start to speak until he is at least a year old. The reason for this, she argues, is that he cannot begin to *acquire* language until his intelligence, his thought, has advanced to a certain level. Thought develops *before* language. In the first year or so of life, as we have already seen, the child is constructing his sensory-motor view of the world. He is coordinating action and its effects, creating, amongst other things, the basis of object permanence. 'How can the child possibly acquire speech to label objects, actions or qualities until he has achieved such constructions?', the Piagetians ask. When he has constructed the object and thereby disassociated the object from his actions on it, then and only then can he begin to have hypotheses about the relationships between speech sounds and aspects of experience. So, language, like perception, is subjugated to action. Throughout the child's development his appreciation of what is said to him, his capacity to understand language will be paced by his stage of intelligence. For example, in the conservation studies already described, it is no use trying to *tell* the child he must consider not only the height of the liquid in the containers, but that he must also look at depth and width—he may indeed be enjoined to look at depth and at width, but since he cannot *coordinate* these experiences mentally he still will not conserve. Nor will he understand verbal expressions like 'as much as' in the same sense as adults, since this comprehension too demands the coordination of different acts of judgement. And it seems indeed to be the case that talking a child through such tasks really does not help him to understand—though here too we face the problem illustrated by Donaldson's and Bryant's work, that we may be dealing more with factors like memory limitations than with a failure of logic *per se*.

So the Piagetians, as we have already seen, place little importance on language in the development of intelligence. Only when the individual enters the formal, operational stage where he becomes capable of thinking about hypothetical states of the world does language become a major tool of thought—after the essential structure of thought has been determined through action. For Bruner, as we have also seen, the child's mental structures arise primarily out of his interactions with others and the 'tools' of their culture. And the child's hypotheses about the meaning of speech *also* resides in social reciprocity (Bruner, 1975). Before the child is able to speak he is controlling the actions of others (although the point at which he becomes *conscious* of so doing is far from clear). He is acting through them to control his environment and his immediate future. And others are controlling him. Bruner argues that when the child comes to attend to and to start to produce speech he derives his hypotheses about the relationships between speech and meaning from such established patterns of interaction. An example should hopefully help to clarify his argument.

Everyday observation, backed up with well designed experimental studies (Collis and Schaffer, 1975), shows that mothers with young babies will often look along their child's line of sight, presumably to get some idea what he is attending to. More surprisingly, very young babies of 6 or so weeks of age start, on occasion, to look where their mothers look (Scaife and Bruner, 1975). In other words, mother and child are occasionally locked onto and attending to the same things, they have achieved, as it were, joint reference in action. Looked at in one way, they are sharing an experience and a mental state—'intersubjectivity' as it has been called. Such sharing of experience is at the heart of language development. In game situations like peek-a-boo which, Bruner argues, are probably universal, this intersubjectivity is extended. Consider what is involved once such a game 'format' is achieved. The mother does something, say, with the expectation based in past experience that the child will respond in a particular way. The child, also knowing what mother's behaviour portends, complies with the expectation and, in so doing, produces the state of affairs where mother can make the next move in the game—and so on. Mother and child, in sharing the 'doing' of a game, are also sharing expectations and interpretations. It is these shared expectations which ultimately underlie the child's capacity to crack the linguistic code. For example, suppose the mother were to point to an object and say 'dolly'. How could the child know what she means? Whether he has achieved object permanence or not, mother could be referring to many things—to the doll, the act of pointing, her own finger, whatever the doll is near; and so on. However, if the object were already part of an established format such that the word 'dolly' was announced with suitable gusto at a juncture in the game where it achieves salience; then the conditions of reference are achieved. The same focal object is the attention of mother and child, ready to be correlated with the word which refers to it.

So the pre-conditions for acquiring language according to Bruner are the establishment of reciprocal behaviour with another. The word is passed on from one generation to the next in the context of shared actions and shared mental states.

The practical implications of these perspectives are quite different and important. Bruner would expect that the child's development of linguistic, communicative and, as we shall see, intellectual skills, will depend upon the quality and duration of adult–child relationships. Chomsky and Piaget would expect, for quite different reasons, no such effect. There is some evidence that intellectual, linguistic and emotional development really do suffer when a child is deprived of continuous contact with a familiar caretaker, but it is also true that such effects are often reversible and vary considerably from child to child (*e.g.* Rutter, 1972). Language retardation in Chomskian terms would presumably signal some underlying neurological problems or some factors impending the operation of the natural language acquisition device. For

Bruner it may well signal some general upset in the child's social and emotional relationships.

But before we can try to reach any conclusions about this debate—and there is, as yet, no proper basis for a confident scientific decision—we need to look further, to proposals and evidence about the relationships between language and thought later in development.

LANGUAGE, INSTRUCTION AND THOUGHT

As the child becomes enmeshed in the activities and mental states of others, he is not merely gaining knowledge of an immediate task or situation. He is also being induced into a particular way of thinking about himself and the world he lives in, being gradually caught up in systems of values and goals and different forms of language use. He is inheriting forms of intellectual life. This general conception of human intelligence has a long and argumentative history in psychology. It was formulated in one particularly provocative and testable way by an American, Benjamin Whorf (1956). Although in some respects his perspective was somewhat narrower than that just outlined, he shared the same basic view that reality is basically a *social* construction and one, furthermore, which can be directly assessed and understood through differences in the structures of *languages*. He observed that no language could be translated *perfectly* into any other. Each language makes a unique set of distinctions—its vocabulary or lexicon contains nuances of meaning not found in any other language, and vice versa. Its syntactic devices differ, and so on. Whorf argued that these differences reveal fundamental variations in perceptions and concepts across cultures, and they imply that peoples from different language groups can only imperfectly understand each other. They can roughly translate their ideas but, in so doing, the distinctions and relationships inherent in their native tongue must be distorted or, at least, blunted.

As you might expect, this important proposition has attracted a good deal of experimental scrutiny (*see* Cole and Scribner, 1974, for a brief but readable review) and, in its strongest form it has been rejected. Different language—cultures, for example, embody quite different colour terms—they carve up the spectrum in a wide variety of ways. As you might expect, Eskimos distinguish many different snow-whites; some people who inhabit jungles tend to articulate the green and blue parts of the spectrum in some detail, and so on. We would expect, given Whorf's hypothesis, that English-speaking people would *fail* to notice differences embodied in the lexicons of other languages, but absent in their own. However, such is not the case. Language does not 'prevent' us from making distinctions for which we have no words. None the less, there are definite relationships between language, perception and memory. For example, although people can distinguish between two colours for which they do not have readily available descriptions, they find it difficult to *remember* them for any length of time. Furthermore, what seems to be important about language is not whether we have available a particular *word* for a given situation, as Whorf suggested, but how easily and reliably we can *describe* that situation—a product of language in use rather than mere vocabulary—not what can be said *per se* so much as the ease with which it can be said clearly. For example, when an individual is asked to describe a situation for another, what he says may or may not be very useful in helping the other person to identify what he is talking about. And, generally speaking, there is a measure of agreement within a language culture as to how reliably a thing *can* be described (*i.e.* if A describes 'X' well and 'Y' poorly, another person B is likely to do the same). Furthermore, when we look at the ability of A or B themselves to remember and identify what they have described, they too show the same pattern of difficulty. In other words, what we find easy to say clearly for another's purposes also relates to the clarity of our own memory. Put yet another way, this implies that the demands of communication which can be most readily met are also reflected in relative ease with which we can recreate our own experiences for others.

Now this is an important and far-reaching conclusion—as we shall see. However, we should caution that the experimental work as yet has been carried out within a very narrow range of situations and we should be careful about accepting this generalization without further research. But such results do fit in well with two other lines of work. These also suggest that the way in which children's actions are described, controlled and evaluated during development becomes internalized, to the extent that they eventually employ similar 'inner dialogues' and evaluations in their own, self-directed mental activity. Let us look at the matter more slowly.

The late Russian psychologists Vygotsky (1962) and Luria (1971) have expressed and explored the view that the essential structure of mind is intimately bound up with that of language. Unlike Whorf, however, they argue that language and thought have biologically and developmentally separate origins. For example, animals and prelingual infants manage to solve many problems mentally without or before the power of speech—thought takes place without language. And, in speaking, we often produce 'new' ideas and thoughts through the power of language to combine past experiences. But language and thought do interact in a fundamental way during the development of intelligence.

When we think through a problem or strive to recall an experience we are aware, at times, of the sequential 'steps' or operations involved as we move from one thought to another. Where do the steps or operations come from? For Piaget, as we have seen, the segments in our stream of consciousness arise from the physical segments of movement, as actions become internalized. But for the Soviet psychologists the stream of behaviour and, hence, consciousness, can be segmented in an indeterminate range of ways. Where different cultures confront their children with differing tasks and problems and a language which has developed to characterize and describe these, then they also impose differing segmentation and structure on behaviour and thought. For example, if, in one society,

the developing child's actions are continually being scrutinized, described and reflected back to him in speech, then his awareness of his own behaviour and the form of that awareness will be shaped, in part, by that language. What he is likely to remember of his experience and the way in which he may evaluate and conceptualize it will reflect these commentaries by others. If, in another culture, the child's learning is not characteristically accompanied by such verbal escorts, then his actions will tend to remain locked in context, not easily remembered, manipulated or communicated.

A good deal of cross-cultural research has now been undertaken to see just how plausible this and competing lines of reasoning are. It is not possible to summarize these adequately here (*see* Cole and Scribner, *op cit.* or Serpell, 1976) except to say that while some 'universals' in human mental development are suggested (*e.g.* Dansen, 1972) it does seem to be the case that the emergence of some forms of thinking is dependent on the relationships between language and learning. To take one single example, Cole and his colleagues report studies of the Kpelle (an illiterate, non-schooled Liberian tribe) who, given problems of the following kind:

'Flumo and Yakpalo always drink cane juice together. Flumo is drinking cane juice. Is Yakpalo drinking cane juice?' provided answers including:
'Flumo and Yakpalo drink cane juice together, but the time Flumo was drinking the first one Yakpalo was not there on that day' (Cole, Gay, Glick and Sharp, 1971, p. 187).

Their replies, though perhaps plausible when checked against their own knowledge of Flumo and Yakpalo, were not logically compelling. Cole *et al.* conclude that the style of logical thinking which is characteristic of scientific, technological man is itself a cultural product. It does not arise spontaneously out of any everyday activity but probably derives from such special cultural experiences as schooling and learning to read, both of which demand that the child think about and represent to himself abstract, imaginary and absent entities. These demands do not exist to anything like the same degree where the child learns always by doing and in practical contexts, as he is likely to do in a non-schooled society. While the researchers do not draw the conclusion that the Kpelle are illogical *per se*, they argue, like Bruner and Donaldson, that particular experiences with language in school are a likely determinant of formal, hypothetical thinking.

There is some evidence, then, that language, cultural institutions and the learning process interact and help shape not only the content but the essential *form* of our thinking.

LANGUAGE AND SOCIAL CLASS

The second line of enquiry into the relationships between language and thought brings us much nearer to home, both in terms of the theories involved and the social issues which they raise. We start with an example.

Suppose we ask children to look at a cartoon strip and describe the action in it. We will find, according to Bernstein and his colleagues (*e.g.* Bernstein, 1961, 1970), substantial differences in the children's linguistic approach depending on their social class. Middle-class children, on average, will speak in such a way that one not sharing their immediate perceptions can understand what is in the cartoon. Working-class children, on the other hand, will tend to talk as though a listener shares their perspective. The language of one is non-egocentric and relatively context free, that of the other—egocentric and context dependent. Suppose we also take children with their mothers and ask mum to help the child solve a problem or execute a task. Here too we will find (idealized) differences which map statistically onto social class. Mothers from a working-class background will tend to give direct orders, may well offer tangible rewards or other extrinsic motivations (do it to please me, *etc*.); they will control the child's actions directly on an act by act basis. The 'average' middle-class mothers, on the other hand, will tend to adopt a less egocentric, less directly controlling mode of interaction inviting the child to consider various lines of action, for example, stressing the longer term relationships between his immediate activity and future or past states of the task and so on. In short, different mothers place their children's actions in qualitatively different procedural and conceptual frameworks, ones which vary in how much initiative the child is given, in the reasons given for doing the task and the clarity and extensiveness of the task analysis offered. Hess and Shipman (1968) argue that these aspects of maternal teaching strategy correlate with various aspects of the child's problem solving capacity and his performance on tests of intellectual capacity. The argument, as you might expect, is that mothers who operate in a de-centred way and use less context dependent 'elaborated code' speech tend to raise children who do better in problem solving than mothers adopting 'restricted code' language.

Bernstein's major proposition is that different class or sub-cultures display different patterns of language use. One culture, adapted to meet the demands of face-to-face work situations which are essentially externally laid down, has created and perpetuates a 'restricted code' language. The other, adapted for the exercise of management and control at a distance and through media, has evolved an elaborated code.

Now this brief and highly idealized view of Bernstein's proposition has attracted many different criticisms, as has the research work based on his ideas (*e.g.* Dittmar, 1976; Labov, 1970). Basically, it is argued that working-class children are not linguistically deprived or lacking in any basic competence. Rather, differences between children tend to reflect their various conceptions of and motivations towards test-like, laboratory and interview situations. None the less, it is precisely in such formal, interview-like and school-type situations that the child's economic and social future is being largely decided (Cole and Bruner, 1971).

At this point we meet two possible lines of thought with important practical implications. First, we might argue that differences in language forms are essentially trivial, and that the reasons for the widely publicized differences in educational achievements of working- and middle-class children are due to secondary, social factors (*e.g.* Stubbs, 1976). There is some evidence, though not without its problems (*see* Pilling and Pringle, 1978) to suggest that the expectations which a teacher has for his or her pupils has a significant effect on what the children learn—these set the 'demand' characteristics of the school environment and supply differing degrees of pressure towards success. It may be the case that teachers and others 'brand' children on the basis of their language in school and this helps determine the teacher's aspiration level for the children. And there is indeed some evidence that a teacher's model of the ideal pupil does vary consistently in middle-class and working-class schools (Brandis and Bernstein, 1974). Generally speaking, the model of the ideal pupil in a middle-class school incorporates expectations that the child will show initiative, ask questions and push himself forward. The working-class child meets a model which seems to emphasize his being attentive and generally more passive.

However, we face there a problem of cause and effect all too familiar in psychology. Are such teacher expectations based simply in prejudice or in a practical working knowledge of how children from the two backgrounds best adapt to the school situation? And, more importantly, it can be argued that language and instruction *per se* are more important than this explanation allows. If techniques of instruction really matter in determining how well and how vigorously a child will master a body of knowledge, and if they relate in some way to forms of language use, then there is clearly a case to be made for helping children to talk about and understand 'elaborated' linguistic descriptions and analyses of their experiences. It may indeed be the case that the child from a low income group does not lack any fundamental competence for particular forms of language use and yet if he does not bring that competence to bear in formal learning or other 'power' situations then his language and thought pertaining to such situations is likely to be arrested.

We have, at present, then, at least two schools of thought about the relationships between language, instruction and thought in relation to intellectual achievement. Both share the optimistic view that sub-cultural differences in achievement are 'man-made' and capable of modification, and both stress the relationships between language and power—both acknowledge a 'hidden curriculum'. But where one argues that the influence is primarily through causal relationships between instruction, language and thought, the other holds that achievement is merely an artefact of expectations based in prejudices about different dialects.

In the next section we come at this problem from a different angle. We ask how far psychologists have provided any evidence that instruction and forms of language use have *predictable* effects on cognitive abilities. This will lead us eventually out of the laboratory to a brief study of the attempts made to act in the real world on the basis of such hypotheses.

INSTRUCTION AND LEARNING

If you ask a 3-year-old to listen to you say a series of digits with a view to repeating them, the odds are that he will manage to handle about three. A 4-year-old may repeat four. Eventually the child will come to handle the seven or so items that adults typically manage. So, as he grows, the child's short-term memory capacity for discrete, arbitrary items increases systematically. Add to this the fact that the child is a novice at life, that in many situations in which he finds himself he is likely to be unsure as to what is going on, where, when and to what effect. And although he understands many words by the time he is 3, his use and comprehension of these is likely to be quite different to the adult's. For words are not simply atoms of meaning which remain unchanged across different contexts of use. Rather they take on fine but important nuances of meaning in given situations.

Imagine yourself learning a complicated skill like skiing or sailing. There may be situations in which you are given an instruction or told to observe something where you may understand every discrete word, have a totally competent grasp of the syntax involved and yet not understand what is being said to you. Look at the matter another way. Suppose that we rid the English language of all the new technical and jargon words added to it over the past 50 years. Now the language we are left with would seem to be the same as that spoken by our grandfathers—nothing has been added. And yet there are surely many things said now and understood by many of us which our grandfathers would find incomprehensible. In other words, language is a living, growing thing which is constantly being fine-tuned to the demands of new situations. A bizarre art nouveau chair may be labelled 'chair' not because it looks like any other chair but because of the context it is found in and the uses it is put to—and it modifies our understanding of the word 'chair'. Verbs like 'compute' take on a new powerful dimension as more of us understand how a computer operates, nouns like 'programme' expand in meaning and lend us new analogues and metaphors and so on. So the young child may often be unknowingly deceiving us when he seems to understand our words. And when we want to make sure he really understands us there is often a need to become involved in the negotiation of the precise meanings of the words through shared actions and problem solving (Wood, Wood and Middleton, 1978). We must bring the words to life by acting alongside the child in the situation until we have negotiated their precise meaning in context.

So, then, the young child differs from us in his short-term memory capacity and in his use and comprehension of some of the words he shares with us. And there is another major difference between us. We actually *see* many situations in qualitatively different terms. But this is also true, of course, of different adults. For example, if a chess grand master is shown a chessboard for just a few seconds, he is able, later, to reproduce perfectly the configuration seen (Van De Groot, 1965; Chase and Simon, 1973), a feat well beyond the untutored eye. Furthermore, he finds it extremely difficult to empathize

with those who can't do the task—he cannot understand why they cannot 'see' what he can. It seems, then, that experience with, and extended thought about, a given task situation leads to highly structured perception and memory. The grand master has achieved an organization of his capacity which enables him to attend to high information points on the board and to remember it in terms of *configurations* of pieces—configurations which he tacitly recognizes as the result of particular moves, rules or strategies of play. Experience thus leads to an economical use of our capacities. In our everyday existence, we too are highly organized and competent in our cognitive activity. We may look at a relatively simple tool or bit of machinery, at a dress or garden, at a football field or even a photograph and 'see' things which are really based in deep inferences about how things go together, how they work and conform to rules and conventions. Looked at in this way, we learn to perceive and remember.

Not surprisingly, then, when adult and child get together in a task situation—particularly in a laboratory type set up where the child is confronted with strange and arbitrary problems—they experience the affair quite differently. They may use the same vocabulary to communicate but with quite different depths of understanding—they may look at the same region of space but see quite different things, they might both reflect on what they have seen but with quite different powers of memory.

If we accept, with Bryant, Donaldson and Bruner, that the young child is not limited in his powers of logic any more or less than adults are, but that they differ in their capacities to bring their competencies to bear on a situation because of their lack of knowledge about it (*e.g.* where to look and when, what to remember and how), then we can ask what the learning process consists in and how the adult as teacher influences that process.

The child is looking at a problem—inherently capable of grasping and comprehending what he sees, but sorely limited in his ability to select, grasp and remember what he needs. If the task is a difficult one and he is left to his own devices he may well become demoralized or disenchanted. An adult steps in to help. Now adults, as Hess and Shipman amongst others have shown, vary tremendously in the way they will go about the helping task. At best, they perform a wide variety of functions for him (*e.g.* Wood, Bruner and Ross, 1976). They highlight those features of the situation which are currently worthy of attention, using actions, gestures, sounds and words to direct him. In so doing, they single out the important from the irrelevant, solving the problem of analysis which, alone, the child could not handle. They enable the child to deploy his limited capacities to the full, acting as external memory aid, literally or metaphorically holding constant aspects of the task which have been done and which will need a return later. They can reduce degrees of freedom for action, breaking down a complex sequence of actions into a manageable series of elements, and so on.

Some parents show a superb capacity to break tasks down in this way so that they are always offering the child problems to solve as he tries to learn something, but problems which are not too difficult (or too easy). When the child starts to experience difficulty they immediately step in and structure the situation more tightly, as he shows signs of success they back off leaving him greater scope for initiative. And, in simple laboratory situations at least, this performance by the parent correlates with the child's ultimate ability to solve the problem alone (Wood and Middleton, 1975). We do not know how far these artificially constrained laboratory exercises represent anything that goes on 'outside' between mother and child, but other, more naturalistic studies, have shown that parents do indeed differ substantially in the time they spend executing these 'teaching' functions with their child at home. Interestingly enough they also suggest that specific materials and contexts in the home—representational material like pictures and stories—are more likely to engender such activities (Dunn and Wooding, 1977). We also know that it is possible to idealize and *imitate* what mothers do in the laboratory to teach *other* children with the same techniques (Wood, Wood and Middleton, 1978). And these have the predicted effects on these children's learning. In other words, the strategy of teaching *does* have a causal influence on the child's learning and we can learn how to teach from observing adults who do it well.

There are also studies of classroom interaction which suggest that teaching techniques really do matter in determining not only the rate but the actual form of what children learn. Nuthall and his colleagues (Wright and Nuthall, 1970; Nuthall and Church, 1973) have found, for example, that where a teacher in the course of a lesson asks his class a large number of what they call 'closed questions' which have a clearly defined right or wrong answer, then his pupils will show a good retention of factual information from the lesson. If he asks few of these, their recall tends to be poor. If, however, he asks a high proportion of open questions—ones which need to be broken down into simpler ones and looked at from several perspectives, then his pupils will show evidence of a much higher incidence of *reasoning* about the lesson. They have also shown that teachers, generally speaking, can spontaneously modify their question formats when asked to teach the children *either* for memory or reasoning. In other words, they know, tacitly, how to teach in order to achieve these different objectives.

There are a growing number of these tantalizing facts about the relationships between teaching and learning and whilst they do not add up to anything approaching an adequate scientific or conceptual analysis of the instructional process they do inspire some confidence that there are systematic, exploitable relationships between teaching and learning. And, with younger children at least, there is some consensus about the nature of the effective learning environment—one which will give the child some zest for tackling difficulty and some skill in managing his own capacities. What seems to be important is not simply the quality of language alone but also the *integrity* and extensiveness of interactions between adult and child. Where they are familiarly locked together in some joint activity, sharing the doing of something, and where control and initiative is partialled out according to the child's

ability, then the child seems to fare well. However, we know little or nothing about the metrics of the situation—we do not know how far children vary in their need for or reliance on such sustained interactions, what constitutes a crucial lower limit for them, nor how late in life children can be profitably exposed to such encounters with adults.

Perhaps the important point to hold on to is that a variety of studies in different parts of the world have established clear and often complementary relationships between techniques of teaching and the nature of what children learn. And where attempts have been made to simulate different techniques to be used in controlled experiments these have had the predicted effects, suggesting that patterns of instruction *per se* are causally involved in the learning process. But it is also true that these studies have only looked at relatively limited, short-term effects of different instructional regimes and often in highly contrived situations. And there are important questions still largely unexplored. We do not know how far children help to shape the teaching capacities of their parents and teachers, for example, although there is some evidence that when they get to school those who already possess a good capacity for communication tend to elicit most communication from teachers, those with poorer capacities less so (Cazden, 1977). In other words, children help to shape their own educational environment, potentially amplifying the differences which already exist between them. And if we are unsure about cause and effect (indeed we are even unsure how to talk about it within an 'intersubjective' framework), our hypotheses about the nature of development can never be tested in the laboratory. Put another way, if we want to test our images of the child and see how far the activities they lead to have the anticipated, desired developmental consequences, then we must bring them to life in the real world. We must intervene in the education of the young. And this is exactly what a large number of social scientists and educationalists are currently trying to do. Ultimately, their success in bringing off the desired ends should measure the usefulness of their guiding theoretical hypotheses. But we seem to be a good way from this apparently straightforward goal, and for reasons that are of themselves of prime theoretical and practical importance.

THE NATURE AND CONSEQUENCES OF INTERVENTION

Early attempts to apply sociological and psychological hypotheses to real-life situations—Headstart in the USA, for example, and our own EPA venture—led to a now familiar general picture. Many interventions engendered the expected changes and improvements in children's linguistic and intellectual achievements thus providing some support for their guiding hypotheses. However, such effects almost always seem to be washed out soon after active intervention ceases (*e.g.* Smith and James, 1975). It may be then that such researchers have failed in their observations and analyses to identify the major factors involved in the intellectual development of children. However, we cannot, as yet, safely reach this conclusion. For we are only just discovering the magnitude and depth of the problem of intervention and changing institutional behaviour.

The aim of a book like the one you are currently reading is to disseminate ideas, knowledge about findings and problems currently occupying the attention of psychologists. It represents one form of psychological intervention. Strangely enough, we know very little about the impact such interventions have. Do you, reader, merely take from these pages that which fits in with and helps to articulate your own ideas and feelings or do you gain any really fresh perspectives and, if so, how do these impinge on your professional and personal life? We do not know the answers to such questions, although we have good reason to be somewhat sceptical about the effects of the abstract written or spoken word on behaviour. Eleanor Duckworth (1974), a graduate student who studied in Geneva amongst frontline Piagetians, reports how it took her several years to see how Piagetian theory was even relevant to her later activities as a teacher of young children. She did eventually manage to marry her abstract theoretical notions with her activities but only after years of hard, sustained effort. Not surprisingly, then, when people try to act out various hypotheses or theories they find it difficult and unfulfilling. To state a hypothesis or theory, however elegantly or precisely, is a far cry from responding in real time and real contexts to one or more (invariably 'atypical') children. One great obstacle to the dissemination process is the contextualization and personalization of knowledge (Bruner, 1976; Wood and Harris, 1977).

Another problem, of a quite different order, is the possibility that practitioners and researchers hold different images of the child and different objectives for his future. It would certainly be very difficult for some psychologists, for example, to accept the following recommendations from one who has been 'intimately involved for some time in the day-to-day activities of children's playgroups'—

'Because he has formed a habit of asking for help, a child on first joining the playgroup, may ask the supervizor for help. But one must remember that if one accedes to his request and is successful in helping him, one will rob him of the satisfaction eventually to be obtained from mastering the thing for himself. One may simply prolong the frustration he feels and, what is more, prevent him from turning to a learning activity with which he could spend his time more satisfyingly.' (Stallybrass, 1974, p. 226).

Working with an adult is not a 'learning experience,' it helps breed frustration and engenders a lack of self-esteem! Stallybrass acknowledges her sympathy with Piagetian views and, presumably, intervention from this source in her particular playgroup might be welcomed. But there is hardly likely to be any immediate sympathy

for the views explored in the last section. People hold different images of the child and this produces something of a procedural problem for the psychologist wanting to test his ideas. Since no scientific conclusion can be reached without intervention this suggests that any participatory research *must* start with an exploration of similarities and differences of attitude and even, perhaps, with a selection of practitioners who share the perspective of the researcher. Although most attempts at intervention have not made this study of images central to their endeavours they have often reported on a clash in perspectives and opinions between researcher and practitioner (*e.g.* Woodhead, 1976). Take this fundamental problem of trying to marry theory and behaviour, the abstract, depersonalized nature of hypotheses, the potential clash of ideologies and add more mundane problems like the different languages and jargons of scientist and teacher and the problem of dissemination starts to take on its proper proportions.

We began this Chapter by talking about growth and change in the individual infant. We end it by posing problems to do with the growth and change of institutions and the behaviour of mature adults. The challenge facing the next generation of developmental psychologists is clearly not simply one of refining and revolutionizing their hypotheses about the nature of human growth. It is perhaps not too preposterous to say that their primary problem will be one of 'giving psychology away'.

CONCLUSION

This Chapter is hardly likely to have resolved any uncertainties a reader might have had about factors which determine the thinking and intelligence of children. It would be satisfying to have given a firm conclusion to at least some of the fundamental problems raised, but the state of our knowledge coupled with a certain humbleness of purpose militates against this. But if we have not advanced very far in problem solving we have, in the past decade or so, made some substantial steps in problem finding—identifying conceptual and practical difficulties facing those who have a concern for the intellectual quality of children's development. Well-articulated, empirically supported alternatives to the great and brilliant Piagetian edifice are now available and, in consequence, a healthier dialogue is taking place about issues like the role of language and the effects of poverty on intellectual growth; the value of schools and teaching; the nature of children's errors, and so on.

The competing images of childhood explored—child in nature and child in culture—have been around for a long time. Philosophers like Plato, Rousseau, Dewey and Russell have long since raised and debated the fundamental issues. And all of them are in a sense true—each tells us something about the problems and joys of childhood, each alerts us to different problems and pitfalls in growth. But where they compete for the explanation of a given phenomenon or in their predictions about the effects of different educational and social regimes then, perhaps, we can ultimately reach some firm ground. But one has the feeling that the images themselves will go on.

REFERENCES

Bernstein, B. (1961). Social class and linguistic development: a theory of social learning. In *Education, Economy and Society*, Ed. Halsey, *et al.*, Glencoe.

Bernstein, B. (1970). A sociolinguistic approach to socialisation with some references to educability. In *Language and Poverty*, Williams, D. (Ed.) Chicago: Markham.

Bower, T. G. R. (1974). *Development in Infancy*, San Francisco: Freeman and Co.

Brandis, W. and Bernstein, B. (1974). *Selection and Control: teacher's rating of children in infant school*. London: Routledge and Kegan Paul.

Brown, R. (1973). *A First Language: The Early Stages*. London: Allen and Unwin.

Bruner, J. S. (1971). *The Relevance of Education*. New York: Norton.

Bruner, J. S. (1972). The nature and uses of immaturity. *American Psychologist*, **27**, 1–22.

Bruner, J. S. (1975). The ontogenesis of speech acts. *Journal of Child Language*, **2**, 1–19.

Bruner, J. S. (1976). Participatory Research—the Oxford Pre-school project. London, *Social Science Research Council Newsletter*, No. 32.

Bryant, P.(1974). *Perception and Understanding in Young Children*. London: Methuen.

Cazden, C. B. (1977). Concentrated versus contrived encounters: Suggestions for language assessment in early childhood education. In *Language and Learning in Early Childhood*, Davies, A. (Ed.). London, Social Science Research Council.

Chase, W. G. and Simon, H. A. (1973). Perception in chess. *Cognitive Psychology*. **4**, 55–81.

Chomsky, N. (1957). *Syntactic Structure*. The Hague: Mouton.

Chomsky, N. (1965). *Aspects of the Theory of Syntax*. Cambridge, Mass.: MIT Press.

Cole, M. and Bruner, J. S. (1971). Cultural differences and inferences about psychological processes. *American Psychologist*. **26**, 867–876.

Cole, M., Gay, J., Glick, J. A. and Sharp, D. W. (1971). *The Cultural Context of Learning and Thinking*. London: Tavistock/Methuen.

Cole, M. and Scribner, S. (1974). *Culture and Thought: a psychological introduction*. New York: Wiley.

Collis, G. M. and Schaffer, H. R. (1975). Synchronization of visual attention in mother–infant pairs. *Journal of Child Psychology and Psychiatry*, **16**, 315–320.

Cromer, R. F. (1974). The development of language and cognition: the cognitive hypothesis. In *New Perspectives in Child Development*, B. Foss (Ed.). London: Penguin.

Dansen, P. R. (1972). Cross cultural Piagetian research: a summary. *Journal of Cross Cultural Psychology*, **3**, 23–39.

Dittmar, N. (1976). *Sociolinguistics: a critical survey of theory and application*. London: Arnold.

Donaldson, M. (1963). *A Study of Children's Thinking*. London: Tavistock Publications Ltd.

Donaldson, M. (1978). *Children's Minds*. London: Fontana/Croom Helm.

Duckworth, E. (1974). Language and thought. In *Piaget in the Classroom*, Schwebel, M. and Raph, J. London: Routledge and Kegan Paul.

Dunn, J. and Wooding, C. (1977). Play in the home and its implications for learning. In *The Biology of Play*, Tizard, B. and Harvey, D. (Eds.). London: Heinemann/S.I.M.P.

Eisenberg, L. (1964). Auditory behavior in the human neonate. *Journal of Speech and Hearing Research*, **7**, 245–64.

Fantz, R. L. (1961). The origin of form perception. *Scientific American*, **204**, 66–72, No. 459.

Harris, P. L. and MacFarlane, A. (1974). The growth of the effective visual field from birth to seven weeks. *J. Exper. Child. Psychol.*, **18**, 340–348.

Held, R. (1965). Plasticity in sensory-motor systems. *Scientific American*. **213** (5), 84–94.

Hess, R. D. and Shipman, V. C. (1968). Maternal influences upon early learning: The cognitive environments of urban pre-school children. In *Early Education*, Hess, R. D. and Bear, R. (Eds.). Chicago: Aldine.

Labov, W. (1970). The Logic of non-standard English. In *Language and Poverty*, F. Williams (Ed.). Chicago: Markham.

Lee, M. and Wood, D. J. (1973). Sensory-motor control problems in a flexible industrial robot system. *Proceedings of the second conference on industrial robot technology*.

Luria, A. R. (1971). Towards the problem of the historical nature of psychological processes. *International Journal of Psychology*, **6**, 259–272.

McNeil, D. (1970). *The Acquisition of Language: The Study of Developmental Psycholinguistics*. New York: Harper and Row.

Nuthall, G. and Church, J. (1973). Experimental studies of teaching behavior. In *Towards a Science of Teaching*, Chanan, G. (Ed.). Slough: National Foundation for Educational Research.

Papousek, H. (1967). Conditioning during early post-natal development. In *Behavior in Infancy and Early Childhood*, Brackbill, Y. and Thompson, S. G. (Eds.). New York: Free Press.

Piaget, J. (1958). In *Discussions on Child Development Vol. III*. Tanner, M. and Inhelder, B. (Eds.) London: Tavistock Publications Ltd., 156.

Piaget, J. (1967). *Six Psychological Studies*. London: London University Press.

Piaget, J. and Inhelder, B. (1956). *The Child's Conception of Space*. London: Routledge and Kegan Paul.

Piaget, J. and Inhelder, B. (1958). *The Growth of Logical Thinking from Childhood to Adolescence*. London: Routledge and Kegan Paul.

Pilling, D. and Pringle, M. K. (1978). *Controversial Issues in Child Development*. London: Paul Elek.

Rutter, M. (1972). *Maternal Deprivation Reassessed*. Harmondsworth: Penguin Books.

Scaife, M. and Bruner, J. S. (1975). The capacity for joint visual attention in the infant. *Nature*, **253**, 265–266.

Serpell, R. (1976). *Culture's Influence on Behaviour*. London: Methuen Essential Psychology.

Sinclair-de-Zwart, H. (1969). Developmental psycholinguistics. In *Studies in Cognitive Development: Essays in Honour of Jean Piaget*, Elkind, D. and Flavell, J. H. (Eds.). New York: Oxford University Press. 315–336.

Smith, G. and James, T. (1975). The effects of pre-school education: some American and British evidence. *Oxford Review of Education*, **1**, 223–240.

Stallybrass, A. (1974). *The Self-Respecting Child*. London: Thames and Hudson.

Stubbs, M. (1976). *Language, Schools and Classrooms*. London: Methuen.

Tronick, E. (1972). Stimulus control and the growth of the infant's effective visual field. *Perception and Psychophysics*, **11**, 373–376.

Van De Groot, A. D. (1965). *Thought and Choice in Chess*. The Hague: Mouton.

Vurpillot, E. (1976). *The Visual World of the Child*. London: George Allen and Unwin Ltd.

Vygotsky, L. S. (1962). *Thought and Language*. Cambridge, Mass.: MIT Press.

Whorf, B. L. (1956). *Language, Thought and Reality*. New York: Wiley.

Wood, D. J., Bruner, J. S. and Ross, G. (1976). The role of tutoring in problem solving. *Journal of Child Psychology and Psychiatry*, **17**, 89–100.

Wood, D. J. and Harris, M. (1977). An experiment in psychological intervention. *Prospects*, Vol. VII, No. 4, 512–527. Paris: UNESCO.

Wood, D. J. and Middleton, D. J. (1975). A study of assisted problem solving. *British Journal of Psychology*, **66**, 181–191.

Wood, D. J., Wood, H. A. and Middleton, D. J. (1978). An experimental evaluation of four face-to-face teaching strategies. *International Journal of Behavioral Development*, **1**, 131–147.

Woodhead, M. (1976). *Intervening in Disadvantage*, Slough: National Foundation for Educational Research.

Wright, C. J. and Nuthall, G. (1970). The relationships between teacher behaviours and pupil achievement in three elementary science lessons. *American Education Research Journal*, **7**, 477–491.

21. INTELLIGENCE

NICOLA MADGE and JACK TIZARD

The concept of 'intelligence' has a central place in developmental psychology and in its clinical application. Intelligence tests have been more widely used than any other scales devised by psychologists—Dockrell (1970) comments that a casual survey of the research journals in education shows that IQ is used as an experimental or control variable in well over half of all studies reported—and IQ scores have been employed to diagnose and to allocate provision or treatment in educational, clinical and occupational settings. At a theoretical level, intelligence and its assessment have probably been more discussed than any other topic in developmental psychology. More controversially, intelligence test scores, at a group rather than an individual level, have been used as evidence to label cultures, and even races, as 'inferior'.

So what is intelligence? Views differ, but one typical definition is that it is 'the broadest and most pervasive cognitive trait, and is conceived of as being involved in virtually every kind of cognitive skill . . . It is a quintessentially high-level skill at the summit of a hierarchy of intellectual skills' (Butcher, 1970).

How fixed is intelligence? Again opinions vary. Earlier writers (*e.g.* Terman, 1919; Sandiford, 1928) claimed that a child was born with a pre-determined intellectual potential which remained relatively constant throughout life, so that IQs on conventional tests administered to the same child at different ages were virtually identical. On the other hand, some contemporary radical psychologists have claimed that intelligence testing is a worse-than-useless reactionary undertaking which merely provides information about an individual's acculturation to middle class values: children become labelled as of low intelligence without the recognition that their failure to do well on the tests might be caused by a disadvantaged background (Ginsburg, 1972).

However, most psychologists take a middle view. As Vernon (1960) points out, it is a myth that intelligence tests measure innate ability. What they do very well is measure a sample of behaviour—and this behaviour will be determined by environment and culture as well as by inherent intellectual potential. In other words, intelligence is what intelligence tests measure—a sample of current intellectual performance.

It is in this sense that the measurement of intelligence is operational: tests are carried out by standardized procedures which permit replication by others; their results are expressed numerically, which permit comparisons with the scores obtained with other subjects; the concurrent and predictive validity of the data can be checked against external criteria, whether the outcomes of other tests or 'real life' behaviour. Finally, and crucially, no single test or measure can be regarded as a pure measure of intellectual ability. If intelligence tests measured relatively fixed innate ability, there would be no explanation for the marked effects of certain environmental changes on test scores—as in some intervention programmes, or when children are transferred from an unstimulating environment—or for differences in average test scores shown by first and second generation immigrants in this country.

If these points are borne in mind, and if tests are used in an operational manner, intelligence measures can provide important information about individual and group differences. They are also invaluable for much clinical work in which decisions have to be made about clients on whom there is little other available information. In practice they can in addition be reasonably good predictors of future cognitive achievement, and, although subject to error, they serve this function better than any other tests yet devised. Moreover, they allow comparisons within and between groups although, as already stressed, any similarities and differences found cannot be directly attributed either to genetical or to environmental characteristics. Intelligence is a classification variable rather than an explanatory variable; and intelligence tests are classification tests rather than diagnostic tests (Kirk and McCarthy, 1961).

MEASURING INTELLIGENCE

We owe the idea of measuring individual characteristics primarily to Francis Galton and Herbert Spencer (Burt, 1940, 1967). However, psychometrics, and in particular the measurement of intelligence, derives principally from the work of Binet in Paris and Spearman in London. The approaches of these men were strikingly different, essentially because their motives for measuring intelligence were quite different.

Binet and his test

Binet became interested in the measurement of intelligence in response to a very practical problem—how to separate out dull and backward children from elementary schools for special education elsewhere, thus allowing teachers to concentrate on the more able pupils. Like his contemporaries he first experimented with tests of sensory and other simple psychological functions in the hope that normal and mentally defective children would perform sufficiently differently to enable him to pick out the dullards. However, this approach led nowhere: first, the measures were unreliable and scores tended to vary from day to day; second, there was a poor correlation between the scores on one type of test and those on another; and third the performance on such measures bore very little relation to academic performance or to teachers' judgements about children's abilities. Evidently some new kind of test was required. In the words of Binet:

... 'Let us recall to mind precisely the limits of the problem for which we are seeking a solution. Our aim is, when a child is put before us, to take the measurement of his intellectual powers, in order to establish whether he is normal or if he is retarded. For this purpose we have to study his present condition, and this condition alone. We have to concern ourselves neither with his past nor his future; as a result we shall neglect entirely his etiology, and notably we shall make no distinction between acquired idiocy and congenital idiocy; and this is all the more reason why we should set aside absolutely all the considerations of pathological anatomy which might explain his intellectual deficiency. So much for the past. As for the future, we shall observe the same restraint; we shall not seek in any way to establish or to prepare a prognosis and we leave the question of whether his backwardness is curable or not, capable of improvement or not, entirely unanswered. We shall confine ourselves to

gathering together the truth on his present condition' (Binet and Simon, 1905).

As can be seen, Binet's attitude to the problem of measuring intelligence was remarkably modern—and the original test he devised is still, even if many times revised, in use in nearly every country of the industrial world. A novel feature of Binet's approach was that his test directly sampled complex rather than simple cognitive skills; and the test items made use of information which it was assumed the normal child would have had ample opportunity to acquire in the course of everyday life. Furthermore, Binet introduced the concept of *mental age* which, at a stroke, cut through the major difficulties of measurement and permitted a comparison of child with child— whether of the same age or not—and of normal with abnormal. Although psychologists subsequently abandoned mental age in favour of quotients expressed in standard deviation units, Binet's approach is still essentially followed. Nearly all the changes that have been made to his original test instrument are mere refinement.

Spearman and 'correlational psychology'

Spearman's interests were very different from those of Binet, Wechsler and other applied psychologists who wanted practical measures to help them in counselling, selection or guidance. For Spearman the fundamental task was to state and measure the dimensions or structures of the mind, and to explain how these worked and how they were inter-related. The earlier attempts of the phrenologists to find anatomical correlates of mental faculties, observable on the surface of the skull, had been discredited and there remained a need to develop an alternative methodology. The most promising means seemed to be to compare different children on the same set of tasks to see whether the *children* could be classified by ability according to differences in performance, and the *tasks* shown to have elements (psychologically speaking) in common. It became feasible to undertake the analyses required for this sort of exercise following the development, at the end of the 19th century, of mathematical techniques to express quantitatively the degree of association, or correlation, between measured attributes of a population or sample.

Spearman observed that when the scores attained by a sample of individuals on a common set of tasks were compared, the correlations were almost uniformly positive: those who did well on one task tended to do well on others. Of more significance he noted that the patterns of correlations tended to constitute a 'stably interconnected hierarchy according to their different degrees of intellective saturation'. And on the basis of some preliminary statistical analyses he concluded that 'all branches of intellectual activity have in common one fundamental function (or group of functions) whereas the remaining or specific elements of the activity seem in every case to be wholly different from that in all the others' (Spearman, 1904).

In other words, according to Spearman, relative performance on any task was determined entirely by two types of factor: a single, general intellective factor (g) which he (Spearman, 1927) likened to 'mental energy' and a second, specific to each task, which he likened to the efficiency of the 'neural machines'. On that analogy, says Thomson (1939, pp. 49–50), 'the energy of the mind is applicable in any of our activities, as the electric energy which comes into a house is applicable in several different ways: in a lighting-bulb, a radio set, a cooking-stove, a heater, possibly an electric razor, etc. Some of the specific machines which use the electric energy need more of it than do others, just as some mental activities are more highly saturated with g. If it fails, they all cease to work; if it weakens, they do not all work equally well: the electric carpet-sweeper may function badly while the electric heater functions well, because of a faulty connection in the (specific) carpet-sweeping machine; while Jones next door (enjoying the same general electric supply) possesses no electric carpet-sweeper. So two men may have the same g, but only one of them possesses the specific neural machine which will enable him to perform a certain mental task.'

Later contributions to the theory of intelligence

Despite Spearman's enormous contribution to the theory of intelligence, it was soon shown, by Burt (1917) among others, that the hypothesis of a single intellective factor (plus an infinite number of 'specifics') failed to account for the correlations found in analysing test scores based on materials having major elements (such as verbal or numerical content) in common. Burt's own conclusion, based on a survey of London children, was that scholastic achievements are apparently determined by pervasive mental factors of two kinds: (a) general intellectual ability—a hypothetical common factor entering into all school work; and (b) 'group' factors, common to special subjects or groups of subjects. In addition, performance on particular tasks was influenced by factors 'specific' to that task and by idiosyncratic or 'error' factors.

A different approach to tests was adopted by Thurstone (1938). Contrary to Burt and others who had postulated a general factor of intelligence, supplemented by group factors of greater or less generality, Thurstone proposed that there exist largely uncorrelated 'primary mental abilities'. (Insofar as scores on tests of these were correlated, the correlations were said to define a 'second order' factor of general intellectual ability.) By multiple factor analysis of results on a battery of group tests, Thurstone at first identified seven primary mental abilities—spatial ability, perceptual speed, numerical ability, verbal meaning, memory, verbal fluency and inductive reasoning—although these were modified somewhat by subsequent analyses.

Thurstone's approach has been greatly expanded by Guilford (1959, 1967) who adopted a three-dimensional definition of intellect. He classified abilities according to: the nature of the *operations* involved (cognition, memory, divergent production, convergent production, evaluation), the *products* of these operations (units, classes, relations, systems, transformations, implications) and the *contents* of the material (figural, symbolic, semantic,

behavioural). The final scheme can be represented by a three-dimensional box with five (operations), by six (products), by four (contents) components: 120 in all. Tests have been constructed for most of these.

INTELLIGENCE TESTS IN PRACTICE

At first sight, intelligence tests seem easy to administer and their scores straightforward to interpret. On the whole, and where properly-trained psychologists are concerned, this is probably true. As Berger (1977, p. 315) has put it: 'The skill and special contribution of the psychologist lies not in the ability to administer tests—most people can quickly master the mechanics of test administration—but in the ability to correctly interpret test findings on the basis of a knowledge of the research literature.' There are, however, particular difficulties in giving tests and in interpreting data obtained from children in certain age, cultural and racial groups.

Testing infants

No meaningful predictions of future intellectual development can be made for a child less than about 18 months whose intelligence falls within the normal range. Before this age correlations between test scores on infant scales of intelligence developed to predict IQs within the normal range (*e.g.* Bayley, 1936, 1969, 1970; Griffiths, 1954) and later IQ are too low to be of any value. In the California Growth Study there was even found to be a slightly negative correlation between scores on tests given in the first year of life and later IQ. Indeed at this age parental IQ is probably a better predictor of cognitive development than infancy tests designed for the purpose.

By two to two-and-a-half years, however, some correlations between IQ or DQ (Developmental Quotient) and subsequent intelligence emerge, although test results are still far from valid predictors of adult functioning (Hindley, 1960; Honzik, 1976). Moreover, misclassification remains common so that it is most important that quotients are not regarded as definitive and that infants are retested when older.

There are several reasons for the failure of infant tests to predict intellectual growth. Test unreliability is not among these: although it is true that infants are particularly variable in performance and distractibility from day to day, test-retest correlations over intervals of a few days are high. Test content at different ages is, by contrast, important. Very young infants, whose functions are very limited, can be tested on only a small range of items relating, on the whole, to sensorimotor abilities. As the child grows older items on social and adaptive behaviours can be introduced, and when he/she becomes older still, verbal ability can be tested. In other words, the older the child the easier it is to construct a test which is both appropriate to current functioning and incorporates items similar to those related to intelligence as it is measured for older groups.

Low correlations between infant and later test scores can also be attributed to the fact that most psychological development occurs *after* early infancy: according to the 'overlap hypothesis' (Anderson, 1939; Bloom, 1964), the less fully a characteristic is developed, the lower its association with comparable characteristics at maturity. Moreover, young children vary enormously in rates of both sensorimotor development and intellectual maturation, so that any predictions made at young ages are based on unstable and unreliable indices of functioning.

A failure to take account of environmental influences on intellectual growth is also partially responsible for the poor predictive power of infant tests. Individual experiences can affect not only later achievement but also early precocity. Thus very young children can learn specific skills—possibly related to those included in intelligence tests—at a much earlier age than normal infants, even those reared in attentive 'child centred' middle-class homes. White and Held (1966), for example, were able to 'teach' institutional babies to reach for objects at a median age of 87 days, as compared with 145 days in a control group. Moreover, this experimental group were markedly further advanced in sensorimotor skills than the home-reared children from academic families studied by Uzgiris and Hunt (1975, p. 33). Nevertheless, infant precocity does not necessarily mean that children remain advanced for their years and, in this way, infant tests may be more sensitive measures of the environment to which the child is currently exposed than of anything else.

Despite their inability to predict future performance from a young age, infant intelligence tests are of value in describing aspects of current functioning. Furthermore, they are better at predicting retardation than normal development (McCall *et al.*, 1972)—although they are no good at predicting above average ability (Rutter, 1970). However, multiple applications of tests do correlate more highly than single testings with later intellect (Bayley, 1965).

Children who present difficulties in testing

Conventional intelligence tests have been developed for use with normally-functioning children and assume a variety of general abilities on the part of testees. Most tests, for example, involve a child in looking, listening, writing, communicating with the tester and concentrating on the task in question for a considerable period of time. These requirements put many children with specific handicaps at an immediate disadvantage, and may cause them to attain lower IQ scores than they would achieve on comparable, but more appropriately structured and constructed, assessment procedures.

Functional handicaps presenting difficulties in the intelligence test situation can, broadly speaking, be divided into the sensory, the neurological and the behavioural (for fuller discussion of area see Bowley and Gardner, 1972; Mittler, 1970; Berger, 1977). Sensory handicaps include deafness and partial hearing, and blindness and partial sight; neurological handicaps refer to brain disorders leading to physical handicap and/or intellectual retardation; behavioural handicaps may arise from central nervous system dysfunction or, more commonly, out of environmental pressures that disturb the personal or social adjustment of particular children. 'Handicapped' children as defined in these terms, are more likely than other children to display characteristics such as distractibility and lack of cooperation (Rutter, Tizard and Whitmore, 1970; Rutter, Graham and Yule, 1970).

There are several general points that can be made about testing functionally-impaired children. First is the importance of developing and maintaining the child's interest and motivation within the test situation. This may be particularly important for groups of children such as the autistic (Clark and Rutter, 1977, 1979). Success depends very much on establishing communication between the tester and the testee right from the start. For deaf, non-verbal and multiply-handicapped children this can be very difficult and calls for experience and versatility on the part of the examiner. Secondly, in administering a test and in interpreting its results, one must take account of any additional handicaps a child may have due to restricted stimulation and experience, both cognitive and emotional.

Testing deaf and partially hearing children has its own special difficulties (*see* Reed, 1970). Verbal tests are often not appropriate, and in practice tests containing tasks such as matching, picture completion and sequencing are frequently employed—although regular tests, standardized on groups of partially-hearing children, can sometimes be used. Particular problems arise in assessing the intellect of non-verbal deaf subjects to whom it is especially difficult to communicate instructions in a comprehensible manner.

Blind children also have difficulties achieving high scores on verbal sections of tests, especially if they have been visually-impaired since birth. In their case a lack of perceptual experience means that they have difficulty with relational concepts such as 'near', 'far', 'large' and 'small' (*see* Langan, 1970). Clearly a further problem with this group is that tests must be presented orally or translated into Braille. The partially sighted also tend to need adapted tests although larger, clearer images and extra time may be their main requirements. They will have greatest difficulty with tasks involving the recall and reproduction of visual patterns, figure-ground discrimination and the isolation of single items from a configuration or a page.

Children with very severe intellectual deficits present different problems again and may require other non-conventional methods of assessment (*see* Reynell, 1970; Shakespeare, 1970; Kiernan and Jones, 1977). This is particularly the case for subjects whose mental age is less than 18 months, as standard tests are inappropriate and unreliable below this level. Systematic observation of general development and skills is frequently the best means of assessment for these lower grade children.

Apart from cognitive dysfunction, many severely handicapped children will present communication problems. In addition a substantial proportion of brain-damaged testees may have behaviour problems, such as marked attention difficulties, that interfere with testing.

Because of these problems inherent in the assessment of abnormal or difficult-to-test children, many psychologists now question the usefulness of giving intelligence tests to just those children for whom earlier writers claimed the information derived from tests would be clinically most useful. We ourselves adhere to what is today perhaps an old-fashioned view, namely that with highly deviant children IQ measures can be extremely informative, both in contributing to individual assessment, and for planning services. The value of psychometric assessment of individual clients is indicated in several ways.

First, constancy of IQ has been shown to be high among, for example (a) the severely retarded (Shapiro, 1970); (b) autistic children (Lockyer and Rutter, 1969); (c) children severely disabled by cerebral palsy (Gardner—personal communication). This may be so even in cases where the psychologist making the original assessment expressed reservations as to the adequacy of their first assessments—as happened in the Rutter and Lockyer follow-up study of autistic adolescents first seen as children in the Maudsley Hospital. Of course there are changes over time in some cases, and only a fool would regard *any* biometric assessment as implying a prognosis which was certain. But the consistency of performance, as measured by the relative standing of severely deviant individuals over time, is impressive.

Secondly, despite the absence of anything approaching an adequate standardization of the relative excellence of performance in clients who score three, four, five or even more standard deviations from the mean there are, surprisingly, real and substantial differences between children and young persons with IQs in the 20s, and those in the 30s and 40s. The distinction has been recognized clinically ever since the time when mental handicap first began to be studied: and the earlier terms idiot, low grade imbecile, high grade imbecile, and moron or feeble minded person, had and still have meaning. And though these terms have today dropped out of use, they have been replaced by euphemisms the meaning of which is still, for epidemiological purposes, best defined in IQ ranges: profound retardation (IQ 0–20); severe (IQ 20–35); moderate (IQ 35–50); mild (IQ 50–70); borderline (IQ 70–85). There are, moreover, marked biological as well as psychological differences between the severely retarded (IQ<50) and the mildly retarded (IQ 50+) (*see* Clarke and Clarke, 1974).

Thirdly, anyone with clinical experience will recall cases in which psychometric assessments which have been markedly at variance with other information about the client have led to a thorough reappraisal: the plausible and well-spoken child whose extraordinarily low IQ leads to a re-examination of his utterances which may indicate that what he says is invariably silly and superficial; the unattractive and sullen child who turns out to have a remarkably high IQ and corresponding keenness and quickness of intellect if you can only get through to him. The *clinical* use of well-standardized assessment measures is an indispensable part of clinical practice; but in clinical psychology as in clinical medicine tests do not obviate the need for judgement and common sense.

Reservations about 'labelling' and about the adequacy of description by IQ have led to a plethora of terms and unstandardized descriptions of children who function cognitively abnormally or subnormally. Ironically, the more vigorous the efforts to avoid classification by IQ, the more difficult it becomes to know just what population or sample of children is being talked about—as can be appreciated by anyone reading literature on mental handicap written by educators or psychologists in Eastern Europe. For descriptive purposes there seems at present to be no useful substitute for classification by IQ. And provided the limitations of the classification are recognized there seems no harm in this either. IQs have fallen into disfavour on political rather than scientific grounds; too much has been, and is still being, claimed for them so there is now a reaction against their use. But for many clinical purposes, and as descriptive categories in epidemiological research and for planning services, they still have a real place.

Testing children of different racial groups

Ethnic minority group children in Britain score consistently lower than their white indigenous peers on both verbal and non-verbal IQ tests (Little *et al.*, 1968; Bhatnagar, 1970; Yule *et al.*, 1975) although the discrepancy is less for children born in this country than abroad (McFie and Thompson, 1970; Yule *et al.*, 1975). In the study by Yule and colleagues for example, 10-year-old West Indian children born in London scored, on average, 8 IQ points higher than their foreign-born compatriots; however their mean measured IQ was still about 10 points below that of indigenous children.

A variety of explanations have been put forward to account for the relatively poor cognitive performance of ethnic minority group children. Clearly cultural adjustment and better schooling would seem important, especially as the IQ of these children rises with time in this country. In general it is quite evident that the environment does play a major role in determining IQ levels. This was demonstrated convincingly for black and inter-racial American children by Scarr and Weinberg (1976) who showed that black children adopted by upper middle-class white families scored, on average, above the mean IQ level of the white population and far above the average for their black non-adopted peers.

The implication is that, like the working classes, minority group children not brought up according to the mores of the dominant culture are disadvantaged on standard tests which are biased towards white middle-class practices and values (Coard, 1971). In particular certain groups may be put at a disadvantage by test content—language, vocabulary, and conventional functions of objects—by the lack of experience of being tested, through problems of establishing rapport and communication with the tester, and because of their characteristic levels of anxiety and motivation.

These difficulties inherent in the use of standard IQ tests with racial minorities (Sattler, 1973; Haynes, 1971) have led to a number of attempts to devise culture-fair tests which can assess learning ability without requiring any specific knowledge on the part of the child. These efforts have not been successful. Non-verbal tests are not as useful with minority groups as was once hoped; even though they do not involve language, they are still based on experience, and in fact both American blacks (Jensen, 1973) and West Indian children living in Jamaica (Hertzig et al., 1972) and in Britain (Yule et al., 1975) tend to score higher on verbal than non-verbal tests. Verbal tests, however, present problems of meaning and assume comparable linguistic experience.

Although it is now generally agreed that there is no such thing as a culture-fair test, there remains a need to differentiate among pupils in a minority group, and to be able to make some prediction about individual progress. Haynes (1971) reports a test developed for this purpose which assesses learning ability rather than IQ. As she points out, any successful test of this kind must fulfil several criteria. It must assume no prior knowledge of English, it must allow the tester to see that the child has understood the test instructions, it must demand learning by *all* children, regardless of ability and experience, it must cover a wide range of ability and it must sample learning skills relevant to the school situation.

The idea of measuring learning ability directly, using tests for this purpose, has been around for a long time; it was first introduced by the Russian psychologist Vigotsky half a century ago (Luria, personal communication). For some purposes (e.g. to measure intellectual deterioration among senile patients or intellectual changes following traumatic brain injuries) it is undoubtedly useful. For children, however, it is no more likely than other methods of assessment to provide an indicator of genetical potential, relatively 'uncontaminated' by environmental influences. The difficulty is that all behaviour is a product of what Harlow (1949) called 'learning sets'. That is, an individual, in the course of his experience, builds up strategies for dealing with *classes* of activity. Of two individuals neither of whom can tackle a particular problem, one may be at the threshold of mastery of it, so that with a little practice he will learn what is required, whereas the other may require a great deal of practice to bring him to that point. The apparent 'ability to learn' will thus be very different. But these differences may arise simply out of the children's prior histories rather than as consequences of their differing learning potential.

A somewhat different approach to the measurement of intelligence using physiological measures of higher nervous activity, has been proposed by electrophysiologists studying EEG responses. Chalke and Ertl (1965), making the not unreasonable assumption that more intelligent people may have faster operating brains, compared the latency of the average evoked potential (AEP) response to brief flashes of light in high IQ subjects with that of a group in the dull to average range. Modest correlations of about -0.33 between latency of response and IQ were found. Subsequent studies have in general confirmed the association though the results are by no means consistent—and are in any case uniformly low. A review of the literature is presented by Halliday and Callaway (1977) who draw attention to the extreme complexity of the evoked potential response, and to the likelihood that relationships with other variables, including IQ, are non-linear, and not normally distributed. It seems not improbable that the problems the earlier psychologists encountered in their attempts to measure complex behavioural functions through psychophysical studies of simpler processes, will be met in a different form by those who seek to replace direct assessments of intelligence through the sampling of complex activities, by indirect measures such as AEP. The argument that such measures are more 'basic' is highly questionable—and may in any case be irrelevant if the functions one is interested in are in this sense less 'basic'. At all events it seems probable that, as Halliday and Callaway themselves say, the usefulness of the AEP will lie in its ability to monitor clinical changes (e.g. following drug administration) rather than in its success in picking successful scholars or measuring the abilities of clients, patients or pupils.

HOW PREDICTABLE IS IQ?

It has been stressed that intelligence test scores are measures of *current* functioning. Nevertheless, IQs are used clinically and educationally with the underlying assumption that they imply something useful about past and future performance, and many studies have been made of the stability of IQ over time. (*See* Thorndike, 1933; Bloom, 1964; Cronbach, 1970; Clarke and Clarke, 1974; Vernon, 1976.) As already pointed out, DQs of children tested under the age of 1 year bear virtually no relation to DQs or IQs a year later, although assessments made at the age of 2 correlate 0·74 with tests given a year later, and about 0·5 with even later testings. Children of 6 years of age or older show fairly marked consistency in IQ: correlations with scores on later tests are 0·8 or higher and show surprisingly little attenuation over time, despite the fact that the specific questions which children are asked three or six years later are likely to be different from those at the threshold of difficulty on first testing.

These findings indicate clearly that measured intelligence becomes more consistent with age. However, as Clarke and Clarke point out, high correlations do not necessarily imply that *all* members of the group tested are showing even growth: a test-retest correlation of almost 0·9 can conceal the fact that two-fifths of the group have shown IQ changes of 12 or more points between testings. This would imply even greater variability in samples in which the retest correlations are much lower.

Consistency and change

The implication is that group data conceal individual patterns of stability and change in intellectual level. When averages are discarded, and individual data are considered, enormous variations in developmental patterns are found. For example, Honzik et al. (1948) showed that of children tested on a number of occasions between the ages of 2 and 18 years only 15% had IQs which remained within a range of 10 points. Overall 58% varied more than 15 points up or down, 9% showed changes of 30 points, and a few children fluctuated by as much as 60 points.

In other words, very idiosyncratic patterns emerge when individual test results are examined over time. As Sontag *et al.* (1958) observed, 'some individuals had periods of loss in IQ followed by a gain, other cases had periods of gain in IQ followed by a period of relatively little change, and others had still different patterns of change'. This means that it is not possible to select a group of children of similar intelligence and predict their later development at all accurately. Dearborn and Rothney (1941) provide a neat illustration of this. They looked at eight girls at age 8 who were 0·9 SD above the mean IQ of 256 girls in the Harvard Growth Study, and followed them up over the next eight years. Whereas they had all been identically bright at the earlier date, their test scores had diverged markedly by the end of the follow-up.

Interpreting consistency and change

Idiosyncratic patterns of intellectual growth, where both the intensities and timings of spurts and plateaux seem to arise out of individual differences rather than as a consequence of any general law of development, imply caution when interpreting intelligence test results, especially if any kind of prediction about the future is being made. The question may be asked, however, whether this manifest variability reflects real change, or whether it is an artefact of the nature of intelligence tests.

Vernon (1976) points out that the extent of real change, as indicated by longitudinal studies, is likely to be exaggerated for a number of reasons. First, as already discussed, intelligence tests used with young children have a quite different content from those used with older children and adults. And, as shown above, the younger the child tested, the lower the predictive power. Second, standardization is uneven so that if two different tests are used at time one and time two, some of the discrepancy in scores may be directly due to different test norms. Third, variances may differ from one age to another so that different numbers of children with very high or very low IQs will be found when consecutive testings span an interval of several years. Fourth, test reliabilities may be low and there may be considerable measurement error due to change in motivation, fatigue and so on of testees. Fifth, practice may lead to increased scores upon retest. Sixth, the extent of test score variation will depend on the ability of the children studied—brighter children show greater fluctuations than those who are duller.* And seventh,

* C. B. Hindley and C. F. Owen (*J. Child Psychology and Psychiatry*, 1978, **19**, 329–350) in a recent paper, 'The extent of individual changes in IQ for ages between 6 months and 17 years in a British longitudinal sample' report that Terman and Merrill's contention that there is a relation between IQ change over time and initial level, high scorers being more likely to show marked changes than low scorers, was probably based on the measure of standardization they employed in calculating IQs. In their own study Hindley and Owen found no such relation when scores were expressed as standard deviation units, nor did an earlier study of Pinneau (*Changes in Intelligence Quotient from Infancy to Maturity*. Boston: Houghton Mifflin, 1961). Hindley and Owen's paper, published too late to be incorporated in the present text, provides an authoritative commentary on the literature on IQ changes and tables drawn from their own sample of 109 cases enable estimates of the likelihood of IQ changes in particular instances to be made.

when several tests are given, maximum differences are typically about 1½ times greater than the median differences between two testings.

All these factors can create individual test-retest differences in IQ. Furthermore, the longer the time interval between the testings, and the more often the tests are repeated, the less consistent, on average, will be an individual's intellectual growth. As Vernon (1976) comments 'Both Honzik's and the other published studies indicate the correlation over, say, 6 to 10 years or 10–17, to be approximately 0·70, and this figure implies that only 17% of children vary 15 IQ points or more for single retests, while 63% stay within ±10 points of the first IQ. However, with repeated retestings, 33% can vary 15 points or more, and 48% stay relatively stable.'

Clinically speaking, the important point is that, over time, one child in three is likely to change by 15 or more points in tested IQ. This will in part be artefactual change, due to the nature of intelligence tests and testing situations, but will also in part be due to external factors directly impinging on the individual. The change will also reflect real or intrinsic changes in the child's rate of intellectual development. As is discussed below, there is an intermesh of genetic and environmental factors that influences patterns of intellectual development. Furthermore, it is not unlikely that, among children referred by schools to child guidance clinics, the proportion whose tested IQ is likely to be highly variable will be higher than that in the general population, simply because clinic children include disproportionate numbers with problems of personal adjustment which are exacerbated by environmental difficulties. This highlights Binet's warning that the IQ should be regarded primarily as a measure of *current* functioning. This is a view now accepted by the American Association on Mental Deficiency (Grossman, 1973) and by the World Health Organization (Tarjan *et al.*, 1972).

Intellectual growth after childhood

Cognitive development shown during childhood does not continue throughout life. Generally speaking, people reach a point beyond which they do not increase their IQ scores. Quite when this peak occurs, however, depends in considerable measure upon their environmental circumstances. According to Vernon (1960) (intellectual) 'growth continues so long as education or other stimulating conditions continue, though probably never beyond 25–30 years, and that when such stimulation ceases decline sets in'.

This thesis is to some extent supported by longitudinal studies that have found that individuals with the least education, and in the least intellectually-demanding jobs, tend to show the earliest halt in mental growth (Bradway and Thompson, 1962; Jones and Conrad, 1933; Kangas and Bradway, 1971; Vernon and Parry, 1949). Nevertheless whether intellectual *decline* necessarily follows the withdrawal of stimulation remains a subject of debate, and the traditional assumption that a loss of mental function is an inevitable concomitant of growing older has recently been called into question.

Baltes and Schaie (1976), for example, argue that although decline does sometimes accompany ageing, it often does not. They stress the shortcomings of searching for 'invariant' and 'unidirectional' developmental functions in adulthood, and maintain that general rules are inappropriate: individuals vary enormously both in their rates of development and in their patterns of abilities. Moreover, a law of development ignores the plasticity of IQ throughout life, and does not take account of any potential effect of environmental change past childhood on intellectual growth and decline. Furthermore, many of the differences found between IQ levels in young and older adulthood are, according to Baltes and Schaie (1976), due to differences in experiences between the generations and are not the reflection of an ontogenetically invariant ageing process.

Low ability groups

The mentally retarded, by definition, score below the average in IQ. An IQ level below about 50 IQ points is considered to define a 'severe' intellectual handicap, and an IQ between about 50 and 70 a 'mild' handicap. Children within these groups may show rather greater consistency in IQ than children whose measured intelligence falls within the normal range. Even so, persons retarded in later life may score normally on an infant test, and the normally intelligent adult may have appeared retarded at a young age.

Beyond infancy, the stability of IQ among the severely handicapped (IQ<50) remains high and, within the IQ range 0–40, test scores correlate quite highly with behavioural competence as assessed by adults who know the children well. This latter observation is noteworthy in that there is no real standardization of test scores for children who differ more than about $2\frac{1}{2}$ standard deviations from the mean. Some variant of a mental age concept has to be used instead to grade the responses to test items.

However, among the mentally retarded, as in the normal population, the relation between IQ and social, educational or occupational adjustment is by no means perfect (see e.g. Tizard, 1974). Furthermore, changes in IQ can and do occur, even in children classified on the basis of very good information as functioning as profoundly subnormal. (A striking case study is given by Williams, 1966; and Clarke and Clarke, 1976, have reported other instances.) Other studies too have shown that a rise in IQ among the mildly retarded can occur in early adulthood, and it seems that often this may be due to a changed environment (Rutter and Madge, 1976).

INTELLIGENCE TESTS AND OTHER ASSESSMENTS

As IQ tests are not the only means of measuring intellectual development, it is important to have some idea of their value relative to other forms of assessment. For instance are they more reliable, are they more predictive and do they give a clearer indication of the specific abilities of an individual? Furthermore, how do they compare in ease of administration?

Testing infants

The problems involved in assessing the intellectual development of infants have already been mentioned. Global measures of general ability are not very informative. Nevertheless, paediatric assessments have proved to be of value in predicting later intellectual retardation. Arnold Gesell, Professor of Paediatrics at Yale, developed one such approach. His aim was to be able to diagnose developmental delay and dysfunction and, as a first step, he undertook normative studies of the development of infants and preschool children. He then devised scales of motor development, language, adaptive behaviour and personal-social behaviour which are still widely used, especially by paediatricians (Knobloch and Pasamanick, 1974; Illingworth, 1971; Egan et al., 1969).

The value of this approach is illustrated by Illingworth (1971) who claimed that, using Gesell measures and clinical insight, he was able successfully to diagnose mental subnormality in infants within the first year of life. In fact, however, as Clarke and Clarke (1974, p. 47) point out, the predictions were not accurate in all cases; only 59% of the survivors were severely subnormal (IQ<50), and 21% of the group were not intellectually retarded on any criterion. Nevertheless the overall record was impressive as 75% of the survivors (65 out of 87) later had measured IQs below 70 and a further 30 who died within 5 or 6 years of birth showed on autopsy that they had gross abnormalities of the brain. The findings are even more striking as Illingworth did not include the more obvious cases of subnormality such as mongolism, hydrocephalus and cretinism in his sample.

Essentially similar findings have been reported by Knobloch and Pasamanick (1967) and by other writers. Such studies vindicate the attempts by Gesell and others to devise measures which will enable predictions of dysfunction and developmental delay to be made in infancy.

Further studies, using other methods of assessment, have traced the course of development of children with known pathology. Carr (1975) reviews the literature and reports a longitudinal study of 45 children with Down's syndrome who were tested seven times on the Bayley Scale between the ages of 6 weeks and 4 years. As Carr points out, a prediction of future developmental status based on clinical diagnosis alone would have been more accurate than predictions made from the test scores. At 6 weeks 68% of the mongol babies had DQs of 80 or more—although their mean DQ was more than 20 points lower than that of a control group. Nevertheless the discriminative power of test scores increased with age so that by 6 months only 34% of the mongol babies had DQs of 80 or above, and by 10 months the figure was only 4%.

Interestingly, however, prediction of individual development was, in Carr's study, more accurate within the normal than within the handicapped group. Thus whereas only 17% of the control group showed variations in DQ of 30 points or more over the course of the study, 49% of the Down's syndrome children had DQs which varied as much as 30 points and 27% showed variations as great as 40 points. Carr adds that these findings may, however, be due to the specific nature of mongolism: the pattern of development of children suffering from this disorder may be not only slower than, but also different from, that of normal children. In particular, mongol children often appear to stay much longer than others at one stage of development. Hence if retested towards the end of a plateau, their DQs would seem to have fallen, whereas if retested when they had just made the step up from a plateau, DQs would appear to have risen. It is possible that more finely graded scales would show a more even development. However, 'milestones' of behaviour, such as sitting age and walking, do undoubtedly represent qualitatively new stages of development. And scales which smoothed out the acquisition of these major accomplishments would need to be justified, both developmentally and psychometrically.

Testing older children and adults

Although they are of limited value with very young children, IQ tests have proved their worth with older children and adults. Their superiority over specific ability tests is due to their greater generality. They sample a wide range of skills and abilities essential for functioning well in school and in other situations; and good test performance is not highly dependent on specialized knowledge. Moreover, as observed by Spearman (1927) and many others, scores attained by individuals on a common set of tasks produce almost uniformly positive correlations. In other words, good performance on one IQ sub-test tends to accompany a good performance on others. In practice tests contain highly, but not perfectly, correlated sub-tests. Some of these are better indicators of the general intellective factor presumed to be measured by the test as a whole than others. As pointed out by Vernon (1976), within the 5 to 25 years age range, it is the verbal comprehension and non-verbal reasoning components of tests that are individually most predictive. By contrast most performance tests, on their own, show little predictive value (block design tests being an outstanding exception).

Tests vary in content. Very often these differences stem from theoretical considerations involved in constructing the instrument, such as the perceived nature of intelligence, and the multiplicity of abilities that it involves. Thus Humphreys (1962, cited Butcher, 1970) commented that Thurstone (although himself a proponent of multiple abilities) supposed he had adequately covered the field with fewer tests than Guilford has factors! And Vernon (*e.g.* 1940, 1970) has repeatedly made the point that general purpose tests work in practice much better than factorially pure tests: 'Binet and his followers chose items very largely from children's everyday life experience regardless of their content, and therefore the test as a whole gives a much better measure of everyday intelligence than would pure tests of unadulterated *g*' (Vernon,

1940, p. 194). Thirty years later Vernon (1970, pp. 99, 100) made essentially the same point, though more forcefully: practising psychologists continue to use tests such as the Terman-Merrill adaptation of the Binet, or Wechsler's tests rather than Thurstone's or Guilford's, because they find the interpretation of 60 or 120 factors 'quite impractical'. Moreover, when they do apply differential batteries, the specific 'pure factor' tests seem to carry little useful information. 'Reasoning components' do almost all the predicting and the other sub-tests add little trustworthy information. 'Hence, in practice, most decisions are based on general plus verbal ability, together with a survey of the person's actual scholastic and/or vocational achievements in different areas' (Vernon, 1970).

In this sense it is a mistake to seek for a test of pure *g*, or to regard Raven's Progressive Matrices, for example, as being necessarily a better test of intelligence than Wechsler's tests, or the Terman-Merrill version of the Binet. It is in this sense too that 'intelligence is what intelligence tests measure'; and the best test of intelligence for any particular purpose is the one which, on the basis of his prior experience, the examiner thinks likely to give the most *useful* information for the purpose for which—rightly or wrongly—he has decided to give the test in the first place. (The use of tests for clinical purposes is well discussed by Berger, 1977.)

The developmental stage approach

Estes (1974), among others, has argued that intelligence is an outdated construct and that instead of administering IQ tests we should be studying underlying intellectual processes. We do not want to grade the child on a scale with a norm of 100: we want to know how he is functioning, both qualitatively and quantitatively. In other words, instead of assuming that intellectual development is a linear progression, it should be seen as a series of stages. When a child achieves competence at one level he passes on to the next.

Piaget (*see* especially Piaget 1936, 1937, 1945 and Hunt, 1961, 1969) has undoubtedly been the most influential proponent of this approach to cognitive development. According to his viewpoint, development is an ordered and invariant process which results from interactions between the organism and its environment. Recently Uzgiris and Hunt (1975—*see also* Uzgiris, 1976, for a brief summary) have attempted to operationalize this concept and measure intelligence as viewed by Piaget. They criticize earlier work founded on the thesis that developmental age can be assessed simply by adding scores on test items which have been selected because they appear to be cognitive in content and because more older, rather than younger, children pass them. In such 'traditional' tests, development is conceived of as a straightforward accretion of behaviour patterns and skills. Any sensorimotor or verbal item may count for a point, irrespective of its sequence in the schemata of normal development.

Uzgiris and Hunt's own starting point, taken from

Piaget, is epigenetic: developments in behavioural competencies follow a consistent sequential order, largely invariant, and largely determined by the outcomes of encounters between the developing child and relevant features of the environment. Insofar as this is true, it should be possible to construct *ordinal* scales of development, that is, scales in which passing a later item implies that the individual can pass an earlier one.

To assess development during infancy (0–2 years) Uzgiris and Hunt and their colleagues have devised seven scales which satisfy criteria of ordinality and which appear relatively independent. The scales are named: object permanence; development of means; vocal imitation; gestural imitation; operational causality; construct of object relations in space; and development of 'schemes'.

Scores on these scales do not depend for meaning upon comparison with the scores obtained by other infants, nor upon their correlation with age. They have 'direct functional significance, or what one might call intrinsic validity' (Uzgiris and Hunt, 1975, p. 139).

Uzgiris and Hunt's achievement is impressive, and there is no doubt that the scale will be widely used in the future to measure the effects of various types of experience upon the development of competencies. Whether it will be possible to develop similar scales for older children is less certain, though attempts to do so have been made by a number of writers (*e.g.* Tuddenham, 1970). Insofar as these are successful they will answer the question first posed by Thomson (*see* pp. 13–14) as to whether the mind can be said to have a 'structure' and, if so, whether we can describe and measure it.

INTELLIGENCE, EDUCATIONAL ACHIEVEMENT AND BEHAVIOUR

Except for very young children, scores on IQ tests correlate fairly well with both achievement—in school, at work—and what might generally be termed 'intelligent' behaviour. Individuals within the middle range of IQ (between 80 and 120) tend to function adequately in society and are able to be independent, have a job, get married and raise children with no more problems than anybody else. Below IQ around 80 however, extra difficulties can arise although severe functional problems can only be expected with any certainty for children and adults with a measured IQ level of about 50 or below.

IQ and educational performance

Although IQ and scholastic progress are correlated, academic success depends of course on many other factors also. On the whole, children with IQs below about 50 are placed in schools or special classes for the severely educationally subnormal, and children with IQs between 50 and 70 are likely to be labelled as 'educable retarded', 'educationally subnormal' or 'slow learners' and placed in special classes or special schools. However, many children with a low measured intelligence manage adequately in normal schools (Rutter *et al.*, 1970) whereas other children with higher IQs cannot cope unless in special provision of some kind. Likewise, some children in mental subnormality hospitals are of normal intelligence (Mittler and Woodward, 1966). Educational attainment thus depends on more than simply what is measured by an IQ test. Sometimes specific behaviour problems, and in other cases specific educational disabilities such as reading retardation (Yule, 1973; Yule *et al.*, 1975) or, more rarely, arithmetic retardation, appear to be more critical factors.

Thus intelligence and scholastic progress are significantly, but not perfectly, related. Interesting in this connection is the suggestion that later school performance can be improved by early educational experience, without any corresponding change in measured intelligence. This appeared to be the consequence of an American preschool intervention project run by Weikart and colleagues (personal communication). Increased stimulation in the nursery years did not lead to significant increases in IQ, but it did seem to be associated with subsequently better school achievement. Some other studies have not however resulted in similar findings—the whole question of long-term effects of early child education is currently under intense discussion. (A recent issue of the *Harvard Educational Review*—May 1978—describes the controversies over the evaluation of the American Project Follow-Through.)

Success in later life

Jensen (1969) suggested that there is a direct association between IQ and achievement both within and between occupations. There is some truth in this—few with IQs below 50 can cope unaided in open employment, although most retardates functioning at an IQ level between 25 and 50 are able to work in a sheltered environment. Waller (1971), studying a normal population, showed for an American sample that the correlation between IQ and occupational status is 0·5. However, the same study found the correlations of occupational status with social origin and education to be 0·32 and 0·72 respectively. In other words, although IQ was associated with type of employment, so were other background factors.

This is borne out by the fact that there are very wide ranges of IQ within each social class (for review of area *see* Rutter and Madge, 1976). It is also supported by Butcher's (1970) account of adults who were very successful despite having shown little promise at school. He cites the cases of Jan Masaryk, briefly confined to an institute for the mentally deficient, and Einstein, who never stood out as a student. Vernon (1976) following Jones *et al.* (1971) asks why, on the one hand, many children who are apparently only average at school become outstanding in their careers while other apparently very able scholars become 'brittle, discontented and puzzled adults whose potentialities have not been actualized'. In Vernon's words, 'Many children react unexpectedly to family and environmental pressures because of differences in temperament or in level of maturity. During their early, and particularly their adolescent, growth they meet many frustrations and traumatic problems, and learn to cope more or less successfully, and thus build up well-adjusted personalities, or the opposite. Throughout this process, their cognitive skills may be enhanced or depressed, and although we can sometimes observe this happening and find plausible explanations in the individual case, we do not know enough about the interplay of individual dynamics with life experiences to be able to control or predict cognitive development, apart from a few rather vague generalizations such as those listed above.'

Creativity

Many children and adults do not 'achieve' at school and in their work or careers as might be predicted by their intelligence, and it has been suggested that this is because the standard IQ test neither allows for the less conventional forms of ability nor for the influences of temperament and motivation. The concept of 'creativity' has been proposed as a better measure of certain forms of achievement (see Freeman et al. (1971) for a review of the research literature).

Guilford (1959) was among the early theorists to incorporate the idea of creativity within his structure of intellect. He distinguished between convergent and divergent thinkers—those who tend to see the 'conventional' answer to a question and those who are more likely to produce their own novel responses. This idea was taken up by other workers who maintained that the traditional IQ tests favoured the convergers and penalized the divergers who might produce answers to questions 'not in the manual'. Accordingly tests were devised where openended questions required the respondent to think of as many uses as possible for a paperclip, or to devise as many problems as possible using a given set of numbers. These were scored in terms of both the number of positive responses and their originality or 'creativity' (e.g. Getzels and Jackson, 1962; Hudson, 1966; Wallach and Kogan, 1965). More recent investigators (e.g. Landau, 1973; Welsh, 1975) have similarly shown that less 'creativity' is found in learning situations that stress the role of memory and the importance of discovering the correct solution.

Nevertheless it is still debated how distinct 'creativity' is from general intellectual ability. Getzels and Jackson (1962), in the most well-known of studies in this area, compared the most intelligent and the most creative of a group of highly-able children (the mean IQs of the two sub-groups were 150 and 127 respectively) and discovered a correlation of only 0·131 between the two types of ability. However, when Hasan and Butcher (1966) replicated the study on a Scottish sample they obtained a comparable correlation of 0·726. Nevertheless, Wallach and Kogan (1965) also achieved a correlation of 0·1, although they did not use identical tests. Generally the studies tend to confirm that the most 'creative' children were the least conformist and did not value conventional modes of success.

Overall it would seem that intelligence and creativity

are highly related, but that the distinct approaches to problem-solving diverge in the upper range of IQ i.e. over an IQ of around 120. Nevertheless the extent to which this distinction is useful for predicting life success is not clear. In Getzels and Jackson's (1962) study, the high IQ and high creativity groups did equally well in school. Hudson (1966) suggested that convergent and divergent thinking is not related to overall attainment so much as to area of interest: he found, among public and grammar schoolboys, that convergers tended to prefer science subjects and divergers were more artistic.

Whatever the implications for general cognition and behaviour, there has recently been considerable emphasis on creativity enhancement programmes. Torrance (1972) reviewed 142 such projects and concluded that the most successful were those which called for both cognitive and emotional effort on the part of the learner and which provided an opportunity for active involvement. Motivation, relaxation and a free atmosphere did not, on their own, promote creative behaviour. Many educationalists also see the value of promoting creativity in the typical school context. Lytton (1971), for example, discusses the issues involved in both teaching creative children and teaching children to be creative.

Personal characteristics

Measured intelligence can be depressed by poor general health; subnutrition and susceptibility to illness during the school years may well mean less learning time at school, and may interfere with learning during critical periods of development, and affect attention, motivation and personality (Birch and Gussow, 1970). At the upper end of the ability range Terman (1919) found that a group of highly intelligent children showed somewhat better health than average and that they had matured physically at an early age. However, within the general population and normal range of intelligence there is probably no strong association between health and intelligence.

Mental health, however, may be more directly related to measured ability. Rutter (1964) reviewed the evidence and concluded that psychiatric disorder was generally associated with a slightly depressed intelligence level although the differences involved were usually quite small, and the relationship depended upon the type of psychiatric disorder concerned. Douglas (1964) found that disturbed behaviour at 11 years, as assessed by maternal reports, school doctors and nurses, predicted for boys and girls from each social class that more time would be lost from school, that scholastic performance would deteriorate and that lower IQ scores would be obtained. By 15 years, the pupils with high ratings for nervousness and/or aggression were still scoring poorly on ability tests (Douglas et al., 1968). Similarly Rutter et al. (1970) found on the Isle of Wight that psychiatric disorder was statistically significantly associated with an IQ level slightly below normal: this held in particular for boys with antisocial disorder and for girls with neurotic disorder. These findings were largely replicated by a parallel study in an inner London borough (Berger et al., 1975).

Delinquent behaviour has also commonly been found to be accompanied by a slightly below average IQ. The general conclusions are that, as a group, delinquents score about 5 IQ points below their peers but that it is persistent delinquents who show the lowest measured abilities (Woodward, 1955; Douglas et al., 1968; West and Farrington, 1973).

Within the more normal range of behaviour it seems unlikely that personality has any important association with IQ although, as Vernon (1965) says, 'We must get away from the notion of intelligence as a definite entity, an autonomous mental faculty, which simply matures as children grow up ... (mental abilities) depend upon personality and motivational factors, organic and social drives, curiosity and interests—and they are channelled by family, cultural and educational pressures.'

INFLUENCES ON INTELLIGENCE

Two distinct questions are involved in asking how intelligent a person is. First what can he do i.e. at what *level* is he functioning and, second, how does he rank on his ability among his peers. The two answers are not necessarily related as it is possible for two people from different cultures to score identically on an IQ test—despite the fact that one is regarded as bright by his compatriots, while the other is considered dull.

Changing levels of intelligence

At the turn of the century, when the eugenic movement was at its most vocal, it was argued that the greater fertility of the working-classes, in combination with their lower IQ, would lead to a national decline in intellectual ability. These fears have proved groundless. Overall there appears to have been little change in national intelligence and where movement has been observed, this has always been in an upward direction. Cattell (1950), for example, tested groups of 10-year-olds in Leicester in both 1936 and 1949 and, although expecting to find a decline of at least one IQ point per 10 years, discovered that levels had risen, on average, by over one point. The Scottish Survey of Intelligence similarly found little change in the individual IQ scores of children tested in 1932 and 1947, although a slight rise in group verbal test scores was found over this period (Scottish Council for Research in Education, 1949).

Interestingly, Garfinkel and Thorndike (1976) have suggested that age-related levels of intellectual attainment may have changed in recent years. He found, in comparing the performances of children on the Terman-Merrill test in 1937 and 1973, that intelligence levels were much higher at the later date for the 2- to 5-year-olds, that there was little difference between 10-year-olds, but that adolescents were again scoring more highly in the 1970s. Whether these age-related differences are 'real' or 'artefactual' is arguable, in that the data themselves are not solid enough to bear the weight of too much interpretation.

All in all it would seem that mean IQ, and presumably 'intelligence' *is* increasing, although not very dramatically. The evidence is insufficient to specify the reason, but it is likely that the small rises observed are due to better education and an improved environment.

INDIVIDUAL DIFFERENCES: GENES OR THE ENVIRONMENT?

One particular difficulty involved in unravelling the relative importance of genetical and environmental factors on cognitive development is that the two kinds of influence both co-vary and interact. Co-variance means, for example, that 'good' genes are likely to go with a 'good' environment and vice versa: bright parents tend to provide a stimulating environment for their children whereas dull parents do not. Interaction effects imply that the strength of genetic factors depends on the nature of the environment—in some situations genetic differences will emerge, whereas in others they will not. For example, Cooper and Zubek (1958) showed that although successive generations of rats reared in standard laboratory conditions could be selected to be either good or bad at running mazes, the differential performance of their offspring were not maintained if they were reared in 'restrictive' or 'enriched' environments.

According to this view an extremely adverse environment is likely to depress mental (and physical) growth. Normally, however, any such effects are quite slight: most ordinary environments contain enough intellectual nourishment to enable children to realize their intellectual potential, and individual differences are thus in very large part consequences of differences in genetical make-up rather than of environmental differences. The evidence for and against this claim is not very strong. (For a critical examination of the arguments *see* Tizard and Plewis, 1977.)

The following sections summarize some of the main lines of evidence relating to the influence of genetical and environmental factors on IQ.

The genetical basis of IQ

Both nature and nurture play a part in determining individual differences in intelligence, although their relative influence is in dispute. The evidence is reviewed by, among others, Jensen (1969, 1973) and Clarke and Clarke (1974). In general the question has been examined by studying groups in which some separation of genetic and environmental influences has been possible. The main strategies adopted have been to compare the IQs of identical twins, who share a common genetic endowment, and who normally also share a common social environment, with those of identical twins separated in infancy; to compare IQs of identical and fraternal twins; to look generally at family patterns of intelligence to discover how closely IQ correlations between sibs, cousins and more distant relatives relate to the degree of genetical similarity; and to compare the intellectual functioning of fostered children with the intelligence of both their natural and their social parents.

Studies such as these give rise to two kinds of data; *correlations* showing degrees of associations between the psychometric attainments of relatives of known genetical similarity, and *mean* scores of individuals and subpopulations growing up in differing environments. The interpretation of the findings has in practice depended largely on which kinds of data are emphasized—genetically minded psychologists have on the whole concentrated on the correlations, the environmentally minded on the means and mean differences. Were it not for its political overtones, the resulting controversy would not have occurred since the questions asked by each of the protagonists are, scientifically, equally legitimate, and since both parties use the same data and employ standard methods of data analysis. The real differences concern the interpretation of data, and the reliance that different investigators are prepared to place on them.

Erlenmeyer-Kimling and Jarvick (1963) have assembled most of the findings relating similarities in IQ to degree of genetical resemblance among relatives. The median correlation between IQs of monozygotic twins reared together is 0·87, whereas that for dizygotic twins (who share only half their genes in common) is only 0·54. The median correlation for different aged sibs reared together, who might be expected to have less similar environments than twin pairs, is 0·40. And when the IQs of unrelated children reared together, who had *nothing* genetically in common, are compared, the correlation is only 0·23. (In all of these comparisons the range of correlations in different studies is quite wide, possibly because of small sample sizes and differences in environmental heterogeneity, as well as because of test, and testing, differences.)

These findings are corroborated by the additional correlations presented by Erlenmeyer-Kimling and Jarvick (1963) relating to identical twins reared together and reared apart. These were 0·87 (based on 14 studies) and 0·75 (based on 4 studies) respectively. Separated monozygotic twins still showed higher correlations in ability than did either fraternal twins or other sib pairs living together.

Studies of fostered or adopted children have led to similar conclusions. In general, IQs of such children have correlated more highly with IQs obtained from their natural, rather than their social, mothers. Furthermore, correlations with *biological* mothers tend to rise as the child grows older, reaching a level of about 0·5 by midchildhood. By contrast there is, at the same age, a correlation of only about 0·2 with the IQs of adoptive parents. This latter figure is much lower than that for the correlation between the IQs of these same foster or adoptive parents and those of their own biological offspring (Freeman *et al.*, 1928; Leahy, 1935), which again suggests a genetic effect; Skodak and Skeels (1949), for example, indicated that even at 13 years the IQs of adopted children still correlate at a level between 0·38 and 0·44 with those of natural mothers. Unless children are consistently placed in families *very* similar to their own, which was not

the case in the Skodak and Skeels study, these studies provide further strong indications of hereditary effects.

Other evidence pointing to the importance of genetical factors as prime determinants of intellectual differences comes from studies of selective breeding, from observations that chromosomal anomalies can be associated with learning difficulties (Jensen, 1969), and from studies showing that IQs tend to regress to the mean across generations (*e.g.* Burt, 1961), in a manner that would be predicted from a genetical model (Jensen, 1973). Similarly it has been shown that institutional children, growing up in a highly uniform environment, none the less show considerable variability in intelligence. Moreover, correlations with parental IQ remain significant (median 0·20) although they are much smaller than those between parent(s) and children living together (median 0·50). Likewise children reared in the same family can show enormous discrepancies in IQ. Maxwell (1969), for example, found that the median difference between the most and least intelligent siblings in a sample of families was 26 IQ points. It seems unlikely that differential treatment from parents, or other environmental factors such as schooling, could account for such variation.

These and other findings have led to the conclusion, widely though not universally accepted, that differences in intelligence have a strong genetical basis. It would be strange if this were not so, since virtually all other biometric attributes can be shown to vary with genetical make-up.

There has been a good deal of criticism of the data on which Erlenmeyer-Kimling and Jarvick's table (and subsequent analyses notably by Jensen, 1973) is based. Kamin (1974) in particular has challenged the validity and even the authenticity of the data presented in the twin and adoption studies—*see* Fulker (1975) for a rebuttal of some of his arguments. More temperate criticisms have come from Clarke and Clarke (1974) and Block and Dworkin (1977).

Heritability

The 'heritability' of a biometric attribute refers to the proportion of the variation in that attribute, among individuals in a population, that is genetically determined. In practice the heritability of a specific attribute is derived from correlations of scores obtained by relatives on measures developed to assess the characteristics in question.

It is not always realized that heritability is a parameter that describes populations, not individuals. Thus among a population of individuals who are genetically identical, but who are reared in diverse environments, all of the resulting variation in development is a consequence of environmental differences: the heritability of any attribute is zero. Likewise, in a genetically heterogeneous population brought up in a completely homogeneous environment, all of the variation in development is due to genetic factors: the heritability of any differences in measured attributes is 100%. In laboratory studies with plants and experimental animals it is possible to approach these limiting conditions and, more generally, to calculate the extent to which, in more natural conditions, genetical differences explain differences in rates of growth and development.

In human populations this type of analysis is much more difficult since, with the exception of twins, it is difficult to be precise about the degree of relevant genetical resemblance among members. More important, there is no metric by which to measure resemblances and differences in the environment: indeed we have very little idea as to what factors in the environment are *relevant* to intellectual development in the first place. In consequence heritability estimates of IQ, if they could be agreed upon, could perhaps be best thought of as providing a rough estimate of the relative influence of non-genetic factors on the development of intelligence. How much difference does it make to a child's intelligence, for example, to be reared in an unstimulating institution, or to be brought up by illiterate or deaf parents?

There are, of course, better and more direct ways of answering specific questions such as these, but if we knew the extent to which intelligence was heritable we might, none the less, so the argument goes, be able to estimate the extent to which changes (*i.e.* improvements) in education and so on might result in improvements in IQ. Jensen's starting point for his own discussion of the use of heritability estimates to explain differences (of about 15 points, or one standard deviation) between the mean IQs of American blacks and whites, is that the average IQ of subpopulations is very stable and difficult to shift because it is a measure of factors which are very largely under genetical control: '... no-one knows how to change IQs appreciably ... except in the case of children reared in almost total social isolation, there is no known psychological or educational treatment that systematically will boost IQs more than the few points' gain that comes from direct practice in taking the tests' (Jensen, 1976, p. 102). Jensen does not deny that there may be other, as yet undiscovered, forms of intervention that might diminish the relative importance of heredity as a determinant of intellectual differences. However, he does believe that both within and between populations the large systematic differences that are found are to be explained in genetical terms, rather than as a result of the contrasting life experiences associated with social class or ethnic background.

Jensen's conclusions are rejected by most psychologists. This is not necessarily because Jensen has been shown to be wrong, but rather that the whole issue is unresolved, and indeed thought to be unresolvable using the type of analysis employed.

There are a number of reasons for this view. In the first place there are serious problems, both statistical and conceptual, involved in deriving heritability estimates *within* a population. Kinships correlations, by their very nature, have dubious validity for the population as a whole. As Burt and Howard (1956) recognized for their own calculations: 'our analysis holds only for a population of the particular type we have sampled, brought up in an environment of a certain restricted character'. Problems of interaction and co-variance become especially critical when attempts are made to *quantify* the relative contributions of genetics and the environment. The crucial point here is that hereditary influences are not independent of their environment—they are most important when the environment is most homogeneous and least important when it varies most.

Secondly, within-group heritability estimates cannot be used to explain differences *between* populations and subpopulations. The first association may make the second more likely; but it certainly does not make it a necessity.

This is clearly shown (Tizard, 1975, 1976), with reference to the highly heritable characteristic of stature. When height data on three generations of London schoolboys collected in 1909, 1938 and 1959 were analysed, it was found that boys were, on average, 10·2 cm taller in 1959 than boys of the same age had been 50 years earlier. These consistent differences between the generations were almost certainly due to better feeding, better material and social conditions, and better medical care. Yet if we were simply presented with the London data as height or IQ measurements obtained from three 'races', and if we accepted Jensen's line of reasoning, an environmental explanation of the differences might well seem very strained. What this means is that the 'probabilistic inference' that the higher the within-groups heritability, the more likely it is that between-groups differences have a genetic basis, is not supported. The genetic model adds nothing to what we already know, or to what we believe on other grounds. But as Jensen, Burt and others have used height data to exemplify the explanatory power and cogency of the genetic model, the London data offer a refutation of its theoretical adequacy.

The race and IQ issue is political as well as scientific, and statements about the intellectual inferiority of racial groups can have dangerous consequences. It is regrettable, however, that most attention has been paid to heritability estimations since these throw no light on the causes of phenotypic differences between subpopulations and detract attention from the critical issue of how environmental factors systematically depress or elevate IQ.

The role of the environment

The potential effect of non-genetic factors on intelligence is best demonstrated by reports of dramatic increases in IQ following massive environmental change. A number of studies have reported how children reared under conditions of extreme privation—such as being locked in a dark attic room until the age of 6—can later attain a normal level of intelligence if moved to a good environment (Davis, 1947; Koluchova, 1972; Mason, 1942). Even removal from poor quality institutions has been shown to promote intellectual growth. A long-term follow-up of 13 children transferred from an orphanage to a more stimulating mental retardation institution revealed marked gains in IQ: within 18 months the children were no longer functioning within the retarded range, and thereafter they showed normal development (Skeels and Dye, 1939; Skeels, 1966). Other studies have reported similar findings (Kirk, 1958; Lyle, 1960; Tizard, 1964).

One important question that arises when considering the influence of the environment on cognition is whether or not effects are more marked at certain ages than others. Some writers stress the importance of 'critical periods' *i.e.* they say that a child's early experiences during the preschool years crucially affect his intellectual development. Indeed this has been the philosophy behind many compensatory education programmes.

Although proponents of this view remain (Pringle, 1974), the existence of critical periods in a strict sense has recently been strongly challenged (Clarke and Clarke, 1976; Rutter, 1979). Nevertheless the issue is hard to resolve conclusively, especially as children of contrasting ages tend to have had experiences differing in both quality and quantity. Moreover, they are likely to have been exposed to relatively advantaged and disadvantaged circumstances for quite different lengths of time.

All the same, some evidence on the matter is forthcoming. First, there are indications that comparable environmental improvements have more impact on younger than older children (Dennis, 1973; Tizard and Hodges, 1978). Second, there are possibilities of marked gains in level of cognitive functioning in middle or later childhood (Koluchova, 1972, 1976; Kagan, 1976). Third, the provision of optimal environmental conditions in early childhood does not necessarily mean that consequent intellectual growth is sustained if such advantage is removed (Fogelman and Goldstein, 1976).

In general it can be concluded that critical periods for the development of intelligence do not exist. Although certain experiences may have more influence on cognitive growth during the early years, it is evident that environmental change can lead to IQ gains and losses at all stages of childhood.

Overall, effects of the environment in other than grossly abnormal situations, and upon individuals functioning with the normal range of intelligence, are limited. They are also difficult to document as advantaging or disadvantaging conditions tend to go together without necessarily independently influencing intelligence. Thus although residence in a particular neighbourhood, a nutritious diet and reading to children at night may all correlate with a high IQ, none may be directly responsible for intellectual growth. A further problem encountered when trying to isolate non-genetic influences on intelligence is that there are a multitude of factors that could possibly be taken into consideration and which might have some, albeit small, independent effect on intelligence. For these reasons discussion of the environment is restricted in this chapter to physical, family and educational factors. The aim is to illustrate how the environment may be important, and not to paint a comprehensive picture of cause and effect.

Physical factors

It has been claimed that intellectual functioning is affected by a variety of physical factors ranging from a mother's smoking in pregnancy (Butler and Goldstein, 1973) to the presence of toxic substances in the environment (Moncrieff *et al.*, 1964; Davie *et al.*, 1972). Two of the factors most frequently examined in this connection are birth circumstances and malnutrition.

Many writers have suggested that hazards surrounding birth *can*, although they do not necessarily, lead to an impairment of later intellectual development (*see* Birch and Gussow, 1970). Of these hazards, a very low birth weight despite a normal gestation period ('small for dates') has most often been related to intellectual retardation (McDonald, 1967; Rutter *et al.*, 1970). Prematurely-delivered babies who are also low birth weight, but who have spent less than 9 months in the womb, are not—unless cerebral palsy is contracted—at the same risk of mental handicap. However, few low birth weight children free from specific sensory or neurological dysfunction are likely to be functioning intellectually at a level much below the average for the general population, and it appears from recent studies that the effect of perinatal factors on IQ is small provided there is not also social disadvantage (Sameroff, 1975). As Birch and Gussow (1970) point out, socially disadvantaged mothers 'tend to be less well fed, less well grown, and less well cared for before they reach child-bearing age. When they reach it, they begin to bear children younger, more rapidly, and more often, and they continue to bear them until a later age. When such a mother is pregnant, both her nutrition and her health will tend to be poorer than that of a woman who is better off, but she will be far less likely to get prenatal care and far more likely to be delivered under sub-standard conditions.'

A variety of observations support this thesis. Certain mothers do have a succession of 'small for dates' babies (Dawkins, 1965; McDonald, 1967) yet, as shown by both Drillien (1964) and Illsley (1966), the relationship between low birth weight and depressed IQ scores is present only in the lowest social classes. This suggests that a 'good' postnatal environment can, except in instances of severe handicap, make up for being underweight at birth. On the other hand, Harper and Wiener (1965) examined the associations between IQ, social class and birth weight and indicated that IQ decreased with social class independent of birth weight and that IQ also declined with birth weight within each social class. Taken as a whole, however, the evidence suggests that there is a small association between IQ and birth weight although the association is less strong than that with social class (Davie *et al.*, 1972).

Nutritional intake, especially during the early years, has also been viewed with interest in relation to intellectual growth. Severe malnutrition has marked effects on cognitive functioning in animals (Cheek *et al.*, 1972; Mönckeberg, 1972), but whether the *sub*nutrition (Lambert, 1964; Lynch and Oddy, 1967) rather than the *mal*nutrition of some children in Britain today has any long-term consequences is less clear. The issue is made more complicated as subnutrition, like low birth weight, is more prevalent in certain social class groups where other factors influencing a child's intellectual development, such as sensory stimulation and maternal IQ, are likely to predict poor cognitive progress (Cravioto and DeLicardie, 1972; Mönckeberg, 1972; Tizard, 1974).

Most studies of nutrition have been in developing countries and have looked at effects of chronic malnutrition (*see* PAHO, 1973). The overall conclusion reached is that any effects on intelligence are largely indirect as a result of interfering with attention, motivation and general psychological development. A study carried out in a developed country also indicated no long-term direct effects on IQ of near-starvation. Stein *et al.* (1972a and b) studied a group of 19-year-old Dutch males who, during gestation, had been exposed to wartime famine. Although it was not possible to quantify the malnutrition suffered by individual members of the group, it was shown that there was no overall difference in intelligence between this and a control group. The conclusion appears to be that acute starvation during gestation has no long-term effects in the context of an otherwise nutritionally good and socially advantaged environment.

Family factors

Family composition—and in particular family size—is among the many aspects of the family situation which have been shown to bear some relationship to intellectual development (*see* Rutter and Madge, 1976). Children with higher IQs, specifically verbal IQs, tend to come from smaller families and, although a less consistent finding, they are likely to be first-borns or only children. However, birth order and family size effects are very small (Belmont and Marolla, 1973; Belmont, 1977). In addition twins and other members of multiple births tend to have lower verbal intelligence than singletons (Rutter and Mittler, 1972).

Interpretations of these findings vary. A number of researchers have suggested that family size is important only through its association with parental characteristics (Oldman *et al.*, 1971; Davie *et al.*, 1972). For example, parents of larger families are likely to be of lower intelligence, to be less concerned with scholastic attainment and to provide their children with fewer material facilities. Other writers have laid more stress on linguistic environment. They suggest that the larger the family the more young children talk to each other rather than to their parents. This, it is assumed, impedes cognitive development (Douglas *et al.*, 1968; Rutter and Mittler, 1972). The same argument is used to explain the depressed verbal intelligence of multiple-birth children.

Birth order effects must, by contrast, be interpreted in terms of the different ways that parents interact with their first and subsequent children. The common explanation is that parents spend more time with the initial child and give him/her more stimulation and greater responsibilities. This develops a need for achievement in the child which is further stoked by competition from younger brothers and sisters.

More generally, parent–child interaction has frequently been cited as a critical factor impeding or promoting intellectual growth. It can be important both in develop-

ing appropriate cognitive strategies and abilities and in fostering educationally relevant attitudes.

Bernstein (1961) has been most influential in Britain in suggesting how socialization practices can affect later intellectual and educational achievement (*see* Chapter 18). Hess and Shipman (1965, 1967) have reported studies of infant children and their mothers which support this idea. Wootton (1974) has shown that middle-class mothers are also more discussive than working-class mothers with their young children. They talk more during play and elaborate more when answering questions.

These and many other studies indicate that there are clear and marked social class differences in the use of language, and suggest that these are likely to influence intellectual growth. Further evidence for this view is provided by a series of studies in institutional nurseries by Barbara Tizard and colleagues (Tizard *et al.*, 1972; Tizard and Rees, 1974), which demonstrated that language development at 30 months was related to the amount, and quality, of communication between the children and the staff. Moreover, by 4 years there were small, but significant, correlations between IQ scores and stimulating experiences, such as outings, of the children.

Overall the family is probably the most important aspect of a child's environment. Not only patterns of family interaction, but also parental attitudes to learning and education are critical (Hertzig *et al.*, 1968). Indeed most investigators who have tried to isolate the effects of different family variables on intellectual growth have found that parental education and aspirations, the encouragement of independence in the child, and the provision of educationally-relevant experiences and materials in an emotionally stable and supportive environment are of most importance (*e.g.* Bayley, 1965; Hoffman and Lippitt, 1960). The critical nature of the home environment—in terms of poverty, crowding and availability of basic amenities—has been pointed out by other writers (Rutter *et al.*, 1970; Davie *et al.*, 1972).

Educational factors

Children who miss schooling tend to score poorly on intelligence tests. Gordon (1923), for example, demonstrated how the IQs of canal boat and gypsy children, who received no formal education, fell beyond the age of 6 years and De Groot (1951) in Holland showed how the generation of children who did not go to school during the Second World War were, on average, about five IQ points below the level expected of them.

Quite how schooling affects intelligence is less clear. Intellectual growth, as reflected by IQ scores, is undoubtedly related to the nature and stimulation of a child's experiences (Hebb, 1949; Bronfenbrenner, 1968), and as such is affected not only by the presence or absence of schooling, but also by its quality (Lee, 1951; Jencks *et al.*, 1973). Nevertheless, as concluded by Coleman *et al.* (1966) in the USA and the Plowden Report (1967) in Britain, it appears that school attributes have a minimal influence on intellectual development when compared with the effects of home and neighbourhood factors. Similar findings have been reported from Poland (Firkowska *et al.*, 1978).

This conclusion is largely borne out by the lack of success of many preschool enrichment programmes which have attempted to accelerate the general development of disadvantaged children, frequently without changing aspects of the home situation. Intervention studies are numerous, especially since the massive Head Start programme was launched in the United States in 1965 for around one million disadvantaged children, and they have been widely reviewed (Bronfenbrenner, 1974; Horowitz and Paden, 1973; Clarke and Clarke, 1974; Rutter and Madge, 1976). A number of general conclusions emerge from the findings.

First, ordinary nursery school experience does not necessarily result in IQ gains or imply better scholastic progress when children start compulsory education. Second, small-scale focused projects, which aim to train specific skills such as verbal ability, can bring about increases in IQ of about 10 to 15 points, and in some cases of up to 20 or 25 points. Nevertheless even these programmes do not mean that IQ gains are maintained into the school years, and thus it is not clear that they compensate the deprived child in any real sense in the long-term. Third, even children who have *not* had preschool education are likely to show IQ gains of 5 to 8 points on starting primary school. Such gains occur most commonly in children from disadvantaged homes. Fourth, there appears to be little influence of the age of the child (at least past the age of 3 years) and the duration of educational intervention at the preschool level and IQ gains. And fifth, some studies have reported more persistent IQ gains when parents are actively involved in the programmes.

Overall the success of pre-school interventions has been disappointing. Some people have argued that compensatory education has failed (*e.g.* Jensen, 1969) and that any IQ gains that have been found are due to practice in IQ test-relevant tasks and do not reflect any change in intelligence proper. However, it is impossible to draw firm conclusions about the potential value of preschool projects when many of those reported have foundered due to unrealistic goals. Very often programmes have had too broad objectives, they have involved the child for only a small proportion of his waking hours, and they have not paid sufficient attention to the importance of either continuing stimulation into the school years or simultaneously altering other aspects of the home and neighbourhood context.

Many of these limitations have been overcome in an important study by Heber and colleagues in Milwaukee (Heber, 1971; Heber *et al.*, 1972; Heber and Garber, 1975; Garber and Heber, 1977). Twenty children were provided with as near total intervention as possible—involving parent training as well as the emotional and educational development of the children—from the age of 3 months, and their cognitive growth was compared with that of 20 control children. It was found that from about 1 year of age the experimental children were more advanced than the controls, and that by 6 years the mean IQs of the two groups were 121 and 87 respectively. At 8

years a third of the control group scored less than 75 IQ points on the WISC (the level at which it is normally accepted that some form of special educational provision is required) whereas all the children from the experimental group, except two, had a tested IQ above 88. Whether these gains will be maintained is not yet known, and probably depends much on the future educational environment of the children. Nevertheless the study is instructive in that it demonstrates that the cognitive growth of even highly disadvantaged children can be encouraged given a sufficiently extensive and comprehensive programme.

CONCLUSIONS

Intelligence tests provide an imprecise but moderately useful way of sorting people out in accordance with what, in everyday terms, is their level of general cognitive ability. Intelligence measurement is subject to a good deal of error, much of it inherent in the manner in which intelligence is assessed. During the last 70 years there has been a good deal of refinement in test construction, but disappointingly small advances towards a theory of intelligence which would take in the empirical findings. Many factors are known to have *some* influence on the growth of measured intelligence; in general, adverse circumstances act synergistically and it is difficult, perhaps impossible, to look at the specific effects upon IQ of any but a few specific and unusual factors.

Much of the research which purports to be on individual differences is in fact concerned with group differences. The mean IQs of children in different social classes and of different ethnic origin have been shown to differ, but in view of the difficulty of sorting out and measuring specific, psychologically relevant factors in the environment it is unrewarding to attempt to explain sub-population differences in measured IQ in genetical or environmental terms.

Intelligence tests are none the less useful because they can give what is otherwise hard-to-get evidence about the general cognitive level of a particular child (albeit in a particular situation). They can also provide educationally relevant indicators by which to describe groups of children. But the concept of measured intelligence, like the concept of health, strength or beauty, is too global and unanalytical to be other than of heuristic value and there is little evidence that refinements in test construction will bring about major advances in our understanding of the nature of cognition or even in our ability to measure 'intelligence' more sensitively or precisely. However, despite their serious limitations—which have been intensively studied and reported on by psychologists—intelligence tests are likely to continue to be used in educational and clinical child psychology for practical reasons.

REFERENCES

Anderson, L. D. (1939). The predictive value of infant tests in relation to intelligence at 5 years. *Child Dev.*, **10**, 203–212.

Baltes, P. B. and Schaie, K. W. (1976). On the plasticity of intelligence in adulthood and old age. *Amer. Psychol.* **31**, 720–725.

Bayley, N. (1936). *The California Infant Scale of Motor Development.* University of California Press, Syllabus Series no. 259.

Bayley, N. (1965). Comparisons of mental and motor test scores for ages 1–15 months by sex, birth order, race, geographical location, and education of parents. *Child Devel., 36,* 379–411.

Bayley, N. (1969). *Bayley Scales of Infant Development: Birth to two years.* New York: Psychological Corporation.

Bayley, N. (1970). Development of mental abilities, pp. 1163–1210. In Mussen, P. H. (Ed.) *Carmichael's Manual of Child Psychology.* New York: Wiley.

Belmont, L. (1977). Birth order, intellectual competence and psychiatric status. *J. Individual Psychology, 33,* 97–104.

Belmont, L. and Marolla, F. A. (1973). Birth order, family size and intelligence. *Science, 182,* 1096–1101.

Berger, M. (1977). Psychological testing. In Rutter, M. and Hersov, L. (Eds.) *Child Psychiatry: Modern Approaches.* Oxford: Blackwell Scientific Publications, pp. 306–333.

Berger, M., Yule, W. and Rutter, M. (1975). Attainment and adjustment in two geographical areas. II. The prevalence of specific reading retardation. *Brit. J. Psychiat., 126,* 510–519.

Bernstein, B. (1961). Social class and linguistic development: a theory of social learning. In Halsey, A. H., Floud, J. and Anderson, C. A. (Eds.) *Education, Economy and Society.* New York Free Press of Glencoe.

Bhatnagar, J. (1970). *Immigrants at School.* Cornmarket Press.

Binet, A. and Simon, Th. (1905). *L'Année psychologique,* vol. **2.**

Birch, H. G. and Gussow, J. D. (1970). *Disadvantaged Children: Health, Nutrition and School Failure.* New York and London: Grune and Stratton.

Block, N. and Dworkin, G. (Eds.) (1977). *The IQ Controversy.* London: Quartet Books.

Bloom, B. S. (1964). *Stability and Change in Human Characteristics.* New York: Wiley.

Bowley, A. H. and Gardner, L. (1972). *The Handicapped Child: Educational and Psychological Guidance for the Organically Handicapped.* Edinburgh: Churchill Livingstone.

Bradway, K. P. and Thompson, C. W. (1962). Intelligence at adulthood: a twenty-five year follow-up. *J. Educ. Psychol., 53,* 1–14.

Bronfenbrenner, U. (1968). Early deprivation in mammals: a cross-species analysis. In Newton, G. and Levine, S. (Eds.) *Early Experience and Behavior.* Springfield: Charles C. Thomas.

Bronfenbrenner, U. (1974). *A Report on Longitudinal Evaluations of Preschool Programs, II. Is Early Intervention Effective?* Washington, D.C., US Department of Health, Education and Welfare, DHEW Publication No. (OHD) 74–25.

Burt, C. (1917). *The Distribution and Relations of Educational Abilities.* London.

Burt, C. (1940). *The Factors of the Mind: An Introduction to Factoranalysis in Psychology.* London: University of London Press.

Burt, C. (1961). Intelligence and social mobility. *Brit. J. Statist. Psychol.,* **14,** 3–24.

Burt, C. (1967). The structure of the mind, pp. 193–217. In Wiseman, S. (Ed.) *Intelligence and Ability: Selected Readings.* Harmondsworth: Penguin Books.

Burt, C. and Howard, M. (1956). The multifactorial theory of inheritance and its application to intelligence. *Brit. J. Statist. Psychol.* **9,** 95–131.

Butcher, H. J. (1970). *Human Intelligence: Its Nature and Assessment.* London: Methuen.

Butler, N. and Goldstein, H. (1973). Smoking in pregnancy and subsequent child development. *Amer. J. Dis. Childh.* **66,** 471–494.

Carr, J. (1975). *Young Children with Down's Syndrome.* London: Butterworths for the Institute for Research into Mental and Multiple Handicap.

Cattell, R. B. (1950). The fate of national intelligence: test of a thirteen prediction. *Eugen. Rev., 42,* 136–148.

Central Advisory Council for Education (England) (1967). *Children and Their Primary Schools.* (Plowden Report). London: HMSO.

Chalke, F. and Ertl, J. (1965). Evoked potentials and intelligence. *Life Sci., 4,* 1319.

Cheek, D. B., Holt, A. B. and Mellitis, E. D. (1972). Malnutrition and the nervous system. In PAHO, *Nutrition, the Nervous System and Behavior.* Proceedings of the Seminar on Malnutrition in Early Life

and Subsequent Mental Development. Scientific Publication no. 251, Washington: PAHO.

Clark, P. and Rutter, M. (1977). Compliance and resistance in autistic children. *J. Autism Child. Schizo., 7,* 33–48.

Clark, P. and Rutter, M. (1979). Task difficulty and task performance in autistic children. *J. Child Psych. Psychiat.,* **20,** 271–285.

Clarke, A. D. B. and Clarke, A. M. (1974). The changing concept of intelligence: a selective historical review. In Clarke, A. M. and Clarke, A. D. B. (Eds.) *Mental Deficiency: The Changing Outlook* (3rd ed.) London: Methuen, pp. 143–163.

Clarke, A. D. B. and Clarke, A. M. (1974). Genetic–environmental interactions in cognitive development. In Clarke, A. D. B. and Clarke, A. M. *Mental Deficiency: The Changing Outlook* (3rd ed.) London: Methuen, pp. 164–205

Clarke, A. D. B. and Clarke, A. M. (1974). Mental retardation and behavioural change. *Brit. Med. Bull., 30,* 179–185.

Clarke, A. M. and Clarke, A. D. B. (Eds.) (1976). *Early Experience: Myth and Evidence.* London: Open Books.

Coard, B. (1971). *How the West Indian Child is made Educationally Subnormal in the British School System,* London: New Beacon Books.

Coleman, J. S., Campbell, E. Q., Hobson, C. J., McPartland, J., Mood, A. M., Weinfeld, F. D. and York, R. L. (1966). *Equality of Educational Opportunity.* Washington, D.C.: Office of Education.

Cooper, R. M. and Zubeck, J. P. (1958). Effects of enriched and restricted early environments on the learning ability of bright and dull rats. *Canad. J. Psychol., 12,* 159–164.

Cravioto, J. and DeLicardie, E. (1972). Environmental correlates of severe clinical malnutrition. In PAHO, *Nutrition, the Nervous System and Behavior.* Proceedings of the Seminar on Malnutrition in Early Life and Subsequent Mental Development. Scientific Publication no. 251. Washington: Pan American Health Organization.

Cronbach, L. J. (1970). *Essentials of Psychological Testing* (3rd ed.) New York: Harper and Row.

Davie, R., Butler, N. and Goldstein, H. (1972). *From Birth to Seven: A Report of the National Child Development Study.* London: Longmans.

Davis, K. (1947). Final note on a case of extreme isolation. *Amer. J. Sociol., 52,* 432–437.

Dawkins, M. J. R. (1965). The 'small for dates' baby. In Dawkins, M. and MacGregor, W. G. (Eds.) *Gestational Age, Size and Maturity.* Clinics in Developmental Medicine no. 19. London: Heinemann.

Dearborn, W. F. and Rothney, J. W. M. (1941). *Predicting the Child's Development.* Cambridge, Mass.: Sci.-Art publ.

De Groot, A. D. (1951). War and the intelligence of youth. *J. Abn. Soc. Psychol., 46,* 596–597.

Dennis, W. (1973). *Children of the Creche.* New York: Appleton-Century Crofts.

Dockrell, W. B. (Ed.) (1970). *On Intelligence: The Toronto Symposium on Intelligence.* London: Methuen.

Douglas, J. W. B. (1964). *The Home and the School.* London: Macgibbon and Kee.

Douglas, J. W. B., Ross, J. M. and Simpson, H. R. (1968). *All Our Future: A Longitudinal Study of Secondary Education.* London: Peter Davies.

Drillien, C. M. (1964). *Growth and Development of the Prematurely Born Infant.* Edinburgh: Churchill Livingstone.

Egan, D. F., Illingworth, R. S. and MacKeith, R. C. (1969). *Developmental Screening 0–5 Years.* Clinics in Developmental Medicine no. 30. London: Heinemann.

Erlenmeyer-Kimling, L. and Jarvik, L. F. (1963). Genetics and intelligence. *Science,* **142,** 1477–1479.

Estes, W. K. (1974). Learning theory and intelligence. *Amer. Psychol.* **29,** 740–749.

Firkowska, A., Ostrowska, A., Sokolowska, A., Stein, Z., Susser, M. and Wald, I. (1978). Cognitive development and social policy. *Science,* **200,** 1357–1362.

Fogelman, K. R. and Goldstein, H. (1976). Social factors associated with changes in educational attainment between 7 and 11 years of age. *Educational Studies, 2,* 95–109.

Freeman, F. N., Holzinger, K. J. and Mitchell, B. C. (1928). The influence of environment on the intelligence, school achievement and conduct of foster children. In *The Twenty-Seventh Yearbook of the Nat. Soc. Stud. Nature and Nurture, Part I, Their Influence upon Intelligence.*

Freeman, J., Butcher, H. J. and Christie, T. (1971). *Creativity: A Selective Review of Research*. Society for Research into Higher Education Ltd., London.

Fulkar, D. W. (1975). Book review of L. J. Kamin, *The Science and Politics of I.Q. Amer. J. Psychol.*, **88**, 505–537.

Garber, H. and Heber, F. R. (1977). The Milwaukee Project: indications of the effectiveness of early intervention in preventing mental retardation. In Mittler, P. (Ed.) *Research to Practice in Mental Retardation*. Vol. I, *Care and Intervention*. Baltimore: University Park Press.

Garfinkel, R. and Thorndike, R. L. (1976). Binet item difficulty then and now. *Child Dev.* **47** (4), 959–965.

Getzels, J. W. and Jackson, P. W. (1962). *Creativity and Intelligence*. New York: Wiley.

Ginsburg, H. (1972). *The Myth of the Deprived Child: Poor Children's Intellect and Education*. Englewood Cliffs: Prentice-Hall, Inc.

Gordon, H. (1923). *Mental and Scholastic Tests Among Retarded Children*. Board of Education. Educ. Pamphlet No. 44.

Griffiths, R. (1954). *The Abilities of Babies*. London: University of London Press.

Grossman, H. J. (1973). *Manual on Terminology and Classification in Mental Retardation*. Spec. Publ. no. 2. Washington, D.C.: AAMD.

Guilford, J. P. (1959). Three faces of intellect. *Amer. Psychol.*, **14**, 469–479. Reprinted in Anderson and Ausubel, 1965.

Guilford, J. P. (1967). *The Nature of Human Intelligence*. New York: McGraw-Hill.

Halliday, R. and Callaway, E. (1977). Average evoked potentials and human intelligence. In Mittler, P. (Ed.) *Research to Practice in Mental Retardation. Biomedical Aspects*. Vol. III. IASSMD. Baltimore: University Park Press, pp. 451–463

Harlow, H. F. (1949). The formation of learning sets. *Psychological Review*, **56**, 51–65.

Harper, P. A. and Wiener, C. (1965). Sequelae of low birth weight. *Ann. Rev. Med.* **16**, 406–420.

Hasan, P. and Butcher, H. J. (1966). Creativity and intelligence: a partial replication with Scottish children of Getzels and Jackson's study. *Brit. J. Psychol.*, **57**, 129–135.

Haynes, J. M. (1971). *Educational Assessment of Immigrant Pupils*. Slough: N.F.E.R.

Hebb, D. O. (1949). *The Organization of Behavior*. New York: John Wiley.

Heber, R. (1971). *Rehabilitation of Families at Risk for Mental Retardation: a progress report*. Madison, Wisconsin: Rehabilitation Research and Retraining Center in Mental Retardation.

Heber, R., and Garber, H. (1975). Progress Report II: An Experiment in the Prevention of cultural-familial retardation. D. A. A. Primrose (ed.) *Proc. Third Int. Congr. Int. Assoc. Scient. Stud. Ment. Defic.* Warsaw: Polish Medical.

Heber, R., Garber, H., Harrington, S., Hoffman, C. and Falender, C. (1972). *Rehabilitation of Families at Risk for Mental Retardation*. December Progress Report, University of Wisconsin.

Hertzig, M. E., Birch, H. G., Thomas, A. and Mendez, O. A. (1968). Class and ethnic differences in the responsiveness of preschool children to cognitive demands. *Mon. Soc. Res. Child Develop.*, **33**, no. 1, Serial no. 117.

Hertzig, M., Birch, H. J., Richardson, S. A. and Tizard, J. (1972). Intellectual levels of children severely malnourished during the first two years of life. *Pediatrics*, **49**, 814–824.

Hess, R. D. and Shipman, V. C. (1965). Early experience and the socialization of cognitive modes in children. *Child Dev.*, **36**, 869–886.

Hess, R. D. and Shipman, V. C. (1967). Cognitive elements in maternal behavior. In Hill, J. P. (Ed.) *Minnesota Symposia on Child Psychology*, Vol. I, Minneapolis: University of Minnesota Press.

Hindley, C. B. (1960). The Griffiths Scale of Infant Development: Scores and predictions. *J. Child Psychol. Psychiat.*, 1, 99–112.

Hindley, C. B. and Owen, C. F. (1978). The extent of individual changes in IQ for ages between 6 months and 17 years in a British longitudinal sample. *J. Child. Psychol. Psychiat.*, **19**, 329–350.

Hoffman, L. W. and Lippitt, R. (1960). The measurement of family life variables. In Mussen, P. H. (Ed.) *Handbook of Research Methods in Child Development*. New York: Wiley.

Honzik, M. P. (1976). Value and limitations of infant tests: an overview. In Lewis, M. (Ed.) *Origins of Intelligence: Infancy and Early Childhood*. London: Wiley, pp. 59–96.

Honzik, M. P., MacFarlane, J. W. and Allen, L. (1948). Stability of mental test performance between 2 and 18 years. *J. Experimental Educ.*, **17**, 309.

Horowitz, F. D. and Paden, L. Y. (1973). The effectiveness of environmental intervention programs, pp. 331–402. In Caldwell, B. M. and Ricciuti, H. N. (Eds.) *Child Development and Policy: Review of Child Development Research*. Vol. 3, Chicago and London: University of Chicago Press.

Hudson, L. (1966). *Contrary Imaginations*. London: Methuen.

Humphreys, L. G. (1962). The organisation of human abilities. *Amer. Psychol.* **17**, 475–483.

Hunt, J. Mc V. (1961). *Intelligence and Experience*. New York: Ronald Press.

Hunt, J. Mc V. (1969). *The Challenge of Incompetence and Poverty: Papers on the Role of Early Education*. Urbana, Illinois: University of Illinois Press.

Illingworth, R. S. (1971). The predictive value of developmental assessment in infancy. *Develop. Med. Child Neurol.*, **13**, 721–725.

Illsley, R. (1966). Early prediction of perinatal risk. *Proc. Roy. Soc. Med.*, **59**, 181–184.

Jencks, C., Smith, M., Acland, M., Bane, M. J., Cohen, D., Gintis, H., Heynes, B. and Michelson, S. (1973). *Inequality: A Reassessment of the Effect of Family and Schooling in America*. London: Allen Lane.

Jensen, A. R. (1969). How much can we boost IQ and scholastic achievement? *Harvard Educ. Rev.*, **39**, 1–123.

Jensen, A. R. (1973). *Educability and Group Differences*. London: Methuen.

Jensen, A. R. (1976). Race and mental ability, pp. 71–108. In Ebling, S. J. (Ed.) *Racial Variation in Man*. Symposia of the Institute of Biology no. 22. London: Institute of Biology.

Jones, H. E. and Conrad, H. S. (1933). The growth and decline of intelligence: a study of a homogeneous group. *Genet. Psychol. Monogr.*, **13**, 223–298.

Jones, M. C., Bayley, N., MacFarlane, J. W. and Honzik, M. P. (1971). *The Course of Human Development*. Waltham, Mass.: Xerox Publishing.

Kagan, J. (1976). Resilience and continuity in psychological development. In Clarke, A. M. and Clarke, A. D. B. (Eds.) *Early Experience: Myth and Evidence*. London: Open Books.

Kamin, L. J. (1974). *The Science and Politics of IQ*. Potomac, Maryland: Lawrence Erlbaum Associates and London: Wiley.

Kangas, J. and Bradway, K. (1971). Intelligence at middle age: a thirty-eight year follow-up. *Develop. Psychol.*, **5**, 333–337.

Kiernan, C. C. and Jones, M. (1977). *Behaviour Assessment Battery*. Windsor, Berks: NFER.

Kirk, S. A. (1958). *Early Education of the Mentally Retarded: An Experimental Study*. Urbana, Ill.: University of Illinois Press.

Kirk, S. A. and McCarthy, J. J. (1961). The Illinois test of psycholinguistic abilities—an approach to differential diagnosis. *Amer. J. ment. Defic.*, **66**, 399–412.

Knobloch, H. and Pasamanick, B. (1967). Prediction from the assessment of neuromotor and intellectual status in infancy. In Zubin, J. and Jervis, G. A. (Eds.) *Psychopathology of Mental Development*. New York: Grune and Stratton, pp. 387–400

Knobloch, H. and Pasamanick, B. (1974). *Gesell and Amatruda's Developmental Diagnosis: The Evaluation and Management of Normal and Abnormal Neuropsychologic Development in Infancy and Early Childhood* (3rd ed.). Hagerstown, Maryland: Harper and Row.

Koluchova, J. (1972). Severe deprivation in twins: a case study. *J. Child Psychol. Psychiat.*, **13**, 107–114.

Koluchova, J. (1976). The further development of twins after severe and prolonged deprivation: a second report. *J. Child Psychol. Psychiat.*, **17**, 181–188.

Lambert, R. (1964). *Nutrition in Britain, 1950–1960*. Occasional Papers on Social Administration, no. 6, London: Bell.

Landau, A. (1973). *Creativity*. Goma, Cherikover.

Langan, W. (1970). Visual and perceptual difficulties. In Mittler, P. J. (Ed.) *The Psychological Assessment of Mental and Physical Handicaps*. London: Methuen.

Leahy, A. M. (1935). Nature-nurture and intelligence. *Genet. Psychol. Monogr.*, **17**, 241–305.

Lee, E. S. (1951). Negro intelligence and selective migration: a Philadelphia test of the Klineberg hypothesis. *Amer. Sociol. Rev.*, **16**, 227–233.

Little, A., Mabey, C. and Whittaker, G. (1968). The education of immigrant children in Inner London primary schools. *Race, 9*, 439–452.

Lockyer, L. and Rutter, M. (1969). A five to fifteen year follow up study of infantile psychoses: III, psychological aspects. *Brit. J. Psychiat.*, **115**, 865–882.

Lyle, J. G. (1960). The effect of an institutional environment upon the verbal development of imbecile children. III. The Brooklands residential family unit, *J. Ment. Defic. Res.*, **4**, 14–23.

Lynch, G. W. and Oddy, D. J. (1967). Are children of the under-paid under-fed? *The Medical Officer*, **117**, 353–354.

Lytton, H. (1971). *Creativity and Education*. London: Routledge and Kegan Paul.

Mason, M. K. (1942). Learning to speak after six and one-half years of silence. *J. Speech and Hearing Dis.*, **7**, 295–304.

Maxwell, J. (1969). *Sixteen Years on: A Follow-up of the 1947 Scottish Survey*. London: University of London Press.

McCall, R. B., Hogarty, P. S. and Hurlburt, N. (1972). Transition in infant sensori-motor development and the prediction of childhood IQ. *Amer. Psychol.*, **27**, 728–748.

McDonald, A. (1967). *Children of Very Low Birth Weight*. MEIU Research Monogr. no. 1. London: Heinemann/S.I.M.P.

McFie, J. and Thompson, J. A. (1970). Intellectual abilities of immigrant children. *Brit. J. Educ. Psychol.*, **40**, 348–351.

Mittler, P. H. (1970). Assessment of handicapped children: some common factors. In Mittler, P. J. (Ed.) *The Psychological Assessment of Mental and Physical Handicaps*. London: Methuen, pp. 343–374.

Mittler, P. (Ed.) (1970). *The Psychological Assessment of Mental and Physical Handicap*. London: Methuen, pp. 343–374.

Mittler, P. and Woodward, P. (1966). The education of children in hospitals for the subnormal: a survey of admissions. *Develop. Med. Child Neurol.*, **3**, 16–25.

Mönckeberg, F. (1972). Malnutrition and mental capacity. In PAHO, *Nutrition, the Nervous System and Behavior*. Proceedings of the Seminar on Malnutrition in Early Life and Subsequent Mental Development. Scientific Publication no. 251. Washington: Pan American Health Organisation.

Moncrieff, A. A., Koumides, O. P., Clayton, N. A., Patrick, A. D., Renwick, A. G. C. and Roberts, O. E. (1964). Lead poisoning in children. *Arch. Dis. Childh.*, **39**, 1–13.

Oldman, D., Bytheway, B. and Horobin, G. (1971). Family structure and educational achievement. *J. Biosoc. Sci.*, Suppl. **3**, 81–91.

Pan American Health Organization (1972). *Nutrition, the Nervous System and Behavior*. Proceedings of the Seminar on Malnutrition in Early Life and Subsequent Mental Development. Scientific Publication no. 251. Washington: Pan American Health Organization.

Piaget, J. (1936). *La Naissance de l'Intelligence*. Neuchatel: Delachaux et Niestlé.

Piaget, J. (1937). Le problème de l'intelligence et de l'habitude: réflexe conditionné, 'Gestalt' our assimilation. *Proc. 11th Int. Congr. Psychol.*, 170–183.

Piaget, J. (1945). *Play, Dreams and Imitation in Childhood*. (Trans. by C. Gattegno and F. M. Hodgson.) New York: Norton (1951).

Pinneau, S. R. (1961). *Changes in Intelligence Quotient from Infancy to Maturity*. Boston: Houghton Mifflin.

Plowden Report—see Central Advisory Council for Education (1967).

Pringle, M. L. K. (1974). *The Needs of Children*. London: Hutchinson.

Reed, M. (1970). Deaf and partially hearing children. In Mittler, P. J. (Ed.) *The Psychological Assessment of Mental and Physical Handicaps*. London: Methuen.

Reynell, J. (1970). Children with physical handicaps. In Mittler, P. J. (Ed.) *The Psychological Assessment of Mental and Physical Handicaps*. London: Methuen.

Rutter, M. L. (1964). Intelligence and childhood psychiatric disorder. *Brit. J. Soc. Clin. Psychol.*, **6**, 71–83.

Rutter, M. L. (1970). Psychological development—predictions from infancy. *J. Child Psychol. Psychiat.*, **11**, 49–62.

Rutter, M. (1979). Maternal deprivation, 1972–78: New Findings, New Concepts, New Approaches. *Child Dev.*, **50**, 283–305.

Rutter, M., Graham, P. and Yule, W. (1970). *A Neuropsychiatric Study in Childhood*. London: Heinemann.

Rutter, M. and Madge, N. (1976). *Cycles of Disadvantage: A Review of Research*. London: Heinemann.

Rutter, M. and Mittler, P. (1972). Environmental influences on language and development. In Rutter, M. L. and Martin, J. A. M. (Eds.) *The Child with Delayed Speech*. Clinics in Developmental Medicine no. 43, London: Heinemann.

Rutter, M., Tizard, J. and Whitmore, K. (Eds.) (1970). *Education, Health and Behaviour*. London: Longmans.

Sameroff, A. J. (1975). Early influences on development: Fact or fancy? *Merrill-Palmer Quart.*, **21**, 267–294.

Sandiford, P. (1928). *Educational Psychology*. New York: Longmans.

Sattler, J. M. (1973). Intelligence testing of ethnic minority-group and culturally-disadvantaged children. In Mann, L. and Sabatino, D. A. (Eds.) *The First Review of Special Education*. Philadelphia, Buttonwood Farms.

Scarr, S. and Weinberg, R. A. (1976). IQ test performance of black children adopted by white families. *Amer. Psychol.*, **31**, 726–739.

Scottish Council for Research in Education (1949). *The Trend of Scottish Intelligence*. London: University of London Press.

Shakespeare, R. (1970). Severely subnormal children. In Mittler, P. J. (Ed.) *The Psychological Assessment of Mental and Physical Handicaps*. London: Methuen.

Shapiro, M. B. (1970). Intensive assessment of the single case: an inductive–deductive approach. In Mittler, P. J. (Ed.) *The Psychological Assessment of Mental and Physical Handicaps*. London: Methuen.

Skeels, H. M. (1966). Adult status of children with contrasting early life experiences. *Mon. Soc. Res. Child Develop.*, **31**, no. 3.

Skeels, H. M. and Dye, H. B. (1939). A study of the effects of differential stimulation on mentally retarded children. *Proceedings and Addresses of the American Association on Mental Deficiency*, **44**, 114–136.

Skodak, M. and Skeels, H. M. (1949). A final follow-up study of one hundred adopted children. *J. Genet. Psychol.*, **75**, 85–125.

Sontag, L. W., Baker, C. T. and Nelson, V. C. (1958). Mental growth and personality development: a longitudinal study. *Mon. Soc. Res. Child Develop.*, **23**, no. 2.

Spearman, C. (1904). General intelligence: objectively determined and measured. Reprinted in Wiseman, S. (Ed.) *Intelligence and Ability: Selected Readings*. Harmondsworth: Penguin Books, 1967.

Spearman, C. (1927). The doctrine of two factors. Reprinted. In Wiseman, S. (Ed.) *Intelligence and Ability: Selected Readings*. Harmondsworth: Penguin Books, 1967. pp. 58–68.

Spearman, C. (1927). *The Abilities of Man*. London: Macmillan.

Stein, Z., Susser, M., Saenger, G. and Marolla, F. (1972a). Nutrition and mental performance. *Science*, **178**, 708.

Stein, Z., Susser, M., Saenger, G. and Marolla, F. (1972b). Intelligence test results of individuals exposed during gestation to the World War II famine in the Netherlands. *T. soc. Geneesk.* **50**, 766.

Tarjan, M. D., Tizard, J., Rutter, M., Begab, M., Brooke, E. M., de la Cruz, F., Lin, T.-Y., Montenegro, H., Strotzka, H. and Sartorius, N. (1972). Classification and mental retardation: issues arising in the fifth WHO seminar on psychiatric diagnosis, classification and statistics. *Amer. J. Psychiat.*, **128**, May Suppl. **11**, 34–45.

Terman, L. M. (1919). *The Intelligence of School Children*. Boston: Houghton Mifflin.

Thomson, G. H. (1939). *The Factorial Analysis of Human Ability*. London: University of London Press.

Thorndike, R. L. (1933). The effect of the interval between test and retest on the constancy of the IQ. *J. Educ. Psychol.*, **24**, 543–9.

Thurstone, L. L. (1938). Primary mental abilities. *Psychomtr. Monogr. No 1*.

Tizard, B., Cooperman, O., Joseph, A. and Tizard, J. (1972). Environmental effects on language development: a study of young children in long-stay nurseries. *Child Dev.*, **43**, 337–358.

Tizard, B. and Hodges, J. (1978). The effect of early institutional rearing on the development of 8-year-old children. *J. Child Psychol. Psychiat.*, **19**, 99–118.

Tizard, B. and Rees, J. (1974). A comparison of the effects of adoption, restoration to the natural mother and continued institutionalization on the cognitive development of four-year-old children. *Child Develop.*, **45**, 92–99.

Tizard, J. (1964). *Community Services for the Mentally Handicapped.* London: Oxford University Press.

Tizard, J. (1974). Early malnutrition, growth and mental development in man. *British Medical Bulletin,* **30,** no. 2.

Tizard, J. (1974). Longitudinal studies: problems and findings. In Clarke, A. M. and Clarke, A. D. B. (Eds.) *Mental Deficiency: The Changing Outlook.* 3rd edition. London: Methuen.

Tizard, J. (1975). Race and IQ: the limits of probability? *New Behaviour, 1,* 6–9.

Tizard, J. (1976). Progress and degeneration in the IQ debate: comments on Urbach. *Brit. J. Phil. Soc.,* **27,** 251–274.

Tizard, J. and Plewis, I. (1977). *Critical Notice* of Broman, S. H., Nichols, P. L. and Kennedy, W. (1975). *Preschool IQ: Prenatal and Early Developmental Correlates.* Hillsdale, New Jersey: Lawrence Erlbaum Associates and London: John Wiley. In *J. Child Psychol. Psychiat.,* **18,** 381–388.

Torrance, E. P. (1972). Can we teach children to think creatively? *J. Creative Behavior,* **6** (102), 114–143.

Tuddenham, R. D. (1970). A 'Piagetian' test of cognitive development, pp. 49–70. In Dockrell, W. B. *On Intelligence: The Toronto Symposium on Intelligence.* London: Methuen.

Uzgiris, C. (1976). Organisation of sensori-motor intelligence, pp. 123–164. In Lewis, M. (Ed.) *Origins of Intelligence: Infancy and Early Childhood.* London: John Wiley.

Uzgiris, I. C. and Hunt, J. McV. (1975). *Assessment in infancy: Ordinal Scales of Psychological Development.* Urbana, Illin.: University of Illinois Press.

Vernon, P. E. (1940). *The Measurement of Abilities.* London: University of London Press.

Vernon, P. E. (1960). *Intelligence and Attainment Tests.* London: University of London Press.

Vernon, P. E. (1965). Ability factors and environmental influences. *Amer. Psychol.,* **20,** 723–733.

Vernon, P. E. (1970). On intelligence. In Dockrell, W. B. (Ed.) *On Intelligence: The Toronto Symposium on Intelligence,* pp. 99–117. London: Methuen.

Vernon, P. E. (1976). Development of intelligence. In Hamilton, V. and Vernon, M. D. (Eds.) *The Development of Cognitive Processes.* London and New York: Academic Press.

Vernon, P. E. and Parry, J. B. (1949). *Personnel Selection in the British Forces.* London: University of London Press.

Wallach, M. A. and Kogan, N. (1965). *Modes of Thinking in Young Children.* New York: Holt, Rinehart and Winston.

Waller, J. H. (1971). Achievement and social mobility: relationships among IQ score, education and occupation in two generations. *Social Biology,* **18,** 252–259.

Welsh, G. S. (1975). *Creativity and Intelligence: A Personality Approach.* Institute for Research in Social Science, University of N. Carolina.

West, D. J. and Farrington, D. P. (1973). *Who Becomes Delinquent?* Second Report of the Cambridge Study in Delinquent Development. London: Heinemann Educational Books.

White, B. L. and Held, R. (1966). Plasticity of sensorimotor development in the human infant. In Rosenblith, J. F. and Allinsmith, W. (Eds.) *The Causes of Behavior: Readings in Child Development and Educational Psychology* (2nd ed.) Boston: Allyn and Bacon.

Williams, C. E. (1966). A blind idiot who became a normal blind adolescent. *Develop. Med. Child Neurol.,* **8,** 166–169.

Woodward, M. (1955). *Low Intelligence and Delinquency.* ISTD.

Wootton, A. J. (1974). Talk in the homes of young children. *Sociology,* **8,** 277–295.

Yule, W. (1973). Differential prognosis of reading backwardness and specific reading retardation. *Brit. J. Educ. Psychol.,* **43,** 244–248.

Yule, W., Berger, M., Rutter, M. and Yule, B. (1975). Children of West Indian immigrants. II. Intellectual performance and reading attainment. *J. Child Psychol. Psychiat.,* **16,** 1–18.

22. ATTACHMENT AND THE DEVELOPMENT OF SOCIAL RELATIONSHIPS

MICHAEL RUTTER

By the time they reach their first birthday infants have usually developed strong and definite attachments to their parents and are acutely distressed if they are forcefully separated from them. People have long been aware of this phenomenon but little serious attention was paid to it until Bowlby (1951) pointed to the importance of mother–infant relationships in his review of maternal deprivation. At first, the main focus was on children's reactions to separation and the need to avoid separations during the preschool years. The films produced by James and Joyce Robertson vividly portrayed the intense emotional disturbance shown by many young children admitted to hospitals and residential nurseries. Together with Bowlby, they pointed to the characteristic sequence of protest—despair—detachment shown following admissions (Robertson and Bowlby, 1952).

However, particularly as a result of Bowlby's writings (*see* Bowlby, 1969) and empirical studies by Schaffer and Emerson (1964) and by Ainsworth (1967), there came a growing awareness of attachment and bonding as developmental features which were important in their own right. The notion of attachment has given rise to a large body of research (*see* Ainsworth, 1973; Bowlby, 1969; Maccoby and Masters, 1970; Rajecki *et al.*, 1978; Rutter, 1978a, 1979a; Schaffer, 1971) and theorists have suggested that an infant's early attachments to his parents may constitute the basis of all later social relationships (Bowlby, 1969). Before discussing how far this is the case, it is necessary to describe how attachments develop and to consider their function and meaning.

THE EARLY MONTHS OF LIFE

Although attachments do not themselves develop until rather later, social relationships have their origins in the early weeks and months of life. The infant's ability to perceive people and to discriminate between them matures; his repertoire of social responses and social imitations increases; and the social dialogue between parent and child grows in complexity.

Perceptual discriminations

At the time of birth, the infant's sensory abilities are already intact and functioning although his powers of perceptual discrimination and sensory integration are quite limited in comparison with the skills shown some months later. Fantz (1965, 1966) showed that a baby's ability to make visual discriminations could be studied by determining whether his gaze was fixed more on one type of stimulus than on another. In this way, he found that from the age of a week patterned surfaces are preferred to plain ones. Neonates are attracted by rather simple stimuli but over the next few months they come to prefer increasing complexity (Brennan, Ames and Moore, 1966; Karmel, 1969). At all ages infants prefer moving to stationary objects (Ames and Silfen, 1965; Haith, 1966), and by 2 months they have come to select three-dimensional over flat objects (Fantz, 1966). Moreover, during the first three or four months, infants develop a definite preference for the human face over other types of visual stimulus (Fantz, 1966; Fantz and Nevis, 1967; Lewis, 1969). Not surprisingly, infants pay more attention to a mobile head than to a stationary one (Wilcox and Clayton, 1968).

Much the same course of development occurs with auditory discriminations. Neonates respond to sounds of all kinds (Brackbill, Adams, Crowell and Gray, 1966) but more so to patterned sounds than to pure tones (Hutt *et al.*, 1968) and most of all to speech sounds (Hetzer and

Tudor-Hart, 1927). Wolff (1963) found that by the fifth week of life the mother's voice was more effective than others in eliciting vocalization.

The infant's ability to recognize his mother as different from other adults has been studied in a variety of ways using heart rate (Banks and Wolfson, 1967), pupillary dilatation (Fitzgerald, 1968), smiling (Wahler, 1967), visual attention (Caldwell, 1965) and changes in behaviour (Yarrow, 1967) as response indicators. It is clear that by the age of 3 months and usually earlier than that, an infant can differentiate his mother from other people. Obviously this constitutes an essential prerequisite to the development of a selective attachment.

Orienting and grasping

At birth babies show a side to side head movement, termed a 'rooting' response which may occur spontaneously but which is especially evoked by touching the baby anywhere near the mouth (Prechtl, 1958). A directed head-turning towards the touch stimulus develops soon afterwards. This movement is most easily elicited when the baby is hungry and obviously it constitutes an integral part of the feeding pattern. However, it also occurs at other times and serves to orient the baby to the person holding him even when there is no feeding (Blauvelt and McKenna, 1961). Babies soon come to orient towards the breast or bottle in anticipation whenever they are held in a nurturing position (Call, 1964). At first holding and position are crucial in the eliciting of the anticipatory orienting, but about the third month the sight of the breast or bottle also begin to play a part (Hetzer and Ripin, 1930).

Neonates already show a grasp reflex but it is not until rather later that reaching and grasping become an integrated response to what the baby sees (White, Castle and Held, 1964). By 2 to 3 months an infant will reach out towards a moving object but it is not until about 4 months that he grasps it. The initially clumsy movements become smoother and babies soon reach and touch the body and face of adults who pick them up. Clinging to the parent develops at about 6 to 9 months and infants come to put out their arms to be picked up whenever their parent approaches (Ainsworth, 1967).

Social signals

However, it would be quite wrong to regard the infant as merely recognizing and responding to adult cues. Babies' cries, vocalizations and smiles constitute important social signals which may attract adult attention and initiate (as well as respond to) social interactions. Wolff (1969) and Wasz-Hockert et al. (1968) both showed that infants had several different types of cry (in particular a hungry cry, an angry cry and a pain cry) which are readily distinguished by parents. Sensory stimulation (Brackbill, 1971) but especially human stimulation (Wolff, 1969) reduces crying. Mechanical rocking (Ambrose, 1969) and, most of all, picking up (Korner and Grobstein, 1966) are particularly effective in producing quietening. Most babies cry fairly frequently and this usually succeeds in

eliciting a maternal response (Moss and Robson, 1968). It is evident not only that crying brings attention from the mother but that the attention then soothes the baby—a rewarding sequence of events for both mother and child. Vocalizations, too, tend to elicit a parental response which in turn proves highly reinforcing of the sounds being produced (Rheingold, Gewirtz and Ross, 1959; Weisberg, 1963; Dodd, 1972). Babbling occurs most frequently in a social context and as early as the second month babies vocalize more with their mothers than with a stranger (Wolff, 1963).

Smiling plays a particularly important role in the development of social relationships as it is so obviously a social signal and is felt by parents as an indication of the baby's pleasure in their interaction. In the early weeks of life experimental studies show that babies smile at a simple pair of eye-like dots, by the third month smiling is more readily elicited by the upper face (in which, of course, the eyes remain crucial); by 5 months the facial expression is important; and by 7 months a smile is elicited only by the faces of certain people familiar to the infant. (Ahrens, 1954; Spitz and Wolf, 1946.) However, even as early as 2 or 3 months babies will smile more often to their mothers than to strangers. Speaking to the child also helps elicit smiling (Wolff, 1963) and institution-reared children tend to be delayed in their development of social smiling (Ambrose, 1961; Gewirtz, 1965). In short, there seems to be a regular progression from spontaneous and reflex smiling to unselective social smiling (usually beginning in the second month) to increasingly discriminating social smiling (Gewirtz, 1965). In the latter two phases babies smile much more when someone smiles back, coos or cuddles them (Brackbill, 1958). Essentially, smiling is a social reciprocal action which serves to prolong and develop any kind of personal interaction. Visual stimuli are particularly important in eliciting smiling but the human voice also plays a role. In blind babies social smiling tends to be delayed and tends not to be present in its normal form until about 6 months of age (Freedman, 1964).

Dialogue between parent and child

The interaction between parent and child, even in the neonatal period, is very much a two-way process in which each is both responding to and influencing the other (see Lewis and Rosenblum, 1974). This is evident in face to face interactions (Brazelton, Tronick, Adamson, Als and Weise, 1975) and in communication patterns (Condon and Sander, 1974; Stern, Jaffe, Beebe and Bennett, 1975). In a very real sense it is a dialogue in which babies and parents smile and vocalize to each other with the same type of flow (initiations, pauses and responses) characteristic of adult conversations. The baby's social behaviour is highly dependent on the appropriate adult response so that vocalizations and smiling die away if the parent merely stands passively watching with an expressionless face. Equally, however, the parent's behaviour is much influenced by the baby's response. This is shown, for example, by differences in the mother's behaviour according to the baby's state when brought for feeding (Levy, 1958) and by the way breast milk flows when the baby cries (Newton, 1951). Mothers also respond differently to premature than to full-term babies, being more active with the less responsive immature infants (Brown and Bateman, 1978). Similarly, mothers who are separated from their babies in the post-natal period tend to be less confident and less competent in some aspects of mothering during the subsequent months. Rather long-lasting changes in mother–child interaction were found by Klaus and Kennell (Kennell, Trause and Klaus, 1975; Klaus, Jerauld, Kreger, McAlpine, Steffa and Kennell, 1972) in groups of socially disadvantaged mothers but more transitory effects were noted by Leiderman and Seashore (1975) and by Whiten (1977).

It has been suggested that these early days after birth constitute a sensitive period for the development of maternal attachment to the baby (Kennell et al., 1975; Hales, Lozoff, Susa and Kennell, 1977). Adequate data to test the hypothesis are lacking so far but at first sight it seems implausible if only because adoptive parents usually develop close relationships with their children in spite of lack of neonatal contact. Nevertheless, what is evident is that events in the post-natal period do play a part in influencing parental responses to their baby. Denial of contact, fears engendered by having a baby placed in special care or the restraints on spontaneous interactions which may stem from hospital practice and structure may all interfere with optimal parenting.

Prospective studies indicate that the interaction between parents and children is truly two-way, with both influencing the other. Clarke-Stewart's findings (1973, 1977), from her cross-lagged analysis of longitudinal data, suggest not only that parents both influence and are influenced by their children, but also that it is a reciprocal relationship which changes in balance and characteristics as the children grow older.

THE DEVELOPMENT OF ATTACHMENTS

Some time about the third quarter of the first year (with considerable individual variation, ranging from 3 to 15 months) there is a further phase in the development of social relationships. Infants come to develop specific *attachments* to particular people. This clinging, 'I want Mummy', phase is familiar to all parents. The infant has now become much more discriminating in his social relationships and there are certain people to whom he will go in preference to all others. Even when much younger he varied in his social interaction according to how other people responded to him. But the difference now is that his selectivity in relationships persists over time and is no longer dependent on the adults' response to him at that moment. The infant will seek his mother even when she is indifferent and ignores him, and he will not go to a stranger even when the person is friendly, smiling and responsive.

This phenomenon occurs in all human cultures and indeed is a feature which is characteristic of the develop-ment of a wide range of animal species including birds, dogs, sheep and subhuman primates (*see* Bowlby, 1969; Cairns, 1966; Rajecki *et al.*, 1978). In all cases the young strive actively to seek the *proximity* of their parents or other specific individuals—the feature which gives rise to the term 'attachment'.

Characteristics specific to attachment

A wide range of attachment behaviours have been described by Ainsworth (1967). These include differential smiling, greeting responses, following, separation, protest, and flight to the person as a haven of safety. These are indeed features of attachment but some are also characteristic of other types of social relationship. Thus, differential responsiveness has been considered a crucial aspect of attachment. Of course, it is a *necessary* part of the attachment process but it is not a *sufficient* criterion for its presence. Babies vary in their smiling, crying, vocalization and looking according to the person they are with (Ainsworth, 1967) but infants are interested in novelty as well as security and differential interest may not indicate attachment. Babies may look at strangers as much as at their parents (Corter, 1973) and even prefer to play with them (Ross and Goldman, 1977). What then *specifically* characterizes attachment? Four main features may be identified; the effects of anxiety, the secure base effect, reduction of anxiety and separation protest.

The effects of anxiety sharply differentiate attachment from other forms of social interaction: whereas social play is *inhibited* by anxiety, attachment is *intensified*. Thus, Lamb (1977a and b) found that when a child was with his parents the entrance of a stranger reduced playful interactions but increased attachment behaviour. Children may prefer to play with peers (Eckerman, Whatley, and Katz, 1975) or even a stranger (Ross and Goldman, 1977) but will nevertheless still prefer to go to a parent for comfort. The same applies to rhesus monkeys (Patterson, Bonvillian, Reynolds and Maccoby, 1975). Similarly, in an unfamiliar situation infants are much more likely to follow their mother than a stranger when both leave the room together out of different doors (Corter, 1973). Following and the seeking of proximity are characteristic of attachment and both tend to increase at times of stress. It should be noted that this differential reaction to anxiety is *not* a consequence of parents being more skilled at providing comfort at times of stress. Harlow and his colleagues showed that infant monkeys clung tightly even to cloth models which repeatedly punished them with a blast of compressed air (Rosenblum and Harlow, 1963) or to deprived mothers who severely abused them (Seay, Alexander and Harlow, 1964). Anxiety seems to increase attachment *regardless* of the response of the attachment-object. Systematic data are lacking for humans but the same seems to apply (Bowlby, 1969).

Play and attachment clearly overlap greatly but they exhibit rather different qualities (Hartup, 1978). The ways children play together (Heathers, 1955) and the ways they interact with a stranger (Ross and Goldman, 1977) are rather different from their style of interaction with parents. Clinging or hugging one another are rarely seen in peer play except in the unusual circumstances of rearing in the absence of parents (Freud and Dann, 1951). The same applies to monkey interactions with peers (Harlow, 1969; Harlow and Harlow, 1972). Thus, play and attachment behaviour have a different style and a different purpose (although, of course, any relationship with one individual may include both components—Rutter, 1979). The key differentiation is that attachment is at its peak at times of stress in contrast to play which is least likely to occur at such times.

Second, attachment provides a 'secure base effect' such that the presence of an attachment object promotes exploration and other adaptive responses (Rajecki et al., 1978). Many workers have noted that infants tend to move away from their mothers on exploratory forays, returning to them at intervals as if for reassurance (Ainsworth, 1967; Anderson, 1972; Rheingold and Eckerman, 1970). Infants play, speak and move about more in their mother's presence than in her absence (Cox and Campbell, 1968) and exploration decreases when she (or some other attachment figure) leaves the room (Ainsworth and Wittig, 1969; Maccoby and Feldman, 1972; Feldman and Ingham, 1975). Infants show more stranger distress when seated a few feet away from their mothers than when held by them (Scarr and Salapatek, 1970; Morgan and Ricciuti, 1969; Sroufe, Waters and Matas, 1974). The presence of a parent reduces stranger anxiety (Kotelchuck, 1976) and infants play more with strangers when their mother is with them. Three features of this secure base effect are particularly noteworthy. Firstly, the presence of the person to whom the child is attached enables him to *move away* more readily. Secondly, the returns are not elicited by adult summonses. Thirdly, this secure-base effect is also seen with inanimate objects such as a blanket (Passman and Weisberg, 1975). Evidently it is the presence of the attachment object which is crucial and *not* the comforting actions of a responsive adult.

The third characteristic of anxiety-reduction is closely related to (and may indeed by synonymous with) the secure base effect. It has long been observed (Arsenian, 1943) that infants are less distressed in a strange or frightening situation if a familiar person is present. This has been repeatedly demonstrated with respect to hospital admission in which case emotional distress is much less if the child is accompanied by a parent (MacCarthy, Lindsay and Morris, 1962; Mićić, 1962; Fagin, 1966). Once again, it seems that it is the mere *presence* of a person to whom the child is attached which is important, rather than adult skills in providing comfort and reassurance. Thus, for example, Heinicke and Westheimer (1965) found the same effect even with the presence of younger sibs. Moreover, if a parent or familiar adult is not available, young children quickly develop new attachments (provided there is the opportunity for continuing personal interactions with the same individual), which then serve the same purpose (Robertson and Robertson, 1971).

The fourth specifically differentiating characteristic of attachment is the phenomenon of separation-protest. Robertson and Bowlby (1952) described the sequence of reactions in young children admitted to sanatoria. At first they were tearful, angry and upset (the phase of 'protest'); they then become more quietly miserable and apathetic ('despair') and finally appear 'detached' and no longer caring about their parents. Similar effects have been observed in healthy children admitted to nurseries (*see* Heinicke and Westheimer, 1965). Schaffer and Callender (1959) found that this response to institution or hospital admission generally developed about the age of 6 or 7 months and was not seen in infants. Yarrow (1963) showed much the same age trend in terms of children's emotional disturbance following transfer from a foster home to an adoptive home—under 3 months none were upset, between 3 and 6 months an increasingly high proportion showed distress and between 7 and 12 months all did so.

The phenomenon of protest may be seen with even very brief separations of a few minutes. In these circumstances separation from an attachment figure (whether father or mother) is very likely to result in protest whereas separation from a stranger less often does so (Cohen and Campos, 1974; Fleener and Cairns, 1970; Kotelchuck, 1976; Stayton, Ainsworth and Main, 1973).

Number and nature of attachment-objects

All studies are agreed that most young infants are most strongly attached to their mother. However, the same studies show that not only is it common for children to be attached to other people in addition or instead, but also it is quite frequent for them to be attached to inanimate objects. Thus, Schaffer and Emerson (1964) found that 55 out of 58 infants developed their initial attachment with their mothers. On the other hand, by 18 months three quarters of the infants were also attached to their fathers. By then nearly all infants showed multiple attachments and in almost a third of cases the most intense attachment was to someone other than the mother. Ainsworth (1967) found much the same. In addition, Schaffer and Emerson (1964) reported that a third of the infants were attached to a specific cuddly object (such as a blanket or teddy). In most cases, these attachments to particular inanimate objects develop during the second year of life, although *non*-differential sucking of a thumb or dummy may have begun much earlier (Stevenson, 1954). It should be noted that multiple attachments and attachments to inanimate objects do *not* appear to be a consequence of a weak bond with the mother—in fact the trend is in the opposite direction. Moreover, institutional children who may be impaired in their development of human attachments are rarely attached to cuddly toys (Provence and Lipton, 1962).

The question arises as to whether all these attachments have the same meaning and constitute the same phenomenon. Bowlby (1969) has suggested that there is an innate bias for a child to attach himself especially to *one* figure and that this main attachment differs in kind from those to other subsidiary figures (hence his use of the term 'monotropy'). However, his concept involves two rather different propositions. The first is that each attachment is specific and not interchangeable. This suggestion is well supported by the findings from several studies which all show that there is a persisting hierarchy among attachments, with some continuing to be stronger than others (Ainsworth, 1967; Schaffer and Emerson, 1964). Even in polymatric institutions, children tend to have their favourite adult to whom they will go in preference to all others, (Burlingham and Freud, 1944; Stevens, 1975).

The second proposition is that the first or main attachment differs *in kind* from all other subsidiary ones. Research findings indicate that this is *not* the case (Rutter, 1978a). In the first place the specific qualities of attachment already discussed have been shown to apply to attachment to sibs (Heinecke and Westheimer, 1965), to peers (Kissel, 1965; Schwartz, 1972), to fathers (Cohen and Campos, 1974; Lamb, 1977a and b; Spelke, Zelazo, Kagan and Kotelchuck, 1973), to adult caretakers in a nursery (Arsenian, 1943) and to inanimate objects (Harlow and Zimmerman, 1959; Mason and Berkson, 1975; Passman, 1977; Passman and Weisberg, 1975) as well as to mothers. It is also crucial that these attachments to other persons function in this way even in children who have developed bonds with their mothers. Furthermore, in most cases the difference in intensity of attachment with the person top of the hierarchy and that with the person second in the hierarchy is no greater than that between the second and third attachments (Stevens, 1975). It may be concluded that multiple attachments tend to have rather *similar* functions in spite of a persisting hierarchy away from them.

Attachment as a unitary concept

In most early writings on attachment there tended to be an implicit assumption that it constituted a unitary behaviour but it is now clear that it is not (Coates, Anderson and Hartup, 1972; Rosenthal, 1973; Stayton and Ainsworth, 1973). At least two distinctions need to be made.

First, there is the difference between the general tendency to seek attachments and the formation of selective bonds which are personal, social and reciprocal (Rutter, 1979b). The importance of this distinction is evident from both monkey and human studies. For example, the early attachments to inanimate objects shown by Harlow's monkeys did *not* lead on to normal social relationships as parent or peer attachments usually do (Harlow and Harlow, 1969; Ruppenthal, Arling, Harlow, Sackett and Suomi, 1976). Also, young children reared in institutions show *more* clinging and following than family-reared children but nevertheless they are *less* likely to show selective bonding or deep relationships (Tizard and Rees, 1975). The findings may mean that the processes involved are different or, more likely, that the nature of the attached object's *response* to the infant will influence the *quality* of the relationship formed and hence its function in relation to later development.

The second distinction is between secure and insecure bonding (Stayton and Ainsworth, 1973). It has often been assumed that the amount of distress on separation is an indicator of the strength of attachment (Schaffer, 1971), but it has been found that this measure does not necessarily agree with other indices of attachment. Thus, strong attachment (as shown by greeting or reunion together with following behaviour) may be accompanied by *less* crying or separation (Stayton and Ainsworth, 1973). It seems that the distress probably reflects *insecurity* of relationships as well as the presence of attachment. It is also pertinent that Hinde and Spencer-Booth (1970) showed that rhesus monkeys' distress after separation was strongly associated with prior maternal rejection and tension in the mother–infant relationship. In these circumstances, intense seeking of proximity may show a strong attachment but a weak secure base effect may reflect high insecurity. In any case, it is evident that the *quality* of attachments as well as their *strength* must be taken into account. Again, the nature of the reciprocal interaction with the infant is probably crucial in this connection.

FACTORS INFLUENCING ATTACHMENT

Because attachment does not constitute a unitary concept it is important in considering the possible factors influencing its development to take into account which aspect of attachment is being influenced by what. Unfortunately, most research reports do not make such distinctions and as a result some of the discussion will have to be somewhat speculative. It will also be necessary to differentiate between factors which influence the timing and intensity of attachment and those which influence the direction of attachments—i.e. to whom they develop.

Factors in the child

While it is evident that infants vary greatly in their characteristics and that the infant plays an important role in initiating and maintaining social interactions, relatively little is known on the nature of these individual features. Freedman (1965), studying a sample of twins, found evidence that smiling and visual fixation were to some extent under genetic control. He also found that Chinese-American babies differed from European-American babies in the ease with which they were comforted (Freedman and Freedman, 1969). Gottesman (1966) and Scarr (1969), in studies of much older individuals, also found evidence of a hereditary component in a factor of sociality. Schaffer and Emerson (1964) found that some infants resisted physical contact. These 'non-cuddlers' were somewhat delayed in their acquisition of attachments but they no longer differed from the cuddlers by age 18 months. Physical disabilities, such as blindness or lack of limbs, which interfere with social signalling may somewhat delay the formation of attachments (evidence on this point is lacking) but certainly they do not prevent bonding (DeCarie, 1969; Freedman, 1964). It is clear that a wide variety of social signals and responses may form the basis of personal interaction.

On the other hand, infants with a severe and general impairment of social signalling are likely both to inhibit parental social approaches and to be delayed in the development of attachments. Retrospective data indicates that this is what happens in the case of infantile autism (Schaffer, 1971; Rutter, 1978b).

Infant state

Quite apart from enduring characteristics of the child, the temporary condition of the child will influence the extent to which he shows attachment behaviour *at that time*. Thus, intense attachment is most likely to be seen when a child is tired, hungry, unwell, in pain or feeling cold (Bowlby, 1969; Maccoby and Masters, 1970). As every parent knows, children are very liable to be clinging and 'mummyish' at such times—wanting to sit on the parent's knee or be cuddled. Attachment behaviour is also increased by fear, anxiety, rebuffs or rejection. When frightened or upset young children tend to rush to a parent to be held. However, if the parent is absent, they will seek to be near whoever is present even if they do not know them (Rosenthal, 1967).

Object characteristics—animal studies

Experimental studies with monkeys (and other animals) provide useful evidence on the characteristics of objects which influence whether infants become attached to them. The principal conclusions are (i) whether or not the object provides food is irrelevant (Harlow and Zimmerman, 1959); (ii) a soft surface facilitates attachment (Harlow and Zimmerman, 1959); and (iii) movement increases the likelihood of attachment (Mason and Berkson, 1975). The effects of severe punishment and maltreatment are somewhat more complicated. First, several studies have clearly shown that maltreatment considerably *increases* attachment behaviour (*see* Harlow and Harlow, 1971 and Rajecki *et al.*, 1978). Thus, indulged and punished young dogs showed stronger attachment than dogs which were indulged but not punished. This is in keeping with the evidence that anxiety intensifies attachment (*see* above). On the other hand, if punished individuals are exposed to two objects only one of which punishes them they are more likely to become attached to the non-punishing object. However, even severe punishment does not prevent attachment occurring. The evidence is by no means clear-cut but the implication is that maltreatment (or stress) greatly increases attachment behaviour but, in these circumstances, if the individual has a 'choice', the less punishing object will be selected.

Institutional care

Several studies of human infants have shown that impersonal institutional rearing with little social interaction delays the acquisition of attachments. This was evident, for example, in Schaffer's (1963) comparison of the development of attachments on return home in infants from a hospital with low levels of interaction and those from a rather better residential nursery. Provence and Lipton (1962) also noted the impaired social responsiveness of institutional babies. Even in an institution with quite good levels of social stimulation, the dispersion of care among a large number of caretakers seems to delay the development of attachments (Stevens, 1975).

Parental characteristics

The main data on the parental characteristics which facilitate attachment are provided by naturalistic studies of parent–child interaction (*see* Ainsworth, 1973 and Bowlby, 1969). It is clear from all studies that feeding and physical caretaking are largely irrelevant in children's selection of attachment-figures. Children frequently develop attachments to adults who play no role in feeding or dressing them. It is also evident that the sheer amount of time in the presence of someone is irrelevant. Not only do children develop attachments to fathers who are out of the home at work all day but also it appears that in Israeli kibbutzim children are usually more strongly attached to their parents than to the nurse who looks after them during the day. On the other hand the amount of time in *active reciprocal interaction* with the child may be relevant. In this connection it is relevant that children in kibbutzim spend more time actively involved with their mother than with their nurse. Moreover, although fathers tend to spend less time than mothers in caretaking, they may be *more* likely to engage in physically stimulating play (Lamb, 1978a and b).

It is relevant, therefore, that studies are agreed in showing that attachments are most likely to develop to people who *actively* interact with the infant (whether in play, comforting or other activities). The *way* a person responds to the infant is also important. Children are most likely to become attached to people who are sensitive and responsive to their cues and signals. These same parental qualities seem to predispose to secure rather than anxious attachments (Blehar, Lieberman and Ainsworth, 1977).

It has been argued on the basis of naturalistic observations that rapid responses to a baby's crying are effective in reducing the amount of crying both immediately and later in the first year of life (Bell and Ainsworth, 1972). On the other hand, there are problems in the interpretation of these observations (Gewirtz and Boyd, 1977) and the findings from other studies have been different (Etzel and Gewirtz, 1967; Sander, 1969; Sander, Stechler, Burns and Julia, 1970) in showing that rapid responses may *increase* babies' crying, and in showing weak correlations between measures of responsiveness in the neonatal period and in later infancy (Dunn, 1975). It is evident that the conceptualization and measurement of 'sensitive responsiveness' continues to pose problems. Probably, optimal responsiveness does not consist of an unthinking and undiscriminating rushing to the baby every time it cries. Babies' cries are of several quite different kinds (*see* above) and it may be that it is the parents' ability to discriminate between these and to respond appropriately which is important. The mode and style of response must be considered as well as the matter of whether there is any response at all. Moreover, as judged by the findings on the reciprocal nature of early parent–child interaction (described above) it seems likely that the way the parent responds to the baby's *positive* signals (smiling, gurgling, babbling, cuddling) may also be important.

Fear of strangers

It has long been observed that about the same time as infants first develop attachments they also first show fear of strangers (so-called 'eight months anxiety'). Spitz (1965) has argued that the two are causally related. However, the empirical evidence suggests that this view is mistaken (Bowlby, 1969). In the first place, in individual children the two do not necessarily develop together; fear of strangers may antedate or postdate the development of attachments. Secondly, fear of strangers is not synonymous with separation anxiety, as shown by the fact that fear may be shown even in the presence of the child's mother (Morgan and Ricciuti, 1969). Moreover, at least in dogs (Scott and Bronson, 1964; Davis *et al.*, 1977), it appears that separation-anxiety and fear reactions can be differentiated behaviourally.

ATTACHMENT AND LATER SOCIAL RELATIONSHIPS

Although there has been a great deal of research on the acquisition of attachments during the infancy period, much less attention has been paid to the course of social development during the middle and later years of childhood. Most writers have suggested that early bonding is likely in some way to constitute the basis for the acquisition of later personal relationships (*see e.g.* Bowlby, 1969; Rutter, 1978a), but there are few empirical data on how far and in what way this is in fact the case.

What is known is that as they grow older children become less closely tied to their parents in the sense that they move away from them more readily and tolerate separations more easily. Thus, Rheingold and Eckerman (1970) studied children aged 1 to 4 years and noted how far they crawled or walked from their mother when left in a large experimental room with her. There was considerable individual variation but the average distance the child went away from the mother rose from 7 metres at 1 year to 15 metres at 2 years and 21 metres at 4 years. Similarly, Shirley and Poyntz (1941) found that at age 2 to 3 years about half the children studied were distressed on separating from their mothers; by $4\frac{1}{2}$ to 5 years the proportion had dropped to one child in five and by age $6\frac{1}{2}$ to 7 years very few children were distressed on separation. Other studies have shown much the same pattern of increasing independence and tolerance of separation (*see* Rheingold and Eckerman, 1970; Bowlby, 1973). However, the meaning of these observations is less certain. Schaffer (1971) described the phenomena in terms of a weakening of bonds and the development of detachment but this may be misleading. As children grow older they become better able to appreciate continuities over time and to realize that, even though they are not at that moment with their parents, nevertheless their parents are still there. Perhaps in this way they become better able to

maintain an enduring bond throughout a period of separation. The strength of a bond is probably better assessed in terms of its power to reduce anxiety in a frightening situation than in terms of the degree of separation-protest (Rutter, 1978a). Unfortunately, the varying strength of bonds as children grow older has not been studied in this way. It is certainly clear that older children are much less upset by separations but this does *not* necessarily mean that the bonds are any weaker. To the contrary, perhaps they are more secure and effective. The empirical data needed to test the various competing possibilities are not yet available.

Two studies (Main, 1973; Matas *et al.*, 1978) have examined the links between measures of attachment in infancy and the qualities of social behaviour six to nine months later. Securely attached infants were found to be more sociable and cheerful than those who had been weakly or insecurely attached. However, the findings refer to a very short period of follow-up and the data allow no conclusions about causal relationships with respect to early bonding.

The issue of how far early selective bonds provide the basis for later social development may also be studied by examining what happens to children with impaired early bonding. Data on this point are provided by Tizard's (Tizard, 1977; Tizard and Hodges, 1978) and Dixon's (1979) studies of children reared in institutions with multiple caretakers.

Tizard (Tizard and Rees, 1975; Tizard and Tizard, 1971) found that, at 2 years, institution-reared children were both more clinging and more diffuse in their attachments than children brought up in ordinary families. At 4 years the institutional children were still more clinging and less likely to have deep attachments than other children. In addition they now tended to be overfriendly with strangers, and unduly attention-seeking. By 8 years less than half the institutional children were said to be closely attached to their housemothers and still they tended to seek affection more than other children. At school the institutional children were more attention-seeking, restless, disobedient and unpopular than family-reared controls.

Dixon (1979) also studied the school behaviour of children reared in institutions from the first year of life. Her interview and questionnaire findings were closely comparable to those obtained by Tizard. Again, the institution-reared children were more disruptive and attention-seeking, they fought more with other children and tended to be less liked by their peers. Systematic time-sampled observations in the classroom confirmed that the institutional children's social interactions were less successful in the sense that they were more likely to behave in unacceptable ways, calling out in class and disregarding teachers' directions. Also they showed more 'off-task' behaviour in the classroom.

It seems probable that this inept social behaviour was a consequence of the children's relative lack of selective bonding in infancy (due in turn to a pattern of upbringing in which each child experienced as many as 50 to 80 caretakers). It is important, in this connection, that Dixon

(1979) found that this pattern of maladaptive social behaviour was much less frequent among foster children born to similarly disadvantaged parents. The fact that the foster children had experienced a stable upbringing in a nuclear family seems to have facilitated their social development.

Of course, the meaning of the institutional children's attention-seeking behaviour remains uncertain. For example, do they lack fundamental social qualities or rather have they merely learned patterns of interaction which were adaptive in the institution but maladaptive in other settings? Similarly, knowledge is lacking on how far the social difficulties at age 8 years are likely to be fore-runners of impaired personality functioning in adulthood.

Monkey studies are also relevant in considering the sequelae of an early failure to form adequate reciprocal bonds. The studies from the Wisconsin laboratory (*see* Ruppenthal *et al.*, 1976 for an overview) clearly indicate the long-lasting effects of early social isolation. The isolated monkeys not only showed gross social and behavioural disturbance during the pre-pubertal years but also they exhibited deviant sexual relationships and markedly impaired parenting (such that the offspring of the isolated mothers were maltreated and sometimes killed). A degree of social recovery in adolescence and adult life has proved possible in some cases (*see* Rutter and Madge, 1976) but the monkeys have remained abnormal to varying degrees in their social, sexual and parenting relationships. The findings certainly suggest important continuities between these different forms of relationship spanning the period from infancy to maturity. However, it is difficult to draw precise conclusions on the nature of the links in view of the rather generalized disturbance resulting from the severe (and unbiological) isolation experienced by the monkeys.

Sensitive periods

Various writers have argued for the existence of some kind of sensitive period for the development of attachments, such that normal bonding is increasingly difficult thereafter. Thus, Hales *et al.* (1977) suggest that mothers have a sensitive period, which lasts only a matter of hours after birth, during which attachment to the neonate develops. Hess (1973), similarly, has maintained that attachment may have a critical period like that which supposedly exists for imprinting in birds. Bowlby (1969), although not proposing such a sharply demarcated period, has also suggested that first bonds need to develop during infancy if normal social relationships are to be possible later. In fact, the notion of an invariant narrowly defined period for imprinting does not stand up to scrutiny even with precocial birds (Bateson, 1974). On the other hand, it is still possible that optimal social development requires that certain events should occur during the early years of life.

There is no doubt that environmental improvement in middle or later childhood can lead to marked social improvement and that a good home in the early years does not prevent damage from psychosocial stresses later (*see*

Clarke and Clarke, 1976; Rutter 1979). Nevertheless, Tizard and Hodges' (1978) findings on late adopted children are consistent with the possibility of a sensitive period for fully normal early socialization. They showed that even children adopted after the age of 4 years usually developed deep relationships with their adoptive parents. As this was so for a few children who had not appeared closely attached to anyone while they were in the institutions, it seems that first bonds can develop as late as 4 to 6 years. However, in spite of this, the late adopted children showed the same social and attentional problems in school as those who had remained in the institution (although the adopted children appeared more normal at home). It may be that although attachments can still develop after infancy, *optimal* social development is nevertheless dependent on early bonding. As the children have only been studied so far up to age 8 years, it is still too early to know whether this is so.

Friendships and intimate relationships in adult life

The course of development of friendships during childhood is described in Chapter 23. It is clear that poor peer relationships are associated with a variety of later problems and disorders (*see also* Rutter, 1978a). Relatively little is known about the role of parent–child ties during the middle years of childhood except that family disharmony is strongly associated with disorders of conduct (Rutter, 1971). This is so even when there have been no parent–child separations or family disruptions. A good (warm and non-critical) relationship with one parent provides an important protective factor in these circumstances. The findings suggest the importance of a close and supportive relationship but evidence is lacking on how far or in what way this is associated with infantile bonding. There is also some indication that good family relationships tend to be associated with high self-esteem and sound social functioning during adolescence but the data are meagre (*see* Bowlby, 1973).

It is also clear that deep attachments and loving bonds are an important feature of adult life. It is not just that such relationships are a universal feature of normal adult life (which they are) but also that they seem to serve a crucial role in maintaining emotional equilibrium (Henderson, 1977).

This is shown by several rather different kinds of observation. First, it is well established that the death of a parent or spouse constitutes a significant precipitant of depressive disorder and of suicide in adults (Bunch, 1972; Parkes, 1972). Death of a spouse also markedly increases the likelihood of the surviving marriage partner's death from natural causes during the following year (Young *et al.*, 1963; Rees and Lutkins, 1967). Secondly, many investigations have demonstrated that the onset of depression in adult life is frequently preceded by acute life stresses (*see* e.g. Paykel *et al.*, 1969; Brown *et al.*, 1975). These stresses may involve a variety of events, but those involving the loss of an important relationship (by death, moving away, or rebuff) are prominent among those associated with depression. Third, a lack of close confiding relationships seems to predispose women to depression (Brown *et al.*, 1975; Roy, 1978; Henderson *et al.*, 1978). In short, there is abundant evidence that social bonds continue to play an important role throughout the whole of life. In many respects these adult ties seem to share many of the properties of infantile attachments but systematic comparisons are lacking.

Little is known about the extent of links between bonding experiences in early childhood and the quality of social relationships in adulthood. Some kind of developmental continuity is circumstantially suggested by the evidence that early parental loss predisposes to depression in adult life (Brown *et al.*, 1975, 1977; Roy, 1978), but the mechanisms involved remain ill-understood. Brown and Harris (1978) have argued that parental loss operates by making people less able to cope with life stresses and hence more likely to develop depression as a consequence of stress, but there are difficulties in adequately testing the interactive effects required for such a vulnerability model (Tennant and Bebbington, 1978).

THEORIES OF ATTACHMENT

The development of attachments has attracted the attention and interest of many theorists and there are a wide variety of quite disparate explanations of attachment behaviour (*see* Rajecki *et al.*, 1978 for a good summary and appraisal). Some, although historically important, no longer warrant serious attention in view of the mass of findings inconsistent with the theory. Thus, Lorenz' (1937) original view of imprinting has had to be greatly modified in the light of research data; Freud's (1946) notion that object relations develop on the basis of feeding and Dollard and Miller's (1950) view of attachment as the result of secondary reinforcement are both inconsistent with the findings showing the irrelevance of feeding and physical caretaking; Schneirla's (1965) epigenetic model lacks empirical support; and Scott's (1971) concept that attachment develops as a response to separation is out of keeping with research findings.

Bowlby (1969) and Ainsworth (1973) have both suggested that infants are born with a biological propensity to behave in ways which promote proximity and contact with their mother-figure. According to their view, attachment then develops as a consequence of parental responsiveness to these innate behaviours during a sensitive period in the first years of life. In this way attachment is seen as a specific phenomenon which differs qualitatively from dependency.

Gewirtz (1961; 1972), in contrast, argues that both develop as a result of differential reinforcement, the difference being simply that positive stimulus control is restricted to a particular person (rather than to a class of objects) in the case of attachment. Cairns (1966), on the other hand, proposes a contiguity conditioning process which does not rely on any rewarding properties of the attached-object. In his view, attachment occurs because a proximate relationship with a salient object predisposes

to conditioning. Hoffman and Ratner (1973) suggest a somewhat different form of conditioning model and Solomon and Corbit (1974) and Salzen (1978) posit a more central role for the child's emotional state.

Theorists are agreed on several crucial issues. Firstly, the process of bonding obviously involves a *reciprocal* interaction between infant and parent in which *both* play an active role (*see e.g.* Bowlby, 1969; Cairns, 1977; Gewirtz and Boyd, 1976). Secondly, maturational as well as environmental factors are important in determining *when* bonding occurs. Thus, the development of selective attachment necessarily presupposes that the child can differentiate between people and has a repertoire of social signals and responses. However, while this is a necessary condition it is not a sufficient one as bonding does not occur until some weeks or months later and may be even further delayed if the environment lacks adequate social opportunities. Thirdly, attachment clearly develops as a result of some form of social learning. Moreover, differential reinforcement manifestly plays an important role in determining the patterning of social interactions (Hinde and Stevenson-Hinde, 1976).

Dispute mainly centres on the question of how far bonding is a process which is qualitatively distinct from other forms of social learning and on the nature and importance of possible innate propensities. Five key observations demand explanation and together these pose problems for all of the theories. First, there is the secure base effect—the fact that the presence of an attachment object makes it more likely that the infant will move *away* and explore. Ainsworth and Bowlby's ethological model accounts best for the phenomenon but it is not at all clear from their theory why inanimate objects should serve this purpose. The various learning theories can only account for the behaviour by making several assumptions that do not arise directly from the theories.

Second, there is the consistent observation that attachment still develops in the face of maltreatment and severe punishment. Ethological theory correctly predicts that stress should enhance attachment behaviour but Bowlby (1969) and Lamb's (1978) emphasis on the importance of an 'appropriate' parental response does not seem to fit easily with the findings. Cairn's contiguity conditioning theory is in keeping but it is difficult to see how Gewirtz' reinforcement model could satisfactorily account for the observations.

Third, there is the observation that attachments develop to inanimate objects. In this instance, the monkey data and human observations seem to be somewhat in conflict. Socially isolated monkeys readily develop attachments to cloth surrogates but it has been found that institutional children (who show impaired human attachments) do not. Indeed it seems that institutional children are *less* likely than family-reared children to be attached to blankets and cuddly toys. On the Bowlby-Ainsworth theory it is easy to see how strongly attached children might 'generalize' their attachments to inanimate objects. On the other hand, if there is a strong biological propensity to seek attachments (as they suggest) it is not at all clear why institutional children do not use cuddly blankets when they lack adequate human bonds. Of course, it might be suggested that the inanimate objects gain their bonding properties through association with the mother (in learning theory terms) or because of their symbolic link with the mother (in psychodynamic terms). This might explain the occurrence in normal children and its lack in institutional children but it does not account for the animal observations, or for the fact that many normal children do *not* become attached to inanimate objects, or for the observation that autistic children (who lack attachments to their parents) show attachments to (usually non-soft) inanimate objects (Marchant, Howlin, Yule and Rutter, 1974). It may be that the mechanisms involved in these different cases are different but, so far, the observations are not well explained by any of the theories.

Fourth, it is necessary to account for the finding that whereas anxiety *inhibits* play it *intensifies* attachment. This is exactly what the Bowlby–Ainsworth theory predicts. The phenomenon in normal individuals is also readily explicable in social learning terms in view of the very different responses elicited by infants in the two situations. On the other hand, it is less obvious in reinforcement terms why the attachment effect should apply to inanimate objects.

Fifth, there are the observations which suggest that not all forms of attachment are equivalent. In particular, it is necessary to explain why the monkey attachments to cloth surrogates do not lead on to normal social relationships in the way that parent and (to a lesser extent) peer attachments usually do. The distinction between secure and insecure attachment has also to be accounted for. In both instances the nature of the attached-object's response to the infant seems crucial. Social learning provides an adequate explanation as part of most of the main theories but the findings are out of keeping with a mechanistic imprinting view.

It may be concluded that none of the theories fully accounts for all the phenomena and theoretical closure is not yet possible. The widespread occurrence of attachment in many animal species certainly suggests some kind of biological propensity, as the ethological theory suggests. Also, as suggested by almost all theories, social learning plays a major role in the process of bonding and in determining the characteristics of the parent–child relationship. However, several crucial questions have still to receive satisfactory answers.

CONCLUSION

Human beings are very much social creatures and the growth of social relationships constitutes a crucial and, in some respects, central feature of human development. The origins of social behaviour are already present in early infancy and it seems likely that the process of attachment and bonding represents an essential beginning for socialization. However, there is a great deal still to be learned concerning the links between attachments in the early years, friendships in middle childhood, and marital (or other) bondings in adult life. Few workers doubt that some kind of links exist but sound data are lacking on the mechanisms and processes involved after the early years of childhood.

REFERENCES

Ahrens, R. (1954). Beitrag zur Entwicklung der Physiognomie-und Mimikerkennes. *Z. exp. angew. Psychol.*, **2**, 412–454.

Ainsworth, M. D. S. (1967). *Infancy in Uganda: Infant Care and the Growth of Attachment*. Baltimore, Md.: Johns Hopkins Press.

Ainsworth, M. D. S. (1973). The development of infant–mother attachment. In B. M. Caldwell and H. N. Ricciuti (Eds.) *Review of Child Development Research, Vol. 3*. Chicago: University of Chicago Press.

Ainsworth, M. D. S. and Wittig, B. A. (1969). Attachment and exploratory behaviour of one year olds in a strange situation. In B. M. Foss (Ed.) *Determinants of Infant Behaviour, Vol. 4*. London: Methuen.

Ambrose, J. A. (1961), The development of the smiling response in early infancy. In B. M. Foss (Ed.) *Determinants of Infant Behaviour, Vol. 1*, London: Methuen.

Ambrose, J. A. (1969), Discussion contribution. In J. A. Ambrose (Ed.) *Stimulation in Early Infancy*. London: Academic Press.

Ames, E. W. and Silfen, C. K. (1965). Methodological issues in the study of age differences in infants' attention to stimuli varying in movement and complexity. Paper to the Society for Research in Child Development, Minneapolis.

Anderson, J. W. (1972). Attachment behaviour out of doors. In N. Blurton-Jones (Ed.) *Ethological Studies of Child Behaviour*. Cambridge: Cambridge University Press.

Arsenian, J. M. (1943). Young children in an insecure situation. *J. Abn. Soc. Psychol.*, **38**, 225–249.

Banks, J. H. and Wolfson, J. H. (1967). Differential cardiac response of infants to mother and stranger. Paper to the Eastern Psychological Association, Philadelphia, cited Schaffer, 1971.

Bateson, P. P. G. (1974). The nature of learning. *Science*, **183**, 740–741.

Bell, S. M. and Ainsworth, M. D. S. (1972). Infant crying and maternal responsiveness. *Child Develop.*, **43**, 1171–1190.

Blauvelt, H. and McKenna, J. (1961). Mother-neonate interaction: capacity of the human newborn for orientation. In B. M. Foss (Ed.) *Determinants of Infant Behaviour, Vol. 1*. London: Methuen.

Blehar, M. C., Lieberman, A. F. and Ainsworth, M. D. S. (1977). Early face-to-face interaction and its relation to later infant–mother attachment. *Child Develop.*, **48**, 182–194.

Bowlby, J. (1951). *Maternal Care and Mental Health*. Geneva: World Health Organization.

Bowlby, J. (1969). *Attachment and Loss, Vol. 1, Attachment*. London: Hogarth Press.

Bowlby, J. (1973). *Attachment and Loss, Vol. 2, Separation, Anxiety and Anger*. London: Hogarth Press.

Brackbill, Y. (1958). Extinction of the smiling response in infants as a function of reinforcement schedule. *Child Develop.*, **29**, 115–124.

Brackbill, Y. (1971). The cumulative effect of continuous stimulation on arousal level in infants. *Child Develop.*, **42**, 17–26.

Brackbill, Y., Adams, G., Crowell, D. H. and Gray, M. L. (1966). Arousal level in neonates and preschool children under continuous auditory stimulation. *J. exp. child Psychol.*, **4**, 178–188.

Brazelton, T. B., Tronick, E., Adamson, L., Als, H. and Weise, S. (1975). Early mother–infant reciprocity. In R. Porter and M. O'Connor (Eds.) *Parent–Infant Interaction*. Ciba Foundation Symposium 33 (New series). Amsterdam: Associated Scientific Publishers.

Brennan, W. M., Ames, E. W. and Moore, R. W. (1966). Age differences in infants' attention to patterns of different complexities. *Science*, **151**, 354–355.

Brown, G. W., Bhrolchain, M. N. and Harris, T. (1975). Social class and psychiatric disturbance among women in an urban population. *Sociology*, **9**, 225–254.

Brown, G. W. and Harris, T. (1978). *Social Origins of Depression: A Study of Psychiatric Disorder in Women*. London: Tavistock.

Brown, G. W., Harris, T. and Copeland, J. R. (1977). Depression and loss. *Brit. J. Psychiat.*, **130**, 1–18.

Brown, J. V. and Bateman, R. (1978). Relationships of human mothers with their infants during the first year of life: effects of prematurity. In R. W. Bell and W. P. Smotherman (Eds.) *Maternal Influences and Early Behaviour*. Holliswood, NY: Spectrum.

Bunch, J. (1972). Recent bereavement in relation to suicide. *J. Psychosom. Res.*, **16**, 361–366.

Burlingham, D. and Freud, A. (1944). *Infants without Families*. London: Allen and Unwin.

Cairns, R. B. (1966). Development, maintenance, and extinction of social attachment behavior in sheep. *J. comp. physiol. Psychol.*, **62**, 298–306.

Cairns, R. B. (1977). Beyond social attachment: the dynamics of interactional development. In T. Alloway, P. Pliner and L. Krames (Eds.) *Advances in the Study of Communication and Affect, Vol. 3*. New York, Plenum.

Caldwell, B. M. (1965). Visual and emotional reactions of an infant to his mother and other adult females. Paper to the Tavistock Study Group on Mother–Infant Interaction, London, cited Schaffer, 1971.

Call, J. D. (1964). Newborn approach behavior and early ego development. *Int. J. Psycho-Anal.*, **45**, 286–294.

Clarke, A. M. and Clarke, A. D. B. (Eds.) (1976). *Early Experience: Myth and Evidence*. London: Open Books.

Clarke-Stewart, K. A. (1973). Interactions between mothers and their young children: characteristics and consequences. Monographs of the Society for Research in Child Development, **38**, Serial No. 153.

Clarke-Stewart, K. A. (1977). The father's impact on mother and child. Paper to the Society for Research into Child Development, New Orleans.

Coates, B., Anderson, E. P. and Hartup, W. W. (1972). Interrelations in the attachment behavior of human infants. *Develop. Psychol.*, **6**, 218–230.

Cohen, L. J. and Campos, J. J. (1974). Father, mother and stranger as elicitors of attachment behaviors in infancy. *Develop. Psychol.*, **10**, 146–154.

Condon, W. S. and Sander, L. W. (1974). Speech: interactional participation and language acquisition. *Science*, **183**, 99–101.

Corter, C. M. (1973). A comparison of the mother's and a stranger's control over the behavior of infants. *Child Develop.*, **44**, 705–713.

Cox, F. N. and Campbell, D. (1968). Young children in a new situation with and without their mothers. *Child Develop.*, **39**, 123–131.

Davis, K. C., Gurski, J. C. and Scott, J. P. (1977). Interaction of separation distress with fear in infant dogs. *Develop. Psychobiol.*, **10**, 203–212.

DeCarie, T. G. (1969). A study of the mental and emotional development of the thalidomide child. In B. M. Foss (Ed.) *Determinants of Infant Behaviour, Vol. 4*. London: Methuen.

Dixon, P. (1979). Paper in preparation.

Dodd, B. (1972). Effects of social and vocal stimulation in infant babbling. *Develop. Psychol.*, **7**, 80–83.

Dollard, J. and Miller, N. E. (1950). *Personality and Psychotherapy*. New York: McGraw-Hill.

Dunn, J. (1975). Consistency and change in styles of mothering. In R. Porter and M. O'Connor (Eds.) *Parent–Infant Interaction*. Ciba Foundation Symposium 33 (New Series). Amsterdam: Associated Scientific Publishers.

Eckerman, C. O., Whatley, J. L. and Katz, S. L. (1975). Growth of social play with peers during the second year of life. *Develop. Psychol.*, **11**, 42–49.

Etzel, B. C. and Gewirtz, J. L. (1967). Experimental modification of caretaker-maintained high rate operant crying in a 6- and a 20-week old infant (Infans tyrannotearus): extinction of crying with reinforcement of eye contact and smiling. *J. Exper. Child Psychol.*, **5**, 303–313.

Fagin, C. M. R. N. (1966). *The Effects of Maternal Attendance During Hospitalization on the Post-Hospital Behavior of Young Children: A comparative study*. Philadelphia: Davis.

Fantz, R. L. (1965). Visual perception from birth as shown by pattern selectivity. *Ann. New York Acad. Sci.*, **118**, 793–814.

Fantz, R. L. (1966). Pattern discrimination and selective attention as determinants of perceptual development from birth. In A. H. Kidd and J. L. Rivoire (Eds.) *Perceptual Development in Children*. New York: International Universities Press.

Fantz, R. L. and Nevis, S. (1967). Pattern preferences and perceptual-cognitive development in early infancy. *Merrill-Palmer Q.*, **13**, 77–108.

Feldman, S. S. and Ingham, M. E. (1975). Attachment behavior: A validation study in two age groups. *Child Develop.*, **46**, 319–330.

Fitzgerald, H. E. (1968). Autonomic pupillary reflex activity during early infancy, and its relation to social and nonsocial visual stimuli. *J. exp. Child Psychol.*, **5**, 470–482.

Fleener, D. E. and Cairns, R. B. (1970). Attachment behaviors in human infants: discriminative vocalization on maternal separation. *Develop. Psychol.*, **2**, 215–223.

Freedman, D. A. (1964). Smiling in blind infants and the issue of innate v. acquired. *J. Child Psychol. Psychiat.*, **5**, 171–184.

Freedman, D. A. (1965). Hereditary control of early social behaviour. In B. M. Foss (Ed.) *Determinants of Infant Behaviour, Vol. 3*. London: Methuen.

Freedman, D. A. and Freedman, N. (1969). Behavioural differences between Chinese-American and European-American newborns. *Nature*, **224**, 1227.

Freud, A. (1946). *The Psycho-analytical Treatment of Children*. London: Imago; New York: International Universities Press, 1959.

Freud, A. and Dann, S. (1951). An experiment in group upbringing. *Psychoanal. Study Child*, **6**, 127–168.

Gewirtz, J. L. (1961). A learning analysis of the effects of normal stimulation, privation and deprivation on the acquisition of social motivation and attachment. In B. M. Foss (Ed.) *Determinants of Infant Behaviour, Vol. 1*. London: Methuen.

Gewirtz, J. L. (1965). The course of infant smiling in four child-rearing environments in Israel. In B. M. Foss (Ed.) *Determinants of Infant Behaviour, Vol. 3*. London: Methuen.

Gewirtz, J. L. (Ed.) (1972). *Attachment and Dependency*. Washington: Winston.

Gewirtz, J. L. and Boyd, E. F. (1976). Mother–infant interaction and its study. In H. W. Reese (Ed.) *Advances in Child Development and Behavior, Vol. 11*. New York: Academic Press.

Gewirtz, J. L. and Boyd, E. F. (1977). Does maternal responding imply reduced infant crying?: A critique of the 1972 Bell and Ainsworth report. *Child Develop.*, **48**, 1200–1207.

Gottesman, I. I. (1966). Genetic variation in adaptive personality tests. *J. Child Psychol. Psychiat.*, **7**, 199–208.

Haith, M. (1966). The response of the human newborn to visual movement. *J. exp. Child Psychol.*, **3**, 235–243.

Hales, D. J., Lozoff, B., Sosa, R. and Kennell, J. H. (1977). Defining the limits of the maternal sensitive period. *Develop. Med. Child Neurol.*, **19**, 454–461.

Harlow, H. F. (1969). Age-mate or peer affectional systems. In D. S. Lehrman, R. A. Hinde and E. Shaw (Eds.) *Advances in the Study of Behaviour, Vol. 2*. New York: Academic Press.

Harlow, H. F. and Harlow, M. K. (1969). Effects of various mother–infant relationships on rhesus monkey behaviours. In B. M. Foss (Ed.) *Determinants of Infant Behaviour, Vol. 4*. London: Methuen.

Harlow, H. F. and Harlow, M. K. (1971). Psychopathology in monkeys. In H. D. Kimmel (Ed.) *Experimental Psychopathology*. New York: Academic Press.

Harlow, H. F. and Harlow, M. K. (1972). The affectional systems. In A. Schrier, H. F. Harlow and F. Stollnitz (Eds.) *Behavior in Non-Human Primates, Vol. 2*. New York: Academic Press.

Harlow, H. F. and Zimmermann, R. R. (1959). Affectional responses in the infant monkey. *Science*, **130**, 421–432.

Hartup, W. W. (1978). Peer relations and the growth of social competence. In M. W. Kent and J. E. Rolf (Eds.) *The Primary Prevention of Psychopathology, Vol. 3, Social Competence in Children*. Hanover, N. H., University Press of New England.

Heathers, G. (1955). Emotional dependence and independence in nursery school play. *J. Genet. Psychol.*, **87**, 37–57.

Heinicke, C. M. and Westheimer, I. J. (1965). *Brief Separations*. London: Longmans.

Henderson, S. (1977). The social network, support and neurosis: the function of attachments in adult life. *Brit. J. Psychiat.*, **131**, 185–191.

Henderson, S., Duncan-Jones, P., McAuley, H. and Ritchie, K. (1978). The patient's primary group. *Brit. J. Psychiat.*, **132**, 74–86.

Hess, E. H. (1973). *Imprinting*. New York: Van Nostrand.

Hetzer, H. and Ripin, R. (1930). Frühestes Lernen des Säuglings in der Ernährungssituation. *Z. Psychol.* **118.**

Hetzer, H. and Tudor-Hart, B. H. (1927). Die frühesten Reaktionen auf die menschliche Stimme. *Quell. Stud. Jugenkinde*, **5.**

Hinde, R. A. and Spencer-Booth, Y. (1970). Individual differences in the responses of rhesus monkeys to a period of separation from their mothers. *J. Child Psychol. Psychiat.*, **11,** 159–176.

Hinde, R. A. and Stevenson-Hinde, J. (1976). Towards understanding relationships: dynamic stability. In P. P. G. Bateson and R. A. Hinde (Eds.) *Growing Points in Ethology*. Cambridge: Cambridge University Press.

Hoffman, H. S. and Ratner, A. M. (1973). A reinforcement model of imprinting: Implications for socialisation in monkeys and men. *Psychol. Rev.*, **80,** 527–544.

Hutt, S. J., Hutt, C., Lenard, H. G., Bernuth, H. V. and Muntjewerff, W. J. (1968). Auditory responsivity in the human neonate. *Nature,* **218,** 888–890.

Karmel, B. Z. (1969). The effects of age, complexity and amount of contour on pattern preferences in human infants. *J. exp. Child Psychol.*, **7,** 339–354.

Kennell, J., Trause, M. A. and Klaus, M. H. (1975). Evidence for a sensitive period in the human mother. *In* R. Porter and M. O'Connor (Eds.) *Parent–Infant Interaction*. Ciba Foundation Symposium 33 (New Series). Amsterdam: Associated Scientific Publishers.

Kissel, S. (1965). Stress-reducing properties of social stimuli. *J. Pers. Soc. Psychol.*, **2,** 378–384.

Klaus, M., Jerauld, R., Kreger, N., McAlpine, W., Steffa, M. and Kennell, J. (1972). Maternal attachment—importance of the first post-partum days. *N. Engl. J. Med.*, **286,** 460–463.

Korner, A. F. and Grobstein, R. (1966). Visual alertness as related to soothing in neonates: implications for maternal stimulation and early deprivation. *Child Develop.*, **37,** 867–876.

Kotelchuck, M. (1976). The infant's relationship to the father: experimental evidence. In M. E. Lamb (Ed.) *The Role of the Father in Child Development*. New York: Wiley.

Lamb, M. E. (1977a). Father–infant and mother–infant interaction in the first year of life. *Child Develop.*, **48,** 167–181.

Lamb, M. E. (1977b). The development of mother–infant and father–infant attachments in the second year of life. *Develop. Psychol.*, **13,** 637–648.

Lamb, M. E. (1978a). Qualitative aspects of mother– and father–infant attachments. *Infant Behav. Develop.*, **1** (in press).

Lamb, M. E. (1978b). Father–infant relationships: their nature and importance. *Youth and Society* (in press).

Leiderman, P. H. and Seashore, M. J. (1975). Mother–infant neonatal separation: some delayed consequences. In R. Porter and M. O'Connor (Eds.) *Parent–Infant Interaction*. Ciba Foundation Symposium 33 (New Series). Amsterdam: Associated Scientific Publishers.

Levy, D. M. (1958). *Behavioral Analysis: Analysis of Clinical Observations of Behavior as Applied to Mother–Newborn Relationships*. Springfield, Ill.: Charles C. Thomas.

Lewis, M. (1969). A developmental study of information processing within the first three years of life: response decrement to a redundant signal. *Monogr. Soc. Res. Child Develop.*, **34,** no. 9 (whole no. 133).

Lewis, M. and Rosenblum, L. A. (Eds.) (1974). *The Effect of the Infant on its Caregiver*. New York: John Wiley.

Lorenz, K. (1937). Über die Bildung des Instinktbegriffes. Naturwissenschaften, **25.** Eng. trsn. 'The Establishment of the Instinct Concept'. In Lorenz, *Studies in Animal and Human Behaviour*, Vol. 1., 1937. Trans. by R. Martin. London: Methuen, 1970.

MacCarthy, D., Lindsay, M. and Morris, I. (1962). Children in hospital with mothers. *Lancet*, **1,** 603–608.

Maccoby, E. E. and Feldman, S. S. (1972). Mother-attachment and stranger reactions in the third year of life. *Monogr. Soc. Res. Child Develop.*, **37,** Serial no. 146.

Maccoby, E. E. and Masters, J. C. (1970). Attachment and dependency. In P. H. Mussen (Ed.) *Carmichael's Manual of Child Psychology*, 3rd edition. New York: John Wiley.

Main, M. (1973). *Exploration, Play and Cognitive Functioning as Related to Mother–Child Attachment*. Unpublished Ph.D. Thesis, Johns Hopkins University. Cited by Bowlby, 1973.

Marchant, R., Howlin, P., Yule, W. and Rutter, M. (1974). Graded change in the treatment of the behaviour of autistic children. *J. Child Psychol. Psychiat.*, **15,** 221–228.

Mason, W. A. and Berkson, G. (1975). Effects of maternal motility on the development of rocking and other behaviors in rhesus monkeys: a study with artificial mothers. *Develop. Psychobiol.*, **8,** 197–211.

Matas, L., Arend, R. A. and Sroufe, L. A. (1978). Continuity of adaptation in the second year: the relationship between quality of attachment and later competence. *Child Develop.* **49,** 547–556.

Mićić, Z. (1962). Psychological stress in children in hospital. *Int. Nurs. Rev.*, **9,** 23–31.

Morgan, G. A. and Ricciuti, H. N. (1969). Infants' responses to strangers during the first year. In B. M. Foss (Ed.) *Determinants of Infant Behaviour, Vol. 4*. London: Methuen.

Moss, H. A. and Robson, K. (1968). Maternal influences in early social visual behavior. *Child Develop.*, **39,** 401–408.

Newton, H. R. (1951). The relationship between infant feeding experience and later behavior. *J. Pediatrics,* **38,** 28–40.

Parkes, C. M. (1972). *Bereavement: Studies of Grief in Adult Life*. London: Tavistock; New York: International Universities Press.

Passman, R. H. (1977). Providing attachment objects to facilitate learning and reduce distress: Effects of mothers and security blankets. *Develop. Psychol.*, **13,** 25–28.

Passman, R. H. and Weisberg, P. (1975). Mothers and blankets as agents for promoting play and exploration by young children in a novel environment: the effects of social and nonsocial objects. *Develop. Psychol.*, **11,** 170–177.

Patterson, F. G., Bonvillian, J. D., Reynolds, P. C. and Maccoby, E. E. (1975). Mother and peer attachment under conditions of fear in rhesus monkeys (macaca mulatta). *Primates,* **16,** 75–81.

Paykel, E. S., Myers, J. K., Dienelt, M. N., Klerman, C. L., Lindenthal, L. J. and Pepper, M. P. (1969). Life events and depression: a controlled study. *Arch. gen. Psychiat.*, **21,** 753–760.

Prechtl, H. F. R. (1958). The directed head turning response and allied movements of the human baby. *Behaviour,* **13,** 212–242.

Provence, S. and Lipton, R. C. (1962). *Infants in Institutions: A Comparison of their Development with Family-Reared Infants during the First Year of Life*. New York: International Universities Press.

Rajeki, D. W., Lamb, M. E. and Obmascher, P. (1978). Toward a general theory of infantile attachment: A comparative review of aspects of the social bond. *Behav. Brain Sciences,* **1,** 417–464.

Rees, W. D. and Lutkins, S. G. (1967). Mortality of bereavement. *Brit. med. J.,* **4,** 13–16.

Rheingold, H. L. and Eckerman, C. O. (1970). The infant separates himself from his mother. *Science,* **168,** 78–83.

Rheingold, H. L., Gewirtz, J. L. and Ross, H. W. (1959). Social conditioning of vocalizations in the infants. *J. comp. physiol. Psychol.*, **52,** 68–73.

Robertson, J. and Bowlby, J. (1952). Responses of young children to separation from their mothers. *Courr. Cent. int. Enf.*, **2,** 131–142.

Robertson, J. and Robertson, J. (1971). Young children in brief separations: a fresh look. *Psychoanal. Study Child*, **26,** 264–315.

Rosenblum, L. A. and Harlow, H. F. (1963). Approach-avoidance conflict in the mother surrogate situation. *Psychol. Rep.*, **12,** 83–85.

Rosenthal, M. K. (1967). The generalization of dependency behaviour from mother to stranger. *J. Child Psychol. Psychiat.*, **8,** 117–133.

Rosenthal, M. K. (1973). Attachment and mother–infant interaction: some research impasses and a suggested change in orientation. *J. Child Psychol. Psychiat.*, **14,** 201–207.

Ross, H. S. and Goldman, B. D. (1977). Establishing new social relations in infancy. In T. Alloway, P. Pliner and L. Krames (Eds.) *Advances in the Study of Communication and Affect, Vol. 3, Attachment Behavior*. New York: Plenum.

Roy, A. (1978). Vulnerability factors and depression in women. *Brit. J. Psychiat.*, **133,** 106–110.

Ruppenthal, G. C., Arling, G. L., Harlow, H. F., Sackett, G. P. and Suomi, S. J. (1976). A 10-year perspective of motherless-mother monkey behaviour. *J. Abnorm. Psychol.*, **85,** 341–349.

Rutter, M. (1971). Parent–child separation: Psychological effects on the children. *J. Child Psychol. Psychiat.*, **12,** 233–260.

Rutter, M. (1978a). Early sources of security and competence. In J. S. Bruner and A. Garton (Eds.) *Human Growth and Development*. London: Oxford University Press.

Rutter, M. (1978b). Diagnosis and definition. In M. Rutter and E. Schopler (Eds.) *Autism: A Reappraisal of Concepts and Treatment.* New York: Plenum.

Rutter, M. (1979a). Maternal deprivation 1972–1978: New findings, new concepts, new approaches. *Child Develop.* **50**, 283–305.

Rutter, M. (1979b). Protective factors in children's responses to stress and disadvantage. In M. W. Kent and J. E. Rolf (Eds.) *Primary Prevention of Psychopathology: Vol. 3: Social Competence in Children.* Hanover, N. H.: University Press of New England.

Rutter, M. and Madge, N. (1976). *Cycles of Disadvantage: A Review of Research.* London: Heinemann.

Salzen, E. A. (1978). Social attachment and a sense of security: A review. *Social Science Information,* **17**, 555–627.

Sander, L. W. (1969). Comments on regulation and organisation in the early infant-caretaker system. In R. J. Robinson (Ed.) *Brain and Early Behaviour.* London: Academic Press.

Sander, L. W., Stechler, G., Burns, P. and Julia, H. (1970). Early mother–infant interaction and twenty-four-hour patterns of activity and sleep. *J. Amer. Acad. Child Psychiat.,* **9**, 103–123.

Scarr, S. (1969). Social introversion-extraversion as a heritable response. *Child Develop.,* **40**, 823–832.

Scarr, S. and Salapatek, P. (1970). Patterns of fear development during infancy. *Merrill-Palmer Q.,* **16**, 53–90.

Schaffer, H. R. (1963). Some issues for research in the study of attachment behaviour. In B. M. Foss (Ed.) *Determinants of Infant Behaviour, Vol. 2.* London: Methuen.

Schaffer, H. R. (1971). *The Growth of Sociability.* Harmondsworth: Penguin Books.

Schaffer, H. R. and Callender, W. M. (1959). Psychologic effects of hospitalization in infancy. *Pediatrics,* **24**, 528–539.

Schaffer, H. R. and Emerson, P. E. (1964). The development of social attachments in infancy. *Monogr. Soc. Res. Child Develop.,* **29**, Serial no. 94.

Schneirla, T. A. (1965). Aspects of stimulation and organization in approach/withdrawal processes underlying vertebrate behavioral development. In D. S. Lehrman, R. A. Hinde and E. Shaw (Eds.) *Advances in the Study of Behavior, Vol. 1.* New York and London: Academic Press.

Schwartz, J. (1972). Effects of peer familiarity on the behaviour of preschoolers in a novel situation. *J. Pers. Soc. Psychol.,* **24**, 276–284.

Scott, J. P. (1971). Attachment and separation in dog and man: theoretical propositions. In H. R. Schaffer (Ed.) *The Origins of Human Social Relations.* London: Academic Press.

Scott, J. P. and Bronson, F. H. (1964). Experimental exploration of the et-epimeletic or care-soliciting behavioral system. In P. H. Leiderman and D. Shapiro (Eds.), *Psychobiological Approaches to Social Behavior.* Stanford: Stanford University Press.

Seay, B., Alexander, B. K. and Harlow, H. F. (1964). Maternal behavior of socially deprived rhesus monkeys. *J. Abn. Soc. Psychol.,* **69**, 345–354.

Shirley, M. and Poyntz, L. (1941). The influence of separation from the mother on children's emotional responses. *J. Psychol.,* **12**, 251–282.

Solomon, R. L. and Corbit, J. D. (1974). An opponent-process theory of motivation: I. Temporal dynamics of affect. *Psychol. Rev.,* **81**, 119–145.

Spelke, E., Zelazo, P., Kagan, J. and Kotelchuck, M. (1973). Father interaction and separation protest. *Develop. Psychol.,* **9**, 83–90.

Spitz, R. A. (1965). *The First Year of Life.* New York: International Universities Press.

Spitz, R. A. and Wolf, K. M. (1946). The smiling response: a contribution to the ontogenesis of social relationships. *Genet. psychol. Monogr.,* **34**, 57–125.

Sroufe, L. A., Waters, E. and Matas, L. (1974). Contextual determinants of infant affective response. In M. Lewis and L. Rosenblum (Eds.) *The Origins of Fear.* New York: Wiley.

Stayton, D. J. and Ainsworth, M. D. S. (1973). Individual differences in infant responses to brief, everyday separations as related to other infant and maternal behaviors. *Develop. Psychol.,* **9**, 226–235.

Stayton, D. J., Ainsworth, M. D. S. and Main, M. B. (1973). Development of separation behavior in the first year of life: protest, following, and greeting. *Develop. Psychol.,* **9**, 213–225.

Stern, D., Jaffe, J., Beebe, B. and Bennett, S. L. (1975). Vocalising in unison and in alternation: Two modes of communication within the mother–infant dyad. *Ann. New York Acad. Sci.,* **263**, 89–100.

Stevens, A. (1975). *Attachment and Polymatric Rearing. A study of attachment formation, separation anxiety and fear of strangers in infants reared by multiple mothering in an institutional setting.* Unpublished DM Thesis, University of Oxford.

Stevenson, O. (1954). The First Treasured Possession. *Psychoanal. Study Child,* **9**, 199–217.

Tennant, C. and Bebbington, P. (1978). The social causation of depression: a critique of the work of Brown and his colleagues. *Psychol. Med.* **8**, 565–575.

Tizard, B. (1977). *Adoption: A Second Chance.* London: Open Books.

Tizard, B. and Hodges, J. (1978). The effect of early institutional rearing on the development of eight-year-old children. *J. Child Psychol. Psychiat.,* **19**, 99–118.

Tizard, B. and Rees, J. (1975). The effect of early institutional rearing on the behaviour problems and affectional relationships of four-year-old children. *J. Child Psychol. Psychiat.,* **16**, 61–74.

Tizard, J. and Tizard, B. (1971). The social development of 2-year-old children in residential nurseries. In H. E. Schaffer (Ed.) *The Origins of Human Social Relations.* London: Academic Press.

Wahler, R. G. (1967). Infant social attachments: a reinforcement theory interpretation and investigation. *Child Develop.,* **38**, 1079–1088.

Wasz–Höckert, O., Lind, J., Vuorenkoski, V., Partanen, T. and Valanne, E. (1968). *The Infant Cry: A Spectrographic and Auditory Analysis.* Clinics in Developmental Medicine, No. 29. London: Heinemann S.I.M.P.

Weisberg, P. (1963). Social and nonsocial conditioning of infant vocalisations. *Child Develop.,* **34**, 377–388.

White, B. L., Castle, P. and Held, R. (1964). Observations on the development of visually-directed reaching. *Child Develop.,* **35**, 349–364.

Whiten, A. (1977). Assessing the effects of perinatal events on the success of the mother–infant relationship. In H. R. Schaffer (Ed.) *Studies in Mother–Infant Interaction.* London: Academic Press.

Wilcox, B. M. and Clayton, F. L. (1968). Infant visual fixation on motion pictures of the human face. *J. exp. Child Psychol.* **6**, 22–32.

Wolff, P. H. (1963). Observations on the early development of smiling. In B. M. Foss (Ed.) *Determinants of Infant Behaviour, Vol. 2.* London: Methuen.

Wolff, P. H. (1969). The natural history of crying and other vocalizations in early infancy. In B. M. Foss (Ed.) *Determinants of Infant Behaviour, Vol. 4.* London: Methuen.

Yarrow, L. J. (1963). Research in dimensions of early maternal care. *Merrill-Palmer Q.,* **9**, 101–114.

Yarrow, L. J. (1967). The development of focused relationships during infancy. In J. Hellmuth (Ed.) *Exceptional Infant, Vol. 1.* Seattle Special Child Publications.

Young, M., Benjamin, B. and Wallis, C. (1963). The mortality of widowers. *Lancet,* **2**, 454–456.

23. PEER RELATIONS AND FAMILY RELATIONS: TWO SOCIAL WORLDS[1]

WILLARD W. HARTUP

The Nature of Peer Relations
   Contextual characteristics
   Developmental Course

Family interaction and peer interaction
   Similarities and differences
   System interdependencies

Conclusion

The social world to which most children are exposed initially is the family—a complex unit varying widely in composition and cohesiveness from family to family as well as from culture to culture. As a social system, the family can be conceived as a constellation of sub-systems defined in terms of kinship and social functions. Divisions of labour between family members define certain sub-units and attachments define others. Each individual is a member of several sub-systems. The socialization of the child begins within this set of sub-systems and is an outgrowth of the child's actions as well as the actions of the other members of the family unit.

Theories of child development have traditionally stressed the primacy of the family in the growth of social competence. Mutually-regulated relations with other individuals and the conditions necessary to their maintenance are first experienced within the family context. The child's initial experiences with the regulation of negative affects occur within the family as well as the initial experiences with prosocial ones. The precursors of perspective-taking and other forms of social reality-testing also occur initially within family relations (Lempers, Flavell and Flavell, 1977). These observations have convinced numerous investigators that family relations dominate the socialization process, both because the child's initial social experiences occur in this context and because more time is consumed in family interaction than in interaction with other social agents—at least during the early years.

Additions, extensions, and elaborations of the competencies emerging from parent–child interaction occur in a second social world—the peer culture. An appreciation of the role of peer interaction in the growth of social competence has emerged only recently (*cf.* Whiting and Whiting, 1975; Hartup, 1976b), although the ubiquity of children's societies has long been recognized. Even now, the contributions of peer interaction to the child's capacities to relate to others, to regulate emotional expression, and to understand complex social events are not well-understood. Most commonly, the scientific litera-ture has emphasized the conflict and contention presumed to exist between the peer culture and the core (adult) culture. Such contentions have been the basis for innumerable treatments of childhood and adolescence in Western fiction. The 'collision' between the world of the family and the world of the peer culture also draws constant attention from the news media.

The school is a third social world of the child, but relatively little is known about it. The American school has been described most clearly in systemic terms by Coleman and his associates (1961). Clearly, unique forces are brought to bear on the individual child in this context for extending and elaborating behaviour patterns originating in other contexts. The literature, however, frequently emphasizes the conflict between the school and the other social worlds of the child—particularly the peer culture—whereas concordance in socialization pressures involving the school and other agencies has drawn much less attention.

Other social worlds of the child are ancillary to these three: some revolve around formal organizations, some around informal enclaves. Their ancillary status, however, should not tempt one to conclude that the contributions of these systems to the child's socialization are secondary or tertiary. To the extent that any social system adds unique variance to children's social competencies, that system has unrivalled significance in the socialization process. Indeed, the aim of modern social science should not be the isolation of sources of variation in the growth of social competence so much as the analysis of the interaction between the various social systems in determining the development of the child.

The purpose of this essay is to examine the relation of family interaction to peer interaction, in order to establish some working hypotheses about the manner in which family relations set the stage for child–child interaction. Certain sequences in social development make it very difficult to argue that no continuities exist between these social systems: peer relations are not encountered until family interaction is well established; the regulation of aggressive impulses is not achieved until 'trust' is established with primary caretakers; the understanding of social rules emerges on the basis of an understanding of how 'to take the role of the other'; friendship relations with child associates emerge after basic attachments within the family. However, the order of events in social development does not necessarily imply causal linkages between them. An early social event may be neither necessary nor sufficient in the determination of a succeeding event. And yet, the major theories of personality development have been epigenetic theories—each assuming carry-over or continuity from one set of social experiences to the next, from one social world to another.

THE NATURE OF PEER RELATIONS

Contextual characteristics

Studies establishing the proportion of children's social activities that occur with child associates are rare. Barker and Wright (1955) reported that about 10% of the social interactions observed in 2-year-old children involved child associates (other infants as well as preschool and school-age children), while this proportion increased to approximately 30% among preschool children and approached 50% among school-aged children. Konner (1975) observed !Kung San infants between the ages of 1 and 2 years and, again, found that approximately 10% of all physical contact involved other children. Cultural variations in these proportions occur, too (Whiting, 1978), but the proportion of the child's social activity that involves other children universally increases through the years of early and middle childhood.

The nature of peer relations cannot be specified without reference to the age of the child and the age difference existing between the child and his associates. In most cultures, the very young child's early exposures to other children are not to agemates, but to older children. Barker and Wright (1955), in their examination of the relation between the ages of the child's associates and the nature of the social activity, found that power assertion by children's companions was inversely related to the child's own age. That is, the older the child, the less the likelihood that other children would engage in power assertion. In addition, older associates were more likely than younger associates to engage in nurturance towards the child but less likely to manifest dependency.

Whiting and Whiting (1975) reported, across six cultures, that interaction with younger children (particularly infants) was, indeed, the social context most likely to elicit nurturant behaviour from a school-aged child—among both boys and girls. On the other hand, interaction with an older individual was the most likely context for the occurrence of dependency. To quote Barker and Wright, 'From older contemporaries, children get chiefly dominance, nurturance, and resistance ... while they reciprocate these with submission, appeal, and resistance; and the reverse may hold for children in their relations with younger contemporaries.' Although the cross-cultural observations of recent years were required to corroborate these results, the earlier observations (conducted with only eight United States children) served to identify some important universals in child–child relations.

One type of social interaction that occurs more commonly in same-age than mixed-age contexts is aggression. Both among non-human primates (cf. Jay, 1968) and among children (cf. Whiting and Whiting, 1975), aggression is less likely to occur with either older or younger children than with children who are close to the child's own age. Aggressive interaction with someone who is markedly older or younger than the child leads to aversive consequences for the younger partner in almost every instance; neither do such encounters provide tremendous gratification for the older child. In either case, the aggress-

ive cues occurring in mixed-age situations would be expected to elicit mutual withdrawal rather than continued social engagement. Aggressive interaction with agemates, however, provokes more moderate aversive consequences to the participants and is modulated in many instances to provide intermittent reinforcement. Such intermittent reinforcement would explain the persistence of the activity.

Children engage in 'sociable' acts more frequently with associates who are similar in age than with associates who are not (Whiting and Whiting, 1975). Frequencies of positive social interaction are also greater when enclaves consist of only same-age children as contrasted to children of different ages (Hertz-Lazarowitz, Feitelson, Hartup and Zahavi, in preparation) and the amount of interaction in same-age dyads is more frequent than in mixed-age dyads among 3-year-old and 5-year-old children (Langlois, Gottfried, Barnes and Hendricks, 1978).

While associative interaction may be more common in same-age situations than in mixed-age situations, the activity may not always be cognitively 'more mature'. Goldman (1976), for example, conducted observations in three classes of 3-year-olds, three classes of 4-year-olds, and three mixed-age classes that included both 3- and 4-year-olds. The 3-year-olds in the mixed-age situations engaged in more solitary play, less parallel play, and less teacher-directed activity than 3-year-olds in same-age situations. The 4-year-olds in mixed-age classrooms also spent more time in solitary play and less time in parallel activity and teacher-directed work. Assuming that solitary play is more 'mature' than parallel play (Rubin, Maioni and Hornung, 1976), it appears that the social activity in mixed-age situations may be more mature than in same-age situations.

Other studies have shown that a variety of sophisticated accommodations in verbal communication are made by preschool-aged children in mixed-age interaction that do not occur in same-age interaction (Shatz and Gelman, 1973; Lougee, Grueneich and Hartup, 1977). In some instances, these accommodations are reflected in shifts towards less complex modes of communication, rather than more complex constructions, such as when 4-year-olds move to simpler linguistic modes when talking to 2-year-olds than when talking to other 4-year-olds (Shatz and Gelman, 1973). In these instances, the use of the less mature linguistic constructions undoubtedly reflect relatively advanced, sophisticated understanding of the needs of the younger child. That is, the surface 'regression' in the mode of communication seems actually to be a reflection of mature, social/cognitive understanding. In short, the mixed-age situation, either with associates who are older or younger, probably exerts a greater variety of demands for mature social accommodations than same-age interaction. But children's preferences for same-age interaction are well documented and are associated with large amounts of sociable activity (Hartup, 1976a).

Children's behaviour with other children must be specified in relation to the age differences existing among them. The term 'peer interaction' is insufficiently differentiated to convey accurately the discriminative nature of the social activity existing between children and other children. The term 'peer' connotes equivalence between the individuals engaged in social intercourse, but interaction with co-equals does not comprise the majority of the child's contacts with his/her contemporaries. In fact, the Barker and Wright observations indicate that 65% of the child's total experience with contemporaries involved children who differed in age from the subject by more than 1 year. Since social activities such as nurturance, dependency, and aggression—each experience essential to successful adaptation—occur in some contexts more frequently than others, it is clear that the contributions of child–child interaction to socialization cannot be specified through all-encompassing references to 'peer interaction'.

Little evidence exists identifying the later outcomes of the sociable interactions occurring under same-age and mixed-age conditions. One can guess, however, that these extend from advances in role-taking (Selman and Jaquette, 1977) to the socialization of aggression. It has been suggested that peer relations provide the child's main opportunity for engaging in 'intimacy', an attribute essential to social adaptation in any context:

> If you will look closely at one of your children when he finally finds a chum—somewhere between eight-and-a-half and ten—you will discover something very different in the relationship—namely, that your child begins to develop a real sensitivity to what matters to another person. And this is not in the sense of 'what should I do to contribute to the happiness or to support the prestige and feeling of worthwhileness of my chum'.... The developmental epoch of preadolescence is marked by the coming of the integrating tendencies which, when they are completely developed, we call love, or to say it another way, by the manifestation of the need for interpersonal intimacy.... (Sullivan, 1953, pp. 245–6).

Similar status would appear to be necessary to the formation of chumships. Whether it is the essential quality facilitating the development of the need for intimacy within those relationships is less certain.

Individual differences are evident in the outcomes of same-age and mixed-age experiences. One recent experiment shows vividly that, with socially-withdrawn children, the outcomes of socializing with younger children are more beneficial than sociable experiences with same-age children—an outcome not necessarily predictable with normally sociable children. Furman, Rahe, and Hartup (in press) located 24 socially-withdrawn preschool children by means of classroom observations extending over a five-to-eight-week period. For one-third of the cases, the child was assigned randomly to a socialization experience with another child who was approximately 15 months younger; for another one-third of the cases, the child was assigned to another child within three months of his/her own chronological age; and the remaining one-third of the children received no treatment. The socialization experience consisted of a series of ten play sessions, conducted outside the regular nursery school classroom, in which the children themselves determined the nature of their interaction. Follow-up observations in the nursery classroom, again extending over five to eight weeks, showed that socialization experiences with both younger and same-age children increased the social activity of the isolates; no change occurred in the 'no treatment' group. Greater increases were obtained, however, in the social activity of the children who were exposed to younger companions than children exposed to same-age companions. Indeed, post-treatment social activity among the isolates who were exposed to younger children was indistinguishable, in total amount, from the general nursery school population. Same-age experiences, on the other hand, were much more variable in their effect.

The play sessions with 'younger therapists' must have provided the isolates with experiences that occurred infrequently in the classroom. These sessions were not marked by inordinately high levels of social activity but provided the isolate child with opportunities to be socially assertive and to practice leadership skills. In this instance, opportunity to interact with a younger child seemed to provide the isolate with opportunities accruing to most children with agemates. Thus, the outcomes of various kinds of child–child interaction may differ considerably from individual to individual. The results also provide a treatment model that is efficient, effective, and easily implemented.

The child development literature indicates that the major contributions of both mixed-age and same-age interaction to adaptation are in the realm of social competence. Effects on intellectual development are less clear. Experimental support for this argument is lacking, since intervention studies of the necessary sort are neither practicable nor ethical in the human case. Nevertheless, correlational studies (in some cases extending over long periods of time) provide presumptive evidence that peer interaction is embedded centrally in aggressive and sexual socialization, the development of moral values, and the development of sociability (Hartup, 1976b). Several long-term studies (cf. Roff, Sells and Golden, 1972; Cowen, Pederson, Babijian, Izzo and Trost, 1973) show that individuals evidencing poor peer relations in childhood are at significantly greater risk for adult psychopathology, anti-social behaviour, and sexual disorders than individuals with effective peer relations. While the possibility exists that a general disposition towards disorder produces both the early disturbance in social relations and the later socioemotional difficulties, the linkage between early peer interaction and later social adaptation is well-established. Peer interaction is central in childhood socialization and in the growth of social competence, and the suspicion grows that such competencies are direct derivatives of early experience in the peer culture.

Developmental course

Peer interaction proceeds from simple organizations in early childhood to complex hierarchies, from loose differentiation in social encounters to discriminative interaction, and from primitive awareness of the needs of others to use of complex social attributions. Certain characteristics, *e.g.* normative activity and hierarchization, may be found in the peer relations of young children as well as adolescents, but the nature of both social interaction and group structures changes greatly with increasing age.

The social interactions of year-old infants are based on both attraction and rejection. Observations conducted in an infant day care centre (Lee, 1973) showed that one individual baby was more consistently approached than the other members, while one other infant was regularly avoided. The 'popular' infant was unusually responsive to the other babies and readily engaged in reciprocal exchanges; the 'unpopular' infant was nearly asocial —responsiveness depended on whether he himself had initiated the interaction. Early social activity is object-centred, as revealed by the centrality of toys in infant social encounters.

One of the most striking changes to occur in the second year is the appearance of complex contingencies in child–child interaction involving imitation, shared responsibilities for the maintenance of the social exchange, and increased dimensionality and complexity in the organization of the exchange. Play interactions in the second half of the second year are marked by reciprocity and complementarity. Role relations emerge (*e.g.* 'giver' and 'receiver'). Social interaction remains largely dyadic, however, in that children interact in twos even when the individuals are members of a larger group (Vandell, 1977; Vandell and Mueller, 1977).

The frequency of social interaction and the nature of the interaction continue to change during the preschool years. Positive social encounters increase, both in dyadic situations and in group settings (Lougee, Grueneich and Hartup, 1977; Charlesworth and Hartup, 1967). Staring, crying, finger sucking, and flight behaviours decrease during this time; talking, rough-and-tumble play, smiling, laughing, and cooperative activity increase (Blurton-Jones, 1972). Rates of aggression increase from 2 to 4 years but then decline; negative activity is less common in children's social interactions than positive exchanges at all ages (Walters, Pearce and Dahms, 1957).

Normative activity becomes visible in child–child interaction in the preschool years. Lakin, Lakin, and Costanzo (in press) studied normative traditions in various Israeli kibbutzim: 1½–2 years; 2–2½; 2½–3; and 3–3½. Their observations showed more frequent use of clear-cut roles, rule-enforcement, and prosocial behaviour in the older groups than in the younger ones. The most extensive norms in social activity during early childhood are related to gender: boys play more frequently with boys; girls play more often with other girls. Play activities vary according to sex. And sex differences in certain social activities, such as physical aggression, also emerge. Elaboration of normative activity extends into middle childhood with both explicit and implicit norms becoming obvious. Normative activity becomes especially evident when children's groups are thrown into competition with one another and when children share common goals (Sherif, Harvey, White, Hood and Sherif, 1961).

Friendships are characteristic of children at all ages, although the stability of these relations change with age. 'Best friend' relations among preschool children are relatively stable over several weeks (Marshall and McCandless, 1957), but friendship choices become much more stable toward adolescence (Thompson and Horrocks, 1947). Friendship networks among boys are likely to be 'extensive' (*i.e.* scattered across a number of individuals) while, among girls, these networks are more likely to be 'intensive' (*i.e.* concentrated on relatively few individuals). Social interaction is more intimate between friends than between acquaintances, both in pleasant amusement situations (Foot, Chapman and Smith, 1977) and in social problem-solving situations (Newcomb, Brady and Hartup, 1979). Children with many friends are likely to be more attractive, in terms of both physical beauty and personality, than low-status children (Hartup, 1978). Most 'best friend' relations in early and middle childhood, even in adolescence, involve children of the same sex.

Developmental changes occur in the expectations that children have about their friends. These evolve in three loose 'stages': (a) a *reward-cost stage* occurring about Grades 2 and 3 marked by an emphasis on common activities, close social contact, and similarity in outlook; (b) a *normative stage* emerging at about Grades 4 and 5 marked by shared values, rules, and sanctions; and (c) an *empathic stage* occurring about Grades 6 and 7 in which understanding, self-disclosure, and shared interests emerge (Bigelow, 1977). Children's conceptions of friendship and the language used to describe friendships also become more complex and well-differentiated as children move into adolescence (Hartup, 1975).

Certain features of group interaction change during adolescence. In one study (Smith, 1960), social activity and task-related behaviour was examined in 20 groups, each including four individuals, from nursery schools, elementary schools, and university classes. The nursery school and elementary school children were less coordinated in the manner in which new ideas were introduced than were the adolescents; the younger children were also less cooperative and more autonomous in individual activity. In a sense, the younger children's groups seemed like aggregates of individuals, whereas the older children showed reciprocity and synchrony in their social relations. The interaction among adolescents was more finely-tuned: acknowledgments were used, opinions of the other members were requested, questions were asked, and signals given that the individuals understand the various social communications. In short, an increased coordination of social interaction occurs in adolescence. Such coordination marks the social activity of delinquent gangs as well as the interaction in more conforming aggregates. Although peer relations assume an increasingly important position in the children's lives as adolescence approaches, these experiences do not signal the end of family relations.

FAMILY INTERACTION AND PEER INTERACTION

Similarities and differences

Maccoby and Masters (1970) concluded that the evidence supports the notion that adult–child and child–child relations constitute separate affectional systems. At that time, the evidence was stronger for certain behavioural sub-systems (e.g. proximity seeking) than for others (e.g. attention-seeking). New evidence shows both similarities and differences in the nature of adult–child and child–child relations indicating that complex models involving interacting social systems fit the facts of social development better than simple, combinatory models.

Children's earliest experiences with other children are both similar and different from their experiences with adults. Eckerman, Whatley and Kutz (1975) studied 14 pairs of same-age toddlers—children who were either 10 to 12, 16 to 18, or 22 to 24 months of age. The children were not previously acquainted with each other and were brought together for 20 minutes, with their mothers, in a laboratory room containing ordinary household furnishings and toys. Peer-related behaviours occurred with high frequency, i.e. in approximately 60% of the observations. The social salience of the child's associates was thus established. Certain behaviours ordinarily occurring in the children's interactions with their mothers, including smiling, vocalizing, and touching, also occurred with the child associates, but not as frequently. Interactions with the toys occurred more often in peer interaction than in mother interaction. These observations thus confirm certain continuities in mode of interaction across target individuals (i.e. smiling, vocalizing, and touching) but also differences (i.e. play). In particular, child–child interaction was more object-centred than interactions between the children and their mothers, an indication that different controlling mechanisms mark the two social systems.

These investigators also compared the nature of child–child interaction with the children's interactions with strange adults. Exchanges between children involved less crying and fussing and more synchronous use of the play materials (e.g. more give-and-take with these materials as well as struggles) than were involved in exchanges with the strange adults. Play activities were better coordinated among the older children in the study, particularly when toys were involved. The fact that imitative use of these materials was observed indicates that the child–child interaction was instrinsically 'social' rather than a derivative of each child's independent involvement with the toys. Additional observations of social interaction in day care centres (Eckerman, 1979) confirm these findings. Play thus differentiates the mother–child system and the child–child system. It should be recalled, however, that the toddlers' initial overtures to strange peers in these studies contained the same communicative elements noted in interaction with the mother. Interdependencies thus exist between these two social worlds of the child as well as differentiation.

A word more about the social context in which play occurs. Observations of non-human primates consistently show that rough-and-tumble play (as well as certain other forms of play interactions) occurs very rarely between parents and their offspring but, instead, occurs universally among the offspring themselves. Rhesus monkey mothers will play with their infants only when caged alone with them (Hinde, 1974; Suomi, 1978, 1979). Observations of young children confirm these results, both in Western and non-Western cultures (cf. Whiting, 1978). Mothers rarely engage in play with their children, doing so only if other children are not available. Mostly, mothers act as observers or supervisors of play interaction. Sustained play activities, on the other hand, are major activities in child–child relations, particularly among agemates. The lack of involvement of mothers in play with their children suggests that mother–child relations are constrained in some manner that inhibits this activity. Such constraints may apply to both mother and child: (a) adult reality-testing is not wholly compatible with the 'suspension of disbelief' required for the mother to participate in long bouts of playful activity. (b) equivalent or near-equivalent cognitive and social status among the participants may be necessary to elicit this activity.

Other studies suggest that adults and children elicit different affective responses in young children. In one instance (Greenberg, Hillman and Grice, 1973), the investigators presented a total of 12 strangers (six adults and six 4-year-old children of both sexes) to 96 8- and 12-month-old infants. Ratings on an 'affect scale' revealed that infants of both ages responded more positively to the child strangers than to the adult strangers. Why? Direct experience could hardly have determined this difference since the infants had not had much opportunity to interact with other children. Perhaps genetic pre-programming is responsible for such early differentiated responses to adults and to children. Alternatively, such results may stem from the operation of an early internalized concept of self. A strange child, being more similar to this self-concept than a strange adult, would be expected to produce a more favourable reaction than a dissimilar adult. Other investigators (cf. Lewis and Brooks-Gunn, 1972) have also found that infants respond more positively to strange children than to adult strangers, although response to neither of these classes of individuals is as positive as the young child's response to the primary adult caretakers. Nevertheless, these differentiations in emotional reactions to strange adults and strange children suggest that unique elements are encompassed in the socio-emotional interaction of children with adults and with other children, beginning in early childhood.

Stressful experiences of a variety of kinds elicit differential reactions to adults and to other children, although evidence with respect to this issue is scarce (Maccoby and Masters, 1970). Both the non-human and human primate literatures indicate that strange situations, or strange moving objects (including strange persons) produce proximity-seeking to the mother. Distress reactions diminish after a period of clinging and looking at the fear-arousing object; exploration of the object then increases. When no mother or mother-surrogate is available, however, distress remains intense and exploration continues to be suppressed (Harlow and Zimmermann, 1959; Ainsworth and Wittig, 1969). Thus, fear-producing stimuli elicit proximity-seeking but the presence of an attachment object serves eventually to reduce the animal's fearfulness and permit exploration of the environment. Only one experiment has been conducted in which fear-producing stimuli were presented when the youngster could choose between proximity to a familiar adult (the mother) or a familiar peer (Patterson, Bonvillian, Reynolds and Maccoby, 1975). In this instance, fear elicited proximity to the mother rather than proximity to the peer. Proximity-seeking elicited by stress is thus another activity differentiating adult–child and child–child relationships.

Children's interactions with adults and with other children become more differentiated in the preschool years. Beginning at this time, children spend less and less time per day in the company of their mothers, and more and more time in the company of siblings and peers (Barker and Wright, 1955). Associated with these changes in the objects of social interaction are changes in the mode of the social activity. Heathers (1955), for example, conducted observations of 20 2-year-olds and 20 4-year-olds in several nursery school classes and found major age changes in behaviour with child associates relative to behaviour with adult associates (teachers): (a) among the older children, social overtures to peers were more common relative to overtures to adults, and (b) attention- and approval-seeking were more common social activities among the older children while affection-seeking was more common among the younger children.

Children use different behaviours to express affection to other children than to adults—e.g. following one another around, engaging each other in conversation, and sometimes offering help. Open, affectionate behaviour (either verbal or physical) occurs infrequently. Likewise, children rarely cry or fuss in the absence of another child. Separation from a long-time friend may prompt questions and concern, but severe stress reactions are reserved for circumstances in which the child has been separated from an adult. Children do not engage in intensive clinging, hugging, or other forms of ventral-ventral contact with their peers, unlike their contacts with adults. Only among laboratory animals who have been socialized with other young animals in 'motherless' conditions is intense clinging seen among them and then it is frequently dorsal-ventral contact rather than ventral-ventral contact (Harlow, 1969). Parallel observations have also been cited in the child development literature: Freud and Dann (1951), in describing the behaviour of six young children who were reared together in a concentration camp during the Second World War, reported much agitated proximity-seeking, clinging, and mutual affection among these children while their attitude towards adults was hostile and anxious. Seemingly, clinging and intense

physical contact is reserved for interactions with adults unless such individuals have not been salient in earlier socialization.

Further differentiation between child–child and adult–child relations occurs in middle childhood. Again, the work of Barker and Wright (1955) provides the earliest data base. First, the child was shown to be an active social agent. Interaction was initiated by the child as frequently as by his/her associates, whether the latter were adults or children. But the modes of interaction differed considerably according to the status of the associate. Adult actions (mostly parents) towards children most commonly consisted of dominance and nurturance. Resistance (non-compliance), appeals (dependency), and compliance occurred less frequently, while aggression and submission were seldom observed. Avoidance of the child almost never occurred, meaning that 'non-avoidance' or 'engagement' ranked among the most frequently-occurring adult actions towards children. The most common actions of the children toward the adults were appeals and submission. In combination, these observations of adult–child interaction in 'Midwest' suggest a concentration on two issues: (a) dependency, and (b) control. Frequent appeals by the children occurred as complements to frequent nurturance by the adults; frequent submission by the children occurred as complements to frequent dominance by the adults. Although the sample was extremely small, there were no differences in the actions of adults with children that were associated with the child's age (which ranged from 2 to 11 years).

Relative frequencies of the actions between child associates were considerably different. Resistance was the most common activity directed towards the subjects by their child associates. Nurturance and dominance occurred with moderate frequency. Appeals (dependency), submission, aggression, and compliance occurred in descending rank-order among the less frequent actions exhibited by the child associates. Avoidance, as with adult associates, occurred infrequently. In turn, the subjects' main action towards their child associates was dominance, followed by appeals and resistance. Child–child relations, then, appear less harmonious than adult–child relations: resistance and dominance seem to complement dominance. But a caveat is contained in this report: the nature of child–child interactions varied so greatly according to the age difference between the target children and their child associates that the small size of the sample precludes meaningful generalizations concerning the characteristics of these interactions. Nevertheless, child–child interactions seem to be constructed on a different motivational base from the child's interactions with adults.

Cross-cultural studies confirm these results. Edwards and Whiting (1977) have found that the nurturance/ dependency complementarity exists primarily in adult–child interaction, but also in interaction between older children and infants. Control (dominance complemented by submission) also occurs in both adult–child interaction and child–infant interaction. Neither sequence constitutes the most frequently-occurring pattern in peer interaction. In peer interaction, sociable, pro-social, and aggressive interactions predominate. While these data indicate that peer interaction may be the locus of a certain amount of conflict, much of the aggression among children consists of horseplay and insults rather than assaults. The occurrence of pro-social activity in this context suggests yet another positive dimension to the child–child social system. These studies with older children thus support further the contention that the peer system is not a duplicate of the parent–child social system in either its topography or its eliciting conditions. Indeed, it can be argued that the motivational base of social behaviour in these systems varies greatly, and that the contributions of each system to the growth of social competence are complementary rather than duplicative.

Sexual socialization was not observed in the foregoing studies. The literature on this matter is scattered and heterogeneous. Early family interaction—through both labelling and the identification process—undoubtedly plays an important role in the development of the child's gender identity. Environments within the household are organized by parents according to the sex of the child (Rheingold and Cook, 1975); parent–child relations are associated with sex-typing (Hetherington, 1965); and father absence (mother-headed families) is associated with sex-typing that differs from the processes that occur in the nuclear family (Hetherington, 1966, 1972). In most respects, though, the contributions of the family are not to sexuality, *i.e.* they are concerned with gender-typing rather than with sexual behaviour.

Sexual behaviour, in contrast, is socialized extensively within the peer culture. To quote Kinsey, Pomeroy and Martin (1948):

> Children are the most frequent agents for the transmission of the sexual mores. Adults serve in that capacity only to a smaller extent. This will not surprise sociologists and anthropologists, for they are aware of the great amount of imitative adult activity which enters into the play of children the world around. In this activity, play though it may be, children are severe, highly critical, and vindictive in their punishment of a child who does not do it 'this way' or 'that way'. Even before there has been any attempt at overt sex play, the child may have acquired a considerable schooling on matters of sex. Much of this comes so early that the adult has no memory of where his attitudes were acquired (p. 445).

Little more needs to be said in regard to this matter. Note, however, that the Kinsey group recognized that play is the context in which sexual styles are learned—another indication that this unique peer mechanism has pervasive consequences in social development.

Play also contributes significantly to the development of moral values. Piaget (1932) recognized the unique value of reciprocal social relations such as those found among agemates, in promoting relativism in children's moral thinking. Children who are leaders exhibit advanced levels of social responsibility (Gold, 1962) and relatively high levels of moral reasoning (Keasey, 1971). Such correlational statements do not, of course, provide definitive evidence that reciprocity in peer relations

'causes' advances in moral thinking, but the two events are clearly linked.

In adolescence, family relations and peer relations anchor both similar and different social values. Basic, 'core culture' norms, such as educational aspirations, emerge concordantly from both social systems, although parents provide the greater influence (Kandel and Lesser, 1972). Friendship choices and personal values (*e.g.* marijuana use) also reflect synergistic socialization pressures, but with the peer culture providing the major influence (Kandel, 1973). Concordance between parent and peer values is sufficiently pervasive that one would never posit social worlds in the life of the adolescent that do not intersect. But, again and again, surveys show that adolescents look to their parents for assistance in solving problems and to their friends for companionship (*cf.* Kandel and Lesser, 1972).

A striking demonstration of this differentiation between social systems in terms of adolescent values is contained in a study of 'cross pressures' (Brittain, 1963). When status norms and identity issues were involved in the test items, peer endorsement was sought. When future aspirations or achievement in school were involved, adult endorsement was salient. Value orientations, then, are directed differentially towards parents and peers according to the value area involved. The nature of this differentiation may vary from culture to culture (Bronfenbrenner, 1967; Kandel and Lesser, 1972), and family adjustment can also affect this delicate balance (Bowerman and Kinch, 1959). But the contribution of family interaction and peer interaction to the development of values is a differentiated rather than a unitary process.

Overall, then, the evidence suggests that children and adolescents live in two social worlds: a familial world and a society of child associates. Socioemotional behaviour in one world bears the partial imprint of behaviour in the other world, and values are integrated across these social systems rather than created in isolation from one another. We turn now to the fragmented evidence that suggests the manner in which these two social worlds interact to influence the growth of social competencies during childhood.

System interdependencies

What kinds of system interdependencies are built into the socialization process? Essentially two models exist to account for the relation between socialization within the family and within the peer culture: (a) *single process theories*, in which social competence is believed to emerge fundamentally in family interaction with the contributions of peer interaction serving to elaborate and extend them; and (b) *dual process theories*, in which certain competencies are believed to emerge more or less independently in one or the other context.

Most major theories of socioemotional development are single process theories. For example, the formation and maintenance of focused relationships—in both affective and instrumental terms—are assumed within psychoanalytic theory to be based on the child's initial relation with the primary caretaker. The initial attachment sets limits, in terms of both affective response and social action, within which the secondary attachments function. Thus, security in the mother–child attachment system should promote effectance in the peer attachment system both through the general strengthening of the ego and the transfer of specific social skills and sensitivities from the primary attachment to the secondary one. Psychoanalytic theory does not contain, in any of its variants, a very complete account of the development of peer relations—it was not intended to. The works of Harry Stack Sullivan (1953) come closest to such an accomplishment but it is clear that, even though peer relations were conceived as unique contributors to human adaptation, these contributions were viewed as elaborations of basic attitudes toward self and others established within the context of mother–child relations.

Little has been written by the social learning theorists concerning the origins of secondary attachments (e.g. friendships), but most writers have assumed that the initial attachment to the mother plays a key role in these developments. That is, children's requests for attention and approval from other people are thought, in a major way, to be generalized aspects of behaviour vis-à-vis their mothers. The theory can also account for the emergence of unique features in the child's interaction with individuals other than family members (e.g. peers) through discrimination learning. But, again, peer interaction is believed to produce elaborations and extensions of adaptive modes acquired earlier, and the peer attachment system is believed to be a derivation based on earlier systems rather than an independent system.

Dual process theories of social development are not identified with any theoretical system or 'school'. In fact, no one espouses a dual process theory in pure form. Harlow and Harlow (1965), in earlier work, advanced the idea that five distinct affectional 'systems' are found in primate development: the mother–infant system, the infant–mother system, the peer affectional system, the heterosexual system, and the paternal affectional system. These affectional systems were believed to dominate primate development at various points in the life cycle and to be reflected by differences in the topography of behaviour, the elicitation of the act, and their consequences. But the Harlows also stressed the interdependencies existing among these systems. The well-known data showing that deprivation in one 'system' results in atypical development in other 'systems' are consistent with this theory—in particular, the studies showing interdependencies between the infant–mother affectional system and the heterosexual and maternal affectional systems in later life.

The early 'deprivation' studies cited above suggested near-independence between the infant–mother affectional system and the peer affectional system. Early peer interaction seemed to contribute primarily to social competence with agemates, with the infant–mother system contributing to the heterosexual and mother–infant systems. One series of studies (cf. Harlow, 1969) was concentrated on the development of rhesus infants raised with peers but without contact with mothers and, in other instances, on the development of infants raised with mothers but without contact with other infants. Animals raised with agemates developed strong attachments to one another and manifested the intense proximity-seeking described earlier. When such rearing involved several same-age animals, affective and instrumental disturbances in subsequent encounters with other animals were not apparent. Social competencies were less well-generalized among animals reared with a single associate, but marked deficiencies were not evident under those rearing conditions, either. Rearing by the mother without peer contact, on the other hand, produced animals who showed both contemporaneous disturbances in play behaviour and long-term disturbances in affective development. Wariness and hyper-aggressiveness were outstanding characteristics. Taken together, the results of these investigations suggest that early experience with agemates constitutes a unique base for learning affective controls and social skills.

Certain limitations exist, however, in interpreting these results. The 'peer deprivation' studies were conducted with mothers and infants caged together—a condition which may have had deleterious effects on the mothers which then transferred to the infants. Such confinements sometimes make the mother irritable with her infant thereby distorting normal socialization processes. In addition, infants who have no access to peers attempt to play with the mother and such overtures tend to elicit negative reactions from her (Hinde, 1974).

Another study from the Wisconsin Laboratories shows that experiences with mothers and with other infants become integrated in very complex ways. Goy and Goldfoot (1973) separated infant rhesus monkeys from their mothers at 3 months of age and then exposed them to other infants for one half-hour every day. These animals were compared with infants reared in larger groups who had unrestricted access to both mothers and other infants. Major differences marked the development of the animals reared under these two conditions: (a) mature sexual behaviour developed in the combined social environment in approximately six months but not in the peer environment for two to three years; (b) aggression/submission interactions predominated in the social behaviour of the animals reared with only peer exposure whereas these behaviours were rarely shown by the animals reared in the combined environment. Peer-rearing thus may bring about a superficially adequate adaptation in adulthood, but the behaviours associated with such rearing conditions are not identical with the actions of animals reared with both mothers and other infants (see also Suomi, 1978). The two social worlds of the child seem actually to interact as a complementary synergism.

The nature of this synergism can be extracted from various literatures, including both the literature on non-human primates and the literature of child development. First, it is obvious that the child's early attachment to the mother serves to provide a 'secure base' (Ainsworth, 1967) which reduces fear in strange situations and promotes exploration of the environment. Among the consequences of this exploration are encounters with other animals. Among non-human primates, these encounters ordinarily do not include sustained associations with adult or sub-adult animals; such animals reject the infant. But, in almost every situation, this exploratory activity brings about contact with agemates. These contacts do not produce rejection but, rather, elicit social interaction in the form of play.

The mother also takes an active role in directing her offspring towards engagements with other infants. First, she rejects play overtures from her own offspring. Second, she ensures proximity between her infant and other infants by remaining close to the members of a larger social unit—the troop. Thus, the attachment bond is both an affective and an instrumental base that ensures the infant's engagement in peer relations. In this way, the infant–mother social system ensures contact with a second social system that, in turn, contributes on its own to the growth of various social competencies.

Correlational studies of children and adolescents suggest that warm, secure conditions within the family are associated with self-confidence, instrumental competence, and success in peer relations. Much of the evidence, though, has been accumulated to support the theory that the competencies emerging in mother–child relations transfer more-or-less directly to other social situations and are then elaborated and extended to fit those situations. Correlational evidence, of course, can be consistent with either traditional notions about system interdependence or the inter-system model being formulated here; correlations merely establish statistical associations between the mother–child and child–child measures and do not demonstrate cause-and-effect relations between them.

In a recent study of 3-year-olds, Lieberman (1977) explored the relation between the security of the child's attachment to the mother and the effectiveness of the child's interactions with an agemate. Previous experience with peers was also included as a predictor variable. This measure was presumed to be an index of the extent to which the mother encouraged peer interaction, since young children do not control their own whereabouts. Observations of mother–child interaction were conducted in the home and observations of behaviour with agemates were conducted in a familiar playroom in the nursery school. Children whose attachments to the mother were rated as 'secure', according to the scale devised by Ainsworth, Bell and Stayton (1971), were more responsive to other children and engaged in more protracted social interactions than did children who were not securely attached. The security of the attachment was correlated mainly with non-verbal dimensions of peer interaction. In addition, those children whose mothers arranged contact with other children in the home were more mature in the verbal dimensions of their interaction with the other child. Although limited deductions can be made from such evidence, it is instructive to know that the security of attachment and provision of peer experiences by the mother were positively correlated with each other in these data. The evidence thus supports the thesis that

secure attachments predict two occurrences: (a) positive and persistent engagement with other children, expressed mainly in non-verbal ways; and (b) the direct use of social communicative skills with other children.

Other evidence shows that, even among 'securely attached' infants, peer interaction varies according to the nature of the mother–child relationship (Easterbrooks and Lamb, 1979). Forty-two 18-month-old infants and their mothers were observed and classified according to whether their interaction was characterized by distal modes (looking, talking, and smiling) or whether distress during the mother's absence and maintenance-of-proximity were dominant. Peer interaction was then assessed when the subject and another baby were brought together in the presence of their mothers. Those infants who were content to interact with their mothers at a distance played more with the other baby, engaged in more positive social interaction, shared materials more, vocalized more frequently, and imitated their peers more often than did the other infants. Thus, the organization of secure attachments with the mother seem clearly to predict early peer interaction and suggest that family relations set the stage for agemate relations.

A prospective study was conducted by Waters, Wippman and Sroufe (1979). In this instance, the security of the child's attachment to the mother ('secure attachments' versus 'anxious attachments') was assessed from videotape recordings of mother–child interaction made when the children were 15 months of age. Peer interactions were assessed by Q-sorts based on five weeks of observer experience with the children when they were enrolled in nursery school (i.e. when their average age was 42 months). Over two years thus separated the observations used to classify the primary attachment and the observations used to measure the child's engagement in peer interaction. As compared to the anxiously attached children, the securely attached children were: socially active rather than withdrawn, sought out by other children, peer leaders, active in making suggestions, sympathetic to peer distress, participative in social activity rather than onlookers, and not hesitant in reacting to overtures from other children. Various measures of ego-strength also differentiated the two groups of children, although measured IQ did not. These data also support the hypothesis that secure attachments within the mother–child social system promote a positive orientation towards other children, active engagement in peer relations, and the child's centrality in the peer group—over a considerable time span. The study does not elucidate the social learning processes involved in each of these social worlds, but it establishes that security in one social system produces successful adaptation in the other.

Correlational research with older children is consistent with the results for younger children. Using interview and sociometric methods with elementary school boys, Winder and Rau (1962) found that both the mothers and fathers of 'likeable' children made few demands for aggression and did not use aggressive punishment extensively. The mothers rarely used deprivation of privileges as a disciplinary technique, had high self-esteem, and were well-adjusted. The fathers of the high status children also were favourably oriented towards their sons' competencies and provided supportive reinforcement. The qualities in parent–child relations of the high status boys thus included discouragement of anti-social behaviour, infrequent frustration and punishment, and supportive reinforcement. Such features suggest that parent–child relations were relatively more 'secure' in the case of the high status boys than among children who were less well-established in the peer culture. Since attachment was not measured directly, however, it must be understood that this interpretation is drawn indirectly from the evidence.

Other correlational evidence comes from studies of instrumental competence by Baumrind (1967, 1971), who found that children rated as self-reliant, self-controlled, and explorative had *authoritative* parents (*i.e.* mothers and fathers who exerted control over the child, expected independence, but who were also warm, rational, and responsive to the child's feelings and point-of-view). Such a child-rearing orientation contrasted sharply with the orientations expressed by the parents of less competent children. Impulsive-aggressive children, for example, were reared by *permissive* parents, while conflicted-irritable children were reared by *authoritarian* parents. These data contribute a subsidiary hypothesis that, in addition to affective security and its implications for exploratory activity, parent–child relations contribute self-confidence and self-esteem to the child—attributes that would maximize chances of success in initial encounters with other children.[2]

Elkins (1958) also found that children whose parents were satisfied with them received higher sociometric scores than children whose parents were dissatisfied with them. Absence of family tension, along with loving and casual parental attitudes have been predictive of high peer status in several other studies (*cf.* Hoffman, 1961). Both maternal and paternal affection are positively correlated with self-confidence, assertiveness, and effective skills in peer interaction. Finally, data from children themselves present much the same picture: well-liked children are more satisfied with their home lives and describe their families as more cohesive than do less well-accepted children (Elkins, 1958; Warnath, 1955). These trends suggest that parent–child relations result in both an affective and an instrumental base conducive to peer interaction.

Once again, caution is needed in evaluating these data. Children who are well-integrated into the world of other children may enjoy comfortable affectional relations with their parents owing to attributes such as attractiveness or brightness—characteristics that everyone evaluates positively. It is risky to conclude, from such evidence, that secure parent–child relations are necessary precursors of success in peer relations. Nevertheless, the correlational data are consistent with the theory at hand, namely, that the child's relations with his/her parents provide the emotional and instrumental base for exploration of the child–child social system and orients the child towards that same system. According to this view of the social worlds of the child, family relations make peer relations possible; the earlier experiences merely maximize the probability that successful peer experiences will ensue.

A small body of evidence that shows the adverse effects of family disruption on social behaviour and development converges with the literature discussed above. In general, these studies show that, following divorce or the death of a parent, children are more likely to manifest acting out, aggressive, antisocial, and expressive behaviours than children from nuclear families. Mostly, the data base consists of parent reports on behaviour occurring within the family context. In general, indications of disturbances within that social system are more extensive when boys are involved than when girls are (*cf.* Hetherington, Cox and Cox, 1978; Rutter, 1971). Family disruption owing to parental death is more likely to involve depression, anxiety, or disturbance in role relations than disruptions owing to divorce (*cf.* Hetherington, 1972).

Until recently, documentation was lacking concerning the manner in which these disruptions affect, in turn, the child–child social system. Now, Hetherington, Cox and Cox (in press) have studied the peer interactions of 24 boys and 24 girls from divorced families (in which the mother had custody of the child) along with a matched sample of boys and girls from nuclear families. Observations in nursery schools were conducted two months, one year, and two years after the divorce. Teacher ratings and peer nominations were also obtained. In common with all children, the play behaviour of the children from divorced families became cognitively and socially more mature with increasing age. Their social activity, however, was very different from the social activity of the children from nuclear families. Sex differences were also evident. First, affective disturbance in the peer relations of both boys and girls were noted two months after divorce: (a) the children were less happy, affectionate, and task oriented and were more depressed, anxious, guilty, and apathetic than children from nuclear families; and (b) the children from divorced families were more antagonistic and aggressive, showing more negative affect than the children from nuclear families. Over time, these differences gradually disappeared for girls; differences in both depression and acting out behaviours had disappeared two years following the divorce. Boys from divorced families were still more hostile and less happy two years after the divorce than were the boys from nuclear families.

Parallel differences were observed in the children's play: at two months after divorce, both boys and girls evidenced more functional play, less imaginative play, less associative-constructive play, and less cooperative-constructive play than children from nuclear families. One year following divorce, the only differences remaining for girls were lowered scores for imaginative play among the children from divorced families. Two years afterward, these differences had disappeared. Among boys, though, differences were observed between children from divorced families and from nuclear families at all three time periods. As contrasted to boys from nuclear families, boys from divorced families showed: (a) more solitary and parallel play with toys; (b) less cooperative, constructive, imaginative, and game play; (c) more onlooker behaviour; (d) shorter play episodes; and (e) over time, increasing contact with younger children and girls. Overall, the longitudinal changes associated with divorce are consistent with the theory of system interdependencies advocated here. Initially, the conflict in the home situation seems to induce affective insecurity and constrict the child's freedom to explore the environment. In turn, the child's engagements with other children are constrained and, over time, retardation occurs in play development.

The social retardation lasts longer, for some reason, in the case of boys than in the case of girls—maybe because girls receive more supportive interactions from their teachers and their mothers. Indeed, such interactions occurred in the Hetherington *et al.* study more commonly with girls than with boys. Such interactions would serve to re-establish secure adult–child relations from which the child, in turn, can return to explorations of the wider social world. The sex differences in the 'recovery' of social competencies in the aftermath of divorce need further exploration, of course.

CONCLUSION

Family relations and peer relations are very different social systems. While the social interaction occurring in each system becomes more complex and more differentiated as children grow older, the nature of the social interaction differs greatly between the two systems.

Parent–child relations, especially the mother–child relationship, produce an affective and instrumental base from which the young primate (including the young child) can explore the wider social world without undue anxiety or distress. Specific competencies, such as language and role-taking skills, as well as self-esteem, may emanate from this system and later be elaborated in other contexts. But the major function of family relations, from early childhood through adolescence, seems to be the provision of a basis for environmental exploration. Exploratory activity then brings the child into contact with many different social objects, among which are other children. Through interaction with these associates, the child then extends his/her competencies in communication and role-taking. These associations also result in the direct acquisition of a constellation of unique attitudes and affects—each essential to social adaptation.

Parents also exercise managerial functions with respect to the social lives of their children, selecting particular sociobehavioural contexts to which the children will be exposed. Mothers determine the timing and circumstances under which their offspring will have contact with child associates, teachers, and other individuals. In most instances, this management maximizes the child's exposure to socializing agents who can extend, elaborate, and multiply his/her adaptive potential—far beyond what the mother could do alone.

While individual differences exist in the sensitivity of parents to the needs of their offspring, the evolutionary evidence indicates that parental 'folkwisdom' results in more than social management by trial and error: the species survives. Individual differences are also evident in the affective security existing within family relations but, again, secure attachments outnumber insecure or anxious attachments. Most commonly, then, family relations provide the child with freedom to explore the social world of the peer culture and make certain that the child comes in contact with that world. These system interdependencies are among the most universal, most essential, and most elegantly-adapted linkages in the course of human development.

ACKNOWLEDGMENTS

1. This essay was written while the author was a Fellow, Center for Advanced Study in the Behavioral Sciences, Stanford, California. Support in the preparation of this material was provided by the Foundation for Child Development (USA) and Grant No. 5 PO1 HD 05027, National Institute of Child Health and Human Development (USA).
2. This suggestion was made by Eleanor E. Maccoby.

REFERENCES

Ainsworth, M. D. S. (1967). *Infancy in Uganda: Infant care and the growth of love.* Baltimore: John Hopkins University Press.

Ainsworth, M. D. S., Bell, S. M. and Stayton, D. J. (1971). Individual differences in strange situation behavior of one-year-olds. In H. R. Schaffer (Ed.) *The Origins of Human Social Relations.* New York: Academic Press.

Ainsworth, M. D. S. and Wittig, B. A. (1969). Attachment and exploratory behavior of one-year-olds in a strange situation. In B. M. Foss (Ed.) *Determinants of Infant Behaviour.* Vol. 4. London: Methuen.

Barker, R. G. and Wright, H. F. (1955). *Midwest and its Children.* New York: Harper and Row.

Baumrind, D. (1967). Child care practices anteceding three patterns of preschool behavior. *Genetic Psychology Monographs*, **75**, 43–88.

Baumrind, D. (1971). Current patterns of parental authority. *Developmental Psychology*, **4**, 1–103.

Bigelow, B. J. (1977). Children's friendship expectations: A cognitive-developmental study. *Child Development*, **48**, 246–253.

Blurton-Jones, N. (1972). Categories of child–child interaction. In N. Blurton-Jones (Ed.) *Ethological Studies of Child Behaviour.* Cambridge: The University Press.

Bowerman, C. E. and Kinch, J. W. (1959). Changes in family and peer orientation of children between the fourth and tenth grades. *Social Forces*, **37**, 206–211.

Brittain, C. V. (1963). Adolescent choices and parent–peer cross-pressures. *American Sociological Review*, **28**, 385–391.

Bronfenbrenner, U. (1967). Response to pressure from peers versus adults among Soviet and American school children. *International Journal of Psychology*, **2**, 199–207.

Charlesworth, R. and Hartup, W. W. (1967). Positive social reinforcement in the nursery school peer group. *Child Development*, **38**, 993–1002.

Coleman, J. S. (1961). *The Adolescent Society.* Glencoe, Ill.: Free Press.

Cowen, E. L., Pederson, A., Babijian, H., Izzo, L. D. and Trost, M. A. (1973). Long-term follow-up of early detected vulnerable children. *Journal of Consulting and Clinical Psychology*, **41**, 438–446.

Easterbrooks, M. A. and Lamb, M. E. (1979). The relationship between quality of infant–mother attachment and infant competence in initial encounters with peers. *Child Development*, **50**, 380–387.

Eckerman, C. O. (1979). The human infant in social interaction. In R. B. Cairns (Ed.) *Social Interaction: Methods, analysis and illustrations.* Hillsdale, N.J.: Erlbaum.

Eckerman, C. O., Whatley, J. L. and Kutz, S. L. (1975). The growth of social play with peers during the second year of life. *Developmental Psychology,* **11,** 42–49.

Edwards, C. P. and Whiting, B. B. (1977). Patterns of dyadic interaction. Paper presented at the biennial meetings of the Society for Research in Child Development, New Orleans.

Elkins, D. (1958). Some factors related to the choice status of ninety eighth-grade children in a school society. *Genetic Psychology Monographs,* **58,** 207–272.

Foot, H. C., Chapman, A. J. and Smith, J. R. (1977). Friendship and social responsiveness in boys and girls. *Journal of Personality and Social Psychology,* **35,** 401–411.

Freud, A. and Dann S. (1951). An experiment in group living. In R. Eisler *et al.* (Eds.) *The Psychoanalytic Study of the Child.* Vol. 6. New York: International Universities Press.

Furman, W., Rahe, D. F. and Hartup, W. W. Rehabilitation of socially-withdrawn children through mixed-age and same-age socialization. *Child Development,* in press.

Gold, H. A. (1962). The importance of ideology in sociometric evaluation of leadership. *Group Psychotherapy,* **15,** 224–230.

Goldman, J. A. (1976). The social participation of preschool children in same-age versus mixed-age groupings. Unpublished doctoral dissertation, University of Wisconsin.

Goy, R. W. and Goldfoot, D. A. (1973). Experimental and hormonal factors influencing development of sexual behavior in the male rhesus monkey. In *The Neurosciences, Third Study Program.* Cambridge, Mass.: Massachusetts Institute of Technology Press.

Greenberg, D. J., Hillman, D. and Grice, D. (1973). Infant and stranger variables related to stranger anxiety in the first year of life. *Developmental Psychology,* **9,** 207–212.

Harlow, H. F. (1969) Age-mate or peer affectional system. In D. S. Lehrman, R. A. Hinde and E. Shaw (Eds.) *Advances in the Study of Behavior.* Vol. 2. New York: Academic Press.

Harlow, H. F. and Harlow, M. K. (1965). The affectional systems. In A. M. Schrier, H. F. Harlow and F. Stollnitz (Eds.) *Behavior of Nonhuman Primates.* Vol. 2. New York: Academic Press.

Harlow, H. F. and Zimmermann, R. R. (1959). Affectional responses in the infant monkey. *Science,* **130,** 421–432.

Hartup, W. W. (1975). The origins of friendships. In M. Lewis and L. A. Rosenblum (Eds.) *Friendship and Peer Relations.* New York: John Wiley.

Hartup, W. W. (1976a). Cross-age versus same-age peer interaction: Ethological and cross-cultural perspectives. In V. L. Allen (Ed.) *Children as Teachers.* New York: Academic Press.

Hartup, W. W. (1976b). Peer interaction and the behavioral development of the individual child. In E. Schopler and R. J. Reichler (Eds.) *Psychopathology and Child Development.* New York: Plenum.

Hartup, W. W. (1978). Children and their friends. In H. McGurk (Ed.) *Issues in Childhood Social Development.* London: Methuen.

Heathers, G. (1955). Emotional dependence and independence in nursery school play. *Journal of Genetic Psychology,* **87,** 37–57.

Hertz-Lazarowitz, R., Feitelson, D., Hartup, W. W. and Zahavi, S. Social interaction and social organization of Israeli five- to seven-year-olds. Unpublished manuscript, University of Haifa.

Hetherington, E. M. (1965). A developmental study of the effects of sex of the dominant parent on sex-role preference, identification, and imitation in children. *Journal of Personality and Social Psychology,* **2,** 188–194.

Hetherington, E. M. (1966). Effects of paternal absence on sex typed behaviors in Negro and white preadolescent males. *Journal of Personality and Social Psychology,* **4,** 87–91.

Hetherington, E. M. (1972). Effects of parental absence on personality development in adolescent daughters. *Developmental Psychology,* **7,** 313–326.

Hetherington, E. M., Cox, M. and Cox, R. (1978). The aftermath of divorce. In J. H. Stevens and M. Matthews (Eds.) *Mother–child, Father–child Relations.* Washington: National Association for the Education of Young Children.

Hetherington, E. M., Cox, M. and Cox, R. Play and social interaction in children following divorce. *Journal of Social Issues,* in press.

Hinde, R. A. (1974). *Biological Bases of Human Social Behaviour.* New York: McGraw-Hill.

Hoffman, L. W. (1961). The father's role in the family and the child's peer-group adjustment. *Merrill-Palmer Quarterly,* **7,** 97–105.

Jay, P. C. (Ed.) (1968). *Primates: Studies in adaptation and variability.* New York: Holt, Rinehart and Winston.

Kandel, D. B. (1973). Adolescent marihuana use: Role of parents and peers. *Science,* **181,** 1067–1070.

Kandel, D. B. and Lesser, G. S. (1972). *Youth in Two Worlds.* San Francisco: Jossey-Bass.

Keasey, C. B. (1971). Social participation as a factor in the moral development of preadolescents. *Developmental Psychology,* **2,** 216–220.

Kinsey, A. C., Pomeroy, W. B. and Martin, C. E. (1948). *Sexual Behavior in the Human Male.* Philadelphia: W. B. Saunders.

Konner, M. (1975). Relations among infants and juveniles in comparative perspective. In M. Lewis and L. A. Rosenblum (Eds.) *Friendship and Peer Relations.* New York: John Wiley.

Lakin, M., Lakin, M. G. and Costanzo, P. R. Group processes in early childhood: A dimension of human development. *International Journal of Behavioral Development* (in press).

Langlois, J. H., Gottfried, N. W., Barnes, B. M. and Hendricks, D. E. (1978). The effect of peer age on the social behavior of preschool children. *Journal of Genetic Psychology,* **132,** 11–19.

Lee, L. C. (1973). Social encounters of infants: The beginnings of popularity. Paper presented at the biennial meetings of the International Society for the Study of Behavioral Development, Ann Arbor, Michigan.

Lempers, J. D., Flavell, E. R. and Flavell, J. H. (1977). The development in very young children of tacit knowledge concerning visual perception. *Genetic Psychology Monographs.*

Lewis, M. and Brooks-Gunn, J. (1972). Self, other, and fear: The reaction of infants to people. Paper presented at the meeting of the Eastern Psychological Association, Boston.

Lieberman, A. F. (1977) Preschoolers' competence with a peer: Relations with attachment and peer experience. *Child Development,* **48,** 1277–1287.

Lougee, M. D., Grueneich, R. and Hartup, W. W. (1977). Social interaction in same- and mixed-age dyads of preschool children. *Child Development,* **48,** 1353–1361.

Maccoby, E. E. and Masters, J. C. (1970). Attachment and dependency. In P. H. Mussen (Ed.) *Carmichael's Manual of Child Psychology,* Vol. 2. New York: John Wiley.

Marshall, H. R. and McCandless, B. R. (1957). A study of prediction of social behavior of preschool children. *Child Development,* **28,** 149–159.

Newcomb, A. F., Brady, J. E. and Hartup, W. W. (1979). Friendship and incentive condition as determinants of children's task-oriented social behavior. *Child Development,* **50,** 878–881.

Patterson, F. G., Bonvillian, J. D., Reynolds, P. C. and Maccoby, E. E. (1975). Mother and peer attachment under conditions of fear in rhesus monkeys (Macaca mulatta). *Primates,* **16,** 75–81.

Piaget, J. (1932). *The Moral Judgment of the Child.* Glencoe, Ill.: The Free Press.

Rheingold, H. L. and Cook, K. V. (1975). The content of boys' and girls' rooms as an index of parents' behavior. *Child Development,* **46,** 459–463.

Roff, M., Sells, S. B. and Golden, M. M. (1972). *Social Adjustment and Personality Development in Children.* Minneapolis: University of Minnesota Press.

Rubin, K. H., Maioni, T. L. and Hornung, M. (1976). Free play behaviors in middle- and lower-class preschoolers: Parten and Piaget revisited. *Child Development,* **47,** 414–419.

Rutter, M. (1971). Parent–child separation: Psychological effects on the children. *Journal of Child Psychology and Psychiatry,* **12,** 233–260.

Selman, R. L. and Jaquette, D. (1977). Stability and oscillation in interpersonal awareness: a clinical-developmental analysis. In C. B. Keasey (Ed.) *The Nebraska Symposium on Motivation,* Vol. 25. Lincoln, Neb.: University of Nebraska Press.

Shatz, M. and Gelman, R. (1973). The development of communication skills: Modification in the speech of young children as a function of listener. *Monographs of the Society for Research in Child Development,* **38,** (Whole No. 152).

Sherif, M., Harvey, O. J., White, B. J., Hood, W. R. and Sherif, C. W. (1961). *Intergroup Conflict and Cooperation: The robbers cave experiment.* Norman, Okla.: University of Oklahoma Press.

Smith, A. J. (1960). A developmental study of group processes. *Journal of Genetic Psychology, 97,* 29–39.

Sullivan, H. S. (1953). *The Interpersonal Theory of Psychiatry.* New York: Norton.

Suomi, S. J. (1978). Differential development of various social relationships by rhesus monkey infants. In M. Lewis and L. A. Rosenblum (Eds.) *The Social Network of the Developing Infant.* New York: Plenum.

Suomi, S. J. (1979). Peers, play, and primary prevention in primates. In M. W. Kent and J. E. Rolf (Eds.) *The Primary Prevention of Psychopathology: Promoting social competence and coping in children.* Hanover, NH: University Press of New England.

Thompson, G. G. and Horrocks, J. E. (1947). A study of the friendship fluctuations of urban boys and girls. *Journal of Genetic Psychology, 70,* 53–63.

Vandell, D. L. (1977). The development and characteristics of early peer social interaction. Unpublished manuscript, University of Texas at Dallas.

Vandell, D. L. and Mueller, E. C. (1977). The effects of group size on toddlers' social interactions with peers. Paper presented at the biennial meetings of the Society for Research in Child Development, New Orleans.

Walters, J., Pearce, D. and Dahms, L. (1957). Affectional and aggressive behavior of preschool children. *Child Development, 28,* 15–26.

Warnath, C. F. (1955). The relation of family cohesiveness and adolescent independence to social effectiveness. *Marriage and Family Living, 17,* 346–348.

Waters, E., Wippman, J. and Sroufe, L. A. (1979). Attachment, positive affect, and competence in the peer group: two studies in construct validation. *Child Development, 50,* 821–829.

Whiting, B. B. (1978). The dependency hang-up and experiments in alternative life styles. In J. M. Yinger and S. J. Cutler (Eds.) *Major Social Issues.* New York: The Free Press.

Whiting, B. B. and Whiting, J. W. M. (1975). *Children of Six Cultures.* Cambridge, Mass.: Harvard University Press.

Winder, C. L. and Rau, L. (1962). Parental attitudes associated with social deviance in preadolescent boys. *Journal of Abnormal and Social Psychology, 64,* 418–424.

24. PLAY

D. B. ROSENBLATT

Although the nature of play has attracted speculation since the ancient Greeks, until recently it has escaped serious and objective testing of its relevance and function in early child development. The topic is still plagued by disputes of definition, so much so that it stands apart from the other chapters in this volume by the sheer elusiveness of the material. Nevertheless, in a therapeutic discipline like psychiatry play has much to offer the clinician, both in terms of understanding the developmental stages of an activity that takes up so much of childhood, and because play itself reveals important elements of the child's ability to organize and make sense of his environment, his linguistic and cognitive skills, and the process of his personality development. Within the limitations of a single chapter it is only possible to sample a few of the many explanations of the reasons children play, the manner in which the skills necessary for play develop, and the variations that occur between children and between different communities and cultures. For those who seek a greater diversity of material, detailed accounts can be found in Tizard and Harvey (1977), Herron and Sutton-Smith (1971), Bruner *et al.* (1976), Garvey (1977), and Millar (1968).

Functions and features of play

It is common to find the word 'play' used almost indiscriminately in everyday life, and even pejoratively, as when a child is scolded for 'playing about' instead of 'getting on with things'. But there are six almost indisputable characteristics of play which derive from Huizinga's classic volume *Homo Ludens* (1947), and which most authors have subsequently accepted: (i) It is voluntary; (ii) pleasurable; (iii) tension enhancing; and that (iv) its immediate consequences are not of biological necessity; (v) it contains elements of quasi-reality, 'as if', or pure fantasy; and finally (vi) it changes qualitatively and quantitatively as the organism matures—it is not static. We could also add another feature to the list which captures the enigma of play, (vii) that it has certain systematic relations to what is not play (Garvey, 1977), such as problem solving, language learning, and so on.

Classical theorists began by looking for the way in which play is useful; the child must rid himself of *surplus energy* (Schiller, 1795; Spencer, 1855) or *practice skills* (Groos, 1899), or even *relive the history of the race* (Hall, 1904). Recent theories would stress the *adaptive* functions of play in accounting for the distinctive human pre-eminence in tool use, in observational learning, and in symbolic transformations (Bruner, 1972; Sutton-Smith, 1971). Lowenfeld succinctly summed up the many contradictory theories and perspectives by her argument that play can never be fitted into a single formula because it means different things at different times, both to the theorist and to the child (1933). Or as Stone (1971) puts it,

'... when we speculate upon the social significance of child's play, we may well be developing hypotheses that have relevance only for a particular and relatively recent era of Western civilisation. I have often wondered whether or not this is the best any social scientist can do—to dramatise effectively his own socio-historical era ...'

Warning in hand, we can examine the structure and form of play, bearing in mind that although we may begin with a discussion of the cognitive requirements, play is essentially social in nature; the child learns about the world through his social interactions with caregivers, and he will progress inevitably towards using this knowledge in more mature forms of interchange in play with his equals.

COGNITIVE ASPECTS OF PLAY

Learning about the world of objects

During the first two years of life much of the infant's time is taken up by learning about, exploring, and playing with the things that make up his environment. His interest in objects is apparent from the first week of life, when he will focus and then follow a brightly coloured object dangled in his line of vision, or turn to the soft sounds of a rattle or bell (Brazelton, 1973; Packer and Rosenblatt, 1979). Boredom sets in on constant exposure to the same stimuli, which is relieved by shifting attention to the surroundings, with only furtive glances back to the object. His attention can be maintained by presenting new stimuli, particularly if they are brightly coloured, complex in design, or moving (Fantz, 1961).

By 3 months he will reach for objects near him, and will kick and pull at a mobile for long periods, seemingly entranced not only by his own ability to reproduce the movement, but by the way in which the figures change as they are moved. Piaget suggests that the infant gradually comes to be interested in the 'means' by which he produces an action on a toy, rather than the goal of actually making it move. He gives an example from his daughter's behaviour, where pursuit of the means itself becomes play:

'J. was sitting in her cot and I hung her celluloid duck above her. She pulled a string hanging from the top of the cot and in this way shook the duck for a moment, laughing. Her involuntary movements left an impression on her eiderdown; she then forgot the duck, pulled the eiderdown towards her ... noticing the movement of her hands she let everything go, so as to clasp and shake them.' (Piaget, 1951)

By 12 months the infant is interested in a great number of toys, which he subjects to a number of 'instrumental' activities, such as banging, waving, and pushing (Sinclair, 1970). Between 13 and 24 months he comes to use these toys in a functional manner, such as drinking from a cup or brushing his hair, and to include adults in these play bouts. Such functional behaviours become more and more 'representational' as the child elaborates simple schemas into imaginative episodes like giving the doll a cup of tea. After about 24 months he becomes increasingly capable of action in the absence of objects, which permits symbolization, pretence, and make-believe. He transfers rituals to new objects, or out of their original context, and pushes a block along the floor as if it were a car. Some of the activity is immediate imitation, such as 'reading' the paper while Daddy does so at breakfast, while 'deferred' imitative play appears in a mid-morning re-creation of the breakfast conversation or events.

A number of recent studies of children's object play at different stages (Fenson and Kagan, 1976; Nicolich, 1977; Sinclair, 1970; Lowe, 1975; Rosenblatt, 1977) identify the following important trends between the first and third year:

(1) From immature responses applied indiscriminately to all toys (such as mouthing or banging), to appropriate actions which require understanding of the object's properties (rolling a ball, pushing a car);

(2) From a random series of responses directed at a new object, to an obvious sequence of 'investigation' (touching, manipulating) followed by play;

(3) From the use of items one at a time, to an appreciation of the combinatorial use of toys in both a logical-mathematical sense (a nest of beakers, a tower of bricks) and in functional and representation relations (cup on saucer, feeding Teddy with a spoon);

(4) From a series of brief attentive episodes to an organized play session in which objects are selected and ordered according to the demands of the dramatic theme (undressing, bathing, and then putting the doll to bed);

(5) From imitation of adult actions on himself (pretending to eat), to acting on the toy (feeding the doll), and finally to complete 'decentralization' in which the child makes one object act on another (one doll feeds another doll);

(6) From the obvious or functional use of a toy (build-

ing with blocks) to 'double knowledge', whereby the child can transcend its function to make it represent something else (the block becomes a car, or bits of paper become sweets);

(7) From dependence on an adult or older child to initiate symbolic episodes, to directing and instructing others to carry out designated aspects of a complex plot.

Object play and other intellectual skills

The development of sophisticated schemas for dealing with objects develops concurrently with other cognitive skills. For example, the infant needs to have an understanding that objects continue to exist even when out of sight, and that a particular object will retain the same shape from one appearance to the next (Piaget, 1952). Infants who achieve the stages of 'object permanence' earlier also seem to play in a more mature fashion, as evidenced by combining toys, fewer stereotyped responses, and a greater variety of schemas (Rosenblatt, 1977).

Imitative skills are also important in play, although Piaget (1952) would define imitations as pure 'accommodation' to the environment, while 'play' consists of 'assimilation' of new stimuli into existing structures. Nonetheless, the infant's representational knowledge develops largely from social interactions in which he watches, mimics, and only then elaborates adult activities. Dunn and Wooding (1977) caution that many of the 'symbolic' acts which observers record are replications of adult demonstrations; that is, simply delayed imitation rather than internalized representations of an event. In early peer play imitation not only serves as a vehicle for initiating interaction—one child copies another's tower building—but seems to promote more elaborate manipulative skills and complex levels of behaviour (Rubenstein and Howes, 1976).

The majority of recent investigations into object play have attempted to specify the relationship between the emergence of symbolic play and the development of language. The Piagetian school views language as being made possible by early symbolic behaviour which grows out of the infant's transaction with the environment (Sinclair, 1970), while Vygotsky (1962) argues that it is language itself which makes such symbolic processes possible. In a study of three Italian children, Bates et al. (1975) observed that referential speech followed shortly after the first instances of symbolic play and the ability to internally represent absent objects. In a somewhat larger group followed longitudinally, Rosenblatt (1977) found that children who used appropriate and representational play at 9 and 12 months were more likely to be rapid language learners in the second year.

Moreover, play styles were reflected in later strategies of language acquisition. Infants who were 'toy-oriented' as opposed to seeking social interaction during the sessions, were more likely to learn words about objects in their first 50 words. If an infant was prone to mixing up toy functions in his play—brushing his hair with a small, handled mirror—then he usually made similar mistakes by 'over-extending' early words to a greater class of objects ('doggie' as a label for many different animals).

Nelson (1973) puts forward the idea that the child learns language by a 'concept matching' model, in which his experiences of object play and social interaction will be encoded in the sort of vocabulary that he develops. Sinclair (1971) goes further than this in suggesting that syntactic elements in language are a direct reflection of the child's organization of space and materials. In the same way that the child uses a toy telephone as an undifferentiated whole, and only later becomes aware of the separate functions of the dial receiver, he comes to use two-word sentences only after a 'holophrastic' period in which one-word utterances function as whole sentences. In addition, she hypothesizes that one of the essential features of language known as 'recursive property of the base', by which an indefinite set of utterances can be generated (The man who had a daughter who had a son who had . . .), is paralleled by the embedding of one action pattern into another; one might say that the child putting one beaker into another is rehearsing a primitive cognitive skill that he will later need in language. Present evidence, therefore seems to support the notion of language developing out of sensori-motor activities, of which play is a direct expression; in fact, several authors have developed scales from which 'symbolic maturity' and language potential can be inferred (Nicolich, 1977; Inhelder et al., 1972). Although Luria and Yudovich (1959) reported an experiment with twins in which systematic speech training led to the development of meaningful play, the twins concerned were already retarded owing to restricted environmental experience, and (to my knowledge) the same hypothesis has not been tested in normal children learning language.

Attempts have also been made to evaluate whether the child's manipulation of objects in exploration and play confers any advantage in learning and problem-solving. Bruner (1974) has suggested that one benefit of play is the 'flexibility' it offers the player by freeing him from the anxieties of attaining a goal, and enabling him instead to combine pieces of behaviour into novel solutions. In examining this hypothesis, Sylva (1977) constructed a situation in which young children had to clamp two sticks together in order to form a tool long enough to remove a piece of chalk from a box. A comparison of the different experimental conditions showed that those children who were allowed 'free play' with the components completed the task as efficiently as those who watched an adult carry out the task, and, in addition, demonstrated more goal directed activity and a more systematic approach to the problem. She emphasizes that the children who were most successful not only explored the objects (such as trying the clamps on the table edge), but also transformed the clamps and sticks into objects which superseded their physical properties—one child constructed a letter 'A', and another re-arranged them into a house. This contrasts with the findings of Hutt (1966), who implies that learning is more likely to be a consequence of the exploring phase when a child is faced with a new object, and only occurs incidentally once the child's responses have become more playful. When she presented preschool children with an intriguing novel toy—a box with a lever attached to four visible counters, a buzzer, and a bell—they were more likely to discover the function of the parts during systematic investigation. Such behaviours then decreased over the next six sessions, to be replaced by playful manipulations of the lever or bell within a game, or using the object 'as if' it were a seat or bridge. If, as one child did, the child begins a game before full investigation, he is unlikely to find all the working parts. However, it may well be that even in Hutt's situation the children profited by the relaxed mood, and greater diversity and variability of activity which was evident in their 'play', but that the results were not assessed in a task situation.

It may also be that play and games substitute more interesting goals and thus promote learning. For instance, Sutton-Smith (1967) used a number game to encourage conservation in children between 5 and 5½ years old. The experimental group improved significantly between pre- and post-test, from which he concludes that 'the game apparently forced the players to pay attention to the cues for number identity or they would lose, be cheated against, be laughed at, and would not win'. A similar advantage was found for games over traditional work-book procedures in improving verbal and number skills (Humphrey, 1965), and in increasing preschool children's fluency on word association tasks (Dansky and Silverman, 1973).

Lastly, play has been investigated for its contribution to creativity. Wallach and Kogan (1965) found that a game-like approach to creativity tests resulted in scores which were different from those on conventional intelligence tests, and that creativity was facilitated by a playful environment. Lieberman (1965) tested 5-year-old children in a kindergarten, and found that those who were more playful were better at devising novel titles, lists, and stories. This kind of thinking, commonly referred to as 'divergent' thinking, was also facilitated by imaginative play by Glasberg (1975). Several other studies have investigated the relationship between socio-dramatic or fantasy play and creativity (Feitelson and Ross, 1973; Smilansky, 1968) within the context of *teaching* children how to play, and so these will be discussed in a later section. Although the majority of studies do not provide overwhelming support that play improves subsequent intellectual performance, they do at least suggest that play is not simply an escape from more fundamental modes of adaptation, but also is pre-adaptive in itself.

Playing with language

Language too can be exploited and transformed in the same manner as toys. The tape recordings which Weir (1972) made of her 2½-year-old son's pre-sleep monologues revealed playful manipulation of the semantic, phonological, and grammatical features of English. At times these sounded like rehearsals for conversations yet to be held, but many of them contained substitutes and nonsensical inventions—'Let Bobo bink. Bink ben bink. Blue kink.'

Garvey (1977) suggests that there are three areas in which the 3-5-year-old child experiments with language. Firstly, he plays with sound, by selecting vocalizations to accompany actions ('ding-a-ling'), or by the transposition of stress patterns in familiar words (Mónday todáy, Tóozday todáy, Wézday tóday Tóozday . . .). Pairs of children often use rhyming sounds and alliteration to maintain 'silly' conversations, such as 'High/ Sky/Bye-bye/ My-my/ Fly-fly/ Lie-lie—you're a líar!' Such sequences are related to the many chants and jump rope songs of the school years, and become part of the oral tradition passed on from child to child (Opie and Opie, 1969; Ritchie, 1965). Garvey's second category includes fantasy and nonsense words, where the children may use silly names for each other (Big nose), employ forbidden words to gain attention (Ho-hum, it's bum-bum here), and deny established fact ('That's a cat-dog' or 'My sister is really my daddy'). Or, thirdly, they may actually alter the 'pragmatic' aspects of language by violating the normal way in which conversations are conducted. This may involve giving facetious answers to real questions, or vice versa, or producing a string of 'assertions and counter-assertions' ('You're out/ No, you're out/No, you're out'). When older, children engage in an endless round of 'Knock-knock' jokes which are very similar. Like other sorts of play these interchanges were inevitably marked with laughter from both partners, or excessive and predictable ritualization, as well as exaggerated or feigned surprise and indignation.

This kind of play provides an obvious example of play as the 'non-literal' treatment of a given behaviour, which occurs in most other cultures (Kirschenblatt-Gimblett, 1976). In Okinawa verbal wit is an integral part of adult recreation, and linguistic play and teasing are common in the children's games (Maretzki and Maretzki, 1963). In the Philippines children pass on very complicated rhymes, usually overladen with double meanings, and this appears to be true in Kau (Pukui, 1943) and amongst the Dau (Roheim, 1943). Garvey concludes that while its contribution to the development of language has not yet been studied, it is likely that the exploration of the boundaries of linguistic convention probably helps in the mastery of complex speech forms and the capacity to use language creatively.

SOCIAL INTERACTION IN PLAY

Mother and infant: the ontogenesis of social play

Developmental psychologists have become increasingly impressed with the sophistication of the young infant, and perhaps even more important, the subtle yet sophisticated way in which mothers elaborate on their infant's skills. There is no doubt that the play even between a newborn infant and his mother illustrates aspects of timing, intentionality, and communication which are echoed more clearly in the sophisticated social interchanges available to the infant when he masters language at the end of the first year. Stern (1977) offers us a detailed account of the change from a routine and seriously goal-oriented feed turned into play—

'... the mother turned her head and gazed at the infant's face ... he turned to gaze back at her ... he let go of the nipple and the suction around it broke as he eased into the faintest suggestion of a smile ... her eyes opened a little wider and her eyebrows raised a little ... The infant did not return to sucking and his mother held frozen her slight expression of anticipation ... until the mother suddenly shattered it by saying "Hey!" and simultaneously opening her eyes wider, raising her eyebrows further and throwing her head up and towards the infant ... the baby's eyes widened. His head tilted up and, as his smile broadened, the nipple fell out of his mouth. Now she said, "Well hello! ... heell o ... heelloooo!" ... With each phrase the baby expressed more pleasure, and his body resonated almost like a balloon being pumped up, filling a little more with each breath ...'

A careless routine action of a mother looking at her infant is seized on by the infant who interrupts his eating and signals that he is ready to play; she captures the moment and they are off. Not only can the infant take 'his turn' but when the action begins to flag he can redeem it—

'... The shared excitement between them ebbed, but before it faded completely, the baby suddenly took an initiative and intervened to rescue it. His head lurched forward, his hands jerked up, and a fuller smile blossomed. His mother was jolted into motion ... moved forward, mouth open and eyes alight, and said "Ooooh ... ya wanna play do ya ... yeah? ... I didn't know if you were still hungry ... no ... nooooo ... no I didn't ...."'

Bruner (1974) has suggested the term 'scaffolding' for the way in which the mother provides for the infant to perform at his best by filling in the details that he cannot manage (Kaye, 1970). As he gets older she withdraws more from the active role, and encourages the infant to show things to her, find things for himself, tell her what it's called, and so on, so that by the end of the second year he will be able to initiate and sustain these dialogues with playmates of his own. Even simple strategies such as pointing to an interesting toy to signal a shift of attention are learned and reinforced in the mother–infant play session (Collis and Schaffer, 1975) and become instrumental overtures in the sharing of objects and elaboration of conversations.

Many advantages are associated with maternal interest in, and stimulation of, infant play. Yarrow (1975) identifies the mother as the 'mediator of stimulation', who directs her infant's attention to his environment and thus makes the properties of these objects more salient. Young children not only need their mothers in the room physically in order to have the confidence to explore and play with a new set of toys (Ainsworth and Bell, 1970), but the quality of these explorations is better if the mothers are responsive to their initiations of interaction, or play fre-

quently and for prolonged periods with them at home as well as in the laboratory setting (Bell, 1970). A harmonious relationship between mothers and their infants even seems to act as a buffer protecting the infants from the detrimental effects of social and economic disadvantage (Bell, 1971).

The mother's involvement seems to be of greatest importance to the development of representational skills. Mothers use more complicated and elaborate speech to their children during a picturebook-reading session than in other sorts of play (Snow et al., 1976; Cross, 1975) and they increase the length of representational play bouts by taking part in them (Dunn and Wooding, 1977).

Play with peers

Recent work suggests that even toddlers are able to sustain brief social contacts, but that the overwhelming interest in such a situation are the toys between them, with the interactive skills developing more slowly. Bronson (1975) observed 40 children as they played with two or three others from the age of 10 months until they were 2 years. There was a consistently low level of interaction between the children, with about half of the encounters involving disagreements or struggles. Parents seem to be a better bet as companions because other toddlers are too unpredictable. Eckerman (Eckerman et al., 1975), also studying foursomes in the same age range, observed that interaction increased markedly after 20 months, when the child began to imitate activities of the peer, as well as share toys and activities. In a study of a small group of boys, Mueller and DeStefano (1978) observed such turn-taking episodes at the slightly earlier age of 18 months. As was mentioned earlier, peer play at this age begins to confer advantages not evident in comparable play with mother (Rubenstein and Howes, 1976). The 19-month-olds in their study played with the same child regularly, and during his visit were much more likely to play with, imitate, and offer objects to him than to mother. These children spent 50% of their time being sociable, although only 20% of the intervals included sustained mutual play or games. In fact, not only did they play *more* with the toy in the peer's presence, but they played *better*.

These studies emphasize how misleading it can be to accept the norms of previous generations of children as still valid; in a classic study Parten (1932) observed that it was not until 3½ that nursery school children began to play cooperatively. However, Parten's study was important as it was the first to develop an adequate methodology for observational work, it focused on children in a group situation, and it categorized the various levels of play before Piaget's work was available. She identified three levels of social play: solitary play, parallel play, and associative play which emerged in that order. Recent replications suggest that lower levels of associative or cooperative play may occur in disadvantaged children and in girls (Barnes, 1971; Rubin et al., 1976), and that it is related to cognitive levels as well (Moore, Evertson and Brophy, 1974). It also seems that solitary play may have been misrepresented in earlier studies as the least mature form of social play, since solitary play experiences are often the most educative and goal-directed (Moore *et al.*, 1974), and children involved in parallel play may be interested in the other children but not learning or contributing much to the situation (Rubin, 1975; Rubin *et al.*, 1976).

It is not surprising that cooperative play is more difficult for young children. For one thing, their communicative skills are less developed (in terms of vocabulary, as well as the ability to structure sentences to express desires, past and future events, etc.), and they are less able to anticipate their playmate's actions and thoughts. As they get older their symbolic and representational play becomes more elaborate and imaginative, and thus creates more fulfilling roles for playmates. Consequently group size increases as children develop. At the age of 3 children seem happiest in groups of two to three, whereas by 5 the cohort may consist of up to five children and forms a more lasting and stable group (Smith, 1977). During the school years children are quite happy playing in larger groups, and in organized sports up to 25 children may cooperate towards a common goal (Eifermann, 1970).

Content of social play

Smilansky has outlined four categories of play which emerge in order: (1) functional play, using simple repetitive muscle movements; (2) constructive play, as the manipulation of objects to construct and create; (3) dramatic play, in which the child takes the roles of others; and (4) games with rules, in which pre-arranged rules govern the pace and goal of the activity (Smilansky, 1968). These categories were largely based on Piaget's (1951) cognitive stages in play, which were sensori-motor (practice) play, symbolic play, and games with rules. Smilansky's categories offer us an advantage here in dealing with areas of social play which have not been covered elsewhere—motor play, and game playing.

Although play involving movement has its roots in the early practising of motor skills in infancy, and the active games between parents and infants (such as throwing the infant into the air), it also re-appears amongst preschool and older children in mirthful and exuberant abundance. As ethologists have pointed out, this 'rough and tumble' play is most like the play of our primate relatives in the juvenile period, although research is now available which demonstrates the similarities between gorilla and human infants in their skilled and playful manipulations of objects (Redshaw, 1978). Fine-grain analysis of rough and tumble sequences in nursery school children is marked by a 'play face' (grimaces, smiles, laughing) similar to the way in which primates signal that the act of aggression, submission, or threatening is not 'for real'. The active ingredients (run, jump, etc.) usually occur together in a short interval, and at distinctly different times from play involving objects (Blurton-Jones, 1972; Smith, 1973). It figured prominently in early theories which regarded play as arising from 'surplus energy' (Schiller, 1795; Spencer, 1855), and even today the exasperated instruction to 'go out and play!' is intended

to encourage the child to go let off steam by running it out of his system.

Play with motion is an ingredient of the games of most children throughout their school career. Children leave the concrete make-believe era of the nursery school and toys become less important than realistic objects and tools (Millar, 1968), particularly to boistrous re-enactments of television cops-and-robbers. Simple games occupy the early school years, wherein goals are few, parts are loosely organized and assigned, and rules can be bent to suit the players and the occasion (Rosenblatt, 1972). Sutton-Smith (1971) has divided games into those of approach-and-avoidance, attack, choice, observation, and impulse control, with the majority of these being prominent at particular ages. At 5 years old the child may play 'Hide and Seek' or 'Tag' in which everyone is responsible for himself and has an equal chance, while by 7 years of age an element of 'capture' might be added, and cumulative time becomes an issue. Between 9 and 12 the play begins to resemble a team effort, with differentiated spaces and a climax when the last player must be caught, or a strong element of cooperation in which two relatively undifferentiated teams pursue each other over a large area but must prevent the other from returning to base ('Prisoner's Base'). Probably one function of this kind of play is to reinforce the stratification of the society, and to allow the child to assimilate the boundaries of such relationships with his peers in play before he becomes fully responsible for his actions. Watson emphasizes that sometimes who is played with, and what is played, can serve to create discontinuities in order to encourage children to aim higher than the aspirations of their parents: 'To follow and obey the rules of the game, to play appropriate roles, and to realize his position in a larger world' (Watson, 1953). Sutton-Smith (1969) stresses that in 'achievement' (rather than 'ascriptive') game cultures of the West, competition, complex and abstract plans, and make-believe play, are all necessary to visualize a better future world.

AFFECTIVE ASPECTS OF PLAY

The role of 'the emotions' in play has attracted a great deal of attention both clinically (Menninger, 1942; Peller, 1952; Call, 1970) and experimentally (Levin and Wardwell, 1962; Henry and Henry, 1944; Erikson, 1950) although many of the studies are of a psychoanalytic orientation and are also quite old. Waelder (1933) presents the way in which psychoanalysts regard the functions of play:

(1) Movement towards a higher level of mastery through responding to challenges posed in the play situation;
(2) Simultaneous statement and symbolic fulfilment of a wish;
(3) Symbolic re-enactment of an overpowering emotional event;
(4) Reversal of roles so that the child makes himself

into the active controlling agent rather than the unwelcome and passive child he may be;

(5) A 'leave of absence' from reality and inner negative dictates;

(6) Centring of fantasies around real objects.

Call (1968, 1970) has delineated the way in which even the newborn infant comes to be emotionally satisfied in play. Firstly, play usually takes place within the warmth and security of the mother's arms or lap. The infant will probably have just been fed, and is therefore physically gratified. Lap and finger games involve explorations of environmental responses, and the development of reciprocal expectations, such that the infant feels pleasure in learning that the mother will take her turn. According to Call (1968),

'... without this kind of consistent richness of sensory motor experience, and the opportunity to crystalize this complex experience in the pleasure of play, it is doubtful that synthetic processes in the ego could develop in an unimpaired fashion.'

Phillips (1967) suggests that later on in infancy 'peep-bo' has an instrumental function in helping the infant to master separation anxiety, as the tension he feels each time she disappears is continually replaced with pleasure and gratification when she reappears. The game disappears from the infant's repertoire when he realizes that people continue to exist, even when out of sight; *i.e.* when he fully achieves object permanence.

Another aspect of Freudian theory is that play is acted-out fantasy, which offers substitute satisfaction when direct expression is not possible. Partial support for this comes from studies of doll play, in which children are given a doll, or group of dolls to play with. Sears (1960) found that preschool children who were severely punished at home showed much more aggression in their doll play, even though their actual behaviour in the nursery was quite inhibited. A similar study was carried out with Pilaga Indian children in Argentina (Henry and Henry, 1944), a culture in which an older child is displaced and ignored after the birth of a new infant. When these children were given a set of dolls named after the family members they made the 'self-doll' very aggressive and hostile towards the other family members and infant, as well as themselves. They also made the self-doll nurse, which was interpreted by the anthropologists as indicative of the desire to become the favourite nurtured infant once more.

Although in general such studies evidence good controls and high inter-observer reliabilities (Levin and Wardwell, 1962), one must not assume that the amount of aggression shown in play is directly proportional to the child's own feelings of hostility. For instance, greater aggression will result if the dolls are arranged in a family or named (Robinson, 1946), if they are presented in an orderly scene (as in a dollhouse) (Pintler, 1945), and if they are not too realistic (Phillips, 1945). Doll play is more likely to facilitate aggressive acting-out if an adult is present, and responds in an encouraging and supportive

manner (Siegel and Kohn, 1959). As Garvey points out, it is also worth remembering that the child knows he is 'playing' and that certain things are 'allowed' in play; also that what may seem quite realistic might also reflect a number of real and imagined events, including scenes from television, companions' play, and distorted memories of a previous event. Only a few studies have exposed children to aggressive material, for instance, in order to see how it affects subsequent play. Yarrow (1948) frustrated pre-school children after one doll play session by giving them difficult tasks to perform, and observed that frustration increased the aggression seen in play. Make-believe play also tends to become less coherent and creative as a result of allowing children to see bright, attractive toys which they were not allowed to handle (Barker *et al.,* 1941). Moreover, children who were most frustrated (those who were most pre-occupied with the barrier in front of the toys) regressed the most during play.

By school age children often bring fantastic and evil figures into their play, and invoke dire consequences to playmates and parents who dare challenge them. This apparently serves to compensate for the child's own feelings of inadequacy, such that he embodies all his fears and resentments in appropriate characters (Bach, 1945). Although these fantasies may not last very long, generally disappearing by 9 or 10, a continued fascination with such characters in fairy tales and myths may be a continuation of this phenomenon. In a study of many cultures, Roheim (1943) suggested that games and stories involving witches also compensate for object loss, sibling hostility, and the withdrawal of food and affection. Hide-and-seek games are another example of resolving anxieties of being lost or abandoned, and are likely to persist without peer or adult censure if anxiety seems a reasonable response to such a situation in that age group (Phillips, 1967). Sutton-Smith has demonstrated that these central-person games of chase, escape, capture and rescue, occur in cultures where children are made anxious about their independence (Roberts and Sutton-Smith, 1962).

SOCIAL AND CULTURAL VARIATION IN PLAY

Sex differences

It would be surprising if play patterns were not in part determined by the environment in which the child grows up, and by the demands and values of those who make up the adult society. In Western communities, for example, adult expectations of sex appropriate behaviour are just as evident in play behaviour as they are in other aspects. Boys are usually discouraged from playing with dolls, even to the extent that by 1 year of age girls are likely to own more dolls and soft toys, but fewer trains and cars than boys, particularly if they come from working-class families (Rosenblatt, 1972). A study of children's rooms in the age range between 1 and 6 years old (Rheingold and Cook, 1975) revealed that none of the girls had motorcycles or boats, while by the age of 3 boys had a collection numbering about 11 vehicles. Boys' rooms generally contained a greater variety of playthings than girls', although in observed situations girls usually demonstrate greater diversity and versatility in their choice of toys. Both of these authors are led to the conclusion that parents set down 'rules' independent of the interests of the child because in each observational situation no sex preferences were evident in the choice or use of toys.

Further support for sex stereotyping comes from laboratory studies of adult–infant play. Even in early infancy parents tend to stimulate more physical activity in infant sons (Fagot, 1974), and give more verbal stimulation to daughters (Maccoby and Jacklin, 1974; Clarke-Stewart, 1973). Frisch (1977) employed a special research design to separate out 'adult' from 'child effects' by having the naïve adult stranger play with a 15 month child who had been designated either a boy or a girl by name and clothing. She found that in general adults played in masculine ways with children whom they believed to be boys, by encouraging their activity and constructional play with blocks, while girls received more interpersonal stimulation and nurturance. The children themselves did not differ significantly in their play styles. Weinraub and Frankel (1977) demonstrated that parents were more likely to sit down, talk to, and engage in play with their same-sexed infants. One reason that female infants receive more verbal stimulation then might be due to this effect, and male infants might be observed to experience this enrichment in play with their fathers—if such naturalistic situations were to be studied as frequently as in the mother–infant dyad (Kotelchuck, 1972).

In older children there is an even greater socialization towards independence and assertiveness in boys than girls, which probably helps to account for preference and skills in particular games. As social mores and attitudes have changed over the generations, so have children's interests. For instance, by the 1960's girls of 10–12 were substantially more like boys than had been the case in the 1920's, and far more so than in 1898—particularly in active games such as tag and leap-frog, or skills games such as tops and marbles (Rosenberg and Sutton-Smith, 1960; Jones, 1959). Boys are also more likely to join 'gangs' and play in larger groups, as well as being less likely to play near adult supervision, but in adolescent recreation patterns this already seems to be changing.

Fantasy and dramatic play also reveals some sex differences, but the data are contradictory. Singer (1973) observed fantasy play to be more common in boys, while Brindley et al. (1973) report the opposite. Smith (1977) concluded that such gross measurements obscure the differences in content, and his finer analysis revealed that girls are more likely to engage in fantasy play with objects while boys had more episodes of rough and tumble fantasy play. Girls are also much more likely to identify with sex appropriate roles in their dramatic play, particularly when it comes to playing 'house', and often make it quite clear to their male peers that 'daddies' do not do mundane chores like the dishes and the ironing, but rather 'have to go to work'. Because children do tend to execute such limited roles in their play when left on their own, it has been suggested that 'free play' in nursery schools might actually be disadvantageous in the encouragement of flexible and creative learning (Tizard and Harvey, 1977). The skilled parent or teacher could use the 'Wendy House' or doll corner to foster greater awareness of the roles and functions that 'mummies' and 'daddies' do perform today.

Cross-cultural studies of play

The values of each culture exert their influence on the infant through the mother's attitudes towards him, and the specifications as to how he should be handled and stimulated in the early months. Early mother–infant interchanges and the child's explorations of objects may be determined by the frequency with which each mother picks up the baby to feed him, or whether he is strapped to a cradle board, or carried on a sibling's back throughout the day. For instance, American Indian children, and to some extent the Nyansongan (LeVine and LeVine, 1963), are bound in pieces of cloth which restricts their hand and feet movements to a far greater extent than the typical American or English child. Some cultures use the feeding or bathing situation to encourage affectionate teasing and games while others restrict these activities to their functional aspects.

Play time is also likely to be severely limited in cultures where the child's labour is an economic necessity. The Nyansongan children of Kenya are assigned regular chores by the age of 3, and responsibility and obedience are emphasized, and transgression severely punished. Toys are rare, except things fashioned by the children themselves, and most of the later play observed in this culture never progressed beyond rough and tumble play —with the exception of two incidents of imaginative games during the two-year study period (LeVine and LeVine, 1963). In contrast, the children of Taira in Okinawa demonstrate a great deal of imaginative play, using empty boxes, stones and leaves to represent trucks and boats, or peas to serve as marbles. (Maretzki and Maretzki, 1963.) Rich and varied fantasy play seems less likely to occur in communities where the adults live narrow, restricted, and isolated lives, and where there is no well-developed artistic and aesthetic sense. Of course, this begs the question of whether children lack imaginative play because creativity is not fostered, or whether the traditions are not encouraged.

Several studies have recently been made of play in Israel, in part because the country encompasses a number of ethnic groups who are new immigrants or who have been absorbed into the existing society. Feitelson (1977) provides a detailed review of the factors which affect representational play, based on her observations of Middle Eastern, North Arabic, or Kurdish Jews. The first of these is 'play space', which refers not simply to the physical space available, but to the area which is granted to children for this purpose, and is in part determined by the value which adults of the society place on their own comfort. Thus Kurdish children were often denied access to the garden and yards which had been created, because parents believed that children should be 'seen but not heard', whereas the girls from Orthodox Jewish families were always observed to be playing even in the most cramped of flats. The second factor determining play is 'legitimate' time in which to develop play themes, or sustain an entire game, rather than having to steal a few minutes from required chores. Thirdly, play objects need to be 'familiar, permanent and freely available whenever needed', so that themes can be continued and re-enacted with the certainty that a particular prop will still be available. This is less likely to happen when natural objects are scarce in the environment, or where implements are in continual use, or where adults consider such objects to be unnecessary or irrelevant to daily life. Lastly, Feitelson draws on studies which stress the learned aspect of representational play, and the active role of adults in encouraging imaginative elements, and thus providing a play-conducive atmosphere. The absence of these conditions may serve to delay the appearance of sophisticated play schemas if it does not prevent them altogether (Smilansky, 1968; Eifermann, 1971).

CLINICAL APPLICATIONS OF PLAY RESEARCH

Diagnostic uses of play

The observation of play serves a particularly useful purpose in the assessment of children who cannot be assessed with more conventional tests; for instance, a child may be too distractible or hyperactive to complete a formal task. If he is presented with a box of toys and given time to explore the contents, however, it might be obvious to the clinician that his motor and social skills outstrip the symbolic use to which he can put the miniature objects. Parents are usually able to furnish information about what sorts of play he enjoys at home, and whether he is able to initiate and sustain cooperative play with a peer. Sheridan's (1969) guidelines on the developmental stages of play have enabled paediatricians to identify children who may be developmentally delayed, even in the course of a busy clinic.

More formal scales are now being developed which place an infant or child in relation to his peers on particular tasks. Knox (1968) combined important characteristics of play gleaned from the literature into four dimensions: space management, material management, imitation, and participation. From this a 'play quotient' can be calculated, and the observer would also take into account the relative balance between the four categories—in much the same way that an intelligence test is used. The subnormal children that she tested were found to be functioning at a level 24 months behind that of the normals, as well as being less likely to engage in peer interaction than would be expected even at that play level. Lowe (1975) has developed an instrument for assessing symbolic development which will be used to predict potential language delay.

Other studies have used play to distinguish between groups of children, or assess long term effects of a particular condition, by the use of a standardized observational situation. 'Free-field' observations which are recorded systematically offer an advantage over the other assessment methods in that frequency or duration of behaviours can be examined. For instance, in the case of 'hyperactive' children it may be important to know the conditions under which it is manifest, and whether it actually interferes with manual dexterity. Ounsted (1955) observed hyperkinetic children to build a tower of bricks twice as fast as normal children did, and to maintain their high level of activity in all situations, leading to play which occurred in brief and unconnected fragments. Kalverboer (1977) also utilized a 'time-sampling' method to investigate the effect of minor neurological conditions in the newborn period. Although few of the original infant diagnoses were found to relate to later play, quantification permitted comparison of the child's play across a variety of conditions, and enabled more specific conclusions. For example, boys with minor neurological problems in the newborn period did much better under conditions where attractive materials were available, and such information might have an impact in optimizing learning conditions in order to minimize handicap.

In a study of the play of normal, autistic, and retarded children, Tilton and Ottinger (1964) observed that the autistic children devoted very little time to combination use of toys, used a smaller repertoire of play acts, and were more oral and repetitive with the toys. The retarded children were more likely to bang toys than normals, as well as making briefer contact with the toys. Immature play was also a feature of a group of mute autistic children between 2 and 5 years studied by Rosenblatt (1971a) in a special nursery class. Those children with the greatest number of 'autistic' symptoms displayed more tactile play—usually self-directed, persevering activities. They chose fewer toys, engaged in more repetition, and rarely combined toys, while another mute child, diagnosed as aphasic, showed well-coordinated toy play, a wider variety in toy choice, and a longer attention span. Studies which do not measure frequencies and duration of behaviour, and rely instead on scales, are less likely to report differences in the play behaviour of these groups (Hulme and Lunzer, 1966; Lovell et al., 1968). The disadvantage of such methods however, is that they are time-consuming to execute, labour-intensive, and produce much more data than may actually be necessary to answer specific clinical questions.

Play as therapy

Historically, Freud is credited with the earliest use of 'play therapy' in the treatment of Little Hans, and in describing the way in which the incessant play of a toddler mirrored his capacity for dealing with the separation and recapture of his absent mother. His explanation of play is now familiar—

'. . . children in their play repeated everything that has made a great impression on them in actual life, so that they thereby abreact the strength of the impression and so to speak make themselves masters of the situation' (Freud, 1955).

The toddler's control of his own situation was achieved by throwing a wooden reel attached to string out of his cot over and over again, accompanied by an indication of gratification and a sound interpreted by his mother to be 'go away'.

Play therapy itself tends to be extremely diverse, partly dependent on the therapist's school, and partly on what he or she feels is most appropriate in a particular case. At one end of the continuum is the non-directive school (Ginott, 1961; Axline, 1947) which considers the child capable of solving his own problems if he is given the unrestrictive and unpressured environment in which to do so. Thus play allows him to bring tensions to the surface, and come to his own conclusions without having to test the reactions of adults around him. The playroom—with a large selection of toys provides him with security and complete acceptance of who he is or what he wants to be. The therapist may reflect his actions and words back to him, but does not interpret them; the acceptance alone contributes to the child's growth in self-confidence. There is a resemblance here to 'child-centred' education (Plowden, 1964), in which the philosophy is that all the child needs to mature is challenging materials, time, and a supportive environment. Axline (1955) says that the child learns about himself 'through self-exploration, self-in-relation-to-others, self-expansion, and self-expression'.

Other therapies involve a more active and structured situation, in which the therapist is more than a passive participant. Levy (1939) felt it important to 'release' a specific problem in the child by structuring a play situation in which the child could play out all the elements of his conflict. In this way the play session had a focus and purpose, making it more economical of time than a lengthy, diffuse series of visits which did not actually confront the patient with his problem. Conn (1948) also developed a structured form of play session, but only after the child had played out the situation did he interpret the behaviour and point out to the child that he was in fact playing out his own anxieties.

Klein (1957) viewed play as the equivalent of free association used in the treatment of adults, and as fundamental to the picture of the child as would be the meanings in adult dreams. The Kleinian therapist is 'directive' in that her interpretation to the child of the meaning inherent in his play is as important as the cathartic effects of the play itself; she will use her knowledge of the conflicts which might be present and make a guess to the child about what his play configurations might represent.

Anna Freud (1946) differed in many ways from Klein. Firstly, she viewed play as secondary to the role of the therapist in presenting the child with a trusted adult who can be used to come to terms with a problem. She also felt that while play was indispensable for treating the very young child, it was erroneous to assume that the spontaneous play of a child is equal to the free associations of adult analysis, or that it should be interpreted in terms of

unconscious symbolism. Solomon (1948) was in agreement with Anna Freud that play basically serves as the 'medium by which the therapist talks to the child', and that therapy will take different forms according to type of disorder presenting.

Winnicott's approach was rather different, in that he stressed the creative alliance of patient and therapist in using space, materials, and toys in forming a 'mutual illusion' into which the patient can reach back and find what he could never before accept. His 'squiggle technique' (1971) involves both child and therapist elaborating on each other's drawings, in which 'Mutual imaginative processes are released which facilitate communications, untie developmental tangles' (Bentovim, 1977).

Play in hospital

The provision of toys and staff for play activity in hospital has received attention in Western Europe recently, along with such other welcome changes as unrestricted parental visiting. There are special reasons for the emphasis on play in these circumstances. To begin with, the child is in an unfamiliar and probably frightening place, separated for long periods from the family and friends that he is close to. These familiar persons are instead replaced by figures in white coats who administer painful procedures, often without explanation. The convalescence will almost certainly involve restriction of his normal freedoms, and even after his own treatment may have finished he will still be surrounded by children whose crying and distress suggest that his own discomfort is not really over. Several reports have stressed that hospital admissions are linked with subsequent emotional trauma or distress (Bowlby, 1951; Robertson, 1970; Douglas, 1975; Hawthorn, 1974), although some of the difficulties may be associated with pre-existing disturbances (Jessner et al., 1952).

In the hospital situation play is viewed as affording the child an outlet for his anxieties and fears (about the damage to his body, death, etc.), a respite from inactivity and boredom, and an opportunity to anticipate or recreate some of the disturbing experiences in manageable and controlled circumstances. The play-leader therefore is expected to be parent, teacher, and therapist all in one, which makes it a particularly demanding and skilful job. In addition, the play-leader can use her position to interpret paediatric information to the parent, and advise the parents of ways in which the child can readjust to normality once he returns home.

No one is altogether certain about how the provision of play ameliorates the distress caused by hospital admission. It may compensate for the break in the mother–child relationship, or it may provide some continuity in the kinds of familiar experience and activity usually available to the child. Surprisingly these causal aspects have attracted little research—such as providing access to toys or directed play before surgery—with the exception of work by Cassell (1965). Although it may be that access to toys alone helps the child to master the disturbing experience, or aids developmental learning, Provence and Lipton (1962) remind us that in the case of institutionalized children the mere provision of toys did not substantially diminish their developmental deprivation. But what might be important is the role of the hospital staff or play-leader in investing such toys with function and meaning. For instance, Dunn and Wooding (1977) noted that the attention span of toddlers was twice as long when the mother involved herself in the symbolic play as when the child's play was solitary. And in Rubenstein and Howes' study (1976), the children showed greater exploration of new toys if the mothers had been more attentive to their play.

Or it may be that play facilitates recovery by setting up familiar routines and predictable contingencies. As it has been suggested that children under 4 are most prone to emotional disturbance (Hawthorn, 1974), then what may be lacking in the hospital setting is the presence of family members and playmates who define the roles and limits which the child expects. Children are drawn to novelty but too great a discrepancy overwhelms the child and prevents exploration. The sterile, starched atmosphere of the hospital might function to disrupt his behaviour, while playing with toys similar to his own just might bridge the gap. Predictable items such as pop-up clowns, books, and sets of typical representational toys allow the toddler to pretend his daddy is really in the car, or re-create a fond breakfast routine with the tea set. It would be relatively simple to test whether familiar or novel toys were more likely to reduce the crying or sleeplessness common during hospital stays.

Psychoanalysts would also argue that the importance of play in hospital is the opportunity to act out anxieties regarding illness and bodily integrity. Painting is seen as a non-threatening medium in which to portray events, and is often the first 'release' that the child has, and one which the therapist or play-leader can use to draw him out (Winnicott, 1971). In the case of a very young child who cannot express his terror at being run over by a car, his (or the therapists) drawing of a child standing on one side and lying on the other side of a road, divided by a car in the middle can lead to cathartic acting-out and subsequent reduction in anxiety.

Re-structuring children's play

Attempts have been made to modify play behaviour in a number of different categories of children who are felt not to be profiting from the normal play situation. In the case of handicapped children, clinicians have tried to establish sensorimotor and symbolic play for its own value, and as a bridge to more mature cognitive and linguistic processes. Bricker and Bricker (1974) reinforced motor and then functional schemas in subnormal toddlers which resulted in successful vocabulary learning. Morehead and Rosenblatt (Rosenblatt, 1971b) 'trained' mute aphasic children between 2 and 5 years of age in Sinclair's (1969) categories of physical, logical, and symbolic knowledge as they could be applied to playthings. Within a few months all children were able to use materials for simple acts relating to themselves, and to a prop such as a doll. There was also some carry-over into vocabulary acquisition. Conditioning procedures and techniques for handicapped children have now been made explicit in several publications on play (Bricker and Bricker, 1974), but to date there is little or no information about how such play training is generalized to other cognitive and social functions, or whether it forms a stepping stone to developmentally more mature forms as in the normal child.

After the publication of a number of studies reporting low levels of fantasy play in disadvantaged children (Smilansky, 1968; Feitelson, 1959; Freyberg, 1973) a number of strategies were employed to increase its quantity and quality. 'Play tutors', as they are often designated, participate in the children's activities and supply materials or toys, and excursions, to provide themes. Tuition has been found effective in enhancing fantasy play itself (Marshall and Hahn, 1967; Feitelson, 1972; Freyberg, 1973), but it is more difficult to establish that the encouragement of sociodramatic play makes a substantial impact on other skills. Feitelson and Ross (1973) found an improvement on tests of creativity when children were tutored in fantasy play, as opposed to untutored toy play, or music instruction. Rosen (1974) gave sociodramatic tuition to two groups of preschool children, while two control groups received non-fantasy play tutoring. The experimental classes demonstrated more fantasy play and better scores on tasks requiring group cooperation construction and role taking. In a comprehensive discussion of these studies Smith (1977) emphasizes that they only really prove the effectiveness of the *tutoring* on other skills, rather than demonstrating that the play itself enhanced them, and that it is necessary to examine which kinds of play tutoring are more beneficial to disadvantaged children, and at what developmental stage they are most appropriate.

Smith also raises reservations about whether fantasy play—which is apparently minimal or missing altogether—is necessary to development or only just useful. Tizard and Harvey (1977) take up a similar argument with regard to the emphasis on 'free play' in nursery schools. This type of play, she argues, is the hallmark of the traditional English nursery school (and many infant schools), consisting of child-initiated, individualized play with objects, instead of social play, or games, or play initiated by and with adults. From their observations of many different kinds of nursery schools she concludes that this kind of structuring may only serve to reinforce existing interests and experiences, because the children are in no way directed to sample novel, and perhaps more enriching, opportunities. Although sociodramatic play would be expected to emerge in such a relaxed atmosphere it proved to occur infrequently, because large peer groups do not foster the familiarity necessary for sustained play themes, and because without appropriate and imaginative adult examples the children often resort to stereotyped themes reminiscent of domestic dramas or the television. It is obvious, therefore, that the values of mother, teacher, or leisure departments, which are reflected in particular methods of organizing the resources for play may in themselves determine the type and quality of play which occurs there.

The effect of teacher attention to children's play has also been recently exploited in an effort to re-direct children's social play patterns in the nursery school away from the usual single-sex groups to mixed playgroups (Serbin *et al.*, 1977). Simply by praising cooperative activities in mixed groups, teachers were able to double the rate of cooperative cross-sex play, without in any way reducing the amount or quality of same-sex play episodes. The authors suggest that by manipulating environmental factors which lead to same-sex play there might be several benefits: (1) a tendency to view opposite sex children as playmates, friends and coworkers; (2) expose boys and girls to behavioural styles and cognitive skills 'typical' of the opposite sex, and thus broaden the scope of development; (3) broaden the type of play activities in which children engage, since many of them are sex stereotyped, and (4) make it more difficult for boys and girls to be treated differently or exposed to different learning experiences by their teachers. The encouragement of cooperative play, and diversification of roles have long been features of societies which foster group care facilities for young children, such as the Soviet Union or Israeli kibbutzim (Spiro, 1965).

CONCLUSION

In sum, play seems to be a natural and necessary part of the child's development from a dependent organism to one who can control, direct, and creatively use the environment and the people who inhabit it. If he is not developing normally then his play is likely to reflect these problems in a number of ways. He may fail to appreciate the functions of objects, or be unable to combine them and elaborate their use in a symbolic fashion. Or, the content of his play may indicate adequate intellectual ability, while his tactile exploration and manipulation suggest that he has some clumsiness or difficulties in executing skilled actions. If he is finding it difficult to accept demands and pressures from his caregivers or the school then the organizational or thematic aspects of his play might alter. Sometimes this will be obvious, as in heightened aggression or uncharacteristic lassitude, there may only be subtle changes in attention, disorganization and ordering of materials, or tempo. Play in a social situation will almost certainly reveal a child's problems in adjusting to peer demands, turn-taking, or communicating and cooperating towards a common goal.

The diversity between individuals, between boys and girls, and between cultures, is impressive however, and should caution us against assigning a label of 'deviant' to any particular style of play. Growing-up means accepting the values and outlook of the social environment in which it occurs, and the child's play will reflect, challenge, and 'toy' with these experiences until he is mature, no matter which culture he is part of. As Norbeck concludes

'Play is a conspicuously striking and universal kind of human behaviour that is genetically based and cultur-ally modified ... play should not be regarded as an interlude in human behaviour, a dispensable if refreshing indulgence, but as a vitally important activity of human life that in fact exists among the members of all human societies although its manifestations are sometimes masked by human conventions so that it is not readily obvious ...' (Norbeck, 1978)

REFERENCES

Ainsworth, M. and Bell, S. (1970). Attachment, exploration and separation: illustrated by the behavior of one-year-olds in a strange situation. *Child Dev.* **41**, 49–67.

Axline, V. (1947). *Play Therapy*. Boston: Houghton Mefflin.

Axline, V. M. (1955). Play therapy: procedures and results: *Am. J. Orthopsychiat.* **25**, 618–626.

Bach, G. R. (1945). Young children's play fantasies. *Psychol. Monog.* **59**, 3–31.

Barker, R. G., Dembo, T. and Lewin, K. (1941). Frustration and regression: an experiment with young children. *Univ. Iowa Studies in Child Welfare.* **18**, 1–314.

Barnes, K. (1971). Preschool play norms: a replication. *Dev. Psychol.* **5**, 99–103.

Bates, E., Camioni, L. and Volterra, V. (1975). The acquisition of performatives prior to speech. *Merrill Palmer Quart.* **21**, 205.

Bell, S. (1970). The development of the concept of objects as related to infant–mother attachment. *Child Dev.* **41**, 291–311.

Bell, S. (1971). Early cognitive development and its relationship to infant–mother attachment: a study of disadvantaged Negro infants. U.S. Office Education. No. 00542.

Bentovim, A. (1977). The role of play in psychotherapeutic work with children and their families. In *Biology of Play*. Tizard, B. and Harvey, D. (Eds.) London: Heinemann S.I.M.P.

Blurton Jones, N. G. (1972). Categories of child–child interaction. In *Ethological Studies of Child Behaviour*. Blurton-Jones, N. G. (Ed.) Cambridge: Cambridge University Press.

Bowlby, J. (1951). *Maternal Care and Mental Health*. WHO Monograph Series No. 2. Geneva: WHO.

Brazelton, T. B. (1973). *Neonatal Behavioural Assessment Scales*. Clinic. Develop. Med. No 50. London: Heinemann S.I.M.P.

Bricker, W. A. and Bricker D. D. (1974). An early language training strategy. In *Language Perspectives—Acquisition, Retardation, and Intervention*. Maryland: Macmillan.

Brindley, C., Clarke, P., Hutt, C., Robinson, I. and Wethli, E. (1973). Sex differences in the activities and social interactions of nursery school children. In *Comparative Ecology and Behaviour of Primates*. Michael, R. P. and Crook, J. H. (Eds.) London: Academic Press.

Bronson, W. (1975). Developments in behaviour with agemates during the second year of life. In *Peer Relations and Friendship*. Lewis, M. and Rosenblum, L. (Eds.) New York: John Wiley.

Bruner, J. (1972). The nature and uses of immaturity. *Amer. Psychol.* **27**, 1.

Bruner, J. (1974). Child's play. *New Scientist* **62**, 126.

Bruner, J. S., Jolly, A. and Sylva, K. (1976). *Play: Its Role in Development and Evolution*. London: Penguin.

Call, J. (1968). Lap and finger play: implications for ego development. *Internat. J. Psychoanal.* **49**, 375–378.

Call, J. (1970). Games babies play. *Psychology Today*, April, 34–37.

Cassell, S. (1965). Effect of brief puppet therapy upon the emotional responses of children undergoing cardiac catherization. *J. Consulting Psych.* **29**, 1.

Clarke-Stewart, K. A. (1973). Interactions between mothers and their young children: characteristics and consequences. *Monog. Society Research Child Develop.* **38**, no. 153.

Collis, G. M. and Schaffer, H. R. (197?). Synchronization of visual attention in mother–infant pairs. *J. Child Psychol. Psychiat.* **16**, 315–320.

Conn, J. H. (1948). The play interview: an investigative and therapeutic procedure. *Nervous Child.* **7**, 257–286.

Cross, T. (1975). Motherese: its association with rate of syntactic acquisition in young children. Paper presented at Child Language Conference, London.

Dansky, J. L. and Silverman, I. W. (1973). Effects of play on associative fluency in pre-school children. *Develop. Psychol.* **9**, 38–43.

Douglas, J. W. B. (1975). Early hospital admissions and later disturbance of behaviour and learning. *Dev. Med. Child Neurol.* **17**, 456.

Dunn, J. and Wooding, C. (1977). Play in the home and its implications for learning. In *Biology of Play*. Tizard, B. and Harvey, D. (Eds.) London: Heinemann S.I.M.P.

Eckerman, C., Whatley, J. and Kutz, S. (1975). Growth of social play with peers during the second year of life. *Develop. Psychol.* **11**, 42–49.

Eiferman, R. (1970). Level of children's play as expressed in group size. *Br. J. Ed. Psych.* **40**, 161.

Eiferman, R. (1971). Social Play in childhood. In *Child's Play*, Herron, R. E. and Sutton-Smith, B. (Eds.) New York: John Wiley.

Erikson, E. H. (1950). *Childhood and Society*. New York: W. W. Norton.

Fagot, B. I. (1974). Sex differences in toddlers' behaviour and parental reactions. *Develop. Psychol.* **10**, 554.

Fantz, R. (1961). The origin of form perception. *Scientific American* **204**, 66–72.

Feitelson, D. (1959). Some aspects of the social life of Kurdish Jews. *Jewish J. Sociology* **1**, 201.

Feitelson, D. (1972). Developing imaginative play in preschool children as a possible approach to fostering creativity. *Early Child Dev. Care* **1**, 181.

Feitelson, D. (1977). Cross-cultural studies of representational play. In *Biology of Play*. Tizard, B. and Harvey, D. (Eds.) London: Heinemann S.I.M.P.

Feitelson, D. and Ross, G. S. (1973). The neglected factor-play. *Human Development* **16**, 202.

Fenson, L. and Kagan, J. (1976). The developmental progression of manipulative play in the first two years. *Child Dev.* **47**, 232–236.

Freud, A. (1946). *The Psychoanalytic Treatment of Children*. New York: I.U.P.

Freud, S. (1955). *Beyond the Pleasure Principle*. Vol. 18. London: Hogarth Press.

Freyberg, J. T. (1973). Increasing the imaginative play of urban disadvantaged children through systematic training. In *The Child's World of Make-Believe*. Singer, J. L. (Ed.) New York: Academic Press.

Frisch, H. L. (1977). Sex stereotypes in adult–infant play. *Child Dev.* **48**, 1671–1675.

Garvey, C. (1977). Play with language. In *Biology of Play*. Tizard B. and Harvey, D. (Eds.) London: Heinemann S.I.M.P.

Ginott, H. G. (1961). *Group Psychotherapy with Children: The Theory and Practice of Play Therapy*. New York: McGraw-Hill.

Glasberg, R. (1975). Imaginative play and the divergent process. McGill University thesis.

Groos, K. (1899). *The Play of Man*. New York: Appleton, Century Crofts. (trans. 1901).

Hall, G. S. (1904). *Adolescence: Its Psychology*. New York: Appleton, Century Crofts.

Hawthorn, P. (1974). *Nurse, I want my Mummy*. London: Royal College of Nursing.

Henry, J. and Henry, Z. (1944). *Doll Play of Pilaga Indian Children*. Amer. Orthopsychiat. Assoc., No. 4, New York.

Herron, R. E. and Sutton-Smith, B. (1971). *Child's Play*, New York: John Wiley.

Huizinga, J. (1947). *Homo Ludens: A Study of the Play Element in Culture*. London: Routledge and Kegan Paul.

Hulme, I. and Lunzer, E. A. (1966). Play, language and reasoning in subnormals. *J. Child Psychol. Psychiat.* **7**, 107.

Humphrey, J. H. (1965). Comparison of the use of active games and language workbook exercises as learning media in the development of language understandings of 3rd grade children. *Percep. Mot. Skills* **21**, 23–26.

Hutt, C. (1966). Exploration and play in children. *Symp. Zoolog. Soc. London* **18**, 61–81.

Inhelder, B., Lezine, I., Sinclair, H. and Stambak, M. (1972). Les débuts de la fonction symbolique. *Archives de Psychologie*. **41**, 187.

Jessner, L., Blom, G. L. and Waldfogel, S. (1952). Emotional implications of tonsilectomy and adenoidectomy in children. *Psychoanalytic Study Child*. **1**, 126.

Jones, M. C. (1959). A comparison of the attitudes and interests of ninth graders over two decades. 25th SRCD Conference. Unpublished.

Kaye, K. (1970). *Mother–Child Instructional Learning*. Harvard University Dissertation.

Kalverboer, A. F. (1977). Measurement of play: clinical applications. In *Biology of Play*. Tizard, B. and Harvey, D. (Eds.) London: Heinemann S.I.M.P.

Kirschenblatt-Gimblet, D. (Ed.) (1976). *Speech Play: Research and Resources for the Study of Linguistic Creativity*. Pennsylvania: University of Pennsylvania Press.

Klein, M. (1957). The psychoanalytic play technique: its history, significance. In *New Directions in Psychoanalysis*. Klein, M., Heiman, P. and Money-Kyrle, R. (Eds.) New York: Basic Books.

Knox, S. H. (1968). A play scale. In *Play as Exploratory Learning*. Reily, M. (Ed.) Los Angeles: Sage.

Kotelchuck, M. (1972). The nature of the child's tie to his father. Unpublished dissertation, Harvard.

Levin, H. and Wardwell, E. (1962). The research uses of doll play. *Psychol, Bull.* **59**, 27–56.

LeVine, R. and LeVine, B. (1963). Nyansongo: A Guisii community in Kenya. In *Six Cultures*. Whiting, B. (Ed.) New York: John Wiley.

Levy, D. M. (1939). Release therapy. *Am. J. Orthopsychiat.* **9**, 713–736.

Lieberman, J. N. (1965). Playfulness and divergent thinking: an investigation of their relationship at the kindergarten level. *J. Genet. Psychol.* **107**, 219–224.

Lovell, K., Hoyle, H. W. and Seddall, N. Q. (1968). A study of some aspects of the play and language of young children with delayed speech. *J. Child Psych. Psychiat.* **9**, 41.

Lowe, M. (1975). Trends in the development of representational play in infants from one to three years: an observational study. *J. Child Psych. Psychiat.* **16**, 33.

Lowenfeld, M. (1933). *Play in Childhood*. London: Gollancz.

Luria, A. R. and Yudovich, F. (1959). *Speech and the Development of Mental Processes in the Child*. London: Staples Press.

Maccoby, E. and Jacklin, C. (1974). *The Psychology of Sex Differences*. Stanford: University Press.

Maretzki, H. and Maretzki, T. (1963). Taira: an Okinawan Village. In *Six Cultures*, Whiting, B. (Ed.) New York: John Wiley.

Marshall, H. R. and Hahn, S. C. (1967). Experimental modification of dramatic play. *J. Person. Soc. Psych.* **5**, 119.

Menninger, K. (1942). *Love against Hate*. New York: Harcourt.

Millar, S. (1968). *The Psychology of Play*. London: Penguin.

Moore, N. V., Evertson, C. H. and Brophy, J. E. (1974). Solitary play: some functional reconsiderations. *Dev. Psych.* **10**, 830–834.

Mueller, E. and DeStefano, C. (1978). Sources of toddler peer interaction in a playgroup setting. *Early Child Dev. Care* (in press).

Nelson, K. (1973). Structure and strategy in learning to talk. *Monog. Soc. Res. Child Develop.* No. 149.

Nicolich, L. (1977). Beyond sensorimotor intelligence: assessment of symbolic maturity through analysis of pretend play. *Merrill Palmer Quart.* **23** (2), 89–99.

Norbeck, E. (1978). The study of play. In *The Anthropological Study of Play*. Lancey, D. F. and Tindall, B. A. (Eds.) New York: Leisure Press.

Opie, I. and Opie, P. (1969). *Children's Games of Street and Playground*. Oxford: Clarendon Press.

Ounsted, C. A. (1955). The hyperkinetic syndrome in epileptic children. *Lancet*, **2**, 303.

Packer, M. and Rosenblatt, D. B. (1979). Issues in the study of social behaviour in the first week of life. In *The First Year of Life*. Shaffer, D. and Dunn, J. (Eds.) London: John Wiley.

Parten, M. B., (1932). Social play among school children. *J. Abn. Soc. Psych.* **28**, 136–47.

Peller, L. E. (1952). Models of children's play. *Mental Hygiene*. **36**, 66–83.

Phillips, R. (1945). Doll play as a function of the realism of the materials and the length of the experimental situation. *Child Devel.* **16**, 123–43.

Phillips, R. (1967). Children's games. In *Motivations in Play, Games and Sports*. Slovenko, R. and Knight, J. (Eds.) Springfield: Charles Thomas.

Piaget, J. (1951). *Play, Dreams and Imitation*. London: Heinemann.

Piaget, J. (1952). *The Origin of Intelligence in the Child*. London: Routledge and Kegan Paul.

Pintler, M. H. (1945). Doll play as a function of experimenter–child interaction and initial organisation of the materials. *Child Dev.* **16**, 146–66.

Plowden (1967). *Children and their Primary Schools.* Central Advisory Council for Education. London: HMSO.

Provence, S. and Lipton, R. (1962). *Infants in Institutions.* New York: I.U.P.

Pukui, M. (1943). Games of my Hawaiian childhood. *Cal. Folklore Quart.* **2**, 205–220.

Rheingold, H. and Cook, K. (1975). The contents of boys' and girls' rooms as an index of parents' behaviour. *Child Dev.* **46**, 459–463.

Redshaw, M. (1978). Cognitive development in human and gorilla infants. *J. Human Evolution* **7**, 133–141.

Ritchie, O. (1965). *Golden City.* Edinburgh: Oliver and Boyd.

Roberts, J. and Sutton-Smith, B. (1962). Child training and game involvement. *Ethology* **1**, 166–185.

Robertson, J. (1970). *Young Children in Hospital.* London: Tavistock.

Robinson, E. (1946). Doll-play as a function of the doll family constellation. *Child Dev.* **17**, 99–119.

Roheim, G. (1943). Children's games and rhymes. *Amer. Anthropologist* **45**, 99–119.

Rosen, C. E. (1974). The effects of socio-dramatic play on problem solving behaviour among culturally disadvantaged pre-school children. *Child Devel.* **45**, 920.

Rosenberg, B. G. and Sutton-Smith, B. (1960). Revised conception of masculine–feminine differences in play activities. *J. Genet. Psych.* **96**, 165–170.

Rosenblatt, D. (1971a). Non-communicating nursery children: an analysis of spontaneous play behaviour. Queen Mary's Hospital: mimeograph.

Rosenblatt, D. (1971b). Language and the representational process: a Piagetian approach to the linguistically deviant child. Stanford Medical School: mimeograph.

Rosenblatt, D. (1972). A fieldstudy of games in street and playground in Scotland. Stanford University: mimeograph.

Rosenblatt, D. (1977). Developmental trends in infant play. In *Biology of Play.* Tizard, B. and Harvey, D. (Eds.) London: Heinemann S.I.M.P.

Rubenstein, J. and Howes, C. (1976). The effects of peers on toddler interaction with mother and toys. *Child Dev.* **47**, 597–605.

Rubin, K. H. (1975). The relationship of social play preferences to role-taking skills in pre-school children. U. Waterloo: unpublished.

Rubin, K. H., Maioni, T. L. and Hornug, M. (1976). Free play behaviours in middle- and lower-class preschoolers: Parten and Piaget revisited. *Child Dev.* **47**, 414–419.

Schiller, F. (1795). *Essays, Aesthetical and Philosophical.* London: George Bell.

Sears, R. S. (1960). Doll-play aggression in normal young children. *Psych. Monog.* **65**, No. 6.

Serbin, L. A., Tonick, I. J. and Sternglanz, S. H. (1977). Shaping cooperative cross-sex play. *Child Dev.* **48**, 924–929.

Sheridan, M. (1969). Playthings in the development of language. *Health Trends Quart. Review* **1**, 7.

Siegel, A. E. and Kohn, L. G. (1959). Permissiveness, permission and aggression: the effect of adult presence or absence on children's play. *Child Dev.* **30**, 131–141.

Sinclair-de-Zwart, H. (1969). Developmental psycholinguistics. In *Studies in Cognitive Development.* Elkind, D. and Flavell, J. (Eds.) New York: Oxford.

Sinclair, H. (1970). The transition from sensory-motor to symbolic activity. *Interchange* **1** (3), 119–126.

Sinclair, H. (1971). Sensori-motor action patterns and a condition for the acquisition of syntax. In *Language Acquisition: Models and Methods.* Huxley, R. and Ingram, T. T. (Eds.) New York: Academic Press.

Singer, J. L. (Ed.) (1973). *The Child's World of Makebelieve.* New York: Academic Press.

Smilansky, S. (1968). *The Effects of Sociodramatic Play on Disadvantaged Preschool Children.* New York: John Wiley.

Smith, P. K. (1973). Temporal clusters and individual differences in the behaviour of preschool children. In *Comparative Ecology and Behaviour of Primates.* Michael, R. P. and Crook, J. H. (Eds.) London: Academic Press.

Smith, P. K. (1977). Social and fantasy play in young children. In *Biology of Play.* Tizard, B. and Harvey, D. (Eds.) London: Heinemann S.I.M.P.

Snow, C. E., Arlman-Rupp, A., Hassing, Y., Jose, J., Joosten, J. and Vorster, J. (1976). Mothers' speech in three social classes. *J. Psycholinguistic Research* **5**, 1.

Solomon, J. C. (1948). Trends in orthopsychiatric therapy: play technique. *Amer. J. Orthopsych.* **18**, 402–413.

Spencer, H. (1855). *The Principles of Psychology.* London: Longman.

Spiro, M. (1965). *Children of the Kibbutz.* New York: Schocken.

Stern, D. (1977). *The First Relationship: Infant and Mother.* London: Fontana.

Stone, G. (1971). The play of little children. In *Child's Play*, Herron, R. E. and Sutton-Smith, B. (Eds.) New York: John Wiley.

Sutton-Smith, B. (1967). The role of play in cognitive development. *Young Children* **22**, 361–370.

Sutton-Smith, B. (1969). The two cultures of games. In *Aspects of Contemporary Sport Sociology.* Kenyon, G. (Ed.) Chicago: Athletic Institute.

Sutton-Smith, B. (1971). Children at play. *Natural History, Dec.* 54–60.

Sylva, K. (1977). Play and learning. In *Biology of Play.* Tizard, B. and Harvey, D. (Eds.) London: Heinemann S.I.M.P.

Tilton, J. and Ottinger, D. (1964). Comparison of the toy play behaviour of autistic retarded and normal children. *Psych. Reports.* **15**, 967.

Tizard, B. and Harvey, D. (1977). *The Biology of Play.* London: Heinemann/S.I.M.P.

Vygotsky, L. S. (1962). *Thought and Language.* Mass.: MIT (transl).

Waelder, R. (1933). The psychoanalytic theory of play. *Psychoanalytic Quart.* **2**, 208–224.

Wallach, M. A. and Kogan, N. (1965). *Modes of Thinking in Young Children: A Study of the Creativity-Intelligence Distinction.* New York: Holt, Rinehart and Winston.

Watson, W. (1953). Play among children in an East Coast mining community. *Folklore.* **54** (53), 397–410.

Wehman, D. (1977). *Helping the Mentally Retarded Acquire Play Skills: A Behavioural Approach.* Springfield, Ill.: C. C. Thomas.

Weinraub, M. and Frankel, J. (1977). Sex differences in parent–infant interaction during free play, departure, and separation. *Child Dev.* **48**, 1240–1249.

Weir, R. H. (1972). *Language in the Crib.* The Hague: Mouton.

Winnicott, D. W. (1971). *Playing and Reality.* London: Tavistock.

Yarrow, L. J. (1948). The effect of antecedent frustration on projective play. *Psychology Monog.* **62**, No. 6.

Yarrow, L., Klein, R., Lomonaco, S. and Morgan, G. (1975). Cognitive and motivational development in early childhood. In *Exceptional Infant.* Friedlander, B. Z., Sterret, G. M. and Kirk, G. (Eds.) New York: Brunner/Mazel.

25. EMOTIONAL DEVELOPMENT

MICHAEL RUTTER

In spite of a vast range of empirical studies and of theoretical writings (*see* Izard, 1977) there is no general agreement on precisely what is meant by emotion. Nevertheless, it is clear that emotions involve at least three components: (a) a feeling state which has immediate meaning and significance for the individual; (b) a bodily expression in terms of vocalization, facial activity and patterning, together with bodily posture and movement; and (c) physiological changes in both the central and the autonomic nervous system.

Many investigations have shown that adults generally agree well on the recognition of some seven to nine categories of emotion as shown in other adults' facial expressions (Ekman *et al*., 1972; Izard, 1971). The emotions include happiness, surprise, fear, anger, sadness, disgust/contempt, interest, and possibly also distress and shame. Interestingly, these facial signals seem to have much the same meaning in most human cultures (Ekman *et al*., 1972) and are expressed similarly by congenitally blind children (Thompson, 1941; Eibl-Eibesfeldt, 1973). However, there is much more cultural variation in the meaning and use of hand gestures and of bodily contact (Graham and Argyle, 1975; Ekman, 1976). While there are some consistencies in the associations between feeling states and physiological responses, autonomic patterns cannot be used to differentiate specific emotions (*see* Mandler, 1962; Hamburg *et al*., 1975). The development of autonomic reactivity is considered in Chapter 15 and will not be discussed further here. Instead, this chapter surveys some of the main findings on the ways in which emotional expression develops and changes during childhood and adolescence; and reviews the chief theoretical explanations put forward for these processes.

EXPRESSION OF EMOTIONS IN INFANCY

The study of infants' emotions has its roots in Darwin's pioneering observations described in his classic text 'The Expression of Emotions in Man and Animals' (Darwin, 1872). It received a further impetus from Watson and Morgan's (1917) strong claim that there were three basic instinctive emotions—fear, rage, and love—which were already evident in infancy; and more recently there has been a resurgence of interest (*see* Lewis and Rosenblum, 1978), which stems in part from the possible significance of separation anxiety and stranger anxiety (*see* Lewis and Rosenblum, 1974) for theories of bonding and attachment (*see* Chapter 22). The investigation of emotion in infants is hampered by the fact that obviously babies cannot tell us what they are feeling. As a result, the picture has to be built up from observations of bodily exhibitions of affect, and from a study of how these are associated with particular circumstances and stimuli.

Smiling

Low intensity smiles, consisting only of a turning up of the corners of the mouth, are evident in the first days after birth. These earliest smiles, which progressively diminish over the first 3 months, appear to be endogenous and spontaneous (*see* Emde and Koenig, 1969; Wolff, 1963; Sroufe and Waters, 1976), in that they mainly occur during the middle phase of REM sleep when cortical activity is at a low level; they are unrelated to factors such as time since feeding; they do not occur when the infant is stirring or for some 5 minutes following startle; they are more frequent in premature babies and have been found in a microcephalic infant (Emde, McCartney and Harmon, 1971; Harmon and Emde, 1972). It seems that endogenous smiles are associated with low oscillating states of excitation, probably of brainstem or limbic system origin. Because they lack an obvious emotional component some workers do not consider these 'true' smiles.

Waking smiles appear at one to 2 weeks, being elicited

by low-level tactile and kinaesthetic stimulation such as light touches, blowing on the skin or gentle jogging. At first they also consist of just a slight turning up of the corners of the mouth and there is a long latency—the smile appearing only about 6 to 8 seconds after stimulation. Between the second and fourth weeks after birth various changes in smiling take place. Smiles gradually become broader, come to include the eyes and develop into an active alert grin. The latency reduces to 3 or 4 seconds (and to a good deal less than that by 3 months of age). To begin with smiling is most easily elicited when the baby is in a drowsy satiated, state, but these smiles appear following stimulation when the baby is alert and active. Initially low level stimulation is most effective in eliciting smiling, then voices (especially the mother's voice which may even interrupt feeding for a smile), and then by vigorous stimulation such as a lively pat-a-cake which may give rise to a smile which is almost a chortle.

About the fifth week voices wane in their effectiveness to elicit smiling. Between 5 and 8 weeks infants seem most responsive to changing visual stimulation (nodding heads, blinking lights, rotating masks). However, increasingly after that *stationary* meaningful visual stimuli, and above all the eyes and later the full face, become much the most potent elicitors of smiling. Smiling occurs after the infant fixates on the eyes, searching the face. The smile no longer appears as a simple response to stimulation; rather it seems a function of the infant's active cognitive engagement. Such smiling is somewhat delayed in institutionalized infants (Gewirtz, 1965).

From then onwards smiling becomes more and more a social behaviour (*see* Vine, 1973). Not only are infant smiles elicited most easily by social stimuli, but also smiles constitute a key component of the infant's greeting behaviour to others, and are most effective in encouraging social engagement with adults. Social smiling becomes highly differentiated and is more evident with attachment figures. Smiling plays an increasingly important role in modulating face to face social interactions and in this way is crucial for the development of social reciprocity (Brazelton *et al*., 1974).

However, smiling is not only a social behaviour. Piaget (1962) described the way smiling involved an infant's pleasure or his mastery and control over the environment. Thus, Watson (1972) found that 8-week-old infants cooed and smiled more at mobiles activated by head turns or leg kicks than by mobiles whose movement was unrelated to their own activity. Similarly, Kagan (1971) reported that 2 year olds smiled following the solution of a problem, and were especially likely to do so after solving a difficult problem. Smiling seems to occur as a result of recognition and mastery (McCall, 1972; Zelazo, 1972). It is influenced by contingent reinforcement but the waxing and waning of smiling is not primarily due to external reinforcement (Zelazo, 1971).

Laughter

There is considerable individual variation in timing but laughter usually first occurs at about 4 months (Sroufe and Wunsch, 1972; Sroufe and Waters, 1976) when vigorous stimulation is the most potent stimulus. Thus, laughing is most readily elicited by vigorous kissing of the baby's stomach or the 'I'm gonna get you' game in which the person looms towards the infant, talking to him and then abruptly finishing with a tickle. During the next 2 months crescendo sounds (such as a swelling 'aah' with an abrupt cut-off) which may have brought about crying when the infants were younger, begin to induce laughter. Between 7 and 9 months tactile and auditory stimuli decline in potency and laughter becomes more easily elicited by active social and visual stimuli such as a silent peek-a-boo game or the covering of the infant's face or by mother shaking her hair at the infant. Several further important changes take place during the last quarter of the first year. As before, a steep gradient of building tension followed by a rapid recovery is most powerful in bringing about laughter. However, cognitive incongruity (as with the mother walking like a penguin or sucking the baby's bottle) becomes increasingly important; and *anticipatory* laughter is first apparent (so that the infant may start laughing as the mother makes the first premonitory movement indicating the beginning of a stomach-kissing game). At the same time, but continuing into the second year, another alteration takes place. Infants come to laugh more with actions in which they participate and are the active agent; so that there is more laughter when they cover someone else's face than when their own face is covered.

Two further features of laughter require mention. Firstly, repeated presentation of the same stimulus leads to a diminishing response (laughter at first but then only smiling). Secondly, from the second half of the first year onwards, depending on context, the *same* stimulus may elicit either crying or laughing (Sroufe *et al*., 1974). For example, Sroufe *et al*. report that a 15-month-old infant laughed when his mother picked him up by his heels but a little while later cried when she did the same again after the baby had been upset by the intrusion of a stranger. Or a mask on a stranger may induce crying whereas a mask on the mother may bring about laughter. In both cases there is an initial cardiac deceleration associated with attention followed by a quickening of the heart rate with the infant's positive or negative affective response. On these bases, Sroufe and Waters (1976) argue that laughter is associated with tension-release in situations in which the context leads to positive rather than negative affect. Macdonald and Silverman's (1978) findings also suggest links between laughter and fear.

Crying and distress

Crying occurs from the time of birth but it is a matter of some days or weeks (there is marked individual variation—Penbharkkul and Karelitz, 1962) before it is accompanied by tears. Wolff (1969) and Wasz-Höckert *et al*. (1968) have both shown that newborns have several distinct types of cry—representing pain, hunger, or pleasure—with definable acoustic characteristics. Various abnormal cries are also recognizable—such as the special cry of the rare 'cri du chat' syndrome and the short shrill cry of the brain damaged infant. Interestingly, neonates will cry in response to the sound of another cry (Sagi and Hoffman, 1976). Obviously this response lacks a cognitive component and presumably it represents some form of reflex but perhaps it constitutes some form of early precursor of later empathy.

Bridges (1932), in an early study of institutional infants, observed that in the first few months of life distress (as shown by crying, muscle tensing and diffuse movements) was most readily elicited by pain or by loud sharp sounds. The babies were most easily comforted by rocking, wrapping in warm blankets and by sucking. Bayley (1932) made a systematic study of infants' crying during testing; physical restrictions and handling were the most frequent causes of crying. The proportion of babies who cried gradually increased over the first year. More recent studies have given broadly comparable findings (*see e.g.* Cohen, 1967; Bridger and Birns, 1963; Gordon and Foss, 1966). In addition it has been shown that young infants tend to exhibit distress with a looming object (Bower *et al.*, 1970), and that they are soothed by continuous sound (*see e.g.* Brackbill, 1971; Weiss, 1934), by a full stomach, by warmth and by swaddling (Wolff, 1966). Fear of darkness is rare during the first year and it is not until the second half of the first year that infants begin to show a fear of novel objects and of strangers (Bronson, 1972; Schaffer and Parry, 1969; Scarr and Salapatek, 1970).

During the first 6 months infants show distress only *after* the eliciting stimulus and there is none of the *anticipatory* apprehension which is the characteristic of true fear. However, about the age of 9 to 12 months anticipatory emotions (both positive and negative) first become apparent. Thus, about then infants begin to laugh in anticipation of the peek-a-boo game and also they begin to cringe and appear apprehensive at the sight of the approaching inoculation needle (Levy, 1951; Izard, 1978) as well as showing distress following inoculation. In addition, they will no longer go back to the nurse who gave them the injection in the way that younger infants will. The cognitive component of distress which characterizes fear and anxiety is now part of emotion.

Wariness and fear of strangers

It is well established from numerous studies that marked changes in infants' responses to strangeness occur during the third quarter of the first year (*see* Emde *et al.*, 1976; Waters *et al.*, 1975; Schaffer, 1974; Ricciuti, 1974; Harmon *et al.*, 1977; Sroufe, 1977), with the development of so-called '8-months-anxiety' ('so-called' because in fact there is considerable individual variation in when and how this occurs—*see* below) (Spitz, 1950). In the early months of life infants show no avoidance behaviour on the basis of unfamiliarity alone. Then they become differentiated in their initial response to people with a wariness to strangers shown by a frown, worried face, gaze aversion and cardiac acceleration. At about the same time infants become cautious and slow to reach for an unfamiliar

object—having tended to approach impulsively and immediately when younger. During the next few months crying and fearful behaviour in relation to the approach of strangers becomes more common. These age-trends have been observed in developing countries as well as in Western cultures (*see* Goldberg, 1972; Konner, 1972).

This course of development with a qualitative shift in the infant's style of response to strangers and to strange objects is a striking one but the notion that most infants become generally fearful of strangers has been criticized on several grounds (*see* Rheingold and Eckerman, 1973). Firstly, there are marked individual differences in both the age of onset of fear and in its intensity. It seems that in part these are a function of temperamental variations in irritability (Bronson, 1972; Kagan, 1974; Harmon *et al.*, 1977). Secondly, at the same age as infants become wary or fearful of strangers they also show a positive interest in them and may smile, offer them toys and enjoy playing with them (Bretherton and Ainsworth, 1974; Rheingold and Eckerman, 1973; Waters *et al.*, 1975). Moreover, in any one episode the *same* infant may show both wary behaviour and approach to strangers. This observation emphasizes that a wariness of strangers is *not* just the opposite of attachment and exploration. Thirdly, infants' responses to strangers and to novel objects vary greatly by situation. At one time this seemed merely to indicate an inconsistency in behaviour but it is now clear that to a considerable extent the variations are predictable and meaningful. Six main variables seem important: (a) the presence/absence of an attachment figure; (b) the strangeness and context of the overall situation; (c) whether the stranger is an adult or child; (d) whether the stranger approaches or intrudes; (e) previous social experiences; and (f) the infant's control over the situation.

Several studies have shown that infants are much less likely to show a fear of strangers when with their mother (Campos *et al.*, 1975; Ainsworth and Bell, 1970), their father (Spelke *et al.*, 1973) or a familiar caretaker (Ricciuti, 1974). To some extent this is probably because the presence of an attachment figure tends to reduce fear in all circumstances. However, it may also reflect the association of the stranger with separation anxiety, in that fear is most marked when the mother *departs* leaving the infant with a stranger.

The importance of context is also evident in the observation that fear of strangers is more common in the laboratory than in the child's own home (Sroufe *et al.*, 1974; Kagan, 1974; Skarin, 1977). Fearful behaviour is also less likely in the context of play or approach with a toy (Rheingold and Eckerman, 1973). Infants show more negative responses to strange adults than to strange children (Lewis and Brooks, 1974) and there is a slight tendency for them to be more wary of male than female strangers (*see* Sroufe, 1977).

The actions of the stranger greatly influence the infant's response. Rapid approach associated with intrusive behaviours (such as touching or picking up the baby) is most likely to elicit negative reactions. Note, however, that it is the combination of approach plus stranger that elicits wariness; the same approach behaviour by the infant's mother is more likely to induce smiling or laughter (McDonald and Silverman, 1978). If the stranger remains at a distance, or if time is allowed for familiarization, or if the infant is left to make the first overture, little or no negative behaviour is seen (Lewis and Brooks, 1974; Campos *et al.*, 1975; Rheingold and Eckerman, 1973; Ross, 1975).

The findings are rather fragmentary and inconclusive but it seems that an infant's previous social experiences probably modify his response to strangers. Many years ago Bayley (1932) noted that the babies who were upset during psychological testing tended to be those who had experienced few social outings. More recently Harmon *et al.* (1977) found a tendency (falling short of statistical significance) for negative reactions to strangers to be more common among infants with little prior experience of adults (other than baby-sitters). It also appears that institutional children tend to be less wary of strangers, but the effects of day care are less consistent. Presumably much depends on whether the infant's previous social experiences were happy ones or not. Any experiences may reduce strangeness but unhappy ones may sensitize the infant to respond with distress. Also, too, the effects are likely to be confounded by the consequences of the experiences for the development of bonding (*see* Chapter 22).

Finally, the infant's response is likely to be affected by his control over the situation. This was most clearly shown with respect to a strange toy by Gunnar-Vongnechten (1978). One-year-old children were presented with a toy monkey which clapped cymbals—activated either by the child or by the experimenter. Girls did not show distress in either condition but in boys their control over the toy much reduced fear. The same may apply in social situations with strange persons (Sroufe, 1977).

Wariness and fear of strangers tend to be considered as different degrees of the same phenomenon. To some extent this is the case but it is striking that fear is apparent at a rather later age than wariness; moreover whereas wariness may be associated with positive approach, fear is not. Bronson and Pankey (1977) argue that whereas wariness represents a cautious response to unfamiliarity, fear involves a categorical negative reaction based on experience.

Separation anxiety

The extensive literature on separation anxiety has been well reviewed by Bowlby (1973). Both naturalistic and experimental studies show that about the age of 6 or 7 months infants begin to show marked distress when their mother departs leaving them alone—especially, but not only, if in a strange environment. The distress is shown by increased crying, decreased exploration, following the mother as far as the infant can and calling for the mother to return. This pattern of separation anxiety, which is not seen in the early months of life, tends to reach a peak about the age of 18 months and then gradually diminishes. Thus, Maccoby and Feldman (1972) found that over half

2 year olds cried when left by their mother, over two-fifths of 2½ year olds did so but only a fifth of 3 year olds. The emergence of separation anxiety is closely allied to the development of specific attachments (*see* Chapter 22). However, there is considerable individual variation in the extent of separation anxiety. In part this appears to be related to the security of the infant's attachments but also in part it seems to be a function of the child's cognitive capacity to appreciate that the separation will be temporary and to maintain a relationship over a period of absence. Thus, Weinraub and Lewis (1977) not only found that distress during the mother's absence was less among the more intelligent 2-year-old children, but also that it was less when the mothers informed the infants that they were leaving and told them what to do while they were away (than if they just departed without saying anything).

Over the age of 3 years children continue to show separation anxiety in some degree but its intensity and persistence get progressively less. Thus, Shirley (Shirley, 1942; Shirley and Poyntz, 1941) found that about half of 2- to 4-year-old children showed distress at separating from their mother at a research centre but the proportion who were upset diminished considerably during the next 4 years. At all ages boys were somewhat more likely than girls to show marked separation anxiety—perhaps in part because boys lag behind girls in their development.

Other emotions

Although Watson and Morgan (1917) had proposed that infants were born with the three unlearned emotions of fear, love and rage, Sherman (1927) found that observers showed only a poor level of agreement in rating emotions in very young infants if they did not know what the preceding stimulus had been. Bridges (1932) maintained that in the neonate only quiescence and excitement could be differentiated; that distress became evident towards the end of the first month; that pleasure was not differentiable until the second or third month; and that the more specific emotions of anger, disgust and fear became manifest at about 6 months.

As we have seen, more detailed studies of smiling and of crying have allowed somewhat finer discriminations to be made but the general pattern of gradually increasing differentiation of emotions during the first year has been broadly confirmed by more recent investigators. Thus, Emde *et al.* (1978) suggest that at age 2½ months infants' facial expressions are rateable along just two dimensions—hedonic tone (pleasure *v.* displeasure) and activation or state (alertness *v.* drowsiness). By 3½ to 4½ months there is more variation in expressions and a third dimension of internally or externally oriented (curious *v.* bored) enters the ratings. Emotions such as fear, surprise and anger only become recognizable in the latter half of the first year with the increasing range of facial expressions which develop between about 6 and 10 months. Lewis and Brooks (1978) argue that the experience of emotional states is heavily dependent upon self-awareness which begins to develop at the end of the first year and is present in almost all infants by 24 months. They suggest that in the first 3 months emotions consist only of unconditioned responses to stimuli such as hunger or loud noises; that conditioned responses to strangers and to incongruity arise between 4 and 8 months; that the specific emotional experiences of fear, happiness and love develop between 9 and 12 months; and that the beginnings of empathy, guilt and embarrassment first appear during the second year.

Oster's (1978) detailed study of facial expressions has added a further dimension to the significance of brow-knitting or frowning in the first 3 months. Previous workers had tended to assume that the furrowed brow was a sign of negative affect (Stern, 1974; Emde et al., 1976) and hence that the frequent sequence of frowning and smiling was in some way paradoxical. Oster's preliminary observations indicate differences between the facial expressions associated with pre-smile and pre-cry frowns. She suggests that the former may represent an attentive effort to make sense of the stimuli—an early equivalent perhaps of the adult frown of puzzlement or difficulty in cognitive activity (Darwin, 1872). On these grounds, she argues that there may be more emotional expression in the first 3 months than is usually credited.

Even so, it is clear that the quality of emotions changes with the infant's greater capacity for cognitive engagement after 3 months and with his increasing ability to anticipate events after 9 to 12 months. The range of emotions at 12 months is much wider than in the neonatal period.

EMOTIONAL DEVELOPMENT DURING CHILDHOOD AND ADOLESCENCE

Emotional recognition

Although data are rather sparse (and biased by an excessive reliance on verbal reports), it seems that children become progressively more aware of emotions in others as they grow older (see Chandler, 1977 for a good review). It is not just that they become better able to recognize the emotions shown in facial expressions or vocalizations (although they do), or even that they become more aware of the emotional connotations of social situations (which again they do), but also that increasingly they come to utilize emotional concepts. Thus, Gilbert (1969) found that first grade children were more likely than those at nursery school to describe pictures in terms of traits such as 'friendly' or 'happy' rather than literal descriptions such as smiling or jumping or bent knee. A variety of investigations have shown that pre-school children rarely use psychological constructs and it is not until well into middle childhood that they do so at all regularly (Gollin, 1958; Whiteman, 1967). On the other hand, even pre-school children show some skills in anticipating what emotions are likely to be experienced by people in particular situations (as shown by their

response to stories—e.g. Borke, 1973). Also often they are moved by the affective responses of others—recoiling from anger and sharing in distress (Murphy, 1937; Staub, 1971). Children are able to recognize and respond to emotions in others from even the early years but their skills in social role-taking and their use of emotional constructs take longer to develop.

Fears

Many studies have shown a general tendency for specific fears to become less frequent as children grow older. Thus, Macfarlane et al. (1954), using maternal reports, found that the peak prevalence of fears was at age 3 years (when over half the children were said to have at least one specific fear), with a slow decline thereafter. Cummings (1944), using teacher reports, found much the same; the rate of specific fears fell from 33% in 2- to 4-year-olds to 13% at 6 to 8 years. Observations of children's responses to experimental situations by Jersild and Holmes (1935) also produced a similar picture; thus a fear of dogs was manifest in 69% of 2-year-olds but only 12% of 5-year-olds.

However, the overall figures for the varying age prevalence of fears conceal important differences according to the type of fear. At least four different groups are discriminable on the basis of age trends (Jersild and Holmes, 1935; Angelino et al., 1956; Shepherd et al., 1971; Bauer, 1976; Hagman, 1932; Macfarlane et al., 1954). First, there are those fears which are most characteristic of infancy—fears of noises, falling, strange objects and strange persons. These reach a peak before age 2 years and rapidly decline during the pre-school years. Secondly, there is the group of fears which are rare in infancy but which rise rapidly during the pre-school years only to fall again during middle childhood. Thus, fears of animals reach a peak at about 3 years, fears of the dark at about 4 to 5 years and fears of imaginary creatures slightly later than that. Thirdly, there are fears with a less consistent age trend. These include both specific fears which are fairly widespread at all ages, such as a fear of snakes, and also those such as a fear of meeting people which are perhaps more closely associated with temperamental features. In addition, there are those 'abnormal' fears which are not part of normal development and which tend to arise later in childhood or during adolescence. This group includes social anxieties and a fear of open or closed spaces (Marks and Gelder, 1966). However, it also includes a particular form of separation anxiety or fear of school which arises during adolescence. Many normal young children show initial anxieties in a new situation and because of this may be fearful of nursery school or infant school. In most cases these fears rapidly diminish over the first few weeks (Slater, 1939) and do not recur. However, during adolescence a state of fear taking the form of school refusal again becomes more common (Rutter et al., 1976); this variety tends to be more persistent and more often it is part of a generalized emotional disorder (Hersov, 1960; Rodriguez et al., 1959).

Irritability, tantrums and anger

Goodenough's (1931) classical study of temper outbursts in young children, which utilized detailed daily reports by parents, provides the most systematic data on developmental changes during the pre-school years. She found that anger outbursts reached their peak frequency during the second year. After age 2 years there was a progressive shortening of the more violent initial stage of angry behaviour but also a lengthening of such after-effects as sulking, whining or brooding. Tempers tended to be more frequent when children were physically unwell, hungry or tired; the diurnal peaks being at the end of the morning, the end of the afternoon and just before bed-time. During all the pre-school years after the first, over a half of the outbursts arose from some conflict with parental authority—not surprisingly the content of the conflict tended to change with age; from issues over toileting and prohibited activities in the second year to refusal to put away toys and clashes over clothing in the fifth year. Disagreements with playmates were infrequent causes of tempers in the first 3 years but accounted for a fifth of outbursts during the fourth and fifth years. Dawe (1934) found that younger nursery school children started more quarrels but the older ones were more likely to become physically aggressive; Appel (1942) also showed that among 2-year-olds quarrels tended to centre around disputes over possessions whereas in older children aggression arose over disputes concerning joint play.

Shepherd et al. (1971) showed that the prevalence of tantrums continues to fall during the school years; 10% of 5-year-old boys but only 2% of 15-year-old boys were said to have weekly tantrums. The fall in frequency was found to occur somewhat later in girls and there was a further increase at age 14 to 15 years. In both sexes there was no consistent age change in *marked* irritability but occasional irritability decreased and placidity increased as the children became older.

Depression and mood swings

The understanding of all emotions necessarily depends to a considerable extent on people's reports of the feelings they are experiencing. The feeling state and its personal meaning to the individual are essential components of emotion. However, this is particularly the case with depression which involves not only misery and unhappiness but also a lowering of vigour and energy, a sense of rejection (Sandler and Joffe, 1965) and a negative self-image (Poznanski and Zrull, 1970). A full appraisal of these components is only possible when children are able both to view themselves in these terms and to describe their feelings to others. As already noted, most children are not able to do so until well into the school years.

Nevertheless, circumstantial evidence strongly suggests that depression may be experienced even as early as the second and third year of life. Thus a variety of studies of infants admitted to institutions (summarized by Bowlby, 1969) have shown that the initial stage of acute distress and crying is often followed by a phase characterized by a diminution of physical activity, quiet monotonous crying (rather than screaming), social withdrawal and a reduction of demands on people in the environment. Robertson and Bowlby have argued that this behaviour seems to connote a feeling of hopelessness and hence have described the state as one of despair. Spitz (1946) had earlier described 'anaclitic depression' in infants being reared in poor quality institutions. His writings on this topic were influential but little reliance can be placed on his findings in view of the serious methodological limitations of the work (see Pinneau, 1955). In particular, it is unclear how far the children's behaviour was a consequence of physical disease and malnutrition. As with Robertson and Bowlby, Gaensbauer et al. (1980) have observed apparently depressive behaviour in abused and neglected infants—with motor retardation, lack of responsiveness, aimless play, downcast facial expression and persistent whimpering.

During the middle years of childhood, feelings of misery and upset are not uncommon (some 12% of 10-year-olds in the Isle of Wight survey were said to have these feelings). Moreover, unhappiness may sometimes be accompanied by a sense of rejection and a negative self-image, both of which are characteristic of depression (Sandler and Joffe, 1965; Poznanski and Zrull, 1970). However, unhappiness in younger children tends to be a less well-differentiated response; and the adult type of depression with self-blame, ideas of reference, psychomotor retardation and suicidal thoughts (although sometimes occurring in the early years) only becomes at all common during adolescence.

Although crying becomes progressively less frequent during the school years, there is some tendency for occasional worrying to increase and among girls, but not boys, there is a sharp increase in moodiness during adolescence (Shepherd et al., 1971). Both clinic (Pearce, 1978) and general population studies (Rutter et al., 1976) also point to a marked increase in misery, depression, and ideas of self-depreciation during adolescence—in both sexes but possibly to a greater extent in girls. Thus, in the Isle of Wight study of 14- and 15-year-olds, more than a fifth reported that they often felt miserable or depressed—a rate well above that in adult life, as shown by the figures for their parents (Rutter et al., 1976). The rate of suicide also rises during adolescence, having been an extremely rare event in earlier childhood (Shaffer, 1974). There are few systematic data on children's reactions to bereavement but what little evidence there is suggests that the grief of younger children is milder and of shorter duration than that of adolescents or adults (Marris, 1958; Burlingham and Freud, 1942). In part, this may be a consequence of the younger child's imperfect concept of death (see e.g. Anthony, 1940; Nagy, 1948; Koocher, 1974) but in part, too, it may reflect the less well developed ability to express depressive feelings. Of course, too, age trends in the expression of grief will be influenced by variations in family responses to the death and in what the loss means in terms of alterations in the child's overall life experiences (see Furman, 1974).

Thus, although depressive feelings can occur from

infancy onwards and although misery and unhappiness are reasonably common during middle childhood, prolonged states of depressive mood with psychomotor slowing, low self-esteem, self-blame and ideas of hopelessness remain relatively infrequent until early adolescence when there is a marked increase in their prevalence. Controversy continues on whether these age differences mean that depressive disorder is uncommon in young children (Makita, 1973; Graham, 1974) or rather whether it is that depression is expressed in a different form in early childhood (Frommer, 1968). To a considerable extent, the disagreements reflect the lack of adequate criteria or concepts of depression in childhood (*see* Schulterbrandt and Raskin, 1977).

Neuroticism

As well as developmental changes in the expression of more specific emotions, there are also age-related alterations in overall 'emotionality'. Eysenck and Eysenck (1975) have developed a self-rating questionnaire for children to measure the hypothesized personality trait of 'neuroticism'. The reliability of the questionnaire is quite low in 7- to 8-year-old children but is better in adolescents. Cross-sectional studies show that in girls, but not boys, neuroticism scores increase with age. Extraversion also goes up with age—in both sexes but more so in girls than in boys.

Sex differences

There are very important, but ill-understood, developmental changes in the sex distribution of different forms of emotional expression and of emotional disorder. Thus, in the early infancy period there are no consistent sex differences with respect to the frequency of crying (*see* Maccoby and Jacklin, 1975). During the nursery school years sex differences are still not marked (and often fail to reach statistical significance), but the trend is for *boys* to be more likely to cry and show emotional distress in new situations or with strange objects (*see* Smith, 1974). Thus, Gunnar-Vongnechten (1978) found that 1-year-old girls were not distressed by a novel toy monkey that clapped cymbals, whereas boys appeared frightened by it; and Smith (1974) found that significantly more boys than girls were distressed when first attending an experimental playgroup.

Landreth (1941) found that boys were more likely than girls to cry as a result of frustration (either over a failure to manipulate some object or as a result of conflict with an adult). Similarly, Goodenough (1931) showed that over the age of 2 years or so boys were twice as likely as girls to have outbursts of anger. The sex difference seems to reflect increasing emotional control in girls rather than increasing volatility in boys.

At the time of first starting ordinary school at age 5 years there is very little difference between boys and girls in their tendency to cry. However, among older children there is an increasingly wide difference between the sexes. The evidence suggests that this is not that boys grow less

likely to become emotionally distressed, but rather that this form of emotional expression becomes less acceptable in boys. Thus, there is little difference between boys and girls with respect to irritability, whining, fear of the dark and worrying (Shepherd *et al.*, 1971). As judged by reports from parents and teachers, there is little difference between pre-adolescent boys and girls in rates of various forms of emotional disturbance, although there is a slight tendency for some to be marginally more frequent in girls (*see* Rutter *et al.*, 1970).

During the adolescent period of transition from childhood to adulthood, the picture on sex differences changes markedly. Thus, the findings from self-report anxiety scales in *later* childhood suggest that girls are somewhat more willing than boys to admit that they feel anxious (*see* Maccoby and Jacklin, 1975). Also, whereas there is no sex difference on neuroticism up to age 10 years, thereafter there is an increasing sex differentiation because of increasing neuroticism in girls and women but not in males (Eysenck and Eysenck, 1975).

Shepherd *et al.* (1971) found a marked adolescent increase in moodiness for girls but not boys. During adult life it is well established from a wide range of community studies that depression and neurosis are very much commoner in women than in men, and that this large and consistent sex difference is not a reporting artefact (*see* Weissman and Klerman, 1977).

In short, there are no consistent sex differences in emotional expression in infancy; there is a possible slight tendency for boys to be more distressed by novel stimuli during the pre-school years; during the pre-adolescent years of childhood sex differences are small but there may be a very minor tendency for girls to show slightly more emotional disturbance; during adolescence mood disturbances become increasingly common in girls; and in adult life depression is twice as common in women as in men.

Various attempts have been made to explore possible reasons for this marked shift in sex ratio from childhood to adult life (*see* Rutter, 1970a; Gove and Tudor, 1973; Weissman and Klerman, 1977). Various suggestions can be ruled out but no entirely satisfactory explanation is available. The findings can *not* be accounted for in terms of sex differences in 'conditionability', in physiologic responses to stress, in frequency of acutely stressful life events or in the perception of stress. Endocrine changes (as in the premenstrual phase, in the puerperium or through the use of oral contraceptives) may influence mood but the differences are not such as to entirely account for the preponderance of depression in women. Genetic factors may well play a role but the evidence so far is insufficient to provide an explanation for the developmental course of sex differences in emotional disorder. It has been argued that the findings may simply reflect a different mode of *expression* of emotional disturbance in men and women (Dohrenwend and Dohrenwend, 1976 and 1977) – in women by depression and in men by alcoholism and personality disorders. However, this does not account for the *change* in sex ratio of emotional disturbance which takes place between childhood and adult life. Moreover, the factors of possible aetiological importance correlated with emotional disorder are rather different from those correlated with antisocial disorder or personality disturbance. There may be something in the idea but it fails to account for many of the findings.

Finally, it has been suggested that women are more prone to depression because they have a disadvantaged status in Western societies (Gove and Tudor, 1973). If this hypothesis is to account for the findings it must explain why this applies to adult life and yet not to childhood. Four findings begin to provide pointers as to why this might be so. First, whereas marriage acts as a protective factor for men it does not do so for women (*see* reviews by Rutter, 1970b and Weissman and Klerman, 1977). Secondly, among working-class women depression appears most frequent among those with pre-school children at home (Brown *et al.*, 1975). Thirdly, in the same group employment outside the home served as a protective factor. All three variables, of course, apply to adults and not to children. Fourthly, whereas boys tend to respond with greater efforts when they receive feedback from adults that they are failing, girls tend to give up and attribute their failure to their own lack of ability (Dweck and Bush, 1976). The sex difference in response to failure feedback from *peers* was in the opposite direction. One of the reasons for girls being more likely to give up seems to lie in the sex-differentiated pattern of feedback from adults. Dweck *et al.* (1978) found that teachers were more critical of boys than girls but also they were more critical of boys in a diffuse way which could readily be perceived as irrelevant to their intellectual performance. In contrast, almost all criticisms of girls referred specifically to their intellectual failings. Conversely, positive feedback tended to be work-specific for boys but diffuse for girls. The pattern is one likely to increase girls' tendency to feel that they cannot succeed. It has been suggested that the increasing experience of feedback from adults during the school years may lead girls to show an increase in 'learned helplessness' during the later years of childhood and adolescence. The potential importance of this lies in the evidence suggesting that experience with uncontrollable events (learned helplessness) may predispose a person to depression (Seligman, 1975 and 1976).

There is insufficient evidence at present to decide how far the disadvantaged status of women is a cause of their greater propensity to depression but it seems likely that this factor plays some part in leading to sex differences. However, it is possible that other factors are also influential and further investigation is especially necessary in the case of genetic and endocrine factors.

CONTINUITIES IN EMOTIONAL EXPRESSION

So far we have been concerned with the general course of emotional development in terms of the features and characteristics shown at different ages. It is now necessary to consider how far there are continuities at an individual level—that is how far, for example, the infants who show extremes of emotional expression at one age are the *same* children who show extremes at a later age. This has been studied through correlations over time for children's responses to specific situations, for temperamental or personality trait ratings and for indications of emotional disturbance.

Responses to specific situations

The findings from studies of children's responses to specific fear-eliciting stimuli provide modest support for a relatively persistent trait of irritability, sensitivity or anxiety in infancy. Maccoby and Feldman (1972), for example, found a correlation of 0.52 between crying on being left by the mother with a stranger at 2 years and crying in the same situation at 3 years. There was much less consistency, however, in the child's tendency to cry when alone. Bronson (1972) showed a moderate consistency at $6\frac{1}{2}$ months over time in children's wariness of strangers (0.75 between 4 months and $6\frac{1}{2}$ months and 0.49 between 4 months and 9 months) and some consistency across situations (*e.g.* at 6 months a correlation of 0.38 between wariness of strangers and an overall reactivity measure based on other stimuli such as a looming object and reactions to bathing). Similarly, Kagan (1971) found that 4-month-old babies who became restless and irritable after several presentations of visual stimuli tended to be more fretful than other babies at 8 months and 13 months and were more likely to cry when left alone by their mothers in a laboratory at 8 months (as part of a separation experiment). However, continuities in irritability were evident in girls but not boys (Kagan, 1974). Similarly, Harmon *et al.* (1977) found that babies who were fussy and irritable during play were twice as likely as non-fussy babies to show avoidance of strangers.

Temperamental traits

Thomas and Chess (1977) have used data from detailed parental informers to assess children in a longitudinal study on 9 temperamental categories (*see* Chapter 9). They found some consistency across periods of 1 year but the correlations between the first and fifth years of life were near zero for all categories including those of mood and of emotional intensity. Other studies have shown similarly low levels of continuity over several years in temperamental attributes when assessed in relation to the early infancy period (*e.g.* Schaefer and Bayley, 1963; Kagan and Moss, 1962). However, there are major methodological difficulties in the interpretation of these findings (*see* Rutter, 1970b) and it should not necessarily be assumed that in actuality there is no temperamental continuity in these early years. In particular the changing context of the child's behaviour may give the same characteristic very different forms of expression at different age periods. This possibility is certainly suggested by the finding that the same temperamental traits which show such limited developmental continuity also show an important degree of heritability (Torgersen and Kringlen,

1978). Interestingly, however, the genetic component is greater at 9 months of age than at 2 months.

Continuities in middle childhood are rather greater. Rachman (1969) argues from a variety of studies that extraversion and neuroticism are stable personality dimensions but the correlations over time have all been quite modest, even if statistically significant. Thus, Bronson (1966a) found some significant correlations (mainly in the 0.40s) between the extent of behaviour problems over the whole 21–42 month period of emotional reactivity in the early school years but rather lower correlations (in the 0.30s) with adolescence. However, the pattern in boys and girls was somewhat different (particularly with respect to early fearfulness which was associated with later high reactivity in boys but low reactivity in girls). Between 5 and 16 years the dimension of outgoing *v.* reserved showed greater temporal stability than that for placid *v.* explosive (Bronson, 1966b). The continuities with adult personality assessments appeared greater for men tnan for women and in general were greater from adolescence than from early childhood (Bronson, 1967).

Emotional disturbance

Studies of both the general population and clinic samples have consistently shown that emotional problems in childhood and adolescence are much less persistent than disorders of conduct (*see* Robins, 1972). Thus, in the Isle of Wight total population survey half of those with an emotional disorder at 10 years (termed neurotic disorder in the original study (Rutter, Tizard and Whitmore, 1970)) were free of significant problems at 14 years, compared with only a quarter of those with conduct problems (Graham and Rutter, 1973). Similarly, in a teachers questionnaire study of London children, 35% of emotional difficulties persisted over a period of 4 years compared with 62% of conduct problems (Rutter, 1977). Also, studies of psychiatric patients have all shown that whereas half to three-quarters of children and adolescents with emotional disorders recover within a few years this is so for only a minority of those with conduct disorders, sociopathy or psychosis (*e.g.* Annesley, 1961; Cunningham *et al.*, 1956; Masterson, 1967; Warren, 1965). Nevertheless, although the outlook for emotional disorders is generally good, these same figures show a significant degree of persistence within the childhood years.

Other studies show that to some extent continuities extend into adult life although the links between emotional disorder in childhood and adult neurosis have usually (but not always—*see* Waldron, 1976) been found to be fairly weak (*see* reviews by Rutter, 1972 and Cox, 1976). The results indicate that: (a) most children with emotional disorder grow up to be substantially normal adults; and (b) many neuroses have their onset in adult life; but (c) compared with general population controls children with an emotional disturbance have about double the risk of psychiatric disability in adult life; and (d) in most cases the adult psychiatric problem takes the form of neurosis, depression or an immature/inadequate personality disorder. Only quite rarely do children with emotional difficulties show an antisocial personality disorder.

Only very limited information is available on the distinctions between the forms of emotional disorder which do and those which do not persist into adult life. Rutter (1972) suggested that psychiatric conditions in childhood might be more likely to be precursors of adult disability if the patterns of childhood behaviour were developmentally atypical. Thus, school refusal has a worse prognosis when it occurs during adolescence than when it occurs in early childhood at a stage when separation anxiety is a normal feature (Rodriguez *et al.*, 1959; Kennedy, 1965). Similarly, Tyrer and Tyrer (1974) found that the link between school refusal and adult neurosis involved adolescent school refusal in over two-thirds of cases. Other findings suggest that there may be differences in the meaning of emotional difficulties before and after adolescence. Thus, Gersten *et al.* (1976) showed moderate continuity (correlations of about 0.40) of emotional disturbance over 5 year periods during the pre-adolescent years and similarly good continuity between adolescence and adult life. However, continuity was quite weak (correlations of about 0.25) for 5 year periods extending across the adolescent period.

THEORIES OF EMOTIONAL DEVELOPMENT

Any comparative appraisal of the various different theories of emotional development is difficult not only because a very large number of theories deal with some aspect of emotional expression, but also because each tends to focus on a different set of issues and because few are specifically *developmental* in orientation. Accordingly, no attempt is made to provide a comprehensive coverage of theories concerned with emotions (*see* Izard, 1977 for a fuller discussion). Rather, a selection of contrasting approaches is considered briefly in order to highlight the strengths and weaknesses of different conceptual frameworks. It is convenient to discuss first those dealing with general dimensions of personality before turning to those postulating more specific mechanisms.

Eysenck's personality theory

Many writers have postulated the importance of personality dimension in determining variations in patterns of emotional response. Most notably, Pavlov (1927) implicated two basic cortical processes of *excitation* and *inhibition*; and Jung (1924) contrasted *introverts* and *extraverts*. Utilizing both these concepts, Eysenck (*see e.g.* Eysenck, 1947, 1967; Eysenck and Eysenck, 1969 and 1975) has developed a theory of personality which sets out to explain one of the central issues in all aspects of development—namely the origin of individual differences. In essence, Eysenck postulates the existence of three major constitutionally determined and stable dimensions of personality; neuroticism (N), extraversion (E) and psychoticism (P). Neuroticism involves greater emotional arousability and is thought to give rise to stronger drive in emotion-producing situations. This may result in either an improvement or worsening of performance according to task difficulty, stress experienced and other variables. Extraversion is considered to be associated with greater central mental fatigue and higher levels of central inhibition. As a result introverts should condition better than extraverts. Psychoticism, or the P factor, encompasses various aspects of 'tough-mindedness' (see Eysenck and Eysenck, 1975; Powell, 1977) which appear to be related to antisocial and delinquent behaviour. Both the 'N' and 'E' factors are thought to be crucial for the development of anxiety, as a conditional fear response.

The theory has given rise to a vast amount of empirical research much of which supports some of the key postulates of the theory (see references to Eysenck's writings above; also Franks, 1961; Martin, 1973). Thus, the E, N and P dimensions of personality are well established, there is evidence that to an important degree they are genetically determined, and the dimensions relate in a predictable way to overt behaviour. However, it is dubious how meaningful it is to talk of a general characteristic of 'conditionability'—as responses to conditioning seem to vary according to both the nature of the unconditioned stimulus and the type of response to be conditioned (see e.g. Davidson et al., 1964; Franks and Franks, 1966; Gray, 1970). Also, there are major problems in the concept of E, N and P as personality dimensions. In the first place, there is little stability in childhood even over periods as short as one year (Eysenck and Eysenck, 1973). In the second place, in adults N scores vary markedly according to improvement or worsening of neurotic conditions in patients (Ingham, 1966). Few data are available on the links between E, N and P scores and emotional disturbance in childhood, but what evidence there is suggests that the associations with neuroticism are much weaker than they are in adult life (Powell, 1977). Of course, each of these drawbacks may reflect the inadequacies of existing measures rather than the weaknesses of the concepts themselves. Nevertheless, for all these reasons, Eysenck's theory of personality provides an inadequate explanation for emotional development. However, as with other major theories, its main limitation is that it fails to account for the various developmental changes in emotional expression discussed earlier in this chapter, rather than it is wrong in itself.

Conditioning and learning

Learning theories have been most strongly invoked with respect to the development and elimination of fears (see Marks, 1969 for a readable summary). Watson and Rayner's (1920) classic case, in which fear of a white rat was created in an 11-month-old infant by pairing the presence of the rat with a loud noise, is often cited in this connection and has been used as a general paradigm for phobias (Eysenck and Rachman, 1965). Other workers' (e.g. English, 1929; Bregman, 1934) failure to replicate the findings are less often mentioned.

There is ample evidence that fears can be created and abolished through conditioning procedures but as a general theory of fear acquisition it is quite inadequate (see Rachman, 1977). Thus, people fail to acquire fears in what are theoretically fear-evoking situations (e.g. air-raids). Secondly, it has proved difficult to produce conditioned fear reactions in human subjects in the laboratory (cf. English and Bregman above). Thirdly, the theory rests on the false assumption that all stimuli have an equal chance of being transformed into fear signals. Clearly they do not. City children are very much more likely to be afraid of snakes than of lambs although they are unlikely to have encountered either. Fears of the dark are common but pyjama phobias are exceedingly rare. Fourthly, in many cases of specific fear no traumatic precipitants can be found. Fifthly, there is good evidence that fears can be acquired vicariously and indirectly without contact with the feared object. Sixthly, according to conditioning theory, unreinforced fear reactions should extinguish quickly whereas in fact some are remarkably persistent and resistant to treatment (see Eysenck, 1976). Eysenck (1976) has suggested an enhancement mechanism, in which conditioned stimuli acquire drive properties, as an explanation for the last observations. However, to deal with the first five objections it is necessary also to accept that modelling and vicarious learning, as well as classical conditioning play a major role in the genesis of fears. Fears may be acquired from other family members and through symbolic associations as well as from acute stresses and traumata. Moreover, it is also necessary to invoke notions of innate fear patterns and of preparedness to explain why some objects but not others commonly constitute the basis of phobias. Personality factors have to be brought in, in addition, to account for individual differences. With these provisos, it is evident that learning processes are indeed important in determining emotional reactions. On the other hand, many things are left unexplained—particularly the age changes in the types of fears shown.

Until recently less attention has been paid to the role of learning in the development of depression. However, particularly in connection with the work of Seligman (1975 and 1976), considerable attention has been paid over the last decade to the possibility that 'learned helplessness' may be central to depression. The crucial notion is that it is not traumata as such which influence mood but rather the individual's lack of control over the traumata. Certainly, there is laboratory evidence that in animals stresses over which the individual has no control and from which he has no escape lead to passivity and maladaptive behaviour in a way that comparable, but controllable, stresses do not. Stomach ulcers are also more likely to occur during uncontrollable than controllable stress (Weiss, 1972). The particular cognitive set engendered seems to be important in determining the individual's emotional and behavioural response. Already the idea of learned helplessness has considerable empirical support and its extension to the development of depression seems plausible (but unproven—see Blaney, 1977). However, many questions remain and so far there have been only limited attempts to apply the theory to developmental issues. Accordingly, no satisfactory explanations are provided for various key features, for example, for the marked increase in depression during adolescence.

Cognitive-affective theories

Many theorists have emphasized perceptual-cognitive processes in emotional development. The need to invoke cognitive factors is certainly obvious in relation to the changes which take place during the infancy period. It is evident, for example, in the shift which takes place from impulsiveness to wariness in the baby's response to strangers (*e.g.* Schaffer, 1974) and in the infant's growing ability to show positive and negative emotions in *anticipation* of various events (*see* above). However, some theorists have gone further in giving perceptual-cognitive processes a fairly central role in emotional development. Thus, Kagan (1974) has interpreted separation anxiety and fear of strangers in terms of 'an unassimilated discrepant event producing uncertainty'. In other words fear is brought about when there is a cognitive discrepancy (something unexpected and unfamiliar) which the infant tries to interpret and assimilate in his cognitive framework but fails to do so. This general model is in keeping with many of the empirical observations of infantile fear but it has to be stretched a good deal to account for all (*see* Sroufe, 1977). Thus, it is not obvious from discrepancy considerations why fear of strangers should be so much less when the baby is sitting on its mother's lap rather than four feet away (Morgan and Ricciuti, 1969). Nor is it evident why a stimulus which has produced smiling earlier should later lead to crying (*see* Macdonald and Silverman, 1978). However, Kagan (1974) has been at pains to emphasize that unassimilated discrepancy is only one of several sources of distress (anticipation of an undesirable event and a recognition of dissonance between or among beliefs are said to be others—both of which involve cognitive considerations); and also that temperamental factors of possibly genetic origin are important in determining individual differences.

Izard (1977 and 1978) is another writer to emphasize the close links between cognition and emotion. He sees the ontogenesis of emotions as mainly a function of age-related biological changes, but the development of affective-cognitive structures as a function of learning. Both perceptual-appraisal processes (dealing with factors such as the assimilation of cognitive discrepancy) and cognitive-interpretative processes (in which there is a concern with imagery and symbolization) are thought to be important. Emotions are thought to play a part in the development of self-recognition and self-concept and, in turn, self-related cognition influences emotion. As a general concept this view has obvious validity with regard to its insistence on the close inter-relationships between different aspects of development. However, for the most part, the notions involved are too general to allow much in the way of specific predictions concerning individual differences in emotional development. By bringing in symbolization this variety of cognitive-affective theory has some links with psychoanalytic concepts.

Psychoanalytic theories

Emotions constitute a central feature in all psychoanalytic theories of development (*see* Bowlby, 1973; Rapaport, 1953 and 1960; and Dare, 1977 for good summaries). However, while Freud's major reformulation of the theory of anxiety in 1926 stimulated a considerable literature it did not bring about either consensus or clarity (*see* Yorke and Wiseberg, 1976). It may be said fairly that anxiety is the most pervasive but least perspicuous of concepts. Nevertheless, certain key concepts differentiate psychoanalytic theories from others: (a) the concept of instinctual drives with an energy component; (b) the intrinsic quality of internal conflicts between these drives deriving from the id and the controls exerted by the ego; (c) the crucial importance of how the effects are dealt with through the system of defence mechanisms such as displacement, repression and projection; (d) the vital links between psychosexual stages and the development of emotions; (e) the concept of unconscious motivation; and (f) the importance for later development of the intrapsychic events of the early years (together with the related concepts of developmental progression, regression and fixation). A distinction is made between neurotic anxiety deriving from internal conflicts and objective anxiety involving foresight of real danger situations. Anna Freud (1963) went on to emphasize the developmental sequence by which different forms of anxiety characterize different stages in the development of object relations. Mahler (Mahler *et al.*, 1975) somewhat similarly linked emotional development to the process of separation—individuation by which the infant develops autonomy from its mother. Melanie Klein (Klein *et al.*, 1952), however, has differed sharply in her emphasis on the struggle between life and death instincts thought to be already operating at the time of birth and which is considered to give rise to persecutory anxiety.

As is apparent from this brief and inadequate summary the ideas are both complex and abstract in ways which make them difficult, and sometimes impossible, to test. They have arisen as part of a set of theories mainly concerned with the origins of psychopathology and deriving from the analysis of patients rather than from the observation of children. Not surprisingly, therefore, they have little to say about the empirical phenomena of emotional development discussed earlier in this chapter. Moreover, very few of the attempts to experimentally test psychoanalytic theory have been concerned with developmental issues—rather they have largely focused on mental mechanisms (*see e.g.* Kline, 1972). As a result, the most serious limitation of psychoanalytic theories of emotional development are their lack of precision and their lack of relevance to many of the observed features of development. In so far as the theories are specific, the hydraulic notion of a fixed energy component is most obviously wrong (*see* Hinde, 1960) and has indeed been abandoned by many analysts. Klein's concepts are almost impossible to test but they make implausible assumptions about the mental life of very young infants; they lack empirical verification; and fail to explain the emergence of separation anxiety (*see* Bowlby, 1973).

Perhaps the main value of psychoanalytic contributions lie in their suggestions concerning psychological *meaning* and on their emphasis on the vital links between emotional development and the growth of social relationships. Psychoanalytic ideas, although greatly modified by biological concepts, have been seminal in leading to the derivation of more specific theories, of which John Bowlby's is the best established.

Bowlby's theory of attachment and loss

Bowlby (1973) recognizes the existence of constitutional factors in susceptibility to fear and includes both cognitive considerations and evolutionary notions in his theorizing. However, the most distinctive feature of his views lies in his argument that a person's tendency to respond with fear is determined in very large part by the perceived availability of attachment figures. In this way, most fears are derivatives of separation anxiety. Similarly anger is thought to arise as a result of repeated separations and of threats of being abandoned. Depression is considered to be a response to loss, with grief and mourning as key features. Secure attachments are thought to constitute the basis for the growth of self-reliance and in turn this self-reliance is considered to provide the basis of emotional equilibrium. Bowlby's views on the emergence of attachments and on their general importance in development are considered in Chapter 22, where it is concluded that they have a fair measure of empirical support with respect to many (but not all) of his postulates. Here I will consider only the implications for emotional development.

As already discussed earlier in this chapter, there is ample evidence in support of the existence of separation anxiety as a crucial feature of early development, and in support of the importance at all ages of the presence of an attachment-figure as a powerful modifying factor with respect to fear. There is also good evidence indicating the importance of loss in the causation of depression (*see* Brown and Harris, 1978a). What is more controversial is the suggestion that almost the whole of emotional development can be explained in this way. Bowlby (1973) is explicit that some isolated phobias such as animal phobias can arise from frightening experiences unconnected with separation anxiety. Thus, although greatly influenced by the presence or absence of attachment figures, fears of novel objects and of strangers are not just a function of separation anxiety (*see* above). Also the age trends shown by different types of fears (*see* above) are not easily explicable in attachment terms; nor are the sex differences and age trends in depression. While it is certainly true that many cases of school 'phobia' are a consequence of separation anxiety, this is not true of all (*see* Hersov, 1977). It seems apparent that it is misleading to consider attachment and loss as the *only* factors in emotional development. Nevertheless, it does appear well established that they are important features which must have a place in any adequate comprehensive theoretical formulation.

Brown's vulnerability and loss model

Thus, Bowlby's ideas on the role of secure attachments and of losses in the development of self-reliance play a major part in Brown and Harris' (1978a) notion of mastery and self-esteem in their model of depression. Bowlby's theory also deals with the genesis of depression and his major exposition on the problems of grief and mourning will be presented in the shortly expected third volume 'Loss' of his important three volume work on 'Attachment and Loss'. Their theory involves four key postulates. First, loss is thought of in terms of a deprivation of sources of value or reward. These sources may involve not only personal relationships but also roles and ideas. Thus, a demotion at work or other life disappointment; or an hysterectomy with its loss of child-bearing potential are all classed as losses. While Brown and Harris see bonds and attachments as very important sources of value their concept of loss seems to extend beyond that of Bowlby's. Secondly, the immediate response to loss is thought to be a specific sense of hopelessness. Thirdly, whether or not this *specific* hopelessness develops into a *general* state of depression depends on the individual's success or failure in working through the situation to find alternative sources of value. This mechanism can operate at any stage of life (after the infant develops the necessary capacities). However, their fourth postulate, which emphasizes the concept of *vulnerability*, is more explicitly developmental. They suggest that the development of self-esteem and of mastery constitutes a crucial element in personality growth by providing a cognitive set which enables (or fails to enable) the individual to deal with later losses. Brown and Harris include a loss of mother in childhood as a factor increasing vulnerability but they give most emphasis to factors operating during adult life to provide a sense of self-esteem (having a job outside the home, a close confiding relationship with the husband, and not having many young children at home).

There is a good deal of evidence to support the importance of the factors they invoke (in women—men were not included in their studies). Their evidence for the concept of vulnerability has been criticized (Tennant and Bebbington, 1978) and more data are required to settle the issue, but the main findings appear to support this suggestion (*see* Brown and Harris, 1978b). The most serious lack at the moment is the absence of empirical evidence on the developmental processes by which self-esteem develops; and on the means by which it modifies the individual's response to loss. What, for example, is the role or importance of positive experiences in childhood (Rutter, 1979) in aiding the growth of self-esteem? And, insofar as cognitive sets are crucial, how far are specific interpersonal problem-solving strategies (as distinct from a sense of self-esteem) important (*see e.g.* Shure and Spivack, 1978)?

CONCLUSIONS

It is evident that no one theory holds all the keys to the process of emotional development, if only because so many rather different issues are involved. Maturational factors, especially those involving cognition, are important in the changes which take place during the infancy period. Learning is crucial at all ages, and any adequate appreciation of emotional development must also take into account the psychological meaning of the emotions and the ways in which they are responded to and dealt with. Individual differences are in part a function of constitutionally determined variations in temperament but also are a consequence of social experiences. Emotions are modified in crucial ways by the presence or absence of attachment-figures and both separation anxiety and loss play a major role in disturbances of emotions. However, a person's response to loss seems to be affected by his cognitive set, his control over events, and his ability to find alternative sources of reward. His overall sense of esteem may well in part determine his vulnerability in this connection. Finally, it must be said that the substantial body of research on emotional expression in adults and the recent burgeoning of research into infantile emotional development stands in sharp contrast to the paucity of empirical observations on the course of development during the middle years of childhood and during adolescence.

REFERENCES

Ainsworth, M. D. and Bell, S. M. (1970). Attachment, exploration and separation: illustrated by the behaviour of 1-year-olds in a strange situation. *Child Develop.*, **41**, 49–67.

Angelino, M., Dollins, J. and Mech, E. V. (1956). Trends in the 'fears and worries' of school children as related to socio-economic status and age. *J. genet. Psychol.*, **89**, 263–276.

Annesley, P. T. (1961). Psychiatric illness in adolescence: presentation and prognosis. *J. mental Science*, **107**, 268–278.

Anthony, S. (1940). *The Child's Discovery of Death*. London: Routledge and Kegan Paul.

Appel, M. H. (1942). Aggressive behaviour of nursery school children and adult procedures in dealing with such behaviour. *J. exp. Educ.*, **11**, 185–199.

Bauer, D. H. (1976). An exploratory study of developmental changes in children's fears. *J. Child Psychol. Psychiat.*, **17**, 69–74.

Bayley, N. (1932). A study of the crying of infants during mental and physical tests. *J. genet. Psychol.*, **40**, 306–329.

Blaney, P. H. (1977). Contemporary theories of depression, critique and comparison. *J. abn. Psychol.*, **86**, 203–243.

Borke, H. (1973). The development of empathy in Chinese and American children between 3 and 6 years of age: A cross-culture study. *Develop. Psychol.*, **9**, 102–108.

Bower, T. G. R., Broughton, J. M. and Moore, M. K. (1970). Infant responses to approaching objects: an indicator of responses to distal variables. *Percept. Psychophysics*, **9**, 193–196.

Bowlby, J. (1969). *Attachment and Loss, I. Attachment*. London: Hogarth Press.

Bowlby, J. (1973). *Attachment and Loss, Vol. 2. Separation: Anxiety and Anger*. London: Hogarth Press.

Brackbill, Y. (1971). Cumulative effects of continuous stimulation on arousal level in infants. *Child Develop.*, **42**, 17–26.

Brazelton, B., Koslowski, B. and Main, M. (1974). The origins of reciprocity: the early mother–infant interaction. In: Lewis, M. and Rosenblum, L. (Eds.) *The Effect of the Infant on Its Caretaker*. New York: Wiley.

Bregman, E. (1934). An attempt to modify the emotional attitudes of infants by the conditioned response technique. *J. genet. Psychol.*, **45**, 169–196.

Bretherton, I. and Ainsworth, M. D. A. (1974). Responses of 1-year-olds to a stranger in a strange situation. In: Lewis, M. and Rosenblum, L. A. (Eds.) *op. cit.*, pp. 131–164.

Bridger, W. H. and Birns, B. (1963). Neonates' behavioral and autonomic responses to stress during soothing. In: Worth, J. (Ed.) *Recent Advances in Biological Psychiatry Vol. 5*. New York: Plenum.

Bridges, K. M. B. (1932). Emotional development in early infancy. *Child Develop.*, **3**, 324–341.

Bronson, G. (1972). Infants' reactions to unfamiliar persons and novel objects. *Monogr. Soc. Res. Child Develop.*, **37**, Serial No. 148.

Bronson, G. W. and Pankey, W. B. (1977). On the distinction between fear and wariness. *Child Develop.*, **48**, 1167–1183.

Bronson, W. C. (1966a). Control orientations: a study of behavior organization from childhood to adolescence. *Child Develop.*, **37**, 125–155.

Bronson, W. C. (1966b). Early antecedents of emotional expressiveness and reactivity-control. *Child Develop.*, **37**, 793–810.

Bronson, W. C. (1967). Adult derivatives of emotional expressiveness and reactivity-control: developmental continuities from childhood to adulthood. *Child Develop.*, **38**, 801–817.

Brown, G. W. and Harris, T. (1978a). *Social Origins of Depression: a study of psychiatric disorder in women*. London: Tavistock Publ.

Brown, G. W. and Harris, T. (1978b). Social origins of depression: a reply. *Psychol. Med.*, **8**, 577–588.

Brown, G. W., Bhrolchain, M. N. and Harris, T. (1975). Social class and psychiatric disturbance among women in an urban population. *Sociology*, **9**, 225–254.

Burlingham, D. and Freud, A. (1942). *Young Children in War-Time*. London: Allen and Unwin.

Campos, J. J., Emde, R. N., Gaensbauer, T. and Henderson, C. (1975). Cardiac and behavioral interrelationships in the reaction of infants to strangers. *Develop. Psychol.*, **11**, 589–601.

Chandler, M. J. (1977). Social cognition: a selective review of current research. In: Overton, W. F. and Gallagher, J. M. (Eds.) *Knowledge and Development Vol. 1. Advances in Research and Theory*. New York and London: Plenum Press, pp. 93–147.

Cohen, D. J. (1967). The crying newborn's accommodation to the nipple. *Child Develop.*, **38**, 89–100.

Cox, A. (1976). The association between emotional disorders in childhood and neuroses in adult life. In: Van Praag, H. M. (Ed.) *Research in Neurosis*. Utrecht: Bohn, Scheltema and Holkema, pp. 40–58.

Cummings, J. D. (1944). The incidence of emotional symptoms in school children. *Brit. J. Educ. Psychol.*, **14**, 151–161.

Cunningham, J., Wasterman, H. H. and Fischoff, J. A. (1956). A follow-up study of patients seen in a psychiatric clinic for children. *Amer. J. Orthopsychiat.*, **26**, 602–612.

Dare, C. (1977). Psychoanalytic theories. In: Rutter, M. and Hersov, L. (Eds.) *Child Psychiatry: Modern Approaches*. Oxford: Blackwell Scientific.

Darwin, C. (1872). *The Expression of Emotions in Man and Animals*. London: John Murray.

Davidson, P. O., Payne, R. W. and Sloane, R. B. (1964). Introversions, neuroticism and conditioning. *J. abn. soc. Psychol.*, **68**, 136–143.

Dawe, H. C. (1934). An analysis of two hundred quarrels of preschool children. *Child Develop.*, **5**, 139–157.

Dohrenwend, B. P. and Dohrenwend, B. S. (1976). Sex differences and psychiatric disorders. *Amer. J. Sociol.*, **81**, 1447–1454.

Dohrenwend, B. P. and Dohrenwend, B. S. (1977). Reply to Gove and Tudor's comment on 'Sex differences and psychiatric disorders'. *Amer. J. Sociol.*, **82**, 1336–1345.

Dweck, C. S. and Bush, E. S. (1976). Sex differences in learned helplessness: I Differential debilitation with peer and adult evaluators. *Develop. Psychol.*, **12**, 147–156.

Dweck, C. S., Davidson, W., Nelson, S. and Enna, B. (1978). Sex differences in learned helplessness: II. The contingencies of evaluative feedback in the classroom, and III. An experimental analysis. *Develop. Psychol.*, **14**, 268–276.

Eibl-Eibesfeldt, J. (1973). The expressive behaviour of the deaf- and blind-born. In: Von Cranach, M. and Vine, I. (Eds.) *Social Communication and Movement*. New York: Academic Press.

Ekman, P. (1976). Movements with precise meanings. *J. Communication*, **26**, 14–26.

Ekman, P., Friesen, W. V. and Ellswork, P. C. (1972). *Emotion in the*

Human Face: Guidelines for Research and an Integration of Findings. New York: Pergamon Press.

Emde, R. N., Gaensbauer, T. J. and Harmon, R. J. (1976). Emotional expression in infancy. *Psychological Issues,* **10,** Whole No. 37.

Emde, R. N., Kligman, D. H., Reich, J. H. and Wade, T. D. (1978). Emotional expression in infancy. I. Initial studies of social signalling and an emergent model. In: Lewis, M. and Rosenblum, L. A. (Eds.) *op. cit.,* pp. 125–148.

Emde, R. N. and Koenig, K. L. (1969). Neonatal smiling and rapid eye movement states. *J. Amer. Acad. Child Psychiat.,* **8,** 57–67.

Emde, R. N., McCartney, R. D. and Harmon, R. J. (1971). Neonatal smiling in R.E.M. states. IV. Premature study. *Child Develop.,* **42,** 1657–1661.

English, H. B. (1929). Three cases of the 'conditional fear response'. *J. abn. soc. Psychol.,* **34,** 221–225.

Eysenck, H. J. (1947). *Dimensions of Personality.* London: Routledge and Kegan Paul.

Eysenck, H. J. (1967). *The Biological Basis of Personality.* Springfield, Ill.: Chas. C. Thomas.

Eysenck, H. J. (1976). The learning theory model of neurosis—a new approach. *Behav. Res and Therapy,* **14,** 251–267.

Eysenck, H. J. and Eysenck, S. B. G. (1969). *Personality Structure and Measurement.* London: Routledge and Kegan Paul.

Eysenck, H. J. and Eysenck, S. B. G. (1975). *Manual of the Eysenck Personality Questionnaire (Junior and Adult).* London: Hodder and Stoughton.

Eysenck, H. J. and Rachman, S. J. (1965). The application of learning theory to child psychiatry. In: Howells, J. G. (Ed.) *Modern Perspectives in Child Psychiatry.* Edinburgh and London: Oliver and Boyd, pp. 104–169.

Eysenck, S. B. G. and Eysenck, H. J. (1973). Test re-test reliabilities of a new personality questionnaire for children. *Brit. J. Educ. Psychol.,* **43,** 126–130.

Franks, C. M. (1961). Conditioning and abnormal behaviour. In: Eysenck, H. J. (Ed.) *Handbook of Abnormal Psychology: an experimental approach.* New York: Basic Books.

Franks, D. M. and Franks, V. (1966). 'Conditionability' as a general factor of man's performance in different conditioning situations. Paper in *Abstracts. Vol 1 p. 331 of XVIII Internat. Congr. Psychol.,* Moscow.

Freud, A. (1963). The concept of developmental lines. *Psychoanalytic Study of the Child.* **18,** 245–265.

Freud, S. (1926). *Inhibitions, symptoms and anxiety.* Standard Edition, vol. 20. London: Hogarth Press.

Frommer, E. A. (1968). Depressive Illness in Childhood. In: Coppen, A. and Walk, A. (Eds.) *Recent Developments in Affective Disorders. Brit. J. Psychiat.* Special Publ. No. 2.

Furman, E. (1974). *A Child's Parent Dies: studies in childhood bereavement.* New Haven and London: Yale Univ. Press.

Gaensbauer, T. J., Mrazek, D. A. and Harmon, R. J. (1980). Emotional expression in abused and neglected infants. In: Frude, N. (Ed.) *The Understanding and Prevention of Child Abuse: Psychological Approaches.* London: Concord Books (in press).

Gersten, J. C., Langner, T. S., Eisenberg, J. G., Simcha-Fagan, O. and McCarth, E. D. (1976). Stability and change in types of behavioral disturbance of children and adolescents. *J. abn. Child Psychol.,* **4,** 111–128.

Gewirtz, J. L. (1965). The course of infant smiling in four child-rearing environments in Israel. In: Foss, B. M. (Ed.) *Determinants of Infant Behaviour,* Vol. 3. London: Methuen.

Gilbert, D. (1969). The young child's awareness of affect. *Child Develop.,* **39,** 619–636.

Goldberg, S. (1972). Infant care and growth in urban Zambia. *Human Development,* **15,** 77–89.

Gollin, C. S. (1958). Organizational characteristics of social judgement. A developmental investigation. *J. Personality,* **26,** 139–154.

Goodenough, F. C. (1931). *Anger in Young Children.* Minneapolis: University of Minnesota Press.

Gordon, T. and Foss, B. M. (1966). The role of stimulation in the delay of onset of crying in the newborn infant. *Quart. J. Exp. Psychol.,* **18,** 79–81.

Gove, W. R. and Tudor, J. F. (1973). Adult sex roles and mental illness. *Amer. J. Sociol.,* **78,** 812–835.

Graham, J. A. and Argyle, M. (1975). A cross-cultural study of the communication of extra-verbal meaning by gestures. *Int. J. Psychol.,* **1,** 57–67.

Graham, P. (1974). Depression in prepubertal children. *Develop. Med. Child Neurol.,* **16,** 340–349.

Graham, P. and Rutter, M. (1973). Psychiatric disorder in the young adolescent: A follow-up study. *Proc. Roy. Soc. Med.,* **66,** 1226–1229.

Gray, J. A. (1970). The psychophysiological basis of introversion–extroversion. *Behav. Res. and Therapy,* **8,** 249–266.

Gunnar-Vongnechten, M. R. (1978). Changing a frightening toy into a pleasant toy by allowing the infant to control its actions. *Develop. Psychol.,* **14,** 157–162.

Hagman, E. R. (1932). A study of fears of children of pre-school age. *J. exp. Educ.,* **1,** 110–130.

Hamburg, D. A., Hamburg, B. A. and Bachas, J. D. (1975). Anger and depression in perspective of behavioural biology. In: Levi, L. (Ed.) *Emotions: Their Parameters and Measurement.* New York: Raven Press.

Harmon, R. J. and Emde, R. N. (1972). Spontaneous REM behaviors in a microcephalic infant. *Perceptual and Motor Skills,* **34,** 827–833.

Harmon, R. J., Morgan, G. A. and Klein, R. P. (1977). Determinants of normal variation in infants' negative reactions to unfamiliar adults. *J. Amer. Acad. Child Psychiat.,* **16,** 670–683.

Hersov, L. A. (1960). Refusal to go to school. *J. Child Psychol. Psychiat.,* **1,** 137–145.

Hersov, L. (1977). School refusal. In: Rutter, M. and Hersov, L. (Eds.) *Child Psychiatry: Modern Approaches.* Oxford: Blackwell Scientific.

Hinde, R. A. (1960). Energy models of motivation. *Symp. Soc. Exper. Biol.,* **14,** 199–213.

Ingham, J. G. (1966). Changes in MPI scores in neurotic patients: a three year follow-up. *Brit. J. Psychiat.,* **112,** 931–940.

Izard, C. E. (1971). *The Face of Emotion.* New York: Appleton-Century-Crofts.

Izard, C. E. (1977). *Human Emotions.* New York: Plenum.

Izard, C. E. (1978). On the ontogenesis of emotions and emotion-cognitive relationships in infancy. In: Lewis, M. and Rosenblum, L. A. (Eds.) *op. cit.*

Jersild, A. T. and Holmes, F. B. (1935). *Children's Fears.* New York: Teachers College.

Jung, J. C. (1924). *Psychological Types.* London: Kegan Paul.

Kagan, J. (1971). *Change and Continuity in Infancy.* New York: Wiley.

Kagan, J. (1974). Discrepancy, temperament, and infant distress. In: Lewis, M. and Rosenblum, L. A. (Eds.) *op. cit.,* pp. 229–248.

Kagan, J. and Moss, H. A. (1962). *Birth to Maturity.* New York: Wiley.

Kennedy, W. A. (1965). School phobia: rapid treatment of 50 cases. *J. abn. Psychol.,* **70,** 285–289.

Klein, M., Heimann, P., Isaacs, S. and Riviere, J. (1952). *Developments in Psychoanalysis.* London: Hogarth Press.

Kline, P. (1972). *Fact and Fantasy in Freudian Theory.* London: Methuen.

Konner, M. (1972). Aspects of the developmental ethology of a foraging people. In: Blurton Jones, N. (Ed.) *Ethological studies of Child Behaviour.* Cambridge: University of Cambridge Press.

Koocher, G. P. (1974). Talking with children about death. *Amer. J. Orthopsychiat.,* **44,** 404–411.

Landreth, C. (1941). Factors associated with crying in young children in the nursery school and the home. *Child Develop.,* **12,** 81–97.

Levy, D. (1951). Observations of attitudes and behaviour in the child health centre. *Amer. J. Public Health.,* **41,** 182–90.

Lewis, M. and Brooks, J. (1974). Self, other and fear: infants' reactions to people. In: Lewis, M. and Rosenblum, L. A. (Eds.) *op. cit.,* pp. 195–228.

Lewis, M. and Brooks, J. (1978). Self-knowledge and emotional development. In: Lewis, M. and Rosenblum, L. A. (Eds.) *op. cit.,* pp. 205–226.

Lewis, M. and Rosenblum, L. A. (Eds.) (1974). *The Origins of Fear.* New York and London: Wiley.

Lewis, M. and Rosenblum, L. A. (1978). *The Development of Affect.* New York and London: Plenum Press.

McCall, L. B. (1972). Smiling and vocalisation in infants as indices of perceptual-cognitive processes. *Merrill-Palmer Quart.,* **18,** 341–348.

Maccoby, E. E. and Feldman, S. S. (1972). Mother-attachment and stranger-reactions in the third year of life. *Monogr. Soc. Res. Child Develop.*, **37**, Serial No. 146.

Maccoby, E. E. and Jacklin, C. N. (1975). *The Psychology of Sex Differences*. Stanford: Stanford University Press.

Macdonald, N. E. and Silverman, I. W. (1978). Smiling and laughter in infants as a function of level of arousal and cognitive evaluation. *Develop. Psychol.*, **14**, 235–241.

Macfarlane, J. W., Allen, L. and Honzik, M. R. (1954). *A Developmental Study of the Behavior Problems of Normal Children Between 21 months and 14 years*. California: University of California Press.

Mahler, M. S., Pine, S. and Bergman, A. (1975). *The Psychological Birth of the Infant*. London: Hutchinson.

Makita, K. (1973). The rarity of 'depression' in childhood. *Acta Paedopsychiatrica*, **40**, 32–44.

Mandler, G. (1962). Emotion. In: Brown, R. W., Galanter, E., Hess, E. H. and Mandler, G. (Eds.) *New Directions in Psychology*. New York: Holt, Rinehart and Winston.

Marks, I. M. (1969). *Fears and Phobias*. London: Heinemann Medical.

Marks, I. M. and Gelder, M. G. (1966). Different ages of onset in varieties of phobia. *Amer. J. Psychiat.*, **123**, 218–221.

Marris, P. (1958). *Widows and their Families*. London: Routledge and Kegan Paul.

Martin, I. (1973). Somatic reactivity: interpretation. In: Eysenck, H. J. (Ed.) *Handbook of Abnormal Psychology (Second Edition)* London: Pitman Medical, pp. 333–361.

Masterson, J. F. (1967). *The Psychiatric Dilemma of Adolescence*. London: Churchill.

Morgan, G. A. and Ricciuti, H. N. (1969). Infants' responses to strangers during the first year. In: Foss, B. M. (Ed.) *Determinants of Infant Behaviour. Vol. 4*. London: Methuen.

Murphy, L. B. (1937). *Social Behavior and Child Personality: An Exploratory Study of some Roots of Sympathy*. New York: Columbia University Press.

Nagy, M. (1948). The child's theories concerning death. *J. genet. Psychol.*, **73**, 3–27.

Oster, H. (1978). Facial expression and affect development. In: Lewis, M. and Rosenblum, L. A. (Eds.) *op. cit.*, pp. 43–76.

Pavlov, I. P. (1927). *Conditioned Reflexes* (Trans. by G. V. Anrep). London: Oxford University Press.

Pearce, J. B. (1978). The recognition of depressive disorder in children. *J. Roy. Soc. Med.*, **71**, 494–500.

Penbharkkul, S. and Karelitz, S. (1962). Lacrimation in the neonatal and early infancy period of premature and full-term infants. *J. Pediat.*, **61**, 859–863.

Piaget, J. (1962). *Play, Dreams and Imitation in Childhood*. New York: Norton.

Pinneau, S. R. (1955). Infantile disorders of hospitalism and anaclitic depression. *Psychol. Bull.*, **52**, 429–452.

Powell, G. E. (1977). Psychoticism and social deviancy in children. *Adv. Behav. Res. Ther.*, **1**, 27–56.

Poznanski, E. and Zrull, J. (1970). Childhood depression: clinical characteristics of overtly depressed children. *Arch. Gen. Psychiat.*, **23**, 8–15.

Rachman, D. (1977). The conditioning theory of fear acquisition: a critical examination. *Behav. Res. and Therapy*, **15**, 375–389.

Rachman, S. (1969). Extraversion and neuroticism in childhood. In: Eysenck, H. J. and Eysenck, S. B. G. (Eds.) *Personality Structure and Measurement*. London: Routledge and Kegan Paul.

Rapaport, D. (1953). On the psychoanalytic theory of affects. *Int. J. Psychoanalysis*, **34**, 177–198.

Rapaport, D. (1960). On the psychoanalytic theory of motivation. *Nebraska Symposium on Motivation Vol. 8*. Lincoln: Univ. Nebraska Press, pp. 173–247.

Rheingold, H. and Eckerman, C. (1973). Fear of the stranger: a critical examination. In: Rease, H. (Ed.) *Advances in Child Development and Behavior. Vol. 8*. New York: Academic Press.

Ricciuti, H. N. (1974). Fear and the development of social attachments in the first year of life. In: Lewis, M. and Rosenblum, L. A. (Eds.) *op. cit.*, pp. 73–106.

Robins, L. N. (1972). Follow-up studies of behaviour disorders in children. In: Quay, H. C. and Werry, J. S. (Eds.) *Psychopathological Disorders of Childhood*. New York and London: Wiley.

Rodriguez, A., Rodriguez, M. and Eisenberg, L. (1959). The outcome

of school phobia: a follow-up study based on 41 cases. *Amer. J. Psychiat.*, **116**, 540–544.

Ross, H. S. (1975). The effects of increasing familiarity on infants' reactions to adult strangers. *J. exp. Child Psychol.*, **20**, 226–339.

Rutter, M. (1970a). Sex differences in children's responses to family stress. In: Anthony, E. J. and Koupernik, C. (Eds.) *The Child in His Family*. New York: Wiley.

Rutter, M. (1970b). Psychological development: predictions from infancy. *J. Child Psychol. Psychiat.*, **11**, 49–62.

Rutter, M. (1972). Relationships between child and adult psychiatric disorder. *Acta psychiatrica Scandinavica*, **48**, 3–21.

Rutter, M. (1977). Prospective studies to investigate behavioural change. In: Strauss, J. S., Babigian, H. M. and Roff, M. (Eds.) *The Origins and Course of Psychopathology*. New York: Plenum.

Rutter, M. (1979). Protective factors in children's responses to stress and disadvantage. In: Kent, M. W. and Rolf, J. E. (Eds.) *Primary Prevention of Psychopathology: Vol. 3: Social Competence in Children*. Hanover, N.H.: Univ. Press of New England.

Rutter, M., Graham, P., Chadwick, O. and Yule, W. (1976). Adolescent turmoil: fact or fiction? *J. Child Psychol. Psychiat.*, **17**, 35–36.

Rutter, M., Tizard, J. and Whitmore, K. (Eds.) (1970). *Education, Health and Behaviour*. London: Longmans.

Sagi, A. and Hoffman, M. L. (1976). Empathic distress in newborns. *Develop. Psychol.*, **12**, 175–176.

Sandler, J. and Joffe, W. G. (1965). Notes on childhood depression. *Int. J. Psychoanalysis*, **46**, 88–96.

Scarr, S. and Salapatek, P. (1970). Patterns of fear development during infancy. *Merrill-Palmer Quart.*, **16**, 54–60.

Schaefer, E. S. and Bayley, N. (1963). Maternal behavior, child behavior and their intercorrelations from infancy through adolescence. *Monogr. Soc. Res. Child Develop.*, **28**, Serial No. 87.

Schaffer, H. R. (1974). Cognitive components of the infant's response to strangers. In: Lewis, M. and Rosenblum, L. (Eds.) *op. cit.*, pp. 11–24.

Schaffer, H. R. and Parry, M. H. (1969). Perceptual-motor behaviour in infancy as a function of age and stimulus familiarity. *Brit. J. Psychol.*, **60**, 1–9.

Schulterbrandt, J. G. and Raskin, A. (Eds.) (1977). *Depression in Childhood: Diagnosis, Treatment and Conceptual Models*. New York: Raven Press.

Seligman, M. E. P. (1975). *Helplessness: On Depression, Development and Death*. San Francisco: W. H. Freeman.

Seligman, M. E. P. (1976). Depression and learned helplessness. In: Van Praag, H. M. (Ed.) *Research in Neurosis*. Utrecht: Bohn, Scheltema and Holkema, pp. 72–107.

Shaffer, D. (1974). Suicide in childhood and early adolescence. *J. Child Psychol. Psychiat.*, **15**, 275–292.

Shepherd, M., Oppenheim, B. and Mitchell, S. (1971). *Childhood Behaviour and Mental Health*. London: Univ. London Press.

Sherman, M. (1927). The differentiation of emotional responses in infants. *J. comp. Psychol.*, **7**, 265–284, 335–351.

Shirley, M. (1942). Children's adjustments to a strange situation. *J. abn. soc. Psychol.*, **37**, 201–217.

Shirley, M. and Poyntz, L. (1941). Influence of separation from the mother on children's emotional responses. *J. Psychol.*, **12**, 251–282.

Shure, M. B. and Spivack, G. (1978). *Problem-Solving Techniques in Child Rearing*. London: Jossey-Bass.

Skarin, K. (1977). Cognitive and contextual determinants of stranger fear in 6- and 11-month-old infants. *Child Develop.*, **48**, 537–544.

Slater, E. (1939). Responses to a nursery school situation of 40 children. *Monogr. Soc. Res. Child Develop.*, **11**, No. 4.

Smith, P. K. (1974). Social and situational determinants of fear in the playgroup. In: Lewis, M. and Rosenblum, L. A. (Eds.) *op. cit.*, pp. 107–129.

Spelke, E., Zelazo, P. R., Kagan, J. and Kotelchuck, M. (1973). Father interaction and separation protest. *Develop. Psychol.*, **9**, 83–90.

Spitz, R. A. (1946). Anaclitic depression. *Psychoanal. Study of the Child*, **2**, 313–342.

Spitz, R. A. (1950). Anxiety in infancy: a study of its manifestations in the first year of life. *Internat. J. Psychoanal.*, **31**, 138–143.

Sroufe, L. A. (1977). Wariness and the study of infant development. *Child Develop.*, **48**, 731–746.

Sroufe, L. A. and Waters, E. (1976). The ontogenesis of smiling and laughter: a perspective on the organization of development in infancy. *Psychol. Rev.*, **83**, 173–189.

Sroufe, L. A., Waters, E. and Matas, L. (1974). Contextual determinants of infant affective response. In: Lewis, M. and Rosenblum, L. (Eds.) *op. cit.*, pp. 49–72.

Sroufe, L. A. and Wunsch, J. P. (1972). The development of laughter in the first year of life. *Child Develop.*, **43**, 1326–1344.

Staub, E. (1971). A child in distress: the influence of nurturance and modelling on children's attempts to help. *Develop. Psychol.*, **5**, 124–136.

Stern, D. N. (1974). The goal and structure of mother–infant play. *J. Amer. Acad. Child Psychiat.*, **13**, 402–421.

Tennant, C. and Bebbington, P. (1978). The social causation of depression: a critique of the work of Brown and his colleagues. *Psychol. Med.*, **8**, 565–576.

Thomas, A. and Chess, S. (1977). *Temperament and Development*. New York: Brunner/Mazel.

Thompson, J. (1941). Development of facial expression in blind and seeing children. *Arch. Psychol.*, **264**, 1–47.

Torgersen, A. M. and Kringlen, E. (1978). Genetic aspects of temperamental differences in twins. *J. Amer. Acad. Child Psychiat.*, **17**, 433–444.

Tyrer, P. and Tyrer, S. (1974). School refusal, truancy and adult neurotic illness. *Psychol. Med.*, **4**, 416–421.

Vine, I. (1973). The role of facial visual signalling in early social development. In: Von Cranach, M. and Vine, I. (Eds.) *Social Communication and Movement: Studies of Men and Chimpanzees*. London: Academic Press.

Waldron, S. (1976). The significance of childhood neurosis for adult mental health. *Amer. J. Psychiat.*, **133**, 532–538.

Warren, W. (1965). A study of adolescent psychiatric in-patients and the outcome six or more years later. II. The follow-up study. *J. Child Psychol. Psychiat.*, **6**, 141–160.

Wasz-Höckert, O., Lind, J., Vuorenkoski, V., Partanen, T. and Valenne, E. (1968). *The Infant Cry: A Spectrographic and Auditory Analysis*. Clinics in Developmental Medicine no. 29. London: Heinemann/ S.I.M.P.

Waters, E., Matas, L. and Sroufe, L. A. (1975). Infants' reactions to an approaching stranger: description, validation and functional significance of wariness. *Child Develop.*, **46**, 348–356.

Watson, J. B. and Morgan, J. J. B. (1917). Emotional reactions and psychological experimentation. *Amer. J. Psychol.*, **28**, 163–174.

Watson, J. B. and Rayner, R. (1920). Conditioned emotional reactions. *J. exp. Psychol.*, **3**, 1–14.

Watson, J. S. (1972). Smiling, cooing and 'the game'. *Merrill-Palmer Quart.*, **18**, 323–340.

Weinraub, M. and Lewis, M. (1977). The determinants of children's responses to separation. *Monogr. Soc. Res. Child Develop.*, **42**, Serial No. 172.

Weiss, J. M. (1972). Influence of psychological variables on stress-induced pathology. In: Porter, R. and Knight, J. (Eds.) *Physiology, Emotion and Psychosomatic Illness*. Ciba Foundation Symposium 8 (new series). Amsterdam: Assoc. Sci. Publ. pp. 253–280.

Weiss, L. A. (1934). Differential variations in the amount of activity of newborn infants under continuous light and sound stimulation. *University Iowa Stud. Child Welfare*, **9**, No. 4.

Weissman, M. M. and Klerman, G. L. (1977). Sex differences and the epidemiology of depression. *Arch. Gen. Psychiat.*, **34**, 98–111.

Whiteman, M. (1967). Children's concepts of psychological causality. *Child Develop.*, **38**, 143–155.

Wolff, P. (1963). Observations on the early development of smiling. In: Foss, B. M. (Ed.) *Determinants of Infant Behaviour Vol. 2*. London: Methuen.

Wolff, P. H. (1966). *The Causes, Controls and Organisation of Behavior in the Neonate*. New York: Int. Univ. Press.

Wolff, P. H. (1969). The natural history of crying and other vocalisations in early infancy. In: Foss, B. M. (Ed.) *Determinants of Infant Behaviour, Vol. 4*. London: Methuen.

Yorke, C. and Wiseberg, S. (1976). A developmental view of anxiety: Some clinical and theoretical considerations. *Psychoanal. Study of the Child*, **31**, 107–135.

Zelazo, P. R. (1971). Smiling to social stimuli: eliciting and conditioning effects. *Develop. Psychol.*, **4**, 32–42.

Zelazo, P. R. (1972). Smiling and vocalising: a cognitive emphasis. *Merrill-Palmer Quart.*, **18**, 349–365.

26. PSYCHOSEXUAL DEVELOPMENT

MICHAEL RUTTER

Psychosexual issues occupy a central place in child development both because of the importance of sexual interests in any consideration of social and emotional behaviour, and because theories of development have so often regarded sexual drive and its focus as causal influences in relation to personality formation. In considering psychosexual development it will be necessary to differentiate between certain key features: *gender identity* (that is a person's concept of themselves as male or female); *sex-typed behaviour* (meaning those gestural and behavioural features which tend to differentiate the sexes); and sexual activities and interests leading on to *sexual object choice* or *sexual orientation* (*i.e.* homosexual or heterosexual). Before discussing the course of development for each of these aspects it is necessary to consider first the physical changes associated with sexual development. The various factors influencing psychosexual development will then be considered in turn and finally these empirical data will be used to review the main theories of psychosexual development.

PHYSICAL CHANGES ASSOCIATED WITH SEXUAL DEVELOPMENT

The human embryo is initially sexually neuter. If a Y chromosome is present (regardless of the number of X's), at about six weeks after conception the primordial gonad differentiates into a testis (Jost, 1972). If there is no Y but there are two X chromosomes, the gonad instead differentiates into an ovary at about 12 weeks (*i.e.* considerably later than the testis).

The newly developed testis then produces two hormones; an androgen which promotes male genital development and another which inhibits the development of the Mullerian duct system. If these hormones are not produced (as in an XO individual without either testes or ovaries or as a result of embryonic gonad removal) the embryo will proceed to differentiate as a morphologic female, regardless of chromosomal sex (*see* Money and Ehrhardt, 1972).

The testis continues to produce androgens during foetal life and this sex difference in circulating male hormones not only leads to the development of male or female reproductive structures but also it is associated with later behavioural differences (evidence reviewed below). These differences imply that there may be a resulting sexual dimorphism in the central nervous system such that the neural structures of males and females are somewhat different (however, the presence and nature of these differences has yet to be determined). The foetal hormones also act on the hypothalamus during a critical period of development to determine later pituitary function with respect to the release of gonadotrophic hormones (Money and Ehrhardt, 1972). Again, feminine differentiation requires only the absence of androgen and not the presence of a feminizing substance.

Androgen production by the testis ceases about the time of birth and thereafter up until puberty there are no sizeable sex differences in sex hormone production. In both boys and girls small amounts of androgens and oestrogens are produced, probably by the andrenals (Tanner, 1962). Pituitary gonadotrophins are present in the blood of children as young as 5 years of age; there is then a rise which antedates the onset of puberty and which leads to the adolescent increase in hormone production by the gonads (Fitschen and Clayton, 1965). The production of androgens increases in both sexes at about 8 to 10 years with a further much sharper increase in adolescence; the increase is very much more marked in boys than in girls. The production of oestrogens gradually rises in both sexes from about age 7 years with a very large and sharp further increase in girls but only a very small increase in boys.

There is very little change in the weight of the gonads in either sex up to the time of adolescence, but then, of course, very considerable development takes place (Tanner, 1962).

In boys, the first sign of impending puberty is usually an acceleration of the growth of the testes and scrotum, accompanied by slight (and later great) growth of pubic hair. At the same time there is development of the penis, a considerable height spurt, enlargement of the larynx and deepening of the voice. About two years after the beginning of pubic hair growth, axillary and facial hair first appear and there are changes in physique associated with an acceleration in the development of muscular strength. There are two main points to notice in relation to the physical changes at adolescence. First, the development spans a period of at least 4–4½ years and second, there is an immense variation in the age at which puberty occurs. For example, the average age of first ejaculation in the Kinsey study was just under 14 years but in 10% of cases it occurred either before 11 or after the 16th birthday (Kinsey et al., 1948). Thus, in normal boys there is a five year range for the age at which puberty is reached. A similar range is found if puberty is assessed by height spurt, pubic hair growth or gonadal development (Tanner, 1962).

In girls, puberty begins some two years earlier and extends over a slightly shorter period (three or four years rather than four or five). However, individual variation is equally great. The average age of menarche is about 13 years but the range extends from 10 to 16½ years. Breast development is usually the first sign of pubescence. This begins between 8 and 13 years, being followed, usually within a year or so, by the appearance of pubic hair, a height spurt and changes in general physique. There is considerable individual variation, however, in the ordering and timing of these physical changes.

In short, physically speaking there is very little sexual development until puberty, the changes at adolescence spread over some four years, there is enormous individual variation in the time of this development, and girls reach puberty 18 months or two years before boys.

PSYCHOLOGICAL SIGNIFICANCE OF TIMING OF PUBERTY

The age when puberty is reached is of some psychological significance. Boys who are late in reaching puberty tend to be less popular, less confident and less assertive, but eager and talkative and attention-seeking (McCandless, 1960; Mussen and Jones, 1957, 1958; Jones and Bayley, 1950). They are also likely to be late in establishing heterosexual behaviour (Schofield, 1965). The Fels longitudinal study suggested that adolescent boys with non-masculine interests during early childhood tended later to be anxious about sexuality and to have less

heterosexual activity (Kagan and Moss, 1962). The possible reasons for this are not hard to find. Manliness and sexual vigour are highly regarded attributes among adolescent males, and boys who have still not reached puberty by 16 years or so may well begin to doubt their masculinity and become anxious and introspective about their development. A further reason is that early puberty is associated with muscular physique (McCandless, 1960; Tanner, 1962), and athletic abilities are highly valued in most adolescent groups. The extent to which late puberty is a handicap in boys varies somewhat in different cultures, emphasizing that the disadvantages are largely due to society's reaction to continuing physical immaturity (Mussen and Bouterline-Young, 1964). To some extent the social disadvantages of late puberty in boys persist into adulthood but they tend to diminish with age (Jones, 1965). A further point is that early maturers of both sexes tend to have a higher IQ and educational attainment at all ages (Douglas and Ross, 1964).

Girls' reactions to early or late puberty are more complex and so far as can be judged from the limited studies available there are not the clear-cut advantages to early maturing that are found in boys (McCandless, 1960). Indeed, very early maturing may sometimes be associated with undue self-consciousness and anxiety together with an attempt to conceal breast development through altered posture.

THE NORMAL DEVELOPMENT OF GENDER IDENTITY

Children soon learn whether they are a girl or a boy. Gesell (1940) found that two-thirds of 3-year-olds knew their own sex (whereas most 2½-year-olds did not). Rabbon (1950) found much the same and showed that correct sex awareness was almost complete by age 4 years. It is a little while later before children correctly recognize other people's sex but by age 4–6 years the great majority of children are clear, not only that they will be a 'mummy' or a 'daddy' when they grow up, but also that this is inevitable and not open to change (Thompson and Bentler, 1973).

At first children use clothing and hair as the features defining sex (Conn and Kanner, 1947; Katcher, 1955; Levin et al., 1972; Thompson and Bentler, 1971). The findings from play interviews and the matching of pictures are agreed in showing that it is not until 7 years or thereabouts that most children are able to discriminate reliably on the basis of genital cues, and it is not until 11 years that there is a full awareness that the genital difference is the dominant characteristic differentiating boys from girls. The development of gender constancy is related to the child's cognitive level, but curiously it does not appear to be related to sex role preferences (Marcus and Overton, 1978). There is considerable individual variation in timing; also the ages when changes occur vary somewhat by socio-cultural group and tend to be rather earlier in girls. What is quite clear, however, is that a child's gender identity is well developed before he or she has a proper appreciation of sex differences generally and long before there is an adequate understanding of the genital basis of sex differences.

Children's reactions to the discovery of genital differences were investigated by Conn (1940; Conn and Kanner, 1947) using his doll play technique. He interviewed 5- to 13-year-olds attending a paediatric clinic and asked all who had had the opportunity of seeing the genitals of the opposite sex about their reaction. A third were able to describe how they felt and responded. Most children accepted the genital difference as natural, although some were surprised and several thought the difference odd and funny. About a third of the children thought at first that the girls had had a penis but had lost it in some way or it had grown small or been cut off. Not all of the third were perturbed by the thought of penis loss and Conn and Kanner (1947) concluded that castration anxiety was an infrequent occurrence. Levy (1940) criticized this view, pointing out how many of the children could not recall how they felt. However, even on Conn's own findings, a third of the children (boys more than girls) had had castration thoughts, which can hardly be regarded as infrequent.

Several studies (see Rutter, 1971) have examined children's sex preferences using a projective technique involving a figure of ambiguous sex called 'It'. Sex preference is considered to be the sex role or name chosen by the child for 'It'. Even as early as age 3 years there is a strong tendency for children to show a same-sex preference and this preference becomes even stronger as children grow older (at least in boys). Preschool children also tend to choose the same sex parent more often than the other sex parent as a model to emulate. It is clear that same-sex preferences are established early and that this preference occurs earlier, more consistently and more strongly in boys than in girls. In our culture it seems that more girls prefer to be male than boys to be female. Almost certainly the reason is that children see many indications that, in general, males are more highly regarded.

In all ordinary circumstances children's gender identity is well established by 3 to 4 years and, even in the case of children with biological anomalies, the Money and Hampson studies (Money, 1961; Hampson and Hampson, 1961) show that it is usually rather difficult to make a change in sex assignment after that age if a firm gender identity has already been established. However, when the physical appearances are ambiguous, the gender identity is often less certain than normal and there are many accounts of successful changes in gender identity after age 3 years (Armstrong, 1966; Dewhurst and Gordon, 1963; Berg et al., 1963; Imperato-McGinley et al., 1974 and 1979). In some of these cases, a change seems to have been possible in spite of a fairly firmly established gender identity.

THE NORMAL DEVELOPMENT OF SEX-TYPED BEHAVIOURS

Both boys and girls vary greatly in their behaviour and there is considerable overlap between the behaviours generally regarded as appropriately 'masculine' and 'feminine'. Nevertheless, there are important differences in both gestures and play. Rekers et al. (1977) found three mannerisms (limp wrist, arm flutter and flexed elbow) to be significantly commoner in girls. These differences were well marked by age 4 to 5 years and did not increase significantly thereafter. Girls also tended to put their hands on their hips in a different way.

By age 3 to 4 years boys show predominantly masculine preferences in toys and activities, and sex differences can be reliably observed as early as a year (see Maccoby and Jacklin, 1975; also Chapters 8 and 24 in this volume). During the preschool year, boys play more with guns, toy trucks, tractors and fire engines whereas girls are more likely to sew, string beads or play at housekeeping. Doll play, dressing-up and artistic activities (cutting, drawing, etc.) are more typical of girls whereas outdoor play, building blocks and rough and tumble physical activity is more boyish. Furthermore, it is clear that even by the age of 2 to 3 years, children have a considerable knowledge of the sex role stereotype prevailing in the adult culture (Kuhn, Nash and Brucken, 1978). The research findings show that from age 4 years or so boys become increasingly more sex-typed than girls in their behaviour, are more likely to avoid sex-inappropriate activity and more likely to prefer activities associated with their own role. Moreover, other children are less tolerant of sex-inappropriate behaviours in boys (Fagot, 1977).

Thus, it is clear that boys and girls differ in their behaviour even before they become aware of their gender identity and that sex-typical behaviour is already well marked during the preschool years. It is also evident that as early as age 4 years children show a tendency to play with children of their own sex. However, this tendency becomes much more marked at about 7 or 8 years (Campbell, 1939).

THE NORMAL DEVELOPMENT OF SEXUAL ACTIVITIES AND INTERESTS

In the male infant, erections of the penis have been noted to occur from birth (Halverson, 1940), the frequency in the first few months of postnatal life ranging from 3 to 11 times per day. At first these erections seem to be largely associated with bladder and bowel distension and, so far as can be judged by the infant's reaction, appear unpleasant in quality. But elimination is then associated with detumescence. Incidentally, this association suggests how anal activities may acquire an erotic component. These early erections are just reflex but infants soon begin to touch and rub their genitals. At first this is just one aspect of general bodily exploration and, probably, touching the genitals occurs no more often than touching other parts of the body. At this stage, it would be misleading to call this infantile sexuality. However, gradually infants learn that genital stimulation may be particularly pleasant and from observations it would seem that genital manipulation then gains a more definitely erotic quality. The exact incidence of genital manipulation in very young children is not known but it is evident from several studies that the rate is quite high. For example, the Newsons (1963) found that 36% of the mothers of 1-year-olds reported genital play in their children. This did not necessarily involve masturbation in the sense of a rhythmic activity, which is probably much less frequent. Pulling the penis by boys was said to be much commoner than genital stimulation by girls. When such activities lead to orgasm-like responses varies greatly from child to child; they have been noted from as early as 5 months but usually it is not until somewhat later (Kinsey et al., 1948, 1953). From Kinsey's (Kinsey et al., 1948) longitudinal observations of boys from infancy up to late childhood, it appears that the later reactions were sufficiently similar to the earlier behaviour to suggest the orgastic nature of some of the infantile experiences. Even so there are clear physiological differences. Obviously, ejaculation does not occur before puberty but also there is not the male post-orgasm refractory period so that boys may have several 'orgasms' in quick succession (Kinsey et al., 1948).

Oral activities are also very common in infancy and it is clear that much pleasure is gained from non-nutritional sucking. To what extent this can be regarded as erotic clearly depends on how wide a definition of eroticism is employed. In psychoanalytic terminology erotic activities are not confined to those with a genital association or aim. Sexuality and eroticism are seen as an intrinsic aptitude to release the genital. Thus, emotional reactions of all kinds—desire, hope, fear, anger—and associated activities may derive from sexuality (Dalbiez, 1941). The same difficulty applies to any attempt to examine changes with age. Thus, thumb-sucking gradually diminishes during the preschool period but, in marked contrast, nail-biting shows a very considerable rise in frequency over the same years (Macfarlane, 1939; Macfarlane et al., 1954; Wechsler, 1931; Billig, 1941).

During the 2–5 year period, genital interest, however defined, evidently increases. In a study of middle-class American preschool children, Sears, Maccoby and Levin (1957) found that about half were reported to indulge in sex play or genital handling. Levy (1928) studying slightly younger children found that masturbatory activities occurred in at least 55% of boys but only 16% of girls. A similar sex difference was reported by Koch (1935) and it may be concluded that manual stimulation of the genitals is much commoner in boys than girls. Thigh rubbing is an alternative source of genital pleasure in girls, but how often this occurs is not known.

Games involving undressing or sexual exploration (often under the guise of 'mothers and fathers' or 'doctors') are common by age 4 years (Isaacs, 1933; Newson and Newson, 1968) although again the frequency is not known. Nevertheless, that sex play is a common occurrence with nursery school children is evident from Susan Isaacs' early studies. She also showed the diverse nature of preschool children's sex games. Exhibitionistic and voyeuristic activities with both other children and adults are characteristic, masturbation occurs, children attempt to fondle their mother's breasts, and it appears from the

nature of their play that urination is associated in children's minds with sex activities.

There has been some controversy over the extent to which sexual pleasure in girls at this age is centred on the clitoris or vagina (Greenacre, 1950). The original psychoanalytic concept of the maturational importance of a shift from clitoral to vaginal sexuality has been dismissed as wrong by many writers on the grounds that in the adult clitoral and vaginal orgasm are physiologically indistinguishable (Masters and Johnson, 1966). Eissler (1977) has rightly pointed out that this misleadingly assumes that physiological responses and psychological meaning are synonymous. Nevertheless, it now seems that the issue probably has little importance.

The years between 5 or 6 and puberty were once thought to be a sexually latent period with a repression of sex interest and little psychosexual development (Fries, 1959). It is now clear that this is very far from the truth. Anthropologists first pointed out that whatever happened in Western societies, in sexually permissive cultures sex play and love-making were common during middle childhood (Malinowski, 1929; Ford and Beach, 1951). In recent years, a number of studies have produced somewhat similar findings for the USA. Although there may possibly still be some greater concealment of sex interest during middle childhood than either before or after, nevertheless overt sex activities and interests are common and widespread (Bernick, 1965; Reese, 1966). Ramsey (1943) found that the accumulative incidence of masturbation in boys rose from about 10% at 7 years to over 80% at 13 years. Heterosexual play in the same survey rose from less than 5% at 5 years to a third of boys at 8 years and two-thirds at 13 years. The rates in the Kinsey study (1948) were lower but the trend was the same—that is, a gradual rise during the pre-pubertal years. Both studies showed also a rise in coital play during the years before adolescence, although this occurred in only a minority of the children.

Similar findings are reported for girls except that the rates of sexual activity are lower at all ages. These results leave no doubt that sexual activity occurs during the so-called latency years, but it should not be concluded from these figures that there is necessarily a continuity between pre-pubertal sex play and adult sex activity (Broderick, 1966). In the early school years sexual activity is a much more sporadic activity than it is later and it has neither the intensity nor complexity of later sex behaviour.

Homosexual play in boys (which mostly consists of mutual handling of genitals) also shows a gradual rise during childhood (Kinsey et al., 1948) reaching 25 to 30% at 13 years. The figures for girls are similar (Kinsey et al., 1953). In this country Schofield (1965) reported lower rates of homosexual behaviour (although he thought his figures an underestimate) but he did note that in both boys and girls homosexual activities were very much commoner in boarding schools than in day schools. This suggests that the development of homosexual behaviour is probably much influenced by the social setting and by the presence or absence of heterosexual opportunities. Whether this transient phase of homosexual activity has any bearing at all on persisting adult homosexuality is doubtful (West, 1968).

The rates of various sexual activities are in themselves of limited interest in view of the known marked differences between different societies. What is much more important is the light thrown on the process of psychosexual development through the information given on age differences. In this connection, Broderick's study of 10–12-year-old children provides some useful findings (Broderick and Fowler, 1961; Broderick and Rowe, 1968). He found that the majority of the children claimed to have a sweetheart and between 10 and 12 years there was a rise in the proportion of children preferring an opposite sex companion in various situations. By 10 years two-thirds of them had been kissed and by 12 years this was so for 5 out of 6 children. Broderick developed a scale of social heterosexuality and showed that in the preadolescent period there was a gradual progression from wanting to marry someone, to having a particular girl-friend, to being 'in love' with this particular girl-friend and finally social activities in the company of this friend.

Schoof-Tams *et al.* (1976) found much the same. Although only 7 to 8% of 11-year-olds had reached their menarché or had had their first ejaculation, two-thirds of both boys and girls reported having been 'in love' and about half had kissed. By 16 years nearly all had been 'in love' and had kissed. Of course, too, the meaning of these experiences changes with maturity. During adolescence, young people's views about sexuality also develop. Thus the traditional concept of sex as mainly for the purpose of procreation, held by most pre-pubertal children, becomes superseded by the view that the main function of sex is to strengthen and deepen affectionate relationships.

Janus and Bess (1976) studied the development of sexual interests and attitudes by asking 3200 children aged 5 to 12 years to write compositions on boys and girls and on seeing and knowing about 'X' rated (adult only) movies. Overtly expressed sexuality increased during this age period from 16% to 56% and the form of its expression also changed and became more sophisticated in older children. The youngest children mainly wrote of sex in terms of kissing, there was then much voyeuristic interest (at first an infantile looking up girls' skirts extending to a fascination with magazines of nudes), while the older children showed an increasing awareness of sex desires and drives.

An early study by Campbell (1939) showed that up to the age of 7 or 8 years children played with both boys and girls, there was then a phase of playing only with children of the same sex as themselves, followed at about puberty by increasing social interaction with the opposite sex. Broderick also found that at age 10–12 years children had many more friends of the same sex than of the opposite sex. However, as already discussed, even during the period while friendships were mostly same-sex there was considerable heterosexual interest and some sexual activity. It may be concluded that same-sex friendships remain a feature of middle childhood but the inference from this that sex is latent is evidently wrong. It is somewhat disguised but still it is obviously active. The latency is

accurate only in so far as it refers to heterosexual social activities rather than sexual interests.

During and after adolescence, however, there is a very marked upsurge in sexual activity in both sexes. In Schofield's English study of teenagers (1965) he found that by the age of 13, a quarter of the boys and almost a third of the girls had had their first date. During the next two years there is a rapid rise in the incidence of dating so that by age 16 years over 70% of the boys and over 85% of the girls had experienced dating. The figures for kissing are closely similar and again boys lag behind girls in the age at which they start. Deep kissing and breast fondling occurs somewhat later, but by 17 years the majority of adolescents have progressed to this stage of sexual activity. After 15 years the curve for sexual experience rises fast. At 15 less than a fifth of the boys have touched the genitals of a girl but by 17 nearly half have done this. By the age of 18, a third of the boys and about 1 in 6 of the girls will have had sexual intercourse.

In keeping with their slower physical development, boys begin sexual activities later than girls, but by 17 years there is no longer any difference. Youngsters of both sexes who start dating and kissing at an early age are also more likely to have early sexual intercourse. However, there are differences between boys and girls in the pattern of sexual activity in later adolescence. Fewer girls have intercourse but once they have started they are more active sexually. The boys have more sexual partners (implying a small core of promiscuous girls) but the girls more often have an enduring sexual association. There are also differences in attitudes to sex. Girls tend to look for a romantic relationship while boys seek a sexual adventure. At the time of Schofield's survey in the early 1960s most adolescents were not using birth control although nearly all had some knowledge of it. About half of them either said that they did not like the idea of contraceptives or could not be bothered with them. It is uncertain how far this is a rationalization of more deep-seated reasons for avoiding contraception.

Of course, the timing of all these changes in sexual activity varies greatly according to the prevailing cultural norms. This was evident in the various anthropological studies of non-industrial societies (*see* Malinowski, 1929; Ford and Beach; 1951) but it is also shown by changes over time in any one society. Thus Schmidt and Sigusch (1972) showed that in Germany during the 1960s there was a marked trend towards earlier sociosexual activities such as kissing, dating, genital stimulation and coitus. A more permissive approach to sexual normality had also developed, but it still remained within a romantic love ideology. Asayama (1976) found similar changes in Japan between the '50s and '70s. The acceleration of sexual awareness and desire for intimacy in girls was particularly striking, with a resulting convergence between the sexes in sexual behaviour.

It is sometimes thought that sexual competence somehow 'comes naturally' and that sexual intercourse is necessarily pleasurable by some innate mechanism, but it is evident that neither is the case. The fact that sexual competence has to be learned and is not instinctively known is shown by Harlow's studies of the long-term effects of extreme social deprivation in infant monkeys (Harlow and Harlow, 1969). Animals reared in total isolation showed little sexual behaviour when adult and such sexual approaches as they made were extremely inept. Males failed to copulate successfully and the females presented themselves so badly that frequently even experienced males could not impregnate them. However, in that the monkeys showed generally disturbed behaviour this may in part represent a disruption of sexual activities rather than a true failure to develop competence. It appeared that social experiences with other animals (either a mother or peers) in infancy were necessary for normal psychosexual development. The findings emphasize both the importance of early relationships for normal social functioning in adult life and also the fact that sexual and social behaviour are closely linked.

Schofield (1965) in his general population study of sexual behaviour in teenagers found that a third of the boys and half of the girls did not like their first experience of sexual intercourse. A fifth of the boys and the majority of the girls failed to reach a climax. Sexual behaviour includes many learned components and depending upon whether a person's first sexual experience is enjoyable or unpleasant he may not try again for many years or he may have intercourse again within a few days and continue to have sex regularly and frequently (Schofield, 1965).

Schofield's (1973) follow-up of the same group into adult life confirmed these findings. He also found that people who first experienced sexual intercourse after age 21 years were less likely to enjoy it than those who did so in their teens. On the other hand, it was also shown that sexual intercourse was most likely to be pleasurable within the context of a loving relationship. It was striking that a fifth of young adults expressed anxiety over their sexual performance and a half had a sex problem of one kind or another.

PSYCHOSEXUAL ANOMALIES

This chapter is not primarily concerned with anomalies of psychosexual development but if the process of development is to be understood it is necessary to give them some consideration. Two general findings are of particular importance.

First, both retrospective and prospective studies clearly indicate moderately strong links between sexuality in childhood and that in adult life. Thus, Whitam (1977), in a study of 206 adult male homosexuals found that two fifths reported having been more interested in girls' toys and activities when a child, a similar proportion had liked dressing in women's clothing and over a quarter had been regarded as cissies. Nearly half the homosexuals reported at least four out of six indicators of female type childhood sexuality compared with none of the exclusively heterosexual men studied. Studies of homosexuals who were psychiatric patients have produced closely comparable findings (Bieber *et al.*, 1962; Saghir and Robins, 1973). Similarly, it has been found that about half adult

male transsexuals had dressed in female clothing as children and more than half had preferred girls' toys. The converse applied to adult female transsexuals (*see* Green, 1974). Half of transvestites also recall cross-dressing as children (Prince and Bentler, 1972). Follow-up studies of strongly feminine boys indicate that about half show psychosexual anomalies as adults (Green, 1974; Zuger, 1966; Lebovitz, 1972). However, the adult pattern varies between homosexuality, transsexuality and transvestism.

This underlines the second general finding—that there is substantial overlap between the various anomalies of psychosexual development. Thus, Bancroft (1972) found that about half the male homosexuals he studied showed evidence of some disturbance of gender identity; Hooker (1965) found that a third considered themselves feminine and a quarter had gone through a transvestite phase; and Randell (1973) found that a third of transvestites were homosexual.

HORMONAL INFLUENCES

Prenatal influences

In 1959, Phoenix *et al.* showed that when pregnant female guinea pigs were injected with a synthetic androgen, there was a *psychosexual*, as well as physiological, masculinization. When adult, these female hermaphrodites showed male mating behaviour. The administration of androgens in adult life, however, had no effect on the sex-type of mating pattern. On the basis of these and similar studies, it was argued by them (Goy, 1968; Young *et al.*, 1964) and others (Harris, 1964) that the gonadal hormones secreted prenatally acted on the developing brain in such a way as to cause the neural structures to be organized along male or female lines. Subsequent investigations, with primates as well as rodents, have broadly confirmed these conclusions (*see* reviews by Money and Ehrhardt, 1972 and by Reinisch, 1974). It is important to note that these hormonal effects were restricted to a critical period during fetal or early neonatal development and that social as well as mating behaviour was influenced. Thus, in the rhesus monkey, physical threats, rough and tumble and chasing play were all altered in a male direction by the prenatal administration of testosterone.

For obvious reasons, human research on this topic is much more limited but the findings suggest broadly comparable effects of fetal hormones on psychosexual behaviour and development. The evidence comes from two main sources: congenital syndromes involving some kind of prenatal endocrine anomaly and situations in which pregnant women have been treated with synthetic hormones.

The adrenogenital syndrome is an example of the former. In this condition, there is an excessive production of androgens by the adrenals leading to a varying degree of virilization which, postnatally, can be controlled by the administration of cortisone. Ehrhardt *et al.* (1968a and b) found that 11 out of 15 girls with this syndrome appeared to be tomboys in that they showed a high energy level and a strong interest in outdoor physical activities together with a minimal interest in doll play, dresses and girls' activities. In their study of 23 older adolescents and adults living as virilized women, it was found that 10 experienced homosexual as well as heterosexual imagery and four had had homosexual experiences. Nevertheless, all reported a female gender identity.

A subsequent, rather better controlled, study by Ehrhardt and Baker (1974), in which 17 fetally androgenized girls were compared with their sisters, confirmed this finding. The girls with the adrenogenital syndrome were significantly more likely to be interested in rough outdoor play and to prefer boys as playmates; and were significantly less likely to be interested in dolls or in jewellery and make-up. Altogether, three fifths had always behaved as tomboys. All the girls showed a normal female gender identity but a third either would have preferred to have been a boy or were undecided on sex preference. None of the normal sisters had a preference to be a boy. The girls were too young for any satisfactory assessment of their sexual object choice but the indications were that they had a heterosexual orientation which was perhaps somewhat delayed in its expression. Boys with the adrenogenital syndrome did not differ from their brothers apart from the one feature of greater energy expenditure in rough outdoor play.

The therapeutic administration of synthetic progestin to pregnant women in order to prevent miscarriage may have a somewhat comparable (although lesser) virilizing effect. Ehrhardt and Money (1967) found an unusually high degree of tomboyism in 10 girls treated prenatally in this way. Reinisch and Karow (1977) compared 16 girls and 10 boys exposed to prenatal progestin with 29 sibling controls (16 boys and 13 girls). They found that the progestin-exposed children appeared more independent, individualistic, self-assured and self-sufficient than their sibs on the Cattell Personality Questionnaires.

Imperato-McGinley et al. (1974 and 1979) have described an inherited form of male pseudo-hermaphroditism in which a decrease in dihydrotestosterone in utero leads to incomplete masculinization of the external genitalia. Prenatal testosterone is normal. They studied 18 boys (XY) with this syndrome. All had been reared as girls but at puberty (when the normal male changes took place) 16 of the 18 shifted to a male gender role and 15 of these showed a male heterosexual orientation.

Two other syndromes (androgen-insensitivity and Turner's) provide data on the effects of a lack of fetal androgens. The androgen-insensitivity syndrome refers to boys who are genetically male (XY) but female in external appearance. The testes produce normal amounts of both androgen and oestrogen but the body responds only to the oestrogen. Masica, Money and Ehrhardt (1971); Money et al. (1968) found that 10 patients with this syndrome were normally feminine in their gender role, gender identity and heterosexual orientation. Money and Ogunro (1974) found that patients with a partial androgen insensitivity (and hence ambiguous genitalia) usually

showed a heterosexual orientation relative to their sex of rearing, which was not necessarily in keeping with their prenatal hormone exposure.

Individuals with Turner's syndrome have a missing sex chromosome (XO), lack gonads of either sex (and therefore lack gonadal hormones) and are phenotypic females. Ehrhardt et al. (1970) studied 15 subjects and matched controls. All the subjects had a normal female psychosexual identity but as a group they were more passive than the controls.

Less is known about the effects of prenatal oestrogens. Yalom et al. (1973) studied non-diabetic boys born to diabetic mothers who had been given oestrogens during their pregnancies. Compared with controls, the sons of hormone-treated diabetic mothers were found to be less aggressive, less assertive and less athletic. It remains uncertain how far this difference was a result of oestrogens as the experimental mothers were much more ill than the controls (and this may have affected their maternal behaviour). However, Reinisch and Karow (1977) found that children exposed to oestrogens prenatally were less individualistic and less self-sufficient on the Cattell scales than their sibs.

The overall consistency of results in animals and in humans strongly suggests that fetal exposure to androgens influences later sex-related behaviours, probably through an effect on neural structures. However, several qualifications to this conclusion are necessary. First, the shift in behaviour is *quantitative*, not qualitative. That is, the prenatal androgens seem to lead to an increase in certain behaviours typically found in boys. But these behaviours also occur in some normal girls and are not present in all boys. Moreover, the shift towards boyish behaviour is not found in all children exposed to prenatal androgens. Probably, what happens is that the prenatal androgens alter the developing brain in ways which *facilitate* the learning of typically male behaviour patterns. Whether such behaviours in fact develop will depend in part on postnatal experience.

Secondly, the role of prenatal oestrogens remains quite uncertain. Certainly the animal research and the observations on individuals with Turner's syndrome indicates that feminine behaviour develops if there is an absence of androgens, irrespective of whether or not there are oestrogens. However, while oestrogens do not appear to be necessary for the development of female-typical behaviour it is possible that they may accentuate its qualities.

Thirdly, the observed behavioural effects of prenatal androgens may not be *solely* due to endocrine influences in that the hormonal changes are inevitably associated with some degree of alteration to the external genitalia (especially clitoral enlargement). While the behavioural effects are evident in children even when the genital anomaly has been corrected in infancy, it is possible that altered family attitudes play some part. On the other hand, it appears that chromosomal sex is irrelevant.

Fourthly, the effects of prenatal androgens are largely on sex-related behaviours rather than on gender identity. Although girls exposed to prenatal androgens tend to be more tomboyish than other girls, nevertheless they regard themselves as girls and most (but not all) are happy to accept this sex status. The male pseudohermaphrodites with an inherited 5 α-reductase deficiency, living in the Dominican Republic, and studied by Imperato-McGinley and her colleagues (1974 and 1979) constitute a major exception to this statement. Their findings indicate that, in a laissez-faire environment, the effects of prenatal testosterone *in combination with the appearance of male genitalia and secondary sex characteristics at puberty* usually prevail over the sex of initial rearing.

Fifth, little is known about the possible effects of prenatal hormones on sexual object choice. Dorner *et al.* (1975) have argued that the animal studies suggest that neonatal androgen deficiency leads to homosexual behaviour. In favour of this view they report that more homosexual than heterosexual men had a rebound increase in serum luteinising hormone following intravenous injection of oestrogen. However, the finding has yet to be replicated by an independent laboratory, the meaning of the phenomenon is in any case uncertain, there is overlap between the homosexual and heterosexual groups and the response found in some homosexual men is weak and delayed compared with that observed in women. No firm conclusions are yet possible.

Postnatal influences

The postnatal effects of sex hormones may be studied with respect to both sexually ambiguous and sexually normal individuals. Examples of the latter are the administration of oestrogens to men with prostatic cancer, the adrenogenital syndrome of late onset in women, and oestrogen-secreting tumours of the testis in men. In all these cases, there is the appearance of incongruous secondary sexual characteristics (breast development in men, beard growth in women) with consequent distress and embarrassment. However, these hormonal changes cause *no* alteration in either gender identity or sex-typical behaviours (Money and Ehrhardt, 1972).

The findings in connection with sexually ambiguous individuals are more variable and contradictory. In most cases they, too, resent any physical changes which are out of keeping with their view of themselves as male or female. Their wish is to have the unwanted characteristics removed rather than to have their gender identity altered (Money and Ehrhardt, 1972). On the other hand, exceptions have been reported. Thus, in the 18 male pseudohermaphrodites studied by Imperato-McGinley *et al.* (1974 and 1979) the normal growth of the phallus and scrotum at puberty together with the accompanying beard development resulted in a shift to a male identity. It should be noted that these individuals had all experienced the usual male prenatal exposure to testosterone (although they had been reared as girls). Of course, in these cases (unlike the situation with sexually normal individuals) the hormones caused major changes in the external genitalia as well as in secondary sexual characteristics. This may constitute an important difference.

Even so, it is clear from other studies that this only sometimes leads to a change in gender identity.

Altogether the evidence indicates that postnatal exposure to sex hormones does not ordinarily play any decisive role in the acquisition of gender identity. However, in cases where the hormones lead to major physical changes involving the external genitalia there *may* be an effect on gender identity (particularly when such identity was previously uncertain or weakly established).

The next issue concerns the effect of sex hormones on libido or sexual drive. It is clear from a variety of studies (*see* Money, 1961; Money and Ehrhardt, 1972) that androgens have an important (but far from exclusive) controlling function on sex drive in the male. They probably have a similar effect in the female, the hormones being secreted by the adrenal.

Pre-pubertal castration in the male generally leads to a degree of sexual apathy although not necessarily to complete lack of libido. However, the very limited available evidence suggests that ordinarily there is no substantial psychosexual feminization and what sex drive there is remains heterosexual in orientation. The same applies to conditions in which there is complete or partial gonadal failure. Thus, Raboch *et al.* (1977) found that adult cryptorchids showed substantially lower levels of plasma testosterone compared with normal men. Their development of heterosexual activity was slightly delayed and their level of sexual activity somewhat below normal or average. Nevertheless, the differences were slight and 80% of the men were married.

Post-pubertal castration in men, such as that consequent upon the use of oestrogens or androgen antagonists, generally leads to some reduction in sex drive. But it does not eliminate libido nor does it alter its direction. In normal ageing there is a gradual reduction in male hormone production which is associated with some diminution in the strength of sexual desire and of potency. However, the effect is mild, gradual and very variable. Most men retain substantial sex drive well into senescence.

Precocious puberty in boys (Money and Alexander, 1969) is associated with an increase in erections, masturbation and sexual urge. However, the psychosexual content tends to be broadly in keeping with the boy's chronological age (although somewhat advanced) and there is no alteration in either gender identity or sexual object choice. The same applies to precocious puberty in girls (Money and Walker, 1971). The unusually early development of adult sexual features has an impact and causes some emotional problems. However, psychosexual interests and activity are influenced by both cognitive level and experience as well as by physiological sexual maturity. Within the normal range, there is some indication, however, that an earlier puberty is associated with both earlier and greater sexual experience (Schofield, 1965).

Androgens also influence libido in women (Money, 1961). Women with excessive androgens (either endogenous or exogenous) often experience an increase in eroticism or sexual desire. Conversely, normal women deprived of their androgens by either adrenalectomy or hypophysectomy experience a lessening or loss of libido. That this does not happen after ovariectomy (which deprives them of oestrogens but not androgens) indicates that it is indeed the male sex hormone which is important in this connection.

The studies on postnatal exposure to androgens which have been discussed so far all refer to *abnormal* increases or decreases in hormone level. The evidence clearly indicates that androgens play an important role in the development of sexual drive. However, it does not necessarily follow from these findings that differences in hormone level account for individual differences in libido within the *normal* range. This issue has been studied by examining variations in sexual interest and activity both within individuals (over time) and between individuals. The latter indicate that variations between men in levels of sexual drive are *not* accounted for by variations in testosterone level (Brown *et al.*, 1978; Kraemer *et al.*, 1976). On the other hand, within individuals, higher levels of testosterone are associated with periods of greater sexual activity (Kraemer *et al.*, 1976). It also seems that the autumnal peak in plasma testosterone roughly coincides in time with a similar rise in levels of sexual activity (Reinberg and Lagoguey, 1978). It may be concluded that there is probably some link between testosterone levels and sexual activity but the association is weak and certainly it does not account for the major variations between individuals in levels of sexual interest and performance.

The same seems to apply to women. Spitz *et al.* (1975) found that self-rated sexual arousal in female undergraduates correlated with the type of heterosexual encounter on a given day rather than with any period of the menstrual cycle; and that intercourse rates were highest immediately after menstruation (rather than mid-cycle when oestrogen and androgen output is highest). Griffith and Walker (1975) found no association between response to erotic stimuli and menstrual cycle phase. It is not possible from these findings to conclude that there is no association between hormonal level and sexual behaviour, if only because of the major individual differences in hormone secretion pattern. However, what evidence there is suggests that hormone levels are most unlikely to be the major determinant of normal variations in sexual drive in humans.

Evidence in subhuman primates suggests that the sexual attractiveness of the female to the male is under hormonal control, one of the mechanisms being the male's smelling of an oestrogen-dependent vaginal pheromone (*see* Gower, 1976). There is probably something comparable in humans (Sokolov *et al.*, 1976) but it is uncertain how much effect it has on variations in levels of sexual arousal.

Animal studies indicate that androgens influence assertiveness and dominance as well as sex drive in both sexes. Thus, Joslyn (1973) reported that androgens injected into infant female rhesus monkeys between 6 and 14 months of age increased their aggressive behaviour so that they replaced males in the top positions of the social hierarchy. Unlike the situation with *pre*natal administra-

tion, however, their sex and play behaviour remained feminine.

The findings indicate that high androgen levels may lead to an increase in social assertiveness. On the other hand, the association between testosterone levels and dominance is complex with effects two ways. Thus, Rose *et al.* (1972) showed that when adult male rhesus monkeys were provided with individual access to a group of receptive females they became more dominant and their testosterone levels increased several-fold. Conversely, when these males were subjected to sudden and decisive defeat by an all male group their testosterone levels fell. Apparently, in humans, too, stress may lead to lower levels of testosterone (Kreuz *et al.*, 1972). It seems that not only can testosterone influence social behaviour but so also can social experiences influence testosterone level.

Many studies have considered the possibility that the directions of sexual object choice may be influenced by postnatal differences in levels of circulating sex hormones (*see* Bancroft, 1977; Meyer-Bahlburg, 1977). However, the evidence (much of poor quality) is generally negative and it seems unlikely that homosexuality in either men or women is due to any postnatal alteration in androgens or oestrogens. Blood levels of testosterone and oestradiol have been found to be closely similar in pairs of monozygotic twins discordant in sexual orientation (Friedman *et al.*, 1976). It remains uncertain (*see* above) whether prenatal changes have an effect on sexual orientation.

SEX CHROMOSOME INFLUENCES

There are major differences between males and females in their rates of physical maturation, in their vulnerability to disease and to trauma, and in their life expectancy (Childs, 1965; Rutter, 1970; Taylor and Ounsted, 1972). The maturational difference is known to be a function of the Y chromosome and many of the other differences are a result of differences between men and women in their physical make-up (although some are a consequence of differing life experiences—Vessey, 1972).

The Y chromosome determines fetal gonadal development with consequent influences on hormonal production and the development of secondary sex characteristics. It might, therefore, be expected that it would also have a major influence on psychosexual development. Obviously, in the normal child it does, simply because in the ordinary course of events not only physical development but also sex assignment at birth and style of rearing will be largely shaped by the child's primary sex characteristics. On the other hand, the behavioural effects appear indirect and it is necessary to consider how far the sex chromosomes influence psychosexual development when chromosomal sex is out of keeping with hormonal sex, physical appearance and/or sex of assignment and rearing. The evidence suggests that psychosexual development is not, in any way, determined by either the X or Y chromosome.

The question may be considered through the study of

sex chromosome anomalies and also through the investigation of individuals with normal chromosomes but whose physical appearance and rearing have for some reason been out of keeping with chromosomal sex. The evidence is clear cut in showing that feminine development can occur in spite of the presence of a Y chromosome or the absence of a second X chromosome. Thus, XY individuals with the androgen insensitivity syndrome and XO individuals with Turner's syndrome usually have a feminine gender role, gender identity and heterosexual orientation. XY males with a congenitally defective penis or a traumatic loss of their penis in infancy have been successfully reared as girls (Money, 1975). Lev-Ran (1974) has reported several cases of XY male hermaphrodites reared as females who showed a normal female gender identity and heterosexual orientation in spite of an obviously large phallus.

It is also evident that a male gender identity can develop in the absence of a Y chromosome. There are well documented reports of XX females with the adrenogenital syndrome who have been successfully reared as boys and whose later heterosexual fantasies have been those of men (Money, 1955; Lev-Ran, 1974).

On the other hand, it does seem that sex chromosome anomalies may predispose to a mixed bag of disturbances of psychosexual development. An additional Y chromosome (47–XYY) has been reported to show some association with homosexuality and a female gender identity (see Buhrich et al., 1978). The same is reported for an additional X chromosome, as in Klinefelter's syndrome (see Stoller, 1974). In both cases, the data are open to sampling biases and do not allow any statistical estimate of the strength of the association. However, in so far as the association exists, it appears to be a consequence of the accompanying bodily changes (males with Klinefelter's syndrome have poorly developed male secondary sexual characteristics, and often show some degree of breast development and a feminine distribution of fat) rather than any specific effect of either X or Y chromosome.

In order to put things into perspective, it also is necessary to point out that the vast majority of homosexuals and of transsexuals show a chromosomal sex in keeping with their physical status and sex of rearing and out of keeping with their preferred gender identity and sexual object choice (Pare, 1956; Pritchard, 1962). In other words almost always homosexual men are XY and homosexual women XX.

OTHER GENETIC INFLUENCES

Possible genetic influences on gender identity and sexual object choice have been examined through the study of monozygotic and dizygotic twins. Kallman's early report (1952) of 100% concordance for homosexuality in monozygotic pairs has not been confirmed by more recent studies (Parker, 1964; Heston and Shields, 1968; Friedman et al., 1976) and it remains quite uncertain how far hereditary influences play a part in the development of homosexuality. There are also several reports of mono-

zygotic pairs discordant for gender identity (Green and Stoller, 1971; Money, 1975).

OTHER BIOLOGICAL INFLUENCES

In the usual course of events a person's gonadal sex and physical appearance play major roles in the development of gender identity if only because they determine the sex of assignment and rearing. Their independent effect can only be assessed through the study of individuals with various sorts of anomalies. Gonadal sex seems to have only a minor direct influence. Hampson and Hampson (1961) found that among 30 patients in whom the sexual status of the gonads disagreed with the sex of assignment and rearing, in all but three cases the gender role was fully concordant with the sex of rearing (and hence discordant with gonadal sex). In the three exceptions the gender role was neither firmly male nor female. Even the external genital appearance seems to have surprisingly little effect on gender role. In a group of 25 hermaphrodites who showed a marked contradiction between assigned sex and genital appearance, in only two cases was the gender role in keeping with appearance and out of keeping with rearing. Lev-Ran (1974) has reported similar findings.

However, these studies necessarily concern very abnormal populations (often with unknown findings on the prenatal hormonal milieu) and it has been suggested that their biological ambiguity may have rendered them more susceptible to the influence of rearing (Diamond, 1965). It is also relevant that there are many reports of individuals who had doubts about their sex of rearing and in whom a later change of sexual assignment was welcomed and rapidly accepted (e.g. Armstrong, 1966; Dewhurst and Gordon, 1963; Berg et al., 1963; Lev-Ran, 1974; Imperato-McGinley et al., 1974 and 1979; Stoller, 1974). In many of these cases the sex of assignment and rearing has lacked the certainty that is present in the normal, but this was not always the case. On the whole, it seems that gonadal sex and external genital appearance are usually less decisive influences than sex of assignment (in the rare instances when they conflict) but they do have an impact which occasionally is over-riding—especially if these coincide with the prenatal hormone exposure.

SEX OF ASSIGNMENT AND REARING

The evidence stemming from the study of anomalous individuals, which has been discussed already, indicates that the sex of assignment and rearing is usually the overriding determinant of gender identity. Money's (1975) study of a monozygotic twin pair emphasizes the point. A normal boy had his penis almost totally destroyed as the result of a surgical mishap at 7 months. Reassignment as a girl took place at 17 months. Follow-up at age 9 years showed the child to have a normal female gender identity in marked contrast to that of the identical twin brother. However, as expected from the prenatal androgen experience, the twin brought up as a girl was definitely tomboyish. Money and Ehrhardt's (1972) comparison of 'matched' pairs of hermaphrodites also indicates that when the sex of assignment is uncertain gender identity may also be ambiguous. They describe how biologically similar patients with the adrenogenital syndrome one of whom elected to be reassigned from a girl to a boy and the other of whom chose reassignment in the opposite direction.

It is evident that it is not only a question of the parents deciding that the child is a boy or girl and giving it an appropriate name, but also the whole style of rearing tends to be sex differentiated (*see* Chapter 8 by Maccoby and Jacklin). In the twin pair described above, Money (1975) noted how the parents treated the boy and 'girl' differently in terms of how to urinate, attitudes to sex, domestic activities, toy play and career intention. As Maccoby and Jacklin describe (Chapter 8) this differential treatment continues at school. Many of the differences between the sexes in behaviour and performance are culturally determined to a very large extent. Nevertheless, the pressures for boys to conform are very considerable even during the preschool years. Those who show consistent cross-gender preferences are criticized by their peers five or six times as often as other children and receive positive feedback a quarter as often (Fagot, 1977). Interestingly, this does not seem to apply to girls who are allowed much greater latitude in their style of play.

There is no doubt, then, that boys and girls are treated differently by their parents, their teachers and their peers. The studies of sexually ambiguous individuals leave no doubt that this differential treatment plays a major role in determining gender identity. What is much less clear is the extent to which particular patterns of rearing lead to anomalies of gender identity, sex-typical behaviours and sexual orientation in physically *normal* individuals.

Green and Stoller (1971) described two monozygotic twin pairs discordant for gender identity. In the first pair the feminine boy was ill for $2\frac{1}{2}$ years from the age of 3—as a consequence he spent much more time with his mother. In the second pair the masculine girl, unlike her sister, had been encouraged to help her father with male-type household repairs and building and was given more boyish toys at birthdays. Green (1974), in his study of feminine boys noted the following features (none present in all cases): parental indifference towards or encouragement of feminine behaviour or cross-dressing, maternal over-protection and dominance, absence of a male model, and rejection by the father. Rosen *et al.* (1977) have reported much the same. However, it is uncertain how far the parental behaviour was a cause of or response to the children's behaviour and in most cases adequate comparative data are lacking.

In many cases the development of homosexual inclinations seems to be related to a person's early life experiences (West, 1968; Bancroft, 1970; Kenyon, 1970). The evidence suggests that poor relationships with parents, perhaps particularly the parent of the same sex, may play a part in the development of homosexual interests. The studies are largely of psychiatric patients or volunteers and most of the data are retrospective so that it is difficult to know how much weight to attach to the findings. However, the results of differing studies are fairly comparable and it seems highly probable that early family relationships constitute one important influence on the development of sexual object choice.

ANOMALOUS FAMILY SITUATIONS AND EXPERIENCES

Parental loss

Numerous writers have argued that the loss of a parent of the same sex is likely to have a distorting influence on psychosexual development (*see* Biller, 1974, for review). However, the empirical findings are contradictory and inconclusive. Certainly, most boys who have lacked fathers during the preschool years acquire normal masculine behaviour. Biller (1974) concluded that, on the whole, they tend to be rather less masculine than other boys; but Herzog and Sudia (1973) reviewing the same body of research argue that the findings provide no adequate base for that conclusion. Birtchnell's (1974) study of 696 adults constitutes one of the largest samples: his results showed no significant relationship between early parent loss and masculinity-femininity of behaviour.

Rearing in a sexually-atypical household

In so far as it has often been considered that modelling plays a major role in psychosexual development, it might be thought that children reared in sexually-atypical households would often develop in anomalous ways. The available evidence is inconclusive but the data certainly suggest that this is *not* the case. Green (1978) described 37 children who were being raised by parents at least one of whom was either transsexual or homosexual. His preliminary observations indicated that psychosexual development appeared typical in at least 36 of the 37 children. The few who were old enough for the matter to be assessed showed an heterosexual orientation.

More systematic data are available from a study by Golombok, Spencer and Rutter who compared the psychosexual development of children being reared in lesbian households with those of children being brought up by their mothers in one-parent families. Most of the children in the former group were living with their mother together with her lesbian partner, but some were in communes or other living arrangements. A very few had been in a lesbian household throughout their life (being born by AID) but most had spent some years with their father and mother. No differences in the masculinity-femininity of either boys or girls was evident on the data from either the mothers or the children themselves. All children showed an appropriate gender identity. There were too few young people past puberty for any reliable assessment of sexual orientation to be made. However, it was evident that most experienced normal heterosexual feelings.

At first sight it may seem surprising that psychosexual development should apparently proceed so normally in spite of rearing in households which were so markedly atypical in terms of current sexual norms. Several points need to be made in this connection. First, almost all the children had considerable contact with men in spite of not being with their fathers (in fact contact was rather greater for those in lesbian households than for those in female one-parent families). Moreover, the great majority had started life in a heterosexual family. The very few reared by two lesbian women from the outset did not seem to have suffered from this but the number studied is far too small to draw firm conclusions about the psychosexual effects. Second, it seems most unlikely from other evidence that psychosexual development proceeds through a process of *copying*. Rather, to the extent that environmental influences play a part, it appears that it is sex differentiated treatment in the early years which shapes gender identity. Sexual orientation, on the other hand, is more likely to be influenced by the balance and quality of family relationships. Our findings indicate that, like other parents, lesbian couples treat boys and girls differently. Furthermore, in most cases the mother and her lesbian partner played rather different roles in the child's life—it was *not* an undifferentiated pattern of relationships. Thirdly, of course, studies of individuals with an anomalous gender identity or sexual orientation show that virtually all are brought up in *heterosexual* households.

The data are still too few and too incomplete to conclude that rearing in a sexually-atypical household is without appreciable effect on psychosexual development. However, all the indications so far are that the great majority of the children in such households show a normal gender identity, normal sex-typical behaviours and (probably, although less certainly) normal sexual orientation.

Early sexual experiences

There is considerable uncertainty about the effects of early atypical sexual experiences on later psychosexual development. Some studies of adults with atypical sexual behaviour have suggested possible links. For example, James and Meyerding (1978) reported that prostitutes were more likely than other women to have experienced incest or sexual advances from an older man. However, such experiences are known to occur to many normal women (Kinsey *et al.*, 1953), the data are retrospective and open to biases of recall, and it is not possible to disentangle the effects of the sexual experiences from the effects of the disturbed family relationships which were also usually present. Gibbens and Prince (1963) found that the immediate emotional disturbance was greatest in the case of children sexually assaulted by relatives—perhaps because this was often associated with serious family difficulties and was frequently followed by the removal of the child from home. In the longer-term, Bender and Grugett (1952) reported that most of the small group of sexually assaulted children whom they studied developed satisfactorily and in particular none showed psychosexual abnormalities. However, far too

little is known for any firm conclusions to be drawn. On the whole, it seems likely that the disturbed family relationship which may precede or the maladaptive adult reactions which may follow the child's experience of sexual assault are more likely to cause emotional disturbance than the acts themselves. But even this conclusion lacks adequate empirical support.

THEORIES OF PSYCHOSEXUAL DEVELOPMENT

Biological

Diamond (1976) has argued that sex differences in the brain are established early in fetal life under the influence of genetic and hormonal factors, so that by four or five weeks after conception crude neural programmes have been organized which eventually will mediate the individual's entire reproductive and sexual patterns. He suggests that related but different sets of neural tissues are involved in the various facets of sexuality—sex-typed behaviours, gender identity, sexual object choice, and sexual mechanisms (erections, orgasm, etc.). Hutt (1978) has argued on somewhat similar lines.

The evidence in favour of this view has been considered already. Most writers now agree on the importance of biological (especially prenatal hormonal) influences on psychosexual development and certainly on sex-typed behaviour. However, there is not agreement on Diamond's relegation of environmental influences to an entirely subsidiary role. He points to the lack of empirical evidence for any consistent societal 'shaping' of children towards sex stereotypes, to the finding that although behavioural treatments may suppress sexual behaviours they do not lead any sexual reorientation, and to the failure to demonstrate clear environmental determinants of atypical psychosexual development (transsexualism, homosexuality, etc.). Studies such as that by Imperato-McGinley (*see* above) are used to demonstrate the overriding importance of biological forces.

On the other hand, in order to hold this view, Diamond has to reject the evidence on the considerable importance of sex assignment and sex of rearing on gender identity. Moreover, it is necessary to overlook the fact that it has been found that the biological variables which have been studied do *not* account for individual differences in the various facets of sexuality. Furthermore, in most cases, empirical studies have *failed* to find any biological factor to account for anomalies of psychosexual development.

Cognitive-developmental approaches

Kohlberg (1967), in contrast, has linked psychosexual development to the process of cognitive organization. According to this view, the acquisition of gender identity is basic (usually resulting from an early physical reality judgement). While this cognitive judgement is crystallizing into a conception of a constant gender identity, the child's sex role may be influenced by various environmental variables. Masculine-feminine values and behaviour develop out of a need to behave in ways which are consistent with a child's concept of himself as male or female. *After* these values have been acquired, the desire to be masculine (or feminine) leads to identification with male (or female) models. These trends follow a regular course which is largely determined by cognitive (rather than physiological) maturity.

There is much to be said for this approach and it seems highly likely that the processes he describes do in fact occur and play an important part in psychosexual development (*see* Kohlberg, 1967 and also Maccoby and Jacklin, 1975). Certainly the empirical evidence supports his view that gender constancy develops gradually in line with cognitive maturity and that children strive to behave in ways which are consonant with their image of themselves. On the other hand, it is clear that (contrary to Kohlberg's theory) sex-typing of behaviour occurs *before* gender constancy normally develops, and hence cannot possibly be a *result* of gender identity. Furthermore, this theory has no adequate explanation for individual differences in psychosexual development and has nothing to say about sexual object choice.

Social learning theories

Social learning theorists (*see* Mussen, 1969; Mischel, 1970) see the course of events as happening in the reverse order to Kohlberg. In other words, imitation of or identification with same-sexed models and differential reinforcement of sex-typed behaviour constitutes the basis for psychosexual development. It is pointed out that sex differences in behaviour are not universal. Not only are there many ways to be a boy or girl, man or woman, but also sex-typed behaviours vary according to culture. These individual differences and societal variations are thought to be explicable in terms of variations in the models available and in patterns of reinforcement.

There is abundant evidence that imitation, identification and differential reinforcement not only occur but play a major role in shaping children's behaviour. Indeed *all* theorists ascribe some part of psychosexual development to social learning. Its importance is not in dispute. However, there are many difficulties in any theory which attributes the *whole* of psychosexual development to this process (*see* Maccoby and Jacklin, 1975). So far as modelling is concerned the main snags are:

(i) children do not closely resemble the same-sexed parent in their behaviour, (ii) preschool children do not characteristically choose a same-sex model (in spite of the fact that their behaviour is strongly sex-typed), and (iii) children's sex-typed behaviours do not closely resemble those of adult models (and may include some which are totally outside the adult repertoire). So far as differential reinforcement is concerned, there is plenty of evidence that it occurs and it seems highly likely that it is important in shaping many aspects of psychosexual development. However, it is necessary also to take into account the strong evidence for biologically determined sex

differences in behaviour (*see* above) and for child influences on parental behaviour (*see* Rutter, 1977). Furthermore, it has to be recognized that there is a *lack* of empirical evidence that anomalies of psychosexual development are associated with (let alone due to) variations in patterns of reinforcement.

Psychoanalytic views

Psychosexual development constitutes the cornerstone of psychoanalytic views of human personality functioning and hence the theoretical formulations have ramifications far beyond psychosexual development itself. It is not possible to consider *the* psychoanalytic view, not only because Freud himself changed his views several times but also because other psychoanlytic theorists have departed considerably from Freud's concepts (*see* Dare, 1977 for a useful summary of similarities and contrasts). However, the key elements may be summarized in terms of psychosexual stages, the notion of libidinal energy, and the processes involved in the determination of gender identity.

The first psychosexual stage is the 'oral', occurring during the first year and in which sexuality is at first autoerotic and then narcissistically incorporative (Abraham, 1927; Buxbaum, 1959; Freud, 1905, 1923). This is followed during the second year by the 'anal' phase in which the child's libidinal pleasure comes to be focused on the anal zone with accompanying sadistic wishes to control. Between the third and fifth years sexuality becomes increasingly genital or 'phallic' in focus. Penis envy in girls and castration anxiety in boys are predominant, associated with the 'Oedipal' complex of sexual rivalry with the same-sexed parent and attachment to the opposite-sexed parent. The period between 5 and puberty is thought to be a 'latent' one in which sexual development shows a real break (Freud, S., 1922; Freud, A., 1947; Fries, 1959). At adolescence there is a resurgence of sexuality and a re-living of the phallic phase leading to an adult capacity for love. The negotiation of this stage is dependent on the earlier manner of resolution of the Oedipus complex.

Libido is seen as sexual energy or drive, a force which has a quantitative element leading to a hydraulic view of energy flow, dam-up or release. This drive operates by 'cathecting' (in a sense energizing) various psychological personality structures.

The negotiation of the Oedipus complex is thought to proceed rather differently in boys and girls (*see* Edgcumbe *et al.*, 1976; Mächtlinger, 1976; Eissler, 1977). The girls' development is considered to be originally masculine with at first a 'negative Oedipal phase' parallel to the boys' 'positive Oedipal phase' (*i.e.* identification with the father). The castration complex with its penis envy initiates the move to a positive Oedipus complex and then to feminine identification. In this way the girl has an extra developmental stage to negotiate and is somewhat later in her resolution of the Oedipus complex. This is accompanied by a shift of cathexis from clitoris to vagina. For boys the central features of the Oedipus complex are his feelings of hostility and rivalry towards his father. The positive Oedipus complex is terminated (rather than initiated as in girls) by the castration complex which leads to his identification with his father as aggressor.

The hydraulic view of libidinal energy runs counter to the empirical findings on motivation (see Hinde, 1960; Hunt, 1960; Barnett, 1963), and Freud's original notion of libido as an energy force has been abandoned or greatly modified by many analysts (Applegarth, 1971; Holt, 1967). While clearly there is a sex 'drive' in the sense that there is a biologically determined sexual motivation, its ebb and flow do not follow the patterns expected on the basis of a hydraulic energy model (see Rutter, 1971).

Empirical findings support some aspects of the psychoanalytic view of psychosexual stages and run counter to other aspects (Chodorow, 1978). The main feature which is clearly wrong is that of sexual latency. Firstly, several studies have shown a progressive increase in sexual activities during the pre-pubertal years (see refs. above). Second, there is also a progression in social heterosexuality (Broderick and Fowler, 1961; Broderick and Rowe, 1968). Thirdly, there is systematic development in sexual awareness and concepts (Janus and Bess, 1976) and fourthly, there are progressive changes in ideas about sexual morality (Schoof-Tams et al., 1976). There can be no doubt that sexual development does indeed continue to proceed during the so-called latency years. This is certainly quite contrary to Freud's views, although contemporary analysts have attempted to reintegrate modern empirical data into Freud's conceptual framework (Shapiro and Perry, 1976).

The concept of an oral phase is accurate in so far as it implies that oral activities are common in infancy, but it is misleading in implying that these are the only or even the most important behaviours at that stage (Rutter, 1971). Moreover, mother–child attachment does not primarily depend on sucking or feeding (Bowlby, 1969) and the attachment process may well be considered the most important development in the first year (see Chapter 22).

The second and third years of life do indeed constitute the age when toilet training begins and this process is a source of interest and exploration for the child. However, there are many other developments during these years (White, 1960) and the empirical findings on Freud's concept of anal character are inconclusive (see Hill, 1976).

The Oedipus complex has proved difficult to examine. Again the evidence is contradictory and unsatisfactory but it seems probable that many children do go through a phase when there is some antipathy to the same-sexed parent (see Rutter, 1971). Also there is some support for the existence of castration anxiety (see above). However, the Oedipus complex does not appear to be universal and the significance of its resolution for later development is uncertain. The psychoanalytic view of adolescence as a revival of Oedipal conflicts also remains largely untested.

Freud's views on girls' psychosexual development have come under particularly severe fire from other psychoanalysts (see Edgcumbe et al., 1976; Eissler, 1977) and it is clear that some modification is essential. In the first place, the feminine gender identity and sex-typed behaviours are clearly evident before age 4 to 5 years and hence their development cannot be primarily due to resolution of the Oedipus complex (Kleeman, 1971; Edgcumbe et al., 1976). Secondly, there is no indication that her recognition of a lack of a penis forces the girl to abandon a masculine position for a feminine one. Rather an awareness of physical differences between the sexes aids both boys and girls in consolidating their sexual identity (Edgcumbe et al., 1976). Thirdly, for a variety of reasons both boys and girls usually remain attached to their mother and this continues alongside sexual aspects of the relationships (Edgcumbe et al., 1976).

Interactional approaches

Money and Ehrhardt (1972) have most clearly and fully put forward an interactional approach to psychosexual development. Basically, they suggest that hormones and other biological determinants play a major role especially during the early stages of psychosexual differentiation. These biological forces influence behavioural and learning propensities but the individual's behaviour, attitudes and values as they actually emerge are very greatly influenced by psychosocial experiences. Bancroft (1972) has suggested a broadly similar model to account for the development of psychosexual anomalies of gender identity, sex-typed behaviour and sexual object choice. The details of the interactions in these models remain uncertain and many features lack adequate empirical support. However, the empirical findings outlined in this chapter obviously force one to some kind of interactional position. No single theoretical explanation adequately accounts for all or even nearly all of the varied phenomena of psychosexual development. Nevertheless, there is good empirical support for the importance of several different mechanisms which contribute to psychosexual development in somewhat different ways.

CONCLUSION

The available evidence does not permit any firm statements on the relative importance of the various different processes involved in psychosexual development. Nevertheless, some tentative conclusions are possible.

At birth, a child's genitalia are obviously the prime determinants of whether he is regarded and treated as a boy or girl. Thereafter, the sex of assignment and rearing are probably the main determinants of gender identity—that is whether a child feels himself to be male or female. In the ordinary course of events gender identity is established by age 3 to 4 years and remains fixed thereafter. However, it may remain uncertain for longer than that and it can change in certain circumstances. The continuing influences on gender identity include sex-typed behaviours (so that if, for any reason, a child behaves strongly in the style expected of one sex he is more likely to feel identified with that sex, either reinforcing the original gender identity or creating pushes towards the opposite one); parental and other influences reinforcing sex role behaviours; and attitudinal changes stemming from the development of sexual characteristics with puberty. Postnatal hormones and sex chromosomes seem to have no direct impact on gender identity.

Prenatal androgens have an important effect in causing a predisposition towards male sex-typed behaviours. However, sex role development is also much influenced by parental responses to the child and by cultural norms generally. The child's behaviour is also likely to be shaped by his own skills and attributes, his gender identity, and by his perceptions of his own physical appearance.

Postnatal androgens play a major role in creating sex drive in both males and females. They also have an effect on social behaviour such that dominance and assertiveness tend to be increased. On the other hand, hormones appear less important with respect to individual differences in sexual interests and activity. Rather, social and sexual experiences seem much more influential in this connection. The reduced levels of androgen in later life probably lead to some diminution in sexual potency but, again, individual variation is great, and due as much to experiential as hormonal influences.

Least is known about the development of sexual object choice. Clearly it is related to, although different from, gender identity and sex role; and anomalies in either are likely to pre-dispose to the development of homosexuality.

Finally, it needs to be emphasized that psychosexual development is closely linked with social and emotional development. Difficulties in interpersonal relationships or social anxiety are likely to have psychosexual consequences; the converse is also the case.

Acknowledgments

I am grateful to Dr D. Taylor for drawing my attention to some of the references used here.

REFERENCES

Abraham, K. (1927). *Selected Papers on Psychoanalysis*. London: Hogarth Press.

Applegarth, A. (1971). Comments on aspects of the theory of psychic energy. *J. Amer. Psychoanal. Assoc.* **19**, 379–416.

Armstrong, C. N. (1966). Treatment of wrongly assigned sex. *Brit. Med. J.* **2**, 1255–1256.

Asayama, S. (1976). Sexual behaviour in Japanese students: a comparison for 1974, 1960 and 1952. *Arch. Sex. Behav.* **5**, 371–390.

Bancroft, J. H. J. (1970). Homosexuality in the male. *Brit. J. Hosp. Med.* **3**, 168–181.

Bancroft, J. (1972). The relationship between gender identity and sexual behaviour. Some clinical aspects. In C. Ounsted and D. Taylor (Eds) *Gender Differences: Their Ontogeny and Significance*. London: Churchill Livingstone.

Bancroft, J. H. J. (1977). The relationship between hormones and sexual behaviour in humans. In J. Hutchinson (Ed) *Biological Determinants of Sexual Behaviour*. London: Wiley.

Barnett, S. A. (1963). *A Study in Behaviour*. London: Methuen.

Bender, L. and Grugett, E. (1952). A follow-up report on children who had atypical sexual experience. *Amer. J. Orthopsychiat.* **22**, 825–837.

Berg, I., Nixon, H. H. and Macmahon, R. (1963). Change of assigned sex at puberty. *Lancet* **2**, 1216–1217.

Bernick, N. (1965). The development of children's sexual attitudes as determined by the pupil-dilation response. Unpublished doctoral dissertation. Univ. Chicago cited Kohlberg (1967).

Bieber, I., Dain, H. J., Dince, P. R., Drellich, M. Q., Grand, H. G., Gundlach, R. H., Kremer, M. W., Rifkin, A. H., Wilbur, C. B. and Bieber, T. B. (1962). *Homosexuality: A Psychoanalytic Study of Male Homosexuals*. New York: Basic Books.

Biller, H. B. (1974). *Paternal Deprivation: Family, School, Sexuality and Society*. Toronto and London: Lexington Books.

Billig, A. (1941). Fingernail biting; its incipiency, incidence and amelioration. *Genet. Psychol. Mon.* **24**, 123–218.

Birtchnell, J. (1974). The effect of early parent loss upon the direction and degree of sexual identity. *Brit. J. Med. Psychol.* **47**, 129–137.

Bowlby, J. (1969). *Attachment and Loss, Vol. 1. Attachment*. London: Hogarth Press.

Broderick, C. B. (1966). Sexual behaviour among preadolescents. *J. Soc. Issues* **22**, 6–21.

Broderick, C. B. and Fowler, S. E. (1961). New patterns of relationships between the sexes among preadolescents. *Marriage and Family Living* **23**, 27–30.

Broderick, C. B. and Rowe, G. P. (1968). A scale of preadolescent heterosexual development. *J. Marriage and the Family* **30**, 97–101.

Brown, W. A., Monti, P. M. and Corrisean, D. P. (1978). Serum testosterone and sexual activity and interest in men. *Arch. Sex. Behav.* **7**, 97–104.

Buhrich, N., Barr, R. and Lam-Po-Tang, P. R. L. C. (1978). Two transsexuals with 47-XYY karyotype. *Brit. J. Psychiat.* **133**, 77–81.

Buxbaum, E. (1959). Psychosexual development: the oral, anal and phallic phases. In D. Levitt (Ed) *Readings in Psychoanalytic Psychology*. New York: Appleton.

Campbell, E. H. (1939). The social-sex development of children. *Genet. Psychol. Mon.* **21**, 461–552.

Childs, B. (1965). Genetic origin of some sex differences among human beings. *Pediat.* **35**, 798.

Chodorow, N. (1978). *The Reproduction of Mothering*. Berkeley: University of California Press.

Conn, J. H. (1940). Children's reactions to the discovery of genital differences. *Am. J. Orthopsychiat.* **10**, 747–754.

Conn, J. H. and Kanner, L. (1947). Children's awareness of sex differences. *J. Child Psychiat.* **1**, 3–57.

Dalbiez, R. (1941). *Psychoanalytic Method and the Doctrine of Freud*. London: Longmans Green.

Dare, C. (1977). Psychoanalytic theories. In M. Rutter and L. Hersov (Eds) *Child Psychiatry: Modern Approaches*. Oxford: Blackwell.

Dewhurst, C. J. and Gordon, R. R. (1963). Change of sex. *Lancet* **2**, 1213–1216.

Diamond, M. (1965). A critical evaluation of the ontogeny of human sexual behaviour. *Quart. Rev. Biol.* **40**, 147–175.

Diamond, M. (1976). Human sexual development: biological foundations for social development. In F. A. Beach (Ed) *Human Sexuality in Four Perspectives*. Baltimore & London: Johns Hopkins Univ. Press.

Dorner, G., Rohde, W., Stahl, F., Krell, L. and Masius, W.-G. (1975). A neuroendocrine predisposition for homosexuality in men. *Arch. Sec. Behav.* **4**, 1–8.

Douglas, J. W. B. and Ross, J. M. (1964). Age of puberty related to educational ability, attainment and school leaving age. *J. Child Psychol. Psychiat.* **5**, 185–196.

Edgcumbe, R., Lundberg, S., Markowitz, R. and Salo, F. (1976). Some comments on the concept of the negative oedipal phase in girls. *Psychoanal. Study of the Child* **31**, 35–62.

Ehrhardt, A. A. and Baker, S. W. (1974). Fetal androgens, human central nervous system differentiation, and behaviour sex differences. In R. C. Friedman, R. M. Richart and R. L. Van de Wiele (Eds) *Sex Differences in Behavior*. New York: Wiley.

Ehrhardt, A. A. and Money, J. (1967). Progestin-induced hermaphroditism; IQ and psychosexual identity in a study of ten girls. *J. Sex. Res.* **3**, 83–100.

Ehrhardt, A. A., Epstein, R. and Money, J. (1968a). Fetal androgens and female gender identity in the early-treated andrenogenital syndrome. *Johns Hopkins Med. J.* **122**, 160–167.

Ehrhardt, A. A., Evers, K. and Money, J. (1968b). Influence of androgen and some aspects of sexually dimorphic behavior in women with the late-treated andrenogenital syndrome. *Johns Hopkins Med. J.* 123, 115–122.

Ehrhardt, A. A., Greenberg, N. and Money, J. (1970). Female gender identity and absence of fetal gonadal hormones: Turner's syndrome. *Johns Hopkins Med. J.* 126, 237–248.

Eissler, K. R. (1977). Comments on penis envy and orgasm in women. *Psychoanal. Study of the Child* 32, 29–84.

Fagot, B. I. (1977). Consequences of moderate cross-gender behavior in preschool children. *Child Develop.* 48, 902–907.

Fitschen, W. and Clayton, B. E. (1965). Urinary excretion of gonadotrophins with particular reference to children. *Arch. Dis. Child.* 40, 16–26.

Ford, C. S. and Beach, F. A. (1951). *Patterns of Sexual Behaviour*. New York: Harper.

Freud, A. (1947). Emotional and instinctual development. In *Indications for Child Analysis and Other Papers 1945–1956 (1969)*. London: Hogarth Press.

Freud, S. (1905). Three essays on the theory of sexuality. In Strachey, J. (Ed) *The Standard Edition of the Complete Works of Sigmund Freud*, Vol. VII, 125–143. London: Hogarth Press.

Freud, S. (1922). Two encyclopaedia articles. In J. Strachey (Ed.) *The Standard Edition of the Complete Works of Sigmund Freud, Vol. 18*. London: Hogarth Press.

Freud, S. (1923). The infantile genital organization of the libido. In *Collected Papers, Vol. 2 (1924)*. London: Hogarth Press.

Friedman, R. C., Wollesen, F. and Tendler, R. (1976). Psychological development and blood levels of sex steroids in male identical twins of divergent sexual orientation. *J. Nerv. Ment. Dis.* 163, 282–288.

Fries, M. E. (1959). Review of the literature on the latency period. In M. Levitt (Ed.) *Readings in Psychoanalytic Psychology*. New York: Appleton.

Gesell, A. (1940). *The First Five Years of Life*. London: Methuen.

Gibbens, T. C. N. and Prince, J. (1963). *Child Victims of Sex Offences*. London: I.S.T.D.

Golombok, S., Spencer, A. and Rutter, M. Paper in preparation.

Gower, D. B. (1976). Behavioral aspects of pheromones. In O. Hill (Ed) *Modern Trends in Psychosomatic Medicine*, 3. London: Butterworths.

Goy, R. W. (1968). Organizing effects of androgen on the behavior of rhesus monkeys. In R. P. Michael (Ed) *Endocrinology and Human Behavior*. London: Oxford Univ. Press.

Green, R. (1974). *Sexual Identity Conflict in Children and Adults*. New York: Basic Books.

Green, R. (1978). Sexual identity of 37 children raised by homosexual or transsexual parents. *Amer. J. Psychiat.* 135, 692–697.

Green, R. and Stoller, R. J. (1971). Two monozygotic (identical) twin pairs discordant for gender identity. *Arch. Sex. Behav.* 1, 321–327.

Greenacre, P. (1950). Special problems of early female sexual development. *Psychoanalyt. Stud. Child.* 5, 122–138.

Griffith, M. and Walker, L. E. (1975). Menstrual cycle phases and personality variables as related to responses to erotic stimuli. *Arch. Sex. Behav.* 4, 599–603.

Halverson, H. M. (1940). Genital and sphincter behaviour of the male infant. *J. Genet. Psychol.* 56, 95–136.

Hampson, J. L. and Hampson, J. G. (1961). The ontogenesis of sexual behaviour in man. In W. C. Young and G. W. Corner (Eds) *Sex and Internal Secretions, Vol. II, 3rd Edn*. Baltimore: Williams and Wilkins.

Harlow, H. F. and Harlow, M. K. (1969). Effects of various mother-infant relationships on rhesus monkey behaviours. In B. M. Foss (Ed) *Determinants of Infant Behaviour Vol. 4*. London: Methuen.

Harris, G. W. (1964). Sex hormones, brain development and brain function. *Endocrinology* 75, 627–648.

Herzog, E. and Sudia, C. E. (1973). Children in fatherless families. In Caldwell, B. and Ricciuti, H. (Eds). *Review of Child Development Research, Vol. 3*. Chicago: University of Chicago Press.

Heston, L. L. and Shields, J. (1968). Homosexuality in twins: a family study and a registry study. *Arch. Gen. Psychiat.* 18, 149–160.

Hill, A. B. (1976). Methodological problems in the use of factor analysis: a critical review of the experimental evidence for the anal character. *Brit. J. Med. Psychol.* 49, 145–159.

Hinde, R. A. (1960). Energy models of motivation. *Symp. Soc. exp. Biol.* 14, 199–213.

Holt, R. R. (1967). Beyond vitalism and mechanism: Freud's concept of

psychic energy. In J. H. Masserman (Ed) *The Ego, Science and Psychoanalysis, Vol. 11*. New York: Grune and Stratton.

Hooker, E. (1965). An empirical study of some relations between sexual patterns and gender identity in male homosexuals. In J. Money (Ed) *Sex Research—New Developments*. New York: Rinehart and Winston.

Hunt, J. M. (1960). Experience and the development of motivation: some reinterpretations. *Child Develop.* 31, 489–504.

Hutt, C. (1978). Biological bases of psychological sex differences. *Amer. J. Dis. Child.* 132, 170–177.

Imperato-McGinley, J., Guerrero, L., Gautier, T. and Peterson, R. E. (1974). Steroid α-reductase deficiency in man: an inherited form of male pseudohermaphroditism. *Science* 186, 1213–1215.

Imperato-McGinley, J., Peterson, R. E., Gautier, T. and Sturla, E. (1979). Androgens and the evolution of male-gender identity among male pseudohermaphrodites with 5 α-reductase deficiency. *New Engl. J. Med.* 300, 1233–1237.

Isaacs, S. (1933). *Social Development in Young Children*. London: Routledge and Kegan Paul.

James, J. and Meyerding, J. (1978). Early sexual enterprise as a factor in prostitution. *Arch. Sex. Behav.* 7, 31–42.

Janus, S. S. and Bess, B. E. (1976). Latency: fact or fiction. *Amer. J. Psychoanalysis* 36, 339–346.

Jones, M. C. (1965). Psychological correlates of somatic development. *Child Develop.* 36, 899–911.

Jones, M. C. and Bayley, N. (1950). Physical maturing among boys as related to behaviour. *J. Educ. Psychol.* 41, 129–148.

Joslyn, W. D. (1973). Androgen-induced social dominance in infant femal rhesus monkeys. *J. Child Develop. Psychiat.* 14, 137–145.

Jost, A. (1972). A new look at the mechanisms controlling sex differentiations in mammals. *Johns Hopkins Med. J.* 130, 38–53.

Kagan, J. and Moss, H. A. (1962). *Birth to Maturity*. New York: Wiley.

Kallman, F. J. (1952). Comparative twin study on the genetic aspects of male homosexuality. *J. Nerv. Ment. Dis.* 115, 283–297.

Katcher, A. (1955). The discrimination of sex differences by young children. *J. Genet. Psychol.* 87, 131–143.

Kenyon, F. E. (1970). Homosexuality in the female. *Brit. J. Hosp. Med.* 3, 183–206.

Kinsey, A. C., Pomeroy, W. B. and Martin, C. E. (1948). *Sexual Behavior in the Human Male*. Philadelphia: Saunders.

Kinsey, A. C., Pomeroy, W. B., Martin, C. E. and Gebhardt, P. H. (1953). *Sexual Behavior in the Human Female*. Philadelphia: Saunders.

Kleeman, J. A. (1971). The establishment of core gender indentity in normal girls. I (a) introduction (b) development of the ego capacity to differentiate. *Arch. Sex. Behav.* 1, 103–116.

Koch, H. L. (1935). An analysis of certain forms of so-called 'nervous habits' in young children. *J. Genet. Psychol.* 46, 139–170.

Kohlberg, L. (1967). A cognitive-developmental analysis of children's sex-role concepts and attitudes. In E. E. Maccoby (Ed) *The Development of Sex Differences*. London: Tavistock, pp. 82–173.

Kraemer, H. C., Becker, H. B., Brodie, H. K. H., Doering, C. H., Moos, R. H. and Hamburg, D. A. (1976). Orgasmic frequency and plasma testosterone levels in normal human males. *Arch. Sex. Behav.* 5, 125–132.

Kreuz, L. E., Rose, R. M. and Jennings, J. R. (1972). Suppression of plasma testosterone levels and psychological stress: a longitudinal study of young men in officer candidate school. *Arch. Gen. Psychiat.* 26, 479–482.

Kuhn, D., Nash, S. C. and Brucken, L. (1978). Sex role concepts of two and three-year-olds. *Child Develop.* 49, 445–451.

Lebovitz, P. (1972). Feminine behaviour in boys: aspects of its outcome. *Amer. J. Psychiat.* 128, 1283–1289.

Levin, S. M., Balistrieri, J. and Schukit, M. (1972). The development of sexual discrimination in children. *J. Child Psychol. Psychiat.* 13, 47–53.

Lev-Ran, A. (1974). Gender role differentiation in hermaphrodites. *Arch. Sex. Behav.* 3, 391–424.

Levy, D. M. (1928). Fingersucking and accessory movements in early infancy: an ethologic study. *Amer. J. Psychiat.* 7, 881–918.

Levy, D. M. (1940). 'Control-situation' studies of children's responses to the difference in genitalia. *Amer. J. Orthopsychiat.* 10, 755–762.

Maccoby, E. E. and Jacklin, C. N. (1975). *The Psychology of Sex Differences*. London: Oxford Univ. Press.

Macfarlane, J. W. (1939). The relation of environmental pressures to the development of the child's personality and habit patterning. *J. Pediat.* **15**, 142–152.

Macfarlane, J. W., Allen, L. and Honzik, M. R. (1954). *A Developmental Study of the Behavior Problems of Normal Children Between 21 months and 14 years*. Berkeley: Univ. California Press.

McCandless, B. R. (1960). Rate of development, bodybuild and personality. In C. Shagass and B. Pasamanick (Eds) *Child Development and Child Psychiatry, Vol. 88*, 42–57. Washington, D.C.: American Psychiatrical Association.

Mächtlinger, V. J. (1976). Psychoanalytic theory: pre-oedipal phases, with special reference to the father. In M. E. Lamb (Ed) *The Role of the Father in Child Development*. New York: Wiley, pp. 277–305.

Malinowski, B. (1929). *The Sexual Life of Savages in North-Western Melanesia*. New York: Harcourt, Brace and Wold.

Marcus, D. E. and Overton, W. F. (1978). The development of cognitive gender constancy and sex role preferences. *Child Devel.* **49**, 434–444.

Masica, D. N., Money, J. and Ehrhardt, A. A. (1971). Fetal feminization and female gender identity in the testicular feminizing syndrome of androgen insensitivity. *Arch. Sex. Behav.* **1**, 131–142.

Masters, W. H. and Johnson, V. E. (1966). *Human Sexual Response*. London: Churchill.

Meyer-Bahlburg, H. F. L. (1977). Sex hormones and male homosexuality in comparative perspective. *Arch. Sex. Behav.* **6**, 297–325.

Mischel, W. (1970). Sex-typing and socialization. In P. H. Mussen (Ed) *Carmichael's Manual of Child Psychology*. New York: Wiley.

Money, J. (1955). Hermaphroditism, gender and precocity in hyperadrenocorticism: psychologic findings. *Bull. Johns Hopkins Hosp.* **96**, 253–264.

Money, J. (1961). Sex hormones and other variables in human eroticism. In W. C. Young and G. W. Corner (Eds) *Sex and Internal Secretions, 3rd Edition, Vol. II*. Baltimore: Williams and Wilkins.

Money, J. (1975). Ablatio penis: normal male infant sex-reassigned as a girl. *Arch. Sex. Behav.* **4**, 65–71.

Money, J. and Alexander, D. (1969). Psychosexual development and absence of homosexuality in males with precocious puberty. Review of 18 cases. *J. Nerv. Ment. Dis.* **148**, 111–123.

Money, J. and Ehrhardt, A. A. (1972). *Man and Woman; Boy and Girl: The differentiation and dimorphism of gender identity from conception to maturity*. Baltimore and London: Johns Hopkins Univ. Press.

Money, J., Ehrhardt, A. A. and Masica, D. N. (1968). Fetal feminization by androgen insensitivity in the testicular feminizing syndrome: effect on marriage and maternalism. *Johns Hopkins Med. J.* **123**, 160–167.

Money, J. and Ogunro, C. (1974). Behavioral sexology: ten cases of genetic male intersexuality with impaired prenatal and pubertal androgenization. *Arch. Sex. Behav.* **3**, 181–205.

Money, J. and Walker, P. A. (1971). Psychosexual development, maternalism, nonpromiscuity, and body image in 15 females with precocious puberty. *Arch. Sex. Behav.* **1**, 45–60.

Mussen, P. H. (1969). Early sex-role development. In D. A. Goslin (Ed) *Handbook of Socialization Theory and Research*. Chicago: Rand McNally.

Mussen, P. and Bouterline-Young, H. (1964). Relationships between rate of physical maturing and personality among boys of Italian descent. *Vita Humana* **7**, 186–200.

Mussen, P. H. and Jones, M. C. (1957). Self-conception motivations and interpersonal attitudes of late and early maturing boys. *Child Develop.* **28**, 243–256.

Mussen, P. H. and Jones, M. C. (1958). The behaviour motivations of late and early maturing boys. *Child Develop.* **29**, 61–67.

Newson, J. and Newson, E. (1963). *Patterns of Infant Care in an Urban Community*. London: Allen and Unwin.

Newson, J. and Newson, E. (1968). *Four Years Old in an Urban Community*. London: Allen and Unwin.

Pare, C. M. B. (1956). Homosexuality and chromosomal sex. *J. Psychosom. Res.* **1**, 247–251.

Parker, N. (1964). Homosexuality in twins: a report on three discordant pairs. *Brit. J. Psychiat.* **110**, 489–495.

Phoenix, C. H., Goy, R. W., Gerrell, A. A. and Young, W. C. (1959). Organizing action of prenatally administered testosterone propionate on the tissues mediating mating behavior in the female guinea pig. *Endocrinology* **65**, 369–382.

Prince, V. and Bentler, P. (1972). Survey of 504 cases of transvestism. *Psychol. Rep.* **31**, 903–917.

Pritchard, M. (1962). Homosexuality and genetic sex. *Mental Sci.* **108**, 616–627.

Rabbon, M. (1950). Sex-role identification in young children in two diverse social groups. *Genet. Psychol. Mon.* **42**, 81–158.

Raboch, J., Mellan, J. and Starka, L. (1977). Adult cryptorchids: sexual development and activity. *Arch. Sex. Behav.* **6**, 413–420.

Ramsey, C. V. (1943). The sexual development of boys. *A. J. Psychol.* **56**, 217–233.

Randell, J. (1973). *Sexual Variations*. London: Priory Press.

Reese, H. W. (1966). Attitudes toward the opposite sex in late childhood. *Merrill-Palmer Quart.* **12**, 157–163.

Reinberg, A. and Lagoguey, M. (1978). Circadian and circannual rhythms in sexual activity and plasma hormones (FSH, LH, Testosterone) of five human males. *Arch. Sex. Behav.* **7**, 13–30.

Reinisch, J. M. (1974). Fetal hormones, the brain, and human sex differences: a heuristic, integrative review of the recent literature. *Arch. Sex. Behav.* **3**, 51–90.

Reinisch, J. M. and Karow, W. G. (1977). Prenatal exposure to synthetic progestins and estrogens: effects on human development. *Arch. Sex. Behav.* **6**, 257–288.

Rekers, G. A., Amaro-Plotkin, H. D. and Low, B. P. (1977). Sex-typed mannerisms in normal boys and girls as a function of sex and age. *Child Develop.* **48**, 275–278.

Rose, R. M., Gordon, T. P. and Bernstein, I. S. (1972). Plasma testosterone levels in the male rhesus: influences of sexual and social stimuli. *Science* **178**, 643–645.

Rosen, A. C., Rekers, G. A. and Friar, L. C. (1977). Theoretical and diagnostic issues in child gender disturbances. *J. Sex. Res.* **13**, 89–103.

Rutter, M. (1970). Sex differences in children's responses to family stress. In E. J. Anthony and C. Koupernik (Eds) *The Child in His Family*. New York: Wiley Interscience.

Rutter, M. (1971). Normal Psychosexual Development. *J. Child Psychol. Psychiat.* **11**, 259–283.

Rutter, M. (1977). Individual Differences. In M. Rutter and L. Hersov (Eds) *Child Psychiatry: Modern Approaches*. Oxford: Blackwell.

Saghir, M. and Robins, E. (1973). *Male and Female Homosexuality*. Baltimore: Williams and Wilkins.

Schmidt, G. and Sigusch, V. (1972). Changes in sexual behaviour among young males and females between 1960 and 1970. *Arch. Sex. Behav.* **2**, 27–45.

Schofield, M. (1965). *The Sexual Behaviour of Young People*. London: Longmans.

Schofield, M. (1973). *The Sexual Behaviour of Young Adults*. London: Allen Lane.

Schoof-Tams, K., Schlaegel, H. and Walczak, L. (1976). Differentiation of sexual morality between 11 and 16 years. *Arch. Sex. Behav.* **5**, 353–370.

Sears, R. R., Maccoby, E. E. and Levin, H. (1957). *Patterns of Child Rearing*. New York: Harper and Row.

Shapiro, T. and Perry, R. (1976). Latency revisited: the age 7 plus or minus 1. *Psychoanal. Study of the Child* **31**, 79–106.

Sokolov, J. J., Harris, R. T. and Hecker, M. R. (1976). Isolation of substances from human vaginal secretions previously shown to be sex attachment pheromones in higher primates. *Arch. Sex. Behav.* **5**, 269–274.

Spitz, C. J., Gold, A. R. and Abrams, D. B. (1975). Cognitive and hormonal factors affecting coital frequency. *Arch. Sex. Behav.* **4**, 249–263.

Stoller, R. J. (1974). *Sex and Gender*. New York: Jason Aronson.

Tanner, J. M. (1962). *Growth at Adolescence*, 2nd Edn. Oxford: Blackwell.

Taylor, D. C. and Ounsted, C. (1972). The nature of gender differences explored through ontogenetic analyses of sex ratios in disease. In C. Ounsted and D. C. Taylor (Eds) *Gender Differences: Their Ontogeny and Significance*. Edinburgh and London: Churchill Livingstone, pp. 215–240.

Thompson, S. K. and Bentler, P. M. (1971). The priority of cues in sex discrimination by children and adults. *Develop. Psychol.* **5**, 181–185.

Thompson, S. K. and Bentler, P. M. (1973). A developmental study of gender constancy and parent preference. *Arch. Sex. Behav.* **2**, 379–385.

Vessey, M. P. (1972). Gender differences in the epidemiology of non-neurological disease. In C. Ounsted and D. C. Taylor (Eds) *Gender Differences: Their Ontogeny and Significance.* Edinburgh and London: Churchill Livingstone, pp. 203–214.

Wechsler, D. (1931). The incidence and significance of fingernail biting in children. *Psychoanal. Rev.* **18**, 201–209.

West, D. J. (1968). *Homosexuality,* 3rd Edn. London: Duckworth.

Whitam, F. L. (1977). Childhood indicators of male homosexuality. *Arch. Sex. Behav.* **6**, 89–96.

White, R. W. (1960). Competence and the psychosexual stages of development. *Nebraska Symposium on Motivation, Vol. 8,* pp. 97–141.

Yalom, I. D., Green, R. and Fisk, N. (1973). Prenatal exposure to female hormones: effect on psychosocial development in boys. *Arch. Gen. Psychiat.* **28**, 554–561.

Young, W. C., Goy, R. W. and Phoenix, C. H. (1964). Hormones and sexual behaviour. *Science* **143**, 212–218.

Zuger, B. (1966). Effeminate behavior present in boys from early childhood. I. The clinical syndrome and follow-up studies. *J. Pediatrics* **69**, 1098–1107.

27. MORAL DEVELOPMENT

PHILIP GRAHAM

The term 'moral' has been used in psychiatry in a much broader sense in the past than is the case now. Thus Prichard (1835) used the phrase 'moral insanity' to describe mental conditions in which delusions and hallucinations did not occur. This would include virtually all neuroses and most affective psychoses. Following Pinel in the early nineteenth century, Tuke developed 'moral treatment' or therapy which was characterized by gentle persuasion and explanation, encouragement to healthy occupation; with avoidance of restraint and organic methods. In accordance with common usage, the use of the word 'moral' in this chapter is limited to those areas of thought and conduct in which issues of right and wrong are concerned. Such areas may be characterized in four main ways. Firstly, they concern conformity to social standards of behaviour. Secondly, they relate to personal principles. While social norms and personal standards of morality overlap greatly for most individuals, they are far from synonymous for some people. Thirdly, the moral area covers those emotions (especially rectitude, guilt and shame) which are specific to feeling right or wrong. Other emotions, such as anxiety, may be related to situations in which moral behaviour is in question, but are not specific to them. Finally, moral behaviour is usually taken to refer to those pro-social activities such as helpfulness, generosity and altruism which are regarded as generally reflecting 'good', *i.e.* praiseworthy and unselfish motivation. It will be evident that apparent altruism is not always unselfish and this issue will be discussed further below. Nevertheless, this type of behaviour falls within our definition.

There is a problem in making a distinction between the socialization of a child, the means by which it is integrated into a social world, and its 'moralization'. Clearly, the attempt to establish moral principles and ensure some degree of social conformity cannot readily be separated from wider aspects of socialization. Yet those parts of upbringing which concern moral values form a substantial contribution to personality development and deserve separate treatment. In particular, there is a need to concentrate on that aspect of personality formation which eventually results in the internalized mental structure responsible for moral beliefs and behaviour known as 'conscience'. A concept such as conscience is necessary to explain how it comes about that individuals, even in the absence of reminders from other members of society, tend to conform to standards of right and wrong when to do so is against their immediate interests.

Explanations of conscience development have been attempted from three main theoretical standpoints—cognitive-developmental, psychoanalytic, and learning theories. Each of these has proved to have considerable explanatory power in one or more aspects of the subject. Yet each is also incapable of providing a satisfactory comprehensive account. In the present review a critical account will be given of the development of moral judgement from a cognitive-developmental point of view. This will be followed by a brief consideration of psychoanalytic and learning theory contributions. The measurement of various aspects of moral behaviour and factors affecting their occurrence will then be discussed. Subsequently, the relationship, often surprisingly tenuous, between moral judgement and moral behaviour will be considered, and finally there is a section on the relevance of social-psychological knowledge in the field of moral development to psychiatric disorders. For more comprehensive reviews the reader is referred to Maccoby (1968), Hoffman (1970) and Lickona (1976).

THEORIES OF MORAL DEVELOPMENT

Cognitive developmental theories of moral judgement

Contemporary study of this subject may be said to have begun with the publication of 'The Moral Judgement of the Child' by Jean Piaget in 1932. Piaget put forward a cognitive developmental theory in which he proposed that, as they matured, children passed through stages of moral thought in an invariant manner. By observing the way in which children played games alone and with each other, and by questioning them about the rules, he concluded that the concept of shared rules did not appear before the age of 7 or 8 years. Before this, the child's behaviour was egocentrically determined—he imitated others but played by himself. Round about the age of 7 years, somewhat vague rules appeared alongside the development of more cooperative play. Rules were regarded as having been provided by adults and as being sacred and untouchable. Later, round about the age of 11–12 years, rules were more clearly codified and at this stage were regarded as arising from the mutual consent of the players who could, if they wished, alter them.

Piaget supplemented his observations of children's games by administering stories to children and asking questions to elicit their concepts of moral responsibility. One series of stories tapped the concept of 'immanent justice'—the notion that wrong-doing inevitably brings with it some form of punishment. For example, he asked children whether a child who cut himself when sharpening a pencil with a knife he had been forbidden to use by his teacher would have suffered this accident if he had not been engaged in a forbidden activity. At 6 years, 86% of children revealed a belief in this form of 'immanent jus-

tice' (unavoidable retribution) whereas only 34% of 11–12-year-olds held this concept. The notion of a just punishment also altered with age. Younger children viewed just punishment purely as expiation for damage done without reference to the intention of the transgressor so that serious unintentional damage should be punished more severely than intentional trivial damage. Older children took the intention of the transgressor into account and tended to favour a punishment which was equitable.

Piaget concluded that at 7–8 years, the child's beliefs regarding the existence of rules were based on heteronomous forces (powers outside himself). At this age the child was at a stage of moral realism—moral rules had an existence independent of himself. Such a view occurred at a time when the child was subjected to adult constraint, and was in a position of 'unilateral respect'—the child respecting the adult view of morality without the reverse being true. As the child grew older cooperative play with peers replaced egocentric activity. Consequently, rules came to be seen as no longer dependent on adult enforcement and the child's own contribution to rule-making as part of a reciprocal relationship with others became apparent to him. Moral subjectivism replaced moral realism; heteronomy was substituted by autonomy.

These Piagetian formulations regarding the nature of the development of moral judgement have been built on by many others and particularly by Kohlberg (1963) who has used a modification of the original method of questioning children to tap moral attitudes in North American children and young adults. Kohlberg administered stories containing different types of moral dilemma and invited his subjects to comment on the considerations which in their view should govern the behaviour of the story characters. For example, one story described the plight of a man whose wife was dying. A local chemist possessed a life-saving drug but refused to sell it for an amount the man could afford. Should the man attempt to steal the drug? On the basis of his subjects' responses Kohlberg concluded that there were three levels of moral judgement which he labelled 'pre-moral', 'the morality of conventional rule-conformity' and the 'morality of self-accepted moral principles'. In the pre-moral stage, motivation was governed mainly by thoughts of reward and punishment. Motivation in the conventional stage was ruled by anxiety about the disapproval of others and a need to avoid censure by authority. The child espoused a 'good boy' morality as a means of maintaining good relationships with others and keeping on the right side of authority. In the post-conventional phase there was, by contrast, an implicit notion of a contract with others and a democratically accepted set of laws, and this was followed by a morality of self-determined individual principles of conscience which could transcend such laws. Here, motivation was determined by the need to maintain community respect and to avoid disrespect and self-condemnation.

The cognitive developmental theories of Piaget and Kohlberg have been subjected to criticism on a variety of grounds. It has been suggested, to some degree unjustly, that Piaget takes little account of the importance of social factors in the development of moral judgement (Bronfenbrenner, 1962). The influence of intelligence, of sex, and of social and cultural factors will be discussed below and in so far as the findings are positive, they are limiting to the notion of an inexorable developmental course in the growth of moral evaluation. As Lickona (1969) has pointed out, however, Piaget was well aware of the importance of such factors and indeed attempts to incorporate them into his explanatory system. Later formulations have attempted to integrate developmental progress and social influences into a single conceptual framework. Garbarino and Bronfenbrenner (1976) for example, propose a fusion of Bronfenbrenner's own descriptive theory based on analysis by types of predominant social influences (self-orientation, authority orientation, peer orientation, collective orientation, and objective orientation) with Kohlberg's stage analysis described above.

In so far as factors such as intelligence and social class can be seen merely to impede or accelerate rates of development, they do not threaten the essential nature of cognitive developmental theories which are more concerned with processes than with the ages at which particular levels are passed. There are, however, more fundamental criticisms. MacRae (1954) in factor-analysing data obtained from asking Piagetian-type questions, was unable to confirm the presence of a general factor corresponding to that originally described. Bandura and McDonald (1963) were able to show that subjects could be systematically trained to give moral judgement both higher and lower than those they spontaneously delivered. Durkin (1961) found that, when tested for reciprocity, children's responses varied according to the type of story involved—whether, for example, the story concerned a transgression involving taking property or refusing to share. The notion of reciprocity varied according to situation a great deal more than would have been predicted on the basis of the original theory. Havighurst and Neugarten (1955) found that in children reared in certain North American Indian tribes, the notion of immanent justice seemed to increase rather than decrease with age, and Kohlberg himself reports regressions rather than smooth progressions in maturity of moral judgements in longitudinal studies he has conducted (Kohlberg and Kramer, 1969).

Kohlberg has also been criticized on methodological grounds (Trainer, 1977) and for over-generalization from his findings (Trainer op. cit.: Peters, 1971). As these critics point out, the area of moral development with which Kohlberg deals is restricted to certain types of moral judgement and his theory can by no means be said to provide a comprehensive account. Further, it is at times difficult to know whether Kohlberg's approach is less descriptive than prescriptive—promoting the notion of a society organized to encourage so-called 'higher' or more mature levels of moral judgement.

It is therefore clear that, although Piagetian and Kohlberg's views represent the most comprehensive attempt yet made to provide a unitary theory of moral judgement, they are not adequate to account for the available phenomena.

Psychoanalytic theories

Where cognitive developmental theories put most emphasis on maturational processes occurring within the child, both psychoanalytic and learning theory approaches emphasize the influence of environmental factors. In contrast to other areas of child psychology, in the field of moral development learning theory and psychoanalysis do not stand in opposition to each other. Indeed, psychoanalytic formulations have provided a rich source of testable hypotheses for experimentalists with a learning-theory. Although some fundamental psychoanalytic assumptions, especially the concept of conscience, would not be accepted by learning theorists, the contributions to knowledge made by the two theories cannot be considered entirely separately. Both theories aim to provide an explanation for the way in which societal and, in particular, parental values and prohibitions are internalized so that the child eventually conforms to parental wishes regardless of whether his parents are there to ensure that he does so.

Freud's original formulation (1914) of the manner in which parental standards were incorporated into a child's mind, although later slightly modified, remained relatively unchanged throughout his life. He viewed the ego-ideal (later the super-ego) as a mental structure which was the outcome of repressed hostility towards a frustrating parent. In order to give meaning to the repression the child adopts parental rules and prohibitions. He internalizes the parental disposition to punish for transgressions, and this results in self-punishment with a feeling of guilt when he himself transgresses. Thus the super-ego is a mechanism for internalizing and identifying with parental standards and evoking guilt. The stronger the feeling of hostility towards the parent the more powerfully would the super-ego punish the self and the greater the guilt experienced. In Freud's original formulation, such hostility to a parent figure was most strongly felt in relation to the same-sexed parent who was seen as a rival for the love of the parent of opposite sex. Such hostility was experienced at 5–6 years which was therefore the most crucial age in conscience development.

Post-Freudian psychoanalysts have modified this formulation in various ways. Suttie (1963) for example, puts emphasis on the love-relationship between mother and child as the basis for identification rather than from the fear of punishment for prohibited impulses. Melanie Klein, whose views on moral development were summarized by Money-Kyrle (1955) and Sandler (1960), viewed conscience as arising in the first year of life as a result of the internalization of fantasy objects perceived by the child as good or bad. The child develops a caring response largely as a result of a need he feels for reparation for his destructive fantasies. Schafer (1960), like Suttie, elaborates on that aspect of the super-ego (barely mentioned by Freud), which involves internalization of the loved and loving aspects of the parent. The super-ego is thus seen by later analysts as a constructive force in the child's life.

Learning theories

From a psychoanalytic point of view, introjection of parental standards is the chief means of internalizing moral values. It can arise either as a means of avoiding anxiety due to the child's prohibited wishes or as a means of maintaining a love-relationship with the parent (Bronfenbrenner, 1960). Learning theorists such as Mowrer (1950), Aronfreed (1968), and Eysenck (1976) concentrate particularly on the positively and negatively reinforcing experiences which mould behaviour into a particular moral framework. Classical and operant conditioning models have both been invoked to describe the way in which behaviour that is socially acceptable comes to be incorporated into the child's repertoire. Thus, Mowrer (1950) suggests that proprioceptive stimuli became associated with responses that had been repeatedly reinforced. In this way proprioceptive stimuli acquired secondary reinforcing qualities, so that the individual became predisposed to behave in a particular way in order to achieve positive feedback. Aronfreed (1968) pointed to the relevance of the affective value of different social stimuli in order to help explain why certain behavioural predispositions became more readily internalized than others, while Eysenck (1976) has suggested that individual differences in moral behaviour may be attributed to genetically determined variation in cortical arousal levels producing variable rates of social conditioning.

In a theory more sophisticated but also more diffuse and therefore less amenable to testing, Hoffman (1975a, 1976) has proposed a process of moral development, which focuses especially on the development of helpfulness, generosity and altruism, and which has elements derived from cognitive-developmental, psychodynamic and learning theories. He suggests that the child has an innate set of cognitive and affective capacities which, in normal development, undergo characteristic changes and transformations. Thus, in the first few months of life, the child experiences empathic feelings consonant with those of the people around him and especially with his mother. His cognitive maturation allows him to achieve 'person permanence' so that he is capable, between 12 and 18 months, of recognizing the continuity of the physical existence of another person. Later he develops the capacity to role-take, i.e. to recognize that others have their own perspective. Although Piaget had suggested that children only develop this skill at 7–8 years, it is clear, both from anecdotal and more systematically gathered evidence (Murphy, 1937; Borke, 1975), that role-taking is achieved to a significant degree at a much younger age than this, certainly by the third year of life. By 1 year the child has become capable of sympathetic distress—the experience of a feeling of concern for the other person as distinct from the self, but his lack of role-taking capacity prevents him from taking active steps to terminate another's distress because he has no intelligent perception of the source of such distress until about 2–3 years of age. Later, between 6 and 9 years, the child develops a capacity to appreciate another person's general situation, rather than just his immediate distress. Subsequently, guilty feelings and thoughts are aroused by sympathetic distress. Although initially such guilt is aroused in relation to perceived distress, as the child moves into adolescence he becomes capable of existential guilt or emotions derived from a sense of personal responsibility for injustices and inequalities which exist in the world even though the individual has done nothing himself to produce them.

Hoffman (1976) suggests that even though this theory might lead one to the view that all altruistic behaviour is basically selfish and motivated by the desire to terminate one's own distress initiated by distress in another, this is an inappropriate view. Altruism can be seen as distinct from egotistic behaviour by virtue of the fact that it is initially stimulated by distress in another, stimulates behaviour designed to help the other rather than the self, and is only seen as successful if the distress of the other is reduced.

Hoffman has attempted to explain pro-social aspects of behaviour by drawing on elements of the three major theories of moral development. Aronfreed (1968) has undertaken a similar exercise in his consideration of the nature of conscience. He defines conscience in terms of those internalized multiple value systems which govern conduct. Much conduct does not require the existence of conscience for its explanation. Control of behaviour may occur, for example, in very young babies or in animals, without the necessity for the application of evaluation and the presence of internalized control. But the regularities which do exist (see below) between aspects of moral behaviour in different situations (Burton, 1963) and the enhancing effect of explanation in promoting moral behaviour (Staub, 1971a) suggest that any comprehensive theory of moral development must include provision of some form of internalized value system. This view is disputed by Bandura (1969) but most writers consider that such a system, although open to modification, and although exercising only imperfect control over conduct because of a host of other influences, is nevertheless necessary to explain behavioural and attitudinal consistencies.

Having discussed cognitive-developmental, psychoanalytic and learning and integrative theories of moral development we shall now go on to examine different aspects of the development of moral behaviour and emotions.

Moral behaviour, or behaviour to which moral standards can most readily be applied, can be subdivided into that which is pro-social in nature such as altruism, generosity and helpfulness, and that which involves transgression of moral standards. Shame and guilt are the emotions with most specific moral connotations although fear, anxiety and love are also emotions likely to be involved when moral values are in evidence.

THE MANIFESTATION AND MEASUREMENT OF MORAL BEHAVIOUR

Altruism, generosity and helpfulness

Generosity and helpfulness are self-explanatory terms and need no definition. Altruism, the other main manifestation of pro-social behaviour, can be said to occur where activity is undertaken which involves cost to one person (the donor) and some gain to another person (the recipient). Children can be observed to show such pro-social behaviour both in natural settings, especially at home and school, and in laboratory situations. Murphy (1937) made direct observations of children aged 28–47 months and noted the frequency of cooperative and helpful behaviour in a nursery school setting.

Other investigators, such as Severy and Davis (1971) and Barrett and Yarrow (1977) have also observed children in naturalistic settings. However, because of the regrettable infrequency with which pro-social behaviour occurs in most natural settings in Western society, artificial laboratory situations have been most used. Thus Staub (1970) sat children aged 5–10 years in a room and gave them a task to perform. He left them alone in pairs to carry out tasks informing them before he left that there was a child in the next room. A tape-recording of a child in distress was placed in the next room and the subjects were observed to determine whether they attempted to help by going to the inter-communicating door which was locked or whether they told the experimenter about what they had heard.

Other investigators (*e.g.* Rosenhan and White, 1967; Rosenhan *et al.*, 1974; Bryan and Walbeck, 1970) have allowed children to win tokens to exchange for sweets or candy and then provided them with varied opportunities to donate some or all of their tokens to charity.

Questionnaire measurements of pro-social behaviour has been developed to a surprisingly small extent. However, factor analysis of the Pittsburgh Adjustment Survey Scale (Ross *et al.*, 1965) which has been used for boys aged 6–12 years revealed a pro-social factor. Weir and Stevenson (1978) have also produced a reasonably reliable and valid questionnaire for assessing pro-social behaviour for use by teachers with 8-year-old children.

Transgression of moral standards

All forms of delinquency represent, by definition, transgression of moral standards defined by society although, at least in some cases, the standards involved are not accepted by the peer group or by other offenders. The transgressions associated with aggressive behaviour are discussed in Chapter 28. Here, discussion will be limited to transgression as it has been observed and measured in laboratory or experimental situations. The first large-scale enquiry of this type was conducted by Hartshorne and May (1928) who investigated the ways in which 11 000 children aged 8–16 years took opportunities to cheat, lie and steal in a variety of artificially induced situations including the class-room, athletics con-tests and party games. Cheating in academic tasks, lying in response to questionnaires, and the stealing of money and small articles were investigated. Since this pioneer investigation, other more modest studies have been mounted using a variety of ingenious techniques. One of the most commonly used is that devised by Grinder (1964) who employed a game involving a ray gun in which the 7–11-year-old subjects were given the opportunity to earn candy if they hit a target. Children were left to report their own scores and the situation was manipulated so that, unless they cheated, they would have little or no success. Aronfreed (1968) has described a series of experiments in which children aged 8–10 years were faced with an attractive and an unattractive toy having been instructed not to play with the attractive one. Their capacity to resist temptation was measured by assessing the number of times they touched or picked up the attractive toy. Similarly, Stein (1967) put children in a task situation and told them not to get up and observe a movie which was being shown just out of sight, while Kanfer and Duerfeldt (1968) asked 7–12-year-olds to guess a number 0–100 written down on a piece of paper in order to win candy. These children were given candy if successful and the number of candies earned was a quantitative assessment of the number of times they cheated. The findings of the studies employing these techniques are described in later sections.

Guilt and shame

Guilt has been viewed as 'a disagreeable emotional condition which directly follows transgression' (Wright, 1971). It is first obviously manifest around the age of 3 years, at which point a child may clearly refer to himself as 'naughty' and show appropriate signs of emotional change following a transgression. Melanie Klein puts the origins of guilty behaviour much earlier than this, in the first year of life, but this assumption is based on inferences difficult to confirm. Shame is an emotion closely linked to guilt by virtue of its occurrence after a real or imagined transgression. With shame, however, the emotional experience has to do with the visibility of the transgression to others. Anecdotal evidence suggests that shame, like guilt, can usually be first identified round about the age of 3 years.

The direct measurement of guilt and shame presents problems because, unlike anxiety, they are emotions often unaccompanied by easily recognizable or assessed physiological changes. Nor does it seem reasonable to think that in the future one might adequately measure these complex feelings by monitoring such parameters as heart rate, blood pressure or urinary metabolites. Measurement has therefore to be indirect and, inevitably, this is fraught with problems of inference.

The most commonly used measures have been story completion tests. The child is given a story about another child who has committed a transgression of some sort and is asked to complete it. Responses which focus on the external consequence to the child in terms of punishment are distinguished from those implying that the central character accepts responsibility and attempts to achieve reparation or reform himself. Although studies using such measures (*e.g.* Aronfreed, 1961; Hoffman and Saltzstein, 1967) do find correlations between this type of measurement of guilt and other variables, their validity (like that of all projective tests) must be closely questioned. It may well be that they are more closely linked to feelings for social desirability than to the probability that in real life the child experiences a certain frequency and intensity of guilt or shameful emotion. Self or parental report of confession have also been used as a measure of guilt (Sears, Maccoby and Levin, 1957; Hoffman and Saltzstein, 1967). Such measures may well be more valid as the person reporting is likely to have been accurate in judging the presence or absence of guilty feelings, but they have the usual methodological problems of retrospective recall.

FACTORS AFFECTING MORAL BEHAVIOUR

Age

There is probably an increase in helpful, generous and altruistic behaviour with age, at least up to the age of 8–9 years (Bryan and London, 1970), after which the frequency of such behaviour may well remain fairly constant. Preschool children are said to give rarely and to give little (Krebs, 1970), but subsequently a rise in frequency occurs. Ugurel-Semin (1952) found a steady rise in children ready to share nuts they were given from 4 years up to the age of 16 years, and Harris (1970) found that 11-year-old children donated more to charity than 10-year-olds. Staub (1970) found a curvilinear effect in a study of 5–10-year-olds attempting to help a child apparently in distress, older and younger children helping least. He attributed the initial rise with age in frequency of helping to a true developmental phenomenon with the subsequent decline caused by the older children feeling that they needed permission to help from an authority figure before they could do so.

Honesty and resistance to temptation do not appear to alter in any significant way with age. Hartshorne and May (1928) found a slight tendency for older children to cheat more than younger, but this was found to be related to their capacity to work (and therefore cheat) faster, and when this was controlled for, the age effect disappeared. However, later reports from this study (Hartshorne *et al.*, 1930) did tend to show somewhat greater consistency with age across tests of honesty or cheating behaviour, the younger children being more variable in their responses. Slight positive correlations of honesty with age have also been found by Grinder (1964) and Kanfer and Duerfeldt (1968). These positive findings have been attributed by Burton (1976) to age-related correlates such as awareness of risk, capacity to achieve without cheating and greater awareness of moral expectations. Evidence on age trends in guilt and shame are lacking.

Sex

Although on most measures involving aspects of socialization girls appear to have the advantage over boys, this does not appear to be the case with altruistic behaviour. Murphy (1937) and Hartup and Keller (1960) found no sex differences in nursery school children in helpful behaviour and cooperativeness, and Ugurel-Semin (1952) similarly found no differences in older children. When sex differences are found however, as in Hartshorne and May's (1928) study of helpfulness and service, and Moore *et al.*'s (1973) study of donating behaviour in 7–8-year-old children, girls tend to show higher levels of altruism. The reason for the small or absent sex differences in this area may lie in the fact that much helpfulness requires an assertive attitude or approach in order to be successful. Barrett and Yarrow (1977) showed that in 5–8-year-olds, assertiveness was related to prosocial behaviour when the capacity to take another person's point of view was controlled for. Girls may, therefore, have greater inclinations to helpfulness but in fact help no more than boys because they are generally less assertive and outgoing.

Similarly, there is no convincing evidence for consistent overall differences between boys and girls in honesty and resistance to temptation. Hartshorne and May (1928) found no clear differences over a wide age range and others (*e.g.* Walsh, 1967; Burton *et al.*, 1961) have found similar results. Where sex differences have been found (*e.g.* Medinnus, 1966), girls tend to show greater honesty but the differences tend to be small and barely reach levels of statistical significance. One problem in interpreting these negative findings is the difficulty in knowing whether the motivation of the two sexes can be regarded as equivalent. Clearly, girls may be less likely to be interested in achieving high scores in a task involving the use of a ray gun and boys less likely to want to achieve success in pencil and paper tasks. If level of temptation varies by sex, according to the nature of the task in question, it is not so surprising that resistance to temptation is found to be inconsistently related to sex.

There is also a tendency for girls to show more guilty responses than boys both in story completion tasks and in their tendency to confess to misdemeanours (Rebelsky *et al.*, 1963; Sears *et al.*, 1957). It is unclear whether the greater tendency for girls to show guilt is produced by greater intropunitiveness or by a more highly developed tendency for closer social relationships. Confessional behaviour tends to be socially binding and to be accompanied by feelings of dependency both of which might result in girls being more likely to experience guilt. However, the fact that girls also show a greater tendency to produce self-punitive responses in story completion tests does suggest that their more highly developed general tendencies to socialize do not provide sufficient explanation.

Intelligence

Rather more consistent findings have been obtained relating intelligence to measures of altruism and honesty, although its relationship to guilt remains uncertain. Murphy (1937) found sympathy to be related positively to intelligence in preschool children and the Hartshorne and

May (1928) studies also found duller children to be less helpful. Kanfer and Duerfeldt (1968) found a relationship between low achievement in class and tendency to dishonesty in test situations, and Hartshorne and May (1928) found a similar relationship in their earlier studies.

In view of the fact that, especially after 10 or 11 years, age is less consistently related to altruism and honesty than intelligence and educational achievement, it seems likely that intellectual dullness and educational backwardness are not linked to dishonesty and selfishness as a purely developmental phenomenon. It is more probable that the effect is mediated at least partly by the level of self-esteem which achieving youngsters feel—high self-esteem being related to helpfulness and resistance to temptation (Eisen, 1972). It may also be that, as far as cheating is concerned, low achievers have more commonly developed habitual responses which are only identified when systematic investigations are carried out.

Social class

Kohn (1959) has suggested that working-class parents are more concerned than middle-class parents with the immediate consequences of their children's behaviour than with enhancing their general moral development; Bronfenbrenner (1962) has also pointed to the probable importance of social class in moral cognitive development. Nevertheless there is little consistent evidence that low socio-economic status affects moral behaviour adversely. Ugurel-Semin (1952) found poor children more generous than those coming from rich families, and Berkowitz and Friedman (1967) found that, compared with the middle class, working-class boys were more affected in their generosity by feelings of reciprocity towards others who had helped them. In tests of honesty (resistance to temptation and guilt) there is a tendency (as seen for example in the Hartshorne and May investigations), for social status to be negatively linked to measures of honesty. One possible mechanism is provided by Pearlin et al.'s (1967) finding that children's cheating was most common when there was the greatest disparity between parental aspirations and current income. This was naturally most likely to occur in working-class highly aspirant parents whose children were more likely to cheat than those of either middle-class or non-aspirant working-class parents.

Family influences

It is generally assumed that home influences exert a considerable effect on moral development; the type and quality of family relationships and parental disciplinary practices have been most emphasized.

(a) Relationships

Early parent–child relationships involved in attachment and bonding processes (*see* Chapter 22) result in the formation or otherwise of trusting and affectionate relationships between parents and children. Longitudinal studies examining the relationship between types of early bonding and later moral development have not yet been carried out, but there are a number of studies suggesting that these early processes are of aetiological importance. Thus, Stayton et al. (1971) examined the interaction between 25 white middle-class infants aged 9–12 months and found that a simple disposition to comply with maternal command and prohibitions was most closely related to maternal sensitivity to the infant's signals and was independent of efforts to train or discipline. Further evidence for the importance of maternal sensitivity and related characteristics comes from the work of Baumrind (1967) who, in a direct observational study of 3- and 4-year-olds, found children high on self-reliance and self-control to have parents who were firm, loving, demanding and understanding, whereas those children low on self-control and self-reliance had parents who lacked control and were only moderately loving. Others (*e.g.* Hoffman, 1975b) have found pro-social factors in 11-year-old children to be related positively to affection from mothers (in boys) as well as strong altruistic value systems in both parents (in girls). Mussen et al. (1970), examining 12-year-old children, found resistance to temptation in the ray gun game to be related to high levels of maternal warmth, affection, nurturance and respect in girls, but not in boys in whom these positive environmental influences were more closely associated with levels of altruistic behaviour. This finding suggested that high levels of warmth were likely to result in child behaviour most consistent with its own sex role. These effects of parental warmth and sensitivity, however, have not been found consistently. Other studies (*e.g.* Sears, Rau and Alpert, 1965; Burton, Maccoby and Allinsmith, 1961) have failed to find any clear-cut relationship between parental attitudinal measures and honesty in test situations. It seems, nevertheless, that high levels of warmth and affection have generally, but not consistently, positive affects throughout childhood on most aspects of moral development, even though the processes involved may vary from age to age and between the sexes. The importance of child behaviour in eliciting positive parental attitudes and behaviour (Bell, 1968) is doubtless also of importance and is discussed in more detail below.

(b) Child-rearing practices

In considering moral development, most attention has been given to the disciplinary techniques of withdrawal of love, assertion of power, and the use of induction or explanation. Power assertion relies on the child's fear of punishment by concentrating on physical methods or on deprivation of material possessions or privileges such as watching television. Withdrawal of love involves techniques such as ignoring the child, refusing or rejecting approaches for affection, and appearing cold and indifferent. Induction means explanation of the consequences of transgression and may take a variety of forms. Two frequent modes of explanation are: (a) those which concern the consequences of transgressions to other people, children and adults, and (b) those which appeal to the child's self-esteem. The latter may, for example, involve telling him that different behaviour is expected of children of his age, and that when he is older he will be expected to behave in a different way. It is also possible to examine the effects of parental consistency, looking to see, for example, whether a child disciplined for a transgression at one point in time is treated similarly for a similar transgression at another. The consistency with which the same method of discipline is used may also be examined, although such studies appear to be rare.

Hoffman (1970) has reviewed 17 studies examining the relationship between various indices of moral development and the disciplinary practices of mothers and fathers. The findings were not entirely consistent. However, in general, power assertion tended to be negatively associated with child morality. Withdrawal of love, and especially the use of induction, tended to be positively associated with various measures of morality including 'internal orientation', guilt intensity, resistance to temptation and confession and acceptance of blame. Positive effects were found over a wide range of ages from 4–20 years and in both sexes. Hoffman and Saltzstein (1967), for example, examined 444 13-year-old children on a variety of measures of child morality including teacher's judgement of overt reaction to transgression and guilt as well as story completion tests. Parental disciplinary techniques were assessed following interviews with both parents and child. Power assertion by the mother was negatively associated with many measures of morality, while positive relationships were found with her use of induction. By contrast, the disciplinary techniques used by fathers appeared to show no consistent relationship with morality levels. Later, Hoffman (1975b) reported on a similar study of 80 11-year-old children in which various measures of altruism were used to compare different types of induction with regard to the consequences of transgression for the victim. In girls, altruism appeared to be related to the use of victim-centred techniques by fathers, and in boys to the use of such techniques by mothers. However, the positive correlations found were rather low and of doubtful practical significance.

Despite the large number of studies which have been carried out in this area, it is difficult to draw any clear-cut conclusions. The measures of parental discipline were usually gained from interviews rather than by direct observation and their validity is in question. In those few studies where direct observations had been carried out the consistency of observations were often not examined and this aspect of reliability remains uncertain. The measures of morality level used such as story completion items and peer evaluations of honesty and helpfulness were also usually poorly validated. Despite these strictures, the methodological problems in this area do not seem insurmountable. There is a need for more naturalistic studies of interaction between parents and children involving the use of disciplinary techniques in the home. Most parents use a range of methods of discipline and there is a need to examine differences, for example, in the transgressions which elicit different modes of discipline within the same family.

Biological factors

Darwin (1871) was the first to suggest that, because social behaviour enhanced the probability of survival, sociability in animals was likely to have evolutionary advantages. This line of thought has its modern-day descendants in the writings of those biologists (summarized by Wilson, 1975) who point to altruistic behaviour as improving overall gene survival. Trivers (1971) has extended the work further by calculating the likelihood of altruism in terms of the closeness of genetic relationship between potential donor and potential recipient.

Eysenck (1976) has proposed a biological theory to explain individual differences in moral development. He suggests that there is a strong relationship between moral behaviour and cortical arousal, and that when arousal is low, impulsive sensation-seeking behaviour may be expected. Indicators of cortical arousal states may be provided by questionnaire measures of extraversion/introversion; extraverts are said to condition more slowly and to be less likely to conform to socialization procedures. Because of the low correlations between conditionability and criminal behaviour, it seems unlikely that conditionability *per se* is responsible for much of the variability in this aspect of social behaviour but other inherited characteristics may nevertheless be of importance. Thus, Scarr (1965) found greater concordance for sociability within identical than within non-identical pairs.

Modelling and imitation

The process (as conceptualized in psychoanalytic theory) whereby external values and behaviour are converted into a mental representation (introjection) with subsequent borrowing of the identity of those other people (secondary identification) on a permanent basis, is known as 'internalization' (Rycroft, 1968). Such a process is likely to produce a long-lasting disposition to believe or behave in a particular way. More temporary influences of the behaviour of one person upon another are considered less important in psychoanalytic theory but form a central part of learning theory in which they are referred to as modelling or imitation.

Modelling has been shown to be effective in altering a wide range of moral beliefs and behaviour. Bandura and McDonald (1963) showed its effectiveness in enhancing levels of moral judgement in 5–11-year-olds tested before and after exposure to Piaget-type stories. Prentice (1972) demonstrated that such training in moral judgement was as effective when techniques involving symbolic modelling (reading stories to the child) were used as when live modelling was employed.

A range of attributes demonstrated by the model, such as the amount of caring behaviour shown, are also important. For example, although Grusec (1971) suggests that subjects exposed to models low in nurturance or caring behaviour tended to show more generosity than those exposed to high-nurturant models, most studies (*e.g.* Rosenhan and White, 1967; Yarrow *et al.*, 1973) suggest that nurturant models are more effective in producing sharing and sympathy. Non-continuous nurturance may be more effective in producing resistance to temptation than continuous nurturance (Parke, 1967).

The vicarious effects on an observer's subsequent behaviour of seeing a model punished and rewarded were first demonstrated by Bandura *et al.* (1963) with filmed aggression. Models which were rewarded or punished inconsistently had an intermediate effect; their influence was less than those of rewarded models but more than those of punished models (Rosekrans and Hartup, 1967). Models, however, tend to be imitated whether they are rewarded or not and the mere fact that they are carrying out activity seen to be intrinsically rewarding is sufficient for them to be imitated (Bryan and London, 1970). Both Stein (1967) and Rosenkoetter (1973) have shown that, as far as resistance to temptation is concerned, models which give way to temptation by cheating in order to achieve reward have a more powerful influence on observers than those resisting temptation.

Other attributes of the model which have been shown to be of importance include the mode of persuasion employed. Bryan and Walbeck (1970) demonstrated that the charitable outcome of a videotaped adult model practising generosity was more effective than the same model preaching generosity in producing charitable behaviour in 7–9-year-old girls. Finally, although it is likely that modelling is more effective when accompanied by other modes of behavioural alteration, Poulos and Liebert (1972), found that charitable behaviour was not enhanced when modelling was linked with verbalization and surveillance.

The tendency of a child to imitate a model must be seen to be influenced by a wide range of factors within the child, within the model, and in the relationship between the two. Some workers (*e.g.* Bandura, 1968) suggest that the phenomenon of generalized imitation has such comprehensive explanatory power as to make an additional concept of 'identification' unnecessary. The concept of identification has remained helpful to others who see it as important to emphasize that the parental figures do exert a singularly powerful influence on his subsequent behaviour; 'imitation' seems a poor word to describe a process by which a child behaves as his father would do even though he has never seen his father in the situation in question. The argument appears a rather sterile one, for surely the primary task is to identify both those factors that influence behaviour which is imitative in content or style and the processes which govern such influences. In this connection, Bronfenbrenner (1960) has usefully discussed the different ways in which the term 'identification' is employed.

Personality characteristics

In so far as temperamental characteristics affect the strength and nature of parent–child relationships (*see* Chapter 9) which are in themselves important in all aspects of moral development, it is likely that such characteristics exert an important indirect effect on the area of behaviour under discussion. However, a number of studies have examined the more direct influence of personality. Thus, self-esteem measured by questionnaire has been shown to be positively related to resistance to temptation in boys (Eisen, 1972) but not in girls, while the opposite sex effect was found in a similar study by Mussen *et al.* (1970). The sex differences may have been due to the fact that resistance to temptation was assessed in a group situation in the first study, and in an individual situation in the second study.

It has already been suggested that assertiveness may play an important part in determining whether generous behaviour occurs or not and Barrett and Yarrow (1977) found this to be the case in their direct observational study of helpful and comforting behaviour in 5–8-year-olds. This seemed to occur especially when the child had a strong inferential capacity to take another person's point of view.

A child's ability to concentrate on the task in hand might also be expected to relate to some aspects of moral development because of the well-recognized deficits in attention and concentration occurring in delinquents. Grim *et al.* (1968) have shown a positive relationship between a child's attentional capacity as assessed by his reaction time to a discrimination test on both experimental and teacher ratings of resistance to temptation. In a related area, Walsh (1969) also showed a small but significant relationship between teacher ratings of self-control and an experimental situation in which a child was told not to touch some attractive toys.

Finally, in this connection it has been suggested that different personality characteristics relate to different aspects of moral behaviour. Schwartz *et al.* (1969) examined the differential effect of two types of personality attributes which they labelled 'Need for Achievement' and 'Need for Affiliation' both of which were assessed by questionnaire measures. They showed that undergraduate students high in need for achievement were low in helpfulness while those high in need for affiliation were more helpful. By contrast, low need for achievement was related to a high rate of cheating in an experimental situation whereas need for affiliation was unrelated to cheating. They concluded that it is not justifiable to generalize regarding the importance of personality characteristics across the moral domain.

Situational factors

The most obviously relevant situational elements likely to be important in moral behaviour are those concerning rewards and punishments. Clearly, resistance to temptation is likely to be reduced and generous helpful behaviour enhanced by the strength of available rewards. Various factors may influence the effectiveness of rewards; Mischel *et al.* (1972), for example, have demonstrated how distracting a child from an immediately available reward, in a way which is interesting to him, may result in a considerable capacity to delay gratification.

The influence of punishment on moral behaviour has been examined especially in relation to resistance to temptation. Intensity of punishment appears to be one of the most important determinants of outcome but a variety of other factors may mitigate or alter its effect. The timing of punishment is relevant. Aronfreed and Reber (1965) and Cheyne (1971) found that punishment administered before a child engages in a forbidden activity is more likely to be effective than if it is administered after he has found pleasure in the activity. Cheyne and Walters (1969), however, showed that if the punishment was carefully paired with a consummatory response, then it was effective even if of low intensity. The type of punishment is relevant and Cheyne (1971) found verbal admonition more effective than a physical punishment in producing resistance to temptation. The consistency of reward and punishment has been examined by a number of workers and many, including Deur and Parke (1970), have found that aggression is least likely to extinguish when it is dealt with by intermittent reward and punishment.

The affective state of the child has been found to influence the likelihood of charitable, generous behaviour and Rosenhan et al. (1974), Moore et al. (1973), Isen et al. (1973) and Mischel et al. (1972) have all found positive affect to produce more helpfulness. In most of these studies, affect has been experimentally manipulated by asking the child to think of something likely to elevate his mood and then measuring his generosity, but clearly it is probable that mood-changes occurring naturally will exert similar effects.

Other workers have considered the importance of self-monitoring and self-control in determining the likelihood especially of resistance to temptation. Bandura and Perloff (1967) showed that 7–10-year-olds worked as hard for rewards they set themselves as they did for externally-regulated reinforcers, and Monahan and O'Leary (1971) showed in younger children that boys encouraged to self-instruct appropriately broke fewer rules than those not given this injunction. On the same lines, Staub (1969) in his two-room experiment described above also showed that children given explicit responsibility for their actions were more likely to give or offer help than those not so instructed.

Staub (1971a and b) has also shown that the labelling of behaviour as permitted or not permitted will subsequently influence helpful behaviour and this situational variable may well have been responsible for the finding of Kanfer and Duerfelt (1968) that children cheated less when they had to write down their results than when they merely said them out loud.

Finally, a situational variable of considerable pertinence which must be mentioned is the presence of peers or adults and the child's perception of the likely effect of his behaviour on other people's attitudes to himself. In adults, Milgram (1963) has shown how a person can contravene his own moral standards to a horrifying degree in deference to an authority figure. Although comparable work has not been carried out with children, other research suggests that children respond to cues concerning behaviours regarded as desirable by adults. It is worth noting that in different cultures the relative importance of peers and adults may vary. Thus, Bronfenbrenner (1970) has demonstrated broad cultural differences in Soviet boarding and day schools in their adult or peer-orientation in relation to cheating; boarders being more adult-orientated than day boys. He suggested that American children were more likely to be similar to day pupils in their strong peer-orientation in this respect. The work of Shelton and Hill (1969) suggests too that if children think their peers are doing better than they are, their tendency to resist temptation to cheat is reduced.

Relationship between moral judgement and behaviour

It might be thought that the level of a child's moral judgement in terms of the stage of pre-moral, conventional, or post-conventional thinking reached, would be a good predictor of moral transgression and of altruism. In fact, this is not the case. Grinder (1964) used the ray gun technique to assess resistance to temptation in 7–13-year-old children and found no correlation between this measure and level of moral judgement as measured from the children's responses to Piagetian stories eliciting concepts of moral realism and immanent justice. His conclusion was that 'behavioural and cognitive characteristics of the mature conscience, especially in boys, may develop independently of one another'. Similarly, Medinnus (1966) found no relationship between cheating on the ray gun test and measures categorizing children as dominated by internal or external controls. Mischel and Mischel (1976) report a low relationship between what children say is the right decision when asked what is the right thing to do (in choosing a rather unattractive toy now, or waiting for a better one later) and what they actually do when faced with this choice. Some workers have found positive correlations between belief and behaviour but these have never been high. Mischel (1968) found an average correlation of about 0·3 over a variety of measures of personality. An isolated positive finding is that of Henshel (1971) who, assessing attitudes to honesty in a questionnaire, found these related quite strongly to cheating in a spelling test (0·78) in 13-year-olds although in younger children the correlations dwindled virtually to zero.

The reasons for the generally low correlations found are probably multiple. The fact that measures of moral judgement correlate poorly with each other, and that a similar situation exists in relation to dishonesty and altruism is one factor. A further reason for the generally low correlation between moral judgement and behaviour may lie not just in the methodological inadequacies of the tests designed to measure these, but in their unsatisfactory nature in a more general sense. The elements that make up a man or woman of high principle are surely unlikely to be closely related to a capacity to achieve a high or 'mature' score in a test of moral judgement more suited to an examination in an undergraduate course in ethics or moral philosophy. The likelihood of a child conforming to social standards in his tendency to cheat or to show helpful behaviour is likely to be linked only tenuously to highly specific laboratory situations in which the child is engaged in a game to win trivial rewards, by an experimenter who is a relative stranger and who leaves him alone with or without some cursory explanation. All the same, the available evidence suggests that, given the best available measures of moral judgement and behaviour, the two are poorly correlated.

This conclusion also raises the question of the relative importance of dispositional tendencies and situational effects. Mischel and Mischel (1976) argue that situational factors are of such considerable importance in the motivation of individuals that their influence may be overriding. Such situational factors may gain their importance, or lack of it, from the subject's previous experience of gratification. When dispositional factors do exist, they may relate to different aspects of moral behaviour (see, for example, the work of Schwartz et al. (1969) already quoted).

In summary, it is not possible to generalize very broadly from belief and level of moral judgement to behaviour, although some dispositional characteristics can be identified which are definite, albeit rather weak, predictors of specific moral behaviour.

Relationship between different aspects of moral behaviour

If there is only a poor correlation between levels of moral judgement and behaviour, is the association between different aspects of moral activity any stronger? For example, do children who cheat in one situation tend to cheat in another? Is there a link between different manifestations of pro-social behaviour or between pro-social behaviour and the experience of the so-called 'moral emotions'? From the standpoint of both psycho-analytic and Piagetian theories it may be inferred that these different aspects of behaviour reflect a unitary process, whereas from a learning theory viewpoint it might be expected that situational contingencies would have a more important effect.

In fact, empirical work suggests that manifestations of the same type of moral behaviour are not strongly correlated with each other, and the different types of moral behaviour are even more loosely connected. Hartshorne and May (1928) found low correlation between measures of honesty and, although Burton's (1963) re-analysis of their data revealed a greater level of consistency than had been originally claimed, the amount of variance explained by a general 'honesty' factor remained relatively low. The associations found in other studies between different measures of resistance to temptation in younger children have been positive but also low (e.g. Sears et al., 1965). Resistance to temptation is poorly or even negatively related to measures of guilt (Burton et al., 1961).

It might reasonably be predicted that there would be strong negative associations between pro-social and anti-social behaviour, and this turns out to be the case. Fesh-bach (1975), for example, quotes unpublished studies showing negative correlations between aggression, and generosity and sympathy, and Weir and Stevenson (1978) obtained similar results.

It may be concluded that while different aspects of the same type of moral behaviour correlate poorly with each other and are, indeed, likely to be largely situationally determined, there is a broad tendency for pro-social behaviour to be negatively correlated with anti-social behaviour. Practical implications of this finding with consideration of the possibility of reducing anti-social behaviour by promoting pro-social activity are discussed below.

RELEVANCE OF MORAL DEVELOPMENT TO PSYCHIATRIC DISORDERS

Anti-social behaviour

Delinquency per se cannot be regarded as a manifestation of a deviation in moral development, as sometimes breaking the law may be governed by high moral principles. Thus, stealing to provide food for a starving friend when no other means of obtaining food is possible might involve a greater degree of altruism and pro-social behaviour than remaining within the law. However, most delinquency does not fall into this category

(a) The situation-specific nature of moral behaviour. Although much has been written about the so-called delinquent personality and the influences on its formation the importance of situational factors in determining anti-social behaviour has been striking. Hartshorne and May's (1928) demonstration of the variability of honesty, cheating and helpfulness from situation to situation has been confirmed in several more recent studies. Environmental contingencies involve both (a) the presence of a model or person to imitate and (b) aspects of a situation which enhance or reduce motivation (such as the rewards tempting transgression, the degree of risk of detection involved, and the likelihood and strength of subsequent punishment).

(b) Next, specific factors in child personality development. The development of empathy and sympathy in early attachments are important factors fostering moral development (Stayton et al., 1971). It is likely that law-abiding behaviour is enhanced by continuous contact with a limited number of adult figures who are sensitive to the individual signals emitted by the child. The parent's capacity to see the world from the child's point of view is likely also to enhance the child's ability to take the perspectives of other people. When these child-rearing conditions are not met, the child may lack sympathy, empathy and guilt responses and be more likely to transgress. In extreme cases, early deprivation of these necessary conditions may result in a virtual absence of moral sense and the disorder sometimes termed 'psychopathy' may arise.

The conditions for satisfactory normal moral development cannot be distinguished clearly from those necessary for other aspects of social development. However, specific attempts have been made to affect certain aspects of moral judgement and behaviour with the aim of reducing delinquent outcome. Thus, Prentice (1972) succeeded in raising the level of certain aspects of moral judgement in a group of 36 13-year-old delinquent boys by procedures involving live and symbolic modelling. The subjects' responses to stories involving moral dilemmas revealed a more mature level of moral judgement after training. However, although the group which received ineffective training showed no change in level of moral judgement, it did not do any worse in terms of delinquency outcome during the nine months follow-up period. Chandler (1973) achieved a more successful result by concentrating on training for improvement in role-perspective and ego-centrism. He first demonstrated that 11–13-year-old delinquents were deficient in this respect, compared with non-delinquents. He then established that delinquents taught by engaging in film-making to see the world from the point of view of another person were less likely to commit delinquent acts subsequently than those not so-treated. This work needs replication.

Moral emotions and psychiatric disorders

Guilt and shame are both emotions elicited by feelings of moral transgression, the former by virtue of the subjective failure to live up to one's own standards, and the latter by concern over the visible nature to others of one's moral failings. In so far as these occur in disorders of emotional life, the developmental factors leading to their occurrence must be relevant to an understanding of etiology.

Although little investigated or discussed, except in lay terms, one aspect of this subject of obvious relevance is the degree of guilt and shame associated with the expression of other emotions. In some societies, and in some families, the expression of grief after a serious loss is regarded as a matter of moral failure, whereas in others the importance of 'grief work' involving the expression of emotion as a necessary preliminary to reconciliation and reintegration following the loss is acknowledged. Children reared in families or societies in which the expression of emotion is strongly discouraged, may be at a disadvantage in subsequent life. Anxiety, especially situation-specific anxiety, is also regarded as a cause for shame in some settings. It may be that inability to communicate anxiety, because of social or cultural factors, results in an incapacity to take steps to overcome the problem. The individual himself may withdraw completely and, for example, fail to go out at all because of shame in admitting a fear of travelling. Others may then be inhibited from helping because of their ignorance of the true reasons for the subject's social withdrawal.

The irrational occurrence of guilt and shame in psychiatric disorders, particularly in reactive or neurotic depression, can also be considered in relation to normal moral development. The association between depression and guilt is by no means invariable, but children and adults under stress (especially that involving loss) often feel irrational guilt for the event's occurrence as well as experiencing sadness, misery or clinical depression. Although such feelings are usually explained in psychodynamic terms, with reference to the turning

inwards of aggression felt towards an external object or person, this explanation seems improbable in a number of cases. In the young child, irrational self-blame may be explained by the child's egocentricity and a tendency to ascribe responsibility for everything that happens in his environment to his own actions. As the child gets older, however, cognitive immaturity of this type no longer provides an adequate explanation. Here it may be helpful to invoke an explanation using Hoffman's model of moral development (1976) summarized above.

According to Hoffman, the child normally moves from a stage in which he experiences empathic distress for another to a stage in which sympathetic distress or true concern for another person is felt. Sympathetic distress can only take place in the context of emotional separation between the sufferer and the person sympathizing. It may be that when early relationships between mothers and children do not allow the establishment of separate identities (either because of the mother's inability to treat the child as a separate person or because the child is anxiously over-attached to his mother) the child is prevented from developing normal sympathetic distress. In this situation the individual may come to attach blame to himself and feel guilt and depression regardless of where the real cause of the external stressful event may lie.

Pathological helpfulness

It has been suggested in this chapter that helpfulness and generosity usually arise as a result of normal mechanisms which, although they may initially depend on the satisfaction of selfish motives, later come to reflect true concern for the other with distinctly less regard for the self. The view of social, as distinct from selfish, behaviour as a reflection of activity carrying evolutionary advantage was first put forward by Darwin (1871); more recently biologists such as Trivers (1971) and Wilson (1975) have produced evidence for altruism between genetically related individuals as a process enhancing gene survival.

Yet pro-social behaviour is, to common observation, not always motivated selflessly and in some instances true concern for the other appears as a subsidiary or absent factor.

It is possible to distinguish false from true altruism by the former's more mechanical quality, the absence of real concern for the other in what may superficially appear to be altruistic behaviour and the inner sense of compulsion experienced by the donor. Such compulsive helpfulness is seen particularly in a variety of types of pathological personality development, but characteristically is evident in many patients with anorexia nervosa. The typical sufferer from this condition is described by Sim (1969) and Ushakov (1971) as a girl with high moral standards who devotes herself to the service of others, and who is self-sacrificing and perfectionist. During the illness itself, these personality traits are often accentuated and focused around food and the need to ensure that others eat abundantly, but the general tendency towards compulsive helpfulness is present in the pre-existing personality. Bruch (1974) has suggested that this type of personality arises during development as a result of the child's incapacity to develop autonomy from its parents. The child does not develop a secure sense of its own identity and acts for others, not because it has any true concern, but because this is the behaviour expected of it. Such children experience themselves as acting only in answer to demands from other people, and their obedience is correspondingly robot-like. Although, doubtless, this personality development is partly constitutionally determined, the evidence suggests that it is mainly produced by (a) the consistent use of highly effective disciplinary techniques; (b) the absence of an affectionate relationship with the parents; (c) a lack of parental sensitivity to the child's own needs, and (d) a failure to encourage the expression of those needs. At the present time this suggestion is speculative, but clinical impressions support the view that this process may be important in some individuals with anorexia nervosa.

The above discussion by no means exhausts the possibilities of exploring the interface between moral development and psychiatric disorder. Links, for example, are often suggested between the moral prohibitions put on the manifestations of aggression and the later development of childhood obsessional disorders (Adams, 1973). Further, the whole question of the development of a sense of personal responsibility which is so relevant to the ethics of psychiatric intervention generally, is one in which information derived from an understanding of moral development is pertinent.

CONCLUSION

In this chapter the three main theories of moral development (cognitive-developmental, behavioural, and psychoanalytic) have been discussed. It has been seen that none of them is capable of providing a comprehensive framework for an understanding of the subject. The low correlations between moral judgement and moral behaviour, and between different aspects of moral behaviour, suggests the importance of situational factors. This suggests that, in understanding causes and developing remediation for much anti-social behaviour, an approach geared to the here-and-now situation with provision of appropriate models, increasing risk of detection etc., may be most effective. However, in order to understand the behaviour of highly deviant personalities (both those showing severely aggressive behaviour with absence of guilt and shame, and those showing pathological helpfulness) an attention to early parent–child relationships may be more profitable.

REFERENCES

Adams, P. L. (1973). *Obsessive Children: a socio-psychiatric study.* London: Butterworths.

Aronfreed, J. (1961). The nature, variety and social patterning of moral responses to transgression. *J. Pers. Soc. Psychol.* **63**, 223–240.

Aronfreed, J. (1968). *Conduct and Conscience.* New York: Academic Press.

Aronfreed, J. and Reber, A. (1965). Internalised behavioural suppression and the timing of social punishment. *J. Pers. Soc. Psychol.* **1**, 3–16.

Bandura, A. (1969). Social-learning theory of identificatory processes. In: *Handbook of Socialization Theory and Research.* D. Goslin (Ed.) Chicago: Rand McNally.

Bandura, A. and McDonald, F. J. (1963). The influence of social reinforcement and the behaviour of models in shaping children's moral judgement. *J. Abn. Psychol.* **67**, 274–281.

Bandura, A. and Perloff, B. (1967). Relative efficacy of self-monitored and externally imposed reinforcement systems. *J. Pers. Soc. Psychol.* **7**, 111–116.

Bandura, A., Ross, D. and Ross, S. A. (1963). Vicarious reinforcement and imitative learning. *J. Abn. and Soc. Psychol.* **67**, 601–607.

Barrett, D. E. and Yarrow, M. R. (1977). Prosocial behaviour, social inferential ability and assertiveness in children. *Child Dev.* **48**, 475–481.

Baumrind, D. (1967). Child care practices anteceding three patterns of pre-school behaviour. *Genet. Psychol. Mon.* **75**, 43–88.

Bell, R. Q. (1968). A re-interpretation of the direction of effects in studies of socialisation. *Psychol. Rev.* **75**, 81–95.

Berkowitz, L. and Friedman, P. (1967). Some social class differences in helping behaviour. *J. Pers. Soc. Psychol.* **5**, 217–225.

Borke, H. (1975). Piaget's mountains revisited: changes in the egocentric landscape. *Dev. Psychol.* **11**, 240–243.

Bronfenbrenner, U. (1960). Freudian theories of their identification and their derivatives. *Child Dev.* **31**, 15–40.

Bronfenbrenner, U. (1962). The role of age, sex, class and culture, in studies of moral development. *Relig. Ed.* **57** (4, Research Supp.), 3–17.

Bronfenbrenner, U. (1970). Reaction to social pressure from adults versus peers among Soviet day school and boarding school pupils in the perspective of an American sample. *J. Pers. Soc. Psychol.* **15**, 179–189.

Bruch, H. (1974). *Eating disorders.* London: Routledge and Kegan Paul.

Bryan, J. H. and London, P. (1970). Altruistic behaviour by children. *Psychol. Bull.* **73**, 200–211.

Bryan, J. H. and Walbeck, N. H. (1970). The impact of work and deeds concerning altruism upon children. *Child Dev.* **41**, 747–757.

Burton, R. V. (1963). Generality of honesty reconsidered. *Psychol. Rev.* **70**, 481–499.

Burton, R. V. (1976). Honesty and dishonesty. In: *Moral Development and Behaviour.* T. Lickona (Ed.) New York: Holt, Rinehart and Winston.

Burton, R. V., Maccoby, E. E. and Allinsmith, W. (1961). Antecedents to resistance to temptation in four year old children. *Child Dev.* **3**, 689–710.

Chandler, M. (1973). Egocentrism and antisocial behaviour. *Dev. Psychol.* **9**, 326–332.

Cheyne, J. A. (1971). Some parameters of punishment affecting resistance to deviation and generalisation of a prohibition. *Child Dev.* **42**, 1249–1261.

Cheyne, J. A. and Walters, R. H. (1969). Intensity of punishment, timing of punishment, and cognitive structure as determinants of response inhibition. *J. Exper. Child Psychol.* **7**, 231–244.

Darwin, C. (1871). *The Descent of Man.* New York: Appleton.

Deur, J. L. and Parke, R. D. (1970). Effects of inconsistent punishment on aggression in children. *Dev. Psychol.* **2**, 403–411.

Durkin, D. (1961). The specificity of children's moral judgements. *J. Gen. Psychol.* **98**, 3–14.

Eisen, M. (1972). Characteristic self-esteem, sex and resistance to temptation. *J. Pers. Soc. Psychol.* **24**, 68–72.

Eysenck, H. J. (1976). The biology of morality. In: *Moral Development and Behaviour.* T. Lickona (Ed.) New York: Holt, Rinehart and Winston.

Feshbach, N. (1975). Empathy in children: some theoretical and empirical considerations. *Counselling Psychologist* **5**, 25–30.

Freud, S. (1914). *On Narcissism: an introduction.* Standard Edition XIV. London: Hogarth Press.

Garbarino, J. and Bronfenbrenner, U. (1976). The socialisation of moral judgement and behaviour in cross-cultural perspective. In: *Moral Development and Behaviour.* T. Lickona (Ed.) New York: Holt, Rinehart and Winston.

Grim, P. F., Kohlberg, L. and White, S. H. (1968). Some relationship between conscience and attentional processes. *J. Pers. Soc. Psychol.* **8**, 239–252.

Grinder, R. E. (1964). Relations between behavioural and cognitive dimensions of conscience in middle childhood. *Child Dev.* **35**, 881–891.

Grusec, J. E. (1971). Power and the internalisation of self-denial. *Child Dev.* **43**, 93–105.

Harris, H. (1970). Development of moral attitudes in white and negro boys. *Dev. Psychol.* **2**, 376–383.

Hartshorne, H. and May, M. A. (1928). *Studies in the Nature of Character. Vol. I. Studies in Deceit.* New York: Macmillan.

Hartshorne, H., May, M. A. and Maller, J. B. (1929). *Studies in the Nature of Character. Vol. II. Studies in Self-control.* New York: Macmillan.

Hartshorne, H., May, M. A. and Shuttleworth, F. K. (1930). *Studies in the Nature of Character. Vol. III. Studies in the Organisation of Character.* New York: Macmillan.

Hartup, W. and Keller, E. D. (1960). Nurturance in pre-school children and its relation to dependency. *Child Dev.* **31**, 681–690.

Havighurst, R. J. and Neugarten, B. L. (1955). *American Indian and White Children: a sociological investigation.* Chicago: University of Chicago Press.

Henshel, A. (1971). The relationship between values and behavior: a developmental hypothesis. *Child Dev.* **42**, 1997–2007.

Hoffman, M. L. (1970). Moral Development. In: *Carmichael's Manual of Child Psychology.* P. H. Mussen (Ed.) New York: John Wiley.

Hoffman, M. L. (1975a). Developmental synthesis of affect and cognition and its implications for altruistic motivation. *Dev. Psychol.* **11**, 607–622.

Hoffman, M. L. (1975b). Altruistic behaviour and the parent–child relationship. *J. Pers. Soc. Psychol.* **31**, 937–943.

Hoffman, M. L. (1976). Empathy, role-taking, guilt and development of altruistic motives. In: *Moral Development and Behaviour.* T. Lickona (Ed.) New York: Holt, Rinehart and Winston.

Hoffman, M. L. and Saltzstein, H. D. (1967). Parent discipline and the child's moral development. *J. Pers. Soc. Psychol.* **5**, 45–47.

Isen, A. M., Horn, N. and Rosenhan, D. L. (1973). Effects of success and failure on children's generosity. *J. Pers. Soc. Psychol.* **27**, 239–247.

Kanfer, F. H. and Duerfeldt, P. H. (1968). Age, class-standing and commitment as determinants of cheating in children. *Child Dev.* **39**, 545–557.

Kohlberg, L. (1963). The development of children's orientation towards a moral order. I: Sequence in the development of human thought. *Vita Humana.* **6**, 11–33.

Kohlberg, L. and Kramer, R. B. (1969). Continuities and discontinuities in childhood and adult moral development. *Human Dev.* **12**, 93–120.

Kohn, M. L. (1959). Social class and parental values. *Amer. J. Soc.* **64**, 337–351.

Krebs, D. L. (1970). Altruism—an examination of the concept and a review of the literature. *Psychol. Bull.* **73**, 258–302.

Lickona, T. (1969). Piaget misunderstood: a critique of the criticisms of his theory of moral development. *Merrill-Palmer Quart.* **16**, 337–350.

Lickona, T. (Ed.) (1976). *Moral Development and Behaviour.* New York: Holt, Rinehart and Winston.

MacRae, D. (1954). A test of Piaget's theories of moral development. *J. Abn. Soc. Psychol.* **49**, 14–18.

Maccoby, E. (1968). The development of moral values and behaviour in childhood. In: *Socialisation and Society.* J. A. Clausen (Ed.) Boston: Little, Brown.

Medinnus, G. R. (1966). Age and sex differences in conscience development. *J. Gen. Psychol.* **109**, 117–118.

Milgram, S. (1963). Behavioural study of obedience. *J. Abn. Soc. Psychol.* **67**, 371–378.

Mischel, W. (1968). *Personality and Assessment.* New York: Wiley.

Mischel, W., Ebbeson, E. G. and Zeiss, A. R. (1972). Cognitive and attentional mechanisms in delay of gratification. *J. Pers. Soc. Psychol.* **21**, 204–218.

Mischel, W. and Mischel, H. N. (1976). A cognitive social-learning approach to morality and self-regulation. In: *Moral Development and Behaviour.* T. Lickona (Ed.) New York: Holt, Rinehart and Winston.

Monahan, J. and O'Leary, K. D. (1971). Effects of self-instruction on rule-breaking behavior. *Psychol. Reports* **29**, 1059–1066.

Money-Kyrle, R. (1955). Psychoanalysis and ethics. In: *New Directions in Psychoanalysis.* M. Klein, P. Heimann and R. Money-Kyrle (Eds.) London: Tavistock Publications.

Moore, B. S., Underwood, B. and Rosenhan, D. L. (1973). Affect and Altruism. *Dev. Psychol.* **8**, 99–104.

Mowrer, O. (1950). *Learning Theory and Personality Dynamics.* New York: Ronald Press.

Murphy, L. B. (1937). *Social Behaviour and Personality.* New York: Columbia University Press.

Mussen, P. H., Rutherford, E., Harris, S. and Keasey, C. B. (1970). Honesty and altruism among pre-adolescents. *Dev. Psychol.* **3**, 169–194.

Parke, R. D. (1967). Nurturance, nurturance withdrawal and resistance to deviation. *Child Dev.* **38**, 1101–1110.

Pearlin, L. I., Yarrow, M. R. and Scarr, H. A. (1967). Unintended effects of parental aspirations: the case of children's cheating. *Amer. J. Soc.* **73**, 73–83.

Peters, R. S. (1971). Moral development: a plea for pluralism. In: *Cognitive Development and Epistemology.* T. Mischel (Ed.) New York: Academic Press.

Piaget, J. (1932). *The Moral Judgement of the Child.* London: Kegan Paul.

Poulos, R. W. and Liebert, R. M. (1972). Influence of modelling, exhortative verbalisation and surveillance on children's sharing. *Dev. Psychol.* **6**, 402–408.

Prentice, N. M. (1972). The influence of live and symbolic modelling on promoting moral judgement of adolescent delinquents. *J. Abn. Psychol.* **80**, 157–161.

Prichard, J. C. (1835). *A Treatise on Insanity.* London: Sherwood, Gilbert and Piper.

Rebelsky, F. G., Allinsmith, W. A. and Grinder, R. (1963). Sex differences in children's use of fantasy confession and their relation to temptation. *Child Dev.* **34**, 955–962.

Rosenhan, D. L., Underwood, B. and Moore, B. S. (1974). Affect moderates self-gratification and altruism. *J. Pers. Soc. Psychol.* **30**, 546–552.

Rosenhan, D. L. and White, G. M. (1967). Observation and rehearsal as determinants of prosocial behaviour. *J. Pers. Soc. Psychol.* **5**, 424–431.

Rosenkoetter, L. I. (1973). Resistance to temptation: inhibitory and dis-inhibitory effects of models. *Dev. Psychol.* **8**, 80–84.

Rosekrans, M. A. and Hartup, W. W. (1967). Imitative influences of consistent and inconsistent response consequences to a model on aggressive behaviour in children. *J. Pers. Soc. Psychol.* **7**, 429–434.

Ross, A., Lacey, H. and Parton, D. (1965). The development of a behaviour check-list for boys. *Child Dev.* **36**, 1013–1027.

Rycroft, C. (1968). *A Critical Dictionary of Psychoanalysis.* London: Nelson.

Sandler, J. (1960). On the concept of superego. *Psychoanalytic Study Child.* **15**, 128–162.

Scarr, S. (1965). The inheritance of sociability. *Amer. Psychologist* **20**, 524.

Schafer, R. (1960). The loving and beloved superego in Freud's structural theory. *Psychoanalytic Study Child.* **15**, 163–188.

Schwartz, S., Feldman, K., Brown, M. and Heingartner, A. (1969). Some personality correlates of conduct in two situations of moral conflict. *J. Personality* **37**, 41–57.

Sears, R. R., Maccoby, E. E. and Levin, H. (1957). *Patterns of Child Rearing.* Evanston, Ill.: Row, Peterson.

Sears, R. R., Rau, L. and Alpert, R. (1965). *Identification and Child Rearing.* Stanford, Ca.: Stanford University Press.

Severy, L. J. and Davis, K. E. (1971). Helping behaviour among normal and retarded children. *Child Dev.* **42**, 1017–1031.

Shelton, J. and Hill, J. P. (1969). Effects on cheating of achievement, anxiety and knowledge of peer performance. *Dev. Psychol.* **1**, 449–455.

Sim, M. (1969). *Guide to Psychiatry.* Second Edition. Edinburgh: Churchill-Livingstone.

Staub, E. (1969). A child in distress: the effect of focusing responsibility on children on their attempts to help. *Dev. Psychol.* **2**, 152–153.

Staub, E. (1970). A child in distress: the influence of age and number of witnesses on children's attempts to help. *J. Pers. Soc. Psychol.* **14**, 130–140.

Staub, E. (1971a). The influence of implicit and explicit 'rules' of conduct on children and adults. *J. Pers. Soc. Psychol.* **17**, 137–144.

Staub, E. (1971b). The use of role playing and induction in children's learning of helping and sharing behaviour. *Child Dev.* **42**, 805–816.

Stayton, D., Hogan, R. and Ainsworth, M. (1971). Infant obedience and maternal behaviour: origins of socialisation reconsidered. *Child Dev.* **42**, 1057–1069.

Stein, A. H. (1967). Imitation of resistance to temptation. *Child Dev.* **38**, 157–169.

Suttie, I. (1963). *The Origins of Love and Hate.* Harmondsworth: Penguin.

Trainer, F. E. (1977). A critical analysis of Kohlberg's contributions to the study of moral thought. *J. Theory Soc. Behav.* **7**, 41–63.

Trivers, R. (1971). The Evolution of Reciprocal Altruism. *Quarterly Rev. Biol.* **46**, 35–57.

Ugurel-Semin, R. (1952). Moral behaviour and moral judgement of children. *J. Abn. Soc. Psychol.* **47**, 463–474.

Ushakov, G. K. (1971). Anorexia Nervosa. In: *Modern Perspectives in Adolescent Psychiatry.* J. Howells (Ed.) Edinburgh: Oliver and Boyd.

Walsh, R. P. (1967). Sex, age and temptation. *Psychol. Reps.* **21**, 625–629.

Walsh, R. P. (1969). Generalisation of self-control in children. *J. Ed. Research.* **62**, 464–466.

Weir, K. and Stevenson, J. (1978). A teacher's questionnaire of children's prosocial behaviour: preliminary findings. Submitted for publication.

Wilson, E. O. (1975). *Sociobiology.* Harvard, Mass.: The Bellknap Press.

Wright, D. (1971). *The Psychology of Moral Behaviour.* Harmondsworth: Penguin.

Yarrow, M. R., Scott, P. M. and Waxler, C. Z. (1973). Learning concern for others. *Dev. Psychol.* **8**, 240–260.

28. THE DEVELOPMENT OF AGGRESSION

DAVID SHAFFER, HEINO F. L. MEYER-BAHLBURG, CORNELIS L. J. STOKMAN

DEFINITION

Aggression may be defined as 'an action which it is intended should inflict harm on another' (Berkowitz, 1974); either psychological or physical (in which case the term 'violence' is appropriate). The notion of intent is necessary to provide clinical meaning although this may cause considerable difficulties in experimental work, especially with animals. A high degree of affective arousal is present in much, but not all, aggressive behaviour; however this is neither a necessary nor sufficient component of aggressive conduct.

Two main questions arise with aggression. Firstly, are there situations (such as the experience of frustration, pain or discomfort or the exposure to violent films on television) which increase the likelihood of aggressive behaviour in a wide range of individuals? Secondly, are there individuals who are characteristically aggressive, either because their threshold for violent response is lower than that of others or because they respond aggressively to a wider range of stimuli? If so, what are the determinants of this characteristic?

AGGRESSION AS A TRAIT: DEVELOPMENTAL CHANGES

Developmental studies of aggressive behaviour are clinically useful to assess the prognostic significance of aggression at different ages. They are also of theoretical value in terms of the light they shed on the notion of an aggressive trait.

Investigations into the stability of aggressive behaviour at different ages are difficult to conduct and interpret as both form and level of aggression change with age. Goodenough's (1931) study illustrates this point. She studied a large group of 2–7-year-old children using both direct observation and parent diaries. She noted that aggressive behaviour outbursts were in general less common in the older children and that the difference between younger and older children was particularly marked for undirected (temper) outbursts. The situations in which aggressive acts occurred also changed. Between the ages of 2 and 3 years aggressive temper outbursts usually arose out of a conflict with parents during the course of 'habit training'. After the age of 4 there was a drop in this form of aggression although there was an increase in retaliatory and instrumental aggression, in line with the shift from parallel to cooperative play. This study was based on cross-sectional observations and although it tells us about changes in the form and frequency of aggressive behaviour at different ages, it does not tell us whether certain children remained more aggressive than others or whether different children went through different aggressive 'phases' at different times.

Kagan and Moss (1962) examined this issue in the Fels Longitudinal Study. This used both interview reports and some direct observations of behaviour. The study found that aggressive behaviour shown before the age of 3 showed little continuity with aggression after that age. However, from the age of 3 onward the stability of aggression towards others was considerable. The children who fought most with others at that age were also those who most often fought and quarrelled at age 14 and in early adult life. The Fels study also noted that aggression directed towards mother fluctuated considerably from time to time and could not be used to predict later aggressiveness.

The continuity of aggressive and violent behaviour in middle childhood and adolescence has also been noted in the Cambridge Study in Delinquent Development (Farrington, 1978), in the California Study of McFarlane, Allen and Honzik (1954), in the New York Study of Lefkowitz *et al.* (1977), and in the very detailed ethological studies of aggressive behaviour in preschool children by Manning *et al.* (1978).

Developmental studies such as these suggest that the number of aggressive or violent outbursts in non-deviant children diminishes between early and middle childhood. This finding could be explained in a number of different ways. It could, for example, be due to the development of alternative mechanisms of expressing affective or hostile feelings; to the development of better control over emotional behaviour in general or simply to a reduction in the number and range of conflictual circumstances in which aggressive responses are likely to occur.

The first of these explanations suggest that there is a greater use of displacement or other defence mechanisms during later childhood with 'aggressive drive' remaining constant. Certainly fantasy aggression, as assessed by projective techniques such as doll play, increases during this period (Fesbach and Singer, 1971). There is similarly, an increasing preference for violent films between the ages of 9 and 13 (Lyle and Hoffman, 1972; Katzmann, 1972). However, all of the studies into fantasy aggression are based on cross-sectional samples and there is no evidence that children who show high levels of aggression during the preschool period and low levels in middle childhood are those who show particularly high levels of fantasy aggression.

Given the evidence that aggressive behaviour persists, at least in some individuals, between early childhood and late adolescence this could be because of some underlying constitutional factor or through a persistent effect of some early formative social-environmental influence. These influences could be acting by interfering with the normal development of non-aggressive coping styles, or in some

other way. Alternatively it might be that there is no underlying trait of aggressiveness but rather that children who show repeated aggressive behaviour are simply those who are repeatedly exposed to frustrating or other provocative stimuli. Clinical experience suggests that this last explanation is unlikely, for aggressive children usually show their behaviour in a number of different settings; such as home, school or institution (Manning *et al.*, 1978).

CONSTITUTIONAL FACTORS

Sex differences

The greater prevalence of aggressive behaviour in males within both human and animal species is strongly suggestive of a constitutional determinant of aggression. Human males have been shown to be more aggressive than females in a variety of different contexts (*see* Oetzel, 1966, and Maccoby and Jacklin, 1974, for extensive reviews). These include physical violence, rough and tumble play, counter-aggression in response to aggression from others, delivering electric shocks to a mock victim on a 'Buss machine', imitation of aggressive behaviour after exposure to a model, and in fantasy, where the intensity and frequency of aggressive dreams is greater in males than females. Clinically, boys are approximately four times as likely as girls to show antisocial behaviour, which frequently includes an aggressive element (Rutter *et al.*, 1970a), and a male predominance in other violent behaviours such as successful suicide (Shaffer, 1974) and in violent crime (Norland and Shover, 1977) has been demonstrated repeatedly and consistently.

Sex differences are apparent in aggressive behaviours at the toddler stage of development and are maintained through childhood and adolescence and across cultures. Omark *et al.* (1973), utilizing time-sampled observations of playground behaviour in the USA, Switzerland and Ethiopia, noted a similar male predominance of hitting and shoving behaviour in all three countries; as did Whiting and Edwards (1973) studying 3- to 10-year-olds in Kenya, Okinawa, India, the Philippines, Mexico, and the USA.

Since the differences in aggression are present in non-human mammals as well (Moyer, 1974), it is tempting to speculate that they are influenced in some way by biological factors. The most prominent biological differences are the sex chromosomes, the gonads with their gender-specific hormones and the hormone-dependent internal and external genitalia.

Sex chromosomes and aggressive behaviour

If the male predominance in aggressive behaviour arises in some way from the genetic material on the Y chromosomes, individuals with an excess of Y material, either in the form of an extra Y or a large Y, should show increased aggressiveness compared to males with a normal XY complement or normal-sized Y chromosomes. Alternatively, if it were the presence of the X chromosome which reduced the likelihood of aggressive behaviour, males with more X material (*e.g.* XXY males) should show less aggressive behaviour than normals.

XXY individuals are found significantly more often than expected in hospitals for the criminally insane and in the security wings of hospitals for the retarded (Hook, 1973). However, given the established incidence of XYY in the general population (approximately 1:1,000 new births), it is clear that the vast majority of XYY individuals are not in such institutions. An epidemiological study in Denmark (Witkin *et al.*, 1976) suggests that deviant behaviour is also found in non-institutionalized XYY males. Published case descriptions of XYY men (reviewed by Owen, 1972) show a preponderance of aggressive psychopathology of explosive, temperlike character which, one might suspect, is the basis for the increased risk for criminality of XYY subjects. However, offences involving violence against the person are not particularly frequent in XYY criminals (Witkin *et al.*, 1976; Meyer-Bahlburg, 1974) and their adjustment in prison may even be superior to that of XY controls (Price and Whatmore, 1967; Street and Watson, 1969). Finally prospective studies of an admittedly small number of clinically unselected XYY children (N = 15) followed from birth to toddler or preschool age (Valentine *et al.*, 1971; Leonard *et al.*, 1974; Nielsen and Sillesen, 1976; Tennes *et al.*, 1977) provide only limited evidence for increased aggressiveness.

The relationship between XYY genotype and deviant behaviour could be a direct one with the extra Y chromosome contributing specifically to deviancy and (possibly) aggression, or it could be due to a general effect of aneuploidy. The former hypothesis can be tested by studying men with large Y chromosomes, the latter by examining XXY men.

Simple 'dose-response' considerations have led to studies of aggressive behaviour in males with long Y chromosomes as well as to the assessment of Y-chromosome length in aggressive and non-aggressive populations. Several studies have found the relative length of the Y chromosome to be greater in adult criminal or psychiatric populations than in controls, but others, possibly because of methodological differences, have not corroborated these findings (*see* Brøgger *et al.*, 1977). An increased prevalence of long-Y genotypes in behaviourally disturbed boys was found by Kahn *et al.* (1969) in English remand homes and by Christensen and Nielsen (1974) in a Danish child-psychiatric hospital. Precise behavioural descriptions were not given but presumably antisocial behaviour was a common feature. An association of Y chromosome length with activity level (apparently including conduct problems) was found in an interview study of 100 boys (Nielsen and Nordland, 1975). The currently available evidence for the effects on behaviour of the larger Y chromosome thus suggests an association with deviancy but, pending standardization of both chromosomal and behavioural measures, it is not conclusive.

The situation with respect to XXY males is clearer.

They are significantly over-represented in secure psychiatric institutions (Hook, 1973) although less so than XYY males. Five studies (*see* Meyer-Bahlburg, 1974) have compared XXY and XYY males from the same penal institutions; in only one did XYY males show a higher rate of violent crime. The epidemiological study by Witkin *et al.* (*see* above) included 16 XXY men. Their rate of criminality was intermediate between the XYY subjects and the XY controls. Three of the four early-childhood studies listed above included XXY boys, and no significant behavioural differences between XYY and XXY children were described. The interaction seems to be different in adults. For instance, Money *et al.* (1974) comparing 12 XYY adult male patients with 12 XXY patients found that the XYY males were characteristically ill tempered and impulsive while XXY males were characteristically inhibited, inert and reclusive.

In summary, aneuploidy of the sex chromosomes in general appears to increase rates of psychopathology and criminality; although the discrepancies in criminality and behaviour deviancy between XXY and XYY males suggests some additional differential effects of the two genotypes.

Several factors mediating between genotype and behavioural deviancy have been investigated. Because of the increased prevalence of XYY individuals among tall males (*see* Borgaonkar and Shah, 1974), tall stature has been suggested as a cause for the high prevalence of XYY subjects in secure psychiatric institutions. This has been ruled out by Hook and Kim (1971), Borgaonkar *et al.* (1972), and Witkin *et al.* (1976). Male sex hormones constitute an important factor in animal aggression and have been implicated in human aggression as well (*see* below); however in many XYY cases, severe aggressive behaviour disorders have been observed many years before the onset of puberty. There is hardly any evidence that XYY men have increased androgen production (Meyer-Bahlburg, 1974) except for as yet unreplicated findings on the Danish cohort sample (Schiavi *et al.*, 1978).

An alternative explanation for psychopathology in XYY males might be the 'intellectual dysfunction hypothesis' put forward by Witkin *et al.* (1976), *i.e.* that susceptibility to behaviour disorders is mediated through either intellectual impairment or a proneness to learning difficulties. Both of these factors are known to be associated with conduct disorders (Rutter *et al.*, 1970b). The Danish cohort study (Witkin *et al.*, 1976) found impaired intelligence in both XYY and XXY males. Moreover, intellectual impairment, educational attainment and the socio-economic level of the parents were found to be accurate predictors of criminality in both XXY and, to some *lesser* extent, XYY individuals. Several cases with borderline intelligence or language difficulties have been identified within the 4 prospective studies of 15 XYY preschoolers mentioned above.

Underlying both the impairment of intellectual functioning and behavioural pathology may be brain dysfunction. Evidence for the latter comes from a variety of neurological and EEG studies of XYY individuals (*see*

Forssman *et al.*, 1975) many of which must be criticized on methodological grounds (Borgaonkar and Shah, 1974). The Danish cohort study, however, presented un-equivocal evidence for a difference in brain function, manifested mainly by more low-frequency alpha activity in XYY males which could not be explained by selection bias, recording artefacts, or lack of blindness in scoring procedures (Volavka *et al.*, 1977a, b).

In summary the role of the sex chromosomes in determining sex dimorphic behaviours, including aggression, has yet to be established. The major function of the chromosomes is to initiate a differentiation of the gonads into either androgen producing testes or oestrogen producing ovaries. Accordingly one might expect to find a constitutional basis for aggression in some relationship between the gonadal hormones and the development of typically male and female behaviours.

Hormones and aggression

In a variety of mammalian species from rodents to sub-human primates, researchers have identified 'critical' or sensitive periods in early development during which the developing brain is particularly responsive to the influences of sex hormones. In primates and probably man this sensitive period occurs before birth. This organizational phase coincides with an active period of gonadal androgen production in the male fetus whilst the ovaries of females seem to remain relatively inactive. During childhood both testes and ovaries are dormant and only enter a second phase of activity during puberty. At that time sex hormones appear to activate previously organized brain systems to lead to the behavioural sex differences typical of adults of a given species. Experimental manipulation—in animals—of sex hormone levels during either the early sensitizing period or puberty and adulthood can have a dramatic effect on sex dimorphic behaviour (*see* Brain, 1977, for a comprehensive review).

Information about the effects of sex hormone levels on human brain function has been derived from three sources: (1) Cases in which sex hormone levels were manipulated during the course of clinical treatment; (2) Studies of patients with endocrinopathies which have resulted in abnormal sex hormone levels; and (3) Correlational studies which have examined relationships between hormone levels and behaviour in normal and deviant subjects.

A number of studies have examined aggressiveness in children who had been exposed to exogenous hormones in utero. These have usually been administered to the mother in order to maintain a threatened pregnancy. Yalom *et al.* (1973) found decreased aggression-assertion (blind ratings of interview data) in 16-year-old sons and decreased assertiveness (blind ratings by teachers) in 6-year-old sons of diabetic mothers who had been treated with oestrogens and progestogens during pregnancy. Because of inadequate controls it is not clear whether these results are to be interpreted as a consequence of the abnormal conditions during pregnancy which first led to

the treatment. Better controlled studies on children whose parents were treated with progestogens for mild disorders of pregnancy have shown no effect on aggression in boys (Meyer-Bahlburg *et al.*, 1977; Zussman *et al.*, 1977) and only slight increases in indirect aggression in girls (Ehrhardt *et al.*, 1977). Aggressiveness has also been studied in girls suffering from Congenital Adrenal Hyperplasia. This syndrome is a consequence of an enzyme defect in the adrenal cortex which results in the overproduction of androgen. Afflicted genetic females have intersexed or male-like external genitalia at birth. Most are identified and corrected and reared as girls. Some go undiagnosed and are reared as boys. Ehrhardt and Baker (1974) and Money and Schwartz (1976) have studied two different samples of such girls. Although their case histories showed a number of male-like behaviours, *e.g.* increased physical activity, peer preference for boys and decreased doll and parent rehearsal play, no increase in aggressiveness was noted. These studies do not therefore provide convincing evidence that prenatal hormone variations contribute to the sex differences in human aggressive behaviour.

Sex hormone production increases rapidly during puberty. However, the effects of increases in hormone levels on behaviour are relatively unresearched except for some anecdotal accounts (*e.g.* Sands, 1954; Johnson *et al.*, 1970) of increases in assertive and/or aggressive behaviour with androgen treatment in psychologically disturbed adolescents. Correlational studies between testosterone levels and aggressive behaviour have been limited to adults. The findings by Persky *et al.* (1971) of high positive correlations between aggression as measured by questionnaire and testosterone levels have not been replicated by other investigators (*e.g.* Meyer-Bahlburg *et al.*, 1974; Monti *et al.*, 1977). However, two studies have shown higher testosterone levels in violent than in non-violent offenders (Ehrenkranz *et al.*, 1974; Rada *et al.*, 1976); and Kreuz and Rose (1972) have found higher levels in adult prisoners who gave a history of violent criminality during adolescence. Kreuz and Rose's hypothesis is that within a population predisposed by social factors to develop antisocial behaviour, levels of testosterone may be an important additional factor leading to violence. This effect could be exerted directly by the CNS or indirectly by testosterone dependent increased muscle mass.

The relationship between body build (in particular muscularity) and aggression has been noted in a number of studies. Perhaps the most convincing of these is that of the Gluecks (1950) who matched violent and non-violent delinquents for IQ and on a large number of social and environmental variables. When this was done, 'mesomorphs' were over-represented among the violent group. Similar observations on muscularity or mesomorphic somatotype and aggression have been made by Sheldon (1949), Davidson *et al.* (1957) and Walker (1962). An explanation for the association could be that muscular children and adolescents will be more successful in early retaliatory encounters with other children. Patterson *et al.* (1967) have shown that chance success of this sort may initiate a chain of reinforcing events which 'shape' aggressiveness in the child.

For a variety of reasons it is appropriate to exert caution in ascribing a causative role to testosterone in violent and aggressive behaviour: (a) hormone distributions of violent and non-violent groups overlap, and the differences are at best modest; (b) although both chemical and surgical castration have been found to be useful in reducing sexual aggression, they are of no value in the treatment of aggression which is unrelated to sex (Bremer, 1958; Meyer-Bahlburg, 1974; Money *et al.*, 1975); (c) sex hormone levels fluctuate and are strongly influenced by stress, social status (at least in non-human mammals), physical exercise and other behavioural or environmental factors. Such state dependent fluctuations considerably increase the methodological difficulties of research in the area. There are the further difficulties of knowing whether the most relevant parameters are production rate, bound versus unbound fractions, tissue sensitivity, etc. none of which have been fully investigated. Much more sophisticated research is needed to rule out or to firmly establish a role for sex hormones in human aggressive behaviour that could also account for differences in aggression between the sexes.

This discussion has left to one side the frequently voiced contention that sex differences in aggressive behaviour are a consequence of different social learning processes. One hypothesis is that aggressive behaviour is treated differently by parents in the two sexes (parental sex-typing). That is, that aggressive behaviour in males, if not expected or reinforced, is at least not punished as systematically or effectively as in girls. There have been few direct studies into this contention although Stein and Friedrich (1975) have found no differences in teacher responsiveness to aggressive behaviour in boys and girls and in an extensive review on the subject Maccoby and Jacklin (1974) note that the studies that have been undertaken do not show parent differences. If anything it seems that boys are punished more for aggressive behaviour than girls. However, even if it could be shown that parents do permit more aggressive behaviour in their male than in their female children, the transactional nature of parenting would have to be taken into account. Parents' responses are determined in part by prior experience with the child. Thus if boys frequently display some variant of aggressive behaviour and if parental or caretaker responses to that behaviour are unsuccessful in modifying the behaviour (either in limiting it at the time or preventing its recurrence) it is likely that the parents' attempts to modify the unwanted conduct will be altered. If, by contrast, little girls are only infrequently aggressive or if their aggression is amenable to intervention then such intervention, seeming to be successful, would be reinforcing for the parent. Most studies on this subject have not controlled for sex differences in the frequency of aggressive behaviour and have relied upon interview rather than observational data.

A second social-learning hypothesis is that the child identifies with and imitates the same sex parent (modelling) and by generalization other same sex models. Such modelling has been established as a crucial type of social learning for a great variety of behaviours. Maccoby and Jacklin (1974), along with earlier writers, make a compelling argument that the acquisition of potentially sex-dimorphic behaviour, especially by young children, is often unrelated to the sex of the model, *i.e.* that their observation-learned behavioural repertoire is comprised of both masculine and feminine behaviour components, but that the actual performance of behaviour is sex-dimorphic, presumably as a consequence of differential reinforcement by parents and peers as well as of 'self-socialization'.

Aggression and the brain

Electrical or chemical stimulation of various parts of the brain (especially the limbic system) in animals can produce a variety of aggressive and rage responses (Bandler *et. al.*, 1972; Hess and Akert, 1955; Hilton and Zbrozyna, 1963; Stokman and Glusman, 1968). On the basis of such findings and of experiments which have shown that different forms of aggressive behaviour appear to be mediated by different neuropharmacological systems, Moyer (1968) and others suggest that there are certain innately organized functional systems in the mammalian brain which permit aggressive responses to be elicited under appropriate stimulus conditions, and conversely that there are other functional systems which can inhibit these behaviours.

The amygdaloid complex, the hypothalamus and the central gray matter of the mesencephalon are thought to be the most important limbic structures in the control of aggression. Destruction of the arcuate nucleus of the hypothalamus results in an enduring state with strong aggressive responses occurring to previously innocuous stimuli—the so-called hypothalamic 'savage' syndrome —(Stokman and Glusman, 1974). The arcuate nucleus is connected directly with the pituitary gland and its destruction results in interference with pituitary hormonal production. The syndrome can in turn be abolished by secondary lesions in the central gray matter of the midbrain (Glusman *et al.*, 1961). These findings demonstrate how complex interactions may occur between different areas of the limbic system and between neural and humoral systems to facilitate or inhibit agonistic behaviour (Egger and Flynn, 1963; De Molina and Hunsperger, 1962; Stokman and Glusman, 1970).

By contrast there is little experimental support for any anatomically localized 'aggression centre', stimulation of which will invariably result in aggressive behaviour. For example, Valenstein (1970) has demonstrated that identical electrical stimulation of the same hypothalamic area may result in quite different behaviours depending on the situation in which the stimulation occurs and the internal state of the animal. In primates at least, aggressive responses to midbrain stimulation are dependent on the animal's hierarchal position and may only be shown in the presence of less dominant animals (Plotnik *et al.*, 1971). The animal's early rearing experience will also influence response to localized stimulation (Valenstein and Phillips, 1970). There is, further, some doubt as to whether aggressive behaviour shown during brain stimulation is a primary phenomenon or is, at least in some cases, a non-specific consequence of noxious stimulation (Plotnik *et al.*, 1971). Very similar responses can be elicited by unpleasant stimulation of peripheral receptors (*e.g.* the skin of the foot).

A *reduction* in aggressive behaviour in sub-primate mammals has been demonstrated following amygdalectomy (Schreiner and Kling, 1953): and after thalamotomy (Spiegel and Wycis, 1949). The response to such destructive procedures performed on sub-human primates in both laboratory and in free-living colonies may vary with the sex of the animal. Whereas males may show a reduction in aggressive behaviour and a fall in the social hierarchy, females may show opposite changes with an uncharacteristic increase in aggressiveness and social rank following amygdalectomy (Kling *et al.*, 1970, 1971). To explain these and other phenomena Kling (1975) has hypothesized that surgically induced damage to the amygdala may impair the social perceptiveness of the animal. Behaviours which would otherwise be perceived as threatening may be interpreted differently after surgery. In support of this explanation is the observation that operated animals may themselves show impairment in socially meaningful behaviour and that they regularly become isolated within the colony and show a generalized reduction in sexual and other affiliative behaviour (Moyer, 1971).

There are few reported examples of aggressive responses to direct brain stimulation in humans. Nor is it clear, when rage behaviour has been produced by brain stimulation, whether this has been a primary response. In one reported case (Heath *et al.*, 1955) the patient also expressed feeling great fear at the time of amygdaloid stimulation which on other occasions has been known to produce pleasurable responses (Heath, 1963).

A number of isolated case records have appeared in the literature reporting lesions in the hypothalamus or amygdyla at post-mortem, among individuals who had shown exceptionally aggressive behaviour during life. However, such isolated case reports are particularly subject to selection bias and there is no reported association between aggressive behaviour and conditions such as post-herpetic, post-kernicteric or Wernicke's encephalopathy, all of which characteristically involve hippocampal and hypothalamic structures (*see* Goldstein, 1974 for a summary).

A relationship between temporal lobe epilepsy or disease and aggressive behaviour has also been suggested. Ounsted (1969) studied children with temporal lobe epilepsy and reported a high prevalence of aggressive behaviour. However, the findings may have been influenced by subject selection, observations were uncontrolled and the behavioural descriptions were far from complete. In a total population study of children with epilepsy and other forms of brain damage (Rutter *et al.*, 1970b) no excess of antisocial behaviour was shown, although sample size was inevitably small.

A relationship between temporal spikes on the EEG and aggressive behaviour was first suggested by Hill and Watterson (1942) who demonstrated the frequent occurrence of temporal theta activity in adult prisoners. However, temporal delta and theta waves occur frequently in children and adolescents (Eeg-Olofsson, 1970) and a systematic study by Stevens and Milstein (1970) failed to find an association between aggressive behaviours and such phenomena. Other electrographic wave forms that have been described in association with aggression in adolescents include the 14 or 6 cycle per second positive spike discharges (Gibbs and Gibbs, 1951). These discharges were attributed to hypothalamic or thalamic epilepsy because of the locus and purported association with autonomic symptomatology. However, subsequent studies in children and adolescents without behaviour problems (Eeg-Olofsson, 1970; Lombroso *et al.*, 1966) have demonstrated that—providing an appropriate recording technique is used—these spike phenomena occur commonly in normal children. Furthermore, when they are found in children with psychiatric difficulties they are not selectively associated with aggressive behaviour (Woerner and Klein, 1974).

Much of the literature linking gross organic abnormality to aggressive behaviour is undoubtedly distorted by sample bias. Kligman and Goldberg (1975) and Harris (1978), reviewing the literature on localized EEG abnormalities and aggressive behaviour conclude that there is no consistent evidence to link the two phenomena.

Whilst it seems clear that brain injury and epilepsy are associated with an increased prevalence of psychiatric problems (Rutter *et al.*, 1970a) there is little evidence from total population studies that antisocial or aggressive behaviours are over-represented in these groups. Furthermore, a study of localized cortical lesions in childhood has failed to note any association between aggressive behaviour and a particular locus of injury (Shaffer, 1977). The notion that aggressive outbursts may occur during epileptic automata has been examined by Gunn and Fenton (1969) who surveyed a group of epileptic prisoners. They were unable to document any examples of such incidents in the survey.

Finally, certain surgical procedures have been demonstrated to reduce the degree and frequency of aggressive behaviour in experimental animals. These findings have formed a basis for a number of neurosurgical techniques which have included thalamotomy, in which the target areas are the central, medial and intralaminar nuclei (Andy, 1970), amygdalotomy (Narabayashi and Mizutani, 1970; Narabayashi, 1972; Heimburger *et al.*, 1966). Hypothalamotomy (Sano, 1975; Schvarcz *et al.*, 1972; Roeder, 1966) has also been used therapeutically, although animal studies would predict that this procedure would increase, rather than diminish aggressive behaviour (Wheatley, 1944; Glusman, 1974). Reduction in aggression has been reported to follow all of these operations although descriptions of behaviour change have tended to be anecdotal rather than systematic. Furthermore, it is not possible to tell from the literature whether post-operative reduction in aggressiveness is specific or is an indirect consequence of a more general affective blunting.

In summary although there is ample evidence that aggressive behaviour can be obtained by artificial stimulation and surgical interference in animal brains it is not easy to translate such findings to human behaviour. A number of difficulties stand in the way. Firstly, there is the problem of interpreting intentional aggression with the ethological methods available to animal researchers. Secondly, even in animal work, it is abundantly clear that both past and current environmental factors modify the display of brain-elicited aggression. Thirdly, there is the difficulty of species specificity. Similar procedures, *e.g.* hypothalamotomy produce an increase in aggression in animals and a decrease in aggression in humans.

Human aggression is clearly less amenable to neuroanatomical or physiological experimentation. The researcher relies upon findings from clinical groups which are all too often the subject of selection bias. These biases tend to exaggerate a relationship between the clinical abnormality and troublesome or intrusive behaviour such as aggression. In studies where selection bias has been circumvented there *does not* seem to be any specific relationship between either generalized or local brain pathology and aggressive behaviour. A caveat must be that epidemiological studies of relatively uncommon conditions deal with small numbers of pathological subjects so that it is often difficult to know whether the sample size has been sufficiently large to draw any reasonable conclusions. Whilst it is clear that brain damage does increase the likelihood of a range of deviant behaviours it does not seem that aggressiveness is over-represented among these.

PSYCHO-SOCIAL INFLUENCES

Apart from the association with sex there is no very convincing evidence that constitutional factors are of direct importance in determining aggressive behaviour. There is, on the other hand, a good deal more to support the significance of social and cognitive influences.

Theories of aggression

Bandura (1973) has broadly, classified the numerous theoretical models that have been developed to explain aggressive behaviour into 'instinctual' theories, 'drive' theories and social learning models.

Instinctual theories can in turn be classified into those deriving from Freud's psychoanalytic theory and those based on assumptions drawn from observations of animal behaviour (ethological theory). Freud laid a good deal of emphasis on the importance of the motive force provided by the 'pleasure instinct' tempered by the instinct of self-preservation, and he acknowledged the difficulty of explaining interpersonal aggression or 'sadism' in this framework. In 1922 he suggested that interpersonal aggression was an outward turning of a 'death instinct' *i.e.*

an instinct towards self-injury or damage. The outward turning was said (1933) to result from the tension which existed between the self-destructive and the erotic and self-preservation instincts. Later psychoanalytic theoreticians such as Hartmann *et al.* (1949), whilst preserving the notion of an aggressive instinct have in many instances rejected the notion of the 'death wish'. Certain analysts, such as Melanie Klein (1957), have been particularly fervent exponents of the importance of aggressive instincts, suggesting that such instincts are present even before birth and that the conflict between the aggressive and loving instinct are a key dynamic in early development.

Konrad Lorenz (1966) has been the most prominent of the ethological theoreticians who suggest that instinctive aggression is present in all beings; that it serves a number of positive biological purposes *e.g.* that it leads to population dispersal and thus to the optimal use of available food resources; and that it sharpens the process of natural selection.

Lorenz suggested that aggressive energy builds up inexorably until released. The precepts upon which Lorenz has based his theory have been criticized in detail by Montagu and others (1968).

By definition instinctual theories are not capable of empirical support. They deal with a non-measurable instinctual 'force' and as they are elaborated and, inevitably, qualified they can be used to provide post hoc explanations for any variety of events although they cannot predict any (*see* Bandura, 1973).

The *drive model* of aggression postulates that aggressive behaviour results from obstruction of goal directed activity (*i.e.* a frustration). The Frustration-Aggression hypothesis will be referred to later in this chapter along with examples of a number of experiments which have used the artificial imposition of a frustration to produce aggressive responses. Although frustrations may induce aggressive responses these may be modified by a prior experience; by individual differences or by the justification presented to explain the frustrating event. Berkowitz (1978) has argued that it is not frustration itself but rather the pain or unpleasantness that accompanies most frustrating events, which acts as a trigger for aggressive behaviour. Bandura (1973) and others have criticized the frustration hypothesis as subsuming such a diverse set of conditions that it no longer has any specific meaning—a not uncommon sequence as theories which become tempered with accretions of empirically derived knowledge. The notion of 'catharsis' is closely linked to that of aggressive drive theory and this is dealt with in more detail below.

Both instinctual and drive theories posit that aggressive behaviours are determined by factors or forces which come from within the individual. Such theories are in many ways inadequate to explain both the great variability (both situation and person specificity) of much aggressive behaviour; and are conceptually unsound because 'the inner determinants are typically inferred from the behaviour they supposedly cause' (Bandura, 1973).

Social learning theories are best represented by Bandura and his colleagues and take the view that 'man is neither driven by inner forces nor buffeted helplessly by environmental influence'. Rather, behaviour is best understood in terms of 'continuous reciprocal interaction between behaviour and its controlling conditions... behaviour partly creates the environment and the resultant environment in turn influences the behaviour'.

By and large it is this last theoretical framework which has guided the authors of the present chapter for it seems the most sensible fashion by which to explain a number of diverse, empirically derived observations viz; (a) that it is possible to elicit aggressive responses in children by imposing 'frustrations', *i.e.* by interfering with goal oriented activities; (b) that aggression can be learned by both modelling and social reinforcement; (c) that aggressive children and adolescents are more likely to have experienced an upbringing by a cold or distant parent, by parents who use excessive physical punishment and by parents who are discordant between themselves; and (d) that aggressive children are more likely than others to be brought up under socially unfavourable conditions.

Aggression and frustration

In 1941 Barker, Dembo and Lewin carried out a classical experiment supporting Dollard *et al.*'s (1939) frustration-aggression hypothesis. They exposed two groups of children to a playroom in which many desirable toys were on display. One group was permitted to remain and play with the toys. The other was led away from the playroom and only allowed to return to play after a delay. The first group played constructively and cooperatively. The second group broke the toys, argued among themselves and used the toys in a generally less constructive fashion.

Dollard had defined frustration as a deprivation or a deflection from a goal directed activity. Barker *et al.*'s demonstration of how frustration, defined in this way may lead to aggression has been replicated repeatedly under a variety of circumstances.

It seems that frustration may not only induce disruptive and aggressive behaviour but may also influence hostile attitudes. Miller and Bugelski (1948) studied teenage boys in a work camp. The boys were promised a 'night out on the town'. Before the promised event their attitudes towards Mexicans and Japanese were gauged by questionnaire. The 'night out' was cancelled without notice and the boys were set to perform a number of tedious tasks instead. Attitudes were reassessed and showed that the boys now attributed significantly more unfavourable values to the minority groups.

Experiments such as these convey a rather artificial notion of aggression. However, other experimental findings could be conceptualized as demonstrating the effects of repeated frustration in a more natural setting. As an example White and Lippit (1960) studied the social organization of a boys club. Three organizational models were set up. In the first, decisions were made openly through participation; the leader acted as a guide, giving

support and advice. In the second, the leader was remote, made decisions without consultation and gave praise or criticism in a seemingly arbitrary fashion. It is not unreasonable to suppose that this setting imposed an exceptional number of frustrations on its members. In a third club, the leader took a passive role and provided information and guidance only when asked. The third model was unpopular and was least effective in meeting certain task oriented goals. However, the second model seemed to generate disturbance. Not only were aggressive attitudes expressed towards the leader but there was a good deal of scapegoating and within-group hostility between the boys.

However, the response to frustrations need not invariably be aggressive. Davitz (1952) studied 10 groups of children. Five of these were systematically praised and rewarded for cooperative, and the other five for aggressive behaviour during a preliminary 'training' period. The children were then subjected to a frustration experiment in which they were promised a film showing and ice cream. At the last minute the promise was withdrawn and the children were ushered into a playroom. Their responses to this situation were in line with the training they had received earlier. Only the groups who had previously been reinforced for aggressive behaviour showed hostile and disruptive responses.

Aggression as a learned behaviour

Aggressive behaviour is subject to increase or diminution by such processes as modelling and social reinforcement.

In an experiment which demonstrated how aggression conforms to the general principles of learned behaviour, Cowan and Walters (1963) used different schedules to reinforce aggressive behaviour in three groups of children. The technique used to measure aggression is one that has been developed by Bandura and his colleagues at Stanford in which attacks on a large inflatable 'Bobo' doll are recorded. Although the undoubtedly artificial nature of such experiments has often been noted and criticized, a recent study by Johnston (1977) found that aggressive behaviour with a 'Bobo' doll correlated well with peer, teacher and self-ratings of aggression among preschool children. In the Cowan and Walters experiment, subjects were divided into three groups. The first was reinforced with a sweet each time it struck the Bobo; the second was reinforced on every third occasion; and the third one time in six. The disappearance (extinction) of aggression was then studied when reinforcement was withdrawn. As predicted from learning theory, extinction occurred most rapidly in the first (FR$_1$) group.

In another key experiment from the same laboratory Bandura, Ross and Ross (1963) demonstrated that vicarious reinforcement or seeing that aggression in others is rewarded will increase aggressive behaviour in children. Three groups of children were exposed to different films in which a child was seen to misbehave. In one version the child was then punished, in another the child was rewarded and in the third the child was treated neutrally.

The children in the audience were then given an opportunity to misbehave themselves. The group that had seen misbehaviour rewarded showed significantly more aggression during this time than the other two groups. Interestingly—and this finding has been replicated in other settings (*e.g.* Liebert and Fernandez, 1970)—witnessing the punishment of aggression did not affect later behaviour in either direction.

This experiment laid the foundation for the very extensive body of research which has shown that exposure of children to scenes of aggression in films and television is likely to lead to an increase in the children's own aggressive behaviour both in a laboratory and in a naturalistic setting (*see* Howitt and Cumberbatch, 1975 and Stein and Freidrich, 1975 for detailed reviews—with different conclusions).

These effects are subject to many modifications and the notion that witnessing fantasy violence increases aggressive behaviour in young viewers has met with a good deal of criticism. The objections of some workers (*e.g.* Howitt and Cumberbatch, 1975) are on the grounds that laboratory findings can not readily be transposed to real life, that they might not be applicable to clinical problems of aggression and that any effect is unimportant in degree and transient in duration. However, the evidence from naturalistic experiments among delinquents (*e.g.* Parke *et al.*, 1977) conducted under the most rigorous methodological constraints suggest that laboratory findings are probably representative, although the importance of the effects is more debatable.

The ways in which aggression can be learned or abolished in a naturalistic setting have been extensively studied by Patterson and his colleagues (Patterson *et al.*, 1967; Patterson and Cobb, 1971; Patterson, 1977). Their technique has been to carry out detailed observations of target children together with their peers of family members in order to examine the occurrences which immediately precede and follow acts of physical aggression and verbal hostility. In a study on 3- to 4-year-old nursery school children Patterson *et al.* (1967) noted that a child who had just entered nursery school might be a victim of an attack by another child and might retaliate successfully. This would then be followed by an increase in aggressive episodes in which the former victim was now the aggressor. It seemed that continued aggressive behaviour was being reinforced by chance success. Both submission and the manifestation of pain by the victim seemed to be particularly reinforcing in this age group—although this is in contrast with older children and adults for whom aggressive behaviour is usually inhibited by the apparent suffering of the victim.

The group has also studied children in their own homes (Patterson and Cobb, 1971; Patterson, 1977). These studies suggest that most acts of physical aggression in children are triggered by aversive behaviours impinging on the child, such as being teased, laughed at or being hit. When such behaviours come from a younger sibling the response is most often some form of physical aggression; when coming from a parent the response is more likely to be one of verbal hostility. The aggressive behaviour of the child is likely, in turn, to lead to further adverse responses by the parents of siblings. Patterson (1977) has demonstrated that these may serve as 'accelerators': *i.e.* that they increase the likelihood of the target child repeating the aggressive behaviour. By contrast, if the aggressive behaviour meets no response it is much less likely to be repeated.

Patterson has emphasized that all of these studies are correlational and that no causal inferences can be drawn from them; experiments to manipulate the observed variables are still needed. However, the findings already have several important implications. The nursery school study, for example, suggests how aggression and muscularity might be linked (*see* above); more muscular children might be more successful in their initial aggressive encounters with peers. The family studies suggest that training parents to avoid responding in aggressive or compliant ways to their children's aggressive behaviour could lead to its diminution. Finally the observation on sibling stimulated aggression should perhaps be considered in trying to understand the apparent relationship between antisocial behaviour and large densely spaced families.

Modifiers of aggression

The extensive work on the effects of televised and filmed violence is interesting, not only because it deals directly with an issue of potentially great consequence, but more generally because it has provided an experimental model to study factors which *inhibit* and *enhance aggressive behaviour*. Aggressive responses to witnessed violence will vary according to the individuals' earlier experiences. Furthermore, manipulation of the content of the film, by, for example, making the aggressive behaviour more or less justified, will influence the impact of the film material on the viewer.

In order to explain this variability Berkowitz (1960) introduced the notion of '*aggression anxiety*', *i.e.* an internalized concern felt by the individual, when there is a possibility of behaving aggressively. It is postulated that this affect may be generated by anxiety over either the external, *e.g.* the likelihood of punishment, reprisal or disapproval, or the internal consequences—*e.g.* shame, guilt, fear of retaliation, etc.—of aggressive behaviour.

Individual differences

A number of studies have looked at how individual children vary in their response to stimuli which would normally be expected to generate aggressive behaviour. Biblow (1973) compared the responses of anxious and non-anxious 11-year-olds. The experiment used artificial frustration as a stimulus to produce an aggressive response. The high anxious children failed to show the expected increase in aggressive behaviour after stimulation, this lack of effect being especially marked in anxious girls. Liebert and Baron (1972) designed an ingenious experiment in which a group of children were shown a violent film. During the showing of the film their facial expressions were observed. They were then offered an opportunity to administer a mock punishment with a 'hurt button'. Aggression—at least as measured in this way—was greatest in the children who had smiled most during the film and was least in those who appeared sad.

It seems likely that children who characteristically show high levels of aggression are also more responsive to the effects of stimulation. Friedrich and Stein (1973) conducted a careful experiment in which the baseline behaviour of nursery school children was systematically observed over a four-week period. Children were then shown either violent, pro-social or neutral films. Significantly greater changes in aggressiveness were shown by the characteristically aggressive children after they had watched a violent film. The behaviour change also persisted longest in this group. Other studies which have taken baseline levels of aggressive behaviour into account (e.g. Parke et al. (1974) have confirmed these findings.

Arousal state

Differences in the viewer's emotional state just prior to experiencing a stimulus to aggression also seem important. Thus, Hartmann (1969) deliberately angered half of a sample of viewers before exposure to a violent film sequence. These angered viewers responded with more aggression to sequences which contained scenes of the victim appearing to suffer pain—a cue which ordinarily diminishes post-viewing aggression (Buss, 1966)—and which did so in controls. This experiment has been interpreted as showing how prior arousal will overcome aggression anxiety.

Repeated exposure to television

The effects of the frequency with which television is watched and the particular context in which aggression is displayed on film or televised material have also been the subject of research. Correlational studies examining the relationship between frequency of television watching and aggressive delinquency are difficult to interpret. Eron et al. (1972) found that aggressive children (as evaluated by peer reports) watched less TV overall than non aggressives, but the television they did watch had a higher percentage of violent material (as judged by mothers' reports). The effects of repeated watching have been studied by Cline et al. (1973) who used psychophysiological measures to assess anxiety during the display of violent films and suggests that anxiety responses diminish with repeated exposure. How these findings can be equated with the more complex notion of 'aggression anxiety' is not clear, although there is an implication that repeated exposure to television reduces the strength of these mechanisms which otherwise act to inhibit post-viewing aggression.

Content and context of stimulus

It is clear from the experiments of Berkowitz (Berkowitz, 1973; Berkowitz et al., 1978) that the context in which aggression is shown is an important determinant of viewer behaviour, at least in adolescents. In particular, when aggression is portrayed as being unjustified, post-viewing aggression is generally reduced. However, these mediators seem to be less important during the preschool and middle childhood years. To illustrate this point Leifer and Roberts (1972) presented a series of films which varied in aggressive content to children of different ages. The films were stopped short of their ending and the children were asked to choose between a violent and a non-violent outcome. In children under the age of 12 the more violent the preparatory film sequence, the more violent the suggested outcome. It was only among older children that responses were identified by whether the witnessed aggression had been justified even though this was made explicit to all subjects.

Catharsis

The catharsis theory proposes that aggression is a unitary drive which may be diverted into either useful, or at least harmless, channels. In so far as it applies to the effects of violence, what other activities may become an acceptable substitute for violent or aggressive behaviour. If, for example, viewing a violent film induces aggressive fantasies which include imaginary punishment of a real individual, this will provide adequate satisfaction and hence drive reduction in a potentially aggressive viewer.

Empirical support for the catharsis through fantasy largely rests upon an experiment by Fesbach and Singer (1971). Children living in different hostels within a single institution were exposed either to a series of non-violent control films or alternatively to aggressive television and film programmes over a period of several weeks. The subjects who saw the non-violent programmes displayed more aggression than those who saw the violent films. This experiment was undertaken without controlling for a number of variables which have subsequently come to be regarded as important. For example, there was no control for base line levels of aggression or anxiety. The content of the two film programmes appeared to differ in interest value, with non-violent films being . . . generally regarded as less interesting. Finally, non-blind raters were used. Wells (1973) has repeated Fesbach's original experiment controlling for these factors and could not replicate the original findings.

These experiments investigate the effects of fantasied catharsis, and treat aggression as a cognitive construct that is relatively independent of a state of arousal. Clearly, much aggressive behaviour is displayed under circumstances of high affective arousal, in the 'heat of the moment'. The failure to demonstrate a role for catharsis through fantasy should not be taken as an indication that measures which act to reduce arousal, might not reduce the potential for aggressive behaviour. Thus Hokanson and Burgess (1962) showed that systolic blood pressure in an angered subject could be reduced more rapidly if the subject was allowed to punish the instigator of his anger. More recently Konecni (1975) has demonstrated reduction in other measures of physiological arousal under similar circumstances. Although these studies suggest that physical exercise during anger produce physiological benefits, they do not address the issue of whether they result in a concomitant reduction in aggressive feelings. Interventions which encourage 'letting off steam' need to be viewed cautiously. Firstly they may only be effective when arousal is already high. It is unlikely that encouraging sporting activity, breaking crockery, etc. will work prophylactically in the absence of tension. Secondly their content needs to be considered. Thus there is some evidence that very competitive activities may actually result in an increase in aggressiveness (Sherif *et al*. (1961)).

Family life and aggression

Using data from the Cambridge Longitudinal Study, which followed a group of 400 boys from age 8 to early adulthood, Farrington (1978) found that boys who were subsequently convicted of violent offences were of lower overall IQ than others, were especially likely to come from poor and overcrowded homes, have parents who were unhappily married and to have fathers who had themselves been delinquent. Most importantly, they had frequently received harsh punishment from their parents during the early years of childhood. These harsh parental attitudes and behaviours were the strongest predictors of later violent delinquency. Fourteen per cent of the boys who were receiving harsh parental discipline at the age of 8 were to become violent delinquents compared with only 3·6% of the remainder. Over 60% of the violent delinquents had been harshly disciplined early in childhood compared with fewer than 30% of non-violent delinquents. The receipt of harsh parental discipline at age 8 was in fact a stronger predictor of later violent delinquency than was aggressive behaviour itself at age 8.

These findings, particularly important because of the prospective design of the study, are broadly consonant with a large body of data that has been collected from essentially correlational studies over the past 20 years. These have been reviewed fully by Martin (1975). Despite the great difficulties in measuring child rearing behaviours (Yarrow *et al.*, 1968) there is an impressive consistency between studies which have used very different methods and population samples. Research has repeatedly shown that aggressive behaviour in children is associated with extremes of punitiveness in parents, especially when coupled with coldness and rejection (*e.g.* Glueck and Glueck, 1950; McCord and McCord, 1959; Rutter, Quinton and Yule, 1980).

Another variable which has been consistently related to aggression is lack of adequate parental supervision. The Gluecks (1950) noted that the parents of delinquents were nearly 10 times more likely to have failed to keep close watch over their children or to have provided for their leisure hours than the parent of non-delinquents. The McCords (1961), contrasting the parents of aggressive and non-aggressive adolescents, found that 54% of the parents of aggressive boys were rated as 'permissive' in the sense of failing to exert adequate supervision compared with only 15% of the non-aggressive group. How-

ever a more complex analysis of these relationships has been carried out by West and Farrington (1973) who noted that inadequate parental supervision was closely linked to poverty and that once family income was taken into account, poor supervision no longer discriminated between the delinquent's and non-delinquent's parents.

In some respects it is puzzling to find an association between parental punitiveness and aggression in the child, for punishment effectively inhibits aggressive behaviour, at least in the short term. Several possible mechanisms can be considered to explain this association. One is that parental punitiveness and/or laxity represents a response to the child's behaviour rather than its cause. Thomas, Chess and Birch (1968) in their longitudinal study of temperament in childhood were able to predict later behaviour problems, including aggressiveness, on the basis of a number of temperamental characteristics (not including aggression) which were apparent early in the child's development. They categorized parental responses to the 'difficult child' as showing one of a number of characteristic patterns. One was to resent the difficulties posed by the child and as a result to become hostile and punitive. Other parents were submissive and appeasing; Baumrind (1967) described essentially similar findings in a study of nursery school children. Children were categorized into a number of groups on the basis of three months direct observations. One of the groups was characteristically aggressive and unfriendly. In a series of direct observation sessions parent–child interactions were noted. The parents of the aggressive children displayed significantly less control and were less persistent in enforcing their demands than the parents of both self-reliant and immature groups of children. Although this study does not rule out the possibility that parental behaviour had led to the characteristics shown by their children when at school, it is clear that parents do respond to aggressive and difficult children in ways which may further impair the social learning opportunities offered to the child.

On balance it seems unlikely that parental responses to child-initiated aggression can be the only explanation for the strong relationship between punitiveness in the parent and aggression in the child. An illustration of this point can be drawn from the McCords' (1959) study which noted that the presence of warmth in at least one parent did a great deal to mitigate the likelihood of aggressive delinquency in the child. Thus, when one parent was punitive and hostile and the other warm the likelihood of problem behaviours was significantly reduced. Rutter (1971) examining the effect on the child of gross marital discord similarly found that a good relationship with one parent could partially make up for a bad relationship with another.

Alternative explanations link the association between parental harshness and punitiveness and child aggression, by proposing that the parent provides a model for aggressive behaviour which the child learns through imitation or identification. The complex dynamics of 'identification with the aggressor' described by Freud (1922) is less open to direct investigation.

A further possibility is that harsh parenting and frequent punishment impose a series of frustrations for which the child is ill prepared. Davitz's experiments (*see* above) show how consistent reinforcement of pro-social behaviours may help equip a child to deal with frustrating experiences. However, it is likely that this is lacking in aggressive children. Recent studies (Snyder, 1977) suggest that the parents of disturbed children spend a good deal of time responding to unwanted antisocial or aggressive behaviours. Many responses consist of an admonition or reprimand and they do not have to be pleasant to have a reinforcing effect.

Despite the strong relationship between parental criminality and childhood aggression there is little to suggest that aggressive children come from a perverse subculture of parents who *approve* of their child's fighting, bullying and destructiveness. Clinical experience suggest that the frequent punishment endured by these children is often administered for just those aggressive behaviours with which we are concerned.

Parental distance and coldness may itself be frustrating. A cold parent may be less motivated to respond to, or may be less sensitive to the imperfectly expressed needs or discomforts of the young child. Such insensitivity may not only lead to frustrations but may also impair identification with mature pro-social behaviours. The characteristics of a powerful and effective model (Bandura and Walters, 1963) include warmth and the provision of nurturance at times of stress and it may be that the absence of these characteristics in an important caretaker impairs the process of socialization.

Group aggression

Group aggression and in particular, gang activity, is a characteristic of youth and childhood. Gross socio-cultural influences seem to be more important in the development of gangs than as factors which lead to individually expressed aggression. Gang violence currently poses less of a problem in the United Kingdom than in the United States. Scott (1956) interviewed 151 juvenile offenders in London and found that only 17 of them belonged to well-defined gangs; these 17 did not differ significantly from other juvenile offenders either in background or in psychopathology.

In an attempt to classify juvenile gang activity, Yablonsky (1962) studied groups on the lower East side of New York. He contrasted 'social gangs' (which were typified by general stability, uniforms, badges, a clear focus of activity and popular leadership), and 'violent gangs'. In the latter, violence was the main activity; it often centred around pseudo-territorial disputes, the members were generally emotionally deprived and the leaders were characteristically disturbed. Membership of these 'violent gangs' was fluid with members joining and then leaving after brief periods.

Traditional hypotheses about gang formation seemed inadequate to explain groups such as these. For example, Thrasher (1929) who derived his observations from youths in Chicago during the 1920s suggested that gangs functioned to provide support and succour to young people who were otherwise rejected by society. Others (Cloward and Ohlin, 1960) have viewed gangs as a form of counter-culture composed of members who feel excluded from opportunity in society. However, the loose organization and fluctuation of membership, the generally conventional values held by members and the elements of personality disturbance described so vividly by Yablonsky do not readily fit this hypothesis. A newer school of sociologists, *e.g.* Cohen (1971), views gang violence as an interactive process at least partially triggered by police or other authorities.

Crowd violence and hooliganism

Children are also common participants in crowd violence, which is distinguished from gang activity by its brief duration. It seems likely that most examples of crowd aggression can be explained in terms of immediate contingencies rather than by the selective congregation of habitually aggressive individuals. This hypothesis is supported by British Home Office Statistics which show that a much higher proportion of individuals, convicted of malicious damage, are first offenders than individuals convicted of any other form of offence. This would suggest that there is no clear relationship between hooliganism and more conventional delinquency and that aggression of this sort is not persistent.

Bandura (1973) suggests that once collective aggression has been begun by an instigator, 'the disinhibiting effects of wide spread modelling and the immediate rewards resulting from aggressive activity may instigate aggressive actions in ordinarily passive individuals'.

If this were so then one would not expect to find individual differences among participants in crowd violence and one might expect that Le Bon's (1952) classical analysis of crowd violence—which held that rioters, mobs and hooligans were composed of riffraff or new immigrants into society without firm social roots or identity would not be supported. This seems to be so. Caplan and Paige (1968) contrasted rioters and non-rioters during the mid-1960 riots in Newark and Detroit. Riot participants (mostly adults in this case) did not differ with respect to income, rate of employment, family background, personality traits, or church attendance. Nor were they weaker adherents of the 'Protestant ethic' of 'reward for ability'. Indeed the rioters on the whole were better educated, more lengthy residents who felt that the standard of life was improving for blacks, but improving more for others than for themselves. Both Caplan and Paige (1968) and Tomlinson (1968) noted that rioters reported feeling 'frozen out' of the economic and social life which they perceived to be within their grasp. However these are feelings that are likely to be shared by a majority of urban blacks and do not support the notion that there are individual characteristics which predispose to participation in crowd violence.

SUMMARY AND CONCLUSION

There is good evidence that there are certain individuals, more often boys than girls, who are characteristically aggressive throughout childhood and adolescence. The incidents which provoke their aggressive behaviour are mainly those which interfere in some way with the execution of an intended action, or else those which caused them pain or humiliation. Such occurrences are more likely to lead to aggressive behaviour if experienced during a state of high arousal, which may include having watched violence on a film or television programme. These are also the main precipitants of aggressive behaviour in 'good' children.

There is as yet no satisfactory explanation for why some children are more aggressive than others. Enquiries into purely biological factors such as the number or size of Y chromosomes, androgen levels, or localized brain abnormalities have not yet revealed any sufficient influence which will predispose to aggression. Frequent aggression is more common in children of low intelligence and among children who have a hostile or disturbed relationship with their parents. It might be that persistent aggression is most likely when a child has a 'difficult' temperament, is brought up under circumstances which do not facilitate learning alternative models of coping or expression and who has in addition experienced, aggressive behaviour to be either instrumentally successful or attention gaining.

ACKNOWLEDGEMENTS

This work was supported in part by NIMH Psychiatric Education Branch Grant No. MH07715/17 and in part by NIMH Center Grant No. MH30906/O1A1.

REFERENCES

Andy, O. J. (1970). Thalamotomy in hyperactive and aggressive behavior. *Confinia Neurologica*, **32**, 322–325.

Bandler, R. J., Chi, C. C. and Flynn, J. P. (1972). Biting attack elicited by stimulation of the ventral midbrain segmentum of cats. *Science*, **177**, 364–366.

Bandura, A. (1973). *Aggression, a Social Learning Analysis*. Englewood Cliffs, N. J.: Prentice Hall.

Bandura, A., Ross, D. and Ross, S. (1963). Vicarious reinforcement and imitative learning. *J. Abn. Soc. Psychol.*, **67**, 601–607.

Bandura, A. and Walters, R. H. (1963). *Social Learning and Personality Development*. New York: Holt, Rinehart and Winston.

Barker, R., Dembo, T. and Lewin, K. (1941). Frustration and aggression. An experiment with young children. *University of Iowa Studies in Child Welfare*, **18**, 1–314.

Baumrind, D. (1967). Child practices anteceding three patterns of preschool behaviours. *Genet. Psychol. Monogs.*, **75**, 43–88.

Berkowitz, L. (1960). Repeated frustration and expectations in hostility arousal. *J. Abn. Soc. Psychol.*, **60**, 422–429.

Berkowitz, L. (1973). Control of aggression. In: Caldwell, B. and Ricciuti, A. N. (Eds.) *Review of Child Development Research*. Vol. 3, Chicago: University of Chicago Press.

Berkowitz, L. (1974). Some determinants of impulsive aggression. Role of mediated associations with reinforcements of aggression. *Psych. Rev.*, **81**, 165–176.

Berkowitz, L. (1978). Whatever happened to the frustration-aggression hypothesis? *Amer. Behav. Scientist*, **21**, 691–707.

Berkowitz, L., Parke, R. D., Leyens, J. P., West, S. and Sebastian, R. J. (1978). Experiments on the reactions of juvenile delinquents to filmed violence. In: Hersov L., Berger M. and Shaffer D. (Eds.) *Aggression and Antisocial Behavior in Childhood and Adolescence*. Oxford: Pergamon.

Biblow, E. (1973). Imaginative play and the control of aggressive behavior. In: Singer J. L. (Ed.) *The Child's World of Make-Believe*. New York: Academic Press.

Borgaonkar, D. S. and Shah, S. A. (1974). The XYY chromosome male—or syndrome? *Progress in Medical Genetics*, **10**, 135–222.

Borgaonkar, D. S., Unger, W. M., Moore, S. M. and Crofton, T. A. (1972). 47,XYY syndrome, height and institutionalization of juvenile delinquents. *Brit. J. Psychiat.*, **120**, 549–550.

Brain, P. F. (1977). *Hormones and Aggression, Vol. 1*. Montreal: Eden Press.

Bremer, J. (1958). *Asexualization. A follow-up study of 244 cases*. Oslo: Oslo University Press.

Brøgger, A., Urdal, T., Larsen, F. B. and Lavik, N. J. (1977). No evidence for a correlation between behavior and the size of the Y chromosome. *Clin. Genet.*, **11**, 349–358.

Buss, A. H. (1966). Instrumentality of aggression, feedback and frustration as determinants of physical aggression. *J. Person. Soc. Psychol.*, **3**, 153–162.

Caplan, N. C. and Paige, J. M. (1968). A study of ghetto riots. *Scientific American*, **219**, 15–21.

Christensen, K. R. and Nielsen, J. M. (1974). Incidence of chromosome aberrations in a child psychiatric hospital. *Clin. Genet.*, **5**, 205–210.

Cline, V. V., Croft, R. G. and Courrier, S. (1973). Desensitisation of children to television violence. *J. Person. Soc. Psychol.*, **27**, 360–365.

Cloward, R. A. and Ohlin, L. E. (1960). *Delinquency and Opportunity—A theory of delinquent gangs*. Glencoe: Free Press.

Cohen, S. (1971). Directions for research on adolescent group violence and vandalism. *Brit. J. Crim.*, **11**, 319–340.

Cowan, P. A. and Walters, R. H. (1963). Studies of reinforcement of aggression. 1. Effects of scheduling. *Child Develop.*, **34**, 163–179.

Davidson, M. A., McInnes, R. G. and Parnell, R. W. (1957). The distribution of personality traits in seven-year-old children. *Brit. J. Educ. Psychol.*, **27**, 48–61.

Davitz, J. (1952). The effects of previous training on post-frustration behavior. *J. Abn. Soc. Psychol.*, **47**, 309–315.

De Molina, F. A. and Hunsperger, R. W. (1962). Organization of the subcortical system governing defence and flight reactions in the cat. *J. Physiol.*, **160**, 200–213.

Dollard, J. E., Doob, A. L., Miller, N., Mowrer, O. and Sears, R. (1939). *Frustration and Aggression*. New Haven: Yale University Press.

Eeg-Olofsson, O. (1970). The development of the electro-encephalogram in normal children and adolescents from the age of one through 21 years. *Acta Paediatrica Scandinavica*, Supplement 208.

Egger, M. D. and Flynn, J. P. (1963). Effect of electrical stimulation of the amygdala on hypothalamically elicited attack behavior in cats. *J. Neurophysiol.*, **26**, 705–720.

Ehrenkranz, J., Bliss, E. and Sheard, M. H. (1974). Plasma testosterone: correlation with aggressive behavior and social dominance in man. *Psychosomatic Medicine*, **36**, 469–475.

Ehrhardt, A. A. and Baker, S. W. (1974). Fetal androgen, human CNS differentiation, and behavior sex differences. In: Friedman, R. C., Richart, R. M. and Vande Wiele, R. L. (Eds.) *Sex Differences in Behavior*. New York: John Wiley, 53–76.

Ehrhardt, A. A., Grisanti, G. C. and Meyer-Bahlburg, H. F. L. (1977). Prenatal exposure to medroxyprogesterone acetate (MPA) in girls. *Psychoneuroendocrinology*, **2**, 391–398.

Eron, L. D., Lefkowitz, M. M., Huesmann, L. A. and Walder, C. O. (1972). Does television violence cause aggression? *Amer. Psychol.*, **27**, 253–263.

Farrington, D. (1978). The family background of aggressive youths. In: Hersov, L., Berger, M. and Shaffer, D. (Eds.) *Aggression and Antisocial Behavior in Childhood and Adolescence*, Oxford: Pergamon.

Feshbach, S. and Singer, R. D. (1971). *Television and Aggression*. San Francisco: Jossey-Bass.

Forssman, H., Wahlström, J., Wallin, L., Åkesson, H. O. and Frey, T. S. (1975). Males with double Y-chromosome. Göteborg: Esselte Studium.

Freud, S. (1922). *Beyond the pleasure principle. Standard Edition*, 23. London: Hogarth Press.

Freud, S. (1933). *New introductory lectures on psychoanalysis*. New York: Morton.

Friedrich, L. K. and Stein, A. H. (1973). Aggressive and prosocial television programs and the natural behavior of preschool children. *Monogs. of the Soc. for Res. in Child Dev.*, **38** (Serial No. 151).

Gibbs, F. A. and Gibbs, E. L. (1951). Electroencephalographic evidence of thalamic and hypothalamic epilepsy. *Neurology*, **1**, 136–144.

Glueck, S. and Glueck, E. T. (1950). *Unravelling Juvenile Delinquent*. Cambridge, Mass.: Harvard University Press.

Glusman, M. (1974). The hypothalamic 'Savage' syndrome. In: *Aggression*, Research Publication A.R.N.M.D., **52**, 52–92.

Glusman, M., Won, W., Burdock, E. I. and Ransohoff, J. (1961). Effects of midbrain lesions on the 'savage' behavior induced by hypothalamic lesions in the cat. *Transactions of the American Neurology Association*, **86**, 216–218.

Goldstein, M. (1974). Brain research and violent behavior. *Archives of Neurology*, **30**, 1–35.

Goodenough, F. L. (1931). *Anger in Young Children*. Minneapolis: University of Minnesota Press.

Gunn, J. and Fenton, G. (1969). Epilepsy in prisons. A diagnostic survey. *Brit. Med. J.*, **5679**, 326–328.

Harris, R. (1978). Relationship between EEG abnormality and aggressive and anti-social behavior—a critical appraisal. In: Hersov, L. A., Berger, M. and Shaffer, D. (Eds.) *Aggression and Anti-social Behaviour in Childhood and Adolescence*. Oxford: Pergamon Press.

Hartmann, H., Kris, E. and Loewenstein, R. M. (1949). 'Notions on the theory of aggression'. *Psychoanalytic Study of the Child*, **3/4**, 9–36.

Hartmann, D. P. (1969). Influence of symbolically modeled instrumental aggression and pain cues on aggressive behaviors. *J. Person. Soc. Psychol.*, **11**, 280–288.

Heath, R. G. (1963). Electrical self-stimulation on the brain in man. *Amer. J. Psychiat.*, **120**, 571–577.

Heath, R. G., Monroe, R. R. and Mickle, W. A. (1955). Stimulation of the amygdaloid nucleus in a schizophrenic patient. *Amer. J. Psychiat.*, **111**, 862–863.

Heimburger, R. F., Whitlock, C. C. and Kalsbeck, J. E. (1966). Stereotaxic amygdalotomy for epilepsy with aggressive behavior. *J. Amer. Med. Assoc.*, **198**, 741–745.

Hess, W. R. and Akert, K. (1955). Experimental data on role of hypothalamus in mechanism of emotional behavior. *Archives of Neurology and Psychiatry*, **73**, 127–129.

Hill, D. and Watterson, D. (1942). Electroencephalographic studies of psychopathic personalities. *Journal of Neurology and Psychiatry*, **5**, 47–65.

Hilton, S. M. and Zbrozyna, A. W. (1963). Amygdaloid region for defense reactions and its efferent pathway to the brainstem. *J. Physiol.*, **165**, 160–173.

Hokanson, J. E. and Burgess, M. (1962). The effects of three types of aggression on vascular processes. *J. Abn. Soc. Psychol.*, **64**, 446–449.

Hook, E. B. (1973). Behavioral implications of the human XYY genotype. *Science*, **179**, No. 4069: 139–150.

Hook, E. B. and Kim, D. S. (1971). Height and antisocial behavior in XY and XYY boys. *Science*, **172**, 284–286.

Howitt, D. and Cumberbatch, G. (1975). *Mass Media, Violence and Society*. New York: Wiley.

Johnson, H. R., Myhre, S. A., Ruvalcaba, R. H. A., Thuline, H. C. and Kelley, V. C. (1970). Effects of testosterone on body image and behavior in Klinefelter's syndrome: a pilot study. *Develop. Med. Child Neurol.*, **12**, 454–460.

Johnston, A., DeLuca, D., Murtaugh, K. and Diener, E. (1977). 'Validation of a laboratory play measure of child aggression'. *Child Develop.*, **48**, 324–327.

Kagan, J. and Moss, H. (1962). *From Birth to Maturity*. New York: John Wiley.

Kahn, J., Carter, W. I., Dernley, N. and Slater, E. T. O. (1969). Chromosome studies in remand home and prison populations. In: West, D. J. (Ed.) *Criminological Implications of Chromosome Abnormalities* (Institute of Criminology, Cambridge).

Katzmann, N. I. (1972). Violence and color television: what children of different ages learn. In: Comstock, G. A., Rubenstein, E. A. and Murray, J. P. (Eds.) *Television and Social Behavior, Television's effects: Vol. 5, Further explanations*. Washington, D.C.: Government Printing Office.

Klein, M. (1957). *Envy and Gratitude*. London: Tavistock Press.

Kligman, D. and Goldberg, D. A. (1975). Temporal lobe epilepsy and aggression. *J. Nerv. Ment. Dis.*, **160**, 324–341.

Kling, A. (1975). Brain lesions and aggressive behavior of monkeys in free living groups. In: Fields, W. S. and Sweet, W. H. (Eds.) *Neural Bases of Violence and Aggression*. St. Louis: Warren H. Green.

Kling, A. and Cornell, R. (1971). Amygdalectomy and social behavior in the caged stump-tailed macaque (M. speciosa). *Folia Primatologica*, **14**, 190–208.

Kling, A., Lancaster, J. and Bemisone, J. (1970). Amygdalectomy in the free-ranging vervet. *J. Psychiat. Res.*, **7**, 191–199.

Konecni, V. J. (1975). The mediators of aggressive behavior: arousal level vs anger and cognitive labelling. *J. Person. Soc. Psychol.*, **32**, 706–721.

Kreuz, L. E. and Rose, R. M. (1972). Assessment of aggressive behavior and plasma testosterone in a young criminal population. *Psychosomatic Medicine*, **34**, 321–332.

Le Bon, G. (1952). *The Crowd*. London: Benn Brothers.

Lefkowitz, M. M., Eron, L. D., Walder, L. O. and Huesmann, L. R. (1977). *Growing up to be Violent. A longitudinal study of the development of aggression*. New York: Pergamon Press.

Leifer, A. P. and Roberts, D. F. (1972). Children's response to television violence. In: Murray, J. P., Rubenstein, E. A. and Comstock, G. A. (Eds.). *Television and Social Behavior, Vol. 2, Television and Social Learning*. Washington, D.C.: Government Printing Office.

Leonard, M. F., Landy, G., Ruddle, F. H. and Lubs, H. A. (1974). Early development of children with abnormalities of the sex chromosomes: a prospective study. *Pediatrics*, **54**, 208–212.

Liebert, R. M. and Baron, R. A. (1972). Some immediate effects of televised violence on children's behavior. *Develop. Psychol.*, **6**, 469–475.

Liebert, R. M. and Fernandez, L. E. (1970). Effects of vicarious consequences on imitative performance. *Child Develop.*, **41**, 847–852.

Lombroso, C. T., Schwartz, I. H., Clark, D. M., Muench, H. and Barry, J. (1966). Steroids in healthy youths. *Neurology*, **16**, 1152–1158.

Lorenz, K. (1966). *On Aggression*. London: Methuen.

Lyle, J. and Hoffman, H. R. (1972). Children's use of television and other media. In: Rubenstein, E. A., Comstock, G. A. and Murray, J. P. (Eds.) *Television and Social Behavior, Vol. 4, Television in day-to-day life: patterns of use*. Washington, D.C.: Government Printing Office.

Maccoby, E. E. and Jacklin, C. N. (1974). *The Psychology of Sex Differences*. London: Oxford University Press.

McCord, W. and McCord, J. (1959). *Origins of Crime: A new evaluation of the Cambridge Somervile Youth Study*. New York: Columbia University Press.

McCord, W., McCord, J. and Howard, A. (1961). Familial correlates of aggression in non-delinquent male children. *J. Abn. Soc. Psychol.*, **63**, 493–503.

McFarlane, J. W., Allen, L. and Honzik, M. P. (1954). *A Developmental Study of the Behavior Problems of Normal Children between 21 Months and 14 Years*, Berkely: University of California.

Manning, M., Heron, J. and Marshall, T. (1978). Styles of hostility and social interactions at nursery, at school and at home. In: Hersov, L., Berger, M. and Shaffer, D. (Eds.) *Aggression and Antisocial Behavior in Childhood and Adolescence*. Oxford: Pergamon.

Martin, B. (1975). Parent–child relations. In: Horowitz, F. D. (Ed.) *Review of Child Development Research*, Vol. 4, Chicago: University of Chicago Press, 463–540.

Meyer-Bahlburg, H. F. L. (1974). Aggression, androgens and the XYY syndrome. In: Friedman, R. C., Richart, R. M. and Vande Wiele, R. L. (Eds.) *Sex Differences in Behavior*. New York: John Wiley, 433–453.

Meyer-Bahlburg, H. F. L., Boon, D. A., Sharma, M. and Edwards, J. A. (1974). Aggressiveness and testosterone measures in man. *Psychosomatic Medicine*, **36**, 269–274.

Meyer-Bahlburg, H. F. L., Grisanti, G. C. and Ehrhardt, A. A. (1977). Prenatal effects of sex hormones on human male behavior: medroxyprogesterone acetate (MPA). *Psychoneuroendocrinology*, **2**, 383–390.

Miller, N. and Bugelski, R. (1948). Minor studies in aggression: the influence of frustrations imposed by the in-group on attitudes towards out-groups. *J. Psychol.*, **25**, 437–442.

Money, J., Annecillo, C., Van Orman, B. and Borgaonkar, D. S. (1974). Cytogenetics, hormones, and behavior disability: Comparison of XYY and XXY syndromes. *Clinical Genetics*, **6**, 370–382.

Money, J. and Schwartz, M. (1976). Fetal androgens in the early treated adrenogenital syndrome of 46,XX hermaphroditism: influence on assertive and aggressive types of behavior. *Aggressive Behavior*, **2**, 19–30.

Money, J., Wiedeking, C., Walker, P., Migeon, C., Meyer, W. and Borgaonkar, D. (1975). 47,XYY and 46,XY males with antisocial and/or sex-offending behavior: antiandrogen therapy plus counselling. *Psychoneuroendocrinology*, **1**, 165–178.

Montagu, M. F. A. (1968). *Man and Aggression*. London: Oxford University Press.

Monti, P. M., Brown, W. A. and Corriveau, M. A. (1977). Testosterone and components of aggressive and sexual behavior in man. *Amer. J. Psychiat.*, **134**, 692–694.

Moyer, K. E. (1968). Kinds of aggression and their physiological basis. *Communications in Behavioral Biology*, **2**, 65–87.

Moyer, K. E. (1971). *The Physiology of Hostility*. Chicago: Markhans Publishing.

Moyer, K. E. (1974). Sex differences in aggression. In: Friedman, R. C., Richart, R. M. and Van de Wiele, R. L. (Eds.) *Sex Differences in Behavior*. New York: John Wiley, 335–372.

Narabayashi, H. (1972). Stereotaxic amygdalotomy. In: Eleftheriou (Ed.) *The Neurobiology Of The Amygdala*. New York: Plenum Press.

Narabayashi, M. and Mizutani, T. (1970). Epileptic seizures and the stereotaxic amygdalotomy. *Confina Neurologica*, **32**, 289–297.

Nielsen, J. and Nordland, E. (1975). Length of Y chromosome and activity in boys. *Clinical Genetics*, **8**, 291–296.

Nielsen, J. and Sillesen, I. (1976). Follow-up till age 3–4 of unselected children with sex chromosome abnormalities. *Human Genetics*, **33**, 241–258.

Norland, S. and Shover, N. (1977). Gender roles and female criminality: Some critical comments. *Criminology*, **15**, 87–104.

Oetzel, R. M. (1966). Annotated bibliography. In: Maccoby, E. E. (Ed.) *The Development of Sex Differences*. Stanford, Cal.: Stanford University Press, 223–321.

Omark, D. R., Omark, M. and Edelman, M. (1973). Dominance hierarchies in young children. Paper presented at International Congress of Anthropological and Ethnological Sciences, Chicago, 1973. Abstract In: Maccoby, E. E. and Jacklin, C. N. 1974. *Op. cit.*

Ounsted, C. (1969). Aggression and epilepsy: Rage in children with temporal lobe epilepsy. *J. Psychosom. Res.*, **13**, 237.

Owen, D. R. (1972). The 47,XYY male: A review. *Psychological Bulletin*, **78**, 209–233.

Parke, R. I., Berkowitz, L., Leyens, J. P., West, S. and Sebastian, R. J. (1977). Film Violence—A field experimental analysis. In: Berkowitz, L. (Ed.) *Advances in Experimental Social Psychology, Vol. 10*. New York: Academic Press.

Patterson, G. R. (1977). Accelerating stimuli for two classes of coercive behaviors. *J. Abn. Child Psychol.*, **5**, 335–350.

Patterson, G. R. and Cobb, J. A. (1971). A dyadic analysis of 'aggressive' behaviors. In: Knutson, J. F. (Ed.) *Minnesota Symposium on Child Psychology, Vol. 5*. Minneapolis: University of Minnesota Press, 72–129.

Patterson, G. R., Littman, R. A. and Bricker, W. (1967). Assertive behavior in children: A step toward a theory of aggression. *Monog. Soc. Res. in Child Devel.*, **32**, 1–43.

Persky, H., Smith, K. D. and Basu, G. K. (1971). Relation of psychologic measures of aggression and hostility to testosterone production in man. *Psychosomatic Medicine*, **33**, 265–276.

Plotnik, R., Mir, D. and Delgado, J. M. R. (1971). Aggression, noxiousness and brain stimulation in unrestrained rhesus monkeys. In: Eleftheriou, B. E. and Scott, J. P. (Eds.). *The Physiology of Aggression and Defeat*. New York: Plenum Press.

Price, W. H. and Whatmore, P. B. (1967). Behaviour disorders and pattern of crime among XYY males identified at a maximum security hospital. *Brit. Med. J.*, **1**, 533–536.

Rada, R. T., Laws, D. R. and Kellner, R. (1976). Plasma testosterone levels in the rapist. *Psychosomatic Medicine*, **38**, 257–268.

Roeder, E. D. (1966). Stereotaxic lesions of the tuber cinereum in sexual deviation. *Confina Neurologica*, **27**, 162–163.

Rutter, M. L. (1971). Parent–Child Separation. Psychological effects on the children. *J. Child Psychol. Psychiat.*, **12**, 233–260.

Rutter, M. L., Graham, P. J. and Yule, W. (1970a). *A Neuropsychiatric Study in Childhood*. London: Heinemann. SIMP.

Rutter, M., Quinton, D. and Yule, B. (1980). *Family Pathology and Disorder in Children*. London: John Wiley. In preparation.

Rutter, M., Tizard, J., Whitmore, K. (Eds.) (1970b). *Education, Health, and Behaviour*. London: Longmans.

Sands, D. E. (1954). Further studies on endocrine treatment in adolescence and early adult life. *J. Ment. Science*, **100**, 211–219.

Sano, K. (1975). Posterior Hypothalamic Lesions in the Treatment of Violent Behavior. In: Fields, W. S. and Sweet, W. H. (Eds.) *Neural Basis of Violence and Aggression*. St. Louis: Warren H. Green.

Schiavi, R. C., Owen, D., Fogel, M., White, D. and Szechter, R. (1978). Pituitary—gonadal function in XYY and XXY men identified in a population survey. *Clinical Endocrinology*, **9**, 233–240.

Schreiner, L. and Kling, A. (1953). Behavioral changes following rhinencephalic injury in cats. *J. Neurophysiology*, **16**, 643–657.

Schvarcz, J. R., Driollet, R., Rios, E. and Betti, O. (1972). Stereotaxic Hypothalamotomy for Behaviour Disorders. *J. Neurology, Neurosurg. Psychiat.*, **35**, 356–359.

Scott, P. (1956). Gangs and Delinquent Groups in London. *Brit. J. Deling.*, **7**, 4–26.

Shaffer, D. (1974). Suicide in childhood and early adolescence. *J. Child Psychol., Psychiat.*, **15**, 275–291.

Shaffer, D. (1977). Brain Injury. In: Rutter, M. L. and Hersov, L. A. (Eds.) *Child Psychiatry: Modern Approaches*. Oxford: Blackwell Scientific Publications.

Sheldon, W. H. (1949). *Varieties of Delinquent Youth*. New York: Harper.

Sherif, M., Harvey, O., White, B., Hood, W. and Sherif, C. (1961). *Intergroup conflict and Cooperation. The Robbers Cave Experiment.* Norman: University of Oklahoma Book Exchange.

Snyder, J. (1977). Reinforcement analysis of interactions in problem and non-problem families. *J. Abn. Psychol.*, **86**, 528–535.

Spiegel, E. A. and Wycis, H . T. (1949). Physiological and psychological results of thalamotomy. *Proceedings of the Royal Society of Medicine*, Supplement, **42**, 84–93.

Stein, A. H. and Friedrich, L. K. (1975). Impact of Television on Children and Youth. E. M. Hetherington. *Review of Child Development Research, Vol. 5*, 183–256. Chicago: University of Chicago Press.

Stevens, J. A. and Milstein, V. (1970). Severe psychiatric disorders of childhood, electroencephalogram and clinical correlations. *Amer. J. Disorders Childhood*, **120**, 182–192.

Stokman, C. L. J. and Glusman, M. (1968). A procedure to quantify hypothalamically elicited agnostic behavior in the cat. *Psychonomic Science*, **11**, 325–326.

Stokman, C. L. J. and Glusman, M. (1970). Amygdaloid modulation of hypothalamic flight in cats. *J. Comparative Physiolog. Psychol.*, **71**, 365–375.

Stokman, C. L. J. and Glusman, M. (1974). Effects of Dopa and Imipramine on agonistic behavior induced by hypothalamic lesions in cats. *Federation Proceedings*, **33**, 464.

Street, D. R. K. and Watson, R. A. (1969). Patients with chromosome abnormalities in Rampton Hospital: A report. In: West, D. J. (Ed.) *Criminological Implications of Chromosome Abnormalities*. Cambridge: U. Cambridge, Institute of Criminology, 61–67.

Tennes, K., Puck, M., Orfanakis, D. and Robinson, A. (1977). The early childhood development of 17 boys with sex chromosome anomalies: a prospective study. *Pediatrics*, **59**, 574–583.

Thomas, A., Chess, S. and Birch, H. (1968). *Temperament and Behaviour in Children*. New York: University Press.

Thrasher, F. M. (1929). *The Gang: A study of 1,313 gangs in Chicago*. Chicago: University Press.

Tomlinson, T. L. (1968). The development of a riot idealogy among urban negroes. *American Behavioural Scientist*, **11**, 27–31.

Valenstein, E. S. (1970). Stability and Plasticity of Motivation Systems. In: Schmitt, F. (Editor-in-Chief) *The Neurosciences Second Study Program*. New York: The Rockefeller University Press, 207–217.

Valenstein, E. S. and Phillips, A. G. (1970). Stimulus-bound eating and deprivation from prior contact with food pellets. *Physiology and Behavior*, **5**, 279–282.

Valentine, G. H., McClelland, M. A. and Sergovich, F. R. (1971). The growth and development of four XYY infants. *Pediatrics*, **48**, 583–594.

Volavka, J., Mednick, S. A., Rasmussen, L. and Sergeant, J. (1977a).

EEG spectra in XYY and XXY men. *Electroencephalography and Clinical Neurophysiology*, **43**, 798–801.

Volavka, J., Mednick, S. A., Sergeant, J. and Rasmussen, L. (1977b). Electroencephalograms of XYY and XXY men. *Brit. J. Psychiat.*, **130**, 43–47.

Walker, R. N. (1962). Body build and behavior in young children: I. Body build and nursery school teachers' ratings. *Monog. Soc. Res. Child Devel.*, **27**, No. 3, Serial No. 84.

Wells, D. (1973). Television and Aggression: Replication of an Experimental Field Study. Unpublished manuscript. University of Chicago Graduate School of Business. Quoted in Stein, A. H. and Friedrich, L. K. (1979). *Op. cit.*

West, D. J. and Farrington, D. P. (1973). *Who Becomes Delinquent?* London: Heinemann.

Wheatley, M. D. (1944). The hypothalamus and affective behavior in cats. A study of the effects of experimental lesions with anatomic correlations. *Archives of Neurology and Psychiatry*, **52**, 296–316.

White, R. and Lippit, R. (1960). *Autoracy and Democracy: An Experimental inquiry.* New York: Harper.

Whiting, B. and Edwards, C. P. (1973). A cross-cultural analysis of sex differences in the behavior of children aged three through 11. *J. Soc. Psychol.*, **91**, 171–188.

Witkin, H. A., Mednick, S. A., Schulsinger, F., Bakkestrøm, E., Christiansen, K. O., Goodenough, D. R., Hirschorn, K., Lundsteen, C., Owen, D. R., Philip, J., Rubin, D. B. and Stocking, M. (1976). Criminality in XYY and XXY men, *Science*, **193**, 547–555.

Woerner, M. G. and Klein, D. F. (1974). Fourteen and six per second positive spike. Developmental and clinical correlates in psychiatric patients and their siblings. *Journal of Nervous and Mental Disease*, **159**, 356–361.

Yablonsky, L. (1962). *The Violent Gang.* New York: Penguin.

Yalom, I. D., Green, R. and Fisk, N. (1973). Prenatal exposure to female hormones. *Arch. Gen. Psychiat.*, **28**, 554–561.

Yarrow, M. R., Campbell, J. D. and Burton, R. V. (1968). *Child Rearing: An inquiry into research and methods.* San Francisco: Jossey-Bass.

Zussman, J. U., Zussman, P. P. and Dalton, K. (1977). Effects of prenatal progesterone on adolescent cognitive and social development. Paper presented at the Third Annual Meeting of the International Academy of Sex Research, Bloomington, Indiana.

THEORIES AND APPROACHES

29. FUTURE TRENDS AND PROBLEMS

MARTIN C. O. BAX

FUTURE TRENDS AND PROBLEMS

Research is, of course, going on in every subject reviewed in this book and I expect and hope to see new findings modifying present opinions. Certain topics are developing steadily—thus in genetic research there is a constant stream of papers expanding our understanding of behavioural genetics while, on the other hand, in other fields, such as the understanding of 'moral development', unsolved theoretical and methodological problems mean that progress is more intermittent than continuous. In this review I want to draw attention to some researches which, while not the subject of chapters in the present volume, will, undoubtedly, become more significant in the future and then consider some of the difficulties that this burgeoning of research has for the practitioner in the field of developmental psychiatry.

New research

There are many basic studies going on at the moment whose immediate relevance to developmental psychiatry is not clear but which I feel must become relevant in the future. The new technical abilities of the neurophysiologist who now readily studies the function of single cortical cells, coupled with an ontogenic approach, has lead to some exciting work.

Blakemore and his colleagues (1969) have made very detailed studies of the relationship between visual function in the cat and morphological characteristics of the visual cortex. Although these studies have been carried out in the cat the findings have important general implications (Blakemore and Campbell, 1969). The experimental studies have involved rearing cats in visually controlled environments so that individual animals experience different types of visual input; *i.e.* they only see vertical as opposed to horizontal stripes. Not only is the kitten's visual function affected by such techniques but more importantly there are morphological changes in the kitten's visual cortex (Garey and Pettigrew, 1974; Blakemore and Van Sluyters, 1975). To quote the former paper, 'The results suggest that there is a population of terminals in the visual cortex of young, visually inexperienced kittens which develop a high concentration of synaptic vesicles *after* stimulation by patterned input' (my italics). The proper caution in this statement does not disguise the fact that the workers are beginning to be able to discern ways in which early environmental change affects the morphological development of the brain. That

functional changes exist follows almost naturally. In a paper entitled 'Modification of the Kitten's Visual Cortex by Exposure to Spatially Periodic Pattern' the authors again summarize cautiously 'The population of neurones in the visual cortex becomes relatively less sensitive to stimuli that were not experienced early in life' (Blakemore *et al.*) Blakemore, in his 1970 paper, again emphasized the importance of early visual input by its very title alone: 'Development of the Brain depends on the Visual Environment'.

Clearly, the relevance of this work to developmental psychiatry, while important, is more theoretical than practical at the moment but when one considers linking this type of work with other fundamental studies the practical implications are more obvious. Using a combination of radioactive labelling of basic metabolies (such as oxygen CO_2 and glucose) together with the latest computerized scanning techniques, very detailed information about cerebral function during very specific activities becomes available. In an elegant series of papers (in *Cerebral Function, Metabolism and Circulation* 1978) Lassen and his colleagues (1977) report studies of cerebral blood flow during a whole range of activities, including movements, listening to music and to a speech, speaking and reading aloud. In one motor test, after the subject had carried out a finger movement, he was asked to think about the same movement but not actually execute the movement. In this latter situation an increase in cerebral blood flow was measured in supplementary motor areas but not in the Rolandic sensori-motor hand area as had occurred when the movement was actually made. Clinical cases so far studied include patients with sensory or motor aphasia.

Although most of the studies so far reported have been done in patients in whom there was a good clinical reason for injecting a radioactive material, the use of radioactive labelled gases with extremely short $\frac{1}{2}$ lives in normal subjects points the way to further, detailed study of normal adults and, one hopes, eventually to normal children.

The technique of axial computerized tomography has so far largely led to reports in patients with clear-cut neurological symptoms but as the CAT scan becomes more widely available and accepted as an everyday clinical tool, more information will become available about patients presenting with behavioural problems. Thus, Bergstrom and Bille (1978) reported such a study of 46 children aged 4 to 15 years who had that rather nebulous diagnosis of minimal brain damage. Remarkably, 15 (32%) of their cases revealed abnormalities consisting of cerebral atrophy, asymmetry or another anomaly. Their criteria for diagnosing minimal brain damage are probably stricter than those used by other authors, but nevertheless the high rate of positive findings is impressive.

Another application of development of computer sciences is subsumed under the name 'neurometrics' (John *et al.* (1977)). The assumption underlying neurometrics is that 'EEG and sensory evoked potentials contain diagnostically valuable information that can be made accessible by quantitative analysis'. Currently the technique involves recording and analysing EEG activity of resting states and of evoked responses from various auditory or visual inputs (for example, the subject looks at the letters 'b', 'd', 'p', and 'q'). The authors state that by using mathematical techniques known as numerical taxonomy 'quantitative neurometric data from many individuals' can be used to construct objective operational classification schemes. They have been using these techniques in children with varying types of learning disorder. Current reports make it difficult to estimate the clinical value of such studies at the moment but again, the technique clearly has potential.

The studies so far mentioned are likely to be significant in understanding basic processes or helping diagnostically, but equally they can be applied to studying behaviour in particular situations and looking at responses to specific treatments. The neurometric workers have reported on different evoked responses when the children were having a variety of different drugs. The use of telemetric devices, to make continuous study of EEG in everyday situations, has long been reported. More recently, on-going biochemical measures have been used to look at human responses to stress. In adults the biochemical patterns of response to a stressful situation (such as driving in a motor race) have been fully studied and the links between the 'stress' of modern life and 'stress' disease, such as coronary artery disease, studied (*see* Caruthers, 1978). Similar studies are being conducted in children; for example children having frequent temper tantrums will have higher levels of urinary steroids and simply by collecting regular specimens a good measure of this type of activity can be obtained.

The research which I have mentioned in this paper has been selected almost at random from studies which have interested me personally, but I have deliberately emphasized studies where technical advance will, I believe, contribute to developmental psychiatry because it has seemed to me that many practitioners ignore these developments, concentrating on more theoretical ideas.

The problem of application

It is obvious that within the field of medicine the widespread application of existing technical knowledge could substantially reduce existing disease particularly in the field of preventive medicine. Thus, widely disparate infant mortality rates suggest that wider application of modern obstetric and paediatric practice could reduce some of the higher rates. Poliomyelitis has been eliminated in those countries using vaccines, but the disease still damages many children in other countries. Despite the dangers of modern medicine (so vigorously overstated by Illyich) inhabitants of poorer parts of the world would benefit from access to the health services enjoyed by wealthier nations.

How much could the application of existing knowledge of child and personality development affect the rates of disturbance in childhood and later adult life? The question is an extremely difficult one as we really know so little about the antecedents of most disturbed behaviour. The positive findings we do have (like the fact that early hospitalization can disturb a child, or a very disturbed family background can cause problems in later life) hardly help us in making guesses about more common and less aberrant adult behaviour. Thus, many people feel that corporal punishment is wrong, but there is nothing really to support this belief, or any evidence that chastized children later become disturbed.

However, to put the problem another way, and in a way which is of more immediate relevance to the practitioner, there is, as this book has displayed, a huge volume of knowledge about development which, at least if one is a professional concerned with children (disturbed or normal), is seemingly relevant. How far is this knowledge currently distributed among those concerned with children?

I have recently adopted Kushlick's classification of those adults who come into regular contact with children (Bax, 1979). The four categories are (1) near full-time contact with the child; *e.g.* the actual parents or substitute parents; (2) regular contact on a daily basis for a specific time; *e.g.* teachers and some therapists; (3) regular contact, but not on a daily basis; *e.g.* again some therapists, some psychologists and doctors attached to specific units; and (4) occasional contact; *e.g.* specialized doctors and psychologists, social workers. This last category might see the child as infrequently as once every three months (at an out-patient consultation). If one reviews the needs in terms of information of these different categories of people it seems to me that category (1) might need most wide-ranging information, whereas gaps in knowledge of category (4) professionals might be less significant. Yet, if one reviewed the present situation, the training and knowledge of those professionals engaged in the field, category (1) individuals are probably least well trained and least well informed in contrast to category (4) who are expensively and possibly well trained.

Of course, I am over-simplifying the issues; there are different kinds of information required and different levels of sophistication desirable. Nevertheless, in penning the final paragraph to this large book, the issue does seem to me a central one and one which itself should be the subject of discussion and research if the benefits of our existing knowledge are to be brought to the aid of children in need.

REFERENCES

Bax, M. C. O. (1979). Children with Multiple Handicaps. Talk given at Vancouver Conference—Care of the Severely Handicapped Child for International Year of the Child. (In Press)

Blakemore, C., and Campbell, F. W. (1969). The Existence of

Neurones in the Human Visual System Selectively Sensitive to the Orientation and Size of Retinal Images. *J. Physiol.*, **203**, 237–260

Blakemore, C. and Van Sluyters, R. C. (1975). Innate and Environmental Factors in the Development of the Kitten's Visual Cortex. *J. Physiol.*, **248**, 663–716.

Blakemore, C., Moushon, J. A. and Van Sluyters, R. C. (1975). Modification of the Kitten's Visual Cortex by Exposure to Spatially Periodic Patterns. *Exp. Brain Res.*, **31**, 561–572.

Blakemore, C. (1970). Development of the Brain depends on the Visual Environment. *Nature*, **228**, 477–478.

Bergstrom, K. and Bille, B. (1978). Computed Tomography of the Brain in Children with Minimal Brain Damage: A Preliminary Study of 46 Children. *Neuropadiatrie*, **9**, 378–384.

Carruthers, M. (1978). Biochemical Responses to Stress in the Environment. *Proc. Roy. Soc. Med.*, **68**, 429–30.

Garey, L. J. and Pettigrew, J. D. (1974). Ultrastructural Changes in Kitten Visual Cortex after Environmental Modification. *Brain Res.*, **66**, 165–172.

Lassen, N. A. *et al.* (1977). Cerebral Function, Metabolism and Circulation. Supplement 64 *Acta Neurologica Scandinavica*.

John, E. R., Karmel, B. Z., Corning, N. C., Easton, P., Brown, D., Ahn, H., John, M., Harmony, T., Prichep, L., Torro, A., Gerson, I., Bartletts, F., Thatcher, R., Kaye, H., Valdes, P. and Schwartz, E. (1977). Neurometrics: Numerical Taxonomy identifies different profiles of brain functions within groups of behaviorally similar people. *Science*, **196**, 1393–1410.

INDEX